Language and Human Understanding

David Braine

Language & Human Understanding

The Roots of Creativity in Speech and Thought

The Catholic University of America Press
Washington D.C.

The paper used in this publication meets the minimum requirements
of American National Standards for Information Science—
Permanence of Paper for Printed Library Materials, ANSI Z39.48-1984.
∞

Library of Congress Cataloging-in-Publication Data
Braine, David. Language and human understanding : the roots of
creativity in speech and thought / David Braine.
pages cm
Includes bibliographical references and index.
ISBN 978-0-8132-3566-0 (pbk : alk. paper) 1. Comparative linguistics
—History. 2. Cognitive grammar—History.
3. Typology (Linguistics) 4. Communication—History.
5. Psycholinguistics—History. I. Title.
P143.B73 2014
401—dc23 2013012079

IN MEMORIAM

Martin Braine

Elizabeth Anscombe

Simon Dik

Gilbert Ryle

Publication is supported
by a grant made verb.

FIGURE FOUNDATION

Contents

Acknowledgments xiii

Introduction and Overview 1

The Plan of This Book 1

The Inspiration and Background of This Study 2

Section 1. Words and Their Dynamism: How We Are Able to Make an "Infinite Use of Finite Means" 7

Section 2. Seeking a Perspective Appropriate to the Phenomena 11

Section 3. The Role of Pragmatics in Semantics at Every Layer of Meaning within Discourse 25

Section 4. Grammatical Structures as a Projection of Semantic Structures 36

Section 5. The Novelty of Chomsky's Conception of Formal Grammar 47

Section 6. The Verbal or "Saying" Character of Speech as the Key to Grammar 59

Prospect 66

PART ONE. **Words and Their Dynamism in the Expression of Meaning**

CHAPTER 1. **Two Levels of Meaning: The Level of Language-Possession and the Level of Language-Use** 71

The Notion of Linguistic Understanding: Preliminary Remarks 71

Section 1. The Two Levels of Linguistic Understanding 75

Section 2. Words and Sentences: The Relation of the Two Levels 81

Section 3. How "Expressing a Sense" Differs from Other Forms of "Expressing" 88

Section 4. Distinguishing *Langue*-Meaning and *Parole*-Meaning as the Key to Escaping Compositionalism 90

Section 5. How We Achieve an "Infinite Use of Finite Means" 105

CHAPTER II. The Salience of Words and Our Adventurousness in Using Them 113
Section 1. Words and Basic Lexical Factors 113
Section 2. Types of Relationship between Different Uses of the Same Word 120
Section 3. The Roots of Creative Analogy in Extending the Concept of Number 140
Summary: The Power of Examples in Demonstration 149
Appendix: Morphology and Its Bearing on Semantics 150

CHAPTER III. Sentences, Sense, and the Objects of Linguistic Science 158
The Concepts of Sentence and Sense Belong at the Speech-Act Level 158
Section 1. The Notions of Sentence and Sense—Sense Not Tied to Truth-Conditions 159
Section 2. The Speech-Act: Convergence of Philosophy and Psychology with an Older Linguistics 168
Section 3. The "Sense" of Subordinate Sentence-Constituents 176
Section 4. Two Opposite Conceptions of Linguistic Science: The Radical Novelty of Chomsky's Approach 193
Summary 210

CHAPTER IV. The Indivisibility of the Human Capacity for Language 219
The Interdpendence of the Various Semantic Structures within Language 219
Section 1. The Unity and Integratedness of Linguistic Capacity: Structure and Self- Reflexivity 221
Section 2. The Importance of This Holism in Semantics: Scrutinizing "Ordinary Language" 227
Section 3. The Role of Language in the Theory of Human Nature 233
Section 4. This Semantic Structure as the Feature Specific to Language of the Human Type 241

CHAPTER V. Scientific Method and the Significance of Mathematics for Linguistics 243
Section 1. Mistaken Presumptions about What "Scientific Method" Requires 243
Section 2. The Informality of the Concept of Rule 250
Section 3. The Unformalizability of Natural Language and the Informality of Its Concepts 253
Section 4. The Concept of Effectiveness and the Place of Mechanical Procedures in Mathematics 260
Section 5. The Relevance of This Consideration of Mathematical Method to Linguistics 279

PART TWO. The Shape of the Psychology Required for Explaining the Learning and Use of Language

CHAPTER VI. Human and Animal Organisms as Systems Dynamically Geared to the Environment 295

Mechanisms in a Holistic and Teleological Framework 295

Section 1. Human Beings as Integrated Unities: Gibson's Work as a Key to Escaping Physicalism 296

Section 2. Mechanical Processes in Living Organisms: "Mechanical" an Ambiguous Word 312

Section 3. Gibson's Treatment of Perception as a Model for the Treatment of Language 322

Appendix: Being Misled by Anomalies in Our Experience of Time and of Sensory *Qualia* 336

CHAPTER VII. Extending the Dynamic and Environment-Geared Model of Human Functioning to the Psychology of Language 346

Section 1. Difficulties in Applying the Idea of Modularity to Language 346

Section 2. The Human Learning of Language Relies on Multi-Modal Perception 352

Section 3. The Shape of an Integrated View of the Language Faculty and Its "Tuning" 356

CHAPTER VIII. Understanding as Essential to Explaining Speech: Resisting the Drag towards Physicalism 366

Section 1. The Incoherence in Dividing the Inner from the Outer in Language 366

Section 2. Conceiving of Sentences or Thoughts as Representing Reality: A Mistake Revived 382

Section 3. Sentence-Meanings Cannot Be Isomorphic with Either External or Internal States 393

Conclusion 396

PART THREE. Rewriting the Philosophy of Grammar and Restoring Unity to the Theory of Language

CHAPTER IX. Explaining the Semantic Unity of the Sentence: The Shared Roots of the Topic/Comment, Subject/Predicate, and Noun/Verb Distinctions 399

Section 1. The Basis for a Theory of How Linguistic Utterances Are Integrated 400

Section 2. Asymmetry between Names and Other Sentence-Factors—"Sense" and "Reference" 407

Section 3. Verbs as Giving Predicates Their "Verbal" Character—The Way Verbs Are Learned 429

Section 4. Negation and Its Special Character 439

CHAPTER X. **The Gulf between Saying and Naming, the Verbal and the Nominal: "Force"-Potential as Integral to "Sense"** **446**

Section 1. Full Sentences Distinguished from Clauses in General: Relation of Force to Sense 446

Section 2. Disagreements about Force: Wittgenstein's Opposition to Frege 453

Section 3. Geach's Arguments 458

Section 4. Dummett's Interpretation of Frege's Notion of *Sinn* and Its Difficulties 471

Section 5. Recovering the Tradition: Saying Is Not Naming 475

CHAPTER XI. **The Notion of Subject and the Functional Organization of the Clause** **487**

Section 1. Disentangling Linguistics from Its Historical Background 488

Section 2. The Notion of Grammatical Subject 496

Section 3. The Notion of Grammatical Object: Different Options in Structuring Speech 518

CHAPTER XII. **Marrying Philosophy and Grammar in Distinguishing Types of Noun Expression** **528**

Section 1. The Varied Types of Meaning of Abstract Nouns 528

Section 2. Unraveling Plato's Problems as the Key to Resolving Problems in Semantics 538

Section 3. The Value of the Notions of Cognate and Cognitional Cognate 553

Section 4. The Notion of Cognitional Cognate and the Incoherence of Representationalism 568

Concluding Remark: Confirmation That to Describe Cannot Be to Represent or Denote 574

CHAPTER XIII. **Varied Systems of Grammaticalization—Reviewing the Phenomena** **575**

Section 1. Thematic Roles and How They Arise 575

Section 2. Making the Way Thematic Elements Are Integrated into the Sentence Explicit 582

Section 3. Parameters and Bracketing 591

Section 4. Comparing Languages and Language Development Instructive for Grammar 603

Section 5. The Treatment of Reference and the Problems of *Wh*-questions 609

Section 6. The Parasentential Level: The Interplay of Logic and Grammar in Modality and Reasoning 622

Section 7. Some Comparisons between Different Types of Grammar: Formal and Functional 632

Section 8. Optimization in Analyzing Sentences Understood in Context 639

CHAPTER XIV. The Verb Gives Sentences Their Dynamic Character and Shapes Their Syntactic Structure **643**

Section 1. The Verb at the Heart of a Clause Gives Structure to the Whole 645

Section 2. Auxiliaries, Semi-auxiliaries, and Adverbial Modifiers 666

Section 3. Complements and Adjuncts, and the Character of Adpositions 677

Section 4. Types of Functional Complement to Verbs 688

Section 5. Clause-Markers and Types of Subordinate Clause 695

CHAPTER XV. The Distorted Treatment of Phrase Theory in Modern Formal Grammar **705**

Section 1. A Preliminary: Kinds of "of"-Phrases 706

Section 2. Three Levels of Isomorphism When a Noun or Adjective Phrase Is Verbally Rooted 715

Section 3. The Misconceptions Embodied in the X-Bar Presentation of Phrase Theory 723

General Conclusion **745**

Bibliography 755

Index of Names 777

Subject Index 783

Acknowledgments

This book has been over twenty-one years in the writing, the fruit of fifty years' preoccupation with language. For the final result, I have to thank first the chief teachers and authors who led me to realize the necessity of achieving an integration of linguistics, psychology, and philosophy if any account of the meaning and structure of language was to carry conviction. Secondly, I have to thank those without whose encouragement or practical help the project would have been stillborn.

In discussing my transition from physical science and history to academic philosophy in 1962, Gilbert Ryle described himself as "a sort of philosophical uncle", and he proved himself a wise first mentor in philosophy. He was at heart an Aristotelian, and I inherited his Aristotelian instincts. He saw that one had to understand that man is an animal, and that animals are not machines, before one could properly grapple with the special character of human beings. Meantime, he had a never-resting concern with language and the nature of thinking. He also saw the need for what Aristotle and Aquinas called analogy in our use of words.

Michael Dummett and Elizabeth Anscombe, the other main philosophical influences upon me in Oxford, stood before me as examples of discipline, terriers never content with a work left in rough sketch only without pursuing every difficulty. Dummett's first impact upon me was through his seminars, first on the philosophy of mathematics from Frege to the intuitionists in 1964 and '65, and then on the philosophy of language in 1971. However, in the latter, while I shared his sense that Davidson's account of meaning in terms of truth-conditions failed to bring us to a grasp of the inner content of propositions, I felt that his substitution of verification conditions brought us no nearer.

It was only after 1971 in Aberdeen that I came to engage with the linguists and linguistic theory. At an early stage Otto Jespersen's *The Philosophy of Grammar* left an indelible mark. Dr. David Cram, Head of Linguistics at Aberdeen, introduced me to Chomsky, and later, as he left Aberdeen for Oxford, to the very different Simon Dik. Simon Dik was one with whose thought I felt an instant *rapport*, struck by his philosophical acumen, and it was through him that I first encountered functionalist approaches in linguistics. Joan Bresnan and Robert van Valin joined Dik in seeing the need to recognize functional as well as configurational parallels between languages. Thus it became evident that there has never been just one scientific linguistics, any more than there has ever been one unified scientific psychology. It was always clear that there is no one "analytic philosophy"— Ryle, Dummett, and Wittgenstein were poles apart from each other in their approaches, and all three poles apart from the transatlantic Quine and Davidson.

Some of the central ideas of the book were presented in the second set of "Gifford Investigations", which I presented in 1985 as a Gifford Fellow of the University of Aberdeen. In 1990, I turned to develop these. Then, as the very first drafts of early chapters took shape, my brother Martin, the psycholinguist, alerted me to key difficulties, while his wife Lila pointed me towards the work of the psychologist J. J. Gibson. Yet by 1998 I found myself compelled to delve far more deeply into linguistics and its different schools—finding myself rewarded in the lengthening task, not by scatter, but by a reinforcement of my conviction that one could attain a unified view of speech and language. This was a view to which linguistics, psychology, and philosophy each contributed in more than one way.

I have to thank the University of Aberdeen Gifford Committee and the University of Notre Dame Center for Philosophy of Religion for their contribution towards secretarial expenses at an early stage. From 1989, as Honorary Lecturer in Philosophy and then Honorary Research Fellow, I have enjoyed the unfailing support of the computer services and library personnel of the University of Aberdeen.

From the time of my motor accident in 1977 onwards Elizabeth Anscombe was a constant source of affection and a support to my spirit. Since I started on the project, David Burrell of Notre Dame and David Cram gave me frequent encouragement, and I was at different times emboldened by Roy Harris of Oxford and by the counsel of Mouton de Gruyter. My perseverance was particularly renewed over a difficult period by the keen help of a very intelligent student, Robert Norris, who with his belief in my work continued to read drafts for years after he left Aberdeen. Since 2004, I have had good counsel and unfailing patience and encouragement from the Catholic University of America Press.

Since I depend on others to do most of the typing required, doing it at my dictation, there have been many generations of students who have helped me. They have helped me not only in keeping me alert to advances in computer technology, but also in raising my spirits by their encouragement as well as extraordinary patience and goodwill. Whereas when I wrote the preface to my 1988 book I was able to list the twenty-five students who had helped me, this is here impractical, since the number runs to far over a hundred. I owe them a huge debt of thanks. As to Hope Bartel, who must have already read the whole of my script at least five times, ever preserving an eagle eye for defective sentences, omitted references, and other flaws, how can I thank her enough for her copy-editing work? Aldene Fredenburg caringly completed this labor.

Elizabeth Anscombe advised me, when I met a good argument in St Thomas, never to acknowledge it, but let the argument be seen to stand on its own feet without authority. Yet it is salutary to see how, although Aquinas's arguments need to be expanded and refurbished, nonetheless his views—that understanding cannot be the operation of a material organ, that no material system can reflect upon itself, and that, where the most general terms are concerned, intrinsic analogies cannot be captured by definitions, but are not a kind of metaphor—each stands the test of time. As to the foundations of grammar, key seeds are to be found in Plato, Aristotle, and, in the East, Panini. Much new develops in human thought, but, when we have refreshed the old, we find it is surprising how far our forebears have anticipated us.

Language and Human Understanding

Introduction and Overview

A right account of language is, I believe, the key to a right account of the nature of human understanding and thought, and thereby the key to a right understanding of human nature as a whole. Yet the whole theory of language is in considerable disorder, and my aim must therefore be first to seek to remedy this. This will take me into the heart of current debates in linguistics, philosophy, and psychology, and lead me to undertake an extended study of grammar. The effect will be to show how language exhibits the ultimate freedom of the human intellect and will from conformity with mechanically applicable rules and from limitations set by neurology. The brain plays a key role in the normal functioning of the human mind, but does not determine or shape linguistic understanding and thinking in the medium of words, as this develops through adaptation to and learning within a social external environment of other speakers and hearers, all within a setting of natural things. Such understanding and thinking have to be considered the activities not of brains or minds, but of human beings as such. In effect the animal becomes intellectual in nature as soon as the brain reaches such malleability in its modes of functioning as to set no restrictions on the animal or person's intellectual operation, allowing autonomy to the mind's operation.

The Plan of This Book

In part one I outline the form which semantics as a theory of the meanings of the words and sentences which figure in our speech and writing should take. Word and sentence are interdependent, and neither is definable in terms of the other, a word in a particular meaning being multi-potential in use, open to many senses or discourse-significances. The way we use concepts in science and mathematics allows a demonstration of the kind of autonomy of mind with which I am concerned—an autonomy of mind seen in common life in the structures of self-reflection, integral to the "semantic syntax" which shapes all human discourse.

In part two I consider the implications of such a semantic theory for the psychology of language use and acquisition, identifying a way of thinking which takes account of the whole range of data with which psychologists and neuroscientists are presented. I indicate how the proper understanding of evolution and of neuroscience is compatible with the autonomy of mind of which I have spoken.

Finally, in part three, I show how a detailed consideration of grammar confirms my general perspective—that it is the understanding actualized in an extended or general logic, together with the conditions of human communication and inquiry, which shape the forms of human speech. I give an account of the "syntax" of sentences ("syntax" named from the Greek *taxis*, meaning "arrangement" or "order") against the background of the basis of the approaches to semantics and psychology laid out earlier. This involves distinguishing between the semantic structure or "semantic syntax" of sentences and their "morphosyntactic syntax". I speak of "morphosyntactic" syntax or structure because grammar concerns the formal ordering both of words and of morphemes as lexical factors more elementary than words.[1] Human beings therefore need a process of "grammaticalization", by means of which semantic syntax becomes more perspicuous by being marked "grammatically" in the way customary within the language community concerned—marked by such means as phrase order, inflections, and appropriate prepositions—that is, marked morphosyntactically. In this way I redefine the word "grammaticalization".

The Inspiration and Background of This Study

In 1992, when I wrote *The Human Person: Animal and Spirit*, I showed that the human being had to be understood as being an animal—not as a body with a spirit attached to it, but as, at the same time, both an animal and an in-

1. Because I write this book in English, with its close approximation of words to lexical factors (not perfect approximation because of surviving inflections), I often speak of "words", meaning "words and lexical factors". In more inflected languages such simplification becomes more misleading, and in agglutinative languages, and in the extreme case polysynthetic languages (where the noun element is incorporated into the verbal one), the oversimplification involved becomes maximal.

tellectual being or spirit. By an animal, I did not mean a physical mechanism, but an integrated, organic whole, characterized at the same time by bodily properties and by activities characteristic of animal life, such as perception and motivated action. One of the virtues of "ordinary language philosophy", as it has come to be called, lay in the way it lent itself to this understanding of the human being as, in this way, a psychophysical unity.

Yet this opens the question as to what differentiates human beings from other animals—in particular from other higher animals, whose behavior also in some way exhibits mind, but which lacks language as the highly structured unitary semantic capacity found in human beings.[2] Such language presents the form of intellectuality distinctive of the human animal. It indeed strikingly exemplifies the integration of the animal and the intellectual, the bodily activities involved in the speaking which expresses our thinking and understanding in integration with the thinking and understanding it expresses. Yet language in this full sense is also special in that, among publicly observable human activities, speech alone has forms which may provide empirical basis for proof that human beings have activities which transcend any limitations which might be set by the body, instead of leaving this a mere matter of faith—reasoned arguments such as I outlined in the second part of *The Human Person*.

However, from my first thinking about language while first getting to grips with philosophy in 1962, I have become ever more aware of the need for a fresh treatment of the theory of language. In my 1992 book I presented only a sketch of the view of language on which my argument depended. However, I did gain some clue as to a possible basis for the unified theory of language which I have come to envisage as a goal.

The development of my thinking about language

Let me begin by giving an impressionistic sketch of the instincts and insights which have driven my thinking about language since 1962, shaping my assessments of other approaches.

Since my earliest studies in philosophy under Ryle, it has been clear to me that a word, even while still being taken just in one dictionary meaning, normally has many different senses or connotations, its implications and significance modulated by its context in discourse. Although it may be harmless to enforce a rigid uniformity in the use of words in the context of a particular task

2. Perception, imagination, memory, desire, and other emotions do not belong to human beings in a quite different sense from that in which they belong to the higher animals, as I explained in *The Human Person: Animal and Spirit* (Notre Dame, Ind.: University of Notre Dame Press, 1992), chap. 9, in this way echoing ideas to be found in Charles Taylor and Merleau-Ponty. If any nonhuman animal did have properly linguistic systems in the full sense, my argument would have the same implications for them as for human beings. However, in fact, nonhuman communication systems do not seem to be fully properly linguistic.

(for example, in analyzing a particular argument), to enforce such uniformity throughout the whole use of a language is to put language into a fatal strait-jacket. Most of the basic concepts of natural language—concepts on which ordinary discourse, self-reflection, argument in law and history, scientific development, and mathematics all depend—require that words should be used informally in ways which such rigidity would exclude. The flexibility in the use of words which we daily experience and on which our use of metaphor and human cultural development depend arises from a kind of understanding which permits words to be used informally and yet still to be well understood by hearer or reader. And much of my earliest study in philosophy was concentrated in areas in which this informality was of key importance—in particular, the informalities in our use of the family of words associated with different types of knowledge, with different kinds of possibility and necessity, and with the ideas of individual, set, and number of importance to the foundations of logic and mathematics.[3]

So from the start I saw it as a second virtue of "ordinary language philosophy" which it recognized how the same word could have a spread of interconnected uses, rescuing philosophy from the idea that words should be used according to formal or mechanically applicable rules, and beginning to do justice to insights pioneered by Aristotle and Aquinas.

This concern with the salience of word-meaning and our informality in using words led me to react sharply against some assumptions with which I first met in seminars of Dummett and of McDowell in Oxford in the summer of 1971, assumptions shared by philosophers as different as Dummett, Davidson, and Quine. Their rival accounts all involved making things at the sentence level (propositions or assertions, commands, and so forth) fundamental in defining and explaining word-meaning. Their explanations always took one back to conditions of truth, conditions of justified assertion or denial, conditions of fulfillment or obedience, experiences reported in sentences, or responses to the sentences of others. Yet such approaches all put direct controls solely on sentence-meaning and use, and so gave only indirect or ex-

3. Thus I found that the word "know" and related words in other languages have a wide spread of uses, between which there are intelligible connections which are not explicable in terms of paraphrase or mechanical rule; and even where some definition is possible, it is in terms of other very general concepts whose application cannot be contained in any mechanically applicable rule; cf. David Braine, "The Nature of Knowledge", *Proceedings of the Aristotelian Society* 72 (1971–72): 41–63. Again, each family of words expressing possibility, impossibility, and necessity generates three spreads of use, reflecting that we speak of them in relation to three quite different kinds of context: one rooting them in natures or causal powers, another rooting them in practical or moral principles or general human goods, and a third rooting them in reasons for judgment; cf. David Braine, "Varieties of Necessity", *Procedings of the Aristotelian Society* suppl. vol. 46 (1972): 139–70. And every proposal for resolving paradoxes, among other problems in the philosophy of mathematics, depends on making distinctions between different types of use of the most general words, even taken in the same meaning.

ternal access to the meanings or significances of words or other sentence constituents. This made them defective in two ways.

First, these accounts failed to explain why words and other lexical factors are indispensable for *expressing* the sense of an utterance as distinct from just *identifying* its sense. But in expressing the sense or content to be understood in one's communications, it is words or other lexical factors in their context which are primary—at the level of understanding, the sentence or complete utterance has sense only through them. If our only access to meaning were via sentence-meaning, the possession of meaning would perhaps be a matter only of the sentences we utter influencing belief, attitude, and behavior. But each such sentence also has to express the intelligible *content* of the thought being communicated, a thought about which people can deliberate, question, or build into a theory or narrative.

Second, such accounts led their adherents to think of the senses of words, within the limits to which they can be shared between speaker and hearer, as something which can be worked out or calculated from sentence-meanings or uses. Yet this required a rigid connection between word-meaning and sentence-meaning which excluded the informality of which I spoke earlier. At the same time I realized that, for very different reasons arising from Chomsky's quite different conception of sentence, the predominant Chomskyan approach to grammar involved a parallel rigidity in the connection between word-meaning and sentence-meaning, each lexical item allowed only one lexical meaning (or only one set of consequences for sentence-meanings). Thus it turned out that recent philosophers and grammatical theorists have both tended to embrace a doctrine of "compositionality", imposing a rigid connection between the meanings of the lexical factors or words of which a sentence is made up, along with their mode of combination, and the meaning of the resulting sentence, despite the different conceptions of sentence.

In this way I discovered that linguists have been strangely apt to recapitulate the same mistakes as philosophers, the same models creating insoluble problems in both fields. Whether one puts a one-sided emphasis upon the sentence or upon the word or lexical factor as the primary locus of meaning, one puts language into an impossible straitjacket.[4]

Accordingly, the challenge is to restore the balance between word and sentence and give a coherent explanation of how word-meaning and sentence-

4. Michael Dummett recognizes the problem when he tells us that sentences are primary in the explanation of meaning and words primary in an account of its recognition, mentioning that Frege is "unwaveringly insistent that the sense of a sentence . . . is made out of the senses of its constituent words"; Dummett, *Frege: Philosophy of Language* (London: Duckworth, 1973; 2nd ed. Cambridge, Mass.: Harvard University Press, 1993; drafted in 1964, see Preface, x–xi), 4. However, he does not explain how words can give recognition of sentence-meaning without our having first gained an understanding of words from our understanding of sentences; see my further discussion in chapter VIII of this volume.

meaning are interdependent and correlative—or, as Simon Blackburn has expressed it, how bottom-up and top-down approaches can be combined. A language does not consist of a definite set of sentences, but of word-like elements, each with a multi-potentiality allowing it to be used in an open-ended variety of ways in speech, yet still intelligible to an audience sharing the same language. Linguist, philosopher, and psychologist have to explain the nature of this multi-potentiality in a way which gives adequate recognition to the salience of the word or lexical factor as what gives content to the sentence, and to do this in such a way as to clarify how the potentiality associated with words is typically such as to be realized in an indefinite multiplicity of ways.

In 1992, with these ideas, I felt philosophically far advanced in my project.

Crossing the barriers to communication between disciplines and schools

However, at this stage, discussions with my brother, the psycholinguist Martin D. S. Braine, quickly disabused me of the idea that I had only philosophers to satisfy. Although we found ourselves grappling with closely related problems and agreed in some of the ideas key to their solution, such as that of "predicate", nonetheless we found that we used much common vocabulary with quite different presumptions, springing from the gulf between our respective backgrounds of argument and concern. The differences in our assumptions were as startling as the lack of overlap in our reading. How foreign the approaches of philosophers, linguists, and psycholinguists could seem to one another was thrust before my eyes in a particularly vivid way. Thus I had to avoid the behavior of the proverbial ostrich, speaking only to the like-minded or to philosophers alone, and grapple with theoretical linguistics at a much deeper level, taking account of functionalist as well as Chomskyan approaches to grammar. Also, I had to consider the relationship between linguistics and neuroscience.

This has proved a long twenty-one-year process. Here my delvings soon made it plain that the approaches of one school of theoretical linguist often appear as alien to linguists of other schools and to experts in particular languages as the discussions of philosophers may seem alien to linguists. And the frequency with which technical terms are used in many different ways, both within linguistics and outside it, has added to the confusion.

Therefore, I need to explain and argue my position, as it were, from scratch, and clarify my usage of any term whenever this is variable, technical, or in some way special, with the aim of making matters clear to the general reader, to whom theoretical linguistics is usually a closed book because of its unexplained technicalities. For clarity I have almost entirely banished acronyms and utilized the index to indicate the place or places in the text where my usage of a term is first or most fully explained.

Section 1. Words and Their Dynamism: How We Are Able to Make an "Infinite Use of Finite Means"

Language presents itself to us under two aspects, *parole*, or speech, and *langue*, the communal resources on which speech depends—*langue* being exercised and exhibited in *parole*, not as a separate object of study. In my presentation I use the terms *langue* and *parole* to enshrine the logical distinction between *langue* as the object of the shared practical knowledge of a language implicit in communal language-possession and *parole* as its realization in language-use and in the active understanding which users of that language have of what they say or hear, write, or read in their acts of speaking, hearing, writing, or reading in that language. (I do not follow Saussure's account of the distinction.)

I explain my use of the term *langue* more closely in chapter I, relating *langue* to the community of language-users and treating the individual's appropriation of his or her own language as something which develops.

As we shall see, with entities at the rank of sentence and above, all branches of linguistic study are concerned with the same objects, all being considered at the level of language-use or speech. By contrast, the situation with words is very different because we have to consider them both at the level of language-possession and at the level of language-use. If words had no meaning in their own right already given at the level of language-possession, but were mere ciphers, they could not be used to express anything or to give anything semantic content.

On the one hand, within a dictionary with a finite vocabulary of words or lexical factors, although some will require the separate itemization of several distinct focuses of meaning, this will still leave us with a finite vocabulary of lexical entries in total. However, on the other hand, we have to recognize that each such lexical item, embodying some particular focus of meaning of a word, is liable to be such as to be open to flexible use within *parole* or speech so as to have different senses or discourse-significances on different occasions of use which cannot be thus listed, not because they are of some particular number larger than any finite number, but because they are indefinite in number, liable to fresh types of use as speakers meet with fresh types of situation. It is our understanding of these basic lexical items at the level of *langue* or language-possession which makes this flexibility and lack of formality possible. A dictionary or lexicon cannot list all the uses, senses, or kinds of discourse-significance of which a word or other lexical factor is capable in speech. Hence, for each constituent lexical factor within an utterance, we need a distinction between the dictionary or *langue*-meaning of that lexical factor and the sense or discourse-significance which it gains in the act of utterance with its distinctive context and intonation.

It is primarily this informality and flexibility in the use of words which enables us in speech, in Von Humboldt's words, to make an "infinite use of finite means"—made possible through the interplay between language-possession and language-use. This gives them a spread of "senses" or "discourse-significances", as explained in chapter III, disciplined through being contained in one overall semantic framework, as indicated in chapter IV. As I show in chapter II, to some extent we can systematize the types of relation which arise between different uses of the same word by using such notions as "focal meaning", "analogy", and "polymorphousness" introduced by Aristotle, Aquinas, and Ryle and by making a more general use of Zermelo's notion of "indefiniteness", originally introduced to escape the paradoxes of logic and set theory.

Thus I set aside the doctrine of "compositionality" whereby one lexical entry has one set of consequences for meaning at the sentence level. This doctrine arose first in philosophy and logic, with the immediate implication that the meaning of a proposition, a command, a wish, or a question is fully determined by its structure and the meanings of its constituents—thereby immediately imposing the rigidity alluded to earlier.[5] But propositions, commands, wishes, and questions are entities at the level of speech or text—that is, the level of the use of language. And in assessing their meaning, we have to take a wide range of contextual knowledge into account, involving much more than the identification of the references of demonstratives and proper names for which the philosophers commonly make room. Indeed, beyond this, the type of understanding of words on which our use of language relies gives us a way of taking into account quite unpredicted situations and changes

5. The doctrine is stated by John Skorupski: "the fact that the meaning of a sentence is a function of the meaning of its constituent expressions" and "the meaning of a sentence is determined by the meaning of its constituents"; Skorupski, "Meaning, Use, Verification", in *A Companion to the Philosophy of Language*, ed. Bob Hale and Crispin Wright (Oxford: Blackwell, 1997), 35, 46. The same doctrine is seen in Bob Hale's argument in *A Companion*, 279–80. It is often called "Frege's principle" on the basis of Frege's 1879 *Begriffsschrift* as revised in his 1893 *Grundgesetze der Arithmetik*; for references to these works of Frege, see David Wiggins, "Meaning and Truth Conditions: From Frege's Grand Design to Davidson's", in *A Companion*, ed. Hale and Wright, 1–3, nn.1–5 on 22; John Lyons, *Language, Meaning and Context* (London: Fontana Press, 1981), 144–46, understands "Frege's principle" in this way. It is a much weaker principle than the principle that a compositional theory is axiomatizable.

The axiomatizability principle makes the sense of any sentence and any word in a language interdependent with the sense of all others. It surfaced in the first two essays of Donald Davidson's collection *Inquiries into Truth and Interpretation* (Oxford: Oxford University Press, 1984; with his useful notes on the provenance of the essays and introduction in the 2nd edition, 2001): "Theories of Meaning and Learnable Languages" (1965) and "Truth and Meaning" (1967), perhaps more influenced by Quine than by Frege. It reappears in Alexander Miller, "Tacit Knowledge", in *A Companion*, ed. Hale and Wright, 146–72, and in the glossary of *A Companion*, 656–57; see also the discussion in chap. V, n. 53 of this volume.

Both these principles are much stronger than the "Context Principle"; see chap. III, sec. 2 (c).

in paradigm in explanation or description. Such a wide range of contextually arising factors is quite outside the scope of the "composition" of a proposition as conceived by those who currently propose the doctrine of compositionality.[6] Indeed, as Chomsky argues in his criticism of Davidson, there could be no way of explaining the full range of interpretations (what I later call "senses" or "discourse-significances") of which an interpreter is capable without developing what Chomsky describes as "a theory of everything"—which is "not a topic for empirical inquiry" of the kind he considers linguistics to be.[7]

Once freed from the rigidities and artifices which arise from misunderstanding the respective roles of grammar and formal logic, we can envisage the richness and power of *Sprache* emphasized by Von Humboldt as arising principally from the interplay between our understanding of words or lexical factors (whatever the level of understanding the person has reached in his learning of his own language) and the challenge of responding to the questions presenting themselves to us by a situation in some way novel. It is in this setting that we find that expressions taken in one meaning at the level of *langue* can be used with informality and flexibility in an indefinite number of discourse-significances or senses in speech and writing—our understanding not being restricted to conformity to mechanically applicable rule.

The relevant kind of infinity in the use of finite means is therefore not the inductive infinity which we attribute to the natural numbers, the rational numbers, and so forth, which arises as a result of recursive operations. For this is the only kind of infinity which could arise from our supposed capacity to iterate language-relevant operations any finite number of times, producing an infinite set of finitely long sentences. Yet, in practice, we make only a relatively small number of such iterations, as I illustrate in chapters I and XIII,[8] and,

6. In the light of chaps. I and II of this volume, Paul J. Hopper and Elizabeth Closs Traugott's remark that to regard the ideal of "one form—one meaning" as "optimal" is "dysfunctional" because of the multiplicity of meanings which require expression; Hopper and Traugott's *Grammaticalization*, 2nd ed. (Cambridge: Cambridge University Press, 2003), 77–78, points towards the heart of the matter.

7. Noam Chomsky, *New Horizons in the Study of Language and Mind* (Cambridge: Cambridge University Press, 2000), 69–70 (note: "passing" is a misprint for "parsing" in *New Horizons*). Compare Szabó's remark, "If it turned out that in order to interpret a sentence we must know all sorts of ephemeral non-linguistic facts we would have to conclude that the fact that we can reliably understand all sorts of unfamiliar sentences is a mystery"; Zoltán Gendler Szabó, "Compositionality", sec. 4.2, in *Stanford Encyclopedia of Philosophy*, ed. Edward N. Zalta (Stanford, Calif.: Stanford University Press, Winter 2008), http://plato.stanford.edu/archives/win2008/entries/compositionality/. This excludes John Searle's view in "Austin on Locutionary and Illocutionary Acts", *Philosophical Review* 77 (1968): 405–24, which incorporates contextual factors into a compositional theory.

8. The idea that a natural language can include sentences of just any finite length is rightly ridiculed by Paul Ziff in "The Number of English Sentences", *Foundations of Language* 11 (1974): 519–32. The formation of a natural sentence comprising more than 10,000 iterations of the operation Merge in Minimalist theory is difficult to envisage. There are as many finite numbers greater than $10^{10,000}$ as there are finite numbers greater than 10,000, and even what a finite number of finite computers processing in parallel can complete in a finite time is finite, and the matter in the universe is finite.

in order to interpret sentences with embedded clauses also involving negation, especially if conditional clauses are involved, and to interpret questions, we depend increasingly on the consideration of their context of utterance as clausal complexity increases. No! the kind of "infinity" with which we are concerned is an indefiniteness of number such as, for instance, is exemplified in the number of possible constructive definitions of real numbers or of members in a mathematical intuitionist's "spread".[9]

It is this indefiniteness in the number of discourse-significances which can arise from the understanding of the same word or lexical factor at the level of *langue* which enables us to use the concepts concerned intelligibly without dependence on or conformity to mechanical rule—in the way I illustrate in chapter I and which makes possible the types of reasoning involving the most general concepts which I survey in chapter V. It is also this which enables us to escape the various kinds of paradox which arise with such general concepts if one treats natural language according to purely formal rules—and, in each case, it even enables us to form some conception of how the paradox arose and so of how it and related paradoxes are to be avoided without introducing false general restrictions on our use of language.

This kind of informality in the use of the more general concepts also enables us to imaginatively and intellectually penetrate unfamiliar paradigms of explanation and evaluation, sometimes appropriating them and sometimes not, so that differences in cultural history do not present any absolute barrier to understanding other peoples. And it enables us to raise ever new questions and in response find ever fresh methods of approach in answering them, sometimes ourselves playing a part in the opening out of new paradigms. It is as a result of this informality in the working of our minds, which we see exhibited in speech, that our knowledge is not limited by the way our concepts are formed in the way Kant supposed.

The only other important source of our capacity to make an "infinite use of finite resources" arises from the way our understanding gives us the capacity to reflect on what we have said about the initial subjects of our discourse and to turn the properties and relations concerned into new topics or subjects in their own right, in this way setting up a hierarchy of subjects, as suggested in section 4 and explained further in chapters XII and XIII. This is the main root of the discrepancy between grammatical and semantic categories—for instance, between that of "noun" and that of "substance" or "thing".

Human beings have the possibility of only a very limited, albeit indefinite, number of checks of an indefinite number of disparate forms, and here computers are unable to imitate them.[10] And since our capacities to survey

9. Cf. chap. I, sec. 4 (b), sec. 5 (a), and n. 44.

10. Moreover, any particular computer's powers of calculation will always be strictly finite; cf. n. 8.

sentences of any great complexity are very limited, the much-vaunted "iterability" of certain linguistic operations is only a very subsidiary factor in our capacity to make a "richer use of finite resources", and is useless in explaining the "infinite use of finite means" of which Von Humboldt spoke.[11]

Section 2. Seeking a Perspective Appropriate to the Phenomena

(a) *Central elements of the shared background of any modern linguistic inquiry*

In human life we are typically presented with language in the form of sentences as utterances in speech or writing, each presenting itself to us as a structured whole and in a wider context.

As linguistic deliverances, sentences are structured in three ways: semantically, morphosyntactically, and phonologically. Through Leonard Bloomfield and Zellig Harris[12] we have been able to develop formal descriptions of

11. Von Humboldt spoke of the same power as being exercised in producing both thought and speech, both activities involving this "infinite use of finite means", in the key passage "Sie muss daher von endlichen Mitteln einen unendlichen Gebrauch machen, und vermag dies durch die identität der Gedanken- und Spracheerzeugenden Kraft". Here the thought and speech are spoken of in parallel as both things which are generated, not as the things which generate; Wilhelm von Humboldt, *Über die Verschiedenheit des menschlich Sprachbaues und ihren Einfluss auf die geistige Entwickelung des Menschengeschlechts* (Berlin: Königlichen Äkademie der Wissenschaften, 1836), 106; see facsimile of original edition, http://www.google.com/books?id=JflkAAAAMAAJ from *German Linguistics in the Eighteenth Century*, ed. Christopher Hutton (London: Routledge, 1994); cf. *Werke* 3: *Schriften Zur Sprachphilosophie*, ed. Andreas Flitner and Klaus Giel (Stuttgart: Wissenschaftliche Buchgesellschaft, 1963), 477.

Although the word *Sprachen* is also used to refer to different languages or "tongues" spoken by different peoples, mostly Von Humboldt treats *Sprache* and *Rede* and cognate verb forms as similar in meaning. Thus, in making the point that speech is not built up from words which have preceded it, but that the words emerge from the totality of speech, Von Humboldt uses *Sprache* and *Rede* with their cognates almost equivalently; see *Sprachbaues* (1836), 74–75. Peter Heath obscured this closeness of meaning in his translation of Von Humboldt, *Sprachbaues* (1836), in *On Language: The Diversity of Human Language-Structure and Its Influence on the Mental Development of Mankind* (Cambridge: Cambridge University Press, 1988), 70–71. Chomsky therefore seems wrong in regarding *Sprache* as analogous to his "competence" rather than to its exercise.

Moreover, Von Humboldt sees the creative and nonmechanical character of the way we generate thought and speech as what allows the maximal development of our mental powers satisfying the variety of demands made upon them, setting it in contrast with the quasi-mechanical character of practical activities; *Sprachbaues* (1836), 8–9; Heath, *On Language*, 26–27. This excludes Chomsky's conception of this generation as mechanical. For Von Humboldt children's language learning is nonmechanical, and morphology likewise, except for inflectional morphology; Heath, *On Language*, 58, 94, 102–4. He regards mechanical accounts of language as lacking actual application; Von Humboldt, *Sprachbaues* (1836), 328.

12. Leonard Bloomfield, *Language* (New York: Holt, 1933); Zellig Harris, *Methods in Structural Linguistics* (Chicago: University of Chicago Press, 1951), and "La genèse de l'analyse des transformations et de la métalangue", *Langages* 99 (September 1990), translated as "The Background of Transformational and Metalanguage Analysis", in *The Legacy of Zellig Harris: Language and Information into the 21st Century*, ed. Bruce Nevin (Amsterdam: John Benjamins, 2002), 1–15.

morphosyntactic structure, or "grammar"—that is, descriptions of how formally identified atomic lexical elements of a language are put together in regular ways to form sentences, the elements being lexical in being relevant to meaning, but identified formally (rather than semantically) through Harris's distributionalist methods—although such methods describe, not determine, the grammatical categories identified.[13] Roughly speaking, the ultimate constituents of utterances can be formally distinguished as the minimum units at a certain level to occur in a certain spread of combinations and, in these combinations, to constitute complete utterances. Such formally distinguished elements can be classified together as falling into categories according to the ways in which they can be combined. Elements are said to be in "syntagmatic" relations to contexts in which they can occur and in "paradigmatic" relation to elements which can be pitted into the same context. Sequences of such constituents are "formally" patterned insofar as these patterns can be described in "formal" terms.

Speaking in terms of the analogy between the type/token distinction which has to be made between, for instance, the twenty-six letter types in a typewriter and the unlimited number of copies or instances of these which typists may print in particular documents, Foley and Van Valin explain the sense in which those who study the grammars and lexicons of different languages are not concerned with performance in these terms: "They do not attempt to predict the actual *tokens* of speech events … the theories seem to describe the interactions of syntax, semantics and pragmatics in *types* of speech activities; they do not try to predict the occurrence of particular constructions in actual speech events".[14] Likewise they are not concerned with what may be conveyed in particular conversations and other interchanges arising out of the particular situations and private relationships and understandings between the particular participants, but only with the modes of speech and their significance so far as these are publicly recognizable within the relevant community sharing the language concerned. Yet, with this as their meaning, they would have done better to say that their concern was with the "structures of speech within a language" than with a "language-system".

The fact that there are many features of experience which we ordinarily discriminate without theory, but for which we need to use abstract or theoretical concepts in order to explain what we have discriminated, has often misled people. We commonly pick out particular aspects or kinds of aspect of these phenomena under various concepts according to some system, but this

13. These methods are conveniently described by John Lyons, *Introduction to Theoretical Linguistics* (Cambridge: Cambridge University Press, 1968), 70–72, 143–52, 182–83.

14. W. A. Foley and Robert D. van Valin, Jr., *Functional Syntax and Universal Grammar* (Cambridge: Cambridge University Press, 1984), 15.

does not make the phenomena described according to these concepts any less real, concrete, and actually occurrent. Therefore, when in a formal grammar we speak of sentences, words, and the like, these do not need to be thought of as "theoretical entities" belonging to an abstract system in the way which the influence of Chomsky has led many to do. "Sentences" and their elements as considered in grammar need not be considered as "theoretical constructs" formed according to the laws of a "language-system", but rather as the concrete entities we experience in speech and writing, considered in respect of certain of their aspects, and generalized about according to these aspects. As Saussure remarks, "Les signes dont la langue est composée ne sont pas des abstractions mais des objets réels"—that is, the sorts of things with which we meet concretely in speech.[15]

What it is meant by a linguistic entity's having real or concrete existence must not be interpreted overly simply. Aristotle observes that we cannot regard the pronounceable syllable "ba" as composed of two separately pronounceable elements "b" and "a"—but it does not follow that the phoneme "b" lacks concrete existence any more than quarks lack concrete existence. Again, in English the plural "-s" modifying words and realized in several different ways phonemically and in writing constitutes a different grammatical morpheme from the possessive phrase-modifier "-s", even though they are realized in the same ways phonemically.

Thus the developments in thinking from Saussure to Bloomfield and Harris in no way require any novel ontology whereby "sentences" and their elements as considered in grammar and lexical semantics are conceived of as abstract entities, "theoretical constructs" within a "language-system", entirely distinct from the concrete entities or objects we experience in speech, writing, and sign language. Rather they invite the conception that these studies are still concerned with these same concrete entities or objects, but concerned with them in each case in respect of only certain of their aspects and generalized about according to these aspects. It has been solely as a misconception under the influence of Chomsky that many recent forms of formal and functionalist grammar have presented sentences as if they were abstract objects within an abstract system, rather than as possible real utterances whose elements and structures are being given formal description, especially when they do not conceive this form of presentation as the most explanatory. Lexical Functional Grammar is one of several grammars of which this latter seems true.[16]

15. Ferdinand de Saussure, *Cours de linguistique générale*, ed. C. Bally and A. Sechehaye, 2nd ed. (Paris: Payot, 1922), 144.

16. Although Lexical Functional Grammar (Joan Bresnan, ed., *The Mental Representation of Grammatical Relations* [Cambridge, Mass.: MIT Press, 1982] took its name from the special role it gives to grammatical functions rather than from connection with functionalist conceptions of the Prague school, over

(b) *The Chomskyan blind alley contrasted with a more attractive approach*

(i) The novel perspective which artificially separates "language-systems" from language-use

Over the last fifty years a model of language as a code in a coding-decoding system, a tool for use in communication, has become standard in the public eye. This establishes a compartmentalization between, on the one hand, the study of the grammar and lexicon or dictionary of a language, its "language-system", and, on the other hand, pragmatics conceived as a matter of the human organism's relying upon this language-system as a tool in communication.

This system of compartmentalization has fixed itself in the minds of many linguists largely as a result of the long predominance of Chomsky's influence, the language-system being conceived as a system of generative formal grammar combined with a lexicon. Yet this system of compartmentalization depends for its plausibility on the system of grammar being conceived of as autonomous, and many of those proposing systems previously have had no reason to commit themselves to this doctrine of autonomy, since this only arose from Chomsky's conception of grammar as presenting an abstract model, not of language use, but of "competence" as a matter of neurological structures in the brain grounding human capacity for language. Apart from this view, it would seem a puzzle as to why the language-system, that is, the grammar and lexicon, of a language should be conceived separately from its use, in abstraction from our use of words and sentences as we meet this use in speech and worldly context, as if "autonomous" in any of the three ways Newmeyer has distinguished.[17]

---

the years the involvement of discourse-functions in Bresnan's exposition of the nature of different grammatical functions has become increasingly explicit, as in Bresnan, *Lexical-Functional Syntax* (Oxford: Blackwell, 2001), 9–10, 94–98, 304–7. Lexical entries include functional indications shaped by a semantic syntax which incorporates pragmatic elements, not primarily configurational indications. It thus combines formal and functionalist features; cf. Bresnan, ed., LFG Mailing List, September 1995, accessed September 4, 2010, http://web.archive.org/web/20050322002328, http://montague.stanford.edu/lfg, and www.essex.ac.uk/linguistics/LFG/LFG-and-functionalism/), and satisfies Van Valin's criteria for being "structural-functionalist" in his contribution "Synopsis of Role and Reference Grammar", in *Advances in Role and Reference Grammar*, ed. Van Valin (Amsterdam: John Benjamins, 1993), 1–164; see 2—that is, LFG is like Van Valin's RRG in regarding syntax as a vehicle of meaning as incapable of being described independently of semantics and pragmatic discourse factors, although not entirely determined by them.

There is no exact "formal"/"functionalist" divide. Christopher S. Butler, *Structure and Function: A Guide to Three Major Structural-Functional Theories* (Amsterdam: John Benjamins, 2003), 1:7, 30–31, 34–36, restricts his attention to Dik, Van Valin, and Halliday. Like William Croft, "Autonomy and Functionalist Linguistics", *Language* 71 (1995): 490–532, and Frederick Newmeyer, *Language Form and Language Function* (Cambridge, Mass.: MIT Press, 2000), 7–19, he fails to do justice to Susumu Kuno and Ellen Prince's perceptions of how function shapes form in their generative functionalism; see Susumu Kuno and Ken-ichi Takami, *Grammar and Discourse Principles: Functional Syntax and GB Theory* (Chicago: University of Chicago Press, 1993), and Gregory Ward, et al, "Ellen Prince" [Obituary], *Language*, 87 (2011): 866–72.

17. Frederick Newmeyer envisages an autonomy of syntax as a system embodied in human cognition

In Chomsky's conception the function of the grammar and lexical semantics is not to tell us about stretches or elements of speech or text and activities in producing, hearing, or reading such speech or text, but only about the state of our brain in virtue of which we are able to produce, hear, or read speech or text—for him, our linguistic competence. His concern is with the mind or brain and its states, and a grammar as giving an abstract model of this. Hence Lyons can say that "utterances never consist of such sentences, but of one or more segments of speech (or written text) which can be put into correspondence with the sentences generated by the grammar"[18]—expressing this by distinguishing the "system-sentences" generated by the grammar from the segments of speech (or written text) which correspond with them, calling the latter "text-sentences".[19] This convoluted way of thinking of "segments of speech or text" as corresponding with "system-sentences" (referred to by Chomsky as "abstract structures") is one which I examine in detail in section 4 of chapter III.

Chomsky's "biolinguistic" conception of linguistics as part of neurology is given its clearest explanation by Jackendoff in terms of grammar's providing language-geared "functional" descriptions of the relevant aspects of the organization and activity of the brain in what we may label a "neurological functionalism", as opposed to a "linguistic functionalism" geared to communication and the expression of thought.[20] In this way of thinking a generative grammar defines the morphosyntactic structure of sentences not as actual or possible utterances, but as constructs generated within a language-system, making both sentences and words or other lexical factors into abstract objects. Hence, for Chomsky, although in practice the primary test of the "descriptive adequacy" of a system of formal grammar lies in the conformity of the sentence-constructs generated by the system with the language-user's intuitions as to which sentential utterances are grammatical, nonetheless a sys-

---

whose primitive terms are nonsemantic and not discourse-derived syntactic elements combining according to principles which make no reference to system-external factors—where such a system need have nothing to do with language or cognition. He speaks next of an automony of "knowledge of language" ("competence") which can and should be characterized independently of language-use and of social, cognitive, and communicative factors contributing to use—yet no reason is given for judging such competence to have to do with language at all. He then speaks of the autonomy of grammar as a cognitive system, telling us that human cognition embodies the system whose primitive terms are particular to language, but whose principles of combination make no reference to system-external factors—yet, except that the primitive terms are said to belong to language, it is not clear why such a system should have anything to do with cognition, language, or grammar; Newmeyer, *Language Form and Language Function*, 23–24.

18. Lyons, *Introduction*, 176. In accord with this, he assigns the study of the use of types of utterance as they arise in particular types of context to pragmatics.

19. Lyons, *Semantics* (Cambridge: Cambridge University Press, 1977), 1:29.

20. Ray Jackendoff elaborates this conception in his *Foundations of Language: Brain, Meaning, Grammar, Evolution* (Oxford: Oxford University Press, 2002), 21–27, 34, 56, passim; cf. his earlier *Patterns in the Mind: Language and Human Nature* (New York: Harvester Wheatsheaf, 1993).

tem of formal grammar should be evaluated only as it confronts reality as a whole.[21] This involves that the system apply to the whole range of human languages, the brain's modes of handling language being presumed to be common to the whole human species.

It is Chomsky's preoccupation with the brain which underlies the attempt to frame autonomous system-internal characterizations of language and individual language-systems and explains why Haspelmath can contrast formal approaches to language as having the goal of a system-internal characterization of language with linguistic functionalist approaches as having the goal of understanding why language is the way it is.[22] Yet the possibility of a system-internal characterization of language depends upon the existence of "Internalized language". But, *insofar as formal approaches share this motivation, they are bound to frustration,* because, as I argue later, there can be no such things as Internalized languages as Chomsky conceives them, and hence no grammar independent of pragmatics.

Moreover, as later chapters show, one can readily conceive a formal grammar concerned with Lyons's "text-sentences"—that is, sentences at the level of language-use. Formal grammar has no need of this baggage of preoccupation with linguistic "competence" as a state of mind or brain occupied with context-independent sentence-models—let alone any need for a concept of "Internalized" language.

The conception that each grammar and language-system should be considered in abstraction from its use has only become predominant under the influence of Chomsky. However, his fixation upon this way of thinking only arose from his conviction that people are innately preprogrammed with the principles of a shared universal grammar, reflecting the ways in which the human brain functions, and that was the only way to explain the human capacity for language learning, given his argument from the "poverty of the stimulus". Yet this argument has been exposed to much recent criticism and, as we shall see in chapter VI, following the psychologist J. J. Gibson, rests upon a misconception of the notion of "stimulus".[23]

21. Here one senses the influence of Willard van Orman Quine's "Two Dogmas of Empiricism", *Philosophical Review* 60 (1951): 20–43, and of certain ways of speaking of mathematical models in physics.

22. Martin Haspelmath, "Why Can't We Talk to Each Other?" *Lingua* 110 (2000): 236, 239.

23. Chomsky's argument was originally published in his "A Review of B. F. Skinner's *Verbal Behavior*", *Language* 35, no. 1 (1959): 26–58. Geoffrey K. Pullum launched a direct attack on the argument in his "Learnability, Hyperlearning and the Poverty of the Stimulus", in *Proceedings of the 22nd Annual Meeting: General Session and Parasession on the Role of Learning in Grammatical Theory*, ed. Jan Johnson, Matthew L. Juge, and Jeri L. Moxley (Berkeley, Calif.: Berkeley Linguistics Society, 1996), 498–513; see also John D. Lewis and Jeffrey L. Elman, "Learnability and the Statistical Structure of Language: Poverty of Stimulus Arguments Revisited", in *Proceedings of the 26th Annual Boston University Conference on Language Development*, ed. B. Skarabela, S. Fish, and A. H. J. Do (Somerville, Mass.: Cascadilla, 2001), 359–70; Geoffrey K. Pullum and Barbara C. Scholz, "Empirical Assessment of Stimulus Poverty Arguments", *Linguistic Review* 19 (2002):

Chomsky's approach has no intrinsic attractions for psychology. The psycholinguist needs to discover how we get to formulate the meaning we intend and how we manage to interpret what another person says. To require a method of exploring the infinite quiver of context-independent sentence-constructs made available by a generative grammar in order to locate sentence-constructs with appropriate lexical meanings—an indefinitely long sidetrack—and then add a check for satisfaction of pragmatic constraints, as if the satisfaction of grammatical constraints had to be pursued prior to or independently of the satisfaction of pragmatic ones, seems an implausible model of utterance construction or interpretation.

The more attractive supposition is that it is through the practice of speaking and hearing speech, schooled through communication with those among whom we live, adapting to the features special to the language they speak at the time concerned, that we learn to speak in a way appropriate to our intentions in the relevant context. Then our utterances are shaped individually by the universal pragmatic and general logical constraints outlined later in this introduction, constraints operative in each act of speech. It is, then, the structures set by pragmatics and general logic which shape grammatical syntax, and perhaps thereby also shape some aspects of brain function, rather than vice versa.

In the development of each language there is much that is adventitious, and this has inspired an approach such as that of Hopper's "Emergent Grammar",[24] but this has the defect of obscuring the effectiveness of the constraints I mentioned in giving structure to any language and giving languages common features which they owe to function and general logic, and not just to history.

(ii) A rival approach which treats pragmatico-semantic structure as primary

It is intellectually much more attractive to develop an account whereby in human beings it is pragmatic and semantic constraints which shape grammar, leaving the human being to utilize the freedoms in thinking and inquir-

9–50; Florence Reali and Morten Christiansen, "Uncovering the Richness of the Stimulus: Structure Dependence and Indirect Statistical Evidence", *Cognitive Science* 29 (2005): 1007–28; Amy Perfors, Joshua B. Tenebaum, and Terry Riegler, "Poverty of the Stimulus? A Rational Approach", in *Proceedings of the 28th Annual Conference of the Cognitive Science Society*, ed. R. Sun and N. Miyake (Mahwah, N.J.: Erlbaum, 2006), 663–68. See Fiona Cowie's discussion of this issue in her attack on Chomsky's nativism in n. 67. The realization outside Chomskyan circles of a need for a more empirical approach is shown in the balanced discussion by Martin D. S. Braine, "Is Nativism Sufficient?" *Journal of Child Language* 21 (1994): 9–31.

24. Hopper, "Emergent Grammar", *Berkeley Linguistics Society* 13 (1987): 139–57, and his second paper "Emergent Grammar", in *The New Psychology of Language: Cognitive and Functional Approaches to Language Structure*, ed. Michael Tomasello (Hove, East Sussex: Psychology Press, 2009), 1:155–76.

ing which this framework leaves open. The result is that speech and thought conform to the kind of general logic which I outline in sections 4 and 6 in this introduction and later on in chapter IV. What is involved is the "broader logic" spoken of by Jespersen, as mentioned in section 6, with all its informality.

Gibson opened out a conception of the workings of the human sensory system according to which this never operates in isolation from human exploratory and other activity; as a result, the human sensory system becomes tuned in use in functional adaptation to the external environment. In chapters VI and VII I extend the same pattern of thought to the case of each human being's development of speech, and in this case the external environment which conditions the development will be the community of language users, sharing the same language, within which the child develops. It is within this setting that the only constraints on the functioning of the brain pertinent to the shaping of grammar will be pragmatic and semantic.

It has been objected that this would mean that all human languages would conform to the same grammar. However, quite the contrary, the pragmatic and semantic constraints of which I speak can be satisfied by a wide range of different types of grammar and are quite compatible with the enormous variety we find among human languages. Yet this does not leave a choice problem, as if each developing human being had to choose his or her own grammar and vocabulary—this would be perfectly useless in communication with others. Rather, each person's linguistic capacity becomes tuned by exercise in coordination with a particular community of language-users speaking primarily one particular language. Accordingly, each person's memory and processing capacity, so far as these are embodied in the brain and its functioning, will become themselves tuned; this will happen as it were incidentally as part of the person's overall linguistic skills being tuned to conform to the pragmatic and linguistic constraints of which I spoke. At this stage I merely sketch the view of which I give full account in the main body of the book.

(c) *The emergence of human transcendence*

The openness to intellect, involving the capacity for autonomous judgment to which I referred earlier, requires an extreme of malleability in the brain's modes of functioning, a kind of malleability scientists have begun to understand in discovering how parts of the brain adapt to different functions in different species and in human beings according to the calls made upon them, whether arising from mode of life or from injury to other parts.

Within psychology the approaches to perception and to the phonetic aspects of language acquisition which we find in Gibson, Stein and Meredith, Andrew Meltzoff, and others have in their different ways begun to show how the detailed modes of functioning of our brain, sense-organs, and whole motor and kinaesthetic system become shaped only in the course of our putting them to use. That is, to a large extent, it is our ways of using these systems which shape their modes of functioning, rather than these modes shaping our ways of using them. For this, of course, they have had to become biologically apt to be shaped to such modes of functioning, which will have depended upon relevant mutations and the processes of evolution.

It is my contention that when we come to language of the type found among human beings, this tendency has reached an extreme, and the brain and any other bodily apparatus subserving our use of language have evolved biologically in such a way as to become so malleable in their modes of functioning as to be open to the workings of intellect.

That is, these modes of functioning have become such as to be shaped by the semantic and pragmatic structures of our speaking and hearing, rather than themselves determining these semantic and pragmatic structures—except when some neurological or other bodily defect causes some defect in linguistic practice. Within this framework it is semantic syntax which shapes the role of particular "mechanisms" in the use of language—for instance, mechanisms for vocabulary structure and recovery, for the setting of inflections, and for other accidents characteristic of particular languages. Thus, overall, it is semantic syntax which shapes morphosyntactic structure at each stage of a child's development and thereby shapes the grammars of particular languages and so determines whatever kind of "universal grammar" there may be.

Among the higher animals we see a development of functional relationships between perception and behavior so as to allow the growth of signaling systems whereby the signals of one animal achieve desired effects on the beliefs or anticipations and behavior of other animals of the same cultural group. However, in the case of the human animal, this kind of development is taken to a further stage in which the way in which certain signals have certain effects is precisely by means of the communication of a content—that is, by the expression of a sense, something made possible by language in the sense in which this book is concerned. Language makes it possible for the content of the message being communicated to be expressed, enabling us to achieve the expression of its sense, the expression of a thought, doing this in such a way that this thought is something which we can bring into relation with other such thoughts and which can be the take-off point for deliberating as to its truth (or in the case of a command, whether or not to obey it) and for the formation of theories and the pursuit of further inquiries.

The arguments in favor of a functionalist approach in linguistics have given me steadily greater reason to insist upon the role of understanding in our use of language and the impossibility of explaining all linguistic processes in terms of mechanisms. This is a consequence of extending to language the holistic and teleological approach which Gibson applied to perception, and so envisaging language functionally in relation to a social environment of other speakers. It is always whole human beings—persons—which think and understand as well as speak and hear, not their brains or any other organs (which are only parts of human beings).

Linguistic understanding and thinking within human life always involve brain processes, but can never consist in them. Many lines of argument, including some from Wittgenstein, converge on the conclusion that a proposition, that is, a sentence of the kind that can be true or false, cannot "represent" or be "isomorphic" with what it purports to report. Equally, it cannot be isomorphic with any state or process in the brain. Equally also, the meanings of such sentences cannot be represented by any state or process in the brain. The same impossibilities Wittgenstein identified in the "picture theory" of meaning of his *Tractatus* also attend any theory in which sentence-meanings are isomorphic with some structure within the brain, whether the phrase "sentence-meaning" is understood in philosophical or in Chomskyan terms, as chapter VIII makes plain.[25] There can be no analogy between the structure of an expression of sense and the structure of a map or model, no analogy between the relationship between the parts of such an expression and the relationship between the parts of a map or model, and therefore no isomorphism between the structure of such an expression of sense with a state of the brain, any more than with any state or feature of the world. The unity of a sentence as the expression of a sense is like the unity of a thought; it is given its unity in the act of a person's expressing it, just as a thought is given its unity in the act of a person's thinking it, and is quite unlike the unity of a map or model. This unitary character of sentences as expressing a complete sense is reflected in the pragmatically shaped semantic syntax which shapes grammar in ways I consider in part three of this book.

When a person makes a judgment, this process or action is not mediated by "representations", whether in the brain or mind or in language, and the function of linguistic expression is *to express* such judgment, *not to represent* it or make it possible to picture it, and not to give it an isomorphic neurological embodiment. This is part of what puts the intellect in command or capable of autonomous judgment, for, as Aristotle says, the understanding needs to be

25. This therefore also stands as an objection to the isomorphism implied when Chomsky represents (I reproduce his phraseology) internalized language systems as generating derivations establishing a representational correspondence between context-free sentential lexical meanings ("Logical Form interpretations at a conceptual-intentional interface") and appropriate articulatory and perceptual performances ("Phonetic Form interpretations at the articulatory-perceptual interface"); Chomsky, *The Minimalist Program* (Cambridge, Mass.: MIT Press, 1995), 219.

"unmixed, as Anaxagoras says, in order that it may master its objects—that is, that it may know them. For the intrusion of anything foreign into it would interfere with this mastery or knowledge".[26] Contrary to Kant's conclusion that, analogously to the way that the sensory system shapes the objects of sense, it is the faculty of knowledge which shapes its objects; a psycholinguistics appropriate to the character of speech and language will clarify how it is possible that the objects of human knowledge can shape the human faculty of knowledge.

It is the way in which human acts of judging and understanding, lacking any isomorphism with any bodily process, exemplify the command of the intellect, not the determinism of the physical, in our linguistic expressions of judgment and understanding which provides our clearest demonstration of how human beings transcend the body. Thus, human beings, their intentional actions shaped by linguistically expressible deliberation and choice, are constituted as not just practical, but theoretical animals. Further, people's theoretical deliberation and judgment are, as we shall see, open in an indefinite variety of ways, an openness peculiarly well-exhibited by our use of language, in the informality and flexibility of the way in which we use words in reporting and describing, and the freedom exhibited in our capacity to use general concepts without being tied to just one model or paradigm. It is not the brain which gives structure to thought or dictates semantic structure, but pragmatics and the general logic and application of understanding which I delineate in section 4.

(d) *The unity of linguistics*

(i) Grammar, semantics, pragmatics, and logic have the same objects at the rank of sentence

What remains certain is that the first place where questions of grammaticality arise is in regard to past and prospective utterances—that is, real linguistic deliverances of the sort we meet with in daily life, whether in the medium of speech, writing, or sign-language, the very same things at the rank of sentence or above with which pragmatics is concerned, and likewise philosophy and logic (e.g., in discussing the adequacy of truth-conditions as criteria of the sense of propositional sentences and in considering the extended use of terms by analogy or metaphor). Chapters I to V show the irrelevance of the compartmentalized approach described earlier for the purposes of considering the actual problems of semantics, while part three shows its unhelpfulness in considering grammar.

26. Aristotle, *De Anima* 429a18–22.

In practice, when we speak, in formulating what we will say we typically have a topic and an area of interest in regard to it already settled in our mind, rather than proceeding entirely at random. Again, when we listen to others, either the context will already have made it clear what they are speaking about, or the concern of their question will help to clarify this. The tasks of formulating what we are going to say or of understanding what is being said to us are never ones which we approach as if our minds were, at any stage in the development of speech, like a blank slate or *tabula rasa,* as if children learned by experiencing sentences only as acoustic wholes and then in stages proceeded to analyze them. Rather, language-learning begins only in a context of social interaction which allows us to appreciate that what has been uttered is a linguistic communication as well as giving us some means of approach towards the understanding of what is being said, typically first by realizing what it is about or what question it is intended to answer.

Here, for the purposes of utterance interpretation, context is relevant to our appreciation, first of whether we are dealing with mere noises or with speech, and second, of sense or meaning at every layer of sentence-structure. Moreover, it is only through the actual hearing of speech and speaking that the structuring and tuning of human linguistic capacity takes place, a hearing of speech and speaking in situations where context is relevant both to sentence formulation and to sentence interpretation—structuring and tuning in several different respects, semantically, morphologically, and phonologically.

In the view I propose, wherever sentences and more extended stretches of discourse are concerned, pragmatics, grammar or semantics, psychology, and general philosophical logic are, all of them, concerned with one and the same linguistic objects—namely, either sentences considered at the level of use (i.e., as linguistic communicational expressions), or else more extended pieces of discourse or linguistic interchange including such sentences—all these linguistic objects being psychosocial realities within a natural and psychosocial environment. This holds whether the concern is with language acquisition or with our understanding and use of language in hearing and speaking, and whether the medium is speech, writing, or sign-language. The different branches of study consider the same objects, but each under a distinct aspect, abstracting from other aspects.

Thus the notion of sentence has never escaped its roots in the *logoi* spoken of by Plato and Aristotle, which included petitions, questions, and definitions as well as the true or false *logoi* called propositions (*apophanses*). In Latin *logos* was translated by the word *sententia,* as in the title "the Sentences," which is the common way of referring to Peter Lombard's collection of the "Sayings" (*sententiae*) of accepted authorities. Accordingly, it is unsurprising that the word "sentence" has been as much at home in philosophy and logic, where

Dummett and Davidson have followed in the path of such figures as Carnap, Tarski, and Ingarden, as in grammar, semantics, or pragmatics.[27] Yet the philosophers' understanding of the word is very distant from that of Chomsky and many linguists close to him, although the philosophers' remarks have not always kept this clear.[28]

(ii) The interconnections between "syntax", "semantics", and "pragmatics"

In the course of modern controversies, none of the terms "syntax", "semantics", and "pragmatics" have been used in just one meaning agreed by all linguistic theorists, let alone by all linguists and all logicians and philosophers.

If one separates pragmatics from semantics by defining pragmatics as the study of cases in which the "significance" or "sense" of an utterance is affected by special features of its context of utterance, the effect of such a definition is to jumble together a ramshackle assortment of things of utterly discrepant kinds—and there can be no science of such a jumble. For such "significance" or "sense" is affected by context within extended discourse, by features of the context of social interaction and custom, by other environmental facts, and in many structurally heterogeneous ways—for instance, context affects interpretation through affecting the phonetic identification of lexical items and their morphological structure, as well as through enabling us to interpret what would be grammatically ambiguous apart from its context, to identify the references to be attributed to names and demonstratives, and to recognize special idioms, plays upon words, and figures of speech through their appropriateness to the context. All use of language involves some dependence on context, and there is no nice "special-feature-free" area within which semantics is tidy, and therefore no neat division between semantics and pragmatics.

On the other hand, as we shall see in chapter III and the note to it, we must not make "pragmatics" something all-sufficient, lest we be left only with a theory of signals which influence the belief or behavior of others, as in Grice's theory of meaning. Talmy Givón's account, echoed by Terrence Deacon, has parallel consequences, leaving the key content-bearing terms unspec-

27. Roman Ingarden, *The Literary Work of Art* (Evanston, Ill.: Northwestern University Press, 1974), 106–25. The treatment of extended discourses which follows may diverge somewhat from mine.

28. In a most revealing sentence Dummett writes, "In a discussion of this sort, it is hard to retain lucidity while making due allowance, in one's formulations, for the phenomenon of indexicality, and I have preferred to aim at lucidity; thus my use of 'sentence' and 'statement' is very inexact," in a note to the first page of his paper "What Is a Theory of Meaning? (II)", 1 n2, in *The Seas of Language* (Oxford: Oxford University Press, 1993); first published in *Truth and Meaning: Essays in Semantics*, ed. Gareth Evans and John McDowell (Oxford: Oxford University Press, 1976). However, he has preserved readability at the expense of clarity, since the phenomenon of indexicality is only one of the many symptoms of the relevance of context to the sense of utterances or sentences as philosophers have to consider them, although the most conspicuous. Yet consideration of context is supposedly set aside in formal treatments of grammar.

ified meanings (corresponding to the figure, either the faces or the vase, in the Rubin vase illusion defined only by an external contour) so that they are defined only in negative terms.[29] For the essence of language lies in its semantic content, in what is to be found within the clause (core with periphery).

In this situation I use the terms "semantics" and "pragmatics" in the following ways. I take the semantics of an expression to embrace whatever belongs to its public significance in the context in which it is used—public, that is, either to all educated speakers who share the language concerned or at least to some open community of specialists (e.g., experts in the particular field concerned, within that general linguistic community), as opposed to any closed-circle meaning such as might be conveyed within conversational situations, job interviews, questionings by the Gestapo, and discussions in closed schools of scholarship. And when the term "pragmatics" is used without qualification, I regard it as an aspect of semantics, rather than something separate, picking out whatever is contributed to the public significance of an expression within a sentence, or a sentence as a whole, by its context of use, including all the kinds of disambiguation indicated earlier. By contrast, I speak of the "private" meanings special to closed groups, conversational situations, and the like and how they arise as the subject of what I call "private-circle pragmatics".[30]

The term "lexical semantics" is also highly ambiguous. It can mean the identification of the public discourse-significance of terms and phrases in the context in which they are used—that is, roughly in the sense deployed by David Alan Cruse in his *Lexical Semantics* of 1986, a lexical semantics of speech. However, many understand the term "lexical semantics" in such a context-independent way that, in the words of Herbert Clark, the "semantic content" of an expression is the mere "composition of the meaning of its parts"[31]—that is, what the philosopher John Austin called its "phatic" content.[32] Notably, Austin himself never spoke of meaning at this phatic level, a level beyond which Chomsky never gets.

The very idea that the meanings of clauses and phrases might be composed of the meanings of their words in the way that a sentence is composed

29. Talmy Givón, *Context as Other Minds: The Pragmatics of Sociality, Cognition, and Communication* (Amsterdam: John Benjamins, 2005) makes use of the figure/ground distinction as used in connection with perception, but his appeal to "abduction" does nothing more to supplement Popper's hypothetico-deductive narrowing of one's conception of how the object of study is to be understood than to supply illustrative examples; cf. Terrence Deacon, "Emergence: The Hole at the Wheel's Hub", in *The Re-Emergence of Emergence*, ed. Philip Clayton and Paul Davies (Oxford: Oxford University Press, 2006), 111–50.

30. Hopper and Traugott provide a helpful statement of the rather confused common usage of the terms "pragmatics" and "semantics" in *Grammaticalization*, 1st ed. (Cambridge: Cambridge University Press, 1993), 69; the original edition of 1993 reveals a picture more open in perspective than Levinson's view as adopted on 76 in the 2nd edition of 2003.

31. Herbert H. Clark, *Using Language* (Cambridge: Cambridge University Press, 1996), 172, 76.

32. John L. Austin, *How to Do Things with Words* (Oxford: Oxford University Press, 1962), 92.

of words, as if mental entities could be put together like an arrangement of qualitatively differing bricks, embodies a superstition involving what Ryle called a "para-mechanical" conception of mind, as if there were a mind-stuff. It involves a crude model, as if sentence-meanings were composed of word-meanings as molecules are composed of atoms or houses of bricks.[33] This superstitious model, involving a ghostly mind-stuff, constantly reappears in expositions of compositional theories of meaning and of the concept of "the language of thought".[34]

Section 3. The Role of Pragmatics in Semantics at Every Layer of Meaning within Discourse

The pragmatics which affects the "sense" or "discourse-significance", as I use the terms in chapter III, of a sentence is such that the semantics which the sentence has in itself is inseparable from it in ways which appear in chapters IX and X. The verb has a dynamic character lacking to the noun, and this is something intrinsic to what we say using verb and noun, even before we ask, "Is it so or not?" Yet this dynamic character is essentially connected with the role of sentences in communication and is something we can only explain by reference to pragmatics. In this and other ways pragmatics and semantics are inseparable.

Since we do not have any nonlinguistic mode of communication with each other such as has been attributed to angels, but learn to speak in a way adapted to a social environment, we should expect semantics to be shaped by pragmatics. Pragmatics shapes the objects at the rank of sentence and above with which grammar, semantics, and logic are concerned, giving sentences, as opposed to names, a dynamic character; we shall see its role at each layer within discourse.

Yet the relevant pragmatics and relevant semantics are inseparable. If we ask a question of the sort "Is so-and-so thus-and-thus?", commonly called a "Yes/No" question, we presuppose that the proposition about which we are asking whether or not it is the case is something, such as "the dog is barking", which is already structured, indeed is already possessed of implicitly verbal structure within which noun-like and verb-like elements are at least implicit. In this way sentences without negatives or interrogatives underlie sentenc-

33. This way of thinking had a strange modern pioneer in G. E. Moore, "The Nature of Judgment", *Mind New Series* 8 (1899): 176–93. Frege had a similarly open conception of *Bedeutung* in his earliest writings.

34. Jerry A. Fodor's modern conception in *The Language of Thought* (Cambridge, Mass.: Harvard University Press, 1975) presents a strange echo of Ockham's language of "Mental" (cf. n. 56) and G. E. Moore's idea of mental composition alluded to in n. 33.

es of more complex form and are presupposed in any questions we ask. The clause already has a content or sense giving it potential direction before assertion makes this actual.

(a) *The role of pragmatics in picking out sentences*

The vital importance of pragmatics or context to semantics is most obvious in our need to distinguish the superior ranks of discourse-unit (whether expositions and narratives presented in prose or verse, conversational, forensic and other debating exchanges, or deductive and other arguments) from the sentences which give them their specifically linguistic character as well as being what these expositions and narratives are composed of.

(i) **Pragmatic unity as the root of the semantic unity of a sentence**

The unity of a sentence qua speech-unit or linguistic deliverance is established at the level of the speech-act or linguistic delivery; in some sentences there are elements which are grammatically disjoint, and this arises with mature language-users, not only with children. The semantic unity of such sentences is established by their pragmatic unity. Their parts have a semantic syntactic connection, but no grammatical syntactic connection. Such sentences are still syntactic unities, but this unity is not grammatically marked.

Other examples of grammatically disjoint expressions are provided by vocatives and expressions like "Ouch!" when they introduce sentences as in "Ouch! It hurt", or as is done by "Lo!" and some imperatives like "Behold!" Vocatives are in no way dependents of the verb (unlike its noun complements and adjuncts), although they may provide a reference providing a "pragmatic anaphor" indicating the subject or being taken up later by a pronoun in the same way a pronoun may take up a reference from a previous sentence.

A conspicuous example of the grammatically disjoint is provided by so-called absolute phrases, such as "Vercingetorix having been defeated" in "Vercingetorix having been defeated, Caesar proceeded to his next plans", which I discuss in chapter XII and in chapter XIV, section 5 (c) (iii). Jespersen rightly rejects the view that they "stand outside the syntactic connexion".[35] But the syntactic connection is semantic, determined by the unity of the sentence at the pragmatic level established in the act of speech or writing, and not marked by concord, order, or connectives indicating subordination or coordination. In such cases, although we can regard the absolute phrase, like the clause which would convey the same information, as semantically adverbial to the main clause, there remains no concord between any element of the abso-

35. Otto Jespersen, *Philosophy of Grammar* (London: Allen and Unwin, 1924), 126–29.

lute phrase and any element of the clause to which it is adverbial. Such lack of morphosyntactic connection is characteristic of children's early utterances. I discuss other examples of the syntactically disjoint later.

Language-users tend to become uncomfortable with such dry stone masonry, and so in such contexts grammatical indications of the syntactic connection frequently develop, as when colloquial German introduces the preposition *mit* ("with") as a connective linking accusative absolute phrases to the main sentence or expresses nominative absolutes with *zu* and the infinitive instead of the participle, or most explicitly by expressing the matter by an adverbial clause, as in "after he had defeated Vercingetorix". Likewise, from the disjoint "Alas!" introducing a sentence, a new form like "Alas that he died" may develop.

(ii) Sentences as units of committed explicit utterance

The discourse analysis involved in picking out sentences involves our observing the synsentential nature of responses like "Yes" and "No" and the connective "Therefore, . . ."

Larger discourse-units often incorporate smaller ones. To say "Yes!" or "No!" in response to a question constitutes a speech-act, but only in the context of a question which gives the "Yes!" or "No!" content.

A cathedral is a cathedral even without a tower or a porch, and if a tower or porch is added it remains that the whole is a cathedral, but neither tower nor porch could have their character in isolation. Consider expressions such as "Yes", "No", "Certainly", "Perhaps", "Surely", "Phew!", "Alas!", and "What!". As these occur in discourse, they are "sentence-dependent", since they cannot occur in isolation.

In a quite different way expressions such as "Therefore, . . ." and "However, . . ." do not occur in isolation, but only because they occur as parts of the sentence containing them (not always as first constituent, since such words as "however" often occur as the second constituent in sentences). They do not add to or change the force of the sentence containing them, but indicate its situation in the stretch of discourse containing the whole sentential utterance. As speech reveals and rules of written discourse sometimes artificially conceal, it is clear that, in the respect we are considering, there are no distinctions of status between any of the following: "Therefore", "Hence", "However", "Moreover", "For", "So", "But", and "And". Some stylists avoid the use of the last four of these as the first words in written sentences.[36]

36. "For" can still, like the Greek *gar*, introduce a sentence, like the sign ∵, meaning "Because" found in mathematical texts, parallel to ∴, meaning "Therefore". In written discourse, sentence division is very much a matter of text-style. In order to move towards shorter paragraphs and still preserve the structure previously seen in long sentences, writers are compelled to upgrade key subsentential connectives to sentential

Therefore, it would seem that the most appropriate definition of "sentence" as a unit of linguistic deliverance is as a complete expression of sense which possesses force or a minimal unit of committed explicit utterance. Beyond this, it is easiest to proceed by example, recognizing statements (propositions), declarations of intention, promises, commands, requests, petitions, explicit wishes, and so forth as sentential linguistic deliverances or "sentences" in the sense we are seeking.

When some segment of speech occurs embedded and without force as a clausal constituent within a sentence proper, an utterance, we call it a clause because it is of a kind which would have been a sentence if it had occurred on its own (given any necessary morphosyntactic adjustment). Indeed, it has the potentiality to function as a sentence in contexts in speech closely related to the original utterance. Hence the symbol "S" as it occurs in the phrase structure diagrams of formal linguists should be replaced by "S_P" to mean "clause", as having this sentence-potentiality, to distinguish it from "S" for sentences, as complete speech-units.

In an oversimplification I imply later that Chomsky's Minimalist Program makes "all explanation" in grammar proceed in an entirely bottom-up direction, all grammatical restrictions rooted in the properties of atomic lexical elements. Yet this is inaccurate. One should rather say "all explanation up until the stage of 'Spell Out'", since it is only at the stage of "Spell Out" that something is ready for morphological, phonological, and, presumably, pragmatic alterations, making the sentence fit for its role in the expression of thought to oneself or communication to others. This hides the teleological character of "sentences" in formal grammar as geared to communication in committed utterances, unlike mere clauses.

(iii) Ambiguities in the notions of committed utterance and speech-act

Sentences and stretches of discourse can have various kinds of incompleteness, although, as a first approximation, a sentence would seem definable as the smallest complete unit of speech, and so to be defined in terms of its relation to speech-acts.

I make the committed explicit utterance "R" when I say "Therefore, R"; but the speech-act is incomplete inasmuch as it can only have been proper to say "Therefore" in the context which includes some preceding argument, so that that the "Therefore, R" has a kind of retrospective incompleteness. This

status. What in speech would have figured as a single flow and unity is liable to reappear in written form as many "sentences", with the pauses in speech which in earlier times would have been represented by a colon and semicolons reappearing in the guise of sentence beginnings such as "as follows:" and "First", "Second", "Third", and so forth, together with "Then", "Next", and such.

does not compromise the character of "R"—here occurring as the assertion of a categorical proposition.

By contrast, although to ask "Is it the case that P?" is to complete the speech-act of asking a question and make a committed explicit utterance, and to do this independently of whether any answer is returned; nonetheless the very sense expressed indicates an incompleteness, a waiting for the satisfaction of an answer. Again, to say "Suppose that P" is again to complete a speech-act (of posing an hypothesis) and make a committed explicit utterance, although here the speech-act itself has a prospective incompleteness, since its very sense and point depends upon one's having some actual disposition to go on, either by saying something like "Then, Q" or "Then, it follows that Q" or, at least, "Then, what will follow?" ("Therefore,..." had an analogous retrospective incompleteness.)

Further, both the question and the supposition additionally convey the suggestion, although not the implication, "Perhaps, it is the case that P". In this way they are rather like "If P, then Q", which by the very mode of its expression seems designed rather as an inference-ticket, licensing one when one is given the categorical information "P" to go forward to the categorical assertion of "Q". Likewise, to be told "P or Q" is in a way tantalizing, since, although it carries the suggestions that perhaps P and perhaps Q, it does no more than limit the field of possibility. In the kind of natural deduction described in chapter XIII, even such explicit negations as "It is not the case that P" and "Neither P, nor Q" are more like the definite closings off of a line of inquiry than advances to positive knowledge or completions of the particular inquiry concerned.

If these utterances and speech-acts have varying kinds of incompleteness, so much the more do assertions—"Perhaps P" and "It is possible that P"—expressing apparent uncertainty. Indeed, idiomatically, it is strange to describe them as asserting anything, let alone as committed utterances. This makes it unsurprising that expressions of modality of the kind called "epistemic" (as expressing degrees of uncertainty or certainty in knowledge, Greek *epistēmē*) should be regarded as one of the most superficial elements in the "layered" structure of a sentence—as its precise function is to express some degree of uncertainty or certainty in respect of the content of some judgement or statement. The clause expressing this content is inside the scope of the epistemic modal operator.

There seem to be no cases of epistemic modal operators inside the scope of indications of non-assertoric illocutionary force of a kind, as can be seen by considering the following interrogatives indicated by word order, as in "Are you going?"; performatives such as "I ask you: Are you going?", "With this ring, I thee wed" and "I bet that you don't beat Smith"; wishes such as "Would that I had not done that!" or "May things go well with you!"; orders such as "Go" or "I order you to go"; or promises such as "I will look after your son when you die", said to the man on his deathbed, or "I promise that I shall look after your son when you die". Therefore, it seems pointless to discuss whether modals or force-indicators are outermost in the layering of the sentence. A condition placed on the making of a bet is a condition on whether or not an act of a certain kind should be deemed to have been performed, and does not affect the kind of act concerned or express an epistemic condition.

For reasons which will appear, it is important that negation as it occurs in natural languages should be recognized as a core operator, an "internal negation", as Van Valin describes it,[37] and distinguished from various kinds of "external" or "second-order" negation, so that the Law of the Excluded Middle does not apply, as when an assertoric sentence is radically rejected because of its lack of any proper constructive meaning. This can arise when an existential presupposition is unfulfilled or a conditional has to be rejected, as we will see in chapter XIII, or some universal statement about a nonfinite set can be proved untrue, a case discussed in chapters II and IV.[38]

(b) *The character of the verb as what gives sentences and verb phrases their dynamic character*

(i) The "verbal" character of sentences as the root of their pragmatic role

The idea that a sentence *expresses* a sense or thought is emphasized in chapter I in order to make a contrast between linguistic utterance and mere signaling, considering the latter as the intentional causing of a belief or action, or at least influencing this, and doing it in a conventionally established way. To express a sense or thought, in terms of Plato's argument in the *Sophist,* is to say something, and to say something is not just to name it or offer a list of names, but requires a "saying" or *logos* (from *legein,* meaning to say, speak, or declare) involving an interweaving (*symplēkon*) of lexical factors of different kinds—in the cases we are most used to, an interweaving which includes at least the articulation together of a name, noun, or nominal element (*onoma*) with a verb or verbal element (*rhēma,* from the verb *rheō* or *erō* [infinitive *eirein*], meaning I speak, tell, or proclaim; the root of *rhētōr,* public speaker), such verbal elements having a "rhetorical" or "speaking" character. We have no expression of sense until our expressions form a nexus, which Jespersen compares to a process or drama, as opposed to a junction, which he compares to a picture;

37. This is to be distinguished from the "nuclear" or "morphological" negation exemplified in such words as "unclean" and "unnatural".

38. See chap. II, sec. 3 (b) (i), and chap. IV, sec. 2.

such a nexus typically contains a verbal element which makes it "living".[39] In Frege's terms, a proposition cannot consist only of complete expressions such as names for objects, but requires a verbal element with the kind of incompleteness or unsaturatedness required of expressions for concepts in order to glue the names together.[40]

We need a dynamic rather than a static conception of the sentence. My point of view can be dramatized by setting it in contrast with Steven Pinker's static model, in which the verb is the chassis onto which every other part of a sentence is built, expressing a static view more appropriate to the context of a language-system of context-independent sentences.[41] What is required instead is a dynamic conception of the "live" verb as the part of a sentence in virtue of connection with which other parts of the sentence have their direction, vigor, and role; as it were, the living heart in virtue of which blood and therewith life reaches other parts of the body; the life, or, in a Chinese conception, the energy or *qi* (sometimes written *chi*, and in Japanese *ki*) in speech, blockage of the flow of which destroys syntactic connection. These are more appropriate metaphors than that of the chassis, and the clue to their nature is provided by the notion of force. Such is the account which I develop with greater precision in chapters X to XIV.

In particular chapters IX, X, and XI show how the difference in character which Plato describes in terms of the difference between "saying", with its dynamic character, and naming is key to understanding the topic/comment, subject/predicate, and noun/verb distinctions. We shall see how this "saying" character carries over from the whole saying to the verb or verbal and, through the verb or verbal, gives life and structure to the rest of the sentence. This explains what is unexplained in other accounts. For instance, according to the doctrine of Chomsky's Minimalist Program, at each stage in the forming of larger structures the operation "Merge" is conceived as the "merging" of a "Head" with a "non-Head" in an operation which still preserves a hierarchy between the merged elements.[42] This hierarchy, its character, and why it is required needs explanation. This is one which hinges upon the subject/predicate or topic/comment distinction highlighted by Jackendoff.[43] In effect,

39. Jespersen, *Philosophy of Grammar*, 97, 114–16.

40. I give an informal explanation of the argument of Gottlob Frege, "Concept and Object", translated by Peter Thomas Geach, in *Translations from the Philosophical Writings of Gottlob Frege*, ed. Geach and Max Black (Oxford: Blackwell, 1952), 42–55.

41. Steven Pinker, *The Stuff of Thought: Language as a Window into Human Nature* (London: Penguin, 2008).

42. In this I summarize the relevant aspects of the discussion in Naoki Fukui, "Phrase Structure", in *The Handbook of Contemporary Syntactic Theory*, ed. Mark Baltin and Chris Collins (Oxford: Blackwell, 2001), 396–406, esp. 396–98.

43. Jackendoff, *Foundations*, 149–51, 252n11.

in every act of merging, the Head has a more verbal character than the non-Head.

It is the character of sentences in the sense I have outlined, as each the issue of an act of intentionally saying something, which gives a "saying" character to all such sentences, or, in modern terms, gives such linguistic deliverances what has come to be called "force" (Frege's *Kraft* and Austin's "illocutionary force"), and *at the same time* gives the verb or what is more verbal in function its special character as what gives structure to the clause, by contrast with the noun or nominal.

In chapter X, I explain how the force or rhetorical character of the sentence and its verbal framework are interdependent and how subordinate or unasserted clauses inherit the same verbal character in virtue of the nature of a clause as something which, if it occurred on its own or in the relevant sense "naked", would have force or proclamatory character in itself, without the addition of any other element.

It is the peculiarity of clauses that, whether they already occur as completed sentences in speech or writing or as sentence-constituents, in either case their sense is such that *if* they were to occur alone as complete linguistic deliverances in their own right, *then* they would have force, the kind of force appropriate to a clause of the kind concerned, and then this force would belong to their sense, giving them their "direction" as complete linguistic deliverances—in Wittgenstein's analogy, like arrows, but extending this analogy to everything Frege treated as having force, whether statements or questions, wishes, or commands. And it is this, I suggest, which gives clauses their special character and thereby also shapes the distinction between the verb or verbal framework and the noun or nominal, setting predicates and verbal expressions in contrast with phrases of a nominal character, even as they arise in clauses. Further, what I say of clauses extends to what is clause-like, as it makes no difference to the verbal character of the verbal element in the expressions concerned whether I say "the man who is eating a huge pizza" or "the man eating a huge pizza", or whether I say "It would be good that I should run fast" or "It would be good for me to run fast". That is, the relevant verbal character extends to participles and to infinitives, but not to gerunds and parallel lexical nominalizations.

It is in this way that pragmatics shapes semantic syntax, the syntax which in turn shapes the development of the forms taken by grammaticalization, both as languages take on their forms in which we find them at particular times and in children's language learning.

(ii) The role of pragmatics in understanding "root" modality, negation, and *wh*-questions

I have indicated the pragmatic character of what gives sentences a "saying" or "verbal" character and of their outer, illocutionary, or epistemic layers which situate them within discourse. These latter should be contrasted with structural features which have a pragmatic aspect, but are internal to the sentence as such.

As I remark in chapter XIV, section 1 (b), language contains many adjectives such as "strong" and "free" which are used non-modally and without verbal complements, but nonetheless call for clausal disambiguation (e.g., the person whose strength is in running may not be strong in weight-lifting, and vice versa, and there are some who are able to run, but are forbidden to do so).

It is here that we need the distinction between real or natural possibility and deontic possibility, each corresponding to different kinds of impossibility and necessity or necessitation. I might have the (natural) possibility of killing a certain person tomorrow, in the sense that it is within the scope of my natural powers and the means at my disposal, despite that (deontically) I could not do it because it would be wrong.

Real, natural, or cause-rooted possibility, impossibility, and necessitation have also been described as dynamic, metaphysical, or factual, and the various kinds of deontic possibility (permissibility), impossibility (prohibitedness), and necessitation (need or obligation, moral, legal, or prudential) also described as volitional or practical. Both these kinds of modality have been spoken of as kinds of "root" modality, to contrast them with the epistemic modality which represents a more external level of layering in propositional structure.[44] Negation can occur both inside and outside the scope of root modal and aspectual operators,[45] and this can arise even though negation can only be learned as a predicate or clause operator (here by "negation", I refer to negations which are neither second-order nor merely "morphological" or "nuclear", like "unwise" discussed in chapter IX).

In the case of both real and deontic modalities, there is a distinction between the time associated with the application of the modal operator and the time associated with what it is in respect of, and the first must always precede or coincide with the second—a time restriction entirely absent in the epistemic case. And, in both the real and the deontic cases, each of the two verbal expressions concerned can be negated with clear differences in the circumstances in which the resulting assertions would be true—as is particularly clear where real

44. Robert D. Van Valin Jr., "Functionalist Linguistic Theory and Language Acquisition", *First Language* 11 (1991): 7–40.

45. Van Valin, "Functionalist Linguistic Theory", 19–22.

or natural possibility is concerned. Thus at a certain time it was possible that I would get to New Zealand before noon of August 31, 2008, and at noon of August 31, 2008, it had already become logically impossible.[46] Likewise, statements about a particular proposed action that it *is* morally permissible, prohibited, or obligatory are nonsensical if made about past actions, although such statements about proposed actions were not nonsensical when the actions were still future (hence, in legal cases, retrospective legislation generates disputes).

Negation is a core operator, whether inside or outside the scope of such real or deontic modal operators, and when it has the scope of the whole assertion, the Law of the Excluded Middle applies for the reasons explained in chapter IX.

It in no way compromises the character of negation as a core operator that when a question inviting the answers "Yes" or "No" is asked, two kinds of presupposition are usually revealed, exhibiting the pragmatic or discourse-related aspect of the distinction between affirmation and negation, symmetrically placed in relation to these simple interrogative questions. Thus if one asks, "Was Homer blind or not?" one presupposes that there was such a poet as Homer, and such presuppositions of existence arise whenever what in logic would be described as a singular term is present. Likewise, the simple statement "Homer was blind" presupposes that Homer exists, and is "about" Homer. However, in another sense of the word "about", the statement is about or in regard to Homer's being blind, since the statement is in regard to or about that. So with simple questions and statements we should distinguish among the topic or topics between the topic as subject and the topic as the point of interest in regard to the subject discussed.

More precisely, if I ask, "Have you stopped beating your wife or not?" or "Have you started beating your wife yet?", although "you" are certainly the topic and the subject "your beating your wife" is presupposed as the point of interest in regard to the subject, since that you had previously been beating your wife or that you would start beating her sometime is presupposed, as well as the existence of both you and your wife. Nonetheless, the question is "stopped or not" or "started or not", not whether or not beating has ever or will ever go on.

Or I might ask, "Are you swimming slowly in order to win a bet?" Here I presuppose that you are in fact swimming slowly and ask whether this is deliberately motivated in a particular way. Various answers might then be given—that you were swimming slowly because you couldn't go any faster, because you were relaxing, because your life had been threatened if you swam fast, or in order to win a bet. All the questions and answers would in one way be

46. See David Braine, "Varieties of Necessity," 160–61.

about you whose existence is presupposed, and also about the activity again presupposed, but in regard to its motivation. Further discussion would reveal the part played by word order, stress, pauses, and intonation in differentiating topics from what the question is about. Words like "focus" and "concern" turn out to be as treacherous as the word "about".

In chapter XIII I indicate how the other main kinds of question, commonly referred to as *wh*-questions, also reveal discourse context as one of the keys to their syntactic analysis.[47]

(iii) The role of pragmatics in understanding content-bearing expressions

Pragmatics or context in the widest sense plays an indispensable part in the interpretation of sentences, not only in coming to bear upon their general character as verbal or speech acts and their outer and intermediate layers of structure, but also through coming to bear on the significance of their inner parts.

Thus context plays a part in enabling us to gauge the range of significance of some predicates, the relevant comparison being made when a certain term is used, and how the comparison is being made and at what level.[48] In scholastic terms, in considering an object—for instance, an Alsatian dog—we can make abstractions in many different degrees or respects, considering it as a dog, as a companion, as a guardian, as dangerous, as large (from this or that point of view or according to the range of objects being compared), as an animal, as a living thing, as an agent of some kind, as a real entity, not an abstract object, or as a subject of discourse; and it will be the context of discourse which guides us in identifying the range of comparison, and thereby derivatively how to gauge the sense of any simile or metaphor. It will be context that guides us in deciding whether the word "loud" is being used to make some comparison in sound volume or in garishness or the tendency to attract attention to itself by being in bad taste or objectionable. Again, a very different level of abstraction is being made when objects are described as lacking food or lacking a certain property, and in the latter case as to whether privation or mere negation is signified. Again, the word "inescapable" might be applied to a prison or a tiger or might be used as an equivalent to "inevitable" or "necessary". It has thus been

47. "*Wh*-questions" are referred to by many linguists accustomed to French and Latin as "Q-questions".

48. This is achieved, to express it in Talmy Givón's terms, through the shared knowledge and beliefs of those involved in the linguistic interchange, their shared and cooperative speech situation determining the significance of "I", "thou", "he", etc., "now" and "then", "this" and "that", as well as the intended reference of names, and their roles, perspectives and concerns, and the shared relevant background of the discourse concerned; Givón, *Mind, Code and Context: Essays in Pragmatics* (Hillsdale, N.Y.: Erlbaum, 1989), 74–76. Later he was to conceive this within the externalist account of meaning, context defining something as an outline defines a figure without expressing what is in it, in Givón, *Context as Other Minds*; see n. 24.

conceivable that, as some scholastics held, every "concept" (*species* or *eidos*) is first given in sense or some experience of the concrete, and that the associated words acquire wider use in ways which context allows us to identify, even coming to play wide structurizing roles in semantic and syntactic structure.

Section 4. Grammatical Structures as a Projection of Semantic Structures

(a) *The idea of semantics as shaping grammar or reflected by it*

I regard grammar as a projection of semantics. For, in the view I propose in this book, describing a sentence grammatically is somewhat analogous to giving the description of a two-dimensional projection of a three-dimensional field taken from a certain vantage point.

The photographic plate in a telescope, if it shows things as close together, presented two-dimensionally, tells nothing of their closeness in reality. Sometimes the things in the photograph are indeed close together in reality, as in a photograph of the cluster known as the Pleiades, but more commonly, as in a photograph of the constellations centered on Orion, the opposite is true: Sirius, Rigel, Betelgeuse, and Aldebaran as we see them are vast distances from each other. Groups of stars with quite different three-dimensional scatters can present the same two-dimensional projection if one views them from a certain standpoint. Analogously, sentences which are semantically heterogeneous can have the same morphosyntactic structure. For there to be grammatical descriptions of sentences is as natural as that there should be two-dimensional projections of three-dimensional fields.

The astronomer who describes the relative positions of stars in the sky without respect to their distance is not thereby speaking of alterations in photographic plates rather than of the stars. Likewise, the syntactician or grammarian describes not abstract grammatical objects called sentences generated within a "language-system", nor imagined objects of linguistic theory modeling structures of brain functioning, but the same utterances whose "sense" or "meaning" is familiar in speech, shared between speaker and hearer and translated by interpreters.

In order to have a projection of a three-dimensional system onto a surface, one has to take up a standpoint outside that surface. In the case of grammar, what we have is a projection of the array we call *parole* from the standpoint made available by the awareness of *langue* which we have in the very act of *parole*, somewhat analogous to the knowledge of how to kick exercised in the act of kicking a football. It is our awareness of such things as sentence structure, distinguishing between subject and predicate, distinguishing word-forms and the like which enables us to discern grammatical structures. But these are not objects of direct attention or of intention in the act of *parole* itself, any more than knowing how to kick is attended to in kicking a football.

(b) *The principal argument for the priority of semantics*

Sometimes there are two spheres, each the subject of study of some apparently well-identified human science, and on examination there appears to be a systematic conformity between the laws operative within one sphere and those operative within the other. The question then arises as to whether the laws or uniformities witnessed in the first sphere are to be explained in terms of their being caused or grounded in the laws and principles operative in the second sphere—or whether it is the other way around. Thus, for instance, Kant inquires as to why there is apparently such a necessary conformity between the laws and types of relation found among the objects which we experience, think about, and regard as in some sense real and the laws and types of relation which obtain among the concepts in terms of which we think about these objects—concepts which carry with them some principles which present themselves to us as necessities of thought.

My present concern is with a different case of apparently necessary conformity—namely, the conformity between the more general grammatical rules applicable to utterances, spoken or written, within this or that particular language and the more general semantic principles such as we locate in logic, taking the word "logic" in a very wide sense—what I call "general logic". Here, by "grammatical rules", I do not mean such "principles" as are referred to in what Chomsky preferred to call "Principles and Parameters Theory", but the "syntax" we meet in received grammars of particular languages—Kennedy's *Revised Latin Primer*, Hammer's *German Grammar and Usage*, or Grevisse's *Le Bon Usage*, to take random and disparate examples.

In 1957 Chomsky observed:

> There are striking correspondences between the structures and elements that are discovered in formal grammatical analysis and specific semantic functions. None of the assertions of (117) is wholly false: some are very nearly true. It seems clear, then, that undeniable though imperfect correspondences hold between formal and semantic features in languages. The fact that the correspondences are so inexact suggests that meaning will be relatively useless as bases for grammatical description. Careful analysis of each proposal for reliance on meaning confirms this.[49]

49. Chomsky, *Syntactic Structures* (Berlin: Mouton de Gruyter, 1957), 101. The proposals instanced on page 117 are of a maximally simplistic kind—e.g., explaining the subject/verb distinction in terms of the actor/action distinction.

In part three I establish that, on the contrary, if one avoids Chomsky's overly simple descriptions of both "what is discovered in formal grammatical analysis" and "semantic functions", careful analysis has the opposite effect to what Chomsky supposed.

(i) General semantic structures—"general logic" and what belongs to it

By "general logic" I mean something which encompasses modal, causal, and temporal distinctions and relations, the distinctions and relations expressed by such words as "possible" and "necessary", "because", "before", "after", and "while", as well as some of the connections reviewed in chapter IV.[50] General logic identifies the distinction between kinds of predicate or verbal phrase according to what the grammarians now label "aspect". This is something recognized at different points by Aristotle,[51] namely, the need to distinguish (a) states from actions and passions, and among the latter between (b) continuous activities not needing an end (e.g., thinking), (c) ones directed to achieving an end (e.g., building a house), and (d) acts or events complete in themselves (e.g., noticing something or winning a race)—a fourfold division codified by Vendler in terms of states, activities, accomplishments (including all processes), and achievements (commonly called acts).[52] It also distinguishes between bodies and surfaces and between surfaces, lines, and points; it includes a theory and calculus adequate to deal with different types of magnitude (i.e., to deal with the magnitudes of different types of thing which we compare in respect of their magnitude)—first, individuals and collections, distinguished by having a least partition, presumed by Aristotle to have a natural number as their measure of magnitude;[53] second, continua, distinguished by having no least partition, and measured by relations involving reference to spatial distances and temporal movement;[54] and third, moral, intellectual, and

50. Cf. Geach, "Some Problems about Time", in *Logic Matters* (Oxford: Blackwell; Berkeley: University of California Press, 1972), 302–18, esp. 311–16.

51. Theoretical grammatical study tends to dissect what schoolbooks call "tense" into "time", "aspect" (whether the verb expresses action continuing, completed, at a moment, customary or frequent, or expresses a state), and "mood". However, the dogma that these features are all separable in the grammatical representation of a sentence, each marked by distinct morphemes, while "voice" (active or passive in the schoolbooks) is to be treated transformationally or by "movement", is quite unrealistic; see chaps. XI and XIV of this volume.

52. Zeno Vendler, "Verbs and Times", *Philosophical Review* 56 (1957): 143–60; cf. Vendler, *Linguistics in Philosophy*, Ithaca, N.Y.: Cornell University Press, 1967), drawing upon Aristotelian ideas traceable in Gilbert Ryle, *The Concept of Mind* (London: Hutchinson, 1949), and Anthony J. Kenny, *Action, Emotion and Will* (London: Routledge and Kegan Paul, 1963).

53. The natural numbers are those we count with—positive, whole, and finite—as opposed to negative numbers and zero, fractions and all the irrational real numbers, and any infinite or nonstandard numbers mathematicians have imagined there might be; cf. chaps. II and V of this volume.

54. Such an account will envisage no need to distinguish between an individual and the unit-set containing it alone, and will consider membership of a collection as a particular case of inclusion in a class. With

emotional states which have no numerical measure, but only order of magnitude. In all this it constitutes a systemization of the logical structure, most of which Aristotle laid out in his *Categories*, *Physics*, and *Metaphysics*—setting aside his syllogistic system of term logic and his more particular views of natural causation.

When I speak of modal distinctions and relations, I mean to cover all of three very different things—namely, (a) real or natural modality; (b) deontic or prudential possibility, relevant to morals and planning, and to both prohibitions and permissions (including specialized applications to law, e.g., "You can keep silent by your right under the Fifth Amendment"); and (c) epistemic or judgmental possibility such as is expressed by "It is possible that the enemy has been here already", in which what is concerned is what our existing state of knowledge or inquiry leaves open, as opposed to what it is certain is not the case.[55]

In each of the three cases we get the coordination of the kind of possibility concerned with the different respective kinds of impossibility and necessity, related respectively to natures and causes (reflected in the causal "because"), to grounds or reasons for knowledge or belief (reflected in the "because" and "therefore" of reasoning), and to laws governing action and ends offered as reasons for action or desire (reflected in "for the sake of" and "in order that"). Attempts have been made to formalize rules in each area; thus in Polish logic, Lewis and Langford, Prior, Kenny, and others, we have seen various adventures in modal, tense, "deontic", and "imperative" logic; and, one should suppose, if a right view were ever attained in each, the resulting structures, along with the rest of general logic, would all be embraced within an adequate linguistic semantics.[56]

Linguists show cognizance of all these distinctions and many others,

---

a class we have something which is made up of discrete items and which therefore has a least partition, and what is expressed is the relation of these least parts or units to the whole. By contrast, lines, as continua, include the sub-lines within them as parts and have no least partition, since points should not be considered as parts of a line, but divides between two sub-lines ("cuts"); cf. chap. II of this volume.

If nothing moved there would be no basis for judgment as to whether space was continuous or discontinuous; but since continuous movement does appear to take place, both space and time must be continuous. All other continua—for instance, velocity, acceleration, forces, and gravitational, electric, and other fields—are compared in size numerically by virtue of some relation to some kind of movement which makes such comparison possible. Theories about the kinds of infinity possessed by the kinds of numbers concerned are at most an ancillary part of this general logic.

55. I fully explained these distinctions in "Varieties of Necessity" in 1972, where I labeled these types of necessity and possibility respectively "Factual", "Judgemental", and "Volitional" as determining or affecting respectively the facts, the judgment, and the will—in this antedating the distinctions made independently by Montague, developed by Dowty, and drawn on by Van Valin; cf. n. 57 in this chapter.

56. Fodor conceives such a general logic as reflecting and dictated by a "language of thought", or "Mental"—as if adding an inner language with the same structures as the outer languages would do anything to explain the structures of the latter; see Geach's criticism of such ideas, in discussing Ockham's inner language, in Geach, *Mental Acts* (London: Routledge and Kegan Paul, 1957), 100–105.

albeit in diverse ways. Thus Foley and Van Valin attempt to build Vendler's distinctions into Role and Reference Grammar (RRG) along lines suggested by the semantic syntax developed by Montague and Dowty,[57] while Jackendoff, with a different way of thinking, nonetheless regards them, along with the distinctions marked by different spatial prepositions, as all equally embodied in the language in which we think about the world.[58] Van Valin considers the predicate/argument distinction and the differentiation between noun-like arguments with a direct relation to the predicate and noun-like expressions linked to it only peripherally to be firmly based in evidence available to the learning child; and that the child also learns to appreciate differences in the aspect of verbs before indications of time, and learns distinctions of "root" modality (both "dynamic" or cause-rooted and "deontic") before learning the language of epistemic modality as he or she reflects upon other statements.[59] These are all distinctions in discourse which arise directly from the exigencies of our engagement with the world and our need to communicate about it rather than from a system we impose upon the world. It seems plain that to regard principles arising from them as contingent empirical truths learned by a blind Humean extrapolation from observed cases to all cases is as mistaken as Mill's view that arithmetical statements are empirical generalizations—predicate and the other notions concerned are equally empirical and a priori, in this like the elementary notion of number. To ascribe these notions and principles to a general logic as things known *through the understanding* as it deals with worldly phenomena is neither to introduce a rationalist innatism nor to impose on the phenomena a structure not adapted to them.[60]

(ii) Principal argument stated

Now, in most of their writings, Chomsky and others sharing his formal conception of grammar seem to suppose that the most general features of a grammar, besides being recognizable in other languages so as to constitute

57. Foley and Van Valin, *Functional Syntax*, 36–74; David Dowty, *Word Meaning and Montague Grammar* (Dordrecht: Reidel, 1979); and Richard Montague, *Formal Philosophy: Selected Papers of Richard Montague*, ed. R. H. Thomason (New Haven, Conn.: Yale University Press, 1974).

58. Jackendoff, *Semantics and Cognition* (Cambridge, Mass.: MIT Press, 1983), 161–211, tried to integrate these distinctions with the ideas about spatial prepositions developed in Jeffrey S. Gruber's PhD diss. (MIT, 1965), incorporated in Gruber, *Lexical Structures in Syntax and Semantics* (Amsterdam: North-Holland, 1976), and John M. Anderson, *The Grammar of Case: Towards a Localistic Theory* (Cambridge, Cambridge University Press, 1971). However, when Jackendoff refers to the structures he has identified as "not a spatial metaphor", but "an abstract organization that can be applied ... in any field" (*Semantics and Cognition*, 210), what he has in view is the way in which descriptions of spatial states, movements, sources, paths, and destinations provide metaphors for describing states and actions in general.

59. Van Valin, "Functionalist Linguistic Theory", 14–17; cf. Butler, *Structure and Function*, 2:402–4.

60. Cf. Ryle, "Mowgli in Babel", in *On Thinking* (Oxford: Blackwell, 1979). Ryle's thinking is reflected in Simon Blackburn's idea of a "homely interpreter" in Blackburn, *Spreading the Word* (Oxford: Oxford University Press, 1984)—the innatism of Chomsky's *Cartesian Linguistics: A Chapter in the History of Rationalist*

what he calls a Universal Grammar, are given to human beings innately. As such they are supposed to constitute a datum, a preestablished framework, enabling children to learn language more expeditiously, and presumed to be established in the neurological structures governing brain activity in speech and writing.

However, this instantly raises the question as to WHETHER, ON ONE ALTERNATIVE, it is due to the operation of some principle equally foreign to grammar, semantics, and pragmatics (e.g., the Darwinian principle of natural selection applied to the efficiency of nervous systems in allowing useful adaptations such as assist clear communication and the capacity for reflection), OR WHETHER, ON THE SECOND ALTERNATIVE, it might be that the semantic and pragmatic structures dictate the grammatical ones so that the supposition of a neurological base is redundant and conformity to the most general grammatical principles identified is a consequence, first, of the conditions set by interpretability (what is audible being assisted by gesture and appropriate intonation) in respect of the structures set by the general logic I delineated, and second, of the conditions required for interpretability in circumstances rendering communication liable to be ambiguous (whether because of obscurities of context and intention such as arise in written communication or in other ways).

IT MIGHT HAVE BEEN IMAGINED THAT THERE IS A THIRD ALTERNATIVE—namely, that grammatical structures dictate the most basic semantic or logical principles. However, if the roots of grammar lie in neurology and not in something homogeneous with pragmatics and semantics, this suggestion is absurd for reasons I now explain.

In the parallel case in epistemology, Kant's alternatives were (a) that objects and concepts corresponded by accident, (b) that the concepts were necessarily determined by the objects, or (c) that the objects were determined or shaped by the concepts. He adopted option (c). Yet the correct option is (b). Kant rejected this on the grounds that we could not know it to be true even if it were so, but in fact examples reveal how objects determine concepts.[61]

However, in the present case we do not seem to have this third alternative, corresponding to the Kantian view, but only the first two, because the third would involve that, for instance, the laws concerning the relation of singular, existential, and universal propositions and all the related propositions stating the relations between numerically definite quantifiers (i.e., between the differ-

---

Thought (Christchurch, New Zealand: Cybereditions, 2002; first published 1966) had been ridiculed beforehand in Wittgenstein, *Philosophical Investigations*, trans. G. E. M. Anscombe, parallel German-English edition (Oxford: Blackwell, 1953).

61. Cf. David Braine, *The Reality of Time and the Existence of God* (Oxford: Oxford University Press, 1988), 239–45; cf. 257–62.

ent natural numbers) should be determined by facts about the brain; but this would seem to be a flight of fancy, wild except to the most extreme idealist. The idea that truth in natural arithmetic is determined neurologically appears wild enough. But if the same were the case with logic, then there would never be any reasons for belief, but only causes.[62] And in that case there would be no reason for any belief whatsoever—not only no reason for belief in substance or personal identity or any other of Hume's fancies of the mind, but also no reason to credit argumentation giving primacy to grammar.

To summarize, if we are presented with a stark choice between grammar dictating basic semantic structures or basic semantic structures dictating grammar, it is only the latter option that is credible. The only way in which the fundamental structures of speech can be "native" or innate is by their being dictated by the very structure of the activity of communication itself and by our understanding of the world so far as it is given in the general logic to which I refer. That is, the only nativism in regard to language which is credible is a semantic nativism—that is, semantics incorporating elements of pragmatics as I have described, not a grammatical nativism—granted that there is some correspondence, some link or other between grammatical and semantic concepts and principles.

Thus in its general structures grammar is essentially a formal projection from semantics. Semantic considerations suffice by themselves to explain how it is that grammatical structures are determined (and this may dictate that, to certain classes of language, something like one of the proposed systems of formal description will apply). There is no need to postulate an innate neurologically dictated mental faculty to explain morphosyntactic structures as if they were independent of semantic syntax. For reasons that will emerge, the semantic starting point gives the speediest access to an explicit grasp of the fundamental concepts of grammar and to the rationale underlying grammatical rules and principles—it being remembered that semantics also sets the underlying constraints on how any particular language can be learned.

Historically it will be found that the penetration of the grammar of each individual language has been achieved by means of semantics and pragmatics helping us distinguish word/lexeme/morpheme, recognize morphological structures and see ways of analyzing large families of utterance along parallel lines before we go on to recognize the formal similarities between different families of utterance within the individual language concerned.

62. A belief may be caused, and coincidentally the cause may be a correct judgment that the belief follows by valid reasoning. But unless there is at some stage a perception of the reasonableness of assessing such judgments to be correct, there will be an infinite regress of causes for such assessments without knowledge or justified assessment ever being reached. Otherwise we have not knowledge, but only, perhaps, convenient convention.

(iii) Types of fundamental semantic category

The general logic I spoke of earlier is liable to contain some framework or categorial concepts which form a closely knit structure centered around the notion of individual substance as a thing or person capable of acting or being acted upon. Let us group this first group of concepts as ones centered on the concrete, such as causal property, nature and natural kind, and place; act, activity, process, or state (these four being distinguished according to their relation to time), then time itself; and, related to time, continuous change and rate of continuous change in respect of anything continuously measurable. However, this general logic is also liable to contain framework or categorial concepts forming a second group liable to arise in connection with any subject-matter, concrete or abstract—namely, singular topic, general topic, predicate, number, or set, together with second-order concepts of which it may be disputed whether they belong only to grammar or also to logic (e.g., the names of grammatical functions and such morphosyntactic categories as noun, adjective, verb, and adverb). This second spread of concepts are ones which I call "topic-neutral" or "topic-universal" in part one.

The fuller account I put forward in part three of this book shows that many of the reasons given for supposing certain grammatical categories and principles to be innate and autonomously rooted (perhaps reflecting the functioning of the brain) melt away upon examination. What sets limits to grammar lies in semantics—not a semantics of signaling or of representing, but a semantics of "*saying*" or, more precisely, "speaking"—a semantics whose framework is set by pragmatics.

As to fundamental semantic categories, I see them as conditions of our functioning as linguistic animals, but not in a Kantian way as if they were dictated by some accidental adjustment ("module") of mind or brain function arising by an accident of nature, issuing from some conspiracy of the survival of the fittest with convenient mutations and cooperation between genes. Rather, they arise in the act of the social, language-using animal engaging with the world, exercising its understanding in communication and engaged in thinking with the world. The structures described in the general logic to which I referred earlier arise in the act of exercising understanding, arising directly from the need for this communication and thought to be functionally adapted *both* to the realities encountered *and* to the requirements of communication, our capacities "tuned" in the way suggested in chapters VI and VII.

(c) *The controversy between semantic and grammatical nativism*

In espousing a semantic nativism with only semantic structures and concepts considered innate to human functioning when explaining grammar, instead of the grammatical nativism preferred by Chomsky and the psycholinguist Pinker, I take the same view as my brother, Martin Braine. For both of us, the semantic distinction between argument and predicate has always underlain all other syntactic distinctions internal to the clause, and thereby any grammatical expressions of these syntactic distinctions. The argument/predicate distinction still belongs to semantics, even if it has to be explained in terms of its connection with the pragmatics of complete utterances in the way I make plain in chapters IX, X, and XI.

The most obvious reason for distinguishing between semantic and syntactic categories, innate or not, has always been the obvious noncorrespondence among even the most general nonformal semantic categories, such as "actor", "thing", "event", "place", and "time" and the syntactic category of "noun".[63] However, this noncorrespondence is readily explained by reference to the links between the concepts of noun and of possible subject or topic.

Moreover, as Aristotle was the first to realize, it is impossible to understand the character of different semantic categories without reference to the way expressions for them enter into semantic syntactic structure. First, there are the ways in which, in connection with every subject-matter, abstract nouns can be generated in the same ways from discourse which does not contain them, but contains only predicates of which they are nominalizations of one of the kinds reviewed in chapter XII. Second, there is the structured array of ways in which designations of actions, events and states, places and times, and the measures of various continuous quantities arise in connection with concrete subject-matters. However, there is no semantic category of object, the nature of whose instances can be understood except by grasping their semantic structural situation within a verb-centered framework. In part three I renew the argument of this introduction and show how it is the verb which dictates the structure of the rest of the sentence (including the structure of clauses) and how a verbal framework is involved in setting the structure even of children's initial linguistic utterances.

Accordingly, since the logicians' idea of "object" or "entity" reflects the idea of "singular subject", it is natural for the central focus of dispute between the semantic and the grammatical nativist to be on the notion of subject, a

63. Succinctly shown by Jackendoff, *The Architecture of the Language Faculty* (Cambridge, Mass.: MIT Press, 1997), 33–36. The mistake involved in treating events as semantically on a par with substances is shown in chap. XII, sec. 2 (b) (ii)–(iv) of this volume; the relevance of the semantic hierarchy of logical categories to grammar is seen in chap. XIII, secs. 1 and 2 (b).

constant in the description of languages in most or all grammatical theories. Yet, although it is difficult to give a satisfactory explanation of what the different uses of the term "subject" have in common, even within syntax alone, I go some way to achieve this end in chapter IX, as further developed in chapter XI.

One traditional tendency has been to see the root of the conception of subject as in the semantic ideas of agent and experiencer, and Schlesinger envisages a process of extension through "semantic assimilation", extending at each stage through an appreciation of family resemblance to new types of case until the early semantic category of subject "grows" into the category of grammatical surface subject.[64] Pinker likewise treats the example of agent as paradigm, but presumes that the child possesses the formal grammatical categories from the start so that, in what he calls "semantic bootstrapping", some small number of semantic clues are needed, but only in order to get the way the whole formal grammatical system applies correct once and for all at the very start.[65] He uses criteria derived from Lexical Functional Grammar to justify regarding the category of "subject" as coextensive with what traditional grammars have counted as subjects. He regards the sameness in the way we are inclined to treat the term "subject" in connection with many very different languages as vindication of the rules set by Lexical Functional Grammar, just as Chomsky might regard his success in the same respect as vindicating the grammars he has suggested. Pinker remarks that such correlation between languages is unlikely to arise again and again in historically unrelated languages unless there is some property in the minds of the speakers of those languages that causes one of the correlated properties to trigger the rest. Thus the Pinker of 1984 joined the Chomsky of 1957 in taking grammatical categories and functions to be possessed innately because imposed by the ways our brains function, ways of which formal grammar should provide a model—whereas I take both to be ultimately rooted in my "general logic", in this transforming and extending the application of "semantic bootstrapping".

Yet, in their accounts of language learning, psycholinguists, whether grammatical nativists or semantic nativists, join in sharing the presumption that "already-acquired rules or patterns are used to analyze new input"—what Martin Braine labeled the "old-rules-analyse-new-material principle" in his key discussion "What Sort of Innate Structure Is Needed to 'Bootstrap' into Syntax?"—that is, into the syntax which we mark morphosyntactically.[66]

64. I. M. Schlesinger, "The Origin of Relational Categories", in *Categories and Processes in Language Acquisition*, ed. Y. Levy, I. M. Schlesinger, and Martin D. S. Braine (Hillsdale, N.J.: Erlbaum, 1988), 121–78.

65. Pinker, *Language Learnability and Language Development* (Cambridge, Mass,: Harvard University Press, 1984).

66. Martin D. S. Braine, "What Sort of Innate Structure Is Needed to 'Bootstrap' into Syntax?" *Cognition* 45 (1992): 77–100, in a view he repeated within a wider discussion of methodological problems in psychology in "Is Nativism Sufficient?"; cf. chap. XIII, nn. 5–6, of this volume.

However, this principle makes the hypothesis of grammatical nativism, itself open to objection from within psychology on the grounds I stated earlier, entirely redundant.[67]

For once this principle is granted, if one has the phrase structure rules and semantic flags necessary to deal with "The dog bit the cats", then the principle will at once suggest a parallel analysis of "The situation justified the measures". In extending the application of this analysis in order to interpret the speech he hears, the child has thereby formed a wider conception of linguistic subject, going beyond the extension of such concepts as "agent" or "subject of concrete attribution" and forming a functionalist concept of grammatical surface subject, roughly coextensive in application with that of subject term in traditional logic. And, as I mentioned earlier, this will not be a concept limited to the concrete, since the pragmatic roots of the subject/predicate distinction provide the foundation for the capacity to generate the further semantic categories of abstract topic as shown in chapters XII and XIII.

At the same time the child will have formed the concept of noun, a grammatical category roughly correlative with the maximally general logical concept of "expression for the argument of a predicate or for the kind of such argument" (one should note that the concept of what is eligible to be such an argument is one which the logicians, commonly using the word "object", have long ago shown to be not containable within any formalized logical system). Developed in a more detailed way, my brother anticipated, such an approach would make it unnecessary to postulate innate grammatical categories. Instead, in order to explain language learning, it suffices to have certain semantic categories as innate and, when meeting new ways of speaking among adults, to apply the "old-rules-analyse-new-material principle".

Let us be clear. On either view grammatical and semantic categories will not coincide in how they apply, and even when they do correspond, they will be defined in different, albeit (I suggest) related ways. What my brother argued and I also argue is that for the purposes of explaining language learning, there is no need to suppose two sets of innate categories, one semantic and one grammatical—innate semantic categories are quite enough.

He was from the first anxious to insist that his view did not involve a discontinuity from a stage at which syntax is ruled solely according by semantics to a stage at which syntax is ruled solely according to morphosyntactic ("grammatical") rules.[68] In the adult use of language pragmatics and seman-

67. Cf. Cowie's well-reasoned critique of Chomskyan nativism in *What's Within? Nativism Reconsidered* (Oxford: Oxford University Press, 1999). Fodor criticized Cowie in "Doing without What's Within: Fiona Cowie's Critique of Nativism", *Mind* 110 (2001): 99–148, to which Cowie gave full reply in an e-symposium at http://host.uniroma3.it/progetti/kant/field/cowiesymp_replytofodor.htm, accessed September 4, 2010.

68. This dilemma, as to whether in language acquisition it is grammatical structure or semantics which

tics play a large part in the following of grammatical rules, while grammar remains pregnant with semantic suggestion.

My brother's inquiries were cut short by his death, leaving a wide range of pertinent matters undiscussed.[69] His approach suffices to explain children's acquisition of grammatical functions and categories bestraddling abstract and concrete subject-matters, although he did not explain children's acquisition of the semantics of the abstract vocabulary which arises by the generative processes I review in chapter XII. I refer to the processes by which, from forms of sentences in which the relevant expressions occur predicatively, other sentences may be formed in which these expressions or lexically related noun-forms occur as abstract subjects—processes of abstraction to which Frege's "contextual definitions" of directions and the natural numbers in his *Foundations of Arithmetic* have suggested one possible approach.

Section 5. The Novelty of Chomsky's Conception of Formal Grammar

(a) *The wide attractiveness of Chomskyan linguistics*

Until 1950 there had been no clear basis for the development of any systematic mathematical approach to language, let alone bringing linguistics into relation with psychological or neurological studies. Behaviorism in psychology seemed barren in approaching linguistic phenomena, and philosophers and logicians offered little hope of initiating such development.

Into this vacuum Chomsky's new avenue of approach appeared as something of a revelation of what might be possible, only becoming widely known with the appearance of his *Syntactic Structures* in 1957. It soon became evident that his approach had two aspects: linguistic and psychoneurological.[70]

---

comes first (the semantics incorporating various functional distinctions, including that of topic-subject and predicate, along with further distinctions between predicates), was resolved by my brother, Martin Braine, in favor of semantics, *vide* "Modeling the Acquisition of Linguistic Structure", 217–59, in *Categories and Processes*, ed. Levy, Schlesinger, and Braine, 250; paper available in manuscript from 1983. He gives reason for rejecting the idea that this involves a discontinuity between a stage in child development at which semantic structure is primary and a second, separate stage at which grammatical structure becomes determinative of how we speak; Martin Braine, "Modeling the Acquisition", 251–52.

69. I argue in detail in chap. III of this volume that an element of pragmatics is integral to semantics and, in chap. XI, I take the pragmatic notion of "discourse topic" as key to our use of the word "subject". My brother took a different view, at least in regard to the notion of "subject" in English; see chap. XI, sec. 2 of this volume. This was never discussed between us.

Again, it is only recently that my views of how to approach "if" have come close to his—see chap. XIII, sec. 6 (c). Previously I had grouped it with modal and related expressions such as "because", therefore having three corresponding types of use.

70. Because of the dominance of behaviorism in psychology in the 1950s, Chomsky was initially reticent as to the concern with psychology inspiring his linguistic ideas, made public in argument only after

On the linguistic side his school of approach to grammar has been held together by his constant capacity to develop a succession of theories, all preserving the same original leading ideas. The "Standard Theory" of his *Aspects of the Theory of Syntax* in 1965 was extended by adding the hypothesis of a common (X-Bar) structure for all phrases headed by nouns, verbs, adjectives, or adpositions (prepositions or postpositions) treated as having the same structure and by recognizing thematic roles (Agent, Patient, Recipient) in the '70s. After the resulting Government and Binding theory of the '80s had received successive extensions, by 1987 Chomsky came to name the integrated account "Principles and Parameters" theory, human languages differing not in their principles, but in the settings of the various parameters they prescribe. Finally he considered these theories superseded in his Minimalist Program of the '90s. At each stage, where he led, others suggested variations that kept the same leading ideas.

Chomsky's personal convictions, that human languages would turn out to share a universal grammar and that this explained the rapidity with which children learn language, were always grounded in his belief that the study of grammar is the study of an aspect of brain function, and this justified his formal approach to grammar. For him the roots of syntax, just as much as of phonetics, lay in biolinguistics. The structures involved arose biologically through some series of mutations in the course of evolution, perhaps originally subserving quite different functions, but at a second stage coming to subserve a new function (or "exapted").

Both the early Bloomfield and Chomsky held to some form of atomistic psychology, in accord with Bloomfield's striking remark, "As language is in its forms the least deliberate of human activities, one in which rationalizing explanations are most grossly out of place, linguistics is, of all the mental sciences, most in need of guidance at every step by the best psychologic insight available".[71] Both the early Bloomfield and Chomsky were influenced in their thinking by a sense of the need to distinguish structures in principle universally shared within the human species from the material and accidental in language.[72] Yet there is a strange contrast between Bloomfield's conception of psychology as guiding linguistics and Chomsky's tendency to view systems of theoretical linguistics as models to guide thought and experiment in psychology. The a priori tendency in Chomsky's thought is seen in the conception

1960. Thus, in *Syntactic Structures*, 50, he presented the idea of a universal grammar only as a methodological tool, even though its importance for psychology was already a key element in his thinking; see n. 87.

71. Bloomfield, *An Introduction to the Study of Language* (New York: Holt, 1914), 323.

72. In speaking of universal accessibility or sharing in this book, all my remarks should be understood in a way which makes allowances for immaturity, impairment from disorders of various kinds, and limitations in ability, as well as the practical lifespan available for thought.

in his Minimalist Program of what it is for a language system to be perfect,[73] which is in stark contrast with the conception I presented in section 4.

In this "bottom-up" compositionalist and atomist ideal of a "bare structure" phrase theory, all grammatical restrictions stem from the grammatical properties or "features" of the basic lexical factors (referred to as "symbolic elements" or "lexical items"), these lexical factors being specifiable in formal ways independent of semantics and pragmatics. Supposedly the features of these atomic building blocks rigidly determine the formation of grammatical sentences from the bottom up according to a humanly universal system of computational derivation,[74] while their meanings rigidly determine the lexical meaning of the sentences which ultimately result. Supposedly these basic elements with their features, together with this system of derivation, correspond to physical elements and systems of physical functioning within the brain, all as yet unidentified, as "genes" were once unidentified.

If this ideal were attained, explanation would proceed in an entirely bottom-up direction so that all grammatical restrictions would be rooted in the properties of these atomic lexical elements. Such a system of explanation leaves no room for anything corresponding to the informality in the use of lexical factors of which I have spoken. The perfection of language in this way of thinking consists in being completely mechanical in operation and in having such an economy as to involve no linguistic structures intermediate between the atomic elements and the resultant sentences, no intermediate structures such as "deep structure". In this way Chomsky came to conceive perfection in a language-system in terms of conforming to an ideal of mechanical economy—mechanical in Turing's mathematical sense, rather than in terms of its being perfectly adapted to the linguistic communication of meaning or to integration with pragmatics.

By contrast, in my own conception presented earlier, a language-faculty will be "perfect" if the brain is sufficiently malleable in its modes of functioning as to set no structural limits on linguistic communication beyond those set by our capacities to articulate and discriminate sounds, singly or in combination. At the level of meaning the only structural limits on linguistic communication will be ones arising directly or indirectly from semantics and the pragmatics of communication.

The effect of his methodology was to drive Chomsky in the direction of this formalized, mathematically mechanical ideal so as to seem to fulfill the vision Roman Jakobson spoke of as "a spectacular *rapprochement* between linguistics and mathematical thought" in the 1950s and '60s, seeking

73. See Chomsky, *Minimalist Program*, 9.

74. Involving successive applications of Select, Merge, and Move operations in prescribed ways.

a description of the "universal invariants" to be revealed in comparing different languages and uncovering how, "amid infinite diversity, all languages are, as it were, cut from the same pattern", ideas anticipated by Leibniz and Helmholtz.[75] Roman Jakobson's idea of mathematizing grammar yields the possibility, granted a lexicon adapted to the grammar, of also, for instance, mathematizing translation. And if grammar must be formalizable, it should be possible to program a machine—a "computer"—to produce a pedantic translation of a series of sentences from one language into another, without, of course, being able to understand either, let alone to assess their truth. Chomsky has thus been the father of a great project, although up to now it has been grammars of different inspiration that have brought what success we now meet with.

However, the primary inspiration of Chomsky's own thought was never mathematical as such, but rather a metaphysical conviction that any universal features of human grammars must have a biolinguistic explanation—in particular, explanation in terms of the neurological functioning of the human brain, with an anticipation that such neurological explanation would be capable of a digitalized model.

(b) *The misconception of an "Internalized language"*

In conceiving linguistics in biolinguistic terms as providing language-geared descriptions of the relevant aspects of the organization and activity of the brain, Chomsky and others came to consider grammar and semantics as concerned only with a supposed "Internalized language" within the mind or brain, belonging to a speaker's "cognitive faculty", and not with any externally observable "Externalized language".[76]

This second development worsens the situation created by compositionalism by representing grammar and semantics and, in Jackendoff, some aspects of pragmatics, as concerned only with an Internalized language, or I-language, within the mind or brain, as if linguistics or biolinguistics were concerned solely with the inner. In chapters VI to VIII, I demonstrate that this Cartesian abstraction of the Inner from the Outer or external cannot be sus-

75. Roman Jakobson, "Implications of Language Universals for Linguistics", in *Universals of Language: Report of a Conference Held at Dobbs Ferry, New York, April 13–15, 1961*, ed. J. Greenberg (Cambridge, Mass.: MIT Press, 1963), 208–10.

76. Strictly speaking, for Chomsky an I-language is such a state of the language faculty and internal to the individual (it is presumed, internal to his brain) and therefore a theoretical entity whose existence depends upon the validity of some Cartesian style division between inner and outer. However, in his informal expositions (e.g., Chomsky, *Minimalist Program*, 6, 15, 132; and Chomsky, *New Horizons*, 26, 69, 118–19), it has a chameleon-like existence as at one moment this theoretical entity in an individual's brain and in the next identified with his idiolect or "way of speaking", which might seem more like a "natural" or even public object.

tained in psychology and violates key insights and often recurring arguments of philosophers, from Aristotle and Aquinas onwards, and notably the whole school of so-called linguistic philosophers, as influenced by the later Wittgenstein, Ryle, Austin, and, in some cases, Merleau-Ponty. The Cartesian supposition that man is composed of an immaterial bit (the mind) along with a load of physical bits, the bits interacting with each other, constitutes the minimal departure from a purely materialistic "atomism"—and to present these as the only alternatives is to depart from the obvious logical possibility that the entities dealt with in physics, biology, or psychology might be of such a nature as to require descriptions of a logically "holistic" character (e.g., because they required accounts of causal agency, animate or inanimate, or holistic explanation). Charles Taylor, like Stuart Hampshire influenced by Merleau-Ponty, has been one of many who have shown that there is nothing intrinsically nonempirical in irreducibly teleological and therewith holistic forms of explanation. In his book *The Explanation of Behaviour* he attacks behaviorism in psychology, using arguments which tell equally against mechanism.[77]

There is no logical or methodological necessity forcing us to accept the "atomistic" presumption that the road to understanding things as they really are is by explaining the behavior of wholes in terms of the nature, relations, and behavior of their parts. One does not have to regard "holistic" approaches explaining these latter partly by reference to the character and behavior of the wholes only as exigencies forced upon us by lack of calculability in deriving chemical truths from their underlying physical basis and our ways of knowing the phenomena—a form of what is called a "weak emergentism". The alternative, that the understanding gained through "holistic" approaches, perhaps incorporating or allowing an atomistic account of some subordinate elements or features, alone conforms to the real nature of the living entities concerned, is logically just as possible. This is Aristotle's position, according to which it is impossible to understand the parts of living beings in the full range and character of their behavior without reference to the wholes, and impossible to understand the wholes without reference to the parts, and, in this, our mode of understanding reflects the real nature of the living beings concerned. This does not involve any causation from future to past, referred to in a piece of spectacular confusion by Terrence Deacon in terms of an "appearance of time-reversal" and a "creating something from nothing".[78] However, it does involve giving status to agent-causality alongside or underlying event-and-state causality.[79]

77. Charles Taylor, *The Explanation of Behaviour* (London: Routledge and Kegan Paul, 1964).

78. Deacon, "Emergence", 119.

79. Contrary to the tendentious account given by Deacon in "Emergence", 119.

There is no incompatibility between understanding human nature in a holistic way and regarding some aspects of speech as conforming to certain formal norms of which a mathematizable study may be made. Analogously, the laws of propositional logic upon which we draw informally in daily life are formalizable within a mathematical system which is complete and possesses a decision procedure for deciding whether a formula is valid or not. However, our knowledge of the validity of these laws is quite independent of this formalizability, while equally this formalizability detracts nothing from this validity. Mathematics is neutral, open to being applied within the human sciences just as readily as within the natural sciences, and the notion of being mechanical belongs to mathematics rather than to physics. Some people have thought that all human linguistic behavior will be ultimately found to conform to patterns which are digitally simulable (mechanical in the mathematical sense). In chapter V we shall see this view to be demonstrably wrong. But even if there were such conformity, it would not be the basis of the good status and validity of intuitively intelligible forms of explanation and linguistic study already well established in the human sciences and already valid in their own right.

Although Chomsky officially disowns any "metaphysical" materialism or physicalism, it does seem that his presumption that, unless one is to set a gulf between man and all other animals and within man between body and mind, any explanation of linguistic phenomena must be rooted in man's biological nature. This means for him that its only ontological realizations must be of an ultimately physical kind, for this is what the unification he speaks of as the ultimate goal in science involves.[80] This appears as the effect of his view that a properly empirical or scientific approach must be "naturalistic", explaining this as follows:

> A naturalistic approach to the mind investigates mental aspects of the world as we do any others, seeking to construct intelligible explanatory theories, with the hope of eventual integration with the "core" natural sciences. Such "methodological naturalism" can be counter-posed to what might be called "methodological dualism", the view that we must abandon scientific rationality when we come to study humans above the neck (methodologically speaking), becoming mystics in this unique domain, imposing arbitrary stipulations and a priori demands of a sort that would never be contemplated in the sciences, or in other ways departing from normal canons of enquiry.[81]

Yet in the same work he had presumed that we can speak of "mental aspects of the world" and "the human mind", loosely picked out as spanning such things

80. Chomsky, *New Horizons*, 106–7.

81. Chomsky, *New Horizons*, 76, cf. 75–85, on the difficulties of defining in what this "naturalism" consists.

as the "visual system, reasoning, language, etc.", without more precise delimitation, although sometimes speaking of the "intentional" and other times of the "intensional" in quite undefined senses; and he then treats it as an empirical hypothesis in considering all these that "the brain ... is the relevant organ", as if one can simply assume that it is possible to consider language separately from speech and the hearing of speech, sight separately from eye and head movement and exploratory activity, and the brain and nervous system as operating without interdependence on other systems within the body. This is surely to build a metaphysics into one's method from the start, not to proceed empirically, disregarding pertinent empirical argument indicating the opposite.[82]

Yet the obscure description quoted above of what he regards as "nonempirical" and as alien to "methodological naturalism" has no bite unless it excludes the presumption that mental states or activities involve some kind of self-awareness, even only retrospectively, and excludes any irreducibly teleological explanations, unlike supposedly merely ad hominem "folk-psychology". Although he may disown a general philosophical doctrine of "mechanism", his account of his own assumptions presumes that all brain activity and human activity are to be accounted for in terms of mechanisms, and his whole methodology is directed towards a model of derivation which is mechanical in Turing's mathematical sense.[83] His statement that it is "not the business of sciences to express the content of ordinary discourse about anything" is a lame excuse covering any deficiency.[84] I give my own account of the proper place of mechanisms in psychology in chapters VI and VII, explaining the ambiguity of the word "mechanical" in chapter V.

(c) *The spread of existing dissent among linguists*

In earlier times it was presumed that all natural languages would be found to share a common grammar, because grammatical structures reflected structures established at the semantic or logical level. Partly because such a universal grammar was expected to conform overly closely to models suggested by such languages as Latin, English, and French, this presumption came to be

82. Alan Shewmon, "The Brain and Somatic Integration: Insights into the Standard Biological Rationale for Equating Brain Death with Death", *Journal of Medicine and Philosophy* 28 (2001): 457–78; and Shewmon, "Is 'Brain Death' Actually Death? An Autobiographical Conceptual Itinerary", *Aletheia* 7 (1996): 1–34, which is extended in Shewmon, "Recovery from 'Brain Death': A Neurologist's Apologia", *Linacre Quarterly* 64 (1997): 30–96.

83. This appears when Chomsky refers to "some set of mechanisms (what we may call his 'language faculty')" in his introduction to *The Logical Structure of Linguistic Inquiry* (New York: Plenum, 1975), 9, which then proceeds to specify a mathematically mechanical model of the kind of generative grammar which is the goal of his method (*Logical Structure*, 113–399). His presumption that there will be "mechanisms" appears in Chomsky, *New Horizons*, 17–18 passim.

84. Chomsky, *New Horizons*, 91.

thought of as imperialistic and non-empirical. Except for reflecting some pragmatic, experiential, and phonological constraints, there would seem to be no a priori reason why grammar should show any universal features. And this seems to have been the background of Bloomfield and Harris's approaches, reflected again in some recent remarks of Martin Haspelmath,[85] rightly conceiving grammars as to be discovered by direct inquiry into the working of particular languages at particular times, considering them as far as possible without preconceptions, in the way pioneered by Franz Boas and Edward Sapir.

(i) Weaknesses in empirical backing

Because of his a priori supposition that human language learning would be impossible without a biolinguistically rooted universal grammar, Chomsky has never shown much interest in the empirical evidence for the existence of a universal grammar such as was put forward by Greenberg in 1961.[86] In the 1950s, when he first conceived his leading ideas, he saw little profit in the psychology he found and thought the engineering models available too underdeveloped for it to be useful to use them to test any psychological hypothesis relevant to language. He therefore held that a linguistic theory should look for empirical support only, first in its capacity to explain the data provided by adult intuitions as to what is grammatical and what is not, the descriptions of sentences filtered according to the primitives of the system (perhaps through a system of distributionalist analysis), and second in capacity to explain how children are able to learn to speak grammatically.[87]

Yet Chomsky does suppose that his methodological ideas will ultimately be supported by the results of their application, and suggests that his ideas of modularity have some recent empirical support in the studies of certain individuals.[88] Yet, within psycholinguistics, psychologists such as Steven Pinker and others have tended to find the structures of Lexical Functional Grammar

85. Haspelmath, "Pre-Established Categories Don't Exist: Consequences for Language Description and Typology", *Linguistic Typology* 11 (2007): 119–32; and earlier in Haspelmath, "Parametric versus Functional Explanations of Syntactic Universals", in *The Limits of Syntactic Variation*, ed. Theresa Biberauer (Amsterdam: John Benjamins, 2008), 1–29.

86. Greenberg, "Some Universals of Grammar with Particular Reference to the Order of Meaningful Elements", in *Universals of Language*, 58–90.

87. Chomsky explains why he initially presented his theory as justified primarily in terms of the methodology of linguistics in his *Syntactic Structures* of 1957 and his writings of 1955–56, as published in 1975 in *Logical Structure of Linguistic Inquiry*, 55–373, rather than in terms of his convictions of its role in psychological explanation, also in *Logical Structure of Linguistic Inquiry*, 9–13, 35–40, 45, and the introduction, which was written in 1973. The importance of the relevance of linguistic theory to language acquisition for his way of thinking became public from the early 1960s onwards in Chomsky, "Explanatory Models in Linguistics", in *Logic, Methodology and Philosophy of Science*, ed. Ernest Nagel, P. Suppes, and A. Tarski (Stanford, Calif.: Stanford University Press, 1962), 528–50; Chomsky, *Aspects of the Theory of Syntax* (Cambridge, Mass.: MIT Press, 1965).

88. He makes particular allusion to Jeni Yamadam, *Laura: A Case Study for the Modularity of Language* (Cambridge, Mass.: MIT Press, 1990), and the study of "Christopher" by Neil Smith and Ianthi-Maria

(LFG) much better adapted to the purposes of explaining language acquisition and development than those of Chomskyan grammars. From the way Pinker and others treat examples, this does not seem unrelated to the original idea of Joan Bresnan in developing LFG that it should have a greater degree of "psychological reality", not in Chomsky's sense of correspondence to neurological processes, but in being better adapted to understanding the cognitive processes involved in actual language-use or performance so far as we have some awareness of them accessible to conscious reflection, and not just in the preconditions of language acquisition.

Moreover, as we shall see, Chomsky's approach to grammar involves a treatment of the lexicon which does not fit the flexibility of natural languages and does not commend itself even within the field of grammar itself. There the systems he proposed earlier grew in extravagant complexity, making them decreasingly attractive in respect of both descriptive simplicity and explanatory power, while his Minimalist Program has made his position ever more distant from such empirical data as we have.[89]

We shall see in chapter XIII that it is the pragmatics of discourse which guides us in parsing complex, many-claused sentences. However, although pragmatics makes the lack of any formal procedure for parsing sentences less important in practice, it is a weakness of Chomskyan grammars that, designed solely for the generation of sentences, they provide no guidance as to the placing of adjuncts, whether in generating or parsing sentences. But parsing is what people need when they hear, read, and interpret what is said, and for this purpose Gerald Gazdar devised his Generalized Phrase Structure Grammar, which influenced Ivan Sag and Carl Pollard in developing their Head-Driven Phrase Structure grammar (HPSG).[90] It is notable that it is not Chomsky's configurational approach, but LFG in conjunction with Optimality Theory and HPSG which are conspicuous for their concern with machine translation, and even before that with accommodation to natural language.[91]

Tsimpli, in "Linguistic Modularity: A Case of a Savant linguist", *Lingua* 84 (1991): 315–51, as well as presuming the helpfulness of the earlier computational-representational (C-R) approaches without any supporting evidence of relevance, either to modularity or to grammatical study as such.

89. Cf. Pinker and Jackendoff, "The Faculty of Language: What's Special about It?" *Cognition* 95, no. 2 (2005): 201–36. They also indicate uncertainty as to whether in the Minimalist Program, with its "principles of economy," such as of "greed", "procrastinate", and "last resort", and the requirement of choices of optimal derivations from among sets of possibilities, we have a properly "formalizable" theory at all.

90. Gerald Gazdar, "Phrase Structure Grammar", in *The Nature of Syntactic Representation*, ed. Pauline Jacobson and Geoffrey K. Pullum (Dordrecht: Reidel, 1982), 131–86, papers presented at Brown University, Providence, R.I., May 1979; cf. Ivan Sag, "A Semantic Theory of 'NP-Movement' Dependencies", in *Nature of Syntactic Representation*, ed. Jacobson and Pullum, 427–66; and Gerald Gazdar, E. H. Klein, Geoffrey Pullum, and Ivan Sag, *Generalized Phrase Structure Grammar* (Oxford: Blackwell; Cambridge, Mass.: Harvard University Press, 1985).

91. Joan Bresnan and Judith Aissen, "Optimality and Functionality: Objections and Refutations", *Natural Language and Linguistic Theory* 20 (2002): 81–95, provides some insight into how, rather than having a

(ii) Nonconfigurational languages and languages with different functional structures

In 1968 Dik had seen that there could be functional parallels or equivalences without corresponding parallels in constituent or morphosyntactic structure and vice versa,[92] which was later to inspire his Functional Grammar as developed between 1978 and 1997.

In this he prefigured the leading idea in Lexical Functional Grammar (LFG) developed by Joan Bresnan from 1978 and consolidated in the principles set forth by her and Ronald Kaplan in *The Mental Representation of Grammatical Relations* in 1982. This particular system has the special interest, whose consequences I remark later, that it can be conceived of in two very different ways. First, it fulfills the criteria for being a formal grammar. However, second, as a result of introducing various functional concepts (of which subject and object are the best known) as primitive terms, it can also be conceived of as a model of language at the level of language-use—that is, at the level of speech and discourse. For, as primitive terms, these functional concepts, undefined within the formal system described in 1982, can be given informal definitions external to it, such as that, as the language has been grammaticalized, the subject is the argument to the verb which serves as default topic within the clause.[93] (In grammar the term "argument" is borrowed from mathematical logic to refer to the nominal dependents of the verb.) There is nothing novel in the primitive concept of a mathematical system being given informal definitions, which seems precisely the function of definitions in Euclid—namely, to indicate how his geometrical system applies to the concrete world.

The same realization, that there could be functional parallels between languages without parallels in constituent structure, motivated Foley and Van Valin in a paper in 1978, anticipating their *Functional Syntax and Universal Grammar* of 1984. For one of the chief inspirations of LFG, like RRG, was to find a means of describing the grammar of nonconfigurational languages, including so-called head-marking languages—that is, ones which place markings for subject and object agreement on the predicate or verb rather than on its dependents, its subject and objects, the word "head" being understood in a functionalist sense, not defined by reference to X-Bar theory. I explore these deeply different conceptions of "head" in chapters XIV and XV.[94]

---

system in which the parameters of choice are between options within generative grammars which are limited to specifying constituent structures with provisions for movement, one should have a system in which the choices between grammars is wider (e.g., allowing for choices of functional structure within the context of greater freedom in constituent ordering).

92. Simon C. Dik, *Functional Grammar* (Amsterdam: North-Holland, 1978), v.

93. Bresnan, *Lexical-Functional Syntax*, 98; cf. 9–13 on argument structure (i.e., thematic structure) and 94–97 on functional structure.

94. This is a difference on which Van Valin has some useful observations: Robert D. Van Valin Jr. and

The weakness of Chomskyan grammars in failing to take grammatical functions such as subject and object as primitive became more widely recognized from work in Relational Grammar beginning in the 1970s,[95] as well as through Dik, Bresnan and Van Valin, and Jackendoff's general reflections.[96] However, both Relational Grammar's elaborate multiplication of strata beyond Chomsky's two levels, LFG needing only one, and the theory of macro-roles in Van Valin,[97] appear to me to result from neglecting to consider connections between the linguistic and logical roles of the notion of subject, as emphasized in chapters IX and XI.

This adaptability to the description of language at the level of speech and discourse seems to be partly anticipated in much of Joan Bresnan's informal discussion. Lexical Functional Grammar's initiator and leading spirit, Joan Bresnan, emphasizes how it "embodies a typically multidimensionalist conception of language" and "is open-ended, allowing extensibility to discourse", and picks out many ways in which its general principles reflect fundamentally functionalist ideas;[98] it is plain that her lexical functionalism is a functionalism in the communication-directed sense.[99] She observes that the formalization of at least its simpler parts and the empirical preoccupations of many of its proponents had produced a misleading impression that LFG was just "an offshoot of the Chomskyan juggernaut".[100] Unlike Chomsky, she presumes that a grammar should contribute to our understanding of language-use and

Randy LaPolla, *Syntax: Structure, Meaning and Function* (Cambridge: Cambridge University Press, 1997), 67–69.

95. Cf. David M. Perlmutter's editorial observations in *Studies in Relational Grammar*, edited by Perlmutter (Chicago: University of Chicago Press, 1983), 1:31, 54–59, a collection which includes the paper by him and Postal, "The Relational Succession Law"; also Perlmutter, "Functional Grammar and Relational Grammar: Points of Convergence and Divergence", in *Perspectives on Functional Grammar*, ed. Teun Hoekstra, Harry van der Hulst, and Michael Moortgat (Dordrecht: Foris, 1981), 319–52. The fundamental ideas began to emerge in Postal's papers from 1976 onwards.

96. Cf. Jackendoff, *Foundations*, 149–51, 248, 252n11, 262.

97. Cf. Barry J. Blake, *Relational Grammar* (London: Routledge, 1990), 140–42.

98. The citations from Bresnan come from LFG Mailing List (web reference, n. 16). Bresnan explains that it arose historically from combining the lexicalist grammar of the 1970s with functional-unification ideas. (Kay and Kaplan considered these in a form modeled by Augmented Transition Networks [ATNs]; cf. John R. Anderson, "Induction of Augmented Transition Networks", *Cognitive Science* 1, no. 2 [1977]: 125–57.) Bresnan describes functional-unification ideas as stemming directly from the functionalist Halliday.

Bresnan instances (LFG Mailing List) Zaenen's "what you see is what you get" (WYSIWYG) principle, as in Ronald M. Kaplan and Annie Zaenen, "Long-Distance Dependencies, Constituent Structure, and Functional Uncertainty", in *Formal Issues in Lexical-Functional Grammar*, ed. Mary Dalrymple, Ronald M. Kaplan, John T. Maxwell, and Annie Zaenen (Stanford, Calif.: CSLI, 1989), 137–65; and her own accounts of economy of expression and nonuniformity of categorization in numerous works, as well as those of others; see LFG Mailing List.

99. Cf. Bresnan, *Lexical-Functional Syntax*, for the crucial importance of discourse functions for understanding and distinguishing grammatical functions; cf. n. 16.

100. See LFG Mailing List, n. 16, in which K. P. Mohanan and Tara Mohanan support Bresnan in noting the functionalist character of LFG's willingness to explain syntactic patterns in terms of the external factors of meaning or linguistic interaction.

of the actual natural psychological processes involved in speaking and comprehension.[101]

By bringing in discourse functions, LFG, like the generality of functionalist grammars,[102] makes the grammar in this broadened sense more adapted, in Bresnan's conception, to "providing a model for performance",[103] inasmuch as the grammatical structures it proposes are so conceived as to dovetail with the structures of speech. Hence, although grammatical constraints on sentence construction are still conceived of as applying in a context-free way, the sentences or utterance-types concerned are conceived in such a way as to be adapted to utterance in determinate types of context—that is, adapted to the level of use in extended discourse, the level of concern to the logician, philosopher, and translator (sufficiently determinate in context for considering truth or falsity, satisfaction or lack of satisfaction, and recognizing perspective).

(iii) The formal approach: a false divorce between grammar and other branches of linguistic study

As indicated in section 1 (b), the worst problem for Chomsky's position lies in the implausibility of its psychoneurological backing. The idea that we first specify a way of generating context-independent sentence-models and then select one which we could put to use, giving its referential terms a reference, is baseless as well as circuitous, since we draw upon context for much more than Chomsky allows. Indeed, the idea that the language faculty or capacity innate in the child before it learns any particular language is a capacity directed towards satisfying morphosyntactic requirements rather than the requirements of semantic structure seems so counterintuitive as to hardly warrant attention, if it had not been proposed.

Yet there is a more general problem. Human beings are concerned with language in a multiplicity of different ways, generating many different branches of study. If one segregates grammar as a study of the supposed "linguistic competence" directed towards Internalized languages, making it part of psychoneurology, one has difficulty in reconnecting it with the whole spectrum of existing branches of study related to public language. I have in mind accounts of the historical development of concepts, of the particular nuances of this or that word or idiom in particular languages and the ways in which these nuances may have changed over time, the reasonably well-established and

101. See Bresnan, "A Realistic Transformational Grammar", in *Linguistic Theory and Psychological Reality*, ed. M. Halle, J. Bresnan, and G. A. Miller (Cambridge, Mass.: MIT Press, 1978), 1–59.

102. Cf. Van Valin, "Functional Linguistics", chap. 13 in *The Handbook of Linguistics*, ed. Mark Aronoff and Janie Rees-Miller (Oxford: Blackwell, 2003), 329–36.

103. Bresnan, "Realistic Transformational Grammar".

readily intelligible ways of distinguishing figures of speech, the theoretical understanding and discriminations in traditional Western grammars, and many contributions to phonetics and prosody. Along with these, there are also the normal canons of intelligible discourse within biography, autobiography, and history, along with historical and literary studies of language and literature, as well as natural history, ecology, and animal behavior, logic, and philosophical analysis. All are parts of the web of human life, presenting data of which psycholinguists as well as linguists in general have to take account and with which linguistic studies have to be integrated.

It is a matter of experience that the Chomskyan approach to grammar has had the effect of turning it into a technical discipline divorced from other studies bearing upon language, and even from the work of those studying particular languages. Chomsky is right in thinking that there is not one science of everything, and would be right in thinking there is not one science of man and one science of human language. However, inasmuch as language is audible or readable, the web of studies relevant to it derives its unity from connection with human communication in the public sphere, rather than from neurology. This does not make the systematic study of linguistics, and in particular the study of grammar, impossible, so long as it is based in the study of language and grammar at the level of use. Chomskyan grammar has presented ideas of permanent value, but, by divorcing grammar from the level of use, it starts from the wrong point for the purposes of psycholinguistic theory, at the same time as becoming comparable to Ptolemaic theory for the number of its epicycles.

Section 6. The Verbal or "Saying" Character of Speech as the Key to Grammar

(a) *Grammar as a "broader logic"*

In my contrasting approach I envisage the semantics of linguistic utterances, in particular their semantic syntax, as what shapes discourse structure. This semantic syntax, understood as partly shaped by pragmatics, embraces the structures of reasoning and of narrative; distinguishes between statement, question, and negation, along with the degrees of certainty and uncertainty and forms of reasoning which arise in answering questions; and distinguishes statement, command, and other types of speech-act. It differentiates the roles of given topic and new topic as well as the various kinds of thing labeled "focus", and distinguishes the thematic roles of arguments (such as Actor, Agent, Patient, and Place). It encompasses a general logic which takes account, not just of proposition, predicate, collection, and number, as well as the distinction between the linguistic and the metalinguistic, but also of cause, time, space, and the distinction between the discrete and the continuous.

In general, as soon as children genuinely speak, their utterances show this same semantic syntax, even though it takes a process of further development in stages for their speech to become grammaticalized according to the forms used by their elders.

It is this overall semantic syntax which has shaped the various ways in which language has become grammaticalized in varying stages as different human groups have spread and developed, with each function and role being capable of being indicated in many different ways. Thus, in English, syntactic connection is mainly achieved through word-order, a small number of auxiliaries and verb-inflections, and the inflection "-ly" on adverbs, while prepositions are used to such extent as to make most case-markings unnecessary, whereas in other languages intonation and a much richer system of inflections make reliance on word-order of less or no significance. Again, emphatic focus may be marked sometimes intonationally by stress on word or phrase and sometimes through being foregrounded as by clefting in a sentence (e.g., "It was his nakedness which ..."), though, as Dik observed, the same may be achieved by being mentioned last, as in "In the room sat a bear".[104] Stress and intonation, often used in connection with topic and focus distinctions, also often mark whether something is a statement, question, or imperative—sometimes reinforcing lexical or syntactic indications and sometimes serving in place of or overriding them, as happens with rhetorical questions.

It is this semantically rooted syntax which constitutes the successor of the Port-Royal *grammaire generale,* looked to by du Marsais, Beauzee, and Beattie,[105] present when Von Humboldt anticipates a close relationship between grammar and logic, and present in the "logic of speech" (1913) conceived of by Jespersen as set within a "broader-minded logic" (1924).[106] For these thinkers, grammar is concerned with speech (i.e., language-use) and its interpretation, and a theory of "language learning" is directed towards learning to speak; strangely, Chomsky slips into thinking of the theory of language

104. Cf. Jackendoff's example of a phenomenon we will often meet later: "And so I fell in love with a prostitute, *me*"; Jackendoff, *Foundations,* 248, using what Dik calls the Tail position.

105. Chomsky, *Aspects,* 5–7, and Chomsky, *Cartesian Linguistics,* chaps. 1 and 3.

106. On Von Humboldt's approach, see Giorgio Graffi, 200 *Years of Syntax* (Amsterdam: John Benjamins, 2001), 20–25, 29, 78; and Jespersen, *Sprogets Logik* [Logic of Speech] (Copenhagen: Oyldendal, 1913); and Jespersen, *Philosophy of Grammar,* 344. Jespersen remarks, "Often enough we shall find that grammatical categories are at best symptoms, foreshadowings of notional categories, and sometimes the 'notion' behind a grammar is as elusive as Kant's 'das Ding an sich'"; Jespersen, *Philosophy of Grammar,* 57. One may note also Uriel Weinreich, "On the Semantic Structure of Language", in *Universals of Language,* ed. J. Greenberg, 114–71.

learning as concerned only with "grammar construction" in its morphosyntactic aspect, and not with how sentences are to be used or understood.[107] It was Jespersen's *Philosophy of Grammar*, with his conception of grammar as a "broader-minded logic", his idea of nexus, and the recognition that linguistics has speech as its primary object of study, which suggested the subtitle "Rewriting the Philosophy of Grammar" for part three of this volume.

As Tomasello remarks, grammar arises from language-use, and many types of grammatical construction, ditransitive formations like "give X to Y" among them, are simply absent in some languages.[108] Yet the functions achieved by many apparently absent constructions remain integral to the potentiality of the unitary speech capacity spoken of in chapter IV, and the way these functions are achieved is often hidden from us if we pay attention only to writing, forgetting that the primary form of language is speech. In speech, stress and stress-pattern, synlinguistic gesture (pointing is an obvious example) or custom (as with giving), relevant association or adjacency within discourse, and extralinguistic context play a vital role. What is needed is a unitary approach which recognizes the way phonological, syntactic, pragmatic, and semantic constraints operate concurrently in the act of speech, the approach embodied in Jackendoff's notions of "unification" and "enriched composition".[109]

107. Chomsky, *Aspects*, 25.

108. Michael Tomasello, ed., introduction to *The New Psychology of Language: Cognitive and Functional Approaches to Language Structure* (Hove, East Sussex: Psychology Press, 2008), 2:5. The variety of ways in which features belonging to general logic may present themselves in different languages is vividly illustrated in the essays in the same volume, especially in Leonard Talmy, "Concept Structuring Systems in Language", in *New Psychology of Language*, ed. Tomasello, 2:15–46.

109. The most obvious examples of accepting elements of pragmatics into one's unified theory of syntax and semantics appear in Jackendoff, *Architecture*, 93–96. The importance of "unification" arises from Jackendoff's replacing the Chomskyan lexical-"insertion"-after- "derivation" procedures by lexical constraints and lexical "licensing". Unification is the operation whereby constraints of all the kinds mentioned are co-applied; Jackendoff, *Architecture*, 83–92, 96; cf. 13, 38–40.

Jackendoff explains "enriched composition" (*Architecture*, 48–49) by contrasting it with the "syntactically transparent semantic composition", which is what Chomsky requires. This latter involves that all elements of content in the meaning of a sentence are found in the lexical conceptual structures (LCSs) of the lexical items composing the sentence and that the way the LCSs are combined is a function only of the way the lexical items are combined in syntactic structure (including argument structure)—with the consequence that neither the internal structure of individual LCSs nor pragmatics plays any role in determining how these LCSs are combined. By contrast, enriched composition involves (a) that a sentence's conceptual structure may contain, besides the conceptual content of its LCSs, other material not expressed lexically, but required for conceptual structure, either to achieve well-formedness in combining LCSs into conceptual structure (Pustejovsky's "coercion") or for the sake of the pragmatics of the discourse or its extra-linguistic context; and (b) that the way the LCSs are combined into a conceptual structure is determined both by the syntactic arrangement of the lexical items and by the internal structure of the LCSs; Pustejovsky's "co-composition", Jackendoff, *Architecture*, 49. Jackendoff shows the importance of this enriched composition in many examples: cf. *Architecture*, 75–82nn11–18 (see 224–26); in connection with reference (anaphor) and quantification, 137–38, 172–73; and in connection with the isolated uses of conventional sounds such as "Ouch!", 93–95.

Our capacity for cross-linguistic generalization often reflects what makes processing easier and is in this sense functionally explicable.[110] In this semantics, encompassing discourse-structure and cause, time, and aspect will always play a key role so that semantic categories influence and largely determine syntactic ones.[111] This is reflected in functionalist grammars and lexical-functional syntax. It is the universality of the general logic indicated in section 3 that largely underlies the possibility of broader cross-linguistic generalization.

Within my account I adopt the notion that subjects are "essentially grammaticalized topics" from Li and Thompson (utilized in Joan Bresnan's Lexical Functional approach and highlighted by Jackendoff in 2002),[112] so that the distinction between subject and predicate arises from the distinction between topic and comment, the subject/predicate distinction assuming a strategic importance for the logic of discourse—even though many languages invent another pre-subject topic position.

The special feature shared by verb, predicate, and comment is they are what gives a clause its "saying" character whereby, when it occurs unembedded and "naked", it *ipso facto* has the force proper to a sentence—that is, to a completed or committed linguistic deliverance. Section 3 (b) showed that two doctrines separated by Frege and others belonged together: first, force belongs only to sentences as committed linguistic deliverances, and second, the "saying" character which belongs primarily to sentences is achieved through the "verbal" character of verbs, predicates, or comments which make their utterance an act of "saying" or, in modern terms, "speaking"—or, in Jespersen's terms, make the sentence a nexus (compared with a drama) rather than a mere junction (compared with a picture). This verbal character accrues to clauses as what makes them eligible to stand on their own as sentences.

A consideration of the types of presupposition which underlie any affirmation or negation brings out what we can take as topics, topics whose identity can be brought to light by *wh*-questions, and their full variety by differentiating the different kinds of *wh*-question. In this way, a careful linguistic or "grammatical" inquiry dovetails with philosophical conceptions of a hierarchy of categories of logical subject, conceptions of an Aristotelian kind, not making class membership the only kind of relationship between them, as in Russell.

We find a convergence between linguistic and logical requirements in

110. Haspelmath, "Parametric versus Functional Explanations".

111. Haspelmath, "Parametric versus Functional Explanations", 20–21n14. Other Haspelmath papers confirm the dependence of what similarities in syntactic category we find on semantic constraints—e.g., "Pre-Established Categories Don't Exist," and "Universals of Causative Verb Formation," paper presented at LSA Institute course, MIT, Cambridge, Mass., August 2, 2005.

112. Charles N. Li and Sandra Thompson, "Subject and Topic: A New Typology of Language", in *Subject and Topic*, ed. Charles N. Li (New York: Academic Press, 1976), 484; cf. Bresnan, *Lexical-Functional Syntax*, 97–98; Jackendoff, *Foundations*, 252n11 and 149–51.

considering the notion of negation, the workings of reference or anaphor, and quantification and scope; and not only these, but also time, aspect, modality, and continuity.

The linguists who suppose that there is a gulf between grammar and logic have overlooked many things. First, it is evident that the existence of a hierarchy of different categories of topic or subject automatically removes any correspondence between the grammatical notion of "noun" and philosophical conceptions of "concrete object" or substance. Second, except that there are more structural distinctions to be taken account of in linguistics than in the logic of propositions, predicates, and sets, many of the kinds of difference in the organization of sentences are as superficial as the differences between Russellian and Polish notations in logic. And to drop indications of the subject of a sentence in contexts in which such indications are superfluous is no more profound a phenomenon than to drop unnecessary brackets. At a deeper level, different languages may come to treat different ranges of feature as peripheral (the agent, the time, the place), and this may influence functional and tense structure. Much Western consideration of grammar has been distorted by concentration upon written prose intended to stand the test of time, and such texts tend to adhere to the "formal register", avoiding the shortcuts and slang of conversation.

(b) *The synchronic and the diachronic*

Saussure was right to emphasize the priority of the synchronic understanding of a language, both for the description of syntactic structure and for lexical semantics, as many had already recognized.[113] Historical development cannot be linguistic theory's primary object of study. Any clarity in thought about languages depends on a recognition that the study and description of the state of a language at a particular time (its synchronic study) has priority over any study of the historical development of the language concerned as a whole (the diachronic study of its development over a series of times). In short, one has to know how a language is used at a particular time or in a particular context in order to appreciate changes before and after that time or in different contexts.

This doctrine must not be understood in a way which neglects the priority of semantic structure ("semantic syntax") at any stage in the historical development of a language and at each stage of a child's learning of his or her first language over the ways in which it is grammaticalized at that stage ("grammat-

113. In 1911 Malthesius stated this with particular clarity and named Wilhelm von Humboldt, Georg von der Gabelentz, Philipp Wegener, and Otto Jespersen as recognizing the same point, while Bloomfield adds mention of Franz Nikolaus Finck.

ical syntax"). Otherwise, there will be no room for Meillet's concept of grammaticalization, no room for a language-user's capacity to understand variant grammatical forms, and no room for any explanation of the stage-by-stage changes in grammatical form in children's learning of language.

For, since it is this overall semantic structure which shapes our grammar, it becomes intelligible how variations in grammar can arise within the same language without communication breaking down or any inappropriateness in the use of language. As a result, the distinction between the synchronic and the diachronic in language can become blurred. The capacities alive within an extended linguistic community cannot be contained in one formal morphosyntactic framework as described in terms of a closely, distributionally defined constituent structure allowing only strictly controlled "movement". We may find that a more functional layer of description, perhaps still counting as formal, underlies multiple forms of the language—still intelligible, though felt to be obsolete or irregular, or in other cases to be archaic, though still open to use or belonging to an unusually polite, formal, legal, or courtly register, or in yet other cases belonging to a dialect variation of the language.

In this way they introduce a scatter into the *état de langue* even as it exists at a particular time, as referred to by Mathesius in 1911 in terms of the "potentialities" of a language—the range of variation the typical language-user can understand even at one particular time.[114] The *état de langue* needs to be conceived as a framework set by pragmatics and semantics, not proceeding by mechanically applicable rule.

The Chomskyan approach does not explain the tendency of languages to permit considerable coexistence between different sentence structures in the same writers and groups of speakers within the same dialect, as well as large liberty in literary use. Moreover, in settled societies, it is usual for children and grandparents to be able to communicate with one another without feeling that they are speaking different languages.

It is therefore very odd to meet the idea that in 1380 a difference between English and Dutch was established in English, because at that time tense and agreement between subject and verb became functional Heads of functional phrases, as if all of a sudden children might cease to understand their parents and vice versa, or at least come to speak a different language,[115] despite the

114. Vilém Mathesius, "On the Potentiality of the Phenomena of Language", translated by J. Vachek, from "O potenciálnosti jevů jazykových", in *Věstnik Král, české společnosti nauk*, Prague, 1911, in *A Prague School Reader in Linguistics*, ed. Josef Vachek (Bloomington: Indiana University Press, 1964), 1–32.

115. E. van Gelderen, *The Rise of Functional Categories* (Amsterdam: John Benjamins, 1993), discussed in Vivian J. Cook and Mark Newson, *Chomsky's Universal Grammar*, 2nd ed. (Oxford: Blackwell, 1996), 185–88. This is an example of a degree of abruptness in their changes of parameter assumed by followers of Chomsky which belies the facts; cf. Hopper and Traugott, *Grammaticalization*, 26, 51, 207; cf. Cook and Newson, *Chomsky's Universal Grammar*, 186–87.

long-continuing acceptability of both modes of speech. For in Chomskyan grammatical theory, our Elizabethan ancestors and even our grandparents spoke a different language because certain parameters would have to be considered as set differently. However, quite old usages such as "Like it?" and even "And he come, I will go" are quite intelligible. Thus it is quite wrong to draw an arbitrary line in the continuum of colloquial, formal, literary, archaic, and obsolete and to declare the usages on one side of this line "grammatical" language and the others "ungrammatical". Many "obsolete" or dialect forms are still intelligible to speakers of the "received" form of the language. Indeed, even novelties produced by beginners in the language (such as "He come, I go") are commonly intelligible. This intelligibility does not establish such usages as normal, but our knowledge of *langue* enables us to understand them.

As Hopper and Traugott remark, "older and newer forms coexist for individual speakers as well as for communities over time. Indeed, A probably never becomes B without an intermediary stage in which A and B co-exist ... such co-existence may last several hundred or more years".[116] For example, one of the most obvious cases of forms coexisting for hundreds of years is that provided by the gradualness with which the use of the auxiliary "do" became compulsory in standard English, allowing "not" to succeed a finite non-auxiliary verb and allowing inversion of verb and subject, each nowadays forbidden. Yet even now the older forms are still intelligible, so that those who say "I did not go" and "Do you like it?" are still able to understand "I went not" and "Like you it?" In the processes of grammatical change, older and newer forms of speech always coexist for some period of time, often very extended.[117]

In the Chomskyan conception, various "triggers" in the stages of neurological processing will have to be applied in a different order, corresponding to one's speaking a sentence in a different language with a different grammar, a language with its grammatical parameters set differently. Yet to attribute exercises of freedom motivated by prosodic, pragmatic, and semantic needs, exercises of literary choice arising in the course of composition, to neurological triggering instead of to stylistic purposes appears a bit topsy-turvy, especially when the idioms conforming to each of several different sets of Chomskyan parameters coexist in the usage of the same community of language-users. It is as if the alteration to the order of application of neurological triggers deter-

116. Hopper and Traugott, *Grammaticalization*, 1st ed., 36; cf. 2nd ed., 46–58, 56 for its discussion of the development on "do" in 1380–1500; cf. n. 117.

117. The reasons for the alienation of students of "grammaticalization" from this approach are well set forth by Hopper and Traugott, *Grammaticalization*, 1st ed., 204–9; the same argument is presented in more truncated form, buried by listing more recent discussions in the 2nd edition, 43–46, where the discussions of 204–9, 34–38, and 45–48 in the 1st edition of 1993 have been consolidated into 43–49 and 56–58.

The way in which sentences with the same constituent structure can pass from being given one interpretation to being given another appears in several studies by Dik, alluded to in chap. XI of this volume, and more recently in Bresnan, *Lexical-Functional Syntax*, 144–79.

mined one's style in speaking or writing rather than vice versa. This makes the deliberate choices of rhetoric and poetry inexplicable.

The informal concept of "a language" found in Dummett and others is one which we cannot avoid using, even if it does put "philosophy, or the empirical study of language and behavior, or both, in deep trouble", as Chomsky alleges.[118] "Pure substances" and "isotopes" have real existence in particular molecules and atoms, but "pure languages" have no such real existence, and so languages cannot be relegated to mere folk-science; but, because of the greater explanatory power of functional grammars, the situation is not as hopeless as a grammar conforming to a Chomskyan straitjacket would suggest.

Once the universal features of grammatical structure are envisaged in functional terms, they come into connection with the thought structures of speech (a connection obscured in Chomskyan grammar), and it becomes intelligible how it is possible for one and the same speaker to have some facility in understanding variants of his or her own language, and indeed in making free with its structures for rhetorical or poetic purposes. It also becomes possible to understand a language at a particular time in a way compatible with language change, thus following the Prague School in explicitly regarding language as a system which is at any moment in motion.[119]

Prospect

The structure for thinking about language outlined above gives one, I believe, a new freedom in analyzing and talking about language and examples of its use. It shows the legitimacy of talking about these things with the informality characteristic of the study of literature, the problems of the translator tussling with idioms foreign to the language into which he is translating, the general linguist, and the philosopher. Such freedom is rooted in the way the understanding exhibited in the use of language is of a kind which is indeed open to review, critical assessment, and decision, but conforms only to such rules as can be stated in informal terms, not ones which are applicable in a mechanical way. This book indicates how such understanding is possible without erecting understanding into any kind of magic power or superstition put forward to fill in gaps in explanation.

Thus my approach has the virtue of showing the legitimacy of the patterns of explanation of ordinary speech which we most naturally accept, as well as showing the place of formal approaches to grammar and the necessary places

118. Chomsky, *New Horizons*, 49.

119. Josef Vachek, *The Linguistic School of Prague: An Introduction to Its Theory and Practice* (Bloomington: Indiana University Press, 1966), chap. 2.

of neuroscience and physiology in a full account of the workings of language. These are the patterns of explanation which give accessibility and intelligibility to the expositions met with in more traditional grammars and which make received dictionaries useful. This approach thus leaves ample room for one to do full justice to the various studies referred to, however formal or informal, whether by linguists or by philosophers and logicians, whether prosodic, morphological, syntactic, semantic, or pragmatic in central concern.

In the perspective I open out, it is semantic and pragmatic constraints, reflected in the principles of the general logic I outlined, which tune and shape the ways our brains function in the relevant respects, not vice versa. They allow resonance to be achieved between speaker and hearer within a linguistic community. The brain is vital to us as bodily beings if our understanding is to find expression in speech and in coordination with perception, imagination, memory, emotion, and action. But the role of the brain is rather to facilitate our expression of understanding and thinking in the medium of words than to embody it. Our thinking is not *embodied* in language, but *expressed* using it; nor is it embodied in neural or imaginative sequences. The activities of understanding, thinking, and questioning, with their nonrepresentational character, combined with our freedom in the exercise of the capacity involved exhibited in the lack of definable limits to the flexibility in our use of words, show that these activities cannot be the work of any bodily organ. This does not make them the work of some other organ, but the activities of the person as such.

It is the way linguistic understanding, thinking, and questioning transcend the body and transcend limitations set by the body which is of peculiar importance for the status of human beings. For, since what acts exists, and these human activities transcend the body, human existence must therefore also transcend the body.[120]

Yet at the same time, of their very nature, these activities are such as to be expressed in speech and coordinated both with the use of the imagination and with the use of the brain—for instance, in its role in the memory of the vocabulary, accidence, and forms of grammaticalization special to the language used—while we draw on experience for the concepts we rely upon. It is this combination of transcendence and dependence, exemplified in understanding and its expression, which makes the nature of speech the key to appreciating the form of life characteristic of human beings. It is this union of understanding and its expression in speech which shows a key part of the character of our form of life, both in the way our thought and existence transcend the body and in the way human nature makes them require the body for their full human expression.

120. Cf. David Braine, *Human Person*, chap. 15, esp. 537–42.

PART ONE

Words and Their Dynamism in the Expression of Meaning

1

Two Levels of Meaning

THE LEVEL OF LANGUAGE-POSSESSION AND THE LEVEL OF LANGUAGE-USE

The Notion of Linguistic Understanding: Preliminary Remarks

In the introduction and overview I gave a key place to our capacity to use a word in a multiplicity of different senses or discourse-significances, even though it was being taken in the same meaning at the level of language-possession. It is the task of this chapter to develop these ideas merely sketched earlier.

(a) *Propositions precede reasoning, and are what determines the character of human understanding*

The primary hallmark of human nature and of the peculiarly human kind of understanding lies not in reasoning from one thought to another, but in the character of the thinking enshrined in the individual thoughts between which reasoning is made, such as is exhibited in speech. The individual premises of a piece of reasoning need to be put together, and each needs to have sense or discourse-significance before there can be any reasoning from them—prototypically, the giving life to a set of words by asserting or denying a predicate of a subject of an appropriate kind. What used to be called composing and dividing precedes any human reasoning. Propositions have to have been formed before there can be reasoning from them.

The primary function of understanding is not to enable us to make insight-inspired leaps, whether from one thought to another, from an experience to a thought, or from a thought to a desire, plan, or decision. Indeed, these latter are things which we find among animals—for instance, among the elephants as well as the apes in their inventiveness in finding new ways of doing things, despite seeming to lack language as the complex structured whole we find among human beings.

Rather, what matters first in grasping the character of human language is the character of our understanding of the individual thoughts between which such leaps or transitions are made, typically linguistically expressible thoughts. It is this understanding, typically expressed in speech or writing, which underlies the other forms of understanding—understanding the natures of things of different kinds and why they behave as they do, understanding people, and so forth. It is this linguistic understanding which gives rationale to our varied forms of reasoning and explains their variety—the variety whereby no pre-set set of mechanical principles determines or limits our capacities for reasoning, whether in mathematics, in physics, in history, or in any other area in which knowledge arises.

When I speak of language I do not mean just any system of communication (e.g., one which might consist only of single-gesture signals). I mean a system with the type of integrated semantic syntax which we find in the varied human languages, spoken of in the introduction and chapter IV. And this complex structure includes the associated capacities for learning and teaching language and the capacities which allow a particular language to develop over time and allow for the types of extension which go with the capacity to understand other languages. And, when I think of the works of language, I think not only of single-sentence utterances, but also of extended works, whether of song, poetry, and story or of literature, history, and science.

(b) *Linguistic understanding is not rule-bound*

The insight fleshed out in this book is an insight into what is involved in linguistic understanding—an understanding which cannot be mechanically simulated because, as later chapters show, it is not formalizable in any relevant way.

It is often supposed that the essence of language is to be governed by rules. Some accounts of logic, many forms of determinism, and artificial intelligence (AI) theories of mind each require that these rules be formalizable in mechanically applicable rules. However, the normal notion of rule in human life is much more open and informal: it is typical for rules (e.g., those applied by judges judging cases according to precedent, and those found in the arguments of lawyers and historians and in logic) to require interpretation or understanding in their application and not to be mechanically applicable, let alone to be in practice mechanically applied. A similar informality is found with all linguistic rules. Our problem is to grasp how this characteristic and indispensable informality arises.

We will find that it is the character of the "linguistic" understanding of what we hear and read, involved in the very act of hearing and reading, which differentiates speech and writing from mere signaling systems; and it is precisely this which frees our use of language from being limited to the requirement of conformity to this or that set or kind of mechanical rules.

In view of my insistence that linguistic understanding is not bound by mechanically applicable rules, it is crucial that the explanation of my fundamental ideas should not be open to the objection that I am erecting this "understanding" into something mystical and uncheckable, mysterious, and useless as an explanation of anything, just as Molière's "dormitive power" was useless as an explanation of sleep—an objection which I refute in chapter V, especially in section 2 of that chapter. At this point I merely announce the nonmechanical character of our use of language so that its relevance should be seen where it underlies my later argument as it unfolds.

The linguistic expression of thoughts in utterances or "sentences" exhibits them as *in themselves* possessing an intelligible content, or "sense". This internal possession of sense—a possession of sense because in context these expressions "express" it (instead of merely, like a signal, externally identifying it)—makes them in themselves objects of understanding. That is, what it is for such expressions to have sense is not just a matter of their being uttered or written and being directed toward producing certain effects. Absolutely not—on the contrary, these linguistic expressions of thought are meaningful in themselves, not merely means by which certain ends are achieved. Their utterance is in itself a complete human act, an act of communication, independently of any further ends which the speaker may hope to achieve by means of it, whether to influence the hearer's belief or behavior, whether by persuasion or provocation.

As the introduction and these first three chapters make clear, it is words which express the meaning of what we say and the understanding which speaker and hearer are to share. Moreover, since our use of words is informal and flexible in ways I review, it is only by the use of understanding in the context of speaking or hearing that we grasp the sense of the words intended by the speaker in each particular utterance—their discourse-significance.

Here we must begin by setting aside two irrelevancies. First, we are not concerned with words as mere phonetic or phonological items (e.g., the sound "log" as it occurs both in the word "log", meaning "logarithm", and in the word "log", meaning "log of wood"), where there is no etymological connection, but only a mere phonetic and written coincidence. Second, we are not concerned with words as etymological items, the etymological connections between different meanings having no surviving influence on the synchronic use of the language, all awareness of these connections having died as an influence on speech—as with "log" as meaning "log of wood" or "ship's log"; or with "bachelor" as meaning respectively "knight bachelor", "man or woman who has obtained his or her first degree at university", and "man who has not yet married". In these cases, synchronically it is as if there were no more connection than in the case of mere phonemic or written coincidence. A child can enunciate a "phonemic word" without its being thereby for him or her a properly "linguistic word".

However, a linguistic word may still have several distinct, but related "focuses" of meaning. Thus, when the word "play" is used as a verb, it can be used intransitively, as when we say "the children were playing", or transitively, as of playing an instrument, or of playing a game, or of playing [performing] a theatrical drama, and derivatively of playing a part in such a drama, the drama itself being spoken of as a play—giving us five focuses of meaning for the verb "play". For the purposes of my discussion in this book I shall speak of each of these five focuses of meaning as a distinct lexical meaning or, as I will use the expression, "*langue*-meaning". By contrast, grasping the "sense" which the word expresses in the context of a particular linguistic utterance—its discourse-significance—belongs to language-use, not language-possession. Out of one focus of meaning typically spring multifarious senses, types of use, or discourse-significances—the use of a particular word in one particular focus of meaning is extended by analogy or in metaphor, giving it many senses or discourse-significances, arising informally in ways that cannot be itemized in any dictionary or lexicon.

Already in the introduction we began to discuss how we get access to the insides of sentences, sentence-constituents which *express* their content instead of merely serving as components of a signal. Our understanding penetrates to the insides of sentences in the very acts of our hearing or speaking these sentences. Theories which make lexical elements into mere ciphers whose only role is to make a difference to the effects which the delivery of the sentences containing them are liable to have on the beliefs, intentions, and attitudes of their hearers or readers give an unbalanced primacy to the sentence, as if our experience were only of sentences as wholes.

This fact that our experience of sentences is not as indivisible, atomic wholes, but as already articulated semantic structures, opened out in chapter III, appears in a particularly important way in chapter IX, where we see that in understanding language, a name has a use only within the context of a verbal or "saying" framework, so that the difference between names, whether singular or general, and the verbal or "saying" framework within which they are given, is given from the beginning. This is a key part of how pragmatics and semantics set the shape of syntax, so that the requirements of grammar are a kind of formal projection of semantics, marking the formal structures which arise from pragmatic and semantic constraints and potentialities. And the more general aspects of grammar are formal reflections of the principles of the general logic roughly described in the introduction, themselves implicit in the integrated semantic structure common to every language, and making the understanding of the structures of speech an essential unity in the way I explain in chapter IV.

In all this we shall see how both language-possession and language-use require to be understood in their social environment of speakers and hearers, where there is no separation between pragmatics, semantics, and syntax.

Section 1. The Two Levels of Linguistic Understanding

(a) *The logical background: the possession of an ability is distinct from the capacity to gain it*

The distinction I was to make between the understanding of *parole* and the understanding of *langue,* using the terms *langue* and *parole* as terms of convenience, is at root logical—namely, the distinction made by Aristotle between a state or disposition and its exercise—and as relevant to linguists as to philosophers such as Gilbert Ryle.[1] I explain the terms, as it were, from scratch to avoid any confusion between my usage and that of Saussure.

I envisage knowledge of a *langue* as the object of the practical knowledge implicit in the possession of the language concerned as exercised and exhibited in *parole,* not as an independent object of knowledge or study. This practical knowledge is in principle accessible to the language-user on reflection, but not in a form to which he could give any technical expression, and is in no way scientific or systematic. Inasmuch as a language is the possession of a community learned over a lifetime, a person can have greater or less knowledge of the *langue* concerned. Some have a wider vocabulary, and not every Frenchman uses or has practical knowledge of the past anterior.[2]

In order to explain the logical distinction concerned, it is easiest to begin

1. Ryle, "Use, Usage and Meaning", no. 31 in *Collected Essays,* vol. 2 of *Collected Papers* (London: Hutchinson, 1971), 407. Ryle regards his distinction between "language" and "speech" to be close to that made by the linguist Alan H. Gardiner in *The Theory of Speech and Language* (Oxford: Oxford University Press, 1932). I speak of *langue* or language-possession as what contrasts with speech and avoid the word "language" because the latter is so often misleadingly used as a translation of *Sprache,* as in Von Humboldt, Jespersen, and Wittgenstein, whose meaning is usually closer to "speech" or *parole.*

2. I avoid Chomsky's terms "competence" and "performance" because of their associations: "competence" with neuroscience and "performance" with the negative attitude inherited from Bloomfield.

by considering a parallel case. We need to distinguish between (i) a capacity for sight, (ii) the possession of sight, and (iii) the exercise of sight. In parallel with this, we must distinguish (i) a capacity to develop knowledge in some area or of some kind, (ii) the possession of this knowledge, and (iii) the exercise of this knowledge. The distinction between the possession of knowledge and its exercise is obvious from the case of memory, where it is a different thing to have a thing in memory and actually to be actively in mind of it. Babies are not born knowing French or English, but learn them as they grow up; but later, even when they have learned some particular language ("have got to know it"), they are still not always using it (indeed they are often asleep); but they are in an immediate position to go in for actual uses of such languages (whether in speaking and writing or merely in thinking). These are our three levels.

These three levels involve two distinctions. The first is between (i) a bottom level of capacity to acquire knowledge, skill, or competence, and (ii) its first level of realization, the level of having actually reached such skill or competence or other advantageous or good state (second-level states or "capacities" in a fuller sense—knowledge, wisdom, and the various moral virtues and vices, to take Aristotle's examples). The second distinction is between all these capacities and dispositions, both of level (i) and level (ii) and (iii) the actual exercise of these second-level states or capacities in acts, activities, and processes in time, things episodic or quasi-episodic in character (realizations of the second-level capacities)—for instance, having the thing actually in memory (whether by its coming spontaneously to mind or as a result of a deliberate effort to remember), or using the language in speech.

The logically second-level abilities are positive states which we possess just as much when we are asleep or otherwise not exercising them as when we are consciously exercising them. They remain, logically, states in the logical sense rather than acts or episodes. Thus they are to be defined in terms of their ultimate exercise in some characteristic activity—just as solubility has to be understood in terms of what it is for a solid to be dissolved in a fluid. Because such states are thus defined in terms of their mode of exercise, many philosophers have also referred to them as "dispositions", using the word "disposition" technically (as a "being disposed" toward a certain kind of exercise or activity). However, the dispositions here concerned are of the kind Ryle called "many-track dispositions", because they are open-ended in the variety of ways in which they are realized, just as the skills and other excellences, intellectual and moral, which Aristotle called *hexeis*, are realized in many different types of way.

Accordingly, what I am calling *parole*, "speech", or "discourse" and the understanding of this discourse or *parole*, stand at level (iii)—that is, the level of performance, the episodic level (the level of acts, activities, or processes in time).

Language-possession—that is, the second-level knowing of a particular language (knowledge of *langue* in respect of that language), as opposed to the understanding we have in the act of using it—comprises all such skill and knowledge of phonetics, grammar, and word-meanings as is involved in our being able to make any full act of speech in that language. It includes the *langue*-understanding of words and other lexical units (what we commonly call understanding or knowing their meanings), along with the *langue*-understanding a language-user needs to have of different constructions and of the working of what were traditionally called "syncategorematic" elements (I will call them "synlexical" in chapter II)—such as prepositions, inflections, conjunctions, auxiliaries, and the copula. What is concerned here is the practical reflection of the knowledge contained in dictionaries and grammars and of the skills of language-users, but which they need not be able to make theoretically explicit, and therefore something essentially different from linguistic science. And, as we saw, understanding in relation to *langue* is essentially a disposition or state obtaining over a period, like the state of having something in memory even when we are not attending to it or exercising the memory concerned.

The general capacity for language, at level (i), possessed at birth, is logically also a state or disposition, but at a different level—as it were a skill to develop skills.

Language-possession (competence in a particular language), at level (ii), in Ryle's terms has the character less of a *knowledge that* than of a *knowledge how*, as a knowledge of how to express what we want to say or to understand what is said to us in the open-ended variety of types of occasion which present themselves. Ryle calls the variety of forms of knowledge "many-track" or "determinable" dispositions, a conception of which he gave a rough explanation in his *Concept of Mind*. Here he conceives a many-track disposition as a capacity, propensity, or excellence,[3] such as mountaineering skill, which is typically acquired by training, and is such that the person who has it is able to perform expertly or well in a variety of possible types of situation, being, like Aristotle's *hexeis* and *dynameis*, definable only by reference, not to just one general hypothetical statement (covering possible cases as well as actual ones) specifying what pieces of behavior will be generated from certain kinds of background, but to some open spread of such hypotheticals, with antecedents of very varied kinds and complexity.[4] Thus it will be impossible to specify a principle enabling their different types to be listed or enumerated. In mathematical terms these types of hypothetical will be non-enumerable, but not

3. Aristotle applied the term *aretē* for "excellence" to intellectual as well as moral excellences or virtues, including arts or *technai* as well as sciences or *epistemai*.

4. Commonly involving defeasible concepts, discussed in sec. 4 (b) (iv) and n. 27.

because of their large number, since they are "infinite" only in the sense of being indefinite in number, there being no system or mechanically applicable rule for enumerating them, in the way explained in sections 4 and 5.[5] The types of situation to be allowed for arise in quite heterogeneous ways, and the types of response and of situation-response relation are yet more heterogeneous. Ryle's concern is to contrast these "many-track" dispositions with what he calls "single-track" or "determinate" dispositions, by which he means capacities which are obtained by rigid drill, shown in giving narrowly defined responses to a systematically listable set of narrowly defined possible orders or tasks. By contrast, he regards skills as typically acquired by training, not by drill. Drill aims at each performance being a replica of its predecessors, whereas training is in skills which grow by a person's learning from experience involving the exercise of his own judgment in new types of situation.[6]

Ryle is rather careless in explaining his distinction between single-track and many-track dispositions, with its long roots in the thought of Aristotle and those influenced by him, a carelessness I attempt to remedy in chapter VIII, where we will see that he is not to be understood in purely behavioristic terms, but requires interpretation in holistic, teleological, and even mentalistic terms. Many of the difficulties in which modern discussions have been ensnared result from the tendency of philosophers such as Kripke and psychologists to use the words "disposition" and "habit" in a more restricted way under the influence of Hume. This fashion is at the root of Chomsky's difficulties in understanding Jespersen and Hockett's more traditional approach to grammar explained in chapter III, section 4.

Dispositions are characterized or identified in terms of the acts which constitute their exercise and the relevant senses of *langue*-understanding and meaning in terms of their senses in regard to their exercise in *parole*.

The understanding of *parole* is essentially that understanding which is internal both to our act when we speak "meaning what we say" and to our act of hearing what others say when we understand what they are saying to us in the very act of hearing, and is therefore localized in time. This *parole*-understanding of words and other expressions is essentially subordinate to the activities of our speaking with understanding and our understanding the speech of others, logically integral and subordinate to it as intending is logically integral and subordinate to acting intentionally.

If we draw on Ryle's conception of logical grammar, the controls on our accounts of *parole* and of *langue* will be provided by giving a careful description of

5. I.e., better understood in terms of "indefiniteness", or the intuitionists' notion of "spread".

6. Ryle, *Concept of Mind*, chap. 2, sec. 7, and chap. 5, sec. 2.

the interconnections between our various uses of the most general concepts of knowledge, intention, expression, speech, hearing, writing, reading, and understanding. For instance, there is an overlap between (a) the things we count as "intended" or "meant" (objects of "intention"), (b) the things we count as "understood" (objects of "understanding"), and (c) the things we count as "said", "heard", and "expressed" as we use these words in regard to communicating something on a particular occasion. The coincidence of these features distinguishes *parole*-understanding (i.e., the understanding of speech in the very act) from other forms of understanding and knowledge, and in this way gives it a contextual definition. Lexical or *langue*-understanding does not have the same relationship to the intention to say something determinate on particular occasions or to the expression of the sense we intend in what we say in speaking.[7]

Explaining any such fundamental notions requires resort to informal contextual definitions. Philosophers such as Ryle and Wittgenstein follow Husserl in speaking of the "logical grammar" of concepts. What we need to understand at this stage is the "logical grammar" of the concept of linguistic understanding. The concepts of *parole*-understanding and *langue*-understanding are key to any theory of speech and language. Yet each language presents a scatter of words, none designed to capture precisely and solely either of the two kinds of understanding concerned. At every stage we have to be wary, for it is not just the word "understand", but also the verb "mean" and the noun "meaning" which Ryle would call "polymorphous".[8] But according to what we have said, it is "mean" and "meaning" as coordinate with *parole* which are fundamental (notions developed from those of "intend" and "intending").

In considering the theory of meaning, it is useless trying to supply a different word for each of the meanings or senses which such words as "know" and "understand" have to carry. In understanding the relations between their different senses or uses, the idea of contextual definition and Ryle's notion of mapping the geography of concepts are two ideas which come to our aid. At earlier stages in the history of philosophy, in response to the question "What is so-and-so?", Plato's Socrates always began by getting his interlocutor to offer examples and then proceeded to ask for something more explanatory—for instance, a definition (an account or *logos*). He then normally proceeded to exhibit the unsatisfactoriness of each definition offered. Wittgenstein also began by offering examples, using the examples rather to show the unsatisfactoriness of the method of seeking an explicit definition, especially with more

7. Such words as "say" and their equivalents in other languages, *phemi* in Greek and *dico* in Latin, have many ambiguities which Austin tried to distinguish in *How to Do Things with Words*. There are levels of understanding and meaning correlative with each use of the verb "say". We have to pick out what is intended and understood at the illocutionary level.

8. Ryle, "Thinking and Language", in *Collected Essays*, no. 19.

general concepts such as understanding and meaning. Instead, he offered a crafted presentation of examples with comment, exhibiting the way such concepts functioned without offering explicit definitions or explanations of their meaning. Such approaches are designed to substitute informal systems of contextual definition for explicit definition.

(b) *Langue has to be related both to the individual and to the community*

Knowledge of *langue*, as a capacity exercised in speech, has to be rooted in the individual. That is, although a *langue* is essentially something shared by a community—the community of those who use that *langue* in speaking with one another—it has to be appropriated by each individual language-user before it can have any determinate influence on his speech or ability to communicate. It is only as appropriated by the individual that the individual, when he speaks, is able to know the meaning of what he says, as it were before or in the act of saying it, rather than, like others, only by listening to himself as if he were in the same position as his hearers—it is a matter of what it is to know what one means oneself.

Nonetheless, while this knowledge of *langue* has to be considered something which logically belongs primarily to the individual language-users, it remains that, in order for this knowledge to be the basis of communication, *langue* as the object of this knowledge is essentially something social, shared by a community.

For evident reasons, the "community" as here spoken of has to be somewhat ill-defined. It cannot be viewed as a democracy of equals as if those learning the language had a knowledge and authority in regard to it equal to the knowledge and authority of those—the wider community, their parents, and mentors—from whom they learn, a democracy within which it would be pertinent to take a sociological survey in order to judge a linguistic question. Nor, for that matter, within that wider community, are particular adult speakers (for instance, a child's parents) authorities against the larger community within which they are set. The idea of linguistic community as a democracy of equals, even equal family groups, presupposed in such statistical approaches, makes progressive language learning impossible. Saussure wisely avoided any attempt at any close definition of the extent and form of the relevant kind of linguistic community, speaking of *la masse parlante* and considering it as complete in no individual, but only *dans la masse*.[9] These difficulties are mitigated

9. See Roy Harris, *Saussure and his Interpreters*, 2nd ed. (Edinburgh: Edinburgh University Press, 2003), 74; cf. 211, 224. Harris notes how Saussure avoids both thinking of *langue* as something "common to *all* speakers of a community" (my italics) and thinking of it as merely some highest common factor within a community.

if we understand the notions of "a language" and *état de langue* in a broad way which allows for the understanding between generations involved in communication with grandparents, understanding old literature, and the understanding of some limited range of dialect variations and deviations arising in the language of beginners and the unskilled. The limits are set by the requirement of mutual intelligibility except in cases of a new word's becoming part of the language or novel usages arising, normal occurrences in the development of a language. *État de langue* should be understood as having an internal fluidity, something of which we catch descriptions in mid-flow, and not tied in any absolute way to reference to the requirements of some particular Chomskyan grammar or state of the lexicon.

Section 2. Words and Sentences: The Relation of the Two Levels

It is important at every stage to respect the contrast between entities at the rank of sentence and above and entities at the level of the word or other lexical factor, as delineated in the introduction and explained more fully in chapter III. Entities at the rank of the sentence or utterance (whether propositions, questions, commands, or whatever) require to be understood and defined primarily at the level of *parole* or language-use, whereas entities at the rank of word, morpheme, or lexeme have to be understood and defined at the level of language-possession, or *langue*, as well as that of language-use, or *parole*. Since the meaning of sentences has to be understood by reference to the meaning of their words and other lexical factors, the problems of understanding the relationships between sentence and word, sentence-meaning and word-meaning, and of understanding the relationships between *langue* and *parole*, language-possession and language-use, are inseparable.

(a) *The temptation to consider words as mere sense-identifiers*

The concentration of recent philosophers such as Davidson and Grice on entities arising at the level of speech or discourse, complete utterances or sentences, has made it possible to regard words as mere ciphers, parts of a code for identifying the intended effect of utterances, with no content in themselves, no significance except one defined by rule backward from their intended effects—mere instruments for the identification of the significance of complete units of discourse. That is, the way in which sentences or complete utterances have been given such complete primacy has left us without any explanation of the function of words, except merely as contributing to sense identification so that, taken with their order and the intonation and context of the whole utterance in which they occur, they allow the identification of the sense of such utterance.

This predicament arises with a whole family of theories of meaning, those of Dummett and his followers as well as of Davidson and Grice, even though this is not at all how they think of words and word meaning, whatever Chomsky's present way of thinking.[10]

In some theories of this kind, the sense of a "proposition" (a true or false sentence) is identified with its truth-conditions, making knowing its sense consist in knowing what it would be for it to be true and what it would be for it to be false. In such an account, the parts of a proposition, their order, and its intonation and context of utterance constitute a means of identifying these truth-conditions and thus identifying the "sense" of the proposition concerned. But this means that, although the way these various contributory sense-identifiers fit together according to a certain structure may give the means to identify the senses of a whole family of propositions, nonetheless such structures remain entirely external to the senses of the propositions concerned—serving like a schema for calculating the identity of the senses of these propositions. Nothing in such accounts need require us to regard the words of the sentence or these structures as serving any such further function as that of expressing a sense. Such accounts often suggest that we have nothing more than a rich system of external constraints on the understanding of the significance of sentences—nothing enabling us to get inside them. In such accounts, the idea of "expressing a sense" is entirely foreign.

A code may identify messages: 0 = the prisoners are safely imprisoned; 1 = the prisoners have escaped; 2 = the enemy has come; 3 = we don't know what's happened. The signals do not express, but only—by previous agreement or "convention"—indirectly identify senses. However complex the code, and however much we *feel* that the code's complexities have begun to reflect the shape of the messages, we have not yet uncovered *what it is* to express the content of the messages rather than merely identify them as members of a list. Thus far the idea that the content or sense of messages in such a code is expressed rather than merely identified is, as I remarked, a wheel on which nothing turns.

Theories in this family sometimes identify "sense" not with conditions of truth, but with conditions of justified assertion—more akin to "verification-conditions" than to truth-conditions. Another such theory might explain "meaning" in terms of "response-conditions", the consequences aimed at in the speech-act—and indeed such theories have arisen in connection with ethics. Yet none of these alternatives alter the basic situation whereby the conditions

10. Cf. Chomsky, *New Horizons*, 132.

on the meaning of utterances as wholes provide the sole guide to what words and other lexical factors might happen to "mean". All such theories place equally external sets of conditions upon the meaning of whole utterances so that these alone possess "meaning" in their own right. Thus all approaches present the same danger of making the "sense" or "meaning" of a sentence alone directly accessible—none allowing any direct access to the insides of a sentence, to the sense of its constitutive parts.

Moreover, those who discuss the learning of language, whether psycholinguists or philosophers from quite different standpoints, lock themselves in the same trap. Quine's predicament in *Word and Object* when envisaging an imagined one-word utterance, "Gavagai", is typical of the consequences of the behaviorist approach to learning theory, in which complete utterances and the circumstances of their utterance are the only empirical data. The upshot is, again, a system in which rules externally dictate when kinds of utterance are appropriate and when not—a system which again makes linguistic communication a form of signaling, its structure described in H. P. Grice's theory of meaning.

As to theories of formal grammar, nothing is absolutely required of such theories beyond that they should produce right predictions as to which "sentences" should ordinarily be accepted as "grammatical". Beyond this, the only desiderata are elegance and simplicity, together with applicability to as wide a range of languages as possible. All available empirical tests are upon sentences as such conceivable sentential utterances as we would judge grammatical—it is of these that the supposedly abstract sentence-constructs generated by the grammar have to provide a model.

Nothing, then, in any of these theories requires us to think of complete utterances or sentences as objects of understanding in any way different from the way in which we think of signals as objects of understanding. There is, as such, nothing more in understanding a signal than understanding what its effect on belief or behavior is intended to be. This would mean that contributory parts or aspects of a signal would not be objects of understanding, as the signal as a whole or its message, but would be mere ciphers. Such an account leaves our understanding of sentences to be judged by its relation to the beliefs, desires, and actions which precede and follow it.[11] It is as if the only difference between speech and ordinary signaling lay in the form and complexity of the coding. But speech is different from signaling in aim or function, not just in form or method, since speech, unlike a mere signal, aims not just to identify the message to be communicated, but to express its content.

11. This is the conception to which Davidson finds himself finally driven; see chap. III, sec. 3 (c) of this volume.

The effect of reducing speech to signaling is to force us to view the question of the meaning of its inner parts or functional features in such a way as to allow them at an initial stage only a physical description, anything beyond this being reconstructed retrospectively once we have associated a meaning with the whole. This violates what we know beforehand of our awareness of the meaning and role of parts of sentences as we hear and speak them. That is, these theories give no account of what it is to *understand* the sense a sentence expresses, or even of what it is for a sentence to *express* a sense—rather than merely for uttering it to have a purpose.

(b) *The need for a conception of words as sense-expressors*

We require a theory which can explain how we get inside sentences so as to associate sense with the parts of sentences in the same way as we associate it with complete sentences—so that we can apply the words "sense" and "meaning" in the same sense to the words or constitutive parts of sentences as to the sentences themselves.

This need is crucial to the theory of language, because if the words of a sentence are nothing more than contributory identifiers of its so-called sense, it becomes scarcely natural to describe the sentence itself as having a sense at all. Mere signaling does not as such require that the parts of a signal have any sense at all—such parts need not express anything, any more than individual letters within syllables express anything. Indeed, although a signal has to convey a message, it is not clear that we should say that even the complete signal has a sense. Neither the whole signal nor its parts need do more than achieve certain intended effects—for instance, generate beliefs or propensities to act in certain ways. And if the parts of a speech-unit were only contributory message identifiers, speech would achieve no more.

Let us dramatize the matter in terms of an example.

Suppose one sets up a list or rule for enumerating strings of speech sounds, some being sentences and some not; thus the 137th string might be "There is a bullock in the garden", and the 643rd string might be "Shoot the bullock in the garden", and the 605,734th string might be "Fetch the police". Provided the sender and recipient of the messages know, either from a list or by some rule, the order of enumeration of these strings, it would be possible to work a system of communication according to which the sender of messages, instead of saying "There is a bullock in the garden", signaled "137", and instead of saying "Fetch the police", signaled "605,734", and so forth. Now, it seems perfectly plain that, although this system might be perfectly successful, there is a distinction to be made.

In the case of language proper, the signals, for instance, "There is a bullock in the garden", *express* the message being communicated. They are able to do this because of their complexity—that is, it is the words thus combined which give the communication a *content*, by (we might say) carrying the sense of the whole signal.

By contrast, "137", "643", and "605,734", in the system I mentioned, do not *express* the messages which are being put over: they serve only to *identify* them. They may serve to *bring about* some new state of knowledge or belief in the hearer, but they do not express this message, nor express this knowledge or belief. And, although the signals are complex (643; 605,734; etc.), and the subordinate parts of them (6, 4, 3, 1, etc.) have a *use* which enables one to identify the messages put over by the complete signals containing them, it still remains that neither the complete signals nor their subordinate parts have any *sense*, because neither the complete signals nor their parts express any sense or specific content. There is no expressing of a sense because the components of such a signal are ciphers without meaning.

By contrast, in the case of speech, our whole utterance expresses a sense in the same act as its constituent parts or words are used to express this sense. And, by the mere utterance of these words with the relevant intonation and in the context concerned, the sense intended has been expressed, the message issued. Our bolt is shot, the complete act performed, whether or not it secures appropriate understanding or "uptake", so long as it was performed in such a way that one had the right to expect understanding, though not necessarily agreement or obedience, from a speaker of the same language.

One can only make Austin's distinction between what is done in the act of saying from what is done by means of it—between the things he called "illocution" and "perlocution"—if the act of saying something in full context, of expressing a sense, is in itself a complete intentional act, independently of whether the hearer is expected to agree. If it is not, then we have not got beyond a theory of signaling. To get beyond a theory of signaling, we have to do justice to the intuitive idea that in committed utterance, one's sentences *express* something. And if a sentence expresses something, this must involve that its words, as uttered in this particular combination and in this particular context, express this sense.

Nobody really doubts this. Everybody uses the word "express" informally and unreflectively, as if all this were so. But the question is as to whether the theories of philosophers and linguists give any place for this being so. We cannot give the idea of "expressing" an explicit definition (explicit in the way the definition of "bachelor" as "man of marriageable age not yet married" is explicit), but have to treat it as a primitive notion within our account of language. It can only have the contextual definition provided by showing its role in the overall structure of our account.

Yet it is no more possible for a sentence to have a sense without its words expressing this sense than for a person to grasp a table without his fingers grasping the table. For sentences consist in their words in a certain order and intonation, sense being given to sentence and words in the same act—the act of being uttered or promulgated in writing or otherwise. It is its words, taken as they occur in use in context, which express the sense of a sentence. Conversely, sentences only express their sense in and through their words. That is, at the conscious level the function of words as *sense-expressors* is primary. And if words with their combinations are only sense-identifiers, then so are sentences, and there is nothing more to a sentence having sense than its serving as a signal intended (perhaps according to convention) to have certain effects on the beliefs and behavior of the receivers of the signal.

Correlative with the understanding of the role of words in sentences as expressing the meanings of these sentences is a certain view of sentences as complete discourse-units. In the act of utterance we select a sentence from an already compiled store of "possible sentences", like an arrow from a quiver, and then put it to use (although in special circumstances, not as a norm, we may reflect on how we are going to express what we want to say). Rather, the sense of the sentence as taken in its context of utterance, and the senses of its words as used in it, are both formed in the act of uttering it, as the sound of a trill or musical sequence is constituted in the act of performance or, to take a more ancient parallel, as the sounds of consonants and vowels are constituted in the act of pronouncing a syllable and vice versa.

We do not speak of expressing in the musical and phonetic cases because there is nothing which stands to the notes and the trill, or to the phonemes and the syllable, as a sense or meaning stands to the words and the sentence. The sentence or discourse-unit and its sense or meaning are, in the same act, not only objects of speech and hearing, but also objects of understanding. It has an intelligible content, and not just a structure or syntax, and we use the words in context to express this content.

(c) *Words and phrases as sentence-constituents, not mere sentence-components*

In the sentence "Every boy loves some girl", we might regard "boy loves", "every", and "some girl" as components, and equally "every", "boy", "loves some", and "girl"—or, more radically, treating of the written word, we might take "Ever", "y boy lov", and "es some girl". That is, considered as an observable spoken or written entity, we may divide the sentence up into components just as we please, and, experienced only as a phonetic, lexical, or graphological entity, it will be from these components that we will, if possible, have to identify its sense.

The role of sentence-factors as sense-expressors, not mere sense-identifiers, requires them to be conceived as constituents, not mere components, of the sentences they go to make up.[12]

Here I adopt the phraseology of Michael Dummett, who explains it by reference to its importance in logic.[13] There it is vital to distinguish, in the example I took before, whether we are dealing with the proposition in regard to every boy, that he loves some girl—something which we might represent "(Every boy) (loves some girl)"—or whether we are dealing with the proposition that in regard to some girl or other, the situation is that every boy loves her—something which we might represent "(Every boy loves) (some girl)". For instance, if it is built up in the first way, it will not contain the *constituent* "Every boy loves", although this could be regarded as a *component* of the sentence. It is only insofar as it plays a part in the building up or construction of the sentence considered as an utterance with sense that a component should be counted as a constituent of a sentence.

Whereas components come as phonetic, lexical, or graphological wholes or continua, constituents very often come in a very different way—in divided form, rather than necessarily unitary phrase, in a sentence or utterance. Thus in the proposition "2 + 3 = 5" we can consider the proposition as having as constituents (i) the predicate "… + \\\ = ///" (or in Frege's representation "$\xi + \upsilon = \zeta$") and (ii) 2, 3, and 5 as arguments.[14] Now, the predicate "… + \\\ = ///" is not visible or audible as a continuous whole, but involves a structure reaching beyond its visible or audible parts, as it were having tentacles reaching to the whole of the clause concerned, or establishes a field of force extending over the whole clause. Likewise, the sign for the function "$\xi + \upsilon$" reaches beyond its visible part "+"—thus, predicates and other such functional expressions must be regarded as intrinsically incomplete in the way examined in chapter IX.

Later on we shall discover that we need to make the same distinction in grammar. Following Ackerman and Webelhuth, we can regard "look at" (the "at" behaving as a preposition) and "phone back" (the "back" behaving as an adverb) as lexical units, even when they occur as discontinuous wholes, as in "look intensely at" and "phone James back".[15] More importantly, we can do the same with verb phrases in German when they occur in divided form, the finite auxiliary as the second phrase in the main clause, and the participle or infinitive at the end. This conception is vital for bracketing as a form of grammaticalization, treated in chapter XIII.

12. I draw the expression "sentence-factor" from Ryle, "Categories", in *Collected Essays*, no. 12.

13. Dummett, *The Interpretation of Frege's Philosophy* (London: Duckworth, 1981), 271–77.

14. Russell was less fussy in allowing letters to perform multiple functions, and so might say that we had as constituents the predicate "x + y = z" along with 2, 3, and 5 as arguments. Or he might say that we have the function "x + y" with the value "2 + 3" for arguments "2" and "3", and the predicate "x = y", with arguments "2 + 3" and "5", and value "(2 + 3) = 5".

15. F. Ackerman and G. Webelhuth, *A Theory of Predicates* (Stanford, Calif.: CSLI, 1998).

Section 3. How "Expressing a Sense" Differs from Other Forms of "Expressing"

(a) *The pivotal role of the notion of expressiveness*

Sentences are articulated, possessed of structure or syntax. They have a "use" or function. However, their primary structure or syntax is a semantic structure, or semantic syntax, and their use is to express a sense, so that the situation is not to be compared with taking a tool out of a tool bag or drawing an arrow from a quiver or a number out of a phrasebook listing by number and putting it to use to achieve an external end (e.g., using the number out of the phrasebook to signal the sentence listed, as if the phrasebook listed coded instructions).

Thus, in one act, a sentence with its words, at once spoken or heard and understood, and the senses both of this sentence and of these words are established as co-cognates, "cognates" of speech or hearing and "cognates" of linguistic understanding. And what I say of what is spoken and heard applies equally to what is written and read.

Our first task is to give an informal account of this primitive notion of "expressing a sense". This notion is strategic to the structure of our ordinary understanding of the functioning of language. The failure to realize this constitutes the underlying defect of most current semantic theory.

(b) *Distinguishing linguistic expressiveness from the expressiveness of the nonlinguistic*

There are many things in the case of which we speak of expressing—emotions, moods, happiness, boredom, pain, and distress—but my concern is not with expressing in general, but with the special case in which we are said to express a sense. A smile is a typical example of a natural expression of emotion, and smiling at someone can serve to signal amusement, sympathy, warmth, support, identification, or other such emotion to someone else, deceptively or truthfully, but not to express it linguistically.[16] What it expresses does not have the logical relationship to the expressing of an intelligible and intended sense or content required for linguistic understanding. It is the lack of this, rather than the arbitrariness of the sign, which makes the smile nonlinguistic.

The linguistic character of some nonvocal conventional gestures requires more careful consideration. (The "gestures" of sign-languages are irrelevant

16. A spontaneous smile of amusement and a smile deliberately "put on" to show that one is amused are logically distinct. A deliberate smile can serve as a pretense, or even as a prearranged signal of some information or instruction unconnected with amusement.

here, since they are linguistic signs in the full sense, sign-languages having syntactic as well as lexical features.)

I have in view such things as nods, head-shakings, quizzical looks, raised eyebrows, gestures to come or go, and any other signs whose significance is conventionally established. Nods and head-shakes introduce no special problem, but should be thought of as "synsentential" signs with the same function as the utterances of "Yes!" and "No!" Acts of pointing are likewise synsentential in character. And other nonvocal signs may be equivalent to the utterance of "Really?" or "Contemptible!" in appropriate intonation, giving synsentential expression to attitudes in reponse to the remarks of others. Such gestures are not linguistic signs in their own right, but, understood synsententially, in relation to some publicly evident thought-content to which they respond, they have a language-related or "linguistic" sense, although problematic cases arise.[17]

Other kinds of one-word utterance, such as "Ow!" and "Alas", fit the same picture. The only reason we have for regarding these as word-utterances is the way they can figure in more plainly linguistic contexts, and this makes it unsurprising that they have an etymology and can be translated. The fuller linguistic contexts seen in such utterances as "Ow! it hurts" and "Alas, all is lost" reveal a diminutive grammar, readily extensible—for example, to "Alas that he has gone". Such expressions are not to be confused with pieces of pain or distress behavior of a nonlinguistic character; they are not elements either of *langue* or of *parole*, such as could require linguistic understanding.

It is, of course, primarily people who express things, not sentences. But they do this in some way or other—for example, by smiles, frowns, flinching, groaning, or grimacing, whether involuntarily or voluntarily, and not only by expressing pleasure or discontent linguistically, as in complaining. But the linguistic cases need to be distinguished from the others in that they involve not just two things, the people and the way they express themselves, but also a third thing, the sense of the linguistic expression as a thought-content. The existence of this third thing is a precondition of the speech-act—as what Aus-

17. The Neapolitan gesture which struck Wittgenstein as not fitting with his picture theory of meaning, according to Scraffa's tale as recounted in Norman Malcolm, *Ludwig Wittgenstein: A Memoir*, 2nd ed. (Oxford: Oxford University Press, 1984), 58, is instructive as to the difficulty of judging whether a particular conventional gesture should be considered a *semantically expressive* sign, with a place in the language of the people concerned, or not. In this gesture, one brushes the underside of one's chin with an outward sweep of the fingertips of one's hand and is understood to signify disregard, disgust, or contempt—whether in regard to ideas, suggestions, or people.

This Neapolitan gesture is a conventional, not a natural, sign, and when made in sight of a companion it has the function which the predicate "is contemptible" would have in regard to the object of contempt—the object being made clear to oneself and one's companion by the context—for instance, an exhibition of poor-spiritedness or of bad taste, or some person just referred to in conversation. (The sign does not belong to speech or writing—as well as lacking the kind of complexity exemplified in letters or syllables.)

tin called an illocutionary act—having the kind of completeness which I explain in chapter III. It is as a result of this that we can distinguish between things internal to the *illocution*—that is, things we do *in* saying what we say (i.e., internal to the act of utterance *qua* utterance of this public expression of meaning),[18] and mere *perlocutions*,—that is, things not internal to the act of utterance, but what we do or contrive to do *by* performing it (e.g., to get a contrary person to do something precisely by asking him not to do it).

Section 4. Distinguishing *Langue*-Meaning and *Parole*-Meaning as the Key to Escaping Compositionalism

In my account, there are two ways in which words are not mere ciphers.

First, it is a matter of the nature of *parole* or discourse itself that words or lexical factors are not contributory sense-identifiers, but sense-expressors, in the way I have just indicated—and thereby that sentences are constituted not by their constituents being in a certain static arrangement, but in the act of using these constituents within the act of linguistic deliverance itself. It is this dynamic anti-compositionalist conception of the sentence which shapes my thought in chapter III and part three of this book. This way of conceiving the matter has the added advantage of bringing our account within linguistic science into closer accord with our experience as we experience it.

Meantime, the fact that words are not just ciphers appears also in a second way, and it is to this which I now come. Consideration of this second way affords not only a disproof of the adequacy of the supposedly scientific mechanistic approach, as I indicate in chapter V, but also a positive insight into how it is that words in their context of use indeed give content to the sentences they make up and express it.

Second, words reveal themselves as more than mere ciphers when we recognize the relations between *langue* and *parole* according to which each focus of meaning of a word as identified at the level of *langue* is liable to constitute a multi-potentiality for an indefinite spread of logically distinguishable uses at the level of *parole*. It is here that we see the ambiguity in Davidson's argument in his early paper, which reveals the root of all his later thinking and of all "compositionalist" theory. He later summarized this argument in these terms: "A satisfactory theory must discover a finite basic vocabulary in the verbal phenomena to be interpreted if it is to be useful to a creature with finite powers. If this is so, there is no escape from the need to treat the semantic fea-

18. This will include whatever is involved in the illocution, and therefore include the locution; see Austin, *How to Do Things with Words*, 101–3; cf. note A appended to chap. X in this volume.

tures of the potential infinity of sentences as owed to the semantic features of the items in a finite vocabulary".[19] The key ambiguity lies in a consideration of whether we are limited to mechanically applicable "extensional" terms in defining the finite powers of the language-users under consideration or whether we may define these powers in non-extensional terms, whose disputed nature I discuss in chapter VIII, section 1. If, as my discussion will make increasingly clear, single focuses of meaning typically give rise to an indefinite number of senses or types of views in speech and writing, then the finite resources provided by a finite lexicon will give rise to an indefinitely large number of functional constituents in use within complete utterances. In order to understand the character of speech we have to think of sentences as linguistic deliverances formed in the act of speech or writing, a lexical factor gaining what sense or discourse-significance it has as a functional constituent in the act of speech or composition.

(a) *Words and their distinct focuses of meaning*

(i) Giving precision to the notion of focus of meaning

I explain the notion of a *focus of meaning of a word* informally as a usage requiring separate itemization in a dictionary. This is instructively instanced if we look at the entry for "bachelor" in *The Shorter Oxford English Dictionary*, as revised in 1973:

> [ME. *bachelor* - OFr. *bacheler* young man aspiring to knighthood:- Rom. **baccalaris*. Ult. source and connections doubtful.] 1. A young knight who followed the banner of another; a novice in arms. [Hence the suggested derivation from *Bas Chevalier*.] Hence, *b. Knight Bachelor*, a simple knight; the full title of a gentleman who has been knighted 1609. 2 (obsolete). A junior member, or "yeoman", of a trade-guild, or City Company - 1809. 3. A man or woman who has taken the first degree at a university. [In this sense latinized as *baccalarius*, and altered by a pun to *baccalaureus*.] ME. 4. An unmarried man (of marriageable age) ME. 5 (obsolete). A single woman. B.JONS.[20]

The predominant modern use of the word is the one listed as 4, arising in late Middle English.

The types of connection between the different meanings of the word "bachelor" in this list are the types of connection which would be of interest

19. Davidson, *Inquiries into Truth and Interpretation*, xv, summarizing "Theories of Meaning and Learnable Languages", essay 1 of that collection, first read in 1964 and first published in 1965.

20. *The Shorter Oxford English Dictionary* (hereafter *Shorter OED*), 3rd rev. ed., 2 vols. (Oxford: Oxford University Press, 1973), with the boldface numberings of the original marked in italics. Hopper and Traugott have a discussion parallel to my discussion, also taking "bachelor" as homonymous, and taking "sad" as their prime example of polysemy in *Grammaticalization*, 1st ed., 69–71.

in studying the history of a language and how it develops *diachronically* (that is, over time)—indeed, just the types of connection which are absent when we speak of logs of wood, ships' log books, and logarithms as "logs" (where it would be better to speak of different words, rather than different usages of the same word). But in this book my concern is not with etymology, but solely with the *synchronic* use of language—what arises from the knowledge of a language-user has at one particular time of the language concerned (presuming an ideal language-user with perfect knowledge of the language, even its most obscure or recondite terms and grammatical usages).

It is important to distinguish focuses of meaning of whose interconnections we are aware in our synchronic use of the language concerned from cases where there is solely an etymological connection.

Thus, in considering the synchronic use of the language it would not matter if there were different words for "man not yet married" and "person with a first degree from a university". True, it is the same kind of *langue*-understanding or skill which enables us to extend the use of words by metaphor in virtue of some kind of likeness or parallelism which also makes the sort of history exemplified in the case of the word "bachelor" intelligible to us retrospectively, enabling us to appreciate the similarities or parallels which invited the earlier extensions of the use of the word concerned prior to their becoming fossilized and isolated from each other. But it remains that these extensions are indeed now fossilized and have long ceased to be part of the contemporary language-user's understanding of the word concerned.

Accordingly, the one etymological word "bachelor" should count as several different words, lexemes, or lexical factors—one for each of the focuses of meaning concerned.

(ii) Some distinct focuses of meaning have a living connection

By contrast, in many other cases, although the separate focuses of meaning of a word are clearly distinguishable, the associations between them are within the range of the common language-user's awareness—hence it would be wrong to regard them as if we might just as well have had a different word, and so have described them as "polysemous" or "homonymous" (having different meanings, though the first of these terms is variably used). Thus we speak of playing games, playing instruments, a theatre company's playing a play and its members playing parts in such plays, and in all these cases the verb "play" suggests some connection with enjoyment and with an activity of a non-utilitarian character. Yet the purposes of a dictionary require that all these uses of the verb "play" be separately itemized, as involving different focuses of meaning, because what it is to play is not one thing as between games, instruments, and dramas—something reflected in grammatical differences in how the verb is used, its forms of translation, and the ways it is paraphrased.

Prepositions which have both spatial and temporal uses provide another case in which we are tempted to say that there is just one focus of meaning. Such prepositions form a family, and the pattern of relationships within the two families is essentially the same (except that the temporal family has no members corresponding to anything implying more than one dimension; e.g., "left" and "right"). So far as prepositions distinguish points and periods, order and direction between points and within periods, there is perfect formal analogy between our use of prepositions in regard to time and our use in regard to space—and so far as continuous time is concerned, there is perfect algebraic analogy. These things have made some argue that the prepositions concerned have the same meaning in the two cases.[21]

Yet these prepositions are used according to entirely different sets of criteria in their two types of use, spatial and temporal; and sentences using the prepositions in a temporal meaning have a whole system of implications in regard to the presence or absence of causal relations and to what is or is not possible, a system quite absent when the prepositions are used spatially. This alone would compel us to admit the presence of two quite different sets of discourse-significances. However, more importantly, underlying these differences is the quite different relation of temporal and spatial prepositional phrases to motion, and this can be seen in their radically different syntactic roles in the two cases. Temporal prepositional phrases have a role logically modifying the whole verbal framework of the sentence in the examples given, commonly embodied within the predicate in a finite verb, a role parallel to that of temporal clauses such as those introduced by "when", "while", "after", and "before". By contrast, "in the garden" in "David is in the garden" complements the verb "to be" and expresses an attribute of David, not of "being", and in "David is lunching in the garden" an attribute not of David, but of his lunching activity. All these considerations force us to recognize that the prepositions concerned are being used not just with different speech-senses arising from their context of use, but in different focuses of meaning, although with some formal analogy between them. However, the analogy is merely formal, whereas with the word "play" mentioned above there was some real analogy through the connection with enjoyment or recreation in paradigm examples of each kind of playing.

The word "since" raises a very different problem. Here we again need to speak of two focuses of meaning, two *langue*-meanings, even though the associations between them are again within the range of the common language-

21. For instance, this contrary position is taken in David C. Bennett, *Spatial and Temporal Uses of English Prepositions: An Essay in Stratificational Semantics* (London: Longman, 1975), 8; see 4–9.

user's awareness, and it would be wrong to regard them as if we might just as well have had a different word. The word "since" used with a temporal meaning enters discourse in an explanatory role (e.g., in such contexts as "He has been weak and confused since a rock fell on his head") so often that it can readily pass from its original temporal meaning to the role of expressing a causal or inferential connection. Now, in judging of the significance of a word in an utterance we are judging what it expresses as part of the significance of the particular utterance concerned—how it is to be understood in use. Thus, in the case of the word "since", it is only after we have understood the utterance under consideration that we can pick out the focus of meaning listed in the dictionary in which the word had been used (i.e., whether it was being used in its temporal meaning or whether to express a causal or inferential connection).

(b) *Each focus of meaning or langue-meaning as the vehicle of an indefinite number of parole-meanings*

I speak of each identified focus of meaning signified by a particular word as a distinct "*langue*-meaning".[22] In a parallel way I speak of the distinct senses which a word expresses as used in speech or discourse as a constitutive part of a linguistic deliverance as distinct "*parole*-meanings", "speech-senses", or "discourse-significances". True, we may use a word in a particular *langue*-meaning while aware of the relation or analogy between this and some of its other *langue*-meanings (i.e., when this relation is within the range of the language's synchronic use). But we need to distinguish a word's having related, but distinct *langue*-meanings from its having a spread of *parole*-meanings even as used in one particular *langue*-meaning.

The potential infinity which we meet with in considering the spread of senses or "discourse-significances" of a given expression in speech or writing is not the potential infinity presented by any system for enumerating the natural numbers in some law-defined order, but more like the indefiniteness of number exemplified by the constructive definitions of real numbers or the members of a mathematical intuitionist's "spread". From the point of view of the logician or philosopher, the number of possible "sentences" is geared to the number of these possible "discourse-significances" or senses of expressions, not to the number of their *langue*-meanings.

22. To treat words alone as identifying focuses of meaning is an oversimplification, since often *langue*-meaning is associated with extended idiomatic phrases rather than just words, and all languages are to some degree inflected or agglutinative so that, strictly speaking, it is a lexical factor or lexeme, rather than a word as such, which identifies a focus of meaning.

(i) General conception

Some examples will help us grasp how a word, expression, or morpheme taken in one *langue*-meaning (one meaning at the level of *langue*) can be used in many different *parole*-meanings or speech-senses (many senses at the level of *parole*). Thus, "show to be true", "prove", and "demonstrate" are expressions which can be used in one *langue*-meaning equally in respect of assertions alike in history, physics, mathematics, and ethics. Each use or type of application of the word or expression concerned will be associated with distinct conditions of truth or different criteria or reasons for application, and so have a different sense from the point of view of philosophers or logicians.

In this setting there is a natural tendency for preferential usages of particular words to develop to the extent that it can come about that one word, expression, or morpheme has several *langue*-meanings, focuses of meaning separately itemizable in a dictionary, but closely related to each other. Thus one word may be preferred in one class of case and tend to be avoided in the others (e.g., the word "prove" is used more in legal cases and mathematics than in others). Or a word may develop distinct uses with different implications (e.g., the word "prove" from meaning simply "show to be true" may come to mean "show to be true on certain hypotheses" or, a yet more specialized case, "derive according to the rules of a given formal system—for instance, of logic, arithmetic, or geometry")—in any full dictionary such specialized usages would be separately noted.

However, the possibility of such specialized usages arises only within the context of the background datum that such expressions as "true" and "show to be true" can be used in one *langue*-meaning according to different types of truth-condition or criteria of application in the case of each of many different kinds of assertion in different subject areas.

In the account I am putting forward, each *langue*-meaning is defined or explained by means of *parole*. Yet the knowledge of *langue*-meaning (what I call *langue*-understanding) which the language-user thereby acquires is the basis of a skill which enables us to use the word concerned with understanding and still be understood by others in an indefinite range of types of use in speech and writing. These uses in speech (i.e., at the level of *parole*) are logically distinguishable, but do not invite or require separate itemization in the dictionary, because the varied types of use involve only one focus of meaning. The understanding with which we thus use a word in any given particular case, the understanding which is shared by others, is an understanding at the level of *parole*.[23] This conception that a word in one focus of meaning at the level of

23. These ideas, supplemented by an account of the special features of kind terms, discussed in chap. IX, sec. 2 (c) (iii), give more precision to the notions with which Ingarden was struggling in *Literary Work*

language-possession may have many different senses or kinds of significance found its first clear statement among twentieth-century linguists by S. Karcevskij, speaking of the need to distinguish different *significations* in 1929.[24]

(ii) Metaphor and figures of speech

My conception is most readily presented in informal exposition by means of examples. With each example, some questions are liable to arise, and I deal with the most obvious or significant objections in later chapters.

The most recognized type of case is that of "metaphor", a word which by etymology should mean "carried-across" or "transferred" meaning, but which in practice implies a transfer in virtue of some likeness. The primary contrast being made is with the "proper" or "literal" meaning (its use *proprie*). We can see the contrast if we consider the use of the word "play". This is a word for which we have seen that we should itemize several different focuses of meaning in our dictionary. Each constitutes a distinct literal meaning in its own right, and none is metaphorical. By contrast, if somebody said that "At first it was John who played golf, but in the end it was golf which played John", we would not expect the second use of the word "play" to be itemized separately in the dictionary, but rather would regard it as a metaphor. In general, metaphors do not invite separate itemization in the dictionary. Rather, we expect the speaker-hearer's shared skill or *langue*-understanding of words to enable both speakers and hearers to understand metaphorical uses of words which are to them quite fresh and new without explanation—indeed, without this, most poetry and normal literary use would be unintelligible.

In general, the number of ways in which deviation from the most typical paradigm use of a word may arise is quite indefinite, both because there is an indefinite variety of types of possible situation to be described and of types of aspect of such situation to pick out and because there is no definite limit to the number of ways which an inventive mind may find to describe them, no definite limit to the range of cases from similarity to which metaphor may be drawn—somewhat as the number of possible configurations of rock face to be dealt with by the rock climber using his skills and the number of ways in which he may see how to surmount the obstacles presented is non-enumerable. This is why it would be misguided to try and list them in a dictionary, because in each case we are still dealing with just one focus of meaning.

There is a multiplicity of cases in which the context of the use of a word is such as to make clear that the speaker cannot be intending it in such a sense

---

of Art, 84–106, especially when he tries to give a sympathetic account of something like a sentence-formed meaning (101–5), in effect trying to do justice to the ideas rejected; see 98–99.

24. S. Karcevskij, "Du dualisme asymetrique du signe linguistique", in *Prague School Reader*, ed. Joseph Vachek, 81–87, and discussed in Vachek, *Linguistic School of Prague*, 30–31.

as would carry its normal implications or associations. Thus, if the optician pushes a pencil up to three inches from our noses and asks us how many pencils we see, we may give him the answer "two pencils" without the implication that there are two pencils, so that the sentence-constituent "... see—" has acquired a quite distinct speech-sense or discourse-significance through its context of use—quite distinct, that is, from the sense of the sentence-constituent "... see—" in its primary or paradigm use, which requires that the object seen exists under the description given in the object-phrase. And, in general, all the main verbs of perception, action, and sensation carry implications which belong to their sense in their paradigm uses but which may—in one implication or another—be absent in some cases in a way which is appreciated by the hearer or reader in the act of hearing or reading the statement concerned without special explanation being needed.[25]

(iii) The inadequacy of Jackendoff's approach

Jackendoff suggests a quite different kind of approach. For instance, he suggests that the meaning of the word "see" is to be explained in the following way: typically it signifies a combination of visual contact with awareness, while exceptionally it signifies visual contact without awareness or, at other times, awareness without visual contact.[26] This observation, that the use of the verb "see" tends to have these two facets, is perfectly in accord with common sense and very serviceable in making the spread of different uses of the verb and the interrelation between these uses more intelligible.

However, this perfectly correct observation is perfectly useless for the purpose of providing a mechanically applicable procedure for deciding how and when the verb should be used. For there is no mechanically applicable list of types of situation within which visual contact should be considered to have occurred. In the case of hallucination, there is no visual contact, but only some delusory belief that there has been such contact or tendency toward such belief, and it is quite obscure whether it should be counted as a case of "awareness".

Jackendoff, presumably with hallucinations in mind, allows for cases of "awareness" without visual contact. Yet removing the requirement of visual contact allows in not only hallucinations, but also all cases of "intellectual seeing" (seeing the point, seeing a theory as a whole, seeing the full range of

25. I present this account in more detail in David Braine, *Human Person*, 89–92.

26. Jackendoff, *Semantics and Cognition*, 150–51. This suggestion shows the inadequacy of his highly sophisticated attempt to resolve the problems concerned above, which he exactly identifies (112–15) by means of what he calls "Preference Rule Systems" (115–88), which he wrongly anticipates that neuronal computational systems will be capable of applying (187); cf. chap. III, sec. 4 (d), and chap. V, sec. 5 (a) of this volume.

meanings of a word, seeing the full potentiality of a particular athlete, seeing a person's character in its complexity for the first time, seeing the wonder of the stars or the mysterious power of the sea, or even, possibly, seeing God), and this shows the ambiguity in his definition. However, even if the requirement were added that the awareness should be such as could imaginably arise from the visual contact, although the criteria he offers might serve to provide an informal method of somewhat limiting our use of the word "see", they still do not supply any mechanically applicable definition, since the phrase "imaginably aware" is at least as informal in its application as the word "know".

Resort to the notion that some concepts are "fuzzy" is quite inadequate to explain the exactness of the *rapport* between the speaker's meaning and the hearer's understanding which we find, a degree of exactness appropriate to the field concerned (e.g., the branch of mathematics, science, history, or the novel). This insufficiency is especially evident when we consider how inconceivable it is that any computational system programmed beforehand should be able to anticipate the unpredictable variety of demands placed upon the human inquirer—the open-ended variety in the situations and problems which have not been met before.

Jackendoff is determined upon his belief that this kind of variety in the use of the same word can be brought under control and made subject to rule, and proposes to achieve this through his Preference Rule Systems, but in chapter V we will find mathematical reason confirming that his attempts are doomed to failure.

(iv) The character of the most general words in a language

Moreover, this phenomenon of a word being used in the same focus of meaning in logically distinguishable ways or according to logically distinguishable criteria arises also in a quite different and more systematic way in connection with all the most general words in the language: words like *entity, set, true, definition,* and *proof.* Of these, the word *true* should be placed alongside such words as *rational, free, voluntary, normal,* and *real,* for which H. L. A. Hart coined the expression "defeasible" because it is symptomatic of how we meet them as terms that we should find that their application is excluded in a spread of heterogeneous cases.[27] What Hart failed to take account of is that in each case there must be some positive concept which guides us in judging what makes us, for example, reject the classification of an action as "free" or "voluntary".

27. H. L. A. Hart, "The Ascription of Responsibility and Rights", in *Logic and Language,* ed. A. Flew (Oxford: Blackwell, 1951), 145–66. The example of "voluntary" was treated in Aristotle and "real" in Austin, *Sense and Sensibilia* (Oxford: Oxford University Press, 1962), chaps. 7–8.

What it is to prove something is, in an informal sense, readily definable and the same thing in all instances: it is to show that the thing concerned is true. But the criteria for counting as "showing to be true" and the implications of connotations of describing something in this way are very different in different areas. Accordingly, the conditions implied to be satisfied by what is claimed to be a "proof" are very different in history and in law courts from those required in the various physical sciences and in the many branches of mathematics, and all these are very different from what might be offered as a proof of the worthwhileness of some end or the rightness of some action. In this way it is natural to say that proof is not just one thing, indeed not even one thing within any of the many fields just indicated. Moreover, in the very restricted part of mathematics we call natural arithmetic, it is demonstrable that there is no one mechanically applicable criterion for what counts as a proof and no consistent system for proof in natural arithmetic which includes all demonstrative proofs in that area—since, granted any such consistent system of proof, we can always by reflection on it produce a finite demonstration of a further arithmetical proposition which could not have been derived in the original system.

Likewise, there is no mechanically applicable criterion for being true, since no formalizable system of propositions can contain its own definition of truth. This is unsurprising, because what it is to be true is so much more varied in history, the different parts of physics, and ethics than it is in natural arithmetic—it would seem plainly wrong to suppose that what it is to be true is the same in history, in physics, in arithmetic, and in ethics—except in the informal sense that with the question whether "P" or "Not-P" is true, the true proposition is the proposition which one would hold if one were in a position of knowledge in regard to the question.[28]

What these commonplaces imply is highly disputed. Here I merely *state* their significance for the relation between *langue*-meaning and *parole*-meaning, leaving further proof of my statement to chapter V.

We have a *langue*-understanding of such words as "true", "prove", and "know", but no one criterion for their application in any of the three cases. The apparent deficiency is not to be dealt with in the dictionary, as if in each new type of case we had a new itemizable focus of meaning—one focus for proof in history, another for proof in physics, and a whole series for proof in mathematics. We do not use the word "prove" in a new focus of meaning in

28. Such an informal definition fits well with ancient and medieval accounts of truth as the good of the intellect and knowledge as intellectual excellence (*aretē*)—since knowledge consists in being in the relevant intellectually satisfactory or good position; cf. David Braine, "Nature of Knowledge", extending the ideas of Bernard Mayo, "Belief and Constraint", *Proceedings of the Aristotelian Society*, New Series, 64 (1963–64): 139–56.

each new extension of proof in arithmetic, or for that matter for each new extension of modes of proof in astronomy. Rather, our *langue*-understanding of the word "prove", with its one focus of meaning and its associated relations to truth and knowledge, puts us in a position to recognize a non-enumerable range of things as counting as proofs.

It is vital to identify my thesis here more exactly.

There are obviously many different levels at which we can distinguish types of use of the same word. At a high level, each focus of meaning corresponds to one type of use. But, evidently, if two people agree in regard to a statement, for instance, "The number four is green", meaning that the soccer player with the shirt numbered four is inexperienced, then we have one type of use of the expressions concerned, but at least two instances of use of these expressions (i.e., one instance of use by each of the two people). In a statement in the same words, but meaning that the soccer player looks ill, we would have a second type of use of the expression "green". But these types of use of the words "four" and "green" are quite different from those uses concerned when one says, "Dumas's musketeers were now four", "Four is the square of two", and "Grass is green". In speaking of the senses and meanings of particular expressions, whether at the level of language-use (*parole*) or language-possession (*langue*), I shall always be speaking of types of use, not examples of use, yet types differentiated at the relevant level.[29]

My thesis is that if we consider *parole*-meanings or senses, each typically instanced in many different sentence or utterance tokens, we will find many *parole*-meanings or senses corresponding to each of the focuses of meaning of all or most words.[30] And, further, for each focus of meaning of a word or expression worth itemizing in a dictionary, there will be no finitely specifiable indication of all its different possible senses or most specific types of use.

This is obvious in the cases where idiosyncratic modes of reference arise, as in Nunberg's example of "The ham sandwich wants some more coffee" said by one waitress to another, where "the ham sandwich" refers to a customer who has asked for a ham sandwich, and so an adventitious circumstance has allowed the expression "the ham sandwich" to refer to the customer.[31] It is also obvious in cases where there are different focuses of meaning in the same word, as when the use of the color word "green" of unweathered fresh vegeta-

29. The significance of my gearing of sense or *parole*-meaning to the level of utterance includes the consequence (chaps. III and IX of this volume) that a difference in the intended reference of a singular term or proper name constitutes a difference in sense.

30. I say "typically" because one need not suppose that such a nonitemizable multiplicity of senses arises with every word. For instance, perhaps the uses of the word "and" are itemizable—e.g., one signifying conjunction only, another meaning "and then" (the "then" meaning "after that"), and others signifying co-membership of a set or co-objects of a relation.

31. Cf. Jackendoff, *Architecture*, 54.

tion allows an extension of usage to mean "inexperienced", or where consideration of color allows it to be used to signify looking unwell. It is these, along with metaphor and the development of specialized idioms, which make it almost impossible to exclude any grammatically formed construct from gaining sense in some context.

However, the freedom of the imagination whereby new metaphorical uses for old words arise, grounded in conceiving of new ways in which different things and situations are similar, involves an indefiniteness in the possible uses of the same expression which does not depend upon quirks of circumstance and all special idiom. Underlying this freedom of the imagination is the breadth of use of the non-metaphorically used and most general terms in human language. This is to be seen in the impossibility of delimiting the applications of such expressions as *individual, set, true,* or *definition,* or the family *show to be true, prove,* and *demonstrate,* or *see* according to mechanically applicable rule. For there can be no one set of criteria covering all the uses of any of these terms, for reasons amplified in chapter V.

(c) *Indirect confirmation of my view from the arguments of Russell and Davidson*

(i) Davidson's treatment of metaphor

The *langue*-meaning of a word is not left behind when it comes to using the word, but the capacity concerned, as it is exercised on each particular occasion, is such as to enable the word concerned to gain a more determinate use-meaning, *parole*-meaning, or sense. However, the need for this distinction between a word's lexical or *langue*-meaning and the *parole*-meaning or sense it gains in use is strikingly confirmed if we consider the arguments of Davidson and Russell.

Russell made it plain that any system which enables us to avoid the paradoxes of logic and set theory, systems such as the various theories of types and of hierarchies of metalanguages, will involve assigning an infinite range of different criteria of acceptance to the attributions of the natural number words "one", "two", and so on, as well as to applications of such expressions as "true" and "show to be true". For Russell, we will count shoes, colors, and numbers with three different types of number. Yet it is counterintuitive to suppose that these expressions have different lexical or *langue*-meanings in such cases. I return to Russell's problems in chapter II.

The need to distinguish between *langue*-meaning and *parole*-meaning (that is, discourse-significance) is especially clear in the case of metaphor.

When Davidson discusses metaphor he has more spontaneous ad hoc cases in mind, rather than such deeply embedded usages as those which allow us to use words such as "see", both in cases of perception and in the more intellectual cases of seeing a truth or seeing what is meant by something said. In regard to spontaneous ad hoc metaphors, he insists that the expression concerned is used literally, meaning by this that it is used in its established *langue*-meaning, and that the difference which arises when the expression is used metaphorically arises at the level of use. In insisting that in one way nothing novel is "said" beyond the literal, he takes advantage of the fact that the appreciation of what is "meant" depends upon deliberately maintaining the same *langue*-meaning, but relies upon the ambiguity of the word "say". Clearly something novel is "meant" at the level of use, and this he implicitly concedes when he insists that metaphor belongs exclusively to the domain of use.[32] However, this remark takes us no further, since it is only at the level of use, of the speech-act (Austin's "illocutionary act") that questions of truth and falsehood, knowledge or attitude-related properties, arise.

Speaking metaphorically is a form of asserting in which the information expressed is expressed by special idiomatic means, as in speaking of wearing a "loud" tie or as "casting" a "bitter" glance. Often metaphors also express the appropriateness of certain attitudes (e.g., disrespect toward Tolstoy as lacking a certain maturity, if he is described as a "moralizing infant"), but this does not remove their character as statements.[33]

Thus Davidson has vindicated the ideas that it is vital that metaphor should involve no new *langue*-meaning—no new literal meaning—and yet equally vital that it should involve a use of the word in a different speech-sense, albeit one parasitic upon its literal use. He has thus vindicated the very distinction between *langue*-meaning and *parole*-meaning which I am making, a distinction needed even in the cases of metaphors deeply embedded in the structure of language, such as seeing and grasping intellectually. It is only his insistence on explaining meaning in terms of truth-conditions, restricting what can count as a truth-condition, and so restricting what counts as belonging to semantics, that forces him to resort to a vague explanation of metaphor

32. Davidson, "What Metaphors Mean", essay 17 in *Inquiries Into Truth and Interpretation*; I cite 246, 247, 259, and 250 respectively.

33. Thus, rightly, "I depend on the distinction between what words mean and what they are used to do"; Davidson, "What Metaphors Mean", 247. However, in speaking of the latter, he blurs a multiplicity of distinctions carefully made by Austin. The essential thing done in any act of communication involves using words to convey a sense, and this is as true in the case of assertions or statements as in any other. However, his suggestion that speaking metaphorically arises at the level of use in the same sort of way as asserting, hinting, lying, promising, and criticizing involves jumbling many different distinctions together—lying, criticizing, and hinting are each different forms of asserting, differentiated by being contrary to the opinion of the speaker, by the negative view he expresses, or by deliberate incompleteness of information he conveys, whereas promising is not a form of asserting at all. Further, he ignores Austin's main distinction—namely, between using words to convey their expected sense in an act of linguistic communication or illocutionary act, of which asserting and promising are different genera, and, on the other hand, using words to contrive a nonlinguistic effect in a perlocutionary use of speech.

in terms of "expressiveness", as if statements were not expressive. Such a restrictive conception of "sense" and semantics is useless for the theory of language.

The retention of the same *langue*-meaning in contexts involving different *parole*-meanings is key to the semantics of idioms and aphorisms. Their constituent expressions have to retain their normal *langue*-meanings, although, evidently, it is the whole idiom or aphorism, rather than any one word by itself, which carries the sense in speech. Thus, "teach", "your", "grandmother", "to suck", and "eggs" retain their normal lexical meanings, although "teach your grandmother to suck eggs" has a quite distinctive sense. In the example considered earlier, "The ham sandwich wants more coffee", every word and the whole expression "the ham sandwich" retain their normal *langue*-meanings, but the whole sentence has a *parole*-meaning making "the ham sandwich" refer to the customer, not the sandwich, the oblique reference made possible by his having ordered a ham sandwich.

We can now dispose of some common mistakes—mistakes in considering words used in the same focus of meaning in figures of speech, and mistakes in considering words used in different, although related focuses of meaning with spatial prepositions. Always when a word is used in ways carrying different implications or suggestions, the word is being used in a different sense.

(ii) Figures of speech involve differences in "sense", not in supposed "pragmatic meaning"

Figures of speech provide a good example of the distinctions I am making. Thus, when the word "scepter" is used metonymically, as in "Her scepter held sway over all the oceans", its *langue*-meaning refers to the ornamental rod held by rulers symbolizing their position of authority, but in this use the word's sense or discourse-significance makes it refer to that authority itself. Likewise, if I order "All hands on deck", the word "hand" has its normal anatomical *langue*-meaning, but here refers to members of a crew receiving the order. Or again, when, in the Bible, Deuteronomy refers to "cities fenced up to heaven", the *langue*-meaning signifies "walls reaching the dome of the sky", but its speech-sense implies only "exceedingly high walls" in the figure of speech called hyperbole.

To proceed like Davidson and make only one distinction in levels of meaning between "pragmatic meaning" and "lexical" or *langue*-meaning, limiting "semantic meaning" to the latter is to make the false assumption that pragmatics and semantics can be separated. His approach to metaphor breaks the essential link between semantics and relevance to truth, verification, and attitude. The notion of sense required in semantics has to embrace not only the lexicon itemizing focuses of lexical meaning, but also any aspect of morpheme, word, or phrase meaning or their context of use which bears upon what makes an utterance true or false, upon methods of deciding its truth or falsity, or upon the actions or attitudes which it invites. All these pertain to "sense" as it concerns philosophers and linguists, as also to paraphrase and translation. Davidson's understanding of the term "pragmatic meaning" is a muddle.

Metaphorical extensions in the applications of words are rooted in analogy, similarity, or some kind of relation. True, metaphor is introduced for communicative, conversational purposes to make language more dramatic or expressive, as when we say that something "lacks" a certain property, or that 36 and 41 "cannot escape" equalling 77. Yet the metaphorical terms achieve their expressive effect by means of their suggestiveness—for instance, here as drawing attention to the analogy with the case of privation or highlighting human impotence to escape from the consequences of logical or arithmetical truths; and they can only be brought into use because it is part of their semantics that they imply the more general concept of which they are being used as surrogates, here the concepts expressed by "not" and "cannot not" respectively (to lack something is "not" to "have" it, while "not to have solidity" is "not to be solid", and if 36 and 41 cannot escape equaling 77, then they "cannot not" equal 77).

(iii) The confusions of the localist theory of case and how spatial prepositions are used

We can now recognize that the localist theory of case, proposing that our ideas of spatial relation are the root of the distinctions between the thematic roles of different noun phrases in a sentence, as indicated by case inflections,[34] involves the same confusion between lexical or *langue*-meaning and sense or semantic significance.[35]

The worst instance of this arises when existence is explained as a matter of being "in" some location.[36] Yet the existence of an entity is a logical presupposition of any statement about that entity and, unlike being in a location, is not

34. John M. Anderson, *Grammar of Case*; and Marilyn E. Jessen, "A Semantic Study of Spatial and Temporal Expressions in English" (PhD diss., University of Edinburgh, 1975). As a matter of the history of language, many of the locational uses of cases and prepositions may be rooted in nonlocative ones rather than vice versa (e.g., the locative use of the ablative or genitive case may arise from the function of these cases as being to express the origin or cause of a thing or as to specify or identify it—and genitive, dative, and ablative can all express association).

35. Possession may be expressed by a preposition such as "of", by the genitive case, or by a verb like "belong", "possess", "have", or "appertain". But the fact that, for instance, "The car belongs to Robert" can be thought of as a way of the car's being "at" (French, *à*) Robert shows that this spatial preposition might be used metaphorically to express the same ideas, but does not show that the idea of possession or the idioms that express it can be explained in terms of such spatial metaphor. Again, knowledge or understanding has been thought of as having something before one, or being close to it, or standing upon, under, or before something (Jessen, "Semantic Study", 174), but these spatial metaphors are non-explanatory.

36. Hume and some later empiricists suggest this, and the idea reappears in Jessen's linguistics. Since

an attribute or logically a predicate, and even though people often attempt to express the presupposition by using a locative expression, what is concerned is not location as such, but availability to be a subject of predication, which needs not be expressed in terms of locability.[37]

Thus, even though extending the application of a spatial preposition by metaphor or analogy may allow some formal, general, or psychological idea to be given a more vivid means of expression, such extension can in no case *explain* such abstract or psychological meanings. For in these cases the sentences making use of the spatial word have no spatial implications, and the spatial words carry spatial associations, but no spatial implications.

Section 5. How We Achieve an "Infinite Use of Finite Means"

(a) *The ambiguity in the word "infinite"—the notion of "indefiniteness"*

I explained in the introduction how our capacity in language to make an "infinite use of finite resources" arises not from our capacity to iterate certain linguistic operations, but from the capacity to use words with the informality and flexibility which I have begun to indicate. It is this which enables us to communicate intelligibly, even when we are dealing with unanticipated kinds of situation or raising fresh problems and dealing with them in unprecedented ways.

True, there is in principle no limit to the number of times various linguistic procedures can be iterated, and this is of importance in certain very complex mathematical proofs,[38] but in practice speech becomes unintelligible

---

the person who says that there is no God is not saying that God is not located in any place in the physical world, Jessen views this approach as depending on a metaphorical extension to a "world" conceived of as without restrictions of space or time—a metaphor for which her approach itself provides no way of explaining. (Whereas most metaphors involve an extrapolation from one example to another still within the spatiotemporal world, this way of speaking involves extrapolation beyond this into domains about whose existence, and even the possibility of asserting it, are being questioned.)

Moreover, the metaphor of "being there" is better understood as expressing availability to know and to act and, accordingly, availability to be spoken of as a real living agent, and so a subsistent subject of predication.

The believer will say "God is there" to mean "God is a reality, a datum, a fact not to be got away from", and if the word "exist" comes from the idea of "standing out" or "having a position distinct from the rest of things", then "God exists" will mean the same as "God is there", and neither will mean that God is in a particular place, let alone in a particular place in a world of his own distinct from ours. The same believer will also say "God is here. God is everywhere. There is no getting away from him", and the theologians tell us that he is "here" as cause of being, causally immediate to each thing that exists, as well as in other ways.

37. Given a subject of affirmative predications, A, whose existence is presupposed by any of these predications, the presupposition of existence is less misleadingly expressed by saying simply "A is" than by saying "A is there". When the impersonal mode of speech—"There is (such a thing as) A" or "There are A's"—is adopted, the "there" is empty, arising simply from the English demand for a morphosyntactic subject, and nothing more is meant than by "A is" or "A's are"; cf. chap. XI of this volume.

38. E.g., in proofs that four colors suffice to secure that any adjacent countries are in a different color when drawing maps, or in the recent proof of Fermat's Last Theorem.

and useless for the purposes of reflection or communication after a very small number of iterations of those procedures which are iterable. Thus, a sentence like "The editor the authors the newspaper hired liked laughed" bring us close to the limits of intelligibility,[39] and it takes only a small number of iterations of the operators "if", "not", and "or" to flummox us. Likewise, the devices provided by natural language for escaping ambiguity when we admix existential and universal quantifiers ("some" and "all") are very inadequate.

Accordingly, our flexibility in using words, while still achieving exactness in communicating our meaning without introducing vagueness, assumes a special importance for understanding the character of language. For this is the main root of our capacity in language to make infinite use of finite resources.

Yet, what is it for there to be no finitely specifiable indication of all the different possible senses or most specific types of use of a word in a given *langue*-meaning?

It is not, in any given case, that these "senses" or types of use are particularly large in number—for instance, more than 100, or more than 10^6, or more than 10^{56} (any given finite number, even 10^{56}, is very small compared with some other finite numbers), let alone more than any finite number whatsoever (i.e., let alone more than any natural number or positive integer). It is rather that they are of no definite number.

However, there are many ways of failing to be of any definite number. Thus, no definite number of grains of sand constitute a heap. But our problem is with a kind of indefiniteness which requires a different explanation, since it arises in a way which has no connection with vagueness.

In particular, more light is shed by considering the mathematical intuitionists' idea of spread, an idea useful to consider in the context of Zermelo's use of the concept of indefiniteness in set theory.[40] In order to avoid the paradoxes of the theory of sets, Zermelo suggested that a predicate is required to be "definite" for the things to which it applies to constitute a set. Thus, in order to avoid both the logical and the semantic paradoxes, one will say that the predicates "is a set", "is a set which does not contain itself as a member", "is a proposition", "is a definition" ("identifying description", "designation"), "is the least set definable in language L in less than twenty words", "is an adjective not describing itself",

39. I consider this extreme example in chap. XIII, explaining how it can be given the meaning "The editor whom the authors which the newspaper hired liked laughed".

40. "A propositional function is definite if the basic relations of the domain concerned, by means of the axioms and the universally valid laws of logic, determine without any arbitrariness whether it holds or not"; Ernst Zermelo, "Untersuchungen über die Grundlagen der Mengenlehre I", *Mathematische Annalen* 65, no. 2 (1908): 263; translated as "Investigations in the Foundations of Set Theory I", in *From Frege to Gödel: A Source Book in Mathematical Logic*, 1879–1931, ed. Jean van Heijenoort (Cambridge, Mass.: Harvard University Press, 1967). This conception was regarded as a weak point in Zermelo's 1908 set theory by Fraenkel, Skolem, and Weyl, but the proposed alternative ways of avoiding the paradoxes, especially the semantic paradoxes, all involve some arbitrariness or are in some way of an ad hoc character.

and "is a predicate not applying to itself" are none of them "definite" predicates.

No better way of avoiding the paradoxes has been found than to rely on some such informal, undefined concept as "definiteness" and "indefiniteness".

However, all the nontrivial examples of predicates, the use of which lead to paradox, arise in cases where the set of things to which the predicates concerned applies is infinite, if there is any such set. Further, consideration of the Richard paradox explained suggests that there may be a close connection between the notion of infinity in mathematics and the notion of indefiniteness.[41] Within mathematics we have (1) the inductive infinity of sets which can be put into one-to-one correspondence with the natural numbers; (2) the particular kind of infinity of those sets which can be put into one-to-one correspondence with the real numbers or with all the sets of natural numbers; and then (3), as an umbrella concept covering the two previous cases and any others there may be, the infinity of any set which cannot be put into one-to-one correspondence either with the natural numbers or with the real numbers, whether because the predicate is indefinite or for some other reason. Whether we can consider "definite" transfinite numbers to form a whole series of which (1) and (2) are only examples is not our present concern.

Cantor had earlier proved that there does not exist a one-to-one correspondence between *the real numbers* and the natural numbers. The interest of the Richard paradox lies in the fact that it suggests a proof that the definitions of *real numbers* cannot be put into one-to-one correspondence with the natural numbers, so that they also are non-denumerable *because* there is no systematic way of enumerating them.[42]

Paradoxically, philosophers have tended to draw quite different conclusions from these two proofs, holding that the real numbers are non-denumerable because they are too many, but that the definitions of real numbers are non-denumerable because there is an indefiniteness in the notion of definition which cannot be eliminated. We might instead suggest that the non-denumerable infinity of the real numbers constitutes a particular way of being indefinite, rather than a particular magnitude or size. This raises a question as to whether Cantor's theory of transfinite cardinal numbers is meaningful at all, first in treating numbers beyond the natural numbers as having an existence independent of being defined or identified, and second in treating

41. See chap. II, sec. 3 (b), and chap. IV, sec. 2. I explored some of the issues in earlier unpublished papers: "Infinite Sets", presented to the Interdisciplinary Seminar on the History and Philosophy of Science, University of Aberdeen, Scotland, 1968, and "Truth and Definiteness", presented at the University of St. Andrews, Scotland, 1976.

42. The problem thus posed by the Richard paradox is much more significant than the one posed by Berry-type paradoxes (e.g., a paradox arises whether we suppose that "the least number not definable in less than fourteen words of the English language" does exist or that it does not). The Berry paradox shows that the criteria for what counts as a definition need to be stricter, whereas the Richard paradox raises a question as to the meaning of the word "infinity".

transfinite cardinal numbers as measures of the size of sets, measures independent of the order in which their members are considered to be enumerated.[43]

The mathematical intuitionists raised the question as to whether it makes sense to think of a real number as existing independently of any way of defining it constructively. To give clarity to their questionings, they thought of real numbers as defined by infinite decimals, each decimal having one of the numbers between 0 and 9 in each place, and being defined progressively, with such-and-such a number in the first decimal place, such-and-such a number in the second place, and so on endlessly. They proposed that if, by relying on some law defining the number, we can, each time a new decimal place is reached, effectively determine what number should occupy it, then we have what they called a "species". But if we do not yet have any such finite specification or law defining a definite number, it is not that there are no more possible real numbers, but rather that the existence or possibility of others is expressed in the existence of what they call the "spread" constituted by the possibility of free choice or open possibility at each stage of progressively defining a still incomplete sequence. In effect, they think of unending decimal sequences as constituting trees branching as each new decimal place is reached, some according to law and some according to free choice.[44]

This notion of *spread* provides us with a very instructive way of thinking of possibilities in other fields—for instance, possibilities in regard to the future, possibilities in regard to types of situations which may present themselves for description, and possibilities in regard to the types of comparison which we might make in order to describe these situations, our descriptions involving fresh uses or "senses" of the same word in the same focus of meaning. In the case of the different uses, senses, or significances in discourse of the same expression, the notion of spread is applicable, not because of free choice, but because it is not determined by mechanically applicable law. We might say that how the spread will open out in new types of situation and as new paradigms of explanation come into play is determined by the understanding, but that this is no more a matter of mechanical law than when the understanding "forces" assent upon scientists as one scientific paradigm supplants another.

This explains how a word in a certain focus of meaning (i.e., a certain *langue*-meaning) can fail to have any definite number of *parole*-meanings or

43. It is plausible that the theorems or postulates relied upon in those parts of mathematics with application in physics, in particular the Least Upper Bound Theorem on which the differential and integral calculus depend, have their ultimate justification in intuitions concerning continuity analogous to the geometrical intuitions represented in Euclid. Newton's idea of a line as the path of a moving point suggests that the theory of the continuous rests on intuitions about physical motions and processes. Paradoxical functions which are "continuous" but at no point differentiable, arising in the conventional approach, will then prove mere delusions.

44. In my use of the words "spread" and "species" I follow A. Heyting, *Intuitionism: An Introduction* (Amsterdam: North-Holland, 1956), but with the reservation that for the unfolding of a spread, my purposes require not free choice, but only the absence of mechanically applicable rule.

logically differentiable senses so that these senses are *potentially infinite* in number, not enumerable, without being *actually infinite* in the sense of being of some definite "number" larger than any natural number (one of Cantor's supposed unending series of transfinite cardinals with $\aleph_0$, the cardinal of the natural numbers as the first and lowest transfinite cardinal, and $\aleph_1$, $\aleph_2$, etc., as its successors).[45]

What I have in mind in speaking of the potential infinity of the indefinite in number, not enumerable but not actually infinite, may be clarified by considering the Richard paradox.

Let us consider the Richard paradox in the following light. Within a natural language there can be only an effectively enumerable and finite number of phonemes and modes of intonation, or in writing a finite number of characters and attached indications (e.g., accents); any sentence must be a finite string of such elements. Alternatively, one can take as a premise that the words and their focuses of meaning within the language are effectively enumerable and finite, and that any sentence must be a finite string of such words in particular focuses of meaning. From either of these premises it will follow that the strings themselves are effectively enumerable (i.e., capable of being put into one-to-one correlation with the natural numbers according to some mechanically applicable rule), and from this that there cannot be more sentences than there are natural numbers. Therefore, since any definition has to be a finite sentence from within the language, within any natural language there cannot be more definitions than there are natural numbers. However, it is provable that given any effectively applicable law for the enumeration of a set of definitions of real numbers, we can by reference to this law effectively formulate the definition of a real number which is not a member of the original set (i.e., would not have been captured by the original enumeration): this is the essence of the Richard paradox. It follows from this that the definitions of real numbers are not effectively enumerable—that is, there is no mechanically applicable law whereby they could be put into one-to-one correspondence with the natural numbers.[46]

(b) *Relocating the root of our capacity to "make an infinite use of finite resources" in speech and thought*

The kind of appreciation of the meaning of a word which we gain in learning *langue* typically constitutes a potential enabling us to use the word in an

45. The notions of indefiniteness, of the potentially infinite and the mathematical intuitionists' notion of spread, both serve the purposes of illustrating the open-endedness of the possible uses or senses of words and the distinct idea of vagueness, as well as the openness of the future—doing this better than any resort to many-valued logic (here the three-valued logic proposed by Lukasiewicz in order to cater for the future is the best known).

46. Within the framework I describe in the text, on the one hand, the least upper bound theorem allows

indefinite number of varied ways, even within relatively simple sentences. In our speaking and writing we typically use each word in an unlimitedly modulated way, each way of modulating the use of the word giving rise to a different sense—a sense instituted in the very act of utterance, as Cruse explains:

> There are two fundamental ways in which the effective semantic contribution of a word form may vary under the influence of different contexts. First, a single sense can be modified in an unlimited number of ways by different contexts, each context emphasizing certain semantic traits, and obscuring or suppressing others; just as a dirty window-pane will allow some parts of the scene beyond it to be seen clearly, and will partially or completely obscure other parts—and a different pane will affect the same scene differently. This effect of a context on an included lexical unit will be termed *modulation*; the variation within a sense caused by modulation is largely continuous and fluid in nature. The second manner of semantic variation concerns the activation by different contexts of different senses associated with ambiguous word forms. This will be termed *contextual selection* (of senses); in the nature of things, this sort of variation proceeds in discrete jumps rather than continuously. The two types of variability are normally operative together; that is, a selected sense is also subject to modulation by the context which forced its selection.[47]

That a word is being used in different senses in different utterances is commonly clear from the contexts of utterance, and will be anyway evident from some differences in what hearers or readers would take to be implied or not implied. In this connection Cruse aptly refers to language's making "an infinite use of finite resources".[48]

The supposition that the main root of this capacity to make an "infinite use of finite resources" is the "recursiveness whereby semantic and syntactic rules operate on their own output" seems highly implausible.[49] Rather, as a source of this infinite capacity, it is of very subsidiary importance.

True, we can say "... ((p and q) and q) and q ..." or "I know that I know that I know that ... that 2 + 2 = 4" or "X knows that Y knows that Z knows that W knows that V knows that U knows that ... that P". And, true, we can form

a proof that the real numbers themselves cannot have a one-to-one correspondence with the natural numbers; on the other hand, we can lay down no definite limits to the different kinds of definition which may be possible, the number of real numbers being thus indefinite; and there is no way that we can put them into one-to-one correspondence with the natural numbers, although our earlier argument suggested that such definitions cannot be greater in number than the natural numbers. Since in a refined account nothing depends upon there being real numbers which are indefinable, this suggests that the non-enumerability of the real numbers may not be a matter of quantity or "greatness" (*magnitudo*) of number, but a particular kind of indefiniteness.

47. David Alan Cruse, *Lexical Semantics* (Cambridge: Cambridge University Press, 1986), 52; I describe Cruse's general perspective in chap. III.

48. Cruse, *Lexical Semantics*, 76.

49. Gareth Evans, "Semantic Theory and Tacit Knowledge", in *Collected Papers*, ed. John McDowell (Oxford: Oxford University Press, 1985), 334.

sentences involving ever more complex grammatical trees—for instance, "When Caesar approached Vercingetorix's camp with its unparalleled size, which was after Caesar's armies had already conquered most of the surrounding country, it became appropriate both for Vercingetorix to be troubled and for Caesar to make his preparations for laying siege to the camp" (this could be rendered more complicated by adding some nested conditional clauses, ablative absolutes, etc.). So, perhaps true, there is no definite limit to human capacity to iterate operations or to form yet more extended trees, and perhaps conscious surveyability may reach to 3, 7, or 20 iterations or branchings along any one line in a tree psychologically, or to many thousands with the help of pieces of paper carefully checked, or many millions with the help of a computer, or some larger number by richer use of the finite matter of the universe.[50]

Yet clearly, even allowing for a multiplicity of combination of types of iteration and branching, the result will be only a small finite number—as we have remarked, even 10^{56} is a small number compared with 10^{112}, and one never gets any nearer to infinity by finite steps. From this and the finiteness of the number of symbols in any possible actual language, it is evident that the number of possible sentences in any such language is finite.

There is a nice appositeness in Baker's application of an argument which Wittgenstein used in dialogue with Turing. Wittgenstein had asked Turing how many numerals he had learned to write down. Turing replied, "Well, if I were not here, I should say $\aleph_0$ [the cardinal number of the natural numbers]". Wittgenstein agreed, but continued: "Now should we say: 'How wonderful—to learn $\aleph_0$ numerals, and in so short a time! How clever we are!'?"[51] Baker asks, considering the reasons given by linguists and philosophers for supposing that by means of the recursive application of a variety of operators, all English speakers have learned to understand $\aleph_0$ sentences, why we should not consider it as equally a joke to ask, "Now should we say: 'How wonderful—to learn to understand $\aleph_0$ sentences, and in so short a time! How clever we are!'?"[52]

Rather, the limitless use of finite resources arises quite differently. That ways of speaking available to us should express an unlimited number of senses is a simple consequence of there being no structure or law governing or limiting the types of way in which new ways of speaking can arise in such a way as to be modulated to deal with an unrestricted variety of types of situation. The prob-

50. Indeed, in the ordinary use of language, psychological surveyability sets a very low limit to the number of iterations of different operators which allow intelligibility—cf. the introduction, n. 8 of this volume, on Paul Ziff.

51. Descartes played with the idea of our being clever in this way in a letter to Marin Mersenne, November 20, 1629, in *Descartes, Rene, Philosophical Letters*, ed., *trans. Anthony Kenny (Oxford: Oxford University Press, 1970)*.

52. Gordon P. Baker, "Following Wittgenstein: Some Signposts for Philosophical Investigations §§. 143–242", in *Wittgenstein: To Follow a Rule*, ed. S. H. Holtzman and C. M. Leich (London: Routledge, 1981), 68–69.

lem is not that the number of situations to be dealt with, senses to be expressed, and idioms to deal with or express is some particularly large cardinal number, *but that there is no system or effective method for enumerating them.*[53] The resources of language are infinite not primarily because they give one the means of enumerating a mathematical infinity of sentences. That they do this is in a way true, but entirely unimportant, since whatever the created mind can grasp will be less than some quite small finite number—and the ordinary mortal can take in only quite short sentences, so his limit is much less, and the same is true even of such a computer as Penrose conceives in *Shadows of the Mind.*[54] Rather, the resources of language are infinite in the sense that there is no definite limit on the number of possible sentences or capacities to find ways of saying what one needs or wishes to say—no barrier limiting linguistic resourcefulness.

To sum up, the main location of this limitlessness lies not in syntactic complexity, but in the ways human beings use the words in a lexicon—to be illustrated in chapter II.[55] The lexicon gives, not rules mechanically fixing the meaning to be understood when a word is used, but only focuses of meaning allowing the speaker-hearer shared skill exercised in the act of understanding to give determinate sense to what is spoken—possibly a new sense, unanticipated in previous linguistic history.

Thus the sense-expressors which figure as sentence-factors are not pre-existing *langue*-entities (lexical factors or lexemes), meanings mathematically determining sentence meaning, but *parole*-entities (sense-expressors), each with a sense formed only in the act of use within a complete utterance.

Each item in the lexicon, identifying just one focus of meaning, opens out an ensemble of senses or types of use, analogous to an intuitionist's "spread" according to the unlimited exigencies of the situations in which speaker and hearer may find themselves and the formally unrestricted creativeness in the ways in which they can express themselves and still be publicly understood.

53. This distinction is vital to one's consideration of the Richard paradox.

If we compare the proof presented in the Richard paradox with the exactly parallel proof by Cantor that the real numbers themselves cannot be put into one-to-one correspondence with the natural numbers, we should realize that the latter proof proceeds by deriving an absurdity from the supposition that there is some law (whether mechanically applicable or not) putting the real numbers into one-to-one correspondence with the natural numbers. It follows that Cantor's proof in fact only demonstrates that there is no law of any kind whereby the real numbers can be put into one-to-one correspondence with the natural numbers; it has not proved that this is because there are more real numbers than natural numbers rather than because of the non-existence of a law or linguistically formulable predicate of a kind to achieve the desired one-to-one correspondence; cf. n. 46.

The Berry paradox raises quite different problems; cf. n. 42.

54. Roger Penrose, *Shadows of the Mind: A Search for the Missing Science of Consciousness* (Oxford: Oxford University Press, 1994), 352–77.

55. Jackendoff envisages the problems of acquiring grammar as paling in comparison with the problems of lexical semantics and of describing or acquiring semantic patterns; Jackendoff, *Foundations*, 377; cf. chap. V, nn. 20, 55, of this volume.

11 ⇜

The Salience of Words and Our Adventurousness in Using Them

Section 1. Words and Basic Lexical Factors

(a) *The strategic situation of words or expressions of comparable rank*

(i) Words as the loci of stability within languages and as roots of linguistic creativity

Units of different "rank", in the way that "narrative", "argument", "conversation", and "exchange" signify units of discourse of higher rank than "sentence" and "utterance", need to be distinguished in analyzing *parole.* Below the sentence, common idiom reckons the "subsentential clause", the "phrase", and the "word" as entering into speech as significant constituents of three successively lower ranks, while such word-formatives or "morphemes" as "cow-" and "-s" in the word "cows" and "kick-" and "-ed" in the word "kicked", or, in a different way, the "un-" with "-accept-" and "-able" in the word "unacceptable", are constituents of lower rank. (Phonological and graphological ideas such as "syllable", "consonant", "vowel", "phoneme", "character", and "letter" have no semantic or lexical standing, and stand outside this classification.)

In chapter III, I establish that entities of the rank of sentence, such as statements, commands, and wishes, have their primary place in linguistics at the level of *parole,* whatever the medium—speech, writing, or sign-language.

Yet it is elements at the rank of word and morpheme which introduce content into our discourse. And this requires these elements to have a double place, at the level of *langue* as well as the level of *parole*. In any utterance there are typically at least two such expressions, articulated together, and it is these expressions which, in the context of utterance, give content to the utterances in which they occur. It is these content-introducing expressions which constitute at the same time the loci of stability, the vehicles of expressiveness, and the roots of language's openness to creative use.

It is striking that, while to philosopher, linguist, and psychologist sentences are often taken as the basic empirical data, to the ordinary person it is words and morphemes which stand out. They recur in many different utterances, sometimes in liaison, sometimes elided, in varied dialect forms and even in different languages, in many forms, singular and plural, in varied tense, sometimes used literally and sometimes metaphorically.[1] Thus it is of the essence of the word or morpheme—in general of the lexical factor—to be recognized under many garbs, phonemic, grammatical, and semantic. In the introduction and in chapter I, I portrayed this informality and flexibility in the use of words, successfully communicating meaning to our hearers as the chief root of the capacity of the language-user to make "infinite use of finite means" in speech, enabling us to express fresh ways of thinking and deal with unanticipated problems and kinds of situation.

(ii) The need for a conception of "lexical factor" wider than "the word"

The attempt to identify words or lexical factors reveals many ambiguities.

We can form a concept of "word-form", defined as a unitary stretch within sentences which cannot be internally rearranged or suffer internal insertions and which remains stable in form while appearing in different verbal contexts, thus defining it distributionally. Here, as Gabriël Nuchelmans observes, we need to give priority to grammatical over phonological features in defining words,[2] as is evident from the phenomena of liaison and elision as well as of slovenliness of speech and acceptable variations in pronunciation. However, besides the concept of word-form, we need a concept of "lexeme", linguistic sign, or "lexical factor" wider than that of the word in order to cope with the phenomena of inflection and agglutination. In traditional presentations of the grammars of inflected languages, verbs and nouns as lexemes—the verb *amo* or the noun *mensa*—are conceived as occurring in word-forms specified in

1. Cf. Dwight Bolinger, "The Uniqueness of the Word", *Lingua* 12 (1963): 113–36, who draws on the ideas of Reichling, the latter influenced by Karl Bühler. None follow Bloomfield's concentration on the morpheme.

2. Gabriël Nuchelmans, "Review Article: R. H. Robins, *General Linguistics*", *Lingua* 16 (1966): 406–9. Strictly speaking the word "phonological" is preferable to the word "phonetic", since what is concerned is not just the acoustic sound, but complexes of phonemes as items functional within the particular language concerned—counting as the same even if pronounced indistinctly. Sound distinctions may be significant in one dialect or language, but not another.

the "accidence" in the grammar of a language, and within the language concerned commonly conforming to a small number of paradigms—respectively conjugations of verb and declensions of noun. This is the basis of R. H. Robin's Word and Paradigm model of grammatical description, as opposed to Item and Process or Item and Arrangement models.[3]

Among languages there is a spectrum between those which are most analytic or word-isolating, in which word and morpheme most closely correspond, such as Vietnamese, Chinese, and English (although no language is purely isolating or completely free from inflection or agglutination), and the many more highly inflected, agglutinative, or polysynthetic languages with successively less such approximation. In inflected languages, lexemes, besides having prefixes, suffixes, infixes, and reduplicated consonants or syllables added to them, may have their vowel quality altered. These mark such things as number, case, and gender with pronouns and nouns, and mark the past/present, continuous/perfect, and mood distinctions, along with person (first, second, or third) and number with verbs. In inflected and agglutinative languages a greater range of complex linking devices arise, parts of speech sometimes taking inflected forms reciprocally with others in a kind of morphological liaison, so that a complex sentence sometimes ends by comprising just a noun complex and verb complex. At the extreme, some agglutinating languages are "polysynthetic" (the noun complex is incorporated into the verbal complex so that, by the structured putting together of morphemes, an entire "sentence" or clause is expressed without anything like a word-division).

Always one needs to distinguish processes of putting together which leave the lexical factors involved semantically intact from cases in which morphological processes of "composition" and "blending" create semantically novel lexical factors. In "composition" a new nuclear lexical factor is formed by putting two whole words together, while in "blending" it is formed by putting together parts of two whole words. Thus the German *Weltanschauung, Sprachwissenschaft, Apfelbaum,* and *Mittagssonne* and the English *world-view* (with or without the hyphen), *spin-doctor,* and *war-monger* are composed forms; and the English *electrocute* (electricity + execute), *brunch* (breakfast + lunch), *travelogue* (travel + monologue), and *paratroops* (parachute + troops) are blends. Such complex forms behave as morphological unities, with appropriate inflections and independently developing meanings,

3. R. H. Robins, "In Defence of WP", *Transactions of the Philological Society* (1959): 116–44, and Robins, *General Linguistics: An Introductory Survey* (London: Longman, 1964), along with Nuchelmans, "Review Article", 406–9; contrast with Charles Hockett, "Two Models of Grammatical Description", *Word* 10 (1954): 210–34. P. H. Matthews, in "Some Concepts in Word-Paradigm Morphology", *Foundations of Language* 1 (1965): 268–89 and in "The Inflectional Component of a Word-and-Paradigm Grammar", *Journal of Linguistics* 1 (1965): 139–71, give support to Robins; cf. Mark Aronoff, *Word Formation in Generative Grammar,* Linguistic Enquiry Monographs 1 (Cambridge, Mass.: MIT Press, 1976), and n. 42 in this chapter.

although marked by their origin. A world-view is not a view and a spin-doctor is not a doctor. As new centers of meaning, such compounds can be the launch-pads of quite new sets of metaphor (e.g., someone might describe the angels as God's paratroopers). These compounds are single words, whereas each of the nouns contained in the noun phrase "a top-quality top-class Oxford University plant science student" retains its original independent status.

As parts or elements within speech, words occur with determinate function and also with determinate form, and are distinguished pragmatically and syntactically as well as semantically: pragmatically in that, in the unfolding of our speech, the juncture before a word is one which leaves us liberty to develop the expression of our thought using other words instead, and the juncture after the word is another such point of liberty; and syntactically in that, given any two consecutive words, not only might either word occur without the other, but also certain other words may be intruded between them.[4]

Here I must insist upon two different points.

First, words or lexical factors are empirical constituents of speech, despite their variable form, and not merely theoretical entities within a system of generative grammar for describing a language which, as such, will have at most an indirect relation to the facts of speech. To account for this recognition of words or lexical factors under different forms, we need Gibson's approach to the concept of stimulus, described in chapter VI. At the same time, the particular forms they take, as distributionally defined grammatical word-forms within speech, are also empirical data.

Second, some of these words or lexical factors are of the "syncategorematic" or "synlexical" kind, mentioned in chapter I and in (c) below, and some are the elements that introduce content into discourse, some called names ("appellatives" or *Nennwörter*, typically nouns or adjectives) and some of a more verbal character.

(iii) Three senses of the term "word" relevant to linguistics and three irrelevant ways of using the term

I deal first with the ambiguities of the word "word" and of the notions of word-form and morpheme.

In linguistics and logic only four senses of the word "word" are of concern to us: (1) a linguistic word as something which may have several distinct focuses of meaning; (2) a word as a lexeme or lexical factor, encapsulating just one focus of meaning, capable of being realized in many word-forms; (3) a "word" as meaning a "word-form"; and (4) a "word" as meaning a "speech-word"—that is, a "word" as it occurs in speech. Different word-forms of the

4. "Speech-word"—"word" in Sapir's sense.

same "word" may coincide both phonetically and as written—as with the example *cut,* which may stand as the simple present tense (except in the third person), as the simple past tense, as the past participle of the verb *cut,* and as the singular of the noun *cut,* so that we have, respectively, two different lexemes, the verb *cut* and the noun *cut;* four syntactically distinguishable "word-forms" such as would be laid out in different places in grammar-book tables showing the declension of nouns or the conjugation and parts of verbs; and four different "speech-words" (i.e., words as they occur as functioning semantic constituents within speech).[5]

In the case of speech-words, we could speak in two ways. As it is, we speak of the twenty-six letters of the alphabet as "types" and the many hundred thousand letters which in sequence compose a book as "tokens". By analogy, we could distinguish word-types and word-tokens and say that in "I hit him and hit him again" we have five speech-word types (the same word-types "hit" and "him" each occurring twice) and seven speech-word tokens. There would remain five word-forms. It will be noted that the noun *sheep* will count as one lexeme occurring in two word-forms, the one singular and the other plural.

It is at this point that the contrast between sentence and lexical factor becomes vital. In the case of sentences (as distinct from mere clauses) it is only our knowledge of them at the level of speech which is essential to their recognition as units, and this dictates the kinds of way we speak of them in grammar, phonetics, and discussions of enunciation or elocution. By contrast in the case of words and other lexical factors, the situation is quite different, and a separately rooted knowledge of words and other lexical factors as things with multiple discourse-significances at the level of speech but with only a very small number of focuses of meaning at the level of *langue* (e.g., its paradigmatic and syntagmatic relations) is equally indispensable. Thus it is at the level of *langue* that notions of lexeme and word-form arise: (1) a lexeme is a word in the sense of semantically distinguishable item in a vocabulary identifying just one distinct focus of meaning, but which may appear in many forms (e.g., the noun *bachelor* in the meaning "man who has not yet married", or the verb *lie* in the meaning "tell an untruth with the intention to deceive"); and (2) a word-form is a word as it occurs in a particular syntactically definite and fully inflected form.

(iv) Basic lexical factors in relation to grammar and philosophical logic

The problem of how these lexical factors, whether taking the form of words or not, are bound together so as to form a unit of speech, the sentence

5. Here I follow Nuchelmans (cf. n. 2) in defining "word-form" primarily with reference to grammar rather than phonology, fitting Joan Bresnan's conception of "functional word" as opposed to "morphological word"; Bresnan, *Lexical-Functional Syntax,* 93.

(what Jackendoff calls the "binding" problem),[6] is central both to linguistics and to the philosophy of language.

(b) *The double standing of linguistic elements of lowest rank*

To recapitulate, the whole theory of *langue* and *parole* involves that words and other lexical factors have a double aspect as, at once, at the level of *langue*, identifying focuses of meaning to be listed as dictionary items and, at the level of *parole*, expressive of different senses in different sentences or speech-units and thereby marking different sentence-factors. Lexical factors (including words) at the level of *langue* and sentences at the level of *parole* are interdependent, but the latter are not definable as sequences of the former. Petrified idiomatic phrases count as lexical factors, while proverbs or aphorisms count as units of *parole* or speech.

It is fundamental to such lesser units as morphemes, lexemes or lexical factors, and word-forms to have a place in linguistic theory, both as elements of *langue* and as factors in *parole*. It is the key feature of all such lesser units that they should enter into language with a double gearing. First, as morphemes and lexical factors taken in particular focuses of meaning and in the particular forms dictated by the accidence of a grammar, they are geared to *langue*.[7] Second, as used in these particular forms in a particular context, they are geared to *parole*, taking on a particular discourse-significance or sense. Features at the level of *langue* or language-possession underlie their role as sentence-constituents in *parole* (their discourse-significances), and, in the case of speech-words, their effect on how speech can unfold. Yet we must always be clear at which level we are speaking. For instance, when we speak of, say, seven or eight "parts of speech" (noun, verb, adjective, etc.), we have in view seven or eight types of word-constituent within speech distinguished primarily according to their function—speech-function shaping the classification of langue-items, not vice versa, as I explain in depth in chapter XIV.

It is a key consequence of this double standing of words and lexical factors, as at once functioning constituents within speech and items of *langue*, both in the awareness of the language-user at the same time, that language is segmentable[8]—involving distinguishable lexical units, each with a multi-potentiality of interrelated senses at the level of *parole*. It is this segmentability into lexical units, each with a particular focus of meaning, which underlies the

6. Jackendoff, *Foundations*, 58–61.

7. Accidence will determine any changes in vowel quality and connective elements agglutinative languages may require, not just inflections and changes in vowel quality within words.

8. As Gordon P. Baker and P. M. S. Hacker point out in *Wittgenstein: Understanding and Meaning* (Oxford: Blackwell, 1980), 280n18, we cannot require that understanding any part of the language demands understanding the whole.

informality of use which permits such critical assessments as, for example, in seeing how to avoid the traditional paradoxes from Zeno to modern logic, as I explain in chapter IV.

(c) *The interdependence of lexical and grammatical knowledge*

Theoretical knowledge of a particular language includes, first, knowledge of its grammar and inflectional morphology; second, lexical knowledge; and, third, knowledge of the phonology of the language, coordinate with the first two.

There is no clean break between the first two of these, as appears most conspicuously with those "synlexical" elements of speech which seem to serve the purpose rather of gluing the content-introducing elements of a sentence together than of supplying content themselves, the elements to which I refer in chapter XIV as "structurizers", elements with an especially intimate relation to the grammar. Thus some words seem to carry content (e.g., "book" and "black" in "The book is black"), while others (like "the" and "is") seem to lack content.

Under the influence of Aristotle's doctrine of categories this distinction has come to be explained as being between "categorematic" terms and "syncategorematic" expressions, and this has had the advantage that, by a series of historical accidents, both names and verbs, and then adjectives and adverbs, were all classified as categorematic, despite the absence of any surviving clear definition of the term. As one casts around for some other explanation of the distinction, one has to recognize that it cannot be right to explain it in terms of whether or not the expression concerned possesses content, as if syncategorematic expressions lack meaning or never have any content,[9] especially since many of them occur morphologically as noninflectional modifiers of content (e.g., the negative "im-" in "impossible" and the spatial "im-" in "immigrate", and many others expressing causal or spatial relation). However, semantically, categorematic expressions are in themselves semantically content-introducing in regard to some topic, theme, or subject-matter, by contrast with the syncategorematic expressions which lack semantic independence, occurring only in connection with categorematic expressions. Accordingly, I call the former "synlexical" as always dependent on their links with definitely "content-introducing" expressions. Thus, the primary role of "syn-

9. I prefer the expression "content-introducing" to such labels as "lexical", "meaningful", and "semantic". These other labels apply equally to the things with which they are being contrasted, such as "is" and other auxiliaries, prepositions, articles, interrogatives, relatives, conjunctions, and negatives of many types, suffixes and prefixes on nouns and verbs, and so forth, since all these have lexical entries of some kind, some kind of meaning, and some kind of semantics. What makes these latter items "synlexical" is that, even when as with some prepositions, they carry some connotation or content; they still cannot introduce this content except in combination with the words they are associated with (as in "look after", "look at", and "attack upon").

lexical" expressions is to indicate the structural relations, semantic and grammatical, between the content-introducing terms, only subsidiarily carrying any content themselves. Synlexical words (e.g., prepositions) are often used to express what in other languages is achieved by adding a different inflection to a noun (using a different "morphological case")—or, when "is" or "have" are used as auxiliaries, to achieve what in other languages or idioms is achieved by inflections of tense or mood, by appropriate word-ordering, or even by intonation.

The question of the status of pronouns and demonstratives as to whether, when they occur in an utterance, they should be considered content-introducing like proper names or synlexical like inflections to verbs in languages in which pronouns are not used unless required to remove ambiguity, will be best considered in connection with the role of proper names in chapter XIII, sections 4 and 5.

Since, as we shall see in chapter IX, no expression can be used linguistically in complete independence of others, the distinction between the content-introducing and the synlexical depends on a proper integration of semantic and syntactic theory.[10] This is particularly obvious if one considers agglutinative languages in which words cannot be isolated. Within such an integrated theory, forms using auxiliaries and prepositions have no privilege over those using single words, and the combination of a synlexical expression with a content-introducing one can be treated as itself content-introducing, as in the cases of "immigrate" and "look at".[11]

Section 2. Types of Relationship between Different Uses of the Same Word

(a) *Historical review of philosophical approaches to the problem of a word's being used in different senses*

In chapter I I showed that language functions without words having a finitely specifiable range of senses or types of use, even despite the fact that the capacity to use a word in such flexible ways has to be learned through a finite process, initially as the realization of the understanding of the word in just one focus of meaning. Such a suggestion may seem scandalous to many or most linguists, psycholinguists, and philosophers. In chapter V I show this sense of scandal to be misplaced.

10. This theory will have to make it plain how one is to treat words such as "meaning", "truth", "define", "object", "set", and "number" in logical and semantic theory (cf. chap. V), or objects such as *one, two, three,* etc., in theories of sets and numbers (cf. chap. XII and chap. XIV, sec. 1 [b]), but not in other contexts.

11. I here make provision for F. Ackerman and G. Webelhuth's theory of predicates, referred to in chap. I, sec. 2 (c).

This idea of the same word being used in different but related ways or senses, polysemously, has constantly recurred within the history of philosophy. Ryle's notion of polymorphousness constitutes a recent philosophical contribution to this discussion.

(i) Older discussion before the problems of modern mathematical logic came into view

The word "metaphor" was one of the first words used to mark that a term was being used in a secondary or derivative, "transferred" sense (fitting with the etymology of *meta* + *phora*), but in such a way that its secondary sense in some way depended on its primary sense. This left the question of the kinds of relation between the primary and secondary uses of the term which make such secondary use possible.

Meantime, at an early time, the use of the word "metaphor" became more restricted, so as to cover not just any case of a derivative, secondary, "transferred" sense, but only ones in which it was felt that the cases in which the word as used in its secondary sense implied some likeness to the cases in which it was used in its primary sense.

However, Aristotle used the word "metaphor" in a yet more restricted way, limiting it to cases in which he regarded the derivative uses of the term concerned as contributing nothing to "science". Hence, for him the label "metaphor" was used with some contempt, classifying being metaphorical with cases of pure equivocation or "homonymy" (implying likeness in name only).

By contrast, Aristotle regarded the idea that a word might have several related meanings as useful in the sciences. His first example of this was that of a word having a spread of uses within which, one use being primary, it develops secondary uses definable from the primary use by means of paraphrase, as when climates and complexions are called healthy as tending to cause or show health, describing this structure of related meanings or uses by the phrase *pros hen* ("relative to one")—cases in which the various derived uses or meanings of a term are to be defined or paraphrased by reference to one primary "focal meaning".[12] The distinction between "sad" as signifying a form of sorrow and "sad" as meaning being evocative of this kind of sorrow would be another example of this. I shall refer to secondary uses of words arising in this way as "relation-based" or "relational" uses. All secondary uses of this kind were to be contrasted with cases of a term being used "univocally"—according to one properly strict definition.

12. G. E. L. Owen, "Tithenai ta Phainomena", in *Logic, Science and Dialectic: Collected Papers in Greek Philosophy*, ed. Martha Nussbaum (Ithaca, N.Y.: Cornell University Press, 1986), 239–51; first published 1961.

However, inasmuch as the only thing which makes this type of extension of use "scientific" is the possibility of substituting a paraphrase, and this makes it capable of elimination in favor of the paraphrase, this step is not very radical. And typically the secondary uses that arise in this way are small in number and commonly distinguished as different focuses of meaning in dictionaries, as in the case of "sad", or as with the case of being healthy in the primary sense and healthy as being conducive to health or symptomatic of it. Likewise, the philosophers' distinction between "good" as meaning (1) intrinsically good, (2) pleasing to know or to experience because of seeming good or giving pleasure, and (3) useful (advantageous or conducive to good) could well appear in a dictionary.

The more recent idea of a word's being used according to "family-resemblance" fares little better in helping us understand how the spread of use of a word could gain any kind of infinity, at least as this "family-resemblance" is commonly explained. The idea of a word's not being used according to one criterion or one set of criteria of application but according to family-resemblance is most usually popularized in terms of Wittgenstein's discussion of our use of the word "game". This is commonly explained in these terms: there are a number of features which are characteristic or typical of the things called *games*, making for a kind of family-resemblance between games, in such a way that a thing is a game if it exhibits some high proportion of these characteristic features. Yet this, if the characteristic features are A, B, C, D, and E, amounts only to this, that to be a game is to exhibit three or four of these features, A, B, C, D, and E. In this way, the term *game* reappears as having a perfectly straightforward disjunctive definition, which again means that nothing very radical has been shown such as might justify saying that a word can be used "literally" in a spread of highly heterogeneous ways. This account may well represent a travesty of what Wittgenstein actually meant by "family-resemblance",[13] but it constitutes the form in which it has been most commonly popularized.

Despite Aristotle's very negative attitude to metaphor, by contrast, he regarded analogy much more positively, giving it a conspicuous place in his discussions of friendship, of the soul, and of form. But he gives no more definition of analogy than he did of metaphor.

Aquinas's main use of the term "analogy" was in regard to cases of what his exponents call "intrinsic analogy"—as implying some likeness. Terms used according to this kind of analogy are used in the meaning "proper" to them,[14] not metaphorically nor in virtue of an extrinsic relation, but so that

13. The late G. E. M. Anscombe, closest to Wittgenstein, regarded this account as a travesty: his aim was to use simple examples to embody a spread of informal linkages, not to provide an exhaustive disjunction.

14. For Aquinas, for a word to be used nonmetaphorically and nonderivatively is for it to be used *proprie*, in its "own" sense (he uses the word *literalis* to make a quite different distinction; see chap. III n. 28 of this volume).

the term is used with its full positive content, despite the disparity between the cases to which it is applied.

However, because of a preoccupation with the need to pick out which ways of using words contributed to science, Aquinas allowed his use of the word "analogy" to be distorted by widening its application to include the relation-based uses referred to earlier, classified by later writers as cases of "extrinsic analogy". For Aquinas, to call a use of a word "analogical" implied that such use contributed to science, by contrast to the "metaphorical" disparaged by Aristotle as not so contributing.

Yet it is the nonrelational case of words being used in their proper meaning, so-called intrinsic analogy, which is of most importance to later philosophy. In cases of such intrinsic analogy we have a wide spread of application of the term, but not according to one scientific definition. If the applications conform to some loose, informal explanation, this explanation will itself rely on analogous terms, and in this sense remain informal, and not make the uses of the term concerned "univocal" or "synonymous". It is this middle, "intrinsic analogy" between the "equivocal" ("homonymous") and the "univocal" which is of special interest.

The closest modern reflection of this idea of intrinsic analogy lies in Gilbert Ryle's idea of a word's being used "polymorphously". In his article "Thinking and Language" he makes out that the word "thinking" is used in such varied ways as to be incapable of capture by any one set of criteria of application, and yet not in such ways as would make it better to introduce a different word. In his general thought the ability to use the words "think" and "thinking" is a "many-track" disposition.

Of the terms I have already discussed, we can at once pick out the expression *play* as a good example of a term used polymorphously, although its separate uses have become fossilized so as to be eligible for listing in a dictionary as distinct focuses of meaning. Indeed, perhaps the most important fact about games is that they are things we play, something seemingly overlooked in Wittgenstein's discussion of the word "game". In brief, games are one of the four distinguishable kinds of formal object of the verb "play" used transitively, alongside instruments, the entertainments we call plays, and roles (including dramatic parts), all possible objects of enjoyment.[15] (I use the term "formal object" technically: games are the formal objects of play as dangers are the

15. This provides the focus of meaning which, first, sets "games" in their proper context as the primary formal object of the verb "to play" (one of its four types of formal object, alongside musical instruments, plays in the dramatic sense, and roles in such dramatic plays), and second, explains the strange variation in the criteria for what is regarded as counting as "a game". As objects of play, games are in their primary role objects of enjoyment (derivatively benefiting psychological health). *Qua* games, they are not geared to any "practical" purpose, but undertaken "for pleasure" or for their own sake—though this end may be frustrated or other motivations may become primary (e.g., health or the entertainment of others).

formal objects of fear.) Thus the variations in what may count as a game arise wholly or largely from variations in what counts as playing and in the types of thing people are said to enjoy. The idea of family-resemblance when applied to the word "play" begins to appear closer to the idea of polymorphous use than when applied directly to the word "game".

(ii) The semantic and logical paradoxes in modern logic have sharpened the discussion

Russell added a further dimension to the discussion with his theory that the objects we speak of are set in an infinite hierarchy of types, with his suggestion that when what appears to be the same predicate is predicated of things of a different logical type, then it is predicated in a different meaning. In particular, number-predicates, like "has two members", predicated of sets, in his theory of types, had a different sense according to the type of the set concerned. Thus if we begin with concrete particulars as objects or individuals of type 1, then sets of such individuals of type 1 will be objects of type 2, and sets of these type-2 objects (sets of sets of concrete individuals) will be objects of type 3, and so on unendingly. Russell called this phenomenon "typical ambiguity". Thus the same arithmetical laws are applied formally in the same way at each new level—for instance, laws such as "Two objects of a kind together with two different objects of the same kind constitute four objects of that kind", but despite this, the expressions "two" and "four" will have a different sense and reference according to the type of the objects concerned. The expressions "thing", "object" (or "individual"), and "set" shared the same ambiguity.

No theory of meaning can be regarded as satisfactory in regard to natural language if it cannot be coherently stated in that language. Therefore, whatever the virtues of either of Russell's theories of types for certain purposes, neither can be accepted as part of the basis of a theory of meaning for natural language. Ramsey distinguished logical paradoxes which arise independently of the use of any psychological or semantic expressions enabling a language to refer to its own statements or terms from the semantic paradoxes which do so depend, and regarded the simple theory of types as providing a satisfactory "object-language" in that it would suffice for one to avoid the logical paradoxes.[16] In this separation between logical and semantic paradoxes and between these two kinds of language, he anticipated Tarski's 1933 distinction between a language and its metalanguage, whereby for any language L_n there will be a metalanguage L_{n+1} which can include reference to the statements and definitions of L_n, their meaning, truth, satisfactoriness, proof, and methods of proof, but which will itself be subject to the same limitation and be un-

16. F. P. Ramsey, "The Foundations of Mathematics", in *The Foundations of Mathematics and Other Logical Essays*, ed. R. W. Braithwaite (London: Routledge and Kegan Paul, 1931), 20–49.

able to discuss the meaning, truth, or satisfactoriness of its own statements or definitions, which could only be discussed in a meta-metalanguage L_{n+2}. Any object-language L_1 must therefore require an unending series of metalanguages—L_2, L_3, L_4, L_5, and so on unendingly, in order to avoid the semantic paradoxes.[17] However, this is again useless as an account of natural languages, which of necessity incorporate their own metalanguages, since they have to use terms such as "meaning", "truth", "proof", "statement", and "definition"—each in one meaning in discussing their own words and sentences.

The problems which we are here confronting arise both with "semantic" concepts such as "truth", "proof", "meaning", and "definition", called semantic because they belong to epistemology and the theory of meaning, and with such "nonsemantic" concepts as "object", "set", and "whole number", belonging to philosophical logic. These concepts are of the kind Ryle called "topic-neutral"[18] in the sense that they apply in the same way to each subject-matter, abstract or concrete. In human discourse we ordinarily try to make statements about only one subject-matter at a time, but we can think of the formal structures identified in logic and set theory (including arithmetical statements, if they are formulated in such forms as "Two objects and two different objects constitute four objects" rather than in such forms as "2 + 2 = 4") as like a hat which applies to each subject-matter separately. There is what we might call a "formal" or "algebraic" analogy between the different applications of these theories and of their terms, such as "object", "set", and "number". It is therefore very appropriate to think of these terms as applying in one and the same literal meaning in regard to each of these subject-matters. However, although the formal analogy is perfect in some respects, lack of formal analogy arises in certain ways. That is, some formal differences arise according to whether (a) the subject-matters are finite; or (b) inductively infinite in the manner of the natural numbers; or (c) not inductively infinite because incapable of being put into correspondence with the natural numbers, yet of undisputed existence because definable by reference to some constructively definable cut in the continuum; or (d) indefinite in any of the other ways we met in chapter I; or else (e) infinite because they include possible things in the future which may or may not ever be actual as well as actual things.

Yet, as we see in chapter V, we cannot produce any adequate set of criteria for the application of any such concepts, nonsemantic or semantic. Howev-

17. Tarski's 1933 paper was translated from Polish into German in 1936, but only appeared in English twenty years later, as Alfred Tarski, "The Concept of Truth in Formalized Languages" in *Logic, Semantics, Metamathematics: Papers from 1923 to 1938*, selected and trans. J. H. Woodger, 152–278 (Oxford: Oxford University Press, 1956).

18. Ryle, *Dilemmas* (Cambridge: Cambridge University Press, 1954), chap. 8, 115–18; also Ryle, *Plato's Progress* (Cambridge: Cambridge University Press, 1966), 277, where he describes topic-neutral notions as "trans-departmental".

er, when words are used according to different criteria of application or with different implications, it is normal for philosophers to consider them as being used in different senses. Accordingly, since in all these cases the words concerned are being used in the same primary meaning, what Aquinas calls their "own" or "proper" meaning, only one focus of meaning being involved, and are being used in formally the same or similar ways, it would seem appropriate and in accord with Aquinas's way of thinking to speak of them as being capable of use in all these different types of application in virtue of "formal analogy". When we call both planets and natural numbers "individuals" (or "objects"), it is not in virtue of any real similarity between them, but only in virtue of the similarity or sameness of the way mention of them enters into our discourse in regard to them. This makes it indeed appropriate to apply the phrase "formal analogy".

To some extent we can think of the "semantic" concepts I mentioned, "truth", "proof", "meaning", "definition", and the like, in their relations to the things true, proved, meant, or defined, as topic-neutral in the same way as the "nonsemantic" concepts of "object", "set", and of each natural number, so that the theories of proof, of modes of definition, and of meaning associated with them will be likewise like hats which apply to each subject-matter similarly. However, since these semantic concepts each have particular relationships to human knowledge and activity, they are liable to show differences in their relationship to certain subject-matters. And, since formal analogy is something which arises only from samenesses or similarities in our modes of speech and thought, it is only in the context of the particular relationships of these semantic concepts to human knowledge and activity that generalizations using the concepts of "object", "set", and "number" which bestraddle all their uses, or comparisons between their uses with different subject-matters when these show formal differences such as I mentioned above, should be considered. For instance, the statement "A set is an object" does not belong to the theory of sets, but is one of its presuppositions, coming from semantic theory: it has the meaning that every set of objects can be taken as a subject of discourse in its own right.

(b) *Shape of an ordered classification of types of variation in the use of words*

(i) Preliminary attempt at a general classification

We have now picked out four different ways in which the same word or expression is used in different, but related senses.

First, we have the case of formal analogy just described, where an expression is used in the same primary meaning, because what it is being used to refer to enters into the structure of our speech in the same way, but in very different types of application—not because of any likeness in the reality spoken of. It seems unnatural to speak of number-words used to count objects of different logical types or categories, or of a word such as *true* as used in respect of different kinds of statement, as being used in different "senses". We can only justify doing this because the sentences in which they are applied in formally parallel ways have such different types of implication and justification, and in this way have very different "discourse-significances"—although each term is being used in just one focus of meaning.

Second, an expression may be used in different, but related senses in virtue of some real likeness or analogy between the situations described. In this second case, there is no way in which we can justify describing one of the uses as secondary if, "literally" applied, it would be false; and in this case of literal application, the descriptions "intrinsic analogy" or "polymorphousness" are appropriate to contrast them both with the case of metaphor and with the cases of extended use in virtue of an external relation considered below. In this case of intrinsic analogy or polymorphousness, it is still sometimes appropriate to distinguish different focuses of meaning, such as can be exhaustively listed in a dictionary; but in other cases, no such listing is possible or appropriate, despite the fact that the expression is still being used according to different criteria or with different implications in different cases of its use. (In some cases, such as that of the sensory or sense-simulating uses of the verb "see" discussed in chapter I, there is one primary or paradigm sense together with a hierarchy of secondary uses or senses of the word which are not metaphors and are not to be explained by means of a paraphrase.)

In the third case the expression is susceptible of being used in two ways, one literal and the other metaphorical, the latter constituting a secondary, derived meaning in virtue of some similarity, often one which we can explain by means of some paraphrase. The derived meaning will be one according to which, taken "literally", its application would be false: here we call the secondary use "metaphorical". Thus only sounds are literally loud, but metaphorically many things are described as loud because they attract attention and jar upon the sensibility (so we speak of certain clothes or colors of clothes as loud).

Fourth, the different types of use of an expression may be "relational", related as primary to secondary, the secondary uses being explicable by paraphrase in relation to the first, the focal meaning. And we can group cases of metonymy and synecdoche here.

(ii) Two areas where metaphor is indispensable

There are some areas where metaphor is indispensable: the first is that of describing cognitive and conative states. Metaphors related to sight (including references to light) and grasp and the ideas of ability and of having a commanding position in regard to something seem to underlie our ways of speaking about knowledge and understanding. And the ideas of being moved by, drawn towards, pointed towards or at, aiming or going towards, or finding rest in seem to underlie most of our speech about the emotions.

Second, there seems to be a linguistically universal tendency to extend the use of words for possibility from stating what nature leaves or makes possible to what the laws and reasons motivating our action allow us to do, and further to what our present knowledge and the evidence we have allow us to think. At the same time it is universal to pass from speaking of causes and of physical force as making things necessary, inescapable, or inevitable to speaking of actions or conclusions as being necessitated or forced upon us by reasons for action or reasons for judgment.[19]

The relations involved in these two families of case, in which we have distinct focuses of meaning (distinct *langue*-meanings) interrelated at the level of reflective awareness in contemporaneous uses, along with the relations between the families of word associated with the different forms of knowledge and understanding and our uses of such words as "mean" and "intend" in connection with our speech and hearing of speech, belong to the semantic structure common to all human languages, as discussed in chapter IV.

(iii) A note on the complexity in our use of prepositions

It is not just content-introducing words, but also some synlexical words which can be used analogously or metaphorically. We have already observed the way spatial prepositions can have their use extended to express a temporal meaning by formal analogy. And such extension is indispensable when we go beyond prepositions to adjectives and nouns—spatial adjectives and nouns, as when we speak of "long ago" and "lengths" or "stretches" of time.

Moreover, as "lack" includes the formal meaning of negation and so can be used metaphorically to express negation, as in "The number 3 lacks the property of being even", so "in" can be used in formal ways. So we speak of people's health or sickness, virtues and vices, knowledge and ignorance, and the like as being "in" the people (e.g., their bravery as "in" their attitudes and brave acts). The immediate springs of an action are "in" the action—so God is spoken of as "in" things as their cause of being. And when we are told that "in God, we live and move and have our being", it seems that God is being thought of as the ground *in* which we are rooted. Also, we use the word "in" in order to express how something is to be delimited or specified (e.g., "Socrates is wise in that he accepts that he knows nothing"). And we also use it to

19. I gave a more extended and nuanced account of the systematic character of this threefold extension in our use of initially physical terms in David Braine, "Varieties of Necessity".

express one of several merely logical relationships (e.g., having an attribute, as in "Alex excelled in fencing" and "John is in health and in full possession of his wits"). Other prepositions, "into", "out of", and "from", as well as "to", have a large spread of nonspatial uses, some extending to causation and motivation.

(c) *Analogy and polymorphousness in the use of words*

In sum, understanding, not mechanical rule, is required for grasping some of the extensions in the use of words to which I referred earlier and to which I will return in subsection (d). However, first and more importantly, the understanding is required in order to grasp the intimate connection of the most generic uses of the more general terms we use, even when these can be considered as constituting distinct focuses of meaning.

(i) **Analogy as one root of the indefinite extensibility in the types of way in which we use words**

Formal analogy is exemplified in our uses of terms like "individual" (meaning "member of a set" or singular subject of predication), "set", "true", "definition", and "proof" which have application within every subject-matter, concrete or abstract—all of them terms of which, as we shall see in chapter V, the impossibility of giving a finitely specifiable indication of all their logically distinguishable types of use can be shown mathematically.

Analogy in use of terms taken in just one focus of meaning, in their "proper" senses, but of a nonformal kind is exemplified in expressions arising only in dealing with concrete subject-matters such as "concrete entity" (meaning, perhaps, subject of active power), "action" (in a sense in which inanimate as well as animate things are agents), "living", "understanding", and "person". In using the term "living" we have to consider the many forms of nonanimal biological life, the varied levels of animal life, and the possible forms of personal life, and to recognize that there is no one set of criteria which distinguish any of these three, let alone a set of criteria embracing all possible ways of being a "living thing". Indeed, we cannot even delimit a priori the possible forms of personal life, bodily, demonic as the pagans conceived it, angelic, or divine; and certainly no one set of criteria embrace all of these. It is not for the philosophy of language, but for science and metaphysics to delimit what is possible in nature. Even in regard to the things with which we are familiar we have no one set of criteria for the use of the concepts I have instanced. A fortiori, we have no such criteria as could limit their application in considering the kinds of thing which are unfamiliar.

There is an interconnection between some of these words used by nonformal analogy, such as the word "understand" and connected uses of the word "know", and our use of some of the terms which I referred to as used by formal analogy because of their application in regard to every subject-matter, such as "prove", "true", and "definition", mentioned earlier. For instance, the open-endedness in meaning of the word "understanding" underlies the open-endedness of our methods of proof in mathematics as well as underlying their open-endedness within the sciences and history, thus enabling us to use terms such as "prove" and "show" in the wider and seemingly less controlled way of which we spoke earlier, doing this even with the term in just one focus of meaning. And it is the open-endedness of our capacity to speak of subjects of thought and discourse of different kinds, and of distinguishing and counting them, which underlies the generality of such topic-neutral words as "object", "individual", and "set".

Again, there seems to be some kind of nonformal intrinsic analogy between the kinds of "positive existence" attributed to persons, living things, and inanimate objects, to matter and energy, to fields, to electric charges, and to anything whose existence consists in the presence of something rather than its absence (e.g., plugs rather than holes, knowledge rather than ignorance, bravery rather than cowardice). This analogy seems to arise from some kind of capacity to exercise active power. It is the analogy in virtue of which we consider the ability to hit a target as an asset, but the "ability" to miss the target only as a bad joke or as an expression of our having free will.

Or, again, as well as this concept of "positive existence" related to having the capacity to act causally, ordinary people also have a concept for which the philosophers' term is "a particular", so that not only individual people and things, but also shadows, rainbows, and after-images, and even events and states of affairs (including ones which consist in the absence of something) are conceived of as particulars; but not colors, numbers, properties, or relations, and not "abstract facts" such as bravery's being a virtue or the number four's being a square. "Particularity" here consists in either being a person, living thing, or inanimate object, or being related to them in ways involving localization in space as well as time.

Our insight into the intimate connection of the more generic uses of terms we use appears even when involving several distinct focuses of meaning, as with the word "play" discussed earlier, but in a more elaborate way with terms such as "knowledge", "emotion", "love", and "awareness" which each take different forms with different kinds of living thing.

In the case of *know*, as we shall see, these focuses are much more numerous than in the case of *play* considered earlier, and some seem closer to each other than others, and therefore it seems best to present this multiplicity of focuses of meaning as a structured array. As I shall detail later, all these forms of knowledge share the character of being in some way "cognitively satisfactory" situations in regard to the object said to be known. But this is no better as a basis for using the word "know" according to a mechanically applicable rule than Jackendoff's suggestion, discussed in chapter I, that "seeing" implies some combination of awareness with visual contact—explaining one concept which is not mechanically applicable in terms of a disjunction of others even further from mechanical applicability.

If we think of intrinsic analogy or polymorphousness as involving some kind of similarity or likeness in properties, then tradition presents us with some examples of supposed analogy which do not easily fit this model. Thus Aristotle's distinction of being intrinsically good in different ways according to the category of predicate concerned, such as being excellent in nature (divine or intellectual), being virtuous, being moderate in food or moderate in exercise, performing well, being gracefully postured, or being well-dressed, is not given any plausibility by trying to conceive these properties as ways of being similar to each other. Rather, these categories of goodness seem similar only in being desirable or appropriate to be desired.[20] The analogy here seems to lie in the rightness or appropriateness with which a thing might fit into the structure of a person's life and therefore be desirable for its own sake, so that the ways things are "intrinsically" good are structurally varied in ways related to the distinction between these categories of predicate. The goodness concerned is described as intrinsic in order to contrast it with the relation-based goodness of things which are good in the sense of being useful or conducive to something intrinsically good, or of being symptoms of intrinsic goodness.

In section 3 of this chapter I discuss other cases of analogy, some entirely formal, but some not entirely formal, inasmuch as they involve some kind of connection with the concrete, as in the attribution and comparison of quantity or amount (*large, small, more, less*) in the case of virtues, vices, emotions, and other such things as do not have a mathematically measurable quantity, as well as to distances, times, velocities, and other things with measurable quantity; not only concrete collections but also, for instance, masses of substance, water, milk, air, steam, or ice.

(ii) A study of our use of the word "know"

The term "know" serves as a paradigm illustration of polymorphousness in the use of words.

Ryle posed the idea of our understanding of a word being a "many-track disposition" in *The Concept of Mind,* taking our use of the words "know" and "understand" as illustrating this before later coining the word "polymorphous".

The word "know" applies both to the sensory perception of objects

20. Aristotle, *Nicomachean Ethics*, bk. I, 6, 1096a23–34; cf. Aristotle, *Topics*, bk. I, 15, 106a4–8.

("knowledge by acquaintance" in Russell's discussions) and to propositional knowledge ("knowledge by description" in Russell), as well as to knowing how to do things, something which Ryle was concerned to contrast with theoretical knowledge. Further, what is involved in theoretical knowledge varies enormously: what it is to have an understanding knowledge is very different in respect of different parts of physical science, or this or that kind and part of history, and each different branch of mathematics. In each case the type of thing understood by the word *knowledge* has different logical features, differences reflected in the different spreads of thing involved at the different stages of learning, in the advance from first beginning to learn to being an expert. Radically different from all these, one finds the case of knowing this or that particular language, with the still further distinction between theoretical knowledge of a language and the ability to speak it, any element of the latter involving an interweaving of "knowledge how" and "knowledge that".

Separately from these kinds of knowledge are the different degrees or kinds of knowledge one may have of a person, from knowing who someone is in the sense that one can recognize him or her (something Russell might have counted as sensory acquaintance), knowing someone as an acquaintance or superficial friend, to knowing him through and through as one might know oneself if one truly knew oneself (leaving aside the archaic usage whereby knowing one's wife is having intercourse with her). Finally, one has the case of knowing emotions, as when one speaks of someone's knowing no fear, or (in each of several senses) of knowing fear.

No one set of criteria will cover all these cases or even any one of them. Of course, it might be alleged that one should use different words for the different uses. Thus Russell's distinction between knowing objects "by description" and knowing them by sensory or perceptual "acquaintance" has been identified with the *savoir/connaître* distinction in French, yet the paradigm purpose of this latter is quite different—namely, to distinguish theoretical or expert knowledge of a subject from knowing persons (being acquainted with them, not merely recognizing them). Moreover, different languages divide the kinds of knowledge in different ways. Thus knowing emotions is grouped with theoretical knowledge as objects of *savoir* in Romance languages and with knowing persons in Celtic. The origins of the vocabulary used to refer to different kinds of knowledge vary considerably from language to language.[21] Taking an overview of many languages suggests that all these idioms should be considered together as involving some kind of knowledge.

The idea that one might explain this spread of uses of the family of knowl-

21. For instance, in the uses of the English verb "know" (of which *ken* is an old form, still common in some dialects) and the corresponding German verb *kennen*, the same transition has been made entirely independently, from meaning to know persons to knowing skills, as in "knowledge how to do something".

edge-words in terms of the notion of family-resemblance seems initially quite attractive, but it gives the wrong explanation of the unity of the family, just as Wittgenstein's account of the concept of *game* fails in this way, in that it omits to take notice of the unity given to the varied kinds called games by their relation to the notion of playing, and of this to enjoyment and to recreation or non-utilitarian purpose. Always we should seek for some root of the unity of a group of states or activities sharing family-resemblance.

In considering this, some of the uses concerned arise with other higher animals. Human beings share many structures of life and consciousness with a wide range of other animals in a way which makes it absurd to refuse to use the word "knowledge" of such animals as well as of ourselves.[22] Seeing how the uses of knowledge-words are set within the context of a large structure of interrelated features of life and consciousness helps us grasp what the different forms of knowledge have in common.

Many things involved in an animal or a human being's behaving appropriately are not regarded as cognitive, though all presuppose some cognitive attitudes (e.g., desire, anger, fear). Human life reveals an integration between different types or aspects of cognition as related to behavior, and these cannot be separated as if some were truly cognitional and others not so. Neither knowing from sight where the edge of the table is so that one can touch it exactly on its edge (despite one's having no exact knowledge of the relevant positions in millimeters) nor recognitional abilities are cases of propositional knowledge. Yet sensory or perceptual knowledge is integrated both with propositional knowledge and with "knowledge how"—and *technē* (expert knowledge of an art or craft) involves both "knowledge how" and theoretical understanding. It seems impossible to uphold the unity of a human being in perception, in its integration with memory, imagination, emotion, and motivated behavior, without conceding that when the same integrated pattern appears among other higher animals, we should regard the same vocabulary as appropriate as in the human case. For instance, it would be absurd to speak of my ability to recognize a certain person as a case of knowledge and to refuse to allow the title knowledge to my dog's recognitional capacities. Descartes was wrong in regarding animals other than man as automata, as if no kind of awareness is involved in animal perception.

What all the kinds of things labeled "knowledge" seem to have in common is that, as "cognitive" states which are "satisfactory enough", they attain the threshold of satisfactoriness making them relevant to the purpose con-

22. Though not with all—since many animals, even the most complex, such as insects with their colonies, appear so automated in their behavior without showing any learning from experience, so that to speak of knowledge, desire, or pain seems to be just as much an anthropomorphism as in the case of plants; cf. David Braine, *Human Person*, 301–10, esp. 306.

cerned, correct and not by mere accident, but not requiring certainty or infallibility.[23] What it is to be satisfactory needs to be contextually defined in terms of its relations to desire, attainment of ends, and adequacy in planning action; and what it is to be cognitive defined in terms of the relations of sureness of belief or acceptance to things like perception, memory, and the communication of knowledge on the one hand, and the planning of action on the other, and it will have to satisfy more demanding criteria in the human case where intellect, reason, choice, and language allowing knowledge upon testimony are involved.

We have, therefore, what is in effect a system of complex informal contextual definition whereby knowledge, pleasure or enjoyment, desire, and action are co-defined. This may explain the unity in the family of knowledge-words, so that nothing alien has entered in, making this unity a mere façade. However, it has no tendency to suggest a "scientific" or effectively applicable definition of "knowledge", no tendency to suggest that it might be defined disjunctively as such and such in the context of one set of interests and one situation, and something else in some other context, and as some third thing in some third context, and so on, as if one might just as well use different terms. This is for two reasons. First, kinds of knowledge are indefinite in number (the kinds of possible object to be known and the variety of ways in which cognitive faculties may be adapted to different kinds of object are not listable or enumerable). Second, there is no reason to suppose that even one of the kinds of knowledge concerned has an effectively applicable definition.[24] If one examines any one of them, one will find that there is a certain informality or lack of mechanical rule in the way language-users attribute knowledge of the kind concerned, not because of any indeterminacy in the application of the term, but because a certain skill and judgment are required in attributing each kind of knowledge.

(d) *Metaphor and relation-based uses of words distinguished*

(i) A comparison of metaphor and relation-based uses, and the interweaving of the two

Where metaphor is concerned, although some metaphors become standard and can be listed in a dictionary, the nature of metaphor is such as to allow an unrestricted freedom in the spontaneous production of new metaphorical uses of the same term, intelligible to other people without explanation, so that no exhaustive listing is possible.

23. I show the appropriateness of bringing the notion of "satisfactoriness" into an informal definition of knowledge in David Braine, "Nature of Knowledge", sec. 5.

24. These criteria for knowledge of the truths of natural arithmetic elude any effectively applicable definition, for the reasons made plain by Gödel, dealt with in more detail in chap. V.

By contrast, relation-based uses arise in a small number of ways, so that the main types of use can readily be listed in a dictionary, indicative of some but not all of the kinds of relation or connection which will allow us to use the word—never an exhaustive list, since we may light upon a fresh relation or connection allowing us quite spontaneously to produce a new use for a word or a new morphological complex.

Where terms are used as modifiers of nouns, for instance, "healthy" or "cricket", we understand their sense by reference to the relation to health or cricket involved. Thus the expressions "cricket" and "batting" as they occur in "cricket-bat", "cricket-ball", "cricket stumps", "cricket pads", and "batting gloves" are clearly used because of their varied connections with the game of cricket and the activity of batting. In these types of case, the offering of a paraphrase indicating the relation involved suffices to give an exhaustive explanation of sense, but what makes the distinct use or sense of the word clear is a customary form of syntax and an understanding of the context of use and the intelligibility of the relation (obviously, a climate might conduce to health, but would not be caused by it).[25] Novel uses of words in such cases commonly need no explanation when first put to use. Such cases certainly do not involve any new focuses of meaning for the words "cricket", "bat", "ball", or "pads". We can speak of a distinct sense or discourse-significance of the morpheme *cricket* only because each phrase ("cricket-bat", "cricket-ball", etc.) requires a different paraphrase.

I now turn to metaphor.

All metaphor involves likeness, commonly one which can be identified by paraphrase.

What loud ties, people who are loud-mouthed, loud colors, and such like have in common is that they have the tendency to draw attention to themselves in a way which is in daring, bad, or questionable taste (the word carries the suggestions of a thing's being striking, strident, or garish), and when a person has appropriated or at least appreciated the culture, he ceases to need explanations of each new metaphorical application of the word "loud". This paraphrase of "loud" serves as a summary of a whole range of metaphorical applications arising from the fact that loud sounds have this character, sounds alone being loud in the literal use of the word. The speakers of a language come to appreciate all the uses of the word "loud" by a process of cultural learning.

Metaphor provides an area of "deviation" commonly involving breaches of semantic "category" restrictions, as with "It is no longer John that plays golf,

25. Clearly cricket-bats are not games and batting gloves do not bat, so these are expressions used in virtue of relations.

but golf that plays John". Here the normal ("non-metaphorical") use of a two-place predicate "... plays—" involves that the first argument position should be filled by expressions denoting persons, who govern what is done; the metaphor arises from suggesting that in the case described it is golf which has assumed this governing role. The recognition of a certain type of lexical norm is a condition of the intelligent understanding of metaphor as that which violates the norm concerned[26]—but this does not imply that the violation needs long-term storage, either in the dictionary or in the mental lexicon.

"Fanaticism killed Buckingham in 1624" is not a case of metaphor, but a case of an action spoken of in relation to its motivation. Yet our way of speaking again violates lexical norms in a way not needing long-term storage in a dictionary or in memory, and again illustrates the free creativity of language.

Once formal parallelisms in the way words are combined as they occur in utterances have been recognized, philosophers and logicians, as well as grammarians, are free to play the game of first producing constructs such as "The number four is green", a formula instanced earlier, or Chomsky's "Colourless green ideas sleep furiously",[27] violating semantic or lexical norms, and then trying to imagine a possible context of utterance and meaning for them. Thus it is easy to think of inexperienced or bilious footballers with shirts marking them as the number four in a team, or of a numeral in a sign in a public place which has been painted green, or to write novel sequences in which people dreaming of leprechauns sleep restlessly and have feelings of aggression while asleep. However, this is a theorist's game irrelevant to grammar and offers a false starting point for thinking about the semantics of category distinctions, a semantics which should not begin with words at the level of *langue*, their sense and reference in speech or *parole* still indeterminate, but only with expressions in use, at the speech-level with sense and reference as determinate as speech requires.

(ii) The different kinds of variety allowed by metaphor

In the literal sense of the word *cut*, we cut something material or imagined as physically continuous (e.g., wood, meat, a vegetable or piece of vegetable, somebody's or some animal's skin, flesh, or bones). But we also speak of cutting through difficulties. And, thinking of the "tense" relations between peo-

26. Dik appropriately comments, "The selection restrictions on argument positions are taken to define the non-metaphorical uses of the predicate in question. They should not be taken as prohibitions on term insertion. However, when some term is inserted which does not conform to a given selection restriction, this is a sign that special interpretation strategies must be called upon in order to arrive at some sort of metaphorical interpretation"; Dik, "Basic Principles of Functional Grammar", in *Advances in Functional Grammar* (Dordrecht: Foris, 1983), 12.

27. The "colourless" in Chomsky's original example imports the irrelevant feature of contradiction into what is otherwise a marvelous amalgam of category confusions.

ple in a room as making the "atmosphere" in a room "restrictive" or "heavy", we speak about "being able to cut the atmosphere with a knife". Again, we can cut a conversation short or speak of cutting left or making a cut for home in explaining a sharp or decisive change in our action or travel. We speak of remarks which are cutting in the sense that they are intended to be decisive and cruel in adverse judgment of something the other person values about himself (his appearance, good sense, or virtue), even so that he has been "cut to the heart" or "cut to the quick [the part which feels]". But we also speak of people whose intellect or courage, it being automatically presumed that good qualities are assets, are "a cut above the average" in an idiom depending on the idea of measuring qualities by making marks on a measuring rod by cuts, the rod being set vertical so that the better quality is the higher one. There are several uses of the word "cut" derived from the activity of cutting cloth in tailoring clothes (e.g., we speak of the cut of a suit or dress to refer to its style, and to cut one's coat according to one's cloth is to adjust one's aim or expenditure to one's means); and to like the cut of a person, his face, or his jaw is to react favorably to his character or appearance being definite in some way.

With metaphors the ideal case is that they should be capable of being used freshly, without introduction, and be intelligible immediately, despite their freshness. Yet often the metaphor satisfies this ideal only for a restricted audience. Thus not to like "the cut of his jib" has the nautical origin of not liking the way a sail is set. In all these cases the same focus of meaning of the word "cut" is involved, and we would not expect all these ways of speaking to be listed in a normal dictionary, although for many people some explanation is still needed (unless they get the right sense by assuming a false etymology—e.g., supposing "the cut of his jib" to mean "the cut of his jaw"). As we have seen, some metaphors depend upon some almost universal idea (of cuts being sharp or causing pain, of making marks by cutting, of measures of value indicated on a vertical scale, of the activity of tailoring), so that even when first used the user might have hoped or expected to be understood without explanation. However, the use of an archaic word (like "quick" meaning "alive" or "having feeling"), or reference to an unfamiliar context (as with "jib") may require reference to some dictionary of phrases. We commonly meet explanations to these in the notes provided by editors of literary works out of the past.[28]

Accordingly, in the fluidity of language, spread over different times and different groups, explanations of meaning have different functions for different people. For one group an explanation of meaning (e.g., by paraphrase) in the dictionary serves the purpose of identifying a separately learned focus of meaning, a new element of *langue*, a second-level ability presupposed in

28. Cf. George Steiner's examples; see chap. III, n. 38.

its exercise in the use of the word. For another group it may be obvious how the idiom relates to already established focuses of meaning, how it fits into a structured array of uses of the word, so that the dictionary explanation tells them nothing new and expresses, at the third level, understanding of meaning, meaning at the level of *parole*.

Accordingly, as children grow older and their experience of life and appreciation of cultural association grow greater, the function of explanations of meaning changes. In this way the learning process is only complete when the explanation of meaning by paraphrase has made the connection of meanings clear so as to restore awareness of how the metaphor works, indeed even so that language-learners come to be able to use the metaphor concerned freely for themselves. At this stage a further group of explanations of meaning will have been made redundant, no longer needed to impart *langue*, but only serving to make a person's understanding of *parole* explicit, understanding as something at the third level, of activity, not mere capacity.

Most words for sensory qualities are fertile sources of metaphor.

"Sharp" is applied not only to objects of touch which are pointed or cutting, but to sounds, tastes, smells, and other experiences, and beyond this to changes and differences of every kind according to the way they stand out from their background, their suddenness of onset, or intensity, while "flat" applies not only to surfaces, but more generally to experiences which are little changing or uninteresting. (The words "sharp" and "flat" have specialized focuses of meaning in respect of the tone of musical notes.)

The words "sweet", "bitter", "sour", and "salt" have a huge array of metaphorical uses. All of these seem to be applicable not only to the objects of taste and smell, but also to every kind of emotion, every kind of change of character, and even to every kind of character, negatively or positively. "Sweet" applies to sounds as well, and has wide use as a general word of favorable evaluation; "bitter" has some parallel uses more suggestive of unhappiness. Strangely, metaphorical uses of color-words are rare, most of their secondary uses arising from the way colors are treated as symbols, arising sometimes from natural associations and often from cultural convention, and color-idioms always require separate dictionary itemization.[29]

29. "Yellow" is used of the jealous, cowardly, or treacherous, its negative connotations perhaps connected with leprosy and jaundice. As associated with the sun and with gold, yellow becomes a symbol of royalty and expression of high value. White symbolizes innocence or purity, as is reflected in "a soul as white as snow". By contrast, red symbolizes danger and martyrdom, but not in language.

Metaphorical uses of color words are few. A certain pallor invites the description "looking green", suggesting a tendency to vomit. Conceivably, turning pale when envious lies behind the expression "green with envy", or, because one's view of things is infected, "green-eyed with envy". However, green is most commonly associated with the freshness of spring and with youth, and, considering the immaturity of wheat when it is still green, with being inexperienced. "Red", "purple", and "white" due to anger (like "white with fear" and "blue with cold") are quasi-literal. "Black" and "blue" make reference to mood, and "black" to evils intended.

(iii) The significance of the phenomenon of metaphor

What matters here is that, whether or not some explanation of the connection between the different uses of the same word by paraphrase is possible, metaphor in a sense implying likeness or relation typically involves no new focus of meaning. This is especially true in the case of those indispensable metaphors which have to do with the understanding, such as those involving *see*, *light*, and *grasp*, where paraphrase is useless and the context dictates how the connection with knowledge or understanding is to be understood and what form the syntax will, as a result, have to take.

However, the absence of any new focus of meaning in any of these highly varied cases of different uses of the same word means that there is nothing recorded in the dictionary which would allow a calculation of the meaning of statements involving such words beforehand. And in chapter I we saw how words whose literal meaning is in connection with concrete subject matters can be used to express the properties of abstract objects, as when we say that a number lacks a certain property, or that two plus two cannot help equaling four.

In other words, the lexical specifications which have to be given in connection with the use of a word on a particular occasion in order for one to be able, assisted by the general rules of an appropriate grammar, to calculate the significance or sense of the resulting utterance would have to be far more determinate than anything one could specify in a dictionary. Whereas the different focuses of meaning of the same word can be set out in a short definite list, displayed either in random order or in a tree structure reflecting their etymological history, the situation is quite different with the variety of uses, the variety of implications, in general the spread of senses the word can carry while still being used in accord with the same focus of meaning. These cannot be listed beforehand, but arise spontaneously in the act of speech, whether in a metaphor (whether well used or fresh, with a range of implications familiar from other cases or with a new range of implications to be appreciated from the context), or in the formation of a new word in a well-established, but not law-bound metaphorical way. Extensions in the use of a term may arise by morphological devices of which a hearer has had no previous experience, but which do not prevent his or her understanding of what a speaker has said. Such freedom in the use of words may arise from the unpredictability of types of variation in the situations which need to be described or accommodated, or from the possibility of finding quite fresh methods of describing them.

Section 3. The Roots of Creative Analogy in Extending the Concept of Number

The notion of number has been developed in three directions: (1) as a measure of quantity or size, whether of aggregates of discrete items (collections) or of continua such as distances in space; in the case of finite collections, this yields an intuitive identification with numerically definite quantifiers; (2) as a measure of cardinality, predicates being of the same cardinality if they identify sets which can be put into a one-to-one correspondence with each other; and (3) as a way of identifying a place in an order (i.e., as the notion of ordinal number, first, second, third, etc.). Each line of development takes us into highly technical areas of mathematics and science, each beautifully illustrating the general picture of creative extensibility in the use of the same word. These are areas rich with examples of the way in which the freedom of the imagination in inventing new uses for old words, grounded in conceiving new ways in which different things and situations can be compared, involves an indefiniteness and unpredictability in the possible uses of the same expression, not as a result of quirks of idiom, but in response to unforeseen aspects of physical reality and to experiments in thought which in some cases find concrete application, while in others do not.

(a) *Two different directions of extension in our use of the concept of number*

Both the concept of number itself and particular number expressions develop a variety of applications in several quite different ways.

The numbers we count with (positive finite whole numbers) are called "natural numbers". The result of counting gives us a measure of the size of a finite set, as in "The apostles were twelve in number". They also serve as quantifiers, as in "Ten men came this way", as well as "Some men came this way" and "Every team member came this way". Because we can count groups of numbers, colors, concrete objects such as people, and any other kind of discrete object, these natural numbers and the theory of sets belong to the same topic-neutral theory as propositional and predicate logic.

Within this topic-neutral theory, for several interlocking reasons the key notions cannot be characterized formally, and "natural number" is one of these.

As numerically definite existential quantifiers, the natural numbers can be reached in a series. Each such quantifier has an immediate successor, and each such successor is reached in a finite number of steps, and so has an immediate predecessor. The natural numbers then correspond, not to the indefinite "some" in "There exists something, x, such that Fx" ("Fx" signifying a thing's having the property F), but to "There exists something, x, such that (Fx and [it is not the case that there exists something, y, such that (Fy and y is not identical to x)])", which expresses, "There exists exactly one thing, x, such that Fx", and so forth unendingly. Such quantifiers are easy to define within a predicate logic with a way of expressing identity. But such a predicate logic affords no way of giving a general characterization of such quantifiers in a noncircular way unless one postulates that any such quantifier corresponding to a finite number must have a successor (i.e., that for any set defined by a property, there must be a property defining a set with one more member, or at least that for any such set defined by a property, there *could* be such a set containing one more member) and then limits oneself to the numerically definite existential quantifiers definable in this way. If one identified the numerically definite existential quantifiers defined in this way with the natural numbers, they would satisfy Peano's axioms, whereby 1 is a natural number, every natural number has an immediate successor, and, if any property (i) is possessed by the natural number 1, and (ii) is such that, if a natural number has it, then the successor of that natural number has it, then this property is possessed by every natural number. But these axioms do not constitute a definition of what it is to be a natural number, or which things are natural numbers, since there are many other series which satisfy these axioms, such as the even numbers, to take a simple example.

(b) *Extensions in the use of the concept of number as a measure of size*

(i) The natural numbers and positive real numbers

The initial concept of number seems to be a notion of size or quantity, making it natural to assign numbers as measures of the sizes of continua such as distances, areas, volumes, masses, and anything which can be defined by reference to these, and so to finite continua, and not only to finite collections.

In both cases we assign a measure to the size of an aggregate. In both cases a unit has to be defined—whether we are counting men, hundreds of men, or divisions within an army, or counting yards, miles, or kilometers, or pints or liters. The difference between a collection of horses and a mass of water arises in the following way. In the case of the collection of horses we have an aggregate which has a minimum partition, so that we can divide it no further into units of the same kind—we can divide the collection no further once we have got to the level of the individual horses. At this stage we can ascribe a natural number to it (e.g., "a hundred horses" or, speaking indefinitely, "many horses")—we cannot go further than the individual horse because a part of a horse is not a horse. By contrast, in considering continuous aggregates such as distances, geometrical lines, surfaces, volumes, or physical masses of water or iron, we speak as if every part of a line is itself a line divisible into shorter lines, and every part of the mass of water is itself a mass of water divisible into smaller masses of water, and at this stage the measures we assign need not be in terms of whole numbers. We speak of lines as two meters long, two and a half meters long, and so on; and likewise with masses of water; we treat the meaning of the word "number" as the same whether the measure of the continuum concerned is specified in natural or whole numbers, or only in rational, algebraic, or other real numbers (e.g., π being introduced to measure circles and spheres, and others being identified through using a large range of functions, trigonometric, hyperbolic, logarithmic, etc.).

This is all possible because, historically, with the development of mathematics, new ways of defining real numbers have arisen progressively, each definition identifying a point at which a continuum such as a line may be cut, so that Dedekind inspired by Eudoxus could conceive a real number as a cut.[30] Thought-experiments relying on the imagination supply some kind of rationale for defining new real numbers, as when one conjectures putting an idealized rope round a circle and then unwinding it along a straight rod, in this way introducing π.[31] We have no rule or algorithm for defining what new ways will be found for defining cuts in the continuum or real numbers or what later thought-experiments may be devised allowing such definitions. In this way mathematics itself presents an example of many ways in which concepts, here the concept of number, can open out to new types of application. Euclidean geometry provides the imagination with a geometrical model fertile for suggesting such new definitions within the arithmetic of the continuous. Further, we can postulate that whenever a series of real numbers has an upper bound, this series itself defines a cut, which will be its Least Upper Bound. This makes the real numbers into what in algebra is called a "complete field", and from this there follows everything necessary to the theory of differentiation and integration. We can consider this postulate as a necessary part of our concept of a continuum grounded in geometrical intuition.[32] It may be

30. See William Kneale and Martha Kneale, *The Development of Logic* (Oxford: Oxford University Press, 1962).

31. Thus, considering a line as defined by a function, $y = f(x)$, we could envisage filling the space between the line as represented on a graph and the x-axis, between certain values of x, to a depth of (say) 1 cm on a z-axis, with an idealized fluid, and then decanting the fluid into a vertical container 1 cm square, and so give reason for considering various integrals to define cuts in the continuum represented by heights of fluid in the container.

32. Otherwise, it might be as if, between the series $1 + \frac{1}{2} + \frac{1}{4} + \ldots$ and the number 2, there might be an infinite series of numbers infinitesimally less than 2 but greater than any in the series $1 + \frac{1}{2} + \frac{1}{4} + \ldots$. Or else it might be that we had a converging series upwards with an upper bound but not a least upper bound, and an infinite series of descending numbers all greater than any of the original series, each series distinguishing extending parts of continuous lines, but never joined up so as to be continuous with each other—even

noted that the Least Upper Bound "Theorem" is much easier to recommend to intuition than the supposed derivation of analysis ("differential and integral calculus") from set theory as conceived by Bolzano, Cauchy, and Weierstrass, now realized to depend upon the axiom of choice for infinite sets and an apparatus of principles of set theory which includes some ad hoc restrictions to avoid the derivation of Russell's and other paradoxes.

In this double use, both of the discrete and of the continuous, the word "number" and the individual number-words are being used, as we might say, "analogously". The analogy between speaking of the size of a collection and speaking of the size of continua can only be considered a case of intrinsic analogy or likeness insofar as the collection is of concrete things and the continuum concerned is concrete; otherwise, all the analogies must be considered formal. Such formal analogies arise because we count abstract entities as well as concrete ones and because we can measure times and frequencies, velocities, accelerations, and so forth by means involving counting events and measuring continuous lengths (including, e.g., the segments of a clock dial).

We have here what is clearly one focus of meaning of the word *number* as assigning size, but many different types of size to be measured, each giving number statements different criteria of truth, different types of implication, and different types of relation to other statements, so that we should speak of different discourse-significances or "senses" in the way that I explain the word "sense" in chapter III.

This strains our ordinary use of the word "sense", but not our use of the word "meaning" (*langue*-meaning). It would be unnatural to require a decision as to whether or not the person who says he was forced to carry two potatoes, weighing two pounds, and to walk two miles at two miles per hour, is in one case using a natural number and in the other cases using rational, algebraic, or real numbers. In assigning measure we cannot say that the word "two" is being used in different focuses of meaning in its different applications.

(ii) The introduction of zero as a number

However, further thought-experiments and further mathematical developments suggest yet other ways in which the concept of number can be given new applications, in ways which ought to be conceived as introducing new, but interrelated focuses of meaning for the term "number" and for terms

---

though no intervening rational point failed to belong to one or other of the extending lines. Once one postulates that there is one continuous line embracing all these extending sublines which converge from above and below, then it will follow that there is a cut or point in this one continuous line, the same cut being defined by each converging series. This follows once one views the concept of continuous line as primary, and that of a point as secondary, defined as a cut in a line, rather than viewing the concept of point as primary and conceiving a line as a set of points.

for individual numbers, not just new applications of the concept of number in the originally given focus of meaning. I say "interrelated focuses of meaning" because the analogies between them are within the awareness of the language-user and not mere matters of etymology.

Thus when we start using whole numbers in accounting, assessing assets and liabilities, surpluses and deficits, it becomes natural to allow for there being measures of negative quantities, and we find this also in measuring electric charge in physics (by contrast with, e.g., mass, frequency, and wavelength, which have only positive measures). We could think of these negative "quantities" as "virtual" quantities (i.e., as pretend quantities postulated for convenience in order to calculate something real, e.g., what has to be sold to bring me into credit, or to calculate the forces between charged particles), but it is inconvenient to consider this to be a pretense in the case of physics.

Again, when we start using continuous quantities to measure distance from a reference axis, it becomes natural to assign negative values to distances in one direction and positive to distances in the other and then to develop the whole system of Cartesian coordinates for assigning positions in more than one dimension, giving a much richer field for systems for assessing lengths, areas, and volumes enclosed by curves and lines, surfaces and planes, making full use of all the resources already mentioned—negative, fractional, and algebraic numbers—supplemented by the full range of measures defined in terms of continuous functions.

Any use of negative alongside positive numbers requires the treatment of zero as a number. The use of a sign for zero as part of system of decimal representation of numerals appears in India from the fifth century, but its use as part of a system of positive and negative numbers is only documented from the seventh century, appearing in highly developed form in the work of Brahmagupta. These developments passed into Western Europe in the eleventh century via the Arabs, so that these representations have become referred to as Arabic numerals.

Philosophically the notion of zero as a number assigning a measure of size has always seemed problematic. To meet no one is not to meet anyone at all and constitutes the denial of any size rather than the assignment of the size zero; the introduction of the conception of a set with no members, a so-called empty set, is the introduction of a highly convenient fiction as an ideal element into set theory.

(iii) Complex numbers as fitting within the same extended system

All these so-called numbers measuring continuous quantity treat it as a scalar quantity—that is, with the numbers set in what mathematicians call simple order (i.e., as if in one dimension). By contrast, positions in a space of two or more dimensions cannot be set in simple order as if each position is greater or less than another absolutely, rather than having the possibility of being greater in one respect and less in another; and sizes correspond to positions in a one-dimensional space. However, positions in a two-dimensional space can be specified by an ordered pair of numbers $< x, y >$, and by a cunning trick this may be represented by "$x + \sqrt{-1}\, y$", the $\sqrt{-1}$ having no real value, no value corresponding to any size, and out of this there arises the mathematics of what, by formal analogy, are called complex numbers. Multiplying can be used to provide a scalar measure of quantity.[33] Moreover, these numbers are of importance in physics, beginning from when we assign a measure to capacitances and impedances, and so give new application to the notion of "virtual" quantity as something which serves as a convenience in calculating real quantities.

(c) *Algebra as providing a method of distinguishing kinds of number*

So far I have distinguished different interrelated focuses of meaning for the word *number* according to the types of application which a kind of number has to concrete subject-matters, as in assigning measure to what can only have a positive measure, and then in assigning either measure or relative position in some other sorts of way with negative and complex numbers.

However, as well as using number-terms as quantity-terms, as in "The road was two and a half miles long", mathematicians often speak of numbers as objects in their own right, each with relations to other numbers. At this stage mathematicians begin to distinguish types of number, the positive rational numbers, the algebraic numbers, and all the real numbers, according to their algebraic properties, considering each kind of number separately and in abstraction from any consideration of number theory's having any application. One is now using the word "number" and particular number-words in a different meaning and introducing a new and separate set of interrelated focuses of meaning.

Thus, considering numbers as objects in relations with one another (addition, multiplication, subtraction, taking the square, taking the square root, etc.), mathematicians have been drawn to consider a different set of analogies: formal analogies consisting in the character of the algebraic relations into which the various species of object called *numbers* enter. Natural numbers can be multiplied and added without restriction, but the converse operations, division and subtraction, are not always possible, division sometimes

33. By contrast, vectors, specified by ordered triples $< x, y, z >$, while useful for indicating position and direction, yield no means for setting volumes in scalar order or any form of strong order.

taking one to numbers which are not whole, and subtraction to negative numbers. Therefore, one can distinguish classes of number as objects according to the kinds of operation in which both the operation and its converse can be performed without taking one outside that species of number. The positive rational numbers allow both multiplication and division unrestrictedly (we say that they are closed under these operations); positive algebraic numbers are closed under exponentiation and the taking of roots. A further problem arises with subtraction, since, having admitted negative numbers for a kind of number to be closed under addition and subtraction, it is only by admitting complex numbers that we can consider all these relations closed, allowing the taking of roots of negative numbers.

I referred earlier to the further way in which completeness may be sought—namely, that if a series of numbers of a certain kind has an upper bound, this series should have a limit among numbers of the same kind—that is, it should have a least upper bound. This ideal of being algebraically a "complete field" is not obtained by the rational or the algebraic numbers, but, as we noted, is attained with the real numbers, corresponding to the cuts which may be made in the real line. It is this last algebraic property which is vital for differentiation and integration, and so for the handling of continuous quantities.

Considering the different kinds of number according to their algebraic properties in this way, independently of their applications in connection with the concrete, the different species of number come to be treated as if they were each "numbers" according to a different focus of meaning of that word, the focuses of meaning having a living interrelation in virtue of these algebraic analogies between them.

(d) *Using the concept of number in comparing collections and sequences*

The mathematician Cantor developed the notion of the "power" or "cardinal number"—I shall say "cardinality" to avoid possible equivocation on the word "number"—grouping sets which can be put into one-to-one correspondence with each other as having the same cardinality, presuming every set to have such a cardinality independent of the order in which its members are considered to be taken. Applied to positive finite whole numbers this notion might seem to be the same as that of natural number, corresponding to the notion of size. However, it is also a notion which can be applied not only to empty sets, but also to infinite sets, where again it loses its intuitive correspondence to the notion of size, since, for instance, the even numbers can be put into one-to-one correspondence with the natural numbers, while the intuitive expectation would be that there should be more natural numbers than even numbers, since there are an equal number of odd numbers alongside the even numbers. Transfinite cardinals or powers include the cardinality of the set of natural numbers, which can be shown, though, to be the same as the cardinality of the sets of rational numbers and of algebraic numbers.

However, the cardinality of the set of real numbers identifying cuts which may be made in a continuum can be shown to be different from this, so that the real numbers are said to be "non-denumerably infinite", not being capable of being put into one-to-one correspondence with the natural numbers. According to the mathematical intuitionists, real numbers do not have any existence independent of their potentiality for being constructively defined, so that their "non-denumerabe infinity" is not at all because they are of larger number or form a bigger set, but because the forms of constructive definition are open-ended or (one might say) "indefinite in number" in a certain particular way.

Cantor also distinguished sets according to their order into different "order-types", and among order-types picked out "ordinal numbers" as order-types of which every subset had a first member, so that finite order-types can be taken one by one in order. He then developed the notion of transfinite ordinal, a notion whose importance in recent discussions of the comparative powers of the human mind and possible computers will appear in chapter V. The notion of transfinite ordinal can be given a constructive interpretation in the case of those ordinals which come first in the sequence Cantor proposed. For instance, if one considered taking the series 1, 1½, 1¼, and so on, then the number 2 would seem to correspond to the first transfinite ordinal ω, and one could pick out a further series of fractions corresponding to $\omega + 1$, $\omega + 2$. In this way we can give a constructive interpretation as corresponding to certain constructively specifiable discontinuous series of cuts in the continuum to any ordinal in the series, including ω, ω_{ω}, $\omega^{\omega^{\omega}}$, . . . , a unending series of ever greater constructively definable ordinals, followed in Cantor and Gentzen's conception by ε_0, the first ordinal beyond this series.[34] E_0 could then be conceived of not as an ordinal, but only as the order-type of the series of constructively definable ordinals, standing to them somewhat as $\aleph_0$ stands to the natural numbers, the latter not itself a measure of size, but the cardinality of all series which can be put into one-to-one correspondence with the natural numbers.

The natural numbers have sometimes been identified with the finite ordi-

34. For instance, if one considered taking the series 1 + ½, 1 + ¾, 1 + ⅞, . . . (tending to the limit 2); 2 + ¼, 2 + ⅛, . . . (tending to the limit 2 + ½); 2 + ½, 2 + ⅝, 2 + 11⁄16, . . . (tending to the limit 2 + ¾); and so on, then the number 2 would correspond to the first transfinite ordinal ω; 2 + ½ to ω times 2; 2 + ¾ to ω times 3; and 3 to ω times ω, i.e., ω^2; and similar methods would make 4 correspond to $\omega\omega$; and so on; cf. Gerhard Gentzen, *The Collected Papers of Gerhard Gentzen*, ed. M. E. Szabo (Amsterdam: North-Holland, 1969), 186–93, 229–32.

nals instead of with the finite cardinals—a fact which reveals the arbitrariness in such identifications. The use of natural-number words as quantifiers, as in "There were ten men", suggests an analogy with the cardinals, while the use of natural numbers in counting (first, second, third, etc.) suggests an analogy with the ordinals.

I now turn to a new departure in the development of idiom.

In mathematics we have a playground for the development of grandiose theories, clear in their formal structure, but of doubtful meaningfulness, as it were, perhaps "castles in the air", and this is how many such developments appear to the mathematical intuitionists and many others. In general these theories gain indisputable meaning only when we see the possibility of their having application in some less abstract sphere. I have mentioned the importance of negative and complex numbers in electrical theory and the special importance of the real numbers as constituting a "complete field" in the algebraic sense.

This latter is not made more certain by the artificial identification of various different types of number with various abstract constructs within set theory, which has the consequence that each succeeding class of number comes to be treated as if it were a class of sets of numbers of the preceding class, as it were a class of entities of different type or level.[35] However, the proofs concerned add no plausibility to "analysis" as the developed theory of differentiation and integration as a whole, since these proofs depend upon postulates far stronger than anything required for establishing the already undoubted Least Upper Bound Theorem, postulates difficult to protect from contradiction and paradox. Their acceptance carries with it acceptance of Cantor's whole "paradise" of transfinite cardinals and of higher transfinite ordinals (ε_0 and beyond), suggesting hypotheses and raising questions of which it is doubtful whether they have any real meaning, a real meaning which in the view of Gödel depended on having some implications in less abstract areas and which in the view of mathematical intuitionists always requires some constructive backing.[36]

35. Here I refer to the common, but artificial mathematical presentation whereby each different kind of number has been identified with a different kind of set, so that number theory is constructed within set theory.

Thus in one common mathematical presentation fractions are considered as ordered pairs of natural numbers, rational numbers as sets of equal fractions, real numbers as sets of converging sets of rationals, each converging set converging to the same limit, with complex numbers as ordered pairs of real numbers. Then, in Russell's terms, they are each of different logical type, as different as individuals from collections, collections from the numbers which mark their sizes, and these from sets of numbers. However, this theory does no more than present a background to the algebraic distinctions between types of "number" and throws no light what warrants them, if so envisaged, being classified as "numbers".

36. Thus Cantor's approach is compatible with there being any number of "powers" ("cardinal numbers") intermediate between the "number" of the natural numbers and the "number" of the real numbers, and, although Cantor conjectured that there were no such cardinals, Paul Cohen has proved that the suppositions that there are and that there are not such cardinals are each logically compatible with the other axi-

Summary: The Power of Examples in Demonstration

In this chapter I have drawn out the consequences of the argument of my first chapter. However complete one's statement of the rules of grammar and lexical morphology, however carefully one states the bearing of context on the syntactic and semantic category of particular words and the identity of what they refer to, however carefully one states the conditions of cooperative discourse, it will still never be possible for the statements of linguistic science to enable one to calculate or compute the linguistically public significance or sense of the utterances we make. The reason for this is not the mathematically infinite reiterability of the operations for generating ever more complex sentences, but the indefinitely large variety of ways in which we can use the same word in the same focus of meaning.

In fact, the indefiniteness involved is more radical than that allowed for in the intuitionists' conception of a spread. For in a spread as intuitionists conceive it, at each stage at which a new free choice may be made in a series of such free choices, the choices to be made are between kinds of thing which are homogeneous, whereas in actual life the choices which we have to make in respect of ways of using a word are not homogeneous.

It is not just that the spread of senses or types of use which a word or expression can carry cannot be listed beforehand because they are too numerous or because they are indefinite in number, so that there simply does not exist any list of senses or of types of use which might be gone through one by one in following out some method of calculating the senses of whole ut-

oms of set theory. Here Gödel suggested that rejecting Cantor's conjecture would leave room for new axioms of set theory more likely to be fruitful in consequences for number theory and elsewhere in mathematics, including for the solution of Diophantine equations (with whatever applications such solutions may have outside mathematics); Kurt Gödel, "What Is Cantor's Continuum Problem?" in *Philosophy of Mathematics: Selected Readings*, ed. Paul Benacerraf and Hilary Putnam, 2nd ed. (Cambridge: Cambridge University Press, 1983), 474–80, 482–85.

However, more radically, it might seem that the existence of such further consequences is a condition of the meaningfulness and not just the truth of axioms in this and related areas of mathematical theory, a constructive basis or a basis in intuitions about the continuum being required. Transfinite induction over the *ordinals* less than ε_0 has an interpretation in terms of constructively definable discontinuous sequences of rational numbers and has been fruitful not only in confirming things which are not in doubt (such as the consistency of elementary number theory), but also in suggesting results (e.g., Goodstein's Theorem; cf. chap. V of this volume) later demonstrated in other ways. Moreover, no cardinal greater than the number of real numbers is of any importance in any known application of mathematics, and this raises the question of whether discussions of large, huge, immeasurable, and inaccessible cardinals are meaningful or concern any set of real objects.

Again, Dedekind suggested that an infinite set should be considered one which could be put into one-to-one correspondence with a proper subset of itself, other sets being finite. However, this leaves it open that there should be finite (noninfinite) sets which are not standard (technically called "nonstandard") in that they cannot be put into one-to-one correspondence with an initial subset of the natural numbers. Yet this supposition may be incoherent, resting as it does on Cantor's supposition that there can be sets without any constructive definition.

terances. It is rather that the skill or competence associated with knowing a particular focus of meaning of a particular word, the skill exercised in using this word in this focus of meaning, the relevant part of our level-(ii) linguistic capacity (a capacity which underlies our level-(iii) activity of using the word in this focus of meaning, but in many varied discourse-significances). But the use of these capacities occurs only in a way affected by context in an indefinite number of ways. Accordingly, the sense of what is spoken is only formed in our exercise of these capacities in context, and so the locus of *parole*-understanding, the third level, the level of activity at which linguistic capacity is realized, is affected by context. Accordingly, we determine or form a sense in the act of speaking or delivering an utterance, understanding what is said to us or thinking the content of the utterance concerned within the relevant context, and the new sense in no way comes before the first use of a word or expression in the new sense, and we understand a sense in the act of such speaking, or thinking, as well as hearing speech.

Appendix: Morphology and Its Bearing on Semantics

(a) *The lessons to be learned from inflectional morphology*

I consider the narrower sphere of inflectional morphology first, taking examples from English, allowing inflectional morphology to indicate how far phonetic distinctions are relevant in distinguishing morphemes.

In speaking, language-users need to have cognizance of words as lexemes and of these lexemes in the word-forms in which they occur in speech—and to be aware of the latter as comprised of word-stems together with their inflections, each word-stem and mode of inflection constituting a functioning constituent within speech.

Because morphemes are being conceived as lexical factors, contributants to meaning, it is convenient to represent them in a distinctive way—for instance, conceiving the plural word-forms "cows" as composed of {cow} and {-s}, and "sheep" of {sheep} and {-s}, the past tense word-form "went" as composed of {go} and {-ed}, the comparative adjectival form "worse" as composed of {bad} and {-er}. The realizations of these morphemes in speech can be very varied; for instance, the plural {-s} is phonetically realized in three regular ways: by an "s" sound, a "z" sound, and an "iz" sound, in writing represented by "-s" in the first two, and "-es" in the last case. The irregular cases are so few as to be learned individually, such as *ox/en*, *brethr/en*, and *childr/en* involving the morpheme {-en}; *kine*, *men*, *women*, *mice*, and *geese*, in which the morpheme could be designated {vowel quality}, and *sheep* inviting representation as if it were composed of {sheep} and (ø), the latter sign signifying "no change".[37] By the theoretical artifice of allowing a zero morpheme, (ø), to appear in our grammars,[38] we avoid any judgment as to whether or not the plural of "sheep" results from the loss of a suffix, "-en" or "-s", or from the loss of an earlier form in which vowel quality was changed.[39] It is integral to the skills of language-users to recognize particular morphemes as the same, as well as to recognize particular words as the same, doing this in the case of each of the three senses of the term "word".

The language-user has to descend from the level of the lexical factor to that of the morphemes within the concrete structured word-forms which we experience for the lexeme to occur in speech in concrete, determinately inflected form. Here it is useful to distinguish within a word-form between the word-stem and the inflections it receives by suffix and prefix or by alteration of the quality of the vowel in the principal part of the word-stem. The word-stems are the embodiments of lexemes, each a dictionary item in just one focus of meaning. The English language-user will have a practical knowledge that *be* and *was* constitute different verb-stems of the verb "to be" and that *go* and *went* are different stems of the verb "to go"—as well more generally of whether a particular verb-stem varies its tense and past participle in a way which requires changes in the quality of the principal vowel ("sing", "sang", and "has sung"); whether prefixes, reduplications of initial consonants, and suitable suffixes are required as in Greek, or suffixes and auxiliaries suffice as in English ("fish", "fished", and "has fished"); and of which tenses and participles are formed from which stem. However, he need not know that "am", "is", and "are", but not "was", are forms of the same verb-stem. In the case of nouns, he will know which term serves both gender-neutral and gender-specific roles (*sheep, duck, goose, chicken, man, dog, pig*) and which only gender-specific (*ram, drake, gander, cock, woman, bitch, sow*), and the phonological variation in ordinary plurals. So he cannot speak without implicitly distinguishing many things for which he need have no terminology, knowledge of *langue* being exercised in every performance, every act of speech. He need not know the meanings of such words as "noun", "plural", or "tense", let alone expressions such as "lexeme", "lexical factor", "morpheme",

37. The OE *cu* (O. Frisian: *ku*) adopted the Italic "c" to represent the Germanic "k" for *cow* with a plural *cy* (cf. German *Kuh, Kuhe*), but in the north *cy* became *kye*, extended to *kyen* in Middle English (ME) in the weak declension (mainly due to late OE gen. pl. *cyna*), from which *kine* descended and still survives; *cows* is first found in 1600. The *men, women, mice, geese,* and *sheep* cases follow the Germanic pattern of altering the quality of the vowel to form the plural, the alteration in quality having disappeared in English in the case of *sheep*, as it has with the German *Schaf, Schafe*.

38. Some of the difficulties in speaking of a zero morpheme are discussed by Sol Saporta and R. H. Robins in "On the Use of Zero in Morphemics", in *Proceedings of the Ninth International Congress of Linguists*, ed. H. Lunt (The Hague: Mouton, 1964), 228–31.

39. Perhaps reflected in the "shep-" of "shepherd"; cf. the German *der Schäffer,* despite the lack of change of quality in the vowel in the word for "sheep" between singular and plural in German as well as English.

"stem", or "inflection". His knowledge is practical, not a matter of having the technical terminology to describe it.

In counting morphemes we do best to be governed by what seems to belong to the language-user's implicit knowledge and to go no further. In the case of the plural, we shall count one lexical factor and four morphemes {-s}, {-en}, {vowel quality}, and ø), the first of these counting as one morpheme at the level of uncritical conscious awareness in speech, despite being realized in three ways (the sounds "s", "z", and "iz") at the level of practical skill. We shall treat the default simple past morpheme {-t} as a distinct morpheme, but {-ed} as another distinct morpheme represented in two ways in writing, "ed" and "d" as in "sold". *Go* and *went* will count as inflections of the same lexeme, the same lexical factor, but we will nonetheless insist that they count as two quite distinct morphemes. In the same spirit we will treat *be, am, is, are,* and *was* as embodying five distinct morphemes.

In such ways as these we can avoid supposing that the ordinary language-user is phonetically so self-conscious as to distinguish the sounds "s", "z", and "iz" in his mind, rather than merely using them correctly. For we need to avoid making language-use depend on any knowledge of etymological history—for instance, that *am* and *is* come from the same root.[40] Likewise, he need not know whether or not the past tense "-t" ending is an etymological variant on the "-ed" ending.

(b) *Inflectional morphology and noninflectional morphology compared*

Our initial notion of morpheme is as the smallest significant unit within discourse, or minimal lexical factor, and as the smallest grammatical unit. In *unacceptable* we have three morphemes, "un-" having been applied to "acceptable" after "-able" had been applied to "accept"—the "un-" and the "-able" each being unable to occur alone, just as the plural ending "-s" is unable to occur alone. When the same morpheme recurs, as with the suffix "-able" and the prefixes "un-" and "dis-" in "undiscoverable" and "undisturbed", the language does not give a general syntactic permission with the content-carrying element that one can add the suffix or prefix concerned, but rather leaves this as a semantic option which may or may not be taken up. Thus we form the word "disobey", but not a word "discommand".

By contrast, when we are considering the inflections of verbs and nouns, we are considering things which, though lexically determined in often ir-

40. They appear to have the same origins as the Latin *sum, es, est, sumus, estis,* and *sunt,* an initial "e" having been lost from the forms beginning with "s". The background of "are" is obscure.

regular ways, are not grammatically optional. This is the field of inflectional morphology and is integral to grammar, even though the distinction it makes belongs to a part of grammar ("accidence") which is accidental in relation to semantics and semantic syntax, as has been pointed out by Aronoff, not just in the individual irregularities recorded, but also in that, for instance, the different systems for declining nouns or conjugating verbs (e.g., the five declensions and four conjugations in Latin), unlike gender, have no effects on phrasal or sentence syntax, and have connections with semantics arising only from etymology,[41] whereas, although there are many irregular cases, as of certain inanimate things being grammatically male or female, and some individual particulars being denoted by plural nouns, in general the root of gender in Latin lies in sexual difference, just as the root of the difference between single and plural lies in number.

In both inflectional and noninflectional morphology we find examples of new words formed by the composition of two morphemes in the so-called Item and Arrangement system, exemplified in the inflectional case when we have "cats" formed by the combination of the plural inflection "-s" with the noun "cat" and in the noninflectional case when we have *writer* formed by the combination of the verb "write" with the suffix "-er"—a system vastly extended in agglutinative languages.

The tendency of a new word formed by some process of composition or blending to take on a new life of its own, so that its originally independently significant parts lose independent significance, means that Bloomfield is mistaken in thinking of morphemes as the minimal semantic units in discourse, since in many cases the role of minimal sign moves up one level, from the level of the word-formative or morpheme to the level of the word, so that, as Aronoff remarks, "the [function of] sign gravitates to the word".[42] In general, in both inflectional and noninflectional morphology, we should distinguish between lexical and synlexical elements in word-formation, so that, for instance, in the cases of *cats* and *writer*, "cat" and "write" constitute the lexical elements and "-s" and "-er" the synlexical. In general morphemes cannot be considered as functional semantic contributors in isolation from words or lexical factors.

41. See Aronoff, *Word Formation*, and the review article by Andrew Spencer, "Morphology", in *The Handbook of Linguistics*, ed. Aronoff and Rees-Miller (Oxford: Blackwell, 2003), 213–37, including its discussion of the rival Item and Process and Item and Arrangement models in morphology.

42. Aronoff, *Word Formation*, 14; in this work Aronoff was the first in the school of generative grammar to call for a word-based morphology and an account of morphemes other than as the minimal units of meaning. In some of his thought he was anticipated by R. H. Robins; see n. 3.

(c) *The partial autonomy of the morphological level*

Strictly speaking, the word-form "sheep" as a plural comprises two morphemes, {sheep} and (ø), whereas as the unmarked singular it comprises only one. Therefore, a distinction has been made between "morphemes" as somewhat theoretical entities and "morphs" as what we actually meet with, just as we have to distinguish between "words as lexemes" and "word-forms", although it is only the latter which we actually meet with in speech. However, within the process of hearing speech-word and morpheme, our linguistic facility develops in such a way that the presence or absence of liaison between syllables or between words, or whether "a" or "an" has been used, come to pass unnoticed except when they stand out as deviant.[43] Thus, for the purposes of grammatical description and of picking out what the language-user becomes trained to pick out in perception as the independent variables of experience relevant to linguistic understanding,[44] our concern is with the morpheme and the lexical factor. The morphological systems whereby we combine morphemes are known by reflection upon customary practice, not as something to which the language-user attends in speaking.

It is useful to make lexical distinctions among morphemes, and it is plain that one should distinguish the morpheme {in-} derived from prepositions meaning "in", "into", or "on" from the morpheme {in-} signifying negation, both of them susceptible to change according to phonetic rules to {il-}, {im-}, and {ir-}. In some cases the compound words concerned are of OE origin (e.g., *inlet, incomer*), in others of Latin origin (sometimes mediated through French, but lacking the French transformation of "in-" to "en-"), in others through a temporary English fashion to prefer {in-} to the native {un-} in forming new words, even when combining with words of non-Latin origin. The language-user does not as such have any of the etymological knowledge concerned, but must be presumed to appreciate the presence of a negative in *impossible, invincible, indispensable,* and *irresponsible,* but not presumed to appreciate the presence of the prepositional {in-} in *illustrate, impregnate,* and *irradiate.* Sometimes language-users might not know which of the two morphemes, negative or prepositional, is present except from their context (e.g., recognizing only retrospectively that the morpheme {in-} in *invade, invasion, invasive, intrude, intrusion,* and *intrusive* comes from the preposition, not from the negative). In any case, {-vinc-}, {-vas-}, and {-trus-} have no more living meaning than {-poss-}, {-vade}, and {-trude}. Again, we use {-er} to distin-

43. Phonetic developments mostly proceed at an independent pace by independent laws. Liaison has its own problems: French has *le hazard* and *l'histoire,* while English has "a hazard" and "a (an) history"—the "an" seeming archaic.

44. Cf. Gibson's treatment of perception, discussed in chap. VI, sec. 3 of this volume.

guish people or things according to occupation or characteristic activity (e.g., *cobbler, butcher, grocer, ironmonger, joiner, farmer, lawyer, geographer*), but such verbs as "butch", "groc(e)", and "mong" do not exist in English, and so these elements do not count as "significant units" within discourse. They have no live role in the language-user's use of current English. The fact that they reflect certain etymologies (Norman/French/Germanic) is irrelevant.

Accordingly, we need to widen the concept of morpheme to include these nonsignificant morphological elements so that it extends to these remainder elements within words along with their prefixes and suffixes, often arising within words derived from other languages with no living significance to the language-user. Shifting the emphasis in thinking about morphemes from semantics to grammar allows us to recognize the unimportance of differences between speakers of the same language as to how far they are appreciative of the syntactic role of many nonsignificant morphemes, and at the same time to recognize that the breakdown into morphemes is relevant to perception in the same way, whether it arises in inflectional morphology or lexical morphology. For these nonsignificant morphemes are objects of recognition in perception—that is, among the types of independent variables to which the perception of speech is geared,[45] alongside the better-appreciated significant morphemes. A person may recognize the presence of distinct word-formatives as opposed to mere collocations of phonemes at a perceptual level without being aware of them as signs.

It is therefore better to treat the morpheme not as a minimal semantic unit or sign, but as covering both minimal morphological units and minimal grammatical units.

(d) *Wider aspects of morphology: lexical morphology and agglutinative languages*

In languages within which words are distinguished (nonagglutinative), the picking out of words is largely coordinate with the appreciation of the grammatical structure of the sentence, words distinguished within phrases, phrases within clauses, adjectival clauses within phrases, and other clause-like structures within the sentence as a whole. With this it is also coordinate with distinguishing between parts of speech such as nouns, adjectives, and verbs. This allows us to pick out numerous other morphemes. Thus {-er} and {-ian}, along with the more specialized {-ist} and {-monger}, when they occur as the terminations of noun-stems, mark the noun concerned as signifying the occupation or characteristic activity of what is spoken of (*cobbler, butcher, grocer,*

45. See chap. III, sec. 3 (c) (ii), and chap. VI, sec. 3, of this volume.

ironmonger, joiner, farmer, lawyer, geographer, warbler, musician, physician, and so forth). Thus, in nonagglutinative languages, even though the morpheme stands as the minimal grammatical unit, nonetheless it is the word which is the basic unit of syntactic structure and what is relevant to its possible contexts of occurrence (syntagmatic relations) and to the determination of what other words can occur in the same contexts (paradigmatic relations). This gives more application to Robins's Word and Paradigm model of grammatical description.

In chapter XIV we shall find that every sentence has to have a structure, in which how its content-introducing elements fit within the same structure together is typically indicated by structurizing elements: inflections, prepositions, indicators of negation, relatives, clause-markers such as *that,* the different kinds of conjunction, and so forth. The less these structurizing features take any phonetic and morphological form, the more word-isolating or analytic the language becomes and the more dependent on word order for its sense to be capable of being made out. Conversely, the more agglutinative the language, the more we can expect a rich supply of structurizing elements taking phonetic morphological form; within such a context, noun-morphemes and verb-morphemes will be distinguishable, with their respective modifiers, noun-phrasal and clausal substructures being picked out, and the structure of the sentence as a whole being understood.

"Monger" as a word is now obsolete, but {-monger} retains a constant meaning as a morpheme in compound expressions like *fishmonger, cheesemonger,* and *ironmonger,* and as a formative, as in *fashion-monger, gossip-monger, scandal-monger,* and *war-monger.* As it never occurs on its own, we could describe it and other such morphological elements as word-factors by analogy with the way we consider words as sentence-factors. We could then distinguish between, for instance, "-monger" as a lexical word-factor alongside the prefix "in-" and the suffixes "-er" and "-able" as synlexical word-factors. Such a way of thinking would be serviceable in helping pick out the different kinds of lexical factor within agglutinative languages. In more agglutinative languages, we can expect order to be more significant when it comes to the placing of synlexical indicators of both agreement and hierarchy between lexical factors.

Thus, if my argument in part three stands, the underlying differences between the fundamental kinds of significant element within speech ("parts of speech", in this sense) are functional rather than formal. This means that we will be able to make the same contrasts in respect of significant morphemes in agglutinative as in nonagglutinative languages, for instance, between those that are content-introducing and those that are synlexical (structurizing and quantitative), and among content-introducing morphemes between noun-morphemes, noun-modifying morphemes, verb-morphemes, and verb-modifying morphemes. Grammatical analysis will serve to pick out the elements of lowest rank so that we can consider the sentence as constituted of these in a structured way. These will have to be considered at the level of *langue* as well as of speech, since we have to make the same kinds of distinction between focuses of meaning of a morpheme to be distinguished within the dictionary as we make with words in nonagglutinative languages, as well as distinguishing senses or ways of using the morpheme where these distinctions can only be made at the level of speech, completing the parallel with words.

(e) *The significance of the conventions of writing*

What happens in writing is of no significance for the theory of speech and hearing, and the written language tends to develop a life of its own, so that in a "cultural linguistic community" members have several registers for written language somewhat as they may have several registers for spoken language according to whether they are speaking respectfully or familiarly.[46] Empirically, "the function of the spoken utterance is to react to a given reality in a distinct and immediate manner, while the written utterance reacts to the same reality in a manner which is preservable and thus permanent".[47] In written prose and verse conventions of sentence division and other punctuation generate notions of sentence-identity and word-identity different from those required by a theory of speech, which can be somewhat arbitrary, and spelling features gain status as independent variables in visual perception within the activity of reading. In most languages, where merely graphemic distinctions are significant, as with *right*, *rite*, and *write*, this arises largely from the historical influence of other languages.[48] Conventions of spelling are learned largely independently, with a somewhat arbitrary relation to phonetics, though they reveal much about etymology, the history of the fashions of language, and the ideals of dominant literary classes at different times inspiring them.

46. Vachek, ed., *Some Basic and Less Known Aspects of the Prague Linguistic School* (Amsterdam: John Benjamins, 1983), 204.

47. Vachek, *Written Language Revisited*, ed., with an introduction by Philip A. Luelsdorff (Amsterdam: John Benjamins, 1989), 107; first published 1939.

48. Chinese is the only significant case in which a script may have originated sufficiently independently of speech for graphemic distinctions to be significant where there is no difference explicable in speech, the grapheme corresponding to the morpheme; Han-liang Chang, "The Legacy of Josef Vachek and its Implications on the Studies of Chinese Script"; Invited Memorial Lecture at Prague Linguistic Circle, Prague, November 4, 1996, http://homepage.ntu.edu.tw/~changhl/changhl/0219.pdf.

III

Sentences, Sense, and the Objects of Linguistic Science

The Concepts of Sentence and Sense Belong at the Speech-Act Level

This chapter draws out the consequences of recognizing that the primary place of the concepts of sense and sentence in linguistic science is at the level of speech and the speech-act.

This is required for the application of logic and by the functional connection of language with communication. It accords with the speech-related approaches of earlier linguists described in section 4, by contrast with Chomsky's novel conceptions, which I show to be both inappropriate to grammar and unhelpful to psychology.

My proposal is also at odds with the artificial restriction whereby semantics draws on the context of utterance only so far as it affects truth-conditions, but no more, so that everything beyond this is to be dealt with in other terms within a supposedly separate area of linguistics labeled "pragmatics".[1] On the contrary, only one absolute division is required. On the one hand, we have what belongs to the "linguistic-communicational expression" as its discourse-significance, or sense according to public conventions governing the use of language in speech-acts, this sense being as precise and determinate or as vague as communication

1. Hence Grice and others wrongly assume *all* "conversational implicatures" to be as such external to what he counts as the "sense" of what is said; cf. Jason Stanley, "Context and Logical Form", *Linguistics and Philosophy* 23 (2000): 391–434.

requires, and including what is publicly implicated within limits I will specify. On the other hand, going outside the sphere of public linguistic meaning or sense as such, we have, first, uses of language limited to a private circle, the concern of "private circle pragmatics", and, second, "perlocutionary" uses of language in which effects are contrived indirectly, as in the manipulation of language to social effect in propaganda.

My position avoids the rigidity imposed by lexical atomism with the principle "one expression, one rule as to how it affects sentence-meanings" of which I spoke earlier, and instead allows the recognition that each expression's particular *langue*-meaning constitutes a multi-potential only realized in the dynamism of actual linguistic deliverance in context. When such multi-potential is realized, what the expression signifies has a sense shaped or re-shaped by its utterance-context, but not in such a way as could be itemized even in the fullest dictionary. It is only by attention to context of utterance, including discourse-context, that we can distinguish the different uses, discourse-significances, or senses in *parole* arising in the act of using the word concerned. It is these senses which make a difference to truth and falsity, to identifying what is commanded or requested, and to the perspectives and emphases with which matters are presented.

Section 1. The Notions of Sentence and Sense—Sense Not Tied to Truth-Conditions

My remarks apply to linguistic communication in general, not just speech and articulated sign-language, although the forms of writing always or almost always depend on those of speech.

However, in most cases, when I refer to speech, speech-acts, utterances, lexical factors, language-possession and language-use, and so forth, my remarks are intended to apply to these things as they arise in any medium of linguistic communication. For a communication to count as linguistic, it does not require all the kinds of complexity peculiar to speech, arising from its phonetic character. Moreover, the contrasts made in the case of speech by differences in stress and intonation are made in different ways with other media. Yet any properly "linguistic" deliverance has at least to show distinctions corresponding to the contrasts (1) between (a) words or lexical factors with meanings rooted in language-possession and (b) sentences formed of such lexical factors, using them nonrigidly and conveying a spread of discourse-significances in acts of linguistic deliverance; and (2) between form and function. Any such system must give the power to express the whole complex of the semantic features involved in the semantic structure sketched in the introduction and integrated in the way explained in chapter IV, from tense and aspect to reflectivity and the expression of the different types of speech-act.

Whatever the medium of communication, there is always a distinction to be made between the act of linguistic delivery and the deliverance itself—for instance, between speaking and what is spoken. And there are ambiguities corresponding to the ambiguity in the word "sentence" between (a) what is uttered considered as a complex sound; (b) what is said considered as this complex is distinguishably linguistic (not just noises or random movements); (c) what is said considered as a complex of lexical factors from within that language; and finally (d) what a speaker says or means in an actual communication taken in the sense he has the right to be expected to have intended. Words as lexical items and words in use are correlative with (c) and (d) respectively. The concern of this book is with sentences at level (d), the level of committed utterance. The hearer also has the right to take the speaker to be committed to whatever such a sentence immediately presupposes or implies.

By "sentence" I mean the sentence as taken in the sense which the speaker or linguistic communicator should expect a competent language-user of the same language to expect him or her (the speaker) to have intended to express and communicate (as opposed to a "system-sentence" generated or constructed within some grammar without regard to context or meaning). "Sentences", as I use the word, all complete linguistic deliverances—are all, in Austin's terms, "illocutions" correlative to some illocutionary act, as such belong to *parole*.

A sentence as a "committed utterance" is not the act of uttering, but what is uttered—the sentence uttered in a speech-act to which the person is committed, taken in its intended significance. If a person says "P and Q" as a committed utterance, then each of the subsentences "P" and "Q" is a committed utterance. Likewise, the "R" as it occurs in "Therefore, R" at the end of an argument also counts as a committed utterance.[2] And there is a certain arbitrariness in how we answer questions as to whether *and, but,* and *so* have any different status from *moreover* or *further, however* or *yet,* or *therefore.* The criteria of sentencehood often seem more obvious than they are, because linguists mistakenly interpret speech according to where modern written texts place their periods, or full-stops.[3]

Clearly the same thing may be uttered more than once, so I count it as the same utterance or sentence if it has the same "sense" or "discourse-significance", terms I will now clarify.

2. Again, "Or" can be used by itself to introduce a speech-act with the same effect as "Again", "Alternatively", or "Or again" (as in providing further examples illustrating a point), comparably to the French *Alors.*

3. William Cobbett's *A Grammar of the English Language* (1818; Oxford: Oxford University Press, 1984) has the virtue of clarity: his concern is explicitly with written sentences only.

(a) *How I use the word "sense" in this book*

(i) "Sense" in speech or writing as correlative with public linguistic intention

We need a theory of meaning applying to utterances as uttered "live", committedly uttered, and as such belonging to *parole,* not to *langue*—not just grammatical constructs. As chapter I explained, to be the expression of a sense is essential to *parole* as what distinguishes it from mere signaling.

Our key choice of terminology concerns the word "sense".

Sense is what is expressed, what requires to be understood by the hearer, and is intended to be so understood. Thus the notion of sense is correlative with the two notions of intending and of understanding. There is an ever-recurring but mistaken conception that the sense of a statement consists in its information content, whereas statements always present states of affairs and events in some particular perspective, such perspective being integral to what translators are occupied with. We find this conception among linguists as well as philosophers, as in thinking of a predicate with arguments in various thematic roles in relation to the predicate as alone fundamental. As a result, given the predicate element [assassinate, past], they would think that, because they have the same information content, the following would all have the same sense: "The conspirators assassinated Caesar in the Senate on the Ides of March"; "Caesar was assassinated by the conspirators in the Senate on the Ides of March"; and "It was on the Ides of March that Caesar was assassinated by the conspirators in the Senate". For a sentence to present the event under an aspect, in a certain perspective, seems a necessity of language as well as of thought. Moreover, if we say "The conspirators assassinated Caesar", grammar forbids us to miss out the word or phrase referring to the conspirators, whereas we can readily say "Caesar was assassinated" without specifying by whom. And, although the date "the Ides of March" might be significant to the superstitious, grammar did not require that the first two examples mention the date. The direction of interest differs in the different sentences. Thus functional or perspectival features of sentences are as integral to the sense expressed as the "thematic roles" of their arguments (such as Agent, Patient, and Place).

Thus, my use of the word "sense" is quite unrelated to Frege's use of the word *Sinn.*

Instead I use the term "sense" to mean "*parole*-meaning", correlative with language-use, as opposed to "*langue*-meaning", correlative with language-possession, although I will use the word "meaning" when I need a more general, undifferentiated, nontechnical term. Otherwise I restrict the word "meaning" to the focuses of meaning of words distinguished in a lexicon, correlative with language-possession, waiting for speech for actualization.

In this way of speaking I treat the term "sense" as a global term covering every aspect of meaning. It therefore embraces *all* the things referred to by such words as "nuance", "connotation",[4] "tone",[5] "color", "emphasis", and "force", as well as "perspective". In this global use, the term covers all complete utterances, such as questions, commands, wishes, and declarations of intention, as well as statements—all may be described as having sense. Thus I set aside any attempt to use the word "sense" to mean "descriptive content" or "propositional content".

As we shall find in section 2, this has the effect that features of discourse-context are also liable to affect the "sense" of words and other expressions subordinate to the total utterance—discourse-contexts such as conversations, law courts, arguments, or acts of pointing. Accordingly, "sense" embraces many aspects of meaning customarily classified by linguists as belonging to "pragmatics", most conspicuously "force" or the potentiality of it. In any case, the notion of "word" as relevant to speech as well as to syntax remains a pragmatic one, since, as Sapir noted, both the point before a word and the point after it are points at which we can pause to consider how to formulate the rest of what we want to say.

Here "pragmatics" needs to be understood in the restricted way explained in section 3. That is, it does not effect "sense" in the case of (1) conversational "implicatures", those which are either (a) *defeasible* (in the case of statements, readily failing to follow) or (b) *private* (i.e., arising from conventions or features of the situation known only to the private person or circle communicated with), and (2) what Austin called *perlocutionary* aspects of meaning[6]—(1) (b) or (2) covering anything turning on social presumptions, not linguistic conventions. This exclusion of certain implicatures and of the perlocutionary fits exactly with what is required by moderate functional grammars such as those of Dik and Van Valin, while also being compatible with Jackendoff's thinking in his psycholinguistic work, instanced as we shall find in section 4 (c) (ii).

Austin's term "rhetic act", explained as the deliverance of a complete utterance or "rheme", exactly fits the conception of this book, with its links with Plato's notion of a *rhema,* the verbal or saying part of an utterance, coming from one of the verbs Aristotle uses to mean "to say" or "to predicate" of a subject. There is no real difference between the "rhetic act" and the "illocutionary act" (as what makes the utterance carry "illocutionary force").[7] Earlier

4. In contemporary English, "connote" often means "suggesting" rather than "strictly implying".

5. Dummett speaks of "tone", where Frege speaks of *Beleuchtung* ("illumination" or "lighting") and *Farbung* ("colouring"); Dummett, *Frege,* 2.

6. See chap. I, sec. 2 (b) of this volume.

7. The two terms arose in different contexts, picking out different aspects of the same acts; cf. chap. X, Note on Austin.

Austin explained that the "rheme" is a unit of speech, the sort of thing whose "typical fault is to be vague or void or obscure, etc.",[8] with which Ryle would associate truth, mode of verification, and the like alongside vagueness.[9]

(ii) The sense of a committed utterance cannot be abstracted from its force

Today the main drive towards excluding the aspect of force from the sense of an utterance in the case of a proposition or statement arises from the arguments of Frege and Geach from the way truth-functional logic works, arguments I refute in chapter X. I entirely accept the notion of "force" ("illocutionary force") as an aspect of the meaning of an utterance which can be abstracted and spoken about separately, but reject it as a deep error to conceive the "sense" of a complete utterance as an abstractable remainder element separate from its force. Certainly a clause "P" has the same sense when it occurs asserted as when it occurs unasserted (e.g., in an embedded context, as the antecedent "P" in the conditional "If P, then Q"). But, as I explain in chapter X, it is the special peculiarity of such embedded clauses that, unlike other sentence-constituents,[10] they alone should have the property that if they had occurred alone and in no special context, they *ipso facto* would have had force simply in virtue of their sense—nothing would need to be added for their sense as such to give them force. This fact, that if they occur "naked" (i.e., not as embedded clauses and not in any fictional or other such special context), they automatically exercise the force distinctive of them, is what distinguishes them from mere phrases and other kinds of sentence-constituent.

One could compare the case with that of a human being or other animal: when, as the upshot of a dynamic process within the factory of God or of nature, a situation has come about that all the elements are together in appropriate active relationship and overall setting for us to have a living being of the appropriate kind before us, nothing extra is required, no process of switching on, no extra shove, none because the thing is already functioning—in both the case of a living human being or animal and the case of an utterance. We speak these words in a certain particular context, and we have willy-nilly delivered an utterance with a particular sense. When we have reached the level of the semantic speech-unit, speech is there, its "illocutionary force" already there, not waiting to be added, context having supplied whatever it needs to supply. Once the sense is there, the force is there, and nothing needs to be

8. Austin, *How to Do Things with Words*, 98; cf. Note on Austin to chap. X.

9. Cf. chap. I, n. 1.

10. Throughout this and later chapters I take words and other sentence-factors precisely as "constituents" rather than mere "components"—a contrast explained in chap. I, sec. 3 (c), following Dummett in *Interpretation*, 271–77.

added. Sense does not preexist use. At this fundamental level, the "pragmatics" of a linguistic deliverance is not something separate from its sense or "semantics".

Let me express the point more dramatically. If man and woman embrace intentionally in an erotic kiss, the act has its significance or force naturally, even if on one side or both it was a lying act done in *mauvais foi*. And so likewise, if I am out walking with my son and, passing the gate of a field, I remark, "There is a dangerous bull in that field", my utterance, besides having the force of a statement, has the force of a warning (the same remarks made in a plane passing above the field would not have the force of a warning). Therefore, if someone imagines a "said-meaning" or a "linguistic meaning" for a complete utterance which does not extend as far as its "meant-force" or to what is "figuratively", "indirectly", or "implicitly" said, or to whatever is implied by aspects of its context of utterance so far as knowledge of these is not restricted to a private circle, then they have instituted a false divide between discourse-significance (i.e., "sense" as the concern of a proper semantics) and what is expressed in the act of linguistic communication. (Likewise, for a particular "private circle" the "said-meaning" will go just as far as the "meant-force" in the relevant application of "private-circle pragmatics".)

(iii) Some inconveniences in this use of the word "sense"

As we have noted, utterances of such forms as "It is true that …" and "There are ten …" have radically different kinds of implication and of justification where different types of subject-matter are concerned and, accordingly, we cannot give any one definition or set of criteria of application for such words as "true" or number-words such as "ten". Yet as I observed in chapter II, it is very unnatural in the idioms of ordinary speech to speak of different "senses" in such cases. For this reason it will often be less confusing to the reader for me to speak of "discourse-significance" or "*parole*-sense" rather than simply "sense".[11]

In seeking for criteria appropriate to judging the sense of what is said, one has to assess this as geared to a certain kind of audience or readership (e.g., twentieth/twenty-first-century English- speakers or readers), and, where this is relevant, a readership in which acquaintance with a particular expertise or subject-matter is to be presumed.

One always has to distinguish whether the speech is directed towards an open audience or readership or only to a closed or private circle. Thus in court, with police, or in other situations where it is not intended to convey

11. Grice and Searle make varied distinctions in respect of the import of sentences as committed utterances. Kent Bach, "Conversational Impliciture", *Mind and Language* 9 (1994): 124–62, distinguishes between what is implicit and what is implicated; see Stanley, "Context and Logical Form"; see also n. 1.

information in a cooperative way, Grice's maxims, whereby speakers should always offer information relevant to the interests of the hearers in a quantity and manner adapted to them and not misleading as to whether one speaks from a position of knowledge or is merely expressing an opinion, do not apply. The defendant in a court, the person who plays bridge or poker, and the person being questioned by police whom he considers to be acting illegitimately will not intend cooperative communication, so that what he intends to convey may be disguised except to a restricted group. The person who sends a message to a private circle of friends in an enemy land saying "the weather is beautiful" may intend to be understood to signal "the operation is on", while to others the message conveys only what it means at face value.

It is what belongs to the open or public sense or discourse-significance which alone belongs to properly linguistic meaning or sense. Any closed "sense" or "discourse-significance" which is intended to be understood only by some private or closed circle is the concern only of "private-circle pragmatics".

It is of course impossible to assess what is being linguistically delivered (in speech or writing) by such a sentence as "Napoleon is now white-haired" without knowing from the context of utterance whether it is Napoleon I, Napoleon III, or Napoleon my cat who was or is being spoken of, and the rough date at which this is said. These therefore belong to the public or open sense or discourse-significance of the deliverance. A remark about my cat may be public in this way, even though of interest to only a very limited group (it is not private or covert). The default meaning in such a case will be identifiable only at the performance level, but still belong to the linguistic sense of the communication, established by reference to public conventions in the use of language, not to anything private.

(b) *My use of the word "sentence"*

We need a term for a complete unit of *parole,* applying independently of the medium of communication, and for this I chose the term "sentence", for the reasons in ancient, medieval, and modern usage described in the introduction.

In common speech the word "sentence" has now developed a different meaning as a technical term belonging to the study of grammar, most accurately explained as an "utterance-type distinguished by shared grammatical, morphological, and lexical features alone". This usage seems to have derived from treating particular utterance-tokens as grammatical models.

However, many linguists make the mistake, described in the introduction, of imagining that this makes the term "sentence" in grammar refer to a construct within what Lyons calls the "language-system", rather than a type of *parole*-unit or utterance. They would only be right if the subject of grammatical study were the examples which are generated in systems of generative grammar or according to the rules of the schoolbooks of earlier teachers of grammar, rather than units within speech and writing. When I refer to these fabricated constructs put together according to grammatical rules, today typically the rules of a system of generative grammar, I call them "system-sentences", following Lyons,[12] or more generally "sentence-constructs". However, questions of grammaticality arise primarily in regard to utterances, such as the examples from French and Latin literature to be found in Grevisse or Kennedy, and it is the grammaticality of actual utterances of a type which determines the grammaticality of artificially constructed system-sentences, not vice versa.

It is because *parole* is thus the primary concern of grammar that I gear my use of the word "sentence", even in grammar, to language-use or *parole*, rather than to language-possession. When grammarians generalize about a type of utterance or sentence, they are generalizing about utterances or sentences of a particular type, often doing this by means of representative examples, comparing them with utterances or sentences of other types in respect of those kinds of likeness and difference which are relevant to their concerns as grammarians. When functionalists (e.g., Foley and Van Valin in their *Functional Syntax and Universal Grammar*) say that the linguist or grammarian is concerned only with constructions as they occur in *types* of speech activity or speech event, not tokens (i.e., not particular examples as they occur), they are liable to misinterpretation. The influence of the Chomskyan conception of "language-systems" invites this kind of remark to be misconstrued as a concern with types as features of such language-systems, whereas these functionalists are describing a way of generalizing about tokens considered in respect of some restricted features. In fact Foley and Van Valin's intention was only to exclude concern with utterances as parts of history in aspects irrelevant to the linguist, such as their motivation, private-circle use, possible perlocutionary use, and predicted use.

To avoid misunderstanding, one has to establish a vocabulary.

I use the word "sentence" only to signify the smallest units of *parole* (except for additions like "therefore", "however" and so forth, as were mentioned earlier) as expressions of sense correlative with what is uttered in a committed way. Accordingly, I regard it as inappropriate to employ the symbol "S" in phrase-structure diagrams where embedded clauses are concerned, and judge it more appropriate to put "S_P"—meaning "clause" considered as something

12. That is, sentences considered as parts of the "language-system" (Lyons, *Semantics*, 1:29)—to make the contrast with the products of particular pieces of linguistic behavior which he calls "text-sentences". I prefer the term "speech-sentence" to Lyons's term "text-sentence" (Lyons, *Semantics*, 1:29) because speech, not writing, is the primary form of *parole*.

with the potentiality to occur on its own as a sentence—reserving the symbol "S" for completed sentences only, or sentences whose only additions are ones that indicate situation in discourse, such as "Therefore, …", "Moreover, …", and their like.

The word "sentence" has other advantages for my purpose. We need to be able to say that the same thing can be uttered or written by different people and/or at different times, so long as the sense expressed and the words used, with their order and intonation, be the same—likewise, in the parallel case of writings, we must be able to allow the same sentence to occur in different copies of a published text. The term "utterance", besides inviting confusion between the act of uttering and the thing uttered, tends idiomatically to refer only to things individual in space and time, so that two different people cannot make the same utterance, nor can one person make the same utterance at different times. The terms "proposition" and "statement" are unsatisfactory, first, because we want a theory which covers questions, imperatives, wishes, and the like, and not statements alone; and second, because they have often been used paralinguistically, allowing the same proposition or statement to be expressed in different idioms or different languages, whereas the word "sentence" clearly denotes something enunciated in the words of a particular language.

(c) *Recapitulating the implications of the primacy of the complete speech-act for the "sense" of sentences*

The sense of an utterance includes much more than the "minimal lexical meaning" determined by the words used and the grammatical construction of a sentence. Such minimal lexical meaning plays no part in how we come to understand a sentence in ordinary discourse, since, as the introduction made plain, we come at sentences not as discrete sound complexes, but as already structured according to various pragmatic and semantic cues which help us recognize the sentence's functional structure, and other things we can gather from the context of utterance and discourse-context, so that from the first each part is given with more than mere lexical meaning. Even when we encounter a tribe new to us and are presented with the utterance "Gavagai" (Quine's example), we realize it to be a phonemic complex with semantic structure and import and are able to draw on pragmatic and semantic cues as to its structure and intent.

To express the matter precisely, the "sentence" expresses whatever we, the utterers or writers, have the right, in virtue of knowing how to use the language and what it requires in the case concerned, to expect the hearers or readers to understand. Henceforward, for the sake of brevity, instead of saying "the right in virtue of knowing how to use the language and what it requires in the case concerned", I shall say more simply "the right arising from language-use requirements". Accordingly, since what a sentence expresses is exactly what we mean by its "sense", the sense of a sentence is precisely whatever we thus have the right in virtue of language-use requirements to expect the hearers or readers to understand, extending from every nuance of meaning to the sentence's force and anything arising from it (e.g., from its character as a statement, command, or wish). And the sense of a sentence is no more determinate than customary understanding would require.

By contrast, many things gathered from the context will be outside or foreign to the public sense of the sentence concerned because not arising from language-use requirements—for instance, arising from the common, but not obligatory presumptions of cooperative discourse, or from conventions of communication limited to a private circle, or from the ulterior motives of those speaking.

When I speak of "ulterior motives" I have in view what Austin called the perlocutionary use of speech as an indirect means of achieving some end, belonging to the sphere of utility or "ulterior purpose". Only what belongs to Austin's rhemes/locutions/illocutions so far as these are public will belong to semantics proper. That is why I said "the right arising from language-use requirements". I said this in order to exclude what we aim to achieve by means of saying what we say (e.g., to persuade people of something, to get them to do something, or to make them angry). Thus people sometimes make statements or give orders in physical manners or linguistic styles which in the social situation concerned are calculated to engender disbelief in what is stated, disobedience to what is commanded, insult, or anger, but where it is not language which requires this response in the hearer. These are perlocutionary acts.

Section 2. The Speech-Act: Convergence of Philosophy and Psychology with an Older Linguistics

(a) *The speech-act as a unitary act at the levels of intention and choice*

The speech-act is a unitary act as the object of intention and choice. By means of it we may achieve other things, as in "perlocutionary acts", but these are not intrinsic to the speech-act. But there are things intrinsic to the speech-act, subordinate to it, which are not themselves speech-acts, such as using certain words, intentional because intended, although only incidentally, as parts of what is involved in performing the speech-act itself.

(i) The speech-act as the level at which sense can be distinguished from contrived effect

The deliverance of such a complete unit of *parole* with its intended sense is as such fully a properly human act, and an act essentially apt to communicate this sense. And for this to be true, it is peculiarly important that, just as a dream is cognate to dreaming, so sentence and sense are each of them cognates to the understanding of *parole* as spoken or heard, written or read, not cognate to the understanding of *langue*.[13] I say "spoken or heard" because speaking and being heard with understanding are correlative.

This realization that the deliverance of a complete unit of *parole* is itself fully a properly human act is the pivot on which Austin's distinction between what we do *in saying* whatever we say and any further things we may hope to contrive *by means of this saying* depends. The "illocutionary force" of a speech-act is internal to it, determining the kind of act it is.

The central argument of chapter I depended upon making it clear that sentences have sense in themselves (semantics being essentially concerned with sense). This requires the utterance of a sentence with sense to be in itself fully a properly human act, specifically a speech-act. Otherwise, meaning or sense would have to be explained as if speech were a means of achieving something else (e.g., as a means of communicating coded signals), which is the effect of Grice's theory of meaning, making language into a system for coding such signals, removing any real distinction between meaning or sense and intended effect.

(ii) The speech-act and the act of understanding it each as fully integrally unified, properly human acts

In order to understand the notion of a properly human act, it will help to grasp a related distinction. When we are talking to someone or listening to what he is saying, we have a consciousness of this talking or listening, some attention or awareness of them, because the talking or listening is deliberate. Yet even if we are fully attentive in our speaking or listening, nonetheless we normally have some awareness of other things in the background to which we are not attending.

When it comes to what is fully a properly human act (e.g., kicking a football), there will be subsidiary elements integral to its performance (e.g., moving one's legs and feet) of which it is normal that we should be conscious or aware at this background or lower level not involving attention. Similarly, when we ask somebody to do something, many things are involved: we use our words with

13. I explain the notion of "cognate" in chap. XII, contrasting a "cognate" with what Brentano and the phenomenologists call an *Objekte*.

a certain sense; in this we utilize these words in certain grammatical ways; in this we use the appropriate sounds combined in certain ways; and at the same time, we breathe and move our mouth, lips, and tongue in relevant ways—just as we have some analogous background awareness of leg and foot movement in the football-kicking case. (By contrast, we are not aware, even at a background level of awareness, of the details or technicalities of sound-formation or muscle movement, let alone of the intricacies of brain and nerve process, or blood circulation involved—at least, not unless some voice defect, muscle strain, or special training is involved.) Out of what we have some background awareness of, only what is integral to the full human act is intentional (voluntary and not unintentional), but only the total unitary deliberate human act fully constitutes a properly human act in the sense I am concerned with, alone giving point to the subordinate acts so as to make them human in any way at all.

Properly human acts of speaking are designed to be correlative with acts of understandingly hearing—again, properly human acts.

Here I refer to a "hearing" of the speech of others to which a "linguistic understanding" of their utterance is integral, constituting the receiving of a linguistic communication in the full human way appropriate to it. This is the "hearing with understanding" which is the obverse of a "speaking with understanding", a hearing to which linguistic understanding is internal in the same way as it is internal to "speaking" in the normal and primary use of the latter word. As with speaking, so with the hearing of speech. When speech is concerned, specifying that a person spoke what he said meaning it to be heard with understanding is as unnecessary as, in the normal case, specifying that a person's walking or running to work was intentional. Likewise it is this "understandingly hearing" which constitutes "hearing" in the normal and primary use of the word where the hearing of speech is concerned, to be presumed present unless there is something in the context which warns the language-user that there is some deficiency in the linguistic transaction concerned. The phrases "meaning it" or "understanding it" are as unnecessary as the phrase "intentionally", because all these are presumed in the primary use of the words "speak", "hear" in respect of speech, "walk", and "run". In the normal act of hearing what a person says in conversation, we, as it were directly, hear their meaning, or hear their words in the sense in which they mean them.

That is, it is not that we hear something else (e.g., a series or pattern of sounds or a grammatical formation generated from certain lexemes) and then go on to *interpret* the series or pattern of sounds as having the full sense with which it was intended.

In this area of dispute it is as if we were here reliving in regard to the case of the hearing of speech the earlier history of mistakes in treating the sense of sight—the mistake of treating ordinary cases of seeing as if what is involved is, for instance, that we see a material thing moving in complex way, with its sundry protuberances moving in a corresponding complex way, or even merely a sinuously moving patchwork of color, and then *interpret* what we see as being a dog running across a field—or in the case of hearing speech, that what occurs is that we hear sundry noises or word series and then *interpret* them, as if, whether subliminally or consciously, the hearing and the interpreting were two distinct acts. This is the mistake we meet in chapter VI, section 3 of this volume, made by Sperber and Wilson following Fodor, himself following in the footsteps of philosophers like Price. It is a mistake requiring correction in the way explained in chapters VI and VII, achieved by following J. J. Gibson's way of thinking about seeing and hearing.

(iii) The rationale of our most common use of the word "statement"

Gibson's approach also explains another subsidiary feature of our ways of speaking. He observed that in explanations shaped by stimulus-response theory, the stimulus is that which has the status of the independent variable.[14] Now, in considering human linguistic behavior in stimulus and response terms, how we specify what is recognized at *parole* level depends upon what is relevant to attend to or to distinguish. Grammar and vocabulary are not attended to as such, indeed quickly forgotten (did the speaker say "He", "Mr. Blair", or "The Prime Minister"; "which" or "that"; "effect" or "consequence"; "Western civilization" or "our civilization"? we may have scarcely noticed among the distractions of the occasion). This is how we come to speak of the same statement independently of its exact formulation.

Accordingly, recognizing the stimulus as the independent variable in our thinking of the relation of stimulus and response, differences in stimulus being what influences or determines differences in the response rather than vice versa, explains how it comes about that we use the word "statement" more informally than the word "utterance". For although what we call statements, utterances, and assertions are all entities of the same rank, and all at the *parole* level, some aspects of utterances or assertions are commonly irrelevant to how the hearer responds to them. Hence, in using the word "statement", we indicate a willingness to discount modes of reference, grammar, and vocabulary when thus irrelevant. Gibson's ideas suggest how this can be catered for within the theory of perception. Hence also, although any differences inviting differential translations into other languages can be counted as differences in sense, nonetheless, unless the change is radical we tend to speak of the same statement as given in each of many languages.

14. J. J. Gibson, "The Concept of Stimulus in Psychology", *American Psychologist* 15 (1960): 694–703; cf. chap. VI, sec. 3 of this volume.

By contrast, the word "utterance" is closely tied to the words actually used, so that one could say, "I know what statement he made, although I do not recall his exact words".

The same approach, of identifying the independent variable in terms of which other things are to be explained, is helpful in understanding our assessments of word-identity, both at the level of speech and of *langue*, and in more than one way at the level of *langue*, as chapter II, section 1, exhibited.

(iv) Sense as constituted in the act of expressing it

In normal human communication we do not have sentences prepared beforehand, like arrows ready in a quiver, each with a language-given meaning, waiting for a context of utterance in which they would be apt to our purpose to use to express our intention. Rather, in each act of utterance, utilizing our command of vocabulary, accidence (noun and verb inflections, rules of agreement), and grammatical construction, we create a new sentence and therewith a new sense. Therefore, what is primary at the rank of sentence is at the level of what Saussure called *parole*, Gardiner "speech", and Hockett "performance", where "function" is primary, not "form",[15] not at the level of *langue* or language-possession.

In thinking about speech and about sentences as speech-units, we should think first of the level of intention and performance, the level at which pragmatics and semantics coincide, the level towards which Jespersen, long before Dik, drew attention. In thinking about speech we are not tempted to suppose that we begin by producing sentences as "grammar-constructs", generated according to the laws of some system, and then look for a use for them, but rather that we aim to express a sense and, in doing this, incidentally conform to the observable regularities described in morphology and grammar. Of course there remains the question of why, when our aim is to express a sense, we turn out also to speak grammatically, but this I leave to part three.

Thus the deep mistake in Chomsky's approach to sentence-generation or production, considered from the point of view of psychological method, is that it poses the wrong question to the psychologist. The primary problem is not how we are able to speak grammatically in a particular language. Rather, the primary problem is how we are able to produce pieces of speech and writing with a sense and reference appropriate to their discourse-setting and to the situation of the speaker or writer vis-à-vis the hearer or prospective reader, which is the topic of semantics and pragmatics rather than of grammar. How in achieving this main task we incidentally come to speak grammatically is considered in part three.

15. I follow Alan Gardiner's use of these terms; cf. chap. I, n. 1.

(b) *Philosophically, the speech-act level is primary for shared speaker-hearer understanding*

We can now recognize the full importance of the parallelism between grammar in linguistics before Saussure and logic in being adapted to sentences as entities whose primary place is at the level of *parole*. This is of immediate relevance to epistemology and the philosophy of mind. For it is here that we gain full grasp of the depth of misconception involved in Chomsky's separation of a so-called Internalized language (I-language) and a so-called Externalized language (E-language) theory (Chomsky took this I-/E-language distinction from his predecessor Bloomfield),[16] and the correctness of the general instincts shown in more functional approaches to language.

However, as later discussion will show, neither linguistic theory nor the psychology of language requires any such Inner/Outer, I/E, distinction. Further, the extent to which any Chomskyan formal theory is descriptively adequate is independent of this distinction.

True, Chomsky conceives his successive theories of grammar as theories of the Internalized (I-)language, thought of as "a system represented in the mind/brain of a particular individual".[17] Chomsky thinks of Externalized (E-) language as something into which research would consider the regularities of actually occurring sentences independently of the properties of mind or of meaning, in a study belonging to sociology or to Skinnerian behaviorism rather than to psychology proper. Many philosophers, notably Quine and some influenced by him, have felt the same choice of alternatives forced upon them.[18] However, although Chomsky disowned "performance" as a concern of grammar, nonetheless his judgments of whether or not particular sentences are grammatical are in practice governed by intuitive judgments and testimony, both reflections of performance. Accordingly, despite incorporating the Cartesian divide between the external and the internal into the rationale of his method, he still depends on communal and personal judgments of grammaticality for empirical evidence.

Thus the I-/E-language distinction is relevant only to the ideology whereby what he is concerned with (the so-called I-language) is a representation of

16. Bloomfield, *Language* (New York: Holt, 1933).

17. Chomsky, *Language and the Problems of Knowledge: The Managua Lectures* (Cambridge, Mass.: MIT Press, 1988), 36.

18. Quine shows this externalist attitude to language in *Word and Object* (Cambridge, Mass.: MIT Press, 1960), and in his treatment of analyticity and synonymy in "Two Dogmas of Empiricism", sec. 2. It influences Hilary Putnam's treatment of classical logic in "Is Logic Empirical?", in *Boston Studies in the Philosophy of Science*, ed. R. Cohen and M. P. Wartofski (Dordrecht: D. Reidel, 1968), 5:216–41, where he discusses replacing the distributive law governing the relations of "and" and "or" in dealing with the statements of quantum mechanics. In his *Frege*, chap. 17, "Original *Sinn*", Michael Dummett gives a masterly account of the troubles which result from this position.

the workings of the mind or brain as something inner.[19] Rejecting this way of thinking still leaves large scope for the formal development of some aspects of syntax, a development for which Dik and many other functionalists explicitly leave room.[20] One can avoid this Chomskyan divorce between the inner and the outer in language and still preserve the possibility of a unified semantics as long as one limits oneself to the confines set by the illocutionary and purges one's account of any trace of the perlocutionary as well as private circle usages, thus keeping only to what is intrinsic to the public use of language.

In conceiving meaning and grammar as both public, Dik is representative of functionalists in grammar and follows in the tradition of the philosophers Ryle, Wittgenstein, and Austin—all free from any conception of grammar as concerned with something "inner".

The importance of escaping from any Inner/Outer, I/E, divorce will become fully apparent in chapter VIII, recognizing the need for an irreducibly holistic psychophysical account of language and the mental.

From the point of view of Wittgenstein and others considered later, language as a phenomenon from the standpoint of hearers (interlocutors who commonly also see the facial movements of speakers) is not something merely physical. Rather, language *as we experience it* is, as we have already seen, an irreducibly psychophysical phenomenon, the use of sound inseparable from meaning and understanding, so that hearing speech (like speaking itself) is a unitary psychophysical act, an "understandingly hearing", not a hearing and understanding separable from each other.

The key to achieving an escape from the Cartesianism which imposes the Inner/Outer, I/E, divorce lies in a recognition that the "I" (the first person) shares the same knowledge, stated in predications with the same meaning, with the other person, the "you" or the "him" or "her". That is, the uses of the words "sentence" and "sense" which I regard as primary in the discussion of language and speech are those which pinpoint what is shared between speaker and hearer in a full human communication. In the position clarified in successive writings influenced by Ryle and Wittgenstein,[21] we find an insistence on the possibility of first-person and other-person knowledge of the same mind-involving fact about a person (e.g., that he has such and such an opinion, belief, or intention, remembered such and such, imagined such and such, or saw or heard such and such), thus avoiding introspectionist and behaviorist

19. This I-language may be conceived more narrowly, as in Chomsky, or more broadly as incorporating an internalized pragmatics, as in Jackendoff; see sec. 4 (c) of this chapter.

20. E.g., in a late statement of his position, Dik, *The Theory of Functional Grammar, Part 1: The Structure of the Clause* (Dordrecht: Foris, 1989), 25; 2nd ed. published posthumously (1997), 27.

21. I demonstrated the incoherence of introspectionist and behaviorist theories of the meaning of expressions with mind-involving content or implications in David Braine, *Human Person*, chap. 5; cf. chap. VIII of this volume.

accounts of the meaning of ascriptions of mind-involving things as explained in chapter VIII.

When I explained this in chapters 1 to 5 of my earlier book, *The Human Person*, I deliberately spread my attention over such things as knowledge, perception, imagination, memory involving imagination, emotion, and action from emotion—things which in nonhuman animals imply mind without thereby implying intellect, deliberation, or judgment—all of which I envisaged as being shared by human beings with the highest other animals, as chapter 9 of that book explained. And I considered how we, human beings, ascribe these things in statements both to ourselves and to others, walking the tightrope identified by Wittgenstein, Strawson, and Malcolm. The same general pattern of the key importance of the possibility of both first-person and other-person ways of knowing the same mind-involving facts which arises in the case of perception, emotion, and action applies also in the most unmistakably intellect-involving cases of speaking, meaning, and the hearing corresponding to this speaking—speaker and hearer with a shared understanding.

This is the background against which we should see the key importance of our having both first-person and other-person knowledge both of what we speak and of what others speak. The coincidence between what is "spoken, understanding and meaning what we say" and what is "heard, understanding what we hear" has to be the norm, along with the coincidence between the sense intended by the writer and the sense understood by the reader. It has to be the norm that the expression of a sense and the sense it expresses are both shared by speaker and hearer.

It is philosophically vital that it is integral intentional responsible human acts of speech and of hearing, sentence and sense involved together by which human beings communicate and where honesty is appropriate. These integral human acts not only involve speech and meaning in one act and hearing and understanding in one act, with a full linguistic "uptake", to use Grice's term, but also their character as full human acts (i.e., "illocutionary acts" in Austin's sense). The introduction allowed for such cases as the way the assertion of "R" occurs as a complete committed and explicit utterance when it occurs in concluding an argument in the form "Therefore, R" or in the way we find other complete committed and explicit utterances as elements within interrogations, narrations, and so forth.

Section 3. The "Sense" of Subordinate Sentence-Constituents

(a) *The "sense" of subordinate sentence-constituents*

(i) The notion of "sense" applies to the parts or features of sentences, not just to sentences as wholes

Every sentence or speech-unit is essentially composite, formed of distinct significant subordinate parts or features which achieve their function only as taken together within the dynamic unity of the whole and have no discourse-significance or sense independently of each other. Their contribution to our understanding of what we hear or read is simply to express the sense of the whole, something which they can achieve only together. Yet the parts and features of these wholes identify a sense only by expressing it—by being "sense-expressors".

True, as incomplete factors within a sentence they carry a sense and direction integral to and integrated within the sense and direction of the whole sentence.[22] But we deliver and hear the sentence in this sense and direction only in virtue of the fact that in the very act of delivering and hearing the sentence in its intonation and context, the sentence's constituents, down to its least lexical factors, are each themselves given sense, direction, and function.

Features of the context which affect the sense of a sentence as a whole also thereby affect the sense of subordinate expressions, including words and lexical factors. Things gathered from the context are pertinent, not just to the sense of sentences as wholes, but to the sense of subordinate expressions and words within the sentence.

I have instanced earlier a variety of cases in which the context of utterance is important in resolving grammatical ambiguities and in clarifying whether the proper name Napoleon is being used to refer to Napoleon I, Napoleon III, or my cat; whether the expression "the number four" is being used to refer to the natural number or to a certain painted numeral sign; and whether "is green" is being used to mean being inexperienced or being of a certain color. We can narrow the ambiguity in each case to the particular expressions I have picked out.

Again, in chapter I, I contrasted the standard case of a person saying "I see two pencils" with the case when it is said in the special circumstances of an optician thrusting a pencil in front of the person with the request "Tell me when you see two pencils". Plainly there is no difference in senses of the

22. Wittgenstein compared a proposition's having sense to an arrow's having direction in *Tractatus Logico-Philosophicus*, translated by David Pears and Brian McGuinness, parallel German-English edition (London: Routledge and Kegan Paul, 1961), 3:144. (The title *Tractatus Logico-Philosophicus* originated with the first parallel edition, not with the German original of 1921.)

pronouns or of the expression "two pencils"; rather, the different sense in the types of statement concerned implies that the structuring sentence-factor or functor "... see ///" is being taken in a different discourse-significance or sense. This appears in the different truth-conditions of what results from filling in the gaps in "... see ///". This functor "... see ///" has a multiplicity of other discourse-significances in other special circumstances (e.g., the various cases of delusion, and where, in its standard metaphorical use, it means "understand").

In sum, whenever we have a logically distinguishable use of an expression such as might invite a different paraphrase or require different definition for its application, or different specification of truth-conditions for the statements containing it, or have a different primary mode of verification, or imply a different attitude, or which might be in any other way relevant to translation, we have a difference in sense.

The whole matter is most obvious when sense is explained by offering paraphrases. We do not have to reproduce whole sentences, but simply say such things as that to be a bachelor is to be a man who is not yet married, or that for "P and Q" to be true is for "P" to be true and "Q" to be true also, or, if Frege is right, then for two sets to be of the same number is for there to be a one-to-one correspondence between their members. In general the purport of an explanation of meaning by paraphrase is always to specify the meaning of one expression "... f —" in terms of another "... y —". And, as we saw in chapter I, some sentence-constituents are of an essentially incomplete character, this incompleteness being represented when we use gap-signs as in "... see —", or use other devices to record the need for a completion. All these are cases where contextual definition is required, or, in Russell's phrase, "definition in use". This way of explaining meaning was anticipated by Frege in his *Foundations of Arithmetic,* section 61, and the early Wittgenstein in his *Tractatus,* 3.3 and 3.314, telling us that a word or expression "has meaning only in the context of a proposition".

The case of the word "if" is of special interest. If we think of conditionals as statements rather than assertions of some other kind, such as "inference-tickets" or "inference licences" in the way explained by Ryle and which I develop in chapter XIII, then in order to understand their discourse-significance or sense we should look at whatever their discourse-context indicates of the type of warrant upon which they were asserted. This commonly indicates that what is being expressed is a connection which holds in virtue of the causal background or factual context of the conditional concerned, in that case the tense of the grammatical antecedent will be the same or earlier than the tense of the grammatical consequent. By contrast, in the context of a guessing game in which there is no other information on which one can rely for an answer except the information given, some of which is given in the form of conditionals, the connection expressed by the "If . . . , —" will be only that if the antecedent be thought true, then this thought would constitute reason for judging the consequent true, and there will be no restriction on tenses. Thus the "sense" of such lexical factors belongs to them only as sentence-constituents taken within their wider discourse contexts.

(ii) The virtues of Cruse's account, exhibiting the same basic conception

In his *Lexical Semantics* David Alan Cruse very clearly presents this way of thinking about the sense of words and other expressions in his full-bloodedly situation-geared understanding of sentences and their sense. Let us quote his words arguing the primacy of the utterance in judging of word-meaning:

> It might seem obvious that, if one is studying word-meanings, one ought to find native speakers' intuitions concerning the meanings of words the most informative. However, this is not so. We shall inquire presently whether we should ask informants what things mean; let us first consider whether words are the most appropriate items of language on which to elicit judgement. As a matter of fact, there is no reason why language-users should be specially attuned to the semantic properties of words. We do not communicate with isolated words; words are not the bearers of messages; they do not, of themselves, "make sense"; they cannot, taken singly be true or false, beautiful, appropriate, paradoxical or original. A linguistic item must in general have at least the complexity of a simple sentence to show such properties. Words contribute, via their own semantic properties, to the meanings of more complex units, but individually they do not occasion our most vivid and direct experiences of language. We communicate with utterances; it seems reasonable to suppose, therefore, that our intuitions concerning utterances will be sharper, clearer and more reliable than those concerning individual words. Consequently, in this book arguments about the meaning of a word will be made to rest, as far as possible, on facts concerning utterances which contain the words in question.[23]

His further comment is also instructive:

> The adoption of the contextual approach to word-meaning outlined in this chapter has certain inescapable consequences that some might consider to be disadvantages. One is that any attempt to draw a line between the meaning of a word and "encyclopaedic" facts concerning the extra-linguistic referents of the word would be quite arbitrary; another is that there is no motivation for isolating "pragmatic meaning" as a separate domain of lexical meaning. Perhaps most importantly, it would seem that we have no grounds for believing that the meaning of a word, when viewed in this fashion, is finitely describable—the meaning of an expression apart from its context in a proposition without se-

23. Cruse, *Lexical Semantics*, 9–10.

> vere circumscription it is an unpromising candidate for formalization, or representation in terms of logical or quasi-mathematical formulae. However, our conception of word-meaning has the advantage of being intuitively plausible: its scope coincides well with the pre-theoretical notion of word-meaning that anyone with a practical interest in meaning—a lexicographer, translator, or language teacher, or even a novelist or poet—is likely to have.[24]

It is no objection that the sense of a word will not be finitely describable. On the contrary, this recommends his account. For, as we saw in chapter I, the possible semantically differentiable types of use of a word are indefinite in number, and it is a logical mistake to ask for a definite number when one is concerned with a class which mixes possible with actual examples.

(b) *Different expressions can have strictly the same sense contrary to Quine's view*

(i) The criteria for strict sameness of sense

Truth-conditional accounts of what it is for sentences to have the same meaning would suggest that, for instance, it would make no difference to their meaning whether the sentence presented were "N is a bachelor" or "N is a man who has not married", or whether (given a statement "P") the sentence were "P", "It is the case that P", or "It is true that P". The differences would not make any difference to conditions of truth or satisfaction.

However, here Carnap's notion of "intensional isomorphism",[25] the property whereby a sentence or phrase has the same structure as another, provides a useful criterion for literal or strict translation and thereby for strict sameness of sense. Thus "N is a bachelor" and "N is a man who has not married" are not intensionally isomorphic. If one is aiming to offer the definition of a word, the difference between "bachelor" and "a man who has not yet married" is obviously crucial. It would be perverse to translate *Homo est animal rationalis* by "Man is man". Two different terms adjoined cannot be "intensionally isomorphic" with a single term. The way or ways definitions are expressed in one language will map onto some way or ways of expressing them in parallel languages.

The way this criterion detects the absence of strict synonymy or literal-

24. Cruse, *Lexical Semantics*, 19–20.

25. Here I use Carnap's term; Rudolf Carnap, *Meaning and Necessity: A Study in Semantics and Modal Logic* (Chicago: University of Chicago Press, 1956), 56–64. According to William Kneale's account, the term "intension" was introduced by the early-nineteenth-century logician William Hamilton to mean the same as "comprehension" (the word used by the Port Royal logicians)—i.e., sense or connotation. The Port Royal logicians had introduced the terms "extension" to refer to the set of things to which a term applies and "comprehension" to refer to the sense of the term (what it implied in regard to these things). However, much earlier, Cardinal Cajetan had distinguished some terms as grouping things more extensively and others more intensely (*intensive*)—i.e., some terms applied to a greater number of things and some terms had more content or implications. In effect, Hamilton's invention of the term originated in a chance phonetic parallelism.

ness in translation appears in many other cases. Thus, for nearly two centuries in "educated" English a double negative has been considered to have the implications of the positive, although in earlier English and in continuing common or dialect English negatives are often repeated for emphasis, as in "I ain't done nothing" or "Nobody nae tell me nothing". Yet, it would be a rare case for "He had not not told me" to be rightly translated in the same way as "He had told me". The first seems evasive and sounds like an admission squeezed out of a person under cross-examination, and as I noted in the introduction, there is an "external" negation connoting more radical rejection of an assertion, where, as in intuitionist logic, a positive does not follow from the double negative.[26] The statements "Not-(Not-P)" and "P" do not have strictly the same sense, because they are not intensionally isomorphic. All such differences are relevant to translation, and certainly any differences inviting different translations into another language should be counted as differences in sense.

More generally, the natural language connectives as they occur in ordinary speech rarely behave according to the patterns seen in modern symbolic logic. Negation does not behave in natural language in the same way as in formal logic when a double negative is implicitly or explicitly involved. And "or" and "and" do not behave in natural languages in the same way as their parallels in logic. The spoken conjunctions can be thought and spoken in two ways, the one as single complex statements (e.g., "P and Q"), but also as two statements ("P" followed by "And Q" where the "and" implies that the "Q" refers backwards by contextually determined "pragmatic anaphor" to the previous statement). In natural speech or thought, "Neither P, nor Q" is conceived as a conjunction, not as the denial of a disjunction (i.e., as meaning "Not P, and also not Q" or "Not P, and not Q either") as is conspicuously apparent when people say "Not P. Nor Q"—or say "Not P", adding "Nor Q" later as an afterthought. Thinking of it as the denial of a disjunction arose only under the influence of formal logic, as if to say "Not [a hiatus in speech] (Either P, or Q)".

I now turn to a different type of case, instructively highlighting the evaluative/non-evaluative distinction.

It is obvious that "P", "It is the case that P", "P is a fact", and "It is true that P" all have the same truth and same verification/falsification conditions. But how should we assess whether or not they have the same sense?

26. To treat it as a condition of two expressions having the same sense that they should be "intensionally isomorphic" is incompatible with regarding them as having the same sense if they have the same truth-conditions. This difficulty is highlighted if we consider Wittgenstein's *Tractatus* 5.512, 5.513, according to which a proposition has the same sense as all other propositions which have the same truth-conditions, i.e., which would be true in the same contingent circumstances. Since his account of logical and numerical laws put them among the many classes of assertion which have a function but no "sense", his problems are less than those whose ambition is to account for the sense of every kind of non-evaluative assertion in terms of truth-conditions.

Here language requires several different functions to be fulfilled.

First, there needs to exist some device for asserting propositions which are identified only indirectly and for generalizing about them: thus, if Jones says that P, instead of simply asserting "P", we might want to assert, "What Jones said is the case"; or, if Jones was infallible, we might want to say "Whatever Jones says is always the case". (And such a device always leaves open the possibility that the device be used redundantly, as when we say "It is the case that it is raining" instead of simply "It is raining"; or merely to cope with the problems presented by schematic letters for conventional English grammar, e.g., saying "know what it is for it to be the case that P" because "know what it is for P" is ungrammatical.)

Second, we may want to register that something, P, which has been said is an object of knowledge or one of the data to be recognized in thinking about other things, and it is natural to think that "P is a fact" is an idiom particularly geared to serving this purpose.

Third, aware of "that P" as a possible object of belief, statement, or judgment—that is, precisely as the possible object of a cognitive act—we may want to register that it is something either which has attained or which has failed to attain the goal of truth, thinking of truth as what the intellect aims at. This suggests that the function of the idiom "It is true that P" is precisely to register that this goal has been attained.

At this stage it is perfectly open to someone to suggest that people commonly use these idioms interchangeably, without any eye to such nuances and possible differences of significance. And indeed, since the statements have the same truth-conditions, it is certainly perfectly open to people to use them in this way, whether this be a matter of carefree utterance, slovenly speech, economy of words, or supposed elegance in speech. Nonetheless, we do require to distinguish these four distinct functions: (a) merely stating "P", (b) stating "P" as within the range of things which it is right to state (saying "It is the case that P"), (c) stating "P" under the aspect of being an object of knowledge (saying "It is a fact that P"), and (d) expressing that in stating, judging, believing, or knowing it one attains the goal of truth (saying "It is true that P"). And the primary idiomatic significance of the idioms I picked out remains to fulfill these functions, even if in practice we use them with less discrimination. This is not a "deflationary view of truth" in the sense that to assert that a statement is true is just to assert the statement itself, but a "relaxed deflationary view".[27]

27. Cf. Dummett, *Frege*, 228–29. We can use "is the case" in order to quantify over propositions—e.g., in "Whatever he said is the case"—and the function of allowing us to quantify over propositions is quite different from the function of expressing an evaluation—e.g., the evaluation that whatever statement, belief, judgment, or thought had "that P" as its content would be one that attained the goal of truth, the goal of the intellect, the goal exemplified when the goal state of the intellect, viz. knowledge, is attained. This constitutes

Again related to evaluation, a difference in "sense" as I have defined this word is certainly implied in the case of many of Grice's examples of "implicature" and in the cases of the differences between "dog" and "cur" and between "negro" and "nigger" discussed by Dummett in connection with the supposed distinction between "sense" and "tone". Many such cases, as with the difference between "is the case" and "is true", arise from differences in evaluative significance.

It should seem obvious that completely to capture what we ordinarily mean by the word "sense" requires one to capture the presence or absence of such isomorphisms and evaluative and other nuances. This provides a better guide to the theory of meaning than many of the theories of the philosophers.

In using the word "literal", one ambiguity needs to be eliminated. In this book, when I speak of the literal sense of a piece of discourse or text, I mean the sense intended by the author, so that if the author intends to tell a parable, the literal sense is the parabolic (i.e., the moral or other teaching intended to be conveyed by the parable concerned), and faithful translation will retain the parabolic method in conveying this teaching.[28]

(ii) No systematic indeterminacy of translation

The idea that any difference relevant to translation expresses a difference of sense may seem problematic. It raises the question as to the extent to which in ordinary life we intend what we say in an entirely determinate sense. It also raises the question as to whether perfect literal translation is ever possible. Here we find that, although perfect synonymy must sometimes, at least in principle, be possible, we can normally offer only a more informal explanation

a more developed exposition of the position Dummett took in his article "Truth", no. 1, in *Truth and Other Enigmas* (Cambridge, Mass.: Harvard University Press; London: Duckworth, 1978); first published in *Proceedings of the Aristotelian Society* 59 (1959).

The view that the function (a), perhaps allowing for (b) as well, exhausts the meaning of the word "true" constitutes the so-called deflationary view of truth, espoused by Daniel Stoljar and Nic Damnjanovic, "The Deflationary Theory of Truth", in *Stanford Encyclopedia of Philosophy*, ed. Edward N. Zalta (Stanford, Calif.: Stanford University Press, Winter 2010), http://plato.stanford.edu/archives/win2010/entries/truth-deflationary/. The word "deflationary" was coined by Hartry Field in 1986 to refer to a spread of views of this general character, first initiated by Frege and Ramsey and becoming more widespread thereafter.

The term "relaxed deflationary view" was coined by Robert Brandom: "But it is one thing to say that whatever is contentful will, in consequence, have truth-conditions. It is quite another to think that one could use the possession of truth-conditions as part of an *explanation* of propositional contentfulness. As Dummett recognized, this latter strategy is forbidden to deflationists, on grounds of circularity. Deflationists ought to acknowledge the general possibility of *expressing* semantic content truth-conditionally, while denying the possibility of *explaining* semantic content truth-conditionally"; Robert Brandom, *Making It Explicit* (Cambridge, Mass.: Harvard University Press, 1994), 329.

28. Cf. chap. II, n. 14 of this volume. Aquinas himself used the word *literalis* only to mean the sense intended by the author, referring to it as *sensus historicus vel literalis*; *Summa Theologiae* I, Q.1, Art.10, including the parabolic sense as an example of this literal sense (cf. his reply to Obj.3)—standing in contrast with the moral or spiritual senses.

of sense. However, the problems of understanding never appear ineradicable in principle in the way that the arguments of Quine and Davidson suggest.

The sense of a sentence, in our account, is that which the customary or established use of a language gives the language-user a right to expect the hearer to understand. (Cases of defective language-use are not our present concern.) If this gives no right to any determinate expectation in a certain respect, then the sense is straightforwardly indeterminate in certain respects. But then this implies that the publicly established sense leaves its implications indeterminate in these respects. Thus it is quite common for people's utterances to be in this or that respect indeterminate in sense. The main argument of chapter I, that utterances or sentences are not things prepared beforehand as arrows in a quiver and then uttered, but are thought or meant in the act of speech itself, depends upon its being the normal case with human speaking that our formulations are not premeditated beforehand. The limits to the determinateness of the sense of an utterance tend to be recognized retrospectively, as happens when we realize that we have made a slip of the tongue. This general view has the consequence that Abraham Lincoln's saying that "You can fool . . . some of the people all the time . . ." need not have been meant by him in a determinate sense (i.e., it need not have been determinate whether he meant that some people are such fools that you can fool them all the time or that on each occasion one can fool somebody or other, different people on different occasions).[29]

Translation raises difficulties for determining sense in a different way. Innumerable cases show that the idioms of languages differ one from another in such a way as to make perfect translation impossible.

However, it nonetheless remains that if there are ever going to be any tautologies of the form "If P, then P" or any application at all for inferences of the form "P; therefore, P", then it must be possible to recognize an expression "P" as having the same sense as used on two different occasions: this is indeed a condition of "P" having any sense at all. And, if we can know that one expression has been used in the same sense on two different occasions,[30] there can be no obstacle in principle to our knowing that two different expressions have been used in the same sense on different occasions of the same kind, whether this arises between different dialects within the same language (so that, e.g., "furze" is an exact synonym of "gorse") or between different languages (as when *cheval* is taken as a synonym of "horse"). Therefore, there can be no absolute or systematic obstacle to the possibility of our ever having an exact translation, and no absolute or systematic inaccessibility of sense.

29. Daniel C. Dennett, *Consciousness Explained* (London: Penguin, 1991), 244.

30. This was something Aristotle recognized as a condition of language having meaning at all, and provided the basis for his dialectical proof of the Law of Non-Contradiction in *Metaphysics*, bk. Gamma.

This argument shows that, although strictly speaking a translation manual does no more than say that two words in different languages mean the same and tells one nothing as to what either word means,[31] it is a corollary of a language's being intelligible to its own users that literal translation should not be in principle always impossible.

However, Quine and others have sometimes been too ready to see differences in sense.

As we shall discover in chapters XIII and XIV, what is conveyed in one language with very little use of inflection and relatively rigid word order may be conveyed in another in ways relying on complex systems of inflection and quite different word order, perhaps open to much more free variation. Rightly analyzed, what appear to be glaringly different grammatical structures may subserve the same intent and share the same semantic and pragmatic structure, the same thought form, semantically the same syntactic structure. Difference in morphosyntactic structure sometimes conceals intensional isomorphism at the level of semantic syntax. Thus we can regard "Look at John" and "Regardez Jean", and "Play the piano" and "Jouez au piano", as intensionally isomorphic. Quine takes the example of the French "ne ... rien" and suggests the possibility of two different interpretations in English, one with "rien" interpreted as "anything" and "ne" as "not", and the other with "rien" interpreted as "nothing" and "ne" as semantically empty (pleonastic), as if the "ne" and the "rien" constituted two distinct lexical units, whereas in fact this is just another example of a lexical unit being realized in a divided morphosyntactic form in one language and a unitary morphosyntactic form in another. In a formal grammar which takes lexical function into account as well as morphosyntactic form and which allows bracketing, there is no difference at the level of semantic syntax.

Cases of this kind, involving relatively superficial differences in forms of grammaticalization, have misled Quine. He regards it as an open question whether his word "Gavagai" denotes a rabbit, an undetached rabbit part, or a rabbit stage (Quine is supposing "Gavagai" to be a common noun constituting a one-word sentence by being understood within a verbal framework provided by the context of utterance, as chapter IX allows). But he is quite wrong to suppose that, in the language of a tribe which one was meeting for the first time, it might be indeterminate whether they counted and distinguished rabbits, collections of undetached rabbit parts, or collections of rabbit stages[32]

31. Cf. Ian Hacking, "The Parody of Conversation", in *Truth and Interpretation: Perspectives on the Philosophy of Donald Davidson*, ed. Ernest LePore (Oxford: Blackwell, 1986), 450–51. In the same collection, note Dummett's remarks on how the need for interpretation is necessarily the exception, not the norm, in "A Nice Derangement of Epitaphs: Some Comments on Davidson and Hacking", in *Truth and Interpretation*, 471–72 (cf. 473–74); cf. chap. VIII, n. 13, and related text in this volume.

32. The principles for gathering together such peculiarly contrived collections are of great complexity,

in such a way as to make it indeterminate whether we had the same *gavagai* or not. Quine's conjecture could not provide a basis for our understanding of our own language since, as we have seen, in order to make any use of a name at all, we need to have already understood what kind of thing it is naming and, where counting is involved, what is being taken as the unit for counting. Thus, in his example taken from Japanese, what matters is the units in terms of which things are being counted, not whether the unit is described as "a cow" or "a head of cattle".[33] This Japanese case presents a nice example of grammatical difference disguising sameness in semantic syntax. Thus Quine has been deceived into supposing that the semantic syntax of sentences can be indeterminate because of superficial differences in forms of grammaticalization.

In chapter XIII, section 2, and in discussing the impersonal "it" in chapter XI, we shall see other cases of superficial differences in forms of grammaticalization which make no difference to sense, unlike the differences in functional structure found in other cases considered.

(c) *The ambiguities of the "Context Principle"*

Many different meanings have been associated with such maxims as "meaning is use" or "a word has meaning only in the context of a proposition" supposedly embodying the contextualism of Wittgenstein and Frege.[34]

These maxims should be considered as concerning words rather than sen-

---

depending on idealized ways of dividing parts and time-stages, in such a way as to presuppose the concept of "rabbit". And it would be far-fetched to suggest that the way the tribes concerned used language was guided by such extraordinarily complex systems for relevant discriminations of rabbit parts or stages without any evidence.

33. Quine, *Word and Object*; Quine, *Ontological Relativity and Other Essays* (New York: Columbia Univeristy Press, 1977), 1–68, noting the grammatical examples given in 35–38. A more general critique of Quine's arguments is also presented in Crispin Wright, "The Indeterminacy of Translation", in *A Companion*, ed. Hale and Wright, 397–426.

34. This attribution has its own difficulties; see F. J. Pelletier, "Did Frege Believe Frege's Principle?" *Journal of Logic Language and Information* 10 (2001): 87–114; cf. Dummett, *Interpretation*, 547 in context of 537–51.

Baker and Hacker make entirely misconceived attacks on contextualism as it occurs in Wittgenstein.

The "contextualism" of the early Wittgenstein's *Tractatus* applies only to elementary propositions (*Tractatus*, 3.3 and 3.314, cf. 3.142), as when he says in 3.318, "Like Frege and Russell, I construe a proposition as a function of the expressions contained in it", and has nothing to do with the idea of language as a calculus.

This "contextualism" of elementary propositions is based on a picture theory in which the simplest sentences picture states of affairs (senses being shown, not calculated; *Tractatus* 4.02–4.0311) and words or names can only enter language joined in a nexus with this pictorial role. Its background lies in Frege's conception of propositions as composed of elements joined by "unsaturated" elements and Russell's idea of "definitions in use"; Baker and Hacker thereby also here misconstrue Frege and Russell.

As to Frege, with whom Baker and Hacker are not directly concerned, the contextualist principle was first enunciated before he had made the distinction between *Sinn* and *Bedeutung*, and he later applied the principle to both *Sinn* and *Bedeutung*; Dummett, *Interpretation*, 360, 369.

tences, and the idea of "using" sentences should be avoided for reasons insisted upon by Austin and Ryle.[35] (To "use" a sentence is to treat it a tool or contrivance in what Austin called a *perlocutionary* use of speech, as when I tell somebody something in order to make him angry.) What we have come to appreciate is the importance of the fact that, except in the case of topic-neutral propositions such as those of arithmetic, the senses of propositions can rarely be understood without reference to their contexts of utterance.

Thus no sentence-constituent has any existence at all in isolation, since outside its sentence-context it cannot make any contribution to the expression of the sense of the whole sentence. Unless and until we appreciate the kinds of incompleteness involved, we have radically failed to appreciate what a sentence-factor is—precisely a constituent of *parole*, not just an item juxtaposed with other items according to the rules of a "language-system". This is the incompleteness important for chapter IX, requiring indication by the gap-signs instanced earlier; these are to be understood as showing the way in which the expression concerned combines with others, and should ideally include markings indicating the way in which each gap should be filled in order to achieve sense semantically ("… $_{\text{(head of an animal)}}$ is bald"), more being required than mere grammatical correctness. And we must go further and insist that it is not just the expression but its sense which is incomplete. That is, the sense of sentence-factors is equally incapable of existence in isolation, incapable of being expressed or thought except in the context of a complete sentence or thought or, when speech or thought is interrupted, in a context which leaves clear some of the types of way in which speech or thought might have been continued.

A word's particular meaning is typically actualized in a multiplicity of different kinds of way, not reducible to any one mechanically applicable rule, obedience to which is formally decidable. Accordingly we cannot define a language or speech system as a definite or enumerable totality, and there is no way of defining the discourse-significances or senses of words or lexical factors by reference to the whole sentence system in the way Davidson has suggested—inflating the Context Principle, whereby a word only has meaning in the context of a proposition, into the grandiose principle that a word has meaning only in the context of all the sentences of the language.

Dummett is right to object to Davidson's view on the grounds that it would remove the language from proper critical review. His objection is that language must be "segmentable", not just in order to be learnable, but in order to be open to critical review. Yet, in chapter IV, we shall see how, under the influence of Davidson, he misconceives this segmentability. In short, the

35. Cf. n. 84.

segmentability concerned does not involve treating a language or parts of it as sets of sentences.

(d) *Paraphrase, translation, and interpretation: the concept of "radical translation"*

In the meantime, as we saw earlier in section 2 (a) (iii), we speak of sense or discourse-significance in one way for all purposes, and this is confirmed by our need to abandon strict criteria of sameness of sense in considering translation.

(i) "Translation" and "interpretation": vocabulary, perspective, and literary genre

As we saw in section 3 (b) (ii), accessibility of sense does not absolutely require the possibility of strict or "literal" translation, but is a matter of the possibility of attaining mutual understanding. And what this depends upon varies in different cases. In some cases some easy explanation of meaning is possible, making some kind of translation or interpretation likewise easy. But in other cases, in order for mutual understanding to be achieved, a great effort may be required, involving willingness at least in the imagination to enter into the culture and thought-forms of other peoples and times. What is required is like the kind of empathy needed to understand how one paradigm may succeed another in science. As the brief survey which follows suggests, the intellect and imagination place no systematic limits on mutual understanding or intersubjectivity. They place no limits themselves on what radical translation may achieve in allowing the linguistic expression of mutual understanding through drawing deeply upon our capacity for the informal and flexible word-use required. Rather, the limits to the achievement of such mutual understanding are of different kinds, some practical, set by available time, linguistic skill, and historical accessibility, and others set by the will, some cultures and belief systems setting low value on inquiries into the advantages or disadvantages of rival systems of explanation and evaluation and others unwilling to waive deep preconceptions, limiting the scope for such inquiry.

How far and in what ways we can identify the sense an author intended and which he could reasonably expect his original audience or readership to be able to pick up, the intended associations and flavor of each word included, can be limited. But in the view I put forward, the difficulty is not that the original "sense" has become inaccessible in principle, but that, because of developments in language and in historical and cultural situation, we can no longer convey an author's intent by a simple "copying" from his language into our own.

We speak of making the same "statement" in each of many languages.

In general we think of the "sense" of a speech-unit, such as a statement, question, command, or prayer, as something which can be expressed and communicated in other languages. When the languages and cultures of speaker and hearer are too far apart to allow literal or "intensionally isomorphic" translation, some kind of faithful translation is commonly still possible. Unsurprisingly, none of the spread of terms for the word "interpreter" in different languages precisely corresponds with the distinction between strict and non-strict translation.[36]

Let me review the quite disparate kinds of difficulty which arise.

The first is seen at the level of vocabulary when one language makes different or more numerous discriminations in a certain field than another. It is relatively rare for content-introducing terms in different languages to have the same meanings, establishing the same range of contrasts; and the resultant variations between languages inspire the structuralism described in section 4. At the extreme, Argentinian gauchos allegedly distinguish two hundred different colorations of cowhide,[37] and it is normal for different peoples to make different distinctions between colors, kinds of animal and plant, occupation, and so forth.

In general, if we want to reproduce argument or information, we will seek a translation duplicating the semantic complexity and structure of the original. The aims of such an accurate information-preserving translation differ from those of a literary translation. To a creative writer with a sense of the feeling associated with the names concerned (in the cowhide case, liable to be compound and full of associations for the gauchos concerned), the obstacles to a stylistically faithful translation are different from those of the scientist.

Faithful translation requires that we preserve the understanding of the original author; for instance, with New Testament texts, refusing to render "a man with a demon" as "an epileptic", or with classical or medieval texts, preserving expressions of the presumption that certain strengths or weaknesses tend to be inherited ("run in the blood").

Cultural settings change. To translate John the Baptist's injunction to soldiers by "Do not add to your wages by extortion and accepting bribes" might be better than to translate it by "Be content with your wages", which now suggests avoiding wage disputes. The translator here attempts to substitute for what scholarly presentations reserve to appended notes. And he will use the modern expression "go before" rather than using the obsolete "prevent". As George Steiner makes plain, such "interpretation" may be necessary even with

36. George Steiner, *After Babel* (Oxford: Oxford University Press, 1975), 251–52; cf. 253–69.

37. I take this example from Steiner, *After Babel*, 87, a work on which I have drawn deeply.

quite recent texts.[38] Even today social differences and differences in the region or country from which the speaker comes may generate the need for some interpretation.

Then there is the problem that for a faithful translation to show empathy (*Einfuhlung*),[39] it commonly needs to exclude literalism, as Steiner shows, presenting a wide scatter of examples. He instances Samuel Beckett's translations of his own works, which, for instance, substitute a sequence of ejaculations and swear-words different in literal meaning when translating between French and English in order to preserve the spirit of what is said in a situation in which each swear word has different nuances, associations, and stress in the different languages with different intonations.[40]

Problems posed by context and special nuances of meaning are exacerbated when languages and cultures are remote from each other, especially with the different sensitivities and expectations associated with friendship and family connections. Accuracy is vital at very many key points, some particularly apparent to political and business interpreters, but literalism may sometimes be fatal because of some quirk of one of the languages concerned, or of different customs or some special feature of the context.[41] In commenting on translation between languages very far remote from each other, as Indo-European languages and Chinese, Steiner sees it as a key criterion of good translation that the original should be recoverable from the translation, not indeed in the same words, but with the same empathy.[42] For there to be real empathy between text and translation, there needs to be a sharing or imaginative penetration of a wide span of the culture and discourse of the community from whose life the text proceeds. At this point we begin to meet deeper obstacles to translation and interpretation, rendering anything resembling literal translation quite impossible and making "radical translation" necessary.

Faithful translation requires the translator to preserve the perspective of his original. Merely configurational differences in syntax do not prevent this in

38. In *After Babel*, 1–17, Steiner takes instances from Jane Austen's *Sense and Sensibility*, Rossetti's sonnets, and Noel Coward's *Private Lives*.

39. Steiner, *After Babel*, 26; cf. 382–93, 407–13. In 361–81, 393–407, Steiner discusses the systematic difficulties of translating between languages which are relatively close to each other. In 407–13 he gives instructive examples of translations by others of their own works.

40. Steiner, *Extraterritorial* (London: Faber and Faber, 1972), 12–21. Steiner gives interesting instances of special devices used in the translation of poetry, such as Michael Longley's using the names of fjords and headlands in Galway to render Homer's description of the night fires of the Greeks waiting to resume their attack on Troy the next day, and Robert Fitzgerald's deftness in translating Homer's *Odyssey*; Steiner, *Language and Silence* (New York: Atheneum, 1976, 216–18; first published London: Faber and Faber, 1967).

41. These points were particularly well exhibited in a series of interviews with great interpreters in international negotiations on the BBC World Service in 1999–2000; cf. BBC Radio 4, 11:30 p.m., December 1, 2001; see also *Minds, Brains, and Science* (1984). Steiner, *After Babel*, 119, is also instructive.

42. Steiner, *After Babel*, 353–61.

prose translation. Yet even the deeper differences of perspective arising with changes in functional structure cannot always be preserved. Some languages allow for a different range of functional structures or have different voice, mood, aspect, and tense systems, making fully faithful translation impossible. For, as this chapter has shown, semantics embraces much more than information content, and differences in perspective constitute differences in sense.

Where possible a faithful translation will also emulate the stylistic economy in words, elegance of statement, or character of literary style shown in the original. One recalcitrant problem is presented by the fact that the literary genres familiar to one culture and time are often different from those familiar in other cultures and times. Jacob Neusner comments on the difficulties of translating the Mishnah in his preface to the Yale edition (1988), but these are dwarfed with those confronting the interpreter of the first eleven chapters of Genesis, and decisions have to be made as to which stage in the process of editing should be reflected in a "canonical" translation. Such problems are endemic in texts in which some central thread and purpose is combined with reverence for traditional material and extended stretches of discourse have been shaped by literary forms such as chiasmus.[43] Different difficulties arise when more is left to be understood from context of utterance, as happens with Confucius's *Analects*, where the original context on which correct interpretation depends is often uncertain: in earlier times an appreciation of the context of utterance would have been presumed. In more recent nonfictional texts, meaning is less dependent on intonation and context, and faithful prose translation therefore is easier.

(ii) Cultural difficulties and "radical translation"

Some of the difficulties of translation discussed by Saint Jerome in translating the Christian scriptures into Vulgar Latin are relevant here. Here he enunciated the principle that in translation one should aim to express the sense according to the sense (*sensum exprimere de sensu*), except that, where the mystery is concerned, one should translate word by word (*verbum e verbo*).[44] This translation "word from word" meant translation in which intensional isomorphism at a semantic (not grammatical) level is insisted upon to the maximum degree achievable, even if this compels the translator to impose a new vocabulary, or a new interpretation of old vocabulary, upon the other

43. Cf. http://chiasmus.com, drawing upon Mardy Grothe, *Never Let a Fool Kiss You or a Kiss Fool You: Chiasmus and a World of Quotations That Say What They Mean and Mean What They Say* (New York: Viking, 1999). The extremes to which such interpretation can be taken, with some Babylonian precedents, appear in Isaac M. Kikawada and Arthur Quinn, *Before Abraham Was* (Nashville, Tenn.: Abingdon Press, 1985).

44. The Septuagint translators of the Hebrew Scriptures followed a quite different policy of seeking intensional isomorphism to the limits of propriety, producing barbaric Greek, and the Greek of the Four Gospels often displays Semitic word order.

language. Many Church dogmas have involved imposing a Hebrew meaning upon preexisting terms in other languages, often by reshaping the interpretation of surrounding vocabulary (e.g., *ousia, physis, persona, mysterion, sacramentum*), such vocabulary being passed on sometimes by transliteration, sometimes by translation. Again, because *substantia* was already established as the accepted translation of *ousia*, it could not be used to translate *hypostasis*, and this latter therefore had to be rendered in some other way (*persona* or, in Aquinas, *subsistentia*). Thus Jerome's policy conspired with other tendencies to bring about a kind of Hebraicization of Hellenistic philosophy in developing the terms in which Christian dogma came to be stated—a Hebraicization in which concepts foreign to Greek thought entered into Western thinking, enlarged concepts of creation and contingency, of personhood as something which is fully realized only relationally, and of the value of the person. In this way "translation" can be used as a method of injecting concepts from one cultural tradition, in this case the Hebrew, into another, the Greco-Roman.

Other issues arise when it is alleged that languages or cultures differ in how the future is thought of—for instance, whether as not yet existing and therefore radically contingent and open, or as established and fixed just as much as the past and present, but entering our perception or knowledge differently.[45] In the latter case a whole culture might seem to be so imbued with fatalism as to reshape whole languages.

Yet there are arguments which suggest that such a language will involve inconsistency or incoherence at a deep level: for instance, it can be argued that the practice of deliberation between alternative actions involves regarding what one does, with some of what arises in consequence of it, as at an earlier stage absolutely contingent; and this can only be if the future relative to the juncture at which decision is made is viewed as not yet established or fixed, either action being possible because at that juncture the future is not yet actual or does not yet exist. The work of discovering whether or not languages imbued with materialism or fatalism are consistent depends upon the kind of nonmechanical use of the understanding of which I speak in chapters IV and V. The same capacity for informal word-use which enables us to achieve some imaginative penetration of different perspectives also enables us to engage in an examination of their consistency.

However, the way differences of evaluative perspective may permeate a language presents much more recalcitrant problems than any differences in respect of time, possibility, or ontology—indeed, in general, supposed differences in the ontologies reflected in different languages mostly reflect mistaken philosophical analyses.

45. Steiner, *After Babel*, 88–91, 130–61.

That languages at different points of cultural history often reveal different systems of evaluation becomes obvious when we consider such terms as "prudent", "happy", and "rights", with their different connotations at different stages of Western cultural history and in different cultures. We have lived with some instances of these problems extraordinarily long before taking notice of them, as with the concepts relating to different forms of love and friendship.[46]

Davidson's reclassifying of evaluative questions from semantics to pragmatics only changes the name of the area of the disagreements between him and Alasdair MacIntyre, and does not remove the question as to how far mutual understanding and discussion between human beings with different cultures and cultural histories can be achieved. Here MacIntyre seems right that the path to be followed is to attempt an imaginative penetration and appropriation of the viewpoint expressed in the language reflecting the variant culture. This process involves a willingness to engage in an empathetic appreciation of the other culture and linguistic features, a process compared by MacIntyre to the processes involved in imaginatively shifting between paradigms in scientific explanation. This is only possible where there is the willingness and patience required. Sometimes, with some peoples, there are what Everett describes as "cultural constraints" restricting this. He instances the Pirahã, who "restrict communication to the immediate experience of the interlocutors", producing shared constraints inhibiting participation in such empathetic learning—this is in people who, if they choose, can readily remove themselves from the tribe and participate in a more Western culture.[47] The process by which MacIntyre supposes that conflicts affecting evaluative perspective are to be resolved is by finding the narrative of the development of the views concerned which is most inclusive, making its rivals maximally intelligible and revealing its own advantages over these rivals by its capacity to do this in a more enlightening way than is done by the narratives proposed from the rival standpoints.[48]

46. The concept of two people being dear to each other (neither implying nor excluding sexual attraction) was expressed by the Greek *agapein* and the Latin *carus*, roots of the nouns *agape* and *caritas*. This idea survives in the French *cher* and Spanish *cariño*. In the Hellenistic period, the general word both for kissing and for the various relationships expressed by kissing, as husband to wife, father to son, friend to friend, companions for pleasure (as in play, eating, and drinking), and colleagues, was *philein* (without any of the sexual connotations of *eros* and *erao*). In modern Europe there is much variation in how far affection and sexuality are understood to be necessarily connected and as to what kinds of thing those described as friends can expect from each other.

47. Daniel L. Everett, "Cultural Constraints on Grammar and Cognition in Pirahã: Another Look at the Design Features of Human Language", *Current Anthropology* 46 (2005): 621n1, 622n2; on the correctness of Boas and Sapir's conception of the inseparability of culture and language and mistakenness of Whorf's determinism, see Everett, "Cultural Constraints," 625–26, 632 and 633–34n19.

48. Alasdair MacIntyre, *Three Rival Versions of Moral Enquiry* (Notre Dame, Ind.: University of Notre Dame Press, 1990), 113–22, 145–48, 170–95, 213–15; cf. MacIntyre, *Whose Justice? Whose Rationality?* (London: Duckworth, 1988), 370–88; and some instructive comment in Tracey Rowland, *Culture*

Section 4. Two Opposite Conceptions of Linguistic Science: The Radical Novelty of Chomsky's Approach

(a) *The conception that the objects of linguistic science are sentences and their features as met in speech*

These early chapters confirm the view presented in the introduction whereby the primary concern of linguistics is with speech and what is said at a level of language-use, and only secondarily with what is involved in language-possession. This is in accord with the thinking of Jespersen, Hockett, and many others.

In the words of Charles Hockett:

> There is only one "object of study": specific acts of speech as historic events, in their behavioral settings, observable in part overtly and in different part introspectively; it includes certain earlier acts of speech observable only through written records .... The linguist seeks theories, which are generalizations from observations, and are about speech; ... [and is] led to posit that the observable regularities of actual speech are a matter of habits, resident in the users of the language, ... [and] calls these habits "language".... It makes no sense to pretend that there can be a separate and distinct theory of language [i.e., a theory of *langue* separate from a theory of *parole*].[49]

Or, as Otto Jespersen tells us in the opening words of his *Philosophy of Grammar*, under the chapter title "Living Grammar", "The essence of language [*Sprache* in his German, for him the subject-matter of linguistics], is human activity—activity on the part of one individual to make himself understood by another, and activity on the part of that other to understand what was in the mind of the first". He goes on to say that this must "never be lost sight of if we want to understand the nature ... of that part of language which is dealt with in grammar", and bids the grammarian to be "ever on his guard" against "pitfalls" arising from considering the language in the "mummified" form of

---

and Thomist Tradition (London: Routledge, 2003), 118–25; Davidson, "On the Very Idea of a Conceptual Scheme", essay 13 in Davidson, *Inquiries into Truth and Interpretation*, xi, 183–98; and Davidson, "Expressing Evaluations", essay 2 in Davidson, *Problems of Rationality* (Oxford: Oxford University Press, 2004), 19–37; essay first published in 1984.

49. Hockett, *The State of the Art* (The Hague: Mouton, 1968), 65–66. He refers to the "error" of "the notion that since we 'have' both speech and language, these are in some way independent 'objects of study'" and thought that "even Saussure was trapped" by this notion, though "he was creatively discovering the distinctions that must be made and is hardly to be blamed if he did not discover them all". Hockett also reckoned that Bloomfield had made the same mistake in his theoretical discussion, "though hardly ever in his handling of actual language data". And the position of functionalists like Foley and Van Valin, as I remarked earlier, is essentially the same, concerned with habits of speech, but *types* rather than *tokens*, and so are still really concerned with speech, despite disowning concern with performance—when one speaks of *types* of utterance or sentence, one is still speaking of the utterances or sentences of the types concerned, not of these "types" as abstract entities.

the written word before "someone imparts life to it by transposing it mentally into the corresponding spoken word".[50] Thus he anticipates Hockett in regarding the properties of grammaticality and meaningfulness as belonging primarily at the level of performance, at the level of exercise, not mere capacity.[51]

In Hockett's consideration of sentences, the grammarian is considering *types of utterance solely insofar as they can be distinguished by reference to grammar, morphology, and the lexicon alone*. But he is still considering utterances as they occur in use (i.e., pieces of performance), even though only from a certain point of view. He is not, for instance, making a science of the constructs of schoolmasters.

Conformity to what Hockett calls "the observable regularities of actual speech", which "are a matter of habits, resident in the users of the language", reflects knowledge of the language, the level-(ii) capacity alluded to in chapter I. Yet it is still "the observable regularities of actual speech" seen in utterances and their make-up with which lexicography, grammar, and morphology need to have concern. As a result, even though it is the job of these sciences to make explicit the consequences of our knowledge of language, they can still only be stated in terms of generalizations about actual examples of performance, the level (iii) alluded to in chapter I.

The "habits" referred to by Jespersen and Hockett are clearly what Aristotle would have called states or *hexeis* and what Ryle would have counted as "many-track dispositions".[52] As explained in chapter I and in further detail in chapter VIII, section 1 (b), this Aristotelian notion of "habit" or skill is not at all what Chomsky would count as "habit" in what he regards as any "sense of 'habit' known to psychology"[53] or "any reasonably well-defined sense of this notion".[54] For, in his earlier writings, encountering the ideas of Jespersen and Hockett as expressed by the Dutch Reichling and Uhlenbeck following in the Prague tradition, the chief reasons Chomsky gives for his contempt for their view that linguistics is concerned with "habits" in speech based on being "familiar" with such sentences stem from his philosophical presumptions about scientific methodology, which would exclude such Aristotelian notions as unscientific. In the background, he thinks that performance is often defective, an objection which is trivial because the corpus of sentences he recognizes as nondefective is so vast, the skills in producing new utterances at need so well established, and the canons for judging between defective and nondefective

50. Jespersen, *The Philosophy of Grammar*, 17–18.

51. Hockett, *State of the Art*, 73.

52. Commonly ones whose antecedents involve so-called defeasible concepts; cf. chap. I, n. 27, and discussed in chap. VIII, sec. 1 (b).

53. Chomsky, *Topics in the Theory of Generative Grammar* (The Hague: Mouton, 1966), 12, first published in *Current Trends in Linguistics*, ed. Thomas Sebeok, vol. 3 (The Hague: Mouton, 1963–72).

54. Chomsky, *Topics*, 13–14, n. 16.

sentences so little disputed in any relevant way. He also writes as if being "familiar" with sentences meant having a knowledge confined to already experienced utterances,[55] even though his antagonist clearly understood what was said to imply knowledge extending to possible and future utterances, not only already experienced ones. In any case he requires his own theories to stand the test of conforming with the empirical evidence provided by our intuitive personal and communal judgments of grammaticality, judgments which extend not only to realistic examples, but also to quite nonsensical ones.

However, his cavillings disguise the real character of the disagreement concerned: one arising from the divide between Chomsky's conception of a grammar, as a language-user–friendly way of describing the functioning of the brain and the traditional descriptive conception of grammar exemplified in Jespersen and Hockett, a conception dovetailing with the idea that the function of language is to communicate, albeit not by mere signaling, but by the expression of what is being communicated.

(b) *Saussure and Bloomfield, with their structuralism, embody the same traditional perspective*

In 1933, despite regarding his behaviorism as having mechanism as its philosophical basis, Bloomfield nonetheless held a descriptivist view of linguistics, judging that "Since that time [1914] there has been much upheaval in psychology; we have learned, at any rate, what one of our masters suspected 30 years ago, namely, that we can pursue the study of language without reference to any one psychological doctrine, and that to do so safeguards our results and makes them more significant to workers in related fields".[56] This emphasis on finding forms of description of linguistic phenomena independent of any particular psychological theory makes it unsurprising that Hockett, like Bloomfield, a descriptivist, should speak in terms so close to those of Jespersen, the descriptivist approach having a long ancestry among linguists with no antipathy to the mental.

Bloomfield's behaviorism involved considering the parts and structure of sentences or utterances in abstraction from their meaning or that of their parts, and from their context of use, except that he distinguished homonyms like "log", meaning logarithm, and "log", meaning log of wood. It did not involve any idea of sentences as a new kind of object generated within an abstract linguistic system. In this sense its concern was with sentences as utterances according to types distinguished only by reference to grammar, morphology, and

55. Chomsky, *Topics*, 4.

56. Bloomfield, *Introduction to the Study of Language*, as cited by Bloomfield, *Language*, vii.

the lexicon. Again, Saussure tells us that linguistic signs are not abstractions but real objects,[57]—that is, the very same objects as occur in our speech or *parole,* albeit considered only under certain aspects. His differentiation between the study of a *langue* as the system of the signs belonging to a language and the study of *parole* was quite compatible with Jespersen's perspective that the "la langue n'existe que dans et par la parole des individus".[58] However, Bloomfield misunderstood Saussure's *parole* to involve the private intentions and motivations of the speaker rather than being limited to what is public.

Saussure's so-called structuralism had the more limited aim of picking out certain essential aspects of the linguistic signs we use in utterances, not to get into a different world from utterances, whether these signs be at the level of the word or other lexical factor or of the phoneme and the syllables phonemes make up. In respect of language the essence of his structuralism lay in the recognition that the units out of which speech is composed at each particular level can be identified only in terms of their relationships with other units at that level in the same language: we cannot first determine what the units are and then later inquire what structural relationships hold between them.

Saussure speaks of the syntagmatic structures into which linguistic signs, or what I have called lexical factors, fit, and of the associative relations between different signs or lexical factors which might fit into the same slot in a syntagmatic structure. Thus, to take the example of words, the word "red" has, first, its "syntagmatic" relations, the linguistic contexts into which it can fit, as "red" fits into such structures as "is red", "became red", "looked red", "a red bowl", "the red bowl", or "ten red bowls". Second, the word has what Saussure called its "associative" relations, which have come to be called its "paradigmatic" relations, which are the relations it has which work with words that could occur in the same context in the same contrasting meaning or in somewhat more generic or specific meanings (e.g., brown, blue, crimson). The importance of contrastive paradigmatic relations is made obvious if one considers the different contrasts of sex established by the word "cat" in English and *chat* in French, and how the family of words "mat", "rug", and "carpet" in English establishes different contrasts from the family of words *tapis, paillasson,* and *carpette* in French.[59]

57. De Saussure, *Cours de linguistique générale,* 144; cf. Roy Harris, *Saussure,* 74 and 73–74 as a whole; and for evidence of his interest in *parole,* 28–30, 229–31, 241–45; and for his obscurities in regard to the *objet* of linguistic science, 45–55.

58. Jespersen, *Linguistica: Selected Papers in English, French and German* (London: Allen and Unwin, 1933), 111, in a reprint of a 1916 review. *Linguistica,* 225, shows him as holding the same opinion in 1933. Yet Jespersen understood Saussure as making *langue* abstract and distant from the utterances of individuals, as if he had meant "the common norm of language for one people (or one ethnic group) that stands outside the individuals and above them: both exist only together and are so intimately interwoven with each other that they cannot even be considered as two sides of the same thing", misunderstanding Saussure, but indicating his own conception of the inseparability of *langue* and *parole.*

59. Cf. Lyons, "Structuralism and Linguistics", chap. 1 in *Structuralism: An Introduction,* The Wolfson College lectures, ed. David Robey (Oxford: Oxford University Press, 1972).

Parallel pairs of relation arise with the sounds which have a function in a particular language, since, just as one color contrast may be noted by a difference of words in one language but not in another, so one sound contrast may be significant in one language (e.g., a "b" sound and a "v" sound), but not in another. Hence, in respect of any language, we have to speak not simply of sounds, but of phonemes, which are sound-units distinguished by the functional contrasts they mark in the language concerned and the settings in which they can occur.

Likewise, different languages make different distinctions of gender and tense, in the latter case some languages separating contrasts in respect of time, of aspect (whether an action or activity is at a moment or continuous, incomplete or complete, repeated, beginning, or ceasing), and of mood (its possibility, inevitability, uncertainty, or desirability) which other languages do not separate. Since the contrasts which are taken account of and the ways units can be combined differ in different languages, it follows that the structures of languages will be relevantly different in these respects.

Such is the core of structuralism as commonly conceived. Thus what Saussure regarded as belonging to *langue* had to do with our habits of speech, not with the constructs of some ideal "language-system", having to do with linguistic signs as "real objects, not abstractions".

When such structuralism distinguishes the meaning of color-words in terms of the system of discriminations which they encapsulate, it is concerned with these words in their root-meaning, not with their metaphorical or symbolic significance as used, for instance, in reference to emotions or virtues. However, even to describe such a root-meaning for a particular word we need to have at least implicitly considered it in connection with some paradigm examples of its use in that particular sense in actual utterances, because it is only when we use the word in speech that its paradigmatic relations and the associated contrasts become clear. And, since structuralist accounts have to leave indeterminate what speech leaves indeterminate, the inherent vagueness of certain types of concept (e.g., how many grains of sand constitute a heap) is not a problem for this structuralism. Thus such structuralism at every point depends on the consideration of speech.

Many problems arise. For instance, in one view the word "dog" in its primary meaning is a sex-indifferent term for the species in contrastive relations with a cat, a horse, a bear, a cow, and so forth, and only secondly a word set in contrast with the word "bitch" as duck with drake and man with woman. Yet language-users typically use words in contexts in which the audience is anticipated to include speakers of many different ages and dialect,[60] so that in actual

60. Cf. Malthesius, "On the Potentiality".

speech speakers have to use words in ways which often awkwardly bestraddle non-artificial distinctions between senses which it is the task of the linguist as well as the logician to distinguish. However, in such cases the artificiality of presuming speakers to have spoken determinately in one sense rather than another is not an objection to the linguist and logician's enterprise—an enterprise of special value when it exposes cases when the ambivalence of what a speaker says is the vehicle of cheating or self-deception. For many purposes, audiences have to be idealized, treated as sharing knowledge, presumptions, and idiom to a greater extent than they commonly do.

Linguistic signs need not be continuous. Some signs are put together in the way instanced phonologically when we put "g … se" together with different vowel sounds to form the syllables "goose" and "geese", and instanced morphologically when "geese" is understood as the plural of "goose", one of the signs signifying the plural in English consisting not in the addition of a morpheme "-s" as a suffix, but in a change in quality of the vowel. Halliday realized that phrases need not consist in continuous sequences of words, but can also consist in discontinuous ones, and so preferred the expression "word-group" to "phrase". Saussure attributed to *langue* every type of *syntagme* constructed according to a regular form, and this allowed of discontinuous *syntagmes*. Moreover, for him the notion of "regular form" was quite compatible with such forms being put together in highly varied ways, so long as "un rapport de solidarite reciproque" was maintained.[61] This phenomenon of "bracketing", familiar in morphology, is also important in grammar, although awkward for Chomskyan grammars, as we observe in chapters XIII and XV.

Thus, where words and their inflections are concerned, Saussure's syntagmatic and paradigmatic relations are key to distinguishing the words according to their distribution and their possible grammatical modes of combination, the heart of distributionalism, so that key elements of Saussure's structuralism are essential to Zellig Harris, and Chomsky's approach to grammar.

As concerned with speech and language as public interpersonal phenomena, linguists following in the tradition which includes Von Humboldt, Jespersen, and Hockett, to instance only a few, are neither directly nor indirectly occupied with neuroscience.

Yet in the normal cases of speaking and of understanding what other people say (normal in that we do not resort to reference books such as dictionaries and grammars in order to speak and understand speech), we speak and understand without any conscious reflection upon the words that we will use and the grammar of our utterance. It is therefore natural to ask what part

61. Hence, Chomsky was wrong to suppose that Saussure's notions of *syntagme* left no room for his notions of transformation or movement; see Roy Harris, *Saussure*, 90, 165–66.

may be played by the brain in facilitating our capacity to speak and understand with the rapidity and skill with which we customarily do without such reflection.

It was a concern with neuroscience, or the structures of mind or brain, which he conceived as making such speech possible, rather than directly with linguistics, which shaped the thinking of Chomsky from the 1950s onwards. This led him to a quite novel way of conceiving linguistics as a part of the psychology of the individual make-up, rather than as among the sciences of what is public and communal.[62] To his approach and that of Jackendoff I now turn.

(c) *The roots of Chomsky's rival conception and the form it takes in Jackendoff*

(i) For Chomsky, grammar concerns competence whose principles operate independently of consciousness

However, Chomsky adopted a quite new way of thinking about what he was studying.

Beginning from Bloomfield's starting point, that he was not concerned with *parole* as such, Chomsky introduced the idea that grammar, rather than being concerned with utterances, had a quite distinctively different aim—namely, to "represent" what he called "competence", a term he explained by reference to earlier psychologists in their regarding it as important to find ways of describing what an organism knows which are not in terms of what the organism does.[63] He conceived this competence in regard to a particular language to be that in our brains which explains our ability to use the language concerned according to its rules; and he presumed competence in any particular language to be rooted in human species–specific structures in the brain (a shared human linguistic faculty) which gave rise to a universal grammar of which particular grammars would be realizations. Here he moved away from Bloomfield's descriptivism, which had led him to set aside the idea of a universal grammar as non-empirical.

Chomsky's concept of competence is quite different from Saussure's idea

62. Dik states the contrast between a linguistic and a psycholinguistic interpretation of the notion of "generative grammar" (whether or not this includes transformations) with particular clarity, in Dik, "Some Critical Remarks on the Treatment of Morphological Structure in Transformational Generative Grammar", *Lingua* 18 (1967): 357–61.

63. The notion of competence appears in George A. Miller and Chomsky, "Finitary Models of Language Users", chap. 13 in *Handbook of Mathematical Psychology*, vol. 2 (New York: Wiley, 1963). For the roots of the concept, Chomsky refers (in "Finitary Models," 326) to K. S. Lashley, *Brain Mechanisms and Intelligence* (Chicago: University of Chicago Press, 1929), 553; Lashley, "The Problem of Serial Order in Behaviour", in *Cerebral Mechanisms in Behaviour*, ed. L. A. Jeffress (New York: Wiley, 1951), 112–36; and E. C. Tolman, *Purposive Behaviour in Animals and Men* (New York: Appleton-Century-Croft, 1932), 364. Chomsky directs one to the *Handbook* in his *Topics*, 9n3; see also Roy Harris, *Saussure*, 160–62.

of knowledge of *langue*. For Saussure *langue* consisted not in sentences, but in a system of signs, be they words, constructions, patterns of intonation, or whatever, things with some content and/or structural role and well within consciousness, the signs being the concrete realities which we meet with in speech. By contrast, for Chomsky, like Bloomfield, the sentence was the only workable starting point for the linguist, and in his view "a person is not generally aware of the rules that govern sentence-interpretation in the language that he knows"; "nor, in fact, is there any reason to suppose that the rules can be brought to consciousness".[64] For Chomsky both sentences and words are parts of the language-system, considered as a "representation" of the human language faculty as adapted to some particular language, so that he counted neither as in any way concrete.

It is vital to realize that this conception of a grammar constitutes a revolution in tradition. Indeed, Chomsky indulged in a self-deceptive rereading of tradition, even conceiving his conception of competence as "an attempt to develop further the Humboldtian notion of 'form of language'", the *innere Sprachform* spoken of by Reichling[65]—not observing that when Von Humboldt spoke of *Sprache*, he emphasized the nonmechanical character of its production or generation.[66]

This is disguised by the way systems of generative grammar still have to survive the test of descriptive adequacy so that the sentence-constructs they generate are simulacra of types of possible utterance or inscription of kinds which we would deem grammatically correct if they arose in speech or writing. Thus Chomsky criticizes Uhlenbeck for assuming that in transformational grammar "the shooting of the hunters" would be derived either from the phrase "shoot the hunters" or "the hunters shoot", and that the ambiguity is to be explained in terms of "extra-linguistic data" (by which Chomsky must mean data concerning the context of use of the two phrases in particular sentences in speech), and Uhlenbeck is reproved for imagining that sentences are ever derived from kernel sentences rather than from, as Chomsky's novel account requires, "the abstract structures that underlie kernel sentences", Chomsky supposing that "one underlying system of grammatical relations" (derivations) underlies "the hunters shoot" and another underlies "shoot the hunters".[67] Chomsky's contempt for Reichling and Uhlenbeck's criticisms is

64. Chomsky, *Topics*, 10.

65. Chomsky, *Topics*, 9n4. For Von Humboldt, any group of languages which shared the modes of thought, reflected in the structures of their speech, were described as having the same *innere Sprachform*. This conception preoccupied Wundt, Anton Marty, and Franz Nikolaus Finck, and underlied the Sapir-Whorf hypothesis whereby different languages mold thought in different ways, an idea with which Reichling was at home.

66. See introduction, n. 5, this volume.

67. Chomsky, *Topics*, 26n3, in the context of 25–30 in discussion of E. M. Uhlenbeck, "An Appraisal of Transformational Theory", *Lingua* 12 (1963): 1–18.

quite unreasonable.[68] This contempt springs from an expectation that readers of that time would share his view that "abstract structures" underlie kernel structures and share his conception of linguistic competence.

However, it remains that, in Chomsky's conception, the sentence-constructs generated by the grammatical system are not thought of as actual or possible utterances or inscriptions arising within the use of the language (i.e., actual or possible parts of *parole*), but as mathematically generated artificial assemblies of elementary units which are themselves merely creatures of the theory. Such elementary units as morphemes and words are considered by Chomsky as merely "constructs which receive their definition from the theoretical work in which they are embedded and whose relation to the fact of speech is at most an indirect one" whose discussion or definition outside of the complete grammar or theory in which they find their place is impossible.[69] Chomsky is not making the quasi-Kantian point that the concepts used to describe various phenomena of experience are constructs, in that that they embody some theory, and taking such grammatical concepts as morpheme and word to apply to the morphemes and words we distinguish in our experience and behavior, but instead taking the objects of grammar to be merely constructs within an abstract model. Thus, for the purposes of our conscious engagement in speech or conscious thought, there is a gulf between Chomsky's grammar and our actual use of language in speech; for him grammar is only very indirectly concerned with the practical intelligibility or acceptability of our utterances. Instead it is presented as a device for describing the unconscious structures of the working of our mind or brain in virtue of which, without needing to know why, we speak as we do—a mathematical device for describing the software of the brain served up to us in a linguistic-theory–friendly fashion.

68. Jackendoff illustrates the confusion mentioned when he speaks of having learned from Chomsky that the first question in studying language was to ask what a person has to know in order to use language so as "to create and understand an unlimited number of utterances"; Jackendoff, "Conceptual Semantics and Cognitive Semantics", *Cognitive Linguistics* 7 (1996): 94. Yet in Chomsky's conception a generative grammar does not generate utterances, but only sentences as parts of a syntactical system. Jackendoff compounded the confusion when he proposed his idea of "Conceptual Structure" as something broader than "syntactic structure", embracing pragmatics along with semantics and syntax, all integral to the *knowledge representation* internal to the mind; it is this which constitutes the "Conceptual Structure" of the I-language in Jackendoff, *Consciousness and the Computational Mind* (Cambridge, Mass.: MIT Press, 1987), 121–22, thus severing pragmatics from externally situated speech, the E-language. Yet as chap. I, sec. 4 (c) (iii), chap. II, sec. 2 (c) (i), and chap. V, sec. 5 (a) (i) of this volume indicate, the infinity of possible utterances still arises from the indefinite multiplicity of discourse-significances that words can gain in context, not from the capacity for iteration.

69. Dik stated the point particularly clearly in "Some Critical Remarks", 356: "the units figuring in a generative grammar are regarded as constructs which receive their definition from the theoretical framework in which they are embedded, and whose relation to the facts of speech is at most an indirect one", referring to Chomsky, "A Transformational Approach to Syntax", in *Proceedings of the Third Texas Conference on Problems of Linguistic Analysis in English*, ed. Archibald A. Hill (Austin: University of Texas Press, 1958), 126, and to Chomsky, "Explanatory Models in Linguistics", 537.

From the first, Chomsky took it that in each of the successive systems of grammar which he proposed he was aiming to penetrate to the structure of the underlying competence or mental capacity, in virtue of which language-users are able first to learn and then to use their respective languages. He regarded this competence as a faculty of mind, making his inquiries mentalistic in character. Although he was strongly of the view that these mental structures would prove to be structures in the neurological functioning of the brain, strictly speaking, he did not regard this as a matter of linguistics. However, for the purposes of what shaped his way of thinking, when he made this concession, it was little more than window-dressing. This appears in the way that he expressed this concession, saying that he does not exclude that the "mind-body problem" would be solved by "invoking principles that seemed incomprehensible or even abhorrent to the scientific imagination", and speaking as if to suppose that there is anything about the functioning of the mind which cannot be explained in terms of the functioning of the brain would be an example of something thus "abhorrent to the scientific imagination".[70] However, he never really anticipated any need to invoke such principles, and at heart never doubted that our knowledge of our own language was something "represented somehow in our minds, ultimately in our brains, in structures that we can hope to characterize abstractly, and in principle quite concretely in terms of physical mechanisms". Hence he commonly omitted such caveats and spoke unreservedly of what is referred to by such terms as mind, mental representation, and mental computation as "keeping to the level of the abstract characterization of the properties of certain physical mechanisms".[71] Thus this supposed rooting of our knowledge of language in brain functioning remained the ground of his belief in the existence of a "universal grammar" and of his conviction that the structures underlying language would have a formalization involving the computability of procedures of grammatical generation or synthesis.

It is therefore unsurprising to find Chomsky and his objectors at cross-purposes from the start. What Chomsky regarded as essentially mentalistic inquiries into the nonconscious workings of the mind appeared to his critics as essentially mechanistic in character, mechanistic both in reflecting the working out of physically determined ways of functioning and in the mathematical sense. For Chomsky the *innere Sprachform* of a language is to be expected to lie in a neurologically embodied competence, not in speech. By contrast, for those who think the center of the linguist's attention should be on speech, the *innere Sprachform* of speech lies in the structure of the system of linguistic signs

70. Chomsky, *Rules and Representations* (Oxford: Blackwell, 1980), 6.

71. Chomsky, *Rules and Representations*, 5. At the same time, he describes these mechanisms as "as yet entirely unknown".

which give content to the utterances we make, the signs which by their semantic and syntactic interrelations enable our speech to reflect our thought.[72]

(ii) Jackendoff's notion of a "Conceptual Structure" shaping both the pragmatic and the grammatical

As to why the ideal of autonomy persists without the support of Chomsky's original arguments from within linguistics, one can only say that it mainly stems from the persistence of the physicalist presumptions we see so plainly in both Chomsky (see introduction, section 5 [b] in this volume) and Jackendoff—independently of the virtues or vices of Chomsky's methodology.

In his *Architecture of the Language Faculty* and his later *Foundations of Language*, Ray Jackendoff sets forth arguments, even from within the confines of the presumption of autonomy, for nonetheless rejecting Chomsky's ideas of deep structure, movement, and lexical insertion, and attacks what he calls Chomsky's "syntacto-centrism". He retains the conception that grammatical studies are concerned only with an inner I-language and hence with mental states that can only have causal, not logical connections with any events or states outside the brain, but wishes to replace Chomsky's "Logical Form" and substitute a "Conceptual Structure" open to enrichment to allow for neurological function (as relevant to language) being shaped by the pragmatics of discourse and its extralinguistic context.

Here what Jackendoff has done is to internalize pragmatics as well as semantics and syntax, in effect enlarging the scope of "Universal Grammar", and so he still shares Chomsky's belief that it is structures in the neurological functioning of the brain which dictate the shape of language—dictating this Conceptual Structure. So for him the grammar of a language still constitutes a "theory of competence in the language" which he explains as a "functional characterization of the 'data structures' stored and assembled in the f-mind in the course of the use of that language", the "f-mind" being explained as the functional organization and activity of the brain.[73] In other words, one is to describe a certain set of features in the organization and activity of the brain according to the limits they set on what sentences the user of that language may regard as grammatical, doing this by setting down rules by means of which such sentences can be generated. The form of these rules and the way they generate such sentences, it is hoped, reflect the actual structures operative in the relevant brain activity.[74]

72. Cf. n. 65.

73. I have adapted Jackendoff's explanation in *Foundations*, 34, in such a way as to make it independent of the view that there is a Universal Grammar underlying all particular human languages; see Jackendoff, *Foundations*, 19–23, 26–27.

74. Jackendoff, *Foundations*, 55–56, considers the view that theoretical linguists might be looking for a

Jackendoff's views, presented in his theory of representational modularity and elsewhere, as will appear in chapter VII, constitute a complex form of Putnam's mind-brain functionalism whereby the mental states correspond to computer-representable programs in the brain, functionally characterized in terms of relations between input and output.[75]

In sum, in considering the divide between those who consider questions of grammatical and semantic or conceptual structure to be questions about speech and those who consider them to be questions about the underlying nonconscious workings of the mind or brain, one need only notice the common-sense assumptions behind some of the distinctions which the first approach allows us to make. For instance, the different mistakes we classify as grammatical are different in character. Some are not such as to prevent communication or the reconstruction of the sense of what is being said to us, and some are very superficial, excluded only by prescriptive convention (e.g., split infinitives in English). On the other hand, some grammatical mistakes create irredeemable nonsense. To attribute grammatical and pragmatic constraints to restrictions set by brain functioning obscures the different character of the different mistakes.

formal description of languages without caring what they have to do with the mind (General Phrase Structure Grammar had this inspiration), but takes the reasonable view that it would be strange if all languages conformed to such a formal description (a Universal Grammar) by mere coincidence rather than because it had some explanation in terms of how our minds function.

75. The essence of Hilary Putnam's functionalism appears in *Mind, Language and Reality*, vol. 2 of *Philosophical Papers* (Cambridge: Cambridge University Press, 1975), as expressed in xiii–xiv and 291–93. It is set forth in greater length in his papers reprinted in *Mind, Language and Reality*: "Minds and Machines" of 1960 (362–85), "Dreaming and Depth Grammar" of 1962 (304–24), "The Nature of Mental States" of 1967 (429–40), and "Philosophy and our Mental Life" of 1973 (291–303). In his view, pain, fear, jealousy, and all other mental states and processes were to be defined solely in terms of functional causal relations between sensory input, motor behavior, and other mental states which they involve, assuming that these functional causal relations (at least in principle) are such as allow the computation of effects from causes. In effect, the functional states thus defined were theoretical entities which may inexplicably correspond to the states to which we testify when we speak, but such conscious states and the persons supposedly having them have no role in the doctrine of mind concerned. In the last of the relevant papers, "Philosophy and our Mental Life", 298–99, Putnam felt bound to qualify his functionalism because of the problems of self-reflection, but appeared to treat this as a technical blip in 302–3.

However, in the papers reprinted in *Mind, Language and Reality*, "Is Semantics Possible?" from 1970 (139–52), "Explanation and Reference" from 1973 (196–214), and "The Meaning of 'Meaning'" from 1975 (215–71), Putnam came to view what one meant by a term as a matter not of a purely internal state of mind, but dependent on our environment and our interaction with it. This and other problems led him to a wholesale rejection of the idea of mental states as functional states representing physical states in Putnam, *Representation and Reality* (Cambridge, Mass.: MIT Press, 1988). This led him to the rounded view expressed in Putnam, *The Threefold Cord: Mind, Body, and World* (New York: Columbia University Press, 1999), in which mental representations have no role either in thinking and the explanation of speech or of perception—in this way coming to the same view of the human being as a psychophysical unity, and the same rejection of representationalism as I express in chapter VIII.

Jackendoff's functionalism in his *Consciousness and the Computational Mind*, 16–17, and *Foundations*, 21–27, shows no such doubts. In *Patterns in the Mind*, 50, he is more reserved, describing his views as functionalist because they suggest experiments by means of which we might test hypotheses about the organization of information and knowledge in the brain—e.g., showing us what types of difference affect the grammaticality of sentences.

(d) *The compositionalism and meaning-atomism of Chomsky and Jackendoff*

Although for Bloomfield and Chomsky alike the linguist's only workable empirical starting point is sentences as met with in utterances (i.e., in actual *parole*), both end up with views of a compositionalist kind, whereby sentences are composed of lexical atoms at the rank of the word or grammatical morpheme—in Bloomfield's case, syntactic atoms, and in Chomsky's case, atoms which are both syntactic and semantic.

The lexical atoms concerned are held to be defined distributionally in terms of their syntagmatic and paradigmatic relations so that their identity emerges as different sentences are compared with each other, and this way of conceiving them makes them secondary relative to the whole set of sentences accepted as grammatical with which a language presents the linguist. However, their status is primary relative to the individual sentences composed of them.

Bloomfield's compositionalism simply reflects his underlying physicalism (what he calls "mechanism"). However, Chomsky extended this compositionalism to his understanding of sentence-meaning, holding a double compositionalism, sentences being composed of their constituents and sentence-meanings composed of their constituent meanings (in the sense of being the resultants of the lexical meanings of their basic lexical factors in their order). The weaknesses in this kind of compositionalism in linguistics, indicated in the introduction, appear in part three, especially in chapters XIV and XV. This linguistic compositionalism must be sharply distinguished from the compositionalism which has revived among analytical philosophers—since it is often forgotten that the word "sentence" has a very different meaning in the two contexts and the doctrine is supported by different arguments.[76]

All the time, the propensity of Chomsky and Jackendoff to look for a compositionalist account is associated with their drive to root language in the structures of biological functioning and their expectation that these will have a physicalist explanation. It is ironic that just as it was physicalism which pushed Bloomfield into behaviorism, so it was physicalism which pushed Chomsky towards a biolinguistic mechanism.

The determination to preserve compositionalism in respect of meaning is particularly conspicuous in Jackendoff. Chapters 7 and 8 of his *Semantics and Cognition* (1983) are devoted to the explanation of his idea of Preference

76. The arguments of so-called ordinary language philosophy from 1930 onwards might have been expected to have killed off any attempt to reinstate lexical atomism in the philosophical treatment of natural language. However, lexical atomism, or an equivalent compositionalism, has crept back into the philosophy of language, unintendedly through Dummett, and consciously in Davidson and Crispin Wright, through their giving a kind of primacy to sentences, yet without allowing words to do their real work, strangely reinstating the principle "one lexical entry, one set of consequences for sentence meanings".

Rule Systems, designed to circumvent the more obvious objections to the compositionalism relied on in his *Consciousness and the Computational Mind* (1987). This compositionalism is presented in the most disarmingly artless manner in *Foundations of Language* (2002), where he tells us, "Nearly everyone thinks that learning anything consists in constructing it from previously known parts, using previously known means of combination"—explaining that although sometimes combination is by concatenation, in other cases the parts are distinctive features which cannot exist except in combination, just as in physics quarks cannot exist in isolation but are, he says, as it were "features of elementary particles".[77]

Here Jackendoff's very explicitness reveals the inescapable flaw in any kind of compositionalism of this kind.[78] For uttered words are not just abstract features, but concrete parts of an utterance or sentence. Therefore Jackendoff has not given an account of how it is that the sentence (or a clause as something which if uttered on its own would be a sentence) has a unity (any more then he has given an account of the special unity of an elementary particle lacking to the quarks which he describes as its "features"). He thereby fails to meet the argument of Aristotle that any part or principle which gives unity to a set of elements cannot itself be just another element, for if it were, then there would have to be a further unifying part or principle joining it to the elements it was meant to combine. What gives unity to a set of elements must be of a different character to the elements it unifies. In chapter IX we will find how Frege introduced the idea of parts of a sentence which are "unsaturated" or "incomplete" to explain how the other parts are to hang together as a unity. Chapters XIV and XV explain how it is precisely the verbal part or framework of a sentence which gives it a "saying" character and unifies it. This is why it is a grave mistake for grammatical theory to assimilate the theory of sentence structure to that of phrase structure.

(e) *The communicational functionalism proposed in this book*

My argument has suggested a quite different approach to that of Chomsky, not that of a "neurological functionalism" in which an autonomous grammar reflects neurological function, but "communicational functionalism", viewing language as directed towards linguistic communication between speakers and hearers, writers and readers[79]—linguistic communication implying the *expression* of a sense, content, or thought.

77. Jackendoff, *Foundations*, 334, 335; cf. 180–81.

78. He tries to back it up by his preference rule systems, whose inadequacy is shown in chap. V.

79. Jackendoff deliberately distances his treatment of grammar from this kind of functionalism in *Foundations*, 21n1, 37.

The idea of "functionalism" came into psychology in the 1890s with William James's considerations of how consciousness enables people to adapt to their environments. It acquired a bad name in the 1950s through association with B. F. Skinner's form of behaviorism, which Chomsky demonstrated to be useless in explaining language learning—useless because of the poverty of its descriptions of so-called stimuli and responses.

However, the kind of functionalism of which I am speaking has its roots in the idea of the essential connection of language with communication, a connection very clear in Saussure, but first made fully explicit in terms of the notion of "function" by the Prague school of linguists founded by Mathesius.[80] It found new life, crystallized in different forms by Halliday, by Simon Dik and the Dutch-centered school of Functional Grammar inspired by him, and by Robert van Valin in his Role and Reference Grammar.[81] For such linguists the aim of using words in speech is to achieve linguistic communication in a way which involves a semantically structured and integrated form, allowing linguistic "stimuli" and "responses" to be described in terms of their intelligible linguistic content, a kind of description not open to Skinner, who excluded notions of understanding or meaning from linguistics and psychology.

When Chomsky first suggested that grammar had an essentially neurological basis, basing his doctrine of the autonomy of grammar on this supposition, he judged that psychological theory was too underdeveloped for it to be profitable to suggest experiments to test this hypothesis, and after he developed his minimalist program, he conceded that the empirical evidence was against him, now conceiving his theory as a bold hypothesis waiting for confirmation, even against the odds. One might propose instead that the problem lay with his linguistic theory, and that when one had developed a different

80. Vachek, *Linguistic School of Prague*, and Vachek, *Prague School Reader*; cf. Paul Garvin, "Czechoslovakia", in *Current Trends in Linguistics*, ed. Thomas Sebeok, 1:499–522; together with Dik's review of *A Prague School Reader in Linguistics*, ed. Vachek, in *Lingua* 18 (1967): 80–89; and E. M. Uhlenbeck, review of *L'école de Prague d'aujourd'hui: Travaux linguistiques de Prague* 1, ed. Josef Vachek, F. Daneš, K. Horálek, V. Skalička, and P. Trost, in *Lingua* 17 (1967): 358–65.

Many of the same ideas appear, cast in a somewhat different form, in the work of M. A. K. Halliday, drawing on ideas from Stratificational Grammar and from Prague to form his own theory of Systemic Functional Grammar within which an "ideational" underlay is influenced in its formulation by constraints arising at the interpersonal and textual (surface expression) levels; cf. Halliday, *An Introduction to Functional Grammar*, 2nd ed. (1985; London: Arnold, 1994). Halliday sometimes gives the impression of failing to distinguish illocution and perlocution when he speaks of forces and motivated choices operating externally upon language material so as to achieve communication. By contrast Dik's is vision more clearly of a piece with the thought of Frege, Ryle, and Austin, in more obvious accord with emphasis upon the unity of the speech-act, so that all the "forces" or "constraints" spoken of are exercised within, not externally upon, the speech-act.

The philosopher William Haas also embraced the functionalist approach, from "On Defining Linguistic Units", *Transactions of the Philological Society* (1954): 54–84, onwards.

81. See two articles by Van Valin: "A Brief Overview of Role and Reference Grammar", *Korean Journal of Linguistics* 6 (1998): 235–72 (cf. http://wings.buffalo.edu/linguistics/research/rrg/RRGpaper.pdf); and, for a general review of functionalist approaches, "Functional Linguistics".

linguistic theory and one which was more on the right lines, one would come to be in a better position to put the right questions to psychology.[82]

In the present case it appears that some form of linguistic functionalism fits better with the ways of thinking suggested by the work of Gibson and of Meredith and Stein in psychology. In the case of perception, as we shall see in chapter VII, Meredith and Stein show that parts of the brain can be highly malleable in their ways of functioning, so as to allow these ways of functioning to be shaped to the requirements of the mammal's environment and its behavior. As chapters VI and VII show, this fits with the appropriateness of Gibson's way of conceiving perception in environment-geared terms, the environment of perception being that of our intentional behavior. Correspondingly, we should consider language and linguistic understanding in relation to an environment of human speakers and hearers within the natural world to which the rest of their behavior is adapted, involving a new kind of functional adaptation between human beings, and envisage the structures of brain functioning as being shaped accordingly.

Therefore, although the brain as a whole is not unrestrictedly malleable in its ways of functioning (i.e., in Jackendoff's terms, it is "not a big general-purpose device") but has parts apt to function in different ways playing different roles within its overall functioning,[83] nonetheless even the differentiation of the roles of different parts is achieved dynamically as the organism interacts with its environment. Accordingly, rather than conceiving the innate structures of the brain as the principal determinants of linguistic structure, we can conceive the relevant structures of neurological functioning as principally determined or "tuned" by the pragmatic and semantic opportunities and constraints arising in communicating with others.

Thus the relationship between the brain and the way we function linguistically can be conceived in a way quite different from that suggested by Chomsky and Jackendoff.

Such communicational or properly linguistic functionalism converges with psychology in a different way from Jackendoff's neurological functionalism.

We can think of development in the structures of the brain at each stage of biological evolution not as the cause of new modes of behavior, new levels of coordination between sense and sense, exploratory behavior and discovery, but as making them possible. When a violin or piano has come into existence, the violin or piano does not cause new kinds of music and resonance,

82. Indeed, Jackendoff himself questions whether Chomsky's thought has been twisted by the underlying intrusion of mistaken psychological or metaphysical presumptions; Jackendoff, *Foundations*, 33–34, and Jackendoff, *Architecture*, 7–11, 19–20, 217–18n3.

83. Jackendoff, *Patterns in the Mind*, 142.

but makes these possible. Likewise, developments in the brain made it possible for biological organisms not just to communicate, but to communicate linguistically, to resonate at the level expressed by language—that is, *Sprache*, speech. Therefore, although some trends in language development over time will be affected by ease in the perceptual recognition of patterns, one should expect the more absolute constraints upon grammatical structure to come from the top downwards, from the pragmatics and semantics of linguistic communication, rather than from the bottom upwards, from the structures of brain functioning.

(f) *Grammar and grammatical theory describe certain aspects of idealized performance*

The idea that our capacity or propensity to speak grammatically has to be ultimately explained in terms of neurology does nothing to explain what the words "grammatical" and "ungrammatical" mean as used by the nonlinguist. Yet the nonlinguist is a person to whom linguists look for judgments as to whether particular sentences are grammatical or ungrammatical, the linguist's only data.

But what does the nonlinguist understand by the words "grammatical" and "ungrammatical" before he meets any linguistic theory?

The common language-user conceives words, constructions, and so forth to be things we use in utterances or sayings, spoken or written. These utterances may be assessed and criticized in many ways, as true or false, proven or unproven, sensible or absurd, as well as grammatical or ungrammatical. These commonplace assumptions are well set forth by Ryle among the philosophers.[84] Grammaticality and ungrammaticality belong primarily to utterances, not to some kind of abstract entity.

We should begin by rejecting the theory that grammatical rules are simply

84. Gilbert Ryle gives a convenient statement of these presumptions in "Use, Usage and Meaning".

When P. F. Strawson, in "On Referring", *Mind* 59 (1950): 320–44, contrasts individual utterances of particular grammatical sentences, what he calls "uses" of such sentences, and such sentences (which he treats as grammatical entities), he is indeed making a distinction—in effect, between utterance-token, utterance-type distinguished according to semantic criteria (including whatever—grammatical, lexical and contextual, or pragmatic—affects sense as philosophers from Frege onwards have treated sense), and utterance-type distinguished only according to formal or grammatical criteria—a distinction vital to semantic theory.

This is the backcloth of Ryle, "Ordinary Language" (1953), 307–12; Ryle, "The Theory of Meaning" (1957), 363–65; and Ryle, "Use, Usage and Meaning" (1961), 412–14, as reprinted in his *Collected Essays*, vol. 2 of *Collected Papers* (London: Hutchinson, 1971), nos. 23, 27, and 31 respectively. In conversation he constantly spoke of Strawson's way of speaking of "uses" of sentences as the only mistake in the latter's "On Referring". Strawson's view turns on distinguishing two ways of distinguishing utterances into "types", one relevant to grammatical assessment and the other semantic. He has no interest in introducing grammatically distinguished types of utterance as entities within a "language-system".

or even largely the results of the exercises of a social authority which excludes perfectly intelligible discourse by arbitrary law. Inspection of examples reveals many cases of successful ungrammatical discourse which get by in virtue of the fact that every normal utterance by its context, combination of words, and intonation contains a large overplus of indications as to its interpretation (which serve to overcome the effects of slovenly speech or bad conditions of hearing). Experimenting with deviations from the "grammatical" reveals that in their main structure they get by because they respect deeper-level pragmatic and semantic constraints. This suggests that they have a quite proper grammar which the grammatical "authorities" do not take account of.

The common language-user can distinguish between different types of departure from custom such as are liable to frustrate the achievement of successful communication, some regarded as matters of infirmity or psychological impairment, some of dialect, some of vocabulary, and some of grammar. This makes it evident that the distinction between grammatical and other kinds of departure from custom is not an invention of pedants or linguistic law makers.

Rather the distinction between the grammatical and the ungrammatical is analogous to a matter of customary law, not the invention of linguistic law makers, and arises *de facto* in the course of maintaining the conditions of successful communication. Too many departures from customary modes of speech prevent successful communication, undermining the conditions of mutual intelligibility. The question as to what distinguishes grammatical departures from other kinds of departure from customary modes of speech will be my concern in part three. I give my most accurate account of ungrammaticality in chapter XIV in terms of blockages to our capacity to understand how more subordinate elements in a sentence are linked to less subordinate ones, and these ultimately linked to the verbal framework of the sentence, normally by being linked to the main finite verb, the main finite verb or verbal framework being what gives the sentence its "saying" character as a piece of speech. Obscurities in regard to how elements are connected will block understanding.

Summary

In sum, I have explained the concepts of "sense" and "sentence" in this chapter in a way which relates them directly to the speech-act and their context in discourse—the context of the speaker-hearer relation. A speech-act is something complete in itself as a human act of saying something. Moreover, it is only against this background of understanding sense and sentence as belonging to speech that we can understand words as sense-expressors, not just sense-identifiers, as explained in chapter I.

In both linguistics and philosophy much recent semantic theory has narrowed the scope of semantics, wrongly conceiving a sentence as a unit with a settled meaning determined by the *langue*-meanings of its grammatical constituents and their mode of combination, a settled meaning determined at the level of *langue*. As a result, context of utterance has been wrongly conceived to make no difference to the meaning of the sentence-factors within it, except insofar as it serves to disambiguate grammatically ambiguous sentences such as "Flying planes can be dangerous" or to identify which lexical item (e.g., "log" as meaning log of wood, meaning a record such as a ship's log, or meaning logarithm) is being deployed, all other distinctions being regarded as at the pragmatic, not semantic, level. Thus, Sperber and Wilson offer a rich account of how further differentiations of meaning arise from the context of utterance at the level of speech or performance—but since they conceive semantics too narrowly, they regard these differentiations as belonging only to pragmatics.

This recent approach is radically misconceived. Sentence constituents from the level of word-like elements upwards have a differential effect upon sense or discourse-significance in ways pertinent to truth and falsity, to tone and perspective, and to other things relevant to translation, not just in disambiguating grammatical structure or identifying lexical items, but in other ways recognized from context within discourse and context of utterance. Likewise, we offer different paraphrases and translations for the same subordinate expression as it arises in different contexts. All this belongs to semantics.

The role of words and word-like elements as sense-expressors absolutely depends on their double standing, a standing at the levels both of speech and of *langue*. By exact contrast with the case of words, sentences are entities only at the level of *parole* or speech, nothing at the sentence level being given or pre-constructed within language or *langue*. The sentences we use do not preexist like items shelved in a store, even a store of possible sentences, between which we wait to select. Even the delivery of aphorisms, famous quotes, songs, and the like is an example of speech; quoting an author, perhaps applying the sentence or sentences in a way he or she would not have done, is not the parroting of a sentence-construct or model.[85]

At the fundamental level the theory of sentences has to explain sentence-form in terms of sentence-function, not vice versa. Indeed, the grammatical markings of sentence-form can be overridden by stress and intonation or situation in discourse, as in the case of rhetorical questions. True, sentences occur within larger units of discourse, but the relation of sentences to larger units of discourse is not analogous to the relation of words or component phrases and clauses to sentences.

85. Cf. chap. I, sec. 4 (c) (i) of this volume.

From the point of view of linguistics as well as of the psychology of human functioning, sentences belong primarily to *parole*, and it is their function, determined by *parole*, which shapes the way in which words are to be understood in their place in the flow of *parole*. It is this which thereby gives the primary determination to the forms which words and morphemes assume and according to which they combine to determine the various kinds of sentence. Neurological mechanisms enabling us to use appropriate vocabulary and inflection have to be exercised in the act of speech, not separately or prior to it. It is how our linguistic ability is realized in particular acts of speech which has to be the primary concern of linguists, psychologists, and logicians—not the antecedent skill, knowledge of meaning, or competence that these require. This is the perspective validated in parts two and three of this book.

Appendix: Grice's theory of meaning and meaning-nominalism

The approach to meaning proposed by Grice,[86] along with that of the meaning-nominalists, removes the means of distinguishing mere signaling from speech-acts proper.

(i) Grice's account applies to signaling in general, rather than linguistic communication

The hallmark of Grice's approach is to propose a definition of meaning (something he calls "non-natural meaning") applicable both to linguistically expressed signals and other signals. Grice's definition as applied to statements amounts to this: U [the utterer], in his issuing *x* to some audience A, means ("non-naturally") that P *if and only if* U intends his issuing of *x* to produce in A the belief that P by means of A's recognizing that U intended by issuing *x* to produce the belief in A that P. (Grice calls it "non-natural meaning" not to imply that it depends on conventions, but only to distinguish it from the meaning alluded to if we say "A red sky 'means' [gives expectation of] good weather".)

Such a definition fits all signals, and not only linguistic utterances. In this way Grice's approach takes what it is to be a meaningful signal as the fundamental thing to be explained. But, as we have seen already in chapter I and earlier in chapter III, much more is required to count as a linguistic utterance.

What is called "meaning-nominalism" is a reaction against Searle's view

86. This approach was presented in Grice's key papers "Meaning", *Philosophical Review* 66 (1957); "Utterer's Meaning, Sentence-Meaning and Word-Meaning", *Foundations of Language* 4 (1968); "Utterer's Meaning and Intentions", *Philosophical Review* 78 (1969); and "Meaning Revisited", from *Mutual Knowledge*, ed. N. V. Smith (London: Academic Press, 1982)— all four of which papers are reprinted in H. P. Grice, *Studies in the Way of Words* (Cambridge, Mass.: Harvard University Press, 1989).

that language essentially depends on convention. The "meaning-nominalists" repeat that "*x* means that *p*" should be explained in terms of "U means that *p* by *x*", rather than vice versa, and in addition regard conventional meaning as to be explained in terms of occasion-meaning, "the significance which accrues to a signal within its individual context", rather than thinking of convention as intrinsic to the notion of meaning.[87] If this requires the appreciation by the receiver that the signal is a signal (i.e., that it is intended by the issuer as such), then the doctrine fits Grice's formula exactly. The intention is to insist on "utterer's occasion-meaning" as "conceptually, the basic kind of meaning" and, having understood this kind of meaning "in general", be at liberty then to "move on to the special case where we can, in a derivative way associate meanings with the sentences uttered, or with the words that make up these sentences".[88] For reasons which will appear in chapter IX, "utterer's occasion-meaning" cannot be the conceptually basic kind of meaning and is not properly linguistic at all. Sentences are not formed by taking such occasion-meanings as building blocks. In any case, meaning-nominalism is open to the same objections as Grice's account.

Crabs and fishes are both sea-animals and have structures geared to submarine life, but they are not thereby of one genus. In like manner nonlinguistic signals and language-dependent expressions of sense both have structures geared to inducing beliefs in others or to bringing about actions on the part of others, but this does not mean that their having such effects defines their nature.

Linguistic communication cannot be distinguished from signaling simply in terms of complexity, even though expanding knowledge of neurological organization might seem to open the way to explanations in these terms. We will establish in chapter VIII that thoughts have no quasi-physical or, as it were, "chemical" structure whereby they could be isomorphic with anything material. Rather they have only an intentional directedness towards their expressions on the one hand and states, events, and acts reported, inquired into, or desired on the other. Complexity in neurological structures cannot as such explain what makes a signal or communication linguistic in character.

Even if we were told that 604302, 604302131, and 131304234604 by convention signaled "John kicked", "John kicked Judy", and "Judy was kicked by John" respectively, and brought arrangements of numbers into correspon-

87. I take this explanation from Jonathan Bennett, "The Meaning-Nominalist Strategy", *Foundations of Language* 10 (1973): 141. He understands this to cover even "one-off" signals. Bennett, *Linguistic Behaviour* (Cambridge: Cambridge University Press, 1976), 7–11, explains the general position further. Michael Beebe, "The Basis of Semantic Structure", *Dialogue* 15 (December 1979): 624–41, provides notable clarification (especially about one-off signals, 637–38).

88. J. R. Cameron, "Critical Study: *Linguistic Behaviour* by Jonathan Bennett", *Philosophical Quarterly* 27 (1977): 340.

dence with messages by a multiplicity of rules, still the production of these numbers to signal these messages would not show what made this system of numbers into a linguistic system. Sperber and Wilson in their book *Relevance* speak of a system of coding and decoding, but, however complex such a system may be, this complexity will not as such make it linguistic.

Against Grice, Searle objects that no account, in particular Grice's, can be satisfactory which does not involve "conventions" as essential to linguistic communication.[89] However, nonlinguistic systems can require conventions, and therefore dependence on convention is still not enough to differentiate linguistic communications from others. Conventional communication systems are more akin to language than are signals in general, but it does not follow that the involvement of convention as such is the key to the peculiar nature of linguistic communication.

Introducing conventions can allow the introduction of the utmost complexity, but it does not itself involve that a signal relying on a use of convention *expresses* a sense. That is, it does not as such involve that in the act of signaling there should be a thought-content or sense which is expressed in the signal. In the many conventional signaling systems, the signal does not express the message communicated.

(ii) The importance of the distinction between mere signaling and expressing a sense

Grice's avowed intention is to characterize statements rather than linguistic utterances in general; for him, what one does in making a statement is in effect to issue a signal, characterized solely in terms of the end aimed at, namely, the production of a belief of a certain kind in the hearer. There is nothing in this definition which requires the end to be achieved by linguistic means.

Grice's approach gives no explanation of the importance of the distinction between what I do in the very act of saying something and what I do by means of saying something, between illocution and perlocution, a defect made particularly clear by Searle.[90] This distinction, fundamental to Austin's thought, was, we may note, what gave motivation to Hare in introducing the idea of "prescriptives" as sayings intended to give a reason to another person for action in an attempt to avoid explaining moral discourse as aimed at mere-

89. Searle sets up the same distinction between two supposed sets of conventions as Dummett, one set of semantic conventions allowing the identification of propositional content and another set determining whether a proposition is asserted. Searle says that the two objections he makes to Grice hang together, Grice neglecting convention (conventions bearing upon propositional content) and neglecting illocution, because it is the sentence that provides the conventional means of achieving the intention to produce a certain illocutionary effect in the hearer; Searle, *Speech Acts: An Essay in the Philosophy of Language* (Cambridge: Cambridge University Press, 1969), 48. But for Searle the two sets of convention are not necessarily separate.

90. This is Searle's second main objection to Grice; Searle, *Speech Acts*, 43–44, 46–48.

ly causing an alteration in the other person's action. It is the same distinction which is neglected when Sperber and Wilson separate the pragmatic aspect of speech from "language" conceived of as a coding/decoding of signals (signals figure in their account as "ostensive stimuli"), even though the pragmatic must include the illocutionary. What we need is an account which makes the illocutionary and the locutionary or expressive aspects of language inseparable. If we state, "The Americans were responsible for the Vietnam War", our hearers must recognize our illocutionary act (that we have made a statement) to have understood us, independently of whether or not we achieve our perlocutionary aim of persuading them of what we say.

This distinction between perlocution and illocution depends upon there being two intermediary things. The speech-act and the linguistic understanding involved require (a) the *expression* of a sense, and (b) a sense to be expressed, in regard to which the hearer is in a position of entertaining or freedom to consider, for instance, whether or not what is said is to be believed or whether or not to obey it. And this is the reason why statement-making cannot be sufficiently characterized in terms of "the intention to induce a belief by means of recognition of the intention to induce such belief".

These intermediary things, the expression and its sense, constitute twin objects ("cognates") of linguistic understanding, intermediary objects absent in the case of nonlinguistic communications. It is in this way that the notion of the expressing of a sense is key to understanding what a sentence itself is.

When I make a statement, ask a question, or give a command, I do not merely issue a signal aimed at the inducing of a belief, the acquiring of knowledge, or the bringing about of an action, but I make a linguistic utterance ("say something") which is the expression of a meaning or sense, and it is only because this stage has been reached that I have accomplished a complete human act. As it were, if my duty was to inform, to question, or to give the command I had authority to give, I have done it, leaving it up to the hearer (one of such relevant language-capacity as to give me a right to expect him to have understood what I said, to have, in the full sense, heard it) to acquiesce or not: the truth has been stated, the question asked, or the command given, whether or not acquiescence has been secured. It is only because there is some act completed in the expressing of a sense, a sense being something with a direction (to use Wittgenstein's metaphor), that a distinction between illocution and perlocution can be made. Since it is only in regard to acts which are in this sense the expressings of a sense that this distinction arises,[91] this distinction does not have a parallel in the case of human actions in general.

91. As explained in chap. I, sec. 3 (b) of this volume, some gestures have synsentential significance, and the gesture's illocutionary significance as an illocutionary act is distinct from its perlocutionary effects—e.g.,

The reason why Grice has omitted to take into account these "intermediary things", the "expression" of a sense and the sense expressed, is that he has failed to recognize the peculiar role of "expressing" something in differentiating a linguistic utterance proper from a mere signal. Grice's explanation of the meaning of "utterances" as the states of mind, such as belief, they are intended to induce by means of the "utterance" being recognized as "uttered" with the intention of inducing the state of mind concerned, takes no account of anything especially linguistic. Indeed, this is the very purpose of his strategy: to dethrone the linguistic from its solitary preeminence and instead represent what is basic to it as consisting only in what it has in common with other communicative acts (i.e., in mere acts of signaling).

It is not that one's purpose is to make a signal (e.g., to signal that so and so), and that one utilizes a linguistic means of doing this, but that one's very purpose is to say something (e.g., in making a statement to communicate something as being true; in asking a question to state one's concerns; in commanding, requesting, or wishing to say what state of affairs or action one would seek or wish to be the case or be done)—that the utterance or expression of sense which one utters is a signal of what it communicates is just a side effect of its expressing the sense which it does. One communicates a sense simply in the act of expressing a sense, "sense" as we are using the term being something which includes "force", so that, for instance, in the case of a statement, understanding its sense includes understanding this to be geared to bringing about a state of belief (not causally, but because the hearer accepts one's testimony, presuming it well-based), or, in the case of a command or request, bringing about an action (not causally, but in virtue of the acceptance of the authority of the commander or of the desire of the requester).

Accordingly the root of the communicativeness in linguistic signals is their expressive character, rather than in the structural behavioral features which linguistic communication transactions share with nonlinguistic communication transactions. And it is their expressive character in which, as we shall see, sense only arises in the setting of force, that *ipso facto* gives sentential linguistic expressions their character as communications.

To repeat: signaling *can* be just a means to an end (e.g., of communicating a message or bringing about some new state of knowledge or belief) without the signal being itself a message, but only a means, a tool used to a certain particular effect.

By contrast, *live linguistic uttering* is not just a means to communicating a message, but *is itself* the communicating of a message. The utterance *expresses*

---

a gesture may signify assent or contempt, but be made with a view to having the effect of making a person angry.

the message, rather than merely identifying it; and it is able to do this only because it has a pragmatically shaped semantic structure, a structure typically seen in its being expressed in a combination of words.

(iii) The dependence of Gricean accounts on a Platonic ontology

The final objection one should make to Gricean approaches is that they depend upon an uncritical return to Platonism. We are regaled not only with propositions, senses, or beliefs, but also with "features", "concepts", or "sets". And any ordinary means of explaining talk of such abstract entities by reference to language and in terms of their quasi-linguistic status has been set aside by treating them as prior to language in the fall of one's account of meaning.

That is, Grice's account sets aside the kind of philosophical commonplace which I explain in chapter XII. Once the unity of "Socrates is wise" has been dissolved, it will be inevitable (if naming is possible independently of contexts of saying) that we will have on our hands two named or identified entities, Socrates and the feature "wisdom", in some unexplained relation to each other.[92]

Grice and his followers themselves recognize that they need to introduce abstract entities (such as senses and beliefs) and are quite game to do this,[93] despite the fact that they have removed the possibility of the most plausible explanation of the nature of such entities. For one's normal way of explaining the nature of such entities, if one gave any explanation at all, would be of the type I offer in chapter XII in my refutation of Platonism.

Further, Gricean accounts heavily involve reference to intensions and extensions (sets)[94] and meaning-features[95] (i.e., reference to things whose nature one would normally try to explain in terms of the predicative structures and functors within speech). For, unless we can treat these "entities" as quasi-linguistic, that is, in an Aristotelian kind of way, we have no means of identifying their natures ("what they are"). But the enterprise of Grice and his following precisely excludes any such Aristotelian approach as involving an alien or premature reference to propositional and predicative structures in explaining the nature of these entities. In this way, in attempting to reduce the intellectual to the behavioral, we find ourselves led into a full-blown Platonism—a Platonism of objects of the intellect alone.

92. We observe the effects of this dissolution of the proposition at the beginning of chap. IX of this volume in noting the failure of the "meaning-nominalist" Michael Beebe to give any account of the "blending" involved in the articulatedness of a sentence.

93. See Grice, "Concluding Note" at the end of "Utterer's Meaning, Sentence Meaning, and Word Meaning" in *Studies*.

94. This is the problem raised by all Grice's papers on meaning; see n. 86.

95. Beebe, "Basis of Semantic Structure"; also Jonathan Bennett, "Meaning-Nominalist Strategy".

We have to avoid what Haas calls "content-entities",[96] conceived of as objects onto which linguistic entities have mappings or are in relations of correspondence, such as those of "meaning" or "expressing". For, as we will see in chapter IX, it is quite wrong to think of the correlations between linguistic objects and the intentions, meanings, beliefs, sets, properties, or features to which they refer as if they were set up prior to the assertive use of language, prior to language "in function", and prior even to the articulatedness of language of which Frege takes some account.[97]

Gareth Evans argues that "it is simply not a possibility for the thought that *a* is *F* to be unstructured—that is, not to be the exercise of distinct abilities".[98] Evans goes on to say that "knowledge of what it is for it [*a* is F] to be true must be the result of two pieces of knowledge".[99] But it is overly simple to speak as if the abilities to identify an object *a* and to pick out a feature *F* are entirely independent.

For it is key to the understanding of the nature of such abilities that each is of a type such that ability of one type cannot be exercised except in one act with an ability of the other type, and that it is some unitary capacity which is involved equally in speaking and in thinking when both abilities are exercised together. That is, the pieces of knowledge concerned should not be conceived of as two separable bits of knowledge of identity, of a thing denoted by *a* and of a feature denoted by F, but as one piece of knowledge—namely, of which thing *a* is, a piece of knowledge which includes knowing of what kind *a* is; and within this includes knowing what it is for things of that kind to be subjects of predicates of the kind "... is F". Knowing what *a* is depends on knowledge of what it is for *a* to have properties of the kind of which F is an example, and knowing what kind of feature F is depends on knowing what it is for an appropriate kind of subject to be F.

The existence of *a* and the existence of the feature F will normally each be contingent, but knowledge of *a* will not be knowledge in the same way or sense as knowledge of F, since *a* and F will not be objects in the same sense unless the word "object" is being used simply to be a subject of discourse. This speaking as if there were two "pieces of knowledge of identity" betrays the presence of an incipient Platonism, to which I explain my full objections in chapter XII.

96. Haas, "Function and Structure in Linguistic Descriptions", in *Functionalism in Linguistics*, ed. René Dirven and V. Fried (Amsterdam: John Benjamins, 1987), 333–55. The war against "content-entities" is one in which the functionalist Haas is in agreement with the nonfunctionalist Bloomfield.

97. Frege, Dummett, and Searle are right in holding that no expression has either sense or *Bedeutung* ("reference") apart from its context in the proposition. But, as I establish in chap. X, they are quite wrong in thinking that there are two quite distinct sets of conventions, one by which the "sense" of propositions, and "reference" along with it, is "established", and another involved in actually asserting, giving orders, and so forth—as if sense is definable separately from and antecedently to the putting of language to "functional" use.

98. Gareth Evans, *Varieties of Reference* (Oxford: Oxford University Press, 1982), 102; cf. 104.

99. Evans, *Varieties of Reference*, 106.

IV

The Indivisibility of the Human Capacity for Language

The Interdependence of the Various Semantic Structures within Language

The many meanings of the word "holism"

The conception of a whole with an essential, not merely accidental, unity was first made explicit by Aristotle in his treatment of the relationships of the whole animal to its matter or material parts[1] and of the spoken syllable to its phonetic elements.[2] By an essential unity or whole is meant a whole in which the nature and behavior of the parts cannot be understood except by reference to the nature and behavior of the whole, and at the same time the nature and behavior of the whole cannot be understood except with reference to the nature and behavior of the parts.

Within language we have already met the holism involved in the relationship of sentence-constituents to the sentences or utterances they make up, as well as that of the spoken syllable. The structuralist way of thinking mentioned in section 4 (b) of chapter III, instanced in differentiating the contrasts established by "mat", "rug", and "carpet" in English and those established by *tapis, paillasson,* and *carpette* in French, constitutes a third example of holism in the coordination of our speech, as seen not in sentences taken individually, but in the range of contrasts exhibited in families of sentences.

This last holism, as a matter of the organic unity of each particular lan-

1. See David Braine, *Human Person*, esp. chap. 8, sec. 2.

2. Aristotle, *Metaphysics*, bk. Zeta, 17, 1041b11–34; Aristotle made no phonemic/phonetic distinction.

guage as it exists at one time, considered synchronically, has become a datum in the thinking of linguists, one especially associated with Saussure. However, we need to move beyond this structuralism in phonetics and lexical relations to something much more far-reaching.[3] We have to see languages as incorporating the key semantic structures embodied in the general logic outlined in the introduction, section 4 (b) (i). At the semantic level any language involves a unitary integrated logical structure in such a way that one could not have any parts of this structure at all if one did not have all of them, and which provides a framework for the rest of our thought and speech.

Thus we could not, I contend, have the parts of the structure of language which relate to the senses, imagination, memory, the emotions, and the will without having the parts which relate to the distinctions between past, present, and future, causal action and causal explanation, knowledge and truth as they concern propositions, various kinds of possibility and necessity, and various kinds of evaluation—and one could not have any of these if one did not have all the others. Even the simplest of statements has sense at all only as an exercise of an underlying linguistic capacity which also allows us to express this whole ensemble of concepts. One cannot have the capacity for peripheral parts of language without having the capacity for this central core, and one could not have the capacity for parts of this core without having the capacity for the whole core. True, at particular stages of language development one might not yet have the vocabulary or linguistic means of making some of the core notions explicit. But if one has the capacity for language at all, this must include the capacity to acquire or develop the means of making all core notions explicit, and one's earlier utterances have senses pregnant with kinds of significance which can only be made explicit in terms of core notions.

This "framework holism" is quite different from what is called "semantic holism", the doctrine whereby the sense or discourse-significance of a word depends upon its context in the whole language (not just its local discourse context), a language being taken to include all the sentences of the language concerned, treated as completely given each in their full sense, a definite totality even though their utterance may be in some cases future or merely possible.[4] Yet any such conception of a language as a completed totality of potentially actual sentences and sentence-senses is quite misconceived and

3. See the introduction in this volume, Jackendoff's semantic studies, and the essays of Uriel Weinreich, Roman Jakobson, and Stephen Ullmann in *Universals of Language*, ed. J. Greenberg.

4. This is the "holism" which Dummett rightly attacks. His concern is that language should not be a closed system which could not be subject to critical questions. I share the concern, but approach it in a quite different way from Dummett, as I outline in sec. 2 of this chapter, objecting equally to Dummett's own position. In my view, the possibility of such critical questioning depends on language being conceived not as a definite set of sentences, but as a system whose openness arises from the multipotentiality of sense of words and lexical factors.

entirely alien to Saussure, as well as to the unitariness of semantic structure which I am about to explain.

This unitariness reaches to a much deeper level than that of the earlier structuralism of paradigmatic and syntagmatic relations at phonetic, lexical, and intonational levels, reaching beyond these to the structures centered on the most general terms and features to be found in the language and different interrelated types of sentence which they involve. It thereby reaches into areas of concern to philosophers and logicians who, in considering the logical and semantic paradoxes, treat sentences as objects of knowledge, evidence, and counter-evidence, truth and falsity, and raise questions about meaning and reference as well as about causality and value in the world to which they refer.

Thus human language holds together as semantically an integrated organic unity, exhibited in the "general logic" described in the introduction. The capacity for properly human language is not something which can come in parts, bit by bit, whether in evolution or child development, but which is present either all at once or not at all. This point is disguised by the fact that, at any particular stage in human development, many aspects of this capacity may not have been realized and the ways of articulating many key concepts not learned or developed; but this leaves the essential unity of the underlying capacity for human language uncompromised. It is the scope of this integrated semantic ensemble, together with the freedom from being restricted to operating according to mechanically applicable rule, which has the implications for human nature which appear in chapter VIII.

Section 1. The Unity and Integratedness of Linguistic Capacity: Structure and Self-Reflexivity

At many stages knowledge of language is liable to involve that knowing how to use one set of idioms is inseparable from or dependent on knowing how to use another set, or at least the capacity to learn or form such another set. I shall give some simple hierarchical examples—for instance, of the capacity to use color-words presupposing the capacity for subject/predicate statements and the possession of the concept of "seeing" and with it the capacity to learn how to use the word "see". We will find some cases of simple hierarchy in which the presupposition is one-way; other cases in which concepts come in groups so that the relation is symmetrical (e.g., different spatial concepts, or different temporal ones); and yet other cases, the most interesting, the most general capacities and concepts, interlocking with one another and presupposed in the exercise of all other, more determinate concepts. These general concepts underlie any language with the complexity and structure specific to human language as such, expressing the human kind of understanding.

Let me sketch some of the most fundamental elements in the structure I have in view.

If a bodily being (e.g., some foreigner or some electronic machine) issues the sounds "That is red", the question arises whether it has made an utterance with the meaning which an English speaker's utterance of the sentence "That is red", made in appropriate context, would have. Most obviously, this latter would have the character of a proposition about which one might ask whether it is true or false, accurate or overly simple, and so forth—rather than the character of a command or a question. To this we will return later.

The next most obvious observation arises from the subject/copula/adjective structure of this sentence in English. Three groups of aspects arise from this: first, the aspect of distinguishing the logical type of the subject (in the case of "That" as subject, this is something only made plain by the context, since the predicate "... is red" could apply equally well to an animal or person, a body, a surface, a speck on a wall, a shadow, the sun, or the sky, things distinguished in logical type by the spread of other sorts of predication to which they are open); second, the aspects involved in the type of verbal structure here exemplified; and third, the aspects associated with the particular predication made.

The first is the most straightforward. It is a sign that the sound "That is red" has not been uttered with the same meaning which "That is red" would ordinarily have if the producer of the sound could not use the predicate "... is red" in a discriminating way of the same range or ranges of different sorts of object (a machine might not be making an utterance at all).

More notable is the second point. For the word "red" to be understood in its normal meaning, one has to be able to understand the subject of this predicate within such a sentence as susceptible of other predications. More particularly, since "is" is a tensed verb, these other types of predication will include ones differing in respect of time (past, present, or future) and aspect (states or episodes of different types reflected in the use, e.g., of continuous, perfective, or aorist "tenses" according to the mode of "placing" in time concerned). Indeed, any use of the present tense presupposes capacities to speak of the past and to speak of the future or the possible.

There is a deep mistake enshrined in Dummett's remark that "We learn the use of the past tense by learning to recognize certain situations as justifying the assertion of certain statements expressed by means of that tense".[5] He speaks here as if there could be a capacity to use the present tense in its proper meaning in the absence of any capacities to speak of the past or the possible future,

5. Dummett, "The Reality of the Past", no. 21, in *Truth and Other Enigmas*, 363.

and as if the capacity to speak differentially about the past were a separable skill—as if, for instance, statements about the past were constructions out of statements about the present which we represented to ourselves as inferences from pieces of evidence in the present to past (now absent) states of affairs. But this picture of our appreciation of the past in its pastness as being something quite external to our appreciation of the present cannot be right, as one can see from what is implicit in common statements about the present. In knowing my hitting someone I know that I have hit him, in knowing that I see a certain thing I know that I have seen it, in knowing that I am moving across a space I know that I have been moving across it, so that always I know the present as a completion or a continuation of some past: it is a juncture to which a certain past has led. Moreover, it is also a juncture out of which I and other agents act, and action involves an orientation towards a future not yet existent or established, a future to be determined by action: in carrying something I bring it about that something is moved; in burning something, in eating something, and in wetting something, in the respective cases I bring it about that respective kinds of change proceed, so that in each case a change is brought about by the action and is liable to persist, be extended, or be reversed as time continues.

Thus the knowledge of the meanings of past tenses, tenses differing in aspect, and tenses marking times or modalities associated with the future, and of the kinds of possibility and of practical desire and hope associated with the latter, is internal to our knowledge in using the present tense and so not a merely external or observer's knowledge, let alone a merely inferential knowledge of these things. When changes occur we commonly know this not solely by observing different states at different times, but by knowing the acting which is the causing of the change and the changing which is its effect. And we know the present as the time of present doing, whether act, process towards a completion, or other activity, and whether on the part of ourselves, other persons or animate agents, or inanimate things. Time and aspect (to use the linguists' terms for different facets of tense) have to be understood as internal to the propositional or utterance structure concerned.

In the third place, in order to understand the sentence "That is red", one needs to be able to make an adequate range of types of contrast: to distinguish the white, the pink, the red, and the black; the yellow, the orange, and the red; the red, the green, and the blue; the red and the brown; and so forth. Moreover, beyond this, one has to understand these as discriminations in respect of color, not brightness, and not pertinent to senses other than sight.

This last brings us to a capital point: if one is understanding the sentence "That is red" in the way English-users understand it, one has to understand the discrimination which it expresses as a discrimination made by sight in respect of objects of sight, as opposed, for instance, to a discrimination made by hearing in respect of objects of hearing. And this means that one has to be able to understand the verb "see" in its contrasts with "hear", "feel (by touch)", "smell", and "taste". And, yet further, one has not understood what it is to use sight as a means of discrimination if one has not therein understood it as a means of knowledge, affording knowledge by memory after the experience has passed. Moreover, if one knows something by sight, one is aware not only of what one sees, but also that one knows it and that it is by sight that one knows it. This self-knowledge is perpetuated in memory. One does not have the concept of knowledge by the senses unless one understands how such knowledge is to be distinguished from, for instance, knowledge on the testimony of others, knowledge by inference, and knowledge of one's own beliefs, intentions, and emotions.

But with the concept of knowledge comes the capacity for an explicit development of concepts of truth, assent, and the ground or warrant for holding something to be true. With these come the conceptions of mistake or error, of reasons for judging that mistake has occurred, and the anticipation of there being some explanation of the mistake.[6] All these are involved in applying the concept of knowledge to properly language-using animals in the sense in which we are using the word "language". For the capacity of human beings for self-reflection includes or is inseparable from a capacity to reflect upon, partly identify, and criticize their procedures for getting or extending knowledge and the particular applications of the procedures.

The consideration of knowledge has brought us full circle to the fact that what we are dealing with in the case I instanced must have the structure and nature of a proposition—that is, a linguistic entity (normally an utterance or piece of writing) of the sort which is by its *parole*-meaning either true or at least put forward as true. For it to be a proposition, it must be of the sort to which it belongs to be true or capable of being put forward as true.

Moreover, "That is red" is a proposition logically of a subject/predicate type and (if understood at all) understood as being of this type. We can therefore go further and insist that, since it is understood semantically as of the logical form "a is F" (the "That" counting as a singular term and so conventionally represented by the lower-case "a", while the predicate is represented by "F"), its assertion, "a is F", presupposes that either it or its negation ("a is not F"), one of the two, must be true, the existence of the subject being presupposed.[7]

6. The idea that some classes of judgment, e.g., perceptual judgments, have a privileged epistemological status, but that their truth is insecure until we have explanations of how and why mistakes occur when they do, reflected in Bradley's "coherence theory" of truth, represents a more sophisticated approach than those associated with Peirce's probabilism and Popper's hypothetico-deductive methods.

7. Presupposed, but sometimes mistakenly, as when the subject does not exist, although mistakenly thought to do so.

That is, for the purposes of the logician, one has to understand "That" as being a singular term or referring expression within a singular subject/predicate proposition and so, like every singular subject/predicate proposition, a proposition carrying the presumption of the applicability of the relevant specific forms of the Law of the Excluded Middle. I mean by a "specific form" of this law a form restricted to one logical kind of proposition—namely, with singular subject terms, referring to identifiable objects.

Thus the supposition that a bodily being which issues the sounds in the utterance "That is red" is engaged in human discourse and uttering a propositional sentence with the meaning which "That is red" would have for a speaker of English involves a very great deal. In particular, it has involved the (at least implicit, i.e., whether or not the appropriate vocabulary has been learned or developed) capacity to express concepts such as knowing by sense, knowledge in general, truth, assent, mistake, and so forth, as well as the concept of bodily being or substance as the subject of knowledge and perception. If it did not involve these, the supposition would be incoherent.

It is not that the person who utters "That is red" with the meaning which it has for an English-speaker must possess all the vocabulary required for fully self-reflective and critical discussions, but that it is part of the linguistic capacity involved in what he or she does that he or she has, or at least has had the capacity to appropriate, the requisite vocabulary. Children may not use the words "time", "thing", "truth", "assent", and so forth, or may not have developed them in their fully adult form, but they have the capacity to appropriate them.

The more specific linguistic capacities (e.g., those associated with particular shades of color, with the specialized taxonomy of animals, or with various highly theoretical branches of study) all presuppose more general capacities which are inseparable from one another and together constitute a single unitary linguistic capacity.[8] Thus linguistic capacity is unitary in its essentials, and these essentials reach deeply into the structure of human life, including the interrelation of perception, action, and emotion and the integration of these with the procedures of deliberation, both "theoretical" and practical. And the recursiveness or self-reflexivity of linguistic operation is only one facet of this structure, however important.

Such, then, is the framework holism with which we are concerned, a holism of the speech system taken as a whole. This defines the peculiar character of human language when taken together with the holism of the sentence

8. Cf. Blackburn, *Spreading the Word*, 35–36.

Further distinctions are needed. Human beings' underlying semantic capacity is realized in stages, first as children appropriate adult means of expression, and second as they learn more about the world or gain new ways of understanding it.

whereby word and sentence are interdependent, words or lexical factors with their *langue*-meaning only gaining determinate discourse significance when used in *parole*. We placed the holism of word and sentence first because it is upon this that our understanding of the expressiveness and creativity of language turns, while depending on this framework holism for its context and for the control of the creativity in thought and speech that language makes possible.

The inseparability of propositional discourse from the capacity to use such concepts as knowledge, assent, and the full range of concepts involved in the assessment of our warrant for giving assent, such as those connected with inference, knowledge by the senses, and testimony, brings home the importance of the self-reflexivity that any use of language involves.

This self-reflexivity has the additional importance that it is only through it that we can give formal proof of the nonmechanical character of linguistic procedure. Thus all the various proofs of the unformalizability of natural language and of the lack of effective calculability in the application of linguistic rules turn upon this reflexivity. And, as chapter V will show, it is these proofs which allow the nonmechanical character of language to be demonstrated in a mathematical, though not a formal, sense.[9] It is these proofs which set the indispensability of understanding in giving us access to what is expressed by the insides of propositions, in enabling us to use the concepts involved with understanding, with its role within the activities of speaking and hearing finally beyond reasonable question.

This structure includes and depends on all the types of relation which we began to sketch in our first three chapters. Thus, first, it depends on man's capacity to use the most universal concepts, respecting the relationships between them. Within the context of an understanding of "many-track" dispositions we can develop a theory of "polymorphous" or "analogous" concepts. Granted that these concepts form a structure or hierarchy, it is the task of a "logical grammar" to describe this structure or hierarchy, and this will be a key element in the account we give of this kind of holism in the theory of discourse and language. Always this kind of holism, embodying the unitary integrated structure of these concepts, needs to be understood within the context of the "articulatedness" of any linguistic act, that primary "holism" of the individual sentence which was my concern in chapters I to III—these two holisms provide the context for any valid theory of the functioning of a lexicon or dictionary.

9. Accepting the proofs concerned as demonstrations depends in each case upon some concession, e.g., with proof or argument from the significance of Gödel's theorem, the concession that elementary natural number theory is consistent. But since such a concession is a necessary truth, the proofs do provide demonstrations.

Section 2. The Importance of This Holism in Semantics: Scrutinizing "Ordinary Language"

The understanding underlying this framework holism, the integrated semantic structure sketched earlier, helps explain our capacity to use our vocabulary informally and flexibly—most importantly the parts of our vocabulary which are most central to the structure of language and thought. It enables us to draw upon this informality in avoiding and seeing how to resolve such paradoxes as would inescapably arise if we used words like "true", "prove", "define", "set", and "individual" with the generality natural language requires in a mechanical, uniform way instead of with an intelligible informality, as well as to avoid paradoxes resulting from atomistic treatments of the continuous, whether by Zeno or by modern mathematicians. The task of unpicking each paradox and discerning how it arises is a public one, accomplished not instantaneously, but through extended reflection and debate.

This unpicking is possible because our human understanding enables us to go further than just to signal something, but to give actual expression, conceptual expression, to a message being communicated, expressing its content, thereby making this content itself available to be reflected upon. Every such expression of a thought-content requires an utterance of some complexity and articulation involving explicitly or implicitly at least two elements, at least one of which expresses a general concept, even if some of its elements, such as proper names, as chapter IX suggests, presuppose rather than express general concepts. That the content of human communications is accessible to reflection and deliberation has the implication that all the general concepts involved in such thought-contents are accessible to reflection and deliberation as to their significance and conditions of their application. This will be true even in regard to the most general concepts, those furthest from having mechanically applicable criteria of appropriate use. Thus the human capacity for reflection, notable for establishing the contrast between human beings and animals not capable of reflection,[10] *ipso facto* also involves a capacity to reflect on how to avoid paradox.

It is not for this chapter or book, in the case of each general concept, to show how it is legitimate to give it as wide an extension as we do, but only to indicate what makes it possible for such extensions to be open to critical question. Each case needs to be dealt with informally, relying upon definitions which are not mechanically applicable and upon reliable judgments whose

10. With those higher animals not capable of reflection, their behavior, emotion, and thought may also extend beyond the limits of what may be defined in a mechanically applicable way, but without their "choices" being rationalized.

reliability cannot be checked according to mechanical rule, but in such a way that whenever questioned some further answer can be given, as envisaged in chapter V, section 5. The integratedness of the overarching semantic structure I have indicated sets limits which make reflection and critical question possible and so provide controls upon such informal reasoning, but, again, not in any mechanically applicable way.

This same integrated semantic structure also enables us to transcend differences in explanatory paradigms and value-systems, making possible the "radical translation" discussed in chapter III. The flexibility concerned enables people to raise new questions and, in response, find ever fresh methods of approach in answering them, in this sometimes themselves playing a part in the opening out of new paradigms in explaining new phenomena, so that our knowledge is never closed in the way Kant supposed. That people have proceeded in this way is evident from the history of mathematics, science, logic, and the philosophy of mathematics. Chapter II showed how much we draw on this flexibility and informality in the use of words in common life, as well as in the development of science and mathematics.

The kind of holism which I propose is poles apart from the "semantic holism" which Michael Dummett attacks on the grounds that it makes the criticism and correction of "naïve ordinary language" impossible by making language so unitary as to be immune to criticism at any point, every "language-game" having been given, as it were, at the same time in one act—that is, in the very act of giving language itself.[11] He argues that even if language involves accepting some truths as linguistically necessary, its structures need to be open to review and revision where necessary to avoid accepting falsehoods as linguistically necessary. We must be able to root out proposed forms of deduction when these are illegitimate. For instance, we must avoid logical operators like the Run-about Inference Ticket invented by Arthur Prior, which would allow one to deduce anything from anything.[12] Concretely, we must avoid terms like "cur": this term is introduced when we infer from being a dog to being a cur, and eliminated by inferring from its being a cur to being contemptible; so that accepting this term into our language gives a false face of legitimacy to the inference from being a dog to being contemptible. The terms "nigger" and "Boche" function in the same way.[13] Such language-games are exceedingly common, allowing creative inferences which are both illegitimate and perverse in their effects. "Democratic" and "fascist" are other such terms.

11. Dummett, "The Justification of Deduction", no. 17 in *Truth and Other Enigmas*.

12. See Arthur Prior, "The Run-about Inference Ticket", *Analysis* 21 (1960): 38–39; cf. Prior, "Conjunction and Contonktion Revisited", *Analysis* 24, no. 6 (1964): 191–95; and Nuel D. Belnap, Jr., "Tonk, Plonk, and Plink", *Analysis* 22, no. 6 (1962): 130–34.

13. These examples are Dummett's; cf. Dummett, *Frege*, 3, 396–97, 453–55.

When Dummett requires that the different aspects of the use of a form of sentence be harmonious, his aim is to avoid such disguised cheating as well as contradiction in methods of argument.[14] Dummett's own particular concern is with the logical operator "not" associated with the principle of bivalence, whereby every statement is either true or not true. This principle underlies indirect proofs of "Something is F" arising when "Nothing is F" leads to an absurdity in the absence of any indication of how direct proof is possible, and he considers that such proofs are creative in an illegitimate way. However, he is wrong to regard the fault as lying with the principle of bivalence, an important application of the Law of the Excluded Middle. For the problem is more restricted; although we have constructive proofs that various sets can be put into a one-to-one correspondence with the natural numbers, it is indeterminate what follows from the impossibility of any such correlation, whether it is because, as Cantor assumes, such a set is of some definite infinite number or because it is simply indefinite in number. Hence the question is primarily that of the significance of such proofs of impossibility in the case considered.

Such criticism of our use of language is only possible if "fragments of a language" can be picked out from the whole—that is, if language is "segmentable". However, Dummett gravely misconceives the kind of segmentability required.

He argues that "individual sentences carry a content which belongs to them in accordance with the way they are compounded out of their own constituents, independently of other sentences of the language not involving those constituents".[15] He treats languages as definite sets of possible sentences and envisages "fragments of languages" as definite subsets of such sets. In his "molecular" theory of language a fragment of a language involving some particular semantic feature will consist in a separable set of "sentences" or "statements" which define its meaning and allow its legitimacy to be considered independently of the rest of the language structure concerned, so that "segmentability" is a matter of this separability of fragments of languages as sets of sentences.[16] He regards this approach to questions of legitimacy as appropriate *independently of the depth of the feature within the language's structure*, and therefore even in the case of negation.

However, with such features as negation, the interrelation of different tenses, modality, the connections between types of knowledge, and other fea-

14. Dummett, "Justification of Deduction", 312–17.

15. Dummett, "The Philosophical Basis of Intuitionistic Logic", no. 14, in *Truth and Other Enigmas*, 222; first published in *Logic Colloquium '73*, ed. H. Rose and J. Shepherdson (Amsterdam: North-Holland, 1975).

16. This conception of considering fragments of a language in isolation from the rest in the effort to establish a "molecular" view of language appears in Dummett, "Philosophical Basis of Intuitionistic Logic", 220–22, and "Justification of Deduction", 302, 313–17.

tures belonging to the overarching semantic structure of language, the situation cannot be considered in this way. Such features are not separable from the rest of language as if sentences involving them could be separated from the rest and disregarded.

This can be done only with sentences involving subordinate features of language such as, for instance, the sense of sight, since in principle there could easily be a language-speaking animal which lacked the sense of sight or the senses of smell and taste. So, in science fiction, some language-speaking animal might be sensitive to magnetism rather than to light. In such an imagined case we should concentrate on the nonexistence of the sense of sight rather than the set of sentences referring to it.

The root of the trouble concerned lies not with sentences, but with abuses of particular words connected with particular words, conspicuously such words as "cur" and "democratic". It may be part of the "language-games" entered into in using these words that they carry the suggestions of contemptibility or of respecting human rights, but to make the suggested inferences is to accept assumptions which are in no way necessary and which ought to be rejected. Such language-games can be taught, but their teachability does not imply their legitimacy.

In my account the understanding of one element of *langue* (e.g., the present tense) is liable to be inseparable from the understanding of another element of *langue* (viz., the past tense). This is an inseparability shown in their co-involvement in the understanding of present-tensed verbs, attributing acts, activities, performances, or states, and that this understanding shows itself in establishing the truth-relations of differently tensed statements involving the various different types of verb and predicate and the ability to discern when these requirements are being violated.

The framework holism of language-use which I propose is one which recognizes the whole structure of elements of *langue* as set in a hierarchy, the more accidental and determinate elements subordinate to and presupposing the more fundamental and general ones—as, for instance, the concept of crimson presupposes the concept of red, red presupposes the concepts of color and sight, and sight presupposes the concept of knowledge.

In this account language must indeed be segmentable[17]—but only in the sense that speech (cognate to the type of understanding I have called *parole*-understanding) must be segmentable into words and lexical factors (cognates of *langue*-understanding) and that these allow an informality of use in precisely such a way as to make the criticism of language from within language possible. Accordingly, the fact that any given language involves many different

17. Baker and Hacker's term in *Wittgenstein: Understanding and Meaning*, 280n18.

interrelated capacities, many facets at the level of *langue*, does not involve segmentability into sets and subsets of sentences in the way Dummett suggests.

The elements of *langue* involving the relation between different tenses, moods, first- or third-person knowledge, sensory and other kinds of knowledge, and so forth all involve relations which can only be exhibited in sentences and the relations of sentences—for, as we have said, the understanding of an element of *langue* is only born in an act of understanding a sentence in *parole* and is only fully exhibited in acts of understanding such sentences. From the consideration of these sentences and their relations we get contextual definitions of meaning, meanings reflected in the validity of certain logical or conceptual laws. Thus any use of the present tense will take one into a structure wherein the present appears as a completion of the past and the point from which the future opens out. Likewise we can recognize the primacy of "real" possibility, with its particular implications for tense, while also understanding its relationships to other types of possibility, not all involving these implications.[18]

When it comes to considering concepts such as sight subordinate to a more general overarching framework, we find that they do not stand alone, but as part of a structure of interrelated elements, elements in contrastive and other paradigmatic relationships, sharing some or all of their syntagmatic relations—that is, their ways of entering into sentences.

But this might mislead us into thinking that this gave us a determination of meaning governed by strict law, ruling out our flexibility in using words. Thus it might tempt us to lay down rules about the relationship of "seeing" to its objects which ruled out the use of the word "see" in deviant ways or about the relation of possibility and tense which excluded talking about epistemic possibility. Such temptation must be resisted, for we can understand variant or deviant ways of speaking, for instance, "Well, it's raining and it's not raining" (in regard to some "spotting" weather) or "It is green and it's blue" (said of something turquoise). The words which we first meet in certain syntagmatic and paradigmatic relations can then be used in metaphor, in relational uses, or in other extended ways adapted to the circumstances of the context being described. If we deal with these cases by simply adding new rules to allow for kinds of deviation, this will leave us unprepared for others (the variety of different ways of being deviant having no set limits).

Thus a consideration of sight reveals a whole spread of various atypical or deviant cases, always involving an animal or person as subject, but also allowing a generalization to cover all kinds of knowledge or understanding, even those of angels and God—besides the possibility of metaphorical extension

18. The structure described in David Braine, "Varieties of Necessity".

to the nonliving and, via the structure examined in information theory, to the inanimate. In this way we have a map which does not give a complete list of types of use, but an idea of some of the principles whereby these varied types of use arise. We have a structure, but still not one which allows a listing or serial enumeration of uses.

Thus there is no general pattern governing the way one treats all elements of *langue*, or lexical items, or the relations between them. The shape of the spread of a word will be very different in different cases.

It remains that criticism can be brought to bear upon all these subordinate elements in the semantic structure of language and to elements alien to the whole structure. Review can be made of any substructure and a critical assessment made of sentences involving it. But none of this can involve an expurgation of any of the more general elements of the language, for reasons which critical review itself reveals. I considered what such review involved in a range of types of case in chapter III, section 2, in discussing the sources of deeper systematic difficulties in translation. We saw one particular illustration of the resulting holism which merits particular attention because of the way it has entered contemporary controversies—namely, the interrelation of past and future with the present. But there is another, yet more general illustration provided by Dummett's mistaken critique of negation. For a critical view would, I believe, see the principle of bivalence as merely a particular instance of the Law of the Excluded Middle and the notion of negation as never employed without a presumption that the Excluded Middle applies, albeit always with something being presupposed to both affirmation and negation. But it is this presupposition which fails in the case of what I would call "indefinite predicates". This assessment of the situation with negation is itself instructive as to the way language can operate by rule without this being by mechanical rule, since the determination of when this presupposition fails, and with it the applicability of the Law of the Excluded Middle, cannot be handled mechanically.

In conclusion, some kind of critical examination of a concept or kind of concept, judgment or kind of judgment, is always possible; and the judgments put forward in such review of concepts are themselves open to such critical examination. But in some cases the critical examination will show the concept considered to be incapable of revision without undermining the structure as a whole and rendering all discourse nonsensical.

But this fact—namely, that rejection of any of its most general features will involve the setting aside of all discourse as nonsense—is not our reason for accepting the structure as a whole or in some of its parts, and thereby by implication as a whole. Rather we begin a posteriori with first-order judgments, and it is within the framework of first-order judgments that our second-order judgments arise inseparably from them. And given any first-order judgment, we will have always already committed ourselves to the structure it carries with it.[19]

Section 3. The Role of Language in the Theory of Human Nature

(a) *The emergence of Homo sapiens: discontinuity underlying apparent continuity*

It is commonly objected that regarding language as uniquely picking out the special character of human beings obscures our close community and continuity with other animals—the community on which I insisted in my earlier work.[20] Further, the development of communication-systems is presumed to proceed continuously in animals lower than man and, accordingly, with parallel continuity to keep on within hominid and human development.

True, we see the development of increasingly efficient communication by contextualized signal among various kinds of mammals involving relationships between situation and behavior, signals and appropriate behavioral responses becoming progressively more analogous to human patterns of communication. We can envisage an extended system of atomic sound signals conveying warnings, commands, indications of types of prey or other object; expressing woe, submission, hunger; registering number (one, two, many); or serving as vocatives. True also, we may be able to trace or infer a steady progress in the development of the organs needed for the vocalization of the spread of sounds necessary for any ready unfolding of linguistic capacity in the medium of speech (as distinct from gestures, making marks, or communicating in other ways).

Yet none of this shows that the animal concerned has language as something enabling the content of the message to be made explicit—that is, given contentful conceptual expression, making it open to critical reflection and involving the integrated semantic system indicated in section 1. No evidence or argument has undermined my argument that this latter could only come all at once as a unity, or not at all.

It is only by discrete steps, distinctive in that they transform the mode of functioning of the physical system concerned, that a circuit comes to include a loop introducing negative feedback; that a network of different kinds of unit becomes capable of functioning as a radio, a television, or a computer—dis-

19. This is the perspective I put forward in "Nature of Knowledge", secs. 4–6; in "Two Kinds of Critical Philosophy", paper presented to Société Belge de Logique et de Philosophie des Sciences, Brussels, November 18, 1972; and in *The Reality of Time and the Existence of God,* 236–48, 257–65.

20. See David Braine, *Human Person,* chap. 4, 164–70; chap. 8, 267–89; and esp. chap. 9.

tinct changes in the physical organization being required before a system is capable of functioning in a new type of way. Accordingly, even if AI theory provided an adequate account of human linguistic capacity, we ought still to anticipate a radical discontinuity between animals with the capacity for language and those without it.

The contrast between the structure of human language, marked by its complex, interknit semantic and syntactic structure and any other animal system, is clearly appreciated by many recent thinkers.[21] The presumption that no radical discontinuity is involved in the emergence of language is ill-supported. It figures more in loose popularizations of science, or else among scientists preoccupied with physiological evolution or with animals' sexual, social, and tool-using behavior, than among those concerned directly with linguistic theory and the semantic structure of language or its unitary character. Certain forms of life invite a developed communication-system, but what matters is not forms of behavior as such (e.g., the use of tools, the making and use of boats, the hiding or burying of the dead, or any other readily observable behavior), but what understanding and reflective thought they imply.

Certainly we should anticipate a progressive development in physical systems, such as those involved in human breath control, speech production, auditory capacity, and the systems in the brain which enable us to be tuned to make and distinguish sounds in the way communication requires.[22] The late stages of the evolution of animal communication-systems will have depended on a succession of mutations or integrated groups of mutation, in each case allowing an advance from a physical basis which allows one structure of behavior to a physical basis inviting a different structure of behavior. Yet the discontinuity involved in appropriating the whole mathematically integrated semantic and syntactic structure distinctive of human speech remains what is crucial, and without this, developments in capacities for sound production and the associated auditory discrimination would be useless.

As chapter V will show, although parallel processing may be useful in connection with the vocabulary and "accidence" (e.g., variable inflections) of languages, it is of no use in simulating the integrated structure of a language as a whole. Rather, my argument suggests that, although key changes in the

21. Steven Pinker particularly insists on this discontinuity and upon the superficiality of arguments from the "intelligent" behavior and communications skills of apes to a simple continuity, in Pinker, *The Language Instinct* (New York: Morrow, 1994; Penguin, 2003), chap. 11.

22. Human linguistic behavior evidently includes the physiological development underlying phonetic capacity with the required breath control. Human linguistic behavior presumably also depends on a large brain with a greatly increased number and complexity of convolutions and an adequate blood supply, perhaps dependent on erect posture facilitating temperature control. However, what matters most is the structural neural organization developed in this context. Some hominids seemingly very similar to the language-speaking human may thus have a form and level of consciousness anticipatory of the human, but lacking reflection.

structures of the brain and its modes of operation may be indispensable to the linguistic expression of thought, this is a matter of their having developed to become capable of being tuned in use to certain communicational and semantic ends so that their use shapes their organization, rather than vice versa. My argument earlier was directed to the more limited point that, even if thought and understanding were thus physically based or determined, one would still anticipate a radical discontinuity between properly human language and any preceding systems of earlier hominid communication.

The picture suggested by linguistic theory is that the last such step must have a different order of significance from the others, involving more radical structural discontinuity. In this last step, relevant adaptations in modes of neurological functioning and an advance in human structures of communication would have subserved and reflected the event of human beings becoming open to the workings of intellect. And thereafter further adaptations in capacities for speech production and discrimination would have been shaped by, rather than opened the way towards, these novel structures. There will have been a whole series of communal developments before and after individual human beings became open to the workings of intellect—that is, both before and after pragmatic and semantic constraints in the setting of problems posed by the environment had in one act reshaped human communication and retuned human modes of neurological functioning in the way indicated in chapter VII. Over the same period there would have been development in systems of speech production and discrimination. Speech requires a community of at least two people, and a language requires learning over more than one generation. The context may have been that intellect and the capacity for speech spread within a community over some generations before being actually exercised.

Of course, discontinuity in the underlying structures of brain-operation in the human species does not mean the instant development of all the language potentialities opened out by it. The same tribal peoples whose native languages have only two tenses, one for present and past and one for the future, the possible, and the hoped-for or feared, and no words or word-forms distinguishing affirmation, denial, question, supposition, or imperative, instead using gestures and intonation to mark the relevant distinctions, will nonetheless be found to have the ability to learn a Western language on encountering it as at an early enough stage. Certain gestures and various intonational or prosodic features are almost always integral to particular spoken languages, and this feature may have been more marked at earlier stages of the use of language. Indeed, as remarked in earlier chapters, we can have a fully linguistic use of signs as in deaf-and-dumb languages, their sequences exhibiting grammaticalization and not just semantics. Therefore, although humankind probably took many tens of thousands of years to develop a language of the complexity of Western or other highly developed languages, these can and should be seen as unfoldings of one and the same underlying capacity for understanding, as we may take to have been present from the first emergence of *Homo sapiens*.

The capacity for the full gamut of linguistic skills exhibited in the most developed countries today can be acquired by children drawn from a background of the linguistically furthest separated groups, African, Australian aborigine, Native American, and modern Western included, corresponding exactly to the spread of genes represented in the mitochondrial DNA and the nuclear DNA of the XY chromosomes of the same groups, indicating a common origin of the order of 150,000–100,000 years ago and no later than 100,000 years ago.[23]

Therefore, it is reasonable to take the human linguistic capacity I have identified as specific to the species *Homo sapiens* rather than to associate it with a wider group taking its origin around 600,000 years ago, the approximate time that the lineage of *Homo sapiens* and the Neanderthals began to separate.[24] Therefore it is simpler to attribute the shared human semantic structure I have described to common origin rather than to parallel development. Besides this, the differentiation of existing human language groups between the African (excluding the Afro-Asiatic groups arising from flow back into Africa) and the Oceanic from before the Toba eruption of around 75,000 years ago, making it reasonable to take the most radical differentiations between the older human language groups to have originated before that time, suggesting that language may have had a previous long history.[25] Signs of symbolic and technical skills traceable from 100,000 to 70,000 years ago may be construed as partly coordinate with this language capacity.[26] Other language groups appear to become differentiated later.

23. The generation length measured by the time between maternal birth and the birth of fertile daughters and that between paternal birth and the birth of fertile sons will differ, and each will have varied according to culture, so that estimates of time based on spread of genetic variation in mitochondrial DNA and nuclear XY-chromosomal DNA are highly speculative.

24. It appears that there was some interbreeding between late Neanderthals (and perhaps some earlier originating "Denisovans") and some Eurasian groups, but with no discernible effect on linguistic development.

25. Greenberg, followed by Merrit Ruhlen, distinguishes between an "Indo-Pacific" group comprising the original languages of Australia, New Guinea, and the Andaman Islands and an "Austric" group in South-east Asia, later spreading to all the islands of the Pacific and Indian oceans, these groups classified together as "Oceanic". Among human languages, the first fundamental divide appears to be between the elder-rooted African languages (supposedly dividing into Khoisan [Bushman and "Hottentot"], Nilo-Saharan, and Niger-Kordofanian subgroups) and all other languages, and then between the "Oceanic" and all the remaining. For evidence on the classification of languages, see the work of Luigi Cavalli-Sforza, L. P. Menozzi, and A. Piazza, *The History and Geography of Human Genes* (Princeton, N.J.: Princeton University Press, 1994); and Merrit Ruhlen, *The Origin of Language* (New York: Wiley, 1994).

We know that the Oceanic peoples reached Australia not less than 40,000–55,000 before the present (BP). And it appears that the ancestral Oceanic language speakers left Africa before the major extinction associated with the Toba earthquake, although not reaching Australia so early.

26. The human use of geometrical symbols associated with the Blombos cave people around 77,000

In sum, since the human language capacity I have identified is coterminous with the genetic spread of *Homo sapiens*, I place it with the inheritance of *Homo sapiens* as such.

Evidently, just as other mammals may give birth to genetically deformed or irregularly reared individuals within whom the capacities belonging to the species concerned are not realized or not properly realized, so also with human beings. Gross prenatal abnormality and deprivation of human company from a very early stage may have the effect that human linguistic capacity is never properly realized. But this does not affect the general argument associating human linguistic capacity with the human species as such.

(b) *The type of thought specific to human beings as inseparable from linguistic capacity*

The idea that the capacity for language is the key differentiating feature of the human species is contested on two different types of objection.

The first type of objection arises from mistaken responses to certain obvious difficulties in associating thought and language too closely. Thus the adult may have thoughts which he has to search for words to express, uncertain whether such words exist.[27] Also it seems plain that the child has thoughts before learning any means to express them linguistically.

To this I reply that whatever thoughts the child or adult has which have the potential of linguistic expression are realizations of the same underlying capacity for linguistically expressible judgment, question, command, wish, and so forth, whose distinctive human mode of expression is linguistic—the mode which would give these thoughts the most unmistakable sense, and the least ambiguous. Accordingly every thought of the specifically human type, even those thoughts which have not been given linguistic expression, is a realization of this underlying form of intellectual capacity, which Pinker calls the "language instinct".[28] This is a quite different matter from that of the kind

---

BP suggests the capacity for language. The significant acceleration in technical development within Africa from 300,000 BP onwards becomes more marked towards 100,000 BP; cf. Rudolf Botha and Chris Knight, eds., *The Cradle of Language* (Oxford: Oxford University Press, 2000), chap. 3 by C. S. Henshilwood and B. Dubreil, chap. 4 by I. Watts, and chap. 7 by K. C. Diller and R. L. Cann.

27. Here, until they find some way of expressing it, it is not clear that they have genuinely had a thought. Bertrand Russell has this anecdote: "William James describes a man who got the experience from laughing-gas; whenever he was under its influence, he knew the secret of the universe, but when he came to, he had forgotten it. At last, with immense effort, he wrote down the secret before the vision had faded. When completely recovered, he rushed to see what he had written. It was: 'A smell of petroleum prevails throughout'"; Russell, *History of Western Philosophy* (London: Allen and Unwin, 1946), 145.

28. Cf. introduction, n. 11, of this volume; Von Humboldt envisaged man's capacity for thought and for speech as unitary. (Thought of a nonlinguistic character among animals lower than man and men enfeebled or drunk, showing itself in sublinguistic tendencies in behavior, is a separate matter. Thus we say, e.g., "He made the dog think he was going to throw something for it to fetch". Dogs do in some sense have thoughts,

of perceptual discrimination which underlies behavior moved by emotion which we observe among nonhuman animals, without its having even potentially a properly linguistic expression.[29]

The relevant question is what kind of expression of thought is especially distinctive of human beings, not whether human beings have thoughts of another kind, which are not of a sort to be linguistically expressible. Conceivably there could be other intellectual animals sharing language with the same kind of integrated semantic structure, realized in a way we do not yet understand. However, the primary human realization of linguistic capacity remains vocal, even though those subject to some impairment may find means of linguistic expression of a nonvocal kind.[30]

Moreover, when human beings find means of realizing their linguistic capacity in other media than the vocal, these can only classify as genuinely realizations of linguistic capacity (rather than merely systems for signaling) because they show the same underlying structure, characterized most obviously by such distinctions as between affirming, denying, and questioning, between naming and saying or predicating, and between lexical meaning at the level of language-possession and discourse-significance or sense at the level of language-use. This last is important because it is what allows flexibility and informality in the use of words, and with it the peculiar exploratory power and capacity for retrospective criticism and response, as well as giving human communication its especial explicitness and capacity for the expression of nuance.

Aging, stroke, aneurism, or injury to the brain may bring some impairment in speech capacity or its total loss, which disguises the continuance of thought of the kind which remains in principle linguistically expressible. The situation with children is more difficult to assess. The question might be raised as to whether or when children pass from thinking in the manner of other animals to thinking in an implicitly linguistic manner. Even when children are at the stage of one-word utterances like "bed", still, if these are taken in connection with an intonation and context which indicates whether they are naming a type of object, expressing a desire for bed or to go to bed, or questioning whether they have to go to bed, such combination suggests that linguistic thought is incipiently present. From this stage what is involved is an exercise of the same capacity as is involved in speech and writing.

---

and we should reject Malcolm's idea that neither dogs nor human beings have dreams, but only behave as if they do.)

29. Cf. chap. VI, n. 12 and related text, anticipated in the introduction, n. 2 of this volume. Steiner's Argentinian gauchos have words for two hundred different colors of cowhide (*After Babel*, chap. 6, n. 37); this implies concepts expressed linguistically in judgment—a different matter from discriminating shades of color by nonlinguistic behavior.

30. The fact that sign-language has genuine linguistic status, involving functional structures and signs as well as lexical ones, is well recognized.

The second type of objection is of a quite different kind. We speak of kinds of understanding, insight, or realization in association with religion, with music, with wonder at nature, and with the understanding of other persons at a personal level—all of them kinds of understanding whose main expression is not linguistic. But these are forms of understanding or thought which, if there be pure spirits, whether angels or Aristotle's pure intelligences, these pure spirits might have in common with human beings, and they would therefore not be forms of understanding specific to man. Likewise our freedom in directing our will cannot be presumed to be unique to man.

However, we are not concerned with angels, but with what is specific to rational animals, of which human beings are the only ones of which we have certain knowledge, and what is specific to human nature is exhibited when human bodily, imaginative, and intellectual faculties attain mature function unimpaired. But the recognition of the importance of these language-transcending kinds of understanding, realizations, and wonder for the ends of life has to be capable of being registered in deliberation and choice in such a way as to be integrated with the rest of such an unimpaired human life, and the paradigm mature human expression of deliberation is linguistically expressible. Linguistically expressible understanding remains what is specific to the human kind of life. Moreover, the precision with which we can describe the expressions and structures of language provides the key to the only possible source of *proof* that man has a certain transcendence of the body such as I proposed in *The Human Person*.

Robbins Burling supposes that it is Chomsky's portrayal of the intricacies of any syntax dependent on an unrestricted capacity for iteration which has lent plausibility to the assumption of discontinuity between human language and earlier communication-systems, and notes that complex digital structures can be developed in stages, and that grammaticalization develops in stages.[31] But we have shown that it is not the intricacies of formal grammar or iteration which are vital, but the intricacies of the prior, implicit, unitary semantic structure of speech, and that it is the capacity for this (not formal grammar as such) which has to be acquired at once or not at all. The concern is not the metaphysical question of the creation of the rational soul, but the question of what is required for the brain to be open to the operation of intellect—that is, apt for the tuning required for the intellect to function and express itself in language, a tuning which requires a community environment.

31. Robbins Burling, *The Talking Ape* (Oxford: Oxford University Press, 2005), chaps. 8–10. E. Reuland, E. Van Gelderen, F. L. Coolidge, and T. Wynn show the same mistaken preoccupation with recursion in their essays in *The Prehistory of Language*, ed. Botha and Knight (Oxford: Oxford University Press, 2009); cf. Pinker and Jackendoff, "Faculty of Language" (2005).

(c) *Stages in the learning of language*

I have implied that we acquire vocabulary bit by bit, but do not acquire linguistic capacity bit by bit. However, there is another "common-sense" objection—namely, that "empirically" the progress of infants shows that linguistic capacity comes in stages.

As chapter XIII will show, children's early utterances have underlying semantic structures shared with adult discourse, although this may be disguised when, for instance, some words which later function as nouns or connectives function in a verb-like way in children's early utterances.[32] The structures realized in two-word discourse are pregnant with the structures realized in adult discourse.

To this it might be objected that key features of adult discourse are absent in young children—saliently, structures exhibiting reflection with the conscious assessment of beliefs as true or false, forms of reasoning involving transitivity, and a grasp of numbers as forming a series with no last member.

However, the structures exhibiting explicit reflection and the questioning of beliefs as to their truth or falsity are implicit from the first, exhibited in many forms of play and actions such as refusal and, as chapter IX, section 3, will show, implicit in the way we learn verbs and the developing part played by imitation in language acquisition. Linguistically explicit forms of assent and dissent unfold in the course of deliberating with others.

Second, the forms of reasoning which arise with transitive relations are not appreciated by children until after a certain age—for instance, the form "A is bigger than B; B is bigger than C; therefore, A is bigger than C" or, expressing class-inclusion, "Every A is a B; every B is a C; therefore, every A is a C" (whether the age be four or later).[33] Yet this is no problem. Groups of statement may be pregnant with implications which children only realize when they learn to consider them together in relevant ways. This would seem to depend more on developments in the way imagination functions and is coordinated with the relevant "putting together" than on any development of linguistic capacity.

Third, the age at which the child grasps the significance not just of two, but of the possibility of any number of iterations, so that he can give sense to "and so on unendingly", does not seem to depend upon the possession of a developed number system. It is possible for a language to have only the number expressions "one", "two", and "many", and yet for its users to have the concepts

32. See chaps. IX and XIII and the studies of Martin Braine referred to in them.

33. Piaget's discussion of this issue was reopened by Martin Braine, "The Ontogeny of Certain Logical Operations: Piaget's Formulation Examined by Nonverbal Methods", *Psychological Monographs* 73, no. 5 (1959), and proved to involve a complex of different issues; the capacity of a child to deal with serialization such as might extend beyond three items—i.e., transitivity as such, or difficulties in handling too much information or in measuring techniques (making a defect in measuring methods appear a defect in reasoning capacity).

"one more" or "yet another", and "again", "again and again", and "without end" in regard to both repeated discrete operations and continued distance and time.[34] On the other hand, the expression of the differences between the number of places at which a line has actually been divided and the number of places at which it could be divided, and thence between actual infinity and potential infinity, depends on questions which arise only in the context of later debate.

In each of these three cases the new developments can be regarded as unfoldings of preexisting linguistic capacity, the first as the realization of some of its presuppositions, the second as the developing of a grasp of the implications of judgments of kinds already made, and the third as a development allowing preexisting linguistic capacity to gain richer or more efficient expression, rather than as external to preexisting linguistic capacity.

Such problems concerning our general linguistic capacity should be treated entirely differently from those which I discussed in chapter III, section 3. The difficulties of understanding different religions may indeed partly depend upon appreciating the relevant "forms of life" and, along with the appreciation of much literature, require a combination of maturity and experience, imagination, and willingness to empathize, but the hurdles concerned are not primarily linguistic—and likewise with the quite different hurdles presented by theoretical physics or musical theory.

Section 4. This Semantic Structure as the Feature Specific to Language of the Human Type

This chapter reveals a much deeper difficulty in the proposal that a computer might simulate human linguistic capacity than those commonly considered—namely, that it would have to simulate the unitary, integrated character of the semantic structure, incorporating all its key features such as I have indicated. The difficulties discussed in chapters I, II, and V, arising from the informality with which we use words, especially the use of certain words in every subject-matter and from self-reflectivity, can now be seen within a wider framework.

The integrated structure which has to be simulated incorporates first of all the self/other distinction and tense. Even the most sophisticated communications of chimpanzees, with their differential responses (such as the utterance of the words "Elizabeth give apple Amy" and the conveying of "Please Roger tickle Lana" by gestures),[35] fail to exhibit this global structure. Hence such utter-

34. Systems for representing numbers are relatively less important—Latin writers readily formed the concept of infinity despite having no better way of representing 10^{300} than, e.g., to write "M" 10^{100} times.

35. R. E. Passingham, *The Human Primate* (New York: W. H. Freeman, 1982), 201–22, esp. 216, 221.

ances of chimpanzees are not to be construed as if pregnant with the meaning that they would have if other utterances exhibiting the whole global structure I have described were to follow naturally in the learning sequence in the way they do in the case of human children. In the absence of the developmental capacity coordinate with such global structure, it is unsurprising that each new verbal or gestural skill is acquired with such difficulty and depends on a determination and skill not required in teaching unhandicapped human children.

Linguistic capacity is something unitary and therefore comes as a single whole or not at all. There will be some structuring of the brain and sensory and vocal organs and some stages in its development correlative with the realization of this linguistic capacity, including stages pertinent to the use of the imagination, as well as to the more obvious linguistic skills, but this does not compromise the unitariness of the capacity.

The way this underlying capacity for language may take many generations to unfold in explicit forms is evident if we contrast modern European languages with those of some so-called primitive peoples. For instance, the only number-words of some "primitive" languages are "one", "two", "three", "four", "five", and "many", or even only "one", "two", and "many", by contrast with modern European languages. Again, modalities and differences in the force of an utterance, from being indicated by intonation and context, may come to be marked by distinct idioms: "I order you to ...", "I ask you to ...", "I suggest that you ...", and so forth. Indeed, many languages lack idioms for expressing something in a merely factual way (e.g., for speaking of the future without at the same time implying necessity, intention, hope, or fear). But children of peoples from groups whose language is more primitive in such respects as these have, as it were, crossed the threshold and, if brought into a different type of context, for instance, a European one, can acquire these more explicit idioms along with the mathematical and critical thought they make possible.

With this integral linguistic capacity we should adopt the same approach as with perceptual consciousness as I described in *The Human Person*.[36] We should presume its presence in the individuals of the species until its absence is evidenced, since the evidence suggests that linguistic capacity belongs to a species as such.

As to other species, it would make no difference to the argument of this book if it turned out that another species shared the capacity for language in the full sense I have described. My argument requires neither to prove nor to disprove that, for instance, dolphins have the capacity for the kind of linguistic understanding involved, although it is clear enough that *Homo sapiens*'s nearer extant relatives lack it.

36. David Braine, *Human Person*, 297–99.

V

Scientific Method and the Significance of Mathematics for Linguistics

Section 1. Mistaken Presumptions about What "Scientific Method" Requires

This chapter shows the indispensability of informal rules to mathematical practice and scientific method and development. The requirement of conformity to mechanically applicable rules arises only in certain specialized contexts. The deceptive plausibility of arguments that such mechanically applicable rules are necessary leads us into a trap, "up the garden path" as it were; this chapter shows the pits, dumps, and general chaos at the end of this garden path.

(a) *My approach contrasted with its rivals*

For many modern philosophers and psycholinguists it is the received "common sense" that in order to know the sense of an utterance, we need first to identify the words and their *langue*-meanings in their order, the intonation, and the context of utterance, envisaged as the elements and features of the total utterance which *identify* its lexical meaning. Then, second, we need to use the knowledge of these elements and features to work out or "calculate" the sense of the whole in an "effective" or reliable way—a view only plausible because "work out" and "effective" are ordinarily such vague terms. Without such "effective" access, it is argued that the speaker could never rely on being understood correctly.

However, many cognitive scientists and AI theorists take a methodological view involving a third supposition—namely, that the only way in which a method of "working out" the senses of whole sentences could be effective is by its being mechanically applicable. They require a mechanical procedure which, in the case of each sentence, would yield a proof that such and such were the sense of the sentence concerned, since, if one follows Church and Gödel, such a mechanical procedure is necessary and sufficient for "effectiveness".[1] In sum, ordinary security in communication within a short finite time requires a mechanically applicable procedure in applying linguistic rules. This third requirement is much more demanding than that the process be finite, since tasks may be accomplishable in a finite number of steps without these steps following according to a mechanically applicable rule.[2]

But I showed in chapter I that in speech we express the sense we intend and that the primary role of words and other sentence factors is as sense-expressors, so that in speaking we know the sense or meaning of what is said with the directness with which in doing something intentionally we know what we are intending to do, rather than knowing it indirectly by external observation. Hence the idea that we know the meaning or sense of what is said in an utterance by *first* identifying the *langue*-meanings of words and other contributory sense-identifiers, and *then* calculating the resultant sense of the whole utterance, is far-fetched—besides which such calculation is impossible. The primary exercise of the capacity to swim is in actual swimming, not in the capacity to explain how to swim, distinguish particular strokes, or describe particular muscle movements. Likewise the understanding of the *langue*-meaning of words has its primary exercise in the understanding of *parole*—that is, in the understanding of the word in use as a functioning part of utterances—along with its companion words *expressing* the sense of the whole utterance, not in the capacity to identify the *langue*-meanings of words and then calculate utterance meaning.

Thus understanding plays an indispensable part, both in enabling us to speak in a way which is meaningful to ourselves and in enabling others to understand the same thing as we do from what we say, here performing a task beyond the power of calculation or the mechanical processing of relevant information.

1. Alonzo Church, *Introduction to Mathematical Logic* (Princeton, N.J.: Princeton University Press, 1956), 52–53. The requirements of effectiveness he lays down are explained in section 4(a) of this chapter.

2. This chapter provides many examples of such finite serial processes—e.g., proofs which are finite but not discoverable by mechanical process, and not of one mechanically specifiable form. Each time, for instance, given a particular axiomatization of natural arithmetic, we prove something by Gödelian reasoning (informal in the sense of not being according to this axiomatization, but arising by reflection upon it, taking the consistency of natural arithmetic as evident), we have produced a proof which is "along particular lines", but not along mechanically specifiable lines. More generally, the search for a proof for an attractive conjecture often continues through centuries, even if, when we find a proof, checking that it is a proof may perhaps be accomplished mechanically.

(b) *Two different types of explanation*

What I am saying amounts to making *understanding* a part of the explanation of our using words in a sense determinate enough for one to be able to say that the sense intended by the speaker is the same as the sense understood by the hearer, without the calculation of the senses of utterances from prior relevant information. But for most "cognitive scientists", if there could be no mechanism for making such calculation, this would imply that for a hearer the sense to be understood would be indeterminate or unknown. And the position I have put forward they regard as treating the "understanding" of words as a faculty whose activities are not open to scrutiny, serving as it were by magic to remove this indeterminacy in hearer-understanding and bridge the gap concerned. In this they neglect the many ways in which the "understanding" concerned has long been open to critical scrutiny indicated in the introduction, chapters II and IV, and, above all, chapter VIII of this volume.

In addition, these various theorists neglect an essential distinction between conceptual, or theoretical, and nonconceptual questions.

One always has to ask what precisely the psycholinguist, philosopher, or other questioner is seeking to explain, because this makes a difference to the type of explanation appropriate. For some matters indeed need explanation, and psycholinguists and others do right to seek it, but without this explanation being in terms of a mechanism or merely empirically discovered connection.

The need for some distinction between types of explanation appears in many areas.

For instance, if somebody asks, "*By what mechanism* (how) does it arise that always a group of two pieces of wood taken with a similar group make a group of four?", the answer is "It does not arise by a mechanism". The same answer should be given if somebody asks such questions as "*By what mechanism* (how) does it arise that if you take a triangle and then measure the angles, it always turns out that they add up to approximately two right angles?" or "*By what mechanism* (how) does it arise that always the area of a square built on a hypotenuse of a right-angled triangle equals the sum of the areas on the other two sides?" and so for any other theorem of Euclid in its natural interpretation.

This does not mean that no answer can be given as to why these things always work out in the mathematically expected way, but that the appropriate answers are from set theory, logic, or geometry. If the question had been, "By what mechanism (how) does it arise that always a distinct group of 23,587 one-penny pieces taken with a group of 89,463 one-penny pieces constitute a group of 113,050 one-penny pieces?", the answer would still have been the same: "Not by a mechanism". In this more complex case, one's answer to the question of why things work out this way could be exhibited in a computation, together perhaps with a demonstration of how the method of computation is grounded in set theory (or predicate logic with identity). In the two Euclidean cases mentioned earlier, one would commonly answer such questions by commenting on a diagram or offering a proof.[3]

We need to distinguish these types of case, in which the appropriate kind of explanation is of this conceptual, "theoretical", or a priori kind—cases in which the question "By what mechanism?" or "How?" is out of place or absurd—from cases in which the reverse is true and things do require causal, mechanical, or historical explanation. For instance, the question of why a group of 23,587 one-penny pieces placed physically together with a group of 89,463 one-penny pieces always make a group of 113,050 one-penny pieces depends on facts about the physical constitution of penny pieces and, for instance, the pressure and temperature at which the two groups are put together, and not just on the set-theoretical truths to which computations (addition sums) give us knowledge.

This distinction between conceptual and nonconceptual questions arises in psychology just as much as in dealing with the physical applications of arithmetical and geometrical truths. For just as arithmetical and geometrical facts are not contingent results of the operation of some causal mechanism but exemplify logical laws or deeply embedded theoretical or conceptual truths, so also there can be facts in psychology whose explanation or necessity arises for conceptual reasons. And in psychology we often find that there are two closely connected questions which require utterly different sorts of answer—questions which often get confused.

The psychology of perception gives a good instance of such connected questions, with different kinds of answer. Thus consider first the question: "How does it come about that the muscle action from spine to fingers is coordinated with changes in the optical system in such a way that a person touches the edge of a table when he or she wants to?" This first question requires empirical inquiry of perhaps three different kinds, the most obvious in terms we expect to involve neurological theory, then another concerning how this whole neurological and behavioral system functioning in the way discovered developed from single cell to complex organism, and a third concerning how

3. We do not proceed by counting different collections of objects to verify arithmetical propositions or measuring the angles of triangles or the sizes of squares on the sides of right-angled triangles to verify well-known geometrical theorems as if we were merely dealing with the cases of very general empirical laws. Physical geometry has an empirical aspect, but the deviations from the Euclidean ideal are assessed through a complex web of theory and corroborated through critical experiments, not mass observation; cf. Michael Polanyi, *Personal Knowledge* (Chicago: University of Chicago Press, 1958), 9–15.

such a system developing in each animal in this way arose, this third perhaps involving evolutionary theory.

The situation of this first question stands in stark contrast with that of a second, closely related conceptual question: "How does a person who sees where a table is and sees its edge, and wants to touch the table on its edge, come to be able to touch the edge of the table?" Here what is meant by being said to "see where the edge of the table is" depends on and is determined by the possession of the behavioral aptitude involved, not the capacity to specify relative positions in linguistic terms. And what we understand by "seeing" is here set by the case of healthy functioning in normal conditions without error, whereas if the word "see" is used with an extended meaning or special context involving abnormal conditions or defective functioning, it has a different sense or discourse-significance. Here we need a philosophical account exhibiting how behavioral aptitude is integral to the nature of perception and avoiding Descartes's divorce between inner experience and outward behavior. This is part of the general philosophical task of avoiding the dualistic mind/body divide[4]—the false divide we met in chapter III and to which I recur in chapters VI and VIII.

In the psychology of thinking, at each stage we have to raise the same query as to which kind of question we are dealing with, conceptual or empirical. If the question is empirical, we should anticipate that several different avenues of enquiry will open out.

The case of the psychology of reasoning presents an obvious case in which a distinction between types of question and explanation needs to be made. It is not just a contingent matter that we should be prone to think that if it is true that P, and true that, if P, then Q, then it will be true that Q—or if we think that Peter possesses one apple and Paul possesses a different apple, also to think that Peter and Paul together possess two apples. It is strange to look for a "mechanism" by which a person should become able to judge the conclusion in these cases if it is granted that he already knows the premises; the ability to reach such conclusions is internal to understanding the word "if" or other terms used to express these inferences.

Likewise, there does not seem to be any mystery as to how a person might come to understand how a range of arguments, not capable of capture within any one formalization, may all count as demonstrations, all equally showing the truth of their conclusions. For instance, Gödel proposes a form of argument whereby for any given axiomatization of natural arithmetic, we can identify some formula which we can (a) show to be true, so long as the axiomatization embodies only valid principles, and (b), so long as this axiomatiza-

4. Cf. David Braine, *Human Person*, pt. 1, esp. chap. 5.

tion is consistent, show to be not derivable within the axiomatization. Every example of such a Gödelian form of argument is finitary (finite in its number of steps) and intuitively demonstrative; and all such arguments have the same form, but the "same form" only in an informal sense. Yet it is provable that no consistent formal system could produce or check all such arguments, and it is theoretically impossible that there should be a machine able to produce or check them, or even perform the lesser task of recognizing them all as of the same form.

Mathematicians desire rigorous argument and anticipate that the form of each particular argument which they use will have a validity clear enough to be made evident by comparison, example, or other explanation in respect of each of its steps. But they do not require such explanations to be strictly formal. As we shall see in section 4, the notion of a mechanical procedure for proof is itself just another specialized mathematical conception, defined mathematically, not physically. The specific interest of this notion arises from its usefulness in demonstrating the powers and limits of formalized methods, methods simulable by idealized physical "machines" not using intelligence in their operations. However, as it happens, mathematicians themselves employ these methods very little, their understanding allowing greater informality. As we shall see, such understanding requires only finitariness in argument, not conformity to preset formal rule.

It is absurd to say that we do not understand what it is that different particular arguments of the same form have in common, whether they be very simple, such as applications of *modus ponens*, or very complex, such as Gödelian arguments of the kind just mentioned. For our grasp of the notion of proof or demonstration requires only that a method of proof or demonstration proceed from premises to conclusions in ways whose truth-preserving character is evident (their aim being to get at the truth).

Moreover, methods of proof or of establishing truth arise in every field of inquiry, so that the family of notions associated with truth and knowledge has application in physics, biology, history, law, and such, as much as in mathematics.

Therefore the absurdity of denying that we have a notion of "showing something to be true" which is applicable in a nonmechanical way over a variety of areas, a notion which the understanding applies in a spread of very disparate ways, not at all by any one mechanically applicable system of rules, should be something quite obvious and beyond controversy. The key importance of the arguments arising out of consideration of the logical and semantic paradoxes and the problems of various kinds of self-reference is that they alone allow mathematically rigorous demonstration of need for a nonmechanical approach to avoid absurdity where unrestricted generalization is made.

Thus when people seek to explain how understanding works—for instance, when it judges whether or not this or that is a proof or demonstration—then, although the answer is often by some procedure of reasoning or computation (rarely formalized), very commonly the answer is that we use no procedure in judging something to be a proof—and even if some check can be made, there is no mechanical procedure which can check all methods of checking. For instance, it is not by means of a mechanism that one judges that if a person takes a group of two pieces of wood together with a distinct similar group, these will always constitute a group of four, even though we can reflect on the underlying reasons why this is so. Even in more complex cases, when some procedure or computation is used in judging whether or not this or that is known (even a mechanically checkable procedure), the fact of our knowing this, once having grasped the relevant computations and proofs, is not the contingent result of the operation of some causal mechanism.

In Martin Braine's theory of a "mental logic", when he refers to it as relying on "mechanisms", he is not occupied with neural mechanisms in the brain, let alone with causal mechanisms in some immaterial mind, but with the need for "natural reasoning procedures", as well as modes of comprehension and heuristic strategies.[5] The approach which he and his colleagues proposed requires this: which reasoning procedures are "natural" is a matter to be determined empirically rather than something to be dictated externally by logicians proceeding entirely a priori. The psychological studies they considered pertinent are not neurological, but proceed by observation of the ways in which subjects tend to approach the solution of different kinds of reasoning problem and these subjects' readiness or unreadiness to reason in various ways. In such studies it is not imagined or assumed that the propensity of subjects to reason in this or that way is unconnected with the validity of the reasoning procedures concerned or with how evident this validity is, but whether reasoning procedures to be described as "natural" are taken to be a matter of empirical inquiry rather than of conformity with the norms of logic. The word "mechanism" connotes "innately based way of proceeding", rather than any particular account of the roots of the innateness of the reasoning procedures, modes of comprehension, and heuristic strategies observed. The word "mechanism" is therefore misleading inasmuch as the studies concerned are in no way occupied with evidence as to whether these roots lie in neurology or in perception of the truth-tending character of such ways of proceeding. The use of the word "mechanism" leaves what kind of explanation is appropriate quite open.

5. Martin D. S. Braine and David O'Brien, eds., *Mental Logic* (Hillsdale, N.J.: Erlbaum, 1998); see esp. chap. 4, "How to Investigate Mental Logic and the Syntax of Thought", and chap. 7, "Evidence for the Theory: Predicting the Difficulty of Propositional Logic Inference Problems".

Section 2. The Informality of the Concept of Rule

Chapter II showed it to be the norm for rules to be understood in an open and informal way so that they require interpretation or understanding in application, and rare for them to be applied mechanically in practice or for this to be required in principle. And chapter II exhibited the impasse which would quickly arise if one were to insist on a wooden use of the lexicon in which every extension in the use of a word had to be accounted for according to mechanically applicable rules, a frequent requirement of philosophers, linguists, or "cognitive scientists".

Thus linguistic rules are not in general applicable in an "effectively calculable" or "mechanical" way.

Dummett provides the most plausible argument that "effective" rules are indispensable to mutual understanding and reasoning:[6]

> The fact that anyone who has a mastery of any given language is able to understand an infinity of sentences of that language, an infinity which is, of course, principally composed of sentences which he has never heard before, is one emphasized not only by the modern school of linguists, headed by Chomsky, but by Wittgenstein himself; and this fact can hardly be explained otherwise than by supposing that each speaker has an implicit grasp of a number of general principles governing the use in sentences of words of the language. If, then, there exist such general principles of which every speaker has an implicit grasp, and which serve to confer on the words of the language their various meanings, it is hard to see how there can be any theoretical obstacle to making those principles explicit; and an explicit statement of those principles an implicit grasp of which constitutes the mastery of the language would be, precisely, a complete theory of meaning for the language.[7]

For the implicit grasp of these principles to be required for a speaker to use the language meaningfully in communication would seem to require effective methods of applying them, and this appears to be how Dummett thinks. Thus he tells us:

> On a platonistic interpretation of a mathematical theory, the central notion is that of truth: a grasp of the meaning of a sentence belonging to the language of the theory consists in a knowledge of what it is for that sentence to be true. Since, in general, the sentences of the language will not be ones whose

6. Dummett's presentation has a less technical style and more general appeal than Davidson's more recondite argument that a theory of meaning be finitely axiomatizable and that each sentence should deliver a theorem stating the circumstances in which the sentence would be true in a way reflecting its semantic structure.

7. Dummett, "Can Analytical Philosophy Be Systematic, and Ought It to Be?" no. 25, in *Truth and Other Enigmas*, 451.

> truth-value we are capable of effectively deciding, the condition for the truth of such a sentence will be one which we are not, in general, capable of recognizing as obtaining whenever it obtains, or of getting ourselves into a position in which we can so recognize it. Nevertheless, on the theory of meaning which underlies platonism, an individual's grasp of the meaning of such a sentence consists in his knowledge of what the condition is which has to obtain for the sentence to be true, even though the condition is one which he cannot, in general, recognize as obtaining when it does obtain.
>
> This conception violates the principle that use exhaustively determines meaning; or at least, if it does not, a strong case can be put up that it does.[8]

But what sort of rules or "principles"? If there are to be rules for "effectively" deciding a question, in what sense are they required to be "effective"?

It is evident that the word "rule" has many uses in human life, and similar concepts, such as law, procedure, and method, among others, are understood so as to need interpretation, or in Kantian phraseology "judgment", in application. Thus for a part of statute law, and not only parts of common law in England and other parts of the world where common law still exists, and in all parts of the world where codified law exists, one finds a need for interpretation by jury, by judges, or by administrative authority, whether minister or tribunal, to decide certain sorts of case, which will still be regarded as according to rule.

In accord with this "informality", Wittgenstein understands the word "rule" as used in regard to the use of words in language as having the same openness, involving the same type of need for interpretation or determination whenever some new class of instances comes into view, without its being an entirely new rule or quite different rule that is involved, rather than the same rule. And Ryle, in making his distinction between habits drilled into us and skills in which we are trained, understands the latter as fulfilled in a variety of ways not coverable by any mechanically applicable rule. Charles Taylor in his book *The Explanation of Behaviour* shows that most of the concepts associated with categorization required for the use of words such as "see", "recognize", and such, even in regard to animals lower than man, likewise lack any operative mechanically applicable definition.

There is a temptation to revert to the position taken up by Wittgenstein in the *Tractatus* according to which certain terms, when introduced, should be introduced according to a law determining all their possible combinations with other terms. This was Frege's position in his objecting to the more informal procedures of earlier mathematicians such as Peano.[9]

8. Dummett, "Philosophical Basis of Intuitionistic Logic", 223–24.

9. Frege, *Grundgesetze der Arithmetik*, vol. 2 (1903), sec. 58, in Frege's footnote; trans. in *Translations from the Philosophical Writings of Gottlob Frege*, ed. Peter Thomas Geach and Max Black (Oxford: Blackwell, 1952), 160–61.

Yet if we require that language accord with rules on whose correct application we can "effectively" check, as this word is commonly understood by mathematicians, then the concepts of "proof", "truth", "definition", "exists", and a multiplicity of others escape us. This leaves us two alternatives.

On the one hand we can insist on keeping a narrow notion of rule (bound to a mechanically applicable decision procedure) and say that the understanding operates in a way not determined by rules—for instance, that linguistic activity is "orderly", but not rule-governed[10]—and dismiss any idea of rules as known "tacitly" or "implicitly" as "mystical".[11] Or we can use the word "rule" in a wider sense and say that the understanding operates in accord with rules, but not rules for which there is an effective decision procedure as to whether they are being conformed to or not, for any checking procedure requires the understanding, supposed to accord with the rules, to be *used* in the very act of applying them. A procedure of this latter kind will be "effective" for the purposes of speakers or hearers with the understanding concerned— "effective" in an epistemological sense, but not in the sense of being mechanically applicable.

My approach will be along the latter lines. The ideas of "rule" and "operating in a way which accords with a rule" neither imply conscious guidance by the rule concerned nor being caused to conform to it. Rather, these concepts are quite open, offering no ready excuse for rejecting the idea that operating in ways which accord with rules is essential to linguistic activity. As chapter II expressed it, the term "rule" is a polymorphous concept used according to intrinsic analogy (the analogy or similarity between its different applications being closer than in "family-resemblance").[12]

In brief, in using language it is the norm for the rules, criteria, or definitions according to which we operate to be statable only by using concepts which are informal in the sense that understanding has to be used in order to apply them; following mechanical rules in applying them would involve losing full generality or else inconsistency.

The most deeply rooted objection to explaining our use of language in terms of "understanding" was first mentioned in chapter I: the objection that this idea erects "understanding" into a mysterious inner power on whose operations there is no check, appeal to which could therefore be invoked to explain anything, and empty like Molière's explanation of sleep in terms of "dormitive power". However, such objection, besides ignoring well-established ways of as-

10. Cf. Hubert Dreyfus, *What Computers Still Can't Do* (Cambridge, Mass.: MIT Press, 1979); revision of *What Computers Can't Do* (New York: Harper and Row, 1972).

11. Chomsky, *New Horizons*, 76; cf. Baker and Hacker, *Language, Sense and Nonsense* (Oxford: Blackwell, 1984), 289, 295–96, 339–45.

12. Cf. my discussion of transgeneric and polymorphous concepts in David Braine, *The Reality of Time and the Existence of God*, 72–76.

sessing and discriminating meanings, depends on the false presumption that there is no third way between introspectionist and behaviorist conceptions of understanding, the introspectionist conception making it uncheckable. But there is a third way, involving the inseparability of the mental and the behavioral, allowing the intuitive to be checked, a third way I describe in *The Human Person* and again in chapter VIII. In any case, both introspectionism and behaviorism have been amply shown to be incoherent, so some third way is absolutely required.

Accordingly we need have no fear when we insist on the indispensability of understanding in the application of linguistic rules. Accord with the rules is not uncheckable, even though checking it involves the use of understanding.[13]

But this type of objection appears in forms not met in earlier chapters, presented in terms of such concepts as "effectiveness" and "mechanical procedure" lying in the overlap between philosophy and mathematics. These two concepts now need examination. The apparently high-minded logical stance of Frege and the early Wittgenstein, insisting upon a type of rigor that they attribute to mathematics, requires us to decide them in terms of logical and mathematical proof theory. There it appears that just as the developments in modern physics have undermined the basis for the attractiveness of the materialistic metaphysics to which many biologists and psychologists adhere in thinking about the brain and its role in human functioning, so developments within logic and mathematics have themselves undermined the assumptions about such concepts as rule, law, and method of proof upon which many linguists and philosophers rely in their arguments. At the same time we find that working mathematicians set less value on proceeding mechanically than these linguists and philosophers.

Section 3. The Unformalizability of Natural Language and the Informality of Its Concepts

(a) *Coherent thought requires the unrestricted application of the most general concepts*

Let us review the most obvious ways in which the informality of the conception of rule has appeared during the course of the history of logic in the last century.

In the first place, the struggle to escape from the logical paradoxes estab-

13. Quine in 1936 provided an instance of this when he showed that we cannot apply logical laws without relying upon at least one of them (*modus ponens*) requiring us to use our understanding, in "Truth by Convention", reprinted in *The Ways of Paradox and Other Essays*, 2nd ed. (Cambridge, Mass.: Harvard University Press, 1976).

lished at least this: that the word "thing", the term "exists", and the term "set", if used in complete generality, cannot be used as if all the common laws of logic applied to the resulting statements without a formal contradiction following, in which the same thing is both asserted and denied in the very same sense. There is no simple way out.

For instance, one cannot sensibly deny the statement "A set is a set", which makes a universal generalization about all sets; one, therefore, cannot outlaw all universal generalizations about sets. Again, one cannot sensibly deny that to say, "Two sets and another two distinct sets constitute four sets", is an application of the law that "Two things and two distinct things constitute four things". That is, it is impossible to restrict the types of things which we count, and also impossible to exclude sets from counting as "things".

Again, there are three types of use of the word "exist" of concern to formal logic, one expressing the non-emptiness of some domain of discourse presupposed whenever quantified statements are made, another expressed by the existential quantifier, and a third expressing the existence of an individual subject presupposed by any singular statement about that subject. However, one cannot refuse the application of any of them in any area: for instance, one can say with truth, "There exists a natural number greater than 4 and less than 6, namely the number 5". Hence, it is incorrect for Geach to conclude that singular existential propositions arise only in connection with the concrete and assert actuality. Also, many intuitively acceptable examples of negative and conditional statements involve type-crossing. Therefore, we find that there are no exceptionless rules or laws by means of which we can avoid these logical paradoxes without arbitrarily outlawing some quite proper and true statements from within ordinary discourse. Thus we have to deal with paradoxes as they arise and diagnose their causes by informal reasoning, drawing upon our understanding of the concepts involved.

In the second place, as we saw, Tarski demonstrated that no formalized language—that is, for our purposes, no language governed by effectively determining rules (rules which might be dubbed mechanically applicable)—can contain an unrestricted concept of truth without contradiction resulting. Yet any natural language, including the language within which a proof such as Tarski's is set out, and any theory of language and meta-language devised to avoid contradiction, must use or presuppose a notion of truth which is not restricted in this way. Likewise the theory of types, devised to avoid logical paradoxes in regard to the notions of "thing" and "set", cannot be stated without violating the restrictions it sets up.[14]

14. Hence Ramsey proposed to resort to the theory that a language cannot include its own metalanguage to avoid the semantic paradoxes—and also avoiding Russell's ramified theory of types. He also saw the simple theory of types as sufficient for avoiding the logical paradoxes.

In the third place, in 1932, as mentioned earlier, Gödel established that, given any list of axioms or methods of proof in arithmetic such that it was effectively ("mechanically", according to his later position) determinable whether or not something was such an axiom or such a method of proof, whether the method of proof available had been conformed to or not, there would be other things capable of being shown by argument, but only by argument not conforming to these rules and restrictions. This implies that by reflection upon the whole set of these rules of this mechanically applicable type, further truths within natural arithmetic follow and further methods of proof in such arithmetic are justified—methods which go beyond anything formally legitimated in the originally given formalized system for generating such methods and truths.[15] If one supposed that the given formalization gave a complete system for natural arithmetic (the arithmetic which has to do with the natural numbers, including general statements such as "a + b = b + a" as well as singular statements like "2 + 2 = 4"), it would be an inconsistent system, and natural arithmetic would be itself inconsistent or self-contradictory. But in the view of Lucas, Penrose, and others, human beings have a conception of natural number adequate for us to have certain knowledge that natural arithmetic is consistent, and therefore these further truths and the validity of these further methods of proof can be taken as demonstrated. And in their view this establishes that in respect to demonstrations in natural arithmetic, human beings have a power which outstrips any computer—that is, it outstrips any mathematically mechanical device, "mathematically mechanical" in the sense explained in section 4.

Putnam and others have questioned whether such argument counts as a demonstration, since no method of establishing that this natural arithmetic is consistent has been supplied. Human beings in Putnam's implausible conception are in no better position to know the consistency of arithmetic than the computer. I will consider this argument later.

15. To set thinking on, e.g., constructive ordinals into axiomatic form with certain rules of inference, is hardly to render that previous thinking "mechanical" (I owe this thought to Professor Angus MacIntyre). A. M. Turing in "Systems of Logic Based on Ordinals", *London Mathematical Society* 45 (1939): 161–228, in regard to Church-Kleene (C-K) formulae regarded himself as having reduced the need for "ingenuity", but at the expense of increasing the role of "intuition", presumably intuition as to whether or not this or that is a C-K ordinal formula. Yet, heuristically, if the desire is not just to derive new things, but to demonstrate them, the need of intuition is as severe an obstacle to a "mechanical discovery procedure" as the need for ingenuity.

When Kreisel takes it that if one is prepared to rely upon a system in order to establish new things, one ought to be prepared to assume the system's consistency, he is obviously treating "systems", not in a formalist way as objects within which derivations proceed indifferently to questions of the truth under some interpretation of the axioms, but as formalizations of systems presumed true under the interpretation which is deemed "natural" (and whose bases are therefore presumed evident under this interpretation). And the supposed formalist would have no reason to regard "inconsistency" as vicious unless he had interpreted some operator as "not" and another as "and", these operators being applicable only to candidates for being true or false. That is, his interest in finitist *derivation* is a disguised interest in finitist *demonstration*.

"Finitist" thinking cannot be "mechanical" if it includes, e.g., the "intuitive" selection of ordinal formulae or any other nonroutine means of selecting or identifying axioms.

Fourth, at a later date it was established that if one defines an algorithm as a mechanically applicable method for determining whether problems of a certain kind are decidable as to whether they are true or false, then, at least in respect of methods of proof dealing with the natural numbers (i.e., positive whole numbers), there is no algorithm for determining whether or not something is an algorithm.[16] For the fourth time one had been forced within the field of logic and of the mathematical development of logic and proof theory to surrender the notion that the type of rigor achievable in mathematics is one which involves that all instances of proof or demonstration be subject to some mechanically applicable test as to whether they conform to some previously given set of formalizable, mechanically applicable rules or not.[17]

Thus we are in the situation in which, to man's surprise, it is demonstrable in the strictest possible sense available—that is, that sense represented in informal mathematical reasoning—that the concepts of "exists", "set", "proof", "truth", and "method of proof", among others, are used by the human mind, even within the field of mathematical questions itself, in a way in which no machine could be constructed to use them without needing ever-repeated further programming. That is, to the surprise of some, mathematics has confirmed what has been evident to common sense and experience and recognized by other philosophers earlier—namely, that the correct and disciplined use of some of the most general human concepts or terms used in discourse guided by the exercise of understanding does not depend on its accord with some mechanically applicable rule.

The rules governing our use of concepts are strict enough. There is nothing indeterminate about the truth of a proposition which an argument of Gödel's type shows to be demonstrable, but not provable within the given axiomatization of arithmetic—not unless one is willing (wrongly) to concede that the arithmetic of the natural numbers might be inconsistent. And in the case of the less general concepts considered later, it is not that indeterminacy arises when a speaker in a novel situation makes a novel use of a familiar word; in the usual case the speaker has the right to expect the hearer to understand him.

The situation is close to the one portrayed by Dummett.[18] In effect, in each area of study, given an initial set of methods of proof or argument, we are forced on reflection to accept other, further methods of proof or argument so

16. See Martin Davis, *Computability and Unsolvability* (New York: McGraw-Hill, 1958), xv–xviii.

17. One may note that even the notion of effective calculability, if extended to the finitary, has obscurities, some of which have been explored by Georg Kreisel, "Hilbert's Programme," in *Philosophy of Mathematics: Selected Readings*, ed. Paul Benacerraf and Hilary Putnam, 2nd ed. (Cambridge: Cambridge University Press, 1983), 207–38; first published 1958.

18. Dummett, "The Philosophical Significance of Gödel's Theorem", no. 12, in *Truth and Other Enigmas*, 200–201.

that we have a branching tree of ever more powerful sets of method of proof or argument, many of whose branches are unending. Such sets constitute a spread in something like the mathematical intuitionists' sense.

(b) *The most general of the terms we apply to concrete subject-matters have a parallel informality*

We must see the unformalizability and lack of mechanical calculability in application of these most general concepts not as an isolated phenomenon which arises solely with them because of their peculiar generality, associated with their "formal" character, but as something shared by all the more structural concepts in human discourse. The peculiarity of these concepts in this connection is only that, because of their "formality", formal proof of this unformalizability and of the lack of effectively applicable criteria of application is possible.

And we must see this "openness", or lack of mechanically applicable definition, associated with all the more structural concepts as what underlies the "openness" of many other concepts.

Let us consider these more structural concepts first. We have already considered both the formal concept "exists" (meaning "exists as a logical subject within the domain of discourse about which generalization is being made", i.e., the existence implied whenever a singular term is used in such a way as to presuppose that it has reference) and the existence implied by existential quantifiers (i.e., by expressions such as "There exists at least one F", "There exists just one F", "There exist just two Fs", and so forth). I explain the impossibility of encapsulating the notion of natural number in a definition in section 3 (b).

Since truth is one of those most formal concepts which we have considered, and it appears that truth is in some way the goal and good of the intellect, the thing sought after in any inquiry, it becomes natural to anticipate that the word "good" will be another term of this kind of openness. This dovetails with the view of those moral philosophers who say that, although there may be a criterion for when a party should be counted as a good party, a friend be counted as a good friend, a farmer as a good farmer, and so forth, there is no general criterion governing what counts as good in general—no one way of being related back to a role in human life and laws of human behavior or to anything of a more general bearing.

Having gotten so far, it seems absurd to be reluctant to accept the conclusions that there may be the same type of informality or spread in the use of the other words we discussed in chapters I and II, the word "know" having an even greater informality than the terms "true" and "prove" (terms applying to propositional knowledge, sensory knowledge, and to the many levels of knowledge of particular languages, of persons, and of particular emotions), along with the term "living" (some living creatures have a kind of life involving the capacity to know, but their different forms of life involve different forms of knowledge).

"Cause", "act", "person", and many other terms likewise have a large spread whereby they are used nonmetaphorically—that is, properly or literally in regard to many different kinds of agent as well as to many different types of situation, without all these situations conforming to one single mechanically identifiable pattern.[19]

In this way we can understand the flexibility observed by Austin in our use of perceptual verbs, exemplified in our capacity to deal with new situations using perceptual verbs such as "see", whose first use is surely in regard to public, touchable material objects, but which has a wide spread of other uses intelligible to hearers, although they refer to types of situation quite new both to speaker and to hearer, a spread of uses extending to the so-called metaphorical uses in regard to intellectual objects. In chapter I we saw how Jackendoff's explanation of this spread of uses takes account of the extent of the variation involved, but offers no likelihood of a mechanically applicable rule governing the word's use, since his explanation involves a term such as "awareness" whose uses are even less subject to rule. The thinkers who reckon on the adequacy of mechanical procedures (usually thought of as nonconscious) do not allow for dealing with generically new situations, but only with situations of generically the same kind, such as being a man or being shaved, whereas what is required is the capacity to deal with situations that are generically new—a capacity in virtue of which a hearer or reader understands a speaker or writer's account of the situation without fresh explanation of the terms used to give this account. Nor do these thinkers allow for the further flexibility in the use of any given word when we raise new questions or find fresh methods of approach in answering them, sometimes opening out new paradigms or "models" in explaining new phenomena, matters spoken of in chapters III and IV. Not even Jackendoff's Preference Rules System can achieve the task of taking the explanation of meaning of each particular word in each particular discourse-significance back to primitives in a way governed by mechanically applicable rule as required by the compositionalist model for extension in the use of particular words.[20] As remarked early in this chapter, the understanding

19. David Braine, *Human Person*, 131–50, 173–74, 533–34, 538–40.

20. It is Jackendoff who has done most to show how, by extending his Preference Rules System, such a task might be achieved; cf. sec. 5 (a) to follow and n. 55 in this chapter. But in *Foundations*, 377, even Jackendoff has begun to show traces of despair in following this approach. And Daniel Dennett's concession in his discussion of the supposed situation of a brain in a vat allows that, whether or not the variety in the possible situations which may challenge our powers of description be infinite, the quantity of information it

of the *langue*-meaning of words (i.e., at the level of language-possession) has to be such as to ground the understanding of the same word in the same node of meaning, but in many senses or discourse-significances—limits being set by critical understanding where mechanical rule is impotent, reflection capable of being brought into play where mechanical rule is helpless.

It was in the introduction that we first met the unrealistic explanation of the "infinite use of finite resources" in language in terms of the generativeness described in Chomskyan grammar and the iterability of certain syntactic operations and sundry logical operators. We found the real root of this infinity instead in the informality and flexibility in word-use typical of natural language, instanced in metaphor, but appearing universally in the structural role of the most general concepts in relation to the rest of human speech, writing, and inquiry—these terms being each demonstrably incapable of being used according to a single set of mechanically applicable set of rules governing their behavior in all contexts.

As I remarked in chapter II, the phenomenon of metaphor is in most cases parasitic upon our capacity to use these general and more structural terms, in that it draws on some kind of similarity that falls within the ambit of some more general term. I have therefore refused to make metaphor the primary starting point of my argument in respect of the flexibility of human discourse. Metaphor, in any case, like every human use of language, depends on the human capacity to use the most general terms, the expression of some of which originates in metaphors which have become dead. The capacity for the use of these general terms is always there even when they are not explicit, since the understanding they make explicit can always be shown to be presupposed if we reflect upon our presuppositions.

The understanding of these general concepts is expressed in some languages through some syntactic feature such as the inflection of a noun or verb or by some feature of word order or intonation, while in other languages by a preposition, auxiliary, or combination of auxiliaries, often assisted by ancillary words such as articles or the copula. But whatever the way it shows itself (to what extent lexically, grammatically, or by context and intonation), such understanding of the most general concepts is always involved in the exercise of any less general concept whatsoever, however specific. And it is just this understanding which it is most systematically impossible to formalize or regard as mechanically rule-bound. Accordingly, it is not just true, but necessarily true, that the understanding expressed when a word is used is not formalizably reconstructed from the rules of some lexicon, but recognized in the very act of the speaker

would be necessary to feed into a computer to allow for this variety to be coped with according to rule would be of an order vastly too large for any practically conceivable computer to simulate; Dennett, *Consciousness Explained*, 3–7.

and the hearer exercising their shared skill or understanding in speech and the hearing of speech because of these presupposed general concepts.

Our informality in the use of words only arises because of the freedoms given by the character of their complex situation as arising within utterances constituted of terms of different categories and functions, these features established in the act of utterance, which gains its sense or discourse-significance only in its context. Part three fills out the picture presented in chapter III.

Section 4. The Concept of Effectiveness and the Place of Mechanical Procedures in Mathematics

(a) *The concept of effectiveness*

Both Dummett and Crispin Wright after him require that the meaning of a sentence should not outrun its "effectively" calculable consequences. For, as we saw in section 2, Dummett wants a theory of meaning to allow the "effective" determination of the meaning of a sentence from the "use" of its components (here including everything relevant to such determination, e.g., order of parts, intonation, and context of utterance).

However, the plausibility of this kind of argument depends on the word "effective" being understood informally in an epistemological sense, such as would extend to any application of rules involving the use of understanding, albeit in a public hearer/reader recognizable way.

When one thinks of rules being applied with understanding, one need not mean "with ingenuity". Consider the logical law *modus ponens*—that "If P, then Q" and "P" together imply "Q". If I apply *modus ponens* I do not need, in order to check my application, to utilize an understanding of "P" and "Q" beyond recognizing "P" to be understood in the same sense in its two occurrences, and similarly with "Q"; but I would be expected to be exercising understanding of the expression "If . . . , then —", of truth, and of implication—especially since, historically, logical laws are applied long before being formulated.[21]

Again, if perception is thought to provide an "effective" means of determining something, "effectiveness" is being understood in an epistemological sense. One's intuitive notion of an effective way of knowing things of a certain kind does not consist in the possession of a mechanical checking procedure.[22] To tie having an effective way of knowing things to having a mechanical pro-

21. Cf. Quine, "Truth by Convention".

22. The situation is exactly the reverse of the case with continuity, where the common mathematical definition seems initially exactly to capture the intuitive notion—until the paradoxical counter-examples appear.

cedure for deciding them seems to embody a certain kind of behaviorism or operationalism.

Thus the logician Church's notion of effectiveness is not this natural epistemological one. True, in Church's explanations he seems to be thinking along much the same lines as Dummett. Thus he proceeds:

> We have assumed the reader's understanding of the general notion of effectiveness, and indeed it must be considered as an informally familiar mathematical notion, since it is involved in mathematical problems of a frequently occurring kind, namely, problems to find a method of computation, i.e., a method by which to determine a number, or other thing, effectively. . . .
>
> The requirements of effectiveness are (of course) not meant in the sense that a structure which is analogous to a logistic system except that it fails to satisfy these requirements may not be useful for some purposes or that it is forbidden to consider such—but only that a structure of this kind is unsuitable for use or interpretation as a language. For, however indefinite or imprecisely fixed the common idea of a language may be, it is at least fundamental to it that a language shall serve the purpose of communication. And to the extent that requirements of effectiveness fail, the purpose of communication is defeated.[23]

And in Church's approach the things which he names as required for effectiveness are precisely those which would be named by Hilbert and his formalist followers as required for absolute rigor in mathematical proof. Thus he goes on:

> Consider, in particular, the situation which arises if the definition of well-formedness is non-effective. There is then no certain means by which, when an alleged expression of the language is uttered (spoken or written), say as an asserted sentence, the auditor (hearer or reader) may determine whether it is well-formed, and thus whether any actual assertion has been made. Therefore the auditor may fairly demand a proof that the utterance is well-formed, and until such proof is provided may refuse to treat it as constituting an assertion. This proof, which must be added to the original utterance in order to establish its status, ought to be regarded, it seems, as part of the utterance, and the definition of well-formedness ought to be modified to provide this, or its equivalent. When such modification is made, no doubt the non-effectiveness of the definition will disappear; otherwise it would be open to the auditor to make further demand for proof of well-formedness.
>
> Again, consider the situation which arises if the notion of a proof is non-effective. There is then no certain means by which, when a sequence of formulas has been put forward as a proof, the auditor may determine whether it is in fact a proof. Therefore he may fairly demand a proof, in any given case, that the sequence of formulas put forward is a proof; and until this supplementary

23. Church, *Introduction to Mathematical Logic*, 52.

> proof is provided, he may refuse to be convinced that the alleged theorem is proved. This supplementary proof ought to be regarded, it seems, as part of the whole proof of the theorem, and the primitive basis of the logistic system ought to be so modified as to provide this, or its equivalent. Indeed it is essential to the idea of a proof that, to anyone who admits the presuppositions on which it is based, a proof carries final conviction. And the requirements of effectiveness (I)–(IV) may be thought of as intended just to preserve this essential characteristic of proof.[24]

Here I must mention certain technicalities. Within mathematics the problem of finding an effective method for proving formulae of a given kind appears to be equivalent to the problem of finding an effective method for computing which number is the value of a certain function. Therefore questions about effective methods of proof are commonly posed in terms of questions about effective methods of computing the values of functions. Church first posed his thesis in 1934 in the form of a conjecture that every effectively computable function was recursive, and in 1939 Turing showed that this requirement was equivalent to the requirement that it be computable by a Turing machine, and in this adapted form Gödel accepted Church's thesis as intuitively acceptable.[25] It is in this form—that to be effectively computable is to be mechanically computable, so that for procedures of proof or for decision to be effective is for them to be mechanically applicable—that "Church's thesis" is commonly stated.

The discussion of "effectiveness" has been plagued by certain key ambiguities.

Three notions need distinguishing: (a) that of a method describable in informal terms which counts as effective, despite being described only informally, an informality which does not require different cases to be brought under one formal rule; (b) that of a method which can be formalized; and (c) that of a mechanically simulable method.

Church's thesis seems to say that (b) is captured by (c), and he seems to ignore (a).

Yet (a) is of vital importance in nonmathematical contexts, not only the obvious cases of perceptual judgments and those arising in legal and historical disputes, but also those characteristic of fundamental decisions in physics. It has been traditional in choosing paradigms of explanation to mix a priori and empirical considerations.

In Aristotle this is conspicuous in the mixture of utterly different types of

24. Church, *Introduction to Mathematical Logic*, 52–53. The requirements of effectiveness (I)–(IV) are those he laid down in 50–51.

25. I here recapitulate Solomon Feferman's presentation in "Kurt Gödel: Conviction and Caution", in *Gödel's Theorem in Focus*, ed. S. G. Shanker (London: Croom Helm, 1988), 110–11.

factor brought to bear in considering continuity: the possibility of an absolute vacuum; whether an atomist can explain the difference between supposedly homogeneous liquids or alloys such as sea water, whisky, and bronze, and colloids and cases of visibly distinguishable particles suspended in liquid; and whether the Earth is round.

The whole theory of fields, electrical, magnetic, and gravitational, arose from Michael Faraday's a priori conviction that nothing could act where it was absent, so that for an electrically charged object in one location to attract or repel an electrically charged object at another location could only happen by the establishment of some field of force established by the first, a field of force in virtue of which other electrically charged things in the area of the field might be acted upon.

Again it is clear that Einstein was influenced more by a priori than by experimental evidence: for instance, the start of the thinking which led him to the special theory of relativity lay in a sense of the inelegance of supposing it made a difference whether one moved a wire with a current relative to a magnet or vice versa, so that, although he learnt of the Michelson-Morley experiment accidentally in reading the works of the physicist Lorentz, this played little part in his development of special relativity theory (1905), but only in other people's accepting it.[26]

Ironically, informal considerations are also vital within mathematics itself, not only in discussing the philosophically most obvious question as to whether there is a method for producing Gödelian formulae (the sort which are supposedly "true, but not derivable-within-the-system-under-consideration"), but also in considering the normal practice of research mathematicians—namely, to seek proofs which of course have to be finitary if human statement and grasp are to make their conclusions certain, but do not have to conform to any previously given mechanically applicable restrictions.

In any case, as mentioned earlier, there is no algorithm for deciding whether something is an algorithm or not. Yet it would seem essential to the usefulness of the idea of an algorithm as a method of deciding certain questions that it be recognizable in this or that case that such and such algorithm will suffice, and this will typically be mediated or critically assessed by informal reasoning of various kinds.

Epistemological effectiveness sets much stronger requirements than Church provides for. Church's criteria only establish whether or not a derivation is in accord with the rules of a particular system and whether or not the system is such that its fitness could be *decided according to a mechanical procedure*. They could not possibly serve to establish whether or not some-

26. Cf. Polanyi, *Personal Knowledge*, 10–11n2.

thing was *effectively demonstrated,* because demonstration requires, first, truth and evidentness in premises and axioms, and, second, evident validity in rules of inference. Moreover, since it is known that valid axioms and/or rules of inference are non-enumerable, so that any detailed criteria of validity will be too restrictive, there will evidently be other things known with certainty to be valid which, taken as axioms or rules of inference, would provide effective demonstration, but no enumerable totality of such things (either these things do not constitute a totality or we should say that such a totality is not enumerable). In sum, there will be other demonstrative or effective proofs not captured by these requirements.

Both the notion of finitary proof studied by Georg Kreisel and the intuitionist notion of constructive proof are fairly exact.[27] Each stage of the finitary proofs in either case would be formalizable in that it has been shown how the constructive proofs proposed by intuitionist mathematicians can be formalized, even though this is not envisaged in intuitionism. Both notions are of far wider extension than any notion of mechanical proof.

(b) *Comparing the powers of the human understanding with those of computers*

We saw earlier that there are many different lines of argument, each sufficient to show that methods of showing things to be true (the underlying meaning of "demonstrating" or "proving") cannot be captured by any set of mechanically applicable rules. In this way the concept of proof outruns any possibility of formalization.

Moreover, to formalize a proof is not to make it a proof, so that even if retrospectively one can describe a formal system in which a proposition appears as a theorem derivable from certain axioms, the formalization of the proof does not make it demonstrative.

It is instructive to see what makes the principles of proofs in different areas intuitively necessary. For instance, the background of the necessity of the axiom that every natural number has a successor seems to be that we can "see" that given a set with a given number, *n*, of members, there could in principle be a set with $n + 1$ members. Again, consider mathematical induction. Here again, considering some particular case, we can "see" that if 1 has a property, and if for any natural number (i.e. positive integer) *n*, *n* has the property, then $n + 1$ has the property, and we will be able to reason that since 1 has the property, so

27. Kreisel, "Hilbert's Programme"; cf. A. Heyting, "The Intuitionist Foundations of Mathematics"; L. E. J. Brouwer, "Intuitionism and Formalism", trans. Arnold Dresden; and Brouwer, "Consciousness, Philosophy and Mathematics", all reprinted in *Philosophy of Mathematics,* ed. Benacerraf and Putnam; see also Heyting, *Intuitionism.*

does 2, and therefore so does 3, and so on unendingly, each time proceeding to the immediate successor; and we can "see" that this will apply in the case of any "definite" property, justifying our holding the principle of mathematical induction at least for "definite" properties—a property being "definite" for this purpose if it is intuitively clear that it will either apply or not apply in enumerable cases. In this way mathematical induction over the natural numbers is confirmed by what William Kneale called "intuitive induction".[28]

I insert the restriction to "definite" properties because intuition is less bold than naive set theory supposes. For instance, if the property is "describable in less than thirteen words of English", it is not intuitively clear that it is a definite question in regard to each number whether it is thus describable or not, because it is not clear what will count as a description for the purpose, conspicuously whether "the least number not describable in less than thirteen words of English" would count as a description of a number. We often meet arguments to the effect that if human beings think, then they must think according to procedures, and that if these are sufficiently powerful, then the human being will be led into contradictions, but these arguments always depend on supposing that if human beings think methodically, they will always follow certain rules woodenly. But human beings, unlike machines, are not limited to following procedures woodenly.[29]

The debate as to how the human mind is comparable to any conceivable computer has commonly centered on a comparison between, on the one hand, the conceptual capacity required for various kinds of proof possessed by human beings and, on the other hand, the capacities for derivation possessed by systems or networks (finite "machines") limited to following a set of mechanical procedures fixed for the machine concerned. And the problem is often posed in terms of their capacity to decide questions in natural arithmetic. This is because of the discoveries made by Gödel, referred to earlier and summarized by Gentzen, who did not doubt the consistency of arithmetic, in these terms: "We can paraphrase it by saying that for number theory no once-and-for-all sufficient system of forms of inference can be specified, but that on the contrary, new theorems can always be found whose proof requires a new form of inference", an incompleteness which did not surprise him, although he did not expect Gödel's procedure for producing new axioms itself to be fruitful of much of interest.[30]

28. William Kneale, *Probability and Induction* (Oxford: Oxford University Press, 1949), 30–37.

29. E.g., in G. L. Bowie, "Lucas' Number Is Finally Up", *Journal of Philosophical Logic* 11 (1982): 279–85, Bowie takes it that he can assume that Lucas followed some procedure in his Gödel-dependent arguments, and from this purports to show that Lucas's procedure will lead him to an inconsistent output. But he gives no reason for supposing that Lucas is following woodenly mechanical procedures.

30. Gentzen, *Collected Papers*, 240.

As Nagel and Newman put it in 1958, Gödel's work reminded us that just as it had been proved that the parallels postulate could not be derived from other Euclidean axioms, "a proof can be given of the impossibility of proving certain properties and propositions within a given system".[31] But they showed that Gödel's work was more far-reaching, inasmuch as "his theorem does indicate that the structure and power of the human mind are far more complex and subtle than any non-living machine yet envisaged",[32] and they said this at a time when it was already established that nothing can be derived by the mechanical application of mechanically applicable rules of derivation which cannot in principle be derived using a Turing machine. J. R. Lucas gave this argument, implicit in Nagel and Newman: that the human person's powers of proof in natural arithmetic in principle outstrip the powers of any computer, an explicit presentation as exact as its necessarily informal character allowed in 1961.[33]

Putnam and others have suggested the response that human beings have no more *knowledge* of the truth of the axioms of natural arithmetic and truth-preservingness of the laws of inference they rely upon in drawing conclusions from these axioms, and therefore no more knowledge of the consistency of arithmetic, than computers.[34] However, this suggestion seems as wrong-headed as Mill's idea that arithmetical truths are empirically based. I say this because the correspondence of the natural numbers to numerically definite quantifiers within predicate logic with identity gives the propositions of natural arithmetic the same kind of necessity as the laws of logic. In applying to every subject-matter, abstract or concrete, they are like the laws of logic, and have the same kind of necessity.[35] The necessity of Peano's axioms and other propositions of

31. Ernest Nagel and James R. Newman, *Gödel's Proof* (London: Routledge and Kegan Paul, 1959), 10.

32. Nagel and Newman, *Gödel's Proof*, 101–2.

33. John R. Lucas, "Mind, Machines and Gödel", *Philosophy* (1961): 112–27.

34. All Putnam's complaints (apart from those concerned with some later, readily rectified technical misstatements in Penrose) turn upon questioning our knowledge of the consistency of our own human procedures in natural arithmetic; see "Minds and Machines" of 1960, as reprinted in Putnam, *Mind, Language and Reality*, 366; and Putnam, review of Penrose's *Shadows of the Mind*, *Bulletin of the American Mathematics Society* 32 (1995): 370–73.

Putnam's arguments in 1995 reveal a suggestion that the human being might be getting its knowledge by reliance upon an internal cybernetic system enormously more complicated than it would be possible for human beings to survey or check, and of whose consistency the human being could have no better knowledge than a computer. Some discussion of this suggestion appears in Lucas, "The Gödelian Argument: Turn Over the Page", Oxford Computing Services personal web page, accessed October 18, 2012, http://users.ox.ac.uk/~jrlucas/Godel/turn.html. However, even if such an enormously more complicated internal cybernetic system were the *cause* of our being *sure* that our procedures in arithmetical reasoning were sound, it could not be the *grounds* of our *knowing* that they are so, and could not legitimate our saying that we can *see* the necessity of the principles concerned. Yet the legitimacy of this precisely characterizes these elementary axioms and rules of inference.

35. Their application is more general than laws concerning the real numbers, which appear to have application only to continua such as can be measured in ways which in some way involve measuring lengths.

natural arithmetic does not depend on intuitions arising from within some particular subject-matter, by contrast with the axioms of Euclidean geometry which seem dependent on spatial intuition.

Moreover, every time we apply one of the propositions of natural arithmetic, whether singular, such as "2 + 3 = 3 + 2", or general, such as "a + b = b + a", we seem to see the necessity of the result, the application seeming to give us insight into why the thing, if true, must be necessarily so, seeing it by the same "intuitive" induction which made the unconditional truth and necessity of Peano's axioms self-evident—even the axiom of mathematical induction over the natural numbers. Gentzen's starting-point in offering his "proof" of the consistency of natural arithmetic lay in accepting Gödel's clear statement of the impossibility of proving the consistency of any formal theory which includes elementary number theory by means proper to this formal theory (given that the theory is really consistent), but this was far from making him doubt the a priori character of natural number theory.[36]

Benacerraf was, of course, right to argue that Lucas's argument relies upon some philosophical premise in that it presumes the legitimacy of using an unformalized notion of proof. He also points out that Lucas also presumes that the mind can legitimately assert its own consistency in presuming that it has knowledge when it accepts the axioms of arithmetic, including mathematical induction.[37] However, each of these presumptions appears entirely reasonable in the light of my earlier remarks that formalization adds nothing to demonstrativeness in a proof (except in assisting checking long proofs), and that Peano's axioms share the necessity and evidentness of logic.

At root the problem arises from the fact that human beings possess the concept of natural number (the positive whole numbers such as are used in counting) and that machines cannot simulate the possession of this concept. As we saw in chapter II, the natural numbers have the properties described in Peano's axioms as a set of things forming a series with a first member and

36. Thus, in his proof, Gentzen (*Collected Papers,* 132–86) cites Gödel's statement at the start (138–39; one may compare Gentzen's earlier remark, 115). He supposed that the same kind of intuitive induction which grounded mathematical induction over the natural numbers also grounded his reliance upon restricted transfinite induction up to the limit ε_0— that is, over all ordinals constructively definable in the way outlined in chap. II, although whether or not this proof should be regarded as itself constructive, let alone "finitary", is open to dispute (Gentzen, *Collected Papers,* 8–12), including a particularly clear statement from his 1936 Paris address (*Collected Papers,* 12, 26n64). Gentzen himself regarded his proof (improved on an earlier version, *Collected Papers,* 8) as in accord with Hilbert's finitist attitudes, and saw himself as relying upon his sharpened *Hauptsatz* (*Collected Papers,* 5–8, 81–115, 176–88), i.e., upon a method which had already proved itself in analogous forms in more elementary fields.

37. Benacerraf, "God, the Devil and Gödel", *The Monist* 51 (1967): 9–32. These two objections are all that can be drawn from his sec. 3, the location of his counter-arguments, although this is rather disguised by his rollicking style of presentation, throughout exuding a certain contempt for what he is attacking. His sec. 4 irrelevantly explores the supposition that the mind has powers *less* than a Turing machine and generates contradictions.

with every member having a unique successor, a series with the further feature that it conforms to the law of mathematical induction, so that if the first number has a certain property, and if the property is always inherited so that if a number has it then its successor has it, then every member of the series must have it. But Peano's axioms cannot provide even an implicit definition of natural number, since these axioms can be satisfied by the even numbers taken alone or by any finite sequence (the inadequacies of this monomorphic axiom-set cannot be remedied by polymorphic sets). Moreover, the application of these axioms has to be restricted to properties expressible by what I called "definite" predicates—although there cannot be any formal criterion of which predicates are thus "definite". If one attempts to restrict the principle by some set of formal criteria for deciding whether or not a predicate is thus "definite", we find that whatever finite set of criteria is proposed, Peano's set of axioms will then be satisfied not only by the natural numbers and sets of things of the same form, but also by what are called "non-standard models", which include items that do not correspond to anything reached by continuing unendingly one by one from the number 1. Gödel's demonstration that any such formalizable set of axioms will fail to prove everything which it is intuitively possible to prove within natural arithmetic is thus a mere symptom of this impossibility of giving the notion of "natural number" implicit definition in terms of formal axioms to which natural numbers conform.[38]

To Penrose and Lucas, as well as to Nagel and Newman, it always seemed evident that Gödel's incompleteness theorem exhibited that the human possession of the concept of natural number gives the human being residual powers to produce new kinds of proof, going beyond any given mechanically applicable definition of proof and, therefore, beyond any conceivable such definition.[39] The identification of particular tasks has been envisaged chiefly as an illustration of this and has left the conviction of human superiority in this particular respect, not in speed, but in conceptual capacity, intact and evident.

Of course, whenever a deficiency is discovered in a system for mechanical proof, the particular defect can be remedied by producing an appropriate new system, which would be the equivalent of producing a new machine in the attempt to simulate human capacity. Thus, as Kreisel points out, if we apply the nonformalizable rule of consistency whereby whenever, by reasoning outside a system, we can show that every proposition of the form "F(a)" is provable

38. Cf. Kneale and Kneale, *Development of Logic*, 387–88, 473–77.

39. This was evident to Roger Penrose since 1952–53: sec. 4.2 of "Beyond the Doubting of a Shadow", *Psyche* 2, no. 23 (1996), reproduced at http://psyche.cs.monash.edu.au/v2/psyche-2-23-penrose.html. It was evident to Lucas before he wrote his 1961 article, as he mentions in "Gödelian Argument" (see n. 34 of this chapter).

within the system (albeit not always in the same way), we can add "(∀x)(Fx)" as an axiom, marking that whenever using the Gödel procedure suggests a new axiom, we can simply move on to this enriched system. But the system for repeating this procedure unendingly is not itself formalizable.

If we consider Turing machines as mathematical entities and allow continuance through the transfinite ordinals, then the same problem will recur again and again unendingly through all the transfinite ordinals. Each time a new transfinite ordinal is properly identified ("named"), we could in principle produce a new machine, but however many new machines with richer capabilities we produce, there is no possibility of producing a single machine combining the capacities of all this endless series of ever-better machines.[40] No ingenuity enables us to get around this.[41]

The flaws in many of the lines of argument presented have been well advertised. Higginbotham's assessment is more moderate than those of Putnam or Benacerraf: "Lucas's original argument to this effect is notoriously suggestive but vague, and critical literature on it has often taken the form of making the argument more precise, and then showing that in the precise form envisaged it fails to prove the case".[42] However, there remains an extensive consensus among the academic community in regard to the two principal theses at stake—namely, first, that the concept of proof cannot be captured by any mechanically applicable set of criteria and indeed is indefinitely extensible in its application, and second, that the concept of natural number is a fertile source of such extensibility. The problem of describing the basis and character

40. The argument is well set forth in Lucas's discussion in the three paragraphs beginning "In this formulation we have essentially, a dialogue between the Mechanist and the Mentalist", in "Gödelian Argument".

41. If by ingenuity we produce what are called Church-Kleene formulae for describing successively later ordinal numbers, we produce each time an axiom giving successively greater powers to mechanical systems of proof to which it is added (see n. 15). But ingenuity is certainly required, since there is no algorithm for naming these transfinite ordinals (this is undisputed; cf. Lucas, "Gödelian Argument", n. 14), and such exercises of ingenuity in order to establish new axioms are not within the capacities of systems limited to operating according to mechanical procedures; cf. Feferman, sec. 3.11, final sentence of "Penrose's Gödelian Argument", *Psyche* 2, no. 7 (1995).

42. J. Higginbotham, "Penrose's Platonism", *Journal of Behavioral and Brain Sciences* 13, no. 4 (1990): 668.

This is much more accurate than Putnam's dismissive remark that "Roger Penrose is perhaps the only well-known present-day thinker to be convinced by Lucas's argument.... The fact that the experts all reject Lucas's infamous argument counts for nothing in Penrose's eyes. He mistakenly believes that he has a philosophical disagreement with the logical community when in fact this is a straightforward case of a mathematical fallacy"; Putnam, review of *Shadows of the Mind*. Putnam's remarks are highly misleading, particularly since Lucas has never been successfully convicted of any mathematical fallacy (except in cases where he readily provided remedy), whatever the philosophical doubts about his argument; see n. 34 of this chapter.

Feferman refers to Alan Ross Anderson, ed., *Minds and Machines* (Englewood Cliffs, N.J.: Prentice-Hall, 1964), for earlier critical discussion. I have dealt with all the points raised in it in earlier footnotes or my text—the fallacies lay in arguments mistakenly attributed to Lucas, and in certain of Penrose's presentations, detailed by secs. 2–3 of Feferman, "Penrose's Gödelian Argument", and confessed and remedied by Penrose, "Beyond the Doubting of a Shadow".

of these concepts' indefinite extensibility is the one which continues to vex academic discussion.[43]

However, many of the arguments skeptical of our possession of any such concepts which a computer could not have stem from a hidden doubt as to whether "understanding" or the "use of concepts" play any role in determining or explaining human linguistic and brain activity at all; that is, they stem from the underlying physicalism discussed in the introduction and chapter VIII.

(c) *The practice of mathematicians*

The concept of being "mechanical" applied to proof procedures has very limited application and is a highly technical mathematical notion, as subsection (f) will show. And the idea that it is a norm for mathematicians to prove things according to such procedures, or even to anticipate that after discovery all their proofs will turn out to have conformed to just one mechanical rule, has no intuitive support if one considers the heterogeneous character of certain recent finitary proofs.

The infinite Ramsey theorem on partitions, previously only a conjecture, has been shown to be equivalent to Gödel's theorem and therefore true, since Gödel's theorem is proven.[44] Goodstein's theorem, which was a straightforwardly statable conjecture about the natural numbers to which no exception had been found, was not given a proof in a finite number of steps until 1982, when it was shown, drawing on Gödel's arguments, that to reject it would imply the invalidity of mathematical induction over the natural numbers.[45] And Fermat's last theorem, a much simpler conjecture about the natural numbers, but for which proof had been sought over a much longer period, was at last proved by Andrew Wiles and Richard Taylor in 1995, with important connections with results which can be generalized to the definition of new classes of curve.[46] But none of these results was reached by mechanical search; and

43. See Dummett, "Philosophical Significance of Gödel's Theorem"; Christopher Peacocke, "Gödel's Theorem: A Problem for Constructivists", sec. 4 of "Proof and Truth", in *Reality, Representation, and Projection*, ed. John Haldane and Crispin Wright (Oxford: Oxford University Press, 1993), 178–82; and "The Philosophical Significance of Gödel's Theorem: Some Issues", in Wright, *Realism, Meaning and Truth*, 2nd ed. (Oxford: Blackwell, 1993), 321–54.

Dummett's problem is as to how we could manifest the possession of such concepts of proof and of natural number in such a way that others might learn our meaning—a difficulty I discuss in chap. VII of this volume.

44. J. Paris and L. Harrington, "A Mathematical Incompleteness in Peano Arithmetic", in *Handbook for Mathematical Logic*, ed. J. Barwise (Amsterdam: North-Holland, 1977), 1133–42.

45. Goodstein proved it by transfinite induction in 1944, but its being a consequence of the validity of the Gödel argument was only shown in 1982 by L. Kirby and J. Paris; see Penrose, *The Large, the Small and the Human Mind* (Cambridge: Cambridge University Press, 1997), 186–92.

46. The excitement of the result can be seen in Horizon Programme, BBC2, 1995–56, broadcast again

examination of the way in which they were actually reached, particularly in the case of Fermat's last theorem, where they involved links between parts of mathematics not known to Fermat and without obvious connection to each other, does not suggest that they could ever have been reached by a mechanical search procedure, except by one devised retrospectively. Within the philosophy of mathematics, the same applies to the proofs that the common systems of set theory are consistent equally with the assertion or the denial of Cantor's Continuum Hypothesis.[47] These examples only highlight the normal situation in mathematics. Being mechanical is a mathematical notion, but not at all a mathematical ideal in seeking proofs, nor indeed, as I will argue, the human ideal in establishing the sense being communicated by particular utterances.

All these proofs are doubly "mathematical", mathematically deductive and mathematical in subject-matter. This does not mean that they cannot be questioned. For instance, the application of the notion of "set" has long been subject to dispute. Some philosophers would argue that sets have no existence independently of there being some predicate or law allowing the identification of their membership. If this is the case, Cantor's proof that there exists no one-to-one correlation between the natural numbers and the real numbers proves nothing more than that there exists no law or predicate correlating the natural numbers one-to-one with definitions of the real numbers; an intuitionist would add the requirement that the laws and definitions be constructive. Arguments as to the validity of argument in such cases are philosophical, not mathematical, even though mathematical in subject-matter.

(d) *The need for informal reasoning to deal with logical, semantic, and other paradoxes*

We need a notion of incomplete formalizability. We can represent the form of arguments without necessarily having mechanically applicable tests as to whether or not arguments satisfy that form. We do not have mechanically applicable criteria of being a statement or a contentful description, let alone of being an axiom or a method of proof. Our way of handling paradoxes is not that of giving a completed set of rules for avoiding them beforehand, but that

December 16, 2010. The final result was published in two papers, Richard Taylor having collaborated with Wiles in remedying the defects in a suggested 1993 proof: Andrew Wiles, "Modular Elliptic Curves and Fermat's Last Theorem", *Annals of Mathematics* 141 (1995): 443–551, and Richard Taylor and Andrew Wiles, "Ring-Theoretic Properties of Certain Hecke Algebras", *Annals of Mathematics* 141 (1995): 553–72. The developments on which the proof depended had wider implications, particularly in the "modularity theorem" presented by C. Breuil, B. Conrad, F. Diamond, and R. Taylor in "On the Modularity of Elliptic Curves over Q: Wild 3-adic Exercises", *Journal of American Mathematical Society* 14, no. 4 (2001): 843–939.

47. Paul J. Cohen, *Set Theory and the Continuum Hypothesis* (New York: W. A. Benjamin, 1966).

of explaining in each case how they arise by a violation of some intuitive rule, perhaps not previously formulated.

The unformalizability of "normal" methods comes out in our need to handle paradoxical cases skillfully. Here we need ingenuity or variety of approach, although not arbitrariness. But there is no possibility of formalizing the system of varied gambits used to explain how different paradoxes arise, thus to justify our way of avoiding it, and with it some family of similar paradoxes. Nor will we say that we follow principles uniformly until we crash. Rather, we follow principles understandingly when following them is routine; and, although aware that the nonroutine may arise, we do not need to check the cases where we have followed the principles understandingly.

It is very commonly presumed that if we proceed to apply the axioms and rules of inference which seem natural, we are led inexorably into paradoxes, both well-known and novel: paradoxes are endemic. And to presume that unless we limit ourselves to some "safe" principles which will not allow us to prove all that we need to prove, we will be able to deal with paradoxes only by means of ad hoc or arbitrary devices as we come upon them ignores the possibility of using the understanding in applying principles.

A formalized language requires such restrictions as were placed on it by Tarski and conformed to within the "derivations within a system" considered in Gödel's proof, including what is required for procedures for identifying well-formed formulae and for checking that supposed derivations conform to the rules of the system to be effective or mechanical. But such a formalized language is impotent to prove that Tarski and Gödel's proofs conform to the axioms and rule of inference on which they rely. And the conclusions of these proofs can be stated in their full generality only in a nonformalized language, a natural language enriched with the necessary mathematical idioms.

Often consideration of a particular example will lead us to make explicit some new presupposition of our axioms or of the applicability of our rules of inference. Thus the realization that, on one interpretation, "Any A is B" and "All A's are B" are compatible with the nonexistence of A's, and so also compatible with "No A is B" and with "It is not the case that some A is B", makes us realize that almost all applications of common systems of predicate logic presuppose that in applying the principles of predicate logic one is speaking of non-empty domains, and in ancient syllogistic logic the traditional statement of the relations in the square of opposition involves the same presupposition.

Thus, in unpredictable ways, the need for additional principles or nonroutine argument, over and above the routine application of basic principles, is always liable to arise.

In this setting attempts are made to enumerate the additional principles drawn upon, in which case effective identification of statements and proofs will be restored, but new paradoxes will remain endemic unless the additional principles have been arbitrarily overly restrictive. If some system is imposed, such as a theory of types or Tarski's principle that no language can include its own meta-language, the result will not apply to natural languages or therefore any language capable of expressing reflective thought. And whatever philosophical principle such systems are erected upon, they are ad hoc in what they ignore and have many counterintuitive consequences. Thus the simple theory of types requires different logical types of number to count each different logical type of thing, and the theory of meta-languages requires that there be different senses of "true", "provable", and so forth in each succeeding meta-language in the hierarchy. And any statement of these theories of types or meta-languages violates the theory concerned. Rather, we want a single type of natural numbers applicable in counting things of whatever kind, abstract or concrete, and a natural language adapted to use by people who can reflect on what is said.

When the same understanding grounds both the acceptance of a system P and some extension of this system, P_1, natural language embraces both. What is arbitrary in adding a rule to a formal system or machine program need not be arbitrary to one who exercises understanding. A good example of an exercise of understanding transcending any formal system or mechanical procedure is provided by Kreisel's proposal that one add a consistency statement to any system which one accepts as itself, under a certain interpretation, true or truth-preserving; this generates an unending series of new principles, but only according to a nonformal principle.

Therefore we need a different perspective involving no completed or constructively enumerable set of principles, but nonetheless no arbitrariness, allowing free reflective application of basic principles, but providing no definiteness in the boundaries between the safe and the unsafe.[48]

Sometimes what is required to resolve a group of paradoxes consists in the realization or making explicit of something which ought to have been obvious in the first place—for instance, when Aristotle realized that it was wrong to try to conceive a line as a set of points, and that instead a point was a cut in the continuous line, not a constituent part or sub-line within it, thereby solving some of Zeno's paradoxes. And Gödel has argued the importance of being open to conceptual advances in order to resolve problems in mathematics.[49] Gödel's arguments reflect the types of consideration of elegance and

48. The boundary between the definite and the indefinite will be itself indefinite, but the requirements of definiteness, having a different rationale from the requirements of intuitionist logic, will be less restrictive.

49. He anticipates that these may enable us to formulate new axioms of set theory, and this underlies his probabilistic arguments that the continuum hypothesis is false (Gödel, "Cantor's Continuum Problem"), which are unlike Russell's arguments for his axiom of reducibility in that Gödel's arguments are at least of

simplicity which are so important heuristically in fundamental physics. And just as there is no precise line between physical and nonphysical argument, so likewise there is no precise line between mathematical and nonmathematical argument.[50] In both cases the line between proof or demonstrative argument and probable reasoning is not set mechanically, but by the fruitfulness and coherence of the resulting overview. To anticipate that such varied types of argument should conform with mechanically applicable rules would be foolish in view of the discoveries mentioned in section 3 and earlier in the present section.

(e) *Teleology and perceiving evident conceptual connections play parts in getting at the truth*

(i) Characterizing the general notion of proving or "showing to be true"

Plainly the general notion of proving or "showing to be true" is wider than the notion of mechanical proof. There will be general principles which apply in either case: for example, "The combination of a proof of P, together with a proof of Q from P, constitutes a proof of Q". But such rules as this are not enough to determine what we should count as a proof in general. There is no formal rule determining what counts as a proof, and it is only in virtue of our understanding that we recognize various general, formally expressed axiom schemas and rules of inference as yielding valid proofs. Moreover, as we have

---

a kind directly appropriate to the type of subject-matter. G. Polya suggests many such types of argument in his book *Mathematics and Plausible Reasoning* (Princeton, N.J.: Princeton University Press, 1954). It is often just such arguments that convince people of a conjecture of which they later find proof, in some cases within some formalizable framework, and in others not so, but still finitary. Gödel envisages that the denial of the continuum hypothesis might well be fruitful in suggesting consequences at some relatively concrete level such as those of natural number theory ("Cantor's Continuum Problem", 485), or solving Diophantine equations, ("Cantor's Continuum Problem", 476–77), whereas the assertion that the continuum hypothesis is true is likely to be fruitless in suggesting any constructive conclusions.

50. I have already instanced an interesting example from Polanyi. Other nice examples are presented by Henri Poincaré, *Science and Hypothesis* (London: Walter Scott, 1905). Older examples appear in Aristotle, e.g., *De Caelo* II, 14; cf. II, 13.

Some of the arguments which are not clearly mathematical are geometrical or spatial rather than philosophical: e.g., what certainty we have that the Least Upper Bound Theorem is true (i.e., that every series of numbers, none of which is greater than a given number, has some number as its Least Upper Bound) derives from its role in proving the existence of gradients (either at all points, or at least at all but a finite number of points) of lines which we intuitively judge geometrically continuous, and from its role in proving that areas enclosed by lines which we intuitively judge continuous have definite and arithmetically comparable areas, a line being intuitively continuous if it constitutes the possible path of a moving point (to use an explanation given by Newton) rather than merely in the sense defined by Cauchy in the nineteenth century. That is, its role in justifying such common procedures as differentiation and integration in connection with applications to concrete subject-matter does much more to establish its truth or validity than the alleged proofs of this theorem from set theory, since in order for set theory to accomplish this proof it needs very strong axioms of whose truth we have much less certainty than the certainty we have in the security of these common mathematical procedures.

seen, given any formally defined system of proof, there will always be things which can be shown to be true, but are not provable according to the limited means specified.

What then should we say in general? Certainly if we artificially restrict the word "rule" to mechanically applicable rules, the notion of proof can be described as used in a "non-rule-bound way", but this will not mean that it is used arbitrarily. Rather, how the term "proof" is applied is definable only by reference to what directs a person proposing a proof towards truth and knowledge, and thereby according to teleologically determined structures or rules. No more formal definition should be expected. I have deliberately stated this definition in the widest terms so that it extends beyond what we count as deductive argument to the arguments we use in seeking truth in natural science, history, courts of law, morals, and ordinary life in general. With varied qualifications in the different cases, my arguments as to the importance of the nonmechanical character of reasoning, the dependence on the use of understanding for discovery and proof, and the relevance of the evidentness of some conceptual connections to the psychological explanation of reasoning which we saw in section 1 (b), along with some cases of considerations of elegance or simplicity, can be extended to arguments in these other fields. However, in this chapter the concern of my discussions is solely with its relevance to deductive argument, although I make no attempt to define the line between deductive and nondeductive argument.

Our informal notion of proof involves using our understanding in reasoning in accord with some principles of which we may be unaware and which remained unformulated until Aristotle or after.[51] Such principles have to be such as to be evidently truth-preserving, but this is something which places no limits on the idioms in terms of which they are expressed. Different terms can have the same sense and the same term can be used in different senses, and it is the sense which determines whether an argument is valid. For a principle to be valid is for it to be truth-preserving, so that if the premises are true, the conclusion will be true also.

Thus we reason informally, "All Greeks are human beings" and "All human beings are mortal", therefore "All Greeks are mortal". However, if we then schematically represented the form of this argument as from "Every A is B" and "Every B is C" to "Every A is C", we generally need pay no attention as to whether "All human beings are mortal", "Every human being is mortal", "Any human being is mortal", or "Man is mortal" were the words used in a particular example, and we would not regard this as a case in which the understanding departed from routine or needed ingenuity, fresh insight, or special thought.

51. Ryle, *Concept of Mind*, 30–31, 47–48; Martin Braine and O'Brien, *Mental Logic*, 137.

However, since what guides thinking is the understanding and not the material rule, rules must not be handled as if nonroutine thinking such as we spoke of in subsection (d) were never needed. Thus, although we may ignore the differences between "All the A's are B", "Every A is B", "Any A is B", and "(The) A is B" for most purposes, on occasion we will have to note that (1) some statements of the form "Any A is B" do not imply the existence of A's; (2) "All the A's weigh 1,000 stone" is susceptible of a collective interpretation (e.g., supposing "A" means "member of a five-a-side football team", it might mean that the whole team, standing on scales together, weighs 1,000 stone), unlike "Every A weighs 1,000 stone", which has to be taken distributively so that each A has this weight; and (3) "(The) A is B" implies that being B is consequent on the "nature" of A's (e.g., one can say "Man is a biped" or "The horse is a quadruped", despite the existence of amputees).

(ii) In what sense is a conclusion "determined" by the premises which lead to it?

We should ask whether, when we proceed routinely, our earlier steps determine the later ones and, in that case, ask what is meant by the word "determine". We neither imply nor exclude a nonteleological explanation of the determining. But if a teleological explanation can be given as to why the next step was taken—for instance, that we can "see" that reasoning in the way concerned will preserve truth, this of itself provides sufficient explanation. Although not conscious of the logical principles to which one in fact conforms, but proceeding as one does simply because of one's understanding or perception that the conclusion follows from the premises, the aim of preserving truth in one's reasoning seems more apt in explaining one's following of the principles concerned than any other.

In such cases the relation of the earlier states which are said to determine the later ones are liable to be described in teleologically dictated terms—that is, in terms of logical rather than physical or linguistic form. Moreover, the decision that something of a certain linguistic form uttered in a certain context had a certain logical form would be nonmechanical or, as we have seen, not limited by the linguistic specifications of the logical forms of the family of arguments concerned, of which the syllogistic example given is the earliest recognized. It is only in order to show the possibility of a mechanical decision procedure in the mathematics of syllogistic argument that it is required that we should be able to reformulate arguments in some canonical linguistic form.

In saying that the earlier steps of an argument do not exclude a nonteleological explanation of the later steps—for example, causal determination of a physical kind—I have in mind that, in the way chapters VI and VII will explain, the malleability of neural function may be such as to subserve rational functioning, modes of neural organization and functioning having become tuned to the preservation of truth. However, the acceptance of something as an axiom or something else as a valid form of argument is not dependent upon the presumption of the possibility of an explanation or description of relevant neural processes in nonteleological, physically causal terms. For it is their truth-preserving character rather than any material or linguistic properties which constitutes the primary explanation of why one argues according to certain logical forms and not others, independently of whether or not there are structures of neural functioning subserving this achievement, perhaps whose existence evolution may explain.

(f) *"Mechanical procedure" as a specialized mathematical concept*

Supposing that grammar is indeed a projection of semantics (a semantics which has many pragmatically formed features) in the way I explain in chapter IX and the rest of part three, it follows that if we observe a certain economy and restrictiveness in our modes of speech, or enforce transformation into certain canonical modes of speech, or regard only one mode of speech as acceptable, being "well-formed" will become a purely formal matter.

This opens out the possibility of a formal system in which we allow certain starting points and rules of proceeding to be followed strictly mechanically. The understanding has to be able to recognize these procedures as both valid and capable of being performed "mechanically". By comparison with the inferences in such a system, we may verify the validity of a wide variety of inferences not stated in canonical form. In this setting we can "see" that an algorithm or mechanical procedure requires different degrees of formalization with different types of problem. In some cases it may be "mess-safe", even though handled relatively informally. A strict need for complete formalization arises only with certain proofs in proof-theory (e.g., ones requiring the arithmetization of syntax, such as Gödel's proof of the incompleteness of natural arithmetic).

It is here that the question arises as to what it means for a procedure to be "mechanical". Plainly this will involve its being routine, uniform, and direct in application. But this is not enough, unless the word "mechanical" is being used purely metaphorically. When we speak of procedures as mechanical we seem to have in view that they are deterministic in the sense that previous states or steps determine later states or steps "mechanically". And the notion of earlier states or steps determining later ones "mechanically" has to prescind from teleological or semantic considerations.

So far I have not offered any positive characterization of how a later stage or step is determined when it is determined "mechanically" by earlier stages or steps. This does not mean determined "causally", whether in the narrow sense of physically or in the wider sense of being "by the action of an agent". Rather, I mean that the later steps are taken in accord with a certain kind of rule, and the question is what kind of rule. The time intervals between the steps (and indeed whether they are taken at all) can be quite random, a feature we do not find in purely physical machines, since it is something which can depend on the will of an operator such as a person using a machine.

In short, the being "mechanical" with which we are concerned is a specialized mathematical concept and not definable in terms of causation or physics. Indeed, physical machines are bad examples of the "mechanical", because for them to operate "mechanically" in the relevant way they must be ideal, never having their parts decay and never in any way malfunctioning—free from the need for repair. Rather, what matters is the nature of the way in which a certain kind of rule determines what later step should follow a sequence of earlier steps, where this has nothing to do with physics.

Since the kind of calculation we are here speaking of is of such a specialized character, we need have no fear in accepting Church's thesis in the form given to it by Turing and, following him, by Gödel, in allowing that what is "mechanically" determinable is Turing-machine-computable, bearing in mind that procedures for computation are always reducible to procedures for decision and vice versa.[52] Indeed, on reflection, we should regard it as self-evident that the upshot of following a mechanical procedure in this highly specialized sense is Turing-machine-computable. Making this concession implies nothing about what it is for the understanding to follow some routine procedure (routine for the human being with the relevant understanding). This concession does not place us in any danger of behaviorism in speaking of understanding, since there is no reason to suppose that the understanding operates mechanically. Moreover, this concession does not imply that what results from following routinely and directly applicable rules of operation is "effectively determinable" in the sense of Turing-machine-computable, since, as we have seen, even routinely and directly applicable rules can be quite informal.

52. See n. 24. If proofs are formalized and premises and methods of proof are enumerable, the question of whether we can decide a question, producing a proof or formal derivation either for the answer yes or for the answer no, is equivalent to the question of whether some corresponding function is computable; cf. S. C. Kleene, *Mathematical Logic* (New York: Wiley, 1967), 227–29. I have therefore not troubled to separate computing numbers from numbers and deriving propositions from propositions.

Kleene and Davis appear to use the word "effective" only of computations—i.e., in the latter way.

Section 5. The Relevance of This Consideration of Mathematical Method to Linguistics

(a) *Cognitive scientists make the achievement of understanding into a gargantuan task*

Many cognitive scientists and philosophers proceed on the methodological assumption that our primary experience of language-use, predominantly the language-use of others, is of what is said in whole speech-acts, commonly treated as represented by written sentences, whereas the precise ways in which sentences are divided up when written are somewhat artificial. It is then a problem in the theory of perception as to how from this we learn to appreciate the significance of the various significant elements and features of such sentences as spoken, including their grammatical modes of construction, intonation, and the spread of ways in which context is relevant to understanding their significance. And there is the question as to how far our capacities for speech-perception are independent of those for speech-production.

However, these problems of perception are for chapters VI and VII.

This chapter is concerned only with the relevance of the consideration of method in mathematics to the task of understanding fresh communications, taking for granted an already established capacity to identify contributory sense-identifying elements and features.

Here many cognitive scientists presume that we get to identify the senses of complete utterances (even if only unconsciously) from their constituent sense-identifying elements and features by means of some subconscious, mechanically effective means of computation or calculation, tending to regard this as a condition of our understanding the communications made to us.[53] However, this view is subject to at least two difficulties.

The first difficulty lies in the gargantuan nature of the task envisaged. For it requires a set of mechanically applicable rules which will enable a hearer to work out, for any linguistic communication in the shared language in use, from an identification of its significant elements and features, what has and what has not been thereby implied by the speaker, given that the speaker and hearer have the same relevant knowledge of any earlier parts of their conversation and of the physical situation and cognitive aptitudes of the speaker.

53. As chap. VII of this volume intimates, cognitive scientists often envisage such computational tasks to be possible.

And some philosophers have argued that it must be possible in principle, at least retrospectively, as part of a "complete theory of meaning" to show the "presuppositions" of this practice; Dummett, "Theory of Meaning (II)". Wright, *Realism, Meaning, and Truth,* follows Dummett in thus reintroducing the axiomatizability principle referred to in the introduction to this volume, n. 5. But neither supposes that anybody actually performs such deductions of meanings from axioms of meaning in order to attain the mutual intelligibility between language-users which we experience.

The second difficulty is that utterances typically involve general concepts which lack mechanically applicable modes of definition. As we have seen, whenever concepts of this kind are involved, it is systematically impossible to calculate the discourse-significance of such terms in the contexts in which they occur.

(i) Examples of difficulty in depending on mechanically applicable rules

To take a typical instance, we met Jackendoff's attempt to explain the meaning of the word "see" in terms of "visual contact" and "awareness". But, as chapter I, section 4 (b) showed, such a definition is of no use for the purpose of providing a mechanically applicable procedure for judging when to use the word. Quite apart from the ambiguities in the expression "visual contact" (e.g., contact need not be cognitive), the idea of explaining the meaning of one problematic general word, "see", in terms of an even more problematic and even more general term, "aware", is very strange, since the difficulties in laying down mechanically applicable criteria for the applicability of a term as general as "aware" are much greater than in the case of "see". The difficulty of laying down mechanically applicable criteria increases with the generality of the term considered, reaching demonstrable impossibility with the most general terms, among them "entity", "set", "truth", "definition", "proof", and "method of proof", and, with them, related terms such as "prove" and "know". Moreover, the norm is for the context to make "A saw B" imply the existence of B, and "A saw that P" imply P, and more generally for the connection of visual contact with the awareness to be nonaccidental and somehow natural and unitary—yet the specification of criteria has to allow exceptions to this norm (I instanced that a person may say "I see two pencils" at some point as the optician thrusts a pencil towards his eyes without implying that there are two pencils), and yet achieve this without mentioning any particular cases, since the variety of possible situations, delusions, and fields of experience to be catered for is non-enumerable, like the situations which confront Ryle's mountaineers, referred to in chapter I.

Steven Pinker, in *Words and Rules*, surmises that family-resemblances, understood by reference to disjunction in the way I explained in chapter II, can be dealt with by parallel processing (following Rumelhart and McClelland and later connectionists), suggesting that they can be dealt with in ways analogous to those applicable in the case of similarities and connections of origin in morphology, an approach which can cope with a certain random indeterminacy. Meantime, he envisages that, as in morphology, the remaining cases of each kind can be dealt with by uniform rule within a sphere of uniform relations and repeatable operations within which the ideals of simpler forms of computing hold sway. Transferring this picture to the learning and use of language considered generally, he anticipates that the meanings of combinations of words will be computable from the meanings of words and the way they are arranged, remarking that "the human mind is a hybrid system, learning fuzzy associations and crisp rules in different subsystems" and that "we have digital minds in an analog world".[54] Since it is the variety in the possible situations thrown up by this "analog world" which leads him to anticipate the usefulness of the vague and the fuzzy, we may take it that the combinations of words of whose meaning he speaks are not just grammatical units or clauses considered in abstraction from the world, but statements or utterances purporting to report any one such situation.

However, Pinker's assumption that all concepts are either of the rough kind, to be preprocessed on connectionist lines, or "classically" well-behaved, so as to have a mechanically determinable application, is untenable. All our linguistic utterances involve in one or more ways the use of concepts with a generality outstripping what can be mechanically determined, concepts whose fault is not vagueness, but this very generality associated with "intrinsic analogy" and "polymorphousness"—a generality extending beyond examples such as "know", "understand", "define", and "prove" to such formal or topic-universal concepts as "true", "object", "set", and "number".

This excludes the theory whereby the brain is analogous to a number of systems producing rival decisions as to how the utterance one has heard is to be interpreted, so that in arriving at its conclusions the brain is analogous to a committee without standing orders or regular procedure, the final decision being ultimately a matter of chance. It is to escape these crudities that linguists such as Ray Jackendoff have produced highly developed theories whereby different hearers can come to agreement on the meaning of a certain utterance of a particular speaker, in particular the Preference Rules System which Jackendoff proposed in *Semantics and Cognition*, elaborating the idea in his later works,[55] which give a more exact presentation of what might lie behind the procedures described informally by Pinker.

Some theorists appear to imagine that, given a very vague definition of a term, vague as a result of roughness or "fuzziness" or as a result of its generality or both, speaker and hearer may arrive at the same relatively determinate interpretation by a method of successive approximation, utilizing their

54. I take these quotations from Pinker, *Words and Rules* (London: Weidenfeld and Nicholson, 1999), 279 and 287 respectively, from a chapter entitled "A Digital Mind in an Analog World", 269–87.

55. Jackendoff, *Semantics and Cognition*, 128–58, responding to the problems he had raised in 109–27; *Consciousness and the Computational Mind*, 135–59; *Semantic Structures* (Cambridge, Mass.: MIT Press, 1990); *Architecture*, chaps. 3–7. Developing the ideas of her previous books, Margaret A. Boden, *The Creative Mind: Myths and Mechanisms* (London: Weidenfeld and Nicolson, 1990; expanded ed., London: Abacus, 1991), shows the same optimism as Pinker and Jackendoff.

shared knowledge of the human and conversational situation which the utterance concerned seeks to report, as well as their shared knowledge, in the case of "see", of the general structures of interrelating perception and action. In some cases one might try bringing in one's knowledge of how words like "see", "light", and "grasp" have their uses transferred from the exercise of the senses in attaining knowledge to the exercise of the intellect in understanding, or the use of "move" and "force" transferred from the physical case to the case of emotional or rational motivation in explaining events.

Yet, although such suggestions can seem very plausible in popularized presentations, in fact they embody the abandonment of mechanical procedure. For they depend upon the flexible application of certain strategies, a flexible application we are able to make only through exercising the understanding, sometimes by so-called lateral thinking ("inspired" guesswork, seeing loose analogies between very disparate cases, its suggestions checked informally afterwards), an understanding reflected in natural language and commonly expressible, but only in informal terms.

(ii) Such computer methods as parallel processing inadequate to resolve these difficulties

At every point we are confronted with the distinction between (a) systems of a kind whose powers are limited to ways of operating laid down beforehand, in regard to which Church's thesis requiring Turing's kind of mechanical determinability will apply, and (b) human or other reflective intellectual beings with the power at any point in their searches to try some quite different method of approach and at any point turn back and reflect upon their previous methods, for instance, in paradigm shifts which lack any definite restrictions, the power which human beings have in virtue of what we call "understanding".

The introduction into discussion of the possibility of introducing parallel processing and "chance" or "random" elements into computer search operations has created false hopes.

As to the first, it suffices to remark that it has been proved that there is no result which can be obtained using parallel processing which could not have been obtained, albeit more slowly, without it. This is a consequence of Turing's result that anything mechanically computable is Turing-machine-computable.

The value of considering parallel processing is in suggesting models for dividing tasks efficiently and so a possible architecture for some aspects of the work of the brain, but in principle it cannot make any new type of task mechanically achievable if it was not so before. And the same applies to the other sophistications of procedure suggested later. In the perspective suggested in chapters VI and VII such sophistications are required for those functionings of the brain which subserve speech and the understanding of speech. But, however complex the system of such sophistications, they do not give the brain itself these powers of speech and the understanding of speech.

As to the introduction of "chance" elements into search procedures, it allows extraordinary achievements, but not ones which help the solution of the problems posed earlier. Thus, by a method of successive approximation, we can identify the value of π, or the shortest trunk road route from John O'Groats to Penzance, or the shortest road route absolutely. When this method is used, as it was in calculating the location of Neptune in the 1840s, it only succeeds if the presumption that the successive approximations will form a converging series is correct (not true if there had been multiple major planets perturbing the orbit of Uranus, not just one). In such cases we can, by this method of successive approximation, approach ever closer to the location we seek. The method proceeds by making a guess within a sufficiently large area within the field and assessing this guess to produce a narrower area of search, and so on indefinitely. For this, first, the field within which a position has to be located is one within which locations can be specified in a uniform way so that their relative position can be computed and finitely specified. Second, the different paths followed in different chance sequences of approximations can be expected to converge on the same conclusion. And third, in each search there is a mechanically applicable criterion for checking that the apparent result of the search is correct. The introduction of "chance" elements into procedures of computer use by these "guesses" does nothing to remove the requirement that the field not be so open and the factors operative not so many as to put the matter in the field of chaos theory.

However, in interpreting the sayings of others, we are involved in locating something which is not set within a field of things specifiable in a uniform way so that the field can be mapped out and mechanically explored, even by successive guesses within ever more limited areas within a field, since the field is indefinitely wide. The ways of avoiding car accidents, ways of describing a sunset with a sun amidst clouds in the tropics, or possible metaphorical applications of a particular word cannot be mapped out in this way.

(iii) The systematic impossibility of accomplishing these tasks by any mechanical procedure

My earlier discussion, taken together with the preceding argument and the considerations put forward in chapters I and II, make it clear that there is no way in which the type of task concerned can be accomplished within the ambit of a single language or single organism relying on mechanical procedures only.

Here I recapitulate the argument of chapter 12 of *The Human Person*. Three impossibilities are involved.[56]

The first two of these can be made vivid by performing the thought-experiment suggested in *The Human Person*.[57] Imagine a computer being put to many uses, each according to a different program, each corresponding to a different speech-sense of a certain word, and a multiplicity of different users, one for each speech-sense, or just one user turning the hardware to all the different uses. Then consider the suggestion that such a computer is an analog of the brain. For the purposes of the thought-experiment, let us treat the environments of the words as a constant for all these different speech-senses (though necessarily this will be contrary to fact)—constant in the sense of not themselves requiring differential programming.

It is here that the first problem arises, because the presentation suggests a definite number of speech-senses for each word corresponding to an enumerable set of uses or programs. But, as chapters I to III made clear, there will be no enumerable set of speech-senses corresponding to a given *langue*-meaning for a word, and therefore no possibility of identifying the speech-sense in a particular case by working through a list of specifications of types of example of speech-sense, but rather an open set of possible uses arising within the open set of possible situations, not enumerable because not definite in number. Nothing in the computer corresponds to such a non-enumerable set, but only a capacity to be used in a non-enumerable variety of ways. One can consider the variety of directions in which a football might be kicked, or the projections which could be taken of a system of physical objects from a variety of distances and directions, and these will correspond to the real numbers, because the directions of projection are distinguishable according to physical, in this case geometrical, concepts. However, the ways of using a computer do not correspond in number either to the natural or to the real numbers, but to the plans of computer users, which are not enumerable because they are mostly not yet determinate but in the realm of the future or possible, indefinite in number, requiring adaptation to a non-enumerable range of possible situations, projects, and systems of cooperation. Thus the "capacity for an indefinite range of use" is not an internal feature of the computer, or even of the computer taken together with any set of already given programs, but reflects the free initiative of the computer user.

The second problem, connected with the first, is that nothing in the computer corresponds to the unity and interconnection between the multiple

56. The first two are referred to in David Braine, *Human Person*, 451, where paragraph (c) is explained more fully in 462–63), and the third on 451, where paragraph (d) is explained more fully in 467–72, cf. 463–64.

57. David Braine, *Human Person*, 462–63.

speech-senses arising from any one *langue*-meaning (meaning fixed in the lexicon). The unity and interconnection lie in the understanding of the computer user and arise because the human being, unlike the computer, can operate informally in a spread of uses of each term arising in a variety of different types of way. Such understanding can be in no way represented or embodied in the computer and its already given programs. The computer is capable of multiple uses, but all uses are given by the computer user, and the various spreads of use associated with particular *langue*-meanings are not represented in it or its given programs. Rather, the capacity of speaker reliably to communicate with hearer, expressing a determinate *parole*-sense to him, is to be explained in terms of their shared understanding of their shared language.

A third difficulty, considered separately in *The Human Person,* is the one arising from those self-reflective capacities of human beings lacking to computers—self-reflective capacities brought out when we considered Gödel's incompleteness theorem and the differences between the way the human understanding approaches paradoxes and the mechanical way in which they have to be dealt with by computers or in formal languages.

However, I have concentrated more particularly on the first two difficulties because they are much neglected and arise with concepts not involving self-reflection, such as "... exists", "... is a set", "... is good of its kind", "... knows —", "... sees —", "... plays —", just as much as those involving self-reflective procedures, of which "... is true", "... is a definition", "... can be shown to be true", "... is a mechanically effective method of determining —" are conspicuous examples. There is no single set of criteria even for the literal application of any of these predicates, involving self-reflection or not.

The *langue*-understanding of each expression as an item of the lexicon is realized in a *parole*-level understanding of an indefinitely varied range of word-functors in speech. It is these uses of the expression in speech which cannot be encapsulated in a mechanically applicable rule. This is a consequence of the unformalizability of natural language. As we saw, this unformalizability was demonstrated by Tarski, drawing on the properties of the expression "... is true", while other demonstrations are available from the consideration of any of the other most general terms enumerated above: "entity", "set", "definition", "proof", and "method of proof". Any mechanically applicable rule either fails to cover the whole range of the use of a word or else generates contradictions and misuses, so that it is only an understanding not capable of encapsulation in such a rule which does or could do the job.

There can be no calculation of the *parole*-meanings of sentences (utterances) from the senses of their contribuants, not because the *parole*-meanings of these elements are private or indeterminate, but because these *parole*-meanings are grasped in the very act of grasping the *parole*-meaning of the total sentence or utterance, and this *parole*-meaning is public. But for calculation of a *parole*-meaning to be possible, it would have to proceed by being based on semantic facts about each of the lexical items given (such "semantic facts" might, of course, be very complex in their specification); however, the ways in which the unformalizability of natural language can be established show that, since there cannot be adequate codification of the relevant "semantic facts" in the case of the most general concepts, whose use is presupposed in any utterance whatsoever, the supposed calculations of the *parole*-meanings of sentences (in effect, complete speech-units) are not only fictitious, but impossible.

(b) *The involvement of understanding in explaining linguistic behavior*

The impossibility of explaining linguistic behavior in terms of the mechanical application of mechanically applicable rules should not distress us. Indeed, there is something quite odd in the attempt to explain understanding the linguistic communications of other people in terms of working out their meaning by calculation, an idea which carries with it the implication of a procedure which is effective in the sense of being mechanically applicable.

It is, of course, quite natural to use the term "effective" in a way quite different from that found in Church and among other mathematical logicians, in such a way that for a method of coming to conclusions to be "effective", all that is required is that it suffices to establish public certainty. This is quite compatible with supposing it to draw on perception, understanding, and the capacity for nuanced judgment in a nonmechanical way.

In Searle's Chinese room thought-experiment, he adopted the Cartesian gambit of imagining that all the outward behavior of language-use could continue independently of understanding, meaning, and mind, these latter being mere extras which we experience in our own case.[58] However, I have shown that there could not be a Cartesian self which functioned in the way Searle envisaged, and that it is wrong to concede that a "machine" could conceivably simulate our outward linguistic behavior. Rather, speaking in a natural language in the context of the particular use concerned cannot be treated in a mathematically mechanical way.

To resort to "the understanding" in explaining human reasoning and the human use of language is not to suppose that we have no empirical check on the presence or absence of such understanding, since we have the possibility of such empirical check, but not one which follows any mechanically applica-

58. Searle, "Minds, Brains, and Programs", *Behavioral and Brain Sciences* 3 (1980): 417–24; Searle, *Minds, Brains, and Science* (London: BBC Publications, 1984).

ble procedure. As I remarked earlier, how a particular piece of discourse is to be understood is a matter quite accessible to our knowledge through natural language learning and the types of explanation of meaning discussed in the introduction, instanced in chapters II and III and treated in depth in chapter VIII, but without these methods being of any mechanically applicable kind. Turing argued that the capacities of machines to "invent" questions are as great as those practically met with among human beings.[59] But here he failed to take proper account of the systematic difference between the capacities of a question-asking physical system confined to asking questions in a preprogrammed way, however complex the program, and the capacities of an organism whose questions are subject to no preset program or order. It is these capacities which are involved in the interpretation of the speech of others as well as in our capacities for mathematical proof examined earlier.

In sum, the problems suggested by numerous mathematical results, of which Gödel's theorem is only the most famous, by paradigm shifts in physics, and by numerous other features of our use of language are in principle beyond the reach of machines primarily because our types of inquiry are indefinite in number, rather than because they are infinite (though being indefinite in number implies nonfinitude).[60] The problem is not one of largeness of number, but of lack of any mechanical, step-by-step method of finding a solution, even by successive approximation. The field of search is not finitely specifiable and, when a solution is suggested, there is no mechanical way of establishing its satisfactoriness or correctness.

Although neither our reasoning nor our understanding of each other's speech is limited to proceeding according to mechanically applicable rules, they can always be checked upon, but often only by reasoning in accord with rules understood informally, in a way which leaves room for dealing with queries as they arise. If the answer first given leaves room for further reasonable query, then this further query can be dealt with by further informal consideration and so on, so far as need arises. This kind of informality does not involve being uncritical, any more than the lack of strict formality in the proofs offered by mathematicians from Euclid to Newton involved their being uncritical.

59. In "Computing Machinery and Intelligence", *Mind New Series* 59 (1950): 433–60, Alan Turing proposed his "Turing Test" as to whether a computer could think—namely, whether a person questioning it could in practice discover whether or not it could think by asking it a finite series of questions.

60. Even in areas such as chess, where the problems are in principle finite but the numbers of possible situations to be envisaged are very large, human beings tend to surpass machines because, unlike machines, they are not limited to proceeding mechanically: Chess gambits cannot be mapped out in a mechanically useful way, and the ways in which chess champions solve problems are unlike those used by their mechanical rivals, which is why, once beaten by a machine, a new checking procedure having been introduced into a machine, human chess champions tend to recover superiority so quickly. Yet a machine speedy enough to survey every possible game up to any length practicable at a particular historical time could in principle defeat any champion at that time.

Such questions as the significance of the word "see" mentioned earlier are ones in the case of which any sufficiently intelligent human being, such as Socrates's slave, for any given set of axioms, can be drawn to prove more by reflection upon them than could be computed mechanically. By "prove" here I mean "show to be true"—that is, it is not that by evolution human beings are by accident programmed at the point concerned to give the same answer, but that they use reasoning which enables themselves and other human beings to see its truth. It is not by accident or because of evolution that human beings agree in concluding "Q" from "P" and "If P, then Q"; rather, we say that they "see" or "grasp" the implication. This is what is involved in the modes of functioning of the brain having the kind of malleability of which I speak in chapter VII—malleability which makes them open to the workings of intellect in such a way as to make the kinds of description and explanation involved in speaking of "seeing" or "grasping" implications appropriate. Likewise, on a more lowly plane, when we have words susceptible of abundant and richly varied metaphorical use, as well as varied uses invented to suit unpredictably varied types of situation, the words do not come with rules allowing us to determine mechanically how they should be used in these situations, and yet we find that when the speaker makes his utterance, the hearer is able to grasp or understand it in the same sense as the speaker intended to be understood. The common reliability of such speaker-hearer agreement, often in cases where truth or falsehood is involved, excludes the supposition that this agreement comes about by chance.

Human heuristic strategies are not confined to following mechanical procedures in solving mathematical problems, and are free from any such confines in resolving problems of linguistic interpretation. And our understanding of words is not something private so that no one can tell whether speakers have it or not. When whether two different language-users have the same understanding of the same word in a particular type of context is questioned, various checks can be brought into play, leaving no systematic obstacle to knowledge that the people concerned possess understanding and the same understanding. There is no system by which a person can guarantee that his pretending will not be discovered, no system by which he can protect himself against unforeseen questions in unforeseen changes of circumstance. Here I touch upon the question as to whether mental states, including those to do with the understanding of language, have some systematic privacy.

My arguments show that there is no such systematic privacy.

We have seen how mechanical procedures play only a small part in the work of mathematicians (limited to some checking procedures and some specialized meta-mathematical proofs); likewise, they play only a small part in our dealing with the lesser problems of understanding what people say in fields less exact than mathematics. (When we do find that some notable task can be achieved by means of a computer, e.g., the task of translating a Russian text into Japanese, then we should inquire into the limits of the task the computer is expected to achieve and into the difference in its methods.)[61]

Ryle compared cognitive skills or excellences ("virtues" in the Aristotelian tradition) to the skills of the rock-climber. These are skills whereby, for instance, when we take a certain handhold, the reasons for taking it are commonly not at the forefront of our minds at the time, neither the particular reasons why we took this handhold nor the general informal rules according to which we operated, as it were conducting theoretical deductions while on the rock face, even though typically we could give some explanation afterwards. Our capacities to understand the speech and thought of others function analogously.

Having this linguistic understanding is explanatory. For instance, if it is queried whether we do genuinely possess the relevant understanding into the connection between two different uses of the same word, our response is normally to give some answer to the question of what the two uses have in common. The possession of the capacity to give such an answer shows that we have a dispositional knowledge (knowledge or understanding as a state realized or exhibited in exercise) of the fact which we state in our answer. We knew what the two uses had in common, even though it was not passing through our mind, just as we may know that Chad is south of Libya at times when we are not thinking about Chad or Libya at all. It would not be true that we "understood" or "saw" the connection between the two uses of the same word being considered unless we knew that we did have this understanding. That is, such linguistic dispositions are "conscious" states or dispositions, unlike dispositions such as solubility, whose exercise when sugar dissolves does not involve sugar's having any knowledge that it is soluble. Moreover, the dispositional knowledge concerned has to be something we are aware of having, this awareness being itself dispositional, not a new mental act, so that no infinite series of acts of answering questions is implied. And what is involved is just one disposition whereby, relying on our understanding, we can answer questions at need, not an infinite series of dispositions in regard to merely possible questions.

(c) *The inappropriateness of this model of how we understand the communications of others*

The strategy of representing communication as depending upon calculation embodies a deeper misconception. For all the processes of calculation envisaged involve treating the *parole*-meaning of a sentence as the value of

61. Cf. chap. VII, sec. 1 (d) (ii), of this volume.

a function of the meanings of its lexical elements and its context of utterance, the former computable from the latter. This involves that the relation of meanings at the rank of sentence and meanings at the rank of its basic meaning-contribuants regarded as objects to be identified is primary, since it is supposed that it is such calculation or computation by the mind or brain working unconsciously which is alone key to the achievement of communication, feelings of having meant something or understood something being, as it were, mere extras—thereby making the role of words in "expressing" sense or thought redundant in the explanation of what goes on, and so making words little more than ciphers.

This deep misconception of the senses or discourse-significances of sentence-constituents as objects to be identified is one I first picked out in chapters I to IV, but whose full character will only emerge in chapter IX and elsewhere. There I show that, although there is no particular similarity between speaking and dreaming, sentences and senses or meanings should, like dreams, be regarded as referring not to things or "objects" in any proper sense, but to what I call "cognates". The mistake is logically comparable to supposing that in dreaming a dream, we first identified the dream and then dreamt it. In other terms, this approach has made communication depend upon supposing that the mind proceeds by first identifying meaning-contribuants, treating them as arguments of a function, "objects" in Frege's sense; and then calculating sentence-meanings (whether at the level of "competence" or of *parole*), regarded as the values of these functions for those arguments, by means of the calculation identifying these sentence-meanings, in Frege's sense also "objects".

This approach gets things exactly the wrong way around. The trouble is not just that such calculation would have to be unconscious, but that the whole process of learning language and the whole process of using it has been misdescribed. In learning and using language, our starting point is not the identifying or picking out of objects called meanings, but from the start beginning by understanding the sense or discourse-significance of some linguistic utterance as a semantically syntactically structured whole. And from the beginning the role of complete linguistic utterances is to *express* sense, thereby expressing thought, not primarily to identify it and not by means of identifying it.

This fact of the coming into "existence" of the sentence or utterance in the act of speech, typically in the mid-flow of discourse, allows for the flexibility in the formation of fresh word-functors, distinguishable in sense, from the same lexeme, the flexibility which was one of our starting points in the introduction and chapter I, the capacity through language to *express* thought, the something excluded by treating linguistic communications as generated according to a calculus. The fresh sense or discourse-significance which arises with each fresh use of a lexeme is the meaning which words have as constituents in speech, not just as items of language-possession. This expressed meaning is not something private to the speaker but a discourse-significance understood by hearer as well as speaker in virtue of the linguistic capacity which they share.

The computational processes often envisaged by cognitive scientists and philosophers do not explain how language works at a conscious level. If we do not consciously carry out the psychologists' proposed calculations, then they play no part in enabling us consciously to see a connection of senses or to understand in the act of speaking how what we say means what we intend it to mean. It is no answer to say that we do not expect the nonconscious processes involved in sight to be in consciousness in the act of seeing, or knowledge of the detail of muscle processes and nervous transmission of pain messages to be in consciousness in the acts of clenching a fist or feeling pain from a hot plate. The case of speech is different, because the understanding of what we are saying is integral to the intentional act of saying it—because integral to our meaning what we mean by what we say in the very act of saying it, unlike those nonconscious processes involved in perceptual seeing, bodily movement, and sensation. Therefore the occurrence of these computational processes cannot count as an explanation of what understanding consists in.

As to learning, each distinct lexical meaning of a word is learned through the appreciation of a variety of cases of use in *parole*, including the learner's own use and correction at early stages. What is acquired in learning language is not a capacity to operate according to mechanically applicable rules, but an appreciation constituting the basis of a skill capable of proper use only in a nonmechanical way, meaning what we say when we speak with proper understanding of what we say. The lexical entry for a typical lexical-factor will not provide any mechanically applicable rule allowing the computation or calculation of the senses of sayings in which the lexical-factor concerned figures. Rather, the skill acquired is one which allows an indefinite range of variation in its types of exercise or application. To apply semantic rules rigidly, "mechanically", or according to formal rule is not to speak but, as we say, to *parrot*—with nothing more than the illusion of understanding.

(d) *Unscientific to represent understanding as redundant to explaining linguistic behavior*

Those who think that our communication actually depends upon and is by means of some such calculus or system of computation as we have referred to might suggest that this does not prevent us conceiving and experiencing words in a different way—for instance, words as lexemes serving as bases of unconsciously conducted calculations while words in use, with their sense or discourse-significance, having the role of expressing sense of which we are conscious. But this view would make the fact that words expressed meaning, instead of merely helping identify meanings from which some communication might be constructed, an extra with no function in communication or in affecting behavior—identifying meanings being substituted for expressing them. Expressiveness, made in this way a mere extra for the purposes of signaling and influencing action, becomes of "psychological", "introspective", or "attitudinal" importance only, a wheel on which nothing turns in the explanation of things. But such an account has made the ideas of understanding and meaning only parts of a self-deceptive "folk-psychology", not science or genuine explanations.

If the real means whereby we communicated with each other was that the hearer's brain decomposed the speech-act according to certain acquired or innate programs into its "meaning-determining" elements and then calculated a "message", it would be superfluous for there to be any connection between the neurological structures underlying our capacity to speak and function as we do and our being aware of our sentences as meaning what they do.[62]

It is remarkable that, if it had been possible to achieve an explanation of the effects of linguistic communications between human beings along these lines, such an explanation would seem to make the possession of understanding of any kind redundant to the explanation of human behavior, making a successful, strong AI theory strangely convergent with behaviorism.

Those who, like Searle, as when he considers his Chinese room thought-experiment, take it that we know that we have an understanding of language and that therefore the concept of meaning also has application, are right to object to these positions, materialist or epiphenomenalist in character, which give understanding no essential role in explaining people's linguistic behavior and its influence on their other behavior. However, as we have observed earlier, the more fundamental objection is not that "we just know we have understanding", but that the alternatives put forward do not and cannot work, but involve systematic impossibilities.

The skeptical question as to the existence of any such thing as understanding at all arises in different ways when Descartes or Turing raise the question whether other supposed people might be mere machines, and Quine or Davidson raise the question as to whether there can be any genuinely shared understanding between speaker and hearer. In this they raise what Aristotle would have considered an unscientific question, effectively the question as to whether linguistics has any subject-matter, analogously to the way those who ask whether motion occurs are questioning whether physics has any subject-matter.

In my next chapter I turn to examine how it is possible to restore a scientific cognitive science of psychology.

62. Cf. Blackburn, *Spreading the Word*, 35.

PART TWO

The Shape of the Psychology Required for Explaining the Learning and Use of Language

VI

Human and Animal Organisms as Systems Dynamically Geared to the Environment

"Mechanisms" in a Holistic and Teleological Framework

The holistic approach of J. J. Gibson and some other recent psychologists is key to understanding the shape of the psychology required for explaining the learning and use of language, including the part played by the brain and by our human evolutionary background.

Gibson's environment-geared or "ecological" model of visual perception makes the cognitive aspect of perception inseparable from the gearing of our motor activity to the natural environment, a model intelligible only in the context of an Aristotelian conception of human unity and function. Gibson's way of thinking about perception provides a model for how we should think about the human use of speech—speech being adapted not just to the natural environment in general, but to the social environment of a community of people speaking the same language. Within this social environment it will be the norm for hearer and speaker to understand the same by what the speaker has said. This norm determines how we describe and assess deficiencies in speech and its understanding.

In this model, speaking and hearing, with the brain functioning relevant to them, are inseparably integrated and geared to express the thoughts and understanding which the speaker wishes to communicate to the hearer. The physical is integral to our linguistic functioning, but semantics and pragmatics, involving intellect, are indispensable both to the description and explanation of our language and to the functional description and explanation of the organization of the brain which this activity involves.

Any scientific account of the workings of the human mind has to recognize the non-computer–simulable character of its operations established in chapter V. Hubert Dreyfus reached the same conclusion in his *What Computers Still Can't Do* of 1979, establishing the same nonmechanistic view of human beings to which my arguments lead. My approach has different starting points, in this chapter applying Gibson's holistic conceptions to identify the shape of the psychology required for explaining the learning and use of language.

Section 1. Human Beings as Integrated Unities: Gibson's Work as a Key to Escaping Physicalism

(a) *The impossibility of any kind of physicalist account, even of a holistic kind*

At the end of chapter III we observed how many linguists and psycholinguists, Chomsky and Jackendoff among them, anticipate or presume that linguistic structures are resultant upon the structures of neurological functioning within the brain, structures of which they say that linguistic theory provides abstract functional descriptions. Such accounts involve difficulties for human identity to which Daniel Dennett has presented the most sophisticated relevant approach.[1] Dennett's suggestions therefore require particular attention.

However, what I argued earlier excludes any such ultimately purely physically based explanation of the workings of speech and language. For in our earlier chapters we saw how the informality with which we are able to use words and yet still be reliably understood by our hearers shows the impossibility of simulating our use of language or thought mechanically in the mathematical sense of the word "mechanical".[2] Rather, the use of understanding

1. Dennett's apparent sophistication in *Consciousness Explained* reflects his response to "linguistic" philosophy of the period 1940–70, including his doctoral supervisor, Ryle. Dennett's treatment of the "reality" of mental patterns (see chap. VIII of this volume) is independent of the issues of identity raised in this chapter.

2. This even excludes simulation through the adoption of a Dynamical Systems approach, although, as Timothy van Gelder points out, such approaches can allow the possibility of digital simulation: "Program (that is, physically configure) a computer (a concrete computational system) so that it produces sequences of symbol-configurations which *represent* points in the state trajectories of the abstract dynamical model under consideration. In such a situation, the computer does not itself constitute a model of the cognitive process, since it does not contain numerically measurable aspects changing over time in the way that aspects of the target system [the real system which it is being attempted to model in terms of dynamical systems

is indispensable in the use of language. Physical explanations are inadequate to explain either the linguistic behavior illustrated in chapters I and II or the open-ended variety and number in the methods of establishing truth in mathematics and other fields seen in chapter V.

This excludes any possibility that the ability reliably (in normal cases) to understand the speech of others operates in a mathematically mechanical way, as it would do if this operation were the mere resultant of the activity of physically interacting material parts. Nor can explanation of a stable relationship between speaker and hearer behavior be achieved by any bringing in of analog features to supplement digital ones, since these can in principle be digitally simulated to any required degree of approximation.[3]

This excludes any form of the fashionable view that human behavior, including linguistic behavior, is ultimately physically explicable. My argument turns on the general character of language, reflecting the whole spread of human understanding's application; it is not a matter solely of rarefied argument turning on the technicalities of mathematical argument about methods of proof in mathematics, of which Gödel's methods provide merely one instance, but of what is involved in understanding quite ordinary utterances.

In subsection (b) I show that any satisfactory psychological treatment of speech and language must have a holistic character, and in (c) that it must exclude dualism.

(b) *Higher animals must be conceived holistically as mind-involving subjects*

If a surface is red, each perceptibly distinguishable part of it is red. If a body weighs ten pounds, then, although each bodily part of it will weigh less, it will still weigh something—that is, have a property of the kind concerned. By contrast, if a man or dog sees, or imagines, or desires, it is not the case that his legs see, imagine, or desire anything; and similarly, if a man understands, it is not the case that the various parts of him, or even that some part of his brain, understands. And if human beings or dogs see something, it is not accurate to say that it is their eyes which see something, though it is by means of their eyes (among other things) that they see.

Therefore human beings and higher animals are unitary beings, not in the sense of not having bodily parts, but in the sense that their mind-involving properties can only be attributed to them as unities—indeed precisely as hu-

theory] are hypothesized to be changing. That is the computer does not realize the abstract dynamical model; rather it *simulates* it"; Van Gelder, "What Might Cognition Be, If Not Computation?" *Journal of Philosophy* 92, no. 7 (1995): 369.

3. Whatever can be explained in analog terms can, it seems, be in a certain sense "simulated" digitally.

man beings or animals. In *The Human Person* I call this their being "focalized subjects" and explain how it is indispensable to our understanding and explanation of much human and animal behavior.[4]

Failure to recognize this indispensability is one of the fatal flaws in what is called the "pandemonium" theory of the human mind put forward by some AI theorists.

(i) The "pandemonium" theory whereby the self has no more than "narrative" identity

In talking to other people and thinking to ourselves, we presuppose an account or narrative of our own experiences and actions in which we figure as the experiencer and the actor. But in the view of Daniel Dennett, along with other cognitive scientists, such as Michael Gazzaniga, the self has no real existence in itself but is, in effect, an illusion created by our belief in this narrative, and in reality there is no "self" underlying this narrative. In his popular presentations Gazzaniga speaks of this story or narrative as a construct of the left hemisphere of the brain, of the "interpretive chip" or a bit of circuitry located in the left hemisphere which, language-based, asks questions, reasons, and generates hypotheses and theories so as to construct a coherent account of our life and the world.

In human life, decisions have to be made as to what the human organism is to do, and these generally presuppose decisions or judgments as to what is the case. AI theorists have to explain such decisions. Here the philosopher Dennett has followed Marvin Minsky and many others in identifying the workings of the mind with the workings of the brain.[5] This brain is represented as composed of a multiplicity of systems, each with its own genealogy and history; metaphorically these systems are "agents" forming a society, so that the history of each becomes in effect a biography in its own right, these "agents" being like the homunculi or demons spoken of by other AI theorists. In Dennett's account it is as if each system or "agent" produces a draft text of what might be true in the view of the human being as a whole. The question then becomes how it is to be decided which "text" or opinion the real life "person" will offer in "speech". This will be treated by others as the master view or standpoint of the organism itself, even though it may enshrine a piece of self-deception, and it is here that, from the point of view of others and thence of oneself, one's self-identity is established.

How has this view arisen?

The value of Dennett's presentation of this form of materialism lies in the

4. David Braine, *Human Person,* 312–20; cf. 320–26.

5. Marvin Minsky, *The Society of Mind* (New York: Simon and Schuster, 1985).

clarity with which he exhibits how the way cognitive scientists think of the relation of mind and brain is rooted in Descartes's view of the self. Cognitive scientists first assume that Descartes's way of thinking about the thinking subject, the subject of *pensées* in a wide sense—including not only propositional thoughts, but also volitions, emotions, pains, and impressions experienced as if from the external senses—is the only possible view of the self. They then find themselves driven to conclude that this supposed self must be a mere illusion created by part of the brain, with no existence apart from the story we construct about ourselves, exhibited in what we tell each other. Yet, since the self does not have to be thought of in this way, this whole way of thinking is just a trap, although its influence is almost omnipresent. (Thus Jackendoff treats Dennett as his authority for the statement that "the notion that there is a unified source of free will is a cognitive illusion".)[6]

In *Consciousness Explained* Dennett begins by seeking the best way of describing the "self" or "consciousness" and our conscious experience. And this, he instantly suggests, is by a monologue consisting of the narrative which the person might imagine presenting to another person in an attempt to describe his "experience". He regards such narratives as providing the theorist with a convenient style of description for the "experience" of the "subject", but only, it turns out, on the proviso that any such narratives may be false, and apparently false in any respect. He suggests that, though some of the statements contained in such narratives may be mistaken, they still yield a description of the subject's experience as he or she conceives himself or herself to experience it. The experience and life of the "self" in his account will then be whatever is portrayed or reported in such narratives independently of their truth. Dennett's "intentional stance" consists in treating the "self" as the subject of such narratives, irrespective of their truth or untruth in regard to the bodily human being concerned as such.[7]

6. Jackendoff, *Architecture*, 217–18n3, where he is arguing against Chomsky and Descartes's belief in free will as a unitary capacity.

For no good reason, Jackendoff suspects that this would involve the localization of the action of will at one geometrical point in the mind, meaning in the brain. He has not explained how this free will could operate on the body via a point rather than through at least a region of the brain (small, but sufficiently big to operate physically on the rest of the human organism), but logically the latter case is no different in principle from its operating through any larger region within the whole human organism.

The credibility of arguments for free will is (supposedly) "dispelled by current views in cognitive science". But current cognitive science has no one view of explanation, and none adequately demonstrated.

7. It is strange that Dennett should have adopted an approach based on the "intentional stance". For he rejects the modern materialists' parallel to Descartes's argument justifying it—namely, the hypothesis that it would be possible in principle for brain surgeons to maintain a deception whereby an entity which was in fact nothing more than a brain in a vat was cunningly fed with nervous inputs in such a way that it thought that it was a full-bodied, normally functioning human being. But Dennett insists at the very start of his book that the variety of situations to be allowed for and handled by rule is beyond the powers of any practically conceivable computer to simulate; cf. chap. V, n. 20 of this volume.

In accepting this intentional stance, uncommitted to the correspondence of our experience with how the world actually is, Dennett has accepted the legitimacy of Descartes's methodology of "bracketing" our experience from how the world is.[8] His aim is to establish the Cartesian conception of conscious experience and of the "self" or "consciousness" as its subject (even if he does this only in order to set them aside later). He has adopted this device of an "intentional stance" in order (a) to avoid the objections made to successive empiricist theories, theories which suggest such candidates as Berkeley's "ideas", Hume's "impressions", or "sense-data" as being internal objects to the mind, and at the same time (b) to escape the criticisms of "linguistic philosophers" such as Ryle and Austin. And he has done this in a way which makes the AI theorists' representation of the mind as analogous to a society of systems or demons, each with its own biography, more plausible.

The strategic point of introducing this "intentional stance" whereby the autobiographical narratives spoken of can be regarded as having no implications as to the person's actual environment and behavior, but instead no more than the status of mere opinions, analogous to draft reports awaiting finalization, is straightforward. Its aim is to show that, as statements in the biography of a supposed "self", they need have no ontological realization beyond the brain of the human being concernedwith its states and processes.

For his design is to show that this supposed "self" is a fiction, purporting to show this by questioning the objectivity of our judgments about time in the way I describe in the appendix to this chapter.

Yet in this very starting point of supposing the legitimacy of the "intentional stance" or "bracketing" lies his root mistake. For there are other conceptions of the person or self than this bracketed "self". This supposition of the legitimacy of the "intentional stance" (supported by such arguments as I instance in the appendix) indeed suffices to show that his bracketed "self" is

8. Descartes introduced the hypothesis of our being without bodies and without any true experience of the world, but merely deceived by a malevolent demon making us think that we had these things. This was the justification Descartes offered for his notion of consciousness and conscious experience. The essence of the "I" was to be an *être pensant*, Descartes counting sensory experiences, emotions, and volitions as well as thoughts, all equally as examples of *pensées*, or what Hume calls "perceptions of the mind", and this "I" being what Hume calls "the self". It was this Cartesian hypothesis that generated the idea of "bracketing" the world, revived in Husserl's phenomenological "reduction" whereby he held that we could describe our experience in a way noncommittal as to the existence of the world. Husserl viewed this as a way of freeing one's thought from any suppositions as to what exists in reality or in itself ("transcendental suppositions"), and getting at the essentials of our subjective experience or psychic life. This stance, noncommittal as to the correspondence of our experience with how the world actually is, is what Dennett calls the "intentional stance" (*Consciousness Explained*, 76). But neither Dennett nor Husserl has any proof that the adoption of this stance is a legitimate option in our systematic thinking, and many of Husserl's followers in phenomenology, Heidegger and Ingarden (Dermot Moran, *Introduction to Phenomenology* [London: Routledge, 2000, 226–28]) and even Merleau-Ponty (here I follow the interpretation of Eric Matthews, *The Philosophy of Merleau-Ponty* [Chesham, UK: Acumen, 2002, 31–34, 67–74, 160–61, 169–71]), along with a long line of "linguistic" philosophers from Ryle, Wittgenstein, and Austin onwards, have rejected it as illegitimate.

a fiction. But it is no basis for rejecting the conception of the human person or being as a unitary or "focalized" subject in the sense explained earlier, combining both mind-involving and physical properties. In (ii) and (iii) I show the depth of Dennett's mistake and begin to open out this more realistic perspective.

The alternative to which he is condemned, the "pandemonium" theory, has to find a way of establishing some hierarchy or rule among the "demons". To avoid the chaos resulting from all the "systems", "demons", or "agents" putting their draft reports forward at the same time, a certain hierarchy has to emerge among the different drafts. Here many suggestions have been put forward, of which Dennett's is only one. What is significant is that all the systems suggested share the feature that none of the "cooperating" systems or "agents" is dominant, so that there is no single thread running through all the successive final drafts, no single thread running through all the successive deliverances of the organism's supposed consciousness. Successive utterances do not constitute a genuine biography of any one person, agent, or system.[9]

This, then, is what Dennett means when he makes out that self-identity consists in nothing more than narrative identity. We are to regard speaking of all these narratives and draft narratives as merely a concession to anthropomorphism, parallel to our speaking of even relatively primitive computers as making judgments or giving answers.

However, against Dennett, and speaking literally and not metaphorically, in reality it is only the speech of the human being himself or herself with other human beings which is in truth speech, and the issuance of what both we and Dennett speak of as a person. And Dennett has supplied no valid justification for regarding this actual speech as having essentially the same status as the imagined draft texts which preceded it, and being the final text only in the sense of being the one heard by other people, and being regarded by them as having the authority of what they think of as a person. Rather, in reality it is the only actual text, and the rest represent only supposed conscious or unconscious forethoughts, not judgments.

In Dennett's view it follows from his argument that if human beings lacked actual language for any appreciable time, then over that time these hu-

9. "Consciousness" so conceived is accomplished by "a distributed society of specialists that is equipped with a working memory, called a global workspace, whose contents can be broadcast to the system as a whole"; Bernard Baars, *A Cognitive Theory of Consciousness* (Cambridge: Cambridge University Press, 1988), 42. Dennett says there is no single definitive stream of consciousness or central headquarters where it all comes together for perusal by a Central Meaner. Instead, he thinks, there are lots of systems, like Shakey as described in n. 70, except much more complex. Michael S. Gazzaniga has portrayed a wealth of data arising from the study of neurological deficits as supporting a view of the mind as a coalition or bundle of semi-independent agencies; see Gazzaniga and Joseph E. LeDoux, *The Integrated Mind* (New York: Plenum Press, 1978); Gazzaniga, *The Social Brain* (New York: Basic Books, 1985).

man beings would lack self-identity. Self-identity would come into existence only as language came into use, intersubjectivity arising when the things we call "persons" speak with each other.

Unsurprisingly, Dennett's materialist view gives the autobiography the person actually offers no better status than the alternative draft narratives which the person would regard as mistaken. This approach allows no account of personal identity beyond that of the human organism identified physiologically.

(ii) The fatal flaw in the "pandemonium" theory

The real identity of things through time plays an essential role in explanation. This is particularly true in the case of personal and animal identity—a fact entirely neglected in the "pandemonium" theory.

The importance of identity through time presents itself first in physical explanation. It is more economical to suppose that it was the same copy of the Bible which lay on a woman's bedside table when she went to sleep as when she woke up than to suppose that someone took it away and replaced it with another, indistinguishable copy while she slept without her knowing. Hume envisages us as using such causal reasoning when thinking about identity. But this identity is merely material.

Dennett can suppose that the self and self-identity through time are fictions only because, in his view, they play no such role in the ultimate explanation of what happens. Statements purporting to report the affairs of the self in his view concern a fictional identity: only physical states whose existence we may infer from autobiographical narratives play any part in the real explanation of our behavior (including our speech itself), while "experiences" and "intentions" such as these statements purport to describe play no such part.[10]

However, we have no access to any of the neurological explanations of the courses of human behavior over stretches of time which he would envisage. Rather, most of our explanations of human and other higher animal behavior depend essentially upon the persistent identity of the subject through the course of the events concerned.

As I observed in my book *The Human Person*, this persistent identity already arises with higher animals other than man.[11] Thus a dog may see his master put meat on a shelf in a larder, and the next day being left on guard in the adjoining room, remembering the meat, may paw at the door of the larder and, finding that the door opens (not being properly closed), proceed to take the meat and consume it. This explanation involves visual perception

10. Here Dennett's view concurs with Jackendoff, *Consciousness and the Computational Mind*: nothing mental has any effect in the physical world.

11. David Braine, *Human Person*, 301–10; cf. 297–99.

and memory, each implying knowledge, along with imagination, the desire of the meat, and the exercise of skill in pawing at the door, the whole activity being "voluntary" (*hekōn*) in Aristotle's sense—that is, proceeding from desire, though not implying will (*boulē*). I have explained elsewhere how this pattern of explanation presupposes the animal's having the capacity to learn and the relevance of emotion (desire, fear, etc., all emotions being responses to things as good or ill) to one's account of what is perceived.[12]

All such explanations involve the persistence of one subject, not only through the whole course of events concerned, the perception, memory, imagination, desire, and "voluntary" actions all being predicated of one and the same subject, but also through the whole life history in which, through experience and various kinds of learning and habituation, the underlying capacities and dispositions involved are acquired. It is only when experiences, decisions, and actions are taken out of the context of an extended life-history that paradoxical cases arise, giving some apparent footing to Dennett's questioning of the possibility of objectivity in our judgments about them in the way examined in the appendix to this chapter—a questioning which neglects what is involved in considering human beings and other animals as dynamic psychophysical systems subsisting over extended periods.

Furthermore, while all these things involve that the subject be bodily and act using bodily organs, they are all of a special kind such as can only be predicated of the subject as a whole. That is, they are not features of a kind which can be predicated, not only of the subject as a whole but also of various of its parts, by contrast with physical and sensory properties: for instance, if a surface is flat and pink, then each part of it is flat and pink, and if a body has a certain weight, its various parts will also have weight, although less, so that the parts at least have properties of the same kind as the whole. In sum we can say that these things—perception, memory, imagination, desire, and "voluntary" action—belong to the subject concerned under an aspect in respect of which it is indivisible—that is, the subject as an animal with mind, "an animal with *mens*"; and any such subject is what I called a "focalized subject".

Under the influence of Descartes the idea of an "animal with consciousness" has come to suggest an "inner theater", as if the essential person or self

12. David Braine, *Human Person*, 305–6. This need to refer to evaluation, correlative with desire or will, in one's account of animal perception was recognized in Aquinas's account of the "estimative" power and Merleau-Ponty's conception of "functional value"—both theories in which the way features of the environment are perceived, and thereby affect discriminatory behavior, is shaped by their relevance to the animal's good or ill; cf. *Human Person*, 306. Such conceptions are also integral to J. J. Gibson's ecological approach with his concept of "affordance", an approach involving a renaissance of functionalism in the theory of perception; cf. Eleanor J. Gibson, ed., *An Odyssey in Learning and Perception* (Cambridge, Mass.: MIT Press, 1991), 557–69. The same conception of the place of motivation in animal behavior and the need to describe what the animal perceives in terms of it appears in Taylor, *Explanation of Behaviour*, 66–69, along with some features special to the human case.

should be understood as a "consciousness" which existed as an inner watcher or listener, not using eyes or ears, watching or listening to "sensory" images presented, as it were, on an inner screen or loudspeaker. The same inner observer, without using mouth or nose, ears, organs of touch, hands to explore, or muscles to feel kinaesthetic sensations, would be immediately conscious of all the experiences which we ordinarily regard as mediated by these physical organs.

Yet no such ways of thinking were involved in the use of the Latin word *mens* in regard to animals with perception (*sentire*) by Saint Augustine and others in earlier times.[13] For this reason I speak of higher animals and human beings as mind-exercising organisms and, in the human case, as intellectual mind-exercising organisms or beings, avoiding the terms "conscious" and "consciousness".

When it comes to human behavior, the explanatory role of mind-involving concepts is clear. Again, it involves the persistence of the subject of mind-involving predicates through the whole course of events under consideration, and again the special kind of subjecthood which I called "focalized". But now we find that the explanations being offered involve the consideration and acceptance of reasons for a certain conclusion, assent to this conclusion, and action in the light of it, and the advent of capacity allowing for language brings with it the capacity for hopes and desires more complex than those attributed to other animals—for instance, the desire for the return of someone in seven days' time.

So it is that, in a multitude of cases, we have one and the same subject following through a long course of argument while engaged in fundamental physics, theories about plate tectonics, complex mathematics, legal proof, archaeology, or history. It does not matter whether the subject concerned is working things out in his or her head, following the argument presented by another person in speech, or examining an argument in print. The same intellectual capacity is involved in all three cases, and in each case the same subject has to consider and weigh the reasons at each stage, give his or her assent at that stage, pass on to the next stage, and so forth until he or she gives his or her final assent. It may take one some hours, or in some cases (e.g., in the recent proving of Fermat's Last Theorem) some eight years, yet one subject has to accomplish all the relevant reading and reflection. In other creative work we find the same requirement: it was the same subject who conceived *The Critique of Pure Reason* who also completed it, the same subject who first envisaged *Pride and Prejudice* who also completed it. In some cases works are completed or

13. By contrast with the Latin *mens*, the Greek *nous* signified only the intellect, normally the theoretical intellect. As to *sentire*, when Aquinas and earlier authors use this word, they are speaking of perception by the outer senses. Physical pain was conceived as a physically caused grief (*dolor*)—i.e., as an emotion, not a sensation, closer to motivation than to cognition.

reedited by other people, but in these two examples, as in many others, there was one person throughout.

As I have mentioned, one particularly notable case of such explanation is provided by the intellectual grasp of the recent proof of Fermat's Last Theorem, both in its elements and in its whole strategy and cogency. Chapter V instanced other notable cases, and they are found in every main field of study. But all these cases in which a single subject is involved in following through an extended argument, and not just the mathematical ones, depend upon the exercise of understanding, and in particular the understanding of concepts which make possible the kind of nonmechanical polymorphous use of words described in chapters I and II. In all such cases it is one and the same subject who has to apply his or her understanding of the concept, unitary over the whole width of its potential application, at each stage of the argument concerned.

I noted how often material identity was crucial to explanation. What we are now finding is that in the case of the higher animals and, most clearly, in the case of human beings, it is the identity of a subject as a "mental organism" which is crucial to acceptable explanations of courses of affairs, not mere material identity. And in the case of human beings it is not just the identity of this subject as a mind-exercising organism, sentient and subject of memory, imagination, desire, and fear, but, beyond this, as also a being with understanding, an intellectual being or "person".

Both in the human and animal cases it is not just that rival explanations in AI terms are currently unavailable (and in certain cases demonstrably impossible), but that they would be extraordinarily lacking in the simplicity, elegance, and predictive capacity associated with our ordinary explanations.[14]

These considerations also remove any plausibility from another of Dennett's suggestions mentioned above—namely, that the question of the identity of these mind-exercising organisms arises only when they begin to speak to one another. But we find explanations involving perception, memory, imagination, desire, and "voluntary" action useful in the case of all the animals, as well as babies, which exhibit these features. And such explanations depend upon the persisting identity of the animal or human being concerned as a mind-exercising organism independently of whether such being has developed speech. Therefore it cannot be right to think of the identity of the animal or human being as arising only when human beings begin to speak to each other.

Moreover, if we apply explanations of kinds involving reasoning and re-

14. The ways in which computers win chess games against great masters, by exploring the upshot of all possible moves for (say) ten moves ahead, bear little relation to the methods of the masters. These depend not on looking so far ahead but on appreciation of different gambits and strategies, an appreciation with which the computer cannot be programmed. The computer requires successive reprogramming, soon to be outwitted at each stage—the advice of chess masters can provide drills, not adaptable skills.

flection to the activities of human beings who speak, then there seems no necessary reason not to apply them to those who are not speaking, unless their not speaking is due to a defect. It is possible to hypothesize that human beings may have gained the genetic capacity for speech with the integrated complex structure of contemporary human languages at the pragmatic, semantic, and syntactic level, phonetically subserved, before exercising this capacity to the full. But there is no reason to suppose that explanations involving identity as intellectual subjects had to wait until speech had fully developed, a process which on this hypothesis might take a number of generations—no compelling reason to suppose that a being with the genetic capacity for language could not deliberate before having developed or learned a language in which to express his or her deliberations.

As I remarked earlier, Dennett's root-mistake lies in his acceptance of "bracketing" or the "intentional stance" with the associated Cartesian idea of "conscious experience". For him, as for Descartes, Hume, and Husserl, "conscious experience" is something which can be described in a way noncommittal as to the correspondence of our experience with how the world actually is. And this is the strategy of modern materialists, who all wish to say that "conscious experiences" have their only realizations in brain states and events. Yet this is the heart of the error. The primary realizations of "conscious experience" are in states and events in the lives of persons as whole sentient animals, mind-exercising bodily organisms, unitary focalized wholes, not in a history of brains or of any supposed "selves" or "consciousnesses" inside people. The intellectual and sentient person is the whole biological organism as a focalized unity, not a brain. The most conspicuous exercises of intellect are in speech and the hearing of speech, writing, and reading, the forms of communication typical of the human species, exhibiting a unity of motor activity, sentience, and understanding, so that it is not being "inner" which makes something intellectual or mental.[15]

What we need is a holistic understanding of human beings in which they are conceived of as focalized subjects, the same subject, intellectual, sentient, emotional, and bodily at the same time. We could call this a "mind-involving holism". And it is this holism that modern materialists conspicuously reject, taking everything conscious to have its only realization in the brain, and this causally linked to what goes on in the body in other parts and respects. The mind/body division has in this way been replaced by an isomorphic brain/body distinction. As I showed in *The Human Person*, all the objections to the first distinction apply equally to the second.

It is because I am concerned with the holism which arises from the char-

15. This is made very clear in Ryle, *Concept of Mind*, chap. 2.

acter of mind-exercising biological beings (that is, from their being focalized subjects) that I have paid less attention to the holistic features of classical and contemporary physics.[16]

(iii) The starting point of Gibson's way of thinking

A long process of cultural deformation has made the Cartesian way of conceiving sensory experiences, emotions, volitions, and thoughts, along with their subjects, the natural and obvious way of conceiving them, assumed by watchers of the television program *Star Trek* as well as by cognitive scientists. Yet there is nothing obvious or natural about it. Rather, all these things have to be viewed as realized not in brain processes, but in episodes in the life of animals considered as wholes, as mental organisms—and in the case of human beings, mental organisms with intellect.

Consider perception first, in particular visual perception, something we share with many other animals. As I walk on a forest road looking about me, I notice a shrub on my left and go over to inspect the shape of its leaves and identify it, perhaps taking a leaf and turning it over to inspect its other side. In such a course of events the description of my "conscious experience" consists in narrating parts of the biography of a sentient bodily being. And from this narrative we can appreciate that, as Gibson argues, "the organs of the visual system" are "First, the lens, pupil, chamber and the retina"; "Second, the eye with its muscles in the orbit . . . an organ both stabilized and mobile"; "Third, the two eyes in the head . . . a binocular organ"; "Fourth, the eyes in a mobile head which can turn . . . an organ for the pickup of ambient information"; and "Fifth, the eyes in a head on a body . . . a superordinate organ for information pickup over paths of locomotion".[17] That is, where sight is concerned, the active experiencing subject operates not just by means of the retina, but by means which involve the operation of two moving eyes in a head constantly moving in a body also moving, so that the bodily organic subject concerned

16. Elements of holism have entered into physics ever more deeply, first with the recognition that the phenomenon of motion involves a conception of the continuous, so that points have to be considered as cuts in a line, not parts of it, so that lines cannot be reduced to sets of points; then with the extension of field theory from the treatment of electricity and magnetism to that of gravitation; and finally with the quantum theory and with what is called "complexity" theory (often drawing on elements from "chaos" theory).

Moreover, to many physical problems, the holistic "Dynamical Systems Theory" approach is more appropriate than a mathematically and physically atomistic or mechanical one. Nice examples of the application of dynamical systems theory to purely physical problems are instanced by Van Gelder, "What Might Cognition Be". The Dynamical Systems approach was introduced to the study of neural networks by Stephen Grossberg in Boston in the 1960s, and its subsequent followers have attempted to develop the mathematics of David G. Luenberger, *Introduction to Dynamic Systems: Theory, Models, and Applications* (New York: Wiley, 1979).

17. J. J. Gibson, *The Senses Considered as Perceptual Systems* (Boston: Houghton Mifflin, 1966), 50, 245; cf. J. J. Gibson, *The Perception of the Visual World* (Boston: Houghton Mifflin, 1950); J. J. Gibson, "The Concept of Stimulus in Psychology", *American Psychologist* 15 (1960): 694–703; and J. J. Gibson, *The Ecological Approach to Visual Perception* (Boston: Houghton Mifflin, 1979).

operates as a unitary whole, varying the direction in which it looks and the position from which it is looking—for instance, as it walks through the forest or bends to examine a particular plant more closely. The subject of such conscious experience is not an inner watcher within the mind confronted with a succession of images or visual presentations, but something essentially bodily—the same subject who intentionally walks and directs his or her gaze this way and that way is also the one who sees.

Next, consider emotion. The character of the distress involved in physical pain cannot be understood without appreciating the types of behavior in which it may be expressed and the character of sensual pleasures, whether of taste or of sex, without reference to the circumstances and activities in which they arise. Hunger cannot be understood without reference to the anticipation of some alleviation by the taking of food, fear without reference to anticipated danger and the impulse to avoid it, and being angry with somebody without reference to an impulse to attack or hurt him or her in some way. With volition the primary expression of will is not a mere intention or decision when one may yet change one's mind, but the intentional action itself.[18] Last, even with thought and understanding, it is characteristic of human beings to express them, both in their own minds and to others, in the medium of words, so that the same subjects both have opinions and put them forward, understand something and explain it. Moreover, it is the language which a group shares in public which shapes the way its members think to themselves.

Perception and emotions such as pain, pleasure, hunger, and fear are characteristic of many animals as well as human beings. Such mind-involving features in animals require being viewed, not as internal to the mind or brain, but as realized in episodes in the life of animals considered as wholes. And this is just as true in the case of features special to human beings, not just in the cases of anger and volition, but also in those of the most obvious workings of intellect—namely, deliberation, self-reflection, and intellectual wonder. We may conduct our debates as to what is true or what to do and may conduct our self-reflection without speaking, but their nature as activities of deliberation and self-reflection is the same, whether we speak out loud and with others or conduct our deliberations without speaking.

We can understand this better by means of a parallel. When we go to the supermarket and put a melon in our shopping cart, we do not watch ourselves doing this or know of our doing it by such watching of ourselves. We know because we do these things intentionally. We are authors of our actions. The same applies with the workings of intellect, even when they are not public. When we deliberate what is true or what to do or reflect upon ourselves, we

18. Cf. David Braine, *Human Person,* chap. 4, sec. 1 on action and sec. 3 on emotion.

do not know the course of our deliberations or reflection by an inner listening, but because we are the author of our thoughts.

Thus our life so far as we are conscious of it, including thoughts, experiences, and feelings, is played out in the real world, the public world of other people and nature. True, much of our conscious life is not public, but when our thoughts, experiences, or feelings are unexpressed, this does not make them parts of the life of a secret, hidden, inner being, the self, rather than of the person active at home and in the market, wandering the world, seeing and engaging with it.

I give prominence to Gibson's approach primarily because it indicates the lines to be taken by viable alternatives to mechanist accounts. Such alternatives must recognize the nonfictional character of personal identity and be holistic in showing the essential role of body and brain together in underpinning mental function—rather than taking the dualistic form of one thing (the mind or brain) interacting with another thing or organized assemblage of things (the body related to the mind or the rest of the body related to the brain).

Thus the existence of the human agent is not a cognitive illusion, and the same human being who acts also sees, hears, talks, and thinks. The expression "the source of human free will" has no relevant meaning unless it means the personal agent himself or herself, the single author of his or her deliberate acts. The human agent is not a "source of control to be found *in* the brain", a "central executive" *within* the brain, or a "narrative *center* of gravity" *within* the brain. Suppositions like these are byproducts of the influence of Cartesian dualism. Contrary to Descartes and to the materialist, the human agent is not a part of the person, whether a Cartesian soul or anything else, located in the brain or anywhere else; rather, it is simply the person as a bodily being as such.

The question we posed earlier now becomes the question as to how the physical functioning of the human body can subserve or underpin the mental, linguistic, and intellectual functioning of the human being as a "focalized" subject. In section 2 I propose to make this question concrete by considering the case of perception, concentrating on the case of visual perception because it is the one which has been most studied.

In sum, I regard that which both perceives and acts from emotion in higher animals without speech, and also both hears and speaks in the case of human beings, as the animals and human beings themselves. Daniel Dennett's "narrative centers of gravity",[19] centers of each human being's tale or autobiography, are not "cognitive illusions", but actual bodily beings, the very human beings we hear speaking to us, knowing the tale they tell, intentional agents exercising active power, in no way fictional—although sometimes they may

19. Dennett, *Consciousness Explained*, 410 passim.

tell lies or be mistaken or in atypical or contrived situations be deceived.

Once we have escaped from the Cartesian way of thinking of persons and instead think of them as organisms whose behavior is functionally related to the environment, we no longer need to suppose that they have the only authoritative account of their own character and motivations. We can, for instance, be in doubt as to "what we really want". We are not perfectly known to ourselves, and do not always know the roots of our insights or emotion. Rather, we are ignorant of our deepest selves.

(c) *The exclusion of dualism*

We have seen that a merely physicalistic account of human nature is excluded by the phenomenon of understanding as exhibited in language, as well as in the open-endedness of the number of ways of establishing truth. However, the dualistic remedy of a soul and body interacting with each other is to be excluded on many grounds. Indeed, dualism might be thought of as a deviant form of materialism, still explaining the behavior of a thing in terms of the natures, relations, and causal interactions of its parts, but just adding one immaterial part (a mind or soul) to an assemblage of material parts.

However, mind/body dualism is to be excluded not only on the grounds of which I have given forceful account elsewhere,[20] but also, more directly, on simple logical grounds. For the body to act on a mind, the body has to be of such a nature as to be capable of so acting, and, for the mind to act upon a body, the body has to be capable of being acted upon by a mind. Each of these requires the bodily parts of the human being to be holistically organized.

It is the first aptitude, of the body to act on the mind, which presents the worst difficulty. A distributed set of material parts, if they act according to physical principles alone, cannot have within it any principle whereby the parts can act in cooperation to secure a mental effect. Indeed, it is easier to conceive the mind or soul nonsensorily knowing the disposition of the parts and responding to this accordingly than to conceive the material acting on the spiritual. It is as if the body would have to be mentalistically organized if it were to act upon a mind or soul.[21] This essentially logical requirement finds indirect recognition in Fodor's requirement that input systems must "so represent the world as to make it accessible to thought"[22] and in Jackendoff's faith that language "data structures", as stored and assembled in the function-

20. David Braine, *Human Person*, pt. 1.

21. Thus, that a body act physically or materially on a pure spirit is evidently more difficult in principle than that a pure spirit, as it were imitating God, should act by a contact of power on a body; cf. Aquinas, *Summa Contra Gentiles* II, c. 56, 2–10.

22. Fodor, *The Modularity of Mind* (Cambridge, Mass.: MIT Press, 1983), 39–46. His requirement that such systems ("compiled transducers" or "input analyzers"; cf. 47–100) should feed the supposed central

ing brain, will be capable of characterization in the form of a grammar.[23] The need for holism in relating the mind to the body inspired Timothy van Gelder to apply Dynamical Systems Theory to this problem—adding, as we shall discover, the realization that one will only find an appropriate description of the mind if one allows one's holism to extend to the relationship between the experiencing and thinking self and its whole physical environment.[24]

There is no logical difficulty in a mind or soul, conceived of as a pure spirit, acting on a body—no evident lack of power. The main difficulty is as to how the body is to be acted upon, since for a body to be acted upon by a spirit, the various parts of the brain and conceivably other parts of the human organism would have to be in highly contrived physical relationships and the spirit would have to act in a coordinated way at many different places in the body to secure its effect—a golfer has no leverage on a golf club if he merely touches it at one point. In order to operate, the will would require at least a region of the brain, not a geometrical point, through which to operate (small, but big enough to operate through physically on the rest of the human organism). This excludes what seems to have been Descartes's own view of the mind as acting on the body at one geometrical point in the brain located in the pineal gland, and free will as a unitary capacity acting solely from this one localized point.[25]

Locke had the flight of fancy that a material body could think independently of any structure (as if perhaps a uniform block of iron would serve). And Anthony Kenny has suggested that it would make no difference to our thinking that a human being has a mind if it turned out that the human head were full of sawdust.[26] Our holistic account of human nature excludes such mad conceptions. The bodily functioning of a being with a highly organized physical constitution must play a key role in underpinning mental functioning.[27] The problem is as to how this is to be explained.[28]

---

processor "in the language in which the machine computes" is only part of what is required of the input to human beings to be fed to human beings in such a way that they can form appropriate beliefs and act appropriately.

23. Jackendoff supposes that the grammar of a language is a "functional characterization of the 'data structures' stored and assembled in the f-mind [i.e., the functional organization and activity of the brain]"; Jackendoff, *Foundations*, 34; see chap. III, sec. 4 (c) of this volume.

24. Van Gelder, "What Might Cognition Be, If Not Computation?"; cf. Robert F. Port and Timothy van Gelder, eds., *Mind as Motion: Exploration in the Dynamics of Cognition* (Cambridge, Mass.: MIT Press, 1995).

25. Jackendoff, *Architecture*, 217–18n3; cf. n. 6 of this chapter.

26. Anthony J. Kenny, *The Metaphysics of Mind* (Oxford: Oxford University Press, 1989), 30.

27. I explained the problem at greater length in *Human Person*, chap. 9, 336–39.

28. I do not discuss the kind of Aristotelian account which introduces the concept of soul and envisages the soul as present at every point of the living bodily being of which it is the organizing principle, maintaining its identity despite the chaotic input it receives from its environment.

Section 2. Mechanical Processes in Living Organisms: "Mechanical" an Ambiguous Word

As different types of organism arise within nature we find that at various stages it becomes economical for the purposes of human description and explanation to use new forms of description and explanation. Such shifts in patterns of explanation do not always have metaphysical implications, as if some absolutely new kind of entity had "emerged". For instance, no one supposes that because the patterns of explanation employed in organic chemistry are not conducted in terms of quarks or the other theoretical entities spoken of in fundamental physics, it follows that some different, nonphysical kind of being is being spoken of. We take it that what is being described and explained in organic chemistry is ultimately determined at the level of the underlying fundamental physics, but that it is impractical to seek predictions or to conduct our explanations by trying to go back to that underlying level. Therefore, when in the course of evolution we speak of new forms of life marked by new types of goal-seeking behavior as emerging, we are making a claim which is primarily empirical and historical, not metaphysical. However, at each stage we should ask the character and spread of the types of goal which economical description and explanation suggest which the organism seeks.

(a) *Proper human functioning involves mechanisms*

The question of the types of ways in which brain and body physiology and functioning may subserve various mental functions, raised at the end of section 1 (b), quickly gives rise to the question of the role of processes commonly counted as mechanical within human functioning. It is here that the notion of modularity has entered into psychology.

The problem of explaining how mechanical processes are integrated into the functioning of living organisms, and human beings in particular, arises in at least three different contexts.

First, some physical systems in the body are so organized that specific types of variation in the stimulation of an organism can effect specific aspects of the experience, behavior, and judgment of the organism as a whole with deceptive results. I have in mind what affects our awareness of things as continuous, the importance of thresholds in stimulation before we observe things, the importance of gate-phenomena in this, and the various phenomena discussed in the appendix.

Second, defective functioning in specific respects on the part of the organism as a whole can in many cases be correlated with specific physical effects in the brain resulting from neurological interventions, injuries, or inherited conditions, disorder in the experience of pain being the best known. The phenomenon of "blindsight" as studied by Milner and Goodale suggests that perception is served by two distinct neural systems, the one directed towards the vision of things as spread in a field of view and the other towards goal-directed action, leading to deceptive effects in cases of impaired function, but in the normal case operating seamlessly, action being set in a context of global planning.[29] Both neural systems are geared to perception as the means of our well-adaptedness to the environment and as involving an inseparability of cognition and awareness of activity, the vision of things as spread out being especially dependent on the awareness of ambulatory activity, head-turning, and so forth, emphasized by Gibson, while the goal-directed action concerned is conspicuous in close-range engagement anticipatory of touch. Blindsight is perhaps better understood than the kinds of aphasia discussed by Steven Pinker in *Words and Rules*.[30]

Third, many features of our use of language may be ascribed to skilled conscious performance—conscious not in the sense of being reflected upon beforehand and produced according to conscious plan, but in the sense that retrospectively we could explain how the effect was achieved, somewhat as soccer players, tennis players, violinists, or opera singers can give some retrospective accounts of how they used their organs and instruments in order to achieve the effects they did, but others, less practiced, are unlikely to be able to provide such account—there is no precise line to be drawn between the types of case. Yet physiological mechanisms are being relied upon throughout.

Thus, clearly, proper human functioning involves so-called mechanisms. I consider the relevant sense of this ambiguous word in (d).

(b) *How to formulate the problem of incorporating "mechanisms" into a holistic account*

The outcome of the operation of a physical mechanism is an effect. Mechanisms, including assemblies of physical mechanisms connected by parallel processing, produce effects, and both these effects and the processes of producing of them are physical in nature. These mechanisms and complexes of mechanisms are not the authors of these effects, since human beings are authors of their speech and actions and other higher animals are authors of their actions, whereas mechanisms and complexes of mechanisms do not look or

29. A. David Milner and Melvyn A. Goodale, *The Visual Brain in Action* (Oxford: Oxford University Press, 1995), and their "Two Visual Systems Re-viewed", *Neuropsychologia* 46 (2008): 774–85. I avoid their word "representation" for reasons evident in sec. 3 of this chapter and chap. VIII.

30. Pinker, *Words and Rules*, 244–68.

explore, watch or observe, listen for or listen to what is spoken; they neither see nor hear nor understand. They are not alive.

We think of what is alive as exercising some kind of initiative. In the human case this reaches to being the author of one's speaking and acting according to intention. But more generally, with the higher animals, looking, exploring, watching, observing, seeing and feeling by touch, listening and hearing are not passive processes in which seeing, feeling, and hearing are simply the passive effects of the working of mechanisms. Aristotle correctly thought of all the higher animals as self-movers, their actions being "voluntary" (*hekōn*), not in the sense of being from will, but as done unimpeded according to wish, even though without having intellect and will to influence, let alone control, their emotions. In these cases the "initiative" of which I speak, still associated with what I called "focalized subjecthood", does not involve a lack of determinedness, but is determined according to emotion or motive, not by a mechanism.

The idea of living organisms as focalized subjects carries with it the idea of their being "authors" of their actions, something whose implications for the question of physical determinism I have discussed elsewhere.[31] In brief, in order to refute the charge that an action was "by chance" or "by accident", it suffices to show that it was in this broad sense "intentionally" done by a living being. The influence of Hume has led us to think of causation as a relation between earlier sets of events and states of affairs and later ones in which the later follow the earlier in conformity to law, "chance" being thought of as the absence of such causation. But the idea of human beings and higher animals as intending their actions takes us to a different model of causation in which causes are not events or states of affairs, but substances with active powers exercising these powers, in these cases acting intentionally or according to desire. Within this latter model beliefs, desires, choices, and so forth play a role in explaining human and animal action, but it is the human beings and animals who are causes or agents in their actions, and—what is pertinent to language—authors of their utterances and thoughts.

By contrast, Dennett conceives human beings as mere complexes of interrelating mechanisms, even though they do not think or speak of themselves in this way, and he would agree that physical mechanisms and complexes of such mechanisms are not genuinely the authors of these effects in the sense that we commonly think, and that such mechanisms and complexes of mechanisms neither look or explore, watch or observe, listen for or to what is spoken, nor see, hear, or understand. Rather, he thinks that these complexes suffer effects from their environment, function so that their behavior may not be wholly

31. David Braine, *Human Person*, 280–83.

determined, and issue utterances which other such organisms treat as speech (also treating much of their other behavior as evidence of judgments), and that any supposed person or self as the author of such speech or maker of such judgments is a mere fiction, or, as Hume would say, "a fancy of the mind"—a mere *façon de parler* within "folk-psychology".[32]

However, the problem is not the one Dennett and many others have addressed—of how, in a complex of interrelating mechanisms, behavior and utterance are determined, or, in his metaphor, of how "final drafts" are made final. Nor is it the problem as to how, presented with "representation" by an input system, a central processor or executive comes to form a cluster of beliefs, or how the beliefs and emotions of this central executive bring about the behavior they do.

Rather, the problem is as to how systems, whether physically locatable (e.g., in the brain) or otherwise, which are mechanical in the sense that their effects are Turing-computable, can be incorporated within a holistic and teleological conception of the functioning of living organisms. We met this problem earlier in speaking of the problem that, in effect, the body would have to be holistically organized in a way orientated towards mind in order to act upon the soul, with its parallels in Fodor's requirement that input systems must "so represent the world as to make it accessible to thought" and Jackendoff's faith that language "data structures" as stored and assembled in the brain will be characterizable in the form of a grammar. What we shall now discover is the rightness of the insights of Gibson and others, with their ideas of resonance between perception and its context, cross-modality in perception, and what is involved in imitation, which I discuss in chapter VII, section 2. These latter authors recognize how mental functioning, including cognition, has to be understood in terms of the relationship between the animal or human being's life and behavior and its environment.

(c) *Some things' behavior has to be understood teleologically in relation of their environment*

(i) Both living and non-living things need describing in terms of relation to their environment

To see how to envisage understanding animal or human functioning in terms of the relationship between the organism's life and behavior and its environment, let us lower our sights to consider what might seem the simpler cases of plants and bacteria.

32. His view implies that even his own "work" is only something resulting in the printing of various marks on volumes of paper, marks to which other human organisms respond in ways popularly described as if he were expressing opinions.

Where emotion is absent, but we still have things acting as organic wholes, as in the case of plants, we still speak as if the thing had life or initiative in a weak sense, inasmuch as it acts according to the nature it has as a whole—so that, for instance, we speak of a plant as needing water and absorbing moisture, growing and healing naturally, being drawn towards the light, and so forth. It acts according to its nature in virtue of various mechanisms and is able so to act because its nature is such as to incorporate these mechanisms. However, many mechanisms are concerned, and the functioning of the organism involves the intricate criss-crossing of the chains of causation involved in their operation, often the same material parts involved in different ways in the different chains concerned. What we need so as to bring order to our understanding is to grasp the functional role of each mechanism in subserving the functioning of the organism as a whole in relation to its environment, so that its behavior is the resultant of the operation of these mechanisms in functional adaptation to its environment.

In a completely different context David Bohm raised the question of how we should describe a cubic meter of space on the hypothesis that it is empty of matter (or, as we might now say, empty of non-dark matter) and not enclosed by matter at its boundaries.[33] Yet electromagnetic radiation is constantly passing through this empty cube of space, and in such a way as to make this cube a kind of microcosm of the whole universe, inasmuch as observers of the radiation which has passed through this cube of space can from their different vantage-points reconstruct a picture of the whole universe. This flux of radiation is a reality, but we can only understand, describe, or specify it by reference to the things at varying distances which these observers observe, the things which give rise to this radiation. We should note that this flux would exist even if there were no observers, but that its array is specifiable only in terms of the effects it would have on the reports, records, and behavior of observers, and its character is understood only so far as their experience and theory make it intelligible.

In a parallel way the flux of radiation approaching the pupil of the eye, ever changing as the organism changes vantage-point, is a reality, but one which is only to be described and understood by reference to the environment seen by the human or animal organism, an environment of objects, shadows, rainbows, blue sky, and so forth. To eliminate the organism as an active observer and to treat the environment which he or she experiences as an inner impression on the retina, or as some equally momentary internal configuration in the brain at some deeper level within the nervous system, isomorphic with

33. David Bohm, "Quantum Theory as an Indication of a New Order in Physics", *Proceedings of the Enrico Fermi International Summer School* (1971): 412–69.

this impression, is to make nonsense of any accounts we give of vision, hearing, and touch—for instance, it abolishes any way of understanding or specifying the flux of radiation approaching the pupils of our eyes from outside, which is the flux which affects what signals pass down the optic nerves, or the variations in this flux resulting from our ambient and exploratory behavior. Further, we would not speak of eyes or systems of visual perception at all if they did not constitute organs and systems of functioning within organisms whose nature is to exhibit possession of these organs and systems in behavior. That is, the organisms belong to species whose members, when free from relevant injury or defect, exhibit their possession of eyes and a system of visual perception in appropriate discriminatory behavior, including, in the human case, giving appropriate reports of what the organism has seen. Until we have a system of functional relationships between certain types of feature of an organism's environment and certain aspects of its behavior, we have no reason to speak of eyes or a visual system at all.

We need to generalize from the need to consider the visual system by reference to functional relationships between an organism's environment and its behavior to the need to consider the life of the organism as a whole in this way.

The life of each kind of living organism involves the functioning of an integrated system of systems, in higher organisms a more complex system of a larger number of systems, in successively lower organisms successively less complex systems of smaller numbers of systems. And in view of the integrated character of the functioning of all the relevant systems together in the life of an organism, we have to say that this life always involves a functional relation between the organism's environment and its behavior.

(ii) Living things as Aristotelian substances despite lack of precise boundaries

Thus we should not think of the brain, or what corresponds to the brain, in abstraction from the whole body and its functioning.[34] And we should never think of the organism in abstraction from its environment. To take trivial instances, such questions as whether it is the pupil of the eye or the retina, the outer ear or the tympanic membrane, which is the external receptor of the sense concerned should be seen as ill-conceived, like the question as to whether the empty space within my mouth when it is open is part of me or not (it is not alive, but has some importance for speaking with one's mouth).[35]

34. The cytoskeleton with centrosome in the paramecium is an instance of something corresponding to the brain; Penrose, *Shadows of the Mind*, 352–77.

35. In the arthropods nothing corresponds to the chambers of vertebrate eyes or their retinal inner surfaces, as J. J. Gibson points out in *Ecological Approach*, 61–62. Retinal images have no privilege in the theory of perception.

The question whether this space is part of the organ of speech or part of my environment is just as ill-conceived as the same question about the auricle and meatus in relation to the external receptor of the sense of sound, or about the lens and vitreous body in relation to the external receptor of the sense of sight.

Yet this does not mean that we should attempt to describe the phenomena of life without bringing in any mention of organisms as wholes, as if in reality there existed only physical chains of causation—spreads of phenomena in the environment causing certain spreads of behavior in the parts of the organisms concerned, all describable in solely physical terms, without bringing in any mention of the organisms as such as integrated wholes, whether human beings, animals, or less developed life forms. Such restriction to physical causation would exclude any full account of biological organisms and much that is essential to accepted descriptions of biological and psychological phenomena, both in ordinary life and in the relevant sciences.

The description of the natural universe requires us to refer to things with the logical character of Aristotelian substances at many levels, from fundamental particles, atoms, and molecules to rocks, planets, and stars, as well as to living organisms. There are reasons for treating fundamental particles, atoms, and molecules and even rocks, planets, and stars as unitary wholes for the purposes of many of the explanations of phenomena which we give. But the imperative character of the need to treat living organisms as unitary wholes requires further comment.

(iii) Living things have their lives and behavior functionally related to their environment

What makes us distinguish living organisms from other things is the indispensable role of the relationship between their environment and their behavior at the heart of explanations of their way of functioning, together with the teleological character of these explanations.

This teleological character depends on viewing each kind of organism as having a certain end—namely, the living of a certain kind of life, defined by the general structure set by the integrated set of activities and capacities for activity characteristic of it.[36]

36. This formulation is taken from Aristotle, but carefully modified in making it more precise: Aristotle, *Nicomachean Ethics* I.7; cf. I.10, I.13 (1097b24–1098a19; cf. 1100b8–20, 1102a5–1103a3).

(d) *The ambiguity: differentiating the mathematically mechanical from the physically mechanical*

I said that the problem is as to how systems, whether physically locatable or otherwise, which are mechanical in the sense that their effects are Turing-computable, can be incorporated within the functioning of living organisms. I saw that we have to consider this in the light of the fact that living organisms all require the relationship between certain types of feature of their environment and certain aspects of their behavior to be explained in a teleological way which allows for the functional character of this relationship.

At this point the ambiguities in the word "mechanical" become relevant. It is one thing for a process to be mechanical in the mathematical sense, and quite another for it to be mechanical in the sense of being explicable purely physically.

On the one hand the process of copying the continuous text of a page of a book, letter, space, or paragraph break, each copied in order as written in the text, is mechanical in the mathematical sense. At each stage the next relevant move of copying is determined. The stages of copying are Turing-computable. However, we have no reason to suppose the process of the human copying to be *physically* mechanical. Our human copyist may get bored and go for a walk halfway through his task. He will almost certainly proceed at an uneven pace, and there is no guarantee built into our description of his situation that he may not get so bored and angry that he resigns from his job when only halfway through it, and even if he continues he may wilfully miscopy the text. On the face of it, there is nothing physically determined about the process of his copying—unless one appeals to some principle of general physical determinism.

On the other hand, to the extent that we can consider processes going on in other physical systems in such a way that the behavior of the systems can be considered as determined by the physical properties of the parts and their interrelations and interactions according to nonteleological laws of behavior, we will have systems whose behavior is both physically determined (machines in the classical or Newtonian sense) and mechanical in the mathematical sense.[37] I oversimplify here, since it is required that the system be considered closed (i.e., free from interaction of any kind from anything else in existence, whether from within the universe or by some *deus ex machina*). In practice, in the case of most machines of a size one might meet in a museum, the processes of physical wear on the parts will make computation of their

37. I have assumed that if any part of the system is continuous, it can be treated as if it were composed of negligibly small particles in such a way as to give the relevant aggregations the appropriate density (cf. n. 4).

behavior over even a short span of years extraordinarily complex, and in any case they will almost certainly succumb to interference from outside within a very few years, decades, or centuries. No physical system has its behavior computable (i.e., mechanical in the mathematical sense) for very long. Both very small and quite large systems are liable to interference from outside in ways no system of computation can take account of.

The question therefore confronts us as to the sense of the word "mechanically" in which mechanisms within the body proceed mechanically.

Because we pick out particular kinds of part of the human body (e.g., cells) as involved in certain aspects of human functioning and consider their operation in this or that measurable respect over quite short spans of time, abstracting from their situation in the human body as a whole, and ignore the processes of decay and regeneration on which failure in uniform function depends, we are able to regard them as analogous to physical machines. But this way of viewing these processes is nothing more than a useful abstraction. Considered absolutely, it is like viewing these processes as if one were intellectually blindfolded. The setting of these processes is within the context of the life of organisms whose behavior is in teleological or functional relation to their environment. And within the organisms themselves it is difficult to avoid considering the structured processes of regeneration and decay without considering them teleologically.

In the light of the distinction between physical mechanisms and processes which are mechanical in a mathematical sense, one can say that in a crucial sense the parts of a human body should not be counted as "merely physical" as if they were analogous to bits of a mechanical construction set in a machine made of parts taken from such a set and powered mechanically—for instance, by the pressure of a continuous flow of water turning a wheel; or, in a static case, to having bits of Lego form a model house such as some child might erect. Neither the cells of the human body nor their organic parts (their external membrane, cytoplasm, nucleus, etc.),[38] are analogous to bits of a mechanical construction set in such a machine as I described. Rather, the cells are living cells, and the processes of decay and regeneration, and in some cases division or replacement, are influenced by relations with other cells and integrated within systems directed towards maintaining the whole body in proper functioning order, the situation of particular cells in particular locations in the body being governed in such a way as to subserve this order. Yet these cells

38. These cells, neurons in particular, must be recognized as having a very complex internal structure, or parts each with their own functional role. Besides the cell soma with nucleus, axons, and dendrites, we may need to recognize the whole external membrane as constituting a cytoskeleton furnished with a multiplicity of microtubules; Penrose, *Shadows of the Mind*, 352–77.

are not themselves living organisms as amoebae or paramecia are living organisms, but only living parts of living organisms. Indeed, when the cells of an organism begin to function autonomously, we have the beginning of a cancer.

Accordingly, we should not say that the "mechanisms" on which proper human functioning depends, which it utilizes in perception, action, imagination, and thinking in words, and which are exercised in emotion and feeling, are "physical mechanisms" in the sense that we meet physical mechanisms in inanimate objects. People have said that for a system to carry out computational processes (mechanical in the mathematical sense) it does not matter whether it be formed of cogs and wheels and so forth or tin cans, electrical components, or biological materials. And this is true. Further, if a system is composed of cogs, wheels, tin cans, electrical components, and so forth, it is natural and in no way misleading to describe it as a "physical mechanism", because the very word "mechanism" suggests something composed of physical parts. However, by contrast, if it is a biological system composed of parts which are themselves living or biological, to describe it as a "physical mechanism" or "physical system" is misleading, tendentious, or false. If we want to state the matter in a way which does not go beyond what science suggests, we should limit ourselves to saying that the Turing-computable or mathematically mechanical processes involved in human functioning are embodied, not in merely physical mechanisms, but in particular aspects of the functioning of particular groups of living parts of the human body.

Plainly each such part has a certain geometrical or topological structure, constituted of subordinate bits, each having a certain physical and chemical character; but this does not make it "just physical" in character, because such a description is false to the fact that understanding the part's behavior as a whole involves considering it in its functional relation to the life and behavior of the organism as a whole. In brief, we call things such as perceptual systems "living", not merely "physical", systems, because they are functioning and functional parts of whole animals.

What we have here fits the essence of Aristotelianism. There is no complete understanding of the nature of the parts of an organism and no complete explanation of the whole range of their behavior except by understanding them in their function as parts of the whole. To consider cells in terms of what they have in common with other cells independently of any whole they make up is to pick out just certain aspects of their behavior, functioning, and composition, rather than to consider their behavior and functioning in all their aspects or their reality as a whole. However, equally plainly (here we have the other aspect of the Aristotelian view), such a consideration of cells and other parts and subsystems must be possible because, conversely, the functioning of the whole human being cannot be understood apart from some partly independently describable aspects of the constitution and functioning of such parts and subsystems, their physics, chemistry, physiology, and so forth.

Accordingly, if the human being is functioning properly in the relevant aspects of life and behavior, it is certain that certain types of part and subsystem will be capable of being considered in abstraction from the whole in this way, and that certain features of the behavior of the subsystems involved will proceed mechanically in the mathematical sense. If a cinema reel is played ever more slowly, it is physical data about how the visual system functions which allow us to calculate how slowly it needs to be played in order for the display to seem discontinuous. Again, data about the grammar and lexicon of the language which a person has learned enable us to anticipate, before he has completed his utterance, certain inflections, word orders, and word combinations he will not use, and sometimes some which he will use. Pinker's *Words and Rules* provides a plausible picture as to how our assigning of correct plurals to nouns and of correct parts (present, simple past, and past participle) to English verbs may involve and depend on a sequence of parallel processing in one part of the brain, followed by nonparallel processing in another.

This conception of what is involved in some psychological processes being mechanical in the mathematical sense leaves full scope for exploration of how far and in what respects connectionist ideas are useful in understanding them. We can understand connectionism here simply in terms of its making use of the idea of parallel processing from computer theory and in neuroscience emphasizing microstructure and taking account of the possibility of neural paths being strengthened simply by repeated exercise. To give this much place to connectionism—and nothing more than this is required for the partial role which Pinker accords it in our assigning correct plurals to nouns and correct parts to English verbs—is in no way to elevate it into a general materialist theory of mind.[39]

Section 3. Gibson's Treatment of Perception as a Model for the Treatment of Language

Allowing a divide between an Internalized language and an Externalized language presents two immediate problems. The first is that of production—as to how we pass from knowledge of meaning or sense to its actual expression or utterance. The second is that of how, confronted with the utterances of others, we get to interpret them.

39. In connectionism as a general materialist theory of mind, the adaptive usefulness of any development plays no part in explaining how any structure or process develops, contrary to the functionalist approach I have outlined—such a theory of mind is as much metaphysics as science.

This second problem is one which cannot be avoided by anyone who adopts an indirect theory of the perception and interpretation of speech, which instantly forces upon us a divide between language as external to the human mind and language as inner to the human mind—that is, between Externalized and Internalized languages.

The way this happens appears in its full starkness in the explanation given by such representative linguists as Sperber and Wilson, who simply assume our perception of speech to be "indirect", involving the activity of a succession of modules of brain processing:

> In other words, a linguistic stimulus triggers an automatic process of decoding. Just as we cannot choose to see the objects around us in black and white rather than in colour, just as we cannot choose not to hear a gun going off nearby, so we cannot choose to hear an utterance in a language we know as merely an unanalysed stream of sounds. We automatically recover its semantic representation, even if we accidentally overhear it and know it was not meant for us, or even (as the evidence on binaural shadowing shows) if we are not conscious of hearing it at all. The linguistic decoding system has all the hallmarks of automatic, reflex perceptual systems such as hearing and vision. In the terms of Fodor (1983),[40] who develops this point at length, it is an input system rather than a central processing system, and this is one reason why it has been so relatively amenable to study. This suggests in turn that if comprehension is defined as a process of identifying the speaker's informative intention, linguistic decoding is not so much a part of the comprehension process as something which precedes the real work of understanding, something which merely provides an input to the main part of the comprehension process.[41]

All this is stated in terms appropriate to an indirect theory of perception according to which energies of a certain intensity and character are generated within the environment and give rise to stimuli at the receiving surface of the sense organ, and it is these stimuli which determine mental representations of the world of such a character as to be accessible to thought, and thereby to play their part in the fixing of judgment or belief.

In this way of thinking, what is spoken with a certain meaning or sense

40. The authors here refer to Fodor, *Modularity*, 61–64.

41. Dan Sperber and Deirdre Wilson, *Relevance: Communication and Cognition* (Cambridge, Mass.: Harvard University Press, 1986), 177. This secondary text misreads Fodor's psychological/philosophical theory as if as if "recover" meant "discern", "make out", or "recognize"; as if "a linguistic stimulus" meant "the utterance as discernible by us"; and as if "automatic [spontaneous, choice-independent, and non-voluntary] process of decoding" meant "activity of distinguishing what has been said". However, for Fodor the "linguistic stimulus", the "process of decoding", and the "recovering" are not conscious at all, and far from the hearing with understanding which pragmatic accounts of conversation require. It is easy to slip into such misreading if one's interest is solely in the importance of pragmatics in linguistic accounts of meaning, the concern of Sperber and Wilson: it is this misreading which gives their combination of a performance-dictated pragmatic account of meaning and their Fodorian idea of language as part of the input system its apparent plausibility.

and what is heard with a certain understanding is no longer conceived of as a single psychophysical and psychosocial reality of utterance, meaning, and understanding together, all set within the social environment of speakers and hearers. Instead, what is spoken and presented to hearing is conceived of as an external physical reality, and this exists in some elaborate relations to what was meant and what is understood from it—making the environment of intended meaning and of understanding not the social world of speakers and hearers, but an environment inner to the mind.

(a) *Direct and indirect theories of hearing are parallel to direct and indirect theories of vision*

In a parallel way, in indirect theories of vision, the objects of the sense of sight have been made inner and, considered in separation from the environment of objects within which we move about, take different views, explore, and sometimes touch and feel the texture of things arousing our curiosity.

Contrary to Fodor, it is not alterations to cells inner to our eyes and ears (our retinas and tympanic membranes counted as "external" receptors of the senses concerned) which we should consider as the stimuli to our senses, but rather the features of our environment which enable us to discriminate what we see and hear. For we should follow Gibson in his observation that, in the standard use of the word "stimulus" in so-called Stimulus-Response theory, the stimulus is that which we treat as the independent variable—that is, as being the thing variations of which are considered as explaining variations in the response to it.[42] From this standpoint it is the room with its furniture and people in it; the countryside with its fields, animals, hedges, trees, streams, and sky above; the clouds, roofs of houses, and, at night, the spread of stars and so forth, which determine what we see—for example, the cues which determine our picking out a surface are out there in the variations of texture shown up by the reflection of light at the surface. And likewise it is variations in the speech and song of other people and of birds, in the music played, and in the sound of movements around us which determine what we hear.[43] The human input system is so integrated as to feed its conclusions directly to consciousness, and it is only when there are hitches that we inquire into the preceding operations of the input system to which we normally pay no attention.

In contemporary jargon, this is to regard the "central processing" internal to perception as that on which judgment and action turn, and to refuse to consider the various alterations to some intermediate receiving surface (the retina

42. J. J. Gibson, "Concept of Stimulus".

43. Cf. David Braine, *Human Person*, chaps. 2 and 3, exhibiting the repetitious emptiness of post-1960 philosophical attempts to revive theories of indirect perception.

or tympanic membrane) as the elemental sensations, sense data, or "stimuli" antecedent to perception. It means getting away from the model of the central processing of multiple bits of information received from such "stimuli" to the retina or the tympanic membrane and restoring the person or animal in its unitariness as a "focalized subject" to centrality in the understanding of perception, unitary in its activity, perception integrated with action and with dispositions to action. In later sections we shall find that we need to let our thought about hearing follow the same lines as the thinking of J. J. Gibson and his wife, Eleanor J. Gibson, in regard to visual perception, with its holistic and teleological character, while at the same time realizing that they recognized judgments as to what one perceives to be quite fallible—as their accounts of various sensory illusions show.[44]

Fodor finds it paradoxical that the conscious subject should experience that which is computationally most distant from the effects on the retina or tympanic membrane, which he counts as the "stimuli". But it is exactly this which makes J. J. Gibson suppose that the stimulus has been wrongly identified. In the cases of vision and hearing, an optician or audiologist occupied in testing sight or hearing without using invasive procedures alters what Fodor would count as the stimulus—that is, the effects in the retina or tympanic membrane—by altering the object of sight or hearing and the way it presents itself (e.g., by introducing an external lens or hearing aid). Accordingly, except perhaps in cases involving touch, what Fodor counts as the stimulus is a theoretical entity, a construct of indirect theories inferred from our knowledge of optics and of the physiology of the eye, or of acoustics and the physiology of the outer and middle ear. For Fodor the "stimulus" is the relevant externally caused change in what he calls the "transducer", adopting this term to refer to the supposedly "external" receptors of the senses, such as the retina. And it would indeed require elaborate processing to get one "from the representation of a proximal stimulus which the retina provides to the representation of the distal stimuli as an array of objects in space", as he remarked in 1983, dismissing Gibson's view in a contemptuous footnote.[45] Yet here he directly begs

44. J. J. Gibson, "Concept of Stimulus"; J. J. Gibson, *Senses Considered;* J. J. Gibson, *Ecological Approach;* Eleanor J. Gibson, *Principles of Perceptual Learning and Development* (New York: Appleton-Century-Croft, 1969); and Eleanor J. Gibson, *Odyssey.*

45. In an endnote, Fodor says, "Strictly speaking, I suppose I should say that this is true according to all current non-Gibsonian accounts. For reasons given elsewhere however (see Fodor and Pylyshyn, 1981), I am deeply unmoved by the Gibsonian claim to have devised a non-computational theory of perception. I propose simply to ignore it in this discussion"; Fodor, *Modularity,* 53n16. His reference to Fodor and Pylyshyn, 1981, is to J. Fodor, Z. Fodor, and Pylyshyn, "How Direct is Visual Perception?" *Cognition* 9 (1981): 139–96. In his main text, thinking in the same way, as if the stimuli were alterations in the retina, making an "output" into the mind, he states, "transducer outputs underdetermine perceptual analyses" (*Modularity,* 68), remarking that "perceptual categories are not . . . definable in terms of transducer outputs" (*Modularity,* 134n22).

the question in dispute, proposing "simply to ignore" Gibson's position, described as "non-computational" in his discussion, thereby ignoring the point at issue—namely, Gibson's taking the location of the stimuli to the visual system to be in the environment, not in the retina.

Strikingly, one finds that many of the "facts" which have led Fodor and other believers in indirect perception to their conclusions fit Gibson's opposite views rather better.

Suppose one has a telescope designed to look at the environment, whether to obtain accurate vision of the plants and faces at the bottom of one's garden or of the more distant trees, hills, mountains, and stars. The intention is that the light from the environment of which one wishes to have accurate sight should come to focus where the observer puts his eye or, in more complicated telescopes, come to focus in the place where one puts the relevant kind of photographic plate, thereby gaining a picture. Affairs can then be described in two quite different ways.

In the first approach one could speak as if the stimuli to the telescope were the photons impinging on its outermost lens, each approaching from a certain direction. This corresponds to supposing that in sensory perception one has to treat the stimulus as that which impinges upon the external surface of the receptor of that organ. This is how Fodor thinks; and then the lens and mirror system of the telescope become the inanimate equivalent of a computational system (analog and/or digital) operating upon the apparently chaotic array of facts specified for each point of the outer lens surface in a form registering the corresponding values of four variables—the point of lens concerned, the wavelength of light, and for each wavelength of light, its direction of approach and intensity as impinging on that point—in order to generate the picture seen in the photographic plate or what is seen by a person when he or she looks through a telescope's eyepiece at the sky or another object. This view corresponds to an indirect theory of perception in which the physical stimuli by means of an input system produce a representation (picture), and the perceiver has no direct perception of what the representations are of.

This approach divides sensation from perception so that first stimuli are registered as sensations, and then the mind produces an enriched picture relying on various devices which Fodor classifies together as "inferential procedures" (such as association, comparison with other remembered experiences, and computation).[46] This theory fits with a causal hypothesis whereby stimuli to the external receptor of the organ cause representations which the mind then enriches to yield what H. H. Price in *Perception* calls "perceptual accep-

46. This is the approach of Richard Gregory, later to be developed by David Marr, *Vision: A Computational Investigation into the Human Representation and Processing of Visual Information* (New York: W. H. Freeman, 1982)—but the approach against which the Gibsons reacted so strongly.

tances". Vast enrichment is needed, as Price showed in his *Hume's Theory of the External World*. Price, whose book *Perception* presents the philosophically most sophisticated available version of this kind of theory, suggests that perceptual acceptance, which is not infallible, is followed by perceptual corroboration or noncorroboration.

For Fodor the "inferential" work involved in "enrichment" is the work of the central processor, but he has so little to say about how this works that AI theorists see no point in the notion of sensation as a conscious intermediary in mental processing.[47]

In the second approach one takes it that the lens and mirrors of the telescope form a system which has been developed so that it can be adjusted according to the distance of the things we wish to see (relatively close, in the middle distance, or far away) and for different backgrounds or light conditions of different intensity and color, in such a way that the invariants of the outer world which we wish to see (faces and plants, people and animals walking towards one or across one's line of vision, books, furniture, trees, forests, hills, stars) are capable of being picked out or "discriminated" when we put our eye to the duly adjusted telescope or take photographic plates of what is to be seen. This corresponds to taking the stimuli in sensory perception to be those things (color, shape, surface texture pattern, relative size) which tend to remain *invariant* as we look away and look back again, or move about and view from different angles, and taking these to be the stimuli by which our sensory system enables our perceptual knowledge to be determined.

The procedures one goes through to adjust one's telescope for the distance of the objects one is looking at and to point it in the direction one intends, along with the types of thing which can go wrong in such adjustment and pointing, are not involved internally in the act of seeing what is to be seen by means of the telescope or in a photographic plate set to record this.

The person who looks through a telescope, directing it in the appropriate direction and adjusting its focus, does not suppose that it has no internal complexity. He is likely to envisage his seeing what the telescope makes him able to see as essentially dependent on this internal complexity of whose details he is often ignorant, and the previous development in the technology of making better telescopes of which he is probably equally ignorant. Likewise, when he uses his eyes unassisted to see, he is likely to suppose that his eyes and what lies behind them have an internal complexity, the details of which he is ignorant, equally essential to his being able to see what he sees. And nowadays he will anticipate that a long process of evolution lies behind this internal system

47. Dennett, *Consciousness Explained*, 260–61, quoting Fodor, *Modularity*, 127, and describing the associated argument.

in its physiology and mode of functioning. None of this prejudices the directness with which he sees what he sees—namely, the room with its furniture and the people in it, the countryside with its fields, animals, hedges, trees, streams, and sky above, the clouds, roofs of houses, and at night the spread of stars, and so forth. And none of it prejudices the fact that it is to seeing such things as these that his sight is adjusted by his exploration or choice of location, direction of look, and other adjustments (e.g., focusing his eyes) at the time and in virtue of evolution. But, equally, none of this brings into doubt the dependence of his ability to see what he sees on the functioning of the enormously complex integrated system of eye and brain.

By adopting this second approach Gibson has restored an environmentally orientated, or "ecological", view of what we perceive, concentrating especially on the case of sight, a view of a more holistic and functionalist kind, both of the perceiver's mode of approach in perception and of the concepts in terms of which the object of perception is perceived.[48] This same second approach, holistic, functionalist, and ecological, is also applicable to the hearing of speech with understanding. This makes it directly relevant to our study in this book—and relevant whichever perceptual faculty is exercised in the linguistic medium of communication concerned (Braille, articulated human sign language, or writing). Where hearing speech is concerned, the effect of this functionalist and ecological approach in the setting of linguistic theory is to require the integration of pragmatics and semantics in the way explained in the introduction to develop further in chapter III and from chapter IX onwards.

In any such functionalist, environmentally orientated view of perception, the perceptual system is geared to picking out invariants within the public world. And learning is a matter of developing the capacity to differentiate *invariants* of new, more complex types. Thus a person becomes able to recognize that it is a woman who is before him or her, both when she walks in open view and when she is barely visible, camouflaged behind a hedge, or to discern the same morpheme within the settings of "mouse" and "mice", or of "break", "broke", and "broken", and to pick out the structure of a relative clause and how it qualifies what it does in the setting of highly complex sentences.

The term "stimulus" introduces much confusion. Gibson's use of the term, reflecting the logic of Stimulus-Response theory, in normal cases (illusion and hallucination being absent) makes the stimuli approximate to what we ordinarily count as the objects of perception: people, tomatoes, furniture, houses, clouds, the stars, and so forth. Fodor's use of the term makes it correspond to the pre-Humean concept of sense impression—that is, to the immediate "im-

48. The functionalist view I present has no connection with Putnam's mind-brain "functionalism", described in chap. III n. 75 of this volume, which has the effect of making personal identity and consciousness into fictions.

print", or *immutatio*, on the external receptor of the sense organ concerned, something of which we have only indirect knowledge and control.[49] As a result Fodor and Pylyshyn argue that stimuli in this sense can cause sensory illusions, a phenomenon of which, as we shall see, Gibson's approach provides a more attractive account.[50]

With both Gibsonian direct and Fodorian indirect approaches, the question arises as to how the perceptual system gets to be as skilled (user-friendly) as it is. In both cases a nativist ("innatist") view may be proposed so that at least some types of feature or structures in the natural world are as if given. In either case there is a question as to how learning is possible. In both cases the idea of *Gestalt* and "set" (from Allport) prove useful. As we shall see, these two ideas fit better with Gibson's approach.

Gibson's approach makes it unproblematic that in the human case, the world of vision is inseparable from the world of movement and touch, as in distinguishing up and down and visual awareness of depth, in recognizing the direction of a visual object's lateral movement invariantly whether one's head is stationary or moving, and in knowing which eye (or both) one is closing. Likewise the world of vision, movement, and touch is the same as the world of sound (as when we are aware that it is our own speech which we are hearing and appreciate the direction of sound), and the world of smell, integrated with what we know by taste, as well as in special relation to sight, in a way more prominent with other animals, but evident in the human, for instance, in the way redness amplifies awareness by smell.

(b) *Direct theories of perception exclude infallibility in perceptual judgment*

(i) The visual system's proper functioning excludes photographic fidelity

This Gibsonian approach, which envisages perception as "direct"—that is, not mediated by the experience of anything else of a less conceptualized kind, such as the often conjectured "sensations"—allows the subject viewing the same spread of environmental contexts ("field") to learn by progressively distinguishing more of the patterns which are shared between them.

The notions of *Gestalt*[51] and "perceptual set", as "a perceptual bias or pre-

49. I say pre-Humean because Hume made a deliberate change in the use of the word "impression" to mean a "perception of the mind" however produced, but of a kind to be contrasted with "ideas"; Hume, *A Treatise of Human Nature*, bk. I, pt. 1, sec. 1, n. 1.

50. Fodor and Pylyshyn, "How Direct Is Visual Perception?", 163.

51. *Gestalt* was a much earlier term introduced by Ehrenfels in 1890, and key to the work of Wertheimer, Köhler, and Koffka in *Gestalt* psychology.

disposition or readiness to perceive particular features of a stimulus",[52] are both helpful in explaining how we become ready to appreciate progressively more complex invariants, and thus fit well within Gibson's account. *Gestalt* processes come into play in a very great number of cases—for instance, when we see a man through a hedge he is standing behind, or, as our skill develops, begin to emulate an experienced deerstalker.

These concepts also fit well with a Gibsonian view of learning in which one envisages an animal as becoming "tuned" to what is functional or adaptive for its species. In the 1950s it was realized that Stimulus-Response conditioning does not arise fortuitously and inevitably just in virtue of frequent repetition, but that some kinds of learning are definitely favored; for instance, animals develop aversions of taste geared to their survival and success.[53] And it is a commonplace that among the higher animals and human beings we find a capacity to develop and appropriately modify complex patterns of skilled behavior according to the experience of the individual animal, a capacity completely absent or little-developed among the insects. If behavior can be subject to adaptive modification both genetically and through learning, then the same should be anticipated of discriminatory capacity in perception.

This "direct" perception theory contains nothing involving any assumption that judgments as to what one perceives are infallible. When a wrong judgment is made as to what one sees with one's eyes, for instance, the judgment "I saw a lion in front of me on High Street", it is withdrawn as soon as the judgment "There was a lion in front of me on High Street" turns out to be false.[54] However, there is a presumption that the perceptual system is so well ordered that it will not engender false judgments as to what one perceives without there being an explanation as to how the error arose.[55] Illusions result from the proper functioning of our perceptual system in special conditions, whereas delusions are rooted in some kind of disorder either interfering with such proper functioning or making us suppose perception when there is none.[56]

52. G. W. Allport, *Becoming—Basic Considerations for a Psychology of Personality* (New Haven, Conn.: Yale University Press, 1955).

53. J. Garcia, et al., "Relation of Cue to Consequence in Avoidance Learning", *Psychonomic Science* 4 (1966), and Garcia, et al., "Learning with Prolonged Delay of Reinforcement", *Psychonomic Science* 5, no. 3 (1966).

54. If one's intention is to describe one's hallucinations and the context makes this clear, then one's initial statement would not imply the presence of a lion on the high street. In the terms of chap. I of this volume, the verb "see" will have a different sense or discourse-significance.

55. Cf. F. H. Bradley, "On Truth and Coherence", chap. 5 in *Essays on Truth and Reality* (Oxford: Oxford University Press, 1914).

56. This dovetails with Austin's recognition in *Sense and Sensibilia* of the significance of the differences between hallucinations ("delusions") and "illusions" as reflected in our ordinary ways of speaking. David Hamlyn's closeness to Gibson appears in Hamlyn, *Psychology of Perception: A Philosophical Examination of Gestalt Theory and Derivative Theories of Perception* (London: Routledge and Kegan Paul, 1957); *Sensation*

It is quite wrong to suppose that an optical illusion has occurred whenever there is a difference between what would be registered in a photograph taken from the "eyepoint" of a camera with a certain acuity and what a person could report as seeing from that point, and not just because of variations according to direction and distance. In the functionalist, ecological, or pragmatic view of how the environment and direction of interest shape our perception, our perceptual system is not designed to give us precision in judgments about matters of no concern, but to be as efficient as is practicable and necessary in informing us about things pertinent to action, anticipation, and judgment, whether our concern is the dispositions and distance of the enemy troops and the state of the intervening ground, the weather, or the honesty and nervousness revealed in a person's eyes, face, or hand movements.

In some respects paintings by Monet, Seurat, and Utrillo suggest different ways in which departure from the photographic can bring an artist closer to a portrayal of things as we see them. Yet this does not make them deceptive. True, the Greek mastery of how things presented to vision end-on are foreshortened compared with the same things presented sideways, and the application of Giotto's ideas of perspective give enormously greater realism or naturalism to the two-dimensional portrayal of the three-dimensional, whether single figures or scenes involving looking into long distances are concerned. But it is wrong to suppose that there is optical illusion whenever human vision departs from ideals of perspective conforming to Pascal's projective geometry.

In general human beings rely on cues and relevant amplification effects, and a wide spread of sizes of books and trees counts as normal, and we do not pick out branches and leaves distinctly enough at any appreciable distance, and so how a ridge in a field, a line of hedge, or a group of trees appears to us provides only the roughest guide to its distance. Accordingly, one of the most common optical illusions arises when we see one piece of ground beyond another without being able to see the dip, or dead ground, between, and then grossly underestimate the distance of the more distant ground. To avoid this in art the artist is liable to make the considerably more distant ground appear even excessively distant by giving it an exaggeratedly small portrayal, an effect strikingly apparent in Benozzo Gozzoli's *The Journey of the Magi to Bethlehem*.[57] Or, again, receding railway lines must *appear* as if parallel, and therefore as becoming ever closer as they recede, but as portrayed will still be kept separate even at the most distant horizon, even though an equivalent-sized photograph of the scene would not keep them separate. In

and Perception (London: Routledge and Kegan Paul, 1961); and *Perception, Learning and the Self* (London: Routledge and Kegan Paul, 1983). All these authors assume perceptual judgment to be fallible.

57. E. H. Gombrich, *The Story of Art*, 16th ed. (London: Phaidon, 1995).

this way the painting *The Avenue at Middelharnis* is true to the modes of human perspective, not of mathematical projective geometry.[58]

(ii) **"Illusions" as a byproduct of the proper functioning of perceptual systems**

Optical illusions arise from the proper functioning of our perceptual system. This proper functioning includes the presumption that the viewer is, if not actually moving his eyes, head, and body, then at least free to do so; typically he or she will be in active movement—for instance, around the room or through a forest. Certain standard types of illusion arise from the absence of such movement: for instance, the Rubin vase illusion, which I describe later, and the reversed hollow mask illusion;[59] or, in the case of people with hemiaopic vision, the seeing of, for instance, a complete circle when only a semicircle is presented. In such cases the readiness to see patterns in accord with certain "sets" or *Gestalten* comes to our notice because of the illusions which they generate in two-dimensional presentations. Such presentations by their nature exclude the movement in a third dimension which would be required to correct one's natural guess, e.g., that it is one vase which is portrayed, when it is in fact two faces. Such illusions commonly involve a dislocation between expectations on the basis of sight and the lack of subsequent explorations by means of touch or movement so as to get a view from a different angle—for instance, an angle which would allow one to discover that the nose of the hollow mask does not begin to protrude as one begins to move diagonally towards the mask so as to begin to see it side on, or with the semicircle longways vertical if one twists so as to look at it with one's head held horizontal instead of vertical.

Many shapes, as of coins, leaves, books, pieces of writing paper, or rooms, are so standard that, for instance, we regard the coin as round and thin and books and rooms as having right angles at the corners, and as looking like this even though the projection presented to the eyes is elliptical or trapezoidal, so that optical illusions arise when coins are not round or papers or rooms not square at the corners.[60] In judging the shapes and dimensions of two-dimensional objects, some static principles will apply—for instance, presuming the sides of a figure to be actually straight or actually equal, although they are in fact only very roughly such. It is possible that in the Muller-Lyer illusion we are deceived not by the central lines as such, but their contexts, the inward-facing fins seeming to constrict the line they enclose and the

58. National Gallery, London, painted 1689 by the Dutch Meindert Hobbema (1638–1709).

59. Richard Gross, *Psychology: The Science of Mind and Behaviour*, 2nd ed. (London: Hodder and Stoughton, 1992), 237–38.

60. I.e., an Ames' room; Gross, *Psychology*, 236–37.

outward-facing fins seeming rather to be stretching the line between them.[61] This interpretation would suggest that this illusion has a different kind of cause (involving *Gestalten* arising with our experience of dynamic plays of force,[62] rather than problems of perspective).[63]

The case of people who are given inverting glasses which initially make them see the world upside-down but who, after a time, make a flip and see things the right way up could be described as a case of suffering from an illusion in the intervening period. But this has a very evident cause in the innate coordination between sight, anticipations of touch or its absence, and appreciations of balance connected with gravity. In Gibson's view the last is the most significant, because he thinks that underlying all is what he calls the orienting system, to which the vestibular organs within the inner ear are key, within the context of the unity of the senses.[64] Visual cliff experiments reveal varied patterns of cooperation between the senses producing an anticipation of the possibility of falling. Illusions can also arise when things are not viewed in the upright position; for instance, our judgments about the relative positions of branches and the symmetry of the foliage of vertical trees are liable to be confused if the tree is viewed from an angle.[65]

Many illusions arise when one lacks adequate freedom to change one's vantage-point and what is concerned is a view of what is actually a three-dimensional object. Thus *Gestalt* phenomena arise when a two-dimensional figure is presented in such a way as to illustrate the figure/ground distinction, exemplified in the two different ways of seeing Rubin's vase, one as a white vase and the other as two mirror-image black faces facing each other, and in the duck-rabbit illusion, when a picture of a duck's head is presented which, if viewed sideways, can be seen as a picture of the head of a rabbit. Where what is concerned is a view of an actually three-dimensional object, the ambiguity is removed if the viewer shifts position.

61. Likewise, in the case of the Titchener circles the innermost circle seems smaller in the case in which it appears constricted, crowded, or dominated by its context; Gross, *Psychology*, 227, fig. 9.1, illustration (e).

62. Phenomenologically, in our appreciation of the concepts of mechanics, the concepts of statics (of being compressed or of being stretched) always have to be understood in terms of tendencies to be moved in some way—i.e., in terms of the concepts of dynamics.

63. The same may apply in the Ponzo illusion in Gross, *Psychology*, 227, fig. 9.1, illustration (c), where two lines symmetrically sloping upward towards each other bestraddle two horizontal lines at different levels (lines actually equal but seeming unequal): it is perhaps the way the upper line so nearly joins the two, leaving such small gaps, while the lower line leaves such huge gaps that it makes us think the lower line shorter. In this approach the illusion does not depend upon an interpretation involving perspective, although this will increase the effect. If the lines and background are still distinguishable because of different colors but the background is as bright as the lines, this might reduce awareness of the gaps as guides to the length of the central lines.

64. J. J. Gibson, *Senses Considered*, 49–50, 53–55.

65. The simplest case of this is provided by rotating the diagram used to present the Poggendorff illusion; Gross, *Psychology*, 226–67. If the broken line is vertical or horizontal, the illusion disappears.

The ambiguities arise when no three-dimensional object is concerned, but only what one construes or is invited to construe as a two-dimensional representation of something, and one is asked what is being represented. To this question there need be no right or wrong answer, and the question has more to do with the theory of representation and the very different skills of representing things unambiguously and of devising ambiguous representations.[66] Their relevance to perception is only in assisting the discovery of some of the skills involved in normal perception. They do nothing to show that the skills concerned are skills in performing inferences subconsciously, since the phenomena are just as well open to the interpretation that our perceptual system is geared to reveal the types of feature of interest in practice, or else the guises in which some things customarily present themselves. The involvement of "mechanisms" in normal human and animal perception and behavior is not in doubt. Where mechanisms are concerned it is as falsely anthropomorphic to speak of inferences as to speak of the lenses or mirrors of telescopes as making inferences.

Evidently, then, the case of "illusions" is the result of the proper working of the human perceptual system and stands in strong contrast with deceptive effects produced by chemical imbalances or drugs or by neurological interventions, injuries, or inherited conditions.

(c) *Indirect views of perception involve impossible systems of inference or "construction"*

Indirect or representational views of perception involve treating every perceptual judgment as the result of inference. But, even in conscious life, the heuristic process of discerning patterns seems to be a matter of relatively random hit-and-miss selection from among a few often very different candidates, rather than an inference resulting from a systematic search through a predefined list.[67]

We have to distinguish three different things: the consideration of whether we are or were, or whether somebody else is or was, in a good position to see and to judge what it is which has or had been seen; the perception itself with the judgments (Price's "perceptual acceptances") and behavioral ap-

66. The same diagram can serve to represent (a) a closed cubical box, (b) a box of this shape with one of its sides missing so as to be open, (c) three adjoining boards such as might have formerly been the visible sides of the box, but still presenting a corner thrusting towards the viewer, (d) a wire frame of the shape formed by the edges of these sides, all these with its one visible corner thrusting towards the viewer. However, with a change of "set" one can view what is presented (e) as if the corner formed by three sides was most distant from one, as if one was looking into the furthest corner of a box from which the nearer sides had all been removed, or the most distant corner of the ceiling of a room, or (f) again a corresponding wire shape.

67. I give a fuller treatment of philosophers' mistakes in this area in *Human Person*, chap. 2.

titudes internal to it (e.g., to seeing where the edge of the table is); and any subsequent examination of corroboratory or disconfirming evidence or any subsequent inferences.

The things entering into the first consideration vary in different cases—for instance, assessments of the light conditions, of the defects or exceptional acuity of a person's sight, or of their practice or expertise in regard to the type of case concerned.

Second, the judgments claimed to be internal to our perception, as the indirect realist would have us believe, cannot be inferences from a multiplicity of experiences out of our past together with the present, experience prompting our current perceptual claim—as if the whole mountain of our former experiences, some parts generating one probabilistic suggestion in one regard, others generating another in some other regard, and so forth, could be brought together to enable us to reach perceptual judgments. By contrast, the direct realist envisages a combination of genetic and individual history, including a multiplicity of experiences, the communications of others, and training, as having put the animal or human being as a sentient or mental organism in a certain state of adaptedness, making it ready to perceive without inference.

Judgments of perception and the assumptions shown by behavior exhibiting supposed perception will sometimes be richly corroborated and sometimes proved false, but in the latter case it will be because the organism was not in as satisfactory a position to make a judgment or assumption as the confidence of its judgment or action suggested. The situation of perceptual judgments is a particular example of the situation with judgments presumed to express knowledge. The whole point of Austin's contrasting the way we answer questions of the type "How do you know such and such?" with the way we answer questions of the type "Why do you believe such and such?" lies in the very different way we answer them. The first type of question is answered by saying that we were in a position to know and, if necessary, explaining how we came to be in that position. We are shown not to be in that position when it emerges that our situation is one in which optical illusions or hallucinations are typical (e.g., seeing mirages may arise from optical illusions due to refraction, or can be delusions resulting from the physiological and psychological effects of extreme dehydration). With perceptual judgment, as with other cases of supposed knowledge, *knowledge that* can be absent because we have made a right judgment by accident, as in the cases instanced by Gettier.[68] Very commonly there is nothing in our own history, as we experience and remember it, which makes our judgment more reasonable in the case when we get it

68. Cf. similar examples in E. L. Gettier, "Is Justified True Belief Knowledge?" *Analysis* 23 (1963): 121–23, and the general position taken in David Braine, "Nature of Knowledge".

right (nothing abnormal having happened) than in the case when our judgment is right, but only by accident (right despite the abnormal having happened).

The lessons of vision must be applied to the hearing of speech.

The parts of the brain whose functioning require them to be tuned are liable to be different and more extensive in the case of the hearing of speech and the processes involved to be of a more varied kind, but the principles that hearing requires the filtering out of "noise" rather than acoustic fidelity and that illusions and mistakes arising in this process are liable to be the results of proper human functioning are analogous to those we have seen in the case of vision. With proper functioning the norm when we hear speech will be the direct understanding of the sense intended by the speaker.

Appendix: Being Misled by Anomalies in Our Experience of Time and of Sensory *Qualia*

Because the human organism is adapted to function in ways making it quick in reaching right judgment, anomalous situations can be contrived where these ways of functioning result in its forming wrong judgments, as with optical illusions (see section 3).

Dennett and others take advantage of this and pick out experiments contrived to wrong-foot our judgments about the timing of experiences in cases where there is no right or wrong judgment about time order. They follow the same strategy where there is no right or wrong judgment as to the sensory qualities of things.

Dennett uses such examples to support his argument that the person or self has no objective reality or identity over and above the narratives he or she offers of his or her life-history.[69] He explains how we might organize comput-

69. This is the idea of "narrative identity" embraced by Jackendoff, *Architecture*, 217–18n3.

In *Consciousness Explained*, Dennett prepares the way for his explanation of his idea of narrative identity by considering how far we can assess the objectivity of a narrative. He points out that if it happens that a party happening on Sunday is reported as involving one's encounter with one other person on Monday and one's encounter with two other people on Tuesday, this might occur because of a false memory affecting one's judgment at the later time, so that Monday's account would be a true one; or by a mistake (perhaps caused by a certain mindset) affecting the Monday report, and corrected after reflection on Tuesday. (He compares the two kinds of explanation for such disagreements as "Orwellian" and "Stalinesque".)

In such cases the true account might be ascertained by reference to other witnesses. But in the case of purely mental events, there is no objective evidence apart from the public statements which honest subjects give on being questioned, and it is only these reports (as physically realized) which have any objective existence.

Dennett (*Consciousness Explained*, 125–26) compares the problem with that of deciding what counts as the "canonical text" of some work. There used to be only prepublication editing and postpublication errata to distinguish, but now works in draft may be the main ones considered by the *cognoscenti* and the date of publication of concern only to the *plebs* and the pedantic.

ers to produce signals purporting to be descriptions of what they are doing as a byproduct of their operation, expressing these descriptions in ways parallel to the way we talk about ourselves. What these computers "say" about themselves plays no part in the explanation of what they do.[70] He regards human beings as in no better situation than these computers. He here agrees with Ray Jackendoff in his *Consciousness and the Computational Mind* of 1987 that the mental, as what we testify to, plays no part in explaining our outward behavior.

I now explain how the various anomalies arise without carrying any implication of subjectivity.

(a) *Problems about the timing of mental and physical events*

(i) The phenomenon of "psychological" time

What we experience as simple, complete human acts (e.g., hitting someone or kicking a football) are experienced as having a certain special kind of unity in time, so as to be experienced as happening at a moment rather than over a period, a "present" called "specious" because its timing is not mathematically point-like. In the words of Robert Port and his colleagues, we must distinguish between "the naïve time in which we think of auditory processes at the cognitive level" and "the continuous time which measures movement through space".[71] Within our life as higher animals each perception, thought, or action has various functional relationships, requiring us to recognize it as after certain bodily movements or external events and before certain others, but, beyond this, no precise place in the continuous time which measures bodily movement.

Events in the "naive" time inherent in our experience of our perceptions and actions are "weakly ordered" in relation to the physically "continuous" time of the movement of bodies through space. Events are "weakly ordered" if we can have an event, E, when considered in relation to a temporal series of

70. In *Consciousness Explained*, chap. 4, sec. 7, Dennett describes a device called "Shakey" which consisted of a box on wheels with a television linked to a large stationary computer by radio. Shakey had a terminal for typing things like "push the box off the platform". After one typed this Shakey would move, "find" the box, "locate" a ramp, "push" the ramp into position, "roll up" the ramp onto the platform, and "push" the box off. He describes how one could readily add in a television screen showing what it was "as if" Shakey was seeing and one could also add in a mechanical voice seemingly capable of describing what Shakey was doing and why, as if Shakey had been a human being. This could then serve to give a fictional account of what went on as if Shakey were some kind of living being (a homunculus).

71. Robert F. Port, Fred Cummins, and J. Devin McAuley, "Naïve Time, Temporal Patterns, and Human Audition", in *Mind as Motion*, ed. Port and Van Gelder, 313–71. They incidentally describe a "mechanism" which one could readily imagine being wrong-footed: "a dynamical model in which an oscillator can automatically latch on to the rhythm of a stimulus signal. This rhythm can then be used as the standard for measuring time relevant to the recognition of input patterns".

events, W, X, Y, and Z, which is after W and before Z, but neither before nor after the events X and Y.[72] By contrast, as mathematicians use the terms, events are "simply ordered": any event, E, must be either before, after, or at the same time as every other event. The special theory of relativity provides an example of weak order in which there is no absolute time order between physical events when there can be no causal relation of a physical nature between them.

When I see something moving, not just that it has moved, but seeing it "as moving in a certain direction", then the path of travel over which I see it must include many points. Yet any awareness of a thing as moving in a certain direction must have a temporal unity within "naive" time, and be definitely after some previous stages of the thing's movement and definitely before certain other stages of this movement, but neither before nor after the spread of physical times within the moving of which it is an awareness.

This point applies to other conscious events—for instance, my having the thought, "Heavens! The post has gone". We imagine having such a thought as involving the words "Heavens", "the", "post", "has", and "gone" passing serially through my mind. Yet unless I had already had some thought about the post having gone, the word "Heavens" would be quite without its relevant point, and similarly with "the" and each of the other words until the end (even after "the post has", the sentence is still open to the continuation "not yet gone"). Such thoughts are unities: they happen at a time ("a moment", as we say) rather than being processes proceeding in stages, taking time ("a period", as we say). They cannot be imagined to happen at a definite instant within physically measurable time; rather, as in the earlier example, the event of having the thought "Heavens! The post has gone" has only weak order in relation to physical time, after some physical events and before certain others.

The times of perceptions, thoughts, and planned actions have a role in explaining behavior, and we should not expect them to have any more determinate place in the physical time sequence than this requires. True, in speech and thought as in playing tennis we frequently execute incomplete movements—for instance, changing plans as the ball bounces in an unexpected way or as we see the possibility of making a different return shot. But the timings of these changes of plan, whether in skilled movement or in speech or thought, will be no more precisely placed in physical time than their explanatory role requires.

No choice or awareness of choice arises against an empty background. Every choice on a particular occasion to act in a certain way occurs against the background of the general flux in our life as deliberating and reflecting animals, so that the inception of action is integrated within this wider frame-

72. Technically this means that the relations "before" and "after" between times of events are transitive, asymmetrical, and reflexive, but not connected. Simple order requires connectedness, as well.

work. If injured persons can be trained so that their choice, something reflected in changes in the brain, leads to action as a result of these changes, even if their action is brought about through the activation of implanted computer chips rather than in the way normal among human beings, these actions will still have the background appropriate to human action. Their structured background is what makes these actions the actions of a person rather than the effects of a change in the brain. Effects of changes in the brain lacking this setting are not actions of which we are the authors.

Modern physics provides some slight analogy. There, to the degree that one fixes a thing's position exactly, one loses all knowledge of its velocity or direction of movement and future influence. In a parallel way, to the extent that one isolates a state or change in the brain, removing it from an integrated situation within the general flux of our human and animal life, one robs it of its human role and significance. Or, just as to the extent that one considers light as composed of photons as particles one becomes unable to understand the interference and diffraction patterns suggestive of the wave character of light, so likewise with human life. The thought-experiments which consider changes in the brain in isolation from their functional setting produce paradox. But, conversely, to the extent that one restores their functional role within a human being, for instance, so that by means of computer chips they serve a therapeutic role enabling human beings to achieve the actions which they would choose, the inception and carrying through of such choices recovers the character of being inceptions of actions of which the human being concerned is the author, at the same time recovering the background of shifting beliefs, thoughts, and intentions, affected by shifts in emotion and by deliberation, characteristic of the inception of other choices and actions.

(ii) Wrong-footing our systems for perceiving continuity and causal action

Dennett also considers special cases of perception.

It is well known that a rapid succession of still pictures can create the impression of motion. However, if two adjacent small spots are lit successively, they will be perceived as one spot moving to and fro; and if the spots are of different color (e.g., the left spot red and right spot green), then the subject will describe the spot as switching from red to green in the mid-course of its supposed journey and register seeing this even before the right spot has actually lit up green.[73] In a parallel way one can imagine billiard balls being moved about by powerful magnets beneath a billiard table in such a way that it looks as if one ball hit another so that an observer will describe himself or herself as seeing the

73. Dennett, *Consciousness Explained,* chap. 5, sec. 2.

first moving ball cause the movement of the second and the impact as causing its own change of direction and speed. All these effects involve skilled efforts at deception, precisely trading upon a normal observer's skills in perceiving the causal action of one thing on another. Verisimilitude might be increased by introducing an independently caused click at the appropriate time, resembling the click when one billiard ball actually hits another, and one could experiment to discover the threshold at which the difference between the timing of the artificial click and the time of the apparent clash of the balls was realized.[74]

(iii) Interfering with sensory and motor systems so as to confuse our judgements of time order

Dennett appeals to Benjamin Libet's researches, which raise further questions of time order.[75] A tingle in the subject's right hand can be caused either in the normal way or by stimulating the relevant point on the left somatosensory cortex. Libet asked his patients which came first, the hand tingle which was caused by stimulating the cortex, or the hand tingle caused normally, and found (a) that in both cases up to around 500 milliseconds of cortical activity were required before "neuronal adequacy" was attained (the point at which the patient was aware of the tingle as a "conscious" experience—that is, aware so that he or she could report it, and (b) that the natural tingle was thought to happen before the brain-stimulated one. Further, in many cases (with timings sufficiently close), if the left cortex was stimulated to cause a tingle felt in the right hand somewhat before a naturally caused tingle in the left hand, the naturally caused left-hand tingle was reported as felt before the right-hand one, as if the registration of the nonnatural tingle had been delayed. Such results suggest that after the brain attains the physical state into which it would normally be brought after certain physical sensory processes, it is as if there were a delay time for checking, allowing for the receiving of rival messages and that, presumably because naturally caused signals come within the integrated context of other naturally caused signals, they receive the okay more rapidly so that the patient is conscious of the experience (and able to report it) more quickly than the ones which result from artificial cortical stimulation.

All these examples fit with the idea that human organisms have their functioning structured so as to behave as unitary wholes and so are capable of awareness of the nonnaturally caused tingles as arriving "too soon".

Our awareness of the timing of voluntary actions raises problems parallel to those raised by our awareness of the timing of sensations.

74. The systems being wrong-footed in such cases as the ones particularly studied by Stephen Grossberg in "Neural Dynamics of Motion Perception, Recognition Learning, and Spatial Attention", in *Mind as Motion*, ed. Port and Van Gelder, 449–89.

75. Dennett, *Consciousness Explained*, chap. 6, sec. 3.

Thus, in 1963, W. Grey Walter tested the hypothesis that certain bursts of cortical activity (brain activity recorded by electrodes implanted in the motor cortex) were initiators of intentional actions. He identified a part of the motor cortex that was active when people pressed a button to advance a slide in a sequence of slides. When the subject decided to press the button, the electrodes recorded and amplified the signal, and this recording caused the slide to change. The buttons supplied were mere dummies, unconnected with the slide apparatus. His patients were startled because it seemed to them that the slide projector was anticipating their decisions. They reported that just as they were "about to" push the button, but before they had actually decided to do so, the projector would advance the slide—and they would find themselves pressing the button but worried that this would advance the slide twice.[76]

These cases involve mistakes of judgment and expectation which arise because the subject mistakenly assumes that his or her voluntarily pressing the button will cause the projector to change slides. Rather it was their decision to press the button (before pressing the dummy button) which involuntarily activated electrodes so as to generate the electrical signals which caused the projector to change slide—pressing the dummy button had no effect.

Dennett draws other evidence from Libet's controversial researches.[77] Libet caused subjects to flex their wrists when they chose, ascertained the part of the cortex electrically active at such times, and compared the time when they thought they chose to flex their wrists (assessed by recording the position which they later reported a spot on a moving disk to have been when they made the choice) with the time of maximum relevant cortical activity. He found that in normal cases the time of maximum cortical activity was 300 to 400 milliseconds before the time at which people thought they had consciousness of a decision, as if the executive self acted before the conscious self—that is, as if decision were made first at a subliminal level before realization at the conscious level which the person could report.

Again, this fits with the idea that human beings as such have their functioning structured in such a way as to behave as unitary wholes, as it were revving up to the choice, not distinguishing the times of the revving up and the choice and the action.

Here the case of Bertrand Russell's telling the Lady Ottoline, "I did not know I loved you till I heard myself telling you so—for one instant I thought 'Good God, what have I said?' and then I knew it was the truth", cited by Dennett, is perfectly typical of human life.[78] I have argued this case elsewhere in regard to action of every type: the choice, the decision, the forming of inten-

76. Dennett, *Consciousness Explained*, chap. 6, sec. 5.

77. Dennett, *Consciousness Explained*, chap. 6, sec. 4.

78. Dennett, *Consciousness Explained*, 246.

tion need not precede the action, and it is only the choosing and intending internal to the intentional action which is essential to its being intentional.[79] With such choices made on the spur of the moment, our motives may be multiple without its being clear which is uppermost or decisive.[80]

The human being as an organism functions as a dynamic unity through time, the physical and the conscious aspects in perception, conation, and action all ordered in a way to be expected of a mental organism with perceptual and conative systems organized in ways functionally adapted to life in the world—a setting within which the possibility of such wrong-footing of our judgments is to be expected. Dennett's problems here all stem from inattention to the possibility of such a holistic approach.

(b) *Arguments for private qualia like those for private language depend on imaginary cases*

The character of higher animals, those to which it is right to attribute perception, memory, imagination, emotion, and action out of emotion, requires that when they perceive things it should be proper to speak of the way this or that looks, sounds, feels, tastes, or smells to them. The relationship between such animals' environment and their behavior has to be understood in functional terms, with how a thing looks to them gauged in terms of the discriminatory behavior that results from it. With animals with no capacity to make and express judgments, their only discriminatory behavior is the behavior which exhibits their plans, emotions, and needs—for instance, in seeking some foods and refusing others, stalking and going for the kill, climbing trees in search of food or safety, or whatever their form of life requires.

However, once the capacity for judgment arises, new forms of outward behavior appear, such as answering questions, and doing this independently of their relevance to possible nonlinguistic action. Usually answers expressing discriminations of color, sound, taste, and so forth receive common agreement. However, just as our condition as language-speaking or intellectual bodily organisms gives rise to the possibility of asking pointless questions about time order, so also it enables us to raise pointless questions as to how things look, sound, feel, taste, or smell—questions to which answers would have no practical, social, or cognitive function.

79. David Braine, *Human Person*, 135–36, 138–43, 156–58; cf. the rest of 151–59.

80. Such indeterminacy of motive can arise even when what action or response we will make has been clear for a period. In *Pride and Prejudice*, Elizabeth Bennett says that she first began to warm towards Mr. Darcy when she first caught sight of Pemberley, but clearly her feelings had begun to change before this. The case is comparable to the indeterminateness of sense instanced in Lincoln's quotable lines about fooling the people of which I spoke in chap. III, sec. 2 (b) of this volume. Neither has any of the skeptical implications drawn by Dennett, *Consciousness Explained*, 244.

Consider the case of describing how things look.

If asked to describe what we saw on a certain occasion, we are liable to say such things as, "The sky was gloriously blue and free from cloud, the sun was shining, and the wet from the recent rain glistened on the grass and the trees". In saying what we see we describe how things are, and only incidentally describe how they look. The ability to make judgments as to the actual color of things implies the ability to make judgments as to how things look, and the norm is that they look as they are. Hence our vocabulary for describing how things look is the same as our vocabulary for describing how things are, and its use in describing how things look arises derivatively from its use in describing how things are.

Here, when a discrepancy arises between the way things look to us and the way they are, the discrepancy needs explanation. Many such explanations are commonplace; for example, the explanation of some optical illusions in terms of refraction is unproblematic, and generally there is no systematic difficulty in finding such explanations. However, the character of our perceptual systems, with their relationships with our memories, attitudes, likes, and dislikes, makes it possible for quite "unreal questions" to arise—questions which there need be no way of resolving because there is no objective question to be settled.

For example, one could raise a question whether the reason I like lime juice and Jones does not is that it tastes the same to both of us, but one likes it and the other does not, or that it tastes different to Jones from how it tastes to me. Yet one of us might be sickly and not in a position to make sound judgments about the taste of things corresponding to how people in good health experience and describe them. Or one of us might be unused to the taste of lime, and the other accustomed and acculturated to it, without it needing to taste different. However, it is the norm that quite healthy people of the same general acculturation like different things, and there is no need to postulate things tasting different or defects in our likes or dislikes.

There can be different causes of changes in our likes and dislikes. Here some philosophical doctrine might suggest that there must always be some explanation of such changes so that in every case one answer would be right and the other wrong. However, nothing in common experience or the meanings of our words in communication requires us to suppose this.

Various effects arise as a result of medical conditions, such as the different kinds of cerebral achromatopsia mentioned by Dennett, or as a result of surgical intervention.[81] In many of these cases it seems quite arbitrary to sup-

81. Dennett, "Quining *Qualia*", in *Consciousness in Contemporary Science*, ed. A. J. Marcel and E. Bisiach (Oxford: Oxford University Press, 1988), 64–66. Dennett presents no other actual cases, only philosophers' imagined problems.

pose that the person's experience is something about which there is an objectively right view—Dennett, like Wittgenstein, takes this view, and we have no reason to disagree with him. And the philosophers have a huge battery of entirely imaginary cases which could be used to support the same conclusion—namely, that in such cases there is no right or wrong answer to the question of how things look, sound, feel, taste, or smell. We need have no argument with them.[82]

However, here there are two mistakes to be avoided.

The first is the one made by the followers of Descartes and the empiricists from Locke and Hume to Ayer and those in the analytic tradition who regard so-called experiences as essentially inner, realized in the brain, parts of "a stream of consciousness", rather than as parts of the history of unitary human organism. This requires the experiences to have qualities (so-called *qualia*) objectively in their own right and generates the unreal questions to which I have been alluding. This mistake has been rightly repudiated.

The second mistake is to take Dennett's overly simple get-out, of simply denying that there is any such thing as how things look or sound, even in ordinary cases, and, along with this, denying the existence of any kind of "consciousness" at all. On Dennett's view, talk about consciousness or any of the things which imply it, or expressing belief in the existence of such things, is simply a pathology of linguistic behavior.

Rather, the possibility of idle or unreal questions as to how things look or sound is a byproduct of the fact that the states of human organisms can only be described and understood by reference to the context of a functional relationship between the organisms' environment and their behavior.

Yet it is necessary, if there is to be any sight, hearing, feeling, tasting, or smelling of a public world existing independently of the individual at all, that things should be experienced as looking, sounding, feeling, tasting, and smelling in particular ways, because otherwise there would be no perception of any of these kinds to form part of the same biography as the rest of human thought, planning, and behavior—no perception without some level of

82. However, while these questions draw on such common experiences as changes in how things taste or appear, philosophers have developed the method of raising questions which are entirely hypothetical, supposing changes in experience independently of any possible cause. For example, they will suppose that I might wake up and the sky, which everyone else says still looks blue, to me now looks green, while the grass, which everyone else says still looks green, to me now looks brown. They will then raise the question whether I would still be having the experience which I would have if the sky were green and the grass brown, although what I say has no correspondence to what other people say; or whether I must have overnight forgotten what blue, green, and brown look like. If it were suggested that I might be right about the sky and the grass and everybody else wrong, this would provide no general solution to the problem, because it would simply convert a problem about my perception into a problem about everybody else's perception.

It is pointless to speculate about the possible causes of such entirely imaginary developments.

"consciousness". (The ambiguous word "consciousness" only introduces confusion into the discussion.)

If human beings or any other animals are to see, hear, and so on at all, there must be such a "thing" as how things look, sound, and so on; but the use of the word "thing" (supposedly a *qualium*) here is idle, a deceptive effect of the requirements of English grammar. So in normal cases there will be an objectively right answer to the question how things look, sound, and so on, and in this sense Dennett is wrong to deny the existence of *qualia*.

However, it is because the human being is a mind-exercising biological organism that biological variations and defects can give rise to situations in which there is no objectively right answer to questions of how things look or sound. Such questions as whether what looks blue to me looks the same to you when there is no reason for either of us to doubt that it is and looks blue, or whether what looked blue to us yesterday and looks blue to us today might in reality look quite different, the mistake arising solely because we had mis-remembered what blue was like, are idle. They are idle, raising no question in regard to which there could be an objectively right answer, for the same reason as arose in the case of the systematic absence of objectively right answers to certain types of question about exact time order—namely, that they are questions which have no bearing on the functional relationship between the organism with its behavior and its environment, physical and social.

In sum, Dennett ends up in a denial of the reality of the "self" because his whole method of approach—namely, that of looking for a mode of description of our conscious mental contents by means of a phenomenological or Cartesian "bracketing"—has the effect of making the "mental" something inner, independent of anything which might be within the world we perceive and within which we act, and therefore independent of anything external to the brain. He is looking for the self in a place where it does not exist. For, in truth, the self is nothing other than the human person, by nature a bodily, sentient, intellectual organism belonging to a certain biological species. This holistic understanding of the human being as a biological organism excludes the view that human experience involves inner presentations within some "Cartesian theater".

VII

Extending the Dynamic and Environment-Geared Model of Human Functioning to the Psychology of Language

Section 1. Difficulties in Applying the Idea of Modularity to Language

(a) *"Module" as in origin an engineering design concept*

In psychology it has become the norm to presume the existence of mechanisms with various roles in advance of any definite knowledge of how they may be physically realized, often referring to them as "modules".

The word "module" was first used to refer to standardized production units of components in electrical design and architecture and then, with rather different connotations, to refer to separable sections of spacecraft such as can operate as independent units. Derivatively, it came to refer to distinct, well-defined units from which a computer program may be built up or into which a complex process or activity can be analyzed, commonly with a view to computer simulation, each unit being complete in itself, but set in a definite relationship to the other units. With these associations taken from computing, the idea of "modularity" passed into psychology, where it has often been supposed to be useful in explanation, as if the word itself had a special magic. But it has no well-defined meaning or uniform use within psychology.

In Fodor's attempt to give a systematic account of how the notions of module and modularity can be applied in psychology, he considered them only in relation to what he called "input systems", particularly the visual system. Initially he tied the application of these terms to supposedly autonomous and computer-simulable brain processes in what he called "weak modularity".[1] But often he required more, a "strong modularity" involving "informational encapsulation"—that is, "not having access to facts that other systems know about". For, in his view, input systems are informationally encapsulated. Yet this cannot hold in regard to perception, because perception has to take account of memories and previous beliefs. Therefore, in his view input systems cannot achive only a vey shallow level of perception, quite inadequate for the fixation of belief required for perception. This is the work of central processes which operate according to Quinean principles—systems which cannot be informationally encapsulated and cannot operate mechanically. His characterization of modules excludes such reliance on parallel processing as might achieve perception mechanically.[2]

However, once the idea of module was introduced into psychology, its uses proliferated. For instance, Michael Gazzaniga views modularity as referring to "functional units that can produce behaviours and trigger emotional responses". In explaining his general approach in considering the effects of brain bisection, he tells us that "the findings suggest that human brain architecture is organized in terms of functional modules capable of working both cooperatively and independently. These modules can carry out their functions in parallel and outside the realm of conscious experience. The modules can effect internal and external behaviours, and do this at regular intervals". Presumably because he thinks of emotions and beliefs as things evidenced in linguistic behavior, he continues his account in these terms:

> Monitoring all this is a left-brain based system called the interpreter. The interpreter considers all the outputs of the functional modules [seemingly some based in the right brain and some in the left] as soon as they are made and immediately constructs a hypothesis as to why particular actions occurred. In fact the interpreter need not be privy to why a particular module responded [e.g., if it was based in the right brain]. None the less, it will take the behaviour at face value and fit the event into the large ongoing mental schema (belief system) that it has already constructed. If a module effects a behaviour that is dissonant with the belief system established through prior interpretive actions, the behaviour will tend to change the belief system.[3]

1. "Some processes which eventuate in perceptual identifications are, doubtless, cognitively penetrated. But this is compatible with the information encapsulation of the input systems themselves"; Fodor, *Modularity*, 76–77.

2. Fodor, *Modularity*, 72–74, 107–12.

3. The citations above are all from Gazzaniga, "Brain Modularity: Towards a Philosophy of Conscious Experience", in *Consciousness in Contemporary Science*, ed. Marcel and Bisiach, 219. The anthropomorphic style of presentation which Gazzaniga adopts in presenting his striking results is in strong contrast with the nonanthromorphic style of Milner and Goodale, *Visual Brain*, referred to earlier.

This text makes it clear how difficult it is to keep control of the extent to which the processes described by Gazzaniga and others are in fact computational when "observational" results are described in such an anthropomorphic way. If modularization means the association of the exercise of particular capacities in the behavior of the whole person with particular localized areas of the brain or patterns of electrical activity in such areas, this is quite different from thinking of them as "modules" in a sense taken from computer science.

The assumption that the various processes considered are physically mechanical is a piece of metaphysics, not science. The extent to which it is misleading to think of these processes in physical terms can be gauged from the speed at which they take place. The longer they take, the more likely it is that they have involved processes of conscious deliberation, requiring us to view them holistically, so that assessing the physical speed of neural processing could not provide even an approximation.[4]

(b) *General structural problems in applying the concept of modularity*

Before considering how, in general, mechanisms can subserve the functioning of teleological systems, we should note some structural problems in recent applications of the concept of module.

Earlier Chomsky spoke of there being a "language faculty"[5] alongside "the number faculty", each of them "mental organs" to be considered alongside the visual system or the system of motor coordination and planning.[6] He always conceived of such a language faculty, occupied with the innate representation or cognition of underlying linguistic principles, as a cognitive faculty.[7] This led Fodor to think of the "language processing module" as another input system feeding on items out of an inventory of morphemes (things structurally defined).[8]

4. The significance of the large differences of order between the times taken by different "psychological" processes is highlighted by Marta Kutas, "Current Thinking on Language Structures", paper 31 in *Cognitive Neuroscience: A Reader,* ed. Michael Gazzaniga (Oxford: Blackwell, 2000); cf. sec. 3 (b) (ii) and n. 30 of this chapter.

5. Chomsky, *Problems of Knowledge and Freedom* (New York: Pantheon, 1971). In 1965, in *Aspects,* he had spoken of a "general linguistic theory" as being "innately represented" in order to explain children's learning of language.

6. Chomsky, *Rules and Representations,* 39.

7. Thus later on in Chomsky, *Knowledge of Language: Its Nature, Origin and Use* (New York: Praeger, 1986), we find that his concern is with an "Internalized (I-) language", not at all with the formulation or production of speech—mere matters of "performance".

8. Fodor's idea that the "output" of the language processing module is functionally defined in such a way that "what perception must do is to so represent the world as to make it accessible to thought" (*Modularity,* 40) should be compared with Chomsky's conception of such output as the input to the centrally located conceptual-intentional Interface, where a sentence received its LF (logical form) representation (roughly, its "semantic interpretation"); Chomsky, *Minimalist Program,* 219.

As a result philosophical readers came to understand this supposed "module" enabling us to understand grammatical speech and distinguish the grammatical from the nongrammatical as the prototypical "module of brain activity". And a module thus relevant to perception and cognition, to the hearing of speech and to reading, would be related only derivatively to a motor system. For Fodor and Chomsky grammar tells us nothing about "performance" in the sense of motor output in speech.[9] Yet it would have been more natural to think of speech as primary and hearing secondary, albeit both involving understanding, and therefore to think of any module concerned with grammar as a module of an "output" system.

Accordingly, the first problem in applying the idea of a "module for grammar" along the lines of Fodor and Chomsky is that it creates a dilemma as to whether the role of grammar is enabling us to speak grammatically, which at the sentence or utterance level requires generation; or whether its role is in helping us come to understand what we hear, something that will need parsing—as to whether its primary role is productive, in speaking, or interpretive and cognitive, in hearing. Strangely Chomsky proposes his grammar in the form of a theory of generation and presents this as cognitive (instead of a theory of parsing geared to comprehension).[10] As to Fodor, he supposes that the perceptual input in speech has to be synthesized by the "central processor", leading to a cluster of beliefs being formed, which is what directs decisions concerning such actions as uttering a reply after the hearing of a question. Thus we find a hiatus between understanding speech and speaking in modular theories developed along these lines.

In the meantime, it seems wrong that linguistics should be lumbered with all the other difficulties of this form of modular theory.

For Fodor's account is subject to all the difficulties of "indirect" or "representational" theories of perception in their dividing between perceptual "input systems" and a "central processing system". He also has the problem of explaining how this "central processor", by "inferences" of no clearly regulated kind, drawing only upon the individual's own experience (e.g., memories), accomplishes the mountain of work required to enable that individual to make the perceptual judgments he or she does.[11] Indeed Dennett and others see no economy in Fodor's separation of an inner "central processor", and see

9. As we saw in chap. VI, sec. 3 of this volume, Sperber and Wilson adopted the idea of a language module as an input system feeding a central processing system, attributing it to Fodor.

10. For Chomsky the primary function of language is internal, in thinking to oneself and its role in communication perhaps an evolutionary accident.

11. Moreover, as we saw at the end of chap. VI, Fodor's way of thinking misdescribes what goes on in normal perception. It is more attractive to suppose that in normal perception we proceed upon a presumption that our situation for making a correct perceptual judgment is satisfactory, so that our judgments are not "inferential" in the way implied, although subject to corroboration or rejection by ourselves or others later.

this supposed central processor as inheriting all the theoretical problems of world-construction which confronted the person or "self" in earlier Cartesian and Humean accounts analyzed by Price, leaving both the person's inner state and his or her "output" ill-explained.

Accordingly, on any acceptable view, modules must be organized in a different way, avoiding this structural division between input systems, a central processor, and output systems. In brief the same intellectual animal which perceives external things must also accomplish intentionally the bodily actions it performs. The receiver of the input must be the same as the producer of the output—namely, the unitary, holistically conceived, "focalized subject" spoken of in chapter VI. It cannot be an intermediary, whether central processor, inner "self", or set of inner systems (demons).

(c) *These problems peculiarly acute if the concept of module is applied to hearing and speech*

The hiatus between supposed cognitive modules of perception and supposed productive modules of action thus presents us with the absurd dilemma of deciding whether the capacities of hearing and speaking involved in language belong to the sphere of cognition or the sphere of outward activity—that is, whether grammar is a module on the cognitive/perceptual side or a module on the practical/productive side. The choice is false.

Chomsky has always placed all these powers on the cognitive side, integral to his "Internalized language". Hence, paradoxically, his generative grammar is not intended to help us produce utterances in actual performance, but only to represent the grammatical aspect of the competence involved in our possession of the Internalized language concerned. This emphasis reflects his preoccupation with the problems of learning language, with the internal conditions of learning the grammar and lexicon of a language from hearing it used uppermost in his mind, rather than the conditions of using it—presenting us with a model of understanding, but, surprisingly, without showing us how to parse what is said to us. Systems of generative grammar are presented as systems for describing the sentence-forms people can produce and enabling us to judge whether the utterances they do produce are grammatical; but they do not give us any way of parsing these utterances. The student of grammar often gathers examples from considering self-constructed sentences, considering them retrospectively, knowing their analysis, since he constructed them; but this does not put him in the position to parse the sentences of others.

Yet two of the ways mentioned in chapter VI in which "mechanisms" seem to enter into human functioning invite quite the opposite way of thinking—namely, that of making speech primary. Thus the second of these arose from the different kinds of aphasia considered by Steven Pinker in *Words and Rules,* which are all primarily defects in speech, not in hearing or interpretation.[12] And the third, the part played by mechanisms in the achievement of correct pronunciation and of correctly formed noun and verb inflections, is again a matter of explaining output. (I have already dealt with the first, the problems raised by illusions.)

Moreover, yet further, logically the hearing and understanding of speech must (it would seem) be secondary, since they always presuppose the speech which needs to be heard and understood. This might suggest that it is the production or motor system which should be considered primary!—even though, without an audience and the possibility of the hearing and understanding of what is spoken, speaking would be pointless.

Linguistic understanding is, of course, as essential to human speaking as it is to the grasp of what is heard. Hearing might seem to have ultimate priority only in the process of learning to speak. Therefore it seems quite appropriate for Dik and his school of Functional Grammar to consider grammar primarily in its role as what Dik calls a production model, directed towards utterance or performance.[13]

In speaking, our goal is to produce context-geared utterances, not to construct or generate context-free examples of "system-sentences" within a formal grammar. Moreover, it is incidental to our purpose whether the utterance be exactly grammatical or not, and so our science of language should, as Dik recognized, embrace the understanding of nongrammatical utterances, whether the departure from supposed "grammaticality" reflects deliberate art, archaism, difference in dialect, sloppiness in speech, or the mistake of a beginner.[14]

Thus, to generalize, both semantics and pragmatics on the one hand, inseparable as shown in the introduction and chapter III, and phonetics on the other should be considered primarily in relation to speech or production. The relevance of hearing is to language learning and to the speaker-hearer relation intrinsic to communication.

Accordingly it was natural for Jespersen and Hockett to present speech as the primary object of linguistic science with morphosyntactics, or gram-

12. Mark C. Baker has an extended discussion of whether the evidence relating to several different kinds of aphasia suggests a loss of what underlies the capacity for the creative aspect of language use (CALU in his paper) and argues forcefully that it does not, considering several kinds of aphasia in detail; Baker, "The Creative Aspect of Language Use and Nonbiological Nativism", sec. 4 in *The Innate Mind* 3: *Foundations and the Future,* ed. Peter Carruthers, Stephen Laurence, and Stephen Stich (Oxford: Oxford University Press, 2007), 233–53.

13. Dik has the conception of a production model (a generator), an interpretation model (a parser), and a store used in both production and interpretation; traditionally grammar and vocabulary might have been regarded as part of the store; however, he aligns grammar firmly with the production model; Dik, *Theory of Functional Grammar: Part* 1, 8, 13–14.

14. Dik, *Theory of Functional Grammar: Part* 1, 6, in response to his Q3.

mar, as a matter of knowledge of "the observable regularities of actual speech" which "are a matter of habits, resident in the users of the language".[15] Such habits reside in the users of the language primarily as speakers, since without speech there is nothing to be linguistically heard and understood, even though speech is pointless without hearers who can understand it.

In any case this dilemma as to whether language capacities belong to the cognitive/perceptual side or to the practical/productive side of the human makeup seems false. The natural presumption is that the capacities to hear speech and to speak are correlative, each a complete human act as argued in chapter III and rooted in some language-sharing community. What we need is an account of the relevant motor activity and perception which allow the same subject directly to act and directly to perceive, to be both a speaker and a hearer.

Section 2. The Human Learning of Language Relies on Multi-Modal Perception

(a) *The multi-modal character of human perception*

In order to understand how children learn language, we need to understand how children learn by imitation, and to understand this we need to understand how much the processes involved depend on what has been called "multi-modal" or "inter-modal" functioning.

Following Gibson, psychologists have increasingly recognized the need to consider not just the visual system, but the human perceptual system as a whole by reference to functional relationships between an organism's environment and its behavior. This way of thinking can be presented in terms of Dynamical Systems Theory, but without understanding this in purely physical terms. As the child develops, in the womb and out of it, its sensory system interacts with the world as a whole, with the result that the child develops with a capacity for "multi-modal" functioning. One should envisage the different parts of the brain as in different degrees adapted to or specialized towards particular functions, but coming to these functions only in the course of development. Development is governed by the requirements of optimizing the efficiency of the relationships between an organism's environment and its behavior, and within this context every advantage is taken of any relevant capacity for being relevantly influenced by more than one of the senses in a way which renders behavior more efficient.

This general perspective has been increasingly confirmed by studies of

15. Citation given chap. III, sec. 4 of this volume.

children's learning. Thus when Meltzoff and Moore speak of cross-modal mapping, they have it in mind that both perceived and performed human acts are apprehended within a shared supramodal framework, envisaging human acts as a "metric" (i.e., a means of comparison) by which the self and other are both appreciated in terms of goal-directed organ transformations.[16] Butterworth thinks of this in terms of the Dynamical Systems approach, which, rather than thinking in terms of cross-modal matching between perception and action, sees both as rooted in a functional, goal-directed system, and sees this as confirmed by studies of neurological functioning in adults, in particular of the mid-brain.[17]

Thus it would appear from the work of Stein and Meredith that the influence of the primary sensory paths within the sensory nervous system is poorly differentiated at birth, so the different senses form a primitive unity, and it is only in the course of interaction with the world, beginning in the womb and continuing after birth, that the objects of the different senses become differentiated to the extent found in maturity. In the organization of vertebrate perceptual systems, the area of the brain called the superior colliculus plays a key role intermediate between the sense organs and the cortex. In the superior colliculus the organization of affects ("maps") in its superficial cell layers corresponds more closely to the organization of affects in the particular sense-organs, but in the deeper layers the neurons appear to show an organization of affects reflecting a multisensory input more corresponding to the world as we are conscious of it and more corresponding to our behavior. Put in terms of the metaphor of "maps", the deeper we go, the greater the correspondence of multisensory maps with maps found in motor systems.[18] Thus, in the superior colliculus, there are sets of neurons which relate both to perception and to action.[19]

16. Andrew N. Meltzoff and M. Keith Moore, "Persons and Representation: Why Infant Imitation Is Important for Theories of Human Development", in *Imitation in Infancy*, ed. Jacqueline Nadel and George Butterworth (Cambridge: Cambridge University Press, 1999), 20–22, 27; cf. Meltzoff and Moore, "Explaining Facial Imitation: A Theoretical Model", *Early Development and Parenting* 6 (1997): 179–92. In these papers they explain their Active Intermodal Mapping (AIM) model whereby (1) the goal or behavioral target is specified visually, (2) infants' self-produced movements provide proprioceptive feedback that can be compared to the visually specified target, and (3) such comparison is possible because both perceived and performed human acts are "represented" within a common supramodal framework.

17. Butterworth, "Neo-natal Imitation: Existence Mechanisms and Motives", in *Imitation in Infancy*, ed. Nadel and Butterworth, 77–78; cf. E. Thelen and L. B. Smith, *A Dynamics Systems Approach to the Development of Cognition and Action* (Cambridge, Mass.: MIT Press, 1993).

18. Barry E. Stein and M. Alex Meredith, *The Merging of the Senses* (Cambridge, Mass.: MIT Press, 1993).

19. Ken Nakayama gives an instructive discussion of the fecundity of the Gibson-inspired approach of seeking neurons sensitive to higher order properties in Nakayama, "James J. Gibson: An Appreciation", in *Cognitive Neuroscience: A Reader*, ed. Gazzaniga (Oxford: Blackwell, 2000), 140–52; cf. Stein and Meredith, *Merging of the Senses*. In the particular case of facial imitation, it might be that the "memory engram" which carries information from facial recognition carries it in such a way as also to direct the corresponding facial action, in the terms of G. Kugiumutzakis, "The Origin, Development and Functions of Early Infant Imitation" (PhD diss., University of Uppsala, Sweden, 1985).

These studies can be thought of as developments of Gibson's idea of "resonance", as when he speaks of the orienting of the organs of perception as governed by the brain in such a way that the whole system of input and output resonates to the external information, perceptual systems being ways of "seeking and extracting information about the environment from the flowing array of ambient energy". His conception was that a perceptual system should not be thought of as directed towards a processing of information received in the sense organs, but as directed towards securing a resonance between the external world and our behavior in respect of it.[20]

Thus the "multi-modal" character of perceptual knowledge extends beyond an integration between the child's seeing, touch, and hearing and the child's "practical" knowledge of his or her own past and prospective actions, all the time developing through learning from adapting to the modes of adult speech in the course of communication with adults. What I have in mind here is that, when we make a bodily movement intentionally, we have a preobservational or practical knowledge of what we are doing simply because we are acting in accord with our intentions. We do not depend for knowledge of what we are doing on observing our actions as they occur, whether observing them externally or "observing" the kinaesthetic ("feeling of movement") sensations which normally accompany them. This kind of preobservational knowledge begins even before birth. The baby in the womb makes many such intentional movements in exercising, experimenting with his or her body, or even in kicking the wall of what contains him or her. He or she continues making bodily movements, experimental and otherwise, after birth. Thus the children in perceiving the world have themselves already moved their legs and arms and pushed at things with them in the womb, not only after they are born, besides having much experience of sound in such a way as to be energized through some sympathy or shared experience and emotion with the mother.

Accordingly, when children see another person doing what they are doing they envisage him or her as doing something a bit like what they themselves do. Therefore the perceptual appreciation of what another person is doing involves children's practical knowledge arising from their own actions. We should anticipate that children apprehend other persons as if they were solid muscular beings—that is, as feeling strains in the similar places when pushing, and as reacting to prodding at muscles in similar ways, not as largely hollow moving toys. Hence the "information" is not just like a picture or photograph or snapshot in the mind (or series of these), but something which is sensorily multi-modal and practical—as, at a simpler level, a child who has

20. J. J. Gibson, *Senses Considered*, 5, 147, 260, chap. 13. R. S. Woodworth, "Reinforcement of Perception", *American Journal of Psychology* 60 (1947): 119–24 suggested that systems "hunt" until they achieve this clarity or resonance. This theory was developed in Eleanor J. Gibson, *Principles of Perceptual Learning*.

been pushing at or grabbing parts of his or her mother (breast or fingers) or moving bits of food, toy wooden bricks, spoons, and dishes, has the practical knowledge that they are in their respective degrees solid, needing stronger or weaker push or grasp to achieve whatever immediate end the child has. Accordingly the information is received by a being (the child) in such a way as to be in itself practical.

Therefore we do not need the convoluted accounts which make the child first learn the correlations between actions and internal and kinaesthetic sensations, and in imitation makes him or her aim to reproduce the sensations such as would result from actions, rather than directly to reproduce actions.[21] Instead we should think in terms of the child correlating the actions of others externally perceived directly with his or her own actions, knowing his or her own past and present actions as it were prospectively before the event, because they were or are what her or she meant or means to do (not just retrospectively through accompanying kinaesthetic sensations).

(b) *The imitation of speech depends on multi-modal perception*

In particular the child achieves a multi-modal integration of his or her hearing of adult speech and seeing of the relevant adult tongue, mouth, lip, and cheek movements with his or her awareness of his or her own actions in producing certain facial and mouth movements and certain sounds. Daniel Stern says, "infants are never in the position of responding only to the external form of a movement, but rather have the sense of internal correspondences from the beginning",[22] and this is true in the sense that the child does not know either his or her or the adult's actions in speaking only as bodily movements, but both as intentional actions, treating the adult's relevant actions as intentional, just as his or her own are intentional.

By the time a child intentionally imitates a sound made by an adult, he or she will already have experimented with making lots of sounds with variable relationships to those he or she hears in adult speech. Quite generally, when the child makes a sound intentionally, he or she has a multi-modal appreciation of what he or she is doing: first, the preobservational knowledge of what he or she intends (the kinaesthetic sensations which come with the

21. E.g., Alison Gopnik and Andrew Meltzoff, "Imitation, Cultural Learning and the Origins of 'Theory of Mind': Comment on Tomasello et al.", *Behavioral and Brain Sciences* 16, no. 3 (1993): 521–22, envisage the child as mapping the externally perceived behavior of the adult whose actions he or she aims to imitate onto his or her own "internal sensations", knowing his or her own movements only through internal and kinaesthetic sensations, and then formulating a plan to execute movements which will give rise to internal sensations appropriate to having imitated the originally perceived behavior of the adult. It seems convoluted to suppose that the aim is the reproduction of the internal sensations rather than the type of behavior imitated.

22. Daniel Stern, *The Interpersonal World of the Human Infant* (New York: Basic Books, 1985), 270.

bodily movements involved being incidental), and second, auditory perceptions. When a child hears an adult make the same sound, he or she has visual perception of the movements of the adult's tongue, mouth, lip, and other facial movements, together with auditory perception of the sound made, these auditory perceptions being slightly different from those he or she has when he or she makes the same sound himself or herself.

Within this setting the process of deliberately imitating a particular sound made by an adult must involve imitating the facial and tongue movements of the adult so far as they are visible to the child, subsidiarily comparing his or her internal auditory perceptions of the sounds he or she makes himself or herself with his or her external auditory perceptions of the preceding adult sound—not a random experimentation satisfied if the resulting auditory perceptions are similar. These things have been abundantly shown by Andrew Meltzoff and others in multiple studies.[23] (I come to the special semantic role of imitation in learning verbs in chapter IX.)

Section 3. The Shape of an Integrated View of the Language Faculty and Its "Tuning"

The cognitive and productive sides of human linguistic capacity can be reunited by conceiving human functioning in terms of the relations it establishes between an organism's environment and its behavior. Here I can only sketch the form that any account of linguistic activity must take if it is to take account of its physical, intellectual or semantic, and social aspects.

23. Patricia K. Kuhl and Andrew N. Meltzoff, "The Intermodal Representation of Speech in Infants", *Infant Behaviour and Development* 7 (1986): 361–81, and continuing in Kuhl and Meltzoff, "The Bimodal Perception of Speech in Infancy", *Science* 218 (1982): 1138–41, showed the importance of seeing other people's articulatory movements in learning to make the sounds used in language. They incidentally noted how the hearing-impaired can distinguish some vowel sounds according to the openness of the mouth and spread of the lips and distinguish certain groups of consonants by the coming together of the lips or positioning of the tongue. In general the role of the visual depended on the child's learning to appreciate the relation between the relevant articulatory movements (e.g., of lips) and the sounds made in his or her own case, so that auditory-articulatory coordination is fundamental. They argued that the relevant visuo-auditory relations are not learned by association.

Meltzoff and Moore, "Infant Imitation", 17–22, extend and summarize researches showing that the capacity for facial imitation is innate (independent of manual exploration of own or other faces), noting the early occurrence of differential responses to tongue and lip protrusion and lip protrusion and lip opening and early distinguishing of head and cheek movements. Also in Nadel and Butterworth, eds., *Imitation in Infancy* (Cambridge: Cambridge University Press, 1999), G. Kugiumutzakis confirms the imitation of tongue protrusion and mouth opening within the first month. Meltzoff and Moore also bring together the evidence that from at least twelve months imitation can take place a day after the action imitated, and soon even four months later; "Infant Imitation", 13–17.

That newborns distinguish between the sound of their own cries and those of another baby crying has been shown by G. B. Martin and R. D. Clark, "Distress Crying in Neonates: Species and Peer Specificity", *Developmental Psychology* 18 (1982): 3–9.

(a) *Seeking an uncontroversial concept of module*

Gibson thought of the visual system as involving a functional relation between the animal's sensory system and the way its behavior becomes adapted to its environment. What we call perception typically involves an integration of the cognitive and the practical. I instanced earlier the case of seeing precisely where the edge of a table is—where the precision of the knowledge is not something we identify in thought or speech, but exhibit in our capacity to touch the edge exactly.[24]

In a parallel way we should think of the auditory system in relation to speech in the same way as the visual system, the environment of speech being the social and natural world as human voices present it to us in the context of this world, and our understanding of what we hear as something displayed in our own linguistic and other behavior. Accordingly the powers of linguistic understanding are neither exclusively cognitive nor exclusively productive, but exercised equally in hearing and speaking. Moreover, it is only by thinking of human functioning in this way, as geared to the social world, that we can understand the phenomena of imitation as important for language learning.

Just as Dik viewed grammar and the lexicon as elements in some store drawn upon or utilized equally in hearing what is said to us and in speaking, and not as belonging to one rather than the other, so it is possible to view all the powers involved in linguistic understanding in this way. Once we have come to view both hearing and speaking as complete acts of the human organism as such, we can envisage the relevant powers, faculties, or modules as exercised or involved in both. Then we can recognize that it is the person, the human being as such, not the "mind" nor the "brain", which exercises linguistic understanding (whether in regard to the semantic structures of discourse and conversation or to grammar and the lexicon) equally in speaking and in hearing. There is no divorce between the cognitive/perceptual and the practical/productive side of human makeup, except when faculties are impaired.

The idea of a module as a part of the brain in which certain kinds of processing relevant to certain functions occur is well established. Thus the system whereby sets of patterned impulses from several different senses can be processed in such a way as to produce appropriate behavior has been shown to depend upon brain activity in a particular part of the mid-brain called the superior colliculus.[25] It is this, the superior colliculus, and not any other part of the brain which is preadapted to perform such processing: as each mammal

24. In chap. VI, sec. 1 (b) (ii), we met the same inseparability between the cognitive and the practical in Gibson's theory of affordances and its precursors in Aquinas and Merleau-Ponty.

25. Stein and Meredith, *Merging of the Senses*.

or other vertebrate has its senses come into efficient functional relation with its behavior by some developmental process. It thus plays a key part in the processing Gibson conceived as enabling a resonance between perceptual operation and the ongoing life of the mammal or vertebrate, contributing to its particular form of life. It is this part of the brain which performs the relevant processing, while related ancillary parts, such as the optical system, become adapted to the more specialized functions which they alone are physiologically able to fulfill.

Evidently this developmental process is governed in a way lending itself to teleological description and to the holistic way of thinking opened out in chapter VI. At each stage at which the environment influences the development and behavior of the organism, it is already determined which parts of the organism can function in this or that way. As the organism interacts with its environment, its different parts turn out to be apt to being tuned to function in ways subserving the well-functioning of the whole organism, fulfilling their respective roles, this tuning being achieved through interaction with the environment, and where language is concerned, the social environment.

The acoustic input to the ears and optic input to the eyes have effects upon inner parts of the brain relevant to the hearing and understanding of speech, while the observation of the lips, tongue, and face is important to children's learning to speak, as well as to hearing all through life, especially for the deaf. The human organism is genetically possessed of an auditory system apt to be acted upon acoustically in differentiated ways so that some sound patterns are liable to have a linguistic function for the organism as combinations of "phonemes". Which sound patterns are relevant to speech is partly determined by the language of the young language learner's human company, and thus already what happens at what is called the "auditory-phonological interface" is partly determined by interaction with adults and so by adult practice. (If one were to compare the system with that of a grid devised to filter the stones in a pile of rubble according to their shape, then it is as if the shapes of the holes in the grid were partly determined by local custom, rather than in all respects natural to holes as such, so that the question of nativism, i.e., of what is determined innately and what is determined culturally or by learning, arises even at the phonological level.) Sound patterns have a linguistic function for the organism if they "resonate" in speaker-hearer exchanges.

Since human beings have the capacity for speech, it must be that in the course of their developing the exercise of this capacity, all those parts and systems in the brain which play particular roles in exercising this capacity become tuned to play these roles.

We may hypothesize, sometimes on the basis of clinical experience, that this or that part of the brain subserves this or that function—for instance, according to Pinker's suggestion, that in speech one part of the brain subserves the function of assigning tense forms and plurals in irregular cases, prior to another part subserving this function in regular cases, each belonging to the accidence as opposed to the syntax of the language. And perhaps in hearing, there are parts subserving the processing involved at each of the acoustic-phonological, the phonological-syntactic, and the syntactic-conceptual interfaces, if Jackendoff's rich theory of "representational modularity" is acceptable.[26]

Jackendoff speaks of the processes at these interfaces as processes of translation, the acoustic or auditory being "translated" into the phonological, the phonological into the syntactic, and the syntactic into the conceptual or "propositional". However, he anticipates that at each interface, before such translation can take place, a different integrative set of processes has to have taken place in a separate module. Such integrative processes "construct a full representation in a particular format, given a collection of fragmentary structures in that format".[27] Presumably in the input case, whereby we hear in such a way as to understand, integrative processes include an element of reconstruction, the data coming towards such interfaces being often defective due to, for instance, noise, slovenly speech, or poor hearing—the reconstruction to be achieved by feedback from the semantic to the syntactic, the syntactic to the phonological, and even the semantic via the syntactic to the phonological.[28]

However, Jackendoff's use of the term "representation" in describing his theory has the implication that at each different interface, the processing depends upon some kind of part-to-part, relation-to-relation isomorphism—in effect, a "material" isomorphism by contrast with the "intentional" isomorphism Aquinas envisages.[29] But these isomorphisms are in different respects at the different interfaces, making it obscure whether the feedback envisaged in this theory of representational modularity undermines his more general view which we saw earlier in chapters I and V, requiring the exclusion of gaps of a kind requiring the understanding to enter in to determine meaning. (His general view allowed an isomorphism between a sentence and its meaning, involving a "material" isomorphism of the kind chapter VIII excludes.)

26. Hence, in Jackendoff, "Fodorian Modularity and Representational Modularity", in *Language and the Brain*, ed. Yosef Grodznisky, Lew Shapiro, and David Swinney (New York: Academic Press, 2000), 3–30, I interpret the diagrams on 14–15 of in the light of 4. His note on 28 makes plain that this paper of 2000 was expressing views he had held since 1991 or before.

27. Jackendoff, "Modularity", 12–13.

28. Jackendoff, "Modularity", 16–17.

29. For Aquinas, the light passing through the pupil of the eye has the form (*species*) in an intentional manner in virtue of this that we see the object possessing the form materially—this *species* intentionally present in the pupil has no material likeness to the object seen.

(b) *How the animal becomes open to the workings of the intellect*

(i) The determinants involved in the "tuning" of brain behavior

If we think of the parts of the brain concerned as analogous to the hardware of a computer, then there will be some constraints set upon what processing can be achieved in each part by its physiology and by its capacities for physiologically differential responses to the input to it, while all other constraints on what processing actually takes place will be semantic and pragmatic—and it is these which achieve the "tuning", any resonance in speaker-hearer exchange having a reinforcing effect.

Further, whereas the parts of the sensory system fulfilling the more external stages in our getting to hearing with understanding—for instance, the ears, the eyes, and the superior colliculus—cannot have other parts of the brain substituted for them when damaged, the "higher" the stage concerned the more possible it is for a different part of the brain to substitute for them and to become tuned to fulfill the required function, and so the fewer the constraints which are set by the hardware, and the more by the structures involved in the "tuning" process. At the highest levels one would anticipate that the only constraints set will be those set by semantics (what I spoke of in the introduction as a "general logic"), including those reflected in the pragmatics of communication, as these are mediated by the particular language and culture of those with which the hearer is engaged. It is presumably from these highest levels also that human beings derive the capacity to substitute one kind of input for another—for instance, to substitute sign-language for speech.

We see even with the superior colliculus an extreme malleability of function, developing very differently in different animal species. And in cases of impairment we may find parts of the sensory cortex normally adapted to one sense instead developing to serve another. This malleability of the brain and its parts reaches an extreme in the case of linguistic activity, a stage when neurology ceases to set any constraint on the semantics of the speech, sign-language, and so forth, so that the only tuning to which it is subject comes from general logic and pragmatics, together with the intellectual tasks by which the human being is challenged. In brief, for linguistic activity to exist, the brain must have become so malleable in its modes of functioning as to enable the animal to be open to the workings of intellect.

If this picture is substantially correct, and if, as I argue in part three, the universal aspects of syntax are a projection of pragmatics and semantics, then Chomsky's case for regarding "universal grammar" as dictated by limitations in the ways in which the neurological hardware of the brain is capable of functioning physiologically will seem very feeble.

In sum, semantic and pragmatic constraints determine any universal features in the shaping of the syntactic analysis of sentences in any integrative processing, the sentence in its syntactic analysis requiring to be geared to interpretation in its context of utterance. By contrast, one might surmise that the determinants of phonological structure, picking out phonemes, will be determined from below by limitations on the sounds human beings can learn to vocalize and auditorily discriminate (learning capacities which decline with age in ways which affect capacities to learn new languages).

We may further surmise that the aspects of linguistic function which are closely tied to neural functioning within limited areas of the brain (though not so that there can be no substitution within these areas) will be those concerned with the less universal features of language—for instance, the memory of vocabulary and the speedy assignment of tense forms and plurals.

The time taken by such procedures is one sign of which features are of such kind. Differentiating phonemes from each other takes only milliseconds. Deciding that "pencilist" is not a word and that one does not herd animals into pencils takes a somewhat longer time (presumably because it is not obvious that the word "pencil" does not have some secondary, specialized meaning, e.g., as applying to long, thin sheep pens). By contrast, the quasi-logical task of dealing with a sentence concerning numerous relative clauses embedded within each other may take many seconds.[30] Likewise, it is again a quasi-logical task correctly to interpret (1) "The men are too stubborn to talk to Bill", (2) "The men are too stubborn to talk", and (3) "The men are too stubborn to talk to"—examples considered by Chomsky and Mark Baker.[31] Understanding these sentences does not proceed by complex reasoning about facts about the language as is suggested, but by recognizing that "The men" here must refer to certain particular men and considering models which would make the sentences true. Sentence (3) means that these men's stubbornness excludes the productiveness of trying to get them to talk. In (1) and (2), evidently there must be other people involved who might want to talk to these men, but the latter's stubbornness means it would be unproductive for Bill in (1) and for a wider group in (2) to try.

(ii) *Character of the constraints set by semantics and pragmatics in tuning human language-use*

The question now becomes that of the kinds of constraint which semantics and pragmatics set upon the human organism, tuning the various parts of

30. See Kutas, "Current Thinking", 431, 441; cf. n. 4 of this chapter. I consider the problem of interpreting embedded constructions in chap. XIII, sec. 3 (c) of this volume.

31. Chomsky, *Some Concepts and Consequences of the Theory of Government and Binding* (Cambridge, Mass.: MIT Press, 1982), 30; and Mark Baker, "Theism and Cognitive Science", in *The Routledge Companion to Theism*, ed. Charles Taliaferro and Stewart Goetz (London: Routledge, forthcoming).

the brain so that they fulfill their roles in our use of language according to its general functional semantic structure.

In the light of the perspectives I have been presenting, it is liable to seem farfetched to suppose that these constraints upon the organism could have a physical description, however complex. The systems of physical description required would have to provide a complex key to the functioning of all the physical subsystems within the organism involved in the learning and use of language, chiefly in the brain—supposedly shaped by genetically given hardware.

Yet such a representation is required by Chomsky when he describes mind, mental representation, mental computation, and so forth as a matter of "keeping to the level of the abstract characterization of the properties of certain physical mechanisms" (the view cited in chapter III), since this implies that conceptual (otherwise described as propositional or semantic) structural descriptions have some kind of extraordinarily complex isomorphism with structured events in the brain. And Jackendoff's conception, in effect, of a "functional characterization [functional in relation to the relevant functioning of the brain] of the 'data structures' stored and assembled in the functional organization and activity of the brain in the course of the use of a language"[32] implies the same kind of isomorphism.

The environment-geared functional approach which I have proposed highlights the difficulties to conceiving relevant forms of isomorphism among living things at any level, but our present concern is only with the obstacles which arise with the capacity to use language. Our concern here is, of course, only with "material", element-to-element, relation-to-relation, not "intentional", isomorphism.

The relevant isomorphisms could not be between an inner mind and, equally inner, the brain. Rather they would have to be isomorphisms between a system of semantic and pragmatic constraints set up within a whole system embracing both the organism and its natural and social environment and a physical system of constraints within the organism and its environment considered purely physically. This presents problems much worse than the "many-body" problem in physics!—it requires something close to the "theory of everything" which Chomsky contemptuously dismissed as alien to science. This problem is exacerbated by the impossibility, identified in chapter VIII, of a system whereby an organism is mentally directed towards objects in its external environment by being represented by a system of physical relations to representations of these objects.

Chapter VIII will also explain four other problems for any physicalist

32. Jackendoff, *Foundations*, 21–27, 34; cf. my introduction, n. 20.

view, problems I identified in chapter 12 of my book *The Human Person*: first, the only undoubted physical correlate of human thinking and understanding has to be its expression, typically in speech, and not some inner state or sequence in the brain; then there are the problems, second, of how we make any use of any general concept at all; third, of how we handle the concepts we use with such generality or flexibility that their use is unformalizable; and fourth, of how we deal with self-reflection and the concepts involved in its exercise.

Accordingly, the conjecture that it is processes in the brain which causally determine, let alone explain, our thoughts and utterances proves farfetched in the extreme. But this will still leave brain processes playing some part in our hearing and speaking, not just in the operation of the senses and motor control of speech organs, but in the operations of memory and morphosyntactic processing geared to what is particular to each language.

(c) *The resulting holistic view of linguistic activity*

The point of view outlined earlier still leaves room for modules of brain functioning adapted to giving us our skills in hearing and speaking, modules conforming to the requirement that they should coordinate auditory perception with oral production in speaking, modules whose individual impairment prejudices the integration of the activity as a whole.

We have seen that the concept of "module" needs to be transformed from being an element in a mechanical theory of brain functioning to being a facet of a holistic theory of the functioning of the organism. It essentially requires a theory of the "tuning" whereby the functioning of the module of the brain concerned becomes shaped in such a way as to make the behavior of the organism concerned in the relevant respect adapted to its external environment. If we allow the conception of module to undergo this radical reinterpretation in the light of Gibson's treatment of visual perception, it will clearly have some role in respect of the hearing of speech. Clearly, just as in distinguishing visual *Gestalten* perceptually, relevant parts of the brain become tuned to enable us to make sensitive perspectival and topographical judgments—for instance, when viewing an extensive undulating landscape marked by patches of woodland, hedge, and so forth in varying conditions of light set by the clouds—so it is evident that in a parallel way relevant parts of the brain must become tuned in auditory perception. Experiments suggest that adults appreciate order-systems within phonetic sequences given without semantic cues, not by a process of hypothesis testing, but by some discovery procedure which is able to set aside the effects of random errors ("noise"), even though the exercise of this discovery procedure is set within a context of habituation in distinguishing phonemes and perhaps intonational patterns particular to the language being used.[33] This involves a capacity to appreciate patterns analogous to that discerned by Gibson in his studies of visual perception.[34] Such capacities play a huge and inadequately studied role in our hearing of language as well as in our hearing of music. We should anticipate there being modules of brain functioning geared to the auditory and visual perception which enable us to recognize phonemes, morphemes, and words in situations involving liaison and affecting stress.

Thus I see large scope for modules of brain functioning pertinent to the perceptual recognition of linguistically relevant patterns, phonetic, morphological, and morphosyntactic, just as there must be such in the case of music—and I would expect our motor productive oral skills, as well as ones related to speedier writing, sign language, and the playing of musical instruments, to utilize the same modules. However, it is uncertain whether and how far these modules need to be innate, although it seems clear that at different ages there are cutoff points after which various different skills become difficult or impossible to acquire.

Meantime, this does not alter the shape of the main picture. The way in which we learn language, at least at the first language stage, depends on the learning and appreciation of language in its pragmatic and semantic aspects, and this shapes semantic syntax, even at stages of lexical-item distinction prior to grammaticalization. Hence, rather than imagining a special, innate module of brain functioning geared to speech, we should conceive the human capacity for speech as "intelligible-content-bearing communication" which precisely depends on the absence of any such module. Many systems in the brain and outside it are indispensable to language-use—concerned with hearing and speaking, with the memory and use of vocabulary and accidence, and so forth. But the whole speech-serving system must allow the structures of speech to be determined not neurologically, but by being tuned solely by pragmatic and semantic constraints and challenges in the context of fellow language-users and of the problems posed by their environment. It is thus that syntax is a projection of semantics and pragmatics, not of neurology, in such a way that the brain introduces no extra constraints upon human speech and thought, but allows the human being to be free to be open to intellect.

Different languages prioritize the various semantic and pragmatic constraints differently as they seek to optimize the resolution of conflicts between different constraints, thereby influencing grammaticalization in ways which

33. The experiments described in Martin Braine, "On Two Types of Models of the Internalization of Grammars", in *The Ontogenesis of Grammar: A Theoretical Symposium*, ed. Dan I. Slobin (New York: Academic Press, 1971), 164–65, demonstrated this. In general, some phoneme sequences are set aside more readily as random "noise", or not even noticed, in picking out general types of pattern.

34. J. J. Gibson, "Concept of Stimulus", and J. J. Gibson, *Senses Considered*.

Optimality Theory attempts to consider. As children develop, their speech comes to reflect these syntactical differences as their habits of speech become accommodated to those of their elders. In chapters XI and XIII I observe some of the multiple ways in which forms of grammaticalization differ and the pressures involved in their development.

Meantime, of course, since there can be no exercise of the syntax of a language without the use of its accidence and vocabulary, the two related somewhat as matter to form, children have to gather these from the speech of their elders.

VIII

Understanding as Essential to Explaining Speech

RESISTING THE DRAG TOWARDS PHYSICALISM

Section 1. The Incoherence in Dividing the Inner from the Outer in Language

In chapters I to III we registered how linguistic understanding of the lexical or *langue*-meanings of lexical factors grounds the linguistic understanding of their sense or discourse-significance as used in utterances in particular contexts, so that linguistic understanding at two levels is always essential to linguistic communication. These two kinds of linguistic understanding are not theoretical entities in the way quarks are theoretical entities, mere postulates in the explanation of phenomena, but are both things of which we are aware in the act of using language and also as entering into the explanation of linguistic phenomena.

We know that we understand in the very acts of speaking and hearing speech, just as we know that we act intentionally in the very act of doing something, and know that we see in the very act of seeing something. These parts of our knowledge do not require the meanings and senses involved, or their understanding, to be objects of experience—any more than they require that, when we see, our seeing should be an object of our sight. Rather, neither the sentence nor its sense, neither linguistic expressions nor meanings, or senses, have any real existence independently of the acts of speech or other forms of communication in which they arise. As we saw in chapter III, they need no more determinateness of sense than the explanatory role of these activities and states requires.[1]

The arguments of chapter VI indicated that in the natural functioning of human beings the mind-involving is irreducibly psychophysical in nature. Twentieth-century thought up to the 1960s added a great variety of arguments converging on this exclusion of the Cartesian conception of the mind as something whose influence is essentially inner to the brain, as well as excluding physicalism and behaviorism as accounts of mind-involving attributes. Such arguments may be found in the independent approaches of the later Wittgenstein, of Ryle, and of J. L. Austin and others influenced by Aristotle, as well as in Merleau-Ponty and later in Anscombe's *Intention*, Strawson's *Individuals*, Stuart Hampshire's *Thought and Action*, Sydney Shoemaker's *Self-Knowledge and Self-Identity*, and Charles Taylor's *Explanation of Behaviour*.[2] Alongside these we have the reflections of Gabriel Marcel and the whole philosophy of Heidegger, as well as Saussure's conception of the linguistic sign of which speakers and hearers as subjects are aware as essentially physicomental.[3] The conceptions of these thinkers exclude physicalism and behaviorism as much as Cartesianism.

These thinkers reinforce the arguments of earlier chapters, absolutely excluding the separation of I-language and E-language required by Chomsky's identification of the mental and the neurological. Any such conception of the mental as having its only ontological realization in the brain involves the Cartesian severance of the mental, thought of as realized only in or through brain states and processes, from the behavioral and perceptual with their aspects outside the brain. The thought of those I mentioned precludes this severance of the mental from the behavioral.

In accord with this, it is integral both to the notion of linguistic understanding as an aspect of language-possession and to the notion of the linguistic understanding of speech (language-use) that these forms of understanding should be integral to the ultimate explanation of the things we do in expressing our judgment—understanding and judgment both being things which involve mind. That is, if any ascriptions of such kinds of understanding are to be considered true, then these must allow that they are integral to explanations

1. Quine's problem as to the determinacy of translation arose from demanding definiteness of sense where public language did not need it; see chap. III, sec. 3 (b) (ii) of this volume.

2. G. E. M. Anscombe, *Intention* (Oxford: Blackwell, 1958); Stuart Hampshire, *Thought and Action* (London: Chatto and Windus, 1959); Sydney Shoemaker, *Self-Knowledge and Self-Identity* (Ithaca, N.Y.: Cornell University Press, 1963).

3. He explains this in one of the recently published cache of notes in his own hand (Simon Bouquet and Rudolf Engler, eds., *Écrits de linguistique generale par Ferdinand de Saussure* [Paris: Gallimard, 2002]), which he was keeping in order to mull over, concerning problems with which at his death he was still struggling (taking the view of Roy Harris, *Saussure*, 220, 229–34). By *figure vocale* Saussure meant "vocal sound" as something purely physical, as opposed to what he called *forme-sens*; Harris, *Saussure*, 218–19.

of why the bodily movements involved in speaking occur, so that there are "causal explanations" which involve teleological features alien to the mathematically mechanistic or purely physicalistic forms which it is fashionable to treat as canonical for causal explanations, causal explanation being reduced to conformity to law.[4] Accordingly, we need to chart the shape of some third way which will consistently avoid this model of explanation derived from Hume and Kant, besides avoiding the pitfalls of the Cartesian internalization of the mind which underlies most current forms of physicalism.

(a) *The need for a third way which avoids both behaviorism and introspectionism*

In Wittgensteinian terms, for these types of understanding to possess an explanatory role is an essential part of their "grammar", and anything we say which violates this "grammar" involves speaking of linguistic understanding in a nonsensical way, or else in a way which needs to be explained again from scratch, or from outside the framework of our language. As we saw in chapter IV, different general semantic features of language are closely interwoven, and if Wittgenstein is rightly understood, he viewed the different parts of our grammar as in many cases interwoven in such a way that in key cases one cannot, from within the grammar of our present languages, develop alternative ways of using the language without the result being "mere nonsense", or else waiting to be given sense from scratch.[5] Therefore, when Wittgenstein says that "essence is expressed by grammar",[6] he is not saying that it has the status of a notation established by stipulation or choice. Wittgenstein never thought that essence was *created* by grammar. For Wittgenstein, for essence to be expressed by grammar, and the character of such human language-games as assertion, both depend upon the "general fact of nature" that situations in which the game would break down are rare.[7]

However, if we suppose ourselves to speak intelligibly at all, we presuppose the applicability of our common conceptions of linguistic understand-

4. By a causal explanation's taking a Humean form, I mean in practice one fitting the account of J. L. Mackie, "Causes and Conditions", *American Philosophical Quarterly* 2 (1965): 245–64, whereby a cause is an insufficient, but necessary member of a set of causal conditions jointly sufficient, but not necessary, to guarantee the effect.

5. P. M. S. Hacker, *Insight and Illusion*, 2nd ed. (Oxford: Blackwell 1986), 201–3; cf. Hacker, *Insight and Illusion*, chap. 8: according to Hacker, Wittgenstein considers solipsism to *require* explanation from within present language, but to be incapable of this in any coherent way.

6. Wittgenstein, *Philosophical Investigations*, I, §371.

7. Anscombe, paper 13, "The Question of Linguistic Idealism", in *Collected Philosophical Papers* (Oxford: Blackwell, 1981), 1:112–33, esp. 133. Hacker, *Insight and Illusion*, 185–94, implies a Kripke-like conventionalist interpretation of Wittgenstein, as if the autonomy of grammar implied arbitrariness, or openness to choice, yet *Insight and Illusion*, 201–3, excludes this.

ing in our very activity. This is not optional and therefore not a part of "folk psychology" which science can put aside. This "folk psychology" involves the older paradigm whereby there are states of the human being or other animals which have an explanatory role of a teleological kind as states in virtue of which actions are directed to certain ends or purposes.

Explanations of these kinds do have explanatory power. It is not merely that they seem intelligible, that we can "empathize" with them. Rather, they bring a certain simplicity or order into the interpretation of the phenomena which might otherwise appear a merely chaotic array. Thus the types of behavior which a criminal may go in for in order to avoid detection of his crime are liable to be exceedingly varied—for instance, wearing gloves in certain tasks, washing or muddying a variety of dead bodies or objects, placing objects in unlikely places (e.g., offensive weapons in rivers or in the drawers of alternative suspects), or inscribing marks on paper and making noises of various kinds (described as writing and speaking). The malfunction of physical machines may well produce heterogeneous effects, but not ones so apt for explanation in teleological terms. And obviously, human linguistic behavior, whether exemplified in short dialogues or in longer works such as Newton's *Principia* or Shakespeare's *Macbeth*, provides good candidates for requiring explanations of this mentalistic teleology-involving kind.

Such explanations in "teleological" terms, implying an end or purpose, rather than in neurological terms, are commonly quite rich in predictive power—for instance, as to how the animal or person may behave in the future.

When behavior is explained as the result of the workings of a mechanism, the ways of describing and grouping the results of these workings are limited by the character of the mechanism and are quite different from the results of thinking of the workings of the animal or human minds as directed towards ends. This becomes particularly evident when we consider such ends as achieving the understanding of something, producing a proof or justification for some proposition, winning a chess game, discovering the truth in regard to some question, or working out which act most accords with human well-being. And my arguments in chapters I and II, brought to a climax in chapter V, suffice to show how human beings' informality in the use of language, conspicuously in their powers of mathematical reasoning, as well as more generally, is beyond the capacity of any machine—rather it absolutely depends upon understanding human thought and behavior in intellectualistic and end-directed terms.[8] The importance of an end-directed or teleological approach for our understanding of our general grammatical capacity by ref-

8. Chap. V of this volume showed that machines lack our capacity to use the most general concepts and any freedom in such use, as well as our capacity to describe and account for novel situations in novel ways. In secs. 4 and 5 I showed the involvement of teleology in our understanding of argument.

erence to pragmatics and semantics, suggested in chapters VI and VII, will be confirmed in part three.

In considering forms of explanation of linguistic behavior which involve teleology, one more general remark is relevant.

As suggested in chapter V, it seems perverse to seek an explanation from neurology for why people who, in particular cases, think that P and are persuaded that if P, then Q, commonly come to conclude that Q—though quite proper to look to neurology for explanations of the malfunctions leading to the failure to conclude that Q. As we have already seen in chapters IV and V, and will see again later, many aspects of language-use appear self-evident to the understanding, as if "open to view". Hence, in context, Putnam's remark that "we are partially opaque to ourselves" in a way that hydrogen atoms are not opaque to us points in a direction opposite of the truth.[9]

States of understanding are not private. Understanding is not a state behind behavior known only introspectively. Rather, other people are commonly better judges of whether we understand than we are. Our mental states may be known in two different ways: in one, they may be known by us noninferentially in the course of, as it were, "living with ourselves"[10] (in this latter case the fact that it counts as knowledge is indicated by the possibility of lying);[11] and in the other they are known to others from our speech or other behavior. Propositional knowledge of such states can be shared by members of a community of speakers and hearers, both by a person's telling others what he or she believes, intends, or means and by their observing his or her behavior, able to check its consistency with what he or she has told them that he or she believes.

It is vital that knowledge of our mental states and dispositions which is reached by others by inference from outward behavior and knowledge of the same states reached without the help of such inference are inseparable. Recognizing this enables us in the same act, first, to reject the Cartesian separation of the mental and the physical and, second, to reject behaviorism. Here I

9. Cf. Putnam, *Meaning and the Moral Sciences* (London: Routledge and Kegan Paul, 1978).

10. The model of self-knowledge as gained by introspectively looking at ourselves is misguided. Rather, the processes involved are not only more various, but much more complex. Thus, although our knowledge of our motivations or meaning in present action or speech is not that of an external observer, but precedes rather than follows the action or speech, it arises in a context of familiarity with our past life and motivations and involves no inner sense.

11. Malcolm, in *Problems of Mind: Descartes to Wittgenstein* (London: Allen and Unwin, 1972), retreated from his earlier denial of the possession of self-knowledge of mind-involving states by human beings, but Hacker, in his literalist interpretation of Wittgenstein, refuses to make this retreat (Hacker, *Insight and Illusion*, 278–84), despite making it plain that what Wittgenstein is concerned to do is reject certain models of sensations and one's knowledge of them, rather than to deny self-knowledge as such. Once one has escaped the introspectionist trap of supposing that self-knowledge is knowledge of something inner, there is no point in distorting epistemology by removing the notion of shared knowledge presupposed in knowledge by testimony.

recapitulate the account I gave in *The Human Person*, where I sought to correct the behaviorist slant sometimes given to the later Wittgenstein by Malcolm and Dummett.[12]

On the one hand linguistic understanding is something we presuppose in our activities of speaking and in normal cases of understanding what we are told, for, as Dummett explains,

> in the normal case, the speaker simply says what he means. By this I do not mean that he first has the thought and then puts it into words, but that, knowing the language, he simply speaks. In the normal case, likewise, the hearer simply understands. That is, knowing the language, he hears and thereby understands; given that he knows the language, there is nothing that his understanding the words consists in save his hearing them. There are, of course, many exceptional cases for the speaker, whenever he uses the word with which he suspects the hearer may be unfamiliar, whenever he very deliberately uses a subtle or humorous figure of speech, when he is conscious of knowing language imperfectly or believes his hearer to do so . . . for the hearer, when the speaker misuses an expression or uses an unfamiliar one, or employs a difficult figure of speech. . . . They [these cases] are, however in the nature of things, atypical cases: if taken as prototypes for linguistic communication, they prompt the formulation of an incoherent theory.[13]

The norm is not to check that we have the relevant understanding before speaking or before grasping what others are telling us, just as when we act intentionally we do not check that we have the intention. We know that we understand what we are saying in the act of speaking, just as we know that we intend in the act of acting intentionally. We have a first-person knowledge of our own possession of understanding, intention, and so forth which does not depend upon our retrospectively observing our own speech and behavior.

This first-person knowledge is something involved in our awareness of the meaning of what we say and its semantic structure (e.g., that we are saying of so and so that it is such and such, so that, e.g., when we say "It is raining" we are aware of not saying anything about something called "it") in the very act of saying it. In this way it underlies the appreciation of all the distinctions between *langue*-meaning and sense or discourse-significance which

12. In David Braine, *Human Person*, chiefly chap. 5, followed up in chap. 9, sec. 5, I show how P. F. Strawson, *Individuals* (London: Methuen, 1959), chap. 3, and the writings of Norman Malcolm help one reach a consistent view from Wittgenstein's questionings and Ryle's informal explanations. Strawson and the later Malcolm envisage the self-ascriptive use of these predicates as statemental so that we will count as having a case here of two methods of verifying the same proposition, one method involving the self-ascription by oneself or others and the other method involving inference from behavior. The idea that the first method is more direct is the Cartesian and empiricist prejudice with which Wittgenstein is at war.

13. Dummett, "A Nice Derangement of Epitaphs: Some Comments on Davidson and Hacking", in *Truth and Interpretation: Perspectives on the Philosophy of Donald Davidson*, ed. Ernest LePore (Oxford: Blackwell, 1986), 471–72; cf. 472–74.

I discussed in earlier chapters, as well as the appreciation of semantic syntax and the grammatical forms to which this gives rise. It is thereby the basis on which native speakers of their own language, including Chomsky, make their intuitive judgments as to the grammaticality or ungrammaticality of particular sentences.

Thus it is part of the way in which the very concept of linguistic understanding enters our thinking that we can ascribe both *parole*-understanding and the presupposed *langue*-understanding to ourselves without any intermediate inference from, or use of criteria based on, behavior. We presuppose both our understanding of *parole* and our understanding of *langue* in the very act of using language, whether in speaking or hearing, writing or reading. It is not presupposed as an external precondition, but as something internal to the acts of speaking and hearing with understanding.

On the other hand, understanding, like belief and intention, must be understood as attributable on the basis of behavior, so that a third person can assess or judge whether a person has the first-person understanding he or she claims and we can assess or judge other people's understanding, treating their linguistic behavior as evidence rather than testimony. The possession of understanding by someone else is something upon which there is a check by others, and which other people are well-accustomed to assess or judge. Thus these two capacities, to know such things about ourselves and to know them about other people, are inseparable. Understanding, like intention, is something of such a kind that, by its very nature and the very meaning of the word for it, we could not have the capacity to apply to ourselves if we did not have the capacity to apply it to others, and vice versa.

However, judging whether or not someone understands something is commonly no simple task. In the hypothetical case of our being presented with a cunningly devised machine, organized to give appropriate answers to the types of question which its inventor or programmer has anticipated, we may have to ask many questions before we expose it as a mere machine, relying, as I noted in chapter V, on the greater capacities for discernment which we have as a result of not being mechanically rule-bound in the types of question we ask, whereas the machine cannot avoid, *qua* machine, operating in a mechanically rule-bound manner. The ways in which machines can be wrong-footed in questioning are quite different from the ways in which people tend to be wrong-footed.

Davidson recognizes this in a reserved way when he speaks of the inadequacy of Turing's test for whether one is talking with a person or interacting with a machine, telling us:

> Turing's test is inadequate because it deprives the human interrogator—the interpreter—of knowledge he must have if he is to decide what the object thinks and means. Behind this inadequacy lies the mistaken thought that the physical realization of a program makes very little difference to its mental powers. On the other hand, Turing was right, in my opinion, in taking as the only test for the presence of thought and meaning the interpretive powers and abilities of a *human* interpreter.[14]

Davidson's reserve arises from his refusal to believe that human beings might be anything else or more than merely physical entities. However, what matters is his recognition that the Turing test does not establish the possession of "the interpretive powers and abilities of a human interpreter". It cannot test for the capacity to ask questions which are not mechanically rule-bound.

Accordingly, a mind-involving state of a person cannot be conceived as a mechanically law-bound disposition to behave in certain mathematically decidable physical ways in certain physical circumstances (however complex their specification), and is not completely manifest in effectively calculable modes of physical behavior. Yet this does not in the least make it into something only privately knowable. When one organism with an intellect-involving state questions another organism of the same kind of capacity, both able to exercise ingenuity in questioning which is not mechanically programmable because it is not on any preset lines, they can recognize each other's character—although in practice this ingenuity is called upon only when the organisms are of a different kind or answer our questions in puzzling ways. In general, linguistic understanding is exercised in a human community speaking and understanding the same language, each member having the same biologically human origin.

In sum, neither of the two forms of understanding here concerned, understanding at the level of language-possession and understanding at the level of speech, are mysterious, unknown, uncheckable, or non-empirical in their nature or their criteria of its ascription to them. Rather both are already familiar to us and commonly readily ascribed both to ourselves and to others. We have no systematic difficulty, either in deciding whether or not another person knows the meaning of a particular word in a language or in deciding whether or not he or she has understood a particular statement or question. Nor do we have any systematic reason for being uncertain in regard to our own knowledge of the meaning of this or that particular word, or as to whether or not we have understood something said to us.

Since we are concerned with linguistic understanding, not with mind-

14. Davidson, "Turing's Test", essay 5, in Davidson, *Problems of Rationality* (Oxford: Oxford University Press, 2004).

involving states and capacities in general, it is unsurprising that most of the relevant behavior is linguistic behavior, albeit taken in its context and in association with other behavior reflective of the same understanding.[15] We would not expect in a normal case to attribute linguistic understanding to a hearer independently of his or her capacity to use language appropriately, or to a speaker independently of his or her capacity to understand and use a normal spread of ways of expressing him or herself linguistically. Accordingly, the idea that linguistic understanding is sufficiently manifested by nonlinguistic behavior, without bringing linguistic behavior into evidence, is quite unreasonable.

(b) *The nature of the capacities and dispositions underlying the use of language*

(i) The large logical generality of the concepts of state and disposition

The primary logical feature of "states" and "dispositions" (in Aristotle's Greek, *hexeis* and *diatheseis*), including states of linguistic understanding, has to do with their relation to time, states being more stable, setting them in contrast with processes or actions of an episodic character.[16] This makes the contrast of states and dispositions *qua* qualities with actions and passions fundamental and underlies the conception, fundamental to Aristotle's later thought, of states and dispositions as "first acts" which stand to "second acts" as knowing or having in memory (a possession, *ktisis*, in Plato) to realizing or remembering at a particular time.[17] In general we understand first acts in terms of second acts; for example, we understand intentions by reference to their realization in intentional action and the having of an opinion by reference to the act of expressing it.

In these primary logical features these concepts are just as applicable to states requiring characterization in teleological terms as to physical states generating behavior mechanically.

Linguistic understanding can be considered both as a state and as an act. As an act it is internal to speaking and hearing, just as intending and having intended an action are internal to intentional action. As the intention may precede the action as well as be internal to it, so linguistic understanding as

15. In Blackburn's terms, the interpreter of language has to be a "homely interpreter" (*Spreading the Word*, 273–81), i.e., himself or herself a language speaker. Many have tried to avoid the need for "homely interpretation", but Dummett's conception of a mental state's being "manifest" or "directly manifest" in behavior (cf. Crispin Wright, *Realism, Meaning, and Truth*) has as many ambiguities as Austin revealed in the idea of "direct perception" in *Sense and Sensibilia*.

16. Aristotle, *Categories* 8b35–9a3.

17. Aristotle, *De Anima* II, 2.

a state commonly both precedes and continues after its expression, but it can come to birth in hearing, continuing afterwards.[18]

(ii) Other features of the traditional concepts of state and disposition

The second main connotation of the Aristotelian notion of state or *hexis* is the idea of being a positive property, by contrast with being a privation (*steresis*).[19] The intellectual and practical virtues and vices are paradigm cases of states (*hexeis*; Latin, *habitus*),[20] and again sightedness is a *hexis*, whereas the privation, blindness, and the absence of sight, where one would not expect it anyway, are not. In thinking of understanding as a *hexis*, or stably established positive disposition, Aristotle envisages it as having a role in explanation and as something in virtue of which its subject is well or satisfactorily, or else badly, disposed.[21] This way of thinking implies that it is in the nature of realizations of such states that they will be subject to standards of rightness or soundness, so that breaches of such standards have to be explained in terms of some supervening defect or deviation. These ideas are illustrated in Gilbert Ryle, who, when he speaks of dispositions, is in practice mostly concerned with states of mind or character, such as the intellectual and practical virtues and vices—that is, "many-track", not "single-track" dispositions—"many-track" in the Rylean sense explained in chapter I.

When such words as "state" are understood in terms of this older tradition, it excludes the comparison of a state with a mechanism whose inner constitution disposes it to behave in the way characteristic of the state. Rather this background would lead one to expect that such states should typically involve a teleological explanation of the relevant behavior in terms of its fulfilling certain ends or functions.

These conceptions of disposition and state are quite different from the new, very restrictive concepts of "disposition" and "state" which have become predominant since the seventeenth century. In this the possession of a dispo-

18. Wittgenstein's remark, "But there is also this use of the word 'to know': we say 'Now I know!'—and similarly 'Now I can do it!' and 'Now I understand!'", Wittgenstein, *Philosophical Investigations*, I, §151 (observations to which §§179–96 recur), might engender a misconception. In Aristotelian and Rylean terms, these cases exemplify the coming to be of a state, but this coming to be is not a process with stages. The *langue*-understanding of a word comes to birth in the act of our first understanding of its exercise in *parole*, each kind of understanding ranking as a *hexis*. Wittgenstein does not reject the logic of our speech, but false models of the "states" concerned, e.g., *Philosophical Investigations*, I, §197 (cf. §184), in rejecting the conception that understanding the meaning of a word involves having all its uses, including all the cases not yet met with, in some way present to the mind.

19. Aristotle, *Categories* 10, 12a26–34.

20. Or, in Aristotle, often *dynamis* as potentiality (e.g., having something in memory when not thinking about something) as distinct from its actualization (as when one has the remembered thing actively in thought)—*dynamis* as often translated *virtus* or *potentia* in Latin (Molière's "dormitive power" appears as *virtus dormitiva* in the text).

21. Aristotle, *Metaphysics*, Delta, 20.

sition is commonly conceived as being the subject of some class of true hypothetical statements stating that the fulfillment of a condition of a determinate kind will be followed by a consequence of a determinate kind—making them "single-track" dispositions. This conception, molded by behaviorist ways of thinking about animal and human behavior, seems to fit the description of how an ideal machine with a certain constitution and configuration would function.

We find this restrictive way of speaking of dispositions even in Wittgenstein, so that he speaks as if only things analogous to machines could possibly have dispositions.[22] The restrictiveness of this conception of disposition compared with the older, Aristotelian conception is very well exhibited in Saul Kripke's discussion of whether understanding is "to be analysed dispositionally, rather than in terms of occurrent mental states".[23] Although his discussion is written to a different purpose, it reveals how mechanist explanations are defective precisely because they cannot admit key features of more traditional conceptions of mental states such as understanding—for instance, the way cognitive dispositions involve within themselves awareness of their own justifiedness, a person's being able to reflect upon his or her own operations so as to assess success in achieving goals and gain cognizance of mistakes or malfunction. Kripke's last argument is of particular interest as indicating that because the reasons for failure are of such different kinds, human beings cannot be coherently conceived as complex machines.[24]

22. Thus he remarks, "If one says that knowing the ABC is a state of mind, one is thinking of a state of a mental apparatus (perhaps the brain) by means of which we explain the *manifestations* of that knowledge. Such a state is called a disposition. But there are objections to speaking of a state of the mind here, inasmuch as there ought to be two different criteria for such a state: a knowledge of the construction of the apparatus, quite apart from what it does"; Wittgenstein, *Philosophical Investigations*, I, §149; cf. *Philosophical Investigations*, I, §§193–94, where Wittgenstein anticipates that one would need an idealized machine.

Wittgenstein speaks in ways quite unlike Aristotle. He is reported as saying that he had never read a single word of Aristotle; see Karl Britton, "Portrait of a Philosopher", in *Ludwig Wittgenstein: The Man and His Philosophy*, ed. K. T. Fann (New York: Dell, 1967), 61. This independence has made the world the richer. But it sets a large question against drawing any anti-Aristotelian metaphysical conclusions from his discussions.

Baker and Hacker have the same restrictive conception of disposition, shared by Hume, Hempel, and Kripke: "A neural or mental state on the other hand could only causally determine a consequence, not normatively or logically. It could not determine whether what is done is right, nor could it suffice to render behaviour an instance of rule following at all" (Gordon P. Baker and Hacker, *Language, Sense and Nonsense*, 283; see 308–9), commenting on what Wittgenstein called "mental states" in *Philosophical Investigations*, I, §§143–56; cf. Baker and Hacker, *Language, Sense and Nonsense*, 279, and Baker and Hacker, *Wittgenstein: Understanding and Meaning*, 595–620.

23. Saul Kripke, *Wittgenstein on Rules and Private Language: An Elementary Exposition* (Cambridge, Mass.: Harvard University Press, 1982), 22.

24. These arguments can be picked out in Kripke, *Wittgenstein*, 23–25, 28–32, and 32–36, respectively. In his last argument, the "program" corresponds to the "machine as symbol" in Wittgenstein, *Philosophical Investigations*, I, §193. The skeptical argument which he wishes to draw from Wittgenstein appears most strongly when he argues that the dispositions which could be learned from a person's finite past performance could only involve the truth of a finite class of hypothetical statements, and these would leave it indeterminate as to how the person would apply a concept in any new case; Kripke, *Wittgenstein*, 23–28. The

(c) *The shape of current discussion*

(i) The bankruptcy of behaviorism and the equal bankruptcy of Cartesianism

For contemporary discussion, the inadequacy of behaviorism has become a datum.

In behaviorism, a mental state is either a disposition directly towards certain behavior in certain circumstances or an inner disposition to be specified in "operationalist" terms—that is, states for whose presence or absence the sole test is by reference to such behavior as can be observed upon experiment. Such dispositions have to be "single-track", so that their possession must consist only in being the subject of limited classes of true hypothetical statements, reflecting certain regularities in behavior without thereby explaining this behavior. For Quine and others the later Wittgenstein appears to be just another behaviorist, as if he had conceived of linguistic capacity as just a "practical ability". Quine misinterprets Wittgenstein's remark that "the common behaviour of mankind is the system of reference by means of which we interpret an unknown language"[25] as an exact expression of his own behaviorism.

But if statements about peoples' mental states or minds imply no more than that these are reflected in behavior in specified ways, this explains no more about mind or the mental than Molière's "dormitive power". Chomsky's "poverty of the stimulus" argument against Skinner in 1959, along with his later criticism of Quine, merely extends this critique.[26] And for those who regard Wittgenstein's approach to language as externalist, "use-based", and so basically behavioristic, it will be open to the same objections and therefore be irrelevant to any scientific or causal explanation of linguistic behavior, such explanations being assumed to consist in conformity to law and not to involve causal agency with persons as agents.

Some interpreters have taken Wittgenstein's rejection of the comparison of a mental state with a mechanism whose inner constitution might explain its behavior as to be understood as adopting an anti-realist or idealist position. Along this line Kripke wrongly interprets Wittgenstein's remark that "essence is expressed by grammar" as implying a radical conventionalism, so that for him, for instance, there is no independent set of objective mental or mind-involving "facts of the matter" which force upon us the "notation" whereby pain is attributed both to ourselves and to others, rather than a "notation" whereby it is only we

phenomena of machines' suffering physical decay and human beings making mistakes exhibit how, for different reasons, neither machines nor human beings satisfy the ideals of dispositional analysis.

25. Wittgenstein, *Philosophical Investigations*, I, §206.

26. Chomsky, "A Review of B. F. Skinner's *Verbal Behavior*"; and Chomsky, "Quine's Empirical Assumptions", in *Words and Objections: Essays on the Work of W. V. Quine*, ed. Donald Davidson and Jaakko Hintikka (Dordrecht: Reidel, 1969), 53–68.

and not others who have pain or other experiences[27]—implying that there are no objective mental "facts of the matter" in virtue of which two people could be said to have in some respect the same linguistic understanding, or one might be right in saying that the understanding of the other was wrong. In taking the lead from such an approach, much recent Anglo-Saxon philosophy has distanced itself from relevance to the actual problems of linguistics and the explanation of linguistic behavior by pursuing abstract problems of "anti-realism".[28]

By contrast, in the Old World orthodoxy reflected in Ryle, Wittgenstein, and Austin, each independently inspired, the mental was viewed as to be attributed to the person only as regarded holistically, and human action was understood in terms of human causal agency as a kind of agency whose effects, even in the case of intentional bodily movements, are not to be *explained* primarily in terms of conformity to physical law. The accidental primarily excludes the absence of intention or reason, not the absence of physical cause.

Yet, over the course of the 1960s and '70s, this Aristotelian understanding has been mostly replaced by what Davidson called "anomalous monism".[29] In this view our ordinary-life system for accepting and assessing testimonies and judgments as to our perceptions, intentions, and other mental or mind-involving states and activities, commonly referred to as "folk-psychology", remains a valid source of true statements. At the same time it regards such mental or mind-involving statements as "anomalous" *in the sense of having no systematic correlation with brain states or systematic coordination with physical law*. However, the mind is still envisaged as leaving our actions physically determined (or else matters of pure chance), still having influence, but only through the brain, despite not affecting the brain in any physically causal way. So understood, this "anomalous monism" is just a sophisticated form of ontological physicalism. In Searle's terms, the only ontological realization of "intentional states", which is how he defines "mental states", is in brain states. If the mental had any ontological realization apart from brain states and processes, such a realization would be a mere epiphenomenon, a ghostly existence without effect in the world. For Dennett, in our "folk-psychology" we are discerning real material patterns in the brain with causal relevance to our behavior or belief[30]—but again not in a way that allows a systematic coordination between relations among these pat-

27. Kripke, *Wittgenstein*, 142–43.

28. In fact, Wittgenstein's meaning was quite different, as we have noted. This misinterpretation of Wittgenstein as essentially anti-realist would have brought him close to Davidson's "anomalous monism".

29. Davidson, "Mental Events", essay 11 in *Essays on Actions and Events* (Oxford: Oxford University Press, 1980), 207, 215.

30. Dennett, "Real Patterns", *Journal of Philosophy* 88 (1991): 27–51. As to Peter Ludlow's approach in *The Philosophy of Generative Linguistics* (Oxford: Oxford University Press, 2012), 47–48, 109–20, it is obscure whether his position is closer to that of Davidson or that of Dennett, but he appears often willing to give excuse for riding two horses at once; Ludlow, *Philosophy of Generative Linguistics*, 162–70. The existence

terns as they are "folk-psychologically" intelligible to us and relations among them according to physical law.

In "anomalous monism" the mental is excluded from any role in the ultimate explanation of any bodily movements, despite our awareness that all outward expressions of the mental depend on and include particular bodily movements. Thus, in this, even if the mental is understood as making these expressions intelligible, this "monism" does not allow the mental any part in the causal explanations of the occurrence of these bodily movements.

In fact, as I argued in chapter VI, teleological explanation can be ultimate.

It is perfectly possible in principle for explanations of later actions and events in terms of earlier states and events which involve teleological features to have explanatory and even predictive power in cases where physical explanation is impossible. We are very familiar with thermostatic and other homeostatic devices involving feedback in which teleological explanation can be reduced to mechanical explanation, but, as Charles Taylor shows in his *Explanation of Behaviour,* and as his and other examples confirm, there is no reason a priori why this should always be so.

It is often thought that, as a matter of methodological preference, if possible one should always avoid bringing in explanation involving the teleological, the intentional, or the mental, on the basis of Ockham's razor—that is, the principle of never multiplying entities beyond necessity. However, whereas one kind of simplicity consists in one's having to postulate a smaller number of types of entity and types of relation between them, there is another kind of simplicity which arises from the simpler form of the explanation suggested. Thus Fermat's suggestion that light always takes the path of least time provides an extraordinarily elegant way of deciding on the path taken by a ray of light in refraction, even though we actually prefer explanation based on Huygens's wave theory. In fact we prefer the latter only because we are convinced a priori that light does not have aims, besides being able to give wave theory a far wider application by using it to deal with radiation in general.

However, in the case of the higher animals, it is more difficult to avoid teleological elements in our explanations. Here, dealing with perception, learning, and behavior among subhuman higher animals, Charles Taylor has effectively demonstrated that teleological accounts are needed in order to explain aspects of perceptual categorization and of learning behavior—behaviorist and operationalist approaches showing no hope of success, and his arguments sufficing to exclude mechanism also.[31]

---

of functionalist linguistics should have passed unnoticed—even though it would have fitted with his desire to leave room for a little informality.

31. Taylor was here developing ideas from Merleau-Ponty's *Structure du Comportement* (1942), also influential on Hampshire, *Thought and Action.*

Despite such arguments as Taylor's, many persist in believing such accounts are still implicitly behavioristic, and this is reflected in the reluctance of Quine's concession that we "must for the present settle" for the "behavioral level" in the absence of any neurological explanation such as would alone satisfy his ideals.[32] However, human beings can direct their activity towards less circumscribed ends than subhuman animals because they possess more general concepts, and this makes the relations between behavior and the evidence for beliefs related to this behavior so heterogeneous as to make even Quine effectively despair of ever discovering neurological explanations, and so by 1985 he had concluded that in the case of human beings we "must make the best of what Davidson has called anomalous monism".[33] Yet in giving no place to the mental as anything which essentially involves mind in the causation of the bodily movements involved in human behavior, no place for persons as causes,[34] this anomalous monism is no better than the epiphenomenalism of Jackendoff's 1987 *Consciousness and the Computational Mind.* The existence of the mental is not denied, as by Rorty and Dennett, but considered to be realized in the brain. However, our ordinary explanations are still left in a functionless relation to physical explanations of our bodily behavior, just as epiphenomenalism leaves our experiences floating above the physical world.

(ii) The drive towards physicalism

For most non-philosophers it seems strange to suppose that understanding has no role in agents causing their speech, no role in its ultimate explanation.

The nature of the two kinds of linguistic understanding of which I have spoken requires a teleological element in our account of speech and our hearing of it, writing, reading, and sign-language. My early chapters have shown that linguistic phenomena leave us no alternative to accepting the teleological role of these kinds of understanding as a datum for any objective explanation of these phenomena. Teleological approaches, it should be noted, are just as much opposed to behaviorism as physicalist approaches.

However, with physicalist paradigms of explanation, anything involving teleology is assumed to be non-empirical and foreign to science.[35] Here, in an-

32. Quine, "Mind and Verbal Dispositions", in *Mind and Language,* ed. Samuel Guttenplan (Oxford: Oxford University Press, 1975), 87. At that time, Quine argued that mind is a matter of verbal and other behavioral dispositions, and these ultimately physiological states of the body.

33. Quine, "States of Mind", *Journal of Philosophy* 83 (1985): 7.

34. Davidson's view depends upon his insistence that causal relations obtain only between states of affairs or events, excluding the treatment of agency as a form of causation. I present a critique of such a view in *Human Person,* chap. 6, 201–27 (cf. chap. 4, 135–45, 151–59), refuting one by one the arguments presented by Donald Davidson in his essays reprinted in *Essays on Actions and Events.*

35. Taking Chomsky's "naturalism" as a form of physicalism; see my introduction to this volume.

ticipating an ultimately neurological explanation of grammatical phenomena, Chomsky is representative of many. And in his formal grammar he presents a mathematically mechanical model of the sentence generation, which he assumes to play a key role in utterance production. And some philosophers have simplistically taken Chomsky's approach to be "the only game in town".[36]

All this is to ignore what linguistic phenomena actually involve in the way explained above, ignore the considerations advanced in chapter V, and ignore the possible alternative approach presented in chapters VI and VII. It is also to ignore the fact that the only "empirical evidence" which can be adduced for any Chomskyan grammar remains people's unreflective judgments as to the grammaticality or ungrammaticality of this or that sentence, and such judgments remain the only available groundbed for a grammatical theory, so that he has not escaped introspectionism. And from the beginning he has also been unashamedly Cartesian in regarding such judgments as rooted in the mental as something inner to the individual, although, unlike Descartes, he presumes it to be embodied neurologically in the brain so that, in linguistics, the grammatical structure of a person's "Internalized-language", or "I-language", provides a functional description of the structures of brain functioning.

In some more recent writing he anticipates that we may gain increasing knowledge of the same neurological structures from direct neurological studies, but, as I observed in the introduction and chapter VII, the evidence for his particular formal approach is very weak.

Yet, as we have seen, no scientific or philosophical account of language-use can do without the notions of linguistic understanding I have presented. And as I observed in chapter VII, it is typical for the forms of explanation of the normal functioning and development of organic systems, for instance, of the growth of muscle tissue through exercise, to be different from the forms of explanation of the failure or absence of normal functioning and development—to take an extreme case, when the muscle tissue is cut through by a sword in battle. And neurology is much better at distinguishing the causes of some of the different types of linguistic malfunction than at providing an integrated view of any linguistic functioning and development which is free of malfunction. In regard to this, it is fair to say that so far as any properly neurological explanation is concerned, after fifty years Chomsky, Pinker, and Jackendoff have got no nearer to providing anything better than promissory notes.

The reasons for this failure require a two-stage explanation. We must see what is wrong with the idea that language "represents" the world in order to

36. Paul Tomassi echoes this in "Linguistic Understanding and the Philosophy of Language", *Minerva: An Internet Journal of Philosophy* 4 (November 2000). He anticipates disputes between connectionists and nonconnectionists in cognitive science, but takes no note of the widening variety of approaches within linguistics.

understand what is wrong with the idea of language's being represented neurologically.

Section 2. Conceiving of Sentences or Thoughts as Representing Reality: A Mistake Revived

The conception that language "represents" features of the world or that it enables the mind to have something within itself through which it can "represent the world to itself" or form a "model" of the world constantly recurs in philosophy—as if for the mind to know or think about external objects, these must be represented to it by internal objects. This semantic representationalism has been strikingly revived by Dummett and his followers.

Against this conception we need to insist that if in thinking the mind is to be directed towards the objects to be known themselves, this cannot be by means of first being directed towards and knowing intermediate objects of awareness contained within the mind itself—since this would involve an infinite regress. For the intellect to operate freely, what we judge or think, whether inwardly or outwardly, must be an *expression* of intellect, not its *object*, for, to repeat Aristotle's words, the understanding needs to be "unmixed, as Anaxagoras says, in order that it may master its objects—that is, that it may know them. For the intrusion of anything foreign to it would interfere with this mastery or knowledge".[37]

To say something is to express it—to express a sense. Sentences *express* a sense, and they do not *represent* anything. Language and thought do not relate to the world by means of sentences or sentence-meanings, as one set of objects, representing "facts", "states of affairs", "things", or "features" in the world, conceived of as another set of objects. Plato insisted that sentences have meanings by expressing them, by "saying", uttering a *logos,* not by identifying them. And, it is not just that they do not name or designate what they mean, but that they do not identify it in any other way, such as by picturing it or symbolizing it. In chapter XII we will find that the relation between "the name 'Smith'" and the name "Smith" is not the same as that between the name "Smith" and Smith himself, and that quoted expressions do not denote the expressions quoted as if the latter were genuine "objects"—indeed, sentences, senses, meanings, and facts are none of them "objects".

Against all representationalist conceptions we have to insist that the role of speech is to *say something,* to *express a sense,* not to name or symbolize, nor to depict anything or even present a model of it.[38] It is in order to say some-

37. Aristotle, *De Anima* 429a18–22.

38. I develop this key objection to approaches favored by computer theorists in detail in *Human*

thing that, in Jespersen's words, a sentence has to be a "nexus", "like a process or a drama", and not a "junction" of descriptions in some way imaging some reality, a reality combining several features (i.e., in Jespersen's terms, not "like a picture").[39]

Of course, truth involves correspondence with "the facts" or "what is the case" in the trivial sense that the thought, statement, judgment, or belief that P is true because P, rather than vice versa, if P is indeed the case. This is because the assertion of truth expresses the evaluative judgment that the thing assessed (the thought, statement, judgment, or belief) has attained its goal, since in thinking, stating, judging, and believing the goal is truth. But correspondence in this trivial sense does not involve any kind of representation.

Ancient and medieval philosophers had a misleading way of speaking according to which, in order for us, for instance, to think of horses, we need to have the *eidos* or "form" of a horse, a "similitude" or "resemblance", within our minds, so that Aristotle spoke of the intellect as capable of receiving the *eidē* of all things. At the same time they insisted that there was nothing "materially" like a horse in the mind, by which they meant that there was nothing which we would today call a mapping, part to part, of this "form of a horse" in the mind and a bodily, material horse. This way of speaking is intrinsically misleading, and Aquinas's distinction between real and intentional existence constituted a major advance. In his conception intentional existence and likeness was exemplified in the way a configuration of light existed in the air, or in a window, or in the lens (or "pupil") of the eye in such a manner as to make it possible for some external object, not the configuration itself, to be seen; and, more generally, the mode of existence of that through which something is known is never itself the direct object of knowledge or attention.[40] (This is quite opposite to Brentano's conception whereby the "intentional" is "the object" towards which the mind is mentally directed.)

(a) *Two types of representationalist theory, the one of sentences and the other of predicates*

Representationalist theories of the relationship of language and the world are ones in which the directedness of what we think and say towards the world is explained in terms of there being some kind of likeness in structure or mathematical isomorphism between certain kinds of whole sentence or utterance

---

Person, chap. 11, sec. 3 (cf. n. 42). In brief, to produce a model B of A is not to say that A is like B, let alone to say that A is like B in this or that respect; and no multiplication of acts of modeling, or of modeling of modeling, transmutes the production of a model into a saying of something.

39. Jespersen, *Philosophy of Grammar*, 116.

40. The image on the retina is irrelevant to Aquinas's account: this image is neither the object of perception nor the "imprint" or "species" by means of which we perceive the object.

and corresponding processes and events or states of affairs in the world. These are representationalist theories of the meaning of sentences.

Such theories involve the mythology seen in the modern preconception that linguistic deliverances or sentences "represent" facts. This mythology lies at the root of the idea of speech or thought as set over against reality—with one set of objects and relations (in language or thought) "representing" or "depicting" another set of objects and relations (conceived of as existing in reality). I explain why I call this "a mythology" in chapter XII.

In some cases these theories of propositions or sentences "representing" facts have involved as part of their structure a second mythology, whereby "common names", figuring as predicate terms, get their meaning in virtue of a supposed resemblance between concepts or ideas in our minds and properties and relations to which they refer. This second mythology involves a representationalist theory of the meaning of general terms. Within the sentences of which I have been speaking, the elements which are vehicles of intelligible content, commonly referred as "general terms", but in any case having features implicitly (as in the case of such expressions as "the Sun" and "the Evening Star") or explicitly general in their meaning, cannot themselves be regarded as having this meaning by picturing, being similar to, or "representing" what they mean.

This second mythology took two very different forms: Platonic and Lockean. In its Lockean form it was attacked by Wittgenstein when he pointed out that having a red mental picture or idea in one's mind would be no help in judging whether external red things were all of the same color: red. For this would still involve comparing one red thing with another, a sample of red as a mental image with the external red things seen by our senses. But it is precisely this capacity to compare things with a view to judging their properties which needs explaining. In general the principle in virtue of which we compare examples of some general property cannot be just another example of the same general property, itself requiring to be compared, since this would involve an infinite regress.[41] This general refutation was provided by Aristotle in refuting Plato's theory of ideas. Moreover, the comparisons required involve expres-

41. The issues concerned here are those of Aristotle's "Third Man" argument; cf. David Braine, *Human Person*, 412–20, 450–52, 458–60 (cf. 420–46), as corrected in the 1994 paperback edition, and David Braine, "The Active and Potential Intellects: Aquinas as a Philosopher in His Own Right", in *Mind, Metaphysics, and Value in the Thomistic and Analytical Traditions*, ed. John Haldane (Notre Dame, Ind.: University of Notre Dame Press, 2002), 18–35. Some of the issues were earlier discussed in Kenny, "Intellect and Imagination in Aquinas", in *Aquinas: A Collection of Critical Essays* (London: Macmillan, 1970), 273–96, where he also pointed out the parallelism between Wittgenstein's argument and Aquinas's more general argument that the *species* or general concepts in the mind in virtue of that we are able to make judgments about, e.g., pigs or red things, cannot function by depending upon any material likeness to the pigs or red things to which the properties are being ascribed in such judgments.

sions in the form of judgments, and what we have said earlier excludes any general term serving as an element within such judgments. As there can be no material likeness or isomorphism between the idea of a horse and a horse, so there can be no likeness or isomorphism between the idea of a horse and any element within the representation of sentence-meaning at the "Logical Interface" within the brain such as Chomsky's account of sentence-meaning requires (cf. chapter XIII, section 7).

(b) *Representational theories violate the principle of the "simplicity" of mental acts*

The first objection to any representationalist accounts of the working of mind, considered as presenting models of how the mental activities are constituted, constructed, or made up, is that they fail to do justice to the "simplicity" of states and acts of understanding and thinking—that is, to their not being composite in anything analogous to something material.

What is at issue here is what I called the "simplicity" of acts or states of understanding and thinking in *The Human Person*,[42] associated with what has been called the unity of a thought. This goes beyond the "focal subjecthood" I spoke of in chapter VI, whereby the subject of mind-involving states and activities, animal or human, has to be considered as *qua* subject indivisible. For, beyond this, this simplicity concerns the states and acts of understanding and thinking themselves—namely, that these cannot be envisaged as divisible into parts, temporal or spatial, in the way that their expressions can be thus divided. Moreover, if they depended upon neurological or other bodily processes, these processes would not be parts of them as the use and movement of one's eyes is a part of seeing or watching something.

The unity of the thought is particularly obvious in such cases as thinking "Heavens! The post has gone". I do not think "Heavens" without being aware of the object of the astonishment expressed or of "the post" without being aware of what it was about the post that concerned me—namely, that it had gone—but I think the thought as a unity.[43] And we are not aware of the words as passing before us as images to be observed by some inner sense, but rather as how we would express what we were thinking.[44] In thinking of complex sequences of thought, we must follow the same rule as applied to their expressions—namely, that they have no more determinateness than their explan-

42. David Braine, *The Human Person*, 453–55; cf. 514–16, 434–45. My arguments in these sections overlap with Descartes's arguments that the mind is indivisible (*Meditations*, 6), but forbid speaking as if a mind or self were an object of inspection to itself in the way Descartes seems to do.

43. Cf. chap. X, sec. 3 (c) of this volume.

44. David Braine, *Human Person*, chap. 11, sec. 4a, pp. 435–40.

atory role requires. We will typically not be able to identify such sequences of thought except by reference to how they might be expressed, but having such sequences of thought does not consist in a progress of successive word-images passing through our minds, and the discrete stages in such a sequence of thought are reflected in the semantic structure (not the phonetic or phonemic structure) of how it would be expressed.[45] So a sequence of thoughts has to be thought of in terms of discrete related stages, not as a continuous process. And we have to think of every case of describing the deepening of understanding in the same way.

(c) *Wittgenstein identifying what is wrong with all representational theories of meaning*

The theory that language or thought is representative of reality, as if statements and thoughts "represented" facts, reappears again and again. The early Wittgenstein used the metaphor of picturing to imply that the statement was in some way "isomorphic" with the fact or state of affairs. Most recently, statements in particular have been held to have a "descriptive content" or "sense" which made them "represent" reality—their "propositional content". Other kinds of utterance have been imagined to have a meaning dependent on these—so that, for instance, if "P" were the statement that P, then the imperative would have the meaning "Make it to be that P". This imperative would have been obeyed if the statement "P" had its truth-conditions fulfilled. The descriptive content or "sense" of imperatives would be limited to this supposed propositional component.

But this is pure myth, as can be seen by considering very simple examples.

We can form representations, or mental pictures, of what is seen, and even of a person or animal looking at it, but not of a person's act of seeing it. Of course we know what it is to see something, and we are tempted to say that this is because we know and can imagine what it would be for us ourselves to see something. But this is a different kind of imagining—not just a visualizing, but a kind of pretend living out of all that is involved in our normal experience of sight; seeing something includes knowing what it would be to reach out to touch it, or to move in among the things seen or reorient ourselves in regard to them. This imagining is no mere "picturing" of the object seen or even of ourselves in the act of looking at it. Likewise, when we imagine others seeing something, we do not just pose to ourselves some picture of the others in certain bodily and spatial relations to the thing seen. Rather, in some way

45. See David Braine, *Human Person*, 434–45; cf. 424–26, 428–31 in respect of the "allusiveness" of thought spoken of on 445.

we seek to place ourselves imaginatively in the place of the see-ers, entering their life-situation in seeing the thing to be seen, not just placing ourselves as it were athwart the thing being seen and the see-er, as we might be athwart the tiger and its prey, as it were as a third party.

Along the same line, we can now go further and say that indeed we know what it is for someone to wish or to order something to be done, but this is not by picturing this wishing or picturing the relation between the persons giving and receiving the orders. How could one make a picture of wishing that the grass would grow? Perhaps by putting a picture of a person begging on the one side and on the other side a picture of a desert conjoined by an arrow with a picture of seemingly the same area covered with grass? But this would not be one picture, but three, the jointure of pictures requiring an interpretation, highlighted in the need for some account of the function of the picture of the arrow. As to picturing one person ordering another to do something, what would this be? Conjoining a picture of somebody being appointed general with a picture of his operating as general? But how would either picture show that this was what was going on, rather than simply one person kneeling and receiving certain documents and another person prancing about on a horse with indicative gestures from his arms? No! Such pictures can only be at most ancillary, and useful only when their place is set within a structure. But here what will matter is not some picture of the structure, which would always be a picture of some example exhibiting the structure, but something non-picturable which dictates the structure. In brief, knowing what it is to wish or to order something to be done is derivative upon knowing the meaning of optative and imperative moods and forms of expression, or of knowing the force of speech-acts involving these, which, at least according to the doctrine we are criticizing, is not part of the "descriptive content" or "sense" of these speech-acts.

The significance of Wittgenstein's *Tractatus* arises from its constituting the most distilled and formal presentation of the minimum requirements of any representational or "picture" theory. In his presentation, for propositions to represent reality requires *solely* that propositions share logical form with reality. For, in the *Tractatus,* in the case of a proposition, *"pictorial form" amounts to nothing more than this.* Accordingly, everything which tells against the *Tractatus*'s picture theory tells against any representational theory whatsoever. Yet the *Tractatus* itself deliberately enumerates, one by one, various classes of statement or assertion which will not fit these minimal requirements of the picture theory: quantified propositions, ascriptions of number, logical laws, modal statements, laws of nature and assertions of causal connection, statements about the self, and evaluations of any kind among them. That it cannot deal with these should itself constitute sufficient refutation of representationalism as an account of how statements or assertions have sense. Indeed, there is no candidate from either scientific or common discourse which appears to conform to the requirements of such a representational theory. And the hindsight of over eighty years' reflection or discussion (Wittgenstein's own and that of others later) should have made us recognize the untenability of any form of representational theory. What finally broke Wittgenstein's own adherence to the picture theory was that it could not even deal with the implications of color incompatibility, together with the folly of supposing that every sense-expressing act, even the Neapolitan gesture of contempt,[46] has a "logical form" in any sense relevant to a representational theory.[47] Thus we have a vast structured spread of assertions to which this minimal representational or picture theory, which requires only that picture and reality share logical form, cannot apply, the spread of which the *Tractatus* itself offered an initial map. Therefore, such theories should be dismissed.

However, representational theories of meaning or sense remain always with us. Thus, in a strange echo of the *Tractatus,* Dummett tells us that "a sentence is a representation of some facet of reality", speaks of attempting to "explain the way in which we contrive to represent reality by means of language", and identifies "the content of a sentence" with "its representative power".[48] Later Crispin Wright speaks of "the realist's idea that depictive powers may outstrip our cognitive capacity".[49] This mythology is the root of the deep error arising when speech or thought is regarded as set over against reality—as if we had one set of objects and relations (in language or thought) "representing" or "depicting" another set of objects and relations (conceived of as existing in reality). This representationalist conception of the relation between language and the world has given extra plausibility to the idea that the primary object of metaphysics is not reality in its own right, but only the relation between thought and the world.[50] In accordance with this preconception whereby language represents the world, Dummett tells us that it is "the theory of meaning" which "lies at the foundation of the whole of philosophy", and Crispin

46. I discuss this case in chap. I, n. 17 of this volume; cf. Baker and Hacker, *Language, Sense and Nonsense,* 110–11.

47. From this he advanced to a view according to which there is an indefinite number of different types of linguistic utterance, each playing a different role in the form of life of language-users and involved in varied language-games in varied ways. The idea of an indefinite number of different types of linguistic utterance was later taken up by Austin, his idea of kinds of illocutionary force being oversimplified by identification with Frege's notion of "force"; cf. chap. X of this volume and Note A on Austin's approach appended to chap. X.

48. Dummett, "Justification of Deduction".

49. Wright, *Realism, Meaning and Truth,* 3. He assumes that the cognitive job of statements is to depict, and for him the question is whether we can always determine whether reality is as a statement depicts it. Wright's exposition is instructive for the way his criticism of Platonism in mathematics depends on this pictorial model.

50. Wright, *Realism, Meaning and Truth,* 1.

Wright describes "the attempt to understand the relation between thought and the world" as "constitutive of metaphysics".[51] In this way the philosophy of language has been put forward as the supposedly primary part of philosophy—replacing epistemology, which had been primary for Descartes, the empiricists, and Kant. And so, in place of the ancient and medieval view that the primary parts of philosophy are metaphysics and general logic considered as having to do with reality or the world in its own right, primacy has instead been given first to epistemology and now to the philosophy of language, each making philosophy fundamentally anthropocentric, as it were to go back from Copernicus to Ptolemy.

The phrase "descriptive content", used by Dummett and many others, might suggest a representational theory of meaning at least of "factual" propositions. But, in the *Tractatus*'s account, to represent reality, propositions require nothing more than to share the same logical form (that is, *pictorial form here amounts to nothing more than logical form*); and the more one registers the significance of this fact the more problematic *any use* of the phrase "descriptive content" must come to seem. For the impossibility of applying the picture theory, realized by Wittgenstein to have been demonstrated by the *Tractatus* even in the case of color-propositions, will apply the moment the facet of reality being supposed to be described has been supposed to "have the same logical form" as a proposition. What we describe are people, animals, flowers, sunsets, the starry heavens, and paintings, and the virtues, weaknesses, and beauties of these and like things, and even, indeed, states of affairs—but not facts which correspond to true "factual" propositions in the way reality is supposed to correspond to them. It is a mistake to think that talking about "representing", "depicting", or "portraying" reality might be an acceptable metaphor or shorthand for explaining the relationship between statements and reality. The best one can say in this connection is that different types of statement contribute in different ways and degrees to enabling the hearer to imagine various facets of reality.

Thus having a model in one's mental view is not judging, whether explicitly or simply, in one's own mind. Having a model in mind is not judging or saying anything, and what is called "entertaining a proposition", conceived of as having the sense of some sentence in or before one's mind, is no better.[52] The sense of a sentence is not something which depicts the world and

51. Dummett, "Justification of Deduction", 309; Wright, *Realism, Meaning and Truth*, 1.

52. "Entertaining a proposition" is a common phrase for a hanging about in the mind with a determinate sense but in no determinate way, either as being questioned as to truth or possibility or as being assented to as possible. On the contrary, I insist that there is no presence of a propositional clause to the mind except in some way identifiable from the kind of speech-act which would be involved in its expression.

hangs about in the mind while being considered as to whether it is true or false or whether it "corresponds" to the facts. If there were a model or picture involved in giving content to a judgment, the most natural way to suppose this to occur would be to suppose that one judged that *the world was like the model in some respect,* so that the two in some way corresponded or fitted, so that the sentence to be considered would be in the style "The world is like this", where "this" was a demonstrative pointing to the model. It is judgments and statements which are true or false, not some other entities called unasserted "senses" with a supposed depictive relation to the world, with "descriptive contents" which fit or "correspond to" states of affairs.

(d) *The alternative to representationalism*

However, this rejection of depictive forms of correspondence theory does not imply any such mad statements as that "there is no connection between language and reality".[53] Of course, if one still speaks of language and reality as if they were twin constellations of objects (constellations of sentences or senses, and constellations of facts) and yet at the same time denies any connection between them, one will have the worst of both worlds—while becoming prey to transcendental idealism and to conventionalism. But the mistake lies in thinking of language and reality as related in this kind of way at all.

Descartes and Kant made the mistake of treating some second-order study—in their case, epistemology—as primary. The later Wittgenstein was not occupied in presenting a rival view, for instance, that some other second-order study—namely, the theory of language—was primary instead of epistemology—the idea we find in Dummett.[54] Rather, mostly proceeding by means of examples, Wittgenstein used language as a means to show something about it; and he took actual uses of language as a guide to any remarks about it, the first-order always being treated as guide to the second-order, not vice versa. His concern in his later works was indeed with language, but only to exorcise false pictures of how it functions, false presumptions as to how its sense is to be understood. These writings were not directed against logic and metaphysics as such, but against any logic or metaphysics which proceeds from certain types of false move, including those exemplified in Descartes and the empiricists.

As to Wittgenstein's earlier approach, we must take seriously his remark that "the *Tractatus* was not all wrong: it was not like a bag of junk professing

53. Hacker imagines Wittgenstein to have supposed this from 1929 onward; Hacker, *Insight and Illusion,* 185. This is a far stronger claim than the claim that there is "no isomorphism between language and reality" (Hacker, *Insight and Illusion,* 186–88), which merely embodies a rejection of a picture or representational theory of the meaning of statements. He misunderstands (Hacker, *Insight and Illusion,* 207) Wittgenstein's description of grammar as "autonomous" and a matter of notation only (see sec. 1 of this chapter).

54. Dummett, "Can Analytical Philosophy Be Systematic?"

to be a clock, but like a clock that did not tell you the right time".[55] When a clock tells you the wrong time, one reason can be that it has been started in the wrong place. For him this false starting point consisted in beginning by considering what are the most general conditions for the possibility of *representation,* conditions of the possibility of a sign-system *representing* reality[56]—and it was this starting point which he later rejected. He thus rejected any consideration of language which began from asking its relation to reality, as if language and reality were two things in some comparative or projective relation to each other—thus rejecting the picture theory of meaning, with the form of nominalism it involves whereby names standing in relation to each other in a structure constitute an isomorphically structured picture of objects standing in relation to each other.[57]

But he did not think "the clock" was "*all* wrong". As we have seen, in his later thought he maintained his earlier contextualism whereby words have meaning only in the context of a sentence.[58] Chapter X will show his rejection of the segregation of sense and force, and how the hierarchy of types of non-proposition in the *Tractatus* invites rather than excludes a theory of varieties of language-game and speech-act. Indeed, these things loom yet larger in my own account, which involves a stronger version of contextualism than the *Tractatus.*

It is by working through the problems of the philosophy of language that one discovers what it is. Instead of beginning with grand inquiries into the relation of "language" to the "world" (however they are conceived), one begins with accessible questions about category structures within speech, including the categorial structures associated with reflexive discourse, or "talking about talk". All this will bring one to a fuller consideration of the ambiguities of the word "object" and the sense in which sentences, senses, and facts are none of them "objects", and therefore none of them objects between which there might be relations. We need to escape this whole inflated ontology, however disguised, of sentences, meanings, and facts—and, along with them, of "features" as entities with a status determined prior to discourse.[59] It is not these, but the things in the world, which we discourse about—things which have a status determined prior to discourse.

So it has become clear that the whole conception of the philosophy of language and the theory of meaning found in Dummett and his followers is mis-

55. Anscombe, *An Introduction to Wittgenstein's Tractatus* (London: Hutchinson, 1959), 78.

56. Baker and Hacker, *Language, Sense and Nonsense,* 39.

57. Wittgenstein, *Tractatus,* 4.0311 and 4.04 highlight this aspect of the picture theory represented in 3.1432 and 4.012, presaged in 2.13 and 2.131.

58. See chap. III, n. 34 of this volume.

59. Davidson disowns any such ontology, but this is mere disguise: he speaks of meanings as if they were *objects* to be *identified* by means of the specification of sets of truth-conditions; cf. chap. III of this volume, including subsection (iii) of Note on Grice appended to that chapter, and chap. XII, sec. 2.

conceived. They envisage it as having an underlying propositional aspect which establishes the structure of the relationship of language and the world, which depends on "propositions" or sentences being in some representational or depictive relation to supposed facts. And this way of thinking is shared by a great many philosophers and psychologists involved with the theory of meaning. However, this is precisely the picture against which the later Wittgenstein set his face so strongly. In my account, sentences, meanings, and facts or possible facts are, none of them, "objects" such as might have external relations between them. The notion that reflections on "the relationship of language to the world" might be foundational for metaphysics is therefore even more farfetched.

The connection between language and reality must be conceived entirely differently.

It is not a matter of linguistic and nonlinguistic entities corresponding with one another. To report a battle or give a linguistic expression of the truth about it is not to give a picture, although it may enable the hearer to picture it. The importance of this, for the learning of language and our understanding of grammar, will appear in chapter IX.

The use of language in a statement (taking account of any ostension and reliance on context, along with the use of intonation, style, or gesture to mark distinctions of purpose, mood, time, and emphasis) requires that the functioning parts or aspects constitutive of one's utterance be of different types, each of a character which includes how it is integrated with the others, each having its own role and significance. Some coincidence of some major semantico-syntactic categories and major metaphysical ones is required for this.

Therefore any philosophy or theory of language has to take cognizance of these categories: notably, distinctions in relation to time, between subjects persisting through time (continuants) and states, episodes, acts, and activities (respectively distinguished by their posture within time), and between these and times themselves (in their way, adverbial); or in relation to space, the distinctions between first substance, shape, size, and place; or in relation to causal agency, the distinctions between (a) first substance, (b) the nature of such a substance or thing as what determines its modes of action and passion, (c) actions and passions, (d) the terminal and intermediate states from which or to which these substances according to these natures are carried by these actions and passions—that is, by which the stages and end-points of changes are marked, and (e) time as that with reference to which change is measured or ordered—and all these distinctions belong to physics or some first-order study wider than physics, as well as to the science of language. In this way, not only does speech tell, but its structure shows something of reality—but not by there being an isomorphism between language and reality as if these were two objects which might be compared as to structure.

It is rather in this way that "the harmony between thought and reality is to be found in the grammar of language".[60]

Thus, although Wittgenstein appears to have been innocent of any influence directly traceable to Aristotle, nonetheless this doctrine that "the harmony between thought and reality is to be found in the grammar of language" can be considered as expressing rather precisely the standpoint taken by Aristotle in his supposedly early work *The Categories* and embodied in parts of Books Delta, Epsilon, and Zeta of *The Metaphysics* and II to IV of *The Physics*, opening out the general logic of which I spoke in the Introduction and chapter IV, wider than the logic of propositions, predicates, and finite sets.

Accordingly, our critique of representational theories of the meaningfulness of speech and of thinking must be more radical. First, as chapter XII will confirm, we must reject the very idea of statements, senses, and facts as objects between which there are relations—there are no such objects in or before the mind because these things are not objects at all, and to suppose that they are is to make a logical mistake. Second, chapter X will show how the notion of sense as something with no implications for force is entirely misconceived, and so the notion of proposition required by these representational theories is likewise misconceived.

Section 3. Sentence-Meanings Cannot Be Isomorphic with Either External or Internal States

(a) *The arguments summarized*

If thoughts or their expressions in sentences cannot represent or be isomorphic with external physical states, so much more the lexical meanings of sentences will not be capable of being isomorphic with brain states or processes (however these are conceived, e.g., as dynamic states or persisting resonances). Any kind of reciprocal isomorphism between lexical meanings and brain states or processes—the lexical meanings of the "sentences" of formal grammar being understood to enshrine the context-free aspect of the content of utterances—will be open to parallel objections to the theory that thoughts or propositions are isomorphic with states in the world.

First, the same reasons which make it impossible for thoughts or statements

60. Wittgenstein, *Philosophical Grammar*, ed. Rush Rhees, trans. Anthony Kenny (Oxford: Blackwell, 1974), 162; translated from *Philosophische Grammatik*, 1969, Wittgenstein's 1931–34 compilation of his 1930–32 notebooks. For Hacker misconstrues "essence is expressed by grammar" as an expression of conventionalism; cf. n. 7 above and related text. Hacker's main example (*Insight and Illusion*, 185–91) is the superficial case of color differentiation rather than deeper structural distinctions such as those embodied, e.g., in Aristotle's eight principal categories.

to "represent", or be materially isomorphic with, states and developments in the external world also make it impossible for any of the language-related entities suggested, including Chomsky's lexical sentence-meanings (LF [logical form] representations) at the supposed inner "conceptual-intentional interface", to be capable of such isomorphism with structures or types of structure in the brain.[61] In brief, if propositions or sentences cannot be isomorphic with states of the material world, then neither can they be isomorphic with brain structures.[62]

Second, if a representationalist theory of the meaning of sentences incorporates a representationalist theory of the meaning of predicates, it involves all the difficulties of the representationalist theories of predicates referred to earlier. Moreover, if a predicate is supposed to be embodied in a brain state, then where these predicates are used with the informality described in chapters I to V, a spread of brain states will be required to correspond to the different senses or discourse-significances of such predicates. To explain what unifies such a family of brain states would require an account which relates them to speech as the activity of persons, not mere brains, and to pragmatics and general logic.

Third, it is not clear how a particular feature of some brain states can enable it to refer to other brain states of the same organism in a way corresponding to the way people reflect on their own thoughts, a feature corresponding to the concept of self-reflection upon one's own thoughts.

Fourth, we saw how thoughts and other mental acts have an essential simplicity. Correspondingly, sentences as speech-units need to have an essential unity, and of this formal grammar provides no explanation, as we saw in the introduction. Explaining this unity requires going outside grammar or neurology to the semantics and pragmatics of so-called folk-psychology.

(b) *The superstition embodied in "para-mechanical" models*

This "simplicity" of acts or states of understanding and thinking of which I am speaking involves rejecting any material or, in Ryle's phrase, "para-mechanical" model. When we think of human beings as beings with a nature or constitution of such a kind that they can acquire and possess understanding and think, we must not conceive of this nature or constitution, or of states and activities such as understanding and thinking, according to a mechanical or physical model, as if in speaking of the "constitution" of the human being

61. This is also a corollary of Davidson's admission that there are no law-like relations between mental states as described in personalistic terms and the neurological or anything described in purely physical terms.

62. The impossibility of such isomorphisms is quite independent of how the mind or brain and its features are supposed to relate to the world.

we were thinking of it as a structured complex of parts.[63] Indeed, when we consider human linguistic behavior as explained in terms of states which have to be understood teleologically, such as understanding and intention, we are not putting forward a physical, pictorial, or mechanical model at all—that is, not modeling mental processes in the way particle and wave behavior model certain physical processes. A teleological account does not present a rival to a constructional model of the human mind, whether neurological or otherwise, because it does not present a picture or constructional model at all.

If one asks how the attribution of linguistic understanding to human beings contributes to the explanation of human linguistic behavior, one might answer: in a way analogous to that in which understanding contributes to the acceptance of mathematical proofs.

Understanding contributes to the explanation of linguistic behavior, not by bringing the phenomena explained together with other phenomena as exhibiting some general law, but in a different way—namely, by indicating the teleological rooting of the phenomena explained. The understanding of *langue* is directed towards the understanding of *parole*, and thus plays its part in discovering what others wish to communicate to us and in enabling us to communicate things to them—for instance, that something is true, required to be done, or desirable. Moreover, the character of the *langue*-understanding of a particular term or way of speaking makes it intelligible why the different utterances making use of the term or way of speaking exhibit the spread of truth or satisfaction conditions which they do. It also makes it intelligible how it is that different utterances can have the same conditions for being true or satisfied, but present the information or required action in a different perspective or manner.

However, the seeming superfluousness of even mentioning understanding in explaining our linguistic interchanges, simply because it is inbuilt or presupposed, indicates something more. In a certain way the mention of human understanding makes it clear why, within a certain context, further explanation seems superfluous—namely, because the matter concerned is evident in itself to one who shares the same understanding. The capacity for such shared understanding is something native to human beings, not just as a particular biological species, but as a species which is intellectual by nature. For, in our account, the peculiarity of the human species among existing animals is that it is in this species that the brain has become so malleable in its ways of functioning as to be open to the operation of intellect. It is this form of nativism that will be supported by the argument of part three.

The reports we express by language do not achieve the end of describing how the world is by sharing "logical form", as understood in the *Tractatus*,

63. Ryle's problems appeared later in Wittgenstein's questioning, thinking of mind as an apparatus; Wittgenstein, *Philosophical Investigations*, I, §149; cf. nn. 22 and 24 of this chapter.

with something in the world; nor do they achieve this through some brain state or process sharing "logical form" with our thought or with the world. Rather, as I suggested in chapter VII, the brain processes involved in hearing, linguistic processing, and speaking play a role in these activities, without these brain processes being structural parts or aspects of their expressions or end-products—that is, structural parts or aspects either of the sentences and their constituents arising in communication, or of the understanding, thinking, judging, wishing, and deciding which they express, all of which have the kind of simplicity or unity indicated earlier.

Conclusion

In sum, in these two sections we have seen why Chomsky, Pinker, and Jackendoff never get beyond promissory notes in explaining how materially particularized processes or features in the brain could account either for sentence-meanings or for our use of general concepts, let alone for the analogically extended use of concepts typical of human language. What they are attempting is systematically impossible, just as squaring the circle is impossible.

More generally, any view whatsoever that proposes that the only way thoughts are realized ontologically is in brain states or processes will be open to the objection that there can be no isomorphism between thoughts and brain states or processes—for the same reasons that there can be no isomorphism between thoughts and states in the world. For speech and thought do not portray the world, but purport to report or describe features of it. Statements are not pictures, even if they sometimes enable us to form pictures. In making a statement or forming a judgment, human beings (although within the world as psychophysical unities) in speech or thought as it were makes a cut, dividing between truth and falsity—by saying that P, excluding whatever is incompatible with it—but portrays nothing. In this, they exercise an act of mastery, not just the mastery of bringing deliberations to conclusions, but being able to do this without having their thinking limited to proceeding along tramlines set by supposed internal limitations set by language, whether stemming from the speech customs of their society or from their neurophysiological make-up.

Grammar at least imposes no such limitations. For, as part three will indicate, the only constraints reflected by syntax are those set by pragmatics and general logic, with these constraints shaping the role of other language-users in learning to speak and molding the parts played by brain processing in the learning and use of language—the processing which allows us, even as we speak, to adopt appropriate vocabulary, inflections, word order, and morphology with such rapidity.

PART THREE

Rewriting the Philosophy of Grammar and Restoring Unity to the Theory of Language

IX

Explaining the Semantic Unity of the Sentence

THE SHARED ROOTS OF THE TOPIC/COMMENT, SUBJECT/PREDICATE, AND NOUN/VERB DISTINCTIONS

Unless there is reason to the contrary, … in speaking, the verb, which is the driving force of a sentence, should have first importance, then the noun, and the adjectives and adverbs would take care of themselves and personal pronouns should never be emphasized except in special circumstances.

—Alec Guinness, *Blessings in Disguise*

In considering the sentence's semantic constituents and understanding how they are interlinked and integrated together, we must proceed in the way outlined in the introduction, taking semantics and pragmatics to shape syntactic structure and taking grammars as concerned with sentences as utterances, not as the "context-free" constructs of a grammatical theory. My studies in part three will suggest that the problems which confront grammatical theory present no obstacle to this approach. To be concerned with certain aspects of utterances is still to be concerned with utterances (as well as thereby also with clauses as having the potentiality to be utterances). It is, it will be recalled, utterances which express judgments and decisions, and it is these, I argued, that exhibit human transcendence—intellect and will in command. In this part we shall find varied attempts at an optimal response to pragmatic and semantic constraints in the differing syntactic structures of different languages, but no reason to conjecture neurological conditioning or constraint.

The basis of every grammar lies in the structures of topic, subject, and predicate together with affirmation, negation, and interrogation—all of which have pragmatic aspects, albeit of different kinds. These structures arise in the same ways in connection with every subject-matter, abstract as well as concrete, so that they have application to subject-matters to which thematic roles such as Actor, Undergoer, Recipient, and Destination are irrelevant.[1] By contrast with these thematic roles, the pragmatic structures retain their semantic relevance, whether their subject-matters are concrete or abstract.

Our first task will be to clarify the notion of "predicate". Predicates "say" something about a subject or topic. That is, they have some "verbal" function, and this function gives its name to the "verb", which is typically the heart or nucleus of the predicate and thereby of the clause, since, as chapter X will show, it is only when the clause occurs naked as a sentence or complete utterance that its verbal or potential saying character is revealed. So it remains that the character of what is innermost to the clause, the verb, is to be explained by reference to force, which might seem, in Van Valin's terms, outermost in the sentence, force being something which belongs only to complete utterances.

Section 1. The Basis for a Theory of How Linguistic Utterances Are Integrated

In chapters I and III we saw that what differentiates a "sentence" as something at the level of language-use or *parole* from a mere signal is, first, that it *expresses* the sense it communicates, rather than merely identifying the message being sent, and second, that it does this by being articulated of parts blended together into an integrated unity in a way appropriate in the context to achieve this.

Sentences as expressing sense can have sense only by their subordinate significant structural parts or features, including their intonation, themselves expressing sense. These sense-expressors occur as "sentence-factors", "constituents" of the sentences in which they figure—as *exercises* of the linguistic capacities concerned, not as elements of *langue*. The inspiration underlying Ryle's conception of "sentence-factor" and Dummett's conception of "con-

1. This shows that Dik and Van Valin must both be wrong in supposing that an adequate language could dispense with the notion of subject; cf. the argument in chap. XI, sec. 1 (b) of this volume, esp. the text relevant to nn. 6, 7, 13; with chap. XI, sec. 2 (b) (iii) and (v) and n. 28.

stituent" is similar to that underlying the Polish logicians' notion of "functor",[2] but differs in applying to names as well as functors proper. All these sentence-factors have some kind of "incompleteness", which is what enables them to liaise, giving the sentence its articulated character.

(a) *The incompleteness or unsaturatedness of subordinate sense-expressors within the sentence*

An example provided by Beebe shows the need for ideas such as those offered by Frege, Jespersen, and Plato. In Beebe's example the communicator shouts "Crippled" in the context of pointing.[3] This could convey, "That is the crippled wolf [that particular wolf we know well, and might call 'The crippled one']" or "That wolf [the one we have located] is crippled [we did not know it to be crippled beforehand]". But, however considered, the example affords no blending between the act of pointing and the act of signifying what is meant by what is said (the sound "Crippled")—nothing corresponding to the blending which occurs in the suggested explanations. And if in ordinary life one pointed and shouted "The crippled one!" or "Crippled", the syntactic character of the word "crippled" would be determined by the way it would occur in fuller utterances.

To understand what is wrong with Beebe's so-called meaning-nominalism, it is instructive to read what Frege has to say in "Concept and Object":

> For not all the parts of a thought can be complete; at least one must be "unsaturated," or predicative; otherwise they would not hold together. For example, the sense of the phrase "the number 2" does not hold together with that of the expression "the concept *prime number*" without a link. We apply such a link in the sentence "the number 2 falls under the concept *prime number*"; it is contained in the words "falls under," which need to be completed in two ways—by a subject and an accusative; and only because their sense is thus "unsaturated" are they capable of serving as a link. Only when they have been supplemented in this twofold respect do we get a complete sense, a thought. I say that such words or phrases stand for a relation. We now get the same difficulty for the relation that we were trying to avoid for the concept. For the words "the relation of an object to the concept it falls under" designate not a relation, but an object; and the three proper names, "the number 2", "the concept *prime number*", the relation of an object to the concept it falls under", hold aloof from one another just as much as the first two do by themselves; however we put them

2. This term is accessibly explained by K. Ajdukiewicz, "Syntactic Connexion", in *Polish Logic, 1920–1939*, ed. Storrs McCall (Oxford: Oxford University Press, 1967), 207–31. Czesław Lejewski's paper "Parts of Speech", *Proceedings of the Aristotelian Society*, suppl. vol. 39 (1965): 191, pointed the attention of Anglo-Saxon philosophers toward Ajdukiewicz and thence to Leśniewski.

3. Beebe, "Basis of Semantic Structure", 637–38.

> together, we get no sentence. It is thus easy for us to see that the difficulty arising from the "unsaturatedness" of one part of the thought can indeed be shifted, but not avoided. "Complete" and "unsaturated" are, of course, only figures of speech; but all that I wish or am able to do here is to give hints.[4]

Thus, instead of conceiving of a proposition as a concatenation of names, we have to conceive of it as a nexus, to use Otto Jespersen's term.[5] As Jespersen says, a nexus "is as it were animate or articulated", and "a junction is like a picture, a nexus like a process or drama"[6]—the very idea of nexus invites the conception of sentence-factors of radically different kinds articulated together.

The idea that it is essential to a sentence to be structured, to be articulated of at least two parts or factors of different kinds, is not modern, but ancient. Its first public appearance is in Plato, notably when the *Sophist* states that every saying (i.e., sentence, *logos*, derived from *legein*, the verb for "say") must be composed of at least two parts: an *onoma* (name, noun, referring expression) and a *rhēma* (a saying part, predicate, or "verb", from a Greek verb meaning "speak" or "proclaim").[7] Ingarden expresses this when he distinguishes nominal expressions from function words, of which finite verbs are representative, each having a meaning which requires completion—function words giving the sentence what he calls its directionality.[8]

The word "functor" is helpfully suggestive in three ways: first, it suggests the fulfilling of a certain *function*, in the informal sense of the word "function"; second, as Frege saw, function signs in mathematics are paradigm examples of incomplete expressions; and, third, the Polish logicians envisaged "functors" as having the incompleteness of Frege's "concept-terms"—in effect, predicate-expressions.

4. Frege, "Concept and Object", 54–55; cf. Frege, "Function and Concept", translated by P. T. Geach, in *Translations*, 24–25, 31. Geach gets to the root of Frege's idea in Geach, "Names and Identity", in *Mind and Language*, ed. Guttenplan, 147–50; cf. Geach in Anscombe and Geach, *Three Philosophers* (Oxford: Blackwell, 1961), 80, 142–46.

5. The early Wittgenstein tells us that "a proposition is not a medley of words. (Just as a theme in music is not a medley of notes.) A proposition is articulated"; *Tractatus*, 3.141. He continues, "only propositions have sense; only in the nexus (*Zusammenhang*) of a proposition does a name have meaning" (*Tractatus* 3.3). And "a sign does not determine a logical form unless it is taken together with its logico-syntactical employment" (*Tractatus* 3.327), understood in relation to 2.0122 and 2.0123. And, most explicitly, "an elementary proposition consists of names. It is a nexus, an interconnection, of names (*Zusammenhang, eine Verkettung, von Namen*)" (*Tractatus* 4.22). Jespersen had used the term earlier, in *Sprogets Logik*, 1913.

6. Jespersen, *Philosophy of Grammar*, 116 in chap. 8; cf. 97 in chap. 7 and chaps. 9–10. (Van Valin later used the words "juncture" and "nexus" in a quite unrelated way.)

7. Both Plato and Aristotle speak of a combination of *onomata* with *rhēmata* in order to form a proposition. In Plato, *The Sophist* 262A–D, and Aristotle, *The Categories* c. 2, it is called interweaving (*symplekēs* or *symplokē*), and in Plato, *Cratylus* 431B, and Aristotle, *De Interpretatione* c. 3, a putting together (*synthesis*). Where we have a mere catalog of expressions without such *synthesis*, Cratylus compares it to making a noise (*psophein*) as by the repeated banging of a bronze pot (*Cratylus* 430A), and earlier to a twanging to no purpose (*Cratylus* 429E).

8. Ingarden, *Literary Work of Art*, 71–84, where he regards being "completion-requiring" as equivalent to being "dependent" in Husserl's sense; Ingarden, *Literary Work of Art*, 82.

What is at issue is the character of the unity of the sentence, not just composed of parts simply juxtaposed, morphological modification allowing them to fit together like parts of a jigsaw, like liaison in phonetics: rather, the unity is more intimate. It is as if every part had one or another different kind of incompleteness, possessing sense only incompletely until completed into the whole. It is only through the complex articulation in the sense of the significant functioning parts or features of sentences that any thought or sense can be *expressed*, in contrast to merely signaled—signals in Morse code formed of dots and dashes, or syllables formed of phonemes or written characters being parts or features with no significance in themselves.

On the one hand, the whole, the utterance, whether spoken or written, is such as to have parts and to have no existence apart from the parts, and a sense expressed by these parts in their context, and only identifiable in virtue of this. On the other hand, as sentence-factors, these parts have no existence apart from the sentence which they constitute in their nexus together, somewhat as for Aristotle, in the single vocable "box" with one peak of sonority associated with the "o", we have four "sound-functors"—namely, the speech-sounds "(b-)", "(-o-)", "(-k-)", and "(-s)", none of which is vocalized separately from the others. Although the "o" and the "s" could have been vocalized separately, they were not in fact vocalized separately, just as in "She killed her husband with a knife", "She killed her husband" could have occurred separately, but did not in fact occur separately.[9] The different status or role of the "o" is analogous to the special status of the verb, giving life, structure, and direction to the sentence somewhat as the "o" gives sound to the syllable.

Frege's conception that in any sentence there has to be some part or feature which is unsaturated or incomplete recapitulates Aristotle's argument that for any whole which has parts forming an essential unity, there has to be a unifying factor which unites the elements, and this factor, whether principle, part, or feature of the whole, cannot itself be an element of the same kind as the others. The character of Frege's distinction between saturated and unsaturated expressions is eloquently explained by Geach.[10] What is essential is the incompleteness of what serves as the hub in a sentence, like an ion with open valence bonds—it is normally the finite verb that has this role, but in some constructions and in some languages what institutes a "verbal framework" may not require a verb. I will attempt greater accuracy later.

As we shall see in chapter XIV, this understanding of what distinguishes the

9. Analogously, in the single word "acceptable", although the "accept" and "able" could occur separately, they would not then be the same lexical factors.

10. Geach, as referred to in n. 5, especially "Frege" in *Three Philosophers*. Dummett failed to appreciate that Frege's distinction was intended by him to apply to all concept-expressions, and represented it as relevant only to complex predicates; Dummett, *Frege*, 30–33.

role of the verb and the verb-like from that of the noun and the noun-like is fundamental to grammar. It is this conception which I try to make precise in the rest of this chapter. Here and in chapter X, I go beyond Frege and relate the unifying "verbal" role of predicates and finite verbs as having a saying character to the pragmatic character of sentences identified in terms of the notion of force.

(b) *Refuting the objection that there could be semantically unstructured sentences*

The idea that there could be simple, unstructured expressions of senses—simple, unstructured sentences or utterances, seems alien to most linguists.[11] But the question is: why should it be alien to properly human language?

Blackburn suggests that "a genuinely expressive but unstructured language is intrinsically unstable".[12] However, the problem is not of the stability of the ways in which expressions are used, but of how they function at all.

Why, then, is it impossible for a language to consist only of names? Such a language is equally impossible whether the names occur on their own or in concatenation, as a series in phonetic sequence, like a list, and equally impossible whether the names be of "things" or of "features" (e.g., properties or relations).[13] The underlying reason is that in order to communicate something using a name, we have to say something about what is named. Thus a name has to be set in a verbal or "saying" framework for what is said to have any sense, direction, or force at all.[14]

The idea that a simple, unstructured utterance might express a sense by stipulation is simply confused.[15] Stipulation or convention can no more make a sound into a sentence, or an expression of sense, or even a name with the role in speech which names have, than listing commands in a phrase book could make "303" express the sense "I have lost my passport". Uttering "303" might serve to achieve a certain effect—for instance, the imparting of a belief or the securing of appropriate action, within the context of a particular signaling system, but this is not to *express* a sense or thought-content.

11. Evans, *Varieties of Reference*, 102, envisages that such unstructured sentences might arise by stipulation—but this would make them function as mere signals, identifying but not expressing the message they convey.

12. Blackburn, *Spreading the Word*, 140.

13. Blackburn, *Spreading the Word*, 139–40 and elsewhere, often reveals the assumption that language users will "think in terms of particular things and features", and so already smuggles in the misguided conception of a preestablished ontology of general objects called "features"; cf. my discussion of Grice in Note appended to Chap. III.

14. This was recognized in Wittgenstein, *Tractatus*, 4.032: "It is only in so far as a proposition is logically articulated that it is a picture of a situation. (Even the proposition, *Ambulo*, is composite [of stem and inflection].")

15. Cf. n. 12.

Indeed, the notion that something unstructured might express a sense involves an absurdity like that of the supposition, considered by Frege, that Julius Caesar, the familiar conqueror of Gaul, is a number, or that a number might be alive.[16] Such suppositions are not directly contradictory or "contrary to our definitions", but absurd at a deeper level. Nothing unstructured could be transformed from direct to indirect speech so as to occur in the way syntactically required for speakers to specify the sense of their own or other speakers' utterances—and if this is impossible, the uttering has been a mere parroting. Any systematic obstacle to expression in indirect speech is a symptom of impossibility in thought.

Against this, people allege that our one-word utterances are unstructured. But this is to misinterpret the situations concerned. Expressions such as "No" are answers to questions, whether explicit or merely implicit, and equivalent to sentential answers using the word "not". Various kinds of expletive are not *semantically* expressive, making some sense or thought-content explicit, but derive their linguistic character either from being grammatically incorporated into sentences, perhaps to give emphasis, or else because their origin as expressing greetings, attitudes, astonishment, and so forth gives them some preliminary role as announcing speech.

Nouns and verbs function in different ways, even in the simplest utterances. Some English words appear both as nouns and as verbs, such as the words "drink", "fire", and "smoke". This highlights the difference between a child saying "Smoke", meaning "there is some smoke over there", saying "Smoke", meaning "those people are smoking", and saying "Smoke" as an imperative. Likewise, "Fire" uttered in order to sound a fire alarm functions like "(There is a) fire" and is a common noun. "Fire" as a command is the second-person present-tense imperative, with the same sense as the imperatives "Do you fire" and "You, fire".

Differences disguised in English may be obvious in other languages. What we find in Hebrew applies generally—namely, that nouns are learned as individual lexical items independently of morphological structure.[17] By contrast, words functioning as verbs are learned differently, appearing in different morphological forms according to their context. Berman notes how Hebrew children learn verbs quite differently from nouns and only as inflected or in connected use with other words, and in various different inflected forms (as

16. Frege, *Foundations of Arithmetic,* translated by John L. Austin (Oxford: Blackwell, 1959), §56. Compare the absurdity involved in G. E. Moore's dream, in which he looked for the number four under a table and woke up when he failed to find it; G. E. Moore, "An Autobiography", in *The Philosophy of G. E. Moore,* ed. P. A. Schilpp (Evanston, Ill.: Northwestern University Press, 1942), 1–41.

17. R. A. Berman, "Language Knowledge and Language Use", in *Categories and Processes,* ed. Levy, Schlesinger, and Martin D. S. Braine, 45–72.

we note in section 3 in regard to Korean and Japanese). Such verb-forms are already complex.

As to Wittgenstein's "language-game" of saying "Slab!" or "Beam!", unless these are understood in connection with the ordinary language which gives these words their ordinary meaning as common nouns, it would not be a "language-game" at all, but only a signaling system with these sounds used as signals, each to secure a different effect, not as linguistic expressions.[18] Names occurring by themselves are more commonly used, according to their context and the type of emphasis, to express some emotion, such as love, hate, anger, or contempt. In the case of desire, a complete utterance "Bed" might in one context express the desire or intent to go to bed and in another an indication of what one desired to acquire. We specify what one-word utterances express by giving in indirect speech what is required in a more grammaticalized expression, and the results indicate the syntactic character of the word used in the one-word utterance concerned.

Naming ceremonies present no difficulty. All they have to achieve is to introduce a noun or noun phrase in such a way as to make it capable of use after the naming ceremony within sentences of a subject/predicate form to identify some available topic or object referred to in them. To do this it has to be clear *what* is being named; for instance, if I point at a person in introducing the name "N", it must be clear whether I am naming the person, the color of his or her tie, or the shape of his or her body. If the intention is to name an X, the kind X must be sufficiently determinate for one to know that the same X is being spoken of when the name is used again.

Formulae used in naming ceremonies commonly express thoughts inviting complex expression (as in the English idiom, "I hereby name this ship, N"), while even in one-word naming ceremonies the name pronounced will have the syntactic character of a noun, since any such ceremonies are precisely intended to give the name concerned the function of identifying an available topic so that the name can later be used as a subject-term in subject/predicate sentences about this topic.[19] That is, it is essential to names, as to all referring expressions, that we can apply a predicate to them, thereby completing them into sentences. Likewise, linguistically isolated vocatives reveal their linguistic character, as distinct from "Hey!" or other means of attracting attention, by their capacity (despite sometimes distinctive case-markings) to be used as

18. Readers approach Wittgenstein's initial example in *Philosophical Investigations*, consisting in saying "Slab" in a certain context, with a fore-understanding of the word "slab" as a common noun, and so tend to think of saying "Slab" as expressing "[Pass me a] slab". Wittgenstein presents the "slab"-game without any such context in order to refute Augustine's view of language; Wittgenstein, *Philosophical Investigations*, I, §1.

19. Or minimally of a kind introducing mention of a topic which figures as an argument to a verb or has the role of argument within a verbal framework.

names of subjects within sentences—hence the use of a name to draw attention or indicate something depends upon its role in sentences.

Thus the capacity to be the subject of a subject/predicate sentence has to be implicit before a name can have any other use. We already presuppose the framework set by the distinctions between singular terms, predicates, general terms, and those expressions such as quantifiers and demonstratives which control the application of predicates to general terms, described in section 2—that is, the framework underlying predicate logic taken with the logic of identity—and we then fix the place of the name concerned in its determinate place within this framework in such a way that it will be determinate when we have the same X again. Accordingly, Quine's word "Gavagai" will not yet have been given any place in a language if it is still an open question whether it denotes a rabbit, an undetached rabbit part, or a rabbit stage, since language requires these things to be determinate as explained in chapter III.[20]

Single enunciables with no such syntactic background and no such appropriate context or phonology cannot constitute parts of an expressive speech system for the reason that I have given, and there is no argument, either a priori or from examples, which suggests that they can. To put the point differently, there would be no way of distinguishing a system of "one-word" utterances from a merely signaling system, no reason to attribute an expressive function to the signals over and above or underlying their mere causal function (i.e., what is achieved by means of them, their "perlocutionary" effect, e.g., in causing belief).

Section 2. Asymmetry between Names and Other Sentence-Factors—"Sense" and "Reference"

As we saw in the introduction and in chapter III, Frege and Wittgenstein were right in regarding the significance of an expression as gained only in its context in a proposition or discourse—that is, as it occurs in use. That is, they insisted on "the interdependence of sense between sentences and subsentential parts of speech".[21] If the meaning of an expression is to be specified or defined for the purposes of the logician, language-user, or translator, it must be by means which determine the sense or discourse-significance of the resulting sentences—not because sentence significance is prior, but because sentence significance and constituent significance are interdependent.

Further, as seen in chapter III, the significance of a sentence-constituent

20. Chap. III, sec. 2 (a) (ii) of this volume.

21. Baker and Hacker, *Wittgenstein: Understanding and Meaning*, 262.

is affected by its context in discourse and the context of utterance of that discourse just as much as the significance of the sentence of which it is a constituent. *Thinking* the sense or meaning of a sentence includes *thinking* the sense or meaning of its constituents in combination and context and vice versa.[22]

Sense, in the meaning of the word "sense" which applies to sentence-constituents, does not belong to word-items as such at all. A word as a dictionary item or considered in isolation has no "sense" or discourse-significance at all. It is only in a live utterance taken in context that words and other sentence-constituents have sense. What carries sense is not the word-item "white", but the word-functor "... (subject)—(tensed copula) white"—that is, this word as used in combination.

(a) *The basis for distinguishing referring expressions or "names" from functors*

(i) Names cannot stand on their own

I use "..." and "—" differentially in order to indicate that the two spaces need not be filled in the same way—that is, to the same purpose as Frege would have used "x" and "f". The general way in which such a space is to be filled I indicate in subscripts. At this stage I use such terms as "subject", "copula", "tense", and "predicate" informally, so that, for instance, a sentence's "subject" is what it is about and the "predicate" is what it says about this subject.

Referring expressions, among them lexically simple names used as names, have been said to have a kind of completeness lacking to predicates and other functors. I shall consider the special character of referring expressions and the limited sense in which some philosophers have spoken of them as "complete" in sub-subsection (iv), but it remains that no sentence-factor means anything, complete or incomplete, in isolation.[23] Just as sense is in general something only achieved within the context of the complete speech-act, so the same is true in the case of reference. If I utter the name "Homer", I utter what happens by usage to be a name applied to a certain Greek poet, as well as to various other people and animals, but I have not mentioned or referred to any of these. I only mention or refer to the Greek poet when I use this name within the context of a complete, live utterance. Thus what achieves reference is not

22. This does not mean or imply that *thoughts* are made up of components analogously to the way *sentences* are made up of words. It therefore does not involve any doctrine of senses composed of senses (Frege), judgments composed of concepts (G. E. Moore, "Nature of Judgment"), or even of "sayings in one's heart" composed of "Ideas" (Geach, *Mental Acts*). We no more think in an inner language such as Ockham's "Mental" than we imagine by viewing an inner screen.

23. Russell would expect any term which is not a "complete symbol" to have only a "definition in use" of this kind; and the discussion of naming in sec. 1 (b) showed that there could be no "complete symbols", definable solely by pointing.

the word-item "Homer", but the occurrence of the name in use—that is, as in the sentence-factor "Homer wrote about 800 B.C.". So even referring expressions and names still require to be situated in the context set by a predicate in order to function as names at all, and this, coupled with an appreciation of what can be said of them without absurdity (the kind that occurs from mismatching, for example, applying the predicate "... is the square root of 16" to "the Moon"), belongs to their sense.

In sum, names remain essentially sentence-constituents and therefore not self-sufficient or "complete" in any completely unqualified sense. Accordingly, names occurring as names, and referring expressions in general, are appropriately symbolized, if not with gap signs, then at least with indices or subscripts indicating a sentential role, even though they are not functors in the strictest original sense. Thus "Socrates is bald" might be represented by "$B(s_H)$", where "$B(\ldots)$" symbolizes the predicate, and "s" stands in place of the ordinary name "Socrates" with a subscript "$_H$" indicating the general kind—namely, human being, to which Socrates belongs. This "$_H$" controls which predicates can sensibly be applied to "Socrates", whether truly or falsely (e.g., the predicate "... is bald" but not the predicate "... is the square root of 16"). Such a symbolism will dovetail with a way of representing the quantifiers which incorporates record of the domain of which they range: thus, "Socrates is mortal", "All Greeks are mortal", and "Some Greeks are mortal" might appear respectively as "Ms_H", "$(\forall x_H)(Gx \rightarrow Mx)$", and "$(\exists x_H)(Gx \,\&\, Mx)$", following the convention that one use lowercase letters as symbols in place of terms referring to singular subjects and uppercase letters for predicates (corresponding to singular and general terms, respectively). Here the subscript "$_H$" indicates the range of generalization or quantification within a singular subject falls, or over-generalizing or quanitifying, in this case "human beings". In this way I signal that the Socrates to whom mortality is ascribed is presupposed to be a human being, and, in the last case, that what is being said is that any human being, if a Greek, is mortal—that is, I am not saying that anything at all, even the number 4, if it were a Greek, would be mortal, because I am not trying to talk about everything at once. These subscripts would therefore normally indicate a "natural kind" or "proper genus",[24] sometimes a species (man, horse, dog, lead, bronze, water) and sometimes more generic (beast, reptile, fish, animal, river, stream, city, metal, liquid)—something natural to take as a topic to generalize about.[25]

24. I mean genera like color, natural number, and shape, rather than like quality, quantity, or relation.

25. Sometimes they will have a more determinate connotation—e.g., a person addressed in the case of a vocative or of spoken of in a sentence such as "You are fat"—or a thing (of such and such a sort) identified (in this or that way, e.g., by pointing) in the case of demonstratives.

(ii) Sentences as the context for names

The sentence is essentially a nexus, dynamically connecting semantic factors in a functionally significant way, the semantic "liaison" achieved in the act of linguistic delivery in speech, writing, or sign—as opposed to a mere adjunction of elements as in a static picture. Without dynamic functional connection, we have no saying or sentence at all.

Semantics and grammar alike always at some stage divided between noun-headed, or nominal, expressions and verbal expressions in "simple" sentences, and it is from considering this most fundamental divide between kinds of sentence-constituent that I begin.

By "simple sentences" I mean ones without the complexity of containing clausal elements as subordinate constituents. By "clausal element" I mean an element which in context expresses the content of a clause—for instance, "him to go" in the context "I wanted him to go". By "clause" I mean an expression which, if it occurred on its own, would be a sentence, as is revealed by questioning, so that here to the question, "What did you want?" one could reply "That he should go", indicating that my want would be satisfied when "He went" or "He did go" was true. In effect a "simple" sentence is one with only one verb.

Considering such simple sentences as composed of a subject, or noun phrase, and a predicate, or verb phrase, the primary difficulty at the semantic level has been to find an acceptable explanation of the asymmetry between subject and predicate, between nominal expressions (from Latin *nomen*, meaning "name" or "noun"; in Greek *onoma*) and verbal expressions (from Latin *verbum*, meaning "saying"; in Greek *rhēma* or *logos*);[26] this is the mystery of why predicates and verbal expressions should be considered more radically incomplete than subject or noun expressions.

(iii) "Verbal" or "saying" expressions

Sentences alone are complete as speech-units with the first and primary kind of completeness to which I refer. The "verbal" or "live" character associated with acts of speech as complete human acts (Austin's "illocutionary acts") constitutes the primary semantic aspect of the sentence and the aspect governing its syntactic structure.

26. The words *onoma* and *nomen* are often said also to mean "word" as well as "name", but this is a mistake which both Plato and Aristotle avoid, both speaking of *onomata* and *rhēmata* as different kinds of spoken sound. When Plato and Aristotle wish to speak of "words", they can only speak of significant spoken sounds, *phōnai*, as opposed to letters and syllables (Aristotle, *Poetics* 20), or mere sound, *psophos* (cf. Aristotle, *De Anima* 426a12). The Latin *verbum* meant utterance or thing uttered (i.e., "word" as spoken of in the English idioms "giving one's word" or "trusting his word", or *logos* as a saying or definition), and came to mean "word" in its normal English sense only derivatively; cf. n. 59.

The idea suggested by Plato's vocabulary whereby the predicate or verbal phrase is called a *rhēma*—that is, the part of a sentence which does the "saying" or makes it "say", "speak", or "sing", seems to be more helpful; the predicate or verb is, one might say, "live" as an electric wire is "live" when the current is passing and is what makes the whole sentence or utterance "live"—comparable to a living finger, not to a dead finger under dissection. In Aristotle's *Categories* 3, a predicate (*rhēma, kategoroumenon*, or *kategoria*) is something which is "said" (*rhēthēsetai*) or "predicated" ("accused", *katēgorhēthēsetai*) in regard to (*kata*) a subject—while, in *De Interpretatione* 3, he described it as a sign of things "said" of something else (*legomena*). This "saying" character of verbal phrases or predicates groups them together with sentences considered as wholes (both referred to *logoi* and as a *rhēmata*) as opposed to names, so that they have sense in the same way as sentences, in virtue of saying something, rather than in whatever ways names or noun phrases have meaning or sense.

Verbal expressions subordinate to simple sentences have varying degrees of incompleteness, but what makes such expressions verbal is that they retain this feature of being "live", and in their incompleteness they are the key features within sentences which make sentences "live" so as to say something, rather than merely to identify some thing or kind of thing. Such verbal expressions are exemplified first in predicates occurring sententially, whose incompleteness consists in their capacity to be completed into sentences by putting "names" (strictly, what we shall call "singular terms") into the "gaps" which mark how and where they are incomplete. The most obvious such verbal expressions are what we ordinarily call "finite verbs"—finite because they include marks of time indication, aspect, and mood which common English idiom calls "tense". The ultimate in incompleteness is encapsulated in the copula "... is —".

We should note that the feature which makes the whole sentence into something "live", saying something rather than naming or identifying, is still present, even when there is no such expression signaling its presence—not even the copula. Thus if we say "Caesar candidus" instead of "Caesar candidus est", we retain the subject/predicate structure, but the incompleteness of a verbal expression is associated with "... candidus", instead of with "... candidus est".

(iv) The completeness of "names"

This shifts the area of mystery to the question as to the different sense in which the expression "Caesar" should be regarded as "complete", albeit in a way depriving it of this "live" or "saying" aspect possessed by predicates. This second kind of completeness is in respect of identifying an object (something which could be taken as a topic), whereas the completeness of a sentence is completeness in respect of saying something. This second kind of completeness, in respect of the static role of identifying logical subjects, candidates for being topics, as it were anchoring our discourse, deprives them of the capacity to fulfill an active verbal or "saying" role. This second kind of completeness is dependent on the first, since using a name is a function performed only within the context of saying, arising only through connection with predicates to form sentences.

The reasons why we should not consider either predicates or sentences as denoting or identifying objects, with this lower-grade completeness, are the same. Neither predicates nor sentences have the kind of "completeness" which names have been supposed to have—failing to have it because they *aim or tend towards* something fuller, the completeness of sentences, and it is only because they have "gaps" in them in the way I indicated that predicates are "incomplete" as sayings or speech-units.

(v) Singular terms, and general terms combined with "applicatives", combine with predicates

In order to pick out "predicates" we need first to pick out singular terms—that is, expressions which denote, refer to, or "name" just one subject in the sense of just one available topic of discourse, available in being already established in the shared knowledge of the relevant speaker(s) and hearer(s) or writer(s) and reader(s) as a possible topic. That is, each denote, refer to, or "name" just one person or thing (in modern idiom, "object"), concrete or abstract, referring to it in such a way as to enable it, in the context of discourse concerned, to be distinguished from other "objects" of the same kind.

Given the capacity to recognize singular terms, we obtain what we call a "predicate" by taking a sentence and omitting one or more such singular terms, creating gaps, commonly indicated by some arbitrary system of symbols—for instance, "..." and "—"; x, f, z; or x, y, z (although the last two systems have been used to different, though interrelated, purposes). Thinking in this way, we shall regard, for instance, "... was blind" as a predicate: this is something which we naturally think of as "said about" Homer as subject when we say "Homer was blind", although in a system of writing in which there are no quotation marks or other equivalent devices such as italics, or if we have a stylistic aversion to such devices, it will also be natural to identify what we said about Homer as "that he was blind". While "... was blind" is a one-place predicate, "... kissed —" is a two-place predicate, "... lies between — and ///" a three-place predicate, and "... is to — as /// is to \\\" a four-place predicate.[27]

27. Equivalently, we may speak of "blindness" as an attribute, "kissing" as a binary relation, and "between-ness" as a ternary relation.

Given such predicates, we find quickly that there is a second way of filling the gaps which mark how they are incomplete. Instead of inserting the singular subject-term "Homer" into the gap in order to form a complete sentence, we can insert a general subject-term governed by what Johnson called an "applicative"—that is, an expression indicating how the predicate applies to the subject—for instance, "some" indicating how "... was blind" applies to "Greek" in "Some Greek was blind".[28] This use of the word "subject" to cover general as well as singular terms, and not just objects but also terms, derives from earlier presentations of Aristotle's logic.[29] This key difference of category between singular subject-terms and general subject-terms arises within every universe of discourse whatsoever, whether we are speaking of horses, people, or numbers. Johnson let the term "applicative" apply not only to the expressions commonly called quantifiers, "every", "no", "some", "most", "at least one", "exactly one", and so forth, but also to expressions forming singular terms from general ones. For if a general term is combined with a demonstrative ("this", "that", or another expression in context achieving the same effect) or with various genitive or possessive forms (as in "Bill's car"), the result is a singular term (also commonly called a "referring expression").

I shall use the term "predicate application controller" in place of Johnson's word "applicative" because the latter has developed other uses in modern grammar.[30] Such predicate application controllers arise as controlling any noun phrases with a "thematic" role—that is, which indicates how what it denotes participates in the activity or state indicated by the verb.

(vi) Determiners as typical quantity and identity indicators, and thus controlling predicate application

The most typical such controllers are the five kinds of noun-phrase determiner distinguished by Bloomfield: (a) definite and indefinite articles, in English "the" and "a" (also in some contexts, e.g., with stuff-terms such as water, uranium, or rice, "some" functions as indefinite article); (b) demonstrative adjectives; (c) interrogative adjectives; (d) quantifiers and quantitative expressions applying both to the discrete and the continuous—namely, "every", "each", and "many" applying only to the discrete, and "any", "some", "no", "one",

28. The term "applicative" was introduced by W. E. Johnson, *Logic, Part I* (Cambridge: Cambridge University Press, 1921), 97; cf. Geach, *Reference and Generality* (Ithaca, N.Y.: Cornell University Press, 1962), 47–48, 178–80, 188–89. In thinking of these "applicative" words as indicating how the predicate applies to the subject, Johnson echoes Aquinas's idea that "some", "every", and so forth indicate the order of the predicate to the subject; *Summa Theologiae* I.a, Q.13, a.12.

29. Thus Aquinas uses the term *subjectum* whenever Aristotle uses the word *hypokeimenon*, and so applies it to whatever is presupposed by or underlies predication, as well as to what underlies change.

30. Application controllers are what Chomsky calls (syntactic) operators; in logic and semantics, the word "operator" has a much wider use—e.g., most commonly in regard to modal and truth-functional operators.

"two" or other natural numbers, "a few", "approximately 2 million", and "most" applying both to the discrete and the continuous, and "a little", "approximately 2.5", and "much" applying only to the continuous; or (e) a possessive, adjectival in form, for instance, "my", "thy", "his", "her", "our", "your", and "their". Context will indicate whether "a" as the indefinite article is serving in place of "one" or "any". Except when nouns or noun phrases occur attributively, as in "... is a man", or as modifiers of nouns, adjectives, or common nouns, they always require a determiner, granted certain qualifications.

Plurals such as "students" are always understood as if they included the plural indefinite article, signifying either "some (more than one)" or "any", and stuff-terms such as "milk" always understood as if they included "some" as indefinite article, as in "we drank milk". We can regard singular terms as including a determiner which in English takes the form of a zero morpheme.

In Greek, proper names and names of abstract objects, which are all singular terms, are marked by the definite article, as happens in English with the names of species, as in "The horse is a quadruped" ("Man is a biped" is an exception). Such determiners mark the absence of need for a predicate application controller, just as there is no need for them in the case of interrogative and relative pronouns which stand within clauses in the same relation to predicates as singular terms. Alternatively, in all these cases, we can regard them having the role of an English zero morpheme referred to earlier.

All such expressions have the general semantic role either of direct indicators of identity, as in "that man", or of quantity indicators. I say "direct" in order to exclude identity or quantity indicators which depend on indications of accidental identifying properties.

(vii) Some complications

However, often such quantity and direct identity indicators are not application controllers.

Thus two distinct functional roles must be distinguished, some phrases serving either role and some only one. True, quantity and direct identity indicators, grammatically modifying noun phrases fulfilling thematic roles in relation to the activity or state indicated by the verb, setting the structure of the whole clause—that is, taking the role of predicate application controllers—are the best known. But these phrases also serve the relatively peripheral function of modifying adjectives used attributively, most commonly adjective and adverb phrases. For instance, "more" counts as an identity and quantity indicator in "more stupid" and "more stupidly". Likewise, the identity indicators we call demonstratives arise not only with noun phrases, but also with adjective and adverb phrases. Thus "that bad" can be used in attributions like "very bad" and "rather bad", and not only like "that man" as a singular term; and "that awful color" can occur both attributively, as in "He was that awful color", and as a singular term, as in "That awful color is mustard". In a parallel way, to "who did it?" seeking the nameable subject of an action, there corresponds "how?" seeking an attribute of the action predicated of the subject, as in "How badly did he do it?"

Phrases such as "the Queen of England's ..." or "the ... who paid the bill" (as in "the Queen of England's corgis" and "the man who paid the bill"), which, like functional expressions in mathematics like "the sum of ... and —", serve to form a singular term, and "all the ... who assassinated a president", which forms a collective term used distributively, also serve as predicate application controllers. Yet this does not of itself justify following Chomsky in counting them as grammatical determiners (though they count as Heads of the Determiner phrases introduced in Abney's theory into Chomskyan grammar, as discussed in chapter XV). I call them indirect identity indicators because they indicate identity of singular terms and collective terms denoting the extensions of predicates by means of accidental identifying properties. Logically, but not grammatically, they are application controllers parallel to "this ..." and "those ..." in "this man" and "those men".

The relative clauses which subserve an identifying function in such application controllers and some quantity indicators can also serve a functionally quite different and merely adjunctive role. Thus, if one said, "The man who paid the bill was John" to mean "The man, who paid the bill [the speaker mentioning it incidentally], was John", where who is being referred to by the expression "the man" is already clear to both speaker and hearer, the "who paid the bill" would be functionally a mere adjunct. Again, if, without ever having mentioned how many men followed me in the discourse-context concerned, I were to say "The very many men who followed me harassed me all the next day", the quantity indication "very many" would be merely adjunctive, just as it would be merely adjunctive in "The men who followed me, who were very many, harassed me all the next day".[31]

(viii) Some general problems in clarifying the notion of "singular term"

The phrases "singular term" and "referring expression" invite three caveats.

First, granted that the definition relies on the notion of referring to or naming "things" or "objects", it relies upon a concept with no content beyond

31. By contrast, if I said "Very many men followed me", "very many" would be both functionally an application controller and semantically a quantity indicator in that sentence, and if I went on to say "The very many men who followed me harassed me for the rest of the day", the expression "the very many men who followed me" would plainly be intending to speak of the same group already referred to, so that "the very many ... who followed me" would be serving as an application controller.

this: that things or objects are subjects of predicates. For, as the introduction and chapter III made plain, there is no category-transcending concept of "object" with any content, such as "ontologically basic object", but a hierarchy of different categories of object.

It is quite arbitrary how we might count the number of things I said in discussion last night or the number of "things" there are in the room where I am working, since it is arbitrary how these might be distinguished.

Further, for the purposes of any inquiry laying down the general conditions for the application of logic in any substantive study, in order to apply the correlative terms "singular term" and "object", one needs to use criteria of identity set by the type or nature of the kind of things being studied.[32] This is true whatever the area of the study—science, history, theology, linguistics, psychology, mathematics, economics, literature, aesthetics, ethics, or any other. In any case, the disciplined use of language requires one to limit oneself to generalizing about one sort of thing at a time or carefully distinguishing separate ranges of thing over which generalization is made (e.g., points, lines, surfaces, and volumes in geometry). The ranges of generalization are typically set by the specialism with which one is occupied. Such ranges often correspond to the limits over which key types of predicate can be sensibly used or types of question asked.

Second, in order to develop a theory of meaning, one has to begin with such maximally indefinite and "formal" conceptions of "object" as a "thing" which might be made the subject of questions. At this stage in developing a theory of meaning we are working with an informal notion of subject in which the discourse-relative ("pragmatic"), the syntactic, and the referential have not been distinguished, so that only the first, the notion of "topic" as the "subject" which the statement or question is "about", is immediately accessible. As our account develops, the notions of topic-identifier, grammatical subject, and logical subject-expression will be become more distinct. Just as the terms "subject" and "subject- expression" have a certain informality when first introduced, so the same is true of the correlative term "predicate".

Third, taking "referring to" and "denoting" as equivalent, we must distinguish between two different senses of being a referring expression. An expression may refer or have referred in the sense that the object to which it purports or purported to refer does actually or did actually exist. To be an expression which actually refers in this way or did do so when used in the speech or text concerned is to be a "referring/denoting expression" in the primary sense. This is what is required for the purposes of logic and philosophy. In these, "referring expressions" have to be (a) singular terms—that is, singular referring expres-

32. For a concept to be a *Begriff,* Frege required that the predicate concerned provide a criterion which allowed counting. This fitted with his idea that *Begriffe,* "concepts", because referred to by incomplete expressions, had identity only in an analogous sense—namely, that they had the same extension (i.e., membership).

sions apt to be subjects of singular subject/predicate propositions believed to be true by the speaker; (b) eligible as subjects of identity statements likewise believed true by the speaker, and sufficiently known to others to allow communication; and (c) occupying positions in sentences which can be occupied instead by suitable general terms combined with application controllers.

However, although a speaker or author may believe or, at the time of speaking or writing, have believed that the object to which the expression purported to refer does or did exist, he or she may be mistaken, and the expression may refer to nothing. Yet in normal conditions none of us is infallible, and so (except for indexical expressions like "I", "here", "now", and others dependent on these, and for number expressions) any of the referring expressions which we use in the belief that what they purport to refer to did exist or does exist may happen not to refer, because what they purport to refer to has never existed—or, at least, this is not contrary to any law of logic. Moreover, the same applies in the case of apparent references made in any past or present piece of speech or text, and we need a semantic theory which we can apply to any piece of discourse or text in any language and from any period independently of any judgments we might make as to the truth of the beliefs expressed or the intentions of the speaker or author concerned. Therefore semantic theory and its application to any discourse or text in any language, and without respect to the validity of the beliefs expressed, requires to use the expression "referring expression" in a second, derived sense. Accordingly, within linguistics, in semantic theory "referring expression" will take up this secondary sense as meaning an expression which is envisaged, imagined, or supposed to refer or have referred—making no assumptions as to whether or not it refers or referred to anything which actually exists or did exist.

Thus when dealing with Egyptian and Greek texts written by believers in Ptah and Apollo, in one's semantic analysis of these texts it is normal to speak of the names "Ptah" and "Apollo" as "referring expressions". When people with the now usual opinions discuss the history of ideas or such texts as these, they will use the names, not as referring expressions in the primary sense belonging to logic, but as specifications of "intentional objects", what they were mentally directed towards (to use Brentano's explanation), what others believed these names actually to refer to, their beliefs often mistaken.

(b) *The usefulness of the notion of functor*

This approach to explaining the asymmetry between names and predicates, suggested by a reading of Plato and Aristotle, dovetails with our common understanding of the sense of typical utterances or sentences. The questions of "which is meant" and "which kind is meant", with the referential aspects which will appear below, arise only with singular and general terms, whereas with sentences, words, and phrases whose meaning can be given by paraphrase we commonly ask "what it means".

(i) The misleadingness of the mathematical conception of function

In explaining the notion of predicate, modern logicians led by Frege have drawn upon the mathematically specialized notion of function. According to this specialization, if "f(...)" is the functional expression identifying the function f(...), and if something *b* is what is called an argument to the function, then the value of the function for this argument is f(b)—that is, some object designated by the expression "f(b)". This approach, found in Frege, Russell, and the early Wittgenstein, has created some confusions which result from failing to take account of the problems dealt with in chapters X and XII, arising from misguidedly treating the relation of an expression used to refer to the expression it refers to as analogous to the relation of the name "Socrates" to the man Socrates.

This approach explains how predicates came to be described as "functors" to set them in contrast with "names"—"names" in the semantic sense of singular and general subject-terms, and "functors" as incomplete expressions requiring to be completed by such "names" (general names requiring what Johnson called an applicative and singular names allowing no more than the zero morpheme). Developing a theory of "names" and "functors" along the lines suggested by Polish logicians drawing on Leśniewski, as presented by Ajdukiewicz, has the advantage of avoiding the confusions connected with the distinction between using and mentioning the name Socrates and other denoting expressions.

(ii) The approach of the Polish logicians

Accordingly I shall present distinctions between different kinds of sentence-factor and their types of sense in terms of the more informal notion of "functor" introduced by the Polish logicians.[33]

The main development of the theory of "names" and "functors" comes from Leśniewski. In Ajdukiewicz's exposition of Leśniewski's ideas,[34] sentences, names or nouns, and functors are each "semantic categories" of linguistic expression, not of entity, and the fact that nouns are not conceived of as expressions for arguments of functions means that functors are not conceived of

33. According to Ajdukiewicz, "Syntactic Connexion", 209, the term "functor" derives from Kotarbinski.

34. He regarded his work as based on Stanislaw Leśniewski's theory of semantic categories; Leśniewski, *Grundzüge eines neuen Systems der Grundlagen der Mathematik*, first printed in *Fundamenta Mathematicae* 14 (1929): 1–81, except that he does not use Leśniewski's special symbolism.

as functions in the clear mathematicians' meaning found in Frege.[35] Rather he explains a "functor" as being a "functional sign", or "unsaturated symbol" with "brackets in it"—that is, precisely as a sign with a "gap" in it—for instance, an expression such as "... is a sheep" or (schematically) "f(...)". His way of thinking of functors is derived from the ways in which Frege thought of predicates: they are "unsaturated" (Frege's metaphor) and "incomplete" in some way in which, by contrast, sentences are supposed to be complete.

True, there are also grammatical conjunctions, connecting sentential clauses in one way or another, and we have also whatever is involved in indirect speech where, seemingly, an individual is directed towards a proposition, question, order, or wish (a person may believe that P, ask whether P or why P, order somebody else to F, or wish to F or that P). In Ajdukiewicz's formal presentation of the situation we will have two or more categories of suprasentential functor, and obviously these will constitute importantly distinct semantic categories.

In sum we need to distinguish at least five kinds of topic-neutral, subject-matter universal, semantic categories: namely, sentences, suprasentential functors, names, subsentential functors (i.e., predicates),[36] and what I called application controllers (quantifiers or quantity-expressions applied to subject-terms being the most typical).

(iii) Three distinctions: singular/general; individual/collective; and concrete/abstract

The Polish logician's vocabulary is apt to make one confuse several different distinctions, especially between singular and general names [terms], and concrete and abstract names, adding unnecessary obscurities to the meaning of the word "abstract".

Ajdukiewicz grouped together, just as I have done, two very different kinds of application controller, calling them "operators": (a) the quantifiers, and (b) identity indicators serving the purpose of identifying either a singular subject or a collection.[37]

35. The concept of "semantic categories" (*Bedeutungskategorie*), as introduced by Husserl, *Logical Investigations*, vol. 2, pt. 1 (1913), is reflected in Ryle's concept of category-mistake as a mismatching of sentence-factors. Husserl's notion of category is close to Russell's notion of type as the range of significance of a given predicate; cf. Fred Sommers, "Types and Ontology", *Philosophical Review* 72 (1963): 327–63.

36. Ajdukiewicz considers the categories of "sentence" and of "name" as "basic" categories ("Syntactic Connexion", 209) and regards the various categories of functor as definable in terms of the other two. Name and subsentential functor are correlative, so that neither could have the character it has independently of the other.

37. Clearly the quantifiers are neither functors nor arguments. However, instead of, e.g., separating singular concrete names and general ones into different categories, Ajdukiewicz treats the quantifiers as what he calls "operators" on the ground that these expressions, along with others such as "the sum of ...", "the product of ...", "the integral of ...", and in general "the one and only ...", are all ones which, when applied to

Meantime, to distinguish only two categories of name, calling them "concrete" and "abstract" instead of "singular" and "general", is to open a way to confusion between general terms such as "man" and so-called abstract terms such as "humanity". I shall deal with the "general" and, associated with it, the "collective" immediately below, dealing with the "abstract" in chapters XII and XIII.

We have seen the distinction between singular and general terms already.

Now, second, in close relation to this first distinction, we are in a position to distinguish two kinds of singular term: individual and collective. What I mean by a collective singular term is a term such as "the Apostles" or "our football team", of which, when it figures as a subject term, there are two kinds of predication: the one collective, as when we say "The Apostles were twelve in number" or "Our football team won the league"; and the other distributive, as when we say "The Apostles were disciples of Jesus" or "Our football team are very tall", meaning "each of the Apostles was a disciple of Jesus" and "each member of our football team is very tall". A distributive predication of a collective singular subject-term is equivalent to a universal proposition with a general subject-term, in these cases the general terms "Apostle" and "member of our football team".

Collective singular terms are not "abstract expressions", whether for "universals", "features", and "relations" or for the things variably referred to as "events" and "states" or as "particularized universals". These need more elaborate discussion involving questions of grammar, morphology, and lexical priority, as well as semantics (see chapter XII).

Sidelights from philosophical history The difficulty that the same term may sometimes be used attributively or predicatively and sometimes be used to denote an abstraction-namely, the attribute predicated—was noticed very early by philosophers. Aristotle in the *Categories,* taken together with the *Analytics,* shows himself quite alive to the logical problems which this generates. From "Socrates is courageous" and "Courage is a virtue" it does not follow that Socrates is a virtue—although the latter proposition implies that "Courageous men are (thereby) virtuous".

There is a form of reasoning "A is B; B is C; therefore, A is C" which often breaks down, but whenever it breaks down some explanation is required: "Socrates (or 'Man') is a biped; bipeds are animals; therefore, Socrates (or 'Man') is an animal"; "Socrates (or 'Man') is courageous; courage is a virtue; therefore, Socrates (or 'Man') is a virtue"; and "Socrates (or 'Man') is white; white is a color; therefore, Socrates (or 'Man') is a color".

an expression with variables, reduce one or more of these variables to the role of apparent variable (= bound variable); Ajdukiewicz, "Syntactic Connexion", 220. Accordingly, he introduces the new title "operators" to embrace all of them.

Aristotle is already aware of the embarrassments concerned. "Socrates is white" and "White is a color", but Socrates is not a color any more than he is a virtue, yet we do not have the convenient change of inflection so that two different word forms are involved, as in "courageous" and "courage". Aristotle's remedy was to deal with the situation as if he had two different types of case. In the first the word "white" is used homonymously in "Socrates is white; white is a color; therefore, Socrates is a color", because the "white" which is said of Socrates is not the same thing as is later said to be a color, since although "white" is predicable of Socrates, its *logos* (definition or essence) "animal" is not thus predicable (whereas, when "man" is predicated of Socrates, the *logos* of "man"—namely, "biped", is also thus predicable). In the second, the term for "courage" is used "paronymously"—that is, with a change of termination or inflection as between "courage" and "courageous".

Aquinas handles these differences in a much more attractive, remarkably modern way.

In the first place he wants to know whether the first term in each premise is singular or general and, if it is a general term, to know the character of the quantity term applying to it, independently of whether this quantity term be implicit or explicit, the function of such quantity term being *to indicate how the predicate applies to the subject*, thereby making it appropriate to call it an "application controller". The relevance of quantity terms is evident if we contrast the valid syllogism "Some A is B; all B is/are C; therefore, some A is/are C" with the invalid "All A is B; some B is/are C; therefore, some A is/are C".

In the second place he wants to know whether the middle term "B" is being used in the same way or not, or, to use his expression, whether it has the same *modus significandi*. When we are confronted with the words "courage" and "courageous" or the noun "white" and the adjective "white", each being a word which declines—that is, has cases unlike verbs—we have to deal with the same underlying lexical morpheme, lexeme, or word-stem, the same "thing signified" (*res significata*) being referred to by the term concerned. But in each of the last two of the three proposed inferences there is a change in the way in which the term is being used, in its *modus significandi*, from the terms concerned being used predicatively, as in "white" and "courageous", to their being used as subject-terms for the abstract forms white, the color, and courage, the virtue, which are not colored or courageous. The terms are being used predicatively or "concretely" in such contexts as "Socrates is white" and "Socrates is courageous", but not in "This color is white", so that "is white" is ambiguous.[38]

38. Aquinas is occupied in distinguishing between the subject terms for the abstract forms "life", "wisdom", and *deitas* and the predicate terms "lives", "wise", and *deus*.

In *Summa Theologiae* I.a, Q.13, Art.3, *corp.*, and replies to objs.1–3, and Art.6, *corp.*, Aquinas does not imagine that, e.g., the predicate "lives" has many modes of signification (on the contrary, he insists that it

(iv) Noun phrases as arguments to verbs distinguished from noun phrases used attributively

My aim is to clarify the ideas of subject and predicate by means of first explaining the notion of a verbal framework and the correlative notion of an argument to a verbal framework. The places for expressions for such arguments have the characteristic of being accessible both to singular terms and to general terms with application controllers.

These argument places have been described as noun-phrase (NP) slots, but in this connection we have to set them strictly apart from the attributive use of such phrases, as in "Leslie is a man". This is not an ill-formulated identity statement—"Leslie is a certain man whom I met the other day"—but to be placed alongside "Leslie is fat", "Leslie is from Yorkshire", "Leslie is in Penzance", and so forth. "Yorkshire" and "Penzance" are the only occupiers of logical argument places in the logicians' sense in these attributive predications, whereas "a man", "fat", "from Yorkshire", and "in Penzance" are not.

The fact that both noun expressions like "a man" and adjectives such as "fat" can occur in attributive statements raises the question of the distinction between noun and adjective, resolvable by registering the capacity of adjectives to modify nouns within subject and other argument expressions when their dependence on nouns appears in their taking on not just the number, but also the case and gender of the nouns which they modify—in some languages they also take on the number and gender concerned when used in attributive statements.[39]

As to the distinction between adjectives and verbs, Aristotle offered some early answer. For Aristotle words such as "white" presented themselves as primarily "things said of a subject"—that is, as predicate expressions to be grouped with what we think of as verbs.[40] Yet adjectives obviously differ from verbs in that they are not subject to inflections specifying voice, mood, tense, or time,

---

is used of God and of creatures in its proper sense, no metaphor or paraphrase being involved, albeit not according to one scientific definition).

However, in Trinitarian doctrine both *deus* (God) and *deitas* (Godhead or divinity) are logically subject terms (*supposita*), and this occasions Aquinas's fullest discussion of the distinction between abstract and concrete terms. We can say God begot God, although not *deitas* begot *deitas* (God's essence begot God's essence), Q. 39, Art. 5, *corp.*, and replies to objs. 1, 3, 4 (cf. Q. 32, Art. 2, reply to obj. 2; Q. 39, Art. 3, reply to obj. 1, Art. 4, reply to obj. 4; Q. 40, Art. 1, *corp.*, and replies to objs. 2–3; and also Q. 36, Art. 4, reply to obj. 7). The three Persons in God are in Aquinas three subjects (*supposita*), called *subsistentiae* (Gk. *hypostases*) because they fulfill Aristotle's definition of first substance in the *Categories*, Q.29, Art.2, *corp.*, and reply to obj.2.

Aquinas's distinctions here are useful to us in another way—namely, in thinking about the difference between participles and the verbal nouns called gerunds, both expressed in English with the ending "-ing". Participles are expressions always used concretely (predicatively), whereas gerunds are abstract terms.

39. But not, for instance, in German.

40. Aristotle spoke of "white" as a *rhēma*; *De Interpretatione* 16a15. This way of speaking appears also in Plato, *Cratylus* 339B and *Sophist* 262B. For Aristotle, the *phōne* (spoken sound) for a *rhēma* is only an *onoma* when taken in isolation.

inflections which are instead placed on verbs—in the case of attributive statements, on the copula "is". Also, adjectives can fill the place of nouns, as when we go from saying "Socrates is wise" via speaking of "the wise Socrates", "wise husbands", and "wise women", to end by speaking of "the wise", and in general take on the types of inflection appropriate to nouns.

(c) *Sense and reference*

In order to know what a sentence means, we have to take account of all the subordinate expressions within the sentence concerned, along with stress, intonation, and context. This will involve our knowing not only (1), in the case of nonreferring expressions, *what* they mean (or meant) but also (2), in the case of expressions occurring as names or other referring expressions, *which* (or who) is (or was) meant by these names or expressions—that is, *which individual* of a certain class it is (or was) intended to refer to by them, or *which kind* it is (or was) intended to refer to by them.

Sorting out what is going on requires us to clarify the distinction between "sense" and "reference", two terms which have not always been used exactly the way they were in Frege;[41] or "connotation" and "denotation", to use Mill's terms. Granted previous discrepancies in the use of these terms, it is better for us to start afresh.

(i) **Introducing the notion of kind-meaning**

As we have remarked, in order to denote or refer to something, a name or other term must have at least some "kind"-meaning, of importance to the sense of the statements concerned. In order to use a name at all, it has to be part of the language. For this, as the later Wittgenstein exhibited, when one explains the meaning of a name by pointing at the object one intends to name, it has to be clear what sort of thing one is intending to name (e.g., a wall, a mark on the wall, or the color of the wall; or a person, his or her head, or the mark on his or her nose), even if the sort is as generic as "middle sized substance" (such as a rock, living thing, or table), and this involves the sense and not just the reference of a general term. Russell further realized that such an attempt to name would also fail if one did not know what type of propositional context it would fit into—that is, the types of predicate which can sensibly, without absurdity, be predicated of it. These requirements coincide; they also

41. We need feel no obligation to use these terms in Frege's ways—for him, in regard to any term, its *Sinn* is what makes a difference to how we determine whether the term applies or not, and *Bedeutung* is what determines whether the term applies or not independently of whether or how we determine this; cf. Dummett's article "Frege, Gottlob", *Encyclopaedia of Philosophy*, ed. Paul A. Edwards (New York: Macmillan, 1967), 2:225–37.

happen to be what Anscombe noticed as being required to make, for instance, history books generally intelligible, despite the unfamiliar names (with an unaccustomed name, what we need to know is what sort of thing it names, e.g., a person, or a river, or a town). In sum, all semantically primary names, including proper names, along with, for instance, names of colors, can only be used if it is presupposed what kind of thing is being referred to; some have argued that this implies that some names will have some sense or connotations as well as reference. They will connote some general kind, therewith conveying some sense, although when as names they occur as subject-terms, they contribute to the expression of the sense of the sentence not by expressing sense but by denoting.

This question as to "which or who is meant" arises not only when one is asking which object or person is picked out by a singular term, but also when one is asking which kind of animal (pig, horse), which color (red, blue), which letter of a certain alphabet (the Greek *alpha*, *beta*, *omega*, or the Hebrew *aleph*, and so forth) or which Chinese character, or which number (one, two, three) is being referred to, as in the case of the terms "pig", "horse", "red", "blue", "one", and so forth.[42] Of these, the case of the names of colors used as singular subject-terms is perhaps the plainest.

In some special cases, while the name can serve as a subject-term, what it denotes can be predicated, and its predicative meaning is primary and is sufficient to determine the denotation of the name concerned. This arises in many of the kinds of "abstract" terms whose formation and meaning are discussed in chapter XII, such as "wisdom" and "courage", "knowledge", "hope" and "fear", numerals, and the names of letters of alphabets.[43]

By contrast, in the case of names of individual concrete particulars, such fixing of kind-meaning is clearly not enough. This is most obvious with the proper names of particular persons, horses, pets, towns, rivers, lakes, planets, stars, and other individuals referred to by concrete expressions. Knowing what it is to be a person, cobbler, athlete, footballer, horse, town, river, lake, planet, or star does not enable us to identify which individual with the properties of the kinds identified is being named.

(ii) How the function of referring is achieved as a contribution to the sense of sentences

The way an expression such as a name, used simply to identify the subject, contributes to the sense of a whole sentence is quite different from the

42. I explain how it comes about that we regard all these as indeed "names" in chap. XII, sec. 2 (d), of this volume.

43. One can say "I fear …", and also say "I am afraid ('afeard') of … ". But as with terms for other emotions, it is the verb which is fundamental.

way it is exemplified in the case of predicates. It contributes to the sense of the sentence, not by means of expressing a sense, but by identifying which kind or which individual of a kind is being referred to. The kind connoted by a name is limited to the properties of the general kind involved. This connoting, although enough to determine the general features of the name's correct use, such as the types of predicate which may be sensibly predicated of it and the syntax of its use, is not enough to explain how names or referring expressions work.

Their particular way of working is precisely that of "referring" or "denoting".

The way this function is fulfilled has often been misconstrued. Thus some philosophers have entertained the strange idea that the "reference" itself—that is, the object referred to—is internal to the sense of the sentence within which the referring expression occurs.[44] On the contrary, the object referred to (the "who or which is meant") is something clearly external to the proposition—in the world, not in speech.[45] Indeed, in certain cases (e.g., when Apollo is spoken of in the text of past devotees who believed in his existence) the object referred to neither is nor ever was "in" any "world" at all (even though some author or speaker may have believed that what he spoke of existed).

Rather, what we must say is that the way in which an expression fulfills the function of "referring" or "denoting" is by its having been used with the intention to refer to or denote the named object or person, but this sense is expressed by their being used in context. The names themselves in isolation from any context do not express this intention. Even in their discourse-context the names themselves do not *express* their reference—do not express either the object or person to which or whom they refer, or even express *that they refer* to this object or person. Rather, it is the name's *being used* in the particular context concerned which expresses the sense-content and achieves the referring.

This phenomenon, that it is the use of a particular word in the context, not the word in itself, which subserves the expression of sense, is not special to names. To take an extreme case of what is not a name, the word "is" in itself does not express a sense or even contribute to sense (indeed, it is peculiarly empty of semantic content), but only the use of this word "is" with other words linked to it.

44. Thus, G. E. Moore, "Nature of Judgment", seems to have conceived a proposition to be composed of Meanings (*Bedeutung*, the German word for "meaning", can mean "thing referred to" as well as "sense"), so that ordinary named objects (not their names) would be parts of a proposition.

45. Indeed, even when sense determines reference, as in the case of expressions for numbers, the number referred to is not a component of the sense. Only the sense-content of the expressions and the intention to refer to the number referred to affect the sense of the proposition.

In sum, what is internal to the "sense" of an expression is the fact that the speaker has or had a right to expect others to have understood him or her to have meant, or "intended", this or that thing or person by the expression concerned. And that a certain object (the person or thing "who or which is, or was, meant") was what was intended to be referred to by a term is internal to this "sense". It is thus that the intending of this "he who", "she who", or "that thing which" is, or was, meant by the expression concerned (the intending directed towards the identifying of the "which [or 'who'] is, or was, meant") does belong to the intending of the sense of the whole sentence involved. In the normal case the whole sentence's having sense depends upon the intention to refer to a real object and sometimes, as when early Greeks intended to refer to Pegasus, does not depend on actually achieving this (since Pegasus never existed). In cases in which the discourse-context makes it plain that the intention is to offer entirely fictional narratives, report or discuss the arguments and plots of philosophical dialogues and historical novels, report Greek myths, or perform a part in a play, these intentions are part of the sense of the sentences concerned.

(iii) The interplay of predicative and denotational aspects of understanding the names of general kinds

Knowledge of reference, that is, knowledge of "which is meant", stands at two levels.

The first level is general and belongs to the general knowledge which we often have independently of knowing which kind or particular thing is being referred to (e.g., the knowledge that a particular name is of the type customarily given to a person, or to a town, or to a species of animal). The second level is that of actual individuation or identification, identifying which kind or particular thing of a kind concerned it is intended to refer to.

The knowledge of identity at this second level is established by a particular speech-act (or speech-acts) or other history establishing a convention in regard to the application of the name. Thus a naming ceremony (itself a speech-act) constitutes the most obvious way of establishing such a convention. However, a custom of using a name in order to refer to an object, even without a naming ceremony, is quite sufficient—such names arising by custom include nicknames used in the lifetime and presence of the person or other object concerned, names arising in some later period (e.g., Charlemagne), and names arising in fiction or myth. What is essential is some publicly accepted way of applying the name, however this custom arose. The ceremonies, customs, customary ways of speaking, or traditions in speech must fix the use of the name in such a way as to leave no leeway for variation in its use to refer to the object concerned in subsequent acts of speech—that is, no variation as to the genus to which the thing intended to be referred to belongs (e.g., as to whether it is a plant, angel, man, woman, country, town, river, sea, star, color, number, or battle), as well as no leeway for variation in respect of its reference—that is, as to which particular thing or species (of the genus concerned) it is intended to refer.[46]

It is against this background that we should consider Baker and Hacker's remarks:

> Meaning is what is given by an explanation of meaning. Explanations of meaning are diverse, and explanation by necessary and sufficient conditions of application is only one kind. In what sense does "This (pointing) is red" do so [specifying its contribution to determination of truth-conditions]? Similar considerations hold for explanations by example, by drawing an object, exemplifying an action, making an appropriate gesture, giving a locative explanation, etc. These explanations do give the meanings of their *explicanda*.[47]

These remarks apply particularly to words for natural kinds and colors as names: there is a referential element in their meaning absent from property-words in general. Austin's example of "pig" is instructive: we certainly do not proceed by giving the necessary and sufficient conditions for applying the predicate "... is a pig" (a procedure we might naturally adopt in explaining the meaning of such words as "bachelor", e.g., as "a man who has not yet married"). Rather we proceed by the consideration of examples of things which are pigs and things which are not so, in such a way also that these will allow us, for instance, to judge that something is like a pig without it being clear whether or not we should so classify it.

We give a more accurate identification of natural kinds according to a skill, rather than some drill. The principles which guide the operation of this skill have been well described by Putnam, and his explanations serve rather exactly to record the referential element in the meaning of such natural-kind terms.[48] These are conveniently presented by Wiggins against the background of Aristotle, Leibniz, and modern approaches in biological and other classification. In brief, in the case of a natural-kind term F, a thing x will be an F if and only if, given good examples of F's, the most explanatory and comprehensive and true theoretical description of the kind which these examples exemplify would group the thing x alongside these good examples; and, as he

46. Or at least if *parole* leaves no cues to the contrary, they are *presumed* to leave no freedom for variation in these respects. Questions may yet arise as to whether they genuinely refer at all, e.g., as to whether there is or was such an intra-Mercurial planet as Vulcan, or such a person as King Arthur (i.e., a unique person in history around whom the later legends accrued), or such a kind of stuff as phlogiston.

47. Baker and Hacker, *Wittgenstein: Understanding and Meaning*, 281; cf. 69–85. They go on to add, "but not by specifying any sentential role", whereas, as we saw earlier, any explanation of meaning must leave it clear what sentential role a word can take, even though this is not the means of explaining its meaning.

48. Putnam, "Is Semantics Possible?" reprinted in *Mind, Language, and Reality*, 139–52.

points out, this means not that reference is prior to sense, but (here contrary to Frege) that we cannot say simply that sense determines reference, but must insist that reference plays a part in determining sense.[49]

Our initial identification of a natural kind—for instance, copper—is according to its properties (reddish-brown, malleable, and ductile), its origin (from a certain kind of ore), and its use (to make electrical wire) or (earlier) a familiar feature of the results of its use (green-covered roofs). In this case explanations of meaning by allusion to these things are the closest we get to a "nominal" definition, and therefore the closest we get to an expression of its primary *langue*-meaning. Closer to a "real" definition would be a statement that copper is the element of atomic number 29 (the atomic number being the number of protons in the nucleus), this being the fundamental property which explains most of its chemical behavior—better still would be a definition combining this with a specification of the number of neutrons in the nucleus of the most common isotope (roughly the difference between atomic weight and atomic number), which helps determine density and radioactive properties. Which of the two, "nominal" or "real", comes nearest to expressing the sense—that is, "discourse-significance"—of the word varies with the context of discourse. Finally, we can give what I would call a "criterial" definition—for instance, defining copper as the element which melts at such and such a temperature at standard atmospheric pressure, which is something we might specify in giving someone a test procedure (e.g., to check purity). All these definitions define the same thing, the stuff called copper, it being the intended reference of the word which affects the sense of sentences containing it.

A referential element is in a parallel way integral to the determination of the sense of the words we use for colors or shades of color. Likewise, reference is relevant to the sense of sentences about letters of an alphabet—for instance, "In English the letter 'y' is sometimes a vowel and sometimes a consonant".

In general it has been the weakness of earlier philosophers to have concentrated solely or primarily on names in their denoting role, and thereby on those terms for which what is relevant to the sense of sentences is "which is meant" as the object denoted, and not "what it means" as the sense of the word concerned as a constituent.[50] Yet the paradigm cases of sense are those exhibited by complete sentences and by merely descriptive nonreferential predicates.[51]

49. Wiggins, *Sameness and Substance* (Oxford: Blackwell, 1980), 78–86, with 83 on Frege.

50. Cf. Ryle, "Theory of Meaning".

51. To say that what "bachelor" means is "man who has not yet married" is the same as to say that any sentence of the form "*x* is a bachelor" means "*x* is a man who has not yet married".

Section 3. Verbs as Giving Predicates Their "Verbal" Character—The Way Verbs Are Learned

(a) *Preliminary remarks*

The fundamental level at which the noun/verb distinction arises is semantic, arising from the roles of different arguments within a verbal framework, both their functional, or "pragmatic", roles in discourse and their "thematic" roles (i.e., participatory roles in the states of affairs or activities, roles which I attempt to list in chapter XIII).

Such arguments to verbs are typically picked out by noun phrases figuring among complements and adjuncts of the verb (including the subject of the verb and its objects, along with arguments not taken as topics, such as agents to a passive verb, means used in the action, destinations, and directions). Every sentence or clause typically gives a privileged place to one of these arguments as its subject, giving the whole sentence or clause a subject/predicate structure. Let us examine the ways in which the primacy of the verb first shows itself.

It has been said that nouns predominate in presyntactic speech, by which is meant speech in which the implicit syntax has not yet found expression in particular grammatical forms. As we shall see, this appearance is somewhat deceptive, the result of concentrating on Indo-European languages in their present forms, and is not confirmed by study of the learning of language in general. It is true that children begin to acquire syntax, in the sense of grammatical forms of representing syntax, by selecting the verbs, prepositions (or postpositions), and adjectives that combine with the nouns they already know. But it is not universally true that initially grammatical categories in early child language are marked only by patterns of order and selection and that inflection always arises at a second stage after nouns. As we shall see, the verbal framework is present from the start, even when it is not yet explicit in a particular grammaticalized form. Agreement on the primacy of verb recognition in establishing the grammaticalized syntactic form of sentences is a common feature of most contemporary approaches.[52]

The verbal framework of sentences most commonly centers on a verb-expression of a content-introducing character, but in some cases without any explicit argument expressions—for instance, because the subject is clear from

52. See Lois Bloom, "The Centrality of Verbs", in *Language Development from Two to Three* (Cambridge: Cambridge University Press, 1991), 26–32 (cf. 56–58), in which the preeminence of the verb is already strongly emphasized, as also in Tomasello, *First Verbs: A Case Study of Early Grammatical Development* (Cambridge: Cambridge University Press, 1992); "Pragmatic Contexts for Early Verb Learning", in *Beyond Names for Things: Young Children's Acquisition of Verbs*, ed. Tomasello and W. E. Merriman (Hillsdale, N.J.: Erlbaum, 1995); and Pinker, *Stuff of Thought*.

the context or sufficiently identified by inflection on the verb, what I call a silent subject. But in some cases the framework may be marked by the presence of a verb which is not of a content-introducing character, such as "is" in English—for instance, the framework set by "... is white". The same framework is present when the argument and predicate are distinguished pragmatically by the context without a verb, as we saw in the sentence "Caesar candidus", giving the framework "... candidus" instead of "... candidus est".

With these provisos we can safely say with Martin Braine that "the default phrase-structure configuration in languages is, as in logic, one in which a predicate and argument are sisters", where the expression "sisters" is understood in a way compatible with there being some hierarchy between predicate and some primary argument.[53] The introduction gave reason for moving towards a discourse-related concept of grammatical surface subject which will have some application in every language, contrary to the views of Dik, Van Valin, and others,[54] as is borne out by my argument in chapter XI.

(b) *Nouns and verbs in one- and two-word utterances*

The imitation of individual sounds produced by those about them and experimentation or play with such sounds has a key part in the child's development of a phonetic capacity adapted to the language of his or her community. However, anything allowing us to attribute words to children requires a context giving the word a setting which has some structural complexity, even if only minimal. Even *papa*, *mama*, and so forth, as single-word utterances, are being used by the child to draw attention to itself or to something it has pointed at, the context supplying some unexpressed imperative, a cry for help, an invitation to kiss, cuddle, or play, or a request to look at something.

Early object words, used as one-word utterances, can be requests ("Bed" expressing the desire to go to bed), comments ("Bed" equivalent to "That is a bed") or attempts to draw attention to things ("Bed" meaning "Look at that bed", said, for instance, when something strange is happening on it or to it).[55] Even here there could be uncertainty as to whether "bed" in the first case had the semantic role of a verb, rather than a noun or object word—among adults, nouns with or without verbal inflection are sometimes used in the role of

53. Martin Braine, et al., "the Development of Categories at the Semantics/Syntax Interface", *Cognitive Development* 8 (1993): 488; cf. Martin Braine, "What Sort of Innate Structure is Needed to 'Bootstrap' into Syntax?", 93–94. This view fits with Woolford's view that the main verb and its noun phrase arguments are sisters in nonconfigurational and VSO languages; see E. Woolford, "VP-Internal Subjects in VSO and Nonconfigurational Languages", *Linguistic Inquiry* 22, no. 3 (1991): 503–40.

54. Bernard Comrie, *Language Universals and Linguistic Typology*, 2nd ed. (Chicago: University of Chicago Press, 1989), cited by Martin Braine, et al., "Development of Categories", 489.

55. Cf. Tomasello, *First Verbs*, 40.

verbs. More evidently, there is a clear distinction between "Fire" with a clearly verbal character as an imperative directing some person or persons to fire a gun, the verb being understood as in the second person, and "Fire" with a clearly nominal character as, for instance, meaning "Beware, there is enemy gunfire" or, in giving an alarm, "There is a fire". The verbal framework is in all these cases set by the speech-act, and already we can distinguish whether the content-carrying element present has the grammatical role of a noun within this speech framework or of a verb, itself setting the framework.

In this way the idea of Gleitman and her colleagues that "verbal meaning cannot come only through observation of the world's events; but the form of language itself acts like a zoom lens, giving perspective on the main event" applies even at the one-word level.[56] This process, described as *syntactic bootstrapping,* occurs "when the child attends to the syntactic frames in which the verb is used".[57] However, the syntactic structure concerned should not be conceived along the formal lines suggested, but regarded as essentially semantic in character, a semantic syntax incorporating elements of pragmatics (e.g., with appreciation of context important for the recognition of the intention of the utterance concerned). It is semantic syntax that comes into play in considering children's first word combinations in chapter XIII.

Especially in recent times, Europeans writing about these matters have tended to write as if the first words to be learned were always names.[58] Locke and Hume, and perhaps Mill, seem to have thought of language as beginning with the naming of objects, typically ostensively. People then think of "red", "loud", and so forth not as adjectives, but names of "properties" or "features" within the world, such as redness and loudness. The word "feature" invites an enormous indiscipline of thought: particular events and circumstances can be counted as "features" in the world, alongside general properties like redness,

56. Some ideas from B. Landau and L. [Lila] R. Gleitman, *Language and Experience: Evidence from the Blind Child* (Cambridge, Mass.: Harvard University Press, 1985), and Anne Lederer, Henry Gleitman, and Lila Gleitman, "Verbs of a Feather Flock Together", in *Beyond Names for Things,* as summarized by R. M. Golinkoff, Kathy Hirsh-Pasek, Carolyn B. Mervis, William B. Frawley, and Maria Parillo, "Lexical Principles Can Be Extended to the Acquisition of Verbs", in *Beyond Names for Things,* ed. Tomasello and Merriman, 209n66.

57. Landau and Gleitman, *Language and Experience.*

58. Aristotle, like Plato, divided spoken sounds (*phōnai*) into two main kinds, the name (*onoma*) and the verb (*rhēma*), attaining truth or falsity by being combined or divided (as in negations, *diaireseis*).

He spoke of each such *phōne,* if significant by convention (*synthēkē*), as an *onoma* (Aristotle, *De Interpretatione* 16a19), but it could be spoken in that way only when taken in isolation—a *rhēma* in combination with an *onoma* is not an *onoma* (*De Interpretatione,* chap. 3). Aquinas spoke of words as *nomina,* but insisted that they had a different way of signifying (*modus significandi*) when they occurred predicatively (a difference he expected usually to be marked morphologically). By contrast, Ockham in effect made predication into a matter of one thing having two names applied to it; see Geach, "Nominalism", in *Logic Matters,* 289–301; see also Anscombe and Geach, *Three Philosophers,* viii, 6–7; and Geach, *Reference and Generality.* Ockham opened the way for the empiricists to treat all categorematic words equally as names.

In such ways, the tendency to treat every case of signifying as a case of naming was established.

and also alongside individual objects in the world. Fortunately, children's learning of language depends on no such confusion. In chapter XII I show the secondary status of abstract terms from the standpoint of semantics and syntactic structure.

A sound cannot be learned *as a name* merely by a naming ceremony—for instance, by pointing accompanied by such words as "Tommy", "kitty", or "wasp", unless as something that occurs in a certain type of way—for instance, in some appropriate combination with other words, such as "Tommy bad", "want kitty", "kitty gone", or "no kitty", which makes clear what kind of thing is being named or pointed at.[59] It is the way in which a sound is used in combination with other expressions that makes it into a name.

The verbal structure or framework of early child utterances, which is so disguised in languages like English, is much more explicit in many other languages, as has been made plain by the studies of Gopnik and Choi in regard to Korean and Japanese.[60]

The presumption that nouns are acquired before verbs and are the dominant lexical category at the earliest stages of language development arises not only from long-rooted philosophical mistakes, but also from the concentration on English in so many studies. All sorts of theories have been offered to explain this supposed finding—for instance, that nouns refer to what is presented in perception; that nouns partition objects into natural categories; that the child innately tends to begin by labeling whole objects, then using the same label for similar objects; that verbs function more language-specifically, so that children to learn verbs need to experience more previous language input; or that the core nature of verbs lies in shared morphosyntactic properties (their being modified by negation, tense, aspect, and voice) so that this is a reason for their being learned later.

Yet the case of English may be misleading or misinterpreted, since children's early English may often use what is an object word in adult language in a quite different function, as well as using such non-nouns as "no", "more", "up", "down", and, to signify failure or success, "uh-ah" and "there". However, the non-nouns of children's English are of a conspicuously small number of kinds, while the relational words are rarely verbs in adult language, presenting a considerable contrast to a language like Korean.

The adult language experienced by Korean and Japanese children in learn-

59. My statement here is reminiscent of Frege's principle that a name cannot have *Bedeutung* ("meaning" as including "reference") outside the context of a proposition.

60. Alison Gopnik and Soonja Choi, "Early Acquisition of Verbs in Korean: A Cross Linguistic Study", *Journal of Child Language* 22 (1995): 497–529; and Gopnik and Choi, "Names, Relational Words, and Cognitive Development in English and Korean Speakers: Nouns Are Not Always Learned before Verbs", in *Beyond Names for Things*, ed. Tomasello and Merriman, 63–80.

ing to speak is very different from the typical Indo-European pattern. Korean and Japanese have a rich verb morphology in which different verb endings make important pragmatic and semantic distinctions, and the verb-final character of these languages make the inflections to the verb more conspicuous. Pragmatic rules allow noun-arguments to remain unexpressed because implied by the context of utterance (what Gopnik and Choi call "massive noun ellipsis"). Parental speech consists in highly inflected verbs and a large verb vocabulary, with a smaller use of a sparser number of nouns.

These morphological and grammatical differences are combined with differences in the practical setting of learning. In Gopnik and Choi's extensive empirical studies, it appeared that an enormously high proportion of the utterances of the Korean mothers were activity-oriented, whereas those of the American mothers were divided roughly equally between activity-oriented and object-oriented. The result of this cultural difference in the context within which language is learned shows up in an enormous difference in the characteristics of the speech of the child concerned.

In this recent study, which counts a "spurt" as meaning the learning of at least ten new words in one category within the same month, the youngest Korean to show a verb spurt did this as early as between 14½ and 15½ months, at the end of which she had 39 words overall. Two others showed a first verb spurt before they had 15 words and four others before 80 words, and before any noun spurt. At the 50-word mark Korean children had 38 percent nouns and 39 percent verbs in their total vocabulary. The diversity of verb types equaled the diversity of noun types at this stage.

Moreover, in a group of nine Korean children, four showed productivity in verb morphology during or before their first spurt—that is, using different suffixes on the same verb, according to whether requests, questions, or statements were concerned, and also according to tense, while two others regularly put negative particles before the verb, all appropriately. At this early stage nouns can be followed by a verb inflection, corresponding to leaving out the copula in English, while the possessive suffix seems to behave like a verb. In the verb spurt period the children developed verb suffixes relating to mood and modality. This suggests that the children differentiated between nouns and verbs and acquired new verbs as verbs in a fully fledged sense. Unsurprisingly, at this early stage no case or plural indicators appeared with nouns.

By contrast, in learning English, nouns were hugely predominant.

With children being brought up in English, the first noun spurt appeared around the 50-word mark, and before any verb spurt, but later than the verb spurts among the young Koreans.

In considering the treatment of learning verbs by Tomasello and others, one has to avoid supposing that a verb is learned by first learning the meaning of a corresponding noun. In teaching verbs the adults always use them in a finite form ("I am spinning, go on", "You spin", "You've done it—you spinned it", "It spinned", "It is spinning"). Thus the adults never choose a distinctively abstract form as if referring to a thing—for instance, as if to say, "This is motion", "This is movement", or "This is a move" (compare "a hug", "a kiss", "a drink"), ways of speaking which come later. They say "this is spinning" at a stage when the child will take "is spinning" as being used to express the continuous present tense.[61]

Even when inflections are unmarked one should construe a child's early single-word utterance "Kiss" as the imperative of a verb rather than as the name of an object. The thought "Kiss me" does not involve having formed a concept of an object being transferred, as if envisaging an analogy between "Give me a kiss" and "Give me a [toy] brick".[62]

A verb may be given with implicit syntax, even if it is just one word. We must not assume that the syntax of a verb is only learned by first finding the different kinds of noun phrase surrounding it. It appears that verb syntax can be appreciated from the pragmatics of adult speech, without the need first to be presented with many-worded statements, with each argument to the verb appropriately placed.

(c) *The mistake of treating events as objects in describing language learning*

In emphasizing the importance of verbs Tomasello says that "it is important to conceptualize a child's early cognition not solely in terms of objects and properties, but in terms of event structures with objects no more prominent than activities and events in which they are embedded", and he then misleadingly continues by saying, "events are as basic and developmentally primary as

61. At the earliest stage children are likely to experience "is-spinning" as one word, the verb "spin" in an inflected form, not at first associating it with the continuous character of the activity concerned, although perhaps appreciating this quite early. Older children may consider "is spinning" as two words composed of "is" and "spinning", with the latter as some non-finite form of the verb, much later realizing that it has the character of a participle rather than an infinitive. At this stage, the "It" in "It is spinning" is understood to refer to the toy, the spinning top, which is spinning.

It requires much more sophistication to see the possibility of interpreting "It is spinning" as an identity statement as if "spinning" were a noun, so as to say "That is what we call 'spinning'", the "It" and the "that" being used, not to refer to the top which is spinning, but to the type of activity, spinning, of which the behavior of the spinning top is the visible example. In that case, the word "spinning" would be being used, not as the participial part of the modern English continuous present, but as a gerund, naming this activity.

In Greek, in Romance languages, and in German, no such ambiguity could arise, since the primary sense of the simple present, morphologically corresponding to "I spin", is to express the continuous present, and to express this meaning by "is" with the participle is either an excrescence or impossible. It was rare in English up to approaching 1600, and became the dominant form only after 1700.

62. One could put parallel examples with "sell" or "bring", or with "Take a kiss from me".

objects, and thus there is no cognitive reason to a child should focus first on either objects or actions".[63]

People often speak as if sometimes we refer to objects and sometimes to events or situations, and these remarks of Tomasello can be misconstrued as if objects and events serve equally well as things to refer to, and as if referring were the same sort of thing in each case. Tomasello and Golinkoff are only two of a great number of others who sometimes treat nouns and verbs indifferently as names or labels, as if they had the same syntactic role.

Golinkoff and her colleagues,[64] particularly influenced by discussions of how we imagine events,[65] attempt to give recognition to the importance of events and situations for children's learning of language by appealing to Gleitman's ideas of the importance for child learning of the syntactic frames within which verbs are presented. Yet, although Gleitman's underlying conception seems right, whereby "the form of language itself acts like a zoom lens, giving perspective on the main event", her formulation misleadingly suggests that what is in the world, the "event", has a pictorial structure of the kind Wittgenstein called logical form. Gleitman's view suggests a portrayal of events and situations as if what was special about them was their possession of syntactic structure, the mistake which Wittgenstein later recognized as having been involved in his earlier pictorial theory of meaning—whereas it is not the events, but reports of them, which have syntactic structure.

Events and objects are given to knowledge interdependently, but only within a structure within which they have radically different roles, so that there is a radical difference between referring to an object and the so-called "referring" to an event or situation which takes place when events or situations are reported or described. Events and situations are given with structures which involve objects internally, since we cannot understand what it is for things to be objects except as syntactic centers around which events and situations cluster. But what has syntactic structure is a report of an event or situation, not an isomorphic picture of it. Events and situations are not objects. We report events and situations, but refer to objects.

Topics of discourse, including concrete objects, can be referred to and spoken about. We can take events as topics and speak about them, saying, for instance, that they happened, or that they happened in 1066, or that they went on for a long time or were over very quickly or were very exciting or dis-

63. Tomasello, "Pragmatic Contexts for Early Verb Learning", 137, where he refers to the work of Jean Piaget, *The Origins of Intelligence in Children* (New York: Norton, 1952); K. Nelson, *Making Sense: The Acquisition of Shared Meaning* (New York: Academic Press, 1985); and J. Mandler, "How to Build a Baby: II: Conceptual Primitives", *Psychological Review* 99 (1992): 587–604.

64. Golinkoff, et al., "Lexical Principles", 185–221, discuss the principles underlying children's early noun learning, in a setting in which their primary concern is with verbs.

65. Influenced by Mandler, "How to Build a Baby".

tressing to watch, or involved lots of pain, blood, and cruelty. Further, we can say that we can remember *that* the Battle of Hastings is dated 1066, and took place over 945 years ago: these are facts such as we might be taught in school. However, this factual memory involves no experiencing of the events concerned. It is not like remembering being tortured on the rack, or our sister's wedding and the dance afterwards, which are things we remember or imagine in a different way; nor even like imagining or remembering our sister sitting in front of us next to the old grandfather clock, which is the remembering of a static situation, rather than an event.

How are we to explain the difference between this imaginative memory, remembering which involves imagining events, goings-on, or situations, and factual or propositional memory?

Surely the first involves that we experienced the event, going-on, or situation as something dynamic, involving action—that is, movement or the liability or active possibility of movement or action, or at least the privation of these as in remembering static situations (like imagining previous events when we came upon the scene of a field strewn with dead bodies after a battle). What is experienced or imagined is structured in such a way as to be in principle capable of being reported or described. The structure of what we experience is not reflected by the structure of the report—that is, by the expression "our sister" occurring in a certain syntactic relation to the expression "the grandfather clock", for instance, before it in speech or on the left of it in an English sentence and on the right of it in a Hebrew sentence, but in what the report reports (the report says nothing about its own structure—that is the concern of the linguist or the literary critic).

That is, although events, goings-on, and situations can be, in Brentano's technical phrase, "intentional objects", things the mind is directed towards or upon, they are not concrete substances. Experiencing or imagining a going-on or situation is not an example of remembering a thing or person, although the going-on may have these as "participants"—for instance, the grandfather clock or one's sister. Nor is it just having a mental image of something. I can easily hold a mental image of something which is not a going-on or situation, but, for instance, the Sun, an expanse of blue sky, a spread of carpet, a map, or an oak table, or the face of my sister as it appeared in a picture of her when she was fourteen and in school clothes. The things or persons we imagine and the contents of mental images (what they are images of) are each intentional objects of a different kind from events, goings-on, and situations. They cannot be specified in sentences which could be reports of them, but only by proper names or descriptive phrases.

For this is exactly what is distinctive of events, goings-on, and situations as kinds of intentional object: that they are precisely those intentional objects which are apt to be specified in sentences which could be reports of them. Here we must distinguish between on-the-spot descriptions of events and histories telling us facts about them. The latter treat events as if they were objects (for example, the Battle of Hastings) of which one had to predicate something. Thus, an on-the-spot description report of a battle might read, "people are fighting each other with swords, and many are falling down with great wounds and blood pouring out, while it continues to rain and the horses are neighing and running about in distress, some limping, all in an area of mud, mush, and mist". By contrast, a report telling one facts about the battle might read, "The Battle of Hastings took place on Senlac Hill where Battle Abbey is today, with its great tapestry picturing the battle and what happened before and after. The battle constituted not only a decisive change of power, but also the movement of the British Isles into the main west European, France-centered orbit and out of the Scandinavian orbit into which it was becoming pulled".

If some animals experience or imagine goings-on or situations, then they experience things apt for language to report. In an animal without structured language, what corresponds to a report would not be a name, but, for instance, a performance in which an event or reminder of an event is followed by a response, for instance, mourning behavior as a response to its companions having been slaughtered.

Golinkoff illustrates how readily psychologists and psycholinguists fall into the same traps as the philosophers: the trap in this case of making the mistake of thinking of events and situations, or "features" of any kind, as on an ontological par with concrete objects.[66] The depth of this mistake will appear fully in chapter XII, section 2.

(d) *Situating words in a verbal framework; the role of imitation in learning verbs*

Among psycholinguists Tomasello is the most conspicuous for appreciating the connection between the key role of verbs and the role played by pragmatics or the context of human interaction in which they are learned.[67] Thus he regards principles treating nouns and verbs on a par as first approximations only, and insists that such principles "do not precede and structure, but rath-

66. In accord with this way of thinking, they also think of the classification of events as somewhat parallel to the classification of objects, and accordingly provide a further nice example of unconsciously following in the footsteps of the philosophers, recapitulating the empiricists' theory of abstraction in the form of a theory of "bleaching"; Golinkoff, et al., "Lexical Principles", 198, 205.

67. E.g., in Tomasello, *First Verbs* (where we can note the striking title of the second chapter, "In the Beginning Was the Verb"); also Tomasello, "The Social Bases of Language Acquisition", *Social Development* 1 (1992): 67–87; and Tomasello, "Pragmatic Contexts".

er follow and derive from, earlier word learning experiences".[68] Others have connected the role of verbs with the predicate/argument structure of simple clauses, but without connecting it with the pragmatic way in which they are learned.

In order to understand this we need to appreciate the special complexity of the way imitation functions in the learning of language.

The description of any act of deliberately imitating the previous action of some adult itself presents problems. However, the problems of describing the process of learning language are systematically greater because they involve a more complex form of imitation. The child has to learn not just to utter certain sounds in sufficiently the same manner as the adult he or she is imitating, but to do this to give them the same kind of grammatical role.

Suppose that an adult sets a top spinning, and that later the child imitates the adult by himself or herself setting a top spinning. So far, no language learning is involved.

But now let us consider the case when the adult spins a top and says, "I spin (it)" and then the child spins the top and says, "I spin (it)", perhaps with a look of triumph. The child is now imitating two things: not just the action of the adult, but also the announcement of his or her action in a primitive sentential form, a form within which the content-introducing element is the verb, setting the framework for the whole utterance. I put the "it" in brackets because such learning may well precede any evidence of the child's having command of any transitive verbal constructions or three-word utterances.

Experiment and observation show that there is no need for the child to spin the top in the company of the same adult, and that his or her own spinning of the top and saying "I spin (it)" may be at a much later time than his or her experience of the same behavior in an adult. In virtue of the same new piece of learning and of the parity between the way he or she understands his or her own intentional action and the way he or she understands the intentional actions of others, the child may even challenge the same or a different adult with the demand, "(You) spin (it)".

The case of learning such a verb is strikingly different from what is involved in learning a new concrete noun. If a child proves his or her success in learning color words or the names of kinds of animal by triumphantly pointing at things or their pictures and saying such things as "Rabbit", "Monkey", "Red", "Green", "Blue", and so forth, what he or she says is indeed a linguistic utterance with a sense which might be expressed, "This is a rabbit" or "This is red", but in no way announces or reports his or her own action—which is the action of giving the right name to something. The content-introducing el-

68. Tomasello, "Social Bases", 74.

ement in the child's one-word utterance is not a verb, but a name, something whose reference and connotations can be given in context by ostension (at a later stage of language learning, the reference of a name may be indicated linguistically—for instance, a person may be told that Juniper is his or her sister's horse).

By contrast, verbs are not words whose meaning can be given by ostension, as if by pointing at objects at the one- or two-word utterance stage of language-use, because at that stage talking about actions (supposedly what verbs signify) as objects such as might be referred to by names or nouns has played no part in the child's language or thought as expressed by language. (At a later stage verbs might be taught by saying "This is eating", "This is drinking", and so forth, but this involves the use of a gerund and presupposes a considerable development in the understanding of derivative non-finite verbal forms.)

Thus verbs are learned in being used as verbs, not by first naming an action, which would be by means of a noun, and then using this noun as a verb.

Section 4. Negation and Its Special Character

(a) *Negation and presupposition*

Negation has a key role in the logical structure which embraces singular and general terms, with applicatives, notably equivalents of "each" and "at least one". Negation and quantity expressions are both modifiers internal to the whole clause which they modify.

This structure is compatible with great variety in the placing of both quantity expressions and negation and with a great variety of forms of constituent structure and functional organization, with only this restriction: their placing should not make it ambiguous what they apply to—for instance, by being interpretable as a modifier to something else.

"Homer was not blind" is equivalently a predicate negation and a proposition negation, reflecting the symmetrical relation of "Homer was blind" and "Homer was not blind" to the interrogative "Was Homer blind?" This pragmatic context of being in response to a question does not place negation in the situation of expressing force, because negation, like tense and unlike force, is always essentially internal to the clause, belonging to it equally when it is embedded and when it is a sentence or committed utterance in its own right.

In insisting on the equivalence of proposition negation and predicate negation, the structures of grammar and formal logic coincide,[69] and this fits

69. Except in retelling ancient myths and legends, in the telling of stories, fables such as Aesop's, and parables, and in writing novels, where we speak as if all the presuppositions normal in logic were fulfilled, without assuming or implying it, and yet without resorting to indirect speech.

both with the evidence of language learning[70] and with psychological studies of the role of predicate (or verb-phrase) negation in natural reasoning.[71]

Parallel equivalences arise with quantified statements, both as they appear in natural language and in formal logic. It is the same thing to achieve sentence negation by quantity-term negation—that is, parsing the sentence as of the form "(Not every) R is F", instead of parsing it as of the form "Every R is not F", as by predicate negation, so that "Not every R is F" is equivalent to "Some R is not F". This marks how the behavior of negation enables one to recognize the predicate.[72] ("Some" in English behaves as a partitive indefinite article like *du, de la, des* in French.)

The negation of "Some X is F" is "No X is F".[73] The contemporary "No!" and "not", and compounds with the Old English *ne* surviving after 1500 ("nor", "neither", "never", "naught", "none"), are the only natural occurrences of negative particles in modern English.

Thus, whatever the placing of negative particles, there are linguistically only three forms of clause negation, the one with a singular subject, in which the clause is negated by negating the predicate, and the other two with a general term as subject, in which what is negated is a quantity expression taken together with the predicate, one in which the predicate is denied to apply to every member of the class concerned ("Not every R is F") and the other in which it is denied to apply to any of the class ("No R is F").

In describing negation as "clause-internal", I mean that true negation is always what Van Valin calls "internal negation". This has the logic that "P" and "Not-P" leave no alternatives, so that it is presumed that all relevant presuppositions have been fulfilled, so that the Laws of Non-Contradiction and of the Excluded Middle have equal application, the position taken in chapter IV—if any relevant presuppositions are unfulfilled, affirmation and negation are both untrue. This "clause-internal" negation must be sharply distinguished from what Van Valin calls "nuclear" negation, instanced when the negative is treated morphologically, modifying not the predicate, but the predicate-term, as in saying "is unwise" instead of "is not wise".[74]

70. Cf. Bloom, *Language Development*, 144–45.

71. See Martin Braine and O'Brien, *Mental Logic*, chaps. 4, 6, 11–13. The importance of the natural language negation which applies to the verb phrase (*Mental Logic*, 87) appears notably later, when the hypothetical syllogism "'P or Q' implies 'If Not-P, then Q'" is naturally reflected in the reasoning "'Every car is a Toyota or a Honda' implies 'Any car which is not a Toyota is a Honda'" (*Mental Logic*, 304–5). That is, in natural reasoning, we handle predicates in the manner of propositions.

72. The equivalence of "Not every R is F" and "Some R is not F" is reflected in the equivalence of "$\neg$ [($\forall$x) (Fx)]" and "($\exists$x) ($\neg$Fx)", where the range of the quantifiers is the Rs. The symbolism "($\exists$x)" arose independently from a way of thinking "there exists a thing, *x*, such that", without respect to questions of the range of the quantifiers.

73. "Not some X is F" is ill-formed, unlike "Some X is not F".

74. This nuclear negation is misleadingly called "predicate negation" by Dik, *The Theory of Functional Grammar, Part 2: Complex and Derived Constructions* (Berlin: Mouton de Gruyter, 1997), 178–80.

It is integral to this structure that in the case of all logically singular subject/predicate propositions, both their affirmation and their negation presuppose the existence of their subjects. Whenever a singular term is used as a subject-expression, the existence of the object it refers to is presupposed as a condition of the truth of any statement about it, whether an affirmation or its denial; and, for instance, "Homer was not blind" is equally a case of proposition negation and a case of predicate negation, and both the affirmation and the negation have the contingent presupposition that Homer existed. It is not a necessary truth that there should have been a man called Homer who wrote the *Iliad* and the *Odyssey* or played the key role in their composition: some have speculated that these works are the works of a school with no one who could be counted as the author, in which case one would say that Homer never existed.

Likewise, presuppositions arise in the semantics of quantified statements: for instance, "Every R is F" and "Not every R is F" both presuppose the existence of Rs; that is, any use of quantifiers presupposes a non-empty domain over which quantification is made. "Not a scrap remained" and "Not a soul was left alive" might seem to lack this presupposition, but the context of such sentences will show that what is being denied concerns not all scraps of food, but just those scraps of concern in the particular location, and not all people ("souls"), but only those involved in the adventure concerned; and that the existence of food and people elsewhere was not being denied.

An affirmation and its negation always stand as two alternative answers to a simple question, and all three have the same presuppositions. Thus "Has John stopped beating his wife?", "John has stopped beating his wife", and "John has not stopped beating his wife" all presuppose that "John had previously beaten his wife", something which, like the fact that Homer existed, is perfectly contingent.

When we deny an existential statement it is in a context of the accepted usage of a name—for instance, "Cerberus" or "Dragons"—and these will have some such situation as "The Greeks once believed that there was an underworld for the dead where a three-headed dog called Cerberus guarded the gates, but this belief is false and there never was such a dog", or "The Mediterranean and Middle Eastern, as well as Teutonic and Chinese peoples, used to believe that there were giant flying lizard-like creatures called 'dragons', but man has never experienced such beings". In addition, a statement such as "Wisdom is not wise" could be construed as meaning "Wisdom is not something of a type to be properly described either as wise or as not wise". Thus the denials of existential statements combine some first-order information about what has been believed by whom with some second-order information presupposing the first as to the use of the names concerned, while statements such as "Wisdom is not wise" seem to be second-order statements about the applicability of certain kinds of predicate to certain kinds of subject, here of predicates appropriate to living things to character traits.

As I argue in chapter XIII, section 6, human languages uniformly regard some propositions as having genuine negations, while others (conditional statements and indiscriminate and indefinite statements of the types "Any A is F" and "A certain A is F" respectively, along with statements with indefinite predicates) lack them.

(b) *The symmetry of affirmation and negation, reductio ad absurdum argument, and intuitionism*

Negation is as important to philosophers as to linguists.

If one thinks of deduction in the way described by William and Martha Kneale (they call it "involution"), according to which the paradigm form of deductive argument is to proceed by a method of exploring the consequences of different (possibly nonexclusive) alternatives presented as possible or at least requiring consideration, it confirms the view that the position of affirmation and negation is symmetrical in respect of Yes/No questions.[75] Accordingly it will also be symmetrical in respect of *reductio ad falsum* or *reductio ad absurdum* arguments.[76] This method of proving a proposition "P" by ruling out all alternatives (exemplified, for instance, in the so-called disjunctive syllogism whereby "P or Q" and "Not-Q" together imply "P") depends on thinking of *reductio* arguments in a way quite different from Dummett and the mathematical intuitionists.

Within this involutionary structure "P" and "Not-P" present themselves as alternatives on a par with each other, with equal candidature for truth. It is then just as natural to take as one's strategy of proof the supposing of "Not-P" in order to disprove it, thereby establishing "P", as to take as one's strategy the supposing of "P" in order to prove "Not-P". This makes the two groups of forms of *reductio* (and associated forms of argument) symmetrical.

That one should conceive "P" and "Not-P" as exhausting the field of possibilities seems integral to the meaning of the word "not" and other expressions of clause negation. That "Not-P" is a negation excluding "P" is obvious; but what makes it different from other propositions excluding "P" is precisely that they mutually exhaust the field. Their exhaustiveness is expressed in the Law of the Excluded Middle and their mutual exclusiveness in the Law

75. Kneale and Kneale, *Development of Logic*; cf. chap. XIII, sec. 6 (b) of this volume.

76. The discussion of "deduction" has tended to confuse (a) identifying "basic" modes of inference, and ordering rules of inference, with (b) considering the strategies for the discovery of new modes of proof, i.e., heuristics. Both areas are of concern to cognitive psychologists; cf. chap. V, sec. 1, n. 4, of this volume.

of Non-Contradiction. Without this mutual exhaustiveness there is no way of explaining the difference between contraries and contradictories—that is, the difference between the relation of "It is red" to "It is not red" and the relation of "It is red" to "It is green". Indeed, without the conception of negation, whether in the form "Not-P" or "It is not the case that P", it is not possible to conceive of two propositions as contraries or as excluding each other, since to be contrary is to imply the negation.

Yet without this understanding of negation there is no basis for regarding the two logical laws named or the two forms of *reductio* as having a special status in systems of deduction. Both then belong to a logic which allows an explicit use of a genuine negation—that is, with "Not-P" being understood as a proposition on a level with "P" and not understood as a second-order, metalogical, or epistemic statement about the proposition "P". This will be a logic which allows use of the Law of the Excluded Middle whenever a proposition has genuine negation, the logic encapsulated in Gentzen's second system of natural deduction. Of course, when a genuine negation exists and the law of the Excluded Middle applies, first, there are always certain presuppositions—for instance, as to the existence of the subject-matter, or as to John having been beating his wife; and second, predicates have to be germane to a particular subject-matter so that enquiries as to whether or not a predicate applies to a certain thing are of a such kind as to be sensible, and the subject-matter has to exist (we do not inquire whether or not all dragons breathe fire, or whether or not the natural number four is under the table). Such a logic applies to one subject-matter at a time, not within a general theory of all things and all sets of things.

Rather than treating the two forms of *reductio* differently in the normal logic applicable to speech in natural languages, one should distinguish a limited part of logic which depends on the notion of implication only and is, as it were, negation-free (or more accurately, negation independent or invariant), so that when "¬ P" is written it is understood as an implicitly second-order, metalogical, or epistemic proposition with some meaning like "P implies an absurdity", "There is a disproof of P", or "P is absurd", so that negation as found in natural languages is not represented. Intuitionist logic, as represented by Gentzen's first system of natural deduction, nicely encapsulates this limited, negation-free part of logic. The intuitionists took this position to avoid nonconstructive proofs of "Some A is F" from proofs that "'All A's are (¬ F)' is absurd", in particular the case of infinite or indefinite sets discussed in chapter IV. One could contrast an "implicative" logic which embraced *modus ponens* and Gentzen's "and" and "or" introduction and elimination rules, along with the commutative, associative, and distributive laws (but excluded "or" elimination by the disjunctive syllogism whereby one infers "P" from "P or Q" and a disproof of "Q"),[77] with the intuitionist system, considering the latter as an extension of such a merely implicative logic in order to embrace the notion of absurdity.

As I indicated in chapter IV, as an alternative to intuitionism, we should draw on some less general principle to exclude the inference to "Some A is F" from a proof that "All A's are (¬ F)" is absurd in the case of sets which are demonstrably not finite. The question for the mathematician should not be that of the sense of negation but, as we have seen in chapters II and IV, of how one is to interpret generalizations over sets which are demonstrably nonfinite, and of the meaning of such terms as "finite", "infinite", and "non-denumerable".

As we have seen, applications of the Law of the Excluded Middle, "P or Not-P", are rarely tautologies, because of presuppositions of existence. However, the law of bivalence, "Either the assertion P is true or the assertion P is not true", which is one of the applications of the Law of the Excluded Middle, has been held to be valid. Rejecting assertions is quite different from denying them by asserting their negations, since if a presupposition is false, the negation is also untrue, and likewise in the case of "The number four is under the table", and also because some assertions, such as conditionals, do not have negations, but yet may be rightly rejected as not true.

"Not-P" is a first-order statement, but "The assertion P is not true", "P is absurd", "P does not have a proof", and "P has a disproof" are all of them second-order statements. Logicians have no power to make second-order operators into first-order ones by fiat.

This fact is reflected in grammar, where the subject is modified by a determiner (for instance, a quantifier) and the verb is distinguished by being the bearer of tense, by agreement with the subject, and by being what is modified by negation. In Chomskyan grammar speculations have arisen as to whether agreement dominates tense (or vice versa), and whether negation dominates tense (or vice versa).[78] None of these speculations leave it quite undoubted that negation is clause-internal, never a second-order operator like "It is certain that" or "It is provable that", and not an indicator of force.

(c) *The way grammar marks negation is very varied*

For Old English, Old High German, and Old French, the insertion of the single negative particle *ne* before the finite verb was enough to achieve the negation of the statement. But, in all three cases, for emphasis, because this particle *ne* was phonologically weak, it came to be supplemented with other

77. Griss's negation-free logic should be considered in this context.

78. See Cook and Newson, *Chomsky's Universal Grammar*, 181–85; cf. 208–15.

words which possessed or took on negative significance, these changes taking place over long periods during which several idioms were acceptable. Thus in Old and Middle English one can find up to three indicators of negation within the same statement, none canceling the effect of the others, but only reinforcing it. In Middle English it became the norm to reinforce *ne* before the verb by placing some variant of *noht* (from *ne* + *aught*) after the verb, preferably after an auxiliary. Next the particle *ne* disappeared, and *noht* became "not". Then in Modern English the introduction of the empty structural auxiliary "do" enabled the placing of "not" after the finite verb to become universal. In parallel fashion, in German, first in addition to and then instead of a particle before the finite verb, *nicht* or alternative negatives came to be introduced late in the sentence followed only by adverbs of manner, any objects to the verb, and the verb's nonfinite part. With French, if one imagines questions such as "Is he fat?", "Will you go?", and so forth, and answers in the style "No, not a bit", "No, not a step", it is then intelligible how negation came to be expressed in different parts of France with *ne* before the verb and *pas* (step), *point* (point), *mie* (crumb, scrap), *goutte* (drop, bead), *mot* (word), *nois* (hazelnut), *pois* (pea), *espi*, *maille* (a small piece of money), *de* (a die), *bouton* (button), *denier* (penny), *pomme* (apple), *grain* (a grain), *festu*, *nient*, *brin* (blade), and so forth, varying according to dialect, until in modern French only the first two remain acceptable except as deliberate archaisms.[79]

In all these languages, since the negative indicator must have relation to one and only one verbally expressible feature of what is said, one verb kernel, the only essential is clarity in respect of which such kernel it relates to—important in the case of semi-auxiliaries (see chapter XIV). We savored the relative lack of regimentation which this left in Old and Middle English. The near-disappearance of inflections in modern English made it more dependent on dry stone masonry, necessitating stricter rules of configuration, even limiting the placing of adverbials like negation. Yet much is still remarkably free. Thus (a) "They are not all of them swimming" can be expressed, "Not all of them are swimming" or "All of them are not swimming"; and (b) "They are, all of them, not swimming" can be expressed, "None of them is swimming" or "They are none of them swimming", reminiscent of the equivalent "Not one of them is swimming" and "They are, not one of them, swimming".

79. Maurice Grevisse, *Le Bon Usage*, 13th ed. (Paris: Duculot, 1993). The evolution in the use of *pas* is well described in Hopper and Traugott, *Grammaticalization*, 65–66; cf. 117–18.

X

The Gulf between Saying and Naming, the Verbal and the Nominal

"FORCE"-POTENTIAL AS INTEGRAL TO "SENSE"

Section 1. Full Sentences Distinguished from Clauses in General: Relation of Force to Sense

On the face of it every complete "speech"-sentence—that is, something whose identity includes its sense and therefore includes everything relevant to sense arising from its context of utterance—is coordinate to an act of utterance or linguistic deliverance—"cognate" to the speech-act in the sense I explain in chapter XII.[1]

As a result, of its very nature, every such sentence has "force", an idea Frege expressed by the word *Kraft* in his article "Negation".[2] It carries its force as part of its sense or "discourse-significance" (shown precisely in its situation in utterance), force being possessed only by complete speech-units—whether

1. In this work, I uniformly use upper case for "P", "Q", and so forth, even when discussing Wittgenstein's *Tractatus* and Anscombe's *An Introduction*. The latter works, together with Dummett in *Frege*, 318, speaking in reference to the *Tractatus*, and Geach in reference to Frege's doctrine, use lower case for "p", "q", and so forth. In other contexts, Geach and Dummett do not maintain uniform practice.

2. Where Frege, "Negation", translated by P. T. Geach in *Frege: Translations*, ed. Geach and Black, has "assertively", the original, "Die Verneinung", *Beitrage zur Philosophie des deutschen Idealismus* 1 (1919), has "with assertive force", with *Kraft* as the word for "force" ("Die Verneinung", 145–46); cf. "Negation", 120, 123, 127, 129, which also has "assertoric force" and "assertorically" on 128–29. Compare "this constituent of its [a sentence's] meaning, which, following Frege, we may call its assertoric "force", in Dummett, *Frege*, 302–3.

statements, commands, questions, suppositions, or wishes. For, in the way we explained in chapter III, the sense of a sentence is best taken to mean its "direction", its discourse-significance as speech or *parole*, arising with language at the level of actual use, embracing every public aspect of meaning, rather than in any more restricted sense such as that of Frege's *Sinn*.

Because every clause is a potential sentence, clauses as such have the potentiality of force as part of their sense, and this is why the verb has a special "saying" character, whether it occurs in a clause or a sentence. This insight must not be subverted by sophistry.

(a) *Two ways in which clauses occur and the special character of clauses*

Force belongs to utterances or "sentences" only as taken as wholes in the situation of the speech-act, whether the force be that of a statement, a command, a request, a wish, or some other kind. By contrast, apart from conjunctions, subordinate clauses have no force, even though if they had occurred naked, not embedded, they would each have had their own distinctive force: "I order . . .", "I appoint . . .", "I warn . . .", ". . . shall . . ." (except in the grammatical first person), "the sentence of the court is . . .", and so forth. As embedded they make no statement, give no order, make no appointment, give no warning, establish no law, deliver no court sentence.

We must now consider the implications of this situation for the "sense" or "discourse-significance" of clauses, even when embedded or expressed without commitment.

For it is the peculiarity of clauses among the many different kinds of utterance-constituent that their sense is such that *if* they were to occur alone as complete linguistic deliverances in their own right, *then* they would have force, the kind of force appropriate to a clause of the kind concerned, and that this force would belong to their sense, giving them their "direction" as complete linguistic deliverances—in Wittgenstein's analogy, like arrows. They would then constitute committed linguistic deliverances in their own right, "speech-units", using the word "speech" in a broad sense including linguistic delivery in writing or any other medium as well as speech. Occurring "naked" in this sense will involve occurring linguistically without such intonations as remove the assertoric character of what is said (e.g., the intonations characteristic of rhetorical questions); not in socially recognized "pretend" or fictional contexts such as are provided by novels, dramatic performances, and story-telling; as well as not as a clause embedded and within a complex statement such as a negation, a question, a disjunction, or a conditional.

Thus what distinguishes clauses, whether they occur in any of these special contexts or whether they occur naked, is the fact that *if* they were to have occurred naked, or had so occurred, or if they do occur naked, *then* the force appropriate to a committed utterance would have belonged, would belong, or does belong to them automatically, independently of human choice, not by any additional semantic convention.[3] It is part of their sense whether they occur naked or in some special context instead. Nothing has to be added to a clause when it occurs naked in order for it to have the force which it then has—nothing, not even Frege's assertion-sign.[4] Indeed, nothing added would have this effect.[5]

It is not that something pragmatic determines the sense of the clause, but that the sense or semantics of the clause determines its pragmatic role or illocutionary force when it occurs naked. The sense of a clause when it occurs naked as an utterance in its own right remains unchanged, but its special role and force arise immediately from its sense as a clause.

The fact that if a clause occurs embedded, it has none of the force which it would have if it had occurred naked, does not imply that its sense changes if from being embedded it becomes unembedded or if from being unembedded it becomes embedded. I assert, "Caesar conquered Gaul" and at another time assert, "Because Caesar conquered Gaul, he had the strength to become master of Rome", or "If Caesar had not conquered Gaul, he would not have had the strength to become master of Rome", and there is no difference in the sense of "Caesar conquered Gaul" on its three occurrences. In order to understand what a clause means when it occurs embedded in the context of a more extended sentence, its sense within the context of this larger utterance, we have to understand what its significance would be if it were to occur naked. It would be foolish to suppose that one could understand the sense of "P" and "Q" as they occur in "If P, then Q" so as to understand "If P, then Q", if one did not understand what "P" and "Q" would each mean if they occurred separately. And in the case of truth-functional utterances such as "P and Q", the same is true. The sense which the clause has when it occurs embedded is just such a sense as would cause it to have assertoric force *if* it had occurred or did occur unembedded, naked, as an assertion.

Further, as I argued in chapter III, it is because of its distinctively verbal character that a clause is precisely that kind of sentence constituent whose sense is such that when it occurs naked, it will have force.[6] And understanding

3. I discuss this suggestion of Dummett and Searle in secs. 4 and 5 (b) of this chapter.

4. Wittgenstein insisted upon this; cf. sec. 2. Dummett shows awareness of the point in *Frege*, 302; cf. 298, 311. Thus we can set aside Frege's primary initial reason for introducing the assertion-sign; Dummett, *Frege*, 310–11. See my general discussion of Dummett's position in sec. 4, and see Dummett, *Frege*, 308.

5. If one added an assertion-sign, or the word "probably", or (perversely) a negation-sign, to every naked indicative clause occurring on its own, it would make no difference to the sense. A sign or convention which alters nothing is redundant, like an expletive.

6. A parallel point applies in respect of predicates as things possibly "true of" subjects. As the sense of

this enables us to grasp the essential connection between the "saying" character of complete utterances, the fact that they possess illocutionary force, and the "verbal" character of clauses, whether embedded or naked.

(b) *Subordinate clauses are quasi-sentential because of their close link with communication*

Clauses are special in that, in their semantic character, they have a strategic role in the maintenance of the connection between what we say and its relation to communication. If, for instance, we were to use a relative clause and command someone to "Eject anyone who is drunk from the premises", we would be implicitly envisaging the possibility of there being someone drunk on the premises, a possibility we could express by the assertion, "Perhaps there will be someone drunk on the premises", and the intelligibility of either the command or the assertion would depend upon our capacity to understand the assertion, "There is someone drunk on the premises", if it were made.

(c) *The verbal character shared by sentences, clauses, predicates, and finite verbs*

It is this link with the act of communication which sets sentences, clauses, and, along with them, predicates and what have been called "live" verbs in contrast with phrases of a nominal character. It is also the clue to why it is that we learn verbs and appreciate the verbal framework of sentences in such a different way from that in which we learn names and name-like expressions, the contrast we saw in chapter IX, section 3.

Once we are released from thinking of the "force" of an utterance as something external to its "sense", or even something requiring to be added to it (to be indicated by special signs or understood dependently upon a separate set of semantic conventions), we can connect up two doctrines of Frege, which for him were quite separate: first, the doctrine that force is something which can only belong to complete utterances, and second, the doctrine that propositions must have parts which are "incomplete" or "unsaturated".

---

a clause is understood from the sense it would have if it occurred naked, so the sense of a linguistic predicate is understood from the sense it would have if actually predicated, asserting something in regard to a subject. There is an ambiguity here: Geach argues that in "If gambling is bad, inviting people to gamble is bad", one *predicates* "bad" of these kinds of act, whether or not one also *asserts* gambling to be bad; Geach, "Ascriptivism", 253: in *Logic Matters* (Oxford: Blackwell; Berkeley: University of California Press, 1972), 250–54. However, if one did not understand what it means to predicate "bad" assertively, one would not understand the meaning of the predicate "bad" in predications of "bad" in embedded contexts; cf. Searle, *Speech Acts*, 122–23.

According to the second of these doctrines, such "unsaturated" predicative or verbal elements or features are essential to the grammatical realization of syntactic connection—that is, essential to the clause's "holding together" (in Frege's phrase). It is such "incomplete" or "unsaturated" predicative or verbal elements or features which make the unities to which they give structure—namely, the clauses, eligible, if they occur naked, to constitute complete utterances. Thus it is this semantic feature, identified in chapter IX, of being given their structure by an essentially incomplete verbal or predicative element or feature which makes the clause eligible to take on the pragmatic role of a complete utterance—that is, of a carrier of force. As one might express it, it is by combining or synthesizing verbs (*rhēmata*) with names or nouns (*onomata*) that one says something (a *logos* or saying being formed)—as opposed to naming anything or denoting it—to take up the ideas of Plato and Aristotle.

Both Geach and Dummett introduce a technical notion of "sense" applicable to only propositions and propositional contents, a "sense" they think can be isolated from other elements in the "meaning" of sentences, including force. However, as I show in section 4, this inescapably reopens the way to treating sentences as identifying and thereby providing designations of "senses", thereby reintroducing a mythology of "senses" as objects.

(d) *Truth and assertoric force*

The main consideration influencing Geach and Dummett is their view that it is to propositions, or what I call propositional clauses, and not to assertions or committed utterances of any kind, that truth and falsity primarily belong. Against this I argue that truth applies to beliefs and judgments just as much as to assertions or statements.

For "true" and "false" are terms of evaluation like "valid", as I recognized in chapter III. Whereas we use the word "valid" in regard to arguments and reasons, the words "true" and "false" are used in evaluating statements, beliefs, judgments, and thoughts.[7] That is, a judgment as to whether something is true or false is of its nature a second-order act or state in regard to whether or not a statement that P, belief that P, judgment that P, or thought that P has obtained its goal in respect of its direction (i.e., as to whether it has the direction it ought to have in regard to the question whether or not P)—in Anscombe's terms, it is a judgment as to whether it is "P" or whether it is "Not P" which is the "winning move". The role of judgments like "It is true that P" is to give an evaluation of statements, beliefs, judgments, and thoughts that P, judging

7. Cf. my discussion of how saying "is true that" essentially involves positive evaluation, in chap. III, sec. 2 (a) (i) of this volume, unlike "is the case that".

"that the statement [belief, judgment, or thought] that P is true", not merely directly to judge "that P". This latter we do more simply by asserting "P". Accordingly, while I insist that the ascription of truth or falsity to asserted sentences, "assertions", or "statements" is prior to its ascription to unasserted clauses, or to their meanings or contents, developing this argument in section 3, I give no priority to its ascription to statements over its ascription to, for instance, beliefs or judgments.

Not just any thought can be subject of truth or falsity: for instance, we can have thoughts which express intentions, imperatives, supposings, or drawing conclusions, such as "I will go running", "I must get some cabbage", "Suppose that I get some cabbage", and "Perhaps I shall get some cabbage". These are statement-like because they express thoughts, but are not actually statements. What makes an utterance, act of mind, or state of mind capable of being a subject of truth or falsity? I answer that it is having regard to a matter in respect of which one could have the same belief at different times in a way reflected in the tensing of such cross-temporal disputes as when one person says at one time, "It *is* necessary that I get some cabbage" and somebody later disputes this with him and says, "It *was* not necessary for you to get some cabbage".[8] For instance, whether or not at a certain time I gave the order to go on a certain mission, which is a matter for belief or judgment in response to a question, is what determines whether statements beforehand that I will give this order, or at the time that I am giving this order,[9] or afterwards that I did give the order are true or false.

What determines the truth or falsity of statements equally determines the truth or falsity of beliefs and judgments in response to a question.[10]

(e) *The primacy of assertion in the use of language*

The reason why, in considering force, it should always be assertions that philosophers take as their guide is closely connected with their capacity for truth.

In Dummett's account satisfaction-conditions in relation to commands are analogous to truth-conditions in the case of statements.[11] His idea is that

8. This gives the notion of belief or assent a certain definitional or explanatory priority (taking the most general notion of belief, not implying any tentativeness, and not implying the absence of knowledge). I first developed this point about cross-temporal questions and belief in relation to the definition of the notion of "statement" in David Braine, "Explanation and Modality" (bachelor's thesis, Oxford University, 1965).

9. I am in Aberdeen, and two people in London, forewarned by copies of the same message, might say, "He is just now giving the order".

10. A judgment has the nature of a response to a question. Therefore, although judging normally proceeds from deliberation, in its widest sense it extends even to judgments evident without argument, such as "2 + 2 = 4", or statements of one's intentions, opinions, or pains.

11. Dummett argued this in "Truth", and again in *Frege*, chaps. 5 and 10.

in thinking and making statements we aim at truth and in giving orders aim at obedience, and the truth of "X will do my shopping" and the satisfaction of the command "X, do my shopping" are both consequent upon X's having done my shopping. Truth of statement and satisfaction of command are both consequent upon what is the case or the fact.

However, the statement and the command are differently related to the fact. Whereas the fact is directly cognate to being stated, its structural relation to commanding is more complex. The statement "X has done my shopping" states this as if it were a fact (to state that it is a fact that X has done my shopping adds nothing to the original statement). By contrast, the command is directed towards bringing it about that "X has done my shopping" is a fact. In brief, the structure of commanding is more complex than that of stating, involving an implicit causative structure, grammatically explicit when expressed by means of a "causative verb". In effect I state, "X will do my shopping", but I command, "Bring it about that you, X, have done my shopping". As a result the notion of satisfaction in regard to commands has to be explained in terms presupposing the notions used to explain the truth of statements (or their lack of truth).

Philosophers commonly treat "imperatives" or "commands" globally, embracing both "commands" in the strict sense and requests, both instructions to do things and instructions to see to it that they are done. In the latter wide sense, "commands" (sometimes expressed in the form "Let ...") overlap with expressions of intention and with wishes. The declaration of will, "Let God destroy them" is not far different from the wish, "May God destroy them", which may have the real meaning, "May you, God, destroy them". But all these are parasitic upon the assertoric in the same way as properly causative cases. If we do not have "Make it be that P", then we have "Let it be that P" or "May it be that P" (= Permit it to be that P, or Would that P). And the "basis" in all these cases, "P", has to be assertoric ("indicative") in underlying form, and we assess the satisfaction or fulfillment of such commands, dispositions of will, or wishes in terms of the truth or falsity of "P" as an assertion; that is, "P" has to be assertoric not just in form, but also in function or role—that is, as it would be understood if actually in use as a statement, "proposition", or "assertoric sentence".[12]

In sum assertoric discourse holds a certain primacy in all discourse (grammatically reflected in the primacy of the indicative among grammatical

12. The use of the word "mood" in describing the grammars of different languages is a poor guide to philosophical analysis, because this word marks such heterogeneous types of distinction. Thus the distinction between the interrogative and the indicative is of a quite different kind than that between the imperative and the indicative. Most uses of the subjunctive in English arise from distinctions in respect of measures of likelihood, certainty, or uncertainty; but other languages express the same meanings in quite different morphosyntactic forms—e.g., in a "conditional mood"; morphosyntactic distinctions are ill-aligned with semantic differences.

moods), somewhat as the present holds primacy among tenses.[13] In each case there is a primary or paradigm mode of speech which may be considered unmarked in use, a mode of speech in relation to which others are marked in the act of use (morphologically or otherwise), differentiating them in this way or that from the primary or paradigm mode of speech.

Section 2. Disagreements about Force: Wittgenstein's Opposition to Frege

(a) *The historical roots of the separation of force from sense*

Frege's thinking about force had two main elements. First, there is the element highlighted by Geach according to which, when I assert "P", "P" has assertoric force, whereas "P" does not have this force as it occurs embedded, as when I assert "It is not the case that P", "If P, then Q", "If R, then P", or "P or Q"—or ask "Is it the case that P?" But second, questions, stipulative definitions, and, above all, the sentences occurring in fiction and drama all lack assertoric force,[14] in contrast, in his view, with statements, commands, and wishes, which Frege thought of as all alike having assertoric force, expressing thoughts or *Gedanken*, the contents of inner acts of mind, which we could consider whether or not we agreed or assented to them.[15] By contrast Geach would deny assertoric force to commands and wishes.

At this stage I should enter a caveat. Austin had none of Frege and Geach's concern with what we should say about unasserted clauses and developed his ideas about force and meaning independently of Frege. Instead, his design was to give systematic development to the idea of different kinds of speech-act, germs of which are to be found in the later Wittgenstein. For him, such performative acts as saying, "I marry you" or "I appoint you Governor", commands, wishes, expressions of intention, promises, verdicts, warnings, and statements are each expressions of different kinds of speech-act, each with its own distinctive kind of "illocutionary force".[16] The force is *il*-locutionary because it

13. When linguists distinguish tense, mood, and aspect, the word "tense" is used to refer to distinctions of time, not of aspect. In most languages simple or aorist formations have priority in meaning (besides being unmarked morphologically except for time) over perfective and imperfective formations, and in perfective formations time and aspect are often inseparable.

14. Dummett, *Frege*, 308–11.

15. This was Frege's final view in "Negation", extending his view of assertions to questions; Dummett, *Frege*, 307–8. For Frege, in assertions and questions, as well, we might add, as in suppositions, the sense is a thought, whereas in imperative the sense is a command.

16. Austin's ideas spread long before publication, and their influence can be seen in R. M. Hare, *The Language of Morals* (Oxford: Oxford University Press, 1949). Austin's uncertainties affected his followers; see Note A appended to this chapter and nn. 86 and 88.

Searle, "Austin", 406, seems to imagine that a "serious literal utterance" of "I am going to do it" could, in

belongs to the act of speech intrinsically, as characterizing what one does *in* saying what one says—by contrast with what one may contrive to achieve *by* (by means of) such a speech-act, its *per*-locutionary aspects.

True, questions, stipulations, fictional utterances, commands, and wishes lack *assertoric* force. And this view of *assertoric* force has become standard among philosophers and linguists, reflected in Lyons and Searle. For them, conjunctions, negations, disjunctions, and conditionals are kinds of assertion, all sharing assertoric force, whereas suppositions, questions, commands, and wishes have each a different type of force.

To this account of speech-acts and to linguistic theory, the assumption that "force" and "sense" are entirely external to each other is an irrelevancy left over from Frege.

(b) *Wittgenstein's rejection of the separation of force from sense*

For Frege it was a datum that negation is something internal to a proposition, but because he thought of assertoric force as external to the proposition and negation as internal to it, this involved an asymmetry between assertoric force and negation.

By contrast, for Wittgenstein affirmation or assertion is as internal to the proposition as negation: "Every proposition must already have a sense; assertion (affirmation) cannot give it one".[17] As Guy Stock put it to me, affirmation

---

Austin's view, uttered in the same context according to the same linguistic conventions in respect of meaning, have the same "meaning" whether it had the force of a promise, a prediction, a threat, a warning, or a statement of intention. But Austin, *How to Do Things with Words*, 100, makes it plain that although the differences in "force" were not typically or generally marked by the phrase "the meanings of words", we would speak of them as differences in "meaning". For Austin, illocutionary acts cannot be classified absolutely precisely; cf. *How to Do Things with Words*, 93, 98, referring to "a not quite definite meaning".

The recognition of the fact that nuances of force belong to "meaning" in the ordinary sense is very clear in Dummett, *Frege*, 298–300, 302: "the fact that the sentence expresses an act of assertion is as much a matter of linguistic convention as is its having the sense it has (in Frege's use of the word 'sense')"; and, in regard to sentences which can be used to perform more than one of a number of linguistic acts, "what constitutes my meaning the sentence ['You will learn a sonnet'] in any one of these ways [as a prediction, as an expression of my intention, or as a command] is my intention to be understood as performing that one of these linguistic acts"; Dummett, *Frege*, 300.

17. Wittgenstein, *Tractatus*, 4.064. Here, as Anscombe observes in *An Introduction*, 58–59, Wittgenstein is attacking Frege's idea that in judging we "advance from a thought to a truth value", as can be seen from the immediately preceding argument in 4.063, and was the background of his remark in 4.442 on the meaninglessness of Frege's assertion-sign or "judgement-stroke"; see Frege, "Sense and Reference", in *Translations from Frege*, ed. Geach and Black, 65. *Tractatus* 4.063 ends with the remark that "the verb of a proposition is not 'is true' or 'is false', as Frege thought: rather, that which 'is true' must already contain the verb". Frege's distinction between the assertion-sign expressing force and the propositional content, or sense, reappears in Hare's later distinction in *Language of Morals* between "neustic", what indicates assent or dissent in respect of a content, either that it was true or false, or that it was prescribed or to be avoided, and "phrastic", meaning the expression signifying this content.

Strictly speaking, the assertion-sign in a properly Fregean account could not be a linguistic sign within a sentence, since any such expression would be part of the expression of a sense, which the assertion-sign is

has to be internal to the proposition in order for negation to be able to reverse it. A sense is like a direction: thus, in *Tractatus* 4.461, Wittgenstein says, "Tautologies and contradictions are without-sense (*sinnlos*). (Like a point from which two arrows go out in opposite directions to each other.) (E.g., I know nothing about the weather when I know that it is either raining or not raining.)". He at once goes on in 4.4611 to say, "Tautologies and contradictions are not, however, unmeaning (*unsinnig*); they belong to the symbolism, but like 'o' belongs to the symbolism of arithmetic".[18]

Accordingly, "P" and "Not-P" have different senses, the one a function of the other (5.2341). In 4.0641 (b) and (c), he says:

> (b) The negating proposition ["Not-P"] determines a logical place different from that of the negated proposition ["P"]. The negating proposition determines a logical place with the help of the logical place of the negated proposition. For it describes it as lying outside the latter's logical place. [In effect, if "P" meant "inside Australia's coastline", "Not-P" would mean "outside Australia's coastline"].
>
> (c) The negated proposition can be negated again [i.e., having denied "P" we can go on and deny "Not-P"], and this in itself shows that what is negated [respectively, "P" and "Not-P"] is already a proposition, and not merely something that is preliminary to a proposition.

All the time he is thinking of complete utterances—that is, in (b) when he speaks of the negated proposition "P" he is thinking of the utterance of which the negating proposition "Not-P" is the denial, and not thinking of "P" as a clause within "Not-P"; and in (c) when he speaks of how the negated proposition can be negated again it is clear that he is not saying that "P", which was described as the particular negated proposition discussed in (b), can be negated, since that would only give one "Not-P" and so no new point would be being made, but rather he is saying that any negated proposition can be negated even if it is the result of negating something else, so that one can negate (i.e., deny) "Not-P" to get "Not-(Not-P)".

The word *Satz* as it occurs in Frege and Wittgenstein is one whose basic meaning in German is "sentence", and this meaning is evident when Frege speaks of interrogative sentences. However, Frege speaks of *Satz* in many places where he and other logicians of his time speak of a judgment or a proposition, and in the *Tractatus* Wittgenstein uses *Satz* as his almost invariable word for proposition.[19] In *Tractatus* 3.5 he states, "a propositional sign, ap-

---

not. The assertion-sign is equivalent to a convention whereby the expression of a sense (where this sense is a "thought") occurring naked (on its own in an unspecialized context) is taken assertively; cf. Dummett, *Frege*, 300.

18. If we compare ways of being intentionless or directionless, a self-defeating plan would be *sinnlos*, while fidgeting would be *unsinnig*.

19. Twice we meet the ordinary word for "statement" (*Aussage*) in apparently the same meaning as

plied and thought through, is a thought", and in *Tractatus* 4, "a thought is a *Satz* (proposition) with a sense (direction)", in 4.001 adding that "the totality of *Sätze* (sentences, propositions) is speech (*Sprache*)". It is plain that wherever *Sprache* appears in the *Tractatus* it means speech (*parole*) in the linguists' sense, and this confirms that we should think of Wittgenstein's *Sätze* (propositions) as among things spoken.

This fits exactly with the idea that for Wittgenstein propositions are symbols with a sense (3.326), not just signs such as might be *unsinnig* (unmeaning marks). The fact that for him propositions are complete utterances is made even clearer by his discussion of truth-functions. For him "Not-(P or Q)", "(Not-P) and (Not-Q)", and any other truth-function of "P" and "Q" equivalent to them all count as notational variants of the same proposition,[20] so that here as elsewhere it is clear that by a particular truth-function he means a particular utterance with a particular sense or direction (in this case opposite to the sense or direction of "P or Q").

Earlier (3.144), Wittgenstein had said, "Situations can be described but not identified (given names). (Names are like points; propositions like arrows—they have sense.)"

In brief, what has sense or "direction" (*Sinn*) is not an object. The proposition (a complete linguistic expression in use, not a mere clause in a disjunction, or occurring in any other subordinate way) leaves no room for supplementation by an assertion-sign, as if the proposition signified something and the assertion-sign did the asserting or saying of this something. We need not state the matter in terms of Wittgenstein's picture theory whereby a proposition *shows* its sense, but can instead say that it *expresses* its sense, and we can say that what it says and what it expresses are the same—namely, that things stand as the proposition says that they stand. In any case he does not allow his picture theory to override the underlying insight we have just stated. He says that a sense is what a proposition shows, but what it shows is "how things stand if it is true", and what it says is "that they do so stand" (4.022). In thinking or saying, "'P' says 'P'" (5.542).

In this Wittgenstein is of course simply reinstating the natural way of thinking, for when we think of two "propositions" as contradicting each other we think of them as "assertions" or "statements", not as things unasserted: indeed, unless they are considered as asserted or affirmed, they are not available to be said to be contradicted.[21] What we have to recognize is that both stating,

Satz, and we meet the verbs "state" and "judge" in their natural connection with propositions, e.g., "A judges 'p'"; Wittgenstein, *Tractatus*, 5.5442.

20. Cf. Anscombe, *An Introduction*, 61–63.

21. Ryle, "Are there Propositions?", no. 2 in *Collected Essays*, 37–38 under (3); cf. 26 under (6); first published in *Proceedings of the Aristotelian Society* 30 (1930).

or asserting, and denying are speech-acts (in Austin's terminology, "illocutionary acts"): in stating, asserting, or affirming that one is not a bastard, one denies that one is a bastard, and vice versa.[22] "The accused is a bastard" and "The accused is not a bastard" have a symmetrical relationship to the question "Is the accused a bastard?", and so Frege was wrong in holding that asserting and denying are in no way parallel to each other. The argument that they cannot each be a kind of speech-act and that denying cannot constitute a distinctive illocutionary force, because affirmations and denials are not mutually exclusive classes,[23] is useless because it is anyway quite plain that classes of illocutionary act need not be mutually exclusive, since here denials are simply a subclass of affirmation (the affirmations of negations), just as some statements are warnings as well as statements, and some are commendations as well as statements (as with "Jim is very knowledgeable about fisheries").[24]

(c) *A point of agreement in the area under dispute*

In order to adopt a vocabulary neutral in regard to the disputes about the nature of "propositions" discussed later and to clarify discussion, I will speak of "propositional clauses" where Geach and others speak of "propositions". What both Geach and I have in view are linguistic entities of some kind.

Geach is right to insist that these "propositional clauses" (his "propositions") must not be regarded as mere strings of words.[25] For the same "proposition" or "propositional clause", although a linguistic entity of some kind, may appear in different guises. Thus, with all such propositional clauses we

22. I do not say that all acts of affirming, asserting, or stating are acts of denying for two reasons: first, because it seems plausible that there are some intrinsically affirmative propositions, even if there are no "atomic" propositions in the sense of the *Tractatus*, and second, because it is difficult to say what asserting "If P, Q" would be a denial of.

23. This mistake of Frege in "Negation" reappears in Dummett, *Frege*, 316–21.

24. The fact that the classes of warning and commending overlap with the class of stating has often been ignored.

The warning I give to a passing rambler "There is a bull in that field" is a statement, even if, following Austin, we say that my utterance "I warn you that there is a bull in that field" is a warning, but not a statement. Yet if in touring my farm with a BBC Radio 4 correspondent for the "On Your Farm" program, I say "There is a bull in that field", I make a statement but am not occupied in giving a warning. Likewise, if I tell a general audience, "This person's act of bravery made him worthy of the Victoria Cross", I praise or commend the man as well as making a statement, even though the utterance "I commend this person for the act of bravery which made him worthy of the Victoria Cross" would be a commendation rather than a statement. Yet if I say, "This person's act of bravery made him worthy of the Victoria Cross," in table conversation with my wife, I am probably just recounting a bit of history, not making a commendation.

The clauses "I warn you that there is a bull in that field" and "I commend this person for the act of bravery which made him worthy of the Victoria Cross" as propositional clauses are true or false dependent on whether I gave such a warning or made such a commendation, and are about me, not solely about alleged bulls or acts of bravery.

25. Cf. Geach, "Kinds of Statement", essay 14 in *Intention and Intentionality: Essays in Honour of G. E. M. Anscombe*, ed. Cora Diamond and Jenny Teichman (Ithaca, N.Y.: Cornell University Press, 1979), 221–35.

have to be able to recognize the "P" and the "Q" which appear as antecedent and consequent in "If P, then Q" when they appear again, for instance, in "P", "Q", "If it were not the case that Q, then it would not be the case that P", "Is it the case that P?", and so forth, for example, to recognize them whether they are expressed in the indicative or the subjunctive so as to be able to deal with various kinds of conditional. And beyond this, we understand them as predicatively structured and tensed, for instance, so as to handle the alternations between first- and second-person inflections on the verb (or between "I/me" and "thou/thee", or in modern idiom "you") in a dialogue, as well as relations of tense between yesterday's question and today's answer to it (consider dialogue by letter). And just as we had to apply Gibson's ideas in order to develop a theory of perception which allows us to "directly perceive" the same dog sitting, lying, walking, or running, so we need to use the same ideas in a yet more sophisticated way in order to recognize the same underlying "propositional clause" whether in the indicative or the subjunctive, with subject and verb inverted or the object given prominence by being mentioned first, and through any other variations consequent on changes in temporal or spatial vantage point, and other clause and speech-act interconnecting relations which pragmatic and semantic relations introduce. Thus, in general, as we saw in chapter III, the idea of phrases, and utterances composed of them, as just strings of words is part of a false theory of perception, and to understand how speaking with understanding and hearing with understanding are possible, we need to envisage pragmatics, semantics, and grammar as inseparable.

Section 3. Geach's Arguments

The possibility of seeing the special significance of the fact that saying is quite unlike naming or referring has been obscured when philosophers or linguists come to treat "force" and "sense" as external to each other and treat this externality as axiomatic in the interpretation of speech. This results from confusions with which I deal in these final sections. These arise whenever linguists regard force as external to sense at the level of the complete sentence or utterance, often also taking sentences, subordinate clauses, and "verbal phrases" as items which can be considered in isolation as if put together by dry stone masonry rather than articulated together in a unity in a context. It is then as if sentences were formed from certain constituents, and at some stage, some clause, simple or complex, having been formed, the human being performed the "speech-act" of giving delivery to this clause, force being given to the clause in the act of communicating so that force has to be considered external to sense.

The same consequences arise with the adoption of certain presumptions about truth and falsity shared by Frege, Geach, and Dummett. I examine Geach first, because his arguments give the purest presentation of the account prevalent today.

(a) *Geach's fallacies*

Geach differs from Frege in regard to commands and wishes, but still draws on his idea that a judgment or assertion must be distinguished from its content, which is the "thought" (*Gedanke*) or sense expressed. It is this supposed "content" which we may judge, assent to, or assert, or which we may "entertain", consider, or question as to its truth. And it is primarily the linguistic entities Geach and Frege call "propositions", appearing in discourse as propositional clauses, not assertions or statements as such, to which propositional contents or "senses" are ascribed. And it is these propositional clauses and their contents, independently of assertion or assent, which he regards as the primary subjects of truth and falsity, and not statements as things asserted, not beliefs, nor judgments, nor anything else implying an attitude in speech or mind.

Such is the "Frege-point" on which Peter Geach has laid such emphasis,[26] underlying his insistence that there must be an element in the speech-meaning of complete utterances which is neutral as to force—an element which he calls "sense", using this word from common discourse to translate Frege's term *Sinn*. Truth and falsity, on this view, belong primarily to clauses in virtue of such "sense".

To many Geach's argument has seemed irresistible.

You make a statement. I question it. Clearly, as I question it, I do not in the same act state it. Therefore (the argument runs) the "it" which I am questioning and which could be supposed, entertained, pondered, or denied, instead of asserted or assented to, cannot be your statement, but must be the "proposition" ("propositional clause"), with the sense, the thought, the propositional content it expresses.

Geach's position involves two things. First, distinguishing an assertion from a clause of the kind which would be an assertion if it occurred in naked use, he associates the title "proposition" with the latter. Second, he insists that truth and falsity belong primarily to "propositions" in this sense.

His view is that what occurs in an unasserted way—for instance, as the antecedent in a conditional statement or as something questioned—must *in its own right*, unasserted, be capable of being said to be true and capable of being said to be false.

26. Geach, "Assertion", in *Logic Matters*, 254–69; first published in *Philosophical Review* 74 (1965).

However, this position cannot be right.

The most obvious reason is that what defines truth is the fact that it is the goal one is seeking when one asks a question sincerely wanting an answer, the object of desire in intellectual enquiry.[27] Because the possession of truth in knowledge is the good or goal of the intellect, it is to true assertions or statements, true beliefs, true judgments, and so forth—that is, to acts of intellect and their expressions, not to unasserted clauses—that truth primarily belongs; for a statement, belief, judgment, or other act of assent to be false is for it to fail of this goal in the most direct way.

To disentangle the issues concerned, let us examine Geach's argument:

> Nor can the idea of only statements's having truth value be reconciled with truth-functional logic by saying that the truth value of a disjunctive sentence used to make a statement in a given context is a function of the truth values that the disjunct would have had if they had been separately used to make statements in the same context. For this is not even plausible unless we mean by "the truth values that the disjuncts would have had" those that they would have had if *without change of sense* they had been used to make statements in the given contexts. But if we can tell what truth values the disjuncts would have had, given the sense they actually had in the context of their occurrence, then a denial that they actually had truth values is quite empty; it just evinces a determination not to *call* unasserted propositions "true" or "false", and this is what Professor Anthony Flew has aptly called a conventionalist sulk.[28]

However, the last sentences of his argument are empty rhetoric. He says, "But if we can tell what truth values the disjuncts would have had, given the sense they actually had in the context of their occurrence, then a denial that they actually had truth values is quite empty; it just evinces a determination not to *call* unasserted propositions 'true' or 'false'". Yet such a determination is reasonable, and one can only tell what truth-values to assign to the disjuncts for the purposes of drawing up a truth-table and working out the truth-value of the disjunction by considering what truth-values the disjuncts would have held if they had occurred naked, directly asserted. And it is only through this that we can know "the sense they actually have in the context of their occurrence"—that is, as embedded, and therefore nothing is to be added by *asserting* that the disjuncts as they occur embedded as disjuncts actually have truth-values, and it is *this* assertion which is empty. For, in order to judge whether a disjunct "P" has the truth-value "true", we have to judge whether the statement or assertion "P" is true. Thus Geach's method of argument is self-defeating.

27. Cf. Dummett, "Truth", 2–4, and Bernard Mayo, "Belief and Constraint".
28. Geach, "Assertion", 258–59.

Thus my position stands—namely, that truth and falsity are primarily the properties of statements or assertions—that is, primarily the properties of certain "moves in the language game", to use Wittgenstein's later phrase, the properties of certain complete pieces of *parole*. If a statement is true, it is, to follow G. E. M. Anscombe, to be compared with a "winning bet"[29] or, as she describes it later in view of a comparison with games, "a winning move", whereas if it is false, it is "a losing move".[30] Now suppose the statement is complex—namely, "P or Q" considered in a case where we don't know whether "P" or "Q" is true: what are we to say about "P" and "Q", which are evidently not moves in the language-game as played on this occasion? Anscombe therefore raises the question, "with what right, or on what grounds, or again, with a view to expressing what, [do] we use the same symbols in all the columns of the truth-table", since it is only in regard to "P or Q" that we make the assessment "winning move", an assessment which we do not make in regard to "P" or "Q", either or both of which, taken on its own, may be false.[31]

We cannot assign truth-values to either "P" or "Q" just by staring at "P or Q". On the contrary, what we do is to ask whether, if a statement "P" had been true, "P or Q" would have been true or false (answering "true"). That is, for the purpose of drawing up a truth-table, we consider the truth-value of "P" had it occurred on its own, naked, as an assertion, as determining its truth-value in the line of the truth-table under consideration; in that line we represent it as having the truth-value assigned to it as if it had occurred on its own, naked. This answers Anscombe's question without bringing in any doctrine making truth and falsity properties of entities other than assertions, beliefs, or judgments.

Thus we have a perfectly good reason for putting "true" and "false" in the columns for "P" and "Q"—namely, that for the purpose of drawing up a

29. Anscombe, *An Introduction*, 52.

30. Anscombe shows how the problem of the nature of truth and falsity arose in Wittgenstein's thought in Anscombe, *An Introduction*, 51–63, which reveals the difficulties of Geach's position. For Baker and Hacker, the separation of sense and force is one of the key places where modern treatments of language have gone astray, e.g., *Language, Sense and Nonsense*, 11–12, 47–120.

31. Anscombe's own discussion at *An Introduction*, 52, takes the form of comparing saying that "P or Q" is true with its being a winning bet, if P and Q were coins for one or the other to come up heads—envisaging, e.g., the possibilities "First coin Heads, second coin Heads", "First coin Heads, second coin Tails", "First coin Tails, second coin Heads" as all "winning moves", and "First coin Tails, second coin Tails" as a "losing move". Her question then amounts to asking why there should be any relation between the idea of being a winning move and a coin coming up heads. Accordingly she remarks (Anscombe, *An Introduction*, 61), "it may be intuitively obvious that there is no equivocation [in using the words 'true' and 'false' both in connection with 'P or Q' in the final column of the truth-table and in connection with the more elementary 'P' and 'Q', whereas it would not have been natural to put 'win' and 'lose' both in a final column and in the preceding columns in a comparable way of setting out bets].... But our questions were reasonable ones; if there is no way of answering them, and we have just to rely on our intuition, that is of itself an important fact—at any rate, it is important for philosophy [even if not for just getting on with the calculus of truth-tables]".

truth-table we suppose "P" to have had a certain truth-value had it occurred naked—that is, as a statement, and likewise "Q", and set down a line in the truth-table accordingly. More than this does not seem required.[32] Thus answering Anscombe's genuine question does not require any "conventionalist sulk".

(b) *A digression into detail: Geach's arguments analyzed*

Geach's arguments require detailed treatment, even though it takes us on a digression from our main argument. He presents two arguments for regarding force as external to sense, even when propositions occur "naked"—that is, neither embedded in a wider sentential context, nor said in a socially specialized context such as the novel, story-reading, or theater, or merely used as a schoolroom example in teaching language. His first argument, turning on what he calls "the Frege-point", is fundamental, whereas the second, treated in (iv), arises from a mistaken way of handling possibility.

(i) The problem of unasserted clauses

Let us consider any particular example of *modus ponens*:

(1) P
(2) If P then Q
(3) Q

The first argument presents the problem of unasserted clauses (discussed above) in its most direct form. "P" has to have the same sense in (1) and in (2), and it is this "sense" which determines whether "P" is true or false. "P" in (2) is not asserted, and so cannot be rightly described as a statement or assertion; and, he argues, therefore, being a statement cannot be part of its sense as it occurs in (2), so that being a statement cannot be part of its sense as it occurs in (1).

I respond, "Yes, but this is an incomplete account of the matter".

We should say this.

"P" in (1) is an assertion, whereas as a component of (2), "P" is not an assertion, but what we may call a propositional clause. "P" occurring naked

32. Alternatively, one could consider the truth-table as expressing the relationships between the truth-values of the assertions (= statements) "P", "Q" and "P or Q", proceeding as if someone had made such assertions, but this approach seems to depend on a bit of a pretense, since, in often considered examples, "P" or "Q" are things it would be absurd to assert. Or, Wittgenstein may have adopted this approach because things which from the perspective of the *Tractatus* would appear radically absurd, as such as "Queen Anne was starved of green numbers" and "The Good is more identical with the Beautiful" (4.003), are there described as *unsinnig*, meaning "outside speech (*Sprache*)" just as "Kmnpqtbg" is outside it, i.e., not statements or propositions at all, whereas "P and not-P" and "P or not-P" are merely *sinnlos*, statements without sense or direction.

has the force of an assertion, whereas when embedded "P" does not have this force. Yet it has the sense that *if* it occurred naked, it *would* have this force. This sense, *that if it occurred naked, it would have this force,* belongs to "P" equally whether it appears naked, or whether it figures in embedded occurrences. This is not mysterious: it is the clause with its sense, not the assertion *as a complete sentence,* which recurs; but understanding the sense of the clause even when it is embedded includes understanding what force the clause would have if it had stood naked.[33] This makes sense essentially connected with force.

Force is not an extra component within sense as if assertive force were a component of sense present in clauses occurring on their own—that is, as sentences, and absent in clauses occurring embedded in wider sentential contexts. Rather the sense of a propositional clause includes that when it occurs naked—that is, without qualifying context, its sense determines that it has the force of an assertion without further indication or marking needing to be added.

If a propositional clause does occur naked, it needs nothing extra to happen to it—for instance, like "being construed as an assertion" or "being asserted", in order to be an assertion—it has this force, when naked, by itself, needing no special marking such as Frege's assertion-sign. Rather it is nonassertive uses which require marking—either by the sentential context in which the clause is embedded or by the special character of its social context of utterance (e.g., a play or novel).

In sum, sense and reference do not accrue to the constituents of a complete propositional sentence without the force of an assertion accruing to the whole. An unasserted propositional clause requires a context—for instance, the context of a conditional, marking it as unasserted. By contrast, a whole conditional, such as, "If the accused was in Rome at the time of the deed, he did not commit the murder", gains assertoric force from the same context which gives what sense or direction and reference they have to its component expressions. Considered by a grammarian merely as a blackboard example, it has no truth-value anyway. It is only as a "speech-sentence", assertion, statement, or judgment that it has any truth-value. It is not the senses or truth-values of the component clauses, each considered in isolation, which determine the truth-value of the whole, but their role and truth-values as taken in the context of the functor "If . . . , —" which structures the whole nexus.

33. Hare, in "Meaning and Speech Acts", *Philosophical Review* 79 (1970): 3–24, appears to have a partial realization of this, proposing that the content-carrying or more descriptive element in a sentence (the "phrastic") arrives already combined with a "tropic" (prospectively indicating attitude) before the supposed "neustic" (the force-carrier, e.g., an assertion-sign) comes in—in Hare's terminology, the "neustic" being what turns the "tropic-phrastic" combination into the actual expression of a speech-act. His introduction of the unity of the "tropic-phrastic" combine constitutes some recognition that sense incorporates more than "descriptive content", being able to embrace a mood expressing evaluative element without this being separated from previously supposedly independent factual or descriptive element, but this still does not go far enough.

In sum, the issue is not one of a merely technical distinction between "assertion" and "propositional clause", but what truth and falsity are primarily to be attributed to. The question is of the capacity in which something is true or false, of what the question of truth and falsity is about. Are statements and assertions true or false only derivatively inasmuch as the clauses which are stated ("asserted" or "affirmed") are themselves true or false? Or, as I am arguing, are these clauses true and false only in a secondary sense in that they would be true or false if they occurred on their own—that is, as assertions, and as assertions, then either themselves intellectual acts or else expressions of intellectual acts? We have propositional clauses on our hands, some naked (assertions) and some not so. There are two questions: (a) Do we explain what a clause is in terms of its capacity to occur naked as a sentence, or do we explain what a sentence is in terms of its capacity to appear as a clause whether naked or not? and (b) Is it assertions or clauses which are prior as subjects of truth and falsity? My answer to (b) is that it is the latter, because it is only in virtue of attaining the goal of the intellect—namely, truth—that assertions are true.

(ii) We need conditionals to explain truth-functional relations, but not a theory of conditionals

When the logician sets forth a line of a truth-table indicating that if "P" is true and "Q" is true, "P or Q" is also true, what he means is that if the statement "P" (i.e., "P" occurring naked, by that fact a statement) were true, and if the statement "Q" were true, then the statement "P or Q" would be true. He need not be speaking of "P", "Q", and "P or Q" as unasserted clauses. There is no way in which one could possibly assess whether "P" *as it occurs within the context* "P or Q" is true or false, except by considering whether "P", that is, "P" as it occurs naked, is true or false; and likewise with "Q".

Against this approach Geach urges that the logic of truth-functions is not secure and well understood, and should not be made to rest upon the ill-understood logic of subjunctive and, in particular, counterfactual conditionals. To this I reply that the understanding of the "logic" (= logical theory) of truth-functions certainly depends upon the first-order capacity to use and understand conditionals, among them subjunctive conditionals, including counterfactual ones, *but not at all upon the understanding or "possession" of something at the second-order level, a supposed "logic" of conditionals.*

The difference between nonsubjunctive and subjunctive conditionals is merely this: that if I say, "If they win the battle, they will win the war", I present their winning the battle as relatively likely (something that may happen), whereas if I say "If they were to win the battle, they would win the war", I present their winning the battle as relatively unlikely (something that only might happen). And counterfactual conditionals belong to the same logic inasmuch as, given the truth of either of the statements just mentioned at the time of utterance, then given also the later fulfillment of the antecedent, it will follow that at that later time, "As they won the battle, they won the war", whereas, given instead that the antecedent is not fulfilled, it will be, "If they had won the battle, they would have won the war" which follows.

Any exposition of the logic of truth-functions certainly involves the use of conditionals; indeed the explanation of the notion of function, and even the specification of what would be the values of the function if certain arguments were taken, that is, any second-order or meta-linguistic statement about a function, will involve the use of conditionals, with their familiar interconnections and relationships, but not a "theory" of conditionals.

In addition the logic of truth-functions involves that the senses of constituent expressions in "P" as it occurs within the context of the assertion "P or Q" should be the same as their senses in the assertion "P" if it were made, or else in the supposition "P" if it were supposed; but this does not require more than that the supposition "P" should be sufficiently determinate in sense and intelligible for inferences to be made from it in a suppositional argument, and not an unmeaning (*unsinnig*) chain of words, but not that it be the possible object of belief, judgment, or assertion. *Reductio ad absurdum* arguments frequently begin by supposing something so evidently absurd or *sinnlos* (directionless in Wittgenstein's conception) as could not be believed, judged, or asserted.

(iii) Confusions in the use of the notion of "function" in the theory of truth-functions

Here we should note a deeper problem in Geach's exposition.

In the expression "the difference between 4 and 5", the *objects* 4 and 5 do not occur and are not components of what we write on paper, but only the *expressions* "4" and "5". By contrast, if in the expression "P or Q", "P" and "Q" are constituents, then it would seem that we had the objects themselves, and not only their designations, appearing in what we write on paper.

Therefore we need to question the whole way of explaining the theory of truth-functions. For it does not fit with the idea that the sense of "P or Q" is the value of the function "P or Q" for the arguments "P" and "Q", since the mathematical and Fregean way of conceiving of functions and their values and arguments depends precisely upon regarding these values and arguments as objects, conceived of as distinct from the expressions which denote, designate, or identify them. Both the conception of a function as a mapping from one set of objects to another and the analogy between the notion of function and the Fregean notion of *Begriff* ("concept" in the sense of "predicate" defining a class) depend on precisely this distinction. Frege's own way out of the problem is objectionable, as we shall now see.

Thus the logical theory of truth-functions contains a deep obscurity which parallels the obscurity in the theory of propositional functions. If the number 1 is the value of the function "the difference between ... and —" for 4 and 5 as arguments (the objects, 4 and 5, being arguments, and "4" and "5" being designations of these arguments), in the proposition "1 is the difference between 4 and 5", the expressions "1", "4", and "5" occur as designations of objects: but 1 is the difference between 4 and 5, not the difference between the designations of 4 and of 5, and we say "1 is the difference between 4 and 5" (not "1" is the difference between "4" and "5"). Frege constructed a formal theory according to which, when we say that the truth-value of "P or Q" is a function of the truth-values of "P" and of "Q", all these were designations of objects called Truth ("the True") and Falsity ("the False"). This theory involved treating propositions (clauses) as names, and as we will see at the end of this chapter, this way of thinking is less easy for expositors of the theory of truth-functions to escape than Dummett (for instance) seems to suppose.

The problem here confronting us is in fact just an example of the entirely general problem as to how we should speak of the linguistic expressions we use, a problem which, as chapter XII will show, is to be resolved precisely by not thinking of such expressions as genuine "objects", but by thinking of them as only what I call "cognates". By this means, in one act we not only resolve this problem, but also resolve the problem of the status of cognates of possible utterances, a problem which also arises with Geach's second argument, considered in (iv).

For the same puzzle arises in the case of truth-functions as with propositional functions. In both, the so-called function is more properly regarded as a "functor"—that is, the truth-functor "... or —" or the propositional functor "... is bold", since the "arguments" and "values" are expressions of which the one is a constituent of the other, whereas the norm for functions (as opposed to functors) is for an argument to be an object referred to by an expression designating it which is a constituent of the expression for the value of the function, both arguments and values being objects distinct from the expressions referring to them.

Thus in both cases the true solution is to substitute the notion of functor for that of function, substitute the notion of completing a functorial expression—that is, a functor, by inserting propositional clauses where the functorial expression is incomplete for the notion of taking propositional contents as the arguments of a function, and regard the result of completing the functorial expression in this way, the resultant propositional clause, as itself the "value" of the functorial expression for this insertion. In this way one is replacing the idea of going from objects called propositional contents, envisaged as arguments of the function concerned, as one's starting points to another object which is its value, a new propositional content, envisaged as one's destination, by the idea that one is going from inserted propositional clause(s) as one's starting point(s) to the expression of the "value" of the functor after the insertion(s) concerned—this value or result being not the designation of an object, but an expression which has the meaning or sense it has by incorporating the expressions for its so-called argument(s). Consequently the role of these "argument"-expressions in determining the sense and truth-value of the whole propositional clause concerned is primarily in expressing what sense they express, and this only derivatively gives them some analogy with the things normally called functions. The expression which results, or "resultant propositional clause" (the "value" of the functor), if it occurs naked, is in that case, of course, in its own right a statement or assertion.

(iv) Geach's second line of argument turns on the status of possible utterances or thoughts

We come now to the second prong of the argument for considering "propositions" as entities which exist quite independently of being asserted or stated to be primary subjects of truth or of falsity, rather than "statements" or "assertions", judgments or beliefs.

This second argument proceeds quite differently and depends on the requirements of a second-order consideration of what is going on in the *modus ponens* argument presented at the start. If I make statements about statements—for instance, the statement that from the statement "P" and the statement "If P, then Q" there follows the statement "Q"—I treat these statements, "P", "If P, then Q", and "Q", in order to give an example of a consequence of a general law (treating "P" and "Q" here as abbreviations or constants). I take such abbreviations in order that the particular case shall exhibit a general rule.[34] However, if, on the other hand, I say instead, "If 'P' is true and 'If P, then Q' is true, then 'Q' would be true as well", I have enunciated "P", "If P, then Q", and "Q" not as statements or complete speech-sentences, but only as cognates of possible acts of stating or supposing. As Aristotle recognized, one can consider the validity of argument from any given premises to a conclusion independently of any assent to the truth of the premises, and it is plain that one can consider such questions without any attention to features of the context of utterance of the premises involved, where these make no difference to the senses of what is involved.[35]

For me to conceive of them as cognates of acts of stating or supposing, so

34. Dummett may think that the word "statement", unlike the word "assertion", does not imply actually being asserted, but there seems little basis for this.

35. So Geach would argue, and, within the limits I have expressed, correctly.

that what I say makes sense, I must have conceived of them as if such things might be stated or supposed.[36]

Geach's argument here turns on considering the cognates of possible acts of stating or supposing, and this introduces a further question, quite alien to Geach, as to whether propositions are interlinguistic, and if they are interlinguistic, whether they are also things we think—that is, thoughts (*Gedanken*) or "propositional contents", and therefore in a way paralinguistic—I mention how this worry should be approached in chapter XII.

(c) *The roots of Geach's passion in separating sense and force: the defense of moral objectivism*

What we need to appreciate is that the roots of the passion with which this dispute is pursued, both by Geach and by others, lie partly outside logic because they mistakenly suppose that the defense of the objectivity of moral truth depends on force being external to sense.

Hare and other philosophers tried to explain the sense of some types of declarative utterance by suggesting that their utterance is not the speech-act of making a statement or true or false assertion, but a speech-act of some other kind. Clearly there are such cases; for instance, when a person says to a man on his deathbed, "I will look after your son", or when a judge says, after hearing the verdict of the court that a person is guilty of murder, "You shall be taken to the place of execution and hung by the neck", we have respectively an act of promising or declaring an intention, and a judicial sentence, not of stating something true or false. However, Hare ventured the idea that moral utterances are a kind of imperative and tried to explain this by making out that to say that something is good is to "commend" it (in more traditional vocabulary, to "praise" it). This is a less obvious case.

To refute any such approach, Geach and others think that they have to make a *universal* denial, insisting that the sense of an utterance can *never* be explained in terms of the type of speech-act which would be made if it were put forward, the force which defines the kind of speech-act to which an utterance belongs being regarded as completely external to its sense.[37] This is argued be-

36. I need not have "attended" to what is involved, actually envisaging interpretations for "P" and "Q", but treated them as pretend abbreviations or constants, albeit adopted not through laziness in inventing examples, but because it is only the form of what is involved in real cases which needs to be perspicuous. Likewise, in judging that being a centaur excludes being a unicorn, I am unlikely to have "attended" to the question of the circumstances in which I would have described something as a centaur or as a unicorn, but it is odd to suppose that I might make this judgment without knowing what centaurs and unicorns have been supposed to look like.

37. Such independence has seemed especially necessary to those who consider that the proper way of defining the sense of propositional clauses is Fregean, in terms of their truth-conditions, or even see this as the only way of defending objectivism in ethics and elsewhere. This seems to be the root of Alasdair

cause what might be commanded or wished, denied or questioned, cannot as such have one force rather than another.

In particular Geach argued that if Hare's account of "good" in terms of commending was used to explain the sense of unconditional declarations that something was good, and if this was because the word "good" gave some special imperative or commendatory force to the utterance, then the account would fail to explain the sense of the word "good" in conditional declarations—for instance, "If A was F or G, A would be good". In effect, explaining "X is obligatory" as like saying "Do X", or "X is dangerous" or "X is prohibited" as like saying "Avoid X", more like imperatives than assertions, caters only for unconditional ascriptions of the terms "obligatory", "dangerous", and "prohibited".

Yet common sense suggests a much simpler way of defending objectivity.

For to commend or praise something is simply to say that the thing is good or excellent, and commonly we praise a thing by stating properties which make it praiseworthy; just as to warn people is simply to say that there is danger, and is commonly done by stating the danger, for instance, "There is a bull in this field". The statements concerned are described as commendations or warnings precisely because they say or illustrate that or how the thing concerned is good or dangerous. It is the type of interest—being a good thing of its kind (a good screwdriver, a good farmer), being worthy, honest, or right, or, on the other hand, being likely or liable to cause harm or pain—which gives these kinds of statement their more specific force, when they are still also statements.

Hence to resort to a theory of "force" in order to characterize meanings of "good" or "dangerous" is simply to get things the wrong way around. Instead of explaining the meaning of the term "dangerous" in terms of the notion of warning and of "good" in terms of the notion of commending, one needs to explain the notion of warning in terms of informing of risk of hurt or harm and commending in terms of stating that something is good or in what ways it is good. It is the sense of these terms which explains the specific force of the utterances concerned, not the force of such utterances which explains the sense of these terms.

Geach's argument is designed to resist commonly proposed substitutes for the idea that moral truth is an object of knowledge.

These "expressivist" views are designed to give moral assertions a logic which still allows for disagreement—developing the idea that treated moral assertions as a special kind of expression of attitude (Stevenson) or of command (Hare).

MacIntyre's embracing of the supposed Frege-point in his "Moral Relativism, Truth and Justification", in *Moral Truth and Moral Tradition: Essays in Honour of Peter Geach and Elizabeth Anscombe*, ed. Luke Gormally (Dublin: Four Courts Press, 1994), 6–24.

There is a difficulty in working out "logics" governing such "moral" assertions. In the case of denials, the subordinate component clauses which figure as negated, or as antecedents or consequents, and so forth have to be assertoric in form. If we try to put a declaration of intention or a command into the antecedent of a conditional, either grammar or logic compels us to dress it up in assertoric form. For example, "Go to Athens; if (Go to Athens), then (Go to a ship); therefore, go to a ship" is ill-formed, and the second premise has to be reexpressed: "If you are to go to Athens, then you must go to a ship". Direct attempts to build a deductive logic of wishes, commands, or statements of intention on this model fail because there are usually different means to achieve an end.[38]

Accordingly the proponents of expressivism have to dress up their arguments in second-order form. Simon Blackburn has made several attempts at this. He rightly accepts that force cannot be a component part of the sense of an embedded clause in a first-order statement, and his remedy to the supposed problem is to ascend to the second order.

In a recent discussion Blackburn's argument runs roughly as follows: if the premises (1) "X disapproves of lying" and (2) "X approves holding that 'X disapproves of lying' implies that 'X disapproves getting one's little brother to tell lies'" are granted, then it will follow that (3) "X disapproves of getting his little brother to tell lies".[39] Blackburn comments, "He is committed to disapproving of getting little brother to lie, because if he does not, his attitudes clash", and goes on to argue that such a person "has a fractured sensibility which cannot itself be an object of disapproval".[40] He explains that a logic of evaluation requires a way of expressing the thought that the mistake involved is logical. (This is his reconstruction of what he earlier presented in a different form: we hold the attitude "boo" to telling lies; we hold the attitude "boo" to combining booing telling lies in general with failing to boo getting one's little brother to tell lies; therefore, if our attitudes are consistent, we hold the attitude "boo" to getting little brothers to tell lies.)

The approach is formally parallel to the one which would arise if one treated "true" as an evaluative term expressing assertive force and then suggested that the sense of "If P, then Q" is that "If the statement 'P' were true, then the statement 'Q' would be true". Such an approach is useless because it explains nothing, but simply introduces a regress, explaining one use of "if" in

38. The way in which a "logic of imperatives" must differ from the "logic of propositions" has been well explained by Kenny, "Practical Reasoning and Rational Appetite", chap. 5 in *Will, Freedom and Power* (Oxford: Blackwell, 1975).

39. Blackburn, *Spreading the Word*, 194–95.

40. Blackburn, *Spreading the Word*, 194–95. He continues by obscurely arguing that "the 'cannot' here follows, not because such a sensibility must be out of line with the moral facts it is trying to describe, but because such a sensibility cannot fulfill the practical purposes for which we evaluate things".

terms of another, leaving us the same problem at the second-order level which we had had at the first-order level.[41]

This mistake of shifting up from first order to second order arises in all attempts to accommodate sentences imagined to be nonassertoric within the logic adapted to propositions. There is no difficulty in accommodating assertoric force within sense in the normal logic of statements and truth-value relations between them—it requires no additional gambit of a resort to the second order. Such a gambit is required only when the attempt is made to bring nonassertoric sentences within the scope of such propositional logic.[42]

These ideas come across very clearly in an earlier discussion by Blackburn, which ultimately involves there being first-order expressions of second-order thoughts involved in the moral case of uses of "if".[43] Indeed, his general rejection of moral realism (or any presumption in favor of moral realism), preferring such quasi-realism, depends upon generalizing this type of analysis.[44]

But the key to such notions as truth and knowledge is that they are the goals of the intellect in asking questions, and therefore they need not be conceived in terms of the intellect's coming into correspondence with some world of situations, events, and activities (called "facts"). Always, "P is true" is true because "P", rather than vice versa; but "P" need not concern facts rather than things consequential on facts.[45] Once one escapes overly simple correspondence theories of truth, contorted theories such as Blackburn's lose what little attraction they ever had.

Section 4. Dummett's Interpretation of Frege's Notion of *Sinn* and Its Difficulties

Dummett offers additional grounds for taking the same view as Geach that sense and force are mutually external,[46] grounds arising from his quite special interpretation of Frege's notion of *Sinn*, albeit also involving that commands and wishes lack assertoric force.[47]

41. This regress is made plain by Quine in "Truth by Convention", and Frege was aware of it, insisting that one always needed at least one rule of inference, as well as one or more premises, in reasoning.

42. Mark van Roojen criticizes Blackburn's various attempts and those of Allan Gibbard to the same effect in Van Roojen, "Expressivism and Irrationality", *Philosophical Review* 105 (1996): 311–35.

43. Blackburn, "Reply: Rule-Following and Moral Realism", in *Wittgenstein*, ed. Holtzman and Leich, 163–90.

44. For him, cognitivism is a separate issue.

45. The kind of consequence is to be explained by developing the idea that moral truth is a matter of judgment in accord with virtue.

46. Dummett shares the presumption that force cannot be a component of sense even in complete assertoric sentences in *Frege*, 327–28.

47. Dummett is perhaps influenced in this by a surreptitiously introduced suggestion that the sense of

Dummett's interpretation gives Frege's term *Sinn*, customarily translated "sense", a technical meaning whereby the *Sinn* of a propositional clause is that which is relevant to how one is to determine whether it is true or false.[48] By contrast, its *Bedeutung* is that which is relevant to whether it is true or false independently of how one might determine it.[49] The conclusion that Frege's "force" (*Kraft*) will be entirely external to *Sinn* is an automatic consequence of this quite special interpretation of the term *Sinn*, an interpretation presupposed throughout Dummett's presentation.[50]

The question as to what determines who or what a certain referring description, for instance, "the Evening Star", refers to—namely, "that most conspicuously bright celestial object which over extended periods appears in the evening and which is named from this"—seems straightforward. Hence, the *Sinn* of the expression "the Evening Star" will be "that most conspicuously bright celestial object which over extended periods appears in the evening and which is named from this". This example illustrates the difference between *Sinn* and *Bedeutung*: the difference between the descriptions "Evening Star" and "Morning Star" mark how we determine the truth or falsity of propositions containing them, while their *Bedeutung* is the object referred to ("meant") by each description: *der Gegenstand, der bedeutet wurde.*

In Dummett's discussion he next announces that "besides sense and tone, we have discovered a third element in what would ordinarily be called the meaning of such a sentence: for it would certainly be regarded as part of its meaning that a sentence was conventionally understood to express an assertion, and not, e.g., a command; but this is not any part of what Frege counts as its sense, i.e. that which determines under what conditions it is true or false". At this stage, however, he introduces the difficulty that it is "at first unclear

a statement is its "descriptive content" (*Frege*, 305, 308), although in other contexts this idea does not feature in his discussion; cf. Dummett, *Frege*, 326–27.

48. If the *Sinn* of a proposition has to be that which makes a difference to how we determine whether this proposition is true or false, it might seem that a proposition and its negation would have the same *Sinn*. More plausibly, we might say instead that the *Sinn* of a proposition is how one might show it to be true, if it is true, and how one might show the proposition to be false, if it is false. This embodies a weak form of verificationism, long unfashionable as a view of meaning—weak in not implying decidability.

49. This view of *Sinn* in its contrast with *Bedeutung* appears most clearly in Dummett's article "Frege, Gottlob", *Encyclopaedia of Philosophy*, edited by Paul A. Edwards (New York: Macmillan, 1967), 2:225–37, as well as in Dummett, *Frege*, where he says that the sense of a predicate is the criterion for recognizing that the predicate applies to a given object (*Frege*, 293), following up the view whereby "to the sense of a sentence belongs only that which is relevant to determining its truth or falsity" (*Frege*, 2) and in general the sense of an expression is the manner in which we determine its reference (*Frege*, 227).

50. Dummett's announcement that "the notions of sense and reference do not suffice for a complete account of language" (*Frege*, 295) makes one look further back, and there what one finds is not that these notions are inadequate without the notion of force, but that the notion of sense has only been defined in the case of statements, viz., as what is relevant to truth-value (*Frege*, 84), by which other passages and writings show he means our methods of getting knowledge of truth-value. At this point in his book this thesis stands only on the authority of Frege (*Frege*, 83).

what element of a sentence of natural language it is which carries this constituent of its meaning, which, following Frege, we may call its assertoric 'force'".[51]

At this stage Dummett raises the puzzle that we could play a game in which expressions had both *Bedeutung* and *Sinn* in the way Frege explains without there being, as it were, any stakes—anything counting as winning or losing, any point in the particular moves of the game. In such a game assertoric sentences (i.e., statemental utterances rather than, for example, imperatives) would be uttered without force. Accordingly, he says, the conventions of language which determine *Sinn* cannot suffice to determine force.[52] Here he shares the same position as Searle—namely, that one set of semantic conventions allows the identification of the propositional content of an utterance and a second, separate set determines whether a proposition has been asserted.

Accordingly Dummett supposes that assertoric sentences have two roles, one realized when given force, the role of asserting ("saying" in Plato), and the other consisting in merely identifying ("expressing") a *Sinn*.

His embarrassment at the way he has made expressing a sense look like a form of identifying or referring appears in his reluctance to regard assertoric sentences as complex singular names and in his suggestion that singular names, predicates defining concepts, and sentences refer in distinctively different ways, even though he has to regard these ways as analogous to each other.[53] But alas, he has no proof of any such difference, no proof that assertoric sentences are not names, only a "reluctance" to regard them in this way—a reluctance seen, for instance, in his setting aside of Frege's view that such sentences are names of objects, called "the True" and "the False".[54] Expressions of reluctance achieve little. But Dummett is in an even stranger position because when he speaks of "assertoric sentences" he means full sentences such as occur on their own in committed utterances, yet not as asserted, but conceived of as things as such devoid of "force". Thus for him there are certain sentences which are of their nature assertoric, so that these "assertoric sentences" constitute identifying designations of their *Sinne* ("senses" as things to which "force" is external).

51. Dummett, *Frege*, 302–3.

52. This key argument is to be found in Dummett, *Frege*, 295–304, its conclusion stated at the top of 305 in the following terms: "Our arguments showed that the account of assertoric sentences in terms of their sense and their reference is not enough by itself to characterize their use: the additional element is the convention governing their employment to make assertions. We have not shown that this feature of their use has to be symbolized by any feature of their linguistic expression. This will be so only if the kind of sense which a sentence has is insufficient to determine which linguistic convention governs its utterance".

53. Dummett, *Frege*, 7, 180–86.

54. Dummett regards this view that propositions denote either the True or the False is unnecessary to the general structure of Frege's thought; see Dummett, "Frege, Gottlob".

He does not even avail himself of Frege's very natural account of how predicates must be treated differently because of their "unsaturated" or "incomplete" character (instead regarding Frege's expressions as concerned only with complex predicates).

Yet, never daunted or unwilling to question his own position, Dummett appreciates from Wittgenstein that there are indefinitely many kinds of assertion, exceedingly variable in their appropriate means of verification.[55] Hence there would be kinds of assertion in the case of which one might reasonably suspect that there is no adequate means of determining whether they are true or false—implying lack of *Sinn*. The possibility of such quasi-assertions raises a doubt as to how well-conceived Frege's ideas of the *Bedeutung* and *Sinn* are, at least as Dummett explains them, since even such quasi-assertions would need some kind of "sense" to be understood. Such quasi-assertions would have to be nonpropositional, so that if they had an intelligible meaning, they would still not have *Sinn* in the technical sense.

To revert to my less technical use of the word "sense", Dummett has not shown that the force of being a statement is not part of its sense (in *my* sense of the word) in the case of a statement, the force of being a command part of its sense in the case of a command, and so forth. He has only shown that such force should be external to Frege's *Sinn*, an exposition making *Sinn* quite remote from our normal conception of sense or meaning, whether applied to complete utterances or to clauses. I shall therefore henceforward substitute the word *Sinn* for the word "sense" understood as Dummett explains it, and reserve the word "sense" for my own usage—that is, as including every aspect of discourse-significance.

Despite the fact that Dummett thinks that an assertoric sentence does not *as such* possess force, he recognizes the fact that, quite remarkably, uttering them on their own in the *Sinn* which he has accorded them and in a naked context is in our normal human practice necessarily as such an act of assertion, and most of his chapter on "Assertion" can be viewed as if it were directed at substantiating this.[56] It seems a strange coincidence that exactly all and only these peculiar assertoric sentences possessed of *Sinn*, but not "force" (separate linguistic or semantic conventions pertinent to force but not to *Sinn* being unnecessary), should be assertions possessed of "sense" as I defined it in chapter III, which included force where complete utterances are concerned. This powerfully suggests that there are not two sets of semantic conventions governing utterances, but only one, the supposed extra set of conventions whereby naked assertoric sentences are given force being redundant. If one expresses the propositional content of such an utterance, with all the further context required to have done this, but nothing more, then one has *ipso facto*

55. Dummett, *Frege*, 356.

56. Cf. Dummett, *Frege*, 310–11, 317–23, 326–27 (Dummett wrongly assumes the validity of his argument in 295–304, when on 327 he says against Wittgenstein, "this is wrong, as we have seen"; but in the sentence beginning "Admittedly" he concedes the point at issue), 327–51. Dummett, *Frege*, 351–63, rather confirms the same general point.

made an assertion—namely, the propositional utterance concerned. That is, in the case of naked propositional clauses, the semantic conventions pertinent to propositional content suffice to determine force.

It is as I said at the end of section 1 (a) of chapter III: if man and woman embrace intentionally in an erotic kiss, the act has its significance or force naturally, even if on one side or both it was a lying act done in *mauvais foi*. And if with appropriate intonation and stress I utter the words, "Your every word is poisonous, your every action is calculated to deceive, and you have not shown a shred of industry or generosity the whole of your life", there is nothing further required to give the utterance the force of a statement and in the same act the force of a condemnation. No further set of conventions is needed beyond the expression of propositional content to give force, in this case the force not only of a statement, but also of a condemnation.

In sum, I regard both Frege's notion of *Sinn* as applied to sentences or clauses and Dummett's notion of a fully assertoric sentence occurring in a committed utterance which is yet not an assertion as ill-founded.

I do not question their notion of force (*Kraft*).

Force is integral to the discourse-significance ("sense", as I use the word) of the utterance in any speech-act and is indispensable to any account of the use of language—on this I am in complete accord with Geach, Dummett, and Searle. Further, Dummett is right to insist that judgment should be regarded as an interiorization of the external act of assertion, rather than assertion regarded as the expression of a judgment or mental attitude.[57] It is as a result of this that assertions have the properties that their truth can be supposed and that they can be uttered in order to deceive.[58] Human discourse about knowledge and assent is shaped by human discourse about its expression.

Section 5. Recovering the Tradition: Saying Is Not Naming

(a) *Sentences do not designate or "name" meanings, but only express them*

The idea of treating expressions such as "The grass is green" and "that the grass is green" as denoting or identifying objects, let alone objects called "senses", ought to be quite foreign to twentieth-century Anglo-Saxon thought about meaning in view of its origins as an escape from Mill's conception, seen in his *System of Logic*, that sentences were a species of complex name and as such denoted something. The recognition that what we say, believe, express, think, and so forth is not an "object" or "thing" in the proper sense constitut-

57. A frequent theme, most fully stated in *Frege*, 362.

58. Dummett, *Frege*, 349; 356–57.

ed one of the key elements in the transformation of Anglo-Saxon philosophy in the early twentieth century. For a time the insight first clarified by Plato, maintained in Aristotle, and carefully respected by Aquinas, but lost sight of by Descartes and the empiricists, was recovered.

Historically philosophers have paraded the peculiarity of the logic of the notions involved by revealing the very simple paradoxes which arise if we speak of what is believed or said, or of what is known, as if it were a thing or "object". First let us consider the so-called objects of knowledge.

The problem was highlighted by Russell when he distinguished between knowledge "by description" and knowledge "by acquaintance". "By acquaintance" is here a philosopher's term of art to refer to such things as perceptual knowledge of objects, images, concepts, "ideas", natures, and so forth (along, possibly, with the experiencing of emotions)—all conceived of as relations to objects, on the model of seeing or contemplating the object concerned. Knowledge by description—that is, knowledge about objects—is an example of "propositional" knowledge—that is, knowledge expressible in the form "that so and so", as in "A knows that P" where "P" is a proposition about the object concerned.

Next, however, we are tempted to think of this propositional knowledge, including all knowledge about objects by description, as another example of knowing objects by acquaintance, so that knowing "that P" comes to be conceived of as a case of acquaintance with an entity called a proposition.[59] But however clearly one might perceive a proposition to be true, what matters for knowledge is that this proposition be known to be true: if "The grass is green" is an object, knowing this object "The grass is green" could never constitute propositional knowledge—what is needed is knowing something about this mysterious object "The grass is green"—namely, that it is true. If its truth were another object, the proposition "that it is true", then knowing this further proposition, "the truth that the grass is green", will do us no good, since what we need to know is that this further object is true, and so on ad infinitum.[60]

The fundamental concern is the nature of what is believed or said.

59. In the *Republic* Plato conceives intellectual knowledge as knowledge of objects, knowledge and belief being distinguished by having different objects. "Ordinary language philosophers" saw this as blindness to Russell's distinction between knowledge by acquaintance and knowledge by description (knowledge that). Plato himself shows awareness of the difficulty when, in the *Theaetetus* 188A–200C, he plays with the suggestion that false judgment might arise through knowing two things and misidentifying the one by mistaking it for the other (he asks if false judgment is like misidentifying birds in an aviary).

Likewise, Descartes confuses acquaintance with ideas (having quite clear and distinct ideas) with certainty in the knowledge of truths. Yet, if the clear and distinct perception is not of propositions as objects, but of ideas such as are identified by certain terms in propositions, then the transition from clear and distinct knowledge of an idea to knowledge of a truth has not been explained (this also introduces confusion into some formulations of ontological arguments for God's existence).

60. Russell avoided this through his conception of knowledge by description. This he conceived of as a

Plato in the *Sophist* distinguished naming and saying and insisted that saying always arose by articulating a name together with a "speaking" part (a "verb" in our translations) to form a sentence. In the *Theaetetus* and the *Sophist* he makes the point that the person who believes or says what is not the case does not believe or say nothing. Accordingly what is believed or said, when we believe or say that Pericles was a Spartan orator, is not an "object". Thus such expressions as "Pericles was a Spartan orator" or "Pericles was not a Spartan orator" *denote* neither propositions nor facts. Believing and saying cannot be conceived of as relations to objects of any kind.

More recent discussions exhibit the confusions which result from treating what is believed or said as an object, and because of his scrupulous precision in exposition, these are most perfectly exhibited in the discussions of G. E. Moore. He painstakingly considered the theory that the object of a belief was a proposition, meaning by the word "proposition" here not any kind of linguistic entity, but some more abstract kind of object, such as might be denoted by a certain kind of complex name—that is, by a certain kind of linguistic entity.[61] On this theory, in the case of a true proposition, the name of the proposition would be the same as the name of the fact to which the proposition referred, but in the case of a false proposition there would be no such fact in existence for the proposition to refer to such as might have the same name as the proposition.[62] So, once again, false belief and false statement could not be analyzed as relations to objects called facts. Later, while continuing to believe in the existence of facts,[63] he dropped the analysis of belief as a relation to propositions, because there were no such objects.[64] Such

complex relation between the subject of the knowledge and the object of the knowledge. Likewise, believing might be conceived of as complex relation between the subject of belief and the object(s) in regard to which belief is had.

61. This fits Mill's theory of complex names, and, despite G. E. Moore's Platonic critique in "Nature of Judgment", parallels Hume's notion of a proposition as a philosophical relation of ideas (Hume, *Treatise*, bk. 1, pt. 1, sec. 5).

62. G. E. Moore, *Some Main Problems of Philosophy* (London: Allen and Unwin, 1953), chap. 14, esp. 260.

63. G. E. Moore, *Some Main Problems*, chap. 15, where it is beliefs rather than propositions which have the unanalyzable and indefinable relation of "correspondence" with the mysterious entities called "facts". This relation would be the one mentioned in the preceding chap. 14 which is *expressed* (G. E. Moore, *Some Main Problems*, 258) by the relation of identity of name between a belief and the fact to which it refers (G. E. Moore, *Some Main Problems*, 256–58).

64. G. E. Moore, *Some Main Problems*, chap. 14, see 265. Moore's remarks in the preface show exemplary humility: "The second point about which I ought to have added a footnote concerns the relation between what I say about *propositions* in Chapter III and what I say about them in Chapter XIV, 265–6, and again in XVII, 309. In III, 56, [written 1910] I say 'There certainly are in the Universe such things as propositions', whereas in XIV (265) [written 1911] I say that I am recommending a view about the *analysis* of belief which may be expressed by saying 'There simply are no such things as propositions', and in XVII (309) I say 'I don't now believe that there are such things as propositions at all'. Now this looks as if, when I wrote XIV and XVII, I had abandoned the very view which in III I had declared to be certainly true; and certainly I had, *if* in III I had been using the expression 'There are such things as propositions' in the same sense in which I was using

discussions typify the way in which the idea of propositions as objects of relations such as knowledge, belief, and assertion dies when belief in such objects dies—a belief which, each time it dies, reemerges later in the madness of philosophical history.

As Wittgenstein remarks, if such forms of proposition as "A believes that p is the case" and "A has the thought p" are considered superficially, it looks as if the proposition, p, stood in some kind of relation to an object, A,[65] whereas as I remarked earlier Wittgenstein compared them with "'P' says 'P'", which is to be understood in the light of the view explained in chapter XII below that to quote an expression is not to designate it.

The Anglo-Saxon escape from taking denotation, or the relation of a name and its bearer, as the model for thinking about meaning occurred in stages, slowed down by the obscurity of the notion of "complete symbol". For Russell there were two kinds of complete symbol, just as for Frege there had been two kinds of "saturated" expression: first, sentential or propositional expressions; and second, "logically proper names". But whereas for Russell the denotative meaning of "logically proper names" is still something given independently of and prior to propositions possessing sense, for Frege and Wittgenstein this was no longer the case, since "it is only in the context of a proposition that words have any meaning" and "only propositions have sense; only in the nexus of a proposition does a name have meaning".[66] Moreover, the latter thesis not only dethrones names, but also implies that propositions are not themselves names.[67] And, in Russell and Whitehead's presentation of logic, "defi-

it in XIV and XVII. But I now feel doubtful whether in III I had been using that expression merely in that sense. I think it is possible that in III I was using it, partly at least, in such a sense that the truth of what it expresses would follow from the mere fact that such expressions as 'I believe the *proposition* that the sun is larger than the moon' are perfectly correct ways of expressing something which is often true—as they certainly are; whereas in XIV and XVII I was using 'There are such things as propositions' in a way which is perhaps more doubtfully correct, namely in such a way that it would not express a truth unless such expressions as 'I believe the *proposition* that the sun is larger than the moon' can be correctly *analysed* in a certain way—which is a very different usage"; G. E. Moore, *Some Main Problems*, xii.

65. In *Tractatus*, 5.541–542. In 5.541, Wittgenstein unfairly represents Russell and G. E. Moore as construing such forms of proposition in this way. On the contrary, when Russell plays with relational analyses of knowledge and belief, the model is of knowing or believing something about something. In considering the nature of believing something about something, we recurrently meet attempts to analyze what is involved as a many-term relation, attempts often inspired by the model of "X thinking of Y as Z"—e.g., between a subject who believes, thinks, or states; an object or topic which a belief, thought, or statement is about; and a concept or feature believed, thought, or stated to be exemplified in the object or topic. Such analyses are never adequate, since something has to express the relation of X, Y, and Z. But from 1911 onward analyses representing believing and stating as relations to propositions disappear: Russell, G. E. Moore, Ryle (in writings from 1930 to 1971), and Austin ("Truth", in *Philosophical Papers*, 117–33 [Oxford: Oxford University Press, 1961]; first published in *Proceedings of the Aristotelian Society* suppl. vol. 24 [1950]) have abandoned them.

66. Frege, *Foundations of Arithmetic*, 73, §62; and Wittgenstein, *Tractatus*, 3.3, respectively; cf. "An expression has meaning only in a proposition" (*Tractatus*, 3.314), and "Names are like points; propositions resemble arrows—they have sense" (*Tractatus*, 3.144); *Tractatus*, 4.23.

67. Frege understood the word *Gedanke* to refer not to psychological events or objects of any kind, but

nition in use"—that is, the definition of the sense of subordinate expressions in terms of the truth-conditions or sense of the propositional wholes in which they are used, took on a predominant role, while "logically proper names" began to lose their function.[68]

Here the key question returned to being that of the character of the propositions or statements, or more generally of the cognates of speech-acts of whatever kind, in terms of whose sense the sense and even the designation of subordinate expressions are to be understood. What was fundamental in the tradition we are speaking of was that they were not names and did not have meaning through naming or otherwise identifying "objects"—whatever the precise meaning of the word "object".

For Plato and for Wittgenstein, as for Jespersen, the key feature of a sentence or a proposition was, as Jespersen put it, that as a nexus it is "animate and articulated".[69] A name does nothing because it says nothing (it lacks, even implicitly, the sentential articulatedness required if something is to be expressive of a sense). Not expressive of sense, it is dead. "Names are like points; propositions like arrows—they have sense", and having sense is like having a direction.[70] And Plato, Frege, Jespersen, Wittgenstein, and Ryle were all alert to the role of the so-called live verb,[71] what Frege called the "unsaturated part" of a sentence, as making it say something.[72] Further, at least for Wittgenstein and Ryle, the "saying" something was *ipso facto* at the linguistic level of "use"—of "function", not "form".[73]

For Ryle and the later Wittgenstein, along with Austin and other writers, it was therefore foundational for their reflection on language that sentences did not refer to, denote, indicate, or mention objects, whether "meanings" or "objects in the world". Rather they expressed meanings ("senses" in an unspecialized sense), as what a hearer had, within the context of utterance, the

---

to things expressed by sentences, namely, their sense (*Sinn*): he never regarded sentences as denoting senses. His peculiar view that they denote two objects, the True and the False, seems to represent an unnecessary excrescence upon his general view, a formal trick having no structural role in the philosophical account he had to offer. However, as the next subsection (b), will show, this peculiar view reveals the structural fault in Frege's account.

68. The most convenient popularization of this is by Ryle, "Theory of Meaning".

69. Jespersen, *Philosophy of Grammar*, 116, cf. 115.

70. Wittgenstein, *Tractatus*, 3.144, 4.461.

71. The word "finite" as applied to the verb only draws attention to its susceptibility to variations of form according to tense, mood, and aspect, and so does not pick out its underlying nature whereby it is what gives the sentence the character of a drama (as Jespersen expressed it), or whereby Plato could call it a *rhema* or "saying"—constitutive of the sentence's being in use (compare the end of Wittgenstein, *Tractatus*, 4.063).

72. As I commented in chap. IX, sec. 1 (a) of this volume, this understanding of Frege, the "incompleteness" as explained by Geach, is lost in Dummett's explanation, making it relevant only to complex predicates.

73. In his paper "Use, Usage and Meaning", Ryle associates his notion of sentence with Alan Gardiner's notion of Speech (contrasted with "Language"), marked by the association of Speech with "function" as contrasted with "form".

right to understand as having been intended to be expressed in the saying of what was said, as we saw in chapter III.

Indeed, in 1928 Ryle saw no need for the distinction between "sentence" or "statement" on the one hand and "proposition" on the other,[74] and such distinctions were largely ignored in Anglo-Saxon philosophical writings, except when contrasting statements or propositions with questions, commands, and so forth. Rarely bothered with "propositions" as abstract objects distinct from statements or sentences, English-bred "linguistic philosophers" like Austin avoided many mistakes by tolerating vagueness in places where it did not seem to matter.

(b) *For propositions to have sense without force is formally equivalent to their being complex names*

Old mistakes can be disguised in new forms.

In Geach and others we saw the reemergence of a theory which envisages entities called propositions or propositional "sentences" ("clauses" for us), along with other entities called propositional contents or *Sinne*. These are held to differ from statements because they do not as such possess assertoric force. They are not given as expressions of assertoric speech-acts, nor indeed as being in any determinate relation to any speech-act. And it is these which are presented as the primary subjects of truth and falsity, instead of statements, beliefs, or judgments.

Moreover, these new-fangled "propositions", propositional clauses, or propositional contents turn out to have some formal parallelism with denoting expressions or names (whereas "statements" or assertions, because of their assertoric force, are not names).

This formal parallelism is seen in the fact that it was possible for Frege to regard them as names of two objects, the True and the False. It is irrelevant to the present point that nothing in the rest of his theory depended on this strange view of "the True" and "the False" as two objects, or that Dummett should have been "reluctant" to accept any such idea of propositions as being names. What matters is the formal parallelism exhibited by the very possibility of such a view. For what this exhibits is that as soon as one has divorced force from *Sinn*, or propositional content, or divided what gives force from what specifies propositional content, one has made what specifies propositional content (a clause) into something formally parallel to a denoting expression, as if to revive Mill's idea of propositions as complex names, an ever recurrent mistake in philosophical history. One has made what says, com-

74. Ryle, "Are There Propositions?"

mands, or wishes something in a sentence into something dead. One is now in a position to treat it as the designation of, or what identifyingly denotes, a "content", *Sinn*, or "sense", making it lose the "live" quality associated with genuine speech or saying as it arises in a speech-act, giving it instead the dead character of a specification of a propositional or "descriptive" content.

One then has to reintroduce force to bring speech to life again.

However, the proper place for the absolutely indispensable notion of force is not as something from outside to give life to something dead, but as an internal aspect of the sense of any explicit committed utterance, integral to its sense, not something added or applied to this sense, nor something such that the sense could be the same without it.

If an utterance has force, asserting something, commanding something, or having some other force, as is required for it to be alive in the way speech-acts are alive, then it is characteristic for it to contain some feature with the function of what is commonly referred to as the "live verb" in its expression, and to require some actual "live verb" or, in Frege's metaphor, some unifying "unsaturated" expression, in any re-expression of its sense. But there is no way of conceptualizing the sense which is had in common by all "live verbs" or "unsaturated expressions".[75]

The appearance that Geach with his propositions, Searle and Lyons with their propositional contents, and Dummett with his *Sinne* have avoided confusing "saying" and "naming" by introducing their technical notions is entirely deceptive. They have associated "sense" with something less than speech in use. In allowing a new species of "object" to creep in, their "propositional contents" or "senses", for propositional clauses to identify or designate, they have mistaken the role of a proposition or clause. This role is not to designate or name, but only to express whatever kinds of meaning it expresses, and if occurring on its own, naked, as a report or statement, to report or state, not to portray or designate.

Moreover, this is vital to any theory in logic or linguistics whose account has to cover embedded clauses and clauses which are not true or may not be true. And as we saw above, although clauses and verbs around which clauses are framed do not as such have force as part of their sense, they do have it as essential to their sense that if they or (in the case of verbs) the clauses framed

75. Where assertions are concerned, we meet Frege's suggestion that the "common predicate" in all assertions is the predicate "actually obtains" (in effect, "is the case"); this predicate is applied to the circumstance (*Umstand*) specified by the propositional clause concerned. However, whatever thus encapsulates the living character of a subject/predicate proposition and gives the predicate the character of making the proposition say something is something unconceptualizable, and it is this upon which Gilson is chiefly concerned to insist, in saying that their kind of existence is unconceptualizable. The obscurities in these philosophers' explanations arise from the truth, which Geach cannot dispute—namely, that what gives assertoric force indeed cannot be conceptualized.

round them occur in no special context (such as a play or work of fiction) and unembedded, then they will have the force they characteristically express. It is precisely this which distinguishes clauses and predicates from other so-called phrases and word groups, and the verbs around which clauses are framed from other parts of speech.

Note A. Austin's approach to speech-acts: the ambiguities of his discussion

Two elements of Austin's thought are required by any theory.

First, he made a vital distinction between what we do in saying what we say, which he calls the illocutionary act involved (now commonly called the speech-act, the directly intended human act involved *in* saying what we say, whether this act be labeled "rhetic", "locutionary", or "illocutionary"), and things we do intentionally *by means of* saying what we say, which he calls perlocutionary acts (e.g., to make people angry or to make people determined to do the opposite of what we ask them to do).

Second, we need his distinction between statemental or "constative" utterances such as, "I married Joan in 1930" and nonstatemental "performative" utterances such as, "With this ring, I thee wed".

Beyond this, accidents of history make Austin's technical terminology unnecessarily complicated. For instance, he had three terms, "rhetic act", "locutionary act", and "illocutionary act", where perhaps one would have sufficed. What we have in *How to Do Things with Words* are 1955 notes published unaltered after his death, its ideas not integrated for publication and, to his death, regarded by him as exploratory and provisional.[76]

In his time the term "speech-act" was not yet current, and his term "locutionary act" is a surrogate, coined as a preliminary to distinguishing the "illocutionary" and the "perlocutionary". The "rhetic" act was conceived in the different setting of contrasting what is proper to speech with (a) the merely "phatic" act, identified by its vocabulary and grammar, the "phatic" being Chomsky's area of concern, and (b) the phonetic act.[77] There was no real difference between a "rhetic" and a "locutionary" act, except in the origin of the terms. The "rhetic act" was the matter of using the constituent expressions

76. Austin's *How to Do Things with Words* was published by Blackwell in 1962, after his death in 1960. The lectures concerned were delivered in 1955 and record a stage in the development of thoughts first begun in 1939, thoughts he regarded as provisional even after 1958—as was very clear to Michael Partridge (Institute for Theology, Imagination and the Arts, University of St. Andrews, a remarkable 1959 postgraduate student of Austin's). The whole text has an exploratory character, full of expressions of uncertainty, strikingly the statement at 148E. Cf., on the uncompleted character of Austin's work, Lyons, *Language, Meaning and Context*, 172–73.

77. Austin, *How to Do Things with Words*, 92–98.

of what one said with a certain more or less definite sense and reference (together equivalent to meaning) so as to utter a "rheme", the unit of speech.[78] In effect, specifying the illocutionary act performed in a particular locutionary act is giving a more specific description of the linguistic act concerned as a linguistic act, whereas specifying the perlocutionary act performed (for instance, making somebody angry) is giving a description which might apply to nonlinguistic acts.

The origin of our difficulties lies in Austin's complete lack of concern with the problems which occupied Frege in "Negation". Austin's ideas were formed within a background in which most uses of the words "meaning", "sense", "reference", and "force" were those of informal English. None of them were used with the preoccupations with logic and truth-conditions which we find in Frege, the early Wittgenstein, Geach, and the like.[79] In respect of whole utterances he always referred to their "meanings", not their "senses". And when he spoke of "illocutionary force" as a facet of the meaning of whole utterances, there is no reason to suppose he had Frege's discussion of *Kraft*[80] (today translated "force") in mind, since his aim was to make far more fine-cut distinctions than Frege.[81] His instances of illocutionary acts include acts of reporting, answering questions, informing, giving assurances, warning, and passing verdicts, commonly cases of delivering propositions. Thus his discussions are more adapted to an extended pragmatics than to the concerns of Frege or Dummett.

However, strangely, even though the rheme was described as a unit of speech and therefore as having a determinate place in whatever discourse was concerned (argument, conversation, lecture, or other), he did not think of these differentiations between kinds of illocutionary act (each marking a different "illocutionary force") as constituting aspects or features of the meanings of rhemes. For at the time of the lectures concerned, it seemed to him, speaking informally, that the "said-meaning" might determine less than the "meant-force"—for instance, so that it might not be clear whether someone was making a statement or giving a warning. However, for him, "said-meaning" and "meant-force", "utterance-meaning" and "utterance-force" were overlapping facets of "meaning", taking the word "meaning" unrestrictedly. He thought of

78. Austin first introduces the concept of rheme (*How to Do Things with Words*, 93), and later tells us that the "rheme" is a unit of speech, the sort of thing whose "typical fault is to be vague, void or obscure, &c." (Austin, *How to Do Things with Words*, 98), and in saying this he is thinking in the same framework as Ryle when the latter identifies Speech as the concern of philosophers, the locus of truth, verification, and the like (in Ryle, "Use, Usage and Meaning").

79. In their thinking about the senses of expressions, English philosophers of his period tended to be more influenced by Mill's distinction between connotation and denotation than by Frege's papers "Sinn und Bedeutung" and "Die Verneinung".

80. Cf. n. 2 in this chapter.

81. Austin, *How to Do Things with Words*, 98–100.

the "said-meaning" of what he called a rheme (a sentence as it occurs in use), as if it were a matter of the sense and reference of its constituents, thinking of them in a rather static way, even though they were in use and therefore better thought of dynamically, with everything included in its "meant-force", so that there would be no difference between a rheme's said-meaning and what he called its meaning taken unrestrictedly. These tensions in his discussion generate obscurities and difficulties in Searle and Hare.[82] Lyons's painstaking exposition in his *Language, Meaning and Context* fails to explain why an utterance's illocutionary force should not be considered part of its sense, and why one should not distinguish differences of force as giving one a way of distinguishing different kinds of locutionary act.[83] The rhetic/locutionary act is not related to the illocutionary act as various bodily movements are related to the act of kicking a penalty shot, with the bodily movements only incidentally intentional. On the contrary, the rhetic act is itself the fully intended human act, of which different illocutionary forces (warning, praising) are aspects in different cases.

Note B. How Searle falls into the same traps as Geach and Dummett

When writing about speech-acts Searle tends to circumvent the slipperiness of the term "sense" by speaking of the "propositional contents" rather than the "senses" of propositional expressions.[84] Supposedly "the *expression* of a proposition" is "neutral as to illocutionary force" so that it does not assert anything, and this makes his position analogous to those of Dummett and Geach.[85]

However, he feels forced to complicate the picture. He tells us that the "literal meaning" or "said-meaning" always incorporates at least some (perhaps exceedingly generic) indication of illocutionary force—in this going beyond its mere propositional content.[86] He also treads in Austin's footsteps,

82. However, several confusions in Searle are certainly absent from Austin. Thus, Austin held that "said-meaning" does not entirely determine "meant-force", but not that "said-meaning" implies nothing as to "meant-force", as Searle thinks him to have done.

Hare developed Austin's ideas differently; cf. nn. 16, 17, 33, and n. 87 of this volume.

83. Lyons, *Language, Meaning and Context*, 184.

84. Whenever two illocutionary acts contain the same reference and predication, provided that the meaning of the referring expression is the same, Searle will say that the same proposition is expressed. He draws in his initial presentation on the second prong of the "Fregean" argument for distinguishing propositions from statements—namely, that they can be talked about without being asserted. He goes on to say, "I am distinguishing between the illocutionary act and the propositional content of the illocutionary act"; Searle, *Speech Acts*, 29–30. The notion of "content" is, of course, thoroughly Fregean: it was a content to which the "judgement-stroke" was applied, the assertion-sign being composed of the "judgement-stroke" and the "content-stroke".

85. Searle, "Austin", 420.

86. Searle notes that "the expression of a proposition" or "propositional act" can only occur in the context of a speech act—i.e., an "illocutionary act". He wrongly imagines ("Austin", 412–13) that Austin thought

reckoning that "said-meaning" gives only incomplete knowledge of "meant-force". Searle's conclusion, "from this semantical point of view we can distinguish two (not necessarily separate) elements in the syntactical structure of the sentence, which we might call the propositional indicator and the illocutionary force indicator", reveals his thought as frozen where Austin, unsatisfied, left it when he died.[87]

Thus Searle's "expressions of propositions" are no different from Geach's "propositions", and both these and "propositional contents" are objects. The inscription one has before one may be a complete sentence or may be, for instance, the antecedent of a conditional or the complement of an imperatival construction. But whichever it is, it will identify a "propositional content" in virtue of which it is true or false, doing this by one set of conventions. Such "inscriptions" (Dummett's "sentences") differ from the linguist's "system-sentences" (grammar-generated constructs) in that their sense is affected by the context of utterance, intonation, and so forth; but along with propositional contents, they are still entities bestraddling types of speech-act, not determinate as to illocutionary force, and so capable of use in contexts in which they would have different forces. Meanwhile, in virtue of some other, quite distinct set of conventions, one will, for instance, assert the proposition concerned (make public commitment to this content), command or request that it be made true, or publicly wish that it be or become true. Searle has made Austin's speculation that "said-meaning" and "meant-force" *can* come apart a new matter of doctrine, and even *conceptually necessary* (even if the first commonly or even invariably curtails the second).[88]

In this way, drawing on ambivalences in Austin, Searle is able to set up the same distinction between two supposed sets of conventions as Dummett, one set of semantic conventions allowing the identification of propositional content and another set determining whether a proposition is asserted. So "logic and language" map signs onto objects called propositional contents (all at the level of linguistic "form"), and "illocutionary conventions" put the speaker into the position of asserting the proposition with the content in question. Expressing a proposition is to asserting as making the mark X is to voting.[89]

Because a propositional content (what makes its expression true or false) does not include the illocutionary force with which its expression is uttered, Searle can regard the illocutionary force associated with it when uttered as a

---

the opposite. Searle's remarks in *Speech Acts*, 122–23, suggest that the "meant-force" might be invariably, not just commonly, indicated at least generically within the "said-meaning".

87. Searle, *Speech Acts*, 30. In his way of thinking in this part of the book *Speech Acts*, Searle's formalization suggests the influence of Hare's distinction between "neustics" and "phrastics" in *Language of Morals*.

88. Searle, "Austin", 418.

89. Cf. Searle, *Speech Acts*, 24.

matter of institutional fact.[90] The institutional conventions involved are supposedly distinct from the conventions identifying the content.

Approaches such as those of Searle and Dummett avoid making saying an example of designating only by mere stipulation. Despite attempts to avoid it, we still have on our hands linguistic entities which serve as identifying designations of the things Searle calls "propositional contents" and Dummett calls *Sinne*.[91] So if they deny that sentences are designations or that saying is designating, their denials are empty. In effect the propositional sentence is simply the most direct way of identifying the propositional content, the thought expressed, or sense of the sentence. There is then no difference between *expressing* a sense and *identifying* this sense in the most direct way, as if by a complex name. Thus the philosophical mistake identified earlier again reappears.

90. Searle, *Speech Acts*, 50–53.

91. If it is said they identify by expressing, I note that the argument of chaps. I–III of this volume requires a distinction between expressing and any kind of identifying.

XI

The Notion of Subject and the Functional Organization of the Clause

We have seen that it is wrong to confine "sense" and semantics to the lexical, and wrong to confine it to what is relevant to a "logic" of matters affecting truth-conditions. Rather all the distinctions presented in Dik's Functional Grammar and the Czech tradition, between Theme, Predication and Tail, Topic and Focus, Given Topic and New Topic, and so forth, reflect perspective and belong to the semantics of discourse, as I use the term "semantics".[1]

Jackendoff observes in a footnote, "Another possibility, however, is that subject-predicate structure arose from Topic-Comment organization in information structure. It subsequently became grammaticalized and overlaid with lots of other grammatical phenomena, so that some languages (including English) came to reinvent another pre-subject topic position".[2] I develop this view further. Speech always presents matters in a certain perspective, and accordingly gives unequal status to the arguments of what modern logic represents as a many-place predicate. To explain this divergence does not require a grammar shaped by Chomskyan phrase theory, nor the idea that "Grammatical Constraints" are rooted in neurology.[3] In my account grammatical functions and the functional organization of the clause have a key importance, reflected in both traditional and some modern formal grammars.[4]

1. Cf. Dik, "Basic Principles of Functional Grammar", 22; and Dik, *The Theory of Functional Grammar, Part* 1, 264–85 (in 2nd ed. of 1997, 309–38).

2. Jackendoff, *Foundations*, 252–53n11.

3. Jackendoff, *Semantics and Cognition*, 13–22, 57–63.

4. Jackendoff, *Foundations*, 9–18, 149–51, 257–59.

Section 1. Disentangling Linguistics from Its Historical Background

(a) *The common root of the topic/comment, subject/predicate, and noun/verb distinctions*

The semantics of sentences as complete utterances incorporates the pragmatic structures basic to communication as well as the priority of certain thematic roles, and it is only through a developing process of grammaticalization that semantic syntactic structure comes to be marked grammatically by varied devices, agreement in inflection and word order among them. Because the main purpose of such devices is thus to make semantic structure clear (some aspects of semantic structure being defined in partly pragmatic terms), I shall often use words like "verb" and "verbal" as if they belonged as much to semantics as to grammar. The logicians' terms "predicate" and "argument" have the advantage of showing their clear connection with logic.

(i) Distinguishing semantic syntactic structure from the way it is grammaticalized: the interdependence of linguistics and philosophical logic

In logic the terms "predicate" and "argument" mark a syntactic distinction within semantic structure. This and other distinctions can be marked in different ways in different logical notations, and these can be thought of as analogous to different systems of grammaticalization. However, in logic, syntax is not just a matter of how differences of scope are marked, or of the size and typescript of symbols used, or the differences between Russell's notation and Polish notation for propositional and predicate logic. For in these cases there is no difference in semantic syntactic structure, but only in the way the same semantic syntactic structure is represented, "marked", or "grammaticalized". Yet even in traditional and classical logic, "Some A is not B" and "Not every A is B" present a difference of perspective and so of sense, giving motive for having both existential and universal quantifiers, despite their being normally interdefinable—a difference seen when the intuitionists reject inferences from the second to the first. As we shall see in chapter XIII, in natural languages we need always to distinguish cases where variation in form of grammaticalization or its absence has no semantic significance (thus the absolute phrase "Caesar having come", grammatically disjoint from the rest of the sentence, has the same significance as the corresponding adverbial clause) and variations which enshrine some real change of perspective and so of sense.

The terms "subject" and "predicate" were brought into use in semantics and grammar by speakers of the so-called nominative/accusative languages which constitute the great majority of the world's languages.[5] With ergative and other less common forms of language touched on later, parallel perspectival distinctions arise.

Many linguists and psycholinguists use the terms "predicate" and "argument" as if they needed no introduction—as if both terms had been already established with a clear meaning. But one has to look to Frege and his thinking of predicates as analogous to mathematical functions, the signs for them being "unsaturated" or "incomplete", waiting for completion by singular terms or variables, for the origin of this use of the word "argument".

Traditional notions of subject and predicate in grammar, with their common origin in Greek discussions of two thousand years ago, are echoed both in modern logic and in pragmatics. It is, therefore, a mistake to think of these notions as purely grammatical, as if they could readily shed their semantic or pragmatic associations. Although Chomsky defines the terms "subject" and "predicate" on a basis supposedly quite independent of any semantic or pragmatic ideas, the plausibility of his "results" depends upon the degree to which they resemble what traditional notional grammars have suggested.

(ii) The inseparability of semantics, pragmatics, and philosophical logic

Chapter X showed how the special semantic character of clauses, and of the verbal elements which typically give clauses this character, is set by the fact that, of all sentence constituents, they alone—after making appropriate grammatical modifications and adjustments of referential or anaphoric indications—are capable of occurring on their own as complete utterances in their own right. And it is only in this setting of the sentence or the clause that what it is to be a "subject" or "topic" is openly exhibited—with the subject as the expression for the topic or what is spoken about, whether singular or general, on the one hand, and the predicate or complete verbal frame figuring as a functional expression or "functor" on the other.

If I sometimes speak of the notion of subject as if there were only simple assertions, commands, and so forth, and not also subclauses within such sentences, then this is only for the purpose of simplicity of exposition. For such notions as clause, subject, predicate, and verb belong primarily to semantics and to the description of the semantic syntax or structure of clauses, whether occurring naked as complete utterances or not. But it is only when we think of the finite verb in such completed sentences as the glue which holds them together as unities that we can recognize the finite verb as having the same

5. Barry Blake, *Case*, 2nd ed. (Cambridge: Cambridge University Press, 2001), 121, suggests that ergative systems make up over 20 percent of the world's surviving languages, most of them spoken by relatively small numbers of people.

gluing function when it occurs in subordinate clauses as the "unsaturated" or "incomplete" expression within them.

(b) *The notions of subject and topic— their nonpsychological character*

It will be recalled that I introduced the notion of the logical subject of a sentence as "what a [declarative] sentence (a "saying", utterance, or statement) is about". Correlatively, I explained the "predicate" of such a sentence as "what is said about the subject", distinguishing carefully between singular subject terms and general subject terms. And any variations in the way we use the term "predicate" will directly affect our use of the term "argument".

However, linguists commonly use this same informal form of words, "what the sentence is about", both to introduce the traditional grammatical notion of subject and to introduce the "pragmatic" notion of "topic"—both notions important for semantics as concerned with "sense" in the broad use of the term explained in chapter III.

Much confusion has arisen from defining "Focus" and "Topic" almost as opposites, "focus" being commonly explained as meaning "new information" or, more generally, "the information which the statement is concerned to supply", and "topic" as something already familiar, some old information being presupposed by this familiarity. As a result the treatment of Focus has distorted thinking about Topic, and thereby also distorted thinking about subject and predicate.[6] However, conceived as a discourse-function, Focus is best thought of as to do with what the speaker intends to direct attention towards or to emphasize, and not as the opposite of Topic as the new to the old.

Indeed, far from Topic and Focus being opposites, the focus and the topic in a sentence or conversational exchange commonly coincide. This happens in the two types of case considered by Dik.[7] First, one can bring a nominal term or adpositionally marked nominal term into focus, making it a topic, as in "It is *the apples* which were rotten", "It was *with Mary* that John went home", "Who is winning?— It is *the Giants* who are winning",[8] or "It was *by the sword* that

6. This confusion appears in Siewieerska's views, whereby *categorial* or *predicative* statements in which the focus is said to be on what is said about a named entity are distinguished from *thetic* statements in which the event or state is reported as a whole; Butler, *Structure and Function*, 2:84.

7. Such cases are discussed in Dik, *Theory of Functional Grammar, Part 2*, 2nd ed., 313–15.

8. Robert van Valin and Randy LaPolla wrongly argue that because "the Giants" is the focus of the answer to a certain question in their example, it cannot be its topic, and that therefore the notion of subject in English is not topic-based; van Valin and LaPolla, *Syntax*, 252.

This tendency to allow ways of thinking about Focus to distort how we apply the clearer and independent notion of Topic appears in Robert D. Van Valin Jr. and Randy J. LaPolla, *Syntax: Structure, Meaning, and Function*(Cambridge: Cambridge University Press, 1998) 206–8. There they associate the notion of Focus with new information as opposed to presupposed information, drawing upon Knud Lambrecht's ideas in

Ann Boleyn was beheaded". Here, Dik means nominally based expressions which by topicalization become functional complements to a verb—putting the focus upon them makes them into the topics of the sentences concerned. Second, one can bring a predicate into focus and make it a topic, as in "*Clumsy* is what she said I was. *Clumsy* is what I am", "*Teach* is what he said I did. *Teach* is what I mean to do", "What did he do? *Teach* is what he did", "It was *towards London*, not away from it, that he was going", or, to give Bresnan's examples, "She said she would meet me, and *meet me* she has", and "*That he was sick* we talked about for days". The second possibility is of special interest because it shows how expressions whose verbal character normally prevents them from being arguments to the verb (we cannot say, "She has meet me" or "We talked about that he was sick") can become arguments to the verb by being topicalized or by the expression for them being left-dislocated, or, on occasion, right-dislocated.

The fact that a sentence may have more than one topic, as when we say, "That yacht of his, he lets it take up the whole of his life", must not deter us from approaching the notion of subject via the notion of what the sentence is about—that is, via the functional notion of "topic". The "he" constitutes the available topic marked as grammatical subject by its concord with the verb, which signals its being the verb's primary argument and fixes its relation to the predicate, the concords with the verb being marked in English by the nominative form of the pronoun and its position in the sentence in relation to the third-person singular verb. Meantime, "that yacht of his" is the immediate topic which grammar has marked as *focus of attention* by giving it the prominence of being placed at the start of the sentence (the *Vorfeld*), in what Dik and the Czechs called the Theme position in the sentence. Having been as it were extracted from the body of the sentence to be in a grammatically disjoint position, it requires a "resumptive" pronoun, "it", appearing later in the clause in order to fix its relation to the action of the verb, in this case as second argument to the verb in the hierarchy of arguments. Such rivalry between two topics, a Theme as a "disjoint topic" and the subject, within a sentence should not seem surprising.[9] It does not mean that such notions as Theme and Topic are merely psychological, since what we count as the "topic" of a sentence in these different ways is not linguistically arbitrary.

Information Structure and Sentence Form (Cambridge: Cambridge University Press, 1994). Then, on the basis of the dogma that Topic and Focus are opposites, they tell us that it is "one of the defining features of a sentence-focus construction" that "the subject is not the topic", so that neither "I", nor "my car", nor "car" can be described as the "topic" of "My car has broken down".

9. A disjoint topic need not occur at the start of a sentence. In some configurational languages in which agreement is marked only on the verb (making it "functional head" so that these languages are called "head-marking"), a "topic" may be distinguished simply by the absence of such head-marked agreement; see Bresnan, *Lexical-Functional Syntax*, chap. 6, 111–12, and examples in chap. 8, 144–79.

Keeping to our speech-orientated notion of sentence as an utterance or saying, it is natural to take the primary meaning of this phrase, "what the sentence is about", to refer to its topic. Yet some sentences—for instance, "It is raining"—very obviously do not mention their topic; in this case perhaps the weather at the place and time of the sentence being uttered, although no term for "weather" occurs in the sentence. Again, to mention a very different difficulty, some languages have been described as "topic-prominent"—for instance, Chinese. In a topic-prominent language one may have sentences such as could be represented, "The trees: the leaves are turning brown and falling" or "The battle: Harold's army fought long and hard, and failed only because Harold was killed". Here "the trees" and "the battle" would be counted as topics, and "the leaves" and "Harold's army" would seem to be paradigm "subjects" as arguments to the verb. Thus it is vital for both philosophical logic and linguistics to clarify the distinction between the more general notion of "topic" and the more specialized notion of "subject", granted that in common speech the terms "subject" and "topic" are almost interchangeable.[10]

The notion of topic as what is spoken about has a more open sense than the term "subject" in logic or linguistics. In English a "new" (i.e., future) topic is often introduced at the end of a sentence, as when a guide says, "As we go round the corner, you will see a great building on your left. There, that is the Radcliffe Camera". "Radcliffe Camera" thus becomes established as an available topic-term or "given topic" in later discussion, alongside the pool of general terms ("man", "dog", etc.) for things of well-known kinds. In this way, a growing pool of established topics becomes available to be spoken about. In a context in which it is already clear which battle is being referred to by an expression like "*the* battle", so that *this* battle is an available topic within the context, other topics become available within the same discourse-context, such as "the end of the battle", "the winning of the battle", or "the result of the battle", all now available as subjects of sentences.

Thus the underlying idea which guides logicians and linguists in their use of the word "subject" is that of "the topic, from among these available topics, which the speaker has selected to say something about and takes to be main argument to the verb (or main argument within the verbal framework)", and, when there is more than one candidate for this role, it is the topic picked out by the grammatical "concord" between it and the verb or predicate-expression. Thus what I will call the "functional grammatical subject" or, in my discussion, for simplicity, just simply "functional subject" is more precise-

10. The intuitive application of the word "topic" is often just as unclear as that of the word "subject" in common speech, where, for instance, one could say that geometry was the subject on which a person was talking, compatibly with saying that his topic or subject was triangles or, more particularly, isosceles triangles.

ly the "available topic selected to be taken as the primary noun-phrase argument within the verbal framework"; in effect, Joan Bresnan's "argument of the verb which serves as discourse topic" in her *Lexical-Functional Syntax*, where the selection of subject within the verbal framework establishes the perspective of the clause.[11] My concern is to maintain the connections of the notions of both subject and predicate with pragmatics, envisaging the predicate as embodying what the clause has in common with the complete utterance, and keeping a connection between the notions of subject and topic. In effect I follow the view of Li and Thompson that "subjects are essentially grammaticalized topics", while allowing for the presence of structure in speech at stages of incomplete grammaticalization, as with children and as in the development of creoles and pidgins.[12]

The conception of subject as the correlate of predicate is in a certain way primary, since a name as identifying a topic cannot be introduced except as a term which can stand as a subject to a predicate. That is, the possibility of using such terms correlatively with predicates is a precondition of using them in any syntactically different way, whether as vocatives (whether used in isolation or in connection with some full sentential utterance), or in the way seen in our hypothetical example, "The trees: the leaves are turning brown and falling".

Thus the topic/comment distinction and form of utterance presuppose the subject/verbal framework distinction and form of utterance, because any expression which identifies a topic has to be capable of occurring as subject expression within a verbal framework.

Moreover, if my argument is valid, pragmatic notions cannot be excluded from the description of a language if the notion of "predicate" is to have any application at all. And when language is applied to abstract subject-matters such as natural numbers, colors, and character traits, the consideration of thematic roles cannot be what determines the application of the notion of subject. Therefore the notion of subject must have some pragmatic basis, even though we will still need some further pragmatic characterization of the situation of disjoint or dislocated topics.[13]

11. Dik has a more psychological conception of the subject as the thing which, either by the speaker's sympathy or interest or by its being better known, is central from the vantage point from which matters are viewed. This explanation of "perspective" wrongly makes psychology, not pragmatics, primary.

12. Li and Thompson, "Subject and Topic", 484.

13. If, as Van Valin and others conceive, thematic roles determine which argument is to be considered the Privileged Syntactic Argument (PSA), we still need to use the notion of subject. We still need ways of distinguishing a syntactic subject from a disjoint topic. And, with abstract subject-matters where notions like actor and undergoer have no application, we still need to apply such notions as singular subject-term, disjoint topic, and general subject-term, e.g., in analyzing "The sum of two and three is five" or "As to the number three, there is no number of which it is the square".

Foley and Van Valin in *Functional Syntax* and Van Valin and LaPolla in *Syntax* ignore such considerations. They envisage a kind of neutrality whereby a core-argument of a subordinate clause can be given the

(c) *Tensions between linguistics and logic*

When the notion of subject was first introduced into thought as the correlate of the notion of "predicate", there was no clear boundary between philosophical logic and grammar.

The initial ideas inspiring predicate logic fit quite well with habitual ways of thinking in traditional grammar, allowing us to distinguish between singular subject terms and general subject terms, between individual and collective singular subject terms, between abstract and concrete subject terms, and between noun phrases functioning as arguments to a verbal framework and noun phrases functioning as attributes.

However, logicians then go further and treat singular terms as identifying argument-places within predicates, even when they do not have the role of grammatical subjects, but of some other kind of object complement or satellite of the verb, arriving at the notion of two or more place predicates and regarding these predicates as expressing or identifying relations. Hence all the singular terms in "William gave Sicily to Robert" would count logically as singular subject terms within the statement, although only "William" would count as grammatical subject, and in its discourse context would be the topic of the sentence (rather than, e.g., "Sicily").

Going yet further and forming a logic which includes both quantity expressions ("quantifiers") and negation (represented by "~" or "¬" in modern logic), they adopt the view that if we have an object, *a*, which is of the kind R, and both a predicate "F(...)" and its converse "~F(...)", then "F(*a*)" and "~F(*a*)" would each imply "*a* exists".[14] This predicate logic does not deal with "*a* exists" and logicians say that the existence of *a* is "presupposed" to avoid the word "implied" in this context, because the logic does not provide for expressing "*a* does not exist" (even though, in fact, a presupposition, as a condition of truth, remains only a special case of an implication). Moreover, if the R's are proposed as the domain of one's generalizations (the domain of

---

position of controlling the whole sentence independently of whether it is an actor or undergoer, or subject or object of any kind, in the subordinate clause. And they take this as implying that the language concerned does not have grammatical relations in the sense that its verbal structures can supposedly be described either without reference to pragmatic roles or without reference to thematic roles. They regard the Austronesian language of Acehnese as of the first kind, with the language's verbal structures describable in terms of what they count as semantic roles only, by which they mean thematic roles only—they do not consider the possible relevance of logical notions to "semantics".

In this, Acehnese is envisaged (Van Valin and LaPolla, *Syntax*, 262) as strangely parallel with the topic-prominent language Mandarin, where, in effect, "Seems: Lisi bought the car" is equivalent both to "The car: Seems Lisi has bought" and to "Lisi: Seems has bought the car", so that what in English would be the object and subject of the subordinate clause are equally eligible for being given the position of the subject of the whole sentence, it being thematic roles which in this case are irrelevant to structural-functional description.

14. Hence "F(*a*)" would imply "At least one R, say *x*, is such that F(*x*)"; and "~F(*a*)" would imply "At least one R, say *x*, is such that ~F(*x*)".

one's quantifiers), this logic provides no means of saying that R's do not exist. Therefore "exists" will not be logically a predicate, whether in "Zeus exists", "Hell exists", or "Tigers exist", and so in these sentences "Zeus", "tiger", and "Hell" will not be logical subject terms. Again, "Zeus" will not be a subject term in "Zeus is the chief of the gods" (if this is understood as describing Greek belief, not the facts, i.e., understood in the sense "In Greek mythology, Zeus is chief of the gods").[15] The functional grammatical subject term will not count as a logical subject in any of these cases.[16]

Accordingly, with existential statements such as "Napoleon did exist" or "Cerberus never existed", we shall have to say that "Napoleon" and "Cerberus" are *semantically* subjects, and "exists" *semantically* a predicate, although not subjects and predicates for the purposes of predicate logic.

I will clarify the distinction between "functional subject" (as "the argument of the verb which serves as discourse topic") and the "morphosyntactic subject" in section 2. It is the functional grammatical subject which we commonly think of as pragmatically the semantic subject. The notion of functional grammatical subject had to come first before, by formal analogy, the term "subject" could come to be applied in the degenerate case of the morphosyntactically required impersonal "it".

In short we need to envisage the many different uses of the word "subject" in human discourse as forming a system of family relationships involving a closely knit web of logically interconnected types of use in logic and grammar, constituting a family of historically developing uses, some very distant from the starting point.[17] The same is true of the terms "predicate" and "argument".

The associated systems of family relationship become even more extended because, speaking loosely, people now commonly depart from Frege's way of speaking and talk of the singular terms themselves rather than the objects they stand for as the arguments of the functions ("predicates") concerned, and talk of general terms in the same way. In a parallel way linguists and psycholinguists have come to speak of the noun expressions concerned, whether singular or general, as arguments to the verbal frameworks in which they occur. Extending the usage of the word "argument" yet further, linguists,

15. Such remarks about existence do not apply if a logical system allows empty names (e.g., Lesniewski's).

16. All these cases involve what logicians call "intentionality" or "referential opacity"—the truth or falsity of the statement being affected by intersubstituting different referring expressions for the same thing.

17. Thus its use in logic and grammar brought it close to the notion of *ousia* as Aristotle used it of "first substance" in the *Categories*, and then, since Descartes, to a way of thinking in which the human person is the paradigm example of a subject, and thence, because of the new preoccupation with epistemology, to varied uses of the pair of words "subject/object" correlative with various uses of the words "subjective" and "objective". Anscombe, in "The Intentionality of Sensation: A Grammatical Feature", paper 1 in *Collected Philosophical Papers*, 2:3–4, comments instructively on the strange history of these terms.

considering such sentences as, "That the earth is round was agreed by every educated person from Greek times" and "To eat is good", have come to speak of clausal and quasi-clausal complements of the kind found in these examples as "arguments", despite their having nothing name-like about them.

In the meantime linguists and others have followed the philosophers in using similar freedoms in speaking of predicates, not heeding whether they use the expression of the predicate as a whole—for instance, "... is white" or "... is a man"—or only the semantic nucleus of the predicate—namely, "white" and "man". Likewise it is useful to speak of "lexical predicates" with the same informality as the philosophers. In the sentences "Socrates is white", "Socrates is a man", and "Socrates looked at Plato", logically we have the predicates "... is white", "... is a man", and "... looked at —". But it is convenient to refer to "white", "man", and, following Ackerman and Webelhuth, "look ... (adverb optional) at" (the "at" behaving as a preposition) and "phone ... (noun or accusative pronoun optional) back" (the "back" behaving as an adverb) as "lexical predicates".[18] In "look ... (optional) at", the sign "... (optional)" indicates that the same lexical predicate is in use even if an adverb such as "intensely" is inserted internally as in "look intensely at".

Section 2. The Notion of Grammatical Subject

At first sight the notions of grammatical functions such as "subject" and "object" may seem quite clear. However, on examination, we find that this is far from the case. Here in section 2 I deal with the problems experienced in applying the notion of grammatical subject, treating them first because they are largely separable from the difficulties in applying the notion of object, with which section 3 is concerned. The latter reflect more general problems about systems of functional organization as seen in languages with different voice-systems organized along varied lines—sometimes with a mixture of nominative/accusative, ergative, and other features.

(a) *The place of the notion of subject in typical grammars for nominative/accusative languages*

In considering the notion of the grammatical function of "subject", I have in view what others call the subject at surface level (independently of whether or not such a thing as "deep structure" exists).

18. I here follow Ackerman and Webelhuth, *Theory of Predicates*, referred to in chap. I, n. 15 of this volume, except that I call them "lexical predicates" to distinguish the use of the word "predicate" in linguistics from that in logic. I discuss the case of "call ... up" in chap. XIII n. 73 of this volume.

Here we have to compare the accounts given by different grammars of why, if a verb has several noun complements and adjuncts ("arguments"), some one particular complement or "argument" should be regarded as privileged relative to any or all of the others.

(i) **The area of agreement between different approaches**

The various grammars, whether Chomskyan or non-Chomskyan, largely agree in their applications of the notion of subject with traditional grammars of configurational languages.

Within LFG, considered as a strictly formal system understood as in principle capable of being described independently of semantics, the grammatical function of subject is regarded as an undefined notion within the grammar as a formal system, but also definable in terms from outside the system as what uniquely combines the properties of being a grammaticalized discourse-function with being an argument function.[19] Thus, although the notion of subject cannot be captured in compositional or configurational terms, it can be explained in pragmatico-semantic terms. It is quite normal for formal systems that their application only becomes fixed by giving an interpretation to their primitive terms, and that their explanatory importance should depend upon the informal explanation given to these primitive terms—in this case, either the term "subject" itself or the discourse-function, "topic". Thus LFG combines being "formal" with being functionalist and avoids reliance on ad hoc devices by applying the notion of "subject" by introducing it as a primitive and then interpreting it in a functionalist way, as that "argument of the verb which serves as discourse topic".

By contrast, although the terms "subject" and "object" appear in Chomskyan grammar, it is essential to Chomskyan theory that all grammatical functions be defined configurationally so that the terms "subject" and "object" become entirely derivative terms, emptied of any independent meaning. As a result the terms "subject", "object", and "predicate" are deprived of any explanatory role,[20] and their role within the grammar becomes solely expository or

19. Bresnan, *Lexical-Functional Syntax*, 97–98. In early expositions of LFG, "subject" is presented as an undefined notion, whereas Bresnan, *Lexical-Functional Syntax*, 98, makes the connection with "topic" explicit and essential.

20. Bresnan expresses the same view, saying, "I don't think you CAN find an external motivation for Chomskyan dependency relations, because they really do not characterize forms of expression of language ..., but only abstract syntax from which actual forms are encapsulated in PF. Abstract dependency relations do not help you identify constituents at all; in fact, they frequently go against classical constituency tests grounded in overt syntax (see, e.g., Pesetsky's *Zero Syntax* on this). If anything, Chomsky in his Minimalist Program rounds even farther away from language.... Hence, his functional motivations are simply internal motivations for an imaginary computational system almost entirely disconnected from language as we know it"; Bresnan, correspondence with Matt Shibatani, http://web.archive.org/web/20050323112435/http://montague.stanford.edu/lfg/www.essex.ac.uk/linguistics/LFG/LFG-and-functionalism/BresShib.

presentational. The term "subject" can only have any explanatory importance for a formal grammar or in relation to what it is applied to if it is a primitive notion within the grammar, and this Chomsky excludes.

In short, if a "scientific" grammar has to be conceived solely in configurational or compositional terms, any semantic and pragmatic ideas drawn on in explaining the rationale of particular grammars of particular languages (some derived from philosophy and logic) will be completely irrelevant to the meaning of the words "subject", "object", and "predicate" in any such scientific grammar. For a Chomskyan grammar the associations these words carry are a matter of the dead history of words, misleading because they might suggest that these grammars are not purely formal—helpful only to those who wish to apply such grammars without thinking about how irrelevant to semantics and formal they are intended to be. In principle it should not matter if we rewrote such formal grammars using the words "subject" and "object" exactly the opposite way around!

However, in order to keep the closeness to traditional ways of speaking which is essential to maintaining the *semblance* of talking about the same discipline, Chomskyan grammars have no choice but to arrange that what they label "subject" and "object" does not disturb traditionally agreed assignments of the terms "subject" and "predicate". Thus the subject appears either as the head of the verb phrase or as in some way what completes the verb phrase within the clause and, however the presentation varies, figures in much the traditional relation to the predicate, if this is identified with "the verb phrase" or its ancestor in a phrase structure diagram. In practice, in Chomskyan grammars, the notion of "subject" requires exhaustive definition in configurational terms and is kept in touch with our normal modes of using the word "subject" by artificially bolstering phrase structure grammar with the conception of "Abstract Case", the principle of "Case Filter", and a complex system of rules governing "Movement". These devices appear artificial, like a system of epicycles, whereas common reasonings about why this or that sentence is grammatical or ungrammatical suggest that some less technical or more user-friendly explanation should be possible. The appearance of explanatoriness of such a formal grammar depends entirely upon its agreeing with traditional notional grammars in almost all its applications of the traditional vocabulary of "subject", "object", "noun", "adjective", "nominative", "accusative", and so forth.

As explained earlier, the uses of the word "subject" should be treated as enjoying a system of family relationships, so that we grasp each use by seeing its relationship to other uses of the term. Ideally we should hope to come to a unified notion of grammatical subject applying to every type of language. Here, I believe that, by drawing on the ideas of LFG and offering a system of related, but distinct lexical entries where different verbal structures are involved, although involving what we ordinarily call the same verb, we can avoid Perlmutter's suggestion that one needs to keep five different notions of grammatical subject in play.[21] In seeking such a unified notion of grammatical subject, the convenient place to begin is to recognize the pragmatic and logical roots of the notion of "subject" in traditional or "notional" grammars adapted to nominative/accusative languages, and how they achieve accord with our speech.

In sum, granted that noun-phrase arguments to the verb or within the verbal framework of the sentence or clause have to be considered as set in a certain hierarchy, the "grammatical subject" is what somehow grammatically presents itself as the primary argument within this hierarchy. And what gives it privilege is its pragmatic character as the already available topic (established as already given, rather than introduced as a new topic) which we are being told about, a notion reflected in predicate logic so that, in the words of Li and Thompson, "subjects are essentially grammaticalized topics". The subject in this sense, or more than one subject in the case of some relational propositions and where there is coordination, as in "Once upon a time, there was a man called Bob and a dog called Rover" (where the general terms "man" and "dog" have been picked out from the mass of other available topics), is then those topics from among the *available* topics, which are distinguished from rival candidates for the role of subjects in this conjunction by functional relation to the verb as arguments of the verb which serve as discourse topics. The subject defined in this functional way is typically also what we may call the morphosyntactic subject, defined as that with which the verb has concord in inflections for person (first, second, or third) and number (typically,

21. For the LFG approach, see Bresnan, *Lexical-Functional Syntax*, 25–40; cf. Geoffrey Horrocks, *Generative Grammar* (London: Longman, 1987), 235–44. LFG offers different lexical entries for related verbal structures, e.g., those exemplified in "I gave a book to Joseph" and "I gave Joseph a book", along with the passives "A book was given to Joseph (by me)" and "Joseph was given a book (by me)". Pinker, *Learnability and Cognition: The Acquisition of Argument Structure* (Cambridge, Mass.: MIT Press, 1989), is instructive in showing the lexical character of our knowledge of the different range of verbal structures allowed by the apparently similar verbs "give" and "donate".

Perlmutter proposes his five notions of grammatical subject in his "Syntactic Representation, Syntactic Levels, and the Notion of Subject", in *Nature of Syntactic Representation*, ed. Pauline Jacobson and Geoffrey K.Pullum (Dordrecht: Reidel, 1982), 283–340; cf. Perlmutter, "Functional Grammar and Relational Grammar", with ideas supported in William D. Davies, "Choctaw Subjects and Multiple Levels in Syntax", in *Perspectives on Functional Grammar*, ed. Hoekstra, Van der Hulst, and Moortgat (Dordrecht: Foris, 1981), 235–71. However, Perlmutter's relational grammar, Dik in his form of functional grammar, and Van Valin in his discussions of the notion of subject all assume that syntactic relations or functions must be independent of both semantic and pragmatic roles. I reject this preconception and, with LFG, insist in connecting the notions of subject and topic, as seen earlier.

I believe the resources of LFG make it possible to develop a Functional Grammar which avoids distinctions of level or stratum and deals with the difficulties raised by the languages considered by Perlmutter, Davies, and Van Valin. Making a connection between the notions of subject and topic also enables one to apply the notion of subject to what Dik calls "states", an application he excluded in his *Functional Grammar*; cf. Perlmutter, "Functional Grammar and Relational Grammar", 325; Davies, " Choctaw Subjects", 255.

singular or plural), and commonly also marked by case or configuration or both; further, only a subject can be the principal argument of a passive- or middle-voice verb or be referred back to by a reflexive pronoun, so as to constitute the principal argument of a reflexive verb.

(ii) The roots of the distinction between nominative/accusative and ergative languages

In what are called nominative/accusative languages, the effect of these definitions is to group the following subjects, (1) and (2), together:

1. The logical subjects of monadic predicates—namely,
   a. the logical subjects of attributions (of state, location, and circumstance),
   b. the logical subjects of the varied kinds of intransitive and reflexive verbs ("snore", "sleep", "fall", and "die", seemingly very different from "walk", "swim", and "jump", capable of being thought of as self-directed or reflexive and analogous to some things expressed in a middle/passive voice); and
   c. the logical subjects of verbs in the passive.
2. The logical subjects of transitive verbs used in the active voice or at least with an active meaning, the subject being the agent of an action expressed by the verb.[22]

By contrast, in purely ergative languages, these two groups, (1) the logical subjects of monadic predicates of non-active kinds and (2) agents of the action expressed by the verb, are separated. In the paradigm case group (1) is in the fundamental unmarked case of the noun, called the absolutive, and group (2) has the agent distinctively marked in a special ergative case. If one applies the notion of subject to ergative languages at all, it appears that what Foley and Van Valin call the "undergoer" is the only grammatically privileged argument of the verb, as section 3 will show, and so paradoxically its subject.

In his studies of children's speech Martin Braine reckoned it important that recognition of the roles of being a "subject of attribution" (of qualities), being an "actor", and being the object of a transitive verb (typically an undergoer) were each independent of the other two.[23] This means that children's learning capacity and possible teaching methods leave it open whether sub-

22. Martin Braine proposes that the "category" of subject in English is formed of the union of these two groups, and envisages the pragmatic notion of topic as more important in regard to some other languages; Martin Braine, et al., "Development of Categories", 489. However, if the question is of what is meant by the word "subject", then there seems no alternative to defining it in pragmatic terms, the approach I introduced in the introduction to this volume.

23. Martin Braine and Robin S. Wells, "Case-like Categories in Children: The Actor and Some Related Categories", *Cognitive Psychology* 10, no. 1 (1978): 100–22.

jects of attribution will be grouped with actors, as in nominative/accusative languages, or grouped with undergoers, as in ergative languages.

Ergative languages (Basque, Georgian, Inuit, and many Oceanic languages among them) utilize this contrast, naming agents of change in what is called the ergative case, while the undergoers of changes such as I listed earlier are named in the so-called absolutive case. If Caesar destroys a city or transports siege equipment from France to Italy, the expressions for city and siege equipment are throughout one and the same case, the absolutive, and Caesar is named in the ergative case as causing these changes. This absolutive case can also be used to name the subject of intransitive verbs, at least when these are not conceived to denote action—for instance, the sleeper who sleeps.

This creates a tension within the ergative system, since many of the same things are both subjects of changing attributes—conspicuously, change of place—and agents of this change; as well as the converse of the problem for nominative/accusative systems—that a self-moving agent as the grammatical subject is also the undergoer being moved. This double role, coupled with the problem of describing "immanent" activities, generates the instability in both systems of functional organization which I discuss at the end of this chapter.

(b) *Applying the notion of subject in nominative/accusative languages: resolving difficulties*

(i) A superficial problem in applying the term "subject" within nominative/accusative languages

In many languages, called "pro-drop" languages, where indication of the subject is unnecessary, it may have no distinct mention, there being no argument expression indicating it, its identity being merely implicit, as when in Latin a person says, "Te amo" meaning "I love you", in which it is the use of the first-person singular of the verb which shows that the statement is about the speaker. Such a sentence has a grammatical subject, but is lexically subjectless in the sense that there is no subject-expression. I call these silent subjects—silent in the sense that their identity is unambiguously indicated by the concord inflections of the verb, or by these together with the context. Allowing for this, we can safely say that by "grammatical subject" is usually meant either the entity (or class, in the case of general or collective terms) indicated by the person and number of the predicate or the argument expression which is designed to pick it out—for instance, "I" in "I love you"; and this fits quite well with the conceptions explained in chapter IX.

We are now in a position to show how the other problems which arise are to be solved.

(ii) A functional "formal grammar" capable of capturing the intuitive notion of subject

In order to follow through this intuitive conception of "argument of the verb which serves as discourse topic", we have to make a distinction between what is functionally the grammatical subject and various merely morphosyntactic subjects. Traditional grammars sometimes describe this distinction as being between a "real (or logical) subject" and a merely "apparent subject".[24] For instance, in the English sentence "It is raining", the word "it" enjoys the same position and concord with a verb as a genuinely pronominal subject, despite not being functionally the grammatical subject of the sentence. The "it" here holds the position of a merely "morphosyntactic subject".

At this point, in considering grammar, and with it the psychology of speech and hearing, we have to ask: is it the workings of the notion of functionally grammatical subject which explain the relevant morphosyntactic rules, or is it the morphosyntactic constraints, pragmatically and semantically empty, which explain the patterns we find? Here we will find below that pragmatically based functional patterns are more deeply embedded in a person's grasp of the *état de langue* at a particular time than the morphosyntactic patterns to which Chomskyan grammars limit their concern—for instance, in (iv) we see how the impersonal uses of "it" and "there" are to be explained in morphosyntactic terms. While the functional patterns suggested by LFG can be seen as refinements of Dik's Functional Grammar, the thorough work of the Lexical Functional school gives ground for confidence that the genuinely functional patterns concerned will be ones which can nonetheless still be regarded as adequately "formal" in the way grammar requires, to be analyzed in the distributionalist terms described in the introduction.

(iii) Dative and other non-nominative subjects

The first and clearest difficulty in following morphosyntactic criteria in deciding what we should count as functionally the subject of a sentence arises when the selected topic seems to be introduced in a case other than the nominative. Where apparent non-nominative subjects arise from the passivization of a transitive verb whose objects are not in the accusative and from intransitive verbs, they should be accepted as such. Chaucer provides a particularly compelling example showing this in *Canterbury Tales*, the Prologue A 785–87:

Us thoughte it was noght worth to make it wys
and graunted him withouten more avys,
and bad him seye his verdit, as him leste.

24. E.g., Maurice Grevisse, *Le Bon Usage*, 13th ed. (Paris: Duculot, 1993), 305–7, which gives a much fuller discussion than the 6th edition (1964), 129.

Here the pronoun *us* is survival of a dative, assimilated in form to the accusative, and is nonetheless allowed to stand as subject to "graunted" and "bad", because these verbs are in conjunction with "thoughte", even though their subject in normal contexts would have been "we".[25] The "thoughte", like the "thinks" in "Methinks she doth protest too much", is a survival from a verb *thunkan* (*thyncan*) meaning "seem", coordinate with a verb *thenkan* meaning "think", so that etymologically "methinks" means "it seems to me".

Parallel examples of dative subjects are to be found in the German "Mir ist kalt" ("I am cold"), "Mir werde geholfen" ("I am being helped"), and "Mir wurde geholfen" ("I was being helped"), where "mir" is a dative and there is no rival for the position of being grammatical subject.[26] In Icelandic, verbs with a dative or even a genitive object in the active voice commonly have their subject in the dative or genitive respectively in passive constructions.[27] There are many parallels in Malayalam and in many other languages.[28]

25. I take this example from Blake, *Case*, 148. He comments beforehand: "In Old and Middle English there were inversion verbs where the dative complement could be treated as a subject from the point of view of co-ordination. In the same sentence within Chaucer '*thoughte*' (OE *thyncan* 'to seem'), where a verb formed by inversion, is conjoined with *graunted*, which is a normal verb". He also notes: "The verb *leste* (OE *lystan* "to please") is also an inversion verb used impersonally, literally 'as to-him it lusted', i.e. 'as it pleased him'".

Such impersonal usages were still very common in Shakespeare's time, out of whose text A. C. Baugh and T. Cable instance "it yearns me not", "it dislikes me", and "so please him come" in *A History of the English Language*, 4th ed. (London: Routledge and Kegan Paul, 1993), 240. In a parallel way, OE had two verbs for "hang": one transitive with active meaning used in order to say that a person hung something in a certain place or on a certain object, and the other with an intransitive meaning conveying that the subject passively hung there.

26. To give a fuller spread of examples in German, one has "Dir [dative] wurde geholfen" ("You were being helped"), "Mir ist kalt" ("I am cold"), and "Mir wird geholfen" ("I am being helped").

A grammatical form which develops in one way may come to be interpreted in another, so that "methinks" might pass from being understood as meaning "it seems to me" to being thought and understood as meaning "I think". One could then construe this second example as having the sense of "She does, methinks [I think] protest too much". Chomskyan grammar could then propose a rival analysis, taking "that she doth protest too much" as the deep structure subject of "It seems to me that she doth protest too much" (in the latter, "it" would be grammatical subject at surface level in virtue of being the "target of movement" for the clause).

27. Icelandic presents one of the richest sources of examples of this phenomenon (Avery D. Andrews, "The Representation of Case in Modern Icelandic", in *Mental Representation*, ed. Bresnan, 461–69; cf. 482), while Thrainsson's work provides the richest source of argument that the grammatical subject should here be identified with the semantic subject (H. Thrainsson, *On Complementation in Icelandic* [New York: Garland, 1979], 462–76) and that the decision not be treated as arbitrary, drawing several supplementary arguments from LFG in support of this conclusion.

28. In the example from Chaucer, in a conjunctive sentence, a topic introduced in the dative as a subject to "thoughte" needed no reintroduction in the nominative before being taken as subject to the verbs "graunted" and "bad". Similar constructions are possible in Icelandic, but not in modern English or in German, where if a topic is introduced as subject in the dative, it is liable to need reintroduction in the nominative, as in "Dir war kalt und du zogst eine Jacke an" ("You were cold and you put on a jacket"); and again in German, if a topic is introduced in the nominative, it needs reintroduction in the dative to be subject to "wurde geholfen" ("was helped"). Thus, in Chaucer and in modern Icelandic the first mentioned subject counts as a "privileged syntactic argument" in Van Valin's sense, but not in modern English or German; Van Valin and LaPolla, *Syntax*, 354; cf. 150, 352–76, in the setting of 317–76. The phenomena are complex, as may be seen from Van Valin, "Synopsis of Role and Reference Grammar", 67, where Van Valin observes that

These cases create little problem. The argument of the verb which is the discourse topic in the sentences or subsentences concerned is not in doubt. And, although both types of case constitute violations of the norms of present day English and German respectively, and although in Chomskyan grammar there is no surface subject in either, nonetheless pragmatic, semantic, and configurational criteria concur in regard to what should be regarded as grammatical subject, which is in some cases by default the only available topic. The problem of other non-nominative subjects is to be resolved in analogous ways.

The same way of thinking enables us to recognize when genitive phrases or their prepositional equivalents, in virtue of their specificatory and identificatory role, are serving as subject or object phrases in certain languages, so that what would be in a word-by-word translation "Of dogs followed him" might mean "Some dogs followed him". Understanding this provides a basis for considering the grammar of such sentences as "Lots of men pursued him" and "He drank a lot of milk", discussed later.

(iv) Identity of the grammatical subject is not arbitrary—problem of impersonal constructions

Functional grammars and formal grammars, such as LFG, in which "subject" is a primitive notion explained by reference to discourse function, allow one to take a different position from Chomskyan grammars as to what should be regarded as the grammatical subject in many cases in which "intuition" (or perhaps early language teaching) provides no clear guidance. Conspicuous among these are sentences such as "There are tigers in my garden", among many other cases in which the active voice is being chosen as the default voice of the verb, rather than to signify action by an actor, a feature of these cases to which I return later. In such cases, what one says is not arbitrary but determined by one's concept of "subject".

In "There are tigers in my garden", a new topic, "tigers in my garden", is being introduced and therefore cannot be conceived of as an already available topic. However, there are two views as to whether this sentence has a

"The money [dative] has been returned to-her [dative]" is acceptable in German, but not in Icelandic. Van Valin and LaPolla's argument on *Syntax*, 356, cannot override the reasons put forward in the introduction and chap. IX of this volume for insisting that pragmatically rooted notions of subject and topic have application to every language.

In Latin and the Germanic languages considered, there is co-reference between the subject of a sentence containing a subordinate *oratio obliqua* construction and the nominative subject of this construction if its verb is finite, or the accusative subject of this construction if it is formed with the infinitive. Icelandic and English allow the contraction of such subordinate finite clauses from "N is boring" to "N boring", but no such contraction (e.g., the omission of an infinitive "to be"/"be") is allowed in the languages with the infinitive construction. Hence, in Icelandic, "They [dative] seem always to have thought Olaf [nominative] boring [with the meaning "boring to them", which would be expressed with "them" in the dative]" is grammatical, whereas German does not allow an equivalent contracted form; "Olaf [nominative] seems always they [dative] to have thought boring [as it were to them]" is also ungrammatical; Van Valin and LaPolla, *Syntax*, 357.

grammatical surface subject: the one, found in the 1973 *Shorter OED,* that "tigers" is the grammatical subject according to the rules of concord, and that the "there" is here an adverb, and the other, that "there" is the grammatical subject. The latter view has been said to follow on Chomskyan principles, "there" being regarded as a nominative plural because its "Abstract Case" principle and number are determined by its indicating a place which is the target of movement for "tigers" and which would be nominative plural after movement.[29] Against this, I show in (v) that such impersonal occurrences serve to preserve the morphosyntactic structure required by English and French, but in no way introduce a true grammatical subject.

Let us consider the effects of seeking to identify "verbally selected available topics" in order to identify functional subjects. In "There are tigers in my garden", the phrase "tigers in my garden" is not a syntactic unity, and so "tigers in my garden" cannot be the subject— "my garden" is merely where the tigers concerned are. The perspective which the sentence suggests is closer to that of "Tigers have come into / are occupying themselves / live in my garden" than that of "My garden is being visited / occupied / lived in by tigers". Accordingly, it would seem quite reasonable to consider "tigers" as the primary noun argument within the verbal framework "there are ... in my —". Therefore this line of approach of searching for the selected topic suggests "tigers" as functional grammatical subject, something for which we shall see further reason later, and allows us to avoid falling back to the position of treating the impersonal "there" or "it" as grammatical subjects. In this way, in deciding what is to be considered the grammatical subject of an utterance, we can keep to noun-searching principles which respect pragmatic structure but still respect the morphosyntactic aspect of the decision.[30] The rationale of departing from criteria of a configurational compositional kind in picking out the grammatical subject thus remains formal, as it has to be, since otherwise there would be no distinction between formal or morphosyntactic criteria of subjecthood and semantic or logical ones.

We must also deal with the cases in which impersonal constructions are used for the sake of what is called topicalization, whose better title would be the focalization of the topic, such as in "It is clumsy that she called me", "It was with the sword that Saint Paul was martyred", "It is these books which John

29. "Abstract Case" for Chomsky is "case" in a sense neither morphologically indicated nor defined through thematic roles.

30. Hence Blake, *Case,* 134, seems mistaken in his discussion of a complaint to a waiter, "There is a fly in my soup". He thinks it obvious that, because the primary intention is not to make a statement about "a fly", "a fly" cannot be the subject in the straightforward way in which it might be the subject of "A fly is in my soup", perhaps said in a different context. Saying, "English grammar demands a subject", he declares that "there" is this subject. However, if one's aim is to find the noun phrase which is discourse argument to the verb, "a fly" will be the subject, just as "tigers" was the subject of "There are tigers in the garden".

bought", and "It is these books which are what John bought". The sense of the last two of these is to draw attention to "these books", somewhat as one does whenever a demonstrative is used for the sake of emphasis and not just for the purpose of identification. It is as if one has said "Look! These are the books which John bought".

The natural view is that in these latter utterances, the focus is on an already identified topic, "these books", and we are being told about them that they are the things which John bought. Something referred to, as here, by ostension (e.g., pointing) counts as an already available topic, therefore eligible to be a subject. According to our reasoning, they are grammatical as well as logical subjects. If one followed the Chomskyan approach instanced earlier, one would have to follow the convoluted line of thinking that the grammatical subject is the "it", on the ground that it indicates a place which is the target of movement for "what John bought", and this would be nominative singular after movement, so that the "it" is to be considered as a nominative singular. By contrast, in any functional approach treating the notion of subject in the same way as LFG, one would regard the expression "these books" as the subject because it is the referring expression which picks out the "argument of the verb which serves as discourse topic".[31]

(v) A general consideration of impersonal constructions

In reference to impersonal constructions in general, we can say for sure that if the impersonal sentence "It is raining" has a topic, this is only implicit, for instance, the weather at the place and time of the utterance, or this place and time. Such sentences are linguistically subjectless, but, again, the 1973 *Shorter OED* considers them as having "it" as their grammatical subject, being guided by the concord of verb with subject, and fitting with Chomskyan grammar.

However, this kind of case arises only because English is a language with a pronoun which is entirely unmarked, capable of being semantically empty because unmarked. If one extends Ackerman and Webelhuth's conception of lexical units composed of more than one word from the lexical predicates considered in chapter I, section 2 (b), then one can consider "I love", "thou lovest", "he loves" as lexical units differing only morphosyntactically from the Latin "amo", "amas", "amat". Indeed, the distinction between the English "it is

31. As we saw earlier, not only referring expressions, but also uniquely identifying expressions whose reference is indeterminate, so long as they have reference, can serve as grammatical subjects. Therefore, in "It is those books, the last four, which you would find at the top right-hand corner of the end bookshelf, which he has bought in the contract", in which a new topic with a means of identification has been introduced by means of a demonstrative expression with the sense of a definite description, not a referring expression, nonetheless the demonstrative expression concerned, "those books, the last four, which you would find at the top right-hand corner of the end bookshelf", would still count as "the grammatical subject", granted the implication of present existence. Similarly, in "It is whoever chatted you up in the street today that we need to find to get your purse back", "whoever chatted you up in the street today" is the grammatical subject.

raining" and the Latin "pluit" becomes nonexistent in speech except in questions, because English has ceased to allow a negative particle to intervene between the pronoun and the finite verb in any of its forms of negation (consider "It rains not", "It is not raining", "It does not rain", and their inverted forms), and nothing else can intrude at this point. "There is" and "there are" have gained the same indivisibility. This is of interest when one considers popular contemporary spoken French, where there is an increasing tendency to think of the pronoun (perhaps along with pronominal clitics) and verb as forming one indissoluble group, with the result that one will say things like "Moi je-pense ..." and "Mon pere il-dit que ..." (my hyphen indicates that these lexical units have begun to be treated as unitary wholes).

True, Old and most Middle English would have had the original "ne" before the finite verb, the "not" being at first introduced only for emphasis. Modern English preserves record of the relevant original syntax only in its written forms and prosody. Nonetheless, the conception of pronoun and finite verb as forming one lexical unit invites the conception that in modern English, in impersonal constructions, the "it" appears only as a canonical part of the finite verb, the form given to it by the language and not for any other reason. The function of this "it" is simply to exclude any referential functions or, in linguists' terms, "anaphor", such as arise with normal pronouns; hence this "it" is grammatically no longer a true pronoun and occupies a pronoun's morphosyntactic place with the effect of excluding a noun or true "pro-noun".

Languages which do not introduce reference to subject unnecessarily (so called pro-drop languages) say, for example, "Pluit" rather than "It is raining". But here no subject pronoun has been dropped, because there is no subject noun-phrase for a pronoun to go proxy for. If we come now to English, we have the singular third-person nominative pronouns "he" (masculine or generic animate), "she" (feminine), and "it" (neuter, going proxy for a baby, lower animal, plant, or inanimate thing, concrete [the Louvre] or abstract [the number 4]). However, English also uses the "it" with these diachronic roots within *langue* in order to mark the verb as being used in a context and way in which it excludes a subject. Accordingly it is actually grammatically *incorrect* to regard the impersonal "it" or "there" as subjects in the utterances concerned—the need to consider what is involved in being a functional subject in order to make the origins of these morphosyntactic forms intelligible shows the artificiality of treating the morphosyntactic conception of subject as in any way fundamental.

This account can be generalized to cover cases of impersonal constructions utilizing pronouns in other languages—for instance, in the French "il y a", "il fait beau", "il fait froid", and such like, in which the "il ... y a" and "il ... fait" can be considered as single lexical units, even though their syntactic complexity still appears in speech, since the negative particle "ne" can intrude, separating the pronoun from its sequel. In written French in the eleventh century, the forms "y a" and even just "a" are attested, as well as "il y a", which confirms that the purpose of the presence of the "il" in this and other impersonal constructions in later times has been solely in order to conform to what was becoming or had become the customary lexical form for the unmarked finite verb.[32]

The situation of the impersonal "it" is analogous to that of the number 0 (zero) as it occurs in the arithmetic of whole numbers (as distinct from its separate function as an element in the notational systems of higher whole numbers, e.g., 10, 1,002, and of the measures of continuous magnitudes, e.g., as in 30.304506 microns; or as the coordinate of an axis in a system of coordinates taking both positive and negative values). Cantor and Frege conceived of the number 0 as the power or cardinal number of the supposed sets of all and only those things which have a particular property where nothing has this property. It is not a number of a kind used in counting or measuring anything which exists. When we count a group of things we assign the number 1 to the first, 2 to the second, and so forth, and if we began by assigning 0, we would always get the wrong answer. There are no collections with no members, no lines of zero length, and, in general, no continua of zero magnitude—such things are not collections and not continua, though they have a status and role analogous to that of Pascal's equally fictional points at infinity in his system of projective geometry.

The "is" is now more puzzling than the "it".

Here we must avoid the mistake of thinking of the verb "to be" simply in terms of uses which conform readily to a subject/predicate pattern, whether the "is" be the copula or "is" of attribution, the "is" of existence, or the "is" of identity. Rather, to express the matter in a banally obvious form, "is" is the elemental or default verb, figuring in a sentence to convey the drama which gives it the character of a sentence. One could picture a precocious but astonished child coming in to its mother and reporting "Is fact (lion in lounge)", where there is no real subject, animate or inanimate, and the child has not learned the impersonal "it".

The impersonal "it is" also figures in such modal expressions as "it is possible …" and in connection with cognitive verbs as in "it seems / is thought / is true that …", as well as in the cleft construction exemplified in "It was Snooks whom I met", commonly described as an example of "topicalization" whose purpose is to put the focus on the topic in a sentence. If one reviews all the various cases of topicalization, some considered later, one finds that it is as if one were expressing a *thought* of a kind one might represent in the form "Is (these books [not those computer games] that John bought)", "Is (clumsy

32. Alain Rey, ed., *Dictionnaire Historique de la langue française* (Paris: Dictionnaires Le Robert, 1992).

that she said I was)", and, in earlier cases, "Is (tigers which are in the garden out there)", and "Is (bucketing rain outside)". The "Is ..." serves semantically to put focus on the topic and on occasion to introduce a new topic, while the round brackets are serving the role of punctuation marking scope.

Thus an adequate grammar has to recognize that the "is" serves a semantic function in these, whereas the function of the "it" is purely morphosyntactic. One may surmise that the insistence in German on placing the finite verb in the second place in the main clause, preceded only by the *Vorfeld* announcing a topic ("Theme") possibly other than the subject, even when it involves separating the auxiliary from the rest of the verb, has its rationale in serving the same function of expressing the dramatic force of the live utterance.

In chapter XIII, section 4, we shall see how easily systems of inflection and word divisions can melt away over time, especially where the spoken form of a language is little controlled by its written form. And we should remember that it is primarily the spoken form of a language at a particular time whose syntax the language-learner and listener have to penetrate. In this process they first learn the workings of pronouns as used referentially and cross-referentially, and only subsidiarily their empty use in some languages to express the default form of the verb in impersonal constructions. It is only because the so-called pronouns in this empty use have the same morphosyntactic relations to the verb as pronouns in their normal referential use that they count as subjects at all, as what I call "morphosyntactic subjects". Thus we have to learn to understand pronouns in their role as functional subjects before we can understand their degenerate impersonal use or see any reason to call them subjects at all. We cannot penetrate the morphosyntactic structure without first establishing the functional one. We are not given the morphosyntactic structure directly. Our access to grammar has to be in this way top-down, the functional explaining the morphosyntactic.

(c) *Problem cases associated with topic-prominence*

(i) The grammatical treatment of existential statements

The effects of our conception of the subject as the "verbally selected available topic" are illustrated when one considers the grammar of the varied existential statements puzzling to logicians. These are problems because, in a limited way, a topic may be mentioned for consideration of evidence or argument as to its existence, since this has to be agreed before it becomes fully established as a topic for further inquiry.[33]

33. As Aristotle makes clear, although we need to know the meaning of the word for a thing (e.g., an eclipse as a darkening) before asserting its existence, we need to know its existence before developing a science of its nature.

Consider such statements as "There are tigers", "There is a God", or "There are dragons" and their negatives. While "there" would seem to figure as morphosyntactic subject according to Chomskyan criteria, "active living being" would seem the available topic, the sentence introducing tigers as a new topic for future inquiry. By contrast the affirmations "Tigers exist", "God exists", "Dragons exist", and "Cerberus exists", representing announcements of something already concluded, present less difficulty. In all these cases we have a grammatical subject, although not a logical subject, for reasons seen earlier.

As to "Tame tigers exist", its proper analysis depends on how it comes into discourse: (a) if it introduces a discussion of the special properties of domesticated tigers, stating their existence as an available and given topic for study, "tame tigers" would be the grammatical surface subject of the statement; (b) if it means "Some tigers are tame", whether "tiger" or "some tigers" is the grammatical surface subject depends on whether a quantifier counts as part of the surface subject or whether, as I argue later, only the general subject term "tiger" counts as grammatical surface subject; (c) as to "There are tigers which are tame", this treats "tiger" as the available topic and grammatical subject, perhaps introducing "tame tigers" as a possible future topic.

(ii) Rivals for the title of subject: resolving the problems presented by "topic-prominence"

The view we have taken makes it quite intelligible that there should be rivals for the title of subject, a difficulty highlighted by the phenomenon of what is called "Left Dislocation"—for instance, "That yacht of his, he wastes all his time on it". The phenomenon is particularly unmistakable in Icelandic, as highlighted by Thrainsson in his discussion of Icelandic, which, unlike English, retains clearly distinct case-inflections: in English one can say, "This ring, Olaf has promised it to Mary", in which "this ring" and "Olaf" are both in the nominative case, while in Icelandic the "it" referring back to this nominative, as the thing promised, is put in the dative, as the Icelandic use of the verb "promise" requires.[34] In this an already given available topic is picked out as what Dik calls Theme or disjoint topic—that is, what the whole saying is about, and this is signaled by its being put into the nominative case and at the beginning of the sentence (the left); yet meantime the whole original predication is left intact, including its own nominative as a rival subject, while a resumptive pronoun in its original non-nominative case refers back to the announced Theme. The case is unusual, but easy to understand. The elected topic from the point of view of the whole discourse setting, the "subject-matter" which the sentence concerned is beginning to tell us about, is differ-

34. Thrainsson, *On Complementation in Icelandic.*

ent from the verbally selected available topic as marked by the formal criterion of what the predicate is in concord with in person and number, which is also naturally thought of as what or whom the sentence is about. Both are already available or given topics, but only the second is grammatically surface subject to the predicate. This exhibits the impossibility of making an absolute divide between subject-prominence and topic-prominence.

We find a parallel difficulty with two candidates for being counted as subjects in the case of interrogatives in English. It is correct to say, "Who did Mary tell that she was breaking off her engagement to him?" where the hearer is ignorant of whom Mary had been engaged to, and also correct to say, with a stress on the "who" (with the consequent pause after it), "Mary told *who* that she was breaking off her engagement to him?" Both questions seek answers such as "Tom", "It was Tom", or "It was Tom who was told by Mary that she was breaking off her engagement to him". In both questions the Theme is indicated by "who", and there is a resumptive pronoun "him" in a non-nominative case. However, we still have a second subject, the grammatical subject who tells and breaks off her engagement: "Mary" and "she" in both questions.

I can now return to consider the problematic case of "In my garden, there are tigers" (analogous to "My garden has tigers in it"), and why one should feel no pressure to regard what Dik and the Prague school identify as the Theme "in my garden" as the grammatical subject. Forced to admit the possibility of rival candidates for being counted as the subject of a sentence, we must insist that anything called "grammar" has to retain some respect for the form of the clause. Accordingly, although in the utterance "In my garden, there are tigers", "my garden" should not be considered as a merely peripheral argument, since the perspective in which the situation is seen makes the garden nonperipheral, it still lacks a sufficiently close relation to the main verb "are" to be regarded as a complement or argument to the verb, even a discourse-argument. The grammatical subject here is "tigers" (or "tiger" as shown later), while "there" is a merely morphosyntactic subject, and "my garden" is a disjoint topic.

(iii) The problems presented by designations of the logically functional form f(a)

Statements introduced by functional expressions of the logical form "f(a)" often present the intuitive difficulties highlighted by Grevisse when he considers how one is to identify the subject of, for instance, "The capital of France is Paris".[35] Here the morphosyntactic criteria suggested by case, concord with the verb, or word order seem misleading.

Normally, with unproblematic subject/predicate statements, if we pick out

35. Grevisse, *Le Bon Usage*, 13th ed., 321.

the main predicate "is F" or "Fs", then, first, the subject will be what is selected if we ask, "Who [or 'Which'] is F [or Fs]?" or "What is F [or Fs]?" and second, since one might expect the subject S to be a point of least focus, one would expect the formula "It is S who [or 'which'] is F [or Fs]" to be well-formed.

However, applying these tests to "The capital of France is Paris", we find, first, that it is very odd to ask "Which is Paris?" and expect the answer "the capital of France", while "What is Paris?" does not call for this answer rather than another, and, second, that "It is the capital of France which is Paris" is very odd. "France" seems closest to being the topic, although evidently not in privileged relation to the verb, and "the capital of France" is only an apparent or morphosyntactic subject. We have three alternatives: to choose the surface subject in accord with purely morphosyntactic criteria as is natural on a purely formal approach; to be led by pragmatic considerations to regard "France" as subject, despite its lack of privileged relation to the verb; or to identify some more attractive way of handling the problem. It should be noted that this problem arises with all functional designations: "The square of 2 is 4", "The father of Isaac was Abraham", and "The capital of France is Paris" are all of the form "f(a) = b".

A much more attractive suggestion is to construe functional designations such as "the capital of France" nonreferringly—that is, as meaning "the city, whichever it is, which is capital of France". That is, the grammatical subject of such sentences will be whatever general term they presuppose, and in the case of "The capital of France is Paris", this will be the general term "city", since clearly the function "the capital of ..." presupposes that it is a city which is being spoken of. The sentence "The capital of France is Paris" would not have been properly understood unless it was realized that it was a city which was being asked about or spoken of. In the case of "the square of 2", the general term concerned will be "number", and all expressions of the form "f(a)", as they occur in identity statements, should be approached in this way. Frege's example of "The Morning Star is the Evening Star" presents a particularly intriguing example of this. On a natural interpretation this means, "That most conspicuously bright celestial object which over extended periods appears in the morning (and which is named from this) is identical with that most conspicuously bright celestial object which over extended periods appears in the evening (and which is named from this)". In the interpretation which makes this an identity statement of the form "g(morning) is g(evening)", it has "bright celestial object" or "star" as its functional subject.

Thus, just as we avoided analyzing "In my garden, there are tigers" as meaning "My garden has tigers in it", we now avoid analyzing "The capital of France is Paris" as meaning "France has Paris as its capital".

However, this case is clear only because, in such statements, such expressions as "the capital of France" are clearly serving only as descriptions and not also as themselves referring expressions. But in nonidentity statements the expressions "f(a)" and "a" as they occur in a statement will both be being used referringly. In such cases "f(a)" will be functionally the grammatical subject.

Very commonly we have to consider context to determine whether the functional expression, and not only its argument, is used referringly. Thus one might say at a dinner, "The winner of the Booker Prize is about to speak", meaning, "The winner [already identified in the situation, e.g., by the impresario] is about to speak", somewhat as we might say, "Quiet, look, the Queen is about to speak", and then functionally the grammatical and semantic subject will be "the winner [of the Booker Prize]". However, one might mean "the winner [whichever of the people sitting around here is the winner] is about to speak", and then functionally the grammatical and semantic subject will be "person", and in "The winner of the Booker Prize is about to speak", the functional expression will not be being used referringly. In neither case is the Booker Prize the topic or the functional or semantic subject of the utterance. Likewise, in "Whoever got to the top of Mount Everest first was either a very tall man or an unjustly treated one", the subject is "person".[36]

However, in other contexts it is not difficult to conceive "the winner of the Booker Prize this year, whoever it is" as the topic of a conversation. Suppose we abridge this expression to "the W". One could imagine the following conversation: "I wonder who the W is."—"The W is bound to be a woman; they haven't chosen a man for years."—"That's not true, and the W is at this table, although they haven't announced who he or she is."—"The W will be young, I bet you… ". If one follows Brentano and describes "what the mind is mentally directed towards" as the "intentional object", one could say that "the W" identifies and refers to an "intentional object". Accordingly there is no obstacle to treating "the W" as functionally the grammatical and semantic subject of the utterance, despite its indeterminacy of reference.

(d) *Specifying the grammatical subject in cases of atypical formations*

Our problems began when it was first observed how, to first appearance, "it", "nobody", and "ten men" all equally look as if they are morphosyntactic subjects in such sentences as, "It is raining", "Nobody came", and "Ten men attacked me", despite such morphosyntactic subjects showing so little correspondence with any intuitive notion of topic or subject of discourse. Different grammars distinguish these cases in different ways, and we have seen how, in particular, it is still possible for a functional grammar to escape this problem

36. "Sir Edmund Hillary or Sherpa Tenzing" is not a name or referring expression; cf. Geach, *Reference and Generality*, 65–70.

while retaining a formal framework for identifying the grammatical subject, instancing LFG in this connection.

(i) How the grammatical subject should be specified

The first question is as to how one should pick out functional grammatical subjects when they are qualified by identity and quantity indicators and are not referring expressions, or else when they refer to collections spoken of distributively (as in "The Government are liars").

We have examined grammatical subject phrases of many kinds. Other cases include all names and all demonstrative expressions, and likewise all possessive expressions formed with possessive pronouns (e.g., "My books") or proper names in possessive form (e.g., "Bill's books") used as semantic subject terms. And along with all these we have expressions using the indefinite article when these have the sense of "A certain X" (as in "A certain Corsican became known as the greatest general of the Enlightenment period"), or "Certain Xs", or, in the case of kinds of material, "Certain X" (as in "Certain uranium was stolen" and "Certain liquid was administered").

In general, whenever we have a question asked by means of a *wh*-interrogative—for instance, "Who did you ask to marry you?" (= You asked *who* to marry you?) and "Whom did you ask to marry you?"—we can form a referring functional expression from it—that is, "the person whom you asked to marry you", eligible to be a grammatical subject.[37] However, in all such cases, one can form a parallel expression, "whomsoever you asked to marry you", still implying existence, but indeterminate in reference, and in this case the grammatical subject will be the presupposed general term "person".[38]

In our functional approach, in statements whose noun subject phrase is formed with quantity terms, it is the general term considered as unmarked, not the quantified expression containing it, which should be counted as grammatical subject: for instance, "ewe" in "Every ewe / no ewe / one ewe / some ewe is less than 40 kg", and equally in "All of the ewes / none of the ewes / some / a few / several / many / most ewes are less than 40 kg" ("some" before a plural noun being a form of the indefinite article, equivalent to "at least two"), and along with these "Two / three / ... / a thousand / ... [and so on indefinitely] ewes are less than 40 kg", while whether the noun is singular or plural will turn on the sense of the quantity term. It has been a commonplace since the encounter of Odysseus with the Cyclops that "nobody" is not the name of anybody, and the same is true of all these parallel expres-

37. These questions differ only in expecting different forms of answer, viz., answers such as "Mary" and answers such as "It was Mary whom I asked to marry me"; cf. chap. XIII, sec. 5 (b), of this volume.

38. In contemporary speech the last two examples given seem archaic, "whom" having become optional except after prepositions, and "whoever" being preferred both to "whosoever" and "whomsoever", the "-so-" particularly obsolete in common use.

sions.[39] It is the stem as determined by the lexicon which should be counted as grammatical subject (e.g., the nominative singular may often be defective—e.g., in Latin *homo* does not include the stem *homin-*, and in Greek *aner* does not include the stem *andr-*, although in such irregular cases as the French *oeil*, plural *yeux*, one should count *oeil* as grammatical subject by default).

A complication arises with the indefinite article "a" when it marks indiscriminateness—that is, when it is equivalent to "any". In a formation "Any A, if it is F, it is also G", the subject term will be A, and the existence of A's will be presupposed. But in the formations "Any F is G", "An F is G", and "No F is G", the existence of Fs may not be presupposed, and one needs to examine the discourse-context in order to identify the selected topic, perhaps some general term more general than F (the need to refer to the context to identify the selected topic is very common: if a sentence begins with "He", it is the context which shows who is being spoken of as subject).

When a collection appears to be referred to, one has to distinguish between cases in which the collection is being spoken of as a unity, in which case the grammatical subject (the relevant lexical complement to the verb) is the whole referring expression or identifying description—for instance, "the Pleiades", "these books", "my books [the books which belong to me]", "Bill's books", "those books, the last four, which you would find at the top right-hand corner of the end bookshelf", "this year's Oscar winners, whoever they are", or "all the ewes [in the area which the discourse context indicates as being spoken of]". However, very often the collection is not being spoken of collectively—that is, as a unity, but distributively, as in "The Pleiades are middle-distance stars",[40] "These/My/Bill's books are novels", "The last four books at the top right-hand corner of the end bookshelf are each priceless", "This year's Oscar winners are men", and "All the ewes [in the area which the discourse context indicates as being spoken of] are under 40 kg".[41] In these it is "star of the Pleiades", "book in the group pointed to", "book belonging to me", "book of Bill's", "book out of the four at the top right-hand corner of the end bookshelf", "Oscar winner this year", and "ewe [in the area which the discourse context indicates as being spoken of]", which should be considered as grammatical subjects, some form of indication of quantity or identity constituting the "application controller" showing how the predicate applies to the general subject concerned.

It is a corollary of regarding a general term as the grammatical subject in a particular example that the application controllers indicating quantity

39. Cf. Geach, "Quine's Syntactical Insights", in *Logic Matters*, 115–27.

40. Contrast "The Pleiades is a middle-distance cluster", which clearly concerns the Pleiades as a collection (such clusters like galaxies, e.g., the Andromeda nebula, and the Magellanic clouds, are physical realities, unlike constellations, whose members are normally at utterly discrepant distances).

41. Contrast "All the ewes [in the area which the discourse context indicates as being spoken of] weigh 4,000 kg", which clearly concerns a whole group taken as a unity.

or identity will influence what is required for concord with the verb; for instance, we say, "Every ... is —", "All ... are —", "The ... which is — is ///", or (in a possible analysis of "my car") "The ... which belongs to me is ///".

(ii) The use of genitives and equivalent prepositional phrases to pick out subjects

To summarize, to first appearance, "it", "nobody", and "ten men" look as if they are all equally morphosyntactic subjects in such sentences as "It is raining", "Nobody came", and "Ten men attacked me". Different grammars distinguish these cases in different ways, and we have seen how a functional grammar can allow us to deal with this problem without giving up the idea that the criteria for being a grammatical subject must be in some sense formal.[42] The same approach enables us to identify a presupposed grammatical general subject, "person", both when pronouns such as "he" and "I" are used and in those languages in which no subject-expression appears where it would be redundant, the inflection on the verb and the context making the identity of the subject unambiguous, as in Caesar's "*Vici*" ("I conquered").

And the same more functional approach enables us to recognize "animal", rather than "kind", as the grammatical subject of "The kind of animal I saw was a rhinoceros". This last case raises the same questions of principle as the specificatory and identificatory genitive phrases (whether expressed by a genitive case-marking or by a preposition) which stand as subject or object phrases in some languages, as if to say, "Of cows were feeding". This last seems to have the structure "Some [animals] of the kind *cows* were feeding", and it is this which brings it into parallel with "Some kind of *mosquito* bit me" and "A lot of *whisky* was drunk".

With phrases such as these, where the nouns "lot" and "kind" have the role of morphosyntactic complements, while "whisky" and "mosquito" are the functional complements of the verb, our functional approach to picking out the grammatical subject comes into full play.[43] In "A lot of whisky can make you sick", "A little (of) whisky may perk you up", and "Some kind of mosquito attacked me", it is the thematic terms "whisky" and "mosquito" which constitute the subjects of the predicate in each sentence, and it is these thematic terms which constitute the lexical complements to the verb in such sentences, "make ... sick", "perk ... up", and "attacked ..."—it is whisky in a large quantity which can make one sick, not some indefinite quantity as such; and I was bitten by a mosquito of a particular kind, a member of that kind or species, not by the abstract entity, the species.

42. By contrast, Chomskyans tend to treat the word given, "ewe" or "ewes", as the surface subject term, using the deep level/surface level distinction (or equivalent minimalist device) to deal with problems ad hoc.

43. "Large/small portion of cake" and "sub-genus of the genus *Anopheles*" need parallel analyses.

It is phrases of this kind in which the same underlying semantic syntax can be grammaticalized in different ways which underlay Quine's argument mentioned in chapter III, section 2 (d) (ii). Certain Japanese phrases are constituted of a numeral, a classifier differing according to the kind of thing to which a number is being assigned, and a term for something to which number can be assigned in some way (cow, wood), and Quine suggests that these phrases could be equally well translated as assigning a number to things of some kind, "five" to "ox" or to "sticks of wood", or as assigning operators "five head of" and "five sticks of" to the mass-terms "cattle" and "wood". However, this seems to be a distinction without a difference, as if one might dispute whether "five crew-members" had a different meaning from "five members of the crew", or construe "Some kind of mosquito bit me" as asserting the existence of a kind of mosquito rather than a mosquito of that kind. The English speaker finds no such indeterminacy in what is meant when one says, "Ten dogs bit me", or "Rex, a dog, bit me", or "Some kind of dog bit me" (meaning that something of the kind "dog" bit him or her).

A wide variety of phrase structures can arise within this framework.

English requires something with the grammatical status of a noun or pronoun at the head of complex phrases occurring as morphosyntactic complements to verbs and prepositions. Thus we may find morphosyntactic complement phrases taking the form either of a direct identity or quantity indicator occurring *pronominally,* as in "Some fell down", "A few fell down", "A little fell down", "The (whole) lot fell down", and "The majority fell down"; or of the combination of a direct identity or quantity indicator occurring *as an operator* with the relevant thematic noun expression, as in "Some of the men fell down", "A few of the men fell down", "Most of the men fell down", "A little of the flour fell down", "A lot of flour fell down", and "The majority of the men fell down"; or of the combination of a direct identity or quantity indicator occurring *as a modifier* with the relevant thematic noun expression, as in "Some men fell down", "Most men fell down", and "A little flour fell down".

The expressions "two", "second", "twice", and "half" each represent different kinds of indicators of quantity. And like the universal quantifier, they are each capable of appearing sometimes as adjectival modifiers and other times as pronouns or adverbs, as the parallelism between "Two men attacked me", "Two attacked me", and "They twice attacked me", on the one hand, and "All men are mortal", "All attacked me", and "They always attack me", on the other hand, shows, while in "The third attacked me", the expression "third", although noun-like, is better regarded as syntactically part of a pronominal expression: "the third man". And just as we can say, "Two attacked me" instead of "Two men attacked me", so we can say, "Give me a half of lager" instead of "Give me a half pint of lager". Here "a pint" comes to stand alongside nouns like "a pound", "a gram", and "a mile", along with the indefinite "a lot", "a little", "the majority", "a deal", "a pile", and so forth. Again, instead of saying, "More men attacked me than didn't", we could say, "Of the men the greater number attacked me," or "The majority of the men attacked me". But it was lager that I drank and men that attacked me, not a pint and not a majority.

Section 3. The Notion of Grammatical Object: Different Options in Structuring Speech

The notion of grammatical object marks quite different aspects of the functional structure of the clause, not connected with the subject/predicate distinction in logic, but important for the perspective in which the state of affairs, event, or action reported is presented.

If one thinks of the "subject" as the primary complement or argument to the verb, it is natural to think of the "direct object" (or, in languages seeming to allow more than one direct object, whichever it is more necessary to mention) as the second in the hierarchy of arguments in the clause under consideration. Secondary objects within the core of the clause will be terms for arguments to the verb successively later in this hierarchy, other arguments being external to the core of the sentence, or "peripheral", except in cases when they have a disjoint topic ("theme") situation. Always, when considering how to apply terms such as "subject", "direct object", and "indirect object", one should address oneself only to the "core" of the sentence, in the sense explained in chapter XIV. As to arguments introduced by a preposition of agency (such as "by", "*par*") or marked by an ergative case inflection, languages vary as to whether or not they treat them as belonging to the core.

It is only the character of nominative/accusative languages which has led us to think that there are two, not just one, privileged arguments to the verb, an object as well as a subject, the subject regarded as in the position and inflection of a nominative, and the object in the position and inflection of an accusative. The absolutive case of ergative systems is better regarded as a pragmatic and functional subject than as serving an accusative function. As a consequence of this, following Li and Thompson in regarding subjects as grammaticalized topics, I do not follow Dik's sharp divide between pragmatic and semantic functions. Therefore, contrary to Dik and Van Valin, I regard the function of "subject" as universal in describing languages because its role in logic reflects its pragmatic function, whereas the function of "object" lacks any universal unambiguous role.[44]

44. Contrast Dik, *Theory of Functional Grammar: Part* 1, 25; 2nd ed., 27.

(a) *Obscurities in the notion of "object" in traditional grammar*

The variety of options in the functional structuring of our speech is obscured by the dominance of nominative/accusative languages. Yet if one only delves a little into the roots of common thinking about the active and passive voices or reexamines the obscurities of the middle voice in Greek or of deponent verbs in Latin, one discovers many little-noticed difficulties.

(i) The problem of actions which are self-reflective or which have an immanent object

Aristotelian physics presented a structure within which the primary place was held by subjects of change. These pass, by processes of coming to be, from nonexistence to existence, and of perishing, from existence to nonexistence. They move from one place to another, for instance, by walking, running, swimming, and flying; and according to standpoint are described as coming or going. They also change in magnitude, size, and quality—not only between degrees of hotness and coldness, dryness and wetness, but also between various states of belief and knowledge, of emotion, and of character, and from possession of a desirable state to its privation.

This picture suggests a fundamental distinction between being an agent of change and being an undergoer of change, going (a) from one location, velocity, size, or quality (shape, color, or other) to another; (b) from one owner or possessor to another or from being of one stuff to another (water to steam, a log to ashes); or (c) from existing to not existing, whether the change be caused by an agent or agents, due to nature, spontaneous or by chance. The wider term "undergoer" is needed, to cover all these cases, since, unlike the word "patient", it does not imply being acted upon, but still does not extend to recipients, beneficiaries, destinations, or other objects aimed at.[45]

This standpoint suggests the possibility of thinking of the active voice as devised for expressing the causing of change and the passive voice as devised for expressing the undergoing of change. However, this is ill-suited to most nominative/accusative languages, even English and French, since people deliberately come and go, walk, run, swim, and so forth from one place to another. And it is a datum for common thought, as well as for Aristotle in his psychology, ethics, and logic, that animals are self-movers, which would make them agents and patients in the same predication.

45. Some linguists distinguish Patients, which are "affected" or alter in quality, from Themes, which are not altered in quality, but, for example, change in place or ownership, but this gives the term "Theme" too many uses.

I reject Van Valin's view that in the so-called dative shift, whereby we say, "Pat gave Chris the book", rather than, "Pat gave the book to Chris", "Chris" has been marked as undergoer; Van Valin, *Exploring the Syntax-Semantics Interface* (Cambridge: Cambridge University Press, 2005), 121. Rather, by losing the dative inflection and lacking a preposition, "Chris" is represented as internal to the action, no longer merely *external to it*.

Moreover, the tendency to treat English or French as the norm has reinforced a way of thinking of the active and passive voices fitting with the Aristotelian physics sketched earlier, the subject of a statement in the active voice of a transitive verb being an agent bringing about a change in the situation of an a undergoer acted upon, and the passive voice being designed to express the same relation with the undergoer as subject.

The first difficulty in this overly simple conception was noticed by Aristotle himself. In his work on fallacies (*De Sophisticis Elenchis*), he judges that ordinary language is semantically misleading in the case of sight, which he tells us is of its nature a passion, although the verbs concerned are in the active (he would say the same with the other external senses).[46] For in perception the change is in the perceiver, not in the thing perceived.

Yet Aristotle's way of thinking of perception is not obvious. It is natural enough to conceive of the exercise of the senses, hearing and listening, smelling and tasting, and feeling by touch, as activities.[47] Most importantly, the close connections of seeing with looking and exploring fortify our tendency to think of it as an example of an activity, seeing and noticing being the achievements which looking and exploring make possible.

The trouble is not with thinking of seeing, hearing, and so forth as acts or activities, but of thinking of this feature of our language according to the model of physical change as if nature had devised language primarily to deal with physics. As Wittgenstein, early and late, Ryle, and Austin insisted, by contrast with Russell, Carnap, and their following, there is nothing wrong with ordinary language as such; what is wrong is our way of understanding it.

The connection of the active voice with action does not lie in its expression of agency in bringing about change, but its expression of animacy, or something analogous to it when inanimate things are said to act.[48] By "actor" I mean the subject of an activity, whether expressed by a transitive verb in the active voice where an agent is described as operating on an external "object" as patient or expressed by such intransitive verbs. "Live", "see", "hear", "remember", "imagine", and "think" in the active voice all express predicates appropriate to an actor.

This wider conception of "actor" and activity is displayed in the need to take account of the great variety in the kinds of expression which grammar-books

46. Aristotle, *De Sophisticis Elenchis* 178a10–20. The chapter concerned provides the earliest statement of the idea of ordinary language's being misleading, the idea so fashionable in the Anglo-Saxon philosophy of the first half of the twentieth century.

47. I.e., we think of perception along the holistic activity-geared-to-environment way of the psychologist Gibson's later work rather than thinking of it as the action of an external stimulus on a physiological machine.

48. Martin Braine and Wells, "Case-like Categories in Children", showed that children's speech revealed a very broad actor category. The actor "does" the action, and the actors are not necessarily animate, even though animacy is a class property of stimuli to which the children were very sensitive. There was evidence that User and Instrument are subcategories of actor differentiated only when a sentence contains both.

count as "objects" of what they call "transitive" verbs. For in many cases we find this "object" is not external. These verbs are not concerned with an agent's bringing about a change in or movement on the part of the "object" of the verb in any way at all. By the "object" of a verb is meant that on which the actor directs or centers concern in the way expressed by the verb, in the case of an activity its "destination", "aim", or "goal" in the most general metaphorical sense as what it is directed towards or against. Thus what we know, understand, see, hear, taste, smell, touch, feel, love, desire, hate, are sorry at, hope, fear, are angry at, think about, imagine, remember, worship, and so forth is the object of the relevant form of knowledge, perception, feeling, emotion, or other faculty, disposition, or attitude.

These activities with an "object" in this extended sense are called *immanent* "activities" because the "activity" remains within the subject or "agent" to which it is attributed. Thus even if the object has external or independent real existence, as when we worship God or see the sun, the activity is in no way "causative", in no way causing change or movement in an external object, unlike the paradigm Aristotelian examples of agents changing things in quality, shape, or position (as by heating or wetting, or pushing, pulling, lifting, or carrying them) or making them change nature (as by eating, killing, or burning them). Comparably, in giving and receiving, selling and buying, although the object remains unaltered, its social situation is caused to change. These are "out-going" or *exeunt* (Spinoza's word), commonly called *transeunt*, activities, as opposed to *immanent* activities. Some of these verbs are morphosyntactically transitive and some intransitive, lacking a direct object in the accusative. In the intransitive case they are classed as "unergative" because they have such an active meaning that in a nominative/accusative language the actor has to take the grammatical role of subject (in an ergative language they would be marked ergatively).[49]

Thus, these so-called immanent activities, where the "activity", even when expressed by a transitive verb, remains in the actor, resemble what is expressed

49. The description "unergative" is much less useful as a classificatory term than the term "unaccusative" discussed later, because the verbs it groups together are of such disparate kinds, only sharing the property that in modern English and Romance languages their perfect tense is always formed with "to have" rather than "to be". Thus many "unergative" verbs constitute disguised transitive formations. Such verb formations as "collaborate with", "flirt with", "reply to", "lie to", and "struggle with" are logically transitive verbs whose object needs to be specified with a prepositional connective, just as in many languages there are transitive formations requiring objects in some other case than the accusative. Some verbs which are obviously transitive in English, such as "telephone" and "cheat", require some non-accusative specification of the object in some other languages, but the object is still external. Likewise, verbs of movement such as "run", "swim", "walk", "stagger", or "travel" classify as "unergative", but there is typically an object toward which movement is expressed, while other unergative verbs have products as external objects (one bleeds blood as one builds buildings). As to hesitation and delay, these tend to be hesitation or delay to do this or that, taking specificatory objects, while when we reply or lie there seem to be both an external object, the person we address, and a specificatory object, what we tell them. Thus such verbs as "smile", "cough", "bark", "buzz", "snore", "tremble", "shout", "yawn", and "joke" have only immanent objects, their cognates, as in smiling a smile.

by "intransitive" verbs, verbs which have no external grammatical object (although they may have cognate objects, as in "I slept a good sleep"); for instance, certainly sleep remains within the sleeper. The grammatical forms in which we signify the "objects" of these "activities" with no external object are often very different from those which fit "out-going" activities; for instance, I may know, remember, imagine, or dream that I am in my own house, or love, hate, desire, or fear to be so, examples in which the object expression takes the form of an appropriate connective (which grammarians commonly call a complementizer) together with a clause or a formation with the infinitive such as are used to express *oratio obliqua* ("indirect speech").

In Latin many immanent activities are expressed by "deponent" verbs, passive in form, but expressed in the active in English—for instance, judging, thinking (*arbitror*), remembering, forgetting, pitying, and enjoying. In different languages the English intransitive is expressed in varied ways, by the middle voice in Greek, the deponent passive in Latin, and reflexive forms in French.

(ii) The double notion of "object to the verb" present in nominative/accusative languages

In order to understand the basis of the accusative case in nominative/accusative languages and of the absolutive case in ergative languages, we need to conceive of the notion of the "object to the verb" as the non-active center or direction of concern of the state or activity indicated by the verb, using the word "object" in a way more at home in medieval than in modern philosophy. This notion captures both the material center of concern or object of an action, the undergoer, and its intentional or directional center of concern or object—what it is aimed at. From now on I shall speak of the "center of concern of an activity or situation" and use the expression "center of concern" to refer to certain range of thematic roles, not to refer to a discourse-function of any kind.

The required notion of undergoer covers only part of this range of thematic roles, what is acted upon when an agent acts upon a patient, what changes hands or moves in giving and taking, buying and selling, bringing and taking away, coming and going—as it were the Aristotelian *hyle*, which stays the same while altering in quality, being moved, or changing ownership. It need not be inanimate, but in the sentence concerned, *qua* undergoer, it must play no active role: persons and slaves are not inanimate, but play no active role in being hit or bought and sold.

If two direct objects are allowable within a language, as in "I gave John a book", each is a focus of the activity. Only "a book" is an undergoer or material center of concern or object of the activity, while "John" indicates the intentional or directional center of concern or object of the activity, its "goal".

The verb sets the perspective in which the state or activity (the "drama") described is presented. The "subject" and the "object to the verb" are sentential grammatical functions of quite different characters. The subject is defined solely by its character as a grammaticalized discourse-function, the object by reference to its thematic role as undergoer or goal of the state or activity picked out by the verb.

In nominative/accusative languages, the nominative is the case of the subject marked by concord with the verb. Meantime, the accusative has become the default case for the object—that is, for the undergoer (except when this has been made the subject) and for the goal, which may be a destination, aim, or antagonist—the default case to which resort is had if no other case serves to indicate some particular meaning—for instance, indications by preposition and/or special case-marking of being object of one of the immanent activities mentioned earlier, or of being recipient, instrument, or companion.

Since metaphorical destinations or goals include things acted upon, attacked, intended, or aimed at, things which the person is mentally directed towards in looking at, searching for, perceiving, worshipping, remembering, imagining, and so forth, it is evident that, unless some preposition is used requiring a different case, the destinative and antagonist cases will disappear into the accusative. Likewise, "that for the sake of which" is naturally the object in the case of motivational verbs, and so their accusative.

If there are two objects, as in "I gave Jane a book", each in its way is the center of concern of the action of the verb, "a book" as in a more literal sense "matter" changing hands like a medium of exchange and "Jane" as recipient counting as "goal". In such cases mention of the undergoer, as it were materially internal to the action, cannot normally be omitted: in many contexts, one can say, "I gave a book" as a complete sentence, but not "I gave Jane" (unless in marriage or slavery), even though "Jane", as recipient, is still focal to the action, and one can form a passive "Jane was given the book by me". The origin of such idioms in English appears to lie in the loss of the dative case-ending on proper names.

(b) *The conception of "voice" and the roots of fluidity in functional organization*

In thinking of active, passive, and other voices, we need to deepen our conception of "voice". In this context the term "voice" itself is less informative than the Greek word *diathesis* (disposition, which we could understand as meaning something like functional direction) of which it was the translation.[50]

50. Cf. Lyons, *Introduction*, 372.

Consideration of the general Indo-European background suggests a less fixed, more open view of the role of the morphosyntactically intransitive middle (or medio-passive), morphosyntactically intransitive in not taking an object in the accusative. The verb in this intransitive form could then be modified by noun phrases characterized by being preceded by a preposition expressing agency (or having an ergative case-ending).[51] The Latin deponent verbs, in which what seems to the English speaker an active meaning is expressed in the Latin passive, appear on this interpretation to be a survival of this original middle or medio-passive. These verbs often have their functional object in some other case than the accusative: for instance, "*utor*", "I use", and "*fruor*", "I enjoy", take the instrumental ablative, while verbs of remembering and forgetting commonly take the dative. In Slavonic languages the passive meaning is liable to be expressed by impersonal constructions with the "agent"-subject not in the nominative.[52]

(i) The active voice as the default voice of the verb

When we attribute qualities, sizes, locations, or owners to things, the Subject of the attribution, as the verbally selected available topic, has the thematic role of an undergoer. Where the subject of attribution is an abstract entity of some kind, a number, a color, a quality or relation, or an event or situation, it cannot be thought of as an undergoer, except in a metaphorical sense, as when a mathematician is said to perform operations upon numbers.

In attributions, not only of qualities, sizes, locations, or owners, but of properties and relations of abstract entities of any kind, the predication of the discourse-subject is typically made in the active voice as the default form of the verb in nominative/accusative languages. In such attributions the verb "to be" has no active connotation, but is in the active voice solely as the default form of the verb.

Alongside attributive statements in English, we should also place most cases of the use of "unaccusative" intransitive verbs. "Unaccusative" statements may be characterized as statements in which the active voice carries no active connotation. Their subject is in the nominative, not because of any connotation of agency, but solely because of its role as discourse subject.

Unaccusative verbs include "exist", "happen", and "turn out," "appear" and "disappear", "suffice" and "arrive", "fall", "die", "collapse", "wither", "faint", "get moldy", "rot", "well up", "leak out", and "blush".[53] It is typical for the perfect

51. Carl Darling Buck, *Comparative Grammar of Greek and Latin* (Chicago: University of Chicago Press, 1933), 237 and note a.

52. I discuss these immanent activities further in chap. XIV, sec. 4 (b) of this volume.

53. The nature of "unaccusativity" was developed by Perlmutter in a succession of papers, beginning with "Impersonal Passives and the Unaccusative Hypothesis", in *Proceedings of the 4th Annual Meeting of the Berkeley Linguistics Society* (Berkeley, Calif.: Berkeley Linguistics Society, 1978), 157–89.

tense of such verbs to be expressed using the verb "to be" so that "I am now arrived" is comparable to "This building is now built", and in French the perfect is expressed with "to be", while in English the archaic "He is arrived" has the meaning of the later "He has arrived". It is noteworthy that in archaic English we can say, "The tree is fallen" with the same meaning as, "The tree has fallen". (In Italian, the perfect tense of all these verbs is expressed by the use of the verb "to be", rather than "to have".)

Reflection on the cases of "The tree is fallen" and "He is arrived" suggests that with the verbs concerned the distinction between "is" expressing the passive and "is" expressing the perfect is rather unreal, because in either case we have the active voice "is" used solely as the default voice of the verb.[54] To generalize, we can say that whenever the verb "to be" is used to express the passive voice in any language, its primary effect is to elevate whatever available topic it is, in concord with to the role of grammatical subject, and to remove the agent, if any, from this position.

We are now in a better position to understand the grammar of "There is a tiger in the garden". By the device of introducing the impersonal "there", the subject-expression "tiger" is demoted both from the role of actor and from that of preestablished topic. Statements often presuppose an unmentioned topic external to the linguistic construction, as the current weather is external to the statement "It is raining", or as the person who could not sleep is external to the linguistic construction in "fire engines last night not have sleep" (in a literal rendering).[55]

However, when, as in ergative languages, there is an undergoer or non-agent as the primary noun argument, this naturally gravitates to the position of grammatical subject, "argument of the verb serving as discourse topic", and in Foley and Van Valin's terms the primary pragmatic pivots, capable of qualification by relative clauses.[56] Foley and Van Valin are quite wrong to deny these pragmatic pivots the title of subjects, doing this on the basis of the mistaken argument that topic and focus are opposites.[57]

(ii) Comparing the accusative with the absolutive case: evolutions in grammatical systems

The notion of "object" explained earlier combines a thematic element, that of being non-active, with a perspectival element, that of being the center of concern of the situation or activity signified by the verb and reported by

54. Against this background, it is unsurprising that the archaic English "is born" should originate from a use of "is" to express the perfect passive of the verb "to bear", and that the Italian "*e nato*" should be regarded as a perfect (past) tense meaning "was born" or "has been born".

55. Hopper and Traugott, *Grammaticalization*, 2nd ed., 28.

56. See Foley and Van Valin, *Functional Syntax*, 99–102, 114–17.

57. See the discussion in sec. 1 (b) of this chapter, with nn. 6, 13, and 28.

the whole sentence. It can take on the role of subject or topic in statements in the passive, and so cannot be defined as the opposite of the topic. Rather the thematic aspect of being non-active makes the "object to the verb" the opposite of an actor or agent, rather than the opposite of the topic.

The nominative/accusative form of language arises by treating the prototypical case of a statement as that in which the subject is an actor, animate or inanimate, being described as engaged in immanent activity, in acting upon an undergoer or in bringing about a state of affairs—for instance, causing the ice to melt or, as we say, "melting the ice", or "moving the mouse". By contrast, an ergative system can arise by leaving the agent unmentioned, or mentioned only incidentally in the ergative case, and treating the undergoer on which the state or activity indicated by the verb is centered (the material object to the verb) as subject, so that the prototypical statement might be "the ice melted" or "the mouse moved".

In most languages there is a tendency for the original grammatical subject of a sentence to become identifiable from the context. Now, in a "subject-prominent" language in which this topic becomes an unmentioned "theme", this has the effect of making first pronouns and then even inflections of the verb for person and number largely redundant. In such a setting it is possible for the object phrase to evolve into being the unmarked or primary noun phrase and for the agent, if mentioned, to be specially indicated by preposition or ergative case-marking. This makes it unsurprising that the "absolutive" of ergative languages should have some correspondence with the accusative as the default case for the object in nominative/accusative languages, at the same time as taking on a role parallel to that of the nominative as the case of subject. This tendency ends in making the object to the verb the properly morphosyntactic subject, as when the verb is marked for number in concord with the number of the undergoer, not the agent.[58]

Many different devices may be used in order to achieve this non-nominative marking of the agent, of which Hopper and Traugott instance two: one the transformation of a verb with a meaning somewhat like the French *faire* in its causative use into a case-marker, and another the shift in function of a case-marker from indicating an instrument to indicating the agent.[59]

From the point of view of discourse the presumption is that what is be-

58. Such an evolution toward combining the roles of non-active focus of the situation or activity reported by the proposition with being its subject (marked in the absolutive case) may be compatible with Du Bois's explanations of the origins of ergative syntax, in John W. Du Bois, "The Discourse Basis of Ergativity", *Language* 63 (1987): 805–55, as treated in Hopper and Traugott, *Grammaticalization*, 2nd ed., 168–71, since the non-active focus of what is expressed by the verb is often what is fresh informatively; cf. Du Bois, "Competing Motivations", in *Iconicity in Syntax*, ed. John Haiman (Amsterdam: John Benjamins, 1985), 343–65, for his remarks on nominative/accusative languages.

59. Hopper and Traugott, *Grammaticalization*, 2nd ed., 167.

ing spoken about or referred to is as close as possible to the speaker and to the speaker-hearer context. Michael Silverstein has described a natural hierarchy of degrees in such closeness, proceeding in order from the speaker or first person to the second person, and then successively to the third person, to a person or kin group picked out by a personal name or kin name, to something picked out in a more general way merely indicating that it is human, to something picked out in a way merely implying that it is animate, and finally to something inanimate.[60] Accordingly the earlier something figures in this hierarchy the less need there is to mark the phrase for it in any distinctive way. Practically all language types show sensitivity to this hierarchy in one way or another. But within a nominative/accusative system, as soon as the lack of need to make explicit reference to the subject becomes the norm, there is the possibility of losing any marking distinguishing the active and the passive. This opens the way to the possibility of an evolution from a nominative/accusative system of grammaticalization within a language through various systems of ergative grammatical organization.

Conversely the pressures towards treating the agent as a topic keeps alive the possibility of a reverse development back towards a nominative/accusative system.[61] Dik speculatively reconstructs how such a complete cycle of development may take place, suggesting examples from Polynesia and Iran which fit his reconstruction.[62]

60. Michael Silverstein, "Hierarchy of Features and Ergativity", in *Grammatical Categories in Australian Languages*, ed. R. M. Dixon (Atlantic Highlands, N.J.: Humanities Press, 1976), 112–71; and Silverstein, "Case Marking and the Nature of Language", *Australian Journal of Linguistics* 1 (1981): 227–44. In the so-called direct-inverse case system of Algonquian languages (the predominant Amerindian group), as described by Blake (*Case*, 129–30), when the noun phrase which is more topical or higher in the hierarchy is the actor, the verb is unmarked, but if the less topical noun phrase is actor, the verb is always marked.

61. In fact, unless there are markings distinctive of the active and the passive on the verb, few languages can be classified as purely ergative or purely nominative/accusative. Lack of marking indicates the default interpretation in a language. The tendencies not to mark the actor unless the actor is passive and to distinctively mark what is more distant from the speaker ("he" rather than "you"; less personal, less animate) only when an agent indicates an accusative tendency when found in an otherwise ergative language. Conversely, the tendency not to mark what is more distant from the speaker when it is an inactive topic, but to mark it distinctively when it is the agent, can be called an ergative tendency when found in a nominative/accusative language. Ergative languages can show deviant accusative tendencies; e.g., the Australian Rembarnga shows an accusative tendency so that the verb requires marking when the object is later in the hierarchy than the agent in "Me *saw* them" ("I was seen by them", as if the verb was in the passive) but unmarked in "Me saw them" ("I saw them")—by contrast with the Papuan Fore, which leaves what is closest to the speaker or closest in kind unmarked as subject, so that in "The pig the man kill" (meaning "The man kills the pig"), the agent being the man and nearest to the speaker does not requiring any marking, but in "*The pig* the man kill" (meaning "By the pig the man is killed") the agent as more distant from the speaker requires to be marked, indicating an ergative tendency; Blake, *Case*, 120, 122.

62. Dik, *Studies in Functional Grammar* (London: Academic Press, 1980), 113–16, 123–25.

XII

Marrying Philosophy and Grammar in Distinguishing Types of Noun Expression

Section 1. The Varied Types of Meaning of Abstract Nouns

(a) *The roots of grammar lie in the semantics of speech: the awareness of langue involved in speech*

In chapter IX we saw that in any semantically structured expressive speech, the subordinate sentence constituents must be of different kinds. The distinction between referring or "naming" expressions and saying or "verbal" expressions, the latter "incomplete" or "unsaturated", was fundamental, because of the overarching functional role of the latter. We also picked out what we called "application controllers" (typically quantifiers), and, within verbal expressions or predicates, we indicated the need to pick out certain key lexical elements as "content-introducing". The capacity to make such logic-inspired distinctions is what enables us to penetrate the grammar of the language.

However, much more is required for the development of grammatical theory.

Some sentence-factors lie on the surface and are easy to identify by simple quotation, sometimes in the split-up form anticipated in chapter I, seen in the lexical predicate "look ... (optional) at" where "... (optional)" indicates the option of intruding some intervening expression, for instance, "intensely" in this case, or "the man" in "phone ... (optional) back". This, crucially, involves understanding the "split-up" sentence-factors concerned as constituents, not mere components, as explained in chapter I. The same understanding of sentence-factors as constituents rather than as components also allows us to count a lexical factor or lexeme such as "break", *qua* lexical factor, as a constituent when we meet "broke" and "broken". And constructions and other structural features, marked by the order of words and the morphological adaptation of lexemes, sometimes assisted by sentence-intonation, are other constituents.

Here we see the importance of the shared practical knowledge of a language implicit in communal language-possession ("knowledge of *langue*") and its accessibility to consciousness. We register the interconnections between "breaks", "broke", the participles "breaking" and "broken", the noun-form gerund "breaking", the infinitive "to break", and the unmarked present "break" in our practical use of this family of words in different utterances, including utterances exchanged between different times or speakers, different combinations with the copula and various auxiliaries, or embedded in varied clausal constructions. The language-user is aware of such lexical connections and of the semantic significance of these features, including intonation, without his or her needing to label or classify them—but their accessibility to reflective awareness provides the basis of the possibility of "grammar" as a part of linguistics. Developing grammars depends on appreciating the ways words and lexemes are used in speech. This appreciation also gives access to the roots of morphology, important for understanding live utterance as well as for morphological creativeness.[1]

(i) The variety of ways of forming nominalizations from predicates or clauses

Thus the fact that *langue* as well as *parole* is present to consciousness so as to be the subject of reflection makes possible the generative capacity which appears most obviously in the way in which new topics of discourse, or new logical subjects, can arise. At least some such generative capacity is involved whenever we single something out—for instance, when we topicalize a presupposition of a "Yes/No" question, or pick it out by the appropriate kind of *wh*-question, and once having thus picked it out, thereby *ipso facto* having made it the subject to the verb "to be". It is this which at an elemental level enables us to single out individual terms or expressions—for instance, proceeding from "He said that I was clumsy" to "Clumsy is what he said I was". In speech and in writing systems without quotation marks, there is nothing marking the fact that here it is an expression of or for something, not the thing

1. I discussed the distinction between lexically significant morphemes and lexically nonsignificant morphemes, the latter important for perception and sometimes for associations derived from their etymology, in the appendix to chap. II, on morphology, in this volume. The distinction is fuzzy, but it is clear that "ante" from Latin and "anti" from Greek both retain productive lexical significance, *vide* "ante-date" and "antioxidants".

referred to, which is being "topicalized"—so that the subject is being spoken of in what logicians now call the formal mode of speech.[2]

This capacity to single out complements of the verb "to be" becomes generative when the subjects thus topicalized are spoken of in what we now call the material mode of speech.[3] Thus, from saying, "This table is brown", we can proceed to say that this table is the color brown, that the color of this table is brown, and that brown is the color of this table; this shows the capacity to speak of colors as objects.[4] We can then discuss how the colors of the rainbow, the primary colors, and so forth are distinguished and related.

In the case of numbers this generative capacity, letting us treat something which is in some respect formally noun-like as a complement which we can make into a subject of new predications, becomes peculiarly important. The double way of speaking which we instanced in the case of colors, their names first used as adjectives and then derivatively as nouns, recurs with numbers; thus we say not only, "the twelve Apostles" and "The Apostles were twelve", but also, "Twelve was the number of the Apostles". This third example is of peculiar importance because of the way it shows the grammatical basis for the grammatical forms of our references to numbers. The first two examples showed how the way opened for the use of number-terms as quantifiers, as in "Two of her sons were red-haired, and the other two sons not so", to be compared with "Some of her sons were red-haired and the other sons not so". The third example showed how we might move on to the next stage and say, "Two sons and then another two sons make four sons", and open the way towards properly arithmetical statements in which we treat numbers as objects—saying, for instance, "Two and two make four", "Two and two are four", and, with Arabic notation, "$2 + 2 = 4$". The Arabic notation opens the way to a rich calculus once the cipher 0 has been introduced (despite its not being used in counting), corresponding to the quantifier "no" as in "no sons". Having thus treated the natural numbers as objects, we can then quantify over them and even introduce algebraic notation in representing universal statements—for instance, "$x + y = y + x$", meaning "$(\forall x)(\forall y)((x + y) = (y + x))$".

(ii) Kinds of abstract subject of discourse indicated by different ways of forming abstract terms

Concrete modes of speech can be drawn upon in order to generate abstract subject expressions in many different ways, some relatively uniform and some not. I take my examples mostly from English, indicating something of

2. The medievals called this *suppositio materialis,* the words occurring only "materially", not in their formal meaning, *suppositio formalis.*

3. Using what the mediaevals called *suppositio formalis.*

4. In "This table is brown in color", the "in color" is an adverbial phrase signifying "in respect of color".

the variety of forms of expression arising. Each language may show a different spread of forms of expression with its own idiosyncrasies.

English exhibits numerous different morphological forms in which verbal forms can be nominalized. Thus the noun "attack" and the gerund "attacking", with their uses in "his attack on Troy", "his attacking Troy", and "his attacking of Troy", are both capable of occurring as subject-expressions, as is also the infinitive "to attack", seen in "to attack Troy will be difficult".[5] The processes of forming nouns from verbs is not always a grammatical one, and I will refer to it in general as "lexical nominalization", intending this phrase to cover nouns and noun phrases formed by inflectional processes according to inflectional rule, as well as nouns and noun phrases for which we have to look in the lexicon.[6] Nominalizations of the second kind are sometimes formed by processes of morphological change which can be exceedingly variable in their mode of formation, the syntactic rules followed in their use, and the relation between their meaning and that of the verb concerned.

Turning to noun expressions semantically arising from verbs, we have "hope", "fear", and "desire". Again, there is no regular rule of formation, and the sameness in the word-form of the noun and the verb in English is accidental. In Latin and French we have changes in word-form in such cases; for instance, the nouns *spes, timor, desiderium, concupiscentia,* and *appetitus* connect with the verbs *speo/spere, timeo/timere, desidero/desidere, concupisco/concupiscere,* and *appeto/appetere* in Latin, and *espérance* with *j'espère/esperer* in French. "Knowledge" and "wedlock", also formed from verbs, provide particularly extreme examples of idiosyncrasy as the only survivors of a long extinct method of forming nouns from verbs in English. Whereas "knowledge", as referring either to the knowing or to what is known, has straightforward meaning relations to the verb "know", meaning relations between abstract nouns and verbs can be very complex, as will appear later.

All these verbal nouns, whether gerunds proper or "cognate-terms" (an expression explained later) such as "knowledge", take articles and, except for "knowledge", form plurals. However, all have uses in which they take no articles and form no plurals—in which they designate either the individual kind of state, activity, or act being referred to; the study or science of this kind of state, activity, or act; or the art or skill of the exercise in the activities or acts concerned.

With nouns formed from adjectives we have some regularity in forma-

5. Gerunds, nominal in character, are sometimes called "gerundives", as by S. P. Abney, "The English Noun Phrase in its Sentential Aspect" (PhD diss., Massachusetts Institute of Technology, 1987), a term traditionally referring to gerundival participles, adjectival in character, e.g., the Latin *amandus,* "appropriate to be loved".

6. The realization that one needs to resort to the lexicon in some cases and cannot rely solely upon inflectional processes was observed by Chomsky, "Remarks on Nominalization", in *Readings in English Transformational Grammar,* ed. R. Jacobs and P. Rosenbaum (Waltham, Mass.: Ginn, 1970), and gave rise to the misbegotten X-Bar theory discussed in chaps. XIII–XV of this volume.

tion, first, in every case with the copula as with "being courageous" and "being wise", and second, in a great number of cases by adding "-ness" or "-ity" to the adjective; the opposite is the case if we consider such examples as "courage" and "wisdom" which follow no regular rule. Where abstract nouns are concerned, the customs for forming plurals are very varied, both within a language and between languages. In English, in most cases we have to introduce words like "type", "species", "kind", "form", "shade", or "branch", as in speaking of types or kinds of courage; types, kinds, or forms of animal; forms or branches of knowledge; or shades of a color. In classical Greek a common noun was used equally to refer to individuals of the kind concerned or to the kind itself, so that such expressions as "the animals" or "the categories" may mean either the individual animals or the species of animal, the predicates or the genera of predicate, whereas in English this is quite rare, although "this red" can mean "this shade of red" (never "this red thing").[7]

It is easy to be deceived. In English (or in comparable examples in Greek) we make remarks like, "We found about ten animals, including three younger ones, browsing at the bottom of the field. These animals were tapirs, a genus more akin to the horse and the rhinoceros than to the cow or the pig", or "This pet of mine is a gerbil, a species of rodent". Clearly particular animals are not genera or species, but individuals, so that in the second proposition it is kinds of animal, rather than individual animals that are being referred to, "animal" in the second proposition being in apposition, with "animal" in the first proposition taken as a predicate term.

However, with these idioms we have only introduced a new abstract object when we start making remarks about the species or genus of kinds which we would not make about the individuals. That is, when we say that the horse is a hooved herbivorous quadruped, we have not yet made any statement about the species of a type which we would not make about individuals, and what we say could be expressed, "Horses are by nature herbivorous hoofed quadrupeds". We have only introduced species or genera as abstract objects when we start distinguishing them and counting them, as in the remark, "The tapir is a genus more akin to the horse and the rhinoceros than to the cow or the pig, to consider five kinds of hooved mammal". Parallel remarks apply when editors or philosophers distinguish between letter-tokens and letter-types, so that one might say, for instance, that there were six hundred thousand letter-tokens in a certain book and yet still only twenty-six letter-types. Here the primary use of such an expression as "e" is that found in a sentence like "The third letter of this sentence is an 'e'", and the types of description which we offer of the letter "e"

7. English forbids "a courage" (as if "courage is a virtue" were parallel to "a horse is a quadruped"), but commonly requires the introduction of an article or other determiner if there is a modifier before or after the abstract noun—e.g., "a remarkable courage", "a courage almost unique", or "an anger without parallel", although forbidding plurals.

in general, for instance, its shape, are descriptions of how such token-examples should appear. We have introduced letters as abstract objects when we make such remarks as that "e" is the fifth letter in the Latin alphabet.

In the case of actions, "his action" sometimes refers to a particular action and sometimes to the type of action concerned, because we can first form a lexical nominalization of a clause and then generalize from the individual case to the type or species. Types of action have only been introduced as a further kind of abstract object when they are distinguished, counted, or described in ways in which individual actions cannot be described.

(b) *The semantic implications of the formal features of morphology and the lexicon*

(i) The role of the lexicon and morphology in the interplay between syntax and semantics

The fact that *langue*, as well as *parole*, is present to consciousness when we speak also enables us, for instance, to appreciate the working of "synlexical" morphemes.

First, there are synlexical morphemes which alter or add to lexical meaning. Of these, some are morphologically and syntactically incapable of occurring separately from the word-stem concerned, such as "un-", "dis-", "mis-", "pre-", "-able", "-ish", and "-like". Others are separable so as to constitute each a distinct word, a distinct syntactic and morphological unit, but still merely synlexical in function, as in the case of the prepositions in "look at", "look for", "think of", "*penser à*", "*jouer à*" (for playing games), or "*jouer de*" (for playing instruments), the resulting combination still constituting a single lexical unit. In most of the latter cases there are lexical rules linking the uses of the verb when used followed by the preposition and its uses when not followed by a preposition, in such a way as coheres, for instance, with our regarding "look" as being used in the same meaning at the level of *langue* in both cases.

However, in other cases, there are very few such links, because we are dealing with a distinct meaning of the verb concerned—for instance, in the case of "look after" in the sense of "take care of", unrelated to perception, rather than the sense of "look in the direction in which the thing looked at is going". The combine "look after" is a single lexical unit and a distinct item in the lexicon, the metaphorically derived verb being taken together with the preposition, and does not include the element "look" as a lexical unit in its own right, unlike "look at", where the nonmetaphorical "look" has the same perception-related meaning whether the preposition follows or not.[8]

8. Here the relevant "lexicon" concerns only synchronic differences and relations—not diachronic developments and variations.

Second, there are synlexical morphemes which achieve their semantic purpose by bringing about a syntactic change.

Let me list here those which are fixed in their effects upon meaning and semantic function, taking examples from English, some formed in a morphologically regular way and others morphologically irregular (often derived from once-regular forms inherited from the past or from other languages). I mention here only the most important. Of these, some are inseparable from the word they modify and some are separated from it by other words or morphemes. Among the former are regular formations, such as the third-person present tense "-s", the past tense "-ed", the "-ing" of continuous tenses, the "-ing" and "-ed" of the participles, the "-ing" of the gerund, the plural "-s" with nouns, the comparatives "-er" and "-est" with adjectives, all of which we call inflections because of their inseparability. With these we may group the regular formations for forming adverbs from adjectives (by adding "-ly") and nouns from adjectives (by adding "-ness"), and the regular formations for forming infinitives and gerunds from verbs. The regular formations of continuous and perfect tenses take a split-up form—namely, "am/art/is/was/wast" with "-ing" or "are/were" with the present participle "-ing" for continuous tenses; and "has/hast/have/had", "am/art/is/was/are/were" with the regular past participle "-ed" for perfect and passive tenses—while the infinitive-marker "to" is separate from the finite stem.

Once the rationale of the word-forms taken by different lexemes in speech has been recognized, we can make semantic sense of the distinctions of grammatical category which applications of formal distributionalist methods would come upon. However, the grammatical must not be defined as the nonsemantic, as if it were independent of the semantics of speech. Grammar will reflect the existence of parallelisms in formal structure between utterances arising in connection with subject-matters of semantically different kinds.

(ii) The anomalies of the English gerund

The English gerund has always been expressed by "-ing" or "-ung", like those of other Germanic languages, the modern form being "-ing". The possibility of confusion between the gerund as a noun and the present participle arose only late in the history of English. In earlier forms of English present participles were all marked by the presence of a dental sound in their ending, like their Germanic and Romance parallels, but these became assimilated into one form and expressed finally by the Modern English "-ing".[9] Participles are essentially verbal adjectives, not nouns, and in the absolute phrases discussed in chapter XIV, section 5 (a) (iii), yield adverbial modifiers of the verb or clause, not noun complements to the verb.

9. See chap. XIII, sec. 4 (a) n. 55, of this volume for detailed discussion.

Yet while the form of the English participle has radically changed, its use has been constant, showing only adjectival and verbal behavior, never that of a noun, even after its change to the "-ing" form. By contrast, in the 1400s the English gerund began to show more mixed behavior; from showing only the purely noun-like behavior which continues to be the case in all other Germanic languages, it began to show some of the behavior of infinitives in other languages, as discussed in chapter XIII.[10] Thus, in the English of today it is plain that, although an expression like "the Greeks attacking Troy" serves as a noun-phrase, so as to be subject of such predicates as "angered some of the gods" or "was a disaster", it is grammatically analogous to phrases using the infinitive in other languages. In such cases, gerunds cannot be put into the plural and are modified by adverbs like "rapidly", not adjectives like "rapid",[11] evidencing their verbal character.

However, when we insert an "of" between the gerund and its grammatical object, as in "the Greeks' attacking of Troy" or "his attacking of Troy", the gerund loses many of its verbal features; for instance, there is no possibility of substituting an accusative such as "the Greeks", "them", or "him" for the possessive. Here it recovers much of the normal behavior of a noun, and of the gerund in other Germanic languages, even though adverbial expressions may still modify the whole phrase (e.g., "their attacking of Troy first, before anywhere else").

Meantime, in "his many doings", "doing" is a noun formed by inflection from the verb, but without any residual verbal behavior, a gerund proper, almost synonymous with deed, and without any trace of the successfully more verbal character of "his doing his duty".

(iii) The reference of the gerund proper

I can now review the different meanings of these verbal nouns, which correspond to the different types of meaning of the finite verbs concerned. The main finite verb of some sentences makes the sentence signify some state of the subject. In other cases it makes the sentence signify some tendency or habit (e.g., his having a tendency to be ill or to drink to intoxication), or some present piece of activity. When activity is signified, it will be of one of six kinds:

1. an activity continuing over time, but not involving a succession of differing stages, nor any incompleteness waiting for a completion—

10. Historically no such verbal aspects appeared until after the participle had begun to take the "verb + -ing" form in the 1300s, under the influence of confusion between the participle and the gerund (phonetically identical by 1400 except in northern dialects). The English use of a gerund without a preposition to connect it with its object reached its fully fledged form only around the 1500s; cf. chap. XIII, sec. 4 (b) (ii), of this volume.

11. I owe clarity on these constructions to Abney, "The English Noun Phrase".

for instance, seeing something wonderful or exercising understanding in regard to an unchanging object consciously present to the mind in memory or in presence;

2. an activity involving a succession of stages, a stage over one subperiod being distinct from its continuance over the next, but without implying an end—for instance, watching, observing, listening, thinking about something, wondering about something, or dreaming;
3. an activity involving incompleteness, waiting for completion—for instance, building a house as currently engaged in;
4. the achievement of having completed of an activity which involved earlier stages of incomplete fulfillment, but is now actually completed, such as winning a race or building a house as something achieved;
5. the process of completing of an activity which has previous and later stages, such as winning a race spoken of while it is still being run, or building a house spoken of while the building is still in progress;
6. an act, considered not as a process taking time, but as an act achieved at a time—for instance, striking someone, asking something, having a thought, being struck by a thought, suddenly thinking, or noticing (hitting a person is considered as an act even though it involves processes of movement, such as of one's fist from one position to another).

Thus, corresponding to these eight kinds of sentence, we have two signifying a state or tendency, and then these six signifying activity in some sense. In sum, a gerund may signify a state, a tendency, a nonuniform activity, a continuous activity, a progressing in a task, a task completed, the completing of a task, or an act. To distinguish which of these meanings is concerned in a particular case, a dictionary never suffices, and one always has to refer to the context.[12]

In a ninth use, what began morphologically as a gerund may lose this character and signify, not a state or activity, although still cognate to a verb, but typically the product of an activity, such as a building.

(iv) "Cognate-terms"

Gerunds with verbal meaning need to be distinguished semantically and in grammatical function from the kind of verbal noun which I call a "cognate-term". I call them "cognate-terms" because in paradigm cases they are objects to verbs of the kind traditional grammarians called "cognate objects", because their names were morphologically formed from the verbs: thus

12. This gives some advantage to clausal constructions: e.g., "that I built the house" can only refer to kind 4, "that I was building the house" to 3, and "that I have built the house" to 5—the English perfect always signifies that the action is completed, but usually suggests completion in the past.

we dream dreams, feel feelings, build buildings, think thoughts, sing songs, state statements, wish wishes, pray prayers, write writings, run runs, race races, see sights, glimpse glimpses, drink drinks, compose compositions, and so forth. However, it is very common for these expressions to appear as grammatical objects to a different verb—for instance, for us to be said to "have" dreams, feelings, thoughts, glances, and glimpses; to "feel" pains, heat, and anger; to "make" statements, requests, wishes, buys, sales, assaults, attacks, and escapes; to "give" orders; to "play" games; to "take" or "snatch" glances; to "catch", "gain", or "snatch" sights and glimpses; to "win" victories, races, and competitions; or to "compose" writings, symphonies, and so forth. The things referred to by cognate-terms I will call "cognates".

Some might complain at my including "pain" in my list of cognate-terms, because the word "pain" is not in any obvious way formed from a verb. I classify it in this way partly because of the close analogy between the phrases "feel pain" and "feel pleasure". Pain seems rather the odd man out in a list of sensations ("pins and needles", itches, tickles), and is better regarded as a form of *dolor* or grief, distinctive in having a physical cause and felt location, the latter giving us extra reason for treating it as a subject in its own right.[13] However, although cognate-terms arise in a variety of ways, it remains clear that they have meaning only in contexts in which they are cognate to a verb.

What I call "cognates" of a verb (representing the verb as having a stem "V-") fall under the following headings:

1. Products
   a. Physical products (e.g., buildings, moldings)
   b. *Parole*-products and products of artistic performance (e.g., statements, questions, commands, pieces of discourse, writings, criticisms, songs, sonatas)
   c. Mental or other upshots of the act of V-ing internal to the act itself (e.g., a thought, a desire, a pain, a sight, a glimpse, a vision, a hallucination, a death, a blow; thoughts, desires, and wonderings have some analogy to *parole*-products, and sometimes the same word, such as "question" is used both of the outward utterance and of the cognate of the mental act)
2. Instruments of use or play (e.g., tools, musical instruments)[14]
3. Objects of an activity signified by the verb "V" which are in no way products of the activity (thus the expressions "sight" or "hallucina-

13. The grouping of feeling physical pain with the external senses resulted partly from the mistake of thinking of the external senses as really having only internal objects and partly from the contingent empirical discovery of pain cells (localized cells whose activation causes local pain).

14. Surgical instruments, like carpenters' tools, are instruments directed towards a product which survives their use. With musical instruments, the end product towards which they are directed is their use.

tion" are sometimes used to refer to what the sights or hallucinations are of, e.g., an oasis)

4. Doings and deeds: activities in the senses listed earlier (e.g., building a house, its completion, and its completing; playing a game, the game itself considered as finished, the finishing of the game; a dream in the sense of the dreaming of it; the sight of something in the sense of the seeing of the thing)

(v) *The complexity of lexical entries for verbal nouns in the lexicon*

Accordingly, many lexical entries for verbal nouns will take one of two forms, including the following information:

1. "N: a gerund; X; V", where N is the noun concerned, "a gerund", X is a specification of the types: a state, a tendency, a nonuniform activity, a continuous activity, a task in progress, a completed task as a whole, the completing of a task, an act; and V is the finite verb concerned
2. "N: a cognate-term; Y; V1, V2", where N is the noun concerned, grammatical object to the verb V1, Y is a specification of the types: product, *parole*-product, a completed task as a whole, an act, the mental or physical achievement in the act of V2-ing; and V2 is the finite verb from which the type of object concerned is named. Thus we might have an entry for the noun "order" like this: "order: a cognate-term; *parole*-product; give, order".

Strictly speaking, "gerund" is a morphosyntactic term, whereas "cognate-term" as I have defined it has a functional and semantic meaning.

Section 2. Unraveling Plato's Problems as the Key to Resolving Problems in Semantics

(a) *Problems to be solved*

Thus, having learned the subject/predicate distinction from cases where the subject is concrete, we go on to use the same distinction with its associated structures in connection with abstract subjects. We now need to consider the relations between concrete subjects and the various kinds of abstract subject. We shall find that this is a task for semantics, not grammatical theory. We need an account which resolves at least the following four problems.

First, such an account must explain how it is that understanding the sense of predicates such as "... is wise" and "... is white" is prior to understanding locutions in which "wisdom" or "the color, white" is spoken of as logical subject.

That is, the predicative use of lexemes such as "wise" and "white" must be taken as semantically prior to the use of such lexemes in derived nouns, as when we say, "Wisdom is a strength" or "White is a color".

Second, the account must make it plain that understanding the sense of statements such as "John's car collided with the wall" or "Alfred struck Bert" is likewise prior to the understanding of locutions in which "collisions" or "blows" are spoken of as logical subjects. That is, the sentential use of expressions reporting events or states of affairs is semantically prior to any noun phrases or clauses referring to them.

Third, the same account must also cater properly for the situation of adverbs. It must justify saying that the adverbial use of the lexical factor "clumsy" is semantically prior to the adjectival uses, so that clumsy persons are ones who act clumsily, and clumsy actions are ones which are done clumsily, and this is the right order of explanation. That is, we need to avoid the semantic artificiality of saying that "John carried the tray clumsily" has the semantic analysis "There is an event [process] *x* such that, at some past time *t*, *x* is a carrying of a tray at *t*, John performed *x* at *t*, and *x* was clumsy at *t*".[15] The predicative expression "... carry the tray clumsily" has, we must say, semantic, grammatical, and in typical cases morphological priority over the nominal "the clumsy carrying of a tray" (this nominal is the subject phrase in "The clumsy carrying of a tray attracted his notice").

Fourth, the account must explain the difference between the case of "white", which, as we shall see in (d), stands as a name within one of the primary classes of names, and of "wisdom", which has no such standing. That is, color-words have this standing as primary names, even though we still need to understand the predicative use of color-words in order to understand what a color is—for instance, to understand what the name "white" refers to.

(b) *Critique of Plato and Davidson*

Grammatical and morphological theory is constantly plagued by mistaken semantic theories. The theory that events are objects invites a grammatical theory that "carry clumsily", "recover quickly", and "kiss twice" are derived from "perform a clumsy carrying", "quick recovery",[16] and "give two kisses",

15. This is the type of analysis to which Davidson would commit us, with most adverbs and adverbial phrases modifying action verbs, in essay 6, "The Logical Form of Action Sentences", 105, and essay 8, "The Individuation of Events", 166–80, esp. 166–67, both in Davidson, *Essays on Actions and Events*, 1980, misinterpreting the linguistic data as I show in subsection (c). My primary objection is as to how it treats events. It is also objectionable in the way it treats times, mistakenly treating adverbs and adverbial phrases indicating time and place as to be analyzed in terms of predicates with events as subjects; cf. Geach, "Some Problems about Time", in *Logic Matters*, 311–16.

16. Jackendoff offers this example (*Semantics and Cognition*, 71), rightly appreciating the relevance of

and this suggests a morphological theory whereby morphological complexity at surface level in grammatical structure reflects something morphologically simpler at some supposed deeper grammatical level. The parallel theory about properties or universals, arising from the parallel grammatical theory that "is wise" is to be analyzed as "exemplifies wisdom", lacks this morphological attractiveness, even though it has a long history, from Plato to Ramsey, and more recently Grice and the meaning-nominalists (see the appendix to chapter III). Let me show what is wrong with both these kinds of theory, beginning with Plato.[17]

These peculiar semantic theories come from philosophers first adopting and then attempting to systematize ordinary people's commonplace misreading of the logic of our normal ways of speaking—ways of speaking common among physicists and psychologists and prominent in the expositions of philosophers.

Here one is encountering the phenomenon of being mesmerized by the abstract noun. In the older mythology of Plato, noun-expressions such as "wisdom" corresponding to predicates such as "... is wise" are treated as denoting the objects later called universals. In a parallel way, in the newer mythology represented in Davidson, noun expressions, such as "Sebastian's stroll through Bologna", "the car's collision with the wall", and "Socrates's being healthy", corresponding with whole statements, such as "Sebastian strolled through Bologna", "The car collided with the wall", and "Socrates was healthy", are treated as denoting events or states.

More elaborately one may summarize the Platonic mythology as involving that whenever a statement mentioning *n* objects attributes a property or relation, its meaning is to be analyzed in terms of a relation between *n* + 1 objects—namely, the original *n* objects plus one extra object, the property or relation originally attributed. Thus "Socrates is wise" has been analyzed as "Socrates is like the wise-itself", "Socrates participates in wisdom", or "Socrates has wisdom". But as soon as this account is proposed as an analysis or form of explanation of the meaning of predicates in general, as I indicate later, it involves an infinite regress. In a parallel way Davidson's mythology involves that whenever a statement mentioning *n* objects (e.g., one object, Sebastian; or two objects, Alfred and Bridget) reports an event, its meaning is to be analyzed in terms of a relation between *n* + 1 objects—namely, the original *n* objects and one extra object, the event; and again, as I indicate, this account involves an infinite regress.

---

his quite valid Grammatical Constraint principle (see *Semantics and Cognition*, 13–16), but applying it in the wrong way seen in subsection (c) of this section.

17. The rest of this section recapitulates and expands some key points in my refutation of Davidson and others in David Braine, *Human Person*, chap. 6; cf. my older discussion in David Braine, *The Reality of Time and the Existence of God*, 112–15.

The refutations of these theories belong not to grammar or morphology, but to semantics, and are matters for philosophical understanding belonging to philosophical logic.

(i) The problem of properties as abstract entities

I consider first the older mythology of properties and relations—or in modern guise, the mythology of concepts, features, and classes. In the earliest Platonic mythology being wise consisted in sharing in an entity called "wisdom" or imitating an entity called "the wise itself" (the paradigm of all wisdom). Being wise, being red, being round, being an "s", and being human are all alike explained as cases of having wisdom, having the color red, having the shape round, being an instance of the letter-type "s", and belonging to the species "human being". In this way we are asked to envisage concrete things as being in such relations as "having", "exemplifying", "instantiating", "exhibiting", or "being a member of" to entities such as virtues, colors, shapes, letter-types, and species, or more generally properties, concepts, features, and classes—or (one might say, speaking yet more generally) in some relation to a "universal" of some kind or other.

In this way all of a sudden the world comes to seem populated not only with concrete objects, but also with these abstract objects—objects in these special kinds of relation to concrete objects. Wherever there is a one-place predicate such as "... is wise" or "... is red", there is now also a two-place predicate such as "... has —" so that "Socrates is wise" is equivalent to and has to be understood in terms of "Socrates has wisdom"—since, it is argued, if we could not first identify the feature called "wisdom", surely we could not understand the original "Socrates is wise".

But how can we give an account of the nature or identity of these supposed abstract objects or an explanation of what this "having", "exemplifying", or "sharing" is? Only, surely, by referring back to the sense of statements such as "Socrates is wise"! Of course, if we know that Socrates is wise, we thereby know that he has what we call wisdom and we can say that he has the feature or property, wisdom; if we did not already know what it is to be wise so as, for instance, to be able to decide whether or not a person is wise (perhaps using what he said and how he behaved as a criterion), we would not know what wisdom is. But we cannot proceed in the opposite order and use whether or not he has wisdom as a criterion of whether or not he is wise as if our task were first to search about for some entity called "wisdom" and then to determine whether it was in the appropriate relation, "being had by", to Socrates.

The question as to what the "having", "exemplifying", or "sharing" is raises a more fundamental problem arising with this general form of explanation. For if every time we have an *n*-place predicate we explain it in terms of an

($n + 1$)-place predicate, the effect is necessarily to produce an infinite regress. However, rather than explaining what it is for Socrates to be wise in terms of Socrates having wisdom and then explaining this first relation of having in terms of some further relation between Socrates, the relation of having, and wisdom, and so on *ad infinitum*, we ought instead to explain what it is for Socrates to be in the relation of "having" to wisdom in terms of Socrates having wisdom and to explain this in terms of Socrates being wise, and then seek to understand what it is for him to be wise.

Consideration of this semantic question about "universals" has been befuddled by F. P. Ramsey's conception of "propositions".

His argument turns on conceiving "propositions" as language-transcendent Platonic entities in such a way that "Wisdom Socratizes", "Socrates has wisdom", and "Socrates is wise" are all equally good expressions of "the same proposition".[18] Strawson accepted this argument without dispute in his book *Individuals* so that, in order to differentiate particulars and universals, he felt obliged to go beyond logic and semantics to find considerations from within epistemology (as well as a consideration of their modes of identification).[19] But Ramsey's conception of "proposition" is foreign to the notion of *propositio, sententia* ("saying"), or "statement" which philosophers have mostly utilized, and is quite inappropriate to the treatment of linguistic and semantic questions, as we saw in chapter III. The notion of sentence, *propositio*, or "statement" which philosophers have most utilized historically (apart from those who reduce sense to truth-conditions) has involved not just sameness in truth-conditions, approach to verification, and consequences of acceptance for will and attitude, but also anything affecting the perspective in which things are being presented, and indeed anything else relevant to translation into another language—including Carnap's "intensional isomorphism"—that is, that content-introducing terms with the same meaning be related in syntactically equivalent ways.

The idea of the equal status of substances and properties has often been bolstered by the argument that just as properties cannot exist without substances (or so it is said), so substances cannot exist without properties, and therefore dependence is mutual.[20] But this rests on mistaking the relevant way in which substances are prior to properties. The question is not of whether

18. Ramsey, "Universals", with following "Note on the Preceding Paper", in *Foundations of Mathematics*, 112–37.

19. Strawson, *Individuals*, chaps. 5–6. He says that the existence of particulars is contingent (a thesis disputable in different ways in respect of God and the Universe) and that the existence of universals is necessary. The latter holds in such cases as the natural numbers as quantifiers transcending any particular subject-matter (ranging over domains of abstract as well as concrete objects), but not, e.g., with colors, whose range, system, and exactness of distinction depend on the existence and contingent conditions of visual perception of a given species, so that whether and which colors exist is contingent.

20. The priority of substances over properties, or the dependence of properties on substances, has often been explained in terms of a supposed ability of substances to exist without properties. Yet neither

Socrates can exist without properties (such as wisdom or bravery), but of whether the primary way of referring to such properties is predicative (e.g., in the form "... is wise") or by a singular term (e.g., "wisdom"). The trouble with the accounts we are criticizing is that they get things the wrong way around: they explain the sense of "... is wise" in terms of the "having" of "wisdom" instead of vice versa. Accordingly, what is required in this case is that the one-place predication of, for instance, "... is wise" be treated as semantically prior to the two-place predication of "... has —".

Of course substances cannot exist without properties, but this leaves the essential point unaffected: for there remains a *semantic priority* of expressions like "... is wise" over expressions like "wisdom", and this gives a *semantic priority* to substances over objects such as wisdom which are in a subordinate category. What we must insist is that in the primary mode of speech, only substances are mentioned by singular terms, and properties only predicatively—so that the other mode of speech in which singular terms such as "wisdom" appear is semantically secondary.

The moment the *semantic* priority of "... is wise" over "wisdom" and, thereby, of substances over their properties is compromised as by Ramsey, so that the expressions "Socrates" and "wisdom" are treated alike as primitives, the result is that substances and properties are treated as standing beside each other in a common pool of objects. And this is the mistake: to treat "objects" as a genus in which all objects of reference belong. To introduce a theory of properties or features as objects as if it were explanatory is to make the mistake of treating subjects of discourse (persons and material objects, shapes, colors, and other properties or features, places and times, and so forth) *as if they were all given together as semantic primitives in some single pool*, all of them "objects" in some single way or sense—which is the way of treating them which leads directly to logical paradoxes such as Russell's. Instead we should recognize that "being" or "object" is not a genus, that the things we speak of belong to different categories, and that the nature and criteria of identity for subordinate categories require to be explained in terms of statements about things in more fundamental categories.

(ii) The problem of events as abstract entities

The formal parallelism mentioned earlier suggests that we should hold the modern mythology of events in the same incredulity as the older mythology of universals. And indeed it can be refuted in a parallel way.

---

substances nor properties can exist without the other, suggesting symmetry of status, although they exist in different senses. Davidson offers a parallel argument for a symmetry of status between the categories of substance and event ("Individuation of Events", 174–75). But neither argument disproves the kind of semantic priority of substances for which I argue.

Evidently the category of mundane substances cannot exist without the categories of properties and of relations, and likewise the category of mundane substances cannot exist without the category of events—Smith's car cannot exist without there being happenings or events involving it. But this is not to the point.[21] What matters is the semantic priority of expressions like "Smith's car collided with the wall" over expressions like "the collision between Smith's car and the wall". The mythology we are attacking involves the grand mistake of *explaining* what it is for Smith's car to collide with the wall by saying that it consists in the existence of three entities at the same time: Smith's car, the wall concerned, and the event of a colliding between Smith's car and the wall. However, this presents a new puzzle—namely, that of the relation among these three entities. So again we have a dilemma: should we explain this relation, constituting a fourth entity, in terms some further relation, making a fifth entity, and so on *ad infinitum*? Rather, we should again proceed in the opposite direction and explain the relation between the event of a colliding, Smith's car, and the wall in terms of what it is for Smith's car to collide with the wall.

The parallelism can be appreciated when we realize that, contrary to what this view suggests, we only know what a collision is from understanding statements in which one thing is said to collide with another, and only know what a stroll is from understanding statements in which, for instance, somebody is said to stroll round the park. Further, we only know the relation between Smith's car, the collision, and the wall or of Sebastian to his stroll through understanding the kinds of statements in which the nouns "collision" and "stroll" do not occur. It is just as in the earlier case when we registered that we only know what wisdom is or what it is to have wisdom from understanding the predicate "... is wise". Thus the theories which represent events as objects as primary are vicious, just as the theories which represent properties or features as objects as primary were vicious. If these things are represented as primary, then they are being treated as "objects" in an indeterminate way, making no categorial discriminations between them, as it were, all in a common pool, cheek by jowl, events and properties with people and billiard balls, each in quite different kinds of relation with the others.

What is involved needs to be recognized for its essential crudity. By a similar logic we could think of "states" as objects, so that, for instance, a change of mind would become the substitution of one object, the intention to do X, by another object called "the intention to do Y" within a place called the mind—in a way formally analogous to the way one might substitute a lump of lead for a lump of iron within a certain place. And this "substitution" of one object for

21. Cf. n. 20 and related text.

another, this change of mind, will be in this heady way of thinking a new object, this time not a "state", but of a different type called an "event", differently placed in time from "states", and relating the two states of mind concerned cross-temporally.

(iii) The conclusion to be drawn from these problems

We can now sum up the situation in a generalization.

There is no one thing which is what it is to be an object. Persons, states, events, and processes are all of different categories—they differ in ways which are not merely formal, and what is involved for each to be an object is different. The concept of object is a purely formal one, correlative to the formal structures of predicate logic with identity, the structures whose applicability it marks: numbers and colors are objects, just as are events, persons, and billiard balls, but there is nothing, no nonformal property, which they have in common—nothing which warrants considering them together in some common pool. "Object" is a formal concept, the concept of something denoted by a singular term, not a genus containing substances, properties, and events together as all alike metaphysical and semantic primitives.

The proposed mythologies are defended on the grounds that we generalize or quantify over properties, classes, and the like, and even distinguish them from each other and count them; and likewise that we generalize or quantify over, distinguish, and count events, states of affairs, and processes. In each case they are, we are told, therefore "entities" or "objects": and it is insisted not only that there is "no entity without identity", but also that there is "no identity without entity".[22]

Of course, it will be *said* that nothing more is meant by saying that events are objects than that they can be generalized about, distinguished, and counted—to be referred to by singular terms. *And this is indeed all that would be meant if, in fact, the term "object" were being used just as a term belonging to formal logic.* But this is not how it is being used. On the contrary, the view we are attacking involves treating events as objects in a much stronger sense, implying not just that they are things capable of being referred to by noun expressions used as singular terms, but that this is the primary way of referring to them. Saying that they are objects is being taken to imply that they have semantic parity with substances as if they lie together in a common pool antecedent to speech, and that singular terms referring to events are just as primitive and just as indispensable as singular terms referring to substances.

It is this mythology of events which we find in Davidson against which I have marshaled the same arguments in this and the next section as I did in

22. Davidson, "Individuation of Events", 164.

chapter 6 of *The Human Person*. It commits the fundamental error of ignoring the lessons Aristotle learned from the mistakes of Plato, the lessons which led Aristotle to envisage a hierarchy of semantic categories in the way I mentioned in the introduction, section 6 (a), and explain in more detail in chapter XIII, section 1 (b) of this volume.[23]

Part of the trouble is that our philosophers normally have a secret agenda. They want to enthrone events in place of substances or agents as alone causes in what they consider the primary sense. Further, since they suppose experiences to be one kind of event, this fits conveniently with the prejudice which would make events rather than substances primary both as causes and as objects of knowledge.[24] But none of this has anything to do with the linguist's analysis of *the structures of speech*—nothing to do with the semantic and grammatical analysis of common discourse, the analysis of perceptual statements and of statements involving causative verbs.

(iv) A subsidiary argument: the problems generated by topicalized questions

The idea that the primary way of referring to events is by noun-expressions, not by sentences or clauses, has also been supported by alleging that it explains the absence of a simple correspondence between true statements and events. But the true explanation of this lies in the grammatical phenomenon of "topicalization" when one is speaking about the past.

No statement about mundane objects is completely determinate in respect of what might make it true. If I say, "Alfred hit Bridget on Tuesday", this leaves open the exact time on Tuesday, the place, whether he hit her with his fist or with a saucepan, the exact route of his fist through the air, and so on.

However, if in the ordinary course of life on a certain occasion Alfred hits Bridget and does it just once, and, knowing this, I ask, after the event, what was the cause of Alfred's hitting Bridget (or, as we say, "Why did Alfred hit Bridget?"), what happened is perfectly determinate as to subjects, time, place, and all other incidental features, and I ask it in a way which presupposes that the event did occur. Therefore, when, after the event, I ask in respect of this episode why Alfred hit Bridget, I ask the cause of a determinate event lying in the past, referring to it in a way which I presuppose to be unambiguous—I presuppose that Alfred did hit Bridget, that he did not hit her twice, and so forth. And it is evident that there is no difference between asking directly why this event occurred and asking why an event of this sort occurred.

23. The mistaken acceptance of such arguments as Davidson's by cognitive scientists is reflected in Jackendoff, *Foundations*, 322.

24. This raises another difficulty. If events have to be at points of space and at instants of time, they are mere mathematical idealizations. But the continuous cannot be explained in terms of the discontinuous.

From this what emerges is that, when used to make true statements, propositional expressions such as "Alfred struck Bridget with his fist in the sitting room at 2:00 p.m." state facts which are always in some respect general. But equally it is evident that the same expressions, used in appropriate circumstances, also serve to refer to events, and constitute the primary way of doing this. Thus the remedy for the difficulty we have located does not lie in resorting to the misconceived theory of events as objects, but simply in distinguishing the ways and circumstances in which propositional expressions are used.[25]

The protagonists of the idea that events are objects in a strong sense fail to make a distinction between two types of question: (1) simple questions "Why ... ?" like, "Why did Alfred hit Bridget?" in which the only contrast is between Alfred's hitting Bridget and Alfred's not hitting Bridget, so that the question has the form, "Why P rather than not-P?"; and (2) topicalized why-questions such as why Alfred hit Bridget on Tuesday rather than on some previous day, or why he hit her at the time he did rather than at a different time on that Tuesday, or why he hit her only once and not several times, or why he hit her with a saucepan rather than with his fist. In every case one is asking for the explanation of a fact stated in terms presupposing that the event did take place, but in these latter cases one's questions are topicalized or concentrated on one aspect of the affair—that is, asking why this or that occurred where the two things are alternatives (contraries like being red and being blue), not simple opposites (contradictories like being red and being not red).[26]

(c) *Problems in the morphology of seemingly simple verbal nouns*

Of the four difficulties I listed in section 2 (a), the third might seem the most difficult.

What we have to fight against is a semantic analysis which suggests that we understand the verb "kiss" from understanding the verb "give" and the noun "kiss", explaining "kissing Barbara" in terms of "giving Barbara a kiss". This is about as foolish as an analysis which suggests that *just because* there is an expression "make a statement" and we can count statements, it follows that understanding the verb "state" is grounded in understanding the verb "make" and the noun "statement"—or one which suggests that we understand the verb "sleep" from the verb "have" and the noun "sleep" just because there exists the expression "have a sleep" and we can count "sleeps" in the sense of counting periods of sleep.

It might seem that I am fighting here against some quite unreal antago-

25. In these last paragraphs I circumvent the troubles raised when Davidson realizes that sentences do not as such identify events; *Essays on Actions and Events,* 129–37, 167–71; cf. 114.

26. Davidson, "Individuation of Events", 171.

nist—since the idea that someone might conceive the nouns "kiss", "statement", and "sleep" as being semantically prior to the verbs "kiss", "state", and "sleep" seems so farfetched. However, this is not how it appears to many philosophers in their reconstruction of semantics, typified by Davidson. Thus he explains that for Sebastian to stroll through the streets of Bologna at 2:00 a.m. is for it to be the case that there is an event *x* such that Sebastian strolled *x*, *x* took place in the streets of Bologna, and *x* was going on at 2:00 a.m.[27] This event is supposed to be of the sort called a stroll, and it is supposed that what one does with strolls is take them, and in parallel discussions it appears that what one does with blows is strike them. Yet presumably, "taking a stroll" is a rather different type of thing from "taking a book" and is semantically more like "strolling a stroll", and, similarly, "striking a blow" is semantically unlike "striking a gong" or "striking a person": strolls and blows are internal accusatives or "cognates", not external objects of acts.

The same things which make Davidson's analysis strange grammatically and morphologically also make it strange semantically. For it makes the intransitive use of the verb "stroll" semantically derivative from a supposedly primary transitive use, "strolled" being explained in terms of "strolled a stroll" or, more idiomatically, "took a stroll". Davidson's contrived language involves yet other curiosities: thus, "there is an event which took place ..." is contradictory, since the "is" in this grammatical context would naturally imply the present, while the "took place" implies "in the past". And both semanticists and syntacticians should be worried that what took place at 2:00 a.m. was not a stroll (a progress with a beginning and an end), but an instant within some continuous strolling—not an event, nor even an activity, since within an instant of time no rest and no motion goes on or is accomplished.

We need to see the semantic process as proceeding in a quite opposite direction so that we begin with verbs like "strike", "dream", "kiss", "state", "sleep", and "stroll", and only at a second stage transmute them either into the same verb together with a logical cognate-term as with "dream a dream" and "strike a blow" or into a suitable formal verb like "give", "make", "have", or "take", together with some noun lexically cognate to the verb. Each such formal verb has its own associations or nuances determining its suitability in the particular case: "make" suggests creativity or production, whereas "have" suggests passivity and "take" perhaps choice (a stroll, a break, or a route) or reception (a blow, a joke). The semantic constraints on the selection of such verbs are comparable with the constraints determining the selection of prepositions in such cases as when we say, "assault of the Norse upon Paris" avoiding the expression "assault of Paris".

27. Davidson, "Individuation of Events", 166–67.

In their semantics Davidson and others appeal to considerations of morphology and syntactic structure as they affect morphology when doing so is convenient and ignore them when inconvenient. Davidson and others wish to justify treating events as objects; this appears convenient if one wants each quantifier to range over all times, treating all times as coexisting and the universe as a set of events—each one, *e*, with dimensional coordinates *x*, *y*, *z*, and *t*. They ignore such awkwardnesses as we have instanced from Davidson's treatment of strolling in Bologna. Davidson's analysis once seemed convenient in treating adverbs, because the popularity of transformational grammatical theories among philosophers made it attractive to attribute semantic priority to events, something already popularized by philosophers of science who would never have dreamt of classifying strolls as events. Making the adjective semantically and grammatically prior to the adverb could be put forward as explaining certain morphological facts, such as that in English and French it is normal for adverbials to be formed from adjectives, "clumsily", "slowly", and "easily" from "clumsy", "slow", and "easy", and likewise "twice" or "two times" from "two".

However, such an overly simple transformational approach has been successively reformulated by Chomsky and abandoned by many other linguists, especially those with a greater concern with the problems of language acquisition and development. And, independently of this, we may observe that there is more parity between adverbs and adjectives in many other languages than in English and French: for instance, in Latin the adverb *facile* is morphologically no more or less derivative than the adjective *facilis*. The right line of approach is to refuse to regard any of the different morphological forms of the morpheme "clumsy" as grammatically primary as if the others arose by grammatical transformation. Rather we should regard the morpheme, which is a theoretical entity in the sort of way the Latin word-stem "*homin-*" is a theoretical entity (i.e., "present" in the nominative *homo* as much as in the accusative *hominem*), as something neutral as to morphological form and as drawn up into different morphological forms according to its grammatical role—that is, according to whether it modifies a predicate (i.e., is adverbial) or qualifies a nominal (i.e., is adjectival).[28] Moreover, particularly if some grammatical features are shaped according to thematic roles, this approach will serve well in other types of case and is therefore attractive in its own right, precisely in accord with Jackendoff's Grammatical Constraint principle[29]—for instance, it serves well to think of nouns (whether in a prepositional context or not) as

28. I here take grammatical categories such as the nominal, the adverbial, and the adjectival as to be defined in terms of the relevant grammatical roles, an approach more adapted to Lexical Functional Grammar than to its Chomskyan rivals.

29. Jackendoff, *Semantics and Cognition*, 13–16.

drawn up into the different morphological forms called "cases" according to their semantic function, here their "thematic roles".

The case of quantifiers, among them numbers, may seem more complex. But here again this approach seems entirely viable.

When John kisses Barbara and then kisses her again, we say he has kissed her twice, or two times,[30] while, since Peter was an apostle and Paul was another apostle, we say Peter and Paul were two apostles. What we have in both cases is the summary of a conjunction in a quantified statement in which the quantity-indicator applies to the predicate indicating that the predicate applies twice, in one case to one subject at different times and in the other case to different subjects. We do not have to analyze "John kissed Barbara" as "John gave Barbara a kiss" in order to understand "John kissed Barbara twice", any more than in order to understand "John kissed Barbara clumsily". Here again, with "two" and "twice", just as with "clumsy" and "clumsily", we have a morpheme which is drawn up into different word-forms in different grammatical contexts, so that we have the same morphological process in both cases, despite the gulf between the semantic settings within which this process comes into play. None of the different morphological forms of such morphemes has grammatical priority, although in this or that language this or that form may be morphologically prior. In such contexts we find different morphological rules governing the relationships between word-forms in different languages.

In considering the case of adverbs, sometimes of radically different kinds, we have been considering the most difficult case. But the perspective with which we approach this more specialized problem is appropriately set by the considerations arising with the first problem.

The process whereby a morpheme is, as I described it, "drawn up into different word-forms in different grammatical contexts", with the result "that we have the same morphological process in both cases despite the gulf between the semantic settings within which this process comes into play", is to be found in many other contexts within language. Cook, describing Chomsky's grammar, identifies the same structural relations, merely describing them in different terms. Thus, where Cook makes out that "if INFL is finite and 'contains' past" the result will be that "play" will "be realized" as "played",[31] I would say that "play" has been "drawn up" into the word-form "played". And when INFL is infinite, Cook tells us that this indicator may be a separate word

30. I advert to this case because it is suggested by Davidson's argument ("Individuation of Events", 167–68). If I did not consider it, my argument would be open to an obvious attack.

31. Cook and Newson, *Chomsky's Universal Grammar*, 53. This, when translated for the ordinary person, means, "if the Inflection Phrase, that is to say the clause or clause-like unit, is finite, that is to say if it has indications of aspect and time, and contains an indicator that it concerns the past, then the lexical item *play* will appear in the form *played*". Here and in my text the italics are Cook's.

preceding the verb—for instance, the "infinitival marker *to*".[32] I discuss the character of the English "to"-infinitive in discussing prepositions in chapter XIV, section 3 (d).

(d) *The problem of morphologically primitive general names*

The fourth and last of the general problems I listed is that of the nature of the contrast between expressions like "the color white" or "the number three" and expressions like "whiteness" or "three-ness". Here we must not compromise what we have already established—namely, that predicative occurrences of color-words, and so of predicates such as "is white" and "is red", are semantically prior to such nominal occurrences as occur in "Red is a color".

But now we have to reckon with the evident fact that understanding "is white" and "is red" depends on understanding the color-words "white" and "red", even though understanding the words "white" and "red" depends on understanding their primary context of use, which is in such predicates as "is red" and "is white".[33] This puts the color-names "white" and "red" in a quite different situation from such nouns as "courage", "wisdom", "whiteness", or "clumsiness", where it is evident that we understand the noun from the predicate.

The special linguistic situation of such words as "white" and "red" appears in the way that color-words do double duty as adjectives and names, whereas words like "wise" do not, as when we say, "The Sun is orange; orange is the color between red and yellow". Predicates like "... is white", "... is red", and "... is orange" are generative of new subject-terms in an extra, quite distinctive way. That is, besides having the possibility of statements of the type "'Red' is what I said he was", parallel to "'Clumsy' is what I said he was", and being able to speak of whiteness, just as we can speak of clumsiness, as a property predicated in propositions, we have a third possibility—namely, that of speaking of colors as subjects in their own right.

Moreover, names of colors are not alone as names of "abstract objects" which stand semantically among the primary classes of name. We find the same in the case of the names of numbers, where we can say, for instance, "The Apostles were twelve, the number of the tribes of Israel, the number whose square is one hundred and forty-four".

Such is the morphological priority of certain word-forms whose essential characteristics include serving both as adjectives and as nouns, even with the noun-use in apposition with the adjectival one—as in my first example, "The

32. Cook and Newson, *Chomsky's Universal Grammar*, 53. Sometimes what can be expressed by the infinitive "to V" can also be expressed by the gerund "V-ing".

33. This way of understanding attributions of color would not be open to those who express them in verbal form, as if to say, "The sky blues" and "The rose reds", as if forms of the activity of shining.

Sun is orange, the color between red and yellow". The words concerned are given in the language as being at one and the same time expressions which serve as adjectival complements to the verb "to be" and as names. This encourages the temptation to regard them as denoting objects as if it were the nature of these objects (colors and numbers) which dictated the possibility of using their names as adjectives. Yet it is no easier to explain the nature of *white* and *two* as objects than to explain the nature of whiteness and two-ness (duality), unless we first grasp the predicative of the words "white" and "two".

We need another way out of the apparent impasse—that of the use as nouns of the words concerned seeming to have a semantically secondary status relative to the adjectival use, and yet this noun-use being given in the same act as the adjectival use, not as derivative from it.

It is a question of identifying the phenomenon which confronts us. And this is essentially no more than the fact that in particular languages, with some adjectives and not others, the predicate predicating the property indicated by the adjective is formed from the adjective. Our concern should not be with the nature of numbers, colors, and so forth, but with the properties of the adjectives referring to them. Thus it is in the nature of numerically definite quantifiers or quantity words that one should be able to take them out of their context and utilize forms of speech which are formally parallel to subject/predicate forms—for instance, going from "Two things plus another two things constitute four things" to "2 + 2 = 4", just as we could go from "Orange things are between yellow things and red things in color" to "Orange is between yellow and red", or from "The robes of Cardinals are red" to "The color of the robes of Cardinals is the color of the blood of the martyrs".

Thus the sense in which numbers and colors are both objects still goes no further than that the ways in which we speak of them are formally parallel in some respects to the ways in which we speak of concrete objects. By "grammatical parallelism" we mean precisely such parallelism in respect of form, seen in our capacity to use the same structures of speech in regard to the natural numbers, identifying them and counting them, as we do in the case of concrete objects; despite the absence of any community of nature between the things named or any similarity between the meanings of the names. This is a much more profound formal parallelism than the more superficial parallelism between "Nobody has blinded me" and "Odysseus has blinded me", or the yet more superficial "It is biting me" and "It is raining".

The kinds of name referring to universals which raise the problems I have been speaking of, whereby a certain kind of morphological privilege is associated with a semantically predicative root meaning, are few, the names of colors and the natural numbers being the most obvious examples in English, and we need to register that these cases are very different.

The picking out of colors appears to require ostension, either to an object of the color concerned or to objects of related colors. More importantly, what colors we count there as being depends upon the contingent matter of the human possession of sight as one of our senses and the general organization of the human visual system.

By contrast, the picking out of the natural numbers is in principle independent of ostension to the natural world. We have not understood natural number terms until we have recognized their relation to identity and their role as quantifiers—for instance, so that "*a* is not the same A as *b*" implies "*a* and *b* constitute two A's" and "There are at least two A's", while "Two men are dead" excludes "No men are dead". Further, in principle, the differentiation of numbers requires no reference to the natural world or real entities—we also count numbers and groups of number, and, once we have picked out one number without referring to the natural world, we can pick out any other number by reference to it in terms of the relation of successor without depending on the existence of a set of that number.

Section 3. The Value of the Notions of Cognate and Cognitional Cognate

(a) *Cognates contrasted with objects in the proper sense*

(i) The notion of cognates in general

In section 1 (b) (iii) I introduced the notions of "cognate-term" and "cognate", contrasting "cognates" with "objects". Cognates are not "objects" in a proper sense at all. To treat them as objects proper (*Gegenstände*) is to succumb to a special mythology created by the logicians themselves, depending upon the logical slipperiness of the word "object".[34]

34. The word "object" originates from the notion of something thrown before the mind, e.g., as an object of perception, imagination, desire, other emotions and states of mind, and intentional actions. We find this use in Descartes when he speaks of the "objective reality" of an idea, meaning what the idea was an idea of, and in phenomenology, following Brentano, when an object towards which the mind is directed is spoken of as an "intentional object"; its being an "object" (*Objekt*) is independent of whether or not it has any real existence, and it is "immanent" in the mental state or action concerned. Meinong offers a fourfold distinction among things or entities (*Gegenstände*) according to whether they correspond to presentation to the mind (*Objekte*), to thought (*Objektive*), to feeling (*Dignitative*), or to desire (*Desiderative*).

However, by 1651 the word had developed a second meaning, that of a thing external to the mental subject (*Shorter OED*, 1973), making it translate *Gegenstand* in Frege, implying real existence. This has given this word "object" its pivotal role in modern logic. Correspondingly, by 1647 the word "objective" had gained the new meaning of being determined by the objects external to the mind (an idea Descartes expressed in 1642 by the word "subjective"), with the potential later of being contrasted with the "subjective" as what proceeds from the thinking subject (1707), what expresses individuality (1767), or whose truth is according to the determination of the individual (1817). These developments in English reflect a European-wide development.

A "cognate", as I defined it, is something which comes to our discourse as being referred to by a "cognate-term". As "cognate-terms" I instanced the verbal nouns "dream", "thought", "song", "prayer", "statement", "glance", "attack", "sale", and so forth, along with terms with grammatically similar behavior, such as "pain". Cognates are the things (dreams, thoughts, songs, prayers, statements, glances, pains, attacks, sales, and so forth) which such verbal nouns enable us to speak of or generalize about.

Where the cognates concerned are cognate to some verb or verbal expression denoting a cognition-related act—for instance, "know", "believe", "wonder", "think", and "understand" in respect of statements and theories; "have" in regard to knowledge, understanding, beliefs, and thoughts; "say", "state", "tell", "utter", and "ask" both in respect of questions and requests; "give" in respect of commands; "make" in respect of statements, promises, wishes, and so forth; "mean" in respect of senses, meanings, and things intended or understood—then I call the cognates concerned "cognitional cognates".

"Deeds" are "done", "dreams" are "dreamt", "thoughts" are "thought", and in all these cases we have a morphological connection between a verb and the noun concerned. In these paradigm cases of "cognate accusatives", the syntactic and semantic relation coincides with an obvious morphological connection. But, as I implied earlier, the same syntactic and semantic relation can be present in the absence of any morphological connection: thus questions are asked, and it is irrelevant to syntax and semantics that the verb "ask" is not formed from the Latin root of the word "question"; orders are given, but the sense of the word "given" has to be understood in the context of the idiom "give an order", not of the giving of gifts; and statements are made, but the sense of the word "made" has to be understood in the context of the idiom "make a statement", not of the making of artifacts. In this way questions, orders, and statements will be cognates to the verbs "ask", "give", and "make", because here the cognates concerned dictate the sense of the verb.

The point of introducing this term "cognate" into philosophy, instead of leaving it to languish in grammar books, becomes quickly plain. A "cognate" in this way of speaking, for instance, a dream or statement, is an "object" only in the trivial, formal sense that it is a topic which we can take as a subject of some particular kind—for instance, a dream, which we can generalize about; it is not an object proper, or "thing" in any ordinary or stronger sense. It enters our discourse only as activity-dependent, with no existence independent of the activity concerned, as dreams, cognates of dreaming them, are activity-dependent.

(ii) Introducing the notion of cognitional cognate

Both "sayings" or "sentences" as defined in chapter III, their senses essential to their identity, and these "senses" are to be understood in the same way—twin cognates to certain verbs—called "cognitional" cognates because they each have this kind of syntactic and semantic coordination with various cognitional verbs and verbal expressions.

Thus sentences are spoken or written and senses are expressed, and this exhibits each of them as "cognates". Neither sentences nor senses are concrete or spatiotemporal objects in the way that substances or the way that speech-acts are concrete or spatiotemporal. Both exist only as different kinds of "accusative" to acts of speech or communicating in any other medium—and they are in an internal relation to each other, the sentence as the expression of a sense. The speech-act is at once the expressing of a sense and the making or uttering of a sentence. The speech-act as a fully human act involves both sense and sentence, or expression of sense. But if life is missing, we have no living body, and if sense or speech-act is missing, we have no sentence.

Just as in the Aristotelian way of thinking the soul is what makes the living body what it is, so the sense of a sentence is what makes the sentence the sentence it is. The sentence and its sense or meaning are not two things externally related, requiring to be related according to some system.[35] Somewhat as soul and body may be thought of as constituted together in the dynamism of an animal's existing, so sense and sentence are constituted together in the dynamism of the speech-act as its twin cognates—as a deed is constituted in the doing, a game in the playing, and a dream in the dreaming.

As we insisted, both sentences and sentence-constituents express senses, rather than identifying them—sentences only constituted in the act of articulating sentence-factors of different types together in an appropriate way, thus integrating them into a unity, as explained in chapter IX.

A note on the use of the words "statement" and "thought" In chapter III, section 1, we saw how the same statement can be made in each of many languages and so spoken of inter-linguistically or cross-linguistically. This informality in using the expression "same statement" arises readily within the context of statements being cognates, rather than physical entities of a certain kind. In the same way we can speak of the same song or hymn as being sung in many languages. This idiom does not arise by an imagined extension of the type/token distinction.[36]

35. Cf. Aristotle, *Metaphysics* Zeta, c. 10, and further explained by his comparison with the unity of a spoken syllable in c. 17.

36. The type/token distinction is drawn from the distinction between the number of types/letters/characters available on a typewriter and the number of exemplars of the results of using such types, and involves a specialized use of the word "type" quite distinct from its use as a synonym for "species" or "sort". When we extend the so-called type/token distinction to the consideration of words, we find ourselves in confusion because the word "*dies*" ("day") in Latin, the word "dies" in English, "log" (as of wood), "log" (as of a ship's log-book), and "log" (meaning "logarithm") constitute, each of them, different words. When the

In a parallel way thoughts are cognates which we are said to "have", "express", or "think". Sentences or sayings in different languages can have the same content, and thoughts also have this content.[37] Thus there can be a thought that P as well as an utterance that P. However, the thought is not a secret utterance made in the privacy of one's own mind and heard inwardly, nor the sense of such an utterance-hankering-to-be-made. As I explained in *The Human Person*, thoughts have no identity as objects of attention in their own right, no existence distinct from the act of thinking them—that is, as cognates of thinking (in the same sense that pains have no existence apart from the having of them).[38]

(b) *The puzzles generated by the common account of talking about talk*

I will turn now to "cognitional cognates". We shall discover that cognitional cognates are not true objects even in the logician's sense, as I shall now show. Realizing this enables one to escape otherwise intractable logical problems. These cognitional cognates include all the things with which we were concerned in chapter VIII: (1) linguistic expressions, including both sentences and sentence-constituents; (2) meanings or senses, thoughts, judgments, and beliefs, commands, requests, and wishes; and (3) properties and relations, along with facts. These are all things of which one has been supposed to represent, or stand for, another. In each case the cognates of the supposed activity of using one to represent the other turn out not to be independent enough of the activities of which they are the twin cognates to stand against each other as one representing the other.

I begin with an informal presentation of the matter before entering into the dry technical analysis required for demonstration.

type/token distinction is applied to utterances, at a first stage "Flying planes can be dangerous" would count as an example of the same sentence-type, whether it meant that flying planes can be dangerous objects or that flying planes can be a dangerous activity. We are already taking liberties with the type/token distinction when we extend it in such a way as to ignore the difference between "Raleigh" and "Ralegh" and other reflections of any relaxation in rules of spelling. However, when we use sameness of meaning as our criterion of identity, e.g., in the form of Carnap's "intensional isomorphism", we have gone far beyond the type/token distinction.

37. When "propositions" are spoken of paralinguistically, as when, in 1930, Ryle spoke of propositions as things thought as well as spoken or written ("Are There Propositions?", 37), or as when they are reckoned to be what is common to all thoughts as well as all propositional signs with the same content, whatever the language and whether spoken or not, it is only intelligible within this framework, and not by a yet further extension of the type/token distinction.

38. David Braine, *Human Person*, 435–40. We can imagine or remember thinking the thought, but we cannot imagine or remember the thought except in remembering what it was that we were then thinking.

(i) Naive view of the relation between expressions and what they denote or stand for

I utter the sentence, a committed explicit speech-unit, “The grass is green”, thereby saying that the grass is green. Does the expression “The grass is green” occurring in this way denote or designate a sentence, or only express it? Certainly, the expression “the sentence ‘The grass is green’” picks out what I uttered and appears to denote an object called “the sentence ‘The grass is green’”, but this second expression is not itself a sentence in the sense of complete speech-unit, the sense of the word “sentence” made clear in earlier chapters. Yet the sentence “The grass is green” is also picked out simply by the expression “The grass is green”. Therefore, just as we said earlier, the expression “The grass is green” has two types of use: a first and primary one in which the sentence “The grass is green” is used to assert that the grass is green, and is not mentioned; and a second and derivative one in which the expression “The grass is green” is used not in order to make this assertion, but in order to mention or speak of the sentence “The grass is green”. But in such cases we are not mentioning or speaking of objects, even in the logician’s sense, but what I shall show to be apparent or “as if” objects (quasi-objects)—what I shall call “pseudo-objects”.

Parallel questions arise when we mention or speak about the name “Smith” and the predicate “... is a fool”.

Let me analyze this situation.

In the first case we are supposed to have, first, the sentence “The grass is green” occurring in use in order to assert that the grass is green, and then also further distinct objects—namely, names or designations of the first supposed object (i.e., names or designations of this sentence), typically names or designations, either of the more explicit type—for instance, “the sentence ‘The grass is green’”—or, more simply, “The grass is green”, as in the assertion “‘The grass is green’ comprises four words”, where the expression “The grass is green” supposedly denotes itself. Similarly, the predicate “... is a fool” will likewise be thought to have two uses, the one as a predicate and the other to refer to itself. These cases have been regarded as parallel to that of the name “Smith” having two uses, one in which it is used to refer to, or stands for, the person Smith, and the other in which it stands for the name “Smith”. Here we encounter the philosopher’s habit of thinking of expressions referring to themselves as having the same relation to themselves as the name Smith has to the person Smith.

This view presents difficulties. It generates a paradox known as Reach’s paradox, presented quite economically by Anscombe,[39] and more amusingly

39. Anscombe, *An Introduction*, 83–85; cf. Anscombe, “Analysis Competition—Tenth Problem”, paper 20 in *Collected Philosophical Papers*, vol. 2 (1981).

by Lewis Carroll in *Alice Through the Looking-Glass* in Alice's dialogue with the White Knight.[40]

The essence of the view concerned consists in holding that there is just one relation, variously called "naming", "denoting", "standing for", "referring to", or "designating", both between ordinary names and the people, towns, rivers, mountains, countries, colors, numbers, and so forth which they are regarded as names of, and between expressions referring to linguistic expressions and these expressions which they refer to. Ordinary names are among the linguistic expressions which we speak of and refer to, and so it follows that these names of commonplace objects are themselves just as nameable as the commonplace objects and that they have the same relation to expressions referring to them as commonplace objects have to names or other expressions referring to them.

The question is as to whether genuinely the same relation is concerned.

In contemporary written English the two styles of referring to linguistic expressions can be described in the following way. In the first we simply put the expression concerned in quotation marks, as "the grass is green", "is a fool", "clumsy", "the Queen of England", "Smith", and so on.[41] In the second we put the expression concerned in quotation marks in apposition with a specification of the sort of thing we are concerned with—for instance, "a clause", "a predicate", "a word", "a definite description", or "a name", specifying what we are speaking of as "the clause 'the grass is green'", "the predicate 'is a fool'", "the word 'clumsy'", "the definite description 'the Queen of England'", or "the name 'Smith'". In this second style we might have said simply, "the expression so and so" in every case, or in the various cases in other sorts of way—for instance, as "the grammatical predicate 'is a fool'", "the logical predicate 'is a fool'", "the adjective 'clumsy'", "the noun phrase 'the Queen of England'", and so forth. Or, again in this second style, we might want to specify what we

40. Lewis Carroll, *Alice Through the Looking-Glass*, chap. 8 (retaining Carroll's punctuation):

"You are sad," the Knight said in an anxious tone: "let me sing you a song to comfort you.... The name of the song is called '*Haddocks' Eyes*.'"

"Oh, that's the name of the song, is it?" Alice said, trying to feel interested.

"No, you don't understand," the Knight said, looking a little vexed. "That is what the name is *called*. The name really is '*The Aged Aged Man*.'"

"Then I ought to have said 'That's what the *song* is called'?" Alice corrected herself.

"No, you oughtn't: that's quite another thing! The *song* is called '*Ways and Means*': but that's only what *it's called*, you know!"

"Well, what is the song then?" said Alice, who was by this time completely bewildered.

"I was coming to that", the Knight said. "The song really is '*A-sitting on A Gate*': and the tune's my own invention."

After this, in Carroll's text, the full, truly melancholy poem follows about a truly aged aged man a-sitting on a gate, at some point mentioning some use for haddock's eyes!

41. Aristotle, instead of using quotation marks, sometimes uses the definite article, as if to say, "the 'the grass is green'", this use of the article giving it to be understood that one is speaking of an expression; e.g. Aristotle, *Metaphysics* 1017a28–30.

intend to speak of in a way which has implications for the discourse-context in which it is used—for instance, specifying it as "the utterance" or "the sentence 'The grass is green'", or, when a definite description is being used either as what the logicians call "a singular term" or as what they call "a collective term"—that is, in either case what many people call "a referring expression", specifying it as "the singular term 'the Queen of England'" or "the collective expression 'the English football team'".

Both ways of referring to the linguistic expressions we use can be found in speech, quotation marks being absent in speech, as when we say, "Clumsy has six letters".

I draw attention to the existence of these two types of style because they are not interchangeable. Because the expressions concerned in the first style of presentation occur as they occur naturally, in use, they are quite liable to fit together to make sense; for instance, we can put the expression "Smith" together with the expression "is a fool" and get "Smith is a fool". By contrast, if we put together the expressions "the name 'Smith'" and "the predicate 'is a fool'", the result "the name 'Smith' the predicate 'is a fool'" makes no sense—its parts do not hang together in any way unless we interpret it as a fragment of a list. In sum, every expression has two modes of use which are not interchangeable, one in which it is used and not mentioned or referred to, and the other in which it is used to refer to itself, and in the latter the expressions used are not freely interchangeable. Thus both "is a fool" and "the predicate 'is a fool'" refer to the expression "is a fool"; but we can say, "Smith 'is a fool'" (quotation marks are not spoken), but we cannot say, "Smith the predicate 'is a fool'".

(ii) The absurdity of this common account of how we refer to our own expressions

In order to consider the question of whether the naive theory described works, I shall, in this subsection only, use double quotation marks within double quotation marks, reverting to the conventions of the rest of the book when this departure from convention has been shown to be pointless.

My task centers around the refutation of an erroneous theory, according to which the relation between a name and the object which it names is a relation between two different entities or "objects", which for the purposes of discourse are to be regarded as having equal status as objects. In order to refute this way of thinking I shall use one system of notation in this sub-subsection (ii), right up until the last paragraph, *using only double quotation marks* where the relation variously called naming, designating, denoting, or standing for is concerned—for instance, putting "X" wherever "X" is supposed to be the name of X, and *avoiding single quotation marks*. Thus the name "Smith" is the name of the person Smith, and one might be told that the object "Smith" stands in the relation of naming to the object Smith. The difficulties for this approach arises when one considers the way one refers to or names expressions of different kinds, for in this view ""Smith"" names the name "Smith", ""is a horse"" names the predicate "is a horse", and ""The grass is green"" names the sentence or utterance "The grass is green".

What I shall show is that, if followed consistently, this approach would make it impossible to understand how we could ever refer to an expression at all.

If we are told that the name or designation "a" designates the man Smith, we need already to understand the word "Smith" in the expression "the man Smith" as designating (naming) the man Smith. Thus, if the mode of introducing reference to an expression involves rehearsing it in the context of its use, it cannot be informative to be told that an expression is being used to refer to itself (except where ambiguity arises[42]).

If what happens when we are told that "Smith" is the name of the man Smith is that we are given to understand that a second object ("Smith") is in the (as yet undefined) relation of "standing for" to the first object (the man Smith), the puzzle remains as to what the designation of this second object might be, since it cannot be simply "Smith", which only stands for the first object, the man Smith—rather it has to be a third object, ""Smith"" (short for the expression "the name "Smith""), which stands for the second object, that is, stands for the name "Smith".

Now we have alongside the person and his name, "Smith", this third object, the name of the name "Smith", that is, ""Smith"". But surely we must at all costs in formal logic avoid ambiguity, and we cannot have the same name naming two different things. Therefore, we now need a fourth object to be the name of this third object, and according to this system of naming, it will be called """Smith""", which is, after all, quite commonsensically, just the name of the name of the name of the name of a person—or perhaps something is wrong with this supposed common sense! Clearly we will have an infinite regress on our hands, since we would now need the name of this fourth object, and so on *ad infinitum*.

The problem is as to how we are to understand this relation of "naming", "standing for", or "referring to" as used in speaking of naming or referring to the expressions we use. If we have a genuine case of naming or denoting, logical clarity requires that different objects should be represented by different names, and so we cannot omit what differentiates the names, and so cannot economize in the number of sets of quotation marks.

42. I have in mind odd cases, as when somebody uncultured says, "Czechoslovakia was long", where the speaker might mean that the country Czechoslovakia was long and thin or that the name was a long one.

I may be told that in order to talk about the name "Smith", I need to incorporate my object-language into its meta-language, and that in order to be able to go on also to talk about ""Smith"", I need to incorporate both into the meta-meta-language. But none of this will deal with my puzzle, but only throw in the extra difficulty that no such general concept as "designation" or "name" can be used in a meta-language of any finite level, since there would need to be another meta-language of yet one higher level. However, fortunately we are speaking a natural language, not a formalized one—within which such multiplication of quotation marks is purposeless.

When we consider the relation between the name "Smith" and the man Smith whom it is being used to refer to, we envisage relation between one object, a linguistic entity, and another, one in the concrete world of real objects—both the name and the object named being objects existing in some world or other which can be identified by pointing or description or some combination of these. Our problem seems to arise from treating the relationship between an expression used to refer to itself and the expression concerned on the same model as that of "Smith" to the man Smith. For we have seen that if we do this, we will have an infinite regress of names of names of names of names ... —and be in the predicament of never being able linguistically to give the name of any expression at all without being involved in a regress of useless names of expressions, names of names of expressions, *ad infinitum*.

The lesson to be learned from all this is that we must not be deceived by the putting of quotation marks around an expression into supposing that we have introduced the name of a distinct object in some relation to that expression. "The expression "The grass is green"", referring to the sentence "The grass is green", and "the expression "... is a fool"" referring to the predicate "... is a fool" are, we are discovering, no more names of genuine objects than "the expression "the name "Smith"", referring to the name "Smith".

The fundamental mistakes are those of seeking to understand the semantic relation between an expression used to refer to itself and the expression it is used to refer to by analogy with the relation between a referring expression or name and the genuine object (e.g., person, town, river, mountain, color, or number) it denotes or refers to; and likewise of seeking to understand the semantic property of being true by analogy with nonsemantic properties.[43] Rather, when we use an expression to refer to itself we have a different purpose from when we use expressions to refer to people, numbers, colors, or things other than cognitional cognates, which is what we do incidentally in giving information about the world external to discourse. For instance, we use

43. This is foundational for the view argued in Brandom, *Making It Explicit.*

the expression "The grass is green" to specify something that has been said to us by a certain person at a certain time.[44]

What we need to recognize is that these referring expressions, "Smith" and "the name "Smith"", "... is a fool" and "the predicate "... is a fool"", and "The grass is green" and "the sentence "The grass is green"", do not refer to objects at all. Rather, they may reasonably be labeled "pseudo-designations".

The reasonableness of labeling them "pseudo-designations" is shown up by the fact that there are no expressions used self-referringly which are intersubstitutable with the respective names *used as names* (i.e., not self-referringly), predicates *used as predicates*, and sentences *used as sentences*—indeed no designations of the respective sentences, names, and predicates at all which are thus intersubstitutable. Thus "... is a fool" is not intersubstitutable with "the predicate "... is a fool""—we can say, "Smith is a fool", but it is nonsense to say, "Smith the predicate "... is a fool"". This is in contrast with the case of designations of genuine objects, such as persons and planets, which are freely intersubstitutable in normal contexts.[45] Clearly there are designations of Smith which are not pseudo-designations, and it is characteristic of these that they should be intersubstitutable with the name "Smith" used as a name in speaking about the person concerned.

What this illustrates is that in the case of the things ordinarily called names, it is perfectly normal for there to be a multiplicity of other ways of referring to the same named object, and correspondingly a multiplicity of referring expressions referring to it, so that there is abundant possibility of intersubstituting the name and these other referring expressions for each other in speaking about the object concerned, and the person or river may have different names for different people, names being arbitrary (unlike descriptions).

By contrast, there is no contingency in ""Smith"" referring to the name "Smith" or ""The grass is green"" referring to the sentence "The grass is green".

In general every linguistic expression has a primary use in which it does not refer to itself, and its use to refer to itself is a special, secondary use, and it is not a use as a name designed to be intersubstitutable for other names or descriptions of what is being referred to. Having recognized this, I shall now resume customary usage, which allows more than one kind of quotation mark.

44. Alternatively, in philosophical discussions we might be told that "The grass is green" is true because the grass is green, saying this in order to express the general form of the view that what is said or is in the mind is true because of how things are in the world rather than vice versa, thereby repudiating a "deflationist" view of truth; see chap. III, sec. 3 (b) (i) and n. 27 of this volume.

45. I say, "in normal contexts", because, for instance, although the person sitting next to the left of you at table may be the president of Ruritania, I may know that the person sitting to the left of you at table is bald, but not know that the president of Ruritania is bald. The context of the designating expression is said to be "referentially opaque" in such settings—it can happen that two designations of the same object cannot be intersubstituted without loss of truth, although they can be intersubstituted without nonsense.

We can now sum up by saying that when linguistic expressions are used to refer to themselves, the primary intersubstitutable expressions are ones involving a general term for a type of linguistic expression (I italicize these)—for instance, for "... is a fool" used to refer to itself we might substitute "the *predicate* '... is a fool'" or "the first *description* offered by this candid friend"; for "The grass is green" used to refer to itself we might substitute "*What he said* to me to convey that the drought was over"; and so forth in other cases. The name "Smith" will be an object-expression as it occurs in "Smith is a fool", but not as it occurs in "Smith has five letters" (the older punctuation did not use quotation marks), perhaps now written "'Smith' has five letters", the name "Smith" being intersubstitutable with the description "the first *word* in the sentence 'Smith is a fool'". Thus the discussion above illustrates yet a third point, a peculiarity of linguistic and other cognitional cognates: that the expressions designating them are not intersubstitutable without change of mode of linguistic use.

(iii) The interpretation of quotation marks

For reasons parallel to those which apply in the case of linguistic expressions, one should likewise regard senses or meanings as cognates, not objects—and at the same time take full advantage of having been freed from thinking of the function of quotation marks as being to form expressions naming or standing for objects, with one object "standing for" another.

For, first, we are in a position to understand how it is that quotation marks can serve the same function as indirect speech (*oratio obliqua*): thus "The fool said in his heart 'There is no God'" need mean nothing different from "The fool said in his heart that there is no God" (or "The fool said in his heart there is no God"); and from these latter formulations we can readily register how in speech, as well as in writing systems lacking quotation marks, no difference need appear. Geach explains that "quotes signalize a special use of the quoted expression", and their use does not involve the mistaken view, taken by many logicians, that the terms "mention" and "use" are "mutually exclusive—as though a 'mentioned' (i.e. quoted) expression were not at the same time being 'used'".[46]

That is, we must join Geach in rejecting the view "that when an expression is quoted, not it but the corresponding quotation is being used; and that, although the quotation is *physically* built up of the quoted expression and a pair of encircling quotes, the quoted expression is not *logically* or *syntactically* a part of the quotation, any more than the 'man' is logically a part of the word 'emancipate', or the variable 'x' of the word 'six'". This means also rejecting the

46. Geach, *Mental Acts*, 81–82.

view that a quotation is "logically speaking a single long word, whose parts have no separate significance".[47] Instead, with Geach we should recognize that "the quotes around a complex expression are to be read as applying to each syntactically distinct part of the expression". This is necessary in order to understand the quotation, to appreciate the content of what is quoted.

Second, this makes it unsurprising that quotation marks should be able to occur without breach of syntax. What I say is not a unitary object towards which I am in the relation of "saying", because it is not an "object" grammatically or semantically at all. Rather, what I say is just an articulated expression of sense, and quoted expressions can be interwoven with the rest of the sentence in a way indicated by quotation marks or by intonation, as in, "Do you realize what he said? He said that you were 'of irregular ancestry' and had gone to a 'male boarding school', and that with 'that background' it was 'hardly surprising' that your 'habits' were 'correspondingly free'. He could not even use normal Anglo-Saxon, prig that he is".

(c) *Senses as cognates of linguistic acts, not objects; and facts as also cognitional cognates*

(i) Senses as cognates, not objects

I said that not only expressions, but also senses or meanings are "cognates", not objects. For, in uttering a sentence, I express a sense and do not mention this sense or in any way refer to it as if it were an object.

It has been suggested that in uttering a sentence, the sense in which I *express* a sense rather than merely *identify* it, is this: in expressing a sense rather than *merely* identifying it, I simply adopt the most direct mode of identifying the thought or proposition, allowing it to be calculated directly,[48] rather than indirectly—for example, as the proposition uttered at such and such a time and place—despite the fact that any direct calculation of the sense of a proposition is impossible anyway for the reasons introduced in chapter I and further explained in chapter V. But no! Here I make a more fundamental point. My objection is that, as a cognate, the sense of a sentence has no identity as an object proper distinct from the activity of uttering (or thinking) it, but is something with existence only as exercised *in the very act* of its being expressed, whether to others or to oneself—that is, in the speech-act itself—in the act of saying, as Plato recognized, a sentence or clause is not a name.

47. Geach, *Mental Acts*, with reference to Quine, *Mathematical Logic* (Cambridge, Mass.: Harvard University Press, 1951), 26.

48. One supposedly does this by adopting a mode of identification which has the structure of the thought concerned. But it is not thoughts, but only their expressions, which are "structured" of parts of which they are composed.

The case of senses needs to be seen in the setting of the whole span of types of cognitional cognate.

(ii) **The variety of cognitional cognates**

Many mistakes and puzzles have come from the view that senses are objects. People have imagined that expressions of the form "the grass is green" denote the senses of statements. Yet knowing the fact that the grass is green, judging or believing that the grass is green, and understanding that the grass is green are not cases of knowing, judging, believing, or understanding senses. The so-called noun clause, "that the grass is green", is not an accusative to the verb in any of these cases. And, in considering the variety of human languages, we should see "He said that the grass is green" as a grammatical variant of "He said 'the grass is green'".

Once the notion of cognate is grasped and accepted, one is at last in a position to sort out the geography of noun expressions which are not designations of objects.

Thus "that the grass is green" sometimes figures as a complement of verbal constructions such as "believe ..." and "say ...", thereby signifying cognates also referred to as "beliefs" and "sayings" ("sentences"); at other times figures as a complement to verbal constructions such as "I mean ..." and "I think ...", then signifying cognates respectively referred to as "senses" and "thoughts"; and at other times as a complement to the verbal construction "I know ...", then signifying cognates also referred to as "facts".

To put the matter in grammatical terms, we can say this: Granted that in English the subject always has the role of topic to the sentence (even though the sentence may have a second distinct topic of the kind called a Theme, as in "His yacht, we have repaired it"), an expression like "that the grass is green" can occur in subject-position, but not in the position of any other object-complement to the verb, but only in that of a clausal complement. By contrast, expressions like "the statement that the grass is green", "the thought that the grass is green", "the belief that the grass is green", "the judgment that the grass is green", "the knowledge that the grass is green", and so forth can appear in the positions of object-complements of any kind. This summary of the grammatical situation fits with Bresnan's explanations in *Lexical-Functional Syntax*, but is not tied to them.[49]

However, there are not just these cognates which can be expressed clausally, but many fresh ones each time a new context for a noun expression arises,

49. See Bresnan, *Lexical-Functional Syntax*, 17, 96–98, passim. Her notion of argument structure as explained on 9–13 and 307–11 fits with her conception of participants within events and situations reflected in a certain hierarchy of thematic roles in our reports.

whether phrase, word, or other expression, each time a context for a new species of linguistic "complement".

Thus, as there are cognates of verbal constructions having to do with language at the level of use or function, such as those which have to do with fully-fledged speaking and hearing, and meaning and understanding at that level, so there are cognates of verbal constructions which have to do with language at the level of "form", with the "elements" (word-stems, inflections, grammatical constructions, and so forth) which are flexibly and skillfully put to use in speaking and which we have to appreciate in understanding what is spoken. And cognates of each and every kind, not just those already discussed, will be open to more than one mode of description. Thus "We understand the meaning of the word *filius*" (Latin for "son"), "We understand the word *filius*", and simply "We understand *filius*" are equivalent. In each we advert to an item of vocabulary, irrespective of grammatical case and irrespective of distinctions between legal, biological, theological, or other uses.

Introducing the notion of "cognate" is intended to distinguish all these linguistic entities (entities in the sense of subjects of discourse and inquiry), whether at the level of "function" or of "form", from so-called abstract objects. To call a thing an abstract object is to represent it as syntactically analogous to such things as numbers and colors, things which are not concrete, but which are nonetheless still subjects of naming and generalization in the way explained in chapter IX.

(iii) Facts as cognates

Cognitional cognates are not all "mental" or "linguistic".

The cognates of knowledge are primarily not true propositions, but facts.

A fact is not a linguistic entity, but an aspect of a situation, state of affairs, activity, or event of a kind to be an object for propositional knowledge—that is, either actually known or of the sort to be known propositionally. It is not an aspect of a situation as it might be seen visually or an object of the other senses, but only of a kind to be known propositionally—that is, of a sort geared to possible linguistic expression.

Therefore, on the one hand, facts do not derive the *status* they have (in opposition to things supposed to be facts, but not actually so) from being cognate to any linguistic acts or to any other second-order or mental act, but from being what is the case. Facts have a status which is prior to language, speech, thought, or knowledge. Knowledge attains its goal when it is knowledge of that which obtains in the right of being that which obtains, not by the right of what obtains being cognate to some linguistic or mental act, although the proper goal of making statements is to state things that are the fact.

Yet, meantime, on the other hand, facts enter thought and speech (gaining their mode of specification) as objects for propositional knowledge—that is, things of the sort to be known propositionally, from their being of a sort geared to possible linguistic expression. Hence certain of the cognates of belief, judgment, assertion, and so forth that we spoke of earlier—for instance, "that Jupiter is the largest planet of the Sun"—figure as complements to true assertions of knowledge.

Yet, crucial to their status, facts can figure as complements to quite different first-order constructions, such as "brought it about . . .", and in these contexts seem to signify either an actual past or established fact, or something which was at some previous time possible in what was then future and which became actual because something brought it about.

However, just as we had to beware of enriching our ontology with objects or entities such as speech-sentences, *langue*-sentences, statements, senses, beliefs, thoughts, and so forth, all distinct from speech-acts and from each other, so also we have to beware of allowing our ontology to include actual facts (let alone merely possible facts). Rather, facts are things whose character involves being of a sort geared to relation to possible language.

Thus "that the grass of that lawn is green" as a complement of certain constructions signifies a fact, or purports to signify a fact, while in the context of certain other constructions it signifies only a possible fact, or desideratum. Thus "I rejoiced that . . .", "I was glad at . . .", "I brought it about that . . .", and "I knew that . . ." all instance a construction of the form "that the grass is green" or some equivalent gerundival or infinitive construction introducing mention of a fact, whereas "It is possible for . . . to . . ." and "I will be glad when . . ." introduce mention of possible or hoped-for facts, which are not subclasses of actual fact.

Even if there were no language-speaking beings, but only God and a world of inanimate created things also exercising active causal power, the typical exercise of causation would be in something "A" with active power exercising this active power, so that it would be appropriate to say, "A brought it about that P", constituting "that P" as a fact. In the early Wittgenstein, facts (*Tatsachen*) are not counted as "objects", but are parts of *Wirklicheit* or "reality",[50] in the case of positive facts consisting in the existence of certain states of affairs and in the case of negative facts consisting in the nonexistence of certain states of affairs.[51] And, strictly speaking, it is not the thing X which is

50. These seem to be the same as Frege's *Umstände*. Ryle may disparage Meinong's "objectives" as if they were "propositions" (Ryle, "Are there Propositions?"), but, like G. E. Moore, he still gives a privileged position to actual facts (Moore still believed in facts; see Moore, *Some Main Problems*, chap. 13, 249–305 passim, after giving up believing in propositions; see *Some Main Problems*, preface). This privilege remains in Anglo-Saxon tradition except among those who identify "facts" with "truths" or adopt conventionalist or subjectivist positions.

51. Meinong recognized the need for this distinction between objects (*Gegenstände*) and what I call

contingent or which is caused, but that X exists, comes to exist, or continues to exist, or, as we say, "X's existence", "X's coming to exist", or "X's continuing to exist". (In creation and upholding in being, God causes a thing X to exist or to continue in being, without God being in a physical relation of "causing" to X, as if X emanated from him somewhat as light emanates from the Sun.)

The fact that it is true that the Sun is an orange star is just as much something we know, a cognate of knowledge, as the fact that the Sun is an orange star, but obviously there is a hierarchy. Yet it is a fact that it is true that the Sun is an orange star because it is a fact that the Sun is an orange star, not vice versa. Therefore the underlying cognates of such expressions as "it came about that" and "brought it about that" form a narrower class than facts in general.

I have spoken elsewhere of the need to distinguish "facts" and "actualities"—that is, the states of affairs, happenings, processes, or activities which exist, happen, unfold, or continue, and of which facts are aspects in the way of which I have spoken.[52] We need to accord "reality" to the "actualities" of which we seek explanation in terms of causal agency, agents acting according to their natures normally within a context of conditions.

Section 4. The Notion of Cognitional Cognate and the Incoherence of Representationalism

(a) *Many ways of falsely separating sentences or senses from actual speech-acts*

In the course of discussion from the introduction up to chapter X, we met wildly differing conceptions of "sentence" and "proposition"—whether the sentences we meet within Dummett and Davidson, Geach's propositions, or the system-sentences generated by formal grammar which we meet in Chomsky. In each case these entities or objects are conceived of as in some way abstracted from being used as complete utterances, existing independently of this, and requiring something extra, ascribed to pragmatics, before we have an act of speech and an actual utterance. It is these entities or objects

actualities (states of affairs, processes, and events), in his distinction between *Gegenstand* and *Objektiv*, since *Objektive* are more like "circumstances" than like "senses", "thoughts", or "propositions". If one were to contrast what is in the mind or in language with what is or might be in the world, then these words refer to the latter. However, when Meinong speaks of an *Objectiv*, he means a "circumstance", not a proposition or thought, but still a merely "possible state of affairs" which may or may not exist or be actual, rather than simply a fact; cf. J. N. Findlay, *Meinong's Theory of Objects and Values*, 2nd ed. (Oxford: Oxford University Press, 1963), 60, 67–69, 83–86.

52. David Braine, *The Reality of Time and the Existence of God*, chap. 5, pt. 2, secs. 9b and 10a–d, 139–43 and 150–58, indicates the variety of considerations which lead one to make such distinctions. Also, *The Reality of Time*, 76–80 and 117–21 indicates the connections which give both facts and actualities roles in answering "why?" questions—actualities "real" in being exercises of active power or the agents of such exercise.

which have been conceived of as isomorphic with or representations either of reality or of states of the brain in ways which chapter VIII showed to be impossible. In each case the objects concerned are conceived of as if they formed some kind of totality prior to their use in speech, as if like arrows in a quiver waiting to be shot, dreams waiting to be dreamt, sights waiting to be seen, or intentions waiting to be had.

The dry analysis of section 3 has established that it is a mistake to conceive of sentences as objects with an existence independent of use in any of these ways. Rather they are cognates, with an existence no more independent of use as complete utterances than the existence of dreams is independent of dreaming.

Rather, we need to adopt something close to the view that Frege rejects—namely, "the view that the judging subject sets up the connection or order of the parts in the act of judging and thereby brings the judgement into existence", modifying it only so far as is required to allow different people to concur in the same judgment.[53] It is an act of linguistic deliverance which gives a spoken utterance or other *parole*-sentence its existence and constitutes it as a cognate, just as it is the dreaming of a dream which is constitutive of the dream. In enunciating an utterance we in one act constitute the *parole*-sentence (or if it is of a sort to be true or false, the "statement" or "proposition") and constitute its sense. As Wittgenstein says, "A proposition must use old expressions to communicate a new sense", contrary to the Platonic conception of propositions as timeless entities.[54]

(b) *The mistake of treating the possible as real*

The conceptions I am attacking can be compared with a Platonic theory of possible oak trees. Actual oak trees have their shape determined by the acorns from which they develop, together with their whole environment of wind and weather, sun and shade, nutritional base (the ground), and so forth, many accidents arising over time, set within a framework of laws of development. We can also conceive of other possible oak trees, and our Platonic philosophers would conceive of these as already given in a totality including all possible determinate oak trees. They will then conceive of the totality of all possible oak trees as neatly listed in the mind of God, as if God were an infinite human mind.

In my more Aristotelian conception I envisage no such totality of possible oak trees and possible geneses of oak trees, but view us rather as primarily

53. Frege, "Negation", 126–27.

54. Wittgenstein, *Tractatus*, 4.03; cf. 4.027, where the newness of the sense is highlighted.

occupied in considering actual oak trees and geneses of actual oak trees, and only in this light able to consider what would arise if an oak tree took root and grew in various different possible situational contexts. There is no proper consideration of oak trees in abstraction from their environments or of geneses of oak trees in abstraction from patterns of changes within changing environments.

Here we mistakenly suppose we can sensibly think about all "possible worlds".

People conceive that statements need to have had some existence as statements in order to be available to be made or stated because of the way we seem to speak of statements, propositions, questions, and the like in abstraction from whether or not they are ever the issue of actual acts of uttering, stating, or asking, or of contexts in which they have been or might be uttered. This is as strange as thinking that dreams need to exist already as dreams prior to being dreamt in order to be available to be dreamt.

There is also the supposition that if something is possible—for instance, the dreaming of a dream—then the cognates which would be constituted in its being actual—that is, in my actually dreaming this dream—must have some existence already, independently of ever being actually dreamt, in order to be available to be dreamt. Even if it has been already conceded that possible actualities cannot form one totality together with actual ones, still somebody might persist in treating the cognates of possible actualities as together in a single pool or "given totality" with the cognates of actual actualities, so that the existence of these cognates would be still treated as independent of whether these possible actualities are ever actual or not.

What we have here is a familiar logical mistake, but made not directly but only indirectly, by implication—as it were, in subtle disguise. It is as if it were imagined that we are still able to treat the dreams which have been dreamt—that is, are cognate to some actual dreaming, as together in one pool with dreams which might have been dreamt but were not. This is like allowing that we cannot treat Polythemus and other Cyclopes together with actual animals as if the actual and the possible formed one totality existing in the same pool, but still remained willing to treat the sentences Polythemus uttered along with their senses, and along with his dreams and his pains, as in one pool along with the utterances of historical persons and the senses of these utterances and these persons' dreams and pains.[55]

However, we will not finally be rid of the mythologies of such logicians and the linguists, supposing that linguistic or quasi-linguistic objects (sen-

55. Speaking technically, one could say that what is going on is an illicit quantification into a referentially opaque context, illicit prenex quantification into a *de dicto* modal context.

tences, phrases, words, and the like) and paralinguistic objects (meanings or senses) subsist in their own worlds prior to and available for relation to human acts of speaking or meaning, until we have also dealt with the mythologies of "facts" and "possible facts", corresponding respectively with true and with possibly true statements. Until it is shown that none of them are in any relevant sense "objects", it is not decisively shown that any of them are not. Therefore it is crucial to go on from considering what it is for sentences and linguistic entities with meanings and senses to be cognates, not objects, to show the same of "facts" and "possible facts".

(c) *The status of expressions referring to expressions*

Lest objectors dispute the real difference between "cognates" and "objects", I supplied fuller explanation in section 3, showing how expressions for these cognates are not freely intersubstitutable, despite being apparently ordinary subjects of discourse.[56]

Therefore, neither expressions of the sorts "The grass is green" nor "that the grass is green" identify genuine objects of any sort whatsoever—whether sentences, propositions, meanings, senses, actual facts, or "possible facts". We have to recover the truth of the ancient commonplace that saying is not naming, and that sentences (or propositions) are not names.

Of all the things of a language-related kind which we sometimes take as grammatical subjects—sentences, propositions, facts, words, concepts and properties, senses and meanings—the point that they are not objects is most evident in the case of words, and it was with the case of the word "clumsy" that I introduced the more general problem earlier.

From sentence (1), "He said that I was clumsy", in which the only functional role fulfilled by the word "clumsy" is that of being an adjectival complement of the verb "to be", we can derive three other sentences: (2) "Clumsy he said I was", (3) "Clumsy is what he said I was", and (4) "What he said I was was clumsy". In all four cases the "I was" requires an adjectival complement, and this is the primary role of the expression "clumsy", something said about me. However, as the expression "clumsy" occurs in examples (2) and (3), it has topicalized in such a way as to be functionally a grammatical subject term and functionally a noun, which latter it remains in (4), which takes the form of an identity statement. In (4), what is now topicalized is "what he said

56. Davidson may insist that his approach does not involve treating meanings as "entities". Yet he does not make clear what he is denying, and certainly something is supposed to be *identified* by a specification of truth-conditions within the context of a complete theory of meaning—and where there is identification, there is (in the relevant sense) entity-hood and the possibility of quantification over the things spoken of ("entities" for Quine and others).

I was", thereby functionally a grammatical subject and therefore a noun expression, and, because (4) takes the form of an identity statement, the second "was" in (4) expresses identity, with its complement, "clumsy", also assuming the function of a noun expression.

Some linguists say that the more complex sentences are derived from the original, simple sentence, "He said I was clumsy", so that "at a deep level" the word "clumsy" is adjectival, even though at the derived, "surface" level it does not figure adjectivally. However, one need not adopt this Chomskyan way of speaking. Rather, as I have just shown, the matter can be explained in different terms, terms involving that an expression be used in two functional roles at the same time, but not involving Chomsky's conception of deep structure. Indeed, nobody has understood (2), (3), or (4) unless he or she has understood that the word "clumsy" can be used with a double function, and that, nonetheless, it is the sense of the expression "clumsy" in its adjectival function seen most clearly in (1), which provides the key to its semantic content. We should say that the expression retains the adjectival sense which goes with the adjectival function whereby it is a complement to "he said I was" as an aspect of its sense, all the while that, in contexts of (2), (3), and (4), it also functions as a noun expression, which becomes an additional aspect of its sense in virtue of the perspectives being presented in these statements. The adjectival sense and function are still there wrapped up within the word, even when it also has the sense and function of a grammatical subject and a noun. Otherwise, "Clumsy he said I was and that upstart's describing my tennis-play in that way made me furious" would make no sense—if that upstart had not intended the word "clumsy" in its normal adjectival sense, but merely mouthed the sound, I would have no reason to be furious.

The term "clumsy" as a grammatical subject here refers to a cognate, cognate to verbs like "say" and "mean", and accordingly a "cognitional cognate". Cognitional cognates have some noun-like designation at the "surface" level (in my account, the only level grammar knows), but their primary designation (in the example taken, the designation "clumsy", and not "the word 'clumsy'", let alone the designation, "what he said I was, indeed the third nasty thing he said I was") is in the type of use in which the word gains its sense, in no way noun-like, but seen as a word functioning predicatively as an adjective.

The mistake we had to eradicate is the mistake of thinking that cognitional cognates, such as "clumsy" when it occurs as functionally a noun expression, refer to objects.

The freedom to say, "Clumsy he said I was" instead of "He said I was clumsy", did not tempt us to consider that the first statement involves an ontological commitment to the existence of an object called "clumsy" in a way that the second one does not. The fact that we can also say, "Clumsy was what he said

I was" and "What he said I was was clumsy"—that is, that we can introduce here the formal structure of an identity statement, identity being a symmetrical relationship of some kind, should not confuse us into admitting any new ontological commitment. It is particularly here that we can see the usefulness of the distinction between "object" and "cognate".

My proposal that we distinguish "objects" and "cognates", even though both are said to "be", amounts to recognizing that there is nothing beyond some formal structure in speech in common to the different things which are said to "be"—hence Berkeley was right in saying that there are cases where "things" have nothing in common except the name "being", together with a very limited shared grammatical or formal structure.[57]

(d) *The significance of saying that sentences, senses, and facts are "cognates" and not "objects"*

Let us demystify the assertion that none of these things are objects, except in a merely morphosyntactic sense, by first seeing the naturalness and advantages of this pruning.

It is evident that the verb "to be" takes many different kinds of complement. Some of them we describe as adjectival and others as noun-like or "nominal", according to their other grammatical features and relations. We have already distinguished between the logical and grammatical status of expressions for possible logical subjects of discourse and so-called intentional objects, respecting the difference in significance between "There was something he ran into (e.g., a lamp-post)" and "There was something he imagined (e.g., a cow, a battle)". In these first two classes of case it is appropriate to use the word "object" and to speak of relations or mental directedness towards "objects". What we are now occupied with is a third class of case: "There was something which he knew but did not tell me", "There were several points he made", "There was something he said", "There was something he meant", "What he said very clearly meant something", "There was something which what he said very clearly meant", and so forth. In this third class of case this is not appropriate, and we should speak not of "objects", but of "cognitional cognates".

Thus there is a wide spread of linguistic expressions (sentences, predicates, names, and other constituent sentence-factors) which have three modes

57. George Berkeley, *A Treatise Concerning the Principles of Human Knowledge* (Oxford: Oxford University Press, 1998), sec. 89. If each kind of cognate had a special type of existence (after all, they do figure as complements to the verb "to be", as in "There was something he said"), this would involve a new spread of Meinongian kinds of "being" or *Sein*—profitless ways of thinking, examples of what Wittgenstein called "language gone on holiday".

of linguistic use: first, they are simply used as what they are—namely, as sentences, predicates, names, and so forth; second, they can be used to refer to or mention themselves; and third, they are used in a wide variety of ways arising out of this second kind of use. This variety includes the use of a sentence to refer to its own sense or meaning, to refer to a belief or a judgment it would express, or to refer to the fact it states or to a circumstance or situation of which it describes an aspect. Again, a predicate expression can be used to refer to its sense or, in a secondary way, to the property or relation the predicate with this sense picks out. And words or expressions are commonly used both to refer to the sense they have in a particular piece of discourse (a *parole*-meaning) and, in a secondary way, to refer to the relevant *langue*-meaning locatable in an adequate dictionary. Only names can refer to objects.

In sum, these expressions, senses, sentences, predicates, and so forth refer to themselves as used at the level of *parole* only as things which exist only in being exercised or actualized in speech. A sense and a sentence, as a complete speech-unit expressing this sense, stand together as having only a "dynamic" existence, inseparable from being put into exercise intentionally by their human speaker, inseparable from his or her act of speech or being heard and understood by others. As deeds do not exist except in the doing of them, dreams in the dreaming of them, and sights in the seeing of them, so senses and sentences have no existence apart from our speaking, hearing, and understanding them.

Concluding Remark: Confirmation That to Describe Cannot Be to Represent or Denote

Accordingly, our critique of representational theories of meaning in chapter VIII needs to be more radical. We must reject the very idea that statements, senses, and facts are "objects" in such a sense that there might be the relations of isomorphism between them in the way required by representational theories—there are no such "objects" in or before the mind, because these things are not objects at all, and to suppose that they are is to make a logical mistake, carrying grammatical mistakes with it. And this accords with what we established in chapter X: saying is not naming, and sentences and senses do not in any way designate or denote objects. The relation of language to reality is not to represent it or denote it, but to make statements about it—such statements may help us form representations, but are not themselves representations.

In chapter XIV we will discover that this chapter's marriage of philosophy and grammar by sorting out the significance of different nominalizations has cleared the path for our later discussion.

XIII

Varied Systems of Grammaticalization—Reviewing the Phenomena

Semantic syntactic structure is set by the verb, by functional or "pragmatic" roles in discourse, and by the "thematic" roles of different arguments within the verbal framework.

Grammar studies the ways in which this structure takes morphosyntactic form and becomes grammatically explicit by such devices as connectives, inflections, and conventions of word order in the process of "grammaticalization", the particular arguments of verbs thereby assuming various grammatical "functions" in the way seen in chapter XI.

Section 1. Thematic Roles and How They Arise

(a) *A preliminary listing of participatory or "thematic" roles*

(i) Some candidate classifications

The "thematic roles" of things referred to by the different noun-phrase arguments of a verb are distinguished according to their different participatory roles in the state of affairs or activity highlighted in the sentence.

We have seen how semantics and pragmatics are inseparable. In particular, the type of reference which occurs when pronouns, along with particles like "there" and "then", are used to refer to people, objects, places, or times understood beforehand in any linguistic exchange—that is, what is called pragmatic anaphor or reference—has its first roots in logic rather than in grammar. The identity of the speaker and the person spoken to or of, and of relevant places or times, will often be presupposed and given no explicit indication by noun or pronoun in children's early utterances, their semantic structure being more fully marked at later stages.

In general, in children's two-word utterances (disregarding vocatives), we find a verb or verbal framework with various noun-like constituents, each such constituent being liable to have a pragmatic and/or thematic role in the utterance or the state or activity it concerns.

The nominal dependents of a verb (what I call its nominal complements and adjuncts in chapter XIV) have been distinguished and ranked in different ways by different authors. Blake offers a distillation of the views of a succession of thinkers about case from Fillmore to Dik. I use his treatment as a foil for my own discussion. He distinguishes the following thematic roles: Patient, Agent, Instrument, Experiencer, Location, Source, Path, Destination, Recipient, Purpose, Beneficiary, Manner, Extent, and Possessor, following the custom of picking out thematic roles by an initial capital letter introduced by Gruber.[1] Arguments with thematic roles include all those things which are capable of being treated as "topics" in a piece of discourse in the sense made precise in chapter XI, section 1(b).

Here he amalgamates the role of Subject of Attribution, as exhibited in attributions of quality and change of quality, with the role of Patient, as the object acted upon by an Agent. "Her mother" and "Jack" exemplify the role of Beneficiary in "She did it for her mother" and "She bought it for Jack". His Experiencers extend to whoever perceives something, has a sensation, or feels an emotion. By Purpose Blake means an object of desire or aim, as in "He went for a takeaway", which would be grouped with "He aimed his shot at the goal" and "He wanted a perfect apple"; yet "Motivator" (object of attraction or aversion) would do better as a term for what moves to action through the emotions (the term "Purpose" seems less appropriate because it picks out the whole phrase "for a takeaway", "to hit the goal", "to obtain the apple", rather than just the object phrase).

Plainly the list is incomplete, because it seems quite wrong to group cognate accusatives and products, such as "a song" in "The bird sang a song", with Patients. Rather, we should take "Cognate" as a distinct thematic role in

1. This list comes from Blake, *Case*, 66–69, the term "thematic role" from Jackendoff, *Semantic Interpretation in Generative Grammar* (Cambridge, Mass, MIT Press, 1972), while the notion itself, along with the capitalization of the initial letters of the names of thematic roles, was introduced into modern grammar by Jeffery S. Gruber, "Studies in Lexical Relations", PhD Dissertation, MIT, 1965, first published as part 1 of *Lexical Structures in Syntax and Semantics* (Amsterdam: North Holland, 1976). My indication of what counts as "arguments" having thematic rules in the next sentence is given in order to circumvent various difficulties raised by Jackendoff, in "The Status of Thematic Relations in Linguistic Theory", *Linguistic Inquiry* 18, no. 3 (Summer 1987): 369–411, and by those working in Lexical Functional Grammar.

its own right, including songs, dreams, statements, orders, pains, and emotions—in the first four cases described as sung, dreamt, made, and given; and felt, had, suffered, or enjoyed in the case of pains and emotions. Also, we need a thematic role of "Percept" to cover objects of perceptual verbs, to capture rainbows, shadows, sounds, smells, and so forth, as well as the physical objects and people we see and hear. The task of distinguishing thematic roles must be recognized as quite distinct from that of distinguishing semantic categories. The same object (e.g., a person) may be mentioned as an Agent in one sentence and as a Patient in another, and the same thing (e.g., a song) may be mentioned as a Cognate in one sentence and as a Percept in another.

Blake's examples of Agents do not include any subjects of intransitive verbs, although his defining of them in terms of performing an activity would seem to allow this. In his studies of early child utterances Martin Braine carefully emphasized that if Agent and Patient are defined as correlative, then there must be a role of Actor distinct from and more generic than that of Agent,[2] a terminology also used by Foley and Van Valin. The thematic roles of Patient and Agent only appear in the utterances of somewhat older children. Moreover, the actions of an Actor include ones later expressed by intransitive verbs such as "walk", "swim", and "jump", as well as ones expressed by transitive verbs. It was this wider concept of Actor which mattered in considering the significance of the active and other voices in chapter XI.

So far, then, we have distinguished the following thematic roles which noun phrases may occupy: Actor, Subject of Attribution, Agent, Patient, Recipient, Beneficiary, Instrument, Experiencer, and Possessor, all clearly roles only capable of being occupied by concrete objects (i.e., Aristotelian primary substances, viz., persons and other living things, with their parts, and inanimate things, including celestial bodies), and in addition to these, Cognate, Motivator, Percept, Manner, and Quantity (Extent). There remain many obscurities, and one has to be careful in one's classification: "illusion", "delusion", and "hallucination" will count as Cognates, not Percepts. It is not proven that there exists any tidy and exhaustive list of thematic roles as they arise in all languages, but this list appears to provide a good start. The roles of Location, Source, Path, and Destination all require recognition, but need more careful consideration.

(ii) Evidence from children's speech

In the early development of children's speech, the pragmatic and thematic roles of the noun-like constituents of an utterance are generally more determi-

2. Martin Braine, "Children's First Word Combinations", *Monographs of the Society for Research in Child Development* 41, no. 1 (1976): 1–104; see 51, 67–69, 84; cf. Martin Braine and Wells, "Case-like Categories in Children", 100–122, passim.

nate than how they will be classified grammatically later. Notably, Martin Braine and his co-researchers have shown that children up to the age of nine are just as liable to separate Actors and Experiencers as to group them together, these children finding this difference in thematic role just as conspicuous as their shared situation as grammatical surface subjects in their parents' language.[3]

It is as true of children's development of language as of adult language development over time that new grammatical forms arise through two processes, which Meillet named respectively analogy and grammaticalization.[4] By "analogy" he meant the process mentioned in the introduction by which already acquired rules or patterns are used to analyze new input,[5] an already established pattern of speaking in a certain way in regard to one type of topic being applied to speaking in the same way in regard to another type of topic. The second process, for which he introduced the term "grammaticalization", is described by him as the passage of an autonomous word to the role of a grammatical element—a process of transition from a constituent's having a primarily content-introducing or lexical meaning to its serving a synlexical role—for example, as an auxiliary or connective. In this book I use the word "grammaticalization" in a wider sense to cover all the morphosyntactic devices by which semantic syntax is made more perspicuous. The advance of grammaticalization is observable as rules of word order and devices for marking connection or concord different constituents in utterances become stabilized in the variety of different ways considered later.

In assessing this advance, we should not assume that a child or a linguistic community is relying on implicit knowledge of some adult category such as grammatical subject until we have evidence that it is not relying upon recognition of some less general category, such as the thematic role of Subject of Attribution or Actor.[6]

In his study "Children's First Word Combinations" Martin Braine picked

3. Martin Braine, et al., "Development of Categories".

4. I owe my remarks on Antoine Meillet to Hopper and Traugott, *Grammaticalization*, 21–26. In their introduction they say, referring to their first edition, "We defined grammaticalization as the process whereby lexical items and constructions come in certain linguistic contexts to serve grammatical functions and, once grammaticalized, continue to develop new grammatical functions"; *Grammaticalization*, xv.

5. Martin Braine notes that the principle that "old rules analyse new material" is accepted on all sides in the discussion of language learning, whether this is thought to be syntax-led, as by Chomsky and Pinker, or semantics-led. He suggests that *the dog bit the cat* could serve as the structural model for *The situation justified the measures*; Martin Braine, "What Sort of Innate Structure Is Needed to 'Bootstrap' into Syntax?", 81–90. In "Is Nativism Sufficient?" he explains that "the child attempts to parse new sentences in terms of the now known rules" (23–26).

6. Martin Braine enunciates the vital principle that one should never assume that a child or linguistic community is relying on implicit knowledge of any more general category than the evidence warrants; "Modeling the Acquisition", in *Categories and Processes*, 236–37, 239–41. In this way we trace the stages of language learning always by first testing the hypothesis that the child or language-user is relying upon some less general concept, e.g., Actor or Subject of Attribution, rather than the concept of grammatical subject in

out ten principal patterns in children's two-word utterances, recognizing these patterns as reflecting semantic relations.[7] All the utterances he considered have one principal noun-like constituent. The patterns he identified are as follows: the first of drawing attention to a thing, identifying it, or identifying it as of a certain kind; the second of attributing some attribute to it; the third of ascribing to it the possession of something; the fourth and fifth of indicating its number, its recurrence, or the appearance of another example of something of the same kind; the sixth and seventh of indicating its disappearance or absence; the eighth of indicating its acting in this or that way; the ninth of indicating its location or having changed location; and the tenth of indicating a desire or request for it. Here the second, third, and ninth patterns exemplify the thematic roles of Subject of Attribution, Possessor, and subject of location. The eighth exemplifies the thematic role of Actor. All the patterns reveal the center of concern as some concrete thing or things, never anything abstract.

(iii) Special problems with the thematic roles of Location, Source, Path, and Destination

If a person goes from Athens to Brindisi through the Corinthian canal, there is no clear answer to whether Athens or Brindisi should be considered things (inanimate things) or places, and the Corinthian canal a thing, place, or path. Clearly there is a distinction between driving my car into the garage in the sense of putting it in a place and driving it into the garage in the sense of making it collide with the garage wall. But the ambiguity is in the "drive into", not in whether the garage is a place or a thing. The connective adposition (preposition or postposition), distinctive case-marking, or contextual setting which allows us to disambiguate the expression "drive into the garage" should be considered part of the verbal framework, not the type of thing indicated by the noun-like expression "garage".

There are parallel problems as to whether "the Olympic games" or "the winter" refer to the goings-on over a period or whether they refer to the period itself.[8] In "He put on his armor for the battle" or "He got ready for the battle", the expression "the battle" does not refer to a period, but to a complex

---

English. The unproven presumption that grammatical categories are innate leads psycholinguists to assume that certain very general categories are forming the child's speech, even at stages at which there is evidence that other, less general categories are in play. Martin Braine's argument is reinforced by evidence adduced later in Martin Braine et al., "Development of Categories".

7. Martin Braine, "Children's First Word Combinations", 36–37, 88. Braine acknowledged that this recognition of their semantic significance constituted a rejection of his earlier assumption in "The Ontogeny of English Phrase Structure: The First Phase", *Language* 39 (1963): 1–13, that what was involved was solely the imitation of adult patterns of speech.

8. Blake ranks "the winter" in "It lasted the winter" as signifying Extent, but according to the logic of his classification it might rather suggest Location. Discussions of places and times as things mathematically identified and of Locations in an absolute space and time belong to another study.

of activities, and the same is true in the case of "He ate dinner before the battle"—the fact that in this case "before" is being used as a temporal preposition does not mean that "the battle" refers to a temporal location. A person in a long-term state of ill health might be said to "have got used to his condition" or "not to have been prepared for this condition". To cover all these cases we need a term which will group together states or conditions with activities such as battles, and I can find no better term than the term "Actuality" to identify the thematic role here concerned.

In thinking about what Blake calls Location, Source, Path, and Destination, it is important to distinguish the spatial cases in which the phrases concerned occur as attributes as in "David is in the garden" or peripherally as adjuncts as in "David is lunching in the garden", and the temporal cases such as "Daddy is coming on Tuesday" or, as a child might say, "Daddy coming Tuesday".

However, the difference the spatial and temporal uses of prepositions is much more radical than the differences in sense mentioned in chapter I, section 4 (a) (ii), which arose from their being used according to different sets of criteria in the two cases—more radical because it arises at a deeper structural and syntactic level. The temporal expressions "Tuesday" and "on Tuesday" have a role logically modifying the whole clause, in the examples given, commonly embodied within the predicate in a finite verb and here in the "is coming" or "coming", having a role parallel to that of temporal clauses such as those introduced by "when", "while", "after", and "before". By contrast, the spatial expression "in the garden" is an attribute in "David is in the garden" and an adverbial description of the action of the verb in "David is lunching in the garden", and in neither case modifies the clause as a whole.

Of course there can be attributive temporal uses of prepositions—for instance, "The collision was [took place] at 2 p.m." or "The motor accident was [happened] in 1999"—but here the predications are arising at a later stage in the construction of language, when we have moved from speaking only about concrete objects, as in saying, "The car collided with the wall", to speaking about abstract objects such as collisions and other events, which I categorized as Actualities, here relevant as having temporal attributes.

(b) *Semantic or ontological categories*

The argument of the introduction and the evidence of chapter XII show that we have to recognize a hierarchy among semantic categories. What is evident is the primacy of the semantic category of concrete object, since it is these which act as Agents, undergo change, and are subjects of such attributes as quality, spatial location, being possessed, or being part of something. This makes it unsurprising that the corresponding thematic roles have the primacy which Martin Braine observed. Once one has sentences predicating such actions and attributes of these people, animals, and things, one can bring in expressions identifying manner, time, or extent in an adverbial way. It is only after this that events, actions, modes of action, and times can be themselves made topics for predication.

As Aristotle was the first to realize, it is impossible to understand the character of different semantic categories without reference to the way expressions for them enter into the structure of sentences or how they can be generated from them, and to the relation of the sentences concerned to statements about substances (Aristotle, *Metaphysics*, Zeta, 1).

Thus there is no semantic category of object the nature of whose instances can be understood except by grasping their structural situation within a verb-centered framework, and in relation to the linguistically fundamental ontological category of "concrete object"—in Aristotelian terms, the category of "substance". And we have seen how it is the verb or verbal framework which dictates the structure of the rest of each sentence or clause, even in children's initial linguistic utterances. Chapter XII showed how different kinds of abstract noun phrase are only intelligible in relation to less abstract modes of speech, and immediately or ultimately by reference to predicates or clauses of which they constitute derived lexical nominalizations—except where they are lexically nominal forms of the adjective (e.g., the color-word), quantity term, or adverbial temporal indication (such as "Tuesday" instanced earlier), the nominal use dependent on the use as adjective, quantity term, or adverb. And the status of places, paths, and directions became clear earlier.

Thus grammatical and logical analysis alone suffices to explain how subjects of discourse of many different categories arise, and therefore why so many semantically different categories of noun phrase arise—and why semantic and syntactic categories do not correspond with each other;[9] for instance, "noun" does not correspond to "concrete object". This is therefore a quite false reason for regarding grammar as autonomous.

Moreover, because the logicians' sense of the word "object" as meaning "value of a bound variable"—that is, anything denoted by a singular subject-term—covers abstract entities and collections just as much as concrete entities or "first substances", there can be no such thing as a semantic or ontological category of "object".[10]

Philosophers have a hankering for such a super-category of "object" wider than "first substances" which will embrace together all subjects of discourse which are fundamental in some respect. For instance, Quine wishes to select

9. Succinctly set forth by Jackendoff, *Architecture*, 33–36.

10. The argument and evidence provided in the introduction, chap. XII, and earlier in this chapter suffice to refute Quine and Davidson's contrary views.

all those things statements about which cannot be restated in terms of other things conceived of as more fundamental, even though they may presuppose the latter and not vice versa.[11]

Jackendoff has the same hankering for fundamental objects, as is shown by his attempt to identify "fundamental ontological categories". These, he thinks, are to be recognized by distinguishing which kinds of thing can be distinguished by ostension or pragmatic anaphor, and he lists these as [Thing], [Place], [Direction] and [Amount], [Manner], [Action], and [Event].[12] Jackendoff shares this preoccupation with objects of ostension with philosophers from Russell to Dummett,[13] as if objects of these types could be identified independently of the way reference to them enters discourse—the conditions of which include, first, its being clear what sort of thing is being named when the name of one of them is introduced and what kinds of predicate may sensibly be asserted or denied of it, as argued in chapter IX, section 2 (c) (i), and second, how statements about it are related to concrete objects of some kind, as was made plain in subsection (a).

Section 2. Making the Way Thematic Elements Are Integrated into the Sentence Explicit

(a) *The varying ways in which thematic roles are marked*

Having identified the verb or verbal framework of a sentence, the content-introducing noun phrase elements within its core, and the noun-phrase nuclei of any adjuncts, the next question is as to how these elements are glued or jointed together within the whole clause. If, as in modern English, the effect is achieved largely by word and phrase order (i.e., by constituent configuration), then this depends on the exact following of some very precise rules, somewhat as when an architect has to rely entirely on dry stone masonry. The

11. Contrary to this, we must insist that the sense of statements about the existence and entity-hood of logical subjects which we distinguish from each other and count, and in regard to which we generalize, is to be gauged from the sense of the statements which assert identity or distinction. Frege's explanations give semantic priority to statements about lines and their relations (e.g., their being parallel to each other) over statements about directions—considered as classes of lines parallel to each other. And likewise his analysis makes statements not referring to numbers as objects semantically prior to statements referring to numbers as objects. Of course, these analyses do not suggest any doubt as to directions and numbers being objects in the sense of being logical subjects to be distinguished or identified, counted, and generalized about. But these analyses equally make clear the direction of explanation whereby statements which do not refer to directions or numbers as objects are semantically prior to statements which do.

12. Jackendoff, *Semantics and Cognition*, 45–56. What Jackendoff calls "pragmatic anaphor" is what philosophers have called *demonstratio ad phantasmata*, the traditional opposite of *demonstratio ad intellectum* (i.e., via description).

13. Dummett, *Frege*, 257–61, 480–82, 485–93. For Dummett's critique of Quine's ontology, see *Frege*, 476–80.

more normal human resort is to inflections and connectives—glue, mortar, bolts, and the like.

This is precisely how prepositions and, in some languages, postpositions enter the picture—the two grouped together as "adpositions". They serve as hinges or connectives connecting noun phrases, most commonly by being linked up to the verb, since, as we shall see, in sentences with a main verb, it is what the verb expresses which gives direction to the sentence. In this way they serve somewhat like certain adverbs or certain prefixes to verbs. As Aristotle says in the *Poetics* (1456b 39–1457a 5), among those sounds in *lexis* (discourse) which are not signs (*asemos*), they are the type of *syndesmos* (connective) which combines two or more significant sounds into one.

Consider the preposition *with* in Anglo-Saxon when used in the meaning "against".[14] In Anglo-Saxon it was as if one could speak in three ways, using *with* as an adverb to the verb in "I stand a foe *with*", as a preposition in "I stand *with* a foe",[15] as or a prefix to the verb in "I *with*stand a foe". Adverbial prefixes to verbs evolved into prepositions in the same way in Greek. We see here the rightness of Aristotle's way of thinking of prepositions as connectives and not as content-introducing lexical elements—in conformity with the picture presented in chapters XIV and XV.

Such variations are quite superficial compared with the differences in functional structure described in chapter XI, and a translator should not regard them as establishing differences of perspective or "sense".

In sum, how sentences are jointed together may be indicated in any of the five ways instanced, by adverbial affixes to verbs,[16] by adverbs, by adpositions to nouns, by case-markings on nouns (affixes, whether case-endings or prefixes), and by word order.

What is basic is "the ways in which noun arguments are related to the verb", which is how the Indian master of linguistic theory, Panini, explained the idea of *karakas*,[17] and how these relations are indicated in particular examples is entirely secondary.

Panini distinguished just six *karakas* or thematic roles, but in fact we need to distinguish many more, each in principle distinguishable by different case inflections. Thus Dik suggests the possibility of eleven different case inflec-

14. The Anglo-Saxon *with* and *wither* had a use corresponding to that of the modern German *wider* as used with the accusative.

15. The use of the preposition "with" to mean "against" is not obsolete, but found in "fight with X", which can mean either "fight against X" or "fight along with X".

16. Usually prefixes in Indo-European languages, as in the Latin adverbial prefix *in-*, which has the effect of adding "going into" to the significance of the verb, and the English *with-* instanced earlier, as in "withstand". Other adverbial prefixes have a quite different function, e.g., *ne-* in Latin, or *un-* in English, signifying negation.

17. Blake, *Case*, 64–66.

tions: possessive, dative, instrumental, partitive, locative, ablative (Source), destinative (allative), oppositive (antagonist), comitative (company), ergative (agentive), and final ("that for the sake of which").[18] Blake adds the perlative (path);[19] others have mentioned an abessive (in Finnish marking, something lacking or absent), an aversive, and any number of spatial cases variously signifying things as being close by, inside, below, above, or entered—given such names as adessive, inessive, subessive, superessive, and illative.[20]

However, although many languages multiply differences of case inflection to indicate gender, few rise to marking even eleven thematic roles in this way, since many of the distinctions concerned are indicated in other ways. It is not just that there is the possibility of resort to the other devices I have mentioned earlier (such as prepositions, word order), but often one inflection or one adposition has two or three meanings or functions. Beyond this, more importantly, as we shall see later, the verbal organization of the sentences within a language always or nearly always gives privilege to one or two case-markings which we can regard as used by default: in nominative/accusative languages, the nominative and the accusative, whether distinguished by case-marking or by word order; and in ergative languages, the absolutive. As we have seen, the accusative tends to take up the functions of a great number of the thematic roles which might otherwise be picked out by a special morphological case.

I spoke of some adpositions as having two or more functions. In most or all languages, it is overly simple to speak of prepositions as determining the relationship of a noun phrase to the verb. In many languages the sense of a preposition is only fixed by the verb and the noun following the preposition concerned, or by the verb and the case of this noun. Thus, in modern English, it is the verb and the following noun and discourse-context which determine whether a "by" signifies agency, location ("beside" meaning "alongside"), or route ("by York" meaning "via York"), and whether "with" signifies instrumentality, company, or opposition. And, to consider a language in which case is significant, Greek prepositions usually have two or three meanings, differing according to the case of the noun, and it is only the case of the noun which allows us to distinguish the meaning in which a preposition is intended. Thus, in Greek, it is often the difference in case-ending, not the difference

18. Dik, *Theory of Functional Grammar: Part 1*, 1st ed., 312–13 (a slightly variant list appears in 2nd ed., 368–69).

19. Blake thinks that a different relationship between verb and noun is involved with "path" than with "location" (*Case*, 68), but commonly the prepositions and case-markings used to indicate a path are also used to mark being an Instrument or a Location.

20. I derive these names from the glossary in Blake's *Case*. The logic interconnecting the multiplicity of spatial and temporal relations which invite expression is outlined in a preliminary way by Gruber, "Studies in Lexical Relations", 1965, and finds its fullest expression in David Bennett, *Spatial and Temporal Uses of English Prepositions*.

in preposition, which distinguishes whether a preposition signifies movement towards a destination (accusative), a movement of separation or origination (genitive), or the state of being at a location (dative). And whether prepositions are being used to signify movement towards a destination or to signify being statically at the location concerned is marked by case in Latin (accusative and ablative respectively) and German (accusative and dative respectively). In early Anglo-Saxon *with* followed by the accusative meant "against" or "towards" and, followed by the dative, meant "instrumentally with" or "in company with".

The way in which prepositions may require disambiguation from their lexical context suggests that in many cases we might expect them to be redundant, and this is quite common. In English we find assimilations resulting from the activity of French scribes of OE, so that in "It is me", "gave me a book", "gave a book to me", and "hit me", we may see the assimilation of emphatic, dative, post-prepositional, and accusative roles in the one form "me". Part of the background of this may lie in the emphatic French *moi*, rooted in the Latin *mihi*.

(b) *The nature of the difference case-markers and adpositions*

I have shown how certain adverbial affixes to verbs, certain adverbs, adpositions to nouns, and case-markings on nouns (affixes, whether case-endings or suffixes, prefixes, or infixes), all serve the same function of expressing the relation a verb and one of its arguments.

Other words can intervene adverbs and the verbs they modify and adpositions and nouns they connect into the clause, and these can be widely separated, as in "At what did you look?", equivalent to the less pedantic and more common "What did you look at?" By contrast, prefixes and suffixes are like clitics, proclitics pronounced as part of the following word, or enclitics pronounced as part of the preceding word. However, these distinctions can readily be blurred. Many postpositions are commonly pronounced with the preceding word like case-endings; the Turkish postposition indicating instrument or accompaniment is usually pronounced like this, although on occasion it is pronounced as a separate word. Again, the English possessive "-'s" modifies phrases, rather than words, and so can be separated from the head noun of the phrase concerned, as in "the Queen of England's corgis". Similarly, the Korean subject-marker, taking the form *-ka* or *-i*, can only be used externally to a phrase coordinated with the conjunction *kwa*.[21] But this does not force one to think of it as a separate word. Both the English possessive and

21. For the Korean and Turkish examples, see Blake, *Case*, 11–12.

the Korean subject-marker serve as inflections, but as phrase infections rather than word inflections.[22]

Grammatical inflections are not the only suffixes and prefixes to serve a connective function. In Japanese, *-jin* and *-go* show that a people and a language are being spoken of, so that one can discern a certain parallelism: *Nihonjin desu* ("I am a Japanese"),[23] *Nihongo-o hanashimasu* ("I speak Japanese"), *Nihon de shigoto-o shimasu* ("I do [the verb (*sh-*)*imas*] work [the noun *shigoto*] in Japan"), *Nihon ni imas* ("I am in Japan"), *Nihon kara kimashita* ("I come from Japan"),[24] and *Nihon-no desu* ("Made in Japan", a grammatically incorrect slang expression referring only to products). Both *-jin* and *-go* are classified as suffixes because they are always pronounced as clitics, while *de*, *ni*, and *no* are regarded as postpositions by analogy with the Indo-European prepositions. All of them show the same proximity to the verb, and, because in Japanese adjectives precede the noun, the link noun and postposition is rarely broken, and the distinction between postposition and suffix is blurred.

Therefore one should not exaggerate the significance of the difference marking the link between noun and verb by a separate word (preposition or postposition) and achieving this by case-inflections or by the use of specialized verbs (often formed with adverbial prefixes).[25]

Whatever comes first in formulating a sentence leaves one some freedom in developing the rest of what one has to say. Using prepositions leaves one free to choose how to describe what follows the prepositions, a freedom lost with postpositions, and, in verb-last languages, with reliance on suffixes to a verb. This may explain why many verb-last languages prefer prepositions, such as German (verb-last in subclauses), and classical Latin and classical Greek (in default, verb-last).[26] When Greek passed from using spatial prefixes on verbs to using adpositions to link noun to verb, it used prepositions, not postpositions.

Within the constituent structure of sentences, different languages use the devices I have identified—namely, certain case-markings on nouns, adpositions to nouns, adverbial affixes to verbs, and certain adverbs, to equivalent effect. Which devices a language uses is determined in its lexicon. It is therefore a mistake for grammars to treat adpositions and adverbs, but not affixes

22. The way English provides two ways of marking the possessor, by the separate word "of" and by the phrase inflection "-'s", is quite parallel to the way Latin provides two ways of expressing conjunction, the word *et* and the phrase inflection *-que*.

23. Or "Watashi-wa nihonjin desu", introducing *watashi*, meaning "I", with *wa* as topic-marker.

24. Literally, "I have come from (*kara*) Japan".

25. These links are all to the verb and do not warrant the distinction of "satellite framed" from "verb framed" languages in Leonard Talmy, "Lexicalization Patterns: Semantic Structure in Lexical Forms", in *Language Typology and Lexical Description*, ed. T. Shopen (Cambridge: Cambridge University Press, 1985), 36–149.

26. By contrast, postpositions are normal in Sanskrit-derived languages.

to nouns or to verbs, as lexical heads rather than connectives. Such grammars require a reform allowing the affixes (case-markings and quasi-prepositional indications such as "in-" in "incoming" and "with-" in "withstand") on a par with the adpositions and adverbs, exhibiting all four as essentially connective in function, synlexical in character in the way chapter XIV explains. Their semantic function is to link complements to a verb, as in "He was going towards London, not away from it", although some have other linking functions, described in chapter XIV.

(c) *The simplification of case-systems in nominative/accusative languages: linguistic variations*

If one begins with a rich enough supply of morphologically marked case distinctions, all other devices will be redundant, even restrictions on word order. To express "cut a cake with a knife", Latin and Greek need no preposition. Where English requires the preposition "with", these languages use different morphological cases: Latin, originally the instrumental, and Greek, the dative.[27] Again, in order to express giving to somebody, Latin and German use the dative without a preposition where the English uses "to".

The trend towards economy which we saw with the wide use of the accusative we will see later with the genitive and its equivalents. Thus, except for purposes of emphasis and nuance, a small number of cases can make most adpositions redundant, apart from the spatiotemporal ones. Commonly, equivalents of "of", "with", "to", and "for", along with various spatial prepositions, can do duty for the whole case-system.

Some languages unnecessarily retain morphological case-markings despite a rich system of prepositions. Greek retained the genitive alongside the dative, and Latin retained the ablative alongside both genitive and dative. Peculiarly, German retained the accusative and genitive, while making ever more extensive use of the dative. The German dative, while retaining its original role in picking out a recipient or beneficiary, is now also used with all prepositions expressing any kind of relevance or connectedness, including all the equivalents of "with", along with all prepositions expressing location or separation, including the preposition *von* (originally meaning "off" or "from"), which now either expresses animate agency (making it equivalent to the English "by") or else means "of", so making the genitive largely redundant.[28]

27. Instrumental and comitative meanings are associated in both Greek dative and classical Latin ablative, with preposition or without.

28. In effect, besides making the genitive largely redundant, the German dative expresses separation, animate agency, comity, instrumentality, and location—like the Latin ablative, except that German expresses inanimate agency by *durch* ("through") with the accusative.

However, when prepositions are made unnecessary by case, if case distinctions also disappear, more and more depends upon word order and intonation. With pronouns as clitics in appropriate order immediate to the verb in the English "gave it her back" and "give it me back", reminiscent of Italian and French, a preposition is unnecessary. In English the morphological difference between accusative and dative has been lost, even with pronouns. Prepositionless equivalents of the dative have likewise disappeared from the Romance languages, except for equivalents of the French weak third-person pronouns, the clitics *lui* and *leur*.

(d) *"Genitive" expressions fulfilling a specificatory or identificatory function*

Phrases modifying nouns or adjectives and introduced by prepositions such as *de, von* (taking the dative), and "of" remove some incompleteness in the identification or specification provided by the noun, as when we say, "the King of England", "Charles V of France", "David's left big toe", "the head of the bird", or "the bird's head". This is a complementary role they share with words or phrases marked by genitive inflections (the English "-'s" provides an example of the latter), since, although the genitive case is popularly associated with possession, in fact in practice it serves a much wider range of purposes corresponding closely with the specificatory or identificatory role I indicate. I shall therefore refer to both kinds of expression as "functionally genitive".

Being part of something and being possessed by somebody or something are expressed by two different morphological cases in Finnish, but both tend to enter into the identification or specification of things. Since in this case the context will show which sense is meant, one morphological case alone, the genitive, suffices. Many Indo-European languages dispense with the partitive/possessive distinction in this way. It is easy to envisage how it came about that the genitive or its prepositional equivalent achieved such dominance in English, the Romance languages, and Greek. The genitive often takes up the functions of the ablative in expressing separation, origin, and cause, and in some cases company or association. Thus the fact that the Agent originating an action or product and the thing or place out of which or from which the things come play so common a role in their identification may well explain why these should be expressed by means of the genitive in Greek (cause and place of origin are, after all, what things are "of" in English). This is perhaps how the Greek prepositions *hypo*, expressing agency, *ek* or *ex*, meaning "from out of" or separation, and *apo*, meaning "from", all came to take the genitive. Likewise many languages commonly identify individuals or families by reference to their place of origin, and in Latin location are expressed by means of the genitive without a preposition in the case of some nouns of the first two declensions. And the most general expression of association in Greek is by *meta* with the genitive (the comitative "with" or "among"), since the company one keeps serves an identificatory role[29] (even though the Greek dative can express "being accompanied by" without a preposition, and *syn* ["with" or "with the help of"] takes the dative).

In late Anglo-Saxon "of", which had once signified separation ("off" or "away from") and thereby origin, came to be used to translate all three of the Latin prepositions *ab, de,* and *ex*. At the same period the preposition *de* had come to be used as the common Romance substitute for Vulgar Latin's genitive case-marking. Finally, in the eleventh century, the English "of" became the uniform translation of this French *de,* so that "of" phrases could be used as alternatives to the increasingly standardized English genitive ending, by 1300 uniformly "-'s". In Japanese the particle or postposition *no* has a similar function. In German phrases formed with the preposition *von,* taking the dative, usurp this specificatory or identificatory function, to the neglect of the morphological genitive.

The same specificatory and identificatory role enables genitive phrases or their prepositional equivalents to take the place of subject or object phrases in many languages, as if to say, "Of dogs followed him" to mean, "Some of the kind dogs followed him", or to say, "He ate of horse" to mean, "He ate a piece of horse". When the genitive (or some other case, such as the dative) serves a specificatory and identificatory role, it is misleading to deny that it has a "structural" (functional) role and instead treat it as if it had a lexical content. The only important distinctions in types of the structural role of "of" are noted in chapter XV.

(e) *The effects of losing nominative and accusative markings in English and French*

In German case-marking remains important to the preservation of freedom of word and phrase order because it enables the difference between subject and object to be marked independently of word order, besides still serving to distinguish between movement towards a destination and being located in a certain place. In English and the Romance languages the disappearance of case-markings except in the case of pronouns has made distinguishing subject and object entirely dependent on configuration—that is, word and phrase order.

Thus the disappearance of any distinction between nominative and accusative from French nouns in the 1300s led straightway to a reinforcement of the custom of putting the subject immediately before the verb (except for

29. Companionship implies distinction as well as association, making the Latin ablative with *cum* natural.

such clitics as *ne, le, lui,* and so forth) in declarative sentences, making articles or other determiners obligatory except with proper names, and making personal pronouns explicit as subjects (lest the object be mistakenly taken as subject). However, the constraints thereby adopted, subject before the verb and objects after it, are not enough to resolve all ambiguities—for instance, in the inverted forms found in questions. Meantime the same loss of case distinctions had occurred even earlier in English, and we find the two languages following opposite strategies, yielding two different semantic perspectives.

On the one hand, one has the strategy followed in modern French—namely, that of locking the subject to the finite verb even when this is the auxiliary[30] and allowing only one direct object—that is, only one prepositionless object noun phrase. That is, whereas in English quantifier expressions and adverbs, although not negatives, can intervene between the subject and the finite verb, even before an auxiliary, in French such expressions cannot intervene between the subject and the finite verb. This has the semantic effect of reinforcing an awareness of the immediacy of the subject which acts or feels to his or her acting or feeling.

By contrast, one has the strategy represented in modern English—namely, of locking direct-object expressions to what I call the terminal part of the verb (the verb or part of the verb which introduces content) in order to contrast it with auxiliaries, taking prepositionless object noun phrases in order according to a strict rule of interpretation if there is more than one, as in "Give Joseph a coat". Now, although in English quantity-expressions and adverbs can come between an auxiliary and the terminal part of the verb, they can never come between the terminal part of the verb and its object(s).[31] This has the semantic effect of reinforcing an awareness of the logical internality of the objects of the verb to the content of its terminal part, locking any prepositionless object(s) to the nature of the action or emotion signified by the verb.[32]

30. One finds some exceptions in cases where no ambiguity is introduced. E.g., instead of *l'homme que Jean a vu,* one can put *l'homme qu'a vu Jean* (a change of order much needed when in place of *Jean* one has some very complex subject phrase)—a case of interest because it demonstrates that *que* is being interpreted as "whom", not "that". Instead of *Où Christine est-elle allée*? one can put *Où est allée Christine*? And, beside *Jean a-t-il donne le livre a David*? one has *Qu'avait dit le medecin*?—in one case forced to keep subject and verb together, and in the other case prevented from doing this.

31. To be more precise, French achieves this by insisting that subject expression and finite verb be separated only by clitics (*ne; me, te, se, nous,* etc.; *le, la, les, lui,* etc.), while English forbids the separation of the thematic or content-containing part of the verb ("breaks" or "broken", as opposed to the "has" in "has broken") from the direct object expression, and if there are two direct object expressions, forbids one's allowing anything to come between them (i.e., "He gave John a book" excludes anything coming between "John" and "a book"). And modern English, in place of the archaic "Like you it?", makes yet another use of the relatively new-fangled auxiliary "do" and says, "Do you like it?" With "do", what began as a tool of emphasis became a syntactic device (therefore unnecessary and never found if any real auxiliary is present) for avoiding separation between the thematic verb and its objects.

32. By contrast, in French, quantifier expressions and adverbs are quite free to intervene between the

The semantic asymmetry has the effect that in French the genitive complement phrases are interpreted as subjective genitives—for instance, *le crainte de David envers des tigres* (identificatory of what possessed, exercised, or performed the disposition, feeling, or action, in this case, David)—while in English they are interpreted as objective genitives—for instance, "David's fear of tigers" (specificatory of what the disposition, feeling, or action is in respect of or in regard to, here, tigers).[33]

This asymmetry between the two languages has had extra interest since Pollock offered it as empirical evidence in support of Chomsky's idea of functional heads and phrases as to be analyzed in terms of X-Bar theory, a misconception exposed in chapter XV. Pollock has mistaken a semantic difference between the languages for a difference in parameter within a formal grammar.

Of course, with immanent "activities" expressed intransitively, such as snoring and sleeping, predictably English and French show no such semantic asymmetry. Snoring and sleeping are in and of the snorer and sleeper.

Section 3. Parameters and Bracketing

(a) *Describing languages in terms of parameters is independent of Chomskyan theory*

In 1977 Chomsky was still using the word "parameter" in its common, nontechnical sense to refer to the types of factor affecting a variable. Soon after he conceived the possibility, mentioned in his Pisa lectures,[34] of couching his whole theory of Universal Grammar in terms of this idea, from 1987 consistently presenting "Government and Binding Theory" as "Principles and Parameters Theory", whereby the supposed Universal Grammar consisted of one universally shared set of principles with finitely many parameters, each language having these parameters set in one way or another uniformly throughout the language.

However, the term "parameter" has a much wider use within linguistics, quite independently of its use by Chomsky—for instance, in specifying the

---

terminal part of the verb and its objects and, if there is no auxiliary, can come after the finite verb, or if there is an auxiliary, equally well either after it or, unless this introduces ambiguity, after the terminal part of the verb.

33. With immanent activities, both languages avoid "for" or *pour* in respect of the tigers, because it suggests not a fear of tigers, but a fear on their behalf, e.g., of evil befalling them, even of their extinction. English allows the use of "of" in regard to the subject if the object is not mentioned.

With outgoing or *transeunt* activities, there is no room for differences between French and English. And with all the relevant verb-rooted nouns, whether in English or in French, the action is "of" (*de*) the object and can be described as "by" (*par*) the subject—and this rule is absolute. If Caesar has destroyed a city, and we try to speak of the destroying of Caesar of the city, this reveals the impropriety.

34. Published as Chomsky, *Lectures on Government and Binding* (Dordrecht: Foris, 1981).

positions of different types of modifier within noun phrases in different languages.

Thus noun phrases may have up to nine different types of modifier: (1) various adjectival forms of a kind which we would classify with determiners (articles, quantifiers, and indicators of numerical identity or reference, e.g., "the same" or "the other" in numerical identity, demonstratives, and pronominal possessives); (2) possessives such as the English "-'s"; (3) adjective phrases; (4) adjunctive noun phrases unmarked for case; (5) adjunctive prepositional noun phrases; (6) noun phrases marked as complements, sometimes by case (e.g., genitive) or by a default preposition (in English, "of"); (7) noun-phrase complements marked in other ways; (8) possessive noun phrases, marked sometimes by the genitive or by some appropriate preposition (such as "of"); and (9) relative clauses. We also have the phenomenon of fixed phrases which behave like simple nouns for all purposes except for inflections of case and number; these fit into three overlapping groups: proper names with epithets, titles, and fixed idioms in which the customary noun-adjective order within a language is reversed: Charles the Great, Philip the Fair (*le Bel*), heir apparent, bishop-elect, Principal Designate, attorney-general, a court martial, the body politic, *un ancien soldat* ("veteran"), *un ancien eleve* ("alumnus"), *l'ancien regime.*

Hawkins observes that some languages put all modifiers after the head noun and some put them all before the head noun.[35] However, all Indo-European languages appear to have a mixed character. It appears that, always, nouns are immediate to their complements (or to, e.g., unitary epithets as in "heir apparent to the throne"), whether immediately before or immediately after, while adjectives, the head noun, prepositional noun phrases, relative clauses, participial phrases, and adjectives in which the adjective is followed by a noun phrase as complement follow in that order. Thus, in English, we could say, "The nervous King of England from Hanover who spoke no English, being unused to English practice, fearful of doing the wrong thing, joined in the toast to the little gentleman in black velvet" (a favorite Jacobite toast) or "The furniture movers from Italy, who were carrying the piano down the stairs, having got drunk in our cellar, unsteady on their feet, dropped the whole thing over the banisters". (Basque appears unusual in placing relative clauses before their nouns.)

In other respects Indo-European languages vary in the standard order they allow. Thus, in English, all adjective phrases which end with the head adjective, and all noun phrases, whether as adjuncts or complements, together with all possessive phrases not introduced by "of", precede the head noun, as in, "The mouse terrified, toffee chewing, long-haired Oxford physics student

35. J. A. Hawkins, *Word Order Universals* (New York: Academic Press, 1983), 2–3.

who carried your bags visited us" (contrast "The Oxford student of physics with long hair who carried your bags, chews toffee, and is terrified of mice visited us"). Non-prepositional possessive phrases not introduced by "of" (such as "Bill's" or "my") serve as application controllers and come first in any string of modifiers within a noun phrase. In placing adjectives before their head noun, English follows other Germanic languages as well as Greek and Hindi. By contrast, although with many exceptions, adjectives come after the noun in Romance languages (as in Celtic languages and Basque), in this following Vulgar Latin of after 300 AD—classical Latin is less uniform.

Thus the idea that one can identify a number of parameters in respect of which each language will standardly behave in just one of the available ways, rather than others, provides a means of economical description of grammars of particular languages. In respect of the parameter concerned, the language will tend to behave in a perfectly uniform way except, on the one hand, for irregularities presented by some of the most common adjectives in a language and, on the other hand, with some frozen, special idioms. Here the most economical explanation of children's learning seems to be that in learning their first language, children will interpret simple clauses and phrases in whatever way fits most easily with their experience of adult utterance and is least open to ambiguity.

In this way, for instance, with English they will learn first that adjectives precede their nouns, and only later the rather specialized exceptions, while with French, as Italian, they will learn first an opposite rule whereby usually adjectives come after their noun, and then discover the special rules whereby a small number of the most common adjectives come before the noun, especially when they have some evaluative meaning when they come first (such as "handsome", "good", "great", "small", and "poor") and a more descriptive meaning when they come after, or else some logical meaning like "(the) only", "(the) other", "unqualified" (*pure*), "nothing else but" (*simple*).[36] Also, some adjectives come before the noun with a specialized frozen meaning, as with *ancien*. The practice in Celtic languages preceded the Romance and was more uniform, so that adjectives preceded the noun only by forming compound nouns, as if to say, "old-man" as one word-stem. Such rules, and then their exceptions or types of exception, are learned by following adult practice.

36. For other indicative examples, after the noun, we have *sale* ("dirty"), *grand* ("tall"), *gros* ("fat"), *propre* ("clean"), *seul* ("lonely"), *pure* ("unmixed"), *simple* ("easy"), and terms indicating religion or nationality. Before the noun, *sale* becomes "nasty" and *gros* becomes "big" (e.g., of effort).

(b) *Bracketing as a fundamental device in grammaticalization*

Once speakers have advanced beyond utterances composed of two semantic units, they can take advantage of one of the most common devices used in grammaticalization—namely, what we might call "bracketing". This natural device allows for constituent phrases to occur in split-up forms, a possibility which, it will be recalled, was allowed for in the very idea of constituent as explained in chapter I, conspicuous in logic as providing for many-place predicates bestraddling the whole of the clause to which they give structure. By contrast components can only occur as unitary continua, or wholes. Thinking of linguistic signs as mere components coheres with thinking of sentences as mere strings of such unitary continua, whereas thinking of them as constituents coheres with thinking of sentences as pragmatically given linguistic communications, uttered or heard as structured, sense-expressing wholes.

In speaking of bracketing, I pick out only one formal aspect of the kind of variation between languages which inspired the development of Dik's Functional Grammar and Lexical Functional Grammar, directed towards discovering "universals" which configurational and nonconfigurational languages share within the spread of variation well described in Bresnan's *Lexical-Functional Syntax*.[37]

To take the simplest case, suppose that we conceive the elemental division in a particular sentence to be between a subject, S, and a predicate phrase, VO (the verb followed by the object to the verb) or OV (the object to the verb followed by the verb); then we can form sentences of the structures S(OV) and the rare (VO)S, as well as the S(VO) familiar to English speakers. However, in the grammar of V(SO) languages, constituting some 9 percent of the world's languages,[38] conspicuously, Celtic languages and the whole Afro-Asiatic group, including all Semitic languages, along with Berber and Coptic, sentences are structured so as to bracket the subject and object phrases together, subject phrase before object phrase. However, no such sentence can be represented by a phrase structure diagram in two-dimensional tree form, since the branches of the tree would have to cross each other. A sentence, or clause as a potential sentence, S_P, would be represented by a tree in which S_P divided into VP, the verb phrase, and NP_1, the noun phrase standing as subject, and this VP then divided into V, the verb, and NP_2, the noun phrase standing as object. Then, to get a VSO sentence, the tree-line joining S_P to NP_1 would have to cross the tree-line joining VP to NP_2. Yet the structure V(SO) is no less natural than the mathematicians f(x,y).

Now, in Chomskyan grammars, all such problems are dealt with by dis-

37. I pick Bresnan, *Lexical-Functional Syntax*, 5–10, 94–98, 113–14, 302–11 for initial attention.

38. Russell S. Tomlin, *Basic Word Order: Functional Principles* (London: Croom Helm, 1986).

tinguishing a deep structure in which lines in a phrase diagram set forth in the form of a tree never cross, and a phrase or "word group" is never allowed to have discontinuous parts at this deep-structure level, from a surface structure arrived at by such devices as the movement of the subject phrase towards the end of the sentence or of the verb toward the beginning.[39] Yet a bracketing structure, once adult structures of speech are appreciated, does not require such phrase "movement", as if one phrase order was deeper or in closer correspondence to meaning than another.

There are many other examples of bracketing, not just as a literary device, but also as a systematic feature of the grammar of a language. Thus in some languages the finite and infinite parts of the verb may be divided in the main clause. For instance, in German, the finite verb (typically the verb "to be" as auxiliary) stands in the second significant place in the main clause, preceded by the *Vorfeld* (Pre-field) whose function is to indicate the point of reference from which the thought expressed takes off, in a phrase identifying what the Prague school and Dik call the Theme—which may be the subject considered as topic or the place or time of the action of concern in the statement. The rest of the main clause is enclosed within the verbal bracket (*Verbalklammer* or *Satzklammer*) formed by the finite auxiliary at the beginning and the nonfinite parts of the verb, participle, or infinitive at the end. Again, English provides an example of the use of this device of bracketing in constructions involving two direct objects. Thus, in "John gave David a book" and "John bought David a book", the indication of the recipient is inseparable from the verb, an inseparability which remains in the question "Did John give David a book?" and with the passive "A book was given David by John"; the indication of the object given cannot be omitted and, except with the passive, has to follow immediately after the indication of the recipient.

Again, bracketing is common in languages where nouns and adjectives agree in gender, case, and number, allowing whole clauses to be sandwiched between such an adjective and its noun, as in Virgil's *Infandum, regina, iubes renovare dolorem* (which, taken word for word, could be rendered in English "Unspeakable, O queen, you order [me, *by contextual implication*] to renew the sorrow" or, more naturally, "Unspeakable, O queen, is the sorrow you order me to rekindle").[40] Appreciating how such freedoms can arise even in relatively configurational languages such as Latin helps us understand the way nonconfigurational languages work, in which inflection may be the only clue to structure.

39. Of course, the requirements of tree structure phrase diagrams can be violated in much simpler ways, e.g., when a sentential connective such as "however" or *etiam* is put after the first phrase of the clause concerned.

40. I take this example from Blake, *Case*, 96.

When we have relative pronouns expressed in phrases, we have the same possibility of bracketing—for instance, so that instead of saying, "the man to whom you gave a penny", we say, "the man whom you gave a penny to", the second way of speaking being more immediately intelligible in conversation because it does not break the phrase "the man whom". And instead of "To whom did you turn for help?" we can say, "Who did you turn to for help?", the form "Who?" being adopted rather than the form "Whom?" to indicate the desired form of answer—namely, "Peter", rather than "To Peter". Thus the problem of "stranded" prepositions is a pseudo-problem.

We should observe that we say, "the man whom you gave a penny to" and "Who did you turn to for help?" but do not say, "the man whom you gave to a penny" or "Who did you turn for help to?" Thus in these bracketing procedures we are selective, enclosing the complement "a penny" within what we bracket, but not "for help", since it is an adjunct outside the core of the phrase. Any such gathering of groups of words together in such a way that other parts of the sentence are not part of the group constitutes a form of bracketing, whether or not it violates the requirements of phrase structure diagrams in tree form. In French we write *Je ai mangé les pommes,* since the *les pommes* is outside the nucleus of the verb phrase, by contrast with *Je les ai mangées,* where, because the pronoun referring to the grammatically feminine apples occurs inside this nucleus, we have to mark agreement. Adjectives in German have to be marked appropriately for gender and number within a noun phrase, but in such attributions as *Die Männer waren gross* ("The men were tall") and *Die Frau war gross* ("The woman was tall") such agreement is not required.

Clitics—that is, particles lacking stress which never occur separately, but are always pronounced either together with the succeeding word or phrase (proclitics) or together with the preceding word or phrase (enclitics)[41]—introduce interesting cases of bracketing when they apply to the whole phrase concerned (whether a single word or not). Thus the English enclitic "-'s" marks the possessive, but applies to phrases rather than to words—for instance, so that "the King of France's clothes" means the clothes of the king, not of France, and we do not say, "the King's of France clothes".

Note on the role of intonational "hiatus" to secure bracketing Negation, quantity expressions, and such other modifiers apply to the predicate as a whole by applying to the finite verb within it. Thus, if the simple auxiliary

41. Cf. *Shorter OED,* 1973. In Latin, *-que, -ve,* and *-ne* are enclitics, although often printed as parts of the preceding word, and in English, accusative pronouns immediately following the verb are enclitics, except where they are equivalents of, e.g., the French *moi.* Jamal Ouhalla divides pronouns into three groups: those he considers standard, strong pronouns (called emphatic), and weak pronouns or clitics, differentiating them according to phonological strength; Ouhalla, *Introducing Transformational Grammar,* 2nd ed. (London: Arnold, 1999), 361.

"had" figures as the finite verb, then it will draw the simple negative "not" to itself so that the "not" modifies the whole relevant predicate phrase (or whole relevant clause, so that "they had not all eaten" is equivalent to "not [they had all eaten], and this equivalent to "not [all of them had eaten]).

However, with all auxiliaries with some semantic content, which therefore constitute a verb kernel distinct from the verb kernel they govern, we can achieve, in speech but not writing, a breaking of this link by means of a phatic pause or intonational "hiatus" between the auxiliary and the "not". Thus when we say, "You may not walk across the grass", we would normally be expressing a prohibition meaning, "You are not permitted to walk across the grass". But, by special intonation, saying, "You may [PAUSE] not walk across the grass", we can convey, "You are permitted not to walk across the grass". The case of "can" suggests that the intrusion of any adverb between the modal verb and the "not" achieves the same effect, as in, "You can easily not swim" or "You can always not swim"). Such cases, where the "not" modifies the second verb kernel "swim", recur whenever we have a syntactically complex expression, and there, if the expression requires the "to"-infinitive, then the "not" applies to the "swim" if it immediately precedes the "to", as in, "You are able not to swim" (contrast "You are not able to swim").[42]

We can achieve the same effects with a phatic pause after the copula occurring with quantity expressions. Thus, although "All of them are not sighted" can mean merely, "Some of them are not sighted", by contrast, "All of them are [PAUSE] not sighted" means, "None of them are sighted" or "All of them are blind", and is negated by saying, "Not all of them are blind" or "Some of them are sighted".[43] Parallel situations with passives arise contextually rather than from intonation. Thus we cannot introduce "not" within "be educated" or within "be built", saying, "be not educated", except facetiously, as in "go to a specialist school of cooking to learn how not to cook", or to express a contrast, as in "be not educated but brainwashed", "being not educated but brainwashed", or even "are not all of them educated".

42. With "need", we have "I need to go" and "I need not go", and the "not" governs the "need" not the "go"; "dare" behaves in the same way. If the negative governs "want" or "desire", we have to say, "do not want" and "do not desire" in modern English, with the same meaning as "want not to go" in older English; and with a phatic pause, one can say, "I desire [PAUSE] not to go" and "I want [PAUSE] not to go". "Ought" is an exception, since in "I ought not to go", the "not" has to grouped with the "go".

43. Without the phatic pause, "All of them are not sighted" and "Everyone is not sighted" normally mean "Not all of them are sighted", "Not everyone is sighted", or, equivalently, "They are not all sighted". These are negated by saying, "All of them are sighted", "Everyone is sighted", "They are all sighted", "They are, every one of them, sighted", or "None of them is blind".

Similarly, "All of them cannot swim", "They cannot all swim", "They cannot swim, not all of them", "Everyone cannot swim", "They cannot, every one of them, swim" usually suggest that probably some, but not all, can swim.

(c) *Restrictions on word and phrase order, and on splitting constituents by embedding*

Sentences which contain many subordinate clauses are liable to become increasingly difficult to understand because of their complexity, and the situation is made worse if there are clauses conjoined by "and" or disjoined by "or" without the scope of the conjunction or disjunction being clear. However, there do not seem to be any absolute limits on the complexity possible. Thus most people require consideration, often involving attempts to find paraphrases, in order to understand the sentences concerned in the two examples given by April McMahon: "The cheese the rat the cat chased ate was rotten" and "That the world is round is obvious is dubious",[44] as with Matthews's example, "The editor the authors the newspaper hired liked laughed".[45]

The last example is intelligible as soon as one realizes that it is the editor who did the laughing, the authors who did the liking, and the newspaper which did the hiring, the editor being the object of the liking and the authors being the object of the hiring. The insertion of "that" in two places does not make interpretation easier. However, the sense intended can sometimes be clarified by using relatives of interrogative origin: "The editor whom the authors which the newspaper hired liked laughed".[46]

McMahon is right in thinking that the difficulty in understanding is the result of embedding subordinate clauses in the center of the sentence, and that in a Subject-Verb-Object (SVO) language like English, which places relative clauses last within any noun phrase, the problem disappears if clauses are embedded to the right, giving, "The cat chased the rat that ate the cheese that was rotten". Her other case could be paraphrased "It is dubious whether it is obvious that the world is round", adopting some reanalysis to bring the clauses involved after what they complement. She shows that embedding clauses centrally raises parallel problems for the Japanese, who place their relative clauses postnominally, but have a Subject-Object-Verb (SOV) language, and that they are solved by embedding relative clauses to the left. In her "cat" ex-

44. April McMahon, *Understanding Language Change* (Cambridge: Cambridge University Press, 1994), 155.

45. I take this example from Bresnan, *Mental Representation*, xliii.

46. This clarification shows how nuances of sense provided by differences between "who/whom" and "which", and between "who" and "whom" where passives are involved ("The editor whom the authors … liked" specifies the subject of "laughed"), give the array "who", "whom", and "which" much advantage over "that"—and why the American preference for "that" increases the pressure for simpler sentences. The use of "that" as a relative pronoun also removes the signal differentiating indirect statements and relative clauses.

The American tendency to use "that" is more immediately adapted to representation in the symbolism of predicate logic, so that "The editor that the authors that the newspaper hired liked laughed" would express the sense "The editor *a*, such that every author, *x*, such that a certain newspaper *b*, hired *x*, liked *a*, laughed", and is convenient for the purposes of formal logic, but not for ready intelligibility.

ample she depends upon the fact that Japanese has a topic-marker *wa* as well as a subject-marker *ga* so as to make it possible to render her Japanese example in a form which might be best represented in English as, "The cat chased the rat that ate the cheese: the cheese was rotten" or "The rotten cheese: the cat chased the rat that ate it"—that is, in a form which exhibits the different analysis exemplified in the Japanese.[47]

However, it seems wrong to regard this kind of complex sentence, with its subordinate clauses center-embedded, as ill-formed, and better to say that the hearer or reader's task of working out the sense of such sentences always becomes at some stage impossible, but that there is no fixed stage at which this happens—although the problem seems more of logical than of perceptual complexity. Kuno shows that the center-embedding of clauses is inevitable in VSO languages with prenominal relatives and in SOV languages with postnominal relatives.[48] Accordingly, it is natural for languages with postnominal relative clauses to evolve from SOV to SVO order,[49] and languages with prenominal relative clauses to evolve from VSO likewise to SVO order.

In sum, in SVO languages, the center-embedding of clauses produces a pile-up of verb phrases at the end of a sentence, such as "chased ate was rotten", "is round is obvious is dubious", and "hired liked laughed" seen in earlier examples, and in SOV languages, a pile-up of noun phrases at the beginning. Each presents a challenge analogous to the challenges of mental arithmetic or chess, rather than exemplifying a grammatical error, and the length of time they take to sort out is of a different order to that taken by ordinary grammatical tasks, a point whose significance was observed in chapter VII, section 1 (d) (iii).

By contrast, a pile-up of prepositions whose linking roles are each in respect of a different noun or verb is instantly ungrammatical. This would arise in any language which combined the use of postpositions with the requirement that, apart from identity and quantity indicators, the head noun should come first in any noun phrase (turning "the color of the flowers in the vase on the table" into "the color the flowers the vase the table on in of"), or the use of prepositions with the requirement that the head noun always come last in its phrase (producing "of in on the table the vase the flowers the color").[50]

47. I am indebted to Lars Larm, now of Lund University, Sweden, for explaining how this example works. McMahon's text in *Understanding Language Change*, 155, appears to contain a misprint, and in *Neko go oikaketa nezumi ga tabeta cheese wa kusatte ita*, *go*- should be *ga*-.

48. S. Kuno, "The Position of Relative Clauses and Conjunctions", *Linguistic Inquiry* 5 (1974): 117–36.

49. McMahon, *Understanding Language Change*, 158, shows one way in which this came about.

50. I here adapt McMahon's examples from *Understanding Language Change*, 156, but I explain the fact that languages with head nouns first in their phrases have prepositions and those with head nouns last in their phrases have postpositions (cf. n. 52) in a quite different way. She takes it that if head nouns come first in noun phrases in a language, adpositions and verbs will come first in their phrases, so that it will be a VSO language—and that if head nouns come last in noun phrases in a language, adpositions and verbs will come last in their phrases, so that it will be typically a SOV language. Here she follows the principle that in any

This strongly confirms my view, which I argue in chapters XIV and XV, that it is wrong to view prepositions and postpositions as lexical heads of phrases. Rather, they are essentially connectives, semantically synlexical, not semantic nuclei in their own right. If they occur as morphosyntactic markers of phrases, it is not as a semantic nucleus, but as the synlexical link between a content-introducing noun, adjective, adverb, or verb and its complement or adjunct. It is wrong to associate the obstacles to structures which would result in a pile-up of prepositions or postpositions with the difficulties in embedding this or that sort of phrase or clause inside another phrase or clause, since one can readily furnish examples of many adjectives modifying the same noun and many adverbs modifying the same verb, alongside the examples of the concatenation of finite verbs and of complete noun phrases given earlier.

Approaches to these problems in Functional Grammar Dik conceived that rules governing constituent order are among our means of achieving expressive communication. He considered that constituent order is only a surface expressive device with a pragmatically rooted role, principles of order of some kind being necessary, but no particular order necessary to natural languages.[51]

Writing earlier than McMahon, he reckons that for any main predicate, there will be an area before it, which he calls the "Pre-field" (corresponding to the notion of *Vorfeld* applied to the space for a single phrase before the finite verb in German grammar), and an area after it, which he calls the "Post-field". In the case of a sentence "The man cut-down the tree", he thinks in terms of there being two rival initial patterns of linguistic representation, a Pre-field pattern (SOV) "man tree cut-down", the subject being in what he called the Theme position, and a Post-field pattern (VSO) "cut-down man tree", the object being in his Tail position, but thinks that the first is less hospitable to more complex constructions and that neither pattern is ever consistently kept to in the general structure of particular languages, pure cases of either kind being rather rare. He envisages both as tending to evolve towards an SVO structure or at least towards showing features to be expected within a SVO framework.[52]

given language, whatever the lexical category, the order between Heads and Complements will be the same, the principle I attack in chap. XV, sec. 3 (e) and (f) of this volume. She therefore expects all VSO languages to be Head-first and to use prepositions, and all OV languages to be Head-last and to use postpositions (as in Japanese and Hindi), and is troubled, in my view quite unnecessarily, by the prevalence of prepositions in many verb-last languages.

51. Dik, *Theory of Functional Grammar: Part 1*, chaps. 16–17; cf. Dik, "Basic Principles of Functional Grammar", 9. I note that Dik's use of the word semantic excludes what he calls expressive, which for me is an integral part of the semantic.

52. Dik reckoned that an SOV ordering would be naturally associated with postpositions, case suffixes, preverbal clauses marked finally, and postverbal marked initially, while an VSO ordering would be naturally

These pragmatic explanations fit the diachronic facts in the history of languages where Chomskyan grammars, not devised to treat diachronic change, offer nothing. These treat any grammatical change as involving essentially a new language with different "parameters", making it mysterious why language-users so readily understand the grammatical forms in play in the speech of their grandparents and even of several centuries earlier.

(d) *The importance of pragmatics for parsing complex sentences involving adverbial clauses*

How a sentence as it occurs in speech should be parsed has to be considered in the light of its context in discourse.

In "In order that he should die, I did not remove the poison", the adverbial clause of purpose is clearly an external modifier to the clause, and outside the clause which includes "not", the adverb of negation. It is a modifier to the auxiliary because we understand the "did" and the "not" as to be taken together, the "not" governing the verb kernel "did remove".

By contrast, "I did not remove the poison in order that he should die" is ambiguous.

According to one analysis (a), the adverbial clause might be intended to modify the main clause taken as a whole (i.e., to modify "I did not remove the poison", including the "not", taken as a whole). Then it will again be outside the scope of the "not", and will have the same meaning as that of the earlier statement—equivalent to "I left the poison in order that he should die". It will be understood in this way, as an answer to the question, "Why did you not remove the poison?", especially if there is a pause emphasizing the divide between the main clause and the clause of purpose. Thus understood, my answer tells my evil purpose in leaving the poison.

However, under another analysis (b) and more commonly, the adverbial clause of purpose would be understood to be inside the scope of the "not", modifying "did remove". In this second case I will be denying the combination of removing the poison and having this motivation. It would be understood in this way if I was being asked why I didn't remove the poison, and I replied to convey either that I did remove it, or that my reason for leaving it was quite different from that suggested by the question. The questioner would be wrongly assuming that the earlier analysis (a) was the correct one.

It is easy to explain the differences in writing by putting in bracketing, contrasting (a) "(I) ([did not remove the poison] [in order that he should die])"

associated with prepositions and case prefixes, but, as we have seen, Indo-European languages show an almost uniform preference for prepositions and for inflections for case and number as suffixes.

with (b) "(I) (did not) (remove the poison in order that he should die)" to represent the two different meanings. But language as treated in Chomskyan grammar lacks such brackets, and the differences would be dealt with in terms of two different deep structures from which, by different movements, one has the misfortune of arriving at the same surface structure. The Chomskyan approach, by its artificial externality to any discourse-situation, leaves it mysterious how the ambiguity of such sentences is to be resolved and how they are to be parsed, despite their naturalness given an appropriate context.

However, if we allow some elements of pragmatics to enter into the determining of the appropriate grammatical analysis, it becomes readily intelligible how such sentences arise, as we saw when we considered what questions the respective sentences might naturally be answers to, and took account of, intonational features.

Syntactically the question is as to whether the clause of purpose is part of the main clause, indeed part of the predicate, modifying the "remove", or whether it is external to the main clause. Parallel ambiguities arise if "had not removed" is substituted for "did not remove".[53]

A comparable example is provided by the ways in which (a) "Because a harmless powder had been substituted for the arsenic with which his wife planned to poison him, he did not die that year" differs from the ambiguous (b) "He did not die that year because a harmless powder had been substituted for the arsenic with which his wife planned to poison him". The twin problems of removing ambiguity from (b) and of parsing (b) are again to be dealt with by resort to pragmatics, as with the previous example.

In "In order that P, I did not remove the poison", "I, in order that P, did not remove the poison", and "I did not remove the poison in order that P", the different phrase orders are grammatically equally acceptable. Again we meet our marvelous freedom from rigidity in using language, albeit that the last formulation leaves more room for ambiguity.

Elaborate problems can arise unconnected with negation if there is more than one subordinate clause. Thus, "While I am here, if he comes, it is safe for you to stay" can only be parsed in one way, with the temporal clause modificatory of the "is safe" at the heart of the main clause, specifying the time of your safety as while I am here, and carrying some hint that I may be needed to protect you from him. However, in "If he comes while I am here, it is safe for you to stay", the temporal clause modifies the verb "come"—that is, specifying the time of his coming if what I say is to be relevant to your behavior, and almost suggests that his coming may secure your safety, even after I have left. In

53. We tolerate sentences which would be ambiguous if grammar were our only guide, because they arise in dialogue settings which make their intended sense clear. The "did" and the "had" examples require different dialogue situations to achieve this disambiguation.

another arrangement, "If he comes, it is safe for you to stay while I am here", the temporal clause modifies the "is safe" as in the original, but the sentence carries other suggestions.

Section 4. Comparing Languages and Language Development Instructive for Grammar

(a) *Two types of inflection on verbs, and how auxiliaries and pronouns reduce reliance on inflection*

The relation of auxiliaries differs radically from that of adpositions, case-endings, and other such connective devices, as chapter XIV will make plain.

Auxiliaries as such do not appear in Aristotle's classification, because classical Greek made so little use of them. Their functions were fulfilled by what I will categorize as "verbal-inflections", because Greek expressed not only the person and number of the subject of the verb, but also its mood, aspect, time, and even voice entirely by variations in the prefixes, infixes, and suffixes affixed to the verb stem. And when Aristotle called them *ptoseis* (sometimes translated "inflections"), he was grouping them with case-markings and with suffixes of kinds which differentiate "courageous" and "courage" or differentiate adjectives and adverbs, as well as the Greek question mark ";". I use the label "verbal-inflections" to separate indications of mood, aspect, time, and voice from "concord-inflections", whether of verb to subject, direct object to verb, adjective to noun, or adverb to verb. Aristotle's grouping of the question mark, which in Greek appears only in written speech, with "inflections" suggests the possibility of classifying the variations in intonation which mark the differences between questions, imperatives, and declaratives as "verbal-inflections". All have to do with the character of what is said, the saying, albeit in different ways, and not with the linking of its parts by indications of concord.

Just as many nouns form plurals by change of quality in a vowel, so many verbs are "strong", forming different tenses in the same way, so that the notion of verb-"stem" has to be extended in the same way as the notion of noun-"stem". This reinforces our sense of the naturalness of extending the notion of "verbal-inflection" beyond being limited to prefixes, suffixes, and infixes.

In Western European languages the distinctions of verb-form, expressing what older grammar books called "tense",[54] including distinctions of aspect—for instance, between continuous or completed action, as well as distinctions of time and mood—have tended to become expressed by auxiliaries rather

54. Cf. this chapter, sec. 4 (c) and chap. XIV, sec. 2 (a) (i) of this volume on the difficulty of disentangling time, aspect, mood, and voice as aspects of tense as lay persons use the word.

than inflections. This is particularly seen in Romance languages. The same development has reached its extreme in English, exceptional among Germanic languages, greatly reducing the need to vary verbal-inflections.

The verbal character of participles, seen in absolute phrases, appears in a more important way in the use the past participle with *to be* and *to have* in perfect noncontinuous tenses, as in "has cut" in the active and "is being cut" in the passive and, in English, the use of the present participle with *to be* in continuous tenses as in "is cutting".[55] In expressing aspect, the participles occur non-adjectivally. In absolute phrases formed of transitive verbs in the active voice, the participles take direct objects in the same manner as the finite verb, without a preposition. But it is only their capacity, along with, for instance, the Latin "gerundives" (*amandus*, to be loved or lovable), to be used as adjectives which differentiates them from other forms of the verb.[56] In "The host has cut the pork" it is not the host, but the pork which is "cut", and the combination of tense-role with adjectival character appears in agreement phenomena in some languages.[57]

(b) *Languages resist attempts to impose rigid laws upon them: English examples*

The extremes to which English has gone in the elimination of noun and verb inflections, preferring prepositions and auxiliaries and, in addition,

55. The formation of the English continuous or progressive tenses by means of combining the simple present or past of the verb *to be* with the present participle is well evidenced in OE, and became slowly more common all through the ME period and afterward, although it only became predominant in the 1700s; Baugh and Cable, *History of the English Language*, 286–88; cf. 240. Originally the participle took all the forms *-inde*, *-ende*, and *-ande*, but first the *-end(e)* and *-inde* became *-eng(e)* and *-in* and then *-ing*, taking the same form as the ME gerunds, and much later *-and(e)* suffered the same fate. But we can find ME examples of continuous tenses formed with all three *-de* forms before the *-ing* became dominant, and so it is wrong to suppose that these tenses derived from combining the verb *to be* with the gerund; W. van der Gaaf, "Some Notes on the History of the Progressive Form", *Neophilologus* 15 (1930): 201–15.

However, in "Summer is a coming in", and the New Testament "I go a fishing" (the KJV and the RV translations of the Greek "I go + the infinitive" in John 21:3), the *OED* gives "a" and "o" as surviving forms of an OE preposition *an* or *on*, surviving also in "go a begging"; cf. ME *were a doing*, and, indicating activities by their place, *was a bed*, *was a field*. But, contrary to Andrew Radford, *Transformational Grammar* (Cambridge: Cambridge University Press, 1988), 58–59, the modern "-ing" is not a gerund in continuous tenses, but a participle.

56. We can speak of "men, dwelling in caves, ...", "gourmets, frying tomatoes, ...", "clothes, washed in machines, ...", from which we can form the compounds "cave-dwelling", "tomato-frying", and "machine-washed", but cannot say, "man-dwelling", "gourmet-frying", or "clothes-washed". The present or continuous participle when used as an adjective always carries an active sense, whereas the past or perfect participle when used as an adjective always carries a passive sense. This has a nice consequence with reflexives, so that we can say both, "He is a self-satisfying, self-pitying, self-indulging, self-serving creep" and "He is a self-satisfied, self-centered, self-indulged braggart".

57. In French, as in Anglo-Saxon, when agreement between participle and noun or pronoun arises, the agreement in gender and number required is with the direct object of the verb, not the subject, e.g., *Je les ai mangées* if the things which have been eaten are grammatically feminine.

eliminating all inflections on adjectives and all markings for gender except in pronouns, has put it into the position of being one of the most isolating (as opposed to inflected or agglutinative) languages in the world.[58] This is perhaps the main source of distortion in modern thinking in linguistics, tempting people towards a configurational and compositional approach as if sentences were constructed by dry stone masonry.

(i) Languages such as French which lose expressiveness in one way find it in another

In contemporary popular spoken French we can trace an opposite trend towards a less isolating language, at the same time taking this spoken French towards a VSO (Verb-Subject-Object) pattern and away from the SVO (Subject-Verb-Object) pattern which has become the norm among Romance languages. Curiously, this arises from a tendency for pronouns to assume the role of inflections where traditional inflections have become mute.

Consider the following: *Moi, je déteste Marie*; *Je déteste Marie, moi*; *Marie, je la déteste*; *Je la déteste, moi, Marie*; *Je l'aime, moi, Marie*; and *Je l'aime, Marie, moi*. All can be said without violating official norms. However, with changes in intonation in popular speech, the pauses between the main sentence and the *moi* and *Marie* in apposition are disappearing. As a result, for instance, in the last two of these examples, the intonation suggests that *je l'aime* is being treated as the verb, producing respectively VSO and VOS order. With the modern use of *on* for "us", one can have *On y va nous a Paris* and think of it as V (*on-y-va*) S (*nous*) Adv (*a Paris*), with a VS or close-to-VSO order. Phonetic developments play an inexorable part in some of these developments. For instance, the reduction of some systems of inflection to insignificance in the spoken language can speed the typological change just described if redundancies arise. Thus, in spoken French, we now have in practice *je porte, tu portes, il/elle porte, on porte, vous portez, ils/elles portent*—that is, a situation in which phonemically there is only one distinctive inflection and all the others have disappeared for this whole conjugation of verbs. The possibility of this development crucially depends upon the disappearance of the clitic *ne* from popular speech and the abandonment of inversion as a way of asking questions, since it is upon these developments that lexical units like the *je-pense* and *il-dit* have come to be capable of being treated as indissoluble units like the *je l'aime* and *on y va* just instanced, the sort of change which was much easier up until the sixteenth century. Yet one sees here a way in which the seeming rigidity of French is misleading, despite the way the hold of official French in public communication and education places an obstacle to any global change in the French language.

58. In this respect it approaches the extremes of Chinese and Vietnamese; see Lyons, *Introduction*, 182.

One also sees how the concepts which motivate Functional Grammars leave open the possibility of gaining some understanding of the diachronic processes of grammatical change, something quite inaccessible on the Chomskyan approach. The elimination of redundancies, such as between a subject pronoun and an inflection for person on the verb, a preposition and a case-ending, a preposition or negative particle and a prefix to a verb, an emphatic (e.g., *moi*) and an ordinary pronoun (e.g., *je*), the presence of two indicators of negation, and so forth, can initiate grammatical change.

Again, if adults consistently use an idiom connoting volition, such as "will", to indicate the future, children may begin to understand the expression concerned as a morphological indicator of future tense, and no longer as having any particular connection with volition, which they will express in other ways.

Likewise one can imagine children's ways of hearing and analyzing their parents and other elders' speech playing a role in the transformation of Old High German *hiu tagu* (the instrumental case of words meaning "this day") into the Modern German *heute* ("today").[59] In consequence Modern German *heute* lacks the double meaning of the earlier form, which may need expression by *an diesem Tage* ("on this day").

Hopper and Traugott give many examples of a cyclical movement in the expression of the future tense,[60] and children's learning processes may play a role in each case at each stage of such movements, both children and adults playing a part in creating new, more expressive or emphatic expanded forms of expression. Thus the activity of speech (*Sprache* in Von Humboldt and *parole* in Saussure), language in use, is the cradle of linguistic development.

(ii) The dynamic use of the verb in English: the continuous tense and the use of the gerund

Some distinctions need to be made in regard even to gradual change within a language. Some changes are of an evidently different character from those discussed at the end of the introduction. In English, in a development taking over five centuries, the acceptable morphological form of the present participle came to share, first locally and then everywhere, the same "-ing" form as the gerund, while retaining all the behavior of the participle. However, this became important only when, in the 1600s and 1700s, after a millennium of very limited use, the continuous forms of the present and past tenses in which

59. Cf. discussions in Hopper and Traugott, *Grammaticalization*, 24. The wider factors in play in the development of a language are well illustrated in R. Anthony Lodge, *French: From Dialect to Standard* (London: Routledge, 1993), and Martin Harris and Nigel Vincent, eds., *The Romance Languages* (London: Croom Helm, 1988).

60. Cf. discussions in Hopper and Traugott, *Grammaticalization*, 9 and 23 (Latin and French), 24 (Greek), and 48 (English).

the auxiliary "be" is used with the present participle became almost the most common forms of present and past tense. Meantime, the norm in European languages has been that the simple present and past should, where possible, carry a continuous meaning, older English being in this no different from Greek,[61] modern German, and modern French. Hence the real change in English waited until around 1700, when English began to refuse a continuous meaning to the simple present and past, the continuous meaning requiring the use of the present participle preceded by the verb "to be" as an auxiliary.[62]

This change, whereby the "-ing" form became capable of a purely verbal, nonnominal meaning as participle in these continuous tenses, even before the use of these tense-forms was very common, may have indirectly accelerated the very rapid grammatical development of the 1400s, whereby the English gerund, while remaining a noun, began to take on many of the verbal properties of an infinitive. As a result, despite the fact that the old syntax it shares with modern German, which is seen when it is followed by "of", remains intact, the gerund in English has come to carry something of the dynamic verbal feeling of an infinitive, especially when the "of" is absent, as in "The Serbs destroying Sarajevo library was a disaster". Indeed the gerund often takes the place of the "to" form of infinitive, the former feeling less stilted: compare "To run is exhilarating" with "Running is exhilarating".

Thus, in English, not only has an "-ing" form of the verb as a participle joined with the auxiliary "is" gained a huge importance in expressing tenses with continuous meaning, but in many contexts it is a gerund and has usurped the role of the infinitive.

(iii) Dethroning grammatical rigidity: literary variations in normal English

Grammar and the lexicon do not prescribe rigid rules which cannot be departed from except at the cost of nonsense. Rather, they set a framework within which linguistic variation of many kinds can take place, some unintentional, but by its existence indicating directions in which language or dialect development can take place. As I suggested in the introduction, and as appeared in chapter XI, section 2 (b), various morphosyntactic variations can be expected to have some explanation at a functional level, thus deepening one's conception of the structure of grammar in the way I explain in section 7.

Grammars, whether traditional or Chomskyan, tend to be excessively

61. Joint Association of Classical Teachers [hereafter JACT], *Reading Greek* (Cambridge: Cambridge University Press, 1980), 310–12. In classical Greek, the present and perfect belonged together as expressing continuous activity (Aristotle tells us that "walks" means the same as "is walking" [*esti badizon*], *Metaphysics*, Delta), whereas the aorist expressed mere factuality.

62. Steiner discusses different ways of thinking of the future in *After Babel*, 157–61; cf. 142–57.

dogmatic. Thus it is said that English is a language in which the "head" of a "phrase" always takes the leftmost position within that phrase so that, for instance, the subject phrase always precedes the predicate, or "verb phrase". Yet many examples violate this rule, but remain perfectly good English. Sells gives these examples: "In the doorway stood my brother", "In the cave there dwells a large ferocious beast", and "In these hills have been found gold and silver coins".[63] None of these examples violates the rule that the subject determines the number and person of the verb.

Koopman and Sportiche are troubled by a type of example, "Bill John will see", which identifies a very common way of speaking, affecting word order without undermining any more fundamental ideas about subjects and case.[64] Thus a coach before a match between two teams, his team A, B, C, D, ... and K, and the opposition Pat, Quentin, Rex, Sam, ... and Zach, might be quite liable to issue instructions in the following form: "Rex A and B will mark—he is a really dangerous player. Pat C will mark. Quentin D will mark... ". And a host or hostess before a party might give instructions in a similar form in specifying who should attend to particularly important guests.

Another particularly common case of subject-verb inversion arises with alternating "he said" and "said he" in reporting conversation. Let me take an example from Humphrey Carpenter's *The Inklings*:

> This was not a new notion to Lewis, since Tolkien was expressing in his own way what Barfield had said before. "Nor", said Lewis, "did it answer his point that myths are lies."
>
> "But", replied Tolkien, "man is not ultimately a liar." Lewis agreed.[65]

Nineteenth-century novelists and modern story-tellers preserve many of the freedoms of their predecessors and their frequent use of such subject-verb inversion is just one of these.[66]

Again, in the setting of a pantomime or play, figures serving same role as the Chorus in Shakespeare's *Henry V* might alter word order in other ways which violate Chomskyan conceptions. Thus, a new Act in a play could be introduced by a prancing Puck-like figure crossing in front of the curtain and in

63. The examples appear in Peter Sells, *Lectures on Contemporary Syntactic Theories* (Stanford, Calif.: CSLI, 1985) 94, 157, 180, respectively. The "stands" follows "my brother" in person and number, and "dwells" has the same concord with "a beast", "have" with "coins", and "Fresno" with "is nice". Note that in variant formulations of the question "Have gold and silver coins been found in these hills?" one could say, "In these hills, have there been found gold and silver coins?" and, if one gave a special stress to mark emphasis, "Have there in these hills been found gold and silver coins?", but not "Have in these hills been found gold silver coins?"

64. H. Koopman and D. Sportiche, "The Position of Subjects", *Lingua* 85 (1991): 211–58.

65. Humphrey Carpenter, *The Inklings: C. S. Lewis, J. R. R. Tolkien, Charles Williams, and Their Friends* (London: Allen and Unwin, 1978), 43.

66. J. R. R. Tolkien discusses the point in *Letters of J. R. R. Tolkien*, ed. Humphrey Carpenter (London: Allen and Unwin, 1981), 225–26.

playful manner announcing, "Falls the night. Comes romance". Or, in a different work, such a Chorus figure might prepare an audience for what was about to be seen by saying

> All now in order—pans and cooking implements lined up and clean—tables all set for preparing meat, vegetables, and other foods—servants spruce and commis-chefs all ready and in line—rightly dressed as well—thus all is prepared just so.
>
> Comes now the cook. What will become? All seems chaos. Yet is it so? On the result does all depend.

This is not poetry—nor would-be poetry, either. If it is "dramatic license", it is a license we always have, although one might ask why drama should invite such ways of speaking. At other times we use "the historic present", again utilizing a certain dramatic way of opening out a narrative. But no account has been given of why putting the finite verb before the subject or why reverting to the present tense should serve the interests of drama. Perhaps the present tense suggests that the things are going on before one's eyes in the present, but what of the verb position? These literary variations are not violations of grammar, but the question remains as to what makes some such exceptional usages legitimate and even "good English" and others illegitimate and almost vicious. These ways of speaking, with their dramatic quality, are not so much archaic as recoveries of a lost freedom, as when a man bound by artificial prison rules realizes his freedom from such rules. As in the first three of Sells's examples, the forward placing of the finite verb, reversing customary English verb-subject order, may perhaps be only incidental to how the dramatic effect is achieved—for instance, the first example makes one feel the juxtaposition "in front of me—my brother" to be almost immediate, as if the "stood" were serving primarily as a copula, its natural meaning almost ignored. These examples show features which Old English shares with German, one of these being the freedom to bring whatever one wants to highlight to the first place in the sentence.

Section 5. The Treatment of Reference and the Problems of *Wh*-questions

(a) *Pragmatics and the problems of reference or anaphor and of long-distance dependency*

Again and again we find the devices of logic put to exactly parallel use in grammar, in what seems a pretense that the grammar is autonomous, since grammar simply reflects semantics and logic, themselves shaped by pragmatic considerations. Each language group evolves its own way of handling the same distinctions.

The fact that the problems of anaphor or reference arise just as much in logic, and just as much in considering extended pieces of discourse—that is, where the pragmatic aspect of semantics is most conspicuous—has one clear implication: namely, that it is a gross mistake to isolate the grammatical consideration of "anaphor" from the semantic treatment of questions of scope or bracketing in logic or to neglect its relevance to wider discourse-contexts.

(i) Constants and variables, and the way proper names function

The grammarians use the word "anaphor" where the philosophers speak of "reference". Hence, in the part of Chomskyan grammars called "Binding" theory, we are told that "Binding principles include: *A*. An anaphor is bound in a local domain. *B*. A pronominal is free in a local domain. *C*. A referring expression is free".[67] By an "anaphor" under *A* is meant a reflexive or reciprocal referring expression (e.g., "himself" or "each other"). Yet the formal logicians have already made the same distinctions, distinguishing different modes of reference and different quantifiers, and removing ambiguities of scope by bracketing.

The "traces" of Chomskyan theory serve the same purpose as the bound variables of logic and achieve the same result of limiting ambiguity. Bound variables, clearly primarily belonging to sense or meaning rather than to grammar, have their formal projection in the grammarians' Binding Theory along with grammatical rules relating to agreement in number and, in other cases, to quantifiers and certain other types of "application controller". The idea that this aspect of grammar is autonomous seems particularly farfetched, since in disambiguating and determining the scope of such words as "some", "every", "all", "any", "a", and so forth when more than one of them occur in a sentence, with many or all natural languages, as with English, we have to consider the context of utterance in most individual cases.

If we realize that pronouns and demonstratives may be free within a sentence, but referring back to something referred to earlier in the discourse-context, the distinction between them and so-called referring expressions becomes blurred. For the use of practically all referring expressions is relative to a discourse-context. The differences arise from the way the discourse-context is defined; for instance, the use of pronouns and demonstratives within a conversation will be set by the bounds of that conversation, and within formal contributions to the proceedings of a trial or debate will be set by such

67. Cook and Newson, *Chomsky's Universal Grammar*, 65, substituting italics for boldface on A, B, and C; cf. Cook and Newson, chap. 7, 235–58, after which they turn to Bounding theory, an area which I treat in terms of pragmatics in subsection (b)(iv).

bounds as would be marked by a faithful official transcript of that trial or debate. By contrast, the reference of a name such as "Homer" will be set by the life history of the poet and the evident intention to discuss him or his works, or by the tradition of some particular modern person called "Homer" and the contextually clear intention to refer to him, or by the fact of thus naming some cat and the evident intention to refer to it. Thus one can consider proper names as bound in a local domain in the sense that, for instance, the name "Napoleon" as referring to the emperor Napoleon I is unambiguous in the context of writing general histories, but might have been misunderstood as used at the court of Napoleon III and, in a different local domain, might refer to a dog. In each case the local domain extends far beyond the individual sentence and commonly beyond the life of a single person. Hence, when a person is known by the name N among one set of people who know one facet of his or her life and the same person is known by the same name N among another set of people who know quite different facets of his or her life, the question can arise as to whether or not the two groups are referring to the same person by this name N.

Thus, what in speech would have figured as a single flow and unity is liable to reappear in written form as many "sentences", with the pauses in speech which in earlier times would have been represented by a colon and semicolons reappearing in the guise of sentence beginnings such as "as follows", "First", "Second", "Third", and so forth, together with "In this town", "In that town", "In a third town", "Then", "Next", and so forth. When this type of apparatus becomes clumsy, we begin to introduce proper names of individual persons, groups of people, tribes, languages and nations, kinds of living thing, and kinds of inanimate thing (along with systems for naming times, whether hours, days, or years, and so forth for other sorts of thing).

(ii) Long-distance dependency and the logical roots of grammatical theories of Binding and of "traces"

Indexical indications such as pronouns, along with "here", "there", "now", then", and so forth, raise a more serious problem for the division of speech-units and therefore for the identification of sentences.

But this is a problem of detail, not of principle. The case of true or direct reference is straightforward. An earlier sentence beginning "Odysseus" or "That man over there" is followed by a later sentence beginning "He", which can be glossed very easily by "[Odysseus]" or "[The man we just referred to]", and similarly in other cases. The case of a sentence beginning, "Any man who wishes to undertake rock-climbing in a serious way must ..." and then followed by another sentence beginning, "He must also ..." presents greater difficulty, but not insuperable: the thought is now, "He [any man who wishes to undertake rock-climbing in a serious way] must also …", and the "also" presents no greater problem than the "And" referred to in chapter III in reference to the pragmatic anaphor which arises when people say, "Not P" and later say, "Nor Q". Relations can involve a greater elaboration in the glosses required—for instance, "The son was a fool [that son we met at the wedding, the son of one of the third cousins of your grandfather's mother-in-law]", but raise no new problem in principle.[68]

Legendary and mythical references present different, but no greater difficulties. In "Cerberus, in Greek belief, was the dog at the gates of Hades. He had three heads", the "He" can be readily glossed as, "He [the dog who in Greek belief stood at the gates of Hades]". This gloss refers not just to what would be in the mind of the speaker, but the meaning the speaker would have a right to expect the hearer to understand. Other cases including fictional and fairy-tale references can be dealt with in parallel ways. The story-teller may leave it open whether his narrative is fictional or not: for instance, although Jonah was a historical figure, much of the point of the story of Jonah does not depend on its historicity.[69] In "A certain man went down to Jericho and fell among thieves.… They robbed him and stripped him and…", the "They" could be glossed "[the thieves among whom the man in my story had fallen]", and the "him" could be glossed "[the man who had fallen among thieves in my story]".

(b) *The importance of pragmatics for the treatment of interrogatives*

(i) The solution of some problems about our use of interrogatives and relatives

Even Chomsky recognized that context is relevant to determining sense, and this dictates the grammatical analysis of "Flying planes can be dangerous", the appropriate analysis depending on whether it means "The activity of flying planes can be dangerous" or "Planes which are flying can be dangerous" (i.e., as things which might hit something or explode). However, the relevance of semantics and pragmatics to grammatical analysis reaches far further than such examples suggest.

We saw how the asking of questions shapes our replies in the case of the Yes/No questions to which the most direct response is by an affirmation or its

68. When we attempt to write down the content of our unspoken thought when our thinking is in the medium of words, similar glosses are necessary in the way I indicated in *Human Person*, chap. 11, sec. 4 (a) and (c), in a way suggested to me by Ryle, "A Puzzling Element in the Notion of Thinking", no. 30 in *Collected Essays*, 400–404 (first published 1971). Such glosses often express presumptions shared by hearer and speaker, and are relevant to understanding the workings of speech, and of Grice's implicatures.

69. The point of the story as originally told may be different from the point of some later allusion to it.

negation. I now turn to consider how the form in which we pose interrogative questions dictates the forms in which we answer them. It may also make the close relation between relatives and interrogatives more intelligible.

Consider first the straightforward question, "Who killed Caesar?", and the information relevant to providing an answer—namely, "The conspirators killed Caesar". Here it is clear that the appropriate answer would be either "The conspirators" or "It was the conspirators who killed Caesar". Next, consider the case of the question, "Who did the conspirators kill?", or in an alternative formulation, "The conspirators killed who?", to which the proper reply would be "Caesar" or "Caesar was the person who the conspirators killed", the "who" being tolerated in the latter because it has the logic of an identity statement (although "Caesar was the person whom the conspirators killed" would be an equally acceptable answer). We do not ask, "Whom did the conspirators kill?" or "The conspirators killed whom?" because "who" is the emphatic form of the interrogative pronoun, here required because of its Topic-prominence (occupying the Theme position, the *Vorfeld*, and in some idioms and languages the corresponding Tail position, spoken of by Dik and the Czech functionalists).

Thus the form of the questions asked dictates our use of relative pronouns in replies.

However, Chomsky and his followers are forced to give the matter a more contrived explanation because they consider the use of relatives in pronominal or adjectival form without regard to the types of question which might explain their form.

For example, Cook's explanation of why one should prefer "The student *who* the examiner failed was Tom" allows for no such appeal to pragmatics, and instead treats "The student who the examiner failed was Tom" as if it reflected a deep structure: "The student [the examiner failed x_1] was Tom_1".[70] Here, the *wh*-word "who" occupies the object position in the deep structure element "[the examiner failed x_1]", the trace "x_1" marking the gap in "the examiner failed ..." at surface structure. This might lead one to expect that the correct expression would be, "The student whom the examiner failed was Tom", reflecting this deep-structure role. However, against the background of the "who" having been moved to indicate its relation to the expression "the student", the doctrine is introduced that the relative "who" supposedly has to agree with "The student" because, according to an idea Cook had stated earlier, "the student" is in the nominative.[71] For, according to Chomskyan doctrine, because "the student" is the "Specifier" of the clause "the student was

70. Cook and Newson, *Chomsky's Universal Grammar*, 203 ex. 56.
71. Cook and Newson, *Chomsky's Universal Grammar*, 202.

Tom",[72] the relative "who" has to agree with it and therefore be itself in the nominative.

My explanation, arising from a conception of grammar orientated towards speech rather than an abstract model, also solves another problem discussed by Chomsky and Jackendoff—namely, why "The man who the boy who the students recognized pointed out is a friend of mine" should be unacceptable.[73] On the other hand, "The man who the boy whom the students recognized pointed out is a friend of mine" would be acceptable, unlike the version discussed by Chomsky and Jackendoff. One could think of this sentence as the result of adding into "The man who the boy pointed out was a friend of mine" the additional information about the boy concerned—namely, that "The boy concerned is the boy who the students recognized". The reason one cannot say, "The man who the boy who the students recognized pointed out is a friend of mine", is that the "the boy who the students recognized" is no longer a term in an identity statement.

In the same context Cook rightly remarks that it is a peculiarity of English that the *wh*-word can be omitted from the surface utterance when it moves out of the grammatical object position. That is, one can understand (1) "The student the examiner failed was Tom" as meaning (2) "The student whom the examiner failed was Tom". Yet (1) can also be understood as meaning (3) "The student which the examiner failed was Tom" or alternatively, as Cook suggests, (4) "The student that the examiner failed was Tom".[74]

Yet this poses the problem of understanding the differences in semantic

72. This Chomskyan conception of the subject of a clause as the Specifier of the clause is key to the example set out by Cook and Newson, *Chomsky's Universal Grammar*, 212. Chomsky uses the term "Specifier" rather arbitrarily (cf. chap. XV, sec. 3, of this volume).

73. Miller and Chomsky suggest that it is grammatical, but unacceptable because of practical strain on working memory, while Jackendoff supposes "the boy who the students recognized" is intonationally awkward. In Jackendoff, *Foundations*, 31–32, this case appears as 3b and is compared with that of 4c. In any case, if "who" and "whom" were alternative forms of the accusative, there would be no problem.

Chomsky and Jackendoff's other case of ungrammaticality (ex. 3a in Jackendoff, *Foundations*, "I called the man who wrote the book that you told me about up") is more straightforward. ("I called the man who wrote the book up" is also objectionable.) Yet, "I called the man up" is acceptable and parallel to "I phoned the man back".

In both cases we have a constraint introduced by the presence of a single lexical unit formed of two words, a verb and an adverb, the one "call ... up" in which the word "call" has its meaning modified (telephoning a person is not calling him in the sense of calling to him, e.g., shouting) and the other "phone ... back" in which the meaning of the verb "phone" is unchanged. These differences parallel the cases in which a verb is combined with a preposition, e.g., "look after" and "look at". Again, in "Talk the man round" we have an adverb which modifies the meaning of "talk", and in "Talk to the man" we have a preposition which does not.

To generalize, there are always stricter constraints on what may intervene between a verb and a modifier considered as a single lexical unit, first, when the modifier alters the meaning of the verb and, second, when the lexical unit is composed with an adverb rather than a preposition. Thus, although if a preposition governs the relative in a relative clause adjectivally qualifying a noun, then the preposition can appear stranded at the end of the clause ("Tell the man whom I spoke to that he is a fool"), the case is quite different with an intervening adverb ("I called the man who wrote the book up").

74. Cook and Newson, *Chomsky's Universal Grammar*, 204 ex. 60.

structure between these three different sentences, and so of understanding their different senses. There is also the puzzle as to why we should have a relative pronoun in case (2) and a relative of adjectival form in case (3).

The answer is not far to seek. One simply has to consider the pragmatic constraints on how it is appropriate to answer various different questions. Formulation (2), "The student whom the examiner failed was Tom", would be an appropriate reply if somebody asked, "Who did the examiner fail?", to which one could also give alternative forms of answer such as, "The student called Tom", "He was a student, and the student was Tom", or "The student who was failed by the examiner was Tom", all answers assuming that the question was as to the identity of the person of whom a certain predicate was true.[75] Formulation (3), "The student which the examiner failed was Tom", would be appropriate if what was asked was, "Which student did the examiner fail?", to which another answer would be, "It was the student Tom", both of which are forms of answers given to questions as to which person, animal, or thing of a certain specified kind was the subject of a certain predicate. Formulation (4), "The student that the examiner failed was Tom", might arise in various discourse-contexts, perhaps to express (4a) "The student that the examiner failed was Tom", an answer close to (2) in sense,[76] or else (4b), "The only student the examiner failed was Tom" (idiomatically close to "There were no students the examiner failed except Tom").

(ii) The stranding of pronouns

"Who were you talking to?" seeks answers such as "John" or "John was the person I was talking to", whereas "To whom were you talking?" seeks answers like, "To John" or "I was talking to John"—the Topic-prominence of the

75. Such "Who?" questions are legitimate because "Who?" is an interrogative; parallel examples appear in "Who did you meet at the party?" and "Who did you kiss?"; Radford, *Transformational Grammar*, 12. However, they are legitimate only in asking an identity question in respect of who was failed, met, or kissed. In speech this Topic-prominent interest could also be shown by intonation.

By contrast, for the use of "who" as a relative, not an interrogative, to be correct, the formulation ought to have been "The student who was failed by the examiner was Tom", because "who" as a nominative has to hold the place of a subject, here of a verb in the passive. I find this more plausible than Radford's account (*Transformational Grammar*, 574). The naturalness of his "He is someone who I think it obvious will be a problem" (*Transformational Grammar*, 119) arises from the increasing tendency in written English, both British and American, to omit punctuation marks, something which intonation would make obvious in speech. The older way of writing would have been, "He is someone who, I think it is obvious, will be a problem" (*Transformational Grammar*, 119), the "it" in the parenthesis being understood to refer to the "he is someone who will be a problem"; this is equivalent to understanding "it" as syntactically marking a place to which the Noun Phrase "that he will be a problem" can be raised.

Radford's "He is someone whom I think it is obvious will be a problem" (*Transformational Grammar*, 122) is an ungrammatical version of the acceptable "He is someone of whom I think it obvious that he will be a problem"—"whom" being the form of the personal relative pronoun appropriate after prepositions. Probably "He is someone who, I think it is obvious, will be a problem", natural in speech, is what one would *say*.

76. This could be represented "The student, x1, such that the examiner failed x1, was Tom"; cf. discussion in n. 77 and related text in this volume.

emphatic "Who" shows a more direct interest in identity.[77] Further, one can say both "You were talking to who?" and "You were talking to whom?" In this setting, while the forms "Who were you talking to?" and "To whom were you talking?" are both acceptable, the form "Whom were you talking to?" is redundant.

Our handling of prepositions appears to be uniform. Thus we can say both "Who was the prize stolen from?" and "From whom was the prize stolen?" and give such replies as "John" or "John was the person who the prize was stolen from" to the first, and "From John" or "The prize was stolen from John" to the second. Exactly parallel examples arise with *by* and other prepositions.

Once one grasps Ackerman and Webelbuth's conception that lexical units such as "look at" can occur as discontinuous and even inverted wholes as in "look intensely at" and "At whom were you looking so intensely?", one should be unsurprised at the phenomena.

To "Whose army defeated the Persians?" the parallel question is "The army that defeated the Persians was whose?", to which the simplest answer is "Alexander's". If one resorted to the passive, one could ask, "By whose army were the Persians defeated?" or "The Persians were defeated by whose army?" and the answer would be the same. I shall spare the reader consideration of other interrogative questions introduced by "Which" and "What", "Where", "Whence", and "Whither", and the very different "When" and "Why".

(iii) The Accessibility Hierarchy

Many of the empirically discovered grammatical constancies of language have never been shown to have any connection with any Chomsky-inspired theory. Thus, for instance, empirically, every language in regard to which the relevant studies have been made appears to conform perfectly to what is called the Accessibility Hierarchy.[78] The hypothesis of a universally applying Accessibility Hierarchy arises when we consider the question of our freedom in forming relative clauses. Compare "I am the one who inspired Jack", "This is the house which Jack built", "Jack was the one to whom they gave the prize", "Jack was the one from whom the prize was stolen", "Jack is the one whose prize was stolen", and "Jack was annoyed because the ability which he did not

77. The discussion in Radford, *Syntactic Theory and the Structure of English* (Cambridge: Cambridge University Press, 1997), 278–80, ignores this type of pragmatic difference in identity and the associated significance of Topic-prominence, making it difficult for Radford to explain the origin of the contrast between his 35a "Who were you talking to?" and 37b "To whom were you talking?"

78. Proposed by Bernard Comrie and Edward L. Keenan, "Noun Phrase Accessibility and Universal Grammar", *Linguistic Inquiry* 8 (1977): 63–99. This view involves a peculiar analysis of Dyirbal lending support to Dik's view of the classification and possible evolution of ergative languages; see chap. XI, n. 62, of this volume.

have more of than Michelangelo was as an architect", and it will be found that the relative pronoun refers respectively to (1) the subject, (2) the direct object, (3) the indirect object, (4) the object of a preposition, (5) a genitive or possessive, and (6) an object of comparison in the relative clause. It is an empirical principle, confirmed as applying in every language that has been studied, that for any number *n* not greater than six, if a language allows clauses such as (6) "Jack did not have more ability as an architect than Michelangelo", that is, penetrating as far as (6) in the list, so as to form a relative clause, then that language will be able to form such clauses, not only with item *n* in the above list, but also with all the items with numbers less than *n*. The principle of the Accessibility Hierarchy is, then, this: for each language, there will be a parameter, *n*, not greater than six, which sets how far that language will allow penetration to go in forming relative clauses.[79]

If we consider only the declarative forms of statement exemplified above, the principle appears to be rather mysterious or a matter of obscure coincidence.

However, if we consider first the interrogative *wh*-questions to which the propositions listed above provide the answers, the matter becomes more intelligible. The circumstance to be inquired into is, let us suppose, that they gave the prize for ability in architecture to Jack in corrupt preference over Dick (so that, in effect, the prize was stolen from Dick).

Consider the following questions: (1) "Who gave Jack the prize?" (2) "What was Jack given?" (3) "Who did they give the prize to?" (4) "Who was the prize stolen from?" (5) "Whose prize was stolen?" (6) "What ability did Jack [supposedly] have more of than Dick?" Notice that the last question is considerably more complex than the more direct inquiry, "What was the prize for?" The successive questions, especially from (4) onwards, require successively greater powers of interpretation, as well as more complex forms of expression.

(iv) Avoiding the convolutions of Chomskyan Subjacency theory and its variants

In the efforts of Chomsky and his followers, from the first beginnings of subjacency theory in 1973 onwards to Rizzi's Relativized Minimality theory of 1990, to devise ever more complex formal rules to govern the use of interrogatives, their insistence on grammar's being regarded as a theory of competence made them blind to the relevance of logic or pragmatics. Yet this is to ignore the commonsense reflection noted in chapter VII that different kinds of task may be distinguished by the time they take.[80] What is required in the

79. Cook and Newson, *Chomsky's Universal Grammar*, 29.

80. Cf. chap. VII, n. 30 and related text, in this volume, with the reference to Marta Kutas.

use of relatives, like the parsing of the complex examples of clause embedding considered earlier, bears much closer analogy to the problems of sorting out the problems of scope which are commonplace puzzles for the logician than to the bread-and-butter problems of the grammarian. On examination, it is precisely logic and pragmatics which yield a more plausible account of the restrictions on our use of interrogatives and relatives, as well as of the way the relevant parts of grammar are appropriated both by first- and second-language learners.[81]

The problems can be conveniently presented in terms of Cook and Newson's discussion and examples, together with some variants.[82] For instance, the question can be raised why (1) "Who did Mary think John saw?" is grammatical, while (2) "Who did John ask when fixed the car?" is not, and (3) "Who did John ask when the car was fixed?" appears defectively formulated, but capable of interpretation.

In pragmatic or logical terms, problems arise when there is ambiguity as to what is being asked. In the first case, if one put (1a) "Mary thought John saw who?", one would be placing the interrogative in the only possible alternative position and asking the same question, exhibiting exactly what question is being posed. However, in the second case, three questions have got confused: that of who John asked some question, who fixed the car, and when this person fixed the car, and it is not clear what the whole question is asking—the whole question is irredeemably defective and the fault is logical. As to (3) "Who did John ask when the car was fixed?", if it is interpreted (3a) "Who did John ask as to when the car was fixed?", it would seem to be clearer than (2).

In each case we consider a variety of types of situation which the terms of the puzzling question posed suggest and attempt to see or guess at what the person was trying to ask. The problem is less of grammar than of logic and pragmatics.

(4) "Who did Mary think that John saw?" is grammatical, but (5) "Who did Mary think that saw John?" is not. This is explicable when one recognizes that (4a) "Mary thought that John saw who?" is related to (4) in the same way as (1a) was related to (1), and again both ask the same intelligible question. By contrast, (5) presupposes that Mary thought something and that somebody saw John and might seem to be trying to ask, (5a) "Mary thought that John was seen by who?" However, because the passive is not used, (5) cannot be interpreted in this way—postulating a missing word between "that" and "saw", or trying different pronouns in place of "that" does not help. Different problems are raised by examples like (6) "Who were you so drunk that Mary went out with?" This seems defective, but designed to ask, "Who did Mary go

81. Van Valin, "Functionalist Linguistic Theory", 22–27.

82. Cf. Cook and Newson, *Chomsky's Universal Grammar*, 258–72.

out with because you were so drunk?"—a question which could be posed in the form "You were so drunk that Mary went out with who?"

(v) The grammar and psychology of the use of relative clauses

As I observe in chapter XIV, section 5 (a), according to one theory, whenever we have a relative pronoun, or "that" used as a stylistic alternative, the situation is best understood if we consider that, as it were covertly, we have both—first the relative and then the "that".[83] More accurately, rather than adopting a Chomskyan system of "ideal elements" (or "traces") and "ideal movements", we should say that our understanding of syntax is such as to allow the potentiality for the presence of each of these things, the relative and the clause-marker, and that what matters is our capacity to recognize a place in clause structure where a subject or object phrase is missing. Thus, if we have "the book which I put on the table", then on this theory when we see the structure "the book I put on the table", we understand it as having been liable to read "the book which that I put on the table", custom prescribing the suppression of either the "which" or the "that" or both, except insofar as the need to avoid ambiguity limits economy in speech. We observe the place in the clause "I put on the table" where something is grammatically missing, namely, the direct object of "put" in the place immediately after "put", and we have the linguistic ability to understand that "the book" is the thing which would fill this empty place, so that we may mark the expression "the book" with the pronoun "which".[84] In the extreme of economy, we could say, "the book I put on the table", and the underlying understanding is the same—namely, first we understand "I put on the table" as occurring as a specificatory or identificatory clause (such as would have been highlighted by a "that"), and second, seeing the empty space calling for an object phrase after "put", we know that that is where "the book" would fit (so that the position could have been earmarked by a "which").

Again, it is the conditions set by the requirement that we be able to recognize the relevant patterns that limit the possible positions of the interrogative pronoun "who" to two, as in "Who did you give the money to?" and "You gave the money to who?"—if the intonation marks the interrogative with a Topic-prominent emphasis, then it is indifferent to case, but if there is no such emphasis, then "whom" is more correct than "who". The functional need that the expression "give the money to" should have an object complement makes it clear what is being asked. The answer takes the form of whatever

83. Note chap. XIV, nn. 62, 64–66, and related text, in this volume.

84. In Chomskyan theory this is stated in terms of a theory of movement whereby in Deep-structure "which" initially held the position after "put" and then migrated to its position in Surface-structure before the Complementizer "that", and the empty space from which it came is marked by an empty resumptive pronoun, designated "O" by Radford in discussing relative clauses in his *Transformational Grammar*.

noun phrase, N, would serve as complement to this "give the money to" in such a way as to convey that "You gave the money to N" is true. To ask the question using "who" suggests that the desired answer will be terse—namely, "N". If we asked "To whom did you give the money?" or "You gave the money to whom?", the appropriate answer would have to take the form "I gave the money to N".[85] One could not ask the question concerned by saying, "Did you who/whom give the money to?" or "Did you give who/whom the money to?" True, in simple cases one might guess what question the questioner was attempting to ask, but only by restoring in one's mind a formulation in which the interrogative pronoun and the noun phrase occurring in the answer were complements to the preposition "to". In more complex cases such a misplacement of interrogatives would yield a mere jumble of words in which one could not identify what was being asked.

Accordingly, the root of the constraints upon the positioning of relative pronouns seems to lie in considerations set by general logic and pragmatics, not by perceptual restrictions on what patterns can be recognized. And, when one comes to consider the problem of interpreting complex sentences involving numerous center-embedded relative clauses such as I discussed in section 2 (c), it becomes evident that the complexity of the problems of unraveling the sense of the sentences concerned presents a deterrent to their use in communication rather than an absolute obstacle. Such sentences cease to occur in a language, not because of ungrammaticality, but for the same sorts of reason that it is difficult to predict possible chess positions more than a few moves ahead.

(vi) Controversies about the importance of ellipsis

Dik rejects any explanation of the syntax of seemingly simplified forms of expression in terms of ellipsis as if they need to be understood as being derived by means of leaving something out, for instance, as if "I met a boy carrying a green uniform" were derived from "I met a boy who was carrying a green uniform" or "I met a boy such that he was carrying a green uniform"; or as if "I consider John unfit for the job" were derived from "I consider John to be unfit for the job", equivalent to "I consider that John is unfit for the job"; or as if "This is the book I bought in Paris" would be better understood by adding a "which" or "that" in the middle.[86] My argument earlier explains how it is that he is right to reject the suggestion that for the hearer to gain understanding, he has, by some nonconscious process, to derive the more explicit form from the contracted form he experiences before he is able to understand the sense of the latter.[87]

85. Cf. n. 46 and related text, in this chapter.

86. Dik, *Theory of Functional Grammar: Part I*, 19–21; and Dik, *Advances in Functional Grammar*, 9 sec. b.

87. On the other hand, in such complex cases as I instanced in n. 50, some derivational process is indeed necessary, but occurs at a level accessible to consciousness.

In general, to be an adjectival expression is to be something whose use in qualifying a head noun is correlative with an attributive use in predication of the head noun as subject, so that neither use is more fundamental. That is, it is essential to our understanding of the use of "green" as a noun-modifier in "green chair" to be able to understand its predicative "attributive" use in "The chair is green". "A fast V-er" can now be analyzed as "a person who V-s fast" (e.g., drives fast), granted that "a driver" is intelligible only as "a person who drives".[88]

Every form of statement says what it says and not something else. Dik's last case, "This is the book I bought in Paris", is equivalent to the artificial form "This is the book. (I bought it [the book] in Paris)"—that is, to "This is the book which I bought in Paris". However, since "This is the book I bought in Paris" has a clear meaning, it is improper to hypothesize as to whether it is a clause-marker or a relative that has suffered ellipsis—there need not have been any ellipsis. At the same time, one should reject the intensional isomorphism of statements using the clause-markers[89] "that" and "such that" with those using the relatives "who/whom/which".

Yet the reconstructions which Dik rejects can have a function, not in one's first understanding of what one hears, but in clarifying how it means what it does, at the same time reducing dependence on understanding the immediate context of discourse and, for instance, what question the statement under consideration may answer.

(c) *The relation between using wh-expressions in wh-questions and using them in relative clauses*

The double use of *wh*-expressions deserves more discussion than it has received.

Even in English it is not essential that the *wh*-constituent of a question be at the beginning or the end of a sentence, since it can perfectly well be left in situ, as in "Your father will put which car in the garage?" The essential characteristic of *wh*-questions is not that the *wh*-interrogative indicator should be in the Theme or the Tail position in the sentence, to use the terms "Theme" and

88. Jackendoff, *Architecture*, 62–66, presents three types of case: adjectives which can be dealt with in ways analogous to "fast", e.g., "sad" and "good"; adjectives which subordinate the nouns to some verb which removes the implication that they apply literally, e.g., "fake", "toy", and "alleged", for each of which he presents a different plausible paraphrase; and adjectives which constrain the interpretation of the noun, e.g., "wooden" (spoon, turtle, etc.). Some adjectives have a special sense when abnormally placed, e.g., before the noun in French (*vieil soldat* means a veteran rather than an old soldier, and *gros fumeur* means a heavy rather than a fat smoker) or after the noun in English (as with "heir apparent")—cf. R. Quirk, S. Greenbaum, G. Leech, and J. Sbartvik, *A Comprehensive Grammar of the English Language* (London: Longman, 1985), 418.

89. See chap. XIV, sec. 5 (a), of this volume.

"Tail" from Czech functional grammar taken over by Dik. Rather, it is that such questions are not seeking an answer which would be given by a statement, but by an identifying expression, an indication of place, or an answer beginning with such words as "because" or "in order to".

It would seem reasonable to suppose that the use of *wh*-expressions in relative clauses has arisen from the connection between *wh*-questions and specifications of identity. I ask, "Which book did I buy in Paris?" You answer, "That one", and I conclude, "So that is the book which I bought in Paris".

Section 6. The Parasentential Level: The Interplay of Logic and Grammar in Modality and Reasoning

(a) *The character and methods of achieving structure at the parasentential level*

In considering the structure of extended discourse containing many main clauses and much that is put forward hypothetically or with a note of uncertainty, we shall find structurizing features—configurational, intonational (the interlocutors laying interrelated stresses), or other. As we have seen, successive sentences tend to be interlinked referentially, and questions tend to be posed in such a way as to shape the form of their replies.

Some structurizers, such as "and" and "or", link clauses together in a way which gives them equal status. "But" and the more complex "On the one hand…, while, on the other hand, …" (Aristotle instances *men* and *de*) suggest equal status, but mark a contrast. Wherever there is such equal status, the clauses are semantically coordinate, not "subordinate".

Other structurizers, particles taking first or second place in a clause, or verbal expressions, mark the clause with a note of uncertainty, certainty, or some particular degree of likelihood—for instance, operators such as "Perhaps …", or "It is possible that …", various devices such as the use of the subjunctive (e.g., "might" instead of "may", and, in conditional constructions, "would" instead of "will") or intonation indicating degrees of uncertainty. The measures of certainty concerned are not private to the speaker, but something he or she would expect to be shared with the hearer or wider discourse group whose cognitive situation and presumptions can be presumed to be shared.

Such structurizing devices can occur in more complex sentences; for instance, I might begin as if to assert something, "P", and then a moment later as an afterthought add "or just possibly Q".

Again, I may assert "Q" categorically, and then continue, "So, necessarily, R", perhaps adding "(For P.)" as a separate sentence, or "(since P)" or "(because P)" inside the sentence, if the circumstances were that "R" only followed from "Q" with the help of the extra premise "P". Here we encounter conjunctions "So" (or "Therefore") and "For", met with at the beginning of statements, and "because" as a coordinate conjunction within it, and the operator "necessarily" used in a contextually relational way corresponding to the "must" in "So, we must conclude, R". The same operator recurs when we reason "Suppose P. From this we must conclude R. Thus, if P, then necessarily R". It is a linguistic mistake to analyze "If P, necessarily R" as if it meant the same as "Necessarily (if P then R)", as if "If P, then R" in general asserted just one kind of relation which might be in some cases necessary and other cases not so. Rather, as we shall see in (c), the function of statements of the form "If P, then R" is not such as to assert any kind of relation, but only to license inference from P to R.

(b) *Reasoning by the method of involution: exploring and excluding possibilities*

Having judged "Possibly, P" and then "Possibly, Q" and "It is impossible that R" in a case where it is plain that R would be the only alternative to P and Q, I might assert "Either P or Q". I might then explore the consequences of each possibility in turn, typically initiating this procedure by exploring the results of supposing P and also exploring the results of supposing Q. The result of my supposing P might be to infer S, and if, by supposing Q, I found I could also infer S, it would be plain that S must be true whichever of P and Q is true, and so follows from "Either P or Q" (this is the method of "or"-Elimination proposed by Gentzen in both his two systems of "natural deduction").

However, exploring the results of supposing, for instance, Q, I might find that, taking Q in conjunction with other information I have, I can infer a conclusion which I know to be false, so that Q must be false, in which case the only possibility left is that P should be true. This type of argument from "Either P or Q" via the exclusion of Q to the truth of P is what the logicians call "the disjunctive syllogism". Philosophers tend to regard absurdities of which direct contradictions are the most undisputed examples as the only things self-evidently "known to be false", and so, when Q is of this nature, this form of argument is called a *reductio ad absurdum*. If we think of P as a positive proposition, the possibility of concluding to it by disproving Q involves reaching a positive from a negative. This involves treating the two kinds of *reductio*, proving a positive by showing that a negative leads to absurdity and proving a negative by showing that a positive leads to absurdity, as on a par—a view associated with accepting the Law of the Excluded Middle, "P or (not-P)", as applicable, as I argued in chapter IX, all presuppositions being satisfied.

This method of proceeding by exploring the consequences of each of what we consider to be an exhaustive list of the possibilities, which is both a method of proof or inference and a common method of discovery (i.e., important in heuristics as well as in confirmatory proof), is the method which William Kneale called "involution" and saw as central in logic.[90] This framework involves several types of speech-act. Just as one can say, "Perhaps P?" with a certain intonation to ask the question whether or not P is so, so one can say, "Suppose P" to raise the question, "What follows from P?"

(c) *The nature of supposing and of conditional statements*

The nature of supposing is in one way unproblematic. As an act in speech it is an example of openly pretending to assert. However, it is not just any pretending to assert, but only that kind which is undertaken within the framework of the patterns of reasoning I have just described—it is meaningless to say, "Suppose P" to somebody without its being in the context of aiming towards drawing out a conclusion in some such way as I have indicated.[91] Supposing P is not a special "mode" of saying P or of asserting P, for, as Ryle says, "a mock-performance may be unitary as an action though there is an intrinsic duality in its description".[92] Supposing P is, one may remark, no more a "way" or "mode" of saying, stating, or asserting P than saying, "If P, Q", "If Q, P", "It is possible that P", "P or Q", "Q or P", "Is it the case that P?" or "Not P" would be such.

If, having supposed P, one is successful (relying on what else is reckoned to be known) in inferring R, then one can state one's conclusion in the form "If P, then R". However, conclusions arrived at in this way are "statements" of a very peculiar kind inasmuch as they imply no more connection between P and R than is exhibited in the way they were concluded to. Thus, if I am a subject in a psychological experiment and the supervisor tells me that the experimenter has left him a note to say that under eight hats, A, B, C, D, E, F, G, and H, he has arranged pieces of fruit so that there is an orange under A, B, or C, a pear under C, E, and G, an apple under B, C, or E, a plum under A, D, or F, and not more than one fruit under any hat, and I infer "If there is an orange under A, there is an apple under E", it does not imply any real connection between the two states of affairs—for instance, that one might be a causal condition of the other. In a quiz, for example, P and R posed as alternatives may relate to quite different times and subject-matters.

90. Kneale and Kneale, *Development of Logic,* 541–47 passim, taking the term from Rudolf Carnap, *Formalization of Logic* (Cambridge, Mass.: Harvard University Press, 1943).

91. Cf. the discussion of supposing in Dummett, *Frege,* 308–10.

92. Ryle, *Concept of Mind,* 247.

We can see from this that the knowledge that "If P, R" may be arrived at in quite different kinds of way, perhaps from knowledge of the probable effect of a particular kind of cause, but perhaps in such accidental ways as I just described. It follows from this that there is no limit to the kinds of reason why their assertion might be justified. It is therefore unsurprising to find that conditional statements do not have a propositional negation. There is nothing determinate in virtue of which they are to be asserted, and therefore nothing determinate to be excluded by denying them. The only definitive reason for saying, "'If P, then Q' is not true", thereby rejecting the sentence at a second-order or "meta" level (natural discourse provides no way of expressing this in a first-order way),[93] arises when P is fulfilled and it turns out that Q is false.[94]

One should therefore inquire as to the function of a statement "If P then Q" as a piece of information, and there seems no better answer than that offered by Gilbert Ryle—namely, that it is an "inference-ticket"[95] whose function is, if we find that P, to allow us straightway to infer that Q. Pieces of reasoning of the form "Suppose P; ... therefore, Q" carried out many years ago, their results recorded in "scientific" or other authoritative papers in the form "If P, then Q", may be useful at a much later time in giving us knowledge that Q.[96]

93. There is nothing which serves as its first-order expression in the way that "Not every man is healthy" and "Socrates was not bearded" serve as logical contradictories of "Every man is healthy" and "Socrates was bearded", respectively.

94. In the case of a future conditional such as "If you go to John's, you will get a good dinner", there are certainly utterances contrary to it—e.g., "I went to John's and did not get a good dinner" said later in reference to the same context, whatever the reason for my not getting a good dinner (perhaps a power failure), or "If you go to John's, you won't get a good dinner", said at the same time and in the same context, said by someone who knows that some third party plans to wreck the meal, while the original statement might have been made because the speaker knew that John was a good cook.

If the original future conditional was valid, there will be two possibilities. The first arises if you went to John's, so that one can say, "As you went to John's, you got a good dinner" (this still leaves it to the context to estimate why it should have been expected to work out that way). Alternatively, if you did not go to John's, if the original speaker was right beforehand, it will be true afterward that "If you had gone to John's, you would have got a good dinner" (this still leaves the reason obscure).

95. Ryle, "'If', 'So', and 'Because'", no. 17 in *Collected Essays*, 239–40; cf. Ryle, *Concept of Mind*, 120–23, Ryle, "Induction and Hypothesis", no. 10 in *Collected Essays*, 131–52, and Ryle, "Predicting and Inferring", no. 28 in *Collected Essays*, 373–80. I find it striking that some of the ideas of Ryle and Kneale are suggested and amplified by psychological studies of natural reasoning written or led by my brother, as they appear in Martin Braine and O'Brien, *Mental Logic*, proposing a theory of "if", supposition, and pretense in chaps. 9–10, and downplaying the consideration of possible worlds or the presumption of decidability.

96. I will confine myself to indicating the general character of Grice's alternative approach to conditionals.

Grice developed his ingenious theory of conditionals as part of his theory of implicatures and developed both in a way forced on him by his very narrow conception of "sense" as requiring to be defined in terms of truth-conditions alone. However, I established in chap. III of this volume that this constitutes a wholly misguided restriction on the notion of sense.

His idea was to try to preserve the identification of "If P, then Q" with "Either P, or not-Q" (so-called material implication) by adding the proviso that the "if" idiom is only used in contexts in which P is some-

(d) *"Any" and "a certain" statements*

"Any"-statements seem to have a similar function—namely, to serve as "inference-tickets". "Any R is G" seems to have the meaning "If a thing (= anything) is R, then it is G". In fact, the more normal way of speaking seems to be "Any R with the property F is G", where R is the range or set or type of thing one is generalizing about, and it seems to have the function, if we meet an R with the property F, of allowing us to infer that it will be G. Thus, if I am told that "Any sheep with horns is a ram", and see a sheep with horns, this "any"-statement allows me to infer from "This sheep has horns" to "This sheep is a ram". This would seem to allow me to assert "Every sheep with horns is a ram" categorically.

"Any"-statements are like conditionals in another way—namely, that natural language provides no straightforward means of giving them a proper negation.[97] "Not any R is G" is far from being straightforwardly the logical contradictory of "Any R is G"; but is construed as one would construe "Not an R is G", with the same meaning as "No R is G", the logical contradictory of "Some R is G".

The truth is that the so-called indefinite article (corresponding in some idioms and languages to the omission of an article) is a device intended to allow different interpretations in different contexts, in some contexts signifying indiscriminateness and equivalent to the "any" discussed earlier, in others signifying "one (not more)", in others signifying "one (not excluding more)", and in others "a certain". "Some" is a form of the indefinite article excluding the implication of indiscriminateness but not indicating how many or how much (it is equivalent to the French partitives *du, de la,* and *des* when used as simple articles, not to mean "of"). When, as in "Any R is G", "any" has the scope of the whole of an assertion, it implies indiscriminateness, which is what makes it possible to derive the categorical universal statements of the form "Every R is G" from them, but when a negative such as "no" has the wider scope, "any" comes to mean nothing more than "a" or "one", conveying mere indefiniteness.

---

thing one might suppose, and then developing an account of the assertion conditions of suppositions; Grice, *Studies*, 58–63, 83–85; cf. 280–82. I heard him develop the essentials of this curious view in seminars in Oxford in 1964, as incredible then as now.

97. As a form for rejecting "Any R is G" we might be tempted to offer "'Any R is G' is not true", a second-order or "meta" rejection. The alternative view, making "Any R is G" parallel to a conditional, would amount to the view that, except in the case "Some R is not G", it is indeterminate whether or not "Any R is G" is true. (For the intuitionists and many others who reject the classical mathematicians' conceptions of real number and of well-orderings as each nonsense, and who hold that for a real number or an ordering to exist, it has to be open to a constructive definition, there will be many cases in which it cannot be asserted that "Any R is G" is either valid or to be rejected.)

(e) *The parallels to "any" and to "a certain" in Gentzen's system of natural deduction*

We can now see an extended parallelism.

In Gentzen's system of natural deduction, supposing P and discovering that on this supposition one can infer Q yields the inference-ticket piece of information, free of supposition, "If P, Q" (the rule for "If"-Introduction). One can then, when given "that P" as new information (no longer merely supposed), conclude "Q" (the rule for "If"-Elimination).

When we use free and bound variable letters in a certain character face and from a certain part of the alphabet, except in certain atypical systems of logic, we presuppose that when we make assertions or statements using them, we are allowing the variables to range over a certain non-empty domain (group, set, or type of thing)—say, the range of things which are R's. Where x is a free variable which can be applied indiscriminately to anything in the range of the R's, the statement "Any R, x, is G" is analogous to setting down the free variable formula "Gx" in a setting in which nothing has tied the application of x down in any way. Moving from the free variable affirmation "Gx" to the bound variable statement "$(\forall x)(Gx)$" is analogous to moving from "Any R, x, is G" to "Every R, x, is G". (For Gentzen, this would be an application of the rule of Universal Quantifier Introduction, commonly called Universal Generalization.)

To take a more typical case, our "Any R with the property F is G" could be expressed "Any R, x, such that x is F, is G", and this will become the free variable affirmation "$Fx \rightarrow Gx$". Now, supposing "Fx" and with this given affirmation "$Fx \rightarrow Gx$", we can infer "Gx" on this supposition, and by the same rule of Universal Generalization we can eliminate the free variable and conclude "$(\forall x)\ (Fx \rightarrow Gx)$". And this is exactly like what is going on in our thought as expressed in natural language which I described earlier. For, if we are told "Any sheep with horns is a ram" and see a sheep with horns, we recognize that this "any"-statement allows us to infer from "This sheep has horns" to "This sheep is a ram"; and we can see that this inference is independent of which sheep with horns was concerned, and that we are therefore in a position to go further and infer "Every sheep with horns is a ram" categorically. The reasoning from "Any sheep with horns is a ram" to "Every sheep with horns is a ram" is analogous to the reasoning whereby, if supposing "x is F" for any random object, x, I can infer x is G, then I can conclude "Everything which is F is G" categorically. In the rule called Universal Generalization, whereby I get from a single indiscriminate example to a universal generalization, the justification for the reasoning precisely lies in the indiscriminateness with which the example was taken.

For quite different reasons, "A certain man met Jones" lacks a logical contradictory, unlike "Some man met Jones". The person stating it seems to be implying that he knows of a particular case, say the man, B, of whom it is true that "B met Jones", but he is hiding who B is or considers it irrelevant (or perhaps the records do not recall it) and so makes a weaker indefinite statement, "A man, *x*, met Jones", which implies "Some man, *x*, met Jones". Within the range of men, this sequence of thought is analogous to the passage first from the singular statement "F*a*" to the free variable affirmation "F*x*", and then from this to the existential statement "(∃x)(F*x*)" (the form of inference called Existential Quantifier Introduction or Existential Generalization).

(f) *Disentangling the semantic and grammatical properties of sentences*

(i) Differentiating tense, person, and number in epistemic and performative utterances

There are different styles of epistemic and imperative utterance, some of which are more statement like than others, and in all of which indications of time and person raise semantic rather than grammatical problems.

When we order someone to post a letter, using the simple imperative, "Post this letter", it is obvious that we are not making a statement, and the same is true if we say, "I will look after your son when you are dead" in solemn promise to a person on his or her deathbed. Likewise, if we say, "I order you to post this letter" or "I promise to look after your son when you are dead", we are not making a statement in either case. However, I am making a statement if I afterwards report my giving of the order or making of the promise, and the same is true if I use the future tense or if others speak of these matters in the third person—and if the matter is spoken of hypothetically, the clause introduced in the conditional is a propositional clause, since the possibility of the giving of an order or the making of a promise is the possibility of a fact and has no savor of either an imperative or a promise.

When it comes to "Perhaps, P", "It might be that P", and "It may be that P", we have expressions of varying degrees of possibility, in that the speaker implies that he has no certainty at the time concerned that P is false, expressing respectively that P is just possible, that it is possible but highly unlikely (conveyed by the subjunctive "might"), and that P is quite on the cards or as likely as not. However, the "may" and "might" in these expressions as expressions of present ignorance of past facts, such as "The Saxons may/might have settled in England before 200 C.E.", have no surviving past tense.[98]

98. The auxiliary "may" in modern English always expresses ignorance, the absence of knowledge of the opposite, and "epistemic possibility", and likewise the subjunctive "might" and "might have"—even though in OE its principal meaning was to predicate the possession of natural ability or power (still referred

"It may be" and "It might be" are said from the standpoint of one's own knowledge and what is certain to oneself, or possibly from the standpoint of the restricted circle which one has to do with personally and to what is certain within that circle. Grammar gives us no way of contradicting such assertions at a later time by means of past tensed statements with direct negation, any-more than we can later countermand an earlier direct imperative. Therefore, these utterances are not only egocentric in the same sort of way as imperatives and declarations of intention, but also, like them, tied to the present time.

If we said, "The Saxons may/might have settled in England before 200 C.E." to an audience of experts, it would be equivalent to "It is possible that the Saxons had settled in England before 200" and "It is not certain that the Saxons had not settled in England before 200", where the uncertainty is uncertainty within an unrestricted circle of contemporaries.[99] And, "In 2007, it was possible that ..." will have reference to what was known at the previous time indicated, and "In 2007, it will be possible that ..." would have had reference to knowledge at some future time.

True, present and nonpresent-tensed assertions of the forms "It is/was/will be possible that ..." are all statements. However, "It is possible that P", "Perhaps P", "It may be that P", and "It might be that P" are all expressions of our assessment of the compatibility of P with what we know now and express elements in our present deliberations so far as they hinge on whether or not P. None are statements about our opinion as to the state of our knowledge of such compatibility. By contrast, when we say, "It was possible that P" or "It will be possible that P", we are expressing assessments of how a person living at the time indicated would have viewed the question of the compatibility of P with the knowledge held at the past time concerned or in the future would view the question of the compatibility of P with the knowledge held at the future time concerned.

Thus the present-tensed statements differ from the past- and future-tensed statements in a way somewhat analogous to the way in which "Go away", "I order you to go away", and "I promise to go away" differ from "I/he ordered you to go away", "I shall/he will order you to go away", "I/you/he promised to go away", and "I shall/you will/he will promise to go away".

One can compare this case with that of the contrast between two different approaches to the question, "Was there a three-headed dog called Cerberus at

to by the noun "might" and adjective "mighty"). The use of the word "might" as a past-tense indicative does survive, but then it concerns not ignorance, but natural ability or possibility, as when a person argues "My mother had pneumonia in September 1939, and nearly died, a year before I was born, and so plainly I might never have existed"—the usual reason for asserting the contingency of existence, whether coming to exist or continuing to exist, lying in our awareness of so many natural possibilities in the case of which we would not come to exist or continue longer.

99. Likewise, "very possible that ..." would be roughly equivalent to "not at all certain that ... not...".

the gates of Hades?" On one approach, the answer is that no such a dog ever existed, whether the gates of Hades existed or not. Alternatively, the question might be more like, "Have I remembered ancient mythology correctly in this respect?" and in context have the sense, "Was it Greek belief that there was a three-headed dog called Cerberus at the gates of what they called Hades?"

So, suppose we give the following account of a bit of Egyptian history: "It was possible that Joseph's interpretation of the dreams was right, and therefore the Pharaoh concerned gathered a third of the grain of the land into his own silos for seven years and one third into the silos of the priests, thereby creating an enormous reserve so that if Joseph was right, then there would be supply for the seven years of famine he predicted, and if he was wrong, no harm would follow". Then, the relevance of "It was possible that Joseph was right" to the explanation of what occurred is not that it was a fact about the weather and flood prospects of the time, but that the Pharaoh made this judgment about Joseph. So, just as we reformulated the question about Cerberus from "Was there a three-headed dog called Cerberus at the gates of Hades?" to "Was it Greek belief that there was a three-headed dog called Cerberus at the gates of what they called Hades?", so also we could remove any ambiguity from the history above by saying, "The Pharaoh judged that it was possible that Joseph had interpreted the dreams rightly, and therefore he gathered a third of the grain of the land into his own silos....".

Again, we could instance a different history: "In 1930 it was possible that the birds as a warm-blooded group had their origin long before the mammals. Since that time fossils of mammals have been found early in the Permian, long before any dinosaur had developed feathers and wings. Accordingly, in the light of present knowledge, it is not possible that the birds took their origin before the mammals". It will be noted that both these judgments, today's judgment about the state of knowledge in 1930 and today's judgment that the 1930 assessment would have been wrong, involve judgments about possibility in respect of events enormously predating the judgments and the time indicated by their tense.

All the cases of statements about possibility and impossibility, necessity and making necessary, which we have been considering concern the presence or absence of knowledge and the kinds of reason which make something necessary or certain. Such statements are of what philosophers call epistemic modality (as relative to *epistemē*, knowledge).

One of the chief characteristics of statements of epistemic modality is that there are no general restrictions on the temporal order between the time of the modality (the time of the presence or absence of knowledge) and the time of the thing which is known or unknown. In this they are in an utterly different situation from statements of what is commonly called natural or real modality—that is, the possibility and impossibility, necessity and making necessary concerned when we are explaining what the natural powers at work in the world at a particular time make possible or impossible at some later time, or bring about by force or compulsion at some later time, or, equally, concerned when we are explaining the effects of people's states of mind (their views as to the facts, their assessments of the law and what is permitted or prohibited, worthwhile or morally wrong) on their decisions and actions. These kinds of possibility, impossibility, necessity, and making necessary are always in respect of what is future relative to the time of the possibility, impossibility, or necessity asserted.

However, there is also a more radical difference between these kinds of statement. True statements in the field of explanation state facts which remain unchanged after the time concerned. If the correct tense in which to state them now is the present, then at later times it will be the past. Thus differently tensed statements of natural or real possibility and the rest will all have the same status. In the vocabulary of the 1950s' *OED*, natural or real possibility is "objective", but epistemic possibility is "subjective"—that is, relative to the time of the knowledge or ignorance of the speaker or his or her contemporaries.

(ii) The problem of describing the grammar of utterances of the types just considered

Grammar is concerned with the form of utterances. Although the whole of this volume has the effect of showing that grammar is a formal projection of semantics, nonetheless it is not concerned with semantic properties as such—for instance, whether or not a statement is true, or whether or not an utterance is a statement, or whether or not this or that exists (consider the case of Cerberus). True enough, it belongs to the way the projection is taken from semantics to get grammar and is a condition of language learning, that it should be the indicative mood which is used for making statements without reference to the quality of our knowledge of them and as expressions of our own beliefs and not, for instance, those of the ancient Greeks. It still does not stop the semantic anomalies I reviewed from arising. For example, the "I promise …" which appeared to be a statement is not statement at all. Again what appeared to be statements about Cerberus and about possibilities both involved implicit reference to the thinking of certain people, viz. to the epistemic status of the judgments in the one case of the Greeks and in the other of people making judgments at the time concerned, so as to be in a certain way both asserted in indirect speech.

Accordingly, we should describe "I order you to …", "I order that …", "I promise to …", "I promise that …", "It may be that …", "It is possible that …", "Cerberus was a three-headed dog", and "Mr. Micawber was an optimist" as all indicative forms, two introducing infinitive phrases, three introducing clauses, and all in direct speech. The fact that the last two would occur in accounts of Greek belief and Dickens's fictional story—that is, semantically as if in indirect speech, is irrelevant to their grammatical analysis and description. That is, the differently tensed versions of all the above, where such versions exist, must be treated in grammatically the same way. Likewise "perhaps" and "possibly" are straightforwardly adverbs adjunctive to the "total saying nexus" of a main clause in the way chapter XIV, section 1 (a) (iii), explains.

Section 7. Some Comparisons between Different Types of Grammar: Formal and Functional

(a) *Types of formal grammar*

The differences between Lexical Functional Grammar (LFG) and Chomskyan grammar are representative of the differences between two radically different families of formal grammar, one open to a functionalist or more utterance-adapted interpretation and the other not. Chomsky's Minimalist Program accentuates rather than removes the contrast.

Chomskyan grammar yields a picture of underlying rigidity. Languages are considered bound by fixed, law-prescribed, configurational patterns at a level of "deep structure" which, by systems of "movement" limited by rules, produce what is apprehended at the level of "surface structure".

The original strategy of this approach was to reduce the number of lexical items, for example, by itemizing the active and passive forms of a verb together, not separately. This economy was at the expense of making lexical entries exceedingly complex, since Chomsky's "Projection Principle" requires every item in the lexicon to be flagged for how it would behave as it approaches any new type of node within a phrase structure diagram. The instructions within lexical entries control what structures are allowable at each higher level.

By contrast, LFG presumes that there is freedom in the placing of elements, except insofar as special constraints arise, normally from the lexicon, but lexical entries are enriched by including specifications of functional indications (Subject, Object, and so forth). This enrichment enables LFG to dispense with the deep/surface distinction and all forms of "movement". It also removes the temptation to extend the X-Bar theory of lexical phrases with lexical heads to supposed "functional phrases" with "functional heads". (As chapter XV shows, LFG introduces such heads only as a convenience of representation to facilitate comparison with other theories.)

The structure of LFG gives language an underlying freedom, allowing variations of phrase order except when prevented by some specific constraint (in this like unification approaches), in a strong contrast with Chomskyan grammars, whose rigidity means that every change in word or phrase order requires permission. This difference stems from LFG's aim of being equally adapted to configurational and nonconfigurational languages—an aim it shares with nonformal functional grammars such as those of Dik and Van Valin, unlike the essentially configurational Chomskyan theories.

The second main advance introduced by LFG among formal grammars is that, despite adequately describing languages in formal terms, it nonetheless leaves room for its primitive syntactic terms to be given informal explanation in terms of the semantic and pragmatic ideas of thematic role and discourse function. As a result, its application can be more readily extended from context-free "sentences" to the utterances of natural languages, sentences properly so called.

(b) *The Minimalist Program does not change this picture*

Chomsky's Minimalist Program leaves these contrasts unaffected.

From the beginning, Chomsky's theories gave a privileged place to the lexicon, insisting on the "Projection Principle" mentioned earlier, whereby "representations at each syntactic level ... are projected from the lexicon, in that they observe the subcategorization properties of lexical items" (their "subcategorization properties" means the properties determining their hierarchical categorization).[100] However, as progress was made in developing this Program, more and more had to be ascribed to the properties of lexical items, and less and less work done by the many different principles and parameters in connection with the various "modules" postulated within the theory. Chomsky's Minimalism fully accepts this, making the lexicon do the whole work previously accomplished both by those modules and by the associated principles and parameters.

Chomsky's Minimalism presents a "bare structure" phrase theory in which the instructions coded into lexical entries, recording "features" of the basic "lexical items", are conceived to determine everything that goes on as these basic items are combined into successively more extended phrases, a process governed by a universally shared computational system. At each stage "Selected" constituents are joined by means of the operation called "Merge" whereby "any word or phrase can be combined with any word or phrase, subject to all applicable constraints".[101] In this way everything is built up from be-

100. Chomsky, *Lectures on Government and Binding*, 29; cf. chap. XV, nn. 35, 36, and related text, in this volume.

101. Jackendoff has an approach in which he specifies the only "rule of grammar" as "UNIFY PIECES",

low, reversing the way in which phrase structure diagrams had been originally presented in Transformational Grammar, as with the rule "sentence → noun phrase + verb phrase", generating sentences from the top.

However, although Minimalism presents a different way of thinking and a fresh system of presentation and may leave openings for some variations of phrase order previously disallowed, the change from its pre-minimalist Chomskyan precursors is much exaggerated. It is still possible to construct phrase diagrams showing the effects of successive applications of the operations Select and Merge, subject to the checking and other procedures which the computational system imposes, and the results show close similarities to the pre-minimalist phrase structure diagrams. Moreover, at each stage in forming larger structures, the operation Merge is conceived as the "merging" of a "Head" with a "non-Head" in an operation which still preserves a hierarchy between the merged elements.[102] And all the variations between the parameters of different languages affecting the order in which structural elements are applied are replicated in Minimalism—for example, parameters prescribing the order in which "Heads" are merged with their "Complements" and other parameters relating to agreement between subject and verb, verb and object, tense, and negation.[103] The labels used in Chomsky's "Principles and Parameters Theory" (often called Government and Binding Theory) make what is going on somewhat more intelligible by their echoes of ideas to be found in traditional or notional grammar. Such labels and structures have the same effect in minimalist theory.

Moreover, the following main presumptions of the Minimalist Program were already present in the previous theory. First, each Internalized language-system consists of a lexicon containing basic atomic lexical items and a computational system by means of which, from these basic lexical items, one can generate (Internal) linguistic expressions; these bring a context-free sentential lexical meaning (what Chomsky calls "a Logical Form interpretation at a conceptual-intentional interface") into combination with "instructions" for appropriate articulatory and perceptual performances ("the Phonetic Form interpretation at the articulatory-perceptual interface").[104] Second, both the basic lexical items and the relevant computational system belong to the Internalized language-system in which competence in a language consists; as "Internal", this consists in elements and modes of brain functioning, and not

where the pieces are stored in a common format dictating what permits unification, which he sees as having some analogies with Chomsky's Minimalism and with Optimality Theory; Jackendoff, *Foundations*, 180; cf. 44.

102. I here summarize the relevant aspects of the discussion in Fukui, "Phrase Structure", 396–98; cf. 398–406.

103. See sec. 2 (e) in this chapter and chap. XV, sec. 3 (c) (i), on Pollock's account of differences between English and French.

104. Cf. Chomsky, *Minimalist Program*, 219.

in anything public outside the brain.[105] Third, the lexical entries recording the features of lexical items via the computational system determine "the Logical Form interpretations of their fully formed combinations"—their sentential lexical meanings.

The differences between Chomskyan multilevel Principles and Parameters theory and Minimalism lie in the shape of the computational system postulated as existing in the brain. Minimalism abandons the idea that computation proceeds from the conceptual to the phonetic interfaces stage by stage via intermediate Deep Structure level to the Surface Structure level representations, or from the phonetic interface via Surface Structure and Deep Structure stages to the conceptual interface. Hence Minimalism can dispense with the so-called Projection Principle only in the sense that intermediate syntactic levels have been abandoned, not because lexical entries determine less.[106] However, just as the stages of movement as one moved upwards in the phrase structure diagrams were recorded by "traces" in the earlier multilevel theories, so within Minimalism some record of "traces" or "copies" is retained when Movement occurs in the process of building up fully interpreted linguistic expressions from basic lexical items. In this way we can say that, fourth, the Minimalist Program preserves the configurational character of Chomsky's earlier theories, marked by an always rule-governed phrase order, and thereby stands in the same contrast as they did with less configurational, and less subject to constraint, systems such as LFG.

(c) *Different systems of formal grammar compared in the light of the way we use language*

It is strange to presume that grammar can be treated as an autonomous feature of language, independent of the pragmatic and semantic framework within which it is set. As I argued in the introduction, it is more economical to suppose that the person has one system of grammar accommodated to the hearing and speaking (both with understanding) of utterances and pieces of discourse or dialogue than to suppose two separate systems, one a grammar geared to context-free "sentences" (sentence-types conceived as independent of context of utterance),[107] and a second geared to the understanding and use of language in individual utterances in their contexts.

105. Taken along with Chomsky's version of sentential lexical meanings ("LF interpretations"), these items and computational system reflect Ockham's "Mental" or "Mentalese"; cf. the introduction, n. 56, of this volume.

106. But see Chomsky, *Minimalist Program*, 189, 220, 241–42.

107. Chomsky's strange conception of linguistics as concerned primarily with this first system is reflected in his idea that the formal grammar he associated with the capacity for recursion might be only accidentally related to communication; see Marc Hauser, Noam Chomsky, and Tecumseh Fitch, "The Faculty of

The inconveniences of the presumption that grammar is autonomous appear in obvious ways. Semantic and pragmatic considerations often play a key part in the interpretation of what one hears. Thus identical grammatical sentence-constructs arise in different ways, whereas the corresponding utterances are normally disambiguated by their context in speech—for instance, "Flying planes can be dangerous" and "The number four is green". It is the intention, which the person addressed can recognize from the context, to say something about the activity of flying airplanes or about a certain soccer player that determines the grammar to be assigned to these utterances. In Nunberg's example, "The ham sandwich in the corner wants some more coffee",[108] it is to be presumed that the waiter addressed knows which customer had previously asked for a ham sandwich. Here a presumption of grammaticality enforces the assignment of the "formal" category "Animate" to the expression "ham sandwich", but this formal grammatical prescription describes rather than explains the forms of our utterances. It is rather the semantics of "want" and the context of utterance which determine the assignment "Animate" as a semantic and not merely grammatical category, and so determine the correct interpretation of what is said. Likewise, since there are no quotation marks in speech, parallel comments apply to the interpretation of the spoken sentence "The greet in the third line of this poem is a dialect verb meaning weep", where a presumption of grammaticality would enforce the assignment of some such "formal" category as "quoted word" to the word "greet" in the utterance concerned with its semantics—again, it is semantic interpretation which determines grammatical judgment, not vice versa.

A contrast needs to be made between the semantic and pragmatic and the phonological. There is no way in which we can learn a language, at least our first language, without its being an appreciation of speech in its pragmatic and semantic aspects which determines what grammar is learned and how it is learned. Hence any module of brain functioning geared to speech, or to hearing speech, will be primarily tuned to reflect functional or semantic structure, determining morphosyntactic structure only derivatively.[109] By contrast, there is no reason to expect phonological structure or the vocabulary special to a particular language to be similarly influenced by semantics or pragmatics; these are semantically arbitrary and accidental.

The view that formal grammars describe structures which are byproducts of semantic and pragmatic constraints has its own economies. The notion of

---

Language: What Is It, Who Has It, and How Did It Evolve?" *Science* 298 (November 2002): 1569–79. Pinker and Jackendoff responded, showing how implausible this position is, in "Faculty of Language" (2005).

108. Jackendoff, *Architecture*, 54.

109. If second-language learning proceeds by specifying the vocabulary of the language while using the grammar of the first language, the pattern of learning is different, giving grammar a quite different role.

the lexical sentential meaning (indispensable to all of Chomsky's presentations) of a context-free sentence, considered as represented or embodied in the brain, has no obvious place in a psychological theory of speech or the understanding of speech. By contrast, my counterproposal fits with the origins of grammar and sets it within the wider context of discourse and "general logic"—with semantics incorporating much of pragmatics and, with it, incorporating "logic" in the narrower sense. The resulting functionalism sets grammar in the context of the purpose of linguistic communication—linguistic in expressing a content, not merely signaling it.

Although grammar is not autonomous, but in its general structures shaped by the pragmatic and semantic structures within which it is set, it remains that in each particular language sentence constituents and their arrangement in sentences must be capable of some formal description of which distributionalist principles allow the identification. Indeed, traditional grammars have always aimed at describing utterances according to what was thought of as their formal structure, analyzing them into clauses and phrases with some elements or features relating these, and the phrases themselves analyzable in terms of various types of parts combining with various others in particular ways. But a purely formal grammar does nothing to explain why languages should share what structures they do.

Chapters IX and XI showed the pragmatic roots of the grammatical functions of predicate and subject. It is here that we see the merits of grammars like LFG which can be presented as formal systems within which, for instance, the notion of subject is primitive in the sense of being undefined within the formal system, just as in Chomskyan grammar the notion of "deep structure" was without definition (the notion of surface structure being obvious by default). For LFG remains a formal system inasmuch as it provides a formal description of the distributionally analyzed grammatical data, and does this with some advantages over rival systems in predictive power, economy, and elegance. Yet, as we have seen, the notion of subject can be given *an informal definition outside this formal system*, one fitting my formulation "argument of the verb with the role of discourse topic"—that is, the functional, rather than the morphosyntactic, grammatical subject.[110] It is the appropriateness of such

110. Cf. the introduction, nn. 17, 98–100, in this volume. When Joan Bresnan says that "although f-structure functions cannot be defined by c-structure categories, and so are 'primitive' in categorial terms they can be derived from more primitive functional properties and so are not primitive in syntactic theory" (*Lexical-Functional Syntax*, 98), she has in mind that relational categories such as subject can be defined in terms of the combination of the two properties of being an argument to a predicator (in her terms, "participants in the event or situation concerned" [cf. Bresnan, *Lexical-Functional Syntax*, 9–10], i.e., in some thematic role in relation to the verb) and of being the grammaticalization of a discourse function; it does not follow that these notions can be applied mechanically, since they are applied with the informality instanced in different "structural expressions of the subject" of which she gives examples at the top of *Lexical-Functional Syntax*, 95.

notional explanations of primitive terms which makes LFG more adapted to the problems of explaining language-use and first-language learning than Chomskyan grammar.[111] As I observed in the introduction, such notional explanations arise with most axiomatizable systems of any interest; thus the definitions in Euclid's system indicate its application by stating its fundamental notions informally.

Because Lexical Functional Grammar, Dik's Functional Grammar, and Van Valin's Role and Reference Grammar were all devised precisely in order to deal with nonconfigurational as well as configurational languages, the bracketing structures I described as typical of language in section 3 above present no problems for them. For this and other reasons, they can cope with such problems as those listed in section 5 (a) to (f) without introducing any categories of "functional Head" within X-Bar phrase structure theory—they need no extension of X-Bar theory to clauses and sentences. In addition, they need no artificial separation between the treatments of problems of scope and reference in grammar and in logic or independent system of traces.

More fundamentally, as we shall see in chapter XIV, a grammar needs to be functional to exhibit that the difference between clauses and other word groups or phrases arises from their more direct relation and similarity to complete utterances, and that what makes the verbal different from the nominal arises from its constitutive role in the clause. Any grammar which fails to explain these things will be defective.

(d) *The hope of finding a universal grammar did not depend on Chomskyan ideas*

The work of Greenberg, of Bresnan in LFG, and of Dik and Van Valin in their more fully functionalist theories, each with their respective coworkers, has done much more to give empirical basis for the hope of developing approximations to a universal grammar than has the work of Chomsky. Moreover, we observed Chomsky's lack of concern with the placing of adjuncts, the difficulties for Chomskyan grammar presented by the quite normal device of bracketing as it occurs in language, and the greater plausibility of explanations drawing on pragmatics and logic in dealing with reference or anaphor and long-distance dependency and with the properties of interrogatives and relatives. These other approaches contrasted favorably with Chomskyan systems with their multiple ad hoc epicycles: Abstract Case, subjacency, Head Movement Constraint, extended reliance on traces, and ever multiplying function-

111. In a personal communication of 2004, Bresnan wrote, "I would welcome such system-external explanations. I view the formal system as a 'model' of (some aspects of) reality, whose properties still need explanation".

al phrases—all supposedly independent of logic, semantics, or pragmatics. However, Chomsky's fundamental mistake lay in basing clause and sentence theory on phrase theory, as chapter XV will show.

The theoretical inventiveness of Chomsky and other linguists in the MIT tradition disguised the defects of his approach.

The incorporation of properly functionalist ideas allows more justice to be done, first, to semantics or what I called general logic, second, to the variety of language types and nonconfigurational languages, and, third, to the distinction between the word and the morpheme. Chomsky's initial concentration upon highly isolating languages such as English made it easier for him to omit any definitions of such units as morpheme, root, stem, affix, derivative, compound, lexeme, and word, discussed in chapter II, definitions required if a system of generative grammar is to be set up. To the degree that a language is inflected, agglutinative, or polysynthetic, it is less easy to talk about "words" and more necessary to make use of such terms as "lexeme" or "lexical factor", raising issues which English examples often allow one to ignore. The grammars presented by Dik, Bresnan, and Van Valin are better designed to show how parallel functional structures can be realized in languages with quite different architectures, some tending towards maximal dependence on configuration and some towards maximal dependence on inflection in indicating structure. These grammars, accustomed to handling more inflected languages, are better adapted to judging how such notions as morpheme, stem, and so forth may be defined.

Section 8. Optimization in Analyzing Sentences Understood in Context

Even when problems are posed in somewhat the wrong way, much may be learned.

In chapter VII, in connection with the development of grammaticalization through language-use, I spoke of semantic and pragmatic constraints or pressures. These do not always pull in the same direction, and, so far as they apply generally, different communities give different priorities to different constraints and seek to minimize the number and seriousness of constraint violations. In this different languages "optimize" the situation in different ways, setting different balances between the different constraints, establishing different prioritizations which are reflected in the grammars of the different languages. This is well explained by Jonas Kuhn, although he is preoccupied with context-free sentences considered purely formally.[112]

112. Jonas Kuhn, *Optimality-Theoretic Syntax—A Declarative Approach* (Stanford, Calif.: CSLI, 2003).

Thus different languages develop different ways of indicating different roles in sentences: the center of attention (the "Theme" of functional grammar); the subject, if that is different; what is informationally novel; types of role in an event or situation; and the various things captured by tense. And if children are to communicate with their elders, they will need to appreciate and follow their habits of speech, which will become ingrained to them, though not innate. The point of each "rule" of optimization is intelligible, even though a different rule might hold in a different language. This preoccupation with optimality has developed in a context of those for whom grammar concerns context-free sentences, but who wish their formalizations to capture the standard features of discourse and information structure. Thus if certain forms of structuring are supposed canonical, one may explain some standard divergences from these forms in terms of what is Prominent and what is New in the context of utterance.[113] Although some prioritizations can be expressed in a formal rule, their function or role will be within reach of reflection, their exercise being a matter of skill, so that, for instance, some formal prioritizations carry no weight when some category difference makes them obviously inapplicable.[114] The variety of types of consideration and contextual circumstance which would make a rule inapplicable cannot be captured mechanically.

Recent followers of Lexical Functional Grammar have postulated two types of algorithm. One supposedly derives constituent structures from functional structures and represents "production", "generation", or "expressive" processes geared toward speech, taking us from meanings to their expressions. The other supposedly derives functional from constituent structures, representing "interpretive" processes of "comprehension" or "recognition".

Thinking in terms of mechanical algorithms, others follow these ways of thinking and repeat the defect of supposing that "working something out" in the mind has to be mechanical in the mathematical sense.[115] Moreover, they impose a false divide between the two kinds of process—for instance, as-

113. Hye-Won Choi, *Optimizing Structure in Context: Scrambling and Information Structure* (Stanford, Calif.: CSLI, 1999), originating from a 1996 PhD diss.; cf. Kuhn, *Optimality-Theoretic Syntax*, 132–36.

114. E.g., operas do not compose people; Kuhn, *Optimality-Theoretic Syntax*, 137–38.

115. Jürgen Wedekind, "Some Remarks on the Decidability of the Generation Problem in LFG- and PATR-Style Unification Grammars", *European Chapter of the Association for Computational Linguistics* (1995): 45–52; Wedekind, "Semantic-Driven Generation with LFG- and PATR-Style Grammars", *Computational Linguistics* 25, no. 2 (1999): 277–81. These papers arose within the context set by Stuart M. Shieber's Unification Grammar developed from 1986 onwards and Ivan Sag's HPSG from 1987, which followed Shieber's "Evidence against the Context-freeness of Natural Language", *Linguistics and Philosophy* 8 (1985): 333–43.

Wedekind's papers introduce the problem of "underspecified inputs" as creating difficulties for parsing relevant to machine translation. The rules of a context-free grammar require "input" to be definable morphologically (even though context may be required to identify morphological input, whether acoustic or written, owing to noise or clutter). Such underspecified inputs are to be expected when functional and other disambiguating information is supplied only by the context of speech (this also infects written reports of

suming that what is given to experience is a sentence with a certain morphological constituent structure, and that in order to understand it, we need an algorithm enabling us to derive its functional structure from this constituent structure.[116]

However, on the contrary, what is given to experience is not primarily a sentence as having a certain constituent structure, but a sentence as already exhibiting a certain functional structure. What is heard is normally heard and grasped in the act of hearing in its patterns or structures. That is, one normally hears the sentences of others as functionally organized in a certain way—and from the point of view of hearing, the appreciation of constituent structure is the product of reflection. When I listen to speech I am commonly more certain of the "substance" or gist of what has been said than of its precise words and intonation, just as when I see a dog running it takes reflection or repeated observation to discern the order in which its back and front legs move. Of course, there have to be determinate words and intonation—just as it is vital that the dog's legs move in some particular way, since the dog cannot run at all without its legs moving in some determinate way, but what we observe is the dog's running, not the detail of its leg movements.

Thus the capacity to get from functional to constituent structures is commonly as much involved in hearing as in speaking. It is therefore unsurprising that Kuhn should find it attractive to explore the formal aspects of combining two different kinds of optimization, one seeking the most harmonic way of expressing some meaning (production-directed or expressive) and the other seeking the most harmonic interpretation of a given utterance (comprehension-directed or interpretive).[117] The concepts of the harmon-

speech, conspicuously such works as the *Analects* of Confucius, where the original context of a saying is lost, so that it is not clear whether we are to respect spirits or avoid meddling with them).

The purpose of the "restriction operator" introduced in Ronald M. Kaplan and Jürgen Wedekind, "Restriction and Correspondence-Based Translation" and "Type-Driven Semantic Interpretation of f-structures", in *Proceedings of the 6th Conference of the European Chapter of the Association for Computational Linguistics*, 193–202 and 404–11, respectively (Utrecht: Association for Computational Linguistics, 1993), is to find a means to allow translation to proceed in maximum independence of these problems. Wedekind and Kaplan, "Squibs and Discussions: Ambiguity-Preserving Generation with LFG- and PATR-Style Grammars", *Computational Linguistics* 22, no. 4 (1996), has the same concern. (The preoccupation with computability is exhibited in the reference to PATR-style grammars. The component "PATR" in the name of this kind of grammar is an abridgement of "PATRICIA tries", "PATRICIA" being an acronym for "Practical Algorithm To Retrieve Information Coded In Alphanumeric" and the word "trie" being taken from a notion of "trie structure", meaning re*trie*val structure; cf. Donald E. Knuth, *Sorting and Searching*, vol. 3 of *The Art of Computer Programming*, 2nd ed. [Redwood City, Calif.: Longman, 1998], 498, 492.)

116. Cf. Bresnan, *Lexical-Functional Syntax*, 56–60.

117. Kuhn, *Optimality-Theoretic Syntax*, 125–72. The word "harmonic" was inherited from the ancestral Harmonic Grammar presented by Geraldine Legendre, Yoshiro Miyata, and Paul Smolensky in several papers in 1990, of which the first was, "Can Connectionism Contribute to Syntax? Harmonic Grammar, with an Application," in *Proceedings of the 26th regional meeting of the Chicago Linguistic Society*, edited by M. Ziolkowski, M. Noske, and K. Deaton (Chicago: Chicago Linguistic Society, 1990), 237–52.

ic and of optimization are realistic in any thinking about our understanding of utterances as spoken and heard in their context—that is, sentences whose sense is essentially context-sensitive—in my parlance, sentences properly so called. That is, the formal approaches stemming from the work of Bresnan, Shieber, and Sag, in being founded on a concern to do justice to the context-sensitive character of natural language, have at least this great advantage over Chomsky and his following.

Indeed, in the actual use of language, little or nothing spoken or written, outside mathematics, has a context-free sense, and the recognition of functional structure is commonly heavily dependent on context. Yet further, any purely formal approach is unrealistic, failing to correspond with psychological reality, since in actual experience human beings are always sensitive to an indefinite variety of pragmatic cues which shortcut relevant formal rules, and literary usage intrudes even into "scientific" and other "factual" accounts. Moreover, the way that human beings approach the understanding of speech shapes the way they approach the understanding of writing; adept readers grasp the sense or direction of written sentences and stretches of text, even when uncertain of their exact words and spelling.

XIV

The Verb Gives Sentences Their Dynamic Character and Shapes Their Syntactic Structure

In this chapter and the next I show how, in grammar, sentence and clause theory shape phrase theory, rather than vice versa. In giving primacy to the sentence and clause, I recognize speech as shaping grammatical form.

By contrast, in the Chomskyan approach sentences are composed stage by stage from words or other basic lexical factors, and sentence structure is represented compositionally in a bottom-up fashion. Thereby the representation of clause structure is modeled upon that of phrase structure. In the "Principles and Parameters" presentation Chomsky came to treat functional elements and features, such as tense, modality, negation, and "agreement" (i.e., concord between subject and verb and between verb and object), as the X-Bar Heads of "functional phrases", analogously to the way in which semantically content-introducing nouns and adjectives occur as the "lexical" heads of phrases in the X-Bar form of lexical phrase theory. As I show in section 1 (d), this approach relies upon an artificial bringing together of several different metaphorical uses of the word "head", metaphors arising in quite independent ways, the word "head" used quite equivocally. The resulting parallelisms are purely formal, like the formal parallelisms which we met in chapter X whereby Frege treated propositions as complex names of "the True" and "the False"—the resulting economies of presentation are artificial and deceptive as explained in chapter X, section 5 (b), and deeply misleading as to how language works.

Treating these functional features as heads of phrases in what is called X-Bar theory, and so as parallel to lexical heads, although labeled "functional" as opposed to "lexical", obscures the character of the verb as to what has these features of agreement, negation, modality, and tense specially linked to it. This approach recognizes these functional features as having a structurizing role within the clause, but does this without exhibiting that these features enter the construction of a sentence only through the verb or some analogue to it.[1] Such an approach obscures the verb's unique structurizing role. As a result, "sentences", considered as context-free constructs, come to be represented as hierarchically organized configurations of atomic semantic elements, including functional atoms alongside lexical atoms. In this way the organizational rules associated with the functional elements allow the construction, commonly by generation, of context-free "sentences".[2] This theory of sentences as language-constructs to be analyzed grammatically into "functional" and "lexical" atoms is not a theory of sentences as the sentential utterances with which the language-user, the language-teacher, and the logician are in practice concerned[3]—utterances in which words in context are integrated into pragmatic and semantic unities in the act of using them. This is the unity which chapter IX explained by drawing on the notions of synthesis, unsaturatedness, and nexus from Plato, Frege, and Jespersen.[4]

In the view I propose, a grammar gains explanatory power by describing the constituent elements and features of sentences in a top-down, pragmatico-semantic fashion, in terms of their functional roles within the clause or sentence—a clause being what is as such eligible to be an utterance complete in its own right, in the way explained in chapter X.

In the conception I open out, the sentence, and within it each clause,

1. When verbs like the copula, and other verbs, like "make" and "let", used quasi-copulatively, are dispensed with, idioms often arise where a noun, adjective, adverb, or spatial preposition functions as a verb—thus prepositions can take on the function of an imperative or infinitive, such as "Into him", "After him", "Upon him", "Off him", and "I will after him". Agreement, negation, modality, and tense are understood from the context when not indicated morphologically; see sec. 1 (b) (ii) of this chapter.

2. This atomization reaches complete explicitness in Jackendoff, *Foundations*, 180–81, 334–35. Jackendoff recognizes the special role of the finite verb as part of the basic "body-plan" of language, equipping it to "express" assertions, thereby identifying situations and events; and contrasts verbs with nouns, which, he supposes, can identify things of every semantic category (*Foundations*, 257–59; cf. 149–51, 252–53n11). But he fails to distinguish identifying or "naming" from the "expressing" which is essential to "saying", i.e., to language *use* as such, and which verbs especially embody.

3. Lexical items and surface structure are both presented by Chomsky as creatures of his grammatical theory, neither brought into any direct relation or comparison with empirical reality. For him, grammatical theories are empirically tested only as wholes.

4. It reveals a blind spot in much of modern grammar that someone as early as Hjelmslev could regard Jespersen's distinction between junction and nexus as one of his less important contributions to thought about language; Louis Hjelmslev, "Otto Jespersen", in *Portraits of Linguists*, ed. T. A. Sebeok (Bloomington: Indiana University Press, 1966), 2:167. In chap. IX, n. 11 of this volume, we observed a parallel blindness in Dummett's failure to appreciate the significance of Frege's distinction in Frege, "Concept and Object".

takes its vigor and structure from the verbal element at its heart. The nature of this verbal element is to be essentially incomplete, as it were achieving its completion in stages, a process only consummated and made concrete in the whole sentence as uttered or thought. In this chapter I consider the structure of a range of kinds of sentence and clause, along with the functional structurizing elements and features within them, including connectives, of which the most familiar are prepositions.

Making sentence theory subservient to phrase theory, Chomskyan grammars treat verbs too much in parity with nouns and adjectives, as just one species of lexical (or "content-introducing") head of phrases among others, a mistake made plain in this and the succeeding chapter. Such grammars thereby fail to give a proper account of what is distinctive about the verb. My task is to show how the character of sentential and therefore also clausal expressions as actual or potential saying expressions depends upon the "unsaturated" character of either their "main verb kernel"[5] or whatever other feature gives them a verbal, predicative, or "saying" character. And it is this difference between such verbal features that gives a sentential or clausal expression the character of a nexus rather than a junction, to use Jespersen's terms.

Section 1. The Verb at the Heart of a Clause Gives Structure to the Whole

In chapter XIII, sections 5 and 6, I analyzed the logical and grammatical structure of discourse as it extends beyond the individual sentence, where points of both grammar and logic turn on the relation of one complete speech-unit (sentence) to another—problems about reference, quotation, interrogatives, and hypothetical clauses among them.

In my presentation I used the terms "subject" and "predicate" in a way which accords with traditional "notional" grammars, as chapter XI proposed. In sum, the subject is the "argument of the verb which serves as discourse topic"—the available topic syntactically selected by concord with the verb, however this concord is indicated.

5. Grevisse speaks of the "kernel" (*le noyau*) of the verb, meaning the whole finite verb, including the content-introducing part, with any auxiliary, and including any indications of concord, aspect, tense, and mood; Grevisse, *Le Bon Usage*, 302.

(a) *The role of the verb*

(i) General framework of understanding

Within a typical simple clause we find a single predicate "... V ...", containing the kernel of the verb, equipped with indications of voice, mood, aspect, time, person, and number, and with a structure allowing of a certain number of expressions, A1, A2, ..., An, as semantic arguments, principally comprising the noun cores of complementary and adjunctive phrases. Some arguments may be expressed by a pronoun, and many languages omit the subject pronoun if the context makes the identity of the subject unambiguous. Besides these noun cores, whatever has a thematic role in relation to the verb may be regarded linguistically as an argument, as can be seen by its being capable of being made a topic in discourse, as when we say "I want to teach", but could say, "To teach is what I want to do".

The intention of a sentence is never to embrace all the aspects of the situation or event it concerns, which would in any case be impossible. Rather, it picks out just one aspect of the situation or event, presenting it in the perspective set by the interest or concern of the speaker. Accordingly, it sets the semantic arguments in a certain hierarchy, privileging one of them as subject, and typically others in the roles of direct object and indirect or other forms of oblique object, with some arguments being inessential to the sense of the verb in its context and therefore, following Dik, classified as satellites.[6] In this way the structure of the sentence is dictated functionally, giving it what has been called a certain information structure, rather than corresponding to the structures suggested by predicate logic, which would have treated the arguments equally. Accordingly, one should not separate "cognitive constraints" from "grammatical constraints" in the way Jackendoff suggests, let alone think of grammatical constraints as dictated by abstract structures such as "X-Bar theory" arising as aspects of a possibly neurologically rooted "competence". Rather, grammar is directly occupied with the structures of speech.[7]

In making the verb thus fundamental I present the background picture of the verb (V) as either constituting a trunk from which subject (S) and object (O) sprout, as in (S)V(O) languages, or bracketing the rest of the clause, as in V(SO) and (SO)V languages.

The inescapable priority of the "predicate" or "verb phrase" as the "say-

6. Dik introduced the notion in *Functional Grammar*, and it appears in its most recent form in Dik, *Theory of Functional Grammar: Part 1*, 86–90. In this later exposition he extended the notion of satellite to cover what he called predicate-satellites, contrasting "They discussed the matter politely" with "They behaved politely". I think it better to speak of "politely" as peripheral to the clause in the first case, and not in the second, and to limit the use of the word "satellite" to objects such as are mentioned in such peripheral adverbials as "with a knife".

7. See chap. XI, the introductory remarks, in this volume.

ing" part of the sentence within this framework will become increasingly unmistakable as our discussion proceeds. But if there is a subject, expressed or not, this function of "saying" is something which the predicate only achieves in the act of exercising its link with the subject, as we saw in chapter IX. How a predicate applies to any general term, general terms being possible subject terms, is indicated by what we there called "predicate application controllers", typically indicators of identity or of quantity, so that any noun or noun phrase is implicitly or explicitly governed by such a controller, except when it is used attributively, as in "... is a man", or as an attributive modifier of a noun, as in "student campaign". If, when predicates apply to singular terms, we deem the noun to be marked by a "zero predicate application controller", we could generalize by defining nouns and noun phrases as those expressions which can be governed by predicate application controllers.

Accordingly, our provisional picture of a typical clause is as constituted of an overarching "saying" framework, giving it its "verbal" character, argument-expressions enfolded within the nexus set by the verb. Such a verb gives the whole clause a dramatic character, communicating this character to other elements in the clause so far as they are integral to the clausal framework. Content-introducing elements thus somehow held, strung, or glued together are each liable to qualification by other modifying elements, perhaps themselves liable to further such qualification, so that the main string, embracing the core elements, may have substrings attached at various points of its length.

As to indicators of identity and indicators of quantity, we have to distinguish between when they have a central functional role within the clause, acting as application controllers upon an argument to the verb, indicating, in Johnson's phrase, "how the predicate applies to it", and when they have merely peripheral roles.[8]

When such indicators of identity and of quantity modify nouns or noun phrases as application controllers indicating how the arguments within a verbal framework fit within that framework, they thereby belong functionally to the core of the clause, as the Chomskyan tradition has come to mark by treating them as Heads of subject phrases (Heads of so-called Determiner Phrases).[9]

By contrast, indicators of identity or of quantity modifying adjective and adverb phrases are syntactically the most peripheral elements within clause and sentence structure. In such cases we can not only introduce comparisons,

8. See chap. IX, sec. 2 (a) (vi), in this volume.

9. Fukui, "A Theory of Category Projection and its Applications" (PhD diss., Massachusetts Institute of Technology, 1986), revised and published as Fukui, *Theory of Projection in Syntax* (Stanford, Calif.: CSLI, 1995); Fukui and M. Speas, "Specifiers and Projection", in *Papers in Theoretical Linguistics*, ed. Naoki Fukui, Tova R. Rapoport, and Elizabeth Sagey (Cambridge, Mass.: MITWPL, 1986), 128–72; Abney, "The English Noun Phrase".

but also apply modifiers to other modifiers, forming chains so as to achieve a baroque complexity, forming such phrases as "a very great deal too much", "very very much too much", "much more courageous than Hercules", "much more than [the amount that] we want", and "a great deal too much more than could possibly fit". The multiplication of indicators such as "very" is so peripheral to the meaning of the sentence as to achieve little more than the addition of expletives.

Examples when there appears to be no application controller arise in two ways. First, there are some of the "impersonal" or subjectless uses of verbs which I discussed in chapter XI. Second, there is the very common case of the subject's being expressed only by a pronoun or only implicitly through the inflection of the verb. Thus when one meets "he" in a text, one has to view the context to discover whether the subject is a singular term, for instance, or whether the reference is general and a universal quantification is implicit, as in the second sentence of the following: "A dictator is always ultimately alone. He [that is, 'every dictator'] has to rely on his own judgment". This exhibits again how the consideration of reference and scope (reflected in what linguists call Binding Theory) makes syntactic analysis subordinate to pragmatics or the consideration of context, as we observed in chapter XIII, section 5, with the ultimate constraints being set by logic.

(ii) The verb as the source of energy unifying the whole sentence: metaphors expressing this

The drawing of the elements of a sentence together, integrating them in such a way as to make the sentence a live utterance, is achieved by "structurizing" features, some intonational and configurational, but some involving the use of particular morphosyntactic forms within some configurational and intonational setting—for instance, the verb "have" when followed by the past participle (e.g., "broken" or "killed") indicating aspect. When a particular feature can be picked out (e.g., "have ... -ed") as subserving this structurizing role, I call it a "clause structurizer". Inflections marking concord between subject and finite verb or between the semantically content-introducing element of the verb and its arguments are "connective structurizers" subserving a structurizing role, "concord linkers". I regard elements or features expressing modality and aspect (inflections, auxiliaries, phrase order, and intonation, including elements or features differentiating statements, questions, commands, and so forth), along with any indicators of negation of the main verb, as "semantic thrust structurizers"—they all have a part in indicating the direction, or thrust, of the utterance or clause concerned. Here one may recall the way Wittgenstein compared sense with direction, thinking of direction as what might be marked with an arrow. This thrust-giving verbal center is the direction-giving and governing feature of a clause, dictating the identity of the subject-phrase.

One could dramatize this conception of the role of the verb in the typical sentence by characterizing the verb as the center or source of the "flow" of the sentence or, taking advantage of a Chinese way of thinking, by speaking of the verbal kernel as the source of *chi* (*ki* in Japanese), or energy, within the sentence as a whole, only able to communicate itself to other parts of the sentence through the presence of appropriate structurizing features—namely, inflections, connectives, configuration, and intonation, which integrate subjects, other complements, and adjuncts with the source of *chi*. The *chi* passes from verb arguments through case markings or adpositions; to adverbs, adverbial clauses, and adverbial phrases modifying verbs through the use of conjunctions, adpositions, or affixes; through the noun arguments to various kinds of modifier in ways that depend in different cases on concord between noun and adjective, word order, and adpositional connectives (modifiers including relative clauses); and through adjectives or adverbs it can pass to other adverbs. It is only by means of these appropriate connectives and affixes, configuration, and intonation that the *chi* can flow. For a sentence to be ungrammatical is for there to be a bar to the flow of *chi*.

All this takes us back to Frege and Plato and the insights of chapters IX and X, developing the perspective of part one of this volume that a sentence cannot be formed by the mere listing or juxtaposition of names or referring expressions. We can form a list of names as complex as we like—Brutus, the relation of killer to killed, Caesar, the relation of acting with others, the position of acting with associates, being an associate, Cassius, Cinna, Trebonius, Metellus, there being others, the position of being in a place, a place being located by being used, the relation of being used for meetings by a group, the Senate, the property of being of a group, and nine relationships of exemplifying—but this list of names is not a sentence: "Brutus killed Caesar, acting with Cassius, Cinna, Trebonius, Metellus, and others as associates, in the Senate as meeting place". The propensity of English speakers to resort to dry stone masonry in putting sentences together, as in, "A top quality top class Oxford University plant science student starved"—joining an article together with five noun phrases (including nine nouns) to form a single noun phrase—is apt to deceive us. The further we go in reducing the external expression of thought to what appears to be a sequence of nouns or names, the greater the complexity of the system of "rules of interpretation" required.

The compositional character of formal grammars, making it natural to think of sentences in terms of principles for putting significant atomic units together, has the misleading effect of making us think of them as if they were built up by dry stone masonry.

When we realize the function of affixes (that is, suffixes and prefixes) to nouns and verbs and of connectives as constituting the glue linking the parts of sentences to one another in a significant way, and linking them to that which we feel to be most alive in the sentence, the finite verb, this enables us to appreciate how grammar can be conceived of as in a more intimate relation to semantics, meaning, and sense than we have become accustomed to conceive of it. Failure to appreciate this gluing and interconnecting function of the elements of language, together with an insistence on approach by formal rule alone, often leads grammarians to give highly technical reasons for ungrammaticality in cases in which the ordinary language-user would feel the reason to be obvious—for instance, as it stands, "Peter seems Mary to like John" has a noun, "Mary", just hanging about in the middle, lacking connection with anything.[10]

We find the same way of thinking in the Japanese grammarian Akira Suzuki (1764–1837)[11] when he puts postpositions among the words which have *zi* (also Romanized *ji*), which he explains as meaning that they "denote nothing", but only attach "a voice of heart or intention" to something with *si* (*shi*). The things with *si* are said to denote something and are, he tells us, of three kinds, nouns, adjectives, and verbs, and it is these alone which I will count as lexical heads in further discussion. Adpositions and case-inflections, like the adverbs and adverbial prefixes discussed in chapter XIII, section 1, have to do with the linkage between a live verb and some argument, and should be counted as synlexical elements in a sentence, like Aristotle's connectives (*syndesmos*), "combining two significant expressions into one".[12] ("Synlexical" is the term I introduced as preferable to the more traditional "syncategorematic".) By contrast, auxiliaries and other speech inflections give "voice of heart" to the verb-stem directly, and are not directed towards linking it to anything else. The finite verb, or auxiliary and rest of the kernel of the verb, expresses what gives life or heart to the whole utterance, what gives it its place in human discourse.

10. Connection would not be restored by substituting the gerund "liking" for the infinitive "to like", but by putting "To Mary, Peter seems to like John" or "It seems to Peter that Mary likes John"—close to "Peter believes Mary to like John" or "Peter believes that Mary likes John" in meaning.

11. Akira Suzuki, *Gengo shishu ron* (On the four categories in language), first published 1824; reprinted *Benseisha Bunkō* 68, 1979, expounded in Keiichi Uchida, "Peripheral Approach in Chinese Linguistics as an Area of Cultural Interaction Studies", *A Selection of Essays on Oriental Studies of ICIS* 1 (2011): 123–37, Institute for Cultural Interaction Studies, Kansai University, available Kansai University Institutional Repository, http://kuir.jm.kansai-u.ac.jp/dspace/bitstream/10112/4350/1/10_UCHIDA.pdf, 132, and referred to in S. Makino, *Some Aspects of Japanese Nominalizations* (Tokyo: Tokai University, 1968), discussed by Abney, "The English Noun Phrase", 63–65. The Hebrew word *nephesh*, for soul (it had a root-meaning "throat" before meaning successively "greed", "life", and "soul"), presents another image for the role of the verbal element in the sentence as making the sentence *say* something.

12. Aristotle, *Poetics* c. 20, 1456b39–57a6.

(iii) The complete saying

By the "complete verbal frame", I have in view what gives "thrust" to the whole saying and determines the character, direction, and scope of this thrust, and therefore constitutes this frame as, as it were, the "heart" of the clause. More precisely, I mean the content-introducing verb-expression, together with whatever auxiliary or semi-auxiliary (to adopt Grevisse's useful term[13]) may govern it, including therefore the finite verb with any indications of mood and aspect; and also including any negative applied to it (since this, by negating the whole predicate, reverses the direction of the whole saying) and any application controller, such as a quantifier, governing the finite verb and therefore governed by this negative, together with any adpositions needed to complete the connection of the content-introducing verb to its arguments in its sentence context. I take any temporal marking to be part of this verbal heart only if it is morphologically integral to the finite verb. The finite verb is either a self-standing content-introducing verb; a semantically synlexical auxiliary, whether with some semantic content, as with modal and other semi-auxiliaries, or without this, as with auxiliaries of aspect, tense, or voice; or else a synlexical copulative verb. Such auxiliary verbs have a synlexical role, not introducing content on their own.

The complete saying is a nexus to which this verb frame gives structure. As such it incorporates the predicate or verb phrase, together with its argument, along with the application-controller expressions which show how the predicate applies to these arguments. But this nexus also includes clauses modifying the verb, or the verb phrase or predicate, or the clause as a whole, traditionally called adverbial clauses, and is unified by the subordination of the tenses of verbs in these adverbial modifiers, whether they modify verb, predicate, or clause, to the tense of the finite verb. Thus if these modifying clauses refer to causes and conditions of the actual or possible state or event recounted in the main clause, or states of knowledge and desire influential on the action there recounted, then the tensing and times referred to must be prior to the time associated with the finite verb; and if they concern the end aimed at or means envisaged in deliberation, then the tensing times they indicate must be future relative to the time associated with the main verb. Even if in some constituent there are quantifiers not governed by the negation contained in the verb frame—for instance, because they contain the "any" or "a certain" discussed in chapter XIII, section 6, or come within a hypothetical clause— they still belong to the complete saying nexus.

13. Grevisse groups *pouvoir*, along with *aller, avoir à, devoir, faillir, manquer, être pour* (= be about to), the causative *faire*, and *laisser, paraitre, sembler, savoir, vouloir* (= want to), when followed by infinitives, as "semi-auxiliaries"; Grevisse, *Le Bon Usage*, 1192–201.

Three types of feature are semantically and structurally outermost in relation to the rest of the saying nexus containing them: (1) conditional clauses and clauses joined by "or"; (2) the anomalous epistemic modal operator "It is possible that" in the present tense, and all its near-equivalents, all treating some clause as hypothetical; and (3) "any" as an application controller signifying indiscriminateness, and "a certain" as the application controller which excludes indiscriminateness but which, by refusing identification, withholds full access to the knowledge to which access is possible.

In chapter XIII, section 6, I explained how "Perhaps, P" expresses epistemic attitude, and how statements of the form "It is possible that P" are designed to summarize the epistemic position within which judgments and decisions on matters connected with P are made rather than state extra non-epistemic facts, so that, along with such statements in past and future tensed forms, they require to be understood semantically as if they were in indirect speech adverting to people's epistemic position at some particular time. In this respect they need to be treated in the same way as statements like "Cerberus was a three-headed dog at the gates of Hades", understood as if implicitly in indirect speech—that is, as meaning "The Greeks believed that Cerberus was a three-headed dog at the gates of Hades".

However, the grammar of such utterances has to be described according to their forms and not considerations of truth and falsity. Accordingly, the same law of subordination of tenses to that of the main verb applies to them as applied to the conditional and disjoined clauses mentioned earlier. Comparably, what Austin called "performative" verbs, such as "order" and "promise", found in present-tense utterances whereby a speaker gives orders and makes promises, which are semantically anomalous in not being statement-making, have to be treated as having the same grammar as the statement-making utterances using these verbs made at other times or by persons other than the speaker. Grammar is interested in the affirmative, negative, interrogative distinctions, but not in the distinctions between statement and nonstatement, fiction and nonfiction, "performative" and statemental ("constative").[14]

(iv) The notions of complement and adjunct are both semantic and functional in nature

Thus the sentence, and within it each clause, takes its vigor and its structure from a verbal element which constitutes its heart. Being essentially incomplete, as if waiting for completion, is part of what it is to be a verbal element.

14. This was Austin's term, distinguishing declaratives whose utterance is statemental from declaratives such as "I hereby appoint you ..." or "I promise to...," whose utterance is the performance of the act signified by the main verb; Austin, *How to Do Things with Words*, 3.

We can analyze each clause and each complete sentence as if it was formed by completing this verbal element stage by stage. The idea of "complement to the verb" has a key place in the functional analysis of clauses.

The verb frames, which I described as the hearts of sentences and clauses, are liable to have other features, some of them internal, such as tense, aspect, mood, and voice, not always separable either semantically or morphologically, and others external—first, their core complements, and, outside the core, the functionally adjunctive elements. Expressions are functionally adjunctive when, as they occur in speech, they present themselves as being structurally external or accidental to an already completed whole or core in the perspective set by their discourse context in the clause.[15]

The distinction between the complements and adjuncts to a verb in a particular involves distinguishing arguments in *rapport* with the meaning of the verb according to its voice, called its complements, from elements peripheral to the core of the clause.[16] The functional rather than simply lexical character of the complement/adjunct distinction where verbs are concerned I explain in detail in section 3 (b).

The complements will include many subject and object expressions, whether or not the phrases introducing them are clausal or else indicative of a sort of activity—see section 2 (b)—and whether or not, in the case of noun phrase complements, a connective or special case-inflection is involved. In each case the kind of complement to the verb concerned is spoken of as fulfilling some grammatical function in relation to the verb and thereby also in relation to the whole clause.

This way of speaking of the complements of the verb, whereby the subject counts as one of the complements, has the virtue of fitting exactly with the way of thinking presented in chapter IX, whereby a singular subject-term is what completes the predicate into a clause (in the case of a general subject-term, together with an applicative, that is, an application or identity controller). Thus the subject is, on the one hand, the sole complement of the predicate (in a defining relation to the predicate); on the other hand, in relation to the verb, it is potentially one of several complements.

The distinction between complements and adjuncts to the verb is instructive when it comes to the consideration of subordinate clauses, where what were traditionally called noun clauses emerge as what we can now recognize as the "clausal complements to the verb". Such subordinate clauses are liable

15. The verb frames at the heart of a clause are also spoken of as its "functional heads", with its noun phrase complements described as "dependents". Agreement is marked either on the dependents, as in "dependent-marking" languages, or on the head, as in "head-marking" ones.

16. Grevisse cites Tesnière as thinking of complements as acting in *rapport* with what Grevisse calls the "kernel" (*le noyau*) of the verb; Grevisse, *Le Bon Usage*, 388; cf. 302; cf. n. 5.

to be linked into the structure set up by the verb and its complements by a connective clause-marker. Thus the verbal framework "he said (that ...)" is completed by "Jones was a fool" into the clause "he said that Jones was a fool", the "that" being the connective clause-marker involved—by far the most common such connective in English. Other kinds of clause are linked into the structure set up by the verb only indirectly, either as modifiers of the verb ("adverbial clauses"), or else as modifying some noun ("relative clauses"), the noun having been already linked into the verbal structure independently: these linkages have some special features I discuss in section 5.

There are two other uses of the word "complement" to consider.

The first is that of the phrases traditionally referred to as complements to the verb "to be". These complete the combination of subject and copula into a clause, or into its core. However, since the copula is sometimes omitted, it is better to think of this kind of complement under the more general description "attributive complement".

We can now generalize in regard to clause and sentence structure. Nouns and noun phrases can be modified by adjectives, and verbs by adverbs. Noun, adjective, and adverb can be modified by indicators of identity or of quantity, as we saw in chapter IX.[17] The verb "to be" can take both noun phrases and adjectives as attributive complements. Beyond this, everything else requires a connective or some other special device to link it into the structure set by the verb.

The second use of the word "complement" which requires mention is the use whereby clause-markers and connectives are supposed to have complements. This is not a case of functional complementation, but of mere morphosyntactic description—involving a use of the one which disguises rather than reveals the true semantic and grammatical structure.

Whenever a noun phrase is added into the structure set by the verb, it brings with it primarily the noun which is its head, but also whatever adjectives modify this noun and whatever noun phrases or verbal expressions are subordinately linked to it by linking devices. Noun phrases and verbal expressions are thus subordinately linked by means of either inflectional indications or connective adpositions, with clauses being linked to them by means of relative pronouns serving as connectives (making clause-markers dispensable). When a noun is modified by an adjective, this adjective may have things linked to it in similar ways, except not by relatives.

Whenever a connective links something to a noun, it links it into the

17. Confusion may result from the fact that determiners are not syntactically adjectives or adverbs. Yet they are morphologically adjective-like or adverb-like: thus the determiners of nouns and noun phrases usually take the same inflections as adjectives (number, case, and gender), while the determiners of adjectives and of adverbs receive some fixed inflection like adverbs.

structure which includes the noun, and likewise whenever a connective links something to an adjective, it thereby links it into the structure which includes the noun which the adjective modifies. Things linked into a larger structure by connectives thereby help complete the clause concerned in some particular core or peripheral respect.

Some linguists, thinking primarily morphosyntactically, conceive such things as complements to the connective concerned, as if, for instance, in the utterance "He was afraid of tigers", we had the structure we may mathematically represent "afraid (of (tigers))", rather than "afraid-of (tigers)"—that is, they wrongly think of *tigers* as mathematically the argument of the prepositional function "of (...)", whereas it is better to think of *tigers* as mathematically the argument of the adjectival function "afraid-of". The linguistic reality is that what is involved is functionally and semantically a complement to the noun or adjective concerned. The word "tigers" is in fundamentally the same semantic relation to the adjective "afraid" as it might be to the noun "fear" in "(fear of) tigers" and to the verb "fear" in "fear tigers". The underlying function of the preposition "of" in these contexts is to indicate the semantic incompleteness of the adjective or noun concerned, an incompleteness in some cases shown by the context of utterance rather than by the presence of "of". Likewise, the underlying function of the clause-marker "that" in such contexts as "knew that ...", or, in archaic constructions, after conjunctions as in "till that ..." or after relative pronouns as in "which that ...", is to mark the incompleteness of the preceding verb, relative pronoun, or connective, as seen in section 5.[18]

If one considers certain restricted parts of clauses, it is evident that whenever one has a connective, it has no function without whatever it connects into the larger structure concerned. Hence, although morphosyntactically what an adposition governs completes the adpositional phrase, and clauses complete clause-markers (labeled "Complementizers" in most formal grammars), as if it were the connective adpositions and clause-markers which were being completed, this is a somewhat myopic way of viewing the situation.

We see here how the notion of complement to a connective arose, despite the deep error in regarding the connective itself as a head from a lexical or semantic standpoint. Such morphosyntactic "heads" are nothing more than morphosyntactic markers indicating how the relevant phrases are linked into a larger whole.

These notions I have identified are all "functional", rather than lexical: "complement to a verb", "subject", "clausal complement to the verb", and "attributive complement".

18. The archaic presence of "that" is illustrated in the *Shorter OED* with several causal and temporal conjunctions; cf. n. 64 and related text, and Radford, *Transformational Grammar*, 486.

(b) *The principal "parts of speech": lexical heads and their complements and modifiers*

(i) Escaping the confusions associated with the word "head" in grammatical theory

Since the Chomskyan school introduced the idea of "functional head" into phrase theory, the use of the words "head" and "phrase" has become undisciplined. Common explanations are often vague—for instance, saying that the head is the "essential" element in the phrase, while also saying that it may lack any morphological realization. Clause-markers such as "that", along with connectives such as relatives and adpositions, have also been counted as "heads" of phrases, whereas the roles concerned seem only those of serving as a connective and providing the equivalent of a certain kind of punctuation. Classifying clauses and even whole sentences as "phrases" has led people to imagine that they all have heads of some kind, by analogy with the lexical heads of X-Bar theory, as if any operator of wider logical scope is thereby a head of some kind.

Yet, in "I told you he hit me", the supposed head of the subordinate clause appears to be a morphological fiction. As to so-called prepositional phrases, in "Give it to John", it would be more accurate to describe "John" as the essential and core element of the prepositional phrase "to John" than to describe "to" in this way, because the "to" is a mere link or connective to the core of the whole sentence. The utterance "Give it John" is grammatically radically less defective than "Give it to". Indeed, clause-markers and connectives can often be omitted, as the clause-marker "that" can be omitted in "I told you that he hit me"—likewise, "that", serving as a relative, has been omitted in "the man I met".

Consideration of phrases with lexical heads suggests that whenever we have a complement, there must be a "head" of which it is complement.

Yet two other, utterly different kinds of syntactic feature have also been labeled "heads".

First, beside the paradigm case of phrases with lexical heads, we have what I called respectively "connectives", which behave like adaptors in electrical systems, allowing us to connect some subordinate piece of apparatus into the main system, ultimately to the heart of the clause, and "clause-markers", which mark something as requiring to be connected. These are heads of phrases only in a morphosyntactic sense, and have no lexical or semantic content. And what are here called complements are semantically complements of what they are connected to, not of these empty elements.

Second, we have synlexical "saying" or "rhetic" elements, first, copulative and auxiliary verbs, and second, what I call constitutive verbs, such as "make" and "have", as when we speak of making statements or having attributes—copula, auxiliary, or constitutive verb, all expressions which lie at the very heart of the clause. In a metaphor, these, along with finite verbs in general, might be thought of as heads of whole clauses rather than of phrases. However, clarity requires confining the use of the word "head" to lexical heads in order to avoid using the word equivocally to apply to features with utterly different syntactic functions—as well as to avoid our applying the term to features which may have no morphological embodiment at all (not even one presupposed in the context, such as could be elicited by a question).

(ii) The priority of the verbal framework remains even when there is no finite verb

The structure of so-called verb phrases is very different from the structures of noun, adjective, and adverb phrases. With noun, adjective, and adverb phrases they are self-contained, except where they require a complement. By contrast, the most essential feature of verb phrases is whatever exhibits their incompleteness of character.

Within the framework I described in subsection (a), the verb "to be" is maximally incomplete. Whether it is serving as a copula or as an auxiliary indicating aspect, tense, or voice, it is semantically synlexical, empty of semantic content, but at the heart of the clause, quite unlike connectives and clause-markers. As with other synlexical elements, it may often be omitted, the discourse or sentence context adequately indicating the verbal framework, as when we meet "... *candidus*" in place of "... *candidus est*" and as in "Look! The plates shattered, the food on the floor, nothing to make another meal, the electricity fused, the kitchen requiring repainting, a complete mess". Again, there is the well-known phenomenon of the "small clause" such as occurs in "I thought him intelligent" (equivalent to "I thought him to be intelligent" and "I thought that he was intelligent") and "The president appointed him ambassador". In such cases, even if the structural character of the context can be made explicit by the provision of the verb "to be" as copula or auxiliary, it remains that such an unnecessary copula or auxiliary would be best described as used synlexically.

In the extreme case of the copula, the verb itself introduces no content whatsoever, and the content-introducing element within the predicate is a noun or adjective expressing an attribute of the subject or a noun within certain kinds of phrase. Thus, consider predicates such as "... is a man", "... is tall", "... is in Athens", and "... is here". In these the content-introducing element within the predicate is respectively a common noun, an adjective, and a location: "a man", "tall", "Athens", and "here". In such cases, in some languages, the saying, "rhetic", or predicative character of the attributive, locative, or other special part of a clause may be understood from the structure or context of the sentence, no copula being used, but the predicative role of such content-introducing parts of a clause being conveniently shown by representing them in a way which indicates their incompleteness: "... a man", "... tall", "... Athens", and "... here". The absence of a verb in such cases does not mean that the overall structure is not "rhetic" or predicative. Rather, within the sentence context, a nonverbal element can here take on a functionally verbal, unsaturated, incomplete, or structurizing character. Jespersen provides some nice examples of this dry stone masonry, or of "nexus without a verb".[19]

I note that participles retain a distinctively verbal character lacking to attributive and locative expressions like those instanced earlier ("... a man", "... tall", "... Athens", and "... here"). The attributive use of a participle is always inseparable from an equivalent use of the verb concerned in a relative clause: the winning teams are the teams which win, while the men running are the men who are running, and the people loved are the people who are loved.

In general, in assessing what belongs to a verb complex, there are two requirements. First, we need to consider the range of related uses of a verb, differentiated according to tense, aspect, mood, and voice, and the parallelism in the behavior of different verbs, by this means identifying what belongs to the verb kernel.[20] Second, we need to consider what has the same structural role within the clause or sentence, this latter enabling us to recognize the synlexical role of auxiliaries and what I will call "semi-auxiliaries" as making them inseparable from the participles and infinitives which go with them, and as sometimes sharing the functions of indicating tense, aspect, modality, and voice traditionally associated with them. Thus a verb complex which takes the form of auxiliary or "semi-auxiliary" together with a participle or infinitive has to be grouped with verb kernels taking the form of a single inflected word, both fulfilling the same "saying" or predicative function.

Because of their incompleteness, I avoid describing the heart of verb phrases in the same way as it is customary to describe noun, adjective, and ad-

19. Jespersen, *Philosophy of Grammar*, 121–22; cf. 86–87, 97, 114–16; cf. John Bowers's desire to introduce Predicate as the name of a functional Head within the framework of Chomskyan grammar, in Bowers, "Predication", in *The Handbook of Contemporary Syntactic Theory*, ed. Mark Baltin and Collins (Oxford: Blackwell, 2001), 299–333, fitting main and small clauses together; cf. also the way Bresnan, *Lexical-Functional Syntax*, 110, 112, in order to deal with certain nonconfigurational languages, feels forced to envisage a form of representation in which a clause S gives privilege to no particular category in its functional structure (in her account, S can dominate varied categories, including NP and AP, as readily as VP).

20. In chaps. VI–VII of this volume, I took up Gibson's insights in conceiving of perceptual systems as being tuned to resonate through use in interaction with their environment, to become able to recognize the same object in many different guises, and applied them to our systems for learning and using language. Here the role and relevant modes of functioning of the brain become shaped through the person's interaction in speaking and hearing with a community of language speakers. As a result the human being becomes able to recognize not only words and lexemes (chap. II) but also more particularly verbs, with their conjugations, parts, irregularities, and related verbal nouns (cf. chaps. XII and XV).

verb phrases. And I avoid any talk of prepositional or other functional verbal heads and their complements, and with it the embarrassments of heads which may have no morphological realization and complements which are not modifiers. Instead I speak of verb kernels within verb kernels or complexes. Then I speak of "might" as the governing verb kernel in relation to "be going to win" in expressions like "might be going to win", "be" in relation to "going to win", and "be going" in relation to "win". Likewise, I regard "will" as the governing kernel in relation to "have been being built" in "will have been being built", and "will have been" in relation to "being built"; and "will have" in relation to "been being educated" in "will have been being educated".

When auxiliaries or semi-auxiliaries occur in such ways, I call the final content-introducing verb the "terminal" verb. Thus "go" is the terminal verb in "I want to go", "I want you to go", and "I want you to send someone to order Jones to go". Many verbs have uses both as semi-auxiliaries and as terminal verbs. Thus the terminal verbs are "want", "want", "send", "order", "exist", and "is", respectively, in "I want an apple", "I might want an apple", "I sent Smith with the message", "I ordered a pizza", "Nobody thought that coelacanths still existed", and "The kangaroo which escaped is [expressing identity] the one you keep in your enclosure".

It is essential to view the character of such verb complexes in this way in order to preserve recognition of the verbal character of the terminal verb as well as of auxiliaries and semi-auxiliaries. For the verbal character to the whole verb complex depends upon the verbal character of the terminal verb, for it is this which constitutes the primary content-introducing semantic nucleus of the typical verb complex.

The complete saying nexus includes the subject with the predicate, including any quantity expression together with negation, if present, modifying the verb kernel and complex.

(iii) Only three kinds of lexical head: nouns, adjectives along with adverbs, and verbs

In his phrase theory Chomsky conceived there to be four kinds of lexical head: the noun, the verb, the adjective, and the adposition, *qua* lexical implied to have semantic content, and gave an artificially neat explanation of there being just these four, representing the noun and the nominal as having the character (+N, –V), the verbal (–N, +V), the adjectival (+N, +V), and the adpositional (–N, –V).

A functionalist, logic-influenced approach to the "parts of speech" allows a less artificial way of viewing what differentiates the different kinds of phrase with lexical heads and their elements.

Thus verbs present themselves as the most incomplete kind of lexical head within the clause, and nouns as the most self-contained. Adjectives can take on the character of a defective noun, as in "The wise declared him innocent" and "They killed the old" ("wise people" and "old people" being respectively referred to), but their essential lexical character is to be semantically content-introducing cores of attributive predicates, such as "is wise" and "is old"—and therefore also capable of being modifiers of nouns or noun phrases, a man who is wise being a wise man. Whereas adjectives and adverbs enter the system only in virtue of their attributive or modificatory role, what distinguishes nouns is their role as the core of phrases identifying the nonverbal complements of verbs, recognizable as such because they are either general terms governed by a predicate application controller, marking how the verb or predicate applies to them, or else singular terms, as it were, governed by zero application controllers.

With adjectives which apply primarily to nouns whose sense arises from lexical connection with a verb, as "slow swimmers" are thus called because they swim slowly, it is not the adjectival, but the adverbial form which is primary, the difference between adjectives and adverbs being here merely morphological. In such cases the primary character of the modifier involved is as a modifier of the verb. Indicators of identity or of quantity can sometimes be used in this adverbial way, as in "He swam thus [said pointing to someone swimming the crawl]", "He was only partly finished", and "He completely succeeded".

As to adpositions, Chomsky's marking them as (–N, –V) is a symptom of their not being lexical in character at all, but essentially synlexical, and arising only as connectives, a fact sometimes concealed in ways discussed later.[21]

In a theory of lexical phrases we should therefore admit only three types of semantically head elements as entering into discourse—namely, nouns, adjectives (with the corresponding adverbs), and verbs. Everything else—whether preposition, postposition, or other connective, determiner, or one of certain verbs, of which the verb "to be" as copula or auxiliary is the most important—serves only some semantically synlexical role.[22] To regard adpositions as lexical heads is to impose on modern theory a straitjacket inherited from schoolbook theories of "government" describing different kinds of concord and how they are indicated in writing.[23]

21. Bresnan recognizes their character as connectives, representing them as (+ transitive) in her un-Chomskyan characterizations of types of phrase head; Bresnan, *Lexical-Functional Syntax*, 120.

22. The view of L. George, "Analogical Generalizations of Natural Language Syntax" (PhD diss., Massachusetts Institute of Technology, 1980).

23. William Cobbett's 1819 *A Grammar of the English Language* (Oxford: Oxford University Press, 1984) is a fine example.

(iv) A review of synlexical expressions

Bresnan and Van Valin distinguish between predicative and nonpredicative adpositions.[24] "Predicative" adpositions are content-introducing (typically with some spatial meaning). Thus "This road is to London" is equivalent to "This road goes to London" or "This road is London-bound", and similarly, "The road to London is long" is equivalent to "The road which goes to London is long"—although some commonly spatial prepositions often take on purely structural roles, "to" being the most obvious example in English. However, such predicative adpositions are just as synlexical as ones with a purely structural meaning. Predicative adpositions can be thought of as like separable affixes to a verb, "goes to" being analogous to "look at" (cf. the French *regarder*), and "lives in" having a similar meaning to "inhabits". Here we must distinguish the attributive use of "in London" after the copula ("He is in London") from its use as an adverbial modifier, as in "He is sleeping in London".

Thus spatial adpositions have content, but can never be heads of phrases, since they remain synlexical. By contrast, modal verbs and other semi-auxiliaries lie in an intermediate position between the auxiliaries indicating aspect, tense, or voice and ordinary verbs, having status as verbs. On the one hand, when modal and other semi-auxiliary verbs and expressions occur as auxiliaries, they are like the auxiliaries of aspect, tense, or voice in being maximally incomplete, like them lying at the heart of the clause, syntactically synlexical, not by being linked to the terminal verb, but rather the terminal verb being linked to them, as in "can swim" and "want to go". On the other hand, they still encapsulate the same semantic content which we meet with lexically related adjectives and verbs. Thus language contains many adjectives and verbs, such as "strong", "powerful", "weak", "need", and "want", which are used nonmodally and without verbal complements, as in "need water" and "want an apple". These are pregnant with the possibility of verbal complementation, but do not require it, unless to avoid ambiguity. The person whose strength is in running may not be strong in weight-lifting, and vice versa, just as some are mighty with the sword and others mighty with the pen. We can gloss "need water" as "need to have water" and "want an apple" as "want to have an apple"; and strength and power are always in respect of some activity or range of activities. Here expressions with a lexical use in their own right, such as "strong "(or "mighty") and "want", come to take on a synlexical use in connection with another verb kernel in which they still retain some or even the whole of their original lexical content.

24. Bresnan, "Control and Complementation", in *Mental Representation*, ed. Bresnan, 282–390, see 302–3; Van Valin, "Synopsis of Role and Reference Grammar", 19. Van Valin and LaPolla, *Syntax*, 52–53, 69, acknowledge the distinction, recognizing nonpredicative adpositions as only marking how certain arguments are linked to the verb in its semantic representation. Halliday also recognizes the structural function of "of", in *Introduction to Functional Grammar*, 2nd ed. (London: Arnold, 1994), 213.

However, the phenomenon of synlexical expressions possessing content, but a content which they could not exercise on their own, arises often with parts of speech other than verbs, conspicuously with words such as "down" and "back" used as adverbs rather than as prepositions, as well as with the prepositions considered earlier.

Here the preposition "in" is of particular interest in philosophical history, comparable to what arises with the verbs "have" and "make". With the latter, uses developed in which nothing was preserved of the original content except the connotation of there being something positive about what is had or made. Thus, in the perfective auxiliary use of "have", what has been done is considered under the aspect of an achievement, and when we speak of "having wisdom" we imply that wisdom is some kind of asset rather than a privation or the absence of something. This can be put beside the long tradition of speaking of attributes, not just as things which are had, but as things "in" or "present in" their subjects, as when saying that changes are in the things that change, not in the causes of these changes.

With the semantically synlexical, constitutive uses of verbs such as "make" and "give", we meet the two most general of the verbs concerned, as in "make statements" and "give orders", where the grammatical (morphosyntactic) objects, "statements" and "orders", are what I called "cognates" in chapter XII. Here, beyond their positive, nonprivative connotation, these verbs have lost their original lexical content, just as happens with adpositions such as "of", "to", and "for" when used in a purely structural way.

The copula and these constitutive verbs exhibit how the essential feature of the verb is to embody the *chi* involved the sentence's being a live linguistic communication. Lexical verbs take on this same role, and this role is associated not just with the finite verb, but the whole finite verb complex, whether it comprises a single verb kernel or, in the case of semi-auxiliaries, two verb kernels.

The "is" of identity has a purely structural function and is empty of semantic content, even though it then has a different structural function from the copula. Verbs used copulatively, and the verb "to be" as expressing identity or existence, are the only verbs which never have any semantic content in the synchronic use of language, whatever the etymology of the particular form in which they appear in a language,[25] although, at the level of discourse-

25. "Will", "shall", and "may" originally expressed respectively desire, owing something or being under necessity, and natural ability or capacity. They are now used only as auxiliaries, but retain connotations from their earlier uses, respectively of intention, imposing necessity, and real possibility. The words "have" and "do" have original meanings in which they were not auxiliaries, but general words respectively for possession and for action, and although it is from these that their uses as forms of copula (and also to express obligation or necessity in the modal "to have to") arose, in these uses they retain no connotations from their origins.

The difference of sense or discourse-significance between the "is" of existence expressing that its gram-

significance or sense, the "is" of identity and the "is" of existence each has many different discourse-significances or senses, according to the different types of significance and implications arising where different kinds of entity are concerned.[26]

The case of determiners is complex.

If we define "determiner" as the kind of modifier which serves as a single-word identity or quantity indicator, it has come to be listed with the traditional "parts of speech", alongside nouns, adjectives/adverbs, verbs, and so forth. However, this is misleading as to how language works. Functionally and semantically, there is no deep distinction between "All the apostles deserted him", "All of the apostles deserted him", and "All [said in a context in which it is plain that the apostles are being spoken of] deserted him". It is the same lexeme "all" which is involved, whether as a modifier or as a pronoun.

Such lexemes control how predicates apply to their arguments. However, in some languages, the indefinite article serves solely as a noun phrase marker in attributive statements, serving to mark noun phrases in the way seen in "John is a wise man".

(v) The generation of what function as fresh head nouns from functional expressions

We are familiar with lexical nouns such as "bravery" and "destruction" lexically arising from adjectives and verbs. More notably, what function as nouns can also arise from functional expressions. The notion of being a lexical expression has been explained in terms of being "content-introducing" involving connection with some particular subject-matter. Where the content involves close connection with some particular concrete subject-matter, the meaning is clear. However, we can take functional expressions, and then by some kind of abstraction make them a subject-matter in their own right, and with the subject/predicate and verb/complements-to-verb, the same phrase structure arises with abstract as with subject-matters.

The fact that we have only three kinds of genuinely lexical heads is quite

---

matical subject is indeed a genuine subject (unlike "it" in "It is raining") and the "is" expressing substantial actuality or positive existence of some kind is a difference to be recognized through philosophical reflection, and not a lexical or *langue*-level difference.

26. Thus, as expressing identity, "is" has different senses according the criteria appropriate for judging the kind of identity being asserted. Thus one's answers will be different according to whether it is asked whether what confronts me is the same *person* as confronted me two years ago, or whether what confronts me is the same *collection of matter* as confronted me two years ago—or, in a different type of dilemma, whether it is asked whether in the respects relevant to physics a flash of lightning is a discharge of electrons, or whether a flash of lightning is the same visual phenomenon as a discharge of electrons. The case of existence requires more elaborate discussion such as I give at the end of my paper "Aquinas, God and Being", in David Braine, *Analytical Thomism: Traditions in Dialogue*, ed. Craig Paterson and Matthew S. Pugh (Aldershot, UK: Ashgate, 2006), 1–24.

compatible with the lexical nominalizations of functional expressions occurring as the lexical heads of noun phrases. Thus, consider "The kind of animal I saw was a rhinoceros—and the rhinoceros is one of the four surviving kinds of even toed ungulate". In the second clause, "kind" is the lexical head of the noun phrase "kinds of even toed ungulate" and "the rhinoceros" occurs as the singular name of a kind, not as a general term. "Eight" occurs as a functional quantity expression in "There are eight major planets" or "Eight major planets go round the Sun". By contrast, "number" is functionally a noun heading the subject phrase "the number of the major planets" in "The number of the major planets is eight"—since this is an identity statement, "eight" is here functionally a noun phrase.

"Eight" occurs adjectivally, expressing an attribute of a collection, in "The major planets are eight in number". The possibility of speaking of collections gives rise to the use of such adjectives as "many-fold", "multiple", "eightfold", "complete", and "incomplete", as in "The group was incomplete", signifying properties of collections, alongside "unique" signifying a property of an individual when this individual can be picked out by a property which nothing else shares, with the result that there is not a collection of things sharing this property. Thus, from functional expressions we can generate yet a further range of what are functionally nouns, such as "multiplicity", "incompleteness", and "uniqueness".

Quite different difficulties are raised by another range of cases.

Each functionally defined type of word group—for instance, quantity and direct identity indicators,[27] temporal indicators, spatial indicators, and so forth—is liable to allow the formation of complex expressions which involve newly formed nouns and adjectives. Nouns like "year" and "day" may come to be used both in expressions of quantity and in temporal indicators, and we can develop systems of nomenclature, so that instead of saying, "in the third year of King Alfred's reign", we can say, "in 874". However, it does not follow from the content-introducing lexical item within a word or word group's being a noun that the word group as a whole is nominal—the word groups "in the third year of King Alfred's reign" and "in 874" are not nominal in function as if candidates for being counted as arguments to a verb. Likewise, semantically, "man", "Athens", "lot", and "tons" are not arguments to a verb as they occur in "Socrates was a man", "He was in Athens", "He drank a lot of milk", and "Ten tons of rock fell upon him".

27. I label articles, demonstratives, and possessives "direct" identity indicators by contrast with ones which depend on relative clauses (the indirect identity indicators in chap. IX of this volume).

(vi) The types of argument of verbs—the situation of adverbs

The semantic structures I have sketched have large implications for syntax, as we shall discover. However, one of these calls for special attention.

From "Gurth reported that Harold had defeated Hardrada", we can form, "That Harold had defeated Hardrada was reported by Gurth". In this way we find that there can be clausal arguments to verbs, in the first example as a specificatory complement to a verb and in the second example as a subject argument.[28]

However, after you have told me that the king is dead, that the council is in session, and that William is advancing on London, I may say, "You told me three things: that the king is dead, that the council is in session, and that William is advancing on London". Yet we cannot treat these clausal arguments to the verb as themselves sentences. "That the king is dead, that the council is in session, and that William is advancing on London" is not a sentence, and none of its three components taken separately is a sentence. As we insisted in chapter IX, reporting facts is not a form of naming or identifying.

Yet the capacity to form clausal arguments to verbs from sentences is essential to our capacity to reflect on what we or others say or think—for instance, to inquire whether what we are told or how many of the things we have been told are true.

And, although saying or reporting a fact it is not identifying or listing an item, nonetheless, whenever we say something, we say it with an awareness of the possibility of its being counted as an item which could be listed as something said or told. Thus we could say, "The king is dead and, something else, William is advancing on London".

This awareness reveals itself not only in our treatment of whole clauses, but also in the treatment of verb phrases and verbs which may be constitutive of their verbal character, and of the adverbial expressions which modify such verbs. Thus we must contrast the case of attributive expressions such as can be complements to the verb "to be" with that of adverbs. If we ask, "Was he brave and courteous?" the reply may be, "He was both"; and if we ask, "Was he brave, courteous, and skilled?" we may be told, "He was all three", and we may put "all three" in apposition with the attribute expressions, saying, "He was all three, brave, courteous, and skilled".

By contrast, if we ask, "Did he fight bravely, skillfully, and with good weapons?", we may accept the reply, "In all three ways", but not the reply,

28. Some verbal constructions can take clausal arguments as subjects, but not as specificatory complements. Thus, "That combustion involved the giving off of phlogiston was refuted by Lavoisier" and "Lavoisier refuted the theory that combustion the giving off of phlogiston" are grammatical, but "Lavoisier refuted that combustion involved the giving off of phlogiston" is not; cf. Bresnan, *Lexical-Functional Syntax*, 17.

"He fought all three". Even "He fought all three, bravely, skillfully, and with good weapons" is unacceptable. We have to understand the reply "In all three ways" by reference to the complete statements we are agreeing with. We have the questions "Did he fight bravely?", "Did he fight skillfully?", and "Did he fight with good weapons?" And it is to these, asked serially, that we reply, "All three", as if saying, "Yes, yes, yes", to the successive questions. We can count the applications of adverbs only by counting the whole statements concerned, because the adverbs belong to the verb "phrases" which do the "saying" in these statements.

Section 2. Auxiliaries, Semi-auxiliaries, and Adverbial Modifiers

(a) *Classifying verbs and distinguishing auxiliaries from semi-auxiliaries*

Finite verbs in the indicative mood in English can be set in seven groups:

1. We have the simple present and past of any content-introducing verb.
2. We have the auxiliaries indicating aspect: "to be" with the present participle indicating continuous action, "to have" (and in archaic idioms "to be") with the past participle indicating perfected action, and "to be about to" with the infinitive or "to be on the point/brink/verge of" with the gerund indicating imminent action.
3. We have the auxiliary "to do" with solely emphatic or morphosyntactic roles—morphosyntactic to preserve such rules as that an auxiliary should precede "not" in negations and negative imperatives, and that an auxiliary should come first whenever subject and verb are inverted, rules only established in normal modern English since the 1500s.
4. We have the auxiliary "to be", together with the past participle, to indicate the passive.
5. We have "will" and "shall" in order to indicate the future, even when they fulfill some other function reflecting obligation, likelihood, or intention at the same time.
6. We have the modal, causative, propensity, and psychological verbs, which I group together as semi-auxiliaries and which I consider in section 2 (c).
7. We have the seemingly paradoxical cases of the constitutive verbs "make" and "have"—that is, transitive verbs used synlexically, as in speaking of having attributes or making statements.

(i) Lexical verbs taking on synlexical functions

In many languages a modal, causative, propensity, or psychological sense becomes inseparable from the expression of tense or voice. In such a case the auxiliary and the terminal verb become inseparable in respect of variation of tense and, as we shall see later, not capable of being separately negated. We can observe this in the behavior of the English auxiliaries "shall" and "will", "should" and "would", and with some complexes which behave as auxiliaries, "is to" and "had to".

The phenomenon of voice introduces other examples. Our notion of voice is excessively influenced by morphosyntactics, whereas to understand the spread of variation within languages, even among those most familiar to us, we need a more functional perspective. Thus it appears that when transitive verbs are used with a reflexive, it is often better to regard what is taking place as the formation of a middle-voice form of the verb, rather than simply the taking of the actor as also the object of the action. We could think of the causative "I moved it" (with the sense "I made it move")—the intransitive "I move" having a kind of anti-causative character somewhat analogous to the anti-passive in ergative languages. This represents a plausible view of the emergence of the intransitive use of *moveor* (= I move; infinitive *moveri*) in Latin.[29]

The question of how far we think of the causative auxiliary "make" as having a distinct content of its own rather than serving a purely structural grammatical function is perhaps analogous to the question of how far we think of the auxiliaries "shall" and "will" (especially in the forms "should" and "would") as having a distinct content of their own beyond indicating future time.

(ii) Synnuclear auxiliaries opposed to modals and other semi-auxiliaries: the importance of scope

The distinction between the auxiliary verbs "be", "have", "do", "will", and "shall", which I count as "synnuclear auxiliaries", and the verbs which, following Grevisse, I group as "semi-auxiliaries", is important when we consider verb complexes which arise with a reduplication of auxiliaries and/or semi-auxiliaries, such as "can swim", "make … go", "can go swimming", "want … to go", "will have been swimming", and "will have been being built". In the case of synnuclear auxiliaries, the auxiliary and the participle or infinitive which introduces the content of the verb form a unity so intimate that adverbs of negation apply to the combination concerned in only one way—namely, as

29. Such phenomena are particularly apparent in Marianne Mithun, *The Languages of Native North America* (Cambridge: Cambridge University Press, 1999), as reviewed by Andrej A. Kibrik in *Linguistic Typology* 6 (2002): 117–21; see also Jane Grimshaw, "On the Lexical Representation of Romance Reflexive Clitics", in *Mental Representation*, ed. Bresnan, 87–148.

semantically adjoined to the whole[30]—except when the "hiatus effect" arises with the negation of passives such as "be built" and "be educated". By contrast, in the case of every verb construction from within the four groups of semi-auxiliary which I mentioned, one can mark parsing divisions like those we can make in such cases as "can/swim", "is able/to swim", "it is possible/for him to swim", and "it is possible/that he swim". With these latter formations, there is free positioning of adverbial modifiers only so far as it is clear which side of the divide the modifier attaches to semantically, except that unitary noun, adjective, and adverb phrases should not be broken. If more than one adverbial modifier is present on either side of the divide, problems arise which I consider separately.

Accordingly, in the cases in which the verb complex constitutes a semantic unity in respect of negation, I follow Grevisse in referring to the verb structures concerned—for instance, "will have been swimming" and "will have been being built"—as "verb kernels". I contrast these with cases where the verb structure concerned can be divided in respect of what is negated. In these latter cases I will speak of a "single verb complex", but of its being constituted of "more than one verb kernel".

This brings us to consider the scope of negation.

Whenever a verb kernel is "governed by negation" (has negation as an adverbial modifier), any other modifier to the same governing verb kernel is determinately either inside the scope of this negative or else outside it. I say this with one reservation: that when auxiliaries and semi-auxiliaries are many-tiered, as in "might be going to win" and "will have been building", it makes no difference to the truth-conditions or grammaticality of the resulting sentence where the "not" is placed. That is, with the empty "do" or the auxiliaries of time or aspect, it is arbitrary after which purely synnuclear auxiliary the "not" is placed. In gen-

30. The contrast between perfect and continuous aspects presents no parallel. Thus one can achieve nothing by changing the parsing of (1) "have not built", e.g., from "have-not built", where a logician might try "(not (have (built)))", to "have not-built", the logician's "(have (not (built)))"; and equally nothing by changing the parsing of (2) "was not walking" from "was-not walking", the logician's "(not (was (walking)))", to "was not-walking", the logician's "(was (not (walking)))". In these two constructions the auxiliary and the content-introducing parts of the verb present each only one verbally expressible condition.

In sum, in these two constructions, the perfect with "have" and the continuous with "be", adverbs of negation are necessarily adjuncts of the auxiliary, and thereby negators of the whole predication, including any subject phrase and application controller, and there is no way of situating them in such a way as to have the effect of making them adjuncts of the subordinate verb only. Likewise, adverbs of negation are adjuncts of the auxiliary when the role of the auxiliary is solely to provide emphasis or set a different grammatical structure ("do" in English) or when time (past, present, or future) is marked by the auxiliary and nowhere else ("will" and "shall" in English, even when they carry additional connotations).

With "will" and "shall", it may be difficult to separate an expression of will from mere prediction. It is usually paradoxical to say, "I shall not do it" and deny "I won't do it", although one can understand, "I shall not do it" said when a task is obviously outside my powers, and the denial of "I won't do it" in such a case because my willingness is irrelevant. "He will not do it" is commonly said simply predictively, but "He won't do it" commonly implies that he would refuse to do it. To disambiguate such cases, one requires elaborate paraphrases. One can still never separate a negative from an auxiliary.

eral negative particles are inseparable from the most incomplete element of a verbal expression to which they apply, so that, for instance, where "did not…" or "had not…" occur, it is as if we had "not (did…)" and "not (had…)". Such customs as writing "cannot" as one word, and forming parallel compounds "can't", "couldn't", "mayn't", "needn't", "haven't", "hadn't", "won't", "shan't", "don't", "didn't", and so forth are symptoms of this inseparability.

Despite their complexity, I would group the complex forms "be about to", "be on the point of", and their equivalents which involve the simple verb "be" used as the copula and some complement formed of a prepositional expression together with the infinitive or gerund and the synnuclear auxiliaries "be", "have", "will" and "shall", and "do". (Comparably, I would group the complex "is able to" with "can"; "able not to go" has the same peculiarity as "can not go". When expressions in which there is a pause between the "able" or the "can" and the "not" replace the normal "not able to go" and "cannot go" signifying inability, what is expressed is not an inability but our belief in free will or an expression of permission).

That is, I think that Grevisse is wrong to regard the auxiliary French *être pour*, along with its English equivalents "is about to A", "is on the point of A", and so forth, as a "semi-auxiliary". On his analysis the auxiliary concerned presents two distinguishable verbally expressed conditions—namely, being in the state of being immediate in time before doing something or other, and the act or activity of doing A. In this case negation occurs in two ways, one as modifying the finite verb, in which case it is indeed inseparable from it in giving the saying its thrust—for instance, in "was not about to eat", and the other as modifying the content-introducing verb—for instance, in "was about not to eat" (as in a demonstration fast when invited to sit next to the president at some celebration one disapproved of). But that this is an anomalous and surprise turn within speech is shown by the pause or hiatus between the "was about" and the "not to eat". It is analogous to the case of introducing a pause before the "not" in "be not educated" discussed earlier.

I consider the auxiliary "is going to A" differently, despite its syntactic similarity, because the state "be going to" cannot be understood in terms of relation to time alone, but includes the notion of propensity or tendency, and so has some semantic content. That is, I group the distinction between "is not going to A" (compare "is not determined to A") and "is going to not A" (compare "is determined not to A") with the distinction between "is not able to A" and "is able not to A".

The difference between auxiliaries marking aspect or tense which lack semantic content and semi-auxiliaries is strikingly brought out by the extra differences between them which appear when we consider the behavior of "not"—for instance, in its relation to quantifiers.

The intrusion of a quantity expression such as "often" between "has" and "not" in "has not kissed" in no way compromises the semantic unity of "has" and "kissed" or the immediacy with which "not" governs the combination. "Often" introduces a generalization about times, being equivalent to "on many occasions" or "at many times". An alteration of the order of the "not" and the "often" affects the scope of "often", but not of "not", scope being conveniently indicated by the brackets of the logician. Thus (a) "John has not often kissed Jemima" means "Of John, it is not the case that (he has kissed Jemima at *t* in respect of many times, *t*)", whereas (b) "John has often not kissed Jemima" means "Of John, in respect of many times, *t*, it is not the case that (he has kissed Jemima at *t*)".

"Often" is here displaying what is characteristic of quantity expressions—namely, that it is significant whether they have wider scope than a negative or whether it is the negative which has the wider scope, and that which has the wider scope can be marked by their order when they both intrude between an auxiliary and the nuclear part of the verb. Thus we can contrast (1) "They are not all of them swimming" with (2) "They are, all of them, not swimming". These mean, respectively, where R is the group whose existence is presupposed and about whom generalization is made, that is, the "range" of the quantifier concerned, that: (1) "(Re: the class of R's) (It is not the case that (in respect of every person, *x*, in R (*x* is swimming)))"; and (2) "(Re: the class of Rs) (in respect of every person, *x*, in R (it is not the case that (*x* is swimming)))".

(iii) Four kinds of semi-auxiliary: some complexities of construction

Verb complexes often have semantically equivalent extended verb complexes. Thus the finite verbs "dream", "strike", "attack", and "murder" have the same functional relation to their object complements as such extended semantically equivalent verb complexes as "dreamt a dream that"; "had a dream that", "strike a blow upon", "make an attack on", and "commit the crime of the murder of". The possibility of such complex semantic equivalents is of special importance with modal and other semi-auxiliaries, where, for instance, "He is able to walk" and "It is possible for him to walk" are parallel to "He can walk".

We can now describe the four groups of semi-auxiliary more precisely. These are verbs which share the property of being able to govern another verb so that one has two distinct verb kernels introducing semantic content, making it worth grouping them together with modals.

First, there are what English works of grammar call modal auxiliaries[31] (as

31. The grammatical use of the word "modal" seems to have arisen by extensions of its uses in logic. In both French and English the original grammatical connotation of "mode" or "mood" was that of a "way" of

we have seen, it is wrong to list "will" and "shall" under this heading), of which in English the chief are "can", "may", "must", "have to", "ought to", "is to", and "need to".[32] These, together with certain particular uses of "will" and "shall", play a varied mix of roles in expressing capacity, knowledge, obligation, and will, or their absence. They should be grouped with forms of assertion whereby intention, command, obligation, request, and desire are expressed by verbal idioms discrete from the verb kernels which complement them, such as "I promise ...", "I guarantee ...", "I order ...", "I request ...", "I have the obligation to ...", "I wish ...", "Would that ..."—together with all the expressions, simple or complex, of possibility, necessity, and impossibility—that is, modality in the philosophers' sense. Complex forms include "*x* is able to ...", "It is possible/easy/difficult for *x* to ...", "It is permissible/lawful/right/obligatory/necessary for *x* to ...", and "It is possible/likely/probable/certain/necessary that ...". In the case of the simple verbs "can", "must", "have", "ought", and "need", when I include "to" in the specification of the verb, it is only to indicate that the "to" form of the infinitive is required in the current state of English idiom,[33] and I do this for the same reason in the case of "be able to" and the propensity and psychological verbs listed under "third" and "fourth".

Second, we have the so-called causative verbs, such as "make", "let", "force", "have", "get", "put", "turn", and "take", which we tend to use in up to three specialized ways: causatively (e.g., "force him to confess", "made him climb the tree", "had him serve the tea", "got him to prune the trees"), permissively (e.g., "let him play in the garden"), and passively (e.g., "had my luggage sent to the wrong airport", "got my hand trapped in the machine"). "Make" and "let" as introducing imperatives exhibit the causative form of all imperatives. Semantically, for something "to force Y to A" is for it "to make it impossible for Y not to A". There are also causative verbs of a kind we might call "preventative", such as "prevent" and "stop".

Third, we have verbs expressing propensity toward some activity: "go"

using the verb, e.g., indicative, imperative, and subjunctive in the case of the finite verb, and infinitive, participle, and gerund for the nonfinite, with variations in different languages (any connection with mood as a form of emotion is sheer coincidence). The name "modal" auxiliary may have arisen by extending the idea of different "ways" of saying something—and then infected logic so that "possible" and even "impossible" are "modal" operators.

32. The *Shorter OED* traces "have to" to an Anglo-Saxon use of "have" meaning "possess" in the case of a duty, the duty being specified by the "to"-infinitive; it is not, therefore, an example of the ME substitution of the auxiliary "have" for the auxiliary "be". "Ought" is a Germanic fixed past tense form of "owe", etymologically unrelated to "have"—the Latin *debeo*, "I owe" has an independent origin, coming from *habeo*, "I have" (owing is a way of not having). To these, I add "is to", treated as a single lexical unit with a modal meaning, arising from the use of the verb "to be" with the preposition "to" used in a purposive meaning introducing a purposive complement, discussed in sec. 4 (d) of this volume.

33. With "need", when there is inversion ("Need we go?") or after "not" ("We need not go"), the "to" is omitted. The "to", when it occurs, is prepositional, and cannot be replaced by "in order to" in any of the constructions mentioned.

and "come", as in "go swimming" and "came visiting", along with the important "be going to", "tend to", and "be liable to".

Fourth, we have such psychological verbs as "dare to",[34] "want to", "be willing to", "be sorry to", "love to", "hate to", "fear to" (= be afraid to), "hope to", "expect to", and "know how to", sharing many of the constructions of "be able to" and "ought to", which seem undisputedly modal in character. "Be capable of" and "despair of" appear to be of the same category, the gerund which follows them having a character similar to a French infinitive.[35]

The question arises as to structure of such statements as, "Dogs can swim", "Dogs are able to swim", "It is possible for dogs to swim", "It is permitted to dogs to swim", "I permit dogs to swim in the lake", "I order you to swim", "I made you swim", "I do not want to be killed by him", and "I do not want him to kill me". The answer is that they have structures which one could represent as follows: "(Nom.) can swim [dogs]"; "(Nom.) are able to swim [dogs]"; "It is possible for (Acc.) to swim [dogs]"; "It is permitted to (Acc.) swim [dogs]"; "(Nom.) permit (Acc.) to swim ('in' Place) [I, dogs, in the lake]"; "(Nom.) order (Acc.) to swim [I, thee]"; "(Nom.) made (Acc.) swim [I, thee]"; "(Nom.) do not want (redundant Acc. reflexive) to be killed (by Agent) [I, me, by you]"; and "(Nom.) do not want (Acc.) to kill (Acc. reflexive) [I, him, me]". In these representations the expressions "(Nom.)", "(Acc.)", and "('in' Place)" indicate how the argument places within the framework set by the verb complex are to be filled. "(Nom.)" signifies a noun expression for the subject, "(Acc.)" an expression for the direct object, and "('in' Place)" indicates the preposition required to link the relevant noun expression into the framework concerned, while the contents of the square brackets list how the respective argument places are to be filled.

The advantage of syntactically more complex forms of expression in all these cases arises chiefly from their extending the range of tenses in which

34. Sometimes this has been grouped with modal verbs because it is often used with the simple infinitive without "to" as in "Dare you go?" or "no man after that durst ask him any question" (Mark 12:34, KJV).

35. I note that French gerunds (called *gerondifs*) have become scarcely distinct from participles. The French gerund proper had a history of continuous use deriving from the ablative of the late Latin gerund, all conjugations reduced to the form *-ando*, and by 1600 to the form *-ant*. Since 1700 it has been used only with prepositions, including *a*, *de*, *par*, *sans*, and *en*, and since 1900 only with *en*; after 1800, determiners (e.g., articles) ceased to be used; Grevisse, *Le Bon Usage*, 1174, 1314. The vestigial use with *en*, "En courant, Philippe ..." is commonly reinterpreted as meaning "while (he was) running, Philip ..." and some grammars now speak of it as a use of the participle; see R. Hawkins and R. Towell, *French Grammar and Usage* (London: Arnold, 1996), 402. Thus in French the so-called gerunds are no longer qualifiable by articles, quantifiers, or plurals, or susceptible of being modified, and so have lost their character as noun expressions, and so cannot be used in the same way as English gerunds (exemplified in "the making of dining room chairs in the workshop"). But English and French both have many nouns serving the same nominal purpose as the gerund: "destruction", "transport", "purchase", and "sale", "gift" and "seizure", "imprisonment" and "enslavement", "conquest" and "rescue". But French has nothing which bestraddles the functions of verbal noun, infinitive, and participle in the way we meet with the English "-ing" formation, where we speak of "his destroying of the city", of "his destroying the city", and of "him destroying the city".

each of the two verb kernels involved may be expressed, sometimes yielding a greater capacity to remove ambiguity. Where we have a more complex form of expression in any of the groups of semi-auxiliary distinguished later, we also have the possibility of what may be thought of as alternative grammatical analyses, not incompatible, but differing in the depth of the analysis proposed.[36]

We also need to represent the underlying structure which remains when a simple expression requires a syntactically complex paraphrase, even in the most "literal" translation. In the present connection it is plainly enlightening to consider "swim" as the verbal complement of "I was able (to)" in "I was able to swim", and "try Mont Blanc" as the verbal complement of "I had been willing (to)" in "For years I had been willing to try Mont Blanc". Treating "able" and "willing" simply as adjectives suggests a more superficial treatment of "able to swim" and "willing to try Mont Blanc" merely as attributes (according to the structure: subject, copula, attribute), failing to recognize the character of "able" and "willing" as parts of semi-auxiliary constructions. Many semi-auxiliary constructions are formed from the copula and an adjective (such as "able" or "willing") followed by some connective (in these cases, the connective "to") linking their respective complements to them. Where the adjective behaves like "possible", the two connectives in the clausal formative "for ... to ///" are appropriate to their respective complements unless epistemic possibility is concerned, as discussed in section 5 (b).

(iv) Two kinds of verbal complement to semi-auxiliaries: sortal and non-sortal

At this point we need to distinguish between two kinds of verbal complement, of the four types of verb (modal, quasi-causative, propensity, and psychological) listed earlier, one "clausal or predicational" and the other "verbally sortal". At this stage I shall explain this distinction only as it works out in respect of real and practical possibility (as opposed to epistemic possibility). I leave questions as to how this distinction arises with other constructions to section 4 (c).

Suppose that on February 20, 2001, one says, "John can get to New Zealand before the end of February 2001". One is generalizing over a definite spread of times—namely, those later than the time of speaking and earlier than the end of February 2001, and what one says can be symbolized, "(Re: John) (it is possible for John that: at some time *t* in the period P, John will arrive in New Zealand at *t*)". I put "(Re: John)" to signify that the existence of John is presupposed; that is, it is a condition both of the truth of the original

36. Further, we need to allow the legitimacy of such double analyses in order to understand the grammar of sentences in which the syntax of what is quoted is integrated with the syntax of the rest of the sentence, as well as to handle the idioms and fixed expressions treated by Jackendoff, *Architecture*, chap. 7.

statement and of its negation (the statement obtained by substituting "cannot" for "can" and "not possible" for "possible"). This possibility is one realized in the event that it turns out that "at some time *t* in the period P, John will arrive in New Zealand at *t*".

Statements of the kind beginning "It is possible for John to …" have a structure involving a complete embedded clause, but the same possibility, just as determinate in its conditions of fulfillment, can also be expressed by idioms of the type "John can get to New Zealand before the end of February 2001" and "John is able to get to New Zealand before the end of February 2001". "It is possible for John to" can be completed predicationally by "get to New Zealand before the end of February 2001"—and understanding what is being said in this way corresponds most closely with the formulations using the expressions "is able to" and "can". However, "for John to get to New Zealand before the end of February 2001" can be thought of as an infinitival clause, so that "It is possible for John to get to New Zealand before the end of February 2001" can be reformulated "It is possible for John that he should get to New Zealand before the end of February 2001"—a formulation in which "It is possible for John" is completed by a finite clause preceded by the clause-marker "that". These are what I refer to as predicational or clausal complements.

By contrast, suppose that one says, "John can swim" or "It is possible for John to swim". One is reporting here a general ability which John has, specified in regard to the *sort* of thing which John is able to do or capable of, but not in regard to any determinate instances in which that ability would be applied. These statements will not be shown to be false if the reason for John's not swimming at a particular time is that there is no readily accessible place with water of appropriate temperature, depth, and situation (e.g., it is not in the middle of a nudist camp or in a firing range), or that John does not want to swim, but to continue an argument, or that John is ill, or that nobody else wants to join him. Normally the evidence for the truth of such statements is some experience of John's past exercise of the ability, and its truth is independent of whether it is ever again actualized, even though it is his present and not his past ability which is being asserted. In the case of such statements there is no double position for temporal qualification: in both cases there may be a capacity at one time which is lost at a later time (in the clausal or predicational cases the possibility will be lost at the end of February 2001, and in the sortal cases the ability may be lost through irreversible trauma, the infirmity of age, or death). Assertions of sortal possibility can be highly complex—for instance, "It is possible for large organic cancers to be remitted very quickly without this having any natural explanation or any historical link with any religion providing hope of miracles". This latter "sortal" possibility is quasi-clausal, inasmuch as it is in relation to a very general sort of situation, rather than "predicational", since it is not predicated of a particular subject in the way that the ability to swim was predicated of John ("quasi-predicational" because the ability is only in respect of a sort of activity, rather than defined in respect of a determinate fulfillment).

They are not properly predicational or clausal in that they do not specify what has to become true in order to be themselves true, so that their complement is not a full clause or predicate. They leave open the range of conditions in which they would be false.

(b) *Classifying expressions modifying the verb (adverbials) and their levels of application*

I discussed the working of negation in modifying predicates in chapter IX. The level at which particular verb modifiers apply within verbal complexes is semantically determined.

I group nonconditional adverbial subordinate clauses into seven kinds, according to whether they express (1) an aspect of the background situation, typically introduced by "as" (used when a condition expressed by "if" has been fulfilled), by the pseudo-locative expressions "in the situation that", or by "granted that" (meaning "it being granted", involving an absolute use of the participle "granted"); (2) causes, typically introduced by the conjunction "because"; (3) results, typically introduced by "so" in the meaning "with the consequence that"; (4) means, typically introduced, for instance, by "by securing that"; (5) ends, typically introduced by "in order that"; (6) temporal clauses, introduced by "before" or "after", or by "when" or "while"; and (7) spatial clauses, introduced by "where". The types of thing which can be expressed by clauses are sometimes indicated by adpositional phrases. When ergative, instrumental, and motivational adpositional phrases are peripheral, not complementary, in relation to the meaning of the verb in the functional perspective set within the context, they can be considered as having the same roles as clauses of kinds 2, 4, and 5, respectively. Thus "gave his life for the cause" should be compared to "gave his life in order to further the cause", whereas "giving" commonly has the sense of effecting the transfer of something from one person to another, so that this "giving" which is for an end has a different sense.

The basis of this sevenfold classification is semantic or logical. My remarks impinge upon grammar or morphosyntactics only so far as they relate to word order and inflection, using English as a source of examples, and to certain of the problems of language learning.

We need to consider the scope of adverbial expressions.

Adverbial clauses and phrases indicating place[37] and adverbial phrases

37. The difference between adverbial indications of place and those of time is made very clear by Geach, "Some Problems about Time", in *Logic Matters*, 312, 314–16.

indicating speed, physical or cognitive aptitude, emotion, or display of these (e.g., “slowly”, “wisely”, “clumsily”, “strongly”, “keenly”, “relaxedly”, “exuberantly”, “flamboyantly”, “extravagantly”) are modificatory of the verb kernel only in virtue of being descriptive of or specifying the attributes of the action or state reported by the terminal verb concerned, and never qualify modal verbs. By contrast, adverbial phrases indicating ease or difficulty are alone in this group in being, like adverbs of degree, able to modify semi-auxiliaries, although normally modifying such terminal verbs.

Some adverbs modify a whole predicate or verb phrase, including indications of motivation (there are times when it takes bravery to kiss someone and other times bravery not to kiss someone), and adverbial expressions descriptive of the action of the verb only in respect of its manner. The former tend to precede the whole verb expression. By contrast, adverbs of manner, such as “clumsily”, “strongly”, “forcefully”, and “flamboyantly”, refer to style of performance or manner of approach, not motivation, and normally come after the verb, as in “Kiss her flamboyantly” or “Do not kiss her flamboyantly”.

Adverbs expressing ease or difficulty and adverbs of degree affect a whole verb phrase and need to be distinguished from adverbs of a more narrowly descriptive type. For instance, the adverb “easily” in its literal sense refers to the manner of the action only in the sense of referring to what affects its modality. This sense is seen in “can easily swim”, “is easily able to swim”, and “is able easily to swim”. Here “easily” has the meaning of “without difficulty”—not the special idiomatic meaning of “relaxedly” (= at ease), which is an adverb of manner of the same kind as “flamboyantly” and “slowly”.

Simple content-introducing adjectives and adverbs tend to be differentiated only morphologically, as by the suffix “-ly” in English or “*-ment*” in French and by the fact that adverbs lack the inflections for gender, case, and number found among adjectives. This “-ly” and such prepositions and case markings are all alike further examples of connective structurizing features—just as, when adjectives modify nouns, their case, gender, and number markings (in languages that have such markings) likewise serve as connective structurizers, linking them with their nouns. According to our metaphor, this allows the *chi* to flow from the verb or noun to the outlying semantic element concerned.

Quite different from the adverbs just considered, there is, last, the group called “adverbs of degree”, such as “very” and “too”, along with “much”, “more”, “most”, and “enough” in their adverbial uses. These are applicable to merely descriptive adverbs of manner; adverbs of place; adverbs in respect of motivation, belief, or knowledge; and adverbs such as “easily”, which can modify both semi-auxiliaries and their equivalents. Adverbs of degree apply to all the adjectives corresponding to the different classes of adverb just listed—for instance, the adjectives “flamboyant”, “brave”, and “easy”. They also apply to present participles used as adjectives, such as "knowing", and in some cases to themselves, as in "very very", "much too", "ten times too", and "quite enough". Since they have the same grammatical relationship to the adverbs and adjectives they modify as quantity and identity determiners have to nouns, they should be counted grammatically as quantity and identity indicators in all three cases. Adjectives may have the same form as the corresponding adverbs, as with "fast", "hard", and "misplaced", as happens also with such quantity and identity indicators as "enough" and "much".

Section 3. Complements and Adjuncts, and the Character of Adpositions

(a) *Preliminary clarifications*

(i) The complements and adjuncts of phrases with lexical heads

I begin by considering the complements and adjuncts of phrases with nouns, adjectives, or adverbs as heads.

Complements of such phrases always serve a specificatory or identificatory role, "of" being the default preposition used to link the complement to its head in English. I call all pronouns, nouns, and noun phrases serving as complements, whether introduced by a structural adposition such as "of" or marked by inflections (typically, genitive case endings), "functionally genitive phrases".

When the complement/head relation arises out of a verbal nexus, the complement may be linked to the head by other adpositions than "of". Thus, out of a verbal nexus expressed in the form "he feared for . . .", there arise expressions such as "he feared for himself", "he was afraid for the future of tigers", and "his fear for the future". In the case of nouns or adjectives rooted in a verbal nexus, arising not from a physical or social, but a "verb-rooted" lexical relationship, the meaning of the noun or adjective being rooted in a verb, their complements should be considered primarily as functionally complementing the verb concerned rather than the noun, behaving semantically as complements to a verb, although morphosyntactically as complements to a noun or adjective.

By contrast, there are complements of nouns which are not thus "verb-rooted". These need not be identifiable, even from the whole discourse context. Thus I might say, "I saw a king", without my knowing or its being specified or understood what this king was king of. Nonetheless, "king" is a relational term, and a king has to be king of something (typically a kingdom or people), and this is a part of the semantics or "lexical meaning" of the word "king". Hence, instead of merely saying, "I saw a king", I may say, "I saw the king of England" or "The Ambassador was accredited to James of England". Here the "of England" is a complement to the head "king" in the phrase "king of England"—and thereby also of James, spoken of in his capacity as king. (By contrast, the "of a big nose" is merely adjunctive in the descriptions "king of a big nose" and "man of the big nose", because noses are not terms of the relation of kingship, and "man" is not a relational term.)

There are many rules applying to the complements of nouns, adjectives, and adverbs which do not apply uniformly to complements of verbs. One of these is the rule that a complement and that to which it is complement should be immediate to each other without any semantically content-introducing expression between them. In complements of nouns and adjectives rooted in a verbal nexus ("his fear of tigers" and "he is afraid of tigers"), no other content-introducing elements can intervene between the head term and its complements. With complements of verbs such rules only arise in special cases.

Thus if complements to nouns are linked to them by prepositions, the prepositional phrase has to come immediately after the noun it complements, as in "teacher of French" or "student of Physics".[38] Or, when prepositionless noun phrases serve as complements, again nothing intrudes between them and their head—as when "the magnificence of the ceremony" and "the teacher of John" become "the ceremony's magnificence" and "John's teacher". However, with prepositionless, uninflected noun phrases in this modificatory role, we are relying upon a kind of dry stone masonry, and the result is liable to be more ambiguous than if prepositions or case-markings are relied upon. Thus "a proportional representation campaign" might mean "a campaign for proportional representation" or "a campaign against proportional representation", and "an Aberdeen Oxford student" mean "a student from Oxford at Aberdeen University" or "a student at Oxford University from Aberdeen".[39]

(ii) A limited descriptive use of X-Bar theory

We are now in a position to state the general structure of noun, adjective, and adverb phrases. Because of the intimacy of such complements with their

38. An apparent exception to this occurs when an adjective is placed after the noun because of some special sense, making it form a unity with the noun. Prince Charles is "heir apparent", not an "apparent heir". Here "to the throne of England" is complement both to "heir" and to "heir apparent", and " England" is complement to "throne of".

39. I have italicized the noun phrase in the sentence "*A tall long-haired student of physics from London who had his two bags carried for him by a porter* got on the train". Within this noun phrase, "of physics" is complement to the head of the noun phrase ("student"), related to it more intimately than its other modifiers. Although we could substitute "physics student" for "student of physics", relying on English dry stone masonry (some other languages might distinguish the phrases by using an adjective in the first case and a genitive in the second), we could not intrude any of the other modifiers between "student" and "physics"—whereas other premodifiers, as well as the prepositional phrase postmodifiers, are order-indifferent.

heads, the head term and its complement taken together can be thought of as a core to which other modifiers may be added successively, either as grammatically external adjuncts or as nonlexical identity or quantity indicators. Thus in noun, adjective, and adverb phrases alike, when identity or quantity indicators are applied, these indicators are applied externally to a core, the core consisting of either (a) a noun, adjective, or adverb; (b) in the case of a noun or adjective, this with a complement, the two taken together forming an expanded core within any more extended phrase; (c) this noun or adjective with or without complement, but with one or more successively applied adjuncts, the addition of each adjunct forming a newly expanded core, each adjunct applied to whatever core is already established; or (d) the result of all this modified by identity or quantity indicators, used in one of the two ways distinguished in section 1 (a) (i). In some cases we find the baroque complexity there mentioned, in each case such indicators applying to an already established core, as in "very very much too many chilies" or "very very much too slow". In "very very much too slow", the first "very" modifies the second, "very very" modifies "much", "very very much" modifies "too", and "very very much too" modifies "slow".

This structure has become customarily described in terms of what is called X-Bar theory. Typically this allows of three levels of phrase for a given type X, with a simple X as its Head at bottom level, represented by an X without any surmounting bar, for which I will put X^0. Distinctions between Head and Complements are made at the bottom level, the combination being a phrase, represented by an X surmounted by one bar, or, as I shall represent it, X^1. Adjuncts can be added at this level, the addition of any one adjunct yielding a more complex phrase, the result still deemed to be at the same level, X^1, this procedure being repeatable an indefinite number of times in the case of nouns (and also of verbs, if the theory is extended to them, and to speak of "verb phrases") so that there is no limit to the number of adjuncts which can be successively added in this way. I avoid the term "Specifier" for reasons seen in my next chapter.

(iii) Adpositions as synlexical connectives

I have portrayed adpositions as functionally connectives or synlexical expressions. In their most important role they serve as connectives within the complements and adjuncts of verbs, connectives indicating how the nominal or verbal core of the complement expression is related to the action of the verb, or how the nominal or verbal core of the adjunctive expression relates to this action (as "with a knife" indicates the instrument, "in the garden" the place, "after the party" what preceded the action, and "before the party" what followed it). In the same phrases they can also serve as the linking elements making such noun phrases the cores of functional complements to the verb "to be", as in "John is in the garden". Adpositions also serve as linking parts within complex quantity indicators which they help to make up; for instance, in the expression "drink a lot of tea", "of" links the semantic complement "tea" of the verb "drink" to "a lot" as the quantity indicator.

However, we must not suppose that adpositions always introduce noun phrases. On the contrary, there are many instances of things naturally classed as prepositions (serving an analogous connective role) introducing verbal expressions and linking them as semantic complements to heads, in some cases verbs, and in others nouns or adjectives. Thus with verbs as heads we have "permit to enter", "fear to enter", "want to go", "promise to go", "need to go", and "dare to go". With nouns as heads we have "permission to enter", "a permit to enter", "a promise to go", and "a need to go". And with adjectives as heads we have "able to swim", "willing to go", "afraid to go", and "eager to go". As a consequence of the latter we also have "ability to swim", "willingness to go", and "eagerness to go". All these cases of verbs, nouns, or adjectives as heads followed by the preposition "to" introducing a verb are cases in which the head verb is a semi-auxiliary or the head noun or adjective is rooted in a semi-auxiliary. "To" can also link a verb to a noun which lacks any such verbal background, such as "way to go", "way to enter", "place to go", "time to go", and "house to be sold". The custom of treating the so-called "to"-infinitive in English as a morphosyntactic unit has had many conveniences, but conceals the fact that the "to" of the infinitive is a preposition of a kind which can readily govern verbs as well as nouns.

Other prepositions introduce verbal formations other than the infinitive or gerund; for instance, the description which uses a gerund, "angry at his kicking his little brother", is equivalent to the description which uses a participial phrase, "angry at him kicking his little brother". Or, to take another example, the statements "Despite his arrival, I shall still stay" and "Despite his coming, I shall still stay" are equivalent to saying, "Despite him coming, I shall still stay", and in this last case the preposition governs the whole participial phrase "him coming", not just the pronoun. In reviewing what I call the situational and purposive complements of the verb "to be" we shall find further examples of uses of prepositions which link verbal forms as well as noun forms into a verbal nexus, of which "for", "to", "with", and "of" are the most common.[40]

40. The archaic preposition "a" survives as a now semantically empty connective of this kind in "go a fishing" (John 21:3, KJV, where the Greek has the infinitive); compare "summer is a coming in".

(iv) The need to consider the syntax of connectives in relation to discourse context

The expressions "in", "on", "out", "up", "down", "forward", "back", "behind", "in front", "before", "after", "at the same time" (the time being spoken of, expressible in Latin and Greek in the single words *simul* and *ama*), and "in between" are often used in ways very unlike prepositions, and as a result are sometimes called particles, sometimes adverbs, and other times conjunctions. "Left" and "right", which seem to be adverbs with a lexical meaning derived from adjectives, belong to the same group. The whole group are capable of use in more than one of the following ways: by themselves, as adverbs or particles; as followed by prepositions; as themselves prepositions; and as conjunctions.

These phenomena misled Emonds into arguing that conjunctions, prepositions, and various adverbial particles should all be grouped together, and Radford gives some nice examples exhibiting the attractiveness of this approach.[41] Thus a sentence which begins with "I haven't seen him ..." can be completed either with "since the party began" or with "since the party", or else simply with "since". Likewise, "I'd never met her ..." can be completed either with "before you held your party" or with "before the party", or else simply with "before". Last, "You can have some chocolate ..." can be completed either with "after you've eaten your dinner" or with "after your dinner", or else simply with "after". He also observes that with such "adverbs" and "adverbial" phrases and clauses adjunctive to the verb of the clause involved, exactly similar temporal phrases qualify their adjunction to it—for instance, "He was unwell a couple of weeks before the party began/a couple of weeks before the party/a couple of weeks before". "Before" (in the temporal sense), "after", and "at the same time as" can be used both prepositionally with noun phrases as complements and as subordinative conjunctions with clauses as complements.

For Radford these examples confirm the view that prepositions are lexical heads of phrases, either with a noun phrase or a clause as complement or else as lexical items on their own (with a null-complement), as the transitive verb "kill" can occur without a complement. However, such syntactic parallels, especially the capacity of the expressions concerned to occur on their own,[42] give a misleading appearance of solidity to the case for the mistaken treatment of prepositions and postpositions as the lexical heads of a fourth fundamental category of lexically headed phrase.

However, these examples and parallels fit much better with the contrary

41. See Radford, *Transformational Grammar*, 133–37, for the argument of this paragraph and the next.

42. The fact that heads can constitute a phrase on their own without a complement misleadingly confirmed Jackendoff in his view of prepositional phrases; see "The Base Rules for Prepositional Phrases", in *A Festschrift for Morris Halle*, ed. S. Anderson and P. Kiparsky (New York: Holt, Rinehart and Winston, 1973), 345–56.

conception that prepositions are functionally connectives, synlexical in character, connecting their functional complements into whatever larger setting is concerned. Their occurring on their own confirms this functionally connective role within discourse; for instance, if one says, "He was unwell a couple of weeks before" with the "before" stranded at the end, there has to be some answer to the question "Before what?" put by someone intruding upon the conversation, and this will have been some later event known to the people conversing from the previous discourse situation.

Thus these examples confirm my very different view of adpositions—namely, as connective structurizers. For the context of utterances in which the relevant expressions occur alone reveal that whenever "since", "before", and "after" occur stranded at the end of a clause as in the previous example, they are being used in a context of dialogue which would make it plain since what, before what, or after what was concerned. "Was it the party which made him unwell?" might elicit the reply, "No! He was unwell a couple of weeks before", the context making it plain that "before the party" was meant. Likewise, one cannot go in without going into something, or out without going out of something, go in front or behind without going in front of or behind something, and the utterances which speak just of going in, out, in front, or behind are all made in contexts which make it clear what one is going into, out of, in front of, or behind. This is an object-lesson in how wrong it is to consider syntax in isolation from context of utterance.

People go, come, and turn in, on, out, up, down, forward, and back, and these ways of speaking indicate direction and in some cases imply an unspecified new location. To "go behind" and "go in front" signify order among people going somewhere. However, the adverbs concerned (e.g., "left", "down") are all such as to imply that the verbs which they modify could have complements connected to them through a preposition (e.g., "left of", "down to"). In this sense these adverbs seem open-ended, "promissory of connectives".

In "I go back to school", "back to" is not a unitary preposition. Rather, "back" is part of a verb "go back", and the same is true of "go down" followed by the adjunct "to the town". In "go down the street" and "go down the hill", the equivalence of "go down" and "descend" exhibits how "down" is here better viewed as an adverb than as a preposition of path, paths or routes being here modifiers of a verb rather than parts of a preposition. On the other hand, in "I phoned the man back" (following Ackerman and Webelhuth), it is perhaps more revealing to consider "back" as part of the verb "phone back" as a lexical unit than to think of "back" as an adverbial modifier of the verb "phone".

Consider the sentence, "I have despised him ever since he made that display of himself at the party". If one views "I have despised him" as having "ever since he made that display of himself at the party" as its functional complement, it is more reflective both of the semantic structure of the whole and of how one hears the utterance concerned than if one considers "I have despised him ever since" as having as the complement "he made that display of himself at the party". Such questions are parallel to the question how one parses "Go into the house" and "Look at the house". If one considers "Go into" and "Look at" as having "the house" as their functional complement and object (compare "Enter the house" and "Regard the house" or "View the house"), this is more reflective both of the semantic structure of the whole and of how one understands the utterance on hearing it than if one considers "Go" and "Look" as verbs linked by prepositions to "the house" as their (oblique) object.

(b) *The functional complements and adjuncts of verbs*

(i) "Complement to a verb" is an intrinsically discourse-orientated or functional notion

We must divide between sentences and clauses which are constituted of a verb and complements, whether object complements or clausal complements, together with adjuncts, and sentences and clauses formed with the verb "to be". I have in mind here attributive statements, existential statements, and identity statements, discussed in section 4 (d).

It is natural to think of the subject and object of a verb as complements to that verb, as natural as to think of nouns and adjectives as having complements. Then, widening one's perspective to consider all the noun phrases set in significant relation to each other by the verb together with relevant case-inflections and/or adpositions, it becomes reasonable to consider all the inflected and adpositional phrases concerned as either complements or adjuncts to the verb.

Here we need to recognize the role of some constructions as being precisely to downgrade one of the arguments of a verb so that this argument is no longer functionally part of the core of the clause and no longer requires to be identifiable for the clause to have sense. Such constructions decrease the number of functional argument places of the verb—that is, its linguistic "valence". Thus the very purpose of the passive construction in which the agent, if mentioned at all, is typically marked by a distinctive adposition ("by", *par, a/ab, von, hypo*) seems to be to exclude such adpositional phrases from the core of the sentence, making them functionally "peripheral" to it, adjuncts introducing noun phrases which denote satellites, not objects of the verb—it has been described as relegating them to the situation of *chômeurs* (= the unemployed).[43] That is, the so-called agent-object of the verb is not a functional

43. Perlmutter, "Relational Grammar", in *Current Approaches to Syntax*, ed. by E. A. Moravcsik and J. Wirth (New York: Academic Press, 1980), 195–229.

object to the verb "... V-ed"—even though in the terms I expressed it earlier, it remains logically an argument to the two-place predicate "... is V-ed by —" ("*a* is V-ed by *b*" reflecting the same event or situation structure as "*b* V-s *a*"), so that one has to distinguish logical from functional or linguistic valence.[44]

Accordingly, although there is lexically a semantic link between "stab" and a person stabbed, this does not make "by Othello" a functional complement of the verb "stab" when in the passive. Such prepositions as "by" here have no relation peculiar to one transitive verb rather than another, unlike the "to" used with "give". Noun phrases with ergative case markings should be regarded as functionally adjuncts peripheral to the core and not functional complements for the same reasons as the prepositional "agent"-phrases just considered.[45]

(ii) Distinguishing complements and adjuncts of verbs: dependence on discourse context

The notion of object to a verb is sometimes explained as covering only those object phrases or pronouns which are essential to the sentence's being grammatical.[46] But this explanation is no use because, for instance, "I gave a book" may be grammatical, even though the indirect object has not been made explicit. Indeed, any complement to a verb may sometimes be omitted in some imaginable context; thus I might say to a person, "Was it that you gave or that he took?" and receive the reply, "I gave". Thus the notion of complement is lexically based, but has a pragmatic aspect, discourse-context having a key influence on it.[47]

44. In passivization, the subject is downgraded to peripheral or *chômeur* status, and it is instructive that in some cases it may be a recipient rather than a patient which is elevated to subject position.

English has some cases in which two direct objects appear, both apparently in the accusative (English no longer possessing a dative), e.g., "I gave Joseph the book", "I gave him it", "I bought Mary a book", and "I bought her it". Each gives rise to two passives—for instance, "Joseph was given the book by me" and "The book was given Joseph by me"—"Joseph", "him", and "Mary" being former or disguised datives. The English rule that nothing should separate a verb from its direct object must allow such former datives as exceptions. The immediate juxtaposition of verb and such former datives ("gave Joseph", "bought Mary") seems to give extra expression to the benefactive intent of the action of the verb. (In languages with a dative inflection distinct from the accusative, there are not usually two such passive formations.)

45. Van Valin questions this in the case of languages in which the ergative "agent" of one statement can reappear in the absolutive as the subject of a corresponding anti-passive statement. Thus, in the anti-passive constructions arising in some ergative languages in which the agent is subject in the absolutive and the undergoer is in the dative, the undergoer remains a functional complement if the argument in Matthew Beach, "Asymmetries between Passivization and Antipassivization in the Tarramiutut Subdialect of Inuktitut", in *The Proceedings of the LFG '03 Conference*, ed. Miriam Butt and Tracy Holloway King (Stanford, Calif.: CSLI, 2003), 1–21, that antipassive constructions do not have a downgrading function analogous to that found with the passive, is correct; see Van Valin, *Exploring the Syntax-Semantics Interface*, 117n16.

46. Martin Durrell, *Hammer's German Grammar and Usage*, 4th ed. (Chicago: McGraw-Hill, 2002), 365–68. Durrell's observations on 368 mark his awareness that his definition is inaccurate, because some complements may not be mentioned.

47. Such sentences as "The original St. Peter's was built", though true, seem very odd in isolation be-

In considering noun, adjective, adverb, or verb phrases, having picked out the content-introducing head of the phrase, we want a way of distinguishing what, if anything, attaches to this head as part of the core or nucleus of the phrase and what is linguistically structurally more accidental to it. What attaches to the head of the phrase as part of the core of the phrase is functionally its "complement", and the other content-introducing modifiers adjuncts.

Unless Joseph is understood to be a slave, "I gave Joseph" is nonsensical as well as ungrammatical. By contrast, "I gave a book" is grammatical. However, in the case of "gave", although the verb "give" should be given different lexical entries in respect of "I gave Joseph a book" and "I gave a book to Joseph" (correspondingly, these entries will distinguish the passive "Joseph was given a book by me" and "A book was given to Joseph by me"), this does not imply that in the latter the "to Joseph" is outside the core and the benefactive aspect a mere circumstance. Rather, the word "gave" always carries a benefactive meaning, even in the simple "I gave a book"—even in routine formal presentations to unknown people, or local voluntary sales in which we have no interest, and certainly in giving one's life for a cause, giving is always to or for something. The lexical meaning of the verb "give" determines that the verb has two objects, both in "I gave a book to Joseph" and in "I gave Joseph a book". Here the same meaning is expressed whether by means of a dative followed by an accusative, as in Greek and Latin or when the recipient is indicated by a dative pronoun, or configurationally, as in the first modern English formation or by means of a preposition, as when English uses the destinational "to" for the recipient.

It is easy to oversimplify. The verb "teach" behaves differently from "give". Consider "Socrates was teaching", "Socrates was teaching Plato", "Socrates was teaching philosophy", and "Socrates was teaching Plato philosophy". Each stands equally well on its own, with Plato the object taught and "philosophy" specificatory of what is taught, while "to Plato" would seem peripheral, with Plato a *chômeur*, in "Socrates taught philosophy to Plato".

The involvement of functional, discourse-related considerations in distinguishing between the complements and adjuncts of verbs explains the relevance of perspective, the aspect of the situation or activity involved which the sentence under consideration is concerned to highlight. Thus every giving is at a certain place and time, and any teaching is a teaching of something to one or more persons, but it does not follow that the place and time and what is taught and who is taught have to be complements of the verbs "give" and "teach".

cause banal and almost tautologous, but in certain contexts make good sense, e.g., while discussing what happened "in Constantine's reign" or what was achieved "by Constantine", occurring in clauses such as "when the original St. Peter's was built".

Thus it is wrong to consider the question of the grammaticality of sentences in isolation from their use or prescribe what object phrases are non-optional in abstraction from discourse-context.

Rather, we should only consider examples conceived as actual pieces of *parole*. We should then consider in each such *parole*-sentence which noun phrases, including what I call genitive complements, "act" in *rapport* with the sense of the verb. The relevant phrases will include ones omitted by ellipsis as in the following dialogue:

PERSON A: "Did you give John the book?"
PERSON B: "I did give it."

The second "give" has "John" as well as "it" as objects. (The sentence "I gave a book" made it plain that questions of grammaticality have to take context into account—here a context making it clear to whom or for what cause I gave a book, semantics revealing a pragmatic aspect that affects grammaticality.)

Further, in identifying the complements of verbs, we should not regard the need of an adposition or case ending to indicate the connection of noun phrase under consideration to the verb as implying that it is not occurring as a complement to the verb. "John" is just as much a complement to the verb "give" as the phrase "a book" in "I gave a book to John"—the idiomatic variation between languages is irrelevant.

"Take from" as the opposite of "give to" should be considered in a parallel way, the "from ..." phrase being as much an object of the verb "take" as the thing taken. And the verbs "buy" and "sell" should be considered in the same way. That is, the phrases introduced by "from" and "to" are complementary to the verbs "buy" and "sell".[48]

This way of thinking rescues one from the unnatural predicament of having to consider "go" and "come" as intransitive in sense. This would be to ignore the fact that they normally appear in such contexts as "go to", "go from", "come to", and "come from". It is no accident that the preposition and/or case ending joining the complement to the simple verb should be directional. Going is always a going away from, which makes the origin more intimate to the verb so that it is often unmentioned, because its identity is already clear from the discourse context as something presupposed; and in the case of coming, the destination has the same position of privilege as something presupposed. Any going is primarily from one place and subsidiarily to another, and any coming is primarily to one place and subsidiarily from another. There is the

48. By contrast, the phrases introduced by "for" indicating beneficiaries are peripheral, as in "I bought a book from David for John". Thus, recipient cases ("I gave John a book" or "I gave a book to John") contrast with beneficiary cases ("I bought John a book" or "I bought a book for John").

same asymmetry between "take from here (to somewhere else)" and "bring to here (from somewhere else)".

(iii) Effects of this approach

From this vantage point we can represent the structure of the following examples, including any preposition within the complement phrase concerned. Noun-centered subject phrases stand first, the noun phrases I have italicized second, and the noun phrases I have indicated by parentheses third in the hierarchy of such complements to the verb, yielding these representations: "I gave *a book*", "I gave (John) *a book*", "I gave *a book to John*", "He gave *his life* (for his country)", "I sold (John) *a book*", "I sold *a book* (to John)", "I bought (John) *some second-hand books*", "I bought *some second-hand books* (for John)", "I bought *some second-hand books* (because I thought they would help with the bonfire)", "He was coming (from Athens)" (compatible with his never arriving), "He came (from Athens)", "He came *hither* (from Athens)", "He came *to London* (from Athens)" (compatible with his having hoped to get to Aberdeen), "He never got *to Aberdeen*", "I went *to Italy*", "I went (from here) *to Italy*", "I went (from Paris) *to Rome*", "I was going *to Italy*", "Constantine built *the original St. Peter's*", "The original St. Peter's was built by Constantine", and "The original St. Peter's was built in Constantine's reign". Coming is primarily a coming toward and only incidentally a coming from, whereas going is a primarily a going from and only incidentally a going toward. In the last two examples the subject is the only complement: "by Constantine" and "in Constantine's reign" are adjunctive, adverbial modifiers of the verb, causal and temporal respectively. In "I was going to go *to Italy*", "(to) Italy" is a noun complement to the second "go", while "was going" is a propensity semi-auxiliary, and has the verbal complement "(to) go to Italy".

Like Dik and Bresnan, I make function-structure a matter of (a) the verb/argument structure arising from the meaning of the verb and its complements identifying the situation or activity concerned, and (b) the perspective in which this is presented. What is important is to distinguish arguments which belong to the core and ones which do not, called *chômeurs* by Perlmutter and satellites by Dik.[49]

Among functional adjuncts to the verb we must distinguish those with a nominal function and those with a purely adverbial relation to the verb. Phrases indicating agents to passive verbs are of the first kind, while the temporal modifier "in Constantine's reign" is of the second. The fact that instrumental phrases (indicating "means") are adverbial adjuncts is particularly evident because the means of performing the action can be expressed not only by such

49. See n. 6 and Bresnan, *Lexical-Functional Syntax*, 9–10, 94.

expressions as "with a knife", but also by phrases introducing gerunds such as "by means of arranging his poisoning" or clauses such as "by securing that his servants would poison him". Moreover, logically, the means is not strictly the knife as such, but doing something with it. What holds with adverbial modifiers indicating means holds equally with those which indicate the manner, motivation, place, or time of the action (e.g., "with a knife", "with certainty", "with a sure hand", "with confidence", "in anger", "in Sparta", "on Tuesday").

Some cases require careful analysis. In "The vandals stripped the branches off the tree", "off the tree" is an oblique object phrase indicating a third term in the relation "... stripped /// off \\\". However, "of its branches" is an adverbial phrase indicating the manner or respect of the stripping of the tree, the tree being the patient, in the action reported in "The vandals stripped the tree of its branches". "The old man walked the streets of the village" and "The old man walked in the streets of the village" reveals a distinction: in both, "the streets of the village" is a unitary phrase ("of the village" being a modifier to "the streets"), in the first statement the object complement to the verb, but in the second only an adjunct peripheral to the core indicating the location of the action, not its object.[50] Instruments, places, or times become functional arguments to the verb only if they are topicalized, as in "It was the President that I sat beside", perhaps said in response to "Who did you sit beside?" Only one adverbial adjunct can be topicalized in any sentence.[51]

Section 4. Types of Functional Complement to Verbs

(a) *The classification of the functional complements of verbs*

The noun phrase complements of a verb include the subject, the verb's primary argument, and any objects. Direct objects stand in contrast with oblique objects, the latter either requiring a connective linking them to the verb in a particular way, or marked by some special case-inflection, or both. The label "indirect object" picks out "oblique objects" which are in functional relationship with the verb.

"Specificatory complements" form a wider class than the functionally genitive phrases referred to earlier.

The term "specificatory" naturally extends to verbal complements, typically expressed by a clause or predicate of a clause—see (b). Some specificatory verbal complements to verbs are only quasi-predicational in the sense

50. I take these "vandal" examples from Blake, *Case*, 134.

51. Bresnan, "Polyadicity", in Bresnan, *Mental Representation*, 149–72; see 164–65, 167, referring to Anthony J. Kenny's emphasis on the optional and indeterminate number of adverbial adjuncts in Kenny, *Action, Emotion and Will*.

explained in section 2 (c), such as "swim" and "to swim" in "I can swim" and "I know how to swim"; and "to go home" in "I want to go home".

(b) *Specificatory genitive object phrases of verbs compared with clausal complements*

In considering examples of immanent activities, there are two ways in which we can indicate their content—namely, either phrasally, as in "dream/think of wild horses" (we also find genitively marked nouns after numerous verbs in numerous languages signifying immanent activities, particularly to do with memory) or clausally, as in "dream/think that wild horses were running over a meadow". We also speak or ask about the same things as we remember, dream of, or think about.[52]

I describe these phrasal and clausal complements as sharing the property of being "specificatory complements to the verb". Also, "make a statement" and "give an order" each belong to the semantically content-introducing part of the complete verb expression, so that "of/about the state of the economy" and "that the state of the economy is good" are both specificatory or identificatory complements. And, as one can have statements about the state of the economy, so also one can have questions about it; and one can consider the problems of infinity, of the age of the universe, or of the relations between Europe and America. All the complements concerned specify, identify, or expound what is dreamt, thought, stated, ordered, or asked about.

The specificatory complements we are concerned with are cases where a sentential role is concerned (unlike the complements of nouns with no verbal rooting)—that is, cases where they are functionally complementary to the verb as "of wild horses" and "that wild horses were running over a meadow" are complementary to "dream" in "I dreamt of wild horses" and "I dreamt that wild horses were running over a meadow"—they have a functional role within clauses such as open "I dreamt . . .".

(c) *Logical and grammatical contrasts between types of imagining*

Whether we look to Plato or to the modern Russell, G. E. Moore, Wittgenstein, Ryle, Geach, or whoever, again and again we meet arguments that such clauses do not stand for entities and should not be thought of as specify-

52. This helps explain why the immanent activities of remembering, forgetting, and pitying expressed by Latin deponent verbs take genitive objects (as do the related adjectives). Latin also has numerous impersonal constructions to express feeling, the person who feels being in the accusative and the object of the feeling in the genitive; cf. B. H. Kennedy and J. F. Mountford, *Kennedy's Revised Latin Primer* (London: Longman, 1962), 138–39, 146–47. Likewise, in English, when one reminds a person of something, the genitive is again used. Some parallels can be found in German and Greek.

ing direct or indirect objects of verbs. Hirst suggested that such clauses should be thought of as adverbial.[53] However, while he thus recognizes that these clauses do not point outward from the act as if to an external object, his idea involves the mistake of representing them as expressing the "how" or manner of the activity instead of its "what" or content.

We can now state the matter more precisely. These so-called noun clauses stand as complements to the verbs concerned, functionally integral to the core of the sentences of which they are parts, and stand in contrast with the adjunctive adverbial clauses instanced at the beginning of section 5, which can also be introduced by "that".

The clausal expression "that there were wild horses running over a rich meadow" as it might occur after such diverse verbs as "dream", "imagine", "think", "suppose", "seem", "believe", "know", "see", "be told", and "hear" is specificatory of what is dreamt, imagined, and so forth. In this way it serves, only more fully, the same kind of specificatory role as genitive phrases like "of wild horses" after the verb "dream", or as the functionally genitive objects of remembering and feeling in various Greek, Latin, and German constructions.[54] If we recognize such clauses as expressing "what specifies or distinguishes" the dreaming, thinking, supposing, seeming, believing, knowing, seeing, telling, and hearing concerned, we do justice to the instinct whereby tradition called them "noun clauses". They are grammatically analogous to grammatical objects to the verbs concerned, and like the genitive objects mentioned are functional complements to these verbs in the sense of being completions to a verb, completions of the sort which this kind of verb requires.

In these cases the connective "that" serves as a clause-marker and, taken together with the following clause, does indeed form a "complement", and therefore deserves its customary title "complementizer". Such "that" clauses are conspicuous in relation to "cognitive" verbs, such as "think" and "believe", along with "say", "hear", and "state", and so are characteristic of reported speech. However, with "wonder" and "ask" we have other clausal complementizers, such as "whether" corresponding to the direct question "Is it so or not?" and *wh*-expressions (referred to as Q-expressions in some non-English works) corresponding to different forms of interrogative, which connect to the clauses they introduce: "who", "whom", and "whose", "which", and "what", either by themselves or preceded by a preposition, and "why", "how", "when", "how long" and "how often", "where", and "how far".[55]

In some cases the verbs concerned can take a direct object as well as a

53. R. J. Hirst, *Perception and the External World* (London: Macmillan, 1996).

54. Cf. chap. XI, sec. 3 (a) (ii), in this volume.

55. In their role as clause-markers, these interrogatives are sometimes preceded by a redundant "about" or "in regard to".

genitive or clausal complement, as when John asks a person whether the classical Romans were the most cruel European people of their times or when the person tells John that this was so, the direct object being the person addressed. When I order, or ask, pray, or beg someone to do something, the case is more complex, since the person addressed is both the direct object of the addressing and the subject of the prospective doing. That is, we can have "ordered that X do A" or "ordered X to do A", the latter when X was addressed directly. Again, we can say, "I promise that I will do A" or "I promise to do A", implying that it is "I" who will be doing A. Accordingly, we have a style of complement of the form "(X) to do A". Comparing the modal case considered in section 2, we should call these complements predicational. These idioms are allied to the causative, permissive, or merely passive-expressing modes of speech I mentioned earlier. We shall find that these also have predicational complements.

Prominent among immanent activities are the emotions. Here again we very often use *that* with a clause in a specificatory role, as when we say, "fear that", "angry that", "hope that", "desire that", "be pleased that", or "be sorry that".

James may be eager for an apple or a game of golf, nonclausally specified objects, and he may also be eager that P, eager for X to F, or eager that he please others (= eager to please). We shall find that in some cases these adjectival ("eager") and verbal ("is eager") expressions have clausal or predicational complements, as when he is eager for something determinate—for instance, to win the election in 2012; and sometimes generic, of a sort specified by a verb or incomplete predicate, for instance, eager to travel.[56] Such verbally sortal, quasi-predicational complements of verbs are exceedingly common, as when we say, "I like to eat out", "Some people dare to go into haunted houses", "It is good to have a good splash", "I want to see castles", "He can swim", and "I know how to swim".

Further, as required in chapter IX, section 3 (c), we must distinguish the knowledge and supposition about situations and events, people, or things from knowing or imagining them (e.g., an apple, a horse, or a person). As a matter of phenomenological or experiential description, to see something move and to see it moving are not the same as to see that it has moved or that it is moving. In knowing or imagining a person or thing moving, fighting, playing, and so forth, the object of the knowing or imagining is neither

56. Being eager is an emotion discussed in recent grammar because of the contrasts to be drawn between the grammatical behavior of "eager" and "easy". By "James is eager to please", we mean that he is eager that others be pleased by him. The case of James being easy to please is quite different. "Easiness" is not an attribute of James, an emotion felt by him like eagerness, but an attribute of the task of pleasing James when this task is undertaken by a person of normal goodwill. Easiness is never an attribute of a substance (an apple or James), but always of some sort of activity (a sortal, rather than clausal, verbal object).

just the activity nor the substance as such, but the substance as in activity, and more particularly the experiencing, remembering, or imagining—for instance, particular pieces of fighting within a battle. It is a mistake to reduce desiring or wanting an apple or a taste of strawberries or the pleasure of feeling the smoothness of silk to cases of desiring or wanting that this or that should be so, even though we can analyze some other cases of desire like this (e.g., for a person to want to be king is for him to desire that he be king).

Accordingly, we must avoid trying to reduce the several different kinds of complement taken by "cognitive" verbs, both syntactically and semantically, to one.

(d) *Types of attribute: functional complements to "to be" as a copula*

The verb "to be" has four uses: the first as a copula empty of content, used to introduce the predication of attributes, and having attributive complements; the second in order to assert existence; the third to express identity; and the fourth as an auxiliary—for instance, in English, one which, used together with the present participle, expresses continuous action.

The copula makes explicit the live character of a clause, advertising the presence of syntactic connection, and supplies tense indication, although sometimes omitted as we saw in section 1 (b) (ii).

Attributive complements of this kind may be of four basic sorts: nominative noun phrases; nominative adjective phrases; noun phrases introduced by an adposition, including nouns or pronouns indicating possession; and purposive verb phrases, in English typically introduced by "to" or "for" followed by a part of the verb which does not take inflections. The same types of attributive complement are taken by verbs closely related to the copula, such as "to remain" ("continue to be"), "to seem" ("seem to be"), and "to become".[57]

Noun phrases which figure as complements to the copula include "Socrates was a man", "Attila was an alien", "Socrates had been a soldier", and "Socrates was the greatest philosopher". "Students are human beings" and "Spartak are eleven men" constitute other examples, the one a distributive predication of a plural subject, and the other a collective predication of a collection, to be contrasted with "Spartak are, all of them, huge men". The presence or absence of the article "a" or "an" marks the presence of a noun—for instance, setting "Attila was an alien" in contrast with "Attila was alien".

Adjectives and adjectival phrases, the head adjective again being in the nominative case or agreeing with the subject, constitute the paradigm cases of

57. Durrell, *Hammer's German Grammar*, 395–96, gives the misleading title "predicate complement" to the complements of the German verbs for "be", "become", "remain", and "seem", with which he includes "be called".

this kind of complement. Such adjectival complements can be simple, composed of an identity or quantity indicator and an adjective, or include a complement, or have both an identity or quantity indicator and a complement, as in "Attila was alien", "The music was very alien", "Winston was afraid of rats", and "Winston was inordinately afraid of rats". ("About" is a locative rather than an adjective in "He is about".)

The adpositional phrases (or, in languages with case-inflections, equivalent noun phrases with the appropriate case marking different from that of the subject) which can follow the verb "to be" are of four kinds, unless group (a) is regarded as a subgroup of (b).

a. Some mark origin (e.g., "from Italy", "by Walter Scott", "off the ship").
b. Some are equivalent to genitives, as in the examples we will meet in chapter XV ("That picture is of me", "This leg is of a primitive bird", "The crime was of murder", "The victim was of Caucasian stock", "His fear was of rats", and "The trial was of Charles I"). Noun possessives (e.g., "Bill's") and pronouns (e.g., "mine", "thine", "his", "hers", "ours", "yours", "theirs") occurring as attributive complements to the copula should be grouped here.
c. Some are locative, not expressing motion (e.g., "in the Lyceum", "on/under(neath)/above/over the table", "outside the city", "He was into Damascus" [in the sense that he had got into Damascus and was now in it, to be contrasted with "He was going into Damascus"], "about", "about on the deck").
d. Others are situational (e.g., "off duty", "on duty", "out of bounds", "at the ready", "at ease", "in readiness"). Likewise, in "He is on the point/brink/verge of shooting" the complement of "is" is situational, although the complement of "point", "brink", or "verge" is verbal, behaving strangely like an infinitive and unlike a gerund, since a determiner cannot be introduced before it and "of" cannot be introduced after it (he can be on the point of shooting or shooting at a fish, but not on the point of the shooting of a fish). These phrases have the same meaning as "He is about to shoot", and the meaning is not locative, but has to do with the timing of an imminent action. As "readiness" is a noun formed from an adjective, "ready", which is attributed to agents in virtue of a relation to prospective action, the complements it takes are specificatory of the type of action, and correspondingly "point", "brink", and "verge" have relevance only as indicative of an edge of time immediately before expected action, and so again their complements are verbal. (By contrast, the meanings of "He is on the point of my sword/brink of a precipice/verge of the lawn" are straightforwardly locative, to be grouped with the examples in [c].)

The last group of attributive complements are those indicative of purpose—for instance, "His action was in/out of revenge for his brother's murder" (in this example, "for" means "in respect of" and the purpose is revenge).

I shall give this last group more extended discussion because they are not well understood and can be introduced by "to" as well as by "for".

Introduction by "for" is common—for instance, "This knife is for the cutting of/for cutting cheese" and "This gift is for Betty". In this last case one would anticipate possible verbal complements to the noun "Betty" saying what she was to do with the gift (e.g., "for Betty to read", "for Betty to eat"). When purposive verb phrases are introduced by "for", as in "The eyes are for us to see with", "to see" is the simple infinitive, and it is the "for" which is expressive of purpose.

However, this is where we should also group the Latin gerundive—for instance, *amandus, amanda, amandum,* meaning "to be loved" (= the subject ought to or must be loved). And in English, purposive verb phrases as complements to the copula are most commonly introduced by the connective "to".[58] Consider the following: "The job to be done is to destroy the guns of Navarone. You, Mallory, are to get the party up the impossible cliff. You, Miller, are to see to the explosives"; "You three are to mark Lomu"; "He is to catch trout"; "We are to pray". Here we have six examples of the form "*a* is to F", and in each F is thereby being implied to be a job to be done by a designated person, *a*. In this context, "to F" is not the normal infinitive, but implies obligation, appointed duty, or at least appropriateness or fittingness. Eyes are to see with as ears are to hear with. Again, we are to value "wisdom more than fine gold" or, equivalently, wisdom is to be valued more than fine gold. In "His action was to revenge his brother", we have a "to"-infinitive expressing purpose.[59]

Syntactically, the simplest way of describing the phenomena seems to be to suppose that we are dealing here with a kind of infinitive different from the infinitives of the indicative mood to which we are accustomed—what we might call an imperative, desiderative, or purposive infinitive. For simplicity I shall call it the purposive infinitive, occurring in two forms, active and passive, "to X" and "to be X-ed". One advantage of this is that it enables us to suppose this infinitive present on many occasions on which the verb "to be" or copula is absent, taking as our criterion that whenever "to" before a verb can be replaced by "in order to", we have this purposive infinitive present. This criteri-

58. I am speaking of the uses of "to" which the 1973 *Shorter OED* lists under "to", under the boldface headings B.I.1.a–c, and B.II.1.b, by contrast with its uses as a simple marker of the infinitive of the verb in the indicative listed under B.III and B.IV.

59. In "His action was in order to revenge his brother", the "in order to" means "for the sake of", both complex prepositional expressions indicating that the whole phrase will indicate purpose—"in order to" followed by "revenge" as a prepositionless infinitive and "for the sake of" by "revenge" as a verb-rooted noun.

on admirably fits Goldsmith's "Fools, who came to scoff, remained to pray"[60] and Tyndale's "a light to lighten the gentyls [Gentiles]". Unsurprisingly, these purposive phrases expressing attributes of a subject after a copula can also modify nouns directly, as in "the job to be done", "the man to mark Beckham", and so forth. This analysis of these attributive phrases explains the origin of the phrasal auxiliary "is to" considered as a single lexical unit.[61] These purposive verb phrases often have equivalents among the purposive prepositional phrases introduced by "for" mentioned earlier.

It will be noticed that in this type of case the connectives "to" and "for" have a trace of semantic content, "to" connoting directedness towards a goal, and "for", like the Latin *pro,* connoting some positive evaluation, whether because of function or purpose, or because on the behalf of or for the sake of somebody or something, or because of mere appropriateness (as in "a time for sowing and a time for reaping", "the time for picking raspberries", and "the time for the harvest").

By contrast, when marking the indicative infinitive, "to" has a purely structural function and lacks any trace of semantic content, and the same holds with "for" used as a disguised clausal marker, discussed in my next section (e.g., "It is possible for him to fail in his quest").

Section 5. Clause-Markers and Types of Subordinate Clause

Within sentences, apart from coordinate clauses, subsentential clauses occur in three ways: first, as complements of verbs or in modal constructions (traditionally called "noun clauses"); second, as adjuncts to predicates or to whole clauses ("adverbial clauses") introduced by connectives variously classified as prepositions or subordinative conjunctions; and third, as modifiers of nouns introduced by relative pronouns as connectives ("relative clauses"). In English all three types of clause have been liable to be introduced by clause-markers such as "that". Such a marker is external to the clause.[62] It marks the clause as what is to be linked in to the sentence, either directly as a specificatory complement to a verb, or indirectly by means of a connective such as a relative pronoun or a conjunction such as "because" so as to modify a noun or verb adjunctively. Such clause-markers have often become optional

60. They each came with the mind or intention to scoff, and stayed with the mind to pray.

61. We find that the only unmistakably subjunctive form of the verb "to be" in modern use is "were" with a future meaning in subjunctive conditionals where German would use the equivalents of "would" or "should". This "were" is invariable for person and number, and when used as an auxiliary it is followed by the "to"-form of the infinitive, without any purposive or imperative connotations.

62. Bresnan, "On Complementizers: Toward a Syntactic Theory of Complement Types", *Foundations of Language* 6 (1970): 297–321; cf. Radford, *Transformational Grammar,* 293–95.

or obsolete, except when they have usurped the place of the connective. In Chomskyan grammars such clause-markers are called "complementizers" and represented by the letter C, and they are often represented as part of sentence structure even when absent morphologically.

(a) *Clauses in general*

(i) Three kinds of clause distinguished through pragmatic, semantic, and morphosyntactic criteria

"Adverbial" clauses can be considered as *adjunctive* to clauses because of the way they arise. Thus I could say, "Caesar crossed the Rubicon", "At that time, no one had power to resist him", "No one had power to resist Caesar when he crossed the Rubicon", and "Because of this, Caesar gained control of Rome", and in summary, "Caesar gained control of Rome, because no one had power to resist him when he crossed the Rubicon".

By contrast, the morphosyntactic complements of these verbs or modal formations, often called noun clauses, are *functionally complementary* to these verbs or modal formations. For instance, the relation of "Caesar was ambitious" to the verb "proclaimed" of which it is the complement should be considered in the context of the relation of "Caesar was ambitious" to "Mark Antony proclaimed —" in "Mark Antony proclaimed (that) Caesar was ambitious". "Mark Antony proclaimed Caesar to be ambitious" is a linguistic variant of this, the infinitive being semantically verbal rather than nominal in character.[63] "It is possible for you to get to New Zealand before Easter" asserts a possibility fulfilled if it turns out that "I got to New Zealand before Easter"; thus "It is possible for — to ///" is the modal formation which has "you" and "get to New Zealand before Easter" as its complements.

Third, relative clauses are used with the function of modifying a noun, so as to be pragmatically or functionally adjectival (compare "the runner" and "the person running" with "the person who was running"), and in phrase diagrams they are represented as subordinate to a nominal phrase (or "Determiner Phrase"), despite their clausal character.

(ii) The large spread of uses of the clause-marker "that"

Grammatically, in English the formative "that" constitutes the default clause-marker of a subordinate clause. It is found in many "adverbial" clauses—for instance, "in order that" expressive of purpose, and "so that" or "with the result that" expressive of results, in this resembling the Latin *ut* and the

63. The infinitive, like the participle and unlike a gerund, is in any case morphosyntactically verbal rather than nominal in character, but it is its semantic character which is relevant to the present discussion.

Greek *oti*; and in medieval English it sometimes appears after the connectives "because" and "if", "after", "before", "when", and "while", all introducing subordinate clauses which, taken with the connectives, constitute adjuncts to the clauses they modify. As I remarked earlier, the "that" indicates the incompleteness of what precedes.

Many examples above show that whenever we want to invent an unambiguous clause introducer, we can do it with the help of "that"[64]—"in the situation that", "granted that", "by securing that", "by providing that", and "by arranging that", along with "it is not the case that". The following symbolism clarifies the structure of common speech: "(Re: John) (it is possible for John that at some time *t* in the period P, John will arrive in New Zealand at *t*"), for "It is possible for John that he should arrive in New Zealand before the end of February 2001". In classical Latin impersonal expressions equivalent to "it is possible that ..." took such forms as Cicero's "potest fieri ut ..." (literally, "it can come about that ...").

The same "that" introduces the complements of epistemic and other modal expressions, for instance, "it is certain that ...", "[personal noun phrase or pronoun] is certain that ...", "it is possible that ...", "it is not certain that ... not ...", "it seems that ...", "it seems to [personal noun phrase or pronoun] that ...", and "it is necessary that ...", which appear parallel to "it is known that ...", "it is known to [personal noun phrase or pronoun] that ...", "it is not known that ... not ...", "it is believed that ...", "it is believed by [personal noun phrase or pronoun] that ...", and "it must be concluded that ...", all followed by a finite verb in the indicative mood.

"That" also appears in the optatives "Oh that ..." and "Would that ...", which can be considered parallel to "I hope that ...". It appears also in some so-called imperatives, permissions, and Kant's "problematic hypothetical imperatives": thus, "it is necessary that ..." said by a judge passing sentence, and "it is permitted that ..." should be considered together with "that" as used after verbs such as "command" and "permit". All these optatives and imperatives, if followed by "that", are properly followed by a finite verb in the subjunctive mood.

The use of "that" with relative clauses presents more puzzles.

According to one theory, whenever we have a relative pronoun (or "that" used as if a relative), the situation is best understood if we think that, as it were covertly, we have both, first the relative and then the clause-marker "that".[65]

64. Under "to", the 1973 *Shorter OED* lists "to the time that" and "to that" as equivalents (last traced by the *OED* in 1575 and 1626 respectively) to the conjunction "until". "Until" arose by combining a Norse or, more generally, Germanic *und, unti, unzi,* meaning "up to", with "till" (or "til"), perhaps deriving from a Germanic word meaning "terminus" or "goal".

65. Argument for this view is well presented by Radford, *Transformational Grammar,* 480–89, includ-

More accurately, we should say that a proper understanding of semantic syntax should allow for the potentiality for the presence of both the relative and the clause-marker.

In French the word *que* has three uses, as meaning "whom" or "which" as object—that is, the accusative of the relative pronoun *qui* ("who" or "which" as subject); as meaning "what?"; and as meaning "that". However, whereas occasionally in medieval and modern English we find both the relative and "that" occurring together, but normally only one, in modern English the relative is used alone, the British tending to use a *wh*-relative, principally using "that" to avoid saying, "who (whom) or which", while in American English "that" is the preferred relative pronoun, except where a *wh*-relative is required to avoid ambiguity. By contrast, in French the *wh*-relative pronoun is never omitted.[66]

(iii) "Absolute" participial phrases equivalent to adverbial clauses—both adjuncts to the clause

The so-called absolute participial phrases of Latin, Greek, German, and English are entirely unlike the various uses of gerunds and other verbal nouns in these languages. All these participial "absolutes" present clear cases of the use of participles as adjectives marked in appropriate case agreement with an appropriate subject noun within the participial phrase, this being the ablative in Latin, the genitive in Greek,[67] the accusative in German,[68] and unmarked in English, the whole phrase having a subject entirely distinct from the subject of the main clause of the utterance, with the result that the whole phrase is without grammatical link with the main clause. Here, as the introduction explained, we have a paradigm example of sentences whose syntactic unity arises only pragmatically in the act of speech, but whose constituents are grammatically disjoint.[69] Past participles are understood in the passive sense,

ing some evidence from examples from all periods of English and from Canadian French and Dutch. However, as my discussion shows, one does not need to explain the phenomena in terms of a theory of movement, and the most problematic French example can be given simpler treatment than Radford proposes (*Transformational Grammar*, 490); cf. my n. 66 and related text in this chapter, and also my remarks on Radford's general treatment of relatives in chap. XIII, nn. 75–77 and related text in this volume.

66. This is the reason why "l'homme qu'a vu Jean" can only mean "the man whom John has seen" ("the man who has seen John" would be "l'homme qui a vu Jean"), whereas if *que* meant "that", the phrase could carry either meaning. This seems the optimal conclusion from the data assembled by Radford, *Transformational Grammar*; R. S. Kayne, "French Relative *que*", in *Current Studies in Romance Linguistics*, ed. F. Henzey and M. Luján (Washington, D.C.: Georgetown University Press, 1976), 255–99; and R. S. Kayne and J.-Y. Pollock, "Stylistic Inversion, Successive Cyclicity and Move NP in French", *Linguistic Inquiry* 9 (1978): 595–621.

67. Greek also has impersonal accusative participial absolutes. These express something's being necessary or being permitted; see *Joint Association of Classical Teachers* [JACT], *Reading Greek*, 147, 211.

68. This accusative absolute expresses something involved in a causal story, whereas the rare German nominative absolute expresses merely accompanying or incidental facts.

69. The participles qualify only their own internal subject noun (with which they are in concord) and do not qualify any ablative, genitive, accusative, or nominative noun or pronoun within the main clause.

while present participles are understood in an active sense and, with transitive verbs, take grammatical objects in the case appropriate to the verb.

As modifiers to the whole clause these absolute phrases are adjunctive to the clause to which they are subordinated and so analogous to adjunctive adverbial clauses, adverbially modifying the main clause of the sentence.

(b) *Problems special to clausal complements of verbs*

(i) Forms of clausal expression with their subject external to the predicate phrase

Consider the family of expressions "It is possible for John to swim two miles", "It is tough/difficult/easy for John to swim two miles", and "It is impossible for John to swim two miles". The predicates parallel to "tough" have been called "tough predicates", although "modal" would have been a better title. The adjective arises from the adverb of manner applied to the verb or adjective expressing modality, as in "can easily swim", "is easily able to swim", and "is able easily to swim", but it is an aspect of manner affecting the degree of natural possibility of accomplishing the task, and hence also its epistemic possibility (i.e., its probability assessed in relation to what our state of knowledge gives reason to expect).

Parallel ways of speaking are found in German with the modal or "tough predicate" followed by *fur* with the accusative, again followed by a predicate phrase in infinitive form, the infinitive introduced by *zu*, the German equivalent of "to". The "for" and the *fur* pick out the subject, that which would be the subject of "John can swim two miles" and "John can easily swim two miles", as in "It is easy for John to swim two miles". The "for" here does not carry its usual connotation of "for the sake of" or "on behalf of", but only the formal significance of "in regard to" or "in respect of".

This general pattern of a subject/verb formation of a clausal character, but with the peculiarity that the subject of the clause stands outside it, either as a subject of the whole sentence ("John can get to New Zealand by Sunday"), or as a direct or indirect object to the preceding verb expression ("He ordered you to X" or "It is possible for John to get to New Zealand by Sunday"), is exceedingly common.

We also find this form of expression, with the subject of a clause in the accusative and its predicate phrase expressed by the infinitive, marked for time and aspect as well as voice, in classical Latin. However, in classical Latin this form of expression extends beyond this range of cases concerned with the future and real or practical possibility, and is also the norm for the indirect or "oblique" expression of reported assertion and of thinking expressed by such assertion, and so is also used with "know" and "certain", along with "possible" as expressing epistemic possibility. But in the Vulgar Latin of Saint Jerome in the Vulgate translation of Christian scripture, this form of expression for reported speech and the objects of "know" and suchlike is almost entirely superseded by *quod, quia,* or *quoniam,* reflecting the Greek clause-marker *oti* and the Hebrew use of direct speech even in reported speech, which is what he was translating, the particle being followed by a nominative subject and finite indicative verb, a pattern kept by the Romance languages and close to English idiom.

In English we meet this noun-infinitive formation in the causative, permissive, or merely passive-expressing modes of speech discussed earlier, where "X" is the direct object phrase and "F" is the infinitive predicate phrase:

1. In "force X to F", "force" requires the marked or "to"-form of the infinitive, as in "Force these clothes to fit into this drawer" and "Force this spy to name his contacts". "Make X F" presumes that the F is of a predicative character, but the copula is omitted, as in "Make the gun serviceable" and "Make the house a ruin", although in the active voice the unmarked infinitive is used: "Make John climb the tree". In the passive a "to"-infinitive is required, as in "John was made to climb the tree".
2. In "allow X F", "allow" requires the marked or "to"-form of the infinitive, as in "Allow the garden to go to ruin" and "Allow the prisoner to escape". "Let" takes the prepositionless infinitive, but with the same resulting meanings, as in "Let the garden go to ruin" and "Let the prisoner escape". When "let" is in the imperative, the resulting forms are often mistakenly counted as first- and third-person imperatives, as in "Let me go" and "Let him go", whereas the only imperative present is the second-person "Let".
3. In "have X F", "have" takes the prepositionless infinitive, as in the imperatives "Have James get the tea" and "Have my luggage found".
4. In "get X to F", "get" requires the "to"-infinitive with the active verb, as in "Get John to prune the trees", yet it takes a passive participle with a passive verb, as in "Get the trees pruned" and "Get my hand trapped", as well as in the non-causative "I got my hand trapped".
5. "Prevent X from R" and "stop X from R", as well as "restrain X from R", are not followed by infinitives, but by gerunds with the behavior of the French infinitive, capable of taking direct objects, but only very rarely a genitive object. Thus we say, "Prevent Napoleon (from) getting his navy across the Channel" (not "from the getting of his navy across the Channel)", "Stop Sam (from) fiddling with the electric plugs" and "Restrain your father from overworking".

In all these we seem to have a complement in the style "X + preposition + F", where F has some predicative element expressive of action or change of state and the preposition is sometimes optional and sometimes excluded. In each case the action or inaction signified is directed towards or has the effect of the coming about of a change in which the object X comes to be in the end state named (serviceable, a ruin, having climbed the tree, having escaped, having pruned the trees, having been pruned, having been trapped) from a previous opposite state.

The close semantic relations between causing a person to do something or making him do it and ordering or commanding him to do it; between demanding, asking, requesting, begging, or praying him to do it and getting him to do it; and between arranging for a person to do a thing or otherwise contriving to get him to do it, perhaps by one of these forms of ordering or requesting, and having him do it or having had it done (by him); between letting a person do something and permitting him to do it; and between preventing a person from doing something and prohibiting him from doing it[70] make it unsurprising that the syntactic forms taken by the reports of all the speech-acts concerned should reflect the syntactic forms associated with these different causative verbs.

The speech-acts concerned are of the kind commonly labeled "prescriptive" or "evaluative", and are uttered in the setting reflected by a wide range of psychological verbs exhibiting the same structure of a subject and a verb with two complements, the one a direct or indirect object in the accusative and the other a predicative phrase in infinitive form. Thus we have "want him to be king", "wish him to be king", "hope for him to succeed", and "trust him to be king". Allied to these are many judgments in which we have a gerund or other verbal noun: "hope for his election", "fear for his life", and "accept his being made king". We can also say, "hope that he will be elected", "fear for him lest he be killed", and "am willing that he be made king". Various kinds of judgment, such as "It is good for him to be king" and "He is worthy to be king", lie in the background of such constructions as "hold him worthy to be king" and "hold that he is worthy to be king".

Whenever the subject of the wanting or other such disposition is the same as its object, we have, as in the case of expressions of intention and promises, a simpler construction, the main verb now needing only the infinitive predicational complement. We say, "I promise that I will be there" and "I intend that I will be there", which can be simplified to "I promise to be there" and "I intend to be there", or simply, according to the weightiness of the matter, "I will

70. Just as "bidden to" means "commanded to", so "forbidden to" is equivalent to "commanded not to", and so we say, "forbidding him to do it", with the *to* having a purely structural meaning, in place of "prohibiting from doing it", where the *from* retains its lexical separational or rejectional meaning.

be there". And we could say, "I want to be king", "I consent to be king", "I am willing to be king", "I hope to be king", or "I fear to be king". Similarly, if the subject of the means is the same as the subject of the end, we can say, "He did it in order to become king" (simpler than "He did it in order that he become king"[71]).

The speech-acts of ordering, requesting, and begging take the "I order/request/beg you to ..." form when the required action is by the addressee, who remains unmentioned when the second person of the imperative mood is used (except in an artificial "Do you ..." form which would allow one to preserve the imagined rule that every sentence have an explicit grammatical subject). As the second person is the implicit subject of the imperative mood, so the second or third person is the subject of "You shall ..." and "He shall ..." formations, which have the meaning, "It is laid down by fate/law/me that you/he will...".

(ii) Predicate-operators and clause-operators: semantic roots of the *de re/de dicto* distinction

There is a place in logic and semantics where we can expect operators which have two different types of use. Sometimes they take a predicate as their complement—that is, modify the predicate and together with the predicate apply to the subject, the modifier being therefore said to apply *de re*. And sometimes they modify a full clause, and are therefore said to apply *de dicto*. We must reject the common presumption that such operators will all behave in the same way.[72]

There are two important cases of this. The first recognizes a divide between such psychological verbs or predicates as "look", "sound", and "appear" used in relation to the senses and "seem" and "appear" used in relation to judgment to express that the judgment is tentative, provisional judgment or such as is initially natural. "Look", "sound", and "appear" are connected respectively with sight, with hearing, and with the senses in general. Thus we say, "Tonight the heavens look and sound angry", "The heavens appear angry", or "The sun appears to have a dark body crossing in front of it", and these have to do with how things appear to the senses. With these statements, a *de re* interpretation is necessary. By contrast, "seem" has to do with judgment, as in "It seems that the sun is an average size normal yellow star, about half way through its life", even though they can be expressed in the form "The sun seems to be an average size yellow star", and "The sun seems to us to be an average size yellow star". With this second group of statements, a *de dicto* interpretation is need-

71. The subjunctive "become" can be weakened to "might become" or strengthened to "should become".

72. E.g., Thrainsson, *On Complementation in Icelandic*, 352–54.

ed—even though they presuppose the existence of the sun, nonetheless it is the provisional character of the complete judgment which is being asserted.

A more important case is presented by modal statements. Negation (except of truth and epistemic propositions), practical possibility, and the various causative and evaluative idioms considered earlier operate *de re*—whereas truth and epistemic idioms apply *de dicto*. This difference reflects deep "general logical" constraints.

The fact that the verb phrase containing the "finite" verb is the "saying" part of the sentence must in any case open the question whether negation, modal, temporal, and causal phrases and adverbial clauses should be considered as modifying the verb phrase or predicate or considered as modifying the whole clause or sentence. These problems are to be solved, not in grammar and not in formal logic, but within a philosophical semantics.

We have already seen how propositional negation always takes a *de re* form if the proposition is of subject/predicate form. Either a predicate is denied to hold of an identified individual ("Julius Caesar was not an emperor"), or it is denied to apply universally to a class ("Not every swan is white" and "Some swans are not white"), or it is denied to apply to any of a class ("Not a scrap was left"), but the existence of the individual or of the class is presupposed. And we find that when a proposition is formed of an adverbial operator and a clause of subject/predicate form, then if the adverbial operator applies *de re,* its denial is also *de re,* while if it applies *de dicto,* its denial is also *de dicto*. This distinction is also important for another reason: because it marks a difference between two different kinds of possibility, represented in English by the epistemic "is possible that" followed by a clause in the indicative mood, requiring a *de dicto* interpretation, and the real or moral/legal "is possible for", requiring a *de re* one.

In general, uses of "possible", "necessary", "certain", and "because" to express states of knowledge or uncertainty or in connection with the making of judgments seem to apply fairly invariably to sentences or to clauses as wholes, *de dicto,* as we saw in discussion of logic at the parasentential level in chapter XIII, section 6. In these uses of modal terms, invariably the "that" form was required—for instance, the combination "possible that" and never "possible for". Further, invariably, there was no restriction, semantic or grammatical, between the time associated with the modal operator expressing the time of judgment and the time of the matter judged about expressed in the clause. And here the denial of the modal statement is *de dicto* also, although the time of judgment expressed by the tense of the modal operator and its temporal modifiers remain overriding.

By contrast, where causal relation, natural ability, and the resulting possibilities and impossibilities, permission, necessitation, obligation, or prohibition are concerned—that is, in what Van Valin calls respectively dynamic and deontic root modality[73]—the modal operator always applies *de re*—that is, adjunctively to the predicate. As a result, its necessary or contingent application to the semantic subject is independent of how the subject is identified.[74] In addition, it is absolutely impossible, engendering grammatical as well as semantic absurdity, for the time associated with the complementary clause to be earlier than that associated with the modal operator. And, although modal assertions of these non-epistemic types commonly use the "for"-construction, nonetheless, if a "that"-construction is used, the same tense requirements have to be kept.

73. Cf. the introduction, secs. 3 (b) (ii) and 4 (b) (i), in this volume.

74. This excludes the context of mention of the subject from being what the logicians call "referentially opaque".

XV

The Distorted Treatment of Phrase Theory in Modern Formal Grammar

In Chapter XIV we saw how discourse and sentence structure shape phrase structure, rather than phrase structure shaping sentence structure.

By contrast, in Chomsky's minimalist approach, beginning with morphemes, in successive stages, ever larger phrasal groups are formed until sentential "phrases" are reached. In this bottom-up approach the properties of each lexical item as set within the lexicon determine the ways it can be joined ("Merge") with other items to form the successive complexes and determine how these can themselves be joined. At various stages in this process certain restricted kinds of "Movement" ("transformations") can occur.

Chomsky has provided successively more sophisticated construction manuals for constructing sentences as static entities, but what we need instead is a grammar which models what is spoken as something live, not as something static. We are deceived through always looking at the written word on paper. Yet even in the act of reading and understanding we have something dynamic.

The constructional model of grammar has been reinforced in two ways.

First, the X-Bar theory of lexical phrases with heads appeared to identify striking parallelisms between noun, adjective, verb, and prepositional phrases.

However, as I show in section 1, noun phrases with complements arise in two quite different ways. A first group express relations—for instance, "the father of Isaac" and "a wing of a bird". The relative terms involved are attributive complements of the copula, as in "Abraham was a father" and "This is a wing".

A second group, along with adjective phrases, recapitulate the structures of verb phrases in which they are both semantically rooted. As for prepositions, we have seen how their essentially synlexical character, linking some other element to a noun, adjective, or verb, makes it quite wrong to treat them as heads of lexical phrases parallel to nouns, adjectives, and verbs. (Whatever I say of prepositions in this chapter applies to postpositions, as well.) Semantic syntax is what is fundamental for each language, and morphosyntactic restrictions consequential.

Second, it was thought fruitful to extend the application of X-Bar theory to supposed "functional phrases" with "functional heads" alongside lexical phrases, and to link the theory of Movement with this larger framework. In this way the earlier mistakes, made possible by Chomsky's conception of the autonomy of syntax vis-à-vis semantics, were compounded.

In section 3 I show that this notion of functional phrases with functional heads is deceptive, since there is no real analogy between lexical heads and so-called functional heads, and it explains nothing which is not better explained in other ways. I discuss Chomsky's ideas in their "Principles and Parameters" form, because the same objections apply *pari passu* to the corresponding ideas presented in minimalist guise for reasons indicated in chapter XIII, section 7 (b).[1]

Section 1. A Preliminary: Kinds of "of"-Phrases

(a) *Two sorts of "of"-phrases*

Complementary phrases can be considered in two different ways: (a) morphosyntactically, whereby the complement concerned (e.g., "tigers") is the complement of a preposition, and the prepositional phrase as a unity (e.g., "of tigers") is considered to be the complement of some noun, adjective, or verb; and (b) semantically, whereby essentially the complement concerned ("ti-

1. In non-transformational formal grammars such as Lexical Functional Grammar (discussed later) and Generalized Phrase Structure Grammar, X-Bar syntax takes varied forms and applies only to lexical phrases. Chomsky never gives it any precise statement, and in itself it explains nothing, as Geoffrey K. Pullum demonstrates in "Assuming Some Version of X-Bar Theory", *Chicago Linguistic Society* 21, no. 1 (1985): 323–53.

In functionalist grammars, it is rejected altogether. Dik has an extended discussion of degrees of nominalization (*Theory of Functional Grammar: Part 2*, 162–68), and regards the verbal "the enemy destroyed the city" as underlying the nominal "the enemy's destruction of the city", the relation to be explained in functional and semantic, not morphosyntactic, terms. The same root and branch rejection of X-Bar syntax even in regard to lexical phrases is to be found in Halliday, *Introduction to Functional Grammar*, 1st ed., 23–29, partly anticipated in Halliday, "Categories of the Theory of Grammar", *Word* 17, no. 3 (1961): 241–92, Van Valin and LaPolla, *Syntax*, 53–67. Van Valin remarks that Role and Reference Grammar "rejects X-bar syntax and assumes instead a multi-projection, semantically based theory of clause structure which permits crossing branches", in "Linguistic Diversity and Theoretical Assumptions", *Chicago Linguistic Society Parasession* 35 (2000): 389–90.

gers") is the complement of the noun, adjective, or verb, and prepositions are mere connectives or linking devices.

Thus, consider "the king of Spain", "a slave of a Roman senator", "a wing of a bird", "a way of cutting cheese", "the way to cut cheese", "his trade in furs", "his trading in furs", "his fear of tigers", "his fear of going out", and "his desire to go". In all these, semantically, the preposition accomplishes a linking to a noun (in other terms, the prepositional phrase modifies a noun). In "afraid of tigers", "afraid of going out", and "afraid to go out", the linking is to an adjective. Third, in "He dreamt of horses", "He went to Seville", "He was in Seville", "He trades in furs", "He feared to go out", and "He desired to go", the linking is to a verb.

In these examples infinitives and gerunds, both syntactically formed from verbs, can be linked both to adjectives and to verbs: thus, morphosyntactically, "to go out" is linked to an adjective in "be afraid to go out" and to a verb in "fear to go out". Meantime, in "be afraid of going out" the verbal expression is linked to an adjective, and in "fear going out" the same verbal expression is linked to a verb.[2]

Approaching the matter semantically, whenever we have two expressions of which one is linked to another, the second being closer to the heart of the clause, the linking is rooted in a relation of some kind. In particular, considered functionally and semantically, genitive or "of" phrases modifying nouns are of two sorts according to the type of relation involved.

With the first sort, which I call semantically nominal, the relation is typically social, biological, or physical—I say, "typically", because mathematical cases such as "a square root of sixteen" also fall here, but do not alter my general argument—and often of a part-whole kind. This is true in the case of the examples "the king of Spain", "a slave of a Roman senator", "the father of Isaac", and "a wing of a bird", given earlier. In these cases the relation on which the verbal link is based is external to language.

In this first sort of case, in which the genitive or "of" phrase arises from a social, biological, or physical relation (we can simplify, since all part-whole relationships fall into these same categories), these relations can be stated in attributive statements such as, "The king is of the Belgians", "The slave is Abraham's", and "The wing is of a bird". In such cases no adjuncts can intrude between the "of"-phrase and what it modifies—for instance, between "king" and "of the Belgians".

2. Many past participles exhibit the same double behavior as "afraid", e.g., "be frightened to go out" where "be frightened" is the passive of the verb "to frighten", or "be frightened of going out" where "frightened" is an adjective in its own right. Paradoxically, one cannot say, "eager of going out" or "eagerness of going out", but only "eager to go out" and "eagerness to go out", as if they came from a verb "to be eager". Many adjectives are like "eager" in showing verb-like behavior; e.g., "keen", "reluctant", "sorry", and "anxious", can likewise only take "to" with the simple infinitive. By contrast, "desirous", like "afraid", can also take "of" with the gerund.

By contrast, the second sort arises from the structure of a clause and is rooted in the relation of a verb to its complements, so that I call it semantically verbal. Thus consider first the case of phrases headed by the nouns "fear" and "desire", which have their meanings rooted in the verbs "to fear" and "to desire": "his fear of tigers", "his fear of going out", and "his desire to go". Here the relations on which the linkage rests are those expressed in "he fears tigers", "he fears to go out", and "he desires to go". Correspondingly, the adjective "afraid" has its meaning rooted in the verb "to fear" and heads such phrases as "afraid of tigers", "afraid of going out", and "afraid to go out". Here again the relations on which the linkage rests are the ones more directly expressed in "he fears tigers", "he fears going out", and "he fears to go out".

All genitive or "of" phrases which modify adjectives are of this second, semantically verbal kind. The linkage expressed by the relevant preposition is grounded in the lexical rooting of the noun or adjective concerned in the relevant verb and arises from the structure of a clause, the linkage rooted in the relation of the complements of the verb to the verb. Further, what is expressed by the verbs in these cases is the content of very varied clauses, such as "he fears tigers" and "he trades in furs". There are therefore a greater variety of prepositions or case-markings expressing linkage to the nouns or adjectives concerned, not just prepositions with a structural function such as "of".

With the subject and the direct object of a verb, there is no preposition connecting them to the verb—for instance, in "David fears tigers" and "The father loves his son". By contrast, if we have a noun or adjective as head of the phrase, we need prepositions to connect the abstract noun-expressions concerned, "fear" or "love", with the expressions "father" and "son", as in "David's fear of tigers" and "the love of the father for his son". In general, if "of" has not already been applied to the subject as the first claimant, it will be applied by default to the direct object of the verbal expression concerned, and thus the noun phrase concerned will reflect the verbal nexus which we see expressed more openly in a clause. And, since English retains the possessive "-'s", in English it is typically the direct object of the verb which is governed by this default "of" in such formations as "David's fear of tigers", echoed in "David is afraid of tigers". However, the French lack of the English possessive "-'s" makes the need of two prepositions arise more often, so that "David's fear of tigers" becomes *le crainte de David envers des tigres,* although the linkages have the same semantic roots. In general, if "of" (or an equivalent) has already been used to express relation to the subject of the action, some alternative preposition is needed to express relation to its object, as in "the assault of the British on Caen".[3]

3. Other examples of prepositions being permitted or excluded can be found in Radford, *Transformational Grammar,* 344–48.

We can now generalize. Since the adjuncts of adjectives are adverbial, and adverbs, as we shall see, cannot take content-introducing adjuncts (not counting identity or quantity indicators), adjectives can take only one content-introducing adjunct. Hence only nouns and verbs are capable of an indefinite series of adjuncts. As section 2 will show, this is of considerable significance in the verb-rooted kind of case, but not in the other.

In the case of verbs alone an adjunct may separate a head from its complement, although, where the subject or object of the verb is concerned, in some languages configurational rules may forbid or limit this.

We have given two types of example: noun phrases in which the relation of the noun to its complement is rooted in a relation external to language, and noun and adjective phrases in which the relation of the noun or adjective to its complement is rooted in the relation of the corresponding verb to its complements. In general, when the terms are linked by discrete words (prepositions or postpositions), the order of the verb phrase—different in different languages, children following the ordering learnt from their elders—will tend to dictate the order of corresponding noun and adjective phrases, and the noun or adjective will be related to its complement and any connective in such a way as to avoid ambiguity and escape confusing complements with other modifiers of the noun or adjective. These last requirements also govern noun phrases in which the relationship of noun to complement is physical or social. The requirements of X-Bar theory are typically satisfied as a byproduct of this. Where connection is made by giving complements genitive inflection or adapting the verb (e.g., by an adverbial prefix), instead of by discrete words such as connectives, configurational requirements are weaker.

Note. Subjective and objective genitives In chapter XI I remarked on how the genitive and in certain cases the dative had taken on a purely identificatory or specificatory role shared by certain prepositions, such as "of", *de*, and *von*. This purely structural role in complementary phrases, so that the inflections and prepositions concerned are entirely devoid of content, is particularly apparent in the cases of so-called subjective and objective genitives, including the degenerate case of "the dreaming of a dream".

No tie is required between a verb and its direct object; there is no relation to be indicated by a preposition and no lexical meaning for such a preposition, the accusative case having no meaning beyond distinguishing the direct object from the subject. And, as there is nothing with lexical content linking the subject to the verb, so there is nothing with lexical content linking the verb to its object. Therefore, we have two purely structural uses of "of": (a) to mark the fact that the "of" phrase is specificatory of what the fear is in respect of or in regard to the object of the fear, as in the case of "fear of mice"; and (b) to mark the fact that in the case of "the love of his father for him" considered earlier, where the love is on the part of the father, the "of" phrase is identificatory of whose love is spoken of, the subject of the love.

The property of the prepositions "of" and *de* whereby they govern whole phrases came to be shared by the English genitive marker "-'s", which has the oddity among genitive suffixes of applying to whole noun phrases rather than solely to nouns as individual words. When "-'s" is used, as in "The father's love for his son", it always expresses a subjective, not an objective, genitive. The equivalent meaning using pronouns is expressed by such means as "my", "thy", "his", "her", and "its",[4] as in "my love for him".

(b) *The variety of prepositions in semantically verbal complements*

The meaning of the relational noun "slave" dictates that its lexical complements signify the slave's master. Where the meaning of a noun is rooted in a verb, the meaning of the verb concerned dictates what complementary object phrases a noun or adjective derived from it may take. And in the case of oblique objects, the preposition occurring in the clausal construction in which the noun or adjective phrase is rooted will be preserved in the noun or adjective phrase concerned. Hence complements can be linked to the verb-rooted noun or adjective they complement by a wide variety of different prepositions and case-markings.

Thus he who trades in furs is a trader in furs and conducts trade in furs. If a man wonders at the beauty of his wife, we can speak of his wonder at his wife's beauty, or of his being struck with wonder at his wife's beauty. The man skillful at gardening has skill at gardening. The woman skillful in getting her own way has skill in getting her own way; and if keen on ornithology, shows keenness for ornithology; if sorry for or at what she did, has sorrow for or at what she did; and if eager for a good result, has eagerness for this. These descriptions are rooted in sentences such as, "The man was skillful at gardening" and "She was sorry for her sins", and the lexically corresponding nouns ("skill" and "sorrow") are rooted in the same verbal nexus.[5]

Again, one gives to people, goes to places, lays siege to cities, trades in furs, sculpts in stone, dotes upon pets, and makes attacks upon the enemy. Thus when other prepositions than "of" are used in expressing the relation of a noun to its complement, the preposition chosen has a semantic character

4. Sometimes called pronominal adjectives, because as determiners of nouns they decline in the same way as adjectives in Indo-European languages.

5. If the object is unspecified ("the skilled man", "the eager man"), the expression is unnatural (as if one could have a skill or eagerness which was entirely general); "a sorry man" is an object of sorrow, not its subject.

reflecting the meaning of the verb. This includes cases such as "look at", discussed earlier, in which the verb and preposition together can also be treated as a genuine lexical unity, although not a morphosyntactic unity. Such prepositions and postpositions enrich or modify meaning, while, like modal verbs, remaining synlexical in character, their role depending on linkage to a lexical head of one of the three types I indicated, senseless alone. If Caesar makes a fierce attack upon the city, he attacks the city fiercely; "make an attack upon the city"[6] is a long way of saying, "attack the city". Semantically, "attacks" are cognates of the verb "make" and not products or objects which we make in the literal sense, any more than "statements" are products in the literal sense.

Note "Cognate genitive" phrases arising from the nexus of a verb with a cognate accusative Some outgoing ("exeunt" or transeunt) acts cannot be defined in terms of being "causative" of changes in physical or social relations. Thus, to define hitting in terms of changing the thing hit from not yet having been hit to having been so would involve circularity. If I hit a wall, I will not hurt it (cause it pain), and perhaps will not alter it at all. If, when I hit people, I deter, insult, hurt, or harm them, still hitting is not to be defined in terms of such effects.

Whereas some causative activities imply changes in physical or social relations, external acts such as hitting are logically self-contained. If a blow is struck or a hit is scored, the act is complete.

With such acts it is particularly important to distinguish between being a semantic object and being a grammatical cognate. The "semantic objects" of acts of hitting or striking are the people or things which are hit or struck. By contrast, the hits we score or blows we strike, along with the sales, rescues, felonies, and murders we achieve or commit, are cognate accusatives, morphosyntactic objects of the verb comparable to those arising with logically intransitive verbs: "dreaming a dream", "sleeping a deep sleep", and "thinking thoughts". If I dream a dream that my house is burning down, "dream a dream" is all part of the extended kernel of the complete verb-expression, and only "that my house is burning down" specifies the semantic complement to the verb "dream". Slayings and rescues are all "of something" (e.g., "of dragons", "of damsels"). The elaborate expression "the committing [commission] of the crime of murder" is equivalent to "the committing [commission] of murder"; both "crime" in the first case and "murder" in the second indicate the act done, "crime" its genus, and "murder" its species. Both these nouns stand as cognates, not objects, whereas it is the person murdered who is the semantic ob-

6. The appropriateness of "upon" or "on" after "attack" may come from a subliminal comparison with the relation of the eagle or the jaguar to its prey.

ject, whether of the verb "murder" or of the cognate noun "murder". Among "of"-phrases modifying nouns, it is only the latter, expressing a relation to the semantic object of an action, which is rooted in a verbal nexus, "Fenton committed the murder of the Duke" being equivalent to "Fenton murdered the Duke". Since Fenton murdered the Duke in a pub, we can speak of the "murder of the Duke in a pub".

With immanent activities, just as with outgoing or transeunt activities, we must avoid giving the status of real relations to mere constructions of language. Just as in the striking of a blow there is no real relation between the striking and the blow, so also if I have a dream or have a thought, there is no special psychological relation of "having" involved. The word "have" here has no more content than the preposition "of". The same empty use of "have" arises when we say, "I have a pain in my thumb" instead of, "I feel pain in my thumb".

(c) *Noun complements rooted in a physical, biological, or social relation, not in a verbal nexus*

The most conspicuous example of relational nouns whose very meaning invites a complement is provided by the names for types of parts of things. Thus we have "the head of Jones", "the head of the butterfly", and "the third finger of the right hand of the man", as well as indefinite expressions like "a finger" and the names of parts of other kinds of animal, tree, and living thing, cars, ships, houses, and so forth. In each case the complement can be specified, but need not be mentioned. In English it can normally be specified in two ways, by means of a prepositional phrase beginning with "of" as in "a wing of a bird" and "the head of Bill", or with an "-'s" as in "a bird's head" or "Bill's head". In these cases the use of the genitive-expression is again rooted in a relation, but the relation is physical or biological, not intralinguistic. Finnish, among other languages, expresses these relations by a partitive case, distinct from the genitive.

Let us consider a typical case of one thing or person being described as "of" another in virtue of a social relation. One cannot be a slave without having a master or, often a very different thing, an owner.

Being a slave must be understood in terms of the social state of being subject to commands in virtue of masterhood or ownership, even though the character of the relationship has been utterly different according to the customs or laws of the society concerned, Mosaic, ancient Roman, and at different times in Brazil. Likewise, being husband and wife naturally includes the practice of sexual intercourse and the care and nurture of resulting children within the context of the human community, but is subject to a variety of customs. "Son" and "daughter" have their meaning with reference to origin in such context and being objects of such responsibility in respect of care and nurture. "Chief" and "king" are words with the original and basic meaning of having the chief role according to custom in governing the whole community, or being honored as having such role (words of similar meaning like "lord" may have a more generic meaning).

Accordingly, we should regard these social states of relationship, each highly variable in character, as grammaticality parallel to those of physical relationships, and again treat the "of" or "-'s" as of the semantically nominal sort, where, for instance, in "son of Charles", "son" is linked to the noun "Charles". These relationships are all rooted in social or physical structures (people may be parents of children, masters of slaves, owners of houses and cattle, or captains of ships), not rooted in a verbal or lexical nexus like the cases considered earlier.

Whenever an X is an X of Y, language provides verbs for expressing both the relation and its converse, and the most general of these verbs must be as formal or empty of content as the preposition "of" itself. The slaves are had by, belong to, or appertain to their master only in the sense that they are "of" him. In this way Charles V's wives, children, and other relatives, empire, kingdoms, duchies, counties, subjects, slaves, and so forth, alongside his possessions, are all "had by" Charles V, the wives as husband, and the subjects as king, and so they all belong or appertain to him in one way or another. Meantime, just as the prow, masts, sails, crew, captain, engines, and lifeboats of a ship all appertain to it in one way or another, so a man's head, hair, legs, kidneys, white blood cells, trousers, and indeed all his parts and accoutrements appertain to him in one way or another.

Note on the ambiguities of the English genitive "-'s" construction If I paint Bill, in trying to represent him in some way, I produce a painting or "picture of Bill", and the "of" here comes out of a verbal nexus. However, if I say, "Bill's picture", I might also mean "a picture painted by Bill" or else "a picture owned by Bill". Thus it is characteristic of the English "-'s" to be open to significantly greater ambiguity than the other genitives we have been looking at.[7] They retain this ambiguity when they come after the head noun: "a picture of Bill" means something quite different from "a picture of Bill's", which would normally mean one owned by him. And "a picture of Rembrandt's" usually means a picture by him (a Rembrandt), not owned by him. The surviving "possessive" pronouns have the same greater ambiguities. I could shout, "That picture is mine" with either meaning, of owning it (a use of the possessive pro-

7. "The King of France" can only mean some actual constitutionally functioning king or claimant to this role, but the phrase "France's King" can instead be understood more informally, e.g., to refer to some handsome brave who is all the rave in film, sport, or music.

noun rooted in the relationship of ownership) or of having painted it (a use of the possessive pronoun rooted in the verbal nexus, "I painted the picture", unconnected with possession). If a picture is of me, I would be more likely to say, "That picture is of me" (which is specificatory of a kind, not an individual, since there may be many pictures of me).[8]

"This leg is of a primitive bird", "The crime was of murder", "The victim was of Caucasian stock", "Winston's fear was of rats", and "The trial was of Charles I" can all be attributed copulatively, just like locatives and ascriptions of agency or origin ("by Rembrandt" and "from Holland"), as in "The picture was by Rembrandt and from Holland".

It is a very different matter to make it clear that a leg which has been touched is one's own living leg. One has to say, "That [what someone is touching] is me" or "That is part of me"—we do not say, "That is of me", or "This leg is of me". The "of" idioms are thus useless for expressing such things, and "This leg is Bill's" is compatible with its being one of Bill's natural living legs, but also with its being a spare prosthetic leg.

(d) *Verbally rooted complements to connectives in phrases adjunctive to clauses*

If Socrates's disciples met later "where Socrates died", this is the same as for them to have met "at the place where Socrates died", or "at the place of Socrates's death". If Jesus was born "when three planets were in conjunction", then he was born "at the time of this conjunction". If Pompeii was destroyed "because Vesuvius erupted", then it was destroyed "because of the eruption of Vesuvius".[9] If I kill Napoleon by arranging that his apartments are painted with arsenic-laden paint, then I have killed him "by poisoning him", "by poison", or "by means of poison". Things done in order that one may have money to support one's family are done "for the family", "on behalf of the family", or "for the sake of the family". And if what is done "has the effect or consequence that one starves", then it is done "with the effect or consequence of one's starving". And actions of politicians have been done "with the consequence of many famines, much starvation, deforestation, and terrible floods". All such uses of "of" invite the explanation that there is a semantic equivalence between a complementizer, such as "that", followed by a clausal formation, and a simple connective, such as "of" (a more complex connective), followed by a noun phrase with a verbal rooting, as "because [that] Vesuvius erupted" is equivalent to "because of the eruption of Vesuvius". A proper treatment of the whole family of cases would require a more extended discussion.

8. "That [picture] is my picture" could equally express ownership or authorship.

9. Here etymology does not lie: "because" derives from "by cause".

Section 2. Three Levels of Isomorphism When a Noun or Adjective Phrase Is Verbally Rooted

(a) *Noun and adjective phrases rooted in verb formations*

(i) A general overview

In considering the structure of clauses, we contrasted the objects of the main verb within the clause and the satellites mentioned in adjunctive phrases. Examination showed that many noun and all adjective phrases have a configuration shaped by correspondence with that of the underlying verb phrase—that is, the clause in which they are semantically rooted. Any qualification in the clausal case is eligible to reappear in its parallel occurrences—for instance, the person who trades in nothing else but furs is a trader in nothing else but furs, or, if he trades in more than furs, a trader in more than furs.

What are called verb "phrases" tend to have several hierarchically ordered complements, configured as each language requires, and any noun and adjective phrase rooted in such a verb phrase can therefore likewise have a set of hierarchically ordered complements. In this capacity to have such a series of complements, rather than just one, noun and adjective phrases rooted in a verbal nexus differ from noun phrases not thus rooted.

Let us consider various groups of example.

One cannot be a trader without trading in something. One may be a general teacher or general trader rather than teacher of or trader in something particular, but in particular cases a teacher of French or a trader in furs. If one has taught anyone at all (rather than being about to teach), there will be someone (e.g., Bill), or some group (e.g., primary school pupils), whom one has taught, and so one will be a/or the teacher of Bill or a teacher of primary school pupils. If one is a receiver of stolen goods, one may specialize and be a receiver of diamonds and be described as "receiving diamonds". If one is a writer, one may be a writer of novels or of sports reports. We have collectors of stamps, drivers of trains, and painters of portraits, and these collect stamps, drive trains, and paint portraits, as well as being described as stamp collectors, train drivers, and portrait painters. Some people train police dogs, and some sheep dogs, and these are trainers of police dogs and of sheep dogs—two kinds of dog trainer. Others love books and so are lovers of books or book lovers. It is better to say, "he sculpts in stone" and "sculptor in stone" than "he sculpts stone" and "sculptor of stone".

The ordering within subjective and objective genitives may differ as between SVO, SOV, and VSO languages. As we have seen, in SVO languages, in "the passionate love of a father for his son", indication of the subject immediately follows the verb-derived noun (including any nuclear adverb) linked by the default preposition ("of") or by being genitively marked, while indication of the direct object will follow, linked by some different semantically appropriate preposition or marking. When such complementary expressions occur before the noun or adjective, they occur without any preposition, so that the student of physics is a physics student, rule by the mob is mob-rule, and to be shy of work is to be work-shy, but when a single word is formed, it can gain a life of its own.

Some verbs are "ditransitive", taking two objects—for instance, "give", "teach", and "employ": one employs someone to do something or as something. With head-nouns formed from ditransitive verbs, the same head-noun may have a double complement. So Socrates was teacher of philosophy to Plato (or teacher of Plato in philosophy), and someone might be the employer of Bill as a chauffeur. When the verb in which the noun involved is lexically rooted is a process-verb, it does not matter whether the activity is still continuing or complete; thus the builder of a house is its builder during its building and after it is complete, and he who fills a jug with water is its filler during as well as after its filling, although the jug is full only after the process is complete.

(ii) Complements of adjectives and nouns referring to emotions and cognition

As philosophers have long recognized, every emotion has an object (e.g., fear is of danger or possible danger, so that any actual fear is of something thought of as possibly dangerous). One cannot fear without fearing something. Likewise, one cannot be angry without being angry at something. If one has pleasure in or at something, then one is said to enjoy it or to be pleased in, at, or by it. A person cannot be emotionally sad without feeling sad, and sadness is always sadness at something.

Some words signify character traits—for instance, jealousy, whose typical exercise is in being jealous of somebody in respect of something, and so I may be jealous of Bill Gates because of his achievement, fame, or wealth. One may be proud of one's books (proud of those one possesses or proud of those one has written), or proud of one's strength, and one can boast of any of these. To have contempt for, hold in contempt, and despise are much the same, and their objects are despised and, if the attitude is appropriate, despicable or contemptible.

Again, parallels arise when we pass from actions and emotions to so-called cognitive states. Those who know about stamps are knowledgeable about or even expert on them, those who know geometry or art history may be experts in them, and those who know how to paint experts at painting. The person who believes in ghosts is a believer in ghosts, if the matter is not trifling for him.

Commonly we accept nouns derived from verbs or verbal expressions as descriptions of people only when they pick out central, rather than peripheral aspects of the person's life. Not everyone who plays cricket is a "cricketer", but only one who is skilled at it. Not everyone who boasts is a braggart, or everyone who drinks a drinker, or mends a shoe a cobbler. Accordingly, some of the nouns corresponding to verbs of action and emotion are missing.

Likewise, there are many adjectives, such as "proud", which correspond to the actions, emotions, and attitudes expressed or identified by a great many verbs and nouns—for instance, "conceit", "arrogance", and "contempt", as well as "pride", but in the cases of which no one verb is privileged. With these reservations we find a constantly recurring correspondence between suitable verbs with their objects, whether these objects are indirect in requiring a preposition or case-marking, and the corresponding nouns and adjectives taking these objects as their complements, the phrase for the complements with the same case-marking or preposition. Often the meaning of the verb "selects" the preposition which will precede the complement of the corresponding noun or adjective—for instance, such prepositions as "in", "at", "on", or "to"; but otherwise the preposition "of" will be used after the corresponding noun or adjective, by default. This last is the invariable case when the noun takes the form of a gerund, as "the killing of Caesar". By contrast, verb-rooted nouns which are not gerunds, such as "destruction", "assault", "wonder", "thought", "dream", "love", "contempt", and "victory", are typically linked to their complements by such prepositions as "on", "at", "about", "for", or "over".

(b) *These isomorphisms support parallel superstructures at two levels*

We have now seen how semantically verbal structures give rise to isomorphic noun and adjective phrases. This allows these phrases, as well as the clause, to use Jespersen's striking contrast, to present a nexus, a process or drama, and not just a picture. We can now advance to grasp the existence of isomorphic structures at two further levels built upon the first.

When we have nouns, adjectives, and verbs which take the same objects or types of objects, with an appropriate preposition when necessary, as complements, these nouns, adjectives, and verbs will then be subject to exactly parallel modifiers, in the case of nouns taking the syntactic form of adjectives agreeing with the noun in case, number, and gender, or in the case of adjectives and verbs the corresponding syntactic adverb (I reserve the descriptions "semantic adverb" and "semantic adverb phrase" for expressions occurring as modifying verbs). The person who has a special, real, enormous, unusual, remarkable, or negligible fear of spiders will be specially, really, enormously, unusually, remarkably, or negligibly afraid of them, and will fear them specially, really, and so forth. The person who trades skillfully, profitably, dishonestly, or independently in furs is a skillful, profitable, dishonest, or independent trader in furs. Again, activities of various kinds can be described as performed carelessly, clumsily, awkwardly, callously, rudely, maliciously, speedily, diligently, and successfully, and as a result we encounter clumsy, awkward, callous, rude, and malicious people, among them waiters, joiners, conversationalists, and husbands.

And sometimes we may speak of the activity not only in regard to its manner, what it is in respect of, its place or time, but in respect of its completion.

He who drives cars is a driver of cars, and he who types may happen to type a particular piece of work, but is not *qua* typist a typist of particular pieces of work, but of documents in general, because being a typist refers to a capacity. But even when the nouns or adjectives do not have the obvious complements, there may be the same interconnection of nouns, adjectives, and verbs; thus, the fast typist is the one who types fast, and likewise the fast driver drives fast, the fast car travels fast, and the fast road is one on which one drives or by which one travels fast;[10] the good knife cuts well, the good fencer fences well and is good at fencing, and the good typist types well and is good at typing; an expert fencer fences expertly and is expert at fencing, and likewise with the typist; the good road is well or expertly made, good or excellent for traveling on, or good as a route between the places it joins. Such analyses are only applicable in the case of head nouns whose meanings require explanation in terms of a characteristic activity, such as "typist", "car", "road", "fencer", "student", and "cobbler". They are useless with the quasi-referential names of natural kinds and colors.

There are no nouns for the persons with certain knowledge of or that something, or sure belief in or that something, but where we have certain knowledge, we know certainly, for certain, and with certainty, while, when we have sure belief that something, we believe it surely and for sure.

He who "proves" Pythagoras's Theorem has a "proof" of it. And he who has proved it for certain has certain proof of it. As a proof has to be a proof of something, so a problem has to be a problem as to something. Hence, if someone "solves" a problem definitively, such as whether or not the prime numbers form an unending series, then something (here Euclid's proof) is its definitive "solution".

The peculiarity of adverbs appears in the fact that the trader, his trade, and his trading may all be skillful and all in furs, and the attacker, his attack, and his attacking may all be brave and on or of the city, but neither the trading in furs nor the attacking of the city can be skillfully. The semantic adverb modifies something semantically verbal and, unlike a noun or an adjective,

10. Cf. Jackendoff, *Architecture*, 62–64, in chap. 2, sec. 1 (e) (i), observing his n. 27.

cannot do duty as a complement to the verb "to be". The trader trades skillfully, and the attacker attacks skillfully, and we can speak of the attacker's "skillfully attacking the city" because the "attacking" is here a verbal form akin to an infinitive. However, we cannot speak of "his skillfully attacking of the city", since the addition of the preposition has removed the verbal character from the noun "attacking": it is now a gerund, and we have to say, "his skillful attacking of the city".

(c) *The second layer of isomorphic superstructure*

Our generalization can be taken further. The second-level isomorphism whereby corresponding adjectives and adverbs serve as modifiers of the earlier corresponding nouns, adjectives, and verbs was built upon the isomorphism between corresponding noun, adjective, and verb phrases. However, upon this second-level isomorphism there is built a third-level isomorphism. In this the same or closely corresponding identity and quantity indicators apply to these adjectives and adverbs[11]—that is, to these corresponding modifiers of nouns (called adjectives), modifiers of adjectives (called adverbs), and modifiers of adverbs (also called adverbs).

We noted that we apply nouns derived from verbs expressing the activity, emotions, attitudes, and qualities of people to the people themselves when they constitute central, habitual, or structural aspects of the person's life. However, even if its clumsiness or continuation is short-lived, we can speak of a person's clumsiness in carrying things, his or her clumsy carrying of things, and his or her clumsy way or manner of carrying things, as well as saying that he or she carries things clumsily. Of the person who speaks really/very/rather/quite/so/too slowly or quickly, we can say that his or her speech is really/very/rather/quite/so/too slow or quick; and he or she might work carelessly in any of these ways or have his or her work described as careless in any of

11. Thus we say, "utter rejection" and "utterly rejecting", and utter-ness is not susceptible of degrees of completeness or thoroughness, and so cannot be qualified by quantity indicators indicating degree. English uses "very" with semantic adjectives and adverbs ("fond", "fondly"), as well as before "very", "much", "many", and "slightly", but not before "too" or "rather". "Much" is used with names for kinds of stuff, by contrast with "many", which is used with count-nouns—we also say, "great courage", as well as "much courage". "Much" is used before "too" and "rather", but not before "very", "many", or "slightly". "Much", many", and "too" are quantity indicators which can be reduplicated any number of times, but only to achieve emphasis, and whose repetition excludes placing any other quantity indicator in front of them. Before "too much" we can put "just", either meaning "simply", i.e., "without qualification", or else "a bit too much"; similarly, in "quite utterly reject", "quite" means "altogether" and cannot mean "a little" or "somewhat", and the repetition is merely emphatic. While "very much more" and "too much more" are acceptable, "very much much more" and "too much much more" are not. Thus the behavior of these words is more complex than Radford (*Transformational Grammar*, 240, 243) indicates, although he is right that, e.g., in Italian *molto* and *tanto* mean "very" as well as "much" and "many", except for variations in inflection for number and gender in the adjectival form, though not with the -*o* of the adverb.

these ways, however we speak of him or her as a speaker or worker in general. The person who is very/more/less indulgent or kind towards Mary has more or less indulgence or kindness towards Mary. In some cases, to certain identity and quantity indicators modifying adjectives—for instance, "very", "as ... as —" (as in, "He did not have as many men serving him as the Persian king"), "so" (implying much more than the norm, as in "so huge an army"), "how" (implying so much more than the norm as to provoke exclamation, as in, "He was astonished at how huge the enemy army was" or "How huge!"), "quite" (meaning more than average, but only a little more, as in "quite a big army"), "too" (meaning excessively), "enough" (meaning sufficiently)—there correspond certain quantity indicators modifying nouns, such as "much", "such", "excessive", and "sufficient".[12]

We mentioned that identity and quantity indicators have two very different roles. We met their role applied to noun phrases as application controllers which show how the verb applies to or governs these noun phrases, and so are central to the structure of the main clause. Then, by contrast, we had identity and quantity indicators serving as the most superficial elements in sentence structure, the identity and quantity indicators modifying adverbs, adjectives, and nouns, as well as modifying abstract nouns formed from the adjectival modifiers of nouns.

These identity and quantity indicators can be gathered so as to constitute a chain of linked elements. Thus, in the string "very very slightly more excitably" in "She performed very very slightly more excitably than her rival", we have four of them hanging on to the "excitably" hanging on to the verb "performed", the first "very" hanging on to the second, and this to the "slightly" and this to the "more", with the "more" morphosyntactically closest to the semantically nuclear adverb "excitably", and its predecessors syntactically more and more distant from the verb. Such an identity and quantity indicator or series of identity and quantity indicators, all syntactically adverbs, can be linked to a semantically nuclear adverb (e.g., "seriously", "intermittently") which is modifying an adjective (e.g., "apprehensive"), or directly to the adjective. But this adjective, if it applies to a abstract noun such as "fear", will only be linked to the main clause by being linked adverbially to a verb ("apprehensively fears"), or if the adjective applies to a concrete noun ("apprehensive man"), it may be linked to the main clause by qualifying the subject or one of the objects of the main verb.

In chains of successively applied identity or quantity indicators, the avoidance of ambiguity strictly requires that the identity and quantity indicators be applied to the word or phrase which they have as head (their core) rigidly in order of their application, grammar strictly following semantics.

12. I adapt these examples from Radford, *Transformational Grammar*, 139, 242–43, 246.

(d) *These two isomorphic levels of superstructure recur with intransitive verbs*

I have concentrated on the structures and the isomorphisms which arise in connection with transitive verbs, whether their objects are direct or oblique, because these are much richer than those arising in connection with intransitive verbs. Nonetheless, intransitive verbs give rise to noun-complement relations with the same character as those we have just been considering, like them arising out of a verbal nexus, something which presents a process or drama, not just a picture. Thus there is the sleeping, the snoring, the flying, the swimming, of the sleeper, the snorer, and so on, and this sleeper is the sleeper of the sleep, and so forth. And insofar as it is thought of not, or not just, as a passivity, but as an activity, it follows that since any such activity is of an agent, it can also be described as by the agent; thus we can speak of the sleeping or snoring by Snooks as well as the sleeping or snoring of Snooks, and even of the death accomplished by Jesus in Jerusalem. In relation to these passivities or activities immanent in a subject, expressed by intransitive verbs, we have much the same range of adverbs as we have already met with, as when we speak of very restless sleeping and of the very brave, slow, or painful dying or death of the man hung, drawn, and quartered.

(e) *Concluding remarks*

Thus, of the kinds of genitive phrase I have spoken of, the ones which have peculiar importance to linguistic theory are those whose use is rooted in a verbal nexus—arising when direct objects and sometimes subjects to verbs become lexical complements to nouns and adjectives semantically related to the verbs concerned.

This first-level isomorphism between the verb/object or verb/subject relation and the noun/complement and adjective/complement relations provides the basis for a second-level isomorphism whereby the adverbial expressions applicable primarily to the verb reappear as adjectival expressions applicable to the nouns and adverbial expressions applicable to the adjectives. Then, at a third level, semantically synlexical adverbs serve as identity and quantity indicators respectively to the adverbial expressions applying to the verbs and adjectives and to the adjectival expressions applying to the nouns, and thence, in an application of further adverbial identity and quantity indicators to these already-present adverbial identity and quantity indicators, the process can be further recapitulated.

The explanatory power of this account appears at many different junctures. Thus it explains how the person who fears tigers just ever so very very slightly more grievously than another person may have just ever so very very slightly more grievous fear of tigers than that other person and be just ever so very very slightly more grievously afraid of tigers! The adjectival phrase "just ever so very very slightly more grievous" corresponds to the adverbial phrase "just ever so very very slightly more grievously", and the two are connected because both the noun phrase "the fear of tigers" and the adjective phrase "afraid of tigers" are rooted in the verb/direct object relation in "he fears tigers".

Again, the same relations are reflected in our different ways of expressing the same information, albeit in ways which set it in different perspectives. Thus, instead of saying, "Very fearful of tigers, he nonetheless continued through the jungle", it is inadequate to say, "He continued very fearfully through the jungle". However, although the simple adverb "fearfully" cannot take a complement however expressed, we can nonetheless express the given information using an adverbial construction, by saying, "He continued through the jungle, despite greatly fearing tigers" (or "despite his being very fearful of tigers" or, again, "despite his great fear of tigers").[13]

The existence of an underlying verbal structure appears in unexpected ways. Consider some interrelated adjective phrases. Thus, in "Acting in character, his aerobatic display was inevitably extravagantly showy", it might look as if the "inevitably" qualifies the "extravagantly showy"; however, its being extravagantly showy is an attribute of the aerobatic display in question, whereas the "inevitably" should be taken as an adverb modifying the verb "was" which heads the clause. We can have combinations like "extravagantly exuberant", "exuberantly extravagant", and "flamboyantly exhibitionist", with adverbs modifying adjectives, but adverbs cannot modify the adverbs parallel to these adjectives. When this appears to happen, the adverbs turn out to be adjoined or attached at grammatically and semantically different points of the verb development, as in, "He can swim slowly easily", which is tolerable because it can be understood as meaning that "he can easily swim slowly if he has to" with the "easily" applying to "can swim slowly", not to "slowly" as such. It is the activity which is performed easily or with ease—it is not the slowness which is being so described. Adverbs applying to activities cannot take complements, any more than they can take adjuncts (unless we treat adverbs indicating quantity or identity, discussed earlier, as adjuncts).

Again, the grammatical requirements reflect the semantics of speech, set by the structural semantic constraints indicated in chapter XIV.

13. "Great" is here a quantity term we often apply to abstract nouns in place of the still used "much". We use "much" with mass-nouns as we use "many" with count-nouns; cf. n. 11.

Section 3. The Misconceptions Embodied in the X-Bar Presentation of Phrase Theory

(a) *X-Bar theory in relation to verb phrases and clauses*

(i) Preliminary remarks

I explained the core of X-Bar theory as it applied to noun, adjective, and adverb phrases in chapter XIV, section 3 (a) (i), explaining it in a form allowing for adjuncts, even though X-Bar theory was not devised to cater for adjuncts in its original conception.[14] The multiple restrictions which particular languages set on the placing of adjuncts are conveniently described in terms of parameters as suggested by Hawkins, but this is external to Chomsky's X-Bar theory, except for the requirements that Head and Complement are inseparable and that what he calls a Specifier cannot come between an adjunct and its Head. Since I regard Chomsky's wider development of the theory, especially in his conception of "functional" heads and complements alongside lexical heads and complements, as questionable, I will use capitals when speaking of Chomskyan X-Bar theory, speaking of "Heads", "Complements", and "Specifiers".

In the form in which Chomsky developed it, X-Bar theory gave one the option of adding a Specifier to cores constituted of a Head, Complements, and Adjuncts. The term "Specifier" was introduced by Chomsky in 1970 in order to complete his description of the structure which he supposed all the principal categories of phrase (noun, adjective, verb) to share. It was a term which, unlike the terms "head", "complement", and "adjunct", had no relevant previous history in grammatical theory. For a time it was common to allow an extra level—for instance, in the case of verbs—to cater for modal verbs, semi-auxiliaries, and their equivalents, generating a fourth level, X^3, but most theorists have now reverted to the original three-level theory, X^0, X^1, and X^2. The maximal level at which the phrase retains the same character, nominal or noun-like, adjectival, or verbal, is customarily described as the maximal projection of the Head concerned, X^0. Thus, in the case of a noun phrase, the kernel noun, X, described as the head of the phrase, stands at the bottom, X^0 level, and the maximal noun-like phrase structured around this noun is described as the "maximal projection of X", which will be at the level X^2 (or, in theories allowing an extra level, X^3). At the stage at which the maximal projection of X is reached, the phrase may be fronted by a "Specifier", a term on which I will comment later.

Until recently every kind of "formal" grammar has incorporated some

14. Cf. Ouhalla, *Introducing Transformational Grammar*, 121–22.

version of X-Bar theory. And in chapter XIV we provided an adequate semantic basis for why X-Bar theory serves as an account of how adjuncts, complements, and heads fit together in noun, adjective, and adverb phrases (and, if it also fits the morphosyntactics of adpositional phrases, this is a byproduct of the way adpositions link their complements to the nouns, adjectives, or verbs to which linkage is made). The application of X-Bar theory to verb phrases and then to so-called functional phrases involves a quite different, much more radical development. Chomsky's whole treatment of the verb depends on his theory of functional Heads of phrases.

(ii) The mistake of extending X-Bar theory to verb phrases and then to clauses

When Jackendoff gave the first systematic account of X-Bar theory in 1977, he represented the sentence or clause as a verb phrase standing at up to three levels above the nonmodal nuclear verb, and the structure was suited to cater for simple modals and other "semi-auxiliaries" and their equivalents, as well as to fit adjuncts into this always verbal structure at an appropriate level. And at each stage the notion of Complement was conceived of, as with lexical phrases, as having a Head which dictated its character.

However, the character of a clause as something which, if it stood on its own, would be a sentence or complete speech-unit constitutes not just a pragmatic or semantic feature, but a grammatical one—otherwise grammar would give no account of when a clause is grammatically complete in such a way as to correspond to a complete utterance. But the verbal character of the core of a clause is a mere echo of the verbal, "rhetic", or "saying" character of speech-units as such, their defining functional, pragmatic, and semantic feature.

Therefore it is deeply misleading for a theory of grammar to attempt to treat verbal "phrases" in the same way as noun, adjective, and adverb phrases, and not at all a virtue as Chomsky and his following have thought. Yet from the first inception of X-Bar theory in 1970, the precise aim of Chomsky and his following has been to explain how, morphosyntactically, as phrases, "the enemy's destruction of the city" and "the enemy destroyed the city" have the same structure, and to regard them as on a par—instead of treating the structure of the sentential or verb phrase as explaining the structure of the noun phrase.[15]

Moreover, it is a grave error to envisage this parallelism as a consequence of the morphosyntactic properties of all "phrases", relying upon a morphosyntactic theory misconceiving of nouns, verbs, adjectives, and prepositions as parallel claimants to the title "lexical head".

15. Fukui, "Phrase Structure", 388–92; cf. Jackendoff, *Semantics and Cognition*, 57, 67, where, strangely, Jackendoff already regards the noun and noun phrase rather than the verb as prototypical, a mistake reiterated in Jackendoff, *Foundations*, 257.

In considering the verb, in contrast with nouns and adjectives, one is considering what lies at the heart of the clause, and the features of agreement-structure, tense, and aspect are internal to this verb, rather than related to it as Heads to a Complement. In analyzing so-called verb phrases, and thence the whole clause, one should consider the role and structure of other elements according to the way they are related to the verb, immediately or indirectly via other elements closer to the verb, in the way outlined in chapter XIV.

In the conception presented in chapter IX and again in chapters X and XIV, it is essential to those constituents of a sentence which have a verbal or "saying" character that they are essentially "incomplete" or "unsaturated", and in no way nominal. It goes with this that the verb kernel of a clause will have among its projections the verb phrase, the whole predicate, and finally the whole clause. It is as head of the clause that verb kernels include the features of agreement-structure, tense, and aspect which belong to the whole clause. This view of the clause as a projection from the verb phrase is anticipated in many presentations of formal grammar, strikingly in those of Jackendoff.[16]

(iii) The two faces of grammars which have both a formal and a functional aspect

Meantime, in many non-Chomskyan systems, symbolisms reflecting the idea of phrases with "functional" Heads are unnecessary and often adopted only as a convenience of representation enabling them to be compared with Chomskyan systems with their different conceptual basis—enabling Lexical Functional Grammar to be more easily thus compared with other systems—for instance, in considering their respective usefulness for the purposes of machine translation.

Accordingly, in discussing what she calls "endocentric languages"—that is, languages in which each phrase incorporates its own head in morphologically realized form—Bresnan invents a ramified version of X-Bar theory incorporating morphologically actual "synlexical" (i.e., syncategorematic)

16. Thus Jackendoff preserves a recognition of this when he represents the sentence as syntactically a projection from the verb phrase and this as a projection of the verb (*Foundations*, 6, 9–10), here developing the perspectives presented in his *X-Bar Syntax: A Study of Phrase Structure* (Cambridge, Mass.: MIT Press, 1977). Jackendoff's account thereby faithfully preserves an imprint of the fact that the function of the verb or predicate is, in notional or traditional terms, the primary functional feature, imposing itself as it were from above at the pragmatic and semantic level, shaping the rest of the grammar of the sentence.

However, strangely, he judges there to be a mismatch between the sentence's syntactic representation and its semantic structure, and thinks that Chomsky's view of the syntax is in better alignment with the semantic facts (Jackendoff, *Foundations*, 10, 14–15), because he shares Chomsky's atomization of the different features of verb, so that it is in a way misleading that tense, negation, and mood should be marked on the verb rather than by operators on the whole clause. Strikingly, he tells us (my italics) that "*everyone agrees that overall there is constituent structure of this sort, and that constituents have heads*" (*Foundations*, 10), despite the fact that whereas this is integral to Chomskyan grammars, it is only a convenience of presentation in Lexical Functional Grammar and absent from most other grammars.

expressions into X-Bar theory, a version in which I^0 is the category of expressions which head verbal expressions (the copula, auxiliaries, and modals), D^0 is the category of expressions which head nominal expressions (determiners and pronouns), and C^0 is a category including expressions (complementizers) which head clausal expressions with either verbal or nominal function, adding the curious explanation that "functional categories are specialized sub-classes of lexical categories", specifically in such a way that I, D, and C have only a synlexical role in the grammar (marking finiteness, nominal role, subordination, and so forth).[17]

These concessions (despite the conveniences already mentioned) violate Bresnan's own insights into what typologically radically different languages have in common, as her willingness to allow for languages which by no plausible contrivance can be represented as endocentric reveals,[18] and so in no way fits with Chomsky's conceptions of X-Bar theory as a theory which embraces verb phrases and clauses, and which makes the patterns of sentence analysis conform to the patterns of lexical phrase analysis. For she reckons on many languages with a different system of organization, which she calls "lexocentric", to which even her own conception of an extended X-Bar theory cannot be applied, but which instead "associates syntactic functions directly with features borne by words rather than with the configurational relations of phrases in syntax", instancing Hungarian, Malayalam, Tagalog, Warlpiri and other Australian languages, and nonconfigurational VSO languages in general.[19]

Moreover, the very way in which Bresnan characterizes her "lexocentric" languages, that their lexocentricity "associates syntactic functions directly with features borne by words rather than with the configurational relations of phrases in syntax", reveals what they have in common with supposedly paradigm cases of so-called endocentric languages, for it is characteristic of many of them that key syntactic functions, in particular time, aspect, subject-verb agreement, and sometimes negation should be associated with markings on a particular word—namely, the verb, and that markings on noun phrases should be directed towards indicating relations to the verb such as subjecthood and being object to the verb.

In sum, to apply a single formalism, that of X-Bar theory, to such discrep-

17. Bresnan, *Lexical-Functional Syntax*, 101. In effect, I-phrases have an essentially verbal character, D-phrases an essentially nominal character, and C-phrases sometimes the one and sometimes the other; *Lexical-Functional Syntax*, 99–101. Bresnan's discussion of 98–109 draws on Jane Grimshaw's idea that functional categories share the categorical features of lexical categories in Grimshaw, "Locality and Extended Projection", in *Lexical Specification and Insertion*, ed. Peter Coupmans, Martin Everett, and Jane Grimshaw (Hillsdale, N.J.: Erlbaum, 1998), 115–33; see Bresnan, *Lexical-Functional Syntax*, 119 for references to Fehri, Postal, Brame, and Falk.

18. Bresnan, *Lexical-Functional Syntax*, 113–14; cf. 5–15.

19. Bresnan, *Lexical-Functional Syntax*, 109–10, introducing 109–14.

ant types of word-group when dealing with configurational languages, and (as we shall see), by the device of introducing "functional" phrases, get to represent the clause and the sentence by the same formalism as the noun phrase, is to belie how language works functionally and semantically.

Rather, one of the most significant general trends in speech organization is that functional indications of time, aspect, subject-verb agreement, and negation should appear as distinctive features of particular verbs or predicates, and not of other lexical items. Clauses themselves are of many kinds, some, like "it is raining", without a subject, and others with a subject, marked for person and number, and a complex argument structure, all centered on a verb typically marked for tense, aspect, and mood.

I, D, and C arose as parts of the Chomskyan construction-kit model of grammar, a construction-kit in which, in Pinker's improved conception, everything is to be built up upon the verb as the chassis. But grammar must not treat the sentence or clause as something static, but as in motion as it occurs in speech, so that what we need is something analogous to a flow diagram, so that, for instance, Chomsky's symbol "INFL" (discussed later) or "I" (for "Inflection") ought have been conceived as an linguist's marker of the source of *chi*, not as a constructional part in deep structure—not as a part of what is modeled, but only something in the diagram of it.

(iv) The stark antithesis between verbal and nonverbal expressions

What we have is a stark antithesis. With noun, adjective, and adverb expressions we begin with a semantically nuclear element and, although many extensions are possible—for instance, by adding adjuncts—at some point the expression becomes closed; that is, we reach a maximum projection, so that any further expansion will take us beyond the sphere of what is respectively noun-like, adjective-like, or adverb-like.

By contrast, it is in the very nature of rhetic or verbal units to be extensible.

Whether a lexical item is to be considered as a rhetic unit or solely as the head or modifier within a non-rhetic phrase can only be judged from its context within the clause or sentence. For instance, the saying or rhetic character of the word "growling" as the content-introducing nucleus of a predicate typically shows itself only by its appearance in combination with the semantically synlexical auxiliary "is"; it is this auxiliary which carries inflections for tense, mood, person, and number (by contrast to "growling" as an adjective, as in "a growling dog"). The verbal or predicative kernel is essentially syntactically complex, whether or not this is morphologically expressed. Again, a so-called verb phrase such as "... is biting the cat" is likewise essentially incomplete, so that it is only with "our dog is biting the cat" that we have the provisional possibility of closure—provisional because such a clause is open to negation or may figure only as a subordinate clause within a more complex sentence. Beyond this, in the case of saying, rhetic, or "verbal" expressions, even when we reach the level of the speech-unit, the cut-off points are largely arbitrary. The sentence commonly arises in the context of an extended discourse and can be continued by coordination, questioning, conditionalization, and so forth.

(b) *The addition of phrases with functional Heads to X-Bar theory*

(i) The strangeness of the Chomskyan treatment of verbs

In order to treat verbs and verb phrases in the same way as nouns and noun and other phrases, Chomsky's followers felt obliged to treat agreement-structure, tense, and aspect, central nonlexical or synlexical features of finite verbs, as Heads in their own right, to which verbal phrases were Complements. In this way they introduced a real conceptual novelty—namely, that alongside phrases headed by nouns, adjectives, and adverbs, there are also these newfangled "functional phrases" with "functional Heads".[20] (The Chomskyans' terminology of "functional Heads", belonging to "functional" categories, has no connection whatever with the idea of grammatical functions such as Subject and Object.)

The chief motivations for introducing the idea of phrases with functional Heads were primarily theoretical—first and most notably, to separate out the five features of INLF: namely, subject-verb concord or coordination (AGR_SP), affirmation/negation, tense or finiteness (or its absence), aspect, and verb-object coordination (AGR_OP), so as to associate them with the whole clause rath-

20. The whole vocabulary of "functional Head" and "functional phrase" only came into in full use in 1986 in Fukui, "Theory of Category Projection"; Fukui, "Deriving the Differences between English and Japanese: A Case Study in Parametric Syntax", *English Linguistics* 5 (1988): 249–70; Fukui and Speas, "Specifiers and Projection"; and Abney, "The English Noun Phrase".

In his *Minimalist Program*, 6 (cf. 54), Chomsky attributes what had then (1995) become common terminology to Borer and Fukui. His first contribution to developing this way of thinking was in "Some Notes on Economy of Derivation and Representation", chap. 2 in Chomsky, *Minimalist Program*; the chapter consisted of a paper reprinted with revision from a collection *Functional Heads and Clause Structure*, ed. I. Laka and A. Mahajan (Cambridge, Mass.: MITWPL, 1989).

In 1970 Bresnan adopted had the term COMP for "Complementizer" from the work of P. Rosenbaum, *The Grammar of English Predicate Complement Constructions* (Cambridge, Mass.: MIT Press, 1967), to pick out clause-markers with clauses as their complements, but the vocabulary of "functional Head" and "functional phrase" did not appear until 1986. In 1981, Chomsky referred to INFL ("inflection") as an "element" heading verb phrases. The same notion is explicit in 1986 in Chomsky, *Knowledge of Language*, 161, as well as often apparent in his symbolism, e.g., *Knowledge of Language*, 157, though it seems in tension with the definition of "phrase" whereby it "consists of a head . . . , and an array of complements determined by the *lexical* properties of the head", since functional heads do not have lexical properties; Chomsky, *Knowledge of Language*, 81; my italics. Geoffrey Horrocks refers to INFLECTION as an "abstract element" in his 1987 *Generative Grammar*. Hagit Borer speaks of "grammatical formatives" in her *Parametric Syntax* (Dordrecht: Foris, 1984).

er than particularly with the verb; and, second, to serve a role in the theory of "Movement" in Chomskyan theories.

The idea of "Phrases" with Heads which are functional, not lexical, appeared to gain some empirical backing when Jean-Yves Pollock utilized these five kinds of phrase in explaining the different placing of negatives and adverbs in French and modern English and the introduction of the auxiliary "do" in English.[21] In "verb movement" the whole finite verb kernel can be left-dislocated in French, but only an auxiliary thus left-dislocated in English. However, in chapter XIII, section 2 (e), I suggested that this was the result of English's having developed a semantic perspective rendering a lexical main verb and its objects inseparable—the need for the empty auxiliary "do" in subject-verb inversion was then a consequence of the main verb's being a lexical verb, and not an auxiliary.

In a disguised way, by this obscure system of representation, Chomskyan theories strikingly preserve a record of the features at the heart of the clause empirically associated with its verb kernel, unintentionally marking it as the "saying" element within the sentence. Thus "Inflection", as the supposed functional Head of a sentence, happens to reflect the character of the finiteness of the verb as the semantic expression of the saying character of the sentence, the infinitive being seen only in various positions logically subordinated to a finite verb. And, whether some or all of the features mentioned above are regarded as elements within "Inflection" considered as a single Head, with only "Negation" treated separately, or whether five distinct functional Heads are involved, what is clear is that this list of "functional phrases" includes all and only those things which belong to what I called the heart of the clause, integral to its thrust in its verbal, rhetic, or saying character. Accordingly, what is presented is an analysis of the heart of the verbal core of each clause, around which everything else within them hangs.

21. Jean-Yves Pollock, "Verb Movement, Universal Grammar, and the Structure of IP", *Linguistic Inquiry* 20, no. 3 (1989): 365–424, expresses ideas further developed by Chomsky in "Some Notes on Economy", chap. 2 in *Minimalist Program*; cf. Cook and Newson, *Chomsky's Universal Grammar*, 181–83, 210–13.

Of the other phenomena which Pollock seeks to explain, the main one is the preposing of *ne pas* and "not" to infinitives, both in French and in English. This is to be explained in terms of the absence of their normal role in the use of the verb, clitic before and emphatic after the finite verb, the English clitic having become obsolete. The clitic in the finite construction lies at the point of least stress, between subject and verb, which is why an emphatic was felt to be needed after the finite verb, both in English and in French. With the infinitive, this role and motivation is lost, and there is no subject-clitic-verb sequence to supplement—rather, the emphatic is needed before the infinitive (after the infinitive is a point of least stress). The other "evidence" Pollock appeals to is theory-dependent.

To place the negative particle after the infinitive would seem appropriate only if it had the status of an adverb of degree; cf. the discussion of the possibility of treating negation as an adverbial satellite in Dik, *Theory of Functional Grammar: Part 2*, 170. In German, *nicht*, coming after all noun complements, precedes other adverbs before the verbs if applying to the adverb-verb complex as such, and in a different class from other adverbs.

However, this has a strange upshot. Although the finite verb kernel may be regarded as having the verb phrase, including the objects and adjuncts of the verb, as a projection, this projection will be only a Complement to some functional Head, and therefore the clause will be the projection not of the verb phrase, but of the functional Head INFL—or else of subject-verb Agreement, or of some other functional Head, such as Negation, Aspect, or Tense. In this way the disintegration or decomposition of the sentence or utterance into parts has been completed—the consummation of Chomskyan atomism in grammar.[22] It is this that we should set in contrast with the philosophical repudiation of atomism in semantics seen in Frege, Jespersen, and others.[23]

To the five functional Heads mentioned earlier, we have to add Bresnan's "Complementizers", such as "that" and "whether", conceived of as having clauses as Complements, and, Abney suggested, "Determiners", conceived of as Heads which have noun phrases as Complements. Beyond these, twelve other functional Heads have been proposed, opening the whole system to new uncertainties.[24]

Yet why should Chomsky and his followers want to make the analysis of this verbal core conform to the pattern of X-Bar theory, a theory devised for analyzing phrases with lexical Heads?

To this the answer is regrettably simple. Chomsky and his followers think of sentence and clause structure in the same way as they think of lexical phrase structure, attempting to represent both configurationally, as structured compositionally of parts (even if some have no morphological embodiment on the surface), at the level of "deep" structure whose theoretical role is supposedly to reflect the logical interface (LF) in the "the brain or mind".

Yet the whole system of building up sentences by "merging" a non-Head with a Head, by this very form of description, implies some hierarchy between the phrases adjoined or concatenated, non-Head somehow subordinate to Head, and the grammar does not itself provide any account of the character or origin of this hierarchy. This insistence upon this hierarchical structure requires explanation from outside Chomskyan grammar. Any attempt to provide

22. Mark Baker coined the name "the Borer-Chomsky Conjecture" for the hypothesis that "all parameters of variation are attributable to differences in the features of particular items (e.g., the functional heads) in the lexicon"; Baker, "The Macroparameter in a Microparametric World", in *The Limits of Syntactic Variation*, ed. Theresa Biberauer (Amsterdam: John Benjamins, 2008), 3. In the setting of the principle "Merge" in Chomsky's minimalism, this amounts to putting grammatical formatives ("functional Heads") cheek by jowl in the lexicon (even though some of the functional Heads may be hidden at surface level (the Phonetic interface, PF), as the ultimate determinatives in a process of composition, paying no heed to context, of meaning.

23. Cf. chap. XIV, n. 4 and related text, in this volume.

24. See Cook and Newson, *Chomsky's Universal Grammar*, 148–58, 173–88, 206–15, 234–41, on functional phrases and Heads. Cf. Ackerman and Webelhuth, *Theory of Predicates*, 30–31, for their sardonic comment on the multiplication of types of functional phrase, each with its new type of functional Head, reaching up to nineteen distinct functional levels in a phrase diagram.

such an explanation will set one on the path to recovery of an understanding of the true role of grammar and its non-autonomous character.

(ii) The anomalous nature of the notion of "Specifier" in X-Bar theory

As X-Bar theory was first conceived it highlighted the appearance that noun, adjective, and verb phrases all share the same formal structure of Head and Complement, possibly with something called a Specifier applied to the unity they form. Within this structure it was possible successively to introduce any number of adjuncts applied to the Head-Complement complex before applying the Specifier "every" to achieve closure of the noun phrase "every tall dark handsome man" and "so" to achieve closure of the adjective phrase "so utterly incompetent". Adverbs, seemingly taking neither Complements nor lexical adjuncts, tended to get little attention. But with both adjectives and adverbs it is obscure how identity and quantity indicator phrases such as "less" and "that" should be classified in view of the analogies between "less big" or "less slowly" and "less rice" as it occurs in "Less rice was distributed", or between "It was that green" or "He did it thus" and "That man hit me". Yet the "less" in "less rice" and the "that" in "that man" belong to the core of the clause lacking to the "less" or the "that/thus" in the other cases.

However, the term "Specifier" has been applied arbitrarily in so many different ways at different times, often in effect simply to provide an optional initial spare place in the phrase. The term has been a convenience allowing one to give the facade of a "theoretical" solution to formal problems of very varied kinds, before some quite different solution of a problem has been preferred, and then some new use for "Specifiers" conjured up.

This is indeed an object-lesson in the evils of introducing terms into grammar with no adequate history, credentials, or explanation, and without their reflecting any features within pragmatic or semantic structure, quite unlike the terms "head", "complement", "modifier", and "adjunct".[25] In fact no special new notion as general as that of "Specifier" is needed to deal with noun, adjective, and adverb phrases, since the notions of identity-indicator and quantity-indicator phrases, with their two different roles, serve the purpose.

Since the Chomskyan conception of "Specifier" is purely formal, it is empty of any hint of positive content beyond that of achieving closure on a type of phrase. In view of this it is unsurprising that the things grouped as Specifiers should have been so heterogeneous, and that their being grouped together should seem so arbitrary, especially arbitrary in the case of verb

25. The only vaguely relevant use of the word "specifier" recorded by the full version of the *OED* is "the word classes: adjective, quantifier, specifier, pluraliser and intensifier respectively", cited from G. Ansre, "The Influence of English on West African Languages", in *The English Language in West Africa*, ed. J. Spencer (London: Longman, 1971), 162.

phrases.[26] Chomsky and his followers were themselves uncomfortable with this arbitrariness. In his earliest theory Chomsky viewed the auxiliaries of verbs as the Specifiers of verb phrases, and in line with this Jackendoff in 1977 still mentioned indicators of aspect as holding this position.[27] Chomsky then introduced the "inflectional" element INFL in 1981 as "Head" of the Verb Phrase, considering INFL as having the features [[± Tense], (AGR)].[28] In 1986 Chomsky came to present the subject phrase as the "Specifier" within this Phrase.[29] In a development suggested by Fukui and Speas, in a preliminary presentation of "Relativized X-Bar theory",[30] the subject figures in deep structure as the Specifier of the verb phrase, making the subject internal to the verb phrase at that level. This captures its role as one of the complements of the verb, at the same time as distinguishing it as open to movement to outside the verb phrase—that is, extraposed (in practice, preposed) for the purpose of assigning nominative case at surface level. Thus extraposed, it came to be regarded as the Determiner Phrase serving as Specifier to the Inflection Phrase.[31] The chief role of the Specifier position had come to be that of a landing site to which whole phrases ("maximal projections") could be "Moved" in movements triggered by elements of the theory of functional phrases.

In particular, this movement of extraposition, "which raises the subject to be Specifier to the rest of the clause", is required, Fukui tells us, "by the need for Case assignment [to the subject]"[32]—that is, by the need to assign nominative case to the subject. For in Chomskyan grammar "subject" is a derived notion, defined internally to the system, not a primitive notion such as might be explained informally in terms external to the formal system as happens in Lexical Functional Grammar. Yet in nominative/accusative languages the subject has to be open to thematic roles as diverse as Undergoer and Agent, as we saw in chapter XI.[33] Therefore, the problem to be solved is that of finding

26. This heterogeneity is made strikingly plain by Fukui's review of the history of the treatment of the notion in Fukui, "Phrase Structure", 379–98, and by *Specifiers: Minimalist Approaches*, ed. David Adger, Susan Pintzuk, Bernadette Plunkett, and George Tsoulas (Oxford: Oxford University Press, 1999), especially in the early chapters.

27. Jackendoff, *X-Bar Syntax.*

28. Chomsky introduced INFL in *Lectures on Government and Binding*, 52, the feature AGR ("agreement") being considered a nominal element, "in some sense the subject when present"; *Lectures on Government and Binding*, 209–10.

29. Cook and Newson, *Chomsky's Universal Grammar*, 146, 206–15.

30. Originating with Fukui and Speas, "Specifiers and Projection", and presented in Fukui, "Phrase Structure", in a way based on Fukui, "Theory of Category Projection" (PhD diss., published as *Theory of Projection in Syntax*). "Phrase Structure" gives further references.

31. Chomsky himself has now developed an alternative, the "bare phrase structure" theory of 1994, within the framework of his minimalist program. In both theories, the main structures of X-Bar theory are preserved, but "Relativized X-Bar theory" and Chomsky's "bare phrase structure" theory now assign Specifiers different formal roles; cf. Fukui, "Phrase Structure", 396–98.

32. Fukui, "Phrase Structure", 390.

33. The voice of the verb becomes clear only after it is clear whether the subject is Undergoer or Agent.

a reason internal to a Chomskyan formal grammar for giving the subject its exceptional place among the noun phrases in *rapport* with the verb.

This fact is quite adequately explained by its character as a "grammaticalized topic", something recognized both in traditional logic, in Lexical Functional Grammar, and in numerous other grammars.

However, Chomskyan theory, with its ideal of autonomy, is compelled to set any such explanation aside. Instead, to use Fukui's phraseology cited earlier, the theory has to resort to this peculiar idea of "raising the subject to be Specifier to the rest of the clause in order to assign [nominative] case to the subject". Yet there are no necessities here from within the grammar, but only from the need to engineer a result in which the sentence-constructs generated resemble what we actually say. The idea that an explanation has been provided is farfetched, since the term "Specifier" has no role outside the theory, and the notion of "Abstract Case" is a construct within the theory. In sum, there is no way of explaining the requirement concerned without going outside the grammar, abandoning the straitjacket of autonomy.

Theories developed to deal with both nonconfigurational and configurational languages have had no use for theories of "Movement", even in describing configurational languages, and therefore no need for the notion of a Specifier position as a target of Movement. In place of the notion of Specifier, it will suffice to differentiate the different roles of identity and quantity indicators according to their position in the structure of the clause.[34]

(c) *Attempts to extend the theory of Movement*

The purpose of "movement" in earlier transformational grammar, this "movement" being limited by highly restrictive rules,[35] was to deal with some real puzzles, such as the relations between how we express declarative sentences and how we express imperative and interrogative sentences, and between active and passive sentences. However, Chomsky's ambitions for Movement grew.

34. The emptiness of the notion of "Specifier", the unsatisfactoriness of having to fabricate roles for specifiers in the case of every kind of lexical phrase, and the awkwardness of the invention of Determiner Phrases as Specifiers, are made very plain by Frank Van Eynde, "NP-Internal Agreement and the Structure of the Noun Phrase", *Journal of Linguistics* 42 (2006): 139–86; see.158–60.

35. See Cook and Newson, *Chomsky's Universal Grammar*, 152–55, 189–98, 206–33, 242–49, on the theory of Movement, the Case Filter, and Abstract Case; cf. nn. 38–39 in this chapter.

Other criticisms of Chomsky's Movement theories, supplementing the general considerations introduced in chap. XIII, sec. 7 (a) of this volume (cf. sec. 3 [b]), can be found in Jackendoff, *Architecture*, esp. 12–19, 100–103, 229n19, referring also to Michael Brody, *Lexico-Logical Form: A Radically Minimalist Theory* (Cambridge, Mass.: MIT Press, 1995); see also Newmeyer, *Generative Linguistics: A Historical Perspective* (London: Routledge, 1996), 166: "the term [movement] seems wholly metaphorical in its usage; there appear to be few processes described in movement that could not be handled just as elegantly through base generation"; cf. *Generative Linguistics*, 189n10—one difficulty had lain in the special problems of relative clauses.

By permitting the Movement of the subject of a clause, or sometimes of its main verb, or else (in topicalization) of some ancillary feature, he reckoned to achieve not only (a) the change of an active into a passive, (b) topicalization (so that "She said I was clumsy" becomes "It was clumsy that she said I was"), and (c) subject raising (so that "It seems that Jane is pining" becomes "Jane seems to be pining"), but also (d) the placing of the finite verb in the second place in the main clause in German and in the first place in Welsh, as well as (e) and (f), arrangements to get *wh*-phrase markers into their right places in the case of relatives and interrogatives.

But these problems can all be resolved without any theory of movement at all and without depending on an X-Bar theory extended to phrases with "functional" Heads, alternative resolutions of most of these problems being seen in chapter XI, section 2, and chapter XIII, sections 3, 5, and 7. A Lexical-Functional approach allows a more satisfactory account of what Bresnan calls "movement paradoxes", such as, "She said that she would meet me, and meet me she has",[36] in which it is the infinitive phrase "meet me" which appears in a focalized topic position in the second clause (the movement of a syntactic element "met me" would not transform "she has met me" into "meet me she has").

Always the purpose of Movement is to get actual lexical elements, morphemes, or phrases into the right order in surface structure. However, the role of introducing "phrases" with functional Heads into X-Bar phrase theory has been to allow Chomsky and his followers to make use of "Movement" rules, not just to deal with the problems for the sake of which the idea of movement was first introduced, but for the purpose of dealing with new problems generated by Chomsky's own post-1980 theories, as it were self-invented problems. The most important case of this arises whenever we have a subject-first language, where Chomskyan grammars encounter the theory-generated problem of getting the subject noun phrase into a forward position outside what we ordinarily call the verb phrase—to get the S to proceed the VO in the typical SVO sentence order. Here "Movement" is being used to deal not with problems presented by the empirical data, but with problems generated by artificialities in the structure of the grammar itself.[37]

This grammar has equal problems with VSO sentences, as we saw when discussing bracketing in chapter XIII. As we noted, the device of bracketing is extraordinarily widespread, to be found in almost every language, and in some

36. I take this example from Bresnan, *Lexical-Functional Syntax*, 18. As remarked earlier, in Lexical Functional Grammar, the symbolism of I, D, and C phrases is a mere convenience of presentation, since LFG makes no use of the idea of movement.

37. It was Pollock's ideas (see n. 21) which made the notion of "Phrases" with heads which are functional, not lexical, attractive as a key to Movement theory, even to working linguists.

languages in every sentence—in a comparable way, classical and Polish notations show some parallel contrasts in logic. And we observed how whenever bracketing is used, no phrase structure tree diagram can be drawn without the branches of the tree crossing each other, so that Chomskyan grammars can only resort to deep structure representations and "Movements" to explain surface structure.

It is a defect in a theory to have to develop such an artificial account of such a common and natural stylistic device as bracketing, in use as soon as human speech develops beyond the two-word or two-morpheme stage. In German we found the device of first announcing the starting point of concern (perhaps the subject, day, or place), and then enclosing the rest of the sentence between the finite verb and the nonfinite part which completes it, the so-called Verbal Bracket, the finite verb being brought to the second place in the main clause for a pragmatic reason, the dramatic drive it gives to the sentence as a whole. In Welsh, as in all VSO languages, the subject always intrudes between the verb and its object, in the structure V(SO),[38] while in English, the recipient or beneficiary of an action is allowed to intrude between a verb and its undergoer object. We observed the Latin literary device of using an adjective and the noun it qualifies as a bracket enclosing the rest of the clause. And in any highly inflected language, one is liable to find such freedom, pragmatic and literary considerations readily overriding almost all others. Thus bracketing devices arise in all the main languages of Western Europe, and so Chomskyans are confronted with the problem long before considering non–Indo-European languages.

The elaborateness of the constructions proposed in Chomsky's Principles and Parameters theory and the apparent arbitrariness of the rules involved—for instance, the Head Movement Constraint rule, which limits how far a word or phrase can be moved, but in a setting in which new applications of the rule can be made successively, appropriate material being picked up at each stage, so that by a cunning magic of leap-frogging everything arrives in the right place in the end[39]—constitute an implausible alternative to the requirements of logical coherence and the avoidance of ambiguity.

It was a condition of the development of the formal conception of grammar that the formal grammarians should begin with an overly simple view of the lexicon as a simple catalogue of signs, analogous to the philosophers' error of thinking of it as a catalogue of names. But now in Chomsky's Principles and Parameters theory and its developments in Minimalism this perspective has

38. A Chomskyan treatment of German and Welsh is described in Cook and Newson, *Chomsky's Universal Grammar*, 216–21.

39. Cook and Newson, *Chomsky's Universal Grammar*, 206–14, 256–67; cf. chap. XIII, sec. 5 (b) of this volume on relatives.

been abandoned, and it is required that every entry in the lexicon should be heavily flagged with prescriptions as to its exact behavior in relation to every so-called module within formal grammatical theory, and how it will behave at each new type of node in a phrase structure diagram.[40] Yet this means that the main motivation for the formal, anti-semantic approach has disappeared, since no justification remains for anticipating an autonomous origin for these prescriptions, rather than one rooted in lexical semantics, which, as we saw in chapter III, takes us back to discourse-significance—that is, a setting in which there is no grasping of the sense of a word outside its whole utterance-context.

As we have seen, the roles served by configuration are in many languages served in quite different ways, a richer set of inflections on verbs serving in place of auxiliaries, a richer set of case-markings serving in place of prepositions, and many roles being served by intonation instead of word order, even with the result that there can be almost totally nonconfigurational languages. Accordingly, many linguists have envisaged the possibility of a formal grammar structured quite differently from the various Chomskyan grammars, instead proceeding along Relational or Lexical Functional lines.[41] With Lexical Functional Grammar (LFG) and other grammars like it in that primitive terms can be given notional content in pragmatic or semantic terms, there is much better hope of picking out the deep community of structure between radically different languages, some with agreement marked on phrases complementing the verb and some on the verb itself, configurational and nonconfigurational, a community of structure of which Chomskyan grammars give no plausible account.[42] Besides accommodating some notions of grammatical functions, such as subject, such a functionalist approach is also open to extension to deal with the grammatical features of dialogue and extended discourse along pragmatic lines of the sort mentioned in the introduction, section 6, some opened out by Dik and some suggested by Jackendoff.

40. This is the effect of the projection principle in an extended form. In effect the nice distinctions of Principles and Parameters theory were abandoned or disguised in Chomsky's 1993 minimalist approach, which increases dependence on the lexicon; see Chomsky and Howard Lasnik, "The Theory of Principles and Parameters", in *Syntax: An International Handbook of Contemporary Research*, ed. J. Jacobs, A. von Stechow, W. Sternefeld, and T. Vennemann (Berlin: de Gruyter, 1993); reprinted in Chomsky, *Minimalist Program*.

In Cook and Newson's account, *Chomsky's Universal Grammar*, 214–16, 316–18, by 1993 Chomsky in his new minimalism had changed his view so as to make it the lexicon that determines verb inflection and its position with its objects relative to different types of adverb in English, thus giving "Movement" an almost fictional character. Chomsky and Lasnik abandon the whole theory of verb movement, and equally in Japanese of *wh*-movement, and instead regard it as dictated by the lexicon rather than by syntax.

41. Bresnan, *Mental Representation*, 12–13; Horrocks, *Generative Grammar*, 230–35.

42. Cf. Mark Baker, "The Natures of Nonconfigurationality", in *Handbook of Contemporary Syntactic Theory*, ed. Baltin and Collins, 407–38, noting 410, 413, 415, and his conclusion on 434 after struggling with the complex array of phenomena.

(d) *Nature and weakness of the evidence for recent Chomskyan conceptions of the shape of grammar*

The suggestion that each language must have phrase structure rules which are the same for all categories comes from T. Stowell.[43] Chomsky in his Principles and Parameters theory presentation suggested a more restricted principle, first in respect of the relative placing of Heads and Complements and second in respect of the relative placing of any phrase and a Specifier to that phrase, so that for each language it is a "principle" either that Complements should precede their Heads for all categories of phrase in that language or that Heads should precede their Complements, this principle applying to verb phrases and their projections, even whole sentences, as well as phrases morphosyntactically headed by nouns, adjectives, adverbs, or adpositions. Whether the rule for all categories of phrase is "Complements before Heads" or "Heads before Complements" will then be a "parameter" for the language concerned. This is the main source of the potential empirical attractiveness of Chomsky's Principles and Parameters theory, ever seeking the simplicity of such generalizations—a delusory source, as we see later.

If Stowell's principle that the phrase structure rules in any language are the same for all categories had indeed applied to every language, whether understood in this unrestricted way or more narrowly, and applied to the various types of adjunct and not just to complements, it would have been theoretically remarkable. It would have seemed an extraordinary coincidence that languages should exhibit such uniformity, a fact for which there was no reason within the structures of language learning and one crying out for explanation, perhaps even in terms of how the brain functions.

However, as applying so generally, as we shall see, it has only superficial plausibility. The great convenience of describing constancies in phrase structure within particular languages in terms of parameters—for instance, the placing of the six or seven types of adjunct within noun phrases—is quite independent of the theory that there are "functional" phrases with "functional" Heads, and provides no evidence for it. And the two notable lacunae of Chomsky's theory are that it offers no systematic account of the placing of adjuncts, especially the clausal adjuncts discussed in chapter XIII, section 3 (d), and no account of how actual sentences, with or without adjuncts, are to be parsed (Gazdar's problem), but only how (possibly useless) context-free sentences are to be generated.

However, the idea that every language conforms to certain principles,

43. T. Stowell, "Origins of Phrase Structure" (PhD diss., Massachusetts Institute of Technology, 1981), 85.

and in particular must either be a Head-last/Complement-first language or a Head-first/Complement-second one, and either a Head-last/Specifier-second language or a Head-second/Specifier-first one, made an attractive beginning for recommending the Principles and Parameters approach.

Moreover, nothing succeeds like success! One whiff of a suspicion that a theory has succeeded in one case has a self-confirming effect, confirming the conception of having universal principles which then merely require that one states the way certain parameters are set in particular languages. We saw how Pollock's explanations of certain differences between English and French had this effect, despite the fact that other explanations suggest themselves.

Therefore, let me review some of the chief parameters proposed, for this will show up the weakness of the case for the "Principles and Parameters" approach.

First, it is suggested that there is a parameter whereby each language will either allow Movement or forbid it altogether. Thus it has been suggested that there is no Movement in Japanese. Yet, in the previous two subsections, we have given reason for rejecting the theory of Movement altogether, a theory which has no application in nonconfigurational languages. In this we would follow the pattern of Lexical-Functional and fully functionalist grammars. Further, since the point of parameters as to whether Agreement dominates Tense or vice versa, or as to whether Negation dominates Tense or vice versa, considering these as functional Heads, turns upon the differences in the Movement that they affect, in rejecting the theory of Movement we remove the motivation for supposing there to be any such parameters or functional Heads.

Second, in *wh*-questions it appears that either the *wh*-word can be placed at the beginning of the question, or it is placed where the corresponding non-interrogative pronoun would occur in the corresponding affirmative statement—and it has been suggested that this is another parameter. But in this matter of the "Movement" of *wh*-expressions, chapter XIII showed that it was more economical to explain the phenomena in pragmatic and semantic terms than by reference to brain function. In such ways all the epicycles of subjacency theory and its successors could be dispensed with.

Third, it appears that every language is either of a "pro-drop" kind allowing of there being no lexical element in subject position (i.e., not requiring unnecessary pronouns), or else such that every finite verb requires a subject, even if it is a pronoun which is really redundant because the inflection of the verb makes clear whether the subject is first, second, or third person and whether singular or plural, and indeed even if the construction is impersonal. Yet, as soon as children have learned from the speech of their elders how to speak in ways which respected the subject/predicate or subject/verb differentiation without confusing subject and object, one would expect them at the same time to have inevitably gathered whether or not these same elders regard explicit reference to the subject as obligatory.[44] This gives strong reason for thinking that children conform the structure of their speech to that of their elders, even when it is situationally or conversationally unnecessary—and semantically pointless in the case of impersonal subject-expressions. In any case, if, inspired by Ackerman and Webelhuth, one conceives "he loves" and *amat* as both lexical units, the question whether a language is "pro-drop" or not becomes lexical, rather than syntactic.[45]

Most important are the two proposed "Head parameters" whereby, in each language, either all Heads come before their Complements or vice versa, and either all Specifiers come before their Heads or vice versa. It was perhaps these examples which first gave the Principles and Parameters approach its superficial attractiveness, both empirically and as posing a simplicity requiring explanation.

Certainly it is a rule in English that the Complements of nouns and adjectives always come after their head within noun and adjective phrases.[46] The noun phrases governed by prepositions (their Complements) come after them, as is natural, since in the absence of case indications one would expect a connective to come between the expressions it connects (for a connective to follow or precede what it connects occurs often, but is less common, as when Latin expresses conjunction by *-que* rather than by *et*). And if one excludes the subjects of verbs from counting as their Complements, then it is only the other objects of verbs which count as Complements, and these do come after the verb. The same rule applies to all the Romance languages.[47] In sum, the verbal frameworks of both English and the Romance languages can be con-

44. I hereby bypass O. Jaeggli and K. J. Safir's more refined formulation of a pro-drop parameter theory (discussed by Cook and Newson, *Chomsky's Minimalist Program*, 284–90); see Jaeggli and Safir, "The Null Subject Parameter and Parametric Theory", in *The Null Subject Parameter*, 1–44 (Dordrecht: Kluwer, 1989). They observe the very different effects of being pro-drop on languages whose present tense is not differentially inflected at all (Chinese and Irish) and on highly inflected languages (Spanish and Latin), and suggest that null subjects are permitted in all and only languages with morphologically uniform inflectional paradigms. This hypothesis involves that if a language has at the least six different inflections for the three persons singular and three persons plural in the present tense, then it will specify a subject only if a pronoun would be inadequate, and otherwise omit pronouns as redundant. At the opposite extreme, if the language provides the same form for every person and number in the present tense (whether or not it has inflections differentiating different tenses), the grammar requires no pronoun, but it depends on the conversation or discourse-situation whether a subject needs specification. In all mixed situations a subject has to be specified, even if it takes an impersonal (expletive) form.

45. Cf. chap. XI, sec. 2 (b) (v) of this volume.

46. Chomsky escapes from thinking of phrasal genitives as Complements by ranking them as "determiners" in his extended use of the label, and so as Specifiers of the noun phrases concerned, so that in the noun phrase "the Queen's corgis", he supposes that the Head noun, "corgi", has no Complement, but only a Specifier.

47. Early modern English worked in the same way, as Radford shows from Shakespeare; Radford, *Syntactic Theory*, 227.

strued as fitting the rules that Heads come before Complements and that in general identity and quantity indicators come before Heads, so that this principle will hold for all categories of lexical phrase in these languages.

Yet as we have seen, the phenomena concerned are explicable in quite different terms.

Further, Korean, Japanese, and Chinese are given as examples of Head-last languages. Thus a noun serving as Complement to the verb has to precede its Head-verb in order to preserve the rule that the verb should come last, and if the noun is linked to the verb by a suffix or connective "postposition", then such postposition will come last in the postpositional phrase. Yet in Japanese all modifiers of nouns precede their nouns, so that adjectives, postpositional phrases, possessives, or relatives, whether Complements or adjuncts, all alike precede their head noun within the phrase concerned, so again Heads come after any Complements or Specifiers.[48] Fukui's studies render it questionable whether Japanese has any such things as Specifiers.[49]

However, although Chinese, in a language group more distant from Korean and Japanese than from Indo-European, is described as essentially Head-last, the Complements of the verb come after the verb, so that one needs to postulate a new ad hoc parametric variation, as it were yet another epicycle in the theory.[50] This makes it questionable whether it is indeed economical to suppose that the same ordering principles apply to all languages, and, in particular, that they apply both to noun phrases and to verb phrases, if one has to invent new parameters to deal with distant language groups.[51]

Let us consider other proposed principles and parameters.

The Principle that what assigns Case must be adjacent to that to which it assigns case (e.g., a verb to its object) suggests the need of an extra parameter to deal with cases such as French where it does not apply. As we have seen, each new functional category or principle that is postulated generates more parameters. Newmeyer judges that Baker's twelve macroparameters would

48. Radford, *Transformational Grammar*, 38.

49. Fukui, "Deriving the Differences"; and Fukui and Hiromu Sakai, "The Visibility Guideline for Functional Categories: Verb Raising in Japanese and Related Issues", *Lingua* 113 (2003): 321–75. Chomsky had regarded Japanese as a nonconfigurational language (despite its evidently having some configurational features) because of its lack of movement rules, making him describe it as having a "flat" structure; Chomsky, *Lectures on Government and Binding*, 132; see 127–34). Cf. Radford's remarks that "flat" structure means that Specifiers cannot be configurationally distinguished from Complements, and that the distinction between Adjuncts and Complements, as well as between Complements and Specifiers, must be lexical rather than syntactical; Radford, *Tranformational Grammar*, 278.

50. Cf. Cook and Newson, *Chomsky's Universal Grammar*, 232, which refers to H. Koopman, *The Syntax of Verbs* (Dordrecht: Foris, 1984), against the background of Chomsky, *Knowledge of Language*, 193.

51. I note that Japanese and Korean fall within the "Eurasiatic" group of languages, along with the Ural-Altaic and Indo-European language groups, all sharing the m-/t- system of marking the first/second person distinction, and each language group having originally made a singular/dual/plural distinction. Indeed, Chinese is deemed to be also more distant than the Semitic, Afro-Asiatic, and Dravidian languages.

prove quite inadequate, and that, allowing for Kayne's microparameters handling the ordering of clitics, the Principles and Parameters approach would involve that the supposed innate Universal Grammar can operate between 8,000 and 8,000,000 triggers.[52] Thus, in general, one cannot easily avoid the feeling that a conjecture from the 1950s[53] is being repeatedly salvaged by the introduction of ever richer systems of extra hypotheses, new principles, and further parameters, like pre-Copernican epicycles. It is evident that language learning cannot be explained in this way. Rather, it is constraints set by general logic and by the needs of communication which must play the commanding role.

In general, we should envisage languages of different types as arising through the adoption of various different stable responses to the various different pragmatic and logico-semantic constraints to which human speech is subject, different stable ways of achieving optimization in the way sketched at the end of chapter XIII.

(e) The variety of resources open to us in communication and the importance of optimization

It is plausible that the special place of Specifiers with the variety of roles which they have served in Chomskyan theory reflects the importance which sentence-initial and sentence-final positions tend to have in any language, and which is, unsurprisingly, reflected in every grammatical theory, formal or functionalist.

It is natural for the placing of an expression in a proximately sentence-initial position in a sentence to give it a special prominence, as is well-recognized in functional grammar.[54] For instance, leaving aside conjunctions and other indications of relation to any preceding discourse, in many languages the first two positions in the main clause of a sentence are taken by, first, the topic or "Theme" highlighted in Dik's Functional Grammar, and, second, the finite verb.

In many languages a question is signaled by the inversion of the subject and a finite auxiliary or other main verb, bringing it into the clause-initial position in a sentence, and in some cases preceded by a *wh*-interrogative, classified

52. Mark Baker, *The Atoms of Language: The Mind's Hidden Rules of Grammar* (New York: Basic Books, 2001); Newmeyer, "Typological Evidence and Universal Grammar", *Studies in Language* 28, no. 3 (2004): 527–48; Mark Baker, "The Macroparameter in a Microparametric World".

53. See the introduction, nn. 49, 70, and 87, and related text in the introduction, secs. 4 (b), 5 (a), and 5 (c) in this volume.

54. Dik notes that various situations within a sentence or clause give a phrase a particular prominence, most obviously the clause initial position, the position immediately before the verb, and the clause final position (Dik, *Theory of Functional Grammar*, 426–27), concluding the more extended typological analysis of *Theory of Functional Grammar*, 391–427.

in Chomskyan tradition as a Specifier.[55] Whichever explanation is adopted, the *wh*-interrogative and the finite verb followed by the subject take the most prominent, clause-initial, positions in the interrogative sentence—although it is possible to yet further prepose an adverbial Adjunct in the initial Theme position, yielding three privileged clause-initial positions, as in "In Scotland, what do they eat?"[56]

In other languages the differences between statements, questions, and commands are signaled by the presence of particles, typically in the initial or final position,[57] or by intonation, instead of by the inversion of the main verb and subject in the case of questions and by inflection of the verb for mood in the case of commands, with which English-speakers are familiar.

In Chomskyan grammar inversion has been represented as extraposing the Head of the verb phrase into the position of Head of a Complementizer phrase,[58] and Radford envisages the declarative, interrogative, and imperative particles which in some languages signal statements, questions, exclamatives, and commands (without inversion) as to be classified as Complementizers formally analogous to "that" and "whether".[59]

Radford's discussion here nicely exhibits the purely formal and nonfunctional character of Chomskyan grammar, in no way discourse orientated.

The Chomskyan approach involves a special form of constituent analysis driven by a theory which excludes consideration of discourse and logico-semantic constraints and challenges. It postulates constituents which exist or achieve their function at hypothetical levels of deep structure or closer to the level of meaning (the "Logical Interface"), but which may be invisible at the surface level—what counts as evidence for their existence and/or function is dependent on the theory.

The result of proceeding from this starting-point has systematic disadvantages.

First, it implies that some of the basic forms of structure in some languages are not shared by other languages. Second, it implies that in some languages more work is done by Movement—that is, configurationally—and so closer to the supposed logical interface or the level of meaning, and in others mor-

55. Cook and Newson, *Chomsky's Universal Grammar*, 199–206; cf. Radford, *Transformational Grammar*, 466–92, 498–508.

56. Richard Hudson, "Trouble on the Left Periphery", *Lingua* 113 (2003): 607–42. Hudson's Word Grammar depends heavily on a parent word having dependents, and limiting tangling between the resulting word groups.

57. Van Valin, "Functional Linguistics", 321–22; cf. Dik, *Theory of Functional Grammar: Part 2*, 237–40.

58. See Radford's account of Auxiliary Inversion in *Transformational Grammar*, 298, 411–17, cf. Cook and Newson, *Chomsky's Universal Grammar*, 151, 208–15.

59. See Radford's account of Main Clauses (*Transformational Grammar*, 295–301); cf. his speculations arising from considering Inversion (*Transformational Grammar*, 411–19).

phologically at a level closer to the supposed phonetic interface,[60] so that there would be no analogy between the ways different developed languages respond to the very same logico-semantic and communicational constraints and challenges. Third, the grammar would still be inapplicable to many languages.

Since these consequences flow chiefly from the separation between the form of constituent analysis proposed and any consideration of pragmatic and general logical constraints, it would seem that a different basis of approach is indicated.

Our starting-point should rather be to seek forms of description which are most adapted to the logico-semantic, communicational, and expressive goals which speech has to confront. What matters is the expression and communication of sense, the sharing of perspective and content through speech, and the understanding of speech.

In learning any particular language as their first language, children will tend to interpret initially simpler and progressively more complex clauses and phrases in whatever way fits most easily with their experience of adult utterance and is least open to ambiguity—learning, for instance, to appreciate the significance of variations in phrase order and ways of expressing agreement in the particular language concerned.

In accord with my earlier suggestion, we should envisage different languages as arising through the adoption of various different stable responses to the various different pragmatic and semantic constraints to which human speech is subject—different stable ways of optimizing clarity of sense, freedom from ambiguity, expressiveness, intelligibility, and aptness to context. The vocabulary, systems of declension and conjugation, and other accidence of a language has a largely chance character from the point of view of the learner. Canonical systems of constituent order, so far as they extend within the language, will have a rationale representing some form of optimization, but not necessarily within reach of the typical user's reflective access.

By contrast, although departures from such a canonical system often have some standard significance,[61] such departures from the canonical order arise in the course of a person's exercise of freedom in speech—that is, the person concerned will be at least retrospectively aware of their point, and for a variety of literary and other purposes the person may either keep the canonical

60. Fukui and Sakai, "Visibility Guideline".

61. Thus in German, canonically the subject comes early in the clause (in subordinate clauses at the start, and in the main clause either before or after the finite part of the verb) and the direct object, indirect object, any other oblique object, and any adjunct follow afterward, before any concluding verb expressions. However, it is normal for what is more prominent to be brought forward in the order, and what it is desired to emphasize in relation to the action of the verb to be placed last, before the concluding verb expressions. Here I simplify matters, avoiding discussing adverbs, and loosening the definition of "New", but mostly follow Choi, *Optimizing Structure in Context*.

order or deliberately depart from it in varied ways. I have illustrated the extent of this freedom directly or incidentally in many examples throughout this book.[62] We exercise freedom in the act of speech, coining new words, introducing new metaphors and so forth, exhibiting grammatical creativity, without ceasing to be intelligible to others. Often such novelties are little imitated, but other times they take root and contribute to the development of language.

In sum, although the brain plays a key part in language processing, this part is shaped by semantics and pragmatics, rather than vice versa, and therefore presents no obstacle to the recognition of the transcendence of human judgment and understanding demonstrated in part one. And it is semantics and pragmatics, social influence, and human freedom and judgment which shape our modes of speech.

62. For instance, in the introduction, sec. 6 (b); in chap. XIII, secs. 3 and 4 (b) (iv); and in many examples in chap. XIV in this volume.

General Conclusion

We saw how language presents itself to us primarily in the activity of speech. Here, from the first acts of understanding speech, our own and that of others, we begin to learn the language spoken—for instance, to learn the meaning and use of particular words. Both language at the level of what is learned, *langue*, and language at the level of use, "speech", are public things appreciated by a community of people using the same language. Thus speech and *langue* are both by nature public and shared.

What belongs to the individual is the understanding of speech and knowledge of *langue* and the capacity for these. However, even these do not come first absolutely, since they are grounded in a more general understanding or intellectual capacity. And it is this underlying intellectual capacity which enables us to go further than mere signaling, to go beyond this to give conceptual expression to what is being communicated—actually to "express" the content being communicated, thereby making this thought-content available to be reflected upon. Moreover, as we saw in chapter IV, once thought-contents have been thus expressed and made open to reflection, we can reflect upon the ways in which we use the general concepts concerned in various different cases and reflect upon the rationale of this use in such a way as to avoid the contradictions resulting from falsely presuming that we use words in rigidly uniform ways.

This underlying understanding includes the grasp of the structures of interpersonal relationship, causal action, motivation, time, possibility and necessity, reflection, argument, and other broad features underpinning the principles of the "general logic" outlined in the introduction. It is this which sets the framework for the flexible and informal use of words characteristic of the human use of language and required by human thought. The possession of this underlying understanding and capacity for dialogue constitutes a kind of "non-biological nativism".[1] Such a nonbiological nativism ought to be conceived, not in rationalist terms as if our knowledge of the principles concerned was gained without reference to experience, but rather in such a way that our statement of the paradigms of speech and thought is refined in the course of reflection upon their use.

The roots of our ability to express an infinite range of thought with a finite vocabulary

Once we distinguish between knowledge of *langue* (a practical knowledge of the tools put to use in speech) and speech itself, the way is open to distinguish between the lexical meaning of any given word or lexical factor—that is, its meaning at the level of language-possession and language-acquisition and its varied discourse-significances or senses at the level of language-use. Words or lexical elements thus have a double situation, one in speech and the other as the learned vocabulary to be woven together in sentences in this speech. This allows a word or lexical factor with only a few focuses of meaning listed in dictionaries to have an indefinite number of discourse-significances, seen in the different types of implication of the utterances using the word or lexical factor concerned. I elaborated this distinction in chapters I and III, providing many illustrations in chapters II and V. This showed its importance for all the most general words in language, including those on which mathematical and scientific advance depend and without which literature would cease to exist.

From the start I made it plain that it is principally in virtue of this double situation of words that language gives us the capacity, in Humboldt's phrase, to "make an infinite use of finite means". (Throughout I speak of "words" for ease of presentation, meaning "words or lexical factors". For, since languages are in varying degrees inflected, or else agglutinative or polysynthetic, the "word" as such is not the universal vehicle of meaning.)

This capacity for the infinite is quite wrongly attributed by Chomsky and others to our capacity to reiterate certain types of linguistic operation—for instance, in multiple uses of words such as "and", "or", and "if" and in forming

1. Mark Baker has a useful discussion of "non-biological nativism" in "Creative Aspect of Language Use". In sec. 4 he argues that "there is no good evidence from aphasia that it is neurologically embodied, no good evidence from developmental disorders that it is genetically encoded", and in sec. 5 observes the impotence of computational methods in searching for "the best overall explanation, when there is no way of knowing in advance what facts will be relevant". But in Baker, "Theism and Cognitive Science", he concentrates on principles of reasoning rather than on the principles presupposed in the composition of the propositions from which reasoning proceeds—the principles of the general logic of which I spoke earlier.

complex structures involving embedded relative clauses as in "The editor that the authors that the newspaper hired liked laughed"—or, in Chomsky's Minimalism, more generally, in the capacity to repeat the operation "Merge". However, in practice such iterative capacity is of small importance for the power of language. It is of very subsidiary importance for understanding the concepts involved in individual propositions and the way they are put together so as to have sense, something presupposed by any reasoning from them—less important for this than for reasoning itself.

Rather, what gives language its power is the informality and flexibility with which human beings use words in individual propositions. This is seen even with quite ordinary words in figures of speech and comparisons of various kinds, but is above all exhibited in the case of the most general terms that we use: whether it be with words like "individual", "collection", and "number", which arise with every subject-matter; with words like "live", "know", "rule", and "possible" as they arise in non-abstract contexts; or in our extensive use of the metaphors of "seeing" and "grasping" in regard to understanding. Our ability to use these more general concepts in a way free from mechanically applicable rule underlies our flexibility in using other words. It is this informality and flexibility which enables human beings to describe and even, to some extent, explain quite unanticipated situations and features of existence, including features at the extremes of the microscopic and macroscopic—opening out new paradigms of thought and methods of approach, raising new questions and finding new ways of answering them. This lack of definite limits in our raising questions and seeking ways of answering them explains why our thinking is not limited in the way Kant supposed. That is, there is nothing in our faculty of understanding restricting us to "naturalism" or the "empirical" in any definable sense, and, as I have shown, certainly no limitations coming from neurology.

(a) Setting aside the Chomskyan blind alley

In connection with speech I made it clear that it is pragmatics and semantics that determine whatever more general features of grammar we find. The idea that grammar is autonomous quickly appeared ill-grounded and far-fetched. I showed that in human language it is not neurology, but semantics, as reflecting understanding, and pragmatics, as reflecting the structures of human communication, which alone set universal limits to "grammatical structure" in any of the ways that this has been commonly understood. Here I took a view quite opposite to that of Chomsky and those others who regard universal grammatical or conceptual structures as reflecting and determined by the structures of human brain functioning. In part three I exhibited some of the key ways in which semantics and pragmatics explain the tendency of various general syntactic features to be shared by different human languages, and how it is that, through appreciating pragmatic and semantic features of what others say, we gain access to its semantic structure and thence its grammar.

Moreover, the purposes of explaining human facility in using language cannot be served by our first gaining a method of generating context-independent grammatical sentence-constructs and then finding a method of selecting just that particular grammatical construct which is apt to express the sense we desire to express in the context of utterance. For there is no general method of finding a sentence-construct fitting our purpose, granted the endless variety of sometimes unanticipated situations, features of existence, and purposes in making communications.

The illusion that grammar is autonomous, initially suggested by the non-correspondence of the categories of "noun" and "concrete object", has been created, first, by a failure to understand our pragmatic capacity to make new topics both of the states picked out by predicates and of the situations and events reported in propositions, enabling us to set up a hierarchy of different categories of subject or topic; and second, by a failure to register the facility with which we grammaticalize semantic structure in many different ways.

(b) The marriage of pragmatics and semantics

What we say has a semantic content, but pragmatics shapes the way we express this content, and this reflects the fact that speech and thought are activities and, as such, have a dynamic character. In chapters VIII, IX, and X I made plain the importance of the "live" or "saying" character of speech—which sets it in contrast with any form of picturing or representing, as well as with naming. Here I echoed the thought of Wittgenstein, Jespersen, and Plato.

The expressiveness of language arises out of the dynamic nature of its articulation, each sentence a drama in a context, not a junction or composition of parts. Sentences as completed utterances are integrated complexes of parts and features of different kinds. The verb is the typical vehicle of the "saying character" of the sentence, giving it its force, dynamism, and structure. Therefore it is the verb, or what has the role of the verb, which dictates the structure of the sentence and in the same act transforms it from a static arrangement of parts or elements into the living utterance we meet in speech. We gain access to this structure set by the verb through sensitivity to the pragmatic and semantic features of which I spoke earlier. Accordingly a grammar is not concerned with static arrangements of elements, but with sentences as utterances. This transforms the shape of a grammar in the way I set forth in chapters XIV and XV, the verb having a quite different role from all other elements in a sentence, and sentence theory being no longer based on phrase theory, but rather vice versa. As speech becomes grammaticalized, nouns and various elements of a more noun-like character come to have their relation to the verb indicated by inflections, prepositions, word-order or configuration, and other "synlexical" features or elements. It is the dynamic character of the grammatically verbal which differentiates clauses from other word-groups within sentences, clauses being unique in their capacity to occur naked as sentences—that is, as complete utterances in their own right.

The structures of speech, with their integration of the semantic and the pragmatic, exhibit the character of human thought as articulate—each thought involving a complex of different concepts in an appropriate way, whether in affirmation or denial—and each thought having a content concerned with the complex realities of the world as well as with evaluation and motivation, the matters of concern to human beings. Accordingly grammar has to incorporate the structures of "general logic". This "general logic" includes, first, the logic of propositions, predicates, sets, and natural arithmetic (the logic which arises with every subject-matter); second, the differentiation of kinds of acts according to their posture in time, and of acts from states, with the logic of causal action and continuity (the use of continuous tenses, continuous time, and continuous space being inseparable), and the logic of motivation and evaluation; and, third, the logic of the reflective thought which evaluates judgments and forms of reasoning. This logic incorporates three modal frameworks: that of what causally can or cannot be brought about or come about, or must happen; that of what reasons for action permit, prohibit, or command; and that of what grounds for knowledge or belief show to be possibly so, certainly not so, or necessarily so.

(c) The unitariness of linguistic capacity and its evolutionary setting

The conceptual expressiveness of language, its essentially dynamic, verbal, and consequently nonrepresentational character, and the character of words as enabling a thought-content to be made explicit and open to shared reflection are inseparable. In chapter IV I highlighted the unitariness of the semantic structure of language. This unitariness excludes the idea of human language as developing either characteristic by characteristic or structural element by structural element, as if by a process of gradual addition of characteristics or structural elements to some preexisting whole, language might have developed bit by bit until it reached the rounded whole shared by all human beings, so far as they are adult and unimpaired in faculties. On the contrary, human beings' simplest judgments, even the judgment "James is eating", would lack the meaning they have if the person were not able to understand the difference between being actual and being merely possible; understand the raising of questions as to truth or falsehood, certainty or uncertainty, implying the capacity to reflect and deliberate; and make the other discriminations mentioned earlier, including those between present and past, continuous and noncontinuous activity, completed and incomplete action. Machines may signal things, but they lack the potentiality for making this whole span of discriminations, as well as lacking the capacity for self-reflection. By contrast the human capacity for speech involves this whole intellectual structure. New forms of experience may be met with and new vocabulary learned and understood, but the framework of understanding into which any judgment about experience fits or within which any vocabulary is utilized is unitary—and the linguistic framework which reflects this understanding likewise unitary.

Thus the understanding on which human language capacity draws, unlike other developments seen in the evolution of human beings, has an all-at-once, or all-or-nothing, character, even though the development of its external realization is dependent on the development of linguistic exchange within a community. Speech and language are essentially community-dependent (it was quite wrong to psychologize linguistics, proposing myths of "Internalized" languages and treating grammar as belonging to psychology). Therefore the presence of the capacity for speech with the underlying understanding I spoke of may have continued over many generations, in gradual stages obtaining more explicit and regular forms of expression in speech, although the *état de langue* remains always in motion. Thus, as linguistic interchange develops, this external realization of the understanding underlying the capacity for language has to unfold, perhaps over many centuries or millennia, as if reaching for whatever the underlying power of understanding makes possible.[2]

In chapters VI and VII I explained the shape of the development towards the human in more detail, applying Gibson's model for the treatment of perception in psychology to the case of the psychology of language-learning and language-use. According to my argument Gibson's model, whereby perception is to be thought of in terms of a functional adaptation between the human being and the natural environment within which he or she moves, provided a blueprint for considering a person's learning and use of a language in terms of functional adaptation to the social environment of speakers of the same language together with the natural environment of the human being concerned. Within this setting each child learns to speak the language of the adults with whom he or she is interacting linguistically, gathering the vocabulary, accidence (e.g., inflections), and modes of clause construction (word order, agreement) of the language being shared, these latter being shaped by the semantic and pragmatic constraints referred to earlier. In the tuning of the child's linguistic capacity through these constraints in this social setting, the

2. I have put my thought setting language in a wider evolutionary framework in David Braine, "Life and Human Life: Their Nature and Emergence", in *The Missing Link* (Lanham, Md.: University Press of America, forthcoming).

child's brain will incidentally be tuned to play its role in memorizing and processing the features particular to the language concerned.

All this depends upon the way that, in the course of the evolution of the vertebrates, and in particular the various mammal groups, the different parts of the brain have become increasingly malleable in function and thereby adapted to their intermediate role of relating the animal to its environment; not to the natural environment alone, but also to the social environment which in the human case involves other speakers and hearers. In the course of this development the malleability of the brain has become maximal, so that the only universal constraints relevant to human language (the limits reflected in shared grammatical structures) are those set by pragmatics and semantics or, properly speaking, what is required by communication and by the understanding of what is spoken—what I refer to as the constraints set by communication and the general logic of which I spoke. Thus when the hominid brain became so malleable in its functioning as to make the hominids concerned open to the workings of intellect, human beings—true persons—came into existence.

(d) The command of the intellect

When a person makes a judgment, this process or action of thought or speech is not mediated by "representations", whether in the brain or mind or in language, and the function of linguistic expression is *to express* such judgment, *not to represent* it or make it possible *to picture* it, let alone to give it an isomorphic neurological embodiment. This allows the intellect to be in command, free of any physical or other determinism alien to independent judgment. It is thus that we can reject Kant's conception that the faculty of knowledge shapes its objects analogously to the way that the sensory system shapes the objects of sense. Instead, a proper psycholinguistics and epistemology will make clear that through the exercise of understanding, the objects of human knowledge shape the human faculty of knowledge.[3]

As we saw, others—Aristotle, Aquinas, and Wittgenstein—have exhibited the nonrepresentational character of human thought by showing the impossibility of giving any general concept a material representation within some supposed physical organ of thinking. Such representation is impossible, whether the concept is of a specialized kind, or of a more general kind applied analogously in many areas, or with applications in every area.

3. Hegel conceives that it is a fair demand "that even the forms of thought must be made an object of investigation". Yet he continues, "Unfortunately there soon creeps in the misconception of already knowing before you know—the error of refusing to enter the water until you have learnt to swim". "What he wants", he says, "is to combine in our process of enquiry the action of the forms of thought with a criticism of them"—so that "in their own action they must determine their limits and point out their defects"; Georg W. F. Hegel, *The Logic of Hegel*, translated by William Wallace (Oxford: Oxford University Press, 1975), IV.II.§41.1:66.

This absence of any isomorphism between human acts of judging and understanding and any bodily process is necessary for human beings to be able to reflect upon themselves without any definite restriction so that the intellect can operate independently. The logico-linguistic consideration of our linguistic expressions of judgment and understanding gave us an opportunity in chapters IV and V to grasp the conditions of any capacity to avoid paradox and to see how we are able to rely upon even our most general concepts, including such second-order concepts as truth, definition, and proof, despite the fact that these concepts are not formalizable or applicable according to mechanical rule.

The metaphor of needing to be in a position of command in order to know is a particularly powerful one, and applies particularly well to the considerations of Gödel, who did indeed find a way of standing outside a particular system to command a view of it as a whole, thereby to put us into a position to assess it and to find proofs outside the particular system concerned, in this case a formal system—while at the same time we noted our well-evidenced ability to shortcut particular systems of proof to arrive at a conclusion more quickly. However, of more general importance, taking advantage of the understanding which enables human beings to use the possibility of drawing upon the openness of concepts and so of using words informally and flexibly, the mathematical examples we considered in chapter V present themselves as merely subsidiary instances of the more general capacity to criticize and in some cases establish new paradigms, new models in thought, so as to see another person or persons, or the world and its context, in a new light.

The understanding and thought exhibited in language display human beings as in nature bodily, while in existence and activity transcending the body

Human understanding is not limited to what is linguistically expressible. Human intellect and will are moved by love and wonder directed towards the good and true, whether this love and wonder be focused on music and art, on the things of nature, on living things, on nature in its unity and our unity with it, on persons, or on the divine. The intellectual therefore runs wider and deeper than what is expressed in language.

However, how such forms of love and wonder affect a human being's life is limited or else opened out by his or her judgments and choices—and, if social customs and forms of upbringing have an influence, these themselves over a period are limited or opened out by many judgments and choices. But in human life judgments and choices are things characteristically expressed or expressible through language. For, as Humboldt had it, it is one and the same power which underlies or generates both thought and speech. It is this which allows the linguistically expressible its governing and liberating role in human life.

Linguistic understanding, thinking, and questioning are activities which cannot be the work of any bodily organ—this is shown by their nonrepresentational character as we saw it in chapter VIII, and by the lack of definable limits to the flexibility in our use of words, a freedom which does not prejudice the objectivity of our judgment and our intellectual command, things seen in chapters I to V. The judgments we make are not limited by any set of mechanically applicable rules capable of representation or embodiment in the workings of a physical organ, and are situated within the setting of the unitary framework of understanding, involving a general logic which cannot be formalized. For, although the natural form of realization of this understanding, thinking, and questioning lies in their linguistic expression, and the word-skills involved make this natural form of realization depend on the use of the brain, ears, and voice, nonetheless the understanding exercised cannot be the work of a bodily organ. This does not make this understanding, thinking, and questioning the work of some other, immaterial organ, but the activities of the person as such. Our thinking is not embodied in speech; nor is it embodied in neural or imaginative sequences. Thus, when we say that a man had the sudden thought, "Heavens! The post has gone!", it is evident that the man has already thought the "has gone" when he thinks "Heavens!", since it is the post having gone which is the object of his surprise; hence it is evident that, although these words express the thought he has had, his having the thought did not consist in saying these words successively to himself; rather, he had the thought in an indivisible act, as if in an instant.

What acts, or is exercised in activity, exists; and therefore, since both the understanding exercised in judgment and speech and the command of view exhibited in judgment transcend the body, human existence must also transcend the body.[4] Yet these activities are at the same time, of their very nature, expressed through speech and coordinated with the use of the imagination, both involving the brain and how its activity is organized, notably in the exercise of memory of vocabulary and accidence, while the acquisition of concepts depends in varied ways on sensory experience. This makes speech activities uniquely important for the appreciation of the special nature of human beings. Here the character of the activity of thought seen in speech exhibits us as having an existence which transcends the body, so that when any new human being comes into existence, a new root of initiative, a new author of thought and action, is operative in the world—even while such thought requires the body for its characteristically human growth and expression.

4. Cf. David Braine, *Human Person*, chap. 15, esp. 537–42.

Bibliography

Abney, S. P. "The English Noun Phrase in its Sentential Aspect". PhD diss., Massachusetts Institute of Technology, 1987.

Ackerman, F., and G. Webelhuth. *A Theory of Predicates*. Stanford, Calif.: CSLI, 1998.

Adger, David, Susan Pintzuk, Bernadette Plunkett, and George Tsoulas, eds. *Specifiers: Minimalist Approaches*. Oxford: Oxford University Press, 1999.

Ajdukiewicz, K. "Syntactic Connexion". In *Polish Logic, 1920–1939*, edited by Storrs McCall, 207–31. Oxford: Oxford University Press, 1967.

Allport, G. W. *Becoming—Basic Considerations for a Psychology of Personality*. New Haven, Conn.: Yale University Press, 1955.

Anderson, Alan Ross, ed. *Minds and Machines*. Englewood Cliffs, N.J.: Prentice-Hall, 1964.

Anderson, John M. *The Grammar of Case: Towards a Localistic Theory*. Cambridge: Cambridge University Press, 1971.

Anderson, John R. "Induction of Augmented Transition Networks". *Cognitive Science* 1, no. 2 (1977): 125–57.

Andrews, Avery D. "The Representation of Case in Modern Icelandic". In Bresnan, *Mental Representation*, 427–503. 1982.

Anscombe, G. E. M. *Intention*. Oxford: Blackwell, 1958.

———. *An Introduction to Wittgenstein's Tractatus*. London: Hutchinson, 1959.

———. "Analysis Competition—Tenth Problem". Paper 20 in *Collected Philosophical Papers*, vol. 2. 1981.

———. *Collected Philosophical Papers*. 3 vols. Oxford: Blackwell, 1981.

———. "The Intentionality of Sensation: A Grammatical Feature". Paper 1 in *Collected Philosophical Papers*, vol. 2. 1981.

———. "The Question of Linguistic Idealism". Paper 13 in *Collected Philosophical Papers*, vol. 1. 1981.

Anscombe, G. E. M., and Peter Thomas Geach. *Three Philosophers*. Oxford: Blackwell, 1961.

Ansre, G. "The Influence of English on West African Languages". In *The English Language in West Africa*, edited by J. Spencer, 145–64. London: Longman, 1971.

Aronoff, Mark. *Word Formation in Generative Grammar*. Linguistic Enquiry Monographs 1. Cambridge: MIT Press, 1976.

Aronoff, Mark, and Janie Rees-Miller, eds. *The Handbook of Linguistics*. Oxford: Blackwell, 2003.

Austin, John L. "Truth". In *J. L. Austin: Philosophical Papers*, ed. J. O. Urmson and G. J. Warnock, 117–33. Oxford: Oxford University Press, 1961. First published in *Proceedings of the Aristotelian Society* suppl. vol. 24 (1950).

———. *How to Do Things with Words.* Oxford: Oxford University Press, 1962.

———. *Sense and Sensibilia.* Oxford: Oxford University Press, 1962.

Baars, Bernard. *A Cognitive Theory of Consciousness.* Cambridge: Cambridge University Press, 1988.

Bach, Kent. "Conversational Impliciture". *Mind and Language* 9 (1994): 124–62.

Baker, Gordon P. "Following Wittgenstein: Some Signposts for Philosophical Investigations §§. 143–242". In Holtzman and Leich, *Wittgenstein: To Follow a Rule,* 31–71. 1981.

Baker, Gordon P., and P. M. S. Hacker. *Wittgenstein: Understanding and Meaning.* Oxford: Blackwell, 1980.

———. *Language, Sense and Nonsense.* Oxford: Blackwell, 1984.

Baker, Mark C. *The Atoms of Language: The Mind's Hidden Rules of Grammar.* New York: Basic Books, 2001.

———. "The Natures of Nonconfigurationality". In Baltin and Collins, *Handbook of Contemporary Syntactic Theory,* 407–38. 2001.

———. "The Creative Aspect of Language Use and Nonbiological Nativism". In *The Innate Mind 3: Foundations and the Future,* edited by Peter Carruthers, Stephen Laurence, and Stephen Stich, 233–53. Oxford: Oxford University Press, 2007.

———. "The Macroparameter in a Microparametric World". In Biberauer, *Limits of Syntactic Variation,* 351–74. 2008.

———. "Theism and Cognitive Science". In *The Routledge Companion to Theism,* edited by Charles Taliaferro and Stewart Goetz. London: Routledge, forthcoming.

Baltin, Mark, and Chris Collins, eds. *The Handbook of Contemporary Syntactic Theory.* Oxford: Blackwell, 2001.

Baugh, A. C., and T. Cable. *A History of the English Language.* 4th ed. London: Routledge and Kegan Paul, 1993.

Beach, Matthew. "Asymmetries between Passivization and Antipassivization in the Tarramiutut Subdialect of Inuktitut". In *The Proceedings of the LFG '03 Conference,* edited by Miriam Butt and Tracy Holloway King, 1–21. Stanford, Calif.: CSLI, 2003.

Beebe, Michael. "The Basis of Semantic Structure". *Dialogue* 15 (December 1979): 624–41.

Belnap, Nuel D., Jr. "Tonk, Plonk, and Plink". *Analysis* 22, no. 6 (1962): 130–34.

Benacerraf, Paul. "God, the Devil and Gödel". *The Monist* 51 (1967): 9–32.

Benacerraf, Paul, and Hilary Putnam, eds. *Philosophy of Mathematics: Selected Readings.* 2nd ed. Cambridge: Cambridge University Press, 1983.

Bennett, David C. *Spatial and Temporal Uses of English Prepositions: An Essay in Stratificational Semantics.* London: Longman, 1975.

Bennett, Jonathan. "The Meaning-Nominalist Strategy". *Foundations of Language* 10 (1973): 141–68.

———. *Linguistic Behaviour.* Cambridge: Cambridge University Press, 1976.

Berkeley, George. *The Principles of Human Knowledge.* Oxford: Oxford University Press, 1998.

Berkeley, George. *A Treatise Concerning the Principles of Human Knowledge.* Oxford: Oxford University Press, 1998. First published 1710.

Berman, R. A. "Language Knowledge and Language Use". In Levy, Schlesinger, and Braine, *Categories and Processes,* 45–72. 1988.

Biberauer, Theresa, ed. *The Limits of Syntactic Variation.* Amsterdam: John Benjamins, 2008.

Blackburn, Simon. "Reply: Rule-Following and Moral Realism". In Holtzman and Leich, *Wittgenstein: To Follow a Rule,* 163–90. 1981.

———. *Spreading the Word.* Oxford: Oxford University Press, 1984.

Blake, Barry J. *Relational Grammar.* London: Routledge, 1990.

———. *Case.* 2nd ed. Cambridge: Cambridge University Press, 2001.

Bloom, Lois. *Language Development From Two to Three.* Cambridge: Cambridge University Press, 1991.

Bloomfield, Leonard. *An Introduction to the Study of Language*. New York: Holt, 1914.

———. *Language*. New York: Holt, 1933.

Boden, Margaret A. *The Creative Mind: Myths and Mechanisms*. London: Weidenfeld and Nicolson, 1990. Expanded ed. London: Abacus, 1991.

Bohm, David. "Quantum Theory as an Indication of a New Order in Physics". In *Proceedings of the Enrico Fermi International Summer School* (1971): 412–69.

Bolinger, Dwight. "The Uniqueness of the Word". *Lingua* 12 (1963): 113–36.

Borer, Hagit. *Parametric Syntax*. Dordrecht: Foris, 1984.

Botha, Rudolf, and Chis Knight, eds. *The Cradle of Language*. Oxford: Oxford University Press, 2000.

———, eds. *The Prehistory of Language*. Oxford: Oxford University Press, 2009.

Bouquet, Simon, and Rudolf Engler, eds. *Écrits de linguistique generale par Ferdinand de Saussure*. Paris: Gallimard, 2002.

Bowers, John. "Predication". In Baltin and Collins, *Handbook of Contemporary Syntactic Theory*, 299–333. 2001.

Bowie, G. L. "Lucas' Number Is Finally Up". *Journal of Philosophical Logic* 11 (1982): 279–85.

Bradley, F. H. "On Truth and Coherence". Chap. 5 in *Essays on Truth and Reality*. Oxford: Oxford University Press, 1914.

Braine, David. "Explanation and Modality". Bachelor's thesis, Oxford University, 1965.

———. "Infinite Sets". Paper presented to the Interdisciplinary Seminar on the History and Philosophy of Science, University of Aberdeen, Scotland, 1968.

———. "The Nature of Knowledge". *Proceedings of the Aristotelian Society* 72 (1971–72): 41–63.

———. "Two Kinds of Critical Philosophy". Paper presented to Société Belge de Logique et de Philosophie des Sciences, Brussels, November 18, 1972.

———. "Varieties of Necessity". *Proceedings of the Aristotelian Society* suppl. vol. 46 (1972): 139–70.

———. "Truth and Definiteness". Paper presented at the University of St. Andrews, Scotland, 1976.

———. *The Reality of Time and the Existence of God*. Oxford: Oxford University Press, 1988.

———. *The Human Person: Animal And Spirit*. Notre Dame, Ind.: University of Notre Dame Press, 1992.

———. "The Active and Potential Intellects: Aquinas as a Philosopher in His Own Right". In *Mind, Metaphysics, and Value in the Thomistic and Analytical Traditions*, edited by John Haldane, 18–35. Notre Dame, Ind.: University of Notre Dame Press, 2002.

———. "Aquinas, God and Being". In *Analytical Thomism: Traditions in Dialogue*, edited by Craig Paterson and Matthew S. Pugh, 1–24. Aldershot, UK: Ashgate, 2006.

———. "Life and Human Life: Their Nature and Emergence". In *The Missing Link*. Lanham, Md.: University Press of America, forthcoming.

Braine, Martin D. S. "The Ontogeny of Certain Logical Operations: Piaget's Formulation Examined by Nonverbal Methods". *Psychological Monographs* 73, no. 5 (1959).

———. "The Ontogeny of English Phrase Structure: The First Phase". *Language* 39 (1963): 1–13.

———. "On Two Types of Models of the Internalization of Grammars". In *The Ontogenesis of Grammar: A Theoretical Symposium*, edited by Dan I. Slobin, 153–86. New York: Academic Press, 1971.

———. "Children's First Word Combinations". *Monographs of the Society for Research in Child Development* 41, no. 1 (1976): 1–104.

———. "Modeling the Acquisition of Linguistic Structure". In Levy, Schlesinger, and Braine, *Categories and Processes*, 217–59. 1988. Available in manuscript from 1983.

———. "What Sort of Innate Structure Is Needed to 'Bootstrap' into Syntax?" *Cognition* 45 (1992): 77–100.

———. "Is Nativism Sufficient?" *Journal of Child Language* 21 (1994): 9–31.

Braine, Martin D. S., and David O'Brien, eds. *Mental Logic*. Hillsdale, N.J.: Erlbaum, 1998.

braine, Martin D. S., P. j. Brooks, N. Cowan, M. Samuels, and C. Tamis-LeMonda. "The Development of Categories at the Semantics/Syntax Interface". *Cognitive Development* 8 (1993): 465–94.

Braine, Martin D. S., and Robin S. Wells. "Case-like Categories in Children: The Actor and Some Related Categories". *Cognitive Psychology* 10, no. 1 (1978): 100–22.

Brandom, Robert. *Making It Explicit*. Cambridge, Mass.: Harvard University Press, 1994.

Bresnan, Joan. "On Complementizers: Toward a Syntactic Theory of Complement Types". *Foundations of Language* 6 (1970): 297–321.

———. *Lexical-Functional Syntax*. Oxford: Blackwell, 2001.

———. "A Realistic Transformational Grammar". In *Linguistic Theory and Psychological Reality*, edited by Morris Halle, Joan Bresnan, and George A. Miller, 1–59. Cambridge, Mass.: MIT Press, 1978.

———. "Control and Complementation". In *Mental Representation*, ed. Bresnan, 282–390. 1982.

———, ed. *The Mental Representation of Grammatical Relations*. Cambridge, Mass.: MIT Press, 1982.

———. "Polyadicity". In *Mental Representation*, ed. Bresnan, 149–72. 1982.

———, ed. LFG Mailing List, September 1995. Accessed September 4, 2010. http://web.archive.org/web/20050322002328, http://montague.stanford.edu/lfg, and www.essex.ac.uk/linguistics/LFG/LFG-and-functionalism/.

Bresnan, Joan, and Judith Aissen. "Optimality and Functionality: Objections and Refutations". *Natural Language and Linguistic Theory* 20 (2002): 81–95.

Breuil, C., B. Conrad, F. Diamond, and R. Taylor. "On the Modularity of Elliptic Curves over Q: Wild 3-adic Exercises". *Journal of American Mathematical Society* 14, no. 4 (2001): 843–939.

Britton, Karl. "Portrait of a Philosopher". In *Ludwig Wittgenstein: The Man and his Philosophy*, edited by K. T. Fann, 56–63. New York: Dell, 1967.

Brody, Michael. *Lexico-Logical Form: A Radically Minimalist Theory*. Cambridge, Mass.: MIT Press, 1995.

Brouwer, L. E. J. "Consciousness, Philosophy and Mathematics". In Benacerraf and Putnam, *Philosophy of Mathematics: Selected Readings*, 90–96. 1983.

———. "Intuitionism and Formalism". Translated by Arnold Dresden. In Benacerraf and Putnam, *Philosophy of Mathematics: Selected Readings*, 72–89. 1983.

Buck, Carl Darling. *Comparative Grammar of Greek and Latin*. Chicago: University of Chicago Press, 1933.

Burling, Robbins. *The Talking Ape*. Oxford: Oxford University Press, 2005.

Butler, Christopher S. *Structure and Function: A Guide to Three Major Structural-Functional Theories*. 2 vols. Amsterdam: John Benjamins, 2003.

Butterworth, George. "Neo-natal Imitation: Existence Mechanisms and Motives". In Nadel and Butterworth, *Imitation in Infancy*, 63–88. 1999.

Cameron, J. R. "Critical Study: *Linguistic Behaviour* by Jonathan Bennett". *Philosophical Quarterly* 27 (1977): 338–52.

Carnap, Rudolf. *Formalization of Logic*. Cambridge, Mass.: Harvard University Press, 1943.

———. *Meaning and Necessity: A Study in Semantics and Modal Logic*. Chicago: University of Chicago Press, 1956.

Carpenter, Humphrey. *The Inklings: C. S. Lewis, J. R. R. Tolkien, Charles Williams, and Their Friends*. London: Allen and Unwin, 1978.

Cavalli-Sforza, Luigi, L. P. Menozzi, and A. Piazza. *The History and Geography of Human Genes*. Princeton, N.J.: Princeton University Press, 1994.

Chang, Han-liang. "The Legacy of Josef Vachek and Its Implications on the Studies of Chinese Script". Invited Memorial Lecture at Prague Linguistic Circle, Prague, November 4, 1996. http://homepage.ntu.edu.tw/~changhl/changhl/0219.pdf.

Choi, Hye-Won. *Optimizing Structure in Context: Scrambling and Information Structure*. Stanford, Calif.: CSLI, 1999.

Chomsky, Noam. *Syntactic Structures*. Berlin: Mouton de Gruyter, 1957.

———. "A Transformational Approach to Syntax". In *Proceedings of the Third Texas Conference on Problems of Linguistic Analysis in English*, edited by Archibald A. Hill, 124–58. Austin: University of Texas Press, 1958.

———. "A Review of B. F. Skinner's *Verbal Behavior*". *Language* 35, no. 1 (1959): 26–58.

———. "Explanatory Models in Linguistics". In Nagel, Suppes, and Tarski, *Logic, Methodology and Philosophy of Science*, 528–50. 1962.

———. *Topics in the Theory of Generative Grammar*. The Hague: Mouton, 1966. First published in *Current Trends in Linguistics*, edited by Thomas A. Sebeok. Vol. 3. Berlin: De Gruyter, 1966.

———. *Aspects of the Theory of Syntax*. Cambridge, Mass.: MIT Press, 1965.

———. *Language and Mind*. New York: Harcourt Brace Jovanovich, 1968.

———. "Quine's Empirical Assumptions". In *Words and Objections: Essays on the Work of W. V. Quine*, edited by Donald Davidson and Jaakko Hintikka, 53–68. Dordrecht: Reidel, 1969.

———. "Remarks on Nominalization". In *Readings in English Transformational Grammar*, edited by R. Jacobs and P. Rosenbaum, 184–221. Waltham, Miss.: Ginn, 1970.

———. *Problems of Knowledge and Freedom*. New York: Pantheon, 1971.

———. *The Logical Structure of Linguistic Inquiry*. New York: Plenum, 1975.

———. *Rules and Representations*. Oxford: Blackwell, 1980.

———. *Lectures on Government and Binding*. Dordrecht: Foris, 1981.

———. *Some Concepts and Consequences of the Theory of Government and Binding*. Cambridge, Mass.: MIT Press, 1982.

———. *Knowledge of Language: Its Nature, Origin and Use*. New York: Praeger, 1986.

———. *Language and the Problems of Knowledge: The Managua Lectures*. Cambridge, Mass.: MIT Press, 1988.

———. *The Minimalist Program*. Cambridge, Mass.: MIT Press, 1995.

———. *New Horizons in the Study of Language and Mind*. Cambridge: Cambridge University Press, 2000.

———. *Cartesian Linguistics: A Chapter in the History of Rationalist Thought*. Christchurch, New Zealand: Cybereditions, 2002. First published 1966.

Chomsky, Noam, and Howard Lasnik. "The Theory of Principles and Parameters". In *Syntax: An International Handbook of Contemporary Research*, edited by J. Jacobs, A. von Stechow, W. Sternefeld, and T. Vennemann. Berlin: de Gruyter, 1993. Reprinted in Chomsky, *The Minimalist Program*.

Church, Alonzo. *Introduction to Mathematical Logic*. Princeton, N.J.: Princeton University Press, 1956.

Clark, H. H. *Using Language*. Cambridge: Cambridge University Press, 1996.

Cobbett, William. *A Grammar of the English Language* [1818]. Oxford: Oxford University Press, 1984.

Cohen, Paul J. *Set Theory and the Continuum Hypothesis*. New York: W. A. Benjamin, 1966.

Comrie, Bernard. *Language Universals and Linguistic Typology*. 2nd ed. Chicago: University of Chicago Press, 1989.

Comrie, Bernard, and Edward L. Keenan. "Noun Phrase Accessibility and Universal Grammar". *Linguistic Inquiry* 8 (1977): 63–99.

Cook, Vivian J., and Mark Newson. *Chomsky's Universal Grammar*. 2nd ed. Oxford: Blackwell, 1996.

Cowie, Fiona. *What's Within? Nativism Reconsidered*. Oxford: Oxford University Press, 1999.

Croft, William. "Autonomy and Functionalist Linguistics". *Language* 71 (1995): 490–532.

Cruse, David Alan. *Lexical Semantics*. Cambridge: Cambridge University Press, 1986.

Davidson, Donald D. *Essays on Actions and Events*. Oxford: Oxford University Press, 1980.

———. "The Individuation of Events". Essay 8 in *Essays on Actions and Events*. 1980. First published in *Essays in Honour of Carl G. Hempel,* edited by Nicholas Rescher. Dordrecht: Reidel, 1969.

———. "The Logical Form of Action Sentences". Essay 6 in *Essays on Actions and Events.* 1980. First published in *The Logic of Decision and Action,* edited by Nicholas Rescher. Pittsburgh, Penn.: University of Pittsburgh Press, 1967.

———. "Mental Events". Essay 11 in *Essays on Actions and Events.* 1980. First published in *Experience and Theory,* edited by Lawrence Foster and J. W. Swanson. London: Duckworth, 1970.

———. *Inquiries into Truth and Interpretation.* 2nd ed. Oxford: Oxford University Press, 2001. First edition 1984.

———. "On the Very Idea of a Conceptual Scheme". Essay 13 in *Inquiries into Truth and Interpretation.* 2001.

———. "Theories of Meaning and Learnable Languages" In *Inquiries into Truth and Interpretation.* 2001. First read 1964; first published 1965.

———. "Truth and Meaning", Essay 2 in *Inquiries into Truth and Interpretation.* 2001. First published 1967.

———. "What Metaphors Mean". Essay 17 in *Inquiries into Truth and Interpretation.* 2001.

———. "Expressing Evaluations". Essay 2 in *Problems of Rationality.* 2004. First published 1984.

———. *Problems of Rationality*. Oxford: Oxford University Press, 2004.

———. "Turing's Test". Essay 5 in *Problems of Rationality.* 2004. First published in *Modelling the Mind,* edited by W. H. Newton-Smith and K. V. Wilkes. Oxford: Oxford University Press, 1990.

Davies, William D. "Choctaw Subjects and Multiple Levels in Syntax". In Hoekstra, van der Hulst, and Moortgat, *Perspectives on Functional Grammar,* 235–71. 1981.

Davis, Martin. *Computability and Unsolvability*. New York: McGraw-Hill, 1958.

Deacon, Terrence. "Emergence: The Hole at the Wheel's Hub". In *The Re-Emergence of Emergence,* edited by Philip Clayton and Paul Davies, 111–50. Oxford: Oxford University Press, 2006.

Dennett, Daniel C. *Consciousness Explained.* London: Penguin, 1991.

———. "Quining *Qualia*". In Marcel and Bisiach, *Consciousness in Contemporary Science,* 42–77. 1988.

———. "Real Patterns". *Journal of Philosophy* 88 (1991): 27–51.

de Saussure, Ferdinand. *Cours de linguistique générale,* edited by C. Bally and A. Sechehaye. 2nd ed. Paris: Payot, 1922.

Descartes, René. René Descartes to Marin Mersenne, November 20, 1629. In *Descartes, René, Philosophical Letters,* edited and translated by Anthony Kenny. Oxford: Oxford University Press, 1970.

Dictionnaire Historique de la langue française. Paris: Dictionnaires Le Robert, 1992.

Dik, Simon C. Review of *A Prague School Reader in Linguistics,* edited by Josef Vachek. *Lingua* 18 (1967): 80–89.

———. "Some Critical Remarks on the Treatment of Morphological Structure in Transformational Generative Grammar". *Lingua* 18 (1967): 352–83.

———. *Functional Grammar.* Amsterdam: North-Holland, 1978.

———. *Studies in Functional Grammar.* London: Academic Press, 1980.

———. "Basic Principles of Functional Grammar". In *Advances in Functional Grammar,* 3–28. 1983.

———. *The Theory of Functional Grammar: Part 1, The Structure of the Clause.* Dordrecht: Foris, 1989. 2nd ed. Berlin: Mouton de Gruyter, 1997.

———. *The Theory of Functional Grammar: Part 2, Complex and Derived Constructions.* Berlin: Mouton de Gruyter, 1997.

———, ed. *Advances in Functional Grammar.* Dordrecht: Foris, 1983.

Dowty, David. *Word Meaning and Montague Grammar.* Dordrecht: Reidel, 1979.

Dreyfus, Hubert. *What Computers Still Can't Do.* Cambridge, Mass.: MIT Press, 1979. Revision of *What Computers Can't Do.* New York: Harper and Row, 1972.

Du Bois, John W. "Competing Motivations". In *Iconicity in Syntax*, edited by John Haiman, 343–65. Amsterdam: John Benjamins, 1985.

———. "The Discourse Basis of Ergativity". *Language* 63 (1987): 805–55.

Dummett, Michael. "Frege, Gottlob". In *Encyclopaedia of Philosophy*, edited by Paul A. Edwards, 2:225–37. New York: Macmillan, 1967.

———. *Frege: Philosophy of Language*. London: Duckworth, 1973; 2nd ed. Cambridge, Mass.: Harvard University Press, 1993.

———. "The Justification of Deduction". No. 17 in *Truth and Other Enigmas*. 1973. First published in *Proceedings of the British Academy* 59 (1973).

———. "Can Analytical Philosophy Be Systematic, and Ought It to Be?" No. 25 in *Truth and Other Enigmas*. 1978. First published as "Ist systematische Philosophie möglich?" in "Hegel-Kongress Stuttgart 1975", edited by Dieter Henrich, supplement, *Hegel-Studien* 17 (1977).

———. "The Philosophical Basis of Intuitionistic Logic". No. 14 in *Truth and Other Enigmas*. 1978. First published in *Logic Colloquium '73*, edited by H. Rose and J. Shepherdson. Amsterdam: North-Holland, 1975.

———. "The Philosophical Significance of Gödel's Theorem". No. 12 in *Truth and Other Enigmas. 1978*. First published in *Ratio* 5 (1963).

———. "The Reality of the Past". No. 21 in *Truth and Other Enigmas*. 1978.

———. "Truth". No. 1 in *Truth and Other Enigmas*. 1978. First published in *Proceedings of the Aristotelian Society* 59 (1959).

———. *Truth and Other Enigmas*. Cambridge, Mass.: Harvard University Press; London: Duckworth, 1978.

———. *The Interpretation of Frege's Philosophy*. London: Duckworth, 1981.

———. "A Nice Derangement of Epitaphs: Some Comments on Davidson and Hacking". In LePore, *Truth and Interpretation*, 459–76. 1986.

———. "What Is a Theory of Meaning? (II)". No. 2 in *The Seas of Language*. Oxford: Oxford University Press, 1993. First published in *Truth and Meaning: Essays in Semantics*, edited by Gareth Evans and John McDowell. Oxford: Oxford University Press, 1976.

Durrell, Martin. *Hammer's German Grammar and Usage*. 4th ed. Chicago: McGraw-Hill, 2002.

Evans, Gareth. *Varieties of Reference*. Oxford: Oxford University Press, 1982.

———. "Semantic Theory and Tacit Knowledge". In *Collected Papers*, edited by John McDowell, 322–42. Oxford: Oxford University Press, 1985.

Everett, Daniel L. "Cultural Constraints on Grammar and Cognition in Pirahã: Another Look at the Design Features of Human Language". *Current Anthropology* 46 (2005): 621–46.

Feferman, Solomon. "Kurt Gödel: Conviction and Caution". In *Gödel's Theorem in Focus*, edited by S. G. Shanker, 96–114. London: Croom Helm, 1988.

———. "Penrose's Gödelian Argument". *Psyche* 2, no. 7 (1995): 21–32.

Findlay, J. N. Meinong's *Theory of Objects and Values*. 2nd ed. Oxford: Oxford University Press, 1963.

Fodor, Jerry A. *The Language of Thought*. Cambridge, Mass.: Harvard University Press, 1975.

———. *The Modularity of Mind*. Cambridge: MIT Press, 1983.

———. "Doing Without What's Within: Fiona Cowie's Critique of Nativism". *Mind* 110 (2001): 99–148.

Fodor, Jerry A., and Z. Pylyshyn. "How Direct Is Visual Perception?" *Cognition* 9 (1981): 139–96.

Foley, W. A., and Robert D. van Valin, Jr. *Functional Syntax and Universal Grammar*. Cambridge: Cambridge University Press, 1984.

Frege, Gottlob. "Concept and Object". Translated by Peter Thomas Geach. In Geach and Black, *Translations from Frege*, 42–55. 1952. Originally published as "Über Begriff und Gegenstand", in *Vierteljahresschrift für wissenschaftliche Philosophie* 16 (1892).

———. "Negation". Translated by Peter Thomas Geach. In Geach and Black, *Translations from*

Frege, 117–35. 1952. Originally published as "Die Verneinung", in *Beitrage zur Philosophie des deutschen Idealismus* 1 (1919).

———. "Function and Concept". Translated by P. T. Geach. In Geach and Black, *Translations from Frege,* 21–41. 1952.

———. "Sense and Reference". Translated by Max Black. In Geach and Black, *Translations from Frege,* 56–78. 1952. Originally published in *Zeitschrift fur Philosophie und philosophische Kritik* 100 (1892).

———. *Foundations of Arithmetic.* Translated by John L. Austin. 2nd ed. Oxford: Blackwell, 1953. Parallel German-English edition of *Die Grundlagen der Arithmetik.* Breslau: Wilhelm Koebner, 1884.

Fukui, Naoki. "A Theory of Category Projection and Its Applications". PhD diss., Massachusetts Institute of Technology, 1986.

———. "Deriving the Differences between English and Japanese: A Case Study in Parametric Syntax". *English Linguistics* 5 (1988): 249–70.

———. *Theory of Projection in Syntax.* Stanford, Calif.: CSLI, 1995.

———. "Phrase Structure". In Baltin and Collins, *Handbook of Contemporary Syntactic Theory,* 374–406. 2001.

Fukui, Naoki, and Hiromu Sakai. "The Visibility Guideline for Functional Categories: Verb Raising in Japanese and Related Issues". *Lingua* 113 (2003): 321–75.

Fukui, Naoki, and M. Speas. "Specifiers and Projection". In *Papers in Theoretical Linguistics,* edited by Naoki Fukui, Tova R. Rapoport, and Elizabeth Sagey, 128–72. Cambridge, Mass.: MITWPL, 1986.

Garcia, J., et al. "Relation of Cue to Consequence in Avoidance Learning". *Psychonomic Science* 4 (1966).

———. "Learning with Prolonged Delay of Reinforcement". *Psychonomic Science* 5, no. 3 (1966).

Gardiner, Alan H. *The Theory of Speech and Language.* Oxford: Oxford University Press, 1932.

Garvin, Paul. "Czechoslovakia". In *Current Trends in Linguistics,* edited by Thomas A. Sebeok, 1:499–522. The Hague: Mouton, 1963.

Gazdar, Gerald. "Phrase Structure Grammar". In Jacobson and Pullum, *The Nature of Syntactic Representation,* 131–86. 1982.

Gazdar, Gerald, E. H. Klein, Geoffrey Pullum, and Ivan Sag. *Generalized Phrase Structure Grammar.* Oxford: Blackwell; Cambridge, Mass.: Harvard University Press, 1985.

Gazzaniga, Michael S. *The Social Brain.* New York: Basic Books, 1985.

———. "Brain Modularity: Towards a Philosophy of Conscious Experience". In Marcel and Bisiach, *Consciousness in Contemporary Science,* 218–38. 1988.

———, ed. *Cognitive Neuroscience: A Reader.* Oxford: Blackwell, 2000.

Gazzaniga, Michael S., and Joseph E. LeDoux. *The Integrated Mind.* New York: Plenum Press, 1978.

Geach, Peter Thomas. *Mental Acts.* London: Routledge and Kegan Paul, 1957.

———. *Reference and Generality.* Ithaca, N.Y.: Cornell University Press, 1962.

———. "Ascriptivism". In *Logic Matters,* 250–54. 1972. First published in *Philosophical Review* 69, no. 2 (1960).

———. "Assertion". In *Logic Matters,* 254–69. 1972. First published in *Philosophical Review* 74 (1965).

———. *Logic Matters.* Oxford: Blackwell; Berkeley: University of California Press, 1972.

———. "Nominalism". In *Logic Matters,* 289–301. 1972. Originally read to Priests' Philosophical Group, London, 1969.

———. "Quine's Syntactical Insights". In *Logic Matters,* 115–127. 1972. First published in *Synthese* 19, nos. 1 and 2 (19682-69).

———. "Some Problems about Time". In *Logic Matters,* 302–18. 1972. First published in *British Academy* 51 (1965).

———. "Names and Identity". In Guttenplan, *Mind and Language,* 139–58. 1975.

———. "Kinds of Statement". Essay 14 in *Intention and Intentionality: Essays in Honour of G. E. M. Anscombe*, edited by Cora Diamond and Jenny Teichman, 221–35. Ithaca, N.Y.: Cornell University Press, 1979.

Geach, Peter Thomas, and Max Black, eds. *Translations from the Philosophical Writings of Gottlob Frege*. Oxford: Blackwell, 1952.

Gentzen, Gerhard. *The Collected Papers of Gerhard Gentzen*. Edited by M. E. Szabo. Amsterdam: North-Holland, 1969.

George, L. "Analogical Generalizations of Natural Language Syntax". PhD diss., Massachusetts Institute of Technology, 1980.

Gettier, E. L. "Is Justified True Belief Knowledge?" *Analysis* 23 (1963): 121–23.

Gibson, Eleanor J. *Principles of Perceptual Learning and Development*. New York: Appleton-Century-Croft, 1969.

———, ed. *An Odyssey in Learning and Perception*. Cambridge, Mass.: MIT Press, 1991.

Gibson, J. J. *The Perception of the Visual World*. Boston: Houghton Mifflin, 1950.

———. "The Concept of Stimulus in Psychology". *American Psychologist* 15 (1960): 694–703.

———. *The Senses Considered as Perceptual Systems*. Boston: Houghton Mifflin, 1966.

———. *The Ecological Approach to Visual Perception*. Boston: Houghton Mifflin, 1979.

Givón, Talmy. *Mind, Code and Context: Essays in Pragmatics*. Hillsdale, N.Y.: Erlbaum, 1989.

———. *Context as Other Minds: The Pragmatics of Sociality, Cognition, and Communication*. Amsterdam: John Benjamins, 2005.

Gödel, Kurt. "What Is Cantor's Continuum Problem?" In Benacerraf and Putnam, *Philosophy of Mathematics: Selected Readings*, 470–85. 1983.

Golinkoff, R. M., Kathy Hirsh-Pasek, Carolyn B. Mervis, William B. Frawley, and Maria Parillo. "Lexical Principles Can Be Extended to the Acquisition of Verbs". In Tomasello and Merriman, *Beyond Names for Things*, 185–221. 1995.

Gombrich, E. H. *The Story of Art*. 16th ed. London: Phaidon, 1995.

Gopnik, Alison, and Soonja Choi. "Early Acquisition of Verbs in Korean: A Cross Linguistic Study". *Journal of Child Language* 22 (1995): 497–529.

———. "Names, Relational Words, and Cognitive Development in English and Korean Speakers: Nouns Are Not Always Learned before Verbs". In Tomasello and Merriman, *Beyond Names for Things*, 63–80. 1995.

Gopnik, Alison, and Andrew Meltzoff. "Imitation, Cultural Learning and the Origins of 'Theory of Mind': Comment on Tomasello et al." *Behavioral and Brain Sciences* 16, no. 3 (1993): 521–22.

Graffi, Giorgio. *200 Years of Syntax*. Amsterdam: John Benjamins, 2001.

Greenberg, J. "Some Universals of Grammar with Particular Reference to the Order of Meaningful Elements". In Greenberg, *Universals of Language*, 58–90. 1963.

———, ed. *Universals of Language: Report of a Conference Held at Dobbs Ferry, New York, April 13–15, 1961*. Cambridge, Mass.: MIT Press, 1963.

Grevisse, Maurice. *Le Bon Usage*. 13th ed. Paris: Duculot, 1993; 6th ed. 1964.

Grice, H. P. *Studies in the Way of Words*. Cambridge, Mass.: Harvard University Press, 1989.

Grimshaw, Jane. "On the Lexical Representation of Romance Reflexive Clitics". In Bresnan, *Mental Representation*, 87–148. 1982.

———. "Locality and Extended Projection". In *Lexical Specification and Insertion*, edited by Peter Coupmans, Martin Everett, and Jane Grimshaw, 115–33. Hillsdale, N.J.: Erlbaum, 1998.

Gross, Richard. *Psychology: The Science of Mind and Behaviour*. 2nd ed. London: Hodder and Stoughton, 1992.

Grossberg, Stephen. "Neural Dynamics of Motion Perception, Recognition Learning, and Spatial Attention". In Port and Van Gelder, *Mind as Motion*, 449–89. 1995.

Grothe, Mardy. *Never Let a Fool Kiss You or a Kiss Fool You: Chiasmus and a World of Quotations That Say What They Mean and Mean What They Say*. New York: Viking, 1999.

Gruber, Jeffrey S. *Lexical Structures in Syntax and Semantics*. Amsterdam: North-Holland, 1976.

———. "Studies in Lexical Relations". PhD Dissertation, MIT, 1965. Later published as part 1 of *Lexical Structures in Syntax and Semantics*. 1976.

Guinness, Alec. *Blessings in Disguise*. London: Penguin, 1997. First published 1985.

Guttenplan, Samuel, ed. *Mind and Language*. Oxford: Oxford University Press, 1975.

Haas, William. "On Defining Linguistic Units". *Transactions of the Philological Society* (1954): 54–84.

———. "Function and Structure in Linguistic Descriptions". In *Functionalism in Linguistics*, edited by René Dirven and V. Fried, 333–55. Amsterdam: John Benjamins, 1987.

Hacker, P. M. S. *Insight and Illusion*. 2nd ed. Oxford: Blackwell, 1986.

Hacking, Ian. "The Parody of Conversation". In LePore, *Truth and Interpretation*, 447–58. 1986.

Hale, Bob, and Crispin Wright, eds. *A Companion to the Philosophy of Language*. Oxford: Blackwell, 1997.

Halliday, M. A. K. "Categories of the Theory of Grammar". *Word* 17, no. 3 (1961): 241–92.

———. *An Introduction to Functional Grammar*. London: Arnold, 1994. First published 1985.

Hamlyn, David. *Psychology of Perception: A Philosophical Examination of Gestalt Theory and Derivative Theories of Perception*. London: Routledge and Kegan Paul, 1957.

———. *Sensation and Perception*. London: Routledge and Kegan Paul, 1961.

———. *Perception, Learning and the Self*. London: Routledge and Kegan Paul, 1983.

Hampshire, Stuart. *Thought and Action*. London: Chatto and Windus, 1959.

Hare, R. M. *The Language of Morals*. Oxford: Oxford University Press, 1949.

———. "Meaning and Speech Acts". *Philosophical Review* 79 (1970): 3–24.

Harris, Martin, and Nigel Vincent, eds. *The Romance Languages*. London: Croom Helm, 1988.

Harris, Roy. *Saussure and his Interpreters*. 2nd ed. Edinburgh: Edinburgh University Press, 2003.

Harris, Zellig. *Methods in Structural Linguistics*. Chicago: University of Chicago Press, 1951.

———. "La genèse de l'analyse des transformations et de la métalangue". *Langages* 99 (September 1990). Translated as "The Background of Transformational and Metalanguage Analysis". In *The Legacy of Zellig Harris: Language and Information into the 21st Century*, edited by Bruce Nevin, 1–15. Amsterdam: John Benjamins, 2002.

Hart, H. L. A. "The Ascription of Responsibility and Rights". In *Logic and Language*, edited by A. Flew, 145–66. Oxford: Blackwell, 1951. First published in *Proceedings of the Aristotelian Society*, New Series, 49, 1948–49.

Haspelmath, Martin. "Why Can't We Talk to Each Other?" *Lingua* 110 (2000): 235–55.

———. "Universals of Causative Verb Formation". Paper presented at LSA Institute course, MIT, Cambridge, Mass. August 2, 2005.

———. "Pre-Established Categories Don't Exist: Consequences for Language Description and Typology". *Linguistic Typology* 11 (2007): 119–32.

———. "Parametric versus Functional Explanations of Syntactic Universals". In Biberauer, *The Limits of Syntactic Variation*, 1–29. 2008.

Hauser, Marc, Noam Chomsky, and Tecumseh Fitch. "The Faculty of Language: What Is It, Who Has It, and How Did It Evolve?" *Science* 298 (November 2002): 1569–79.

Hawkins, J. A. *Word Order Universals*. New York: Academic Press, 1983.

Hawkins, R., and R. Towell. *French Grammar and Usage*. London: Arnold, 1996.

Heath, Peter. *On Language: The Diversity of Human Language-Structure and Its Influence on the Mental Development of Mankind*. Cambridge: Cambridge University Press, 1988. Translation of Wilhelm von Humboldt, *Über die Verschiedenheit des menschlich Sprachbaues und ihren Einfluss auf die geistige Entwickelung des Menschengeschlechts*. Berlin: Königlichen Ākademie der Wissenschaften, 1836.

Hegel, Georg W. F. *The Logic of Hegel*. Translated by William Wallace. Oxford: Oxford University Press, 1975.

Heyting, A. *Intuitionism: An Introduction*. Amsterdam: North-Holland, 1956.

———. "The Intuitionist Foundations of Mathematics". In Benacerraf and Putnam, *Philosophy of Mathematics: Selected Readings*, 52–61. 1983.

Higginbotham, J. "Penrose's Platonism". *Journal of Behavioral and Brain Sciences* 13, no. 4 (1990): 667–68.
Hirst, R. J. *Perception and the External World*. London: Macmillan, 1966.
Hjelmslev, Louis. "Otto Jespersen". In *Portraits of Linguists*, edited by T. A. Sebeok, 2:158–73. Bloomington: Indiana University Press, 1966.
Hockett, Charles. "Two Models of Grammatical Description". *Word* 10 (1954): 210–34.
———. *The State of the Art*. The Hague: Mouton, 1968.
Hoekstra, Teun, Harry van der Hulst, and Michael Moortgat, eds. *Perspectives on Functional Grammar*. Dordrecht: Foris, 1981.
Holtzman, S. H., and C. M. Leich, eds. *Wittgenstein: To Follow a Rule*. London: Routledge, 1981.
Hopper, Paul J. "Emergent Grammar". *Berkeley Linguistics Society* 13 (1987): 139–57.
———. "Emergent Grammar". In Tomasello, *New Psychology of Language*, vol. 1, chap. 6, 2009.
Hopper, Paul J., and Elizabeth Closs Traugott. *Grammaticalization*. 2nd ed. Cambridge: Cambridge University Press, 2003. First edition published in 1993.
Horrocks, Geoffrey. *Generative Grammar*. London: Longman, 1987.
Hudson, Richard. "Trouble on the Left Periphery". *Lingua* 113 (2003): 607–42.
Husserl, Edmund, *Logical Investigations*. 2 vols. London: Routledge and Kegan Paul, 1970. Translated by J. N. Findlay from *Logische Untersuchungen*. 2nd ed. Halle: M. Niemeyer,1913.
Ingarden, Roman. *The Literary Work of Art*. Evanston, Ill.: Northwestern University Press, 1974.
Jackendoff, Ray. *Semantic Interpretation in Generative Grammar*. Cambridge, Mass.: MIT Press, 1972.
———. "The Base Rules for Prepositional Phrases". In *A Festschrift for Morris Halle*, edited by S. Anderson and P. Kiparsky, 345–56. New York: Holt, Rinehart and Winston, 1973.
———. *X-Bar Syntax: A Study of Phrase Structure*. Cambridge, Mass.: MIT Press, 1977.
———. *Semantics and Cognition*. Cambridge, Mass.: MIT Press, 1983.
———. *Consciousness and the Computational Mind*. Cambridge, Mass.: MIT Press, 1987.
———. "The Status of Thematic Relations in Linguistic Theory". *Linguistic Inquiry* 18, no. 3 (Summer 1987): 369–411.
———. *Semantic Structures*. Cambridge, Mass.: MIT Press, 1990.
———. *Patterns in the Mind: Language and Human Nature*. New York: Harvester Wheatsheaf, 1993.
———. "Conceptual Semantics and Cognitive Semantics". *Cognitive Linguistics* 7 (1996): 93–129.
———. *The Architecture of the Languagxe Faculty*. Cambridge, Mass.: MIT Press, 1997.
———. "Fodorian Modularity and Representational Modularity". In *Language and the Brain*, edited by Yosef Grodznisky, Lew Shapiro, and David Swinney, 3–30. New York: Academic Press, 2000.
———. *Foundations of Language: Brain, Meaning, Grammar, Evolution* Oxford: Oxford University Press, 2002.
Jacobson, Pauline, and Geoffrey K. Pullum, eds. *The Nature of Syntactic Representation*. Dordrecht: Reidel, 1982.
Jaeggli, O., and K. J. Safir. "The Null Subject Parameter and Parametric Theory". In *The Null Subject Parameter*, 1–44. Dordrecht: Kluwer, 1989.
Jakobson, Roman. "Implications of Language Universals for Linguistics". In Greenberg, *Universals of Language*, 208–19. 1963.
Jespersen, Otto. *Sprogets Logik* [Logic of Speech]. Copenhagen: Oyldendal, 1913.
———. *Philosophy of Grammar*. London: Allen and Unwin, 1924.
———. *Linguistica: Selected Papers in English, French and German*. London: Allen and Unwin, 1933. Reprint of a 1916 review.
Jessen, Marilyn E. "A Semantic Study of Spatial and Temporal Expressions in English". PhD diss., University of Edinburgh, 1975.
Johnson, W. E. *Logic, Part I*. Cambridge: Cambridge University Press, 1921.

Joint Association of Classical Teachers [JACT]. *Reading Greek.* Cambridge: Cambridge University Press, 1980.

Kaplan, Ronald M., and Annie Zaenen. "Long-Distance Dependencies, Constituent Structure, and Functional Uncertainty". In *Formal Issues in Lexical-Functional Grammar,* edited by Mary Dalrymple, Ronald M. Kaplan, John T. Maxwell, and Annie Zaenen, 137–65. Stanford, Calif.: CSLI, 1995.

Kaplan, Ronald M., and Jürgen Wedekind. "Restriction and Correspondence-Based Translation". In *Proceedings of the 6th Conference of the European Chapter of the Association for Computational Linguistics,* 193–202. Utrecht: Association for Computational Linguistics, 1993.

———. "Type-Driven Semantic Interpretation of f-structures". In *Proceedings of the 6th Conference of the European Chapter of the Association for Computational Linguistics,* 404–11. Utrecht: Association for Computational Linguistics, 1993.

Karcevskij, S. "Du dualisme asymetrique du signe linguistique". In Vachek, *Prague School Reader in Linguistics,* 81–87. 1964. First published 1929.

Kayne, R. S. "French Relative *que*". In *Current Studies in Romance Linguistics,* edited by F. Henzey and M. Luján, 255–99. Washington, D.C.: Georgetown University Press, 1976.

Kayne, R. S., and J.-Y. Pollock. "Stylistic Inversion, Successive Cyclicity and Move NP in French". *Linguistic Inquiry* 9 (1978): 595–621.

Kennedy, B. H., and J. F. Mountford. *Kennedy's Revised Latin Primer.* London: Longman, 1962.

Kenny, Anthony J. *Action, Emotion and Will.* London: Routledge and Kegan Paul, 1963.

———. "Intellect and Imagination in Aquinas". In *Aquinas: A Collection of Critical Essays,* 273–96. London: Macmillan, 1970.

———. "Practical Reasoning and Rational Appetite". Chap. 5 in *Will, Freedom and Power.* Oxford: Blackwell, 1975.

———. *The Metaphysics of Mind.* Oxford: Oxford University Press, 1989.

Kibrik, Andrej A. Review of *The Languages of Native North America,* by Marianne Mithun. *Linguistic Typology* 6 (2002): 117–21.

Kikawada, Isaac M., and Arthur Quinn. *Before Abraham Was.* Nashville, Tenn.: Abingdon, 1985.

Kleene, S. C. *Mathematical Logic.* New York: Wiley, 1967.

Kneale, William. *Probability and Induction.* Oxford: Oxford University Press, 1949.

Kneale, William, and Martha Kneale. *The Development of Logic.* Oxford: Oxford University Press, 1962.

Knuth, Donald E. *Sorting and Searching.* Vol. 3 of *The Art of Computer Programming.* Redwood City, Calif.: Longman, 1998.

Koopman, H. *The Syntax of Verbs.* Dordrecht: Foris, 1984.

Koopman, H., and D. Sportiche. "The Position of Subjects". *Lingua* 85 (1991): 211–58.

Kreisel, Georg. "Hilbert's Programme". In Benacerraf and Putnam, *Philosophy of Mathematics: Selected Readings,* 207–38. 1983. First published 1958.

Kripke, Saul. *Wittgenstein on Rules and Private Language: An Elementary Exposition.* Cambridge, Mass.: Harvard University Press, 1982.

Kugiumutzakis, G. "The Origin, Development and Functions of Early Infant Imitation". PhD diss., University of Uppsala, Sweden, 1985.

Kuhl, Patricia K., and Andrew N. Meltzoff. "The Bimodal Perception of Speech in Infancy". *Science* 218 (1982): 1138–41.

———. "The Intermodal Representation of Speech in Infants". *Infant Behaviour and Development* 7 (1986): 361–81.

Kuhn, Jonas. *Optimality-Theoretic Syntax—A Declarative Approach.* Stanford, Calif.: CSLI, 2003.

Kuno, S. "The Position of Relative Clauses and Conjunctions". *Linguistic Inquiry* 5 (1974): 117–36.

Kuno, Susumu, and Ken-ichi Takami, *Grammar and Discourse Principles: Functional Syntax and GB Theory.* Chicago: University of Chicago Press, 1993.

Kutas, Marta. "Current Thinking on Language Structures". Paper 31 in Gazzaniga, *Cognitive Neuroscience.* 2000.

Laka, I., and A. Mahajan, eds. *Functional Heads and Clause Structure.* Cambridge, Mass.: MITWPL, 1989.

Lambrecht, Knud. *Information Structure and Sentence Form.* Cambridge: Cambridge University Press, 1994.

Landau, B., and L. R. Gleitman. *Language and Experience: Evidence from the Blind Child.* Cambridge, Mass.: Harvard University Press, 1985.

Lashley, K. S. *Brain Mechanisms and Intelligence.* Chicago: University of Chicago Press, 1929.

———. "The Problem of Serial Order in Behaviour". In *Cerebral Mechanisms in Behaviour,* edited by L. A. Jeffress, 112–36. New York: Wiley, 1951.

Lederer, Anne, Henry Gleitman, and Lila Gleitman. "Verbs of a Feather Flock Together". In Tomasello and Merriman, *Beyond Names for Things,* 277–98. 1995.

Legendre, Géraldine, Yoshiro Miyata, and Paul Smolensky. "Can Connectionism Contribute to Syntax? Harmonic Grammar, with an Application". In *Proceedings of the 26th Regional Meeting of the Chicago Linguistic Society,* edited by M. Ziolkowski, M. Noske, and K. Deaton, 237–52. Chicago: Chicago Linguistic Society, 1990.

Lejewski, Czesław. "Parts of Speech". *Proceedings of the Aristotelian Society suppl. vol.* 39 (1965): 189–204.

LePore, Ernest, ed. *Truth and Interpretation: Perspectives on the Philosophy of Donald Davidson.* Oxford: Blackwell, 1986.

Leśniewski, Stanislaw, *Grundzüge eines neuen Systems der Grundlagen der Mathematik.* First printed in *Fundamenta Mathematicae* 14 (1929): 1–81.

Levy, Y., I. M. Schlesinger, and Martin D. S. Braine, eds. *Categories and Processes in Language Acquisition.* Hillsdale, N.J.: Erlbaum, 1988.

Lewis, John D., and Jeffrey L. Elman. "Learnability and the Statistical Structure of Language: Poverty of Stimulus Arguments Revisited". In *Proceedings of the 26th Annual Boston University Conference on Language Development,* edited by B. Skarabela, S. Fish, and A. H. J. Do, 359–70. Somerville, Mass.: Cascadilla, 2001.

Li, Charles N., and Sandra Thompson. "Subject and Topic: A New Typology of Language". In *Subject and Topic,* edited by Charles N. Li, 457–90. New York: Academic Press, 1976.

Lodge, R. Anthony. *French: From Dialect to Standard.* London: Routledge, 1993.

Lucas, John R. "Mind, Machines and Gödel". *Philosophy* (1961): 112–27.

———. "The Gödelian Argument: Turn Over the Page". Oxford Computing Services personal web page. Accessed September 27, 2003. http://users.ox.ac.uk/~jrlucas/Godel/turn.html.

Ludlow, Peter. *The Philosophy of Generative Linguistics.* Oxford: Oxford University Press, 2012.

Luenberger, David G. *Introduction to Dynamic Systems: Theory, Models, and Applications.* New York: Wiley, 1979.

Lyons, John. *Introduction to Theoretical Linguistics.* Cambridge: Cambridge University Press, 1968.

———. "Structuralism and Linguistics". Chap. 1 in *Structuralism: An Introduction.* The Wolfson College lectures, edited by David Robey. Oxford: Oxford University Press, 1972.

———. *Semantics.* Vol. 1. Cambridge: Cambridge University Press, 1977.

———. *Language, Meaning and Context.* London: Fontana Press, 1981.

MacIntyre, Alasdair. *Whose Justice? Whose Rationality?* London: Duckworth, 1988.

———. *Three Rival Versions of Moral Enquiry.* Notre Dame, Ind.: University of Notre Dame Press, 1990.

———. "Moral Relativism, Truth and Justification". In *Moral Truth and Moral Tradition: Essays in Honour of Peter Geach and Elizabeth Anscombe,* edited by Luke Gormally, 6–24. Dublin: Four Courts Press, 1994.

Mackie, J. L. "Causes and Conditions". *American Philosophical Quarterly* 2 (1965): 245–64.

Makino, S. *Some Aspects of Japanese Nominalizations.* Tokyo: Tokai University, 1968.

Malcolm, Norman. *Problems of Mind: Descartes to Wittgenstein.* London: Allen and Unwin, 1972.

———. *Ludwig Wittgenstein: A Memoir.* 2nd ed. Oxford: Oxford University Press, 1984.

Mathesius, Vilém. "On the Potentiality of the Phenomena of Language". Translated by J. Vachek. From "O potenciálnosti jevů jazykových", in *Věstnik Král, české společnosti nauk*. Prague, 1911. In Vachek, *A Prague School Reader in Linguistics*, 1–32. 1964.

Mandler, J. "How to Build a Baby: II: Conceptual Primitives". *Psychological Review* 99 (1992): 587–604.

Marcel, A. J., and E. Bisiach, eds. *Consciousness in Contemporary Science*. Oxford: Oxford University Press, 1988.

Marr, David. *Vision: A Computational Investigation into the Human Representation and Processing of Visual Information*. New York: W. H. Freeman, 1982.

Martin, G. B., and R. D. Clark. "Distress Crying in Neonates: Species and Peer Specificity". *Developmental Psychology* 18 (1982): 3–9.

Matthews, Eric. *The Philosophy of Merleau-Ponty*. Chesham, UK: Acumen, 2002.

Matthews, P. H. "The Inflectional Component of a Word-and-Paradigm Grammar". *Journal of Linguistics* 1 (1965): 139–71.

———. "Some Concepts in Word-Paradigm Morphology". *Foundations of Language* 1 (1965): 268–89.

Mayo, Bernard. "Belief and Constraint". *Proceedings of the Aristotelian Society* 64 (1963–64).

McMahon, April. *Understanding Language Change*. Cambridge: Cambridge University Press, 1994.

Meltzoff, Andrew N., and M. Keith Moore. "Explaining Facial Imitation: A Theoretical Model". *Early Development and Parenting* 6 (1997): 179–92.

———. "Persons and Representation: Why Infant Imitation Is Important for Theories of Human Development". In Nadel and Butterworth, *Imitation in Infancy*, 9–35. 1999.

Miller, Alexander. "Tacit Knowledge". In Hale and Wright, *Companion to the Philosophy of Language*, 146–72. 1997.

Miller, George A., and Noam Chomsky. "Finitary Models of Language Users". Chap. 13 in *Handbook of Mathematical Psychology*. vol. 2. New York: Wiley, 1963.

Milner, A. David, and Melvyn A. Goodale. *The Visual Brain in Action*. Oxford: Oxford University Press, 1995.

———. "Two Visual Systems Re-viewed". *Neuropsychologia* 46 (2008): 774–85.

Minsky, Marvin. *The Society of Mind*. New York: Simon and Schuster, 1985.

Mithun, Marianne. *The Languages of Native North America*. Cambridge: Cambridge University Press, 1999.

Montague, Richard. *Formal Philosophy: Selected Papers of Richard Montague*. Edited by R. H. Thomason. New Haven, Conn.: Yale University Press, 1974.

Moore, G. E. "The Nature of Judgment". *Mind New Series* 8 (1899): 176–93.

———. "An Autobiography". In *The Philosophy of G. E. Moore*, edited by P. A. Schilpp, 1–41. Evanston, Ill.: Northwestern University Press, 1942.

———. *Some Main Problems of Philosophy*. London: Allen and Unwin, 1953.

Moran, Dermot. *Introduction to Phenomenology*. London: Routledge, 2000.

Nadel, Jacqueline, and George Butterworth, eds. *Imitation in Infancy*. Cambridge: Cambridge University Press, 1999.

Nagel, Ernest, and James R. Newman. *Gödel's Proof*. London: Routledge and Kegan Paul, 1959.

Nagel, Ernest, P. Suppes, and A. Tarski, eds. *Logic, Methodology and Philosophy of Science*. Stanford, Calif.: Stanford University Press, 1962.

Nakayama, Ken. "James J. Gibson: An Appreciation". In Gazzaniga, *Cognitive Neuroscience*, 140–52. 2000.

Nelson, K. *Making Sense: The Acquisition of Shared Meaning*. New York: Academic Press, 1985.

Newmeyer, Frederick. *Generative Linguistics: A Historical Perspective*. London: Routledge, 1996.

———. *Language Form and Language Function*. Cambridge, Mass.: MIT Press, 2000.

———. "Typological Evidence and Universal Grammar". *Studies in Language* 28, no. 3 (2004): 527–48.

Nuchelmans, Gabriël. "Review Article: R. H. Robins, *General Linguistics*". *Lingua* 16 (1966): 399–412.

Ouhalla, Jamal. *Introducing Transformational Grammar*. 2nd ed. London: Arnold, 1999.

Owen, G. E. L. "Tithenai ta Phainomena". In *Logic, Science and Dialectic: Collected Papers in Greek Philosophy*, edited by Martha Nussbaum, 239–51. Ithaca, N.Y.: Cornell University Press, 1986. First published 1961.

Paris, J., and L. Harrington. "A Mathematical Incompleteness in Peano Arithmetic". In *Handbook for Mathematical Logic*, edited by J. Barwise, 1133–42. Amsterdam: North-Holland, 1977.

Passingham, R. E. *The Human Primate*. New York: W. H. Freeman, 1982.

Peacocke, Christopher. "Gödel's Theorem: A Problem for Constructivists", sec. 4 of "Proof and Truth". In *Reality, Representation, and Projection*, ed. John Haldane and Crispin Wright, 178–182. Oxford: Oxford University Press, 1993.

Pelletier, F. J. "Did Frege Believe Frege's Principle?" *Journal of Logic Language and Information* 10 (2001): 87–114.

Penrose, Roger. *Shadows of the Mind: A Search for the Missing Science of Consciousness*. London: Random House, 1995. First published Oxford: Oxford University Press, 1994.

———. "Beyond the Doubting of a Shadow". *Psyche* 2, no. 23 (1996). Reproduced at http://psyche.cs.monash.edu.au/v2/psyche-2-23-penrose.html.

———. *The Large, the Small and the Human Mind*. Cambridge: Cambridge University Press, 1997.

Perfors, Amy, Joshua B. Tenebaum, and Terry Riegler. "Poverty of the Stimulus? A Rational Approach". In *Proceedings of the 28th Annual Conference of the Cognitive Science Society*, edited by R. Sun and N. Miyake, 663–68. Mahwah, N.J: Erlbaum, 2006.

Perlmutter, David M. "Impersonal Passives and the Unaccusative Hypothesis". In *Proceedings of the 4th Annual Meeting of the Berkeley Linguistics Society*, 157–89. Berkeley, Calif.: Berkeley Linguistics Society, 1978.

———. "Relational Grammar". In *Current Approaches to Syntax*, edited by E. A. Moravcsik and J. Wirth, 195–229. New York: Academic Press, 1980.

———. "Functional Grammar and Relational Grammar: Points of Convergence and Divergence". In *Perspectives on Functional Grammar*, 319–52. Dordrecht: Foris, 1981.

———. "Syntactic Representation, Syntactic Levels, and the Notion of Subject". In Jacobson and Pullum, *The Nature of Syntactic Representation*, 283–340. 1982.

———, ed. *Studies in Relational Grammar*. Vol. 1. Chicago: University of Chicago Press, 1983.

Perlmutter, David M., and Paul M. Postal. "The Relational Succession Law". In *Studies in Relational Grammar*, vol. 1, chap. 2, ed. David Perlmutter. 1983.

Piaget, Jean. *The Origins of Intelligence in Children*. New York: Norton, 1952.

Pinker, Steven. *Language Learnability and Language Development*. Cambridge, Mass.: Harvard University Press, 1984.

———. *Learnability and Cognition: The Acquisition of Argument Structure*. Cambridge, Mass.: MIT Press, 1989.

———. *Words and Rules*. London: Weidenfeld and Nicholson, 1999.

———. *The Language Instinct*. New York: Morrow, 1994; Penguin, 2003.

———. *The Stuff of Thought: Language as a Window into Human Nature*. London: Penguin, 2008.

Pinker, Steven, and Ray Jackendoff. "The Faculty of Language: What's Special about It?" *Cognition* 95, no. 2 (2005): 201–36.

Poincaré, Henri. *Science and Hypothesis*. London: Walter Scott, 1905.

Polanyi, Michael. *Personal Knowledge*. Chicago: University of Chicago Press, 1958.

Pollock, Jean-Yves. "Verb Movement, Universal Grammar, and the Structure of IP". *Linguistic Inquiry* 20, no. 3 (1989): 365–424.

Polya, G. *Mathematics and Plausible Reasoning*. Princeton, N.J.: Princeton University Press, 1954.

Port, Robert F., and Timothy van Gelder, eds. *Mind as Motion: Exploration in the Dynamics of Cognition*. Cambridge, Mass.: MIT Press, 1995.

Port, Robert F., Fred Cummins, and J. Devin McAuley. "Naïve Time, Temporal Patterns, and Human Audition". In Port and van Gelder, *Mind as Motion*, 313–71. 1995.

Prior, Arthur. "The Run-about Inference Ticket". *Analysis* 21 (1960): 38–39.

———. "Conjunction and Contonktion Revisited". *Analysis* 24, no. 6 (1964): 191–95.

Pullum, Geoffrey K. "Assuming Some Version of X-Bar Theory". *Chicago Linguistic Society* 21, no. 1 (1985): 323–53.

———. "Learnability, Hyperlearning and the Poverty of the Stimulus". In *Proceedings of the 22nd Annual Meeting: General Session and Parasession on the Role of Learning in Grammatical Theory,* edited by Jan Johnson, Matthew L. Juge, and Jeri L. Moxley, 498–513. Berkeley, Calif.: Berkeley Linguistics Society, 1996.

Pullum, Geoffrey K., and Barbara C. Scholz. "Empirical Assessment of Stimulus Poverty Arguments". *Linguistic Review* 19 (2002): 9–50.

Putnam, Hilary. "Is Logic Empirical?" In *Boston Studies in the Philosophy of Science,* edited by R. Cohen and M. P. Wartofski, 5:216–41. Dordrecht: D. Reidel, 1968. Reprinted as "The Logic of Quantum Mechanics" in *Mathematics, Matter and Method.* Vol. 1 of *Philosophical Papers.* Cambridge: Cambridge University Press, 1975.

———. "Dreaming and Depth Grammar". In *Mind, Language and Reality,* 304–24. 1975. Reprinted from *Analytical Philosophy, edited by* Ronald J. Butler. *First Series.* Oxford University Press, 1962.

———. "Explanation and Reference". In *Mind, Language and Reality,* 196–214. 1975. Reprinted from *Conceptual Change,* edited by Glenn Pearce and Patrick Maynard. Dordrecht: D. Reidel, 1973.

———. "Is Semantics Possible?" In *Mind, Language and Reality,* 139–52. 1975. Reprinted from *Metaphilosophy* 1 (July 1970).

———. "The Meaning of 'Meaning'". In *Mind, Language and Reality,* 215–71. 1975. Revised from "Meaning and Reference". *The Journal of Philosophy* 70 (1973).

———. *Mind, Language and Reality.* Vol. 2 of *Philosophical Papers.* Cambridge: Cambridge University Press, 1975.

———. "Minds and Machines". In *Mind, Language and Reality,* 362–85. 1975. Reprinted from *Dimensions of Mind,* edited by Sidney Hook. New York: New York University Press, 1969.

———. "The Nature of Mental States". In *Mind, Language and Reality,* 429–40. 1975. Originally printed as "Psychological Predicates", in *Art, Mind, and Religion,* edited by W. H. Capitan and D. D. Merrill. Pittsburgh: Pittsburgh University Press, 1967.

———. *Meaning and the Moral Sciences.* London: Routledge and Kegan Paul, 1978.

———. *Representation and Reality.* Cambridge, Mass.: MIT Press, 1988.

———. Review of *Shadows of the Mind,* by Roger Penrose. *Bulletin of the American Mathematics Society* 32 (1995): 370–73.

———. *The Threefold Cord: Mind, Body, and World.* New York: Columbia University Press, 1999.

Quine, Willard van Orman. *Mathematical Logic.* Cambridge, Mass.: Harvard University Press, 1951.

———. "Two Dogmas of Empiricism". *Philosophical Review* 60 (1951): 20–43.

———. *Word and Object.* Cambridge, Mass.: MIT Press, 1960.

———. "Mind and Verbal Dispositions". In Guttenplan, *Mind and Language,* 83–95. 1975.

———. "Truth by Convention". In *The Ways of Paradox and Other Essays.* 2nd ed. Cambridge, Mass.: Harvard University Press, 1976. First published in *Philosophical Essays for A. N. Whitehead,* edited by O. H. Lee. New York: Longman, 1936.

———. *Ontological Relativity and Other Essays.* New York: Columbia University Press, 1977.

———. "States of Mind". *Journal of Philosophy* 83 (1985): 5–8.

Quirk, R., S. Greenbaum, G. Leech, and J. Sbartvik. *A Comprehensive Grammar of the English Language.* London: Longman, 1985.

Radford, Andrew. *Transformational Grammar.* Cambridge: Cambridge University Press, 1988.

———. *Syntactic Theory and the Structure of English.* Cambridge: Cambridge University Press, 1997.

Ramsey, F. P. *The Foundations of Mathematics and Other Logical Essays.* Edited by R. W. Braithwaite. London: Routledge and Kegan Paul, 1931.

———. "The Foundations of Mathematics". In *The Foundations of Mathematics and Other Logical Essays,* 1–61. 1931.

———. "Note on the Preceding Paper ["Universals"]". In *The Foundations of Mathematics and Other Logical Essays,* 136–37. 1931.

———. "Universals". In *The Foundations of Mathematics and Other Logical Essays,* 112–35. 1931.

Reali, Florence, and Morten Christiansen. "Uncovering the Richness of the Stimulus: Structure Dependence and Indirect Statistical Evidence". *Cognitive Science* 29 (2005): 1007–28.

Rey, Alain, ed. *Dictionnaire Historique de la langue française.* Paris: Dictionnaires Le Robert, 1992.

Robins, R. H. "in Defence of WP". *Transactions of the Philological Society* (1959): 116–44.

———. *General Linguistics: An Introductory Survey.* London: Longman, 1964.

Rosenbaum, P. *The Grammar of English Predicate Complement Constructions.* Cambridge, Mass.: MIT Press, 1967.

Rowland, Tracey. *Culture and Thomist Tradition.* London: Routledge, 2003.

Ruhlen, Merrit. *The Origin of Language.* New York: Wiley, 1994.

Russell, Bertrand. *History of Western Philosophy.* London: Allen and Unwin, 1946.

Ryle, Gilbert.

———. *The Concept of Mind.* London: Hutchinson, 1949.

———. *Dilemmas.* Cambridge: Cambridge University Press, 1954.

———. *Plato's Progress.* Cambridge: Cambridge University Press, 1966.

———. "Are There Propositions?" No. 2 in *Collected Essays.* 1971. First published in *Proceedings of the Aristotelian Society* 30 (1930).

———. "Categories". No. 12 in *Collected Essays.* 1971. First published in *Proceedings of the Aristotelian Society* 38 (1938).

———. *Collected Essays.* Vol. 2 of *Collected Papers.* London: Hutchinson, 1971.

———. "'If', 'So', and 'Because'". No. 17 in *Collected Essays.* 1971. First published in *Philosophical Analysis,* edited by Max Black. Ithaca, N.Y.: Cornell University Press, 1950.

———. "Induction and Hypothesis". No. 10 in *Collected Essays.* 1971. First published in Proceedings of the Aristotelian Society, suppl. vol. 16 (1937).

———. "Ordinary Language". No. 23 in *Collected Essays.* First published 1953.

———. "Predicting and Inferring". No. 28 in *Collected Essays.* 1971. First published in *Observation and Interpretation in the Philosophy of Physics: Proceedings of the Ninth Symposium of the Colston Research Society,* edited by Stephan Korner and M. H. L. Price. New York: Dover, 1957.

———. "A Puzzling Element in the Notion of Thinking". No. 30 in *Collected Essays.* 1971. First published 1958.

———. "The Theory of Meaning". No. 27 in *Collected Essays.* 1971. First published in British Philosophy of the Mid-Century, edited by C. A. Mace. London: Allen and Unwin, 1957.

———. "Thinking and Language". No. 19 in *Collected Essays.* 1971. First published in *Proceedings of the Aristotelian Society* suppl. vol. 25 (1951).

———. "Use, Usage and Meaning". No. 31 in *Collected Essays.* 1971. First published in *Proceedings of the Aristotelian Society* suppl. vol. 35 (1961).

———. "Mowgli in Babel". In *On Thinking.* Oxford: Blackwell, 1979.

Sag, Ivan. "A Semantic Theory of 'NP-Movement' Dependencies". In Jacobson and Pullum, *The Nature of Syntactic Representation,* 427–66. 1982. Papers presented at Brown University, Providence, R.I., May 1979.

Saporta, Sol, and R. H. Robins. "On the Use of Zero in Morphemics". In *Proceedings of the Ninth International Congress of Linguists,* edited by H. Lunt, 228–31. The Hague: Mouton, 1964.

Schlesinger, I. M. "The Origin of Relational Categories". In Levy, Schlesinger, and Braine, *Categories and Processes*, 121–78. 1988.

Searle, John. "Austin on Locutionary and Illocutionary Acts". *Philosophical Review* 77 (1968): 405–24.

———. *Speech Acts: An Essay in the Philosophy of Language*. Cambridge: Cambridge University Press, 1969.

———. "Minds, Brains, and Programs". *Behavioral and Brain Sciences* 3 (1980): 417–24.

———. *Minds, Brains, and Science*. London: BBC Publications, 1984.

Sebeok, Thomas, ed. *Current Trends in Linguistics*. Vols.1–3. The Hague: Mouton, 1963–66.

Sells, Peter. *Lectures on Contemporary Syntactic Theories*. Stanford, Calif.: CSLI, 1985.

Shewmon, Alan. "Is 'Brain Death' Actually Death? An Autobiographical Conceptual Itinerary". *Aletheia* 7 (1996): 1–34. Reprinted in extended form as "Recovery from 'Brain Death': A Neurologist's Apologia". *Linacre Quarterly* 64 (1997): 30–96.

———. "The Brain and Somatic Integration: Insights into the Standard Biological Rationale for Equating Brain Death with Death". *Journal of Medicine and Philosophy* 28 (2001): 457–78.

Shieber, Stuart M. "Evidence against the Context-freeness of Natural Language". *Linguistics and Philosophy* 8 (1985): 333–43.

Shoemaker, Sydney. *Self-Knowledge and Self-Identity*. Ithaca, N.Y.: Cornell University Press, 1963.

The Shorter Oxford English Dictionary. 3rd rev. ed. 2 vols. Oxford: Oxford University Press, 1973.

Silverstein, Michael. "Hierarchy of Features and Ergativity". In *Grammatical Categories in Australian Languages*, edited by R. M. Dixon, 112–71. Atlantic Highlands, N.J.: Humanities Press, 1976.

———. "Case Marking and the Nature of Language". *Australian Journal of Linguistics* 1 (1981): 227–44.

Skorupski, John. "Meaning, Use, Verification". In Hale and Wright, *Companion to the Philosophy of Language*, 29–59. 1997.

Smith, Neil, and Ianthi-Maria Tsimpli. "Linguistic Modularity: A Case of a Savant Linguist". *Lingua* 84 (1991): 315–51.

Sommers, Fred. "Types and Ontology". *Philosophical Review* 72 (1963): 327–63.

Spencer, Andrew. "Morphology". In Aronoff and Rees-Miller, *Handbook of Linguistics*, 213–37. 2003.

Sperber, Dan, and Deirdre Wilson. *Relevance: Communication and Cognition*. Cambridge, Mass.: Harvard University Press, 1986.

Stanley, Jason. "Context and Logical Form". *Linguistics and Philosophy* 23 (2000): 391–434.

Strawson, P. F. "On Referring". *Mind* 59 (1950): 320–44.

———. *Individuals*. London: Methuen, 1959.

Stein, Barry E., and M. Alex Meredith. *The Merging of the Senses*. Cambridge, Mass.: MIT Press, 1993.

Steiner, George. *Extraterritorial*. London: Faber and Faber, 1972.

———. *After Babel*. Oxford: Oxford University Press, 1975.

———. *Language and Silence*. New York: Atheneum, 1976. First published London: Faber and Faber, 1967.

Stern, Daniel. *The Interpersonal World of the Human Infant*. New York: Basic Books, 1985.

Stoljar, Daniel, and Nic Damnjanovic. "The Deflationary Theory of Truth". In *Stanford Encyclopedia of Philosophy*, edited by Edward N. Zalta. Stanford, Calif.: Stanford University, Winter 2010. http://plato.stanford.edu/archives/win2010/entries/truth-deflationary/.

Stowell, T. "Origins of Phrase Structure". PhD diss., Massachusetts Institute of Technology, 1981.

Suzuki, Akira. *Gengo shishu ron*. 1824. Reprinted *Benseisha Bunkō* 68, 1979. Expounded in Keiichi Uchida, "Peripheral Approach on Chinese Linguistics as an Area of Cultural Interaction Studies", *A Selection of Essays on Oriental Studies of ICIS* 1 (2011): 123–37, Institute for Cultural Interaction Studies, Kansai Universsity. Available at Kansai University Institutional Repository, http://kuir.jm.kansai-u.ac.jp/dspace/bitstream/10112/4350/1/10_UCHIDA.pdf, 132.

Szabó, Zoltán Gendler. "Compositionality". In *Stanford Encyclopedia of Philosophy,* edited by Edward N. Zalta. Stanford, Calif.: Stanford University, Winter 2008. http://plato.stanford.edu/archives/win2008/entries/compositionality/.

Talmy, Leonard. "Lexicalization Patterns: Semantic Structure in Lexical Forms". In *Language Typology and Lexical Description.* Vol. 3, *Grammatical Categories and the Lexicon,* edited by T. Shopen, 57–149. Cambridge: Cambridge University Press, 1985.

———. "Concept Structuring Systems in Language". In Tomasello, *New Psychology of Language,* vol. 2, chap. 1, 15–46. 2008.

Tarski, Alfred. "The Concept of Truth in Formalized Languages". In *Logic, Semantics, Metamathematics: Papers from 1923 to 1938,* translated by J. H. Woodger, 152–278. Oxford: Oxford University Press, 1956.

Taylor, Charles. *The Explanation of Behaviour.* London: Routledge and Kegan Paul, 1964.

Taylor, Richard and Andrew Wiles. "Ring-Theoretic Properties of Certain Hecke Algebras". *Annals of Mathematics* 141 (1995): 553–72.

Thelen, E., and L. B. Smith. *A Dynamics Systems Approach to the Development of Cognition and Action.* Cambridge, Mass.: MIT Press, 1993.

Thrainsson, H. *On Complementation in Icelandic.* New York: Garland, 1979.

Tolkien, J. R. R. *Letters of J. R. R. Tolkein.* Edited by Humphrey Carpenter. London: Allen and Unwin, 1981.

Tolman, E. C. *Purposive Behaviour in Animals and Men.* New York: Appleton-Century-Croft, 1932.

Tomasello, Michael. *First Verbs: A Case Study of Early Grammatical Development.* Cambridge: Cambridge University Press, 1992.

———. "The Social Bases of Language Acquisition". *Social Development* 1 (1992): 67–87.

———. "Pragmatic Contexts for Early Verb Learning". In Tomasello and Merriman, *Beyond Names for Things,* 115–46. 1995.

———, ed. *The New Psychology of Language: Cognitive and Functional Approaches to Language Structure.* Vol. 2. Hove, East Sussex: Psychology Press, 2008. First published by Erlbaum, 2003.

———, ed. *The New Psychology of Language: Cognitive and Functional Approaches to Language Structure.* Vol. 1. Hove, East Sussex: Psychology Press, 2009. First published by Erlbaum, 1998.

Tomasello, Michael, and W. E. Merriman, eds. *Beyond Names for Things: Young Children's Acquisition of Verbs.* Hillsdale, N.J.: Erlbaum, 1995.

Tomassi, Paul. "Linguistic Understanding and the Philosophy of Language". *Minerva: An Internet Journal of Philosophy* 4 (November 2000).

Tomlin, Russell S. *Basic Word Order: Functional Principles.* London: Croom Helm, 1986.

Turing, Alan M. "Systems of Logic Based on Ordinals". *London Mathematical Society* 45 (1939): 161–228.

———. "Computing Machinery and Intelligence". *Mind New Series* 59 (1950): 433–60.

Uhlenbeck, E. M. "An Appraisal of Transformational Theory". *Lingua* 12 (1963): 1–18.

———. Review of *L'école de Prague d'aujourd'hui: Travaux linguistiques de Prague* 1, edited by Josef Vachek, F. Daneš, K. Horálek, V. Skalička, and P. Trost. *Lingua* 17 (1967): 358–65.

Uchida, Keiichi, "Peripheral Approach on Chinese Linguistics as an Area of Cultural Interaction Studies". In *A Selection of Essays on Oriental Studies of ICIS* 1 (2011): 123–37, Institute for Cultural Interaction Studies, Kansai University, available Kansai University Institutional Repository, http://kuir.jm.kansai-u.ac.jp/dspace/bitstream/10112/4350/1/10_UCHIDA.pdf

Vachek, Josef. *The Linguistic School of Prague: An Introduction to Its Theory and Practice.* Bloomington: Indiana University Press, 1966.

———. *Written Language Revisited.* Edited and with an introduction by Philip A. Luelsdorff. Amsterdam: John Benjamins, 1989. First published 1939.

———, ed. *A Prague School Reader in Linguistics.* Bloomington: Indiana University Press, 1964.

———, ed. *Some Basic and Less Known Aspects of the Prague Linguistic School.* Amsterdam: John Benjamins, 1983.

Van der Gaaf, W. "Some Notes on the History of the Progressive Form". *Neophilologus* 15 (1930): 201–15.

Van Eynde, Frank. "NP-Internal Agreement and the Structure of the Noun Phrase". *Journal of Linguistics* 42 (2006): 139–86.

Van Gelder, Timothy. "What Might Cognition Be, If not Computation?" *Journal of Philosophy* 92, no. 7 (1995): 345–81.

Van Gelderen, E. *The Rise of Functional Categories*. Amsterdam: John Benjamins, 1993.

Van Roojen, Mark. "Expressivism and Irrationality". *Philosophical Review* 105 (1996): 311–35.

Van Valin, Robert D., Jr.,

———. "Functionalist Linguistic Theory and Language Acquisition". *First Language* 11 (1991): 7–40.

———. "Synopsis of Role and Reference Grammar". In *Advances in Role and Reference Grammar*, 1–164, edited byRobert Van Valin. Amsterdam: John Benjamins, 1993

———. "A Brief Overview of Role and Reference Grammar". *Korean Journal of Linguistics* 6 (1998): 235–72.

———. "Linguistic Diversity and Theoretical Assumptions". *Chicago Linguistic Society Parasession* 35 (2000): 373–91.

———. "Functional Linguistics". Chap. 13 in Aronoff and Rees-Miller, *Handbook of Linguistics*, 329–36. 2003.

———. *Exploring the Syntax-Semantics Interface*. Cambridge: Cambridge University Press, 2005.

Van Valin, Robert D., Jr. and W. A. Foley. *Functional Syntax and Universal Grammar* (Cambridge: Cambridge University Press, 1984.

Van Valin, Robert D., Jr., and Randy LaPolla. *Syntax: Structure, Meaning and Function*. Cambridge: Cambridge University Press, 1997.

Vendler, Zeno. "Verbs and Times". *Philosophical Review* 56 (1957): 143–60.

———. *Linguistics in Philosophy*. Ithaca, N.Y.: Cornell University Press, 1967.

Von Humboldt, Wilhelm. *Über die Verschiedenheit des menschlich Sprachbaues und ihren Einfluss auf die geistige Entwickelung des Menschengeschlechts*. Berlin: Königlichen Äkademie der Wissenschaften, 1836. Facsimile of original edition, http://www.google.com/books?id=J-flkAAAAMAAJ. From *German Linguistics in the Eighteenth Century*, ed. Christopher Hutton. London: Routledge, 1994. Reprinted *Werke* 3: *Schriften Zur Sprachphilosophie*, edited by Andreas Flitner and Klaus Giel, 368–756. Stuttgart: Wissenschaftliche Buchgesellschaft, 1963. Translated by Peter Heath as *On Language: The Diversity of Human Language-Structure and its Influence on the Mental Development of Mankind*. Cambridge: Cambridge University Press, 1988.

Ward, Gregory, et al. "Ellen Prince". Obituary. *Language* 87 (2011): 866–72.

Wedekind, Jürgen. "Some Remarks on the Decidability of the Generation Problem in LFG- and PATR-Style Unification Grammars". *European Chapter of the Association for Computational Linguistics* (1995): 45–52.

———. "Semantic-Driven Generation with LFG- and PATR-Style Grammars". *Computational Linguistics* 25, no. 2 (1999): 277–81.

Wedekind, Jürgen, and Ronald M. Kaplan. "Squibs and Discussions: Ambiguity-Preserving Generation with LFG- and PATR-Style Grammars". *Computational Linguistics* 22, no. 4 (1996).

Weinreich, Uriel. "On the Semantic Structure of Language". In Greenberg, *Universals of Language*, 114–71. 1963.

Wiggins, David. *Sameness and Substance*. Oxford: Blackwell, 1980.

———. "Meaning and Truth Conditions: From Frege's Grand Design to Davidson's". In Hale and Wright, *Companion to the Philosophy of Language*, 3–28. 1997.

Wiles, Andrew. "Modular Elliptic Curves and Fermat's Last Theorem". *Annals of Mathematics* 141 (1995): 443–551.

———. and Richard Taylor. "Ring-Theoretic Properties of Certain Hecke Algebras". *Annals of Mathematics* 141 (1995): 553–72.

Wittgenstein, Ludwig. *Philosophical Investigations.* Translated by G. E. M. Anscombe. Parallel German-English edition. Oxford: Blackwell, 1953.

———. *Tractatus Logico-Philosophicus.* Translated by David Pears and Brian McGuinness. Parallel German-English edition. London: Routledge and Kegan Paul, 1961.

———. *Philosophical Grammar.* Edited by Rush Rhees. Translated by Anthony Kenny. Oxford: Blackwell, 1974. Translated from *Philosophische Grammatik,* 1969. Wittgenstein's 1931–34 compilation of his 1930–32 notebooks.

Woodworth, R. S. "Reinforcement of Perception". *American Journal of Psychology* 60 (1947): 119–24.

Woolford, E. "VP-Internal Subjects in VSO and Nonconfigurational Languages". *Linguistic Inquiry* 22, no. 3 (1991): 503–40.

Wright, Crispin. *Realism, Meaning and Truth.* 2nd ed. Oxford: Blackwell, 1993.

———. *Tractatus Logico-Philosophicus.* Translated by David Pears and Brian McGuinness. Parallel German-English edition. London: Routledge and Kegan Paul, 1961. "The Indeterminacy of Translation". In Hale and Wright, *A Companion to the Philosophy of Language,* 397–426. 1997.

Wright, Crispin. "The Philosophical Significance of Gödel's Theorem: Some Issues". In Wright, *Realism, Meaning and Truth.* 1993.

Yamada, Jeni. *Laura: A Case Study for the Modularity of Language.* Cambridge, Mass.: MIT Press, 1990.

Zermelo, Ernst. "Untersuchungen über die Grundlagen der Mengenlehre I". *Mathematische Annalen* 65, no. 2 (1908): 261–281. Translated as "Investigations in the Foundations of Set Theory I", in *From Frege to Gödel: A Source Book in Mathematical Logic,* 1879–1931, edited by Jean van Heijenoort. Cambridge, Mass.: Harvard University Press, 1967.

Ziff, Paul. "The Number of English Sentences". *Foundations of Language* 11 (1974): 519–32.

Index of Names

Abney, S. P., 531n5, 535n11, 650n11, 755; "Determiner phrases", 415, 647n9, 728n20. *See also in Subject Index* Heads and phrases in Chomskyan grammar
Ackerman and Webelhuth: lexically divided verb forms, 87, 121n11, 496, 506, 616, 682, 739; multiplication of functional phrases, 730n24
Adger, David, 732n26, 755
Ajdukiewicz, K., 401n2, 418, 419
Allport, G. W., 329, 330n52
Anaxagoras, 20–21, 382
Anderson, Alan Ross, 269n42
Anderson, John M., 40n58, 104
Anderson, John R., 57n98
Andrews, Avery D., 503n27
Anscombe, G. E. M., xiii, xiv, xv, 367, 424, 495n17, 557n39; in regard to Wittgenstein's later works, 40n60, 122n13, 368n7; on Wittgenstein's *Tractatus*, 391n55, 450, 454n17, 456n20, 461, 462
Ansre, G., 731n25
Aquinas, xiii, xv, 4, 8, 122–23, 126, 182n28; conception of predication, 413n28, 421; estimative power, 303n12, 357n24; holism, 51, 310n21; intentionality, 359, 383, 384n41, 751; "literal" meaning, 122n14, 182n28; *modus significandi*, 421; pain (*dolor*) not example of *sentire*, 304n13; subject, 413n29, 421
Aristotle, 4, 239; active and passive distinction, 519–20; analogy, xiii, 8, 122; continuity, 262–63, 273; general logic, 38–39, 43, 392–93; holism, 13, 206, 219, 403; inflection and paronymy, 421; intellect in command, 20–21, 382, 751; living beings, 51, 318, 321, 367; logic and scientific method, 39, 183n30, 262–63, 275, 292, 467; metaphor, 121–23, 131; notion of connective, 583, 650; notion of inflection, 603; nouns and verbs, 402n7,411, 422n40, 431n58, 450; proposition, 22; pure intelligences, 239; relation-based connections of word use, 8, 121, 123, 131; saying or predicating, 162, 411; semantic categories, 44, 392; states (*hexeis*) 51, 78, 194, 374–76; subject, 413; terms in categories as content-introducing, 119; "Third Man" argument against Plato, 384n, 541–42; voluntariness, 98, 303, 305, 314
Aronoff, Mark, 115n2, 153
Austin, John L., 24, 32, 51, 79n7, 85, 90n18, 98n27, 102, 160, 162, 163, 168, 169, 174, 175, 186, 207n80, 214, 258, 300, 330n56, 335, 367, 374n15, 378, 388n47, 410, 453–54, 457, 478n65, 479, 480, 482–85, 520, 652

Baars, Bernard, 301n8
Bach, Kent, 164n11
Baker, Gordon P., 111. *See also* Baker and Hacker
Baker, Mark C., 351n12, 361, 730n22, 736n42, 740, 741n52, 746n1
Baker and Hacker, 427, 461n30; interpreting Wittgenstein, 118n8, 185n34, 230n17, 252n11, 376n22, 388n46, 391n56, 407n21
Baugh and Cable, 503n25, 604n55
Beach, Matthew, 684n45
Beebe, Michael, 213n87, 217, 401
Belnap, Nuel D., Jr., 228n12
Benacerraf, Paul, 267, 269
Bennett, David C., 93n21, 584n20
Bennett, Jonathan, 213n87
Berkeley, George, 300, 573
Berman, R. A., 405. *See also in Subject Index* verb kernel

Blackburn, Simon: bottom-up and top-down approaches, 6, 225n8, 292n62; 404; expressivism, 470–71; homely interpreter, 40n60, 374n15
Blake, Barry J., 489n5, 503n25, 505n30, 527nn60–61, 576–77, 579n8, 580, 583n17, 584, 585n21, 595n40, 688n50; on Relational Grammar, 57n97
Bloom, Lois, 429n52, 440n70
Bloomfield, Leonard, 11, 13, 48, 54, 75n2, 173, 195–96, 199–200, 205, 218n96; changed view of psychology and linguistics, 48, 195; determiners, 413–15; priority of morpheme, 114n1, 153. *See also in Subject Index* determiners; Internalized Language
Boas, Franz, 54, 192n47
Boden, Margaret A., 281n55
Bohm, David, 316
Bolinger, Dwight, 114n1
Borer, Hagit, 728n20, 730n2
Bowers, John, 658n19
Bowie, G. L., 265n29
Bradley, F. H., 224n6, 330n55
Braine, David: biographical, xiii–xv, 2–8; on *The Human Person,* 2–3, 175, 239, 242, 253, 284–85, 298, 302, 306, 345, 363, 371, 384n41, 385–86, 540n17, 546, 556, 568n52, 753n4; on truth as goal of belief, 451n8
Braine, Martin D. S., xiv, 6, 45, 240nn32–33; centrality of predicate/argument distinction, 44, 46n68, 430; method in psycholinguistics, 16n23, 45–47, 578nn5–6; notion of subject, 500, 520; pattern recognition in phoneme sequences, 364n33; thematic roles, 500, 520, 577–79; theory of mental logic, 249, 275n51, 440n71, 625n95
Brandom, Robert, 181–82n27, 561n43
Bresnan, Joan, xiv, 13n16, 55, 56–58, 62, 65n117, 493, 497n19, 20, 499n21, 594, 598n45, 637n110, 638, 639, 641n116, 642, 658n19, 687, 728n20, 730, 736n40; adverbial adjuncts, 688n51, 695n62; movement paradoxes, 491, 665n28, 734; notion of functional word, 117n5; prepositions, 660n21, 661; X-Bar theory, 725–26
Britton, Karl, 376n22
Brody, Michael, 733n35
Brouwer, L. E. J., 264n27
Buck, Carl Darling, 524n51
Burling, Robbins, 239
Butler, Christopher S., 13n16, 40n59, 490n6
Butterworth, George, 353

Cameron, J. R., 213n88
Carnap, Rudolf, 23, 179, 520, 542, 555n16, 634n90
Carpenter, Humphrey, 608
Cavalli-Sforza, Luigi, 236n25
Chang, Han-liang, 157n48
Choi, Hye-Won, 640n113, 743n61
Choi, Soonja, 432–33
Church, Alonzo, 244, 261–63, 286
Clark, G. B., 356n
Clark, H. H., 24
Cobbett, William, 160n3, 660n23
Cohen, Paul J., 148n36, 271n47
Comrie, Bernard, 430n54, 616n78
Cook, Vivian J. *See* Cook and Newson.
Cook and Newson, 64n115, 444n78, 550–51, 610n, 613, 614, 617n79, 618, 729n21, 730n24, 732n29, 733n35, 735nn38–39, 736n40, 739n44, 740n50, 742n55, 742n58
Cowie, Fiona, 17n13, 46n67
Croft, William, 14n16
Cruse, David Alan, 24, 110, 178–79

Damnjanovic, Nic, 182n27
Davidson, Donald D.: on anomalous monism, 378–80, 394n61; meaning, xiii, xiv, 4, 8n5, 9, 23, 81–82, 83n11, 90–91, 183, 186–87, 192, 205n76, 250n6, 292, 391n59, metaphor, 101–4; theory of events, 539–40, 543n20, 544–49, 581n10; Turing test, 372–73
Davies, William D., 499n21
Davis, Martin, 256n16, 278n52
Deacon, Terrence, 23–24, 51
Dedekind, 142, 149n36
Dennett, Daniel C., 296, intentional stance, 258n20, 298–304, 305–6, 309, 314–15; misleading anomalies, 336–37, 339–45; no construction of the world from sensations, 327n47, 349–50; theory of "real patterns" in the mind, 378–79
Descartes, Rene, 111n51, 133, 247, 292, 299–300, 303, 306, 309, 311, 344, 381, 385n42, 389, 390, 476, 495n17, 553n34
Dik, Simon C., xiv, 56, 57, 60, 65n117, 136n26, 162, 172, 174, 199n62, 201n69, 207, 351, 357, 400n1, 430, 440n74, 487, 490–91, 493n11, 499n21, 502, 510, 511, 518, 527, 576, 583-84, 594, 595, 600, 613, 616n78, 620–22, 633, 638–39, 646, 687, 706n1, 729n21, 736, 741; functional parallels between languages, 56
Dowty, David, 39n55, 40
Dreyfus, Hubert, 252n10, 296
Du Bois, John W., 526n58
Dummett, Michael, xiii, xiv, 4; assertion and assertion-sign, 448n4, 450–53, 472–75, 480–82; compositionalism, 5n4, 82; concept of a language, 66; concept of sentence, 23; contextualism, 185n34; effectiveness, 250–51, 260–61; evils of "semantic holism", 228–32;

force, 446n2, 479; language as basis of philosophy, 290; mental states as directly manifest, 374n15, 382, 388, 391–92; methods of proof form a spread, 256–57, 269n43; misinterpreting Frege's "unsaturatedness", 403n10, 479n72, 644n4; need for speech interpretation as the exception, 184n31, 371; negation, 442; notion of sentence constituent, 87, 163n10, 400–401, 403n10; on propositions as complex names, 473, 480–81, 486; on refutation of Quine, 173n18; representationalism in, 382–85, 388–90, 391–92; segmentability of language, 186; *Sinne* as objects, 473, 480–81, 486; on supposing, 624n91; theory of *Sinn* (sense), 450, 471–75; theory of truth, 181n27; tone as aspect of meaning, 162n5, 182, 482–84; view of past tense, 222–23

Euclid, 56, 108n45, 142, 245–46, 266–67, 287, 638, 718
Eudoxus, 142
Evans, Gareth, 110, 218, 404n11
Everett, Daniel, 192

Feferman, Solomon, 262n25, 269n41–42
Fitch, Tecumseh, 635n107
Fodor, Jerry A.: accessibility of the world to thought, 310, 315; all perception indirect, 171, 323–29; language of thought, 25n34, 39n56; modularity, 346–49
Frege, Gottlob, xiii; assertion-sign, 448, 463; compositional treatment of meaning, 5n4, 8n5, 25n33, 569; Context Principle, 8n5, 185, 407, 432n59, 478; contextual definitions, 47, 62, 582n11; definition of number, 177, 251, 405; facts (*Umstände*), 567n50; ideal of rigor, 253; identity, 512; influence on meaning of "argument" by linguists, 489, 495; notion of force, 32, 163, 446, 453–57, 459–60, 462, 475, 483; object as a *Gegenstand*, 290, 472, 473, 478, 553n34; *Sinn* (sense), 161, 447, 471–72; tone and other aspects of meaning, 162n5; "True" and "False"as objects, 466, 473, 475, 479n67, 480–81, 643; truth, theory, 181n27; unsaturated expressions, 31, 87, 206, 401–3, 408, 416n32, 418–19, 450, 465–66, 479, 481, 644, 649, 730
Fukui, Naoki: account of functional phrases with functional heads, 647n9, 728–31; description of Chomsky's bare structure theory, 31n42, 634n102; identifies Chomsky's key aim on nominalizations, 724n15; proposed remedial strategy, 732–33; treatment of different languages, 740, 742–43. *See also* Speas

Garcia, J., 330n53
Gardiner, Alan H., 75n1, 172, 479n73
Gazzaniga, Michael S., 298, 301n9, 347–48
Geach, P. T.: applicatives 413n28; existence, 254; force, 163, 445n2, 448n6, 450, 453, 458–464, 468–69; incompleteness, 402n4, 403; against Mental or "language of thought", 39n56, 408n22 431n58; misconceived "Frege-point", 459–60, 462; propositions as entities whether asserted or denied, 464–68, 480–82, 483, 484–85, 568; propositions not mere word strings, 457; non-unitary expressions, 513n36, 515n39; on quotations, 563–64; symbolism for propositions, 445n1; on time, 38n50, 539n15, 675n37
Gentzen, 147, 265, 267, 443, 623, 627
George, L., 660n22
Gettier, E. L., 335
Gibson, E. J., 303n12, 325, 354n20
Gibson, J. J., xiv; concept of the stimulus, 16, 18, 116, 154n44, 171, 208, 307, 309, 313, 315, 324–30, 333, 352–54, 520n47; enviromental approach to perception as model for language, 20, 171, 295–96, 458, 658n20, 750; notion of resonance, 357–58, 363–64
Givón, Talmy, 23, 24n29, 35n48
Gleitman, Lila, 431, 435
Gödel, Kurt, 134n24, 148, 149n36, 226n9, 224, 247–48, 255–56, 262–63, 265–70, 272–74, 277–78, 285, 297, 752
Golinkoff, R. M., 431n56, 435, 437
Gopnik, Alison, 355n21, 432–33
Graffi, Giorgio, 60n106
Greenberg, J., 54, 236n25, 638
Gregory, Richard, 326n46
Grevisse, *Le Bon Usage*, 37, 166, 445n79, 502n24, 511, 645n5, 651, 667, 668, 669, 672n35
Grice, H. P.: Platonic ontology involved, 217, 391n59, 404n13, 540; theory of implicatures, 158n1, 164n11, 165, 182, 612, 625n96; theory of meaning as signaling in general, 23, 81–82, 83, 169, 175, 212–16
Grimshaw, Jane, 667n, 726n17
Gross, Richard, 332–33nn59-61, 333n63, 333n65
Grossberg, Stephen, 307n16, 340n74
Grothe, Mardy, 190n43
Gruber, Jeffrey S., 40n58, 576
Guinness, Alec, 399

Haas, William, 207n80, 218
Hacker, P. M. S.: interpretation of Wittgenstein, 368n5, 368n7, 370n11, 390n53, 393n60. *See also* Baker and Hacker
Hacking, Ian, 184n31
Halliday, M. A. K., 57n98, 198, 207, 661n24

Hamlyn, David, 330n56
Hammer's German Grammar and Usage, 37, 684n46, 692n57
Hampshire, Stuart, 51, 367
Hare, R. M., 453n16, 454n17, 463n33, 468–69, 481, 484n82, 485n87
Harrington, L., 270n44
Harris, Martin, 606n59
Harris, Roy, 80n9, 196n57, 198n61, 367n3
Harris, Zellig, 11–13, 54, 198
Hart, H. L. A., 98
Haspelmath, Martin, 16, 54, 62
Hauser, Marc, 635n107
Hawkins, J. A., 592
Heath, Peter, 11n11
Hegel, Georg W. F., 751n3
Heidegger, Martin, 300n8, 367
Heyting, Arend, 108n44, 264n27
Higginbotham, J., 269
Hirst, R. J., 690
Hjelmslev, Louis, 644n4
Hockett, Charles, 78, 115n3, 172, 193–95, 198, 351
Hopper, Paul J., 17
Hopper and Traugott, 9n6, 24n20, 65, 91n20, 445n79, 525n55, 526, 578n4, 606
Hudson, Richard, 742n56
Husserl, Edmund, 79, 300n8, 306, 402n8, 419n35

Ingarden, Roman, 23, 95n23, 300n8, 402

Jackendoff, Ray, 40, 44n63, 50, 55n89, 57, 61, 100, 112n55, 162, 174n19, 201n68, 203–6, 208, 220n3, 299, 302n10, 336n69, 337, 359, 380, 396, 546n23, 581n9, 582, 635n107; atomization, 206, 633n101, 644n2, 725n; contributions to grammar, 31, 60n104, 62, 118, 487, 549, 576n1, 614, 621n88, 633n101, 646, 673n36, 681n42, 718n10, 736; f-mind, functional descriptions, data structures, 15, 203, 209, 296, 310–11, 315, 362; Grammatical Constraint principle, 487; movement theory criticized, 733n35; perceptual verbs, 97–98, 131, 280; Preference Rules System, 258, 281; X-Bar theory, 724, 725, 732
Jakobson, Roman, 49–50, 220n3
Jerome, 190–91, 700
Jespersen, Otto, xiv, 18, 26, 30, 31n39, 60–61, 62, 63n113, 75n1, 78, 172, 192–96, 198, 351, 383, 401, 402, 479, 644–45, 658, 717, 730, 748
Jessen, Marilyn E., 104–5nn35–36
Johnson, W. E., 413, 418, 647

Kant, Immanuel, 10, 21, 37, 41–42, 43, 60n106, 201, 228, 251, 368, 389, 390, 697, 747, 751
Kaplan, Ronald M., 56, 57n98, 641n15
Karcevskij, S., 96
Kayne, R. S., 698n66, 741
Kennedy's Revised Latin Primer, 37, 166, 689n5
Kenny, Anthony J., 38n52, 39, 311, 384n, 470n38, 688n51
Kikawada, Isaac M., 190n43
Kirby, L., 270n45
Kleene, S. C., 278n52
Kneale, William, 142n30, 179n25, 265, 268n38, 442, 624, 625n94
Knuth, Donald E., 641n115
Koopman, H., 608, 640n50
Kreisel, Georg, 255n15, 256n17, 264, 268, 273
Kripke, Saul: on dispositions, 78, 376; interpretation of Wittgenstein, 368n7, 377–78
Kuhl, Patricia K., 356n23
Kuhn, Jonas, 639, 640nn113–14, 641
Kuno, Susumu, 14n16, 599. *See also in Subject Index* functionalism in linguistics
Kutas, Marta, 348n4, 361n30, 617n80

Lambrecht, Knud, 498n8
Landau, B., 451n56
Langford, C. H., 39
Lashley, K. S., 199n65
Lederer, Anne, 431n56
Legendre, Geraldine, 641n17
Leśniewski, Stanislaw, 401n2, 438, 495n15
Lewis, C. I., 39
Lewis, John D., 16n23
Li, Charles N., 62, 493, 499, 518
Lincoln, Abraham, 183, 342n80
Locke, John, 311, 344, 384–85, 431
Lodge, R. Anthony, 606n59
Lucas, John R., 255, 265n29, 266–69
Ludlow, Peter, 378n30
Luenberger, David G., 307n16
Lyons, John, 15–16, 165–66, 196n59, 454, 481, 484

MacIntyre, Alasdair, 192, 468n37
MacIntyre, Angus, 255n15
Mackie, J. L., 368n4
Makino, Suzuki, 650n11
Malcolm, Norman, 175, 238n28, 370n11, 371
Malhesius, Vilém, 64, 207
Mandler, J., 435n63, 435n65
Marcel, Gabriel, 367
Marr, David, 326n46
Martin, G. B., 356n23
Matthews, Eric, 300n8
Matthews, P. H., 115n3, 598
Mayo, Bernard, 99n28, 460n27
McDowell, John, 4
McMahon, April, 598–600

Meillet, Antoine, 64, 578
Meinong, 567–68nn50–51, 573n57
Meltzoff, Andrew, 18, 353, 355n21, 356
Meredith, M. Alex. *See* Stein and Meredith
Merleau-Ponty, Maurice, 3n2, 51, 300n8, 303n12, 357n24, 367, 379n31; influence on Hampshire and Taylor, 51
Miller, Alexander, 8n5
Miller, George A., 199n63, 614n73
Milner and Goodale, 313
Minsky, Marvin, 298
Mithun, Marianne, 667n29
Montague, Richard, 39n55, 40
Moore, G. E., 25n33, 405n16, 408n22, 425n44, 477–78, 567n50, 689
Moore, K. *See* Meltzoff

Nakayama, Ken, 353n19
Nelson, K., 435n63
Newmeyer, Frederick, 14, 733n35, 740
Newson, Mark. *See* Cook and Newson
Nuchelmans, Gabriel, 114, 115n3, 117n5

Ouhalla, Jamal, 596n41, 723n14
Owen, G. E. L., 121n12

Panini, xv, 583
Paris, J., 270nn44–45
Partridge, Michael, 482n76
Passingham, R. E., 241n35
Peacocke, Christopher, 270n43
Pelletier, F. J., 185n34
Penrose, Roger, 112, 255, 266n34, 268, 269n42, 317n34, 320n38
Perlmutter, David, 57n95, 499, 524n53, 683n43, 687
Piaget, Jean, 240n33, 435n63
Pinker, Steven, 31, 44, 45, 54–55, 234n21, 237, 280–81, 313, 322, 359, 381, 396, 429n52, 499n21, 578n5, 635n107, 727
Plato, xv; knowledge, 476n59; method, 79; *rhema*, 22, 30, 162, 401–4, 410–11, 422n40, 431n58, 450, 479, 649; sentence, 22, 30–31, 382, 473, 476, 477, 644, 689, 748; states as possessions, 274; theory of ideas, 384, 538–42
Poincaré, Henri, 274n50
Polanyi, Michael, 246n3, 263n26, 274n50
Pollard, Carl, 55
Pollock, Jean-Yves, 591, 634n103, 698n66, 729, 734n37, 738
Port, Robert F., 311n24, 337n71
Prior, Arthur, 39, 228
Pullum, Geoffrey, 16n23, 55n90, 706n1
Putnam, 173n18, 204, 255, 266, 269, 370, 427
Quine, W. van O., xiv, 4, 8n5, 83, 167, 173, 253n13, 260n21, 292, 347, 377, 380, 471n41, 564n47, 581, 582n13; indeterminacy of translation, 184–85, 367n1, 407, 517; influence on Chomsky, 16n21; influence on Davidson, 8n5; interpretation of Wittgenstein, 377
Quirk, R. S., 621n88

Radford, Andrew, 604n55, 615n75, 616n77, 619n84, 655n18, 681, 695n62, 697n65, 698n66, 708n3, 719n11, 720n12, 729n47, 740nn48–49, 742
Ramsey, F. P., 124, 181n27, 254n14, 270, 540, 542–43
Reichling, Anton, 114n1, 194, 200–201
Robins, R. H., 115n3, 151n38, 153n42, 156
Rowland, Tracey, 192n48
Ruhlen, Merrit, 236n25
Russell, Bertrand: attitude to ordinary language, 520; categories, 62; complete symbol, 478, 582; contextualism, 185n34, 423; definitions in use, 177, 408n23; forms of knowledge, 132, 476; mysticism, 237n27; notations, 63, 87n14, 488; paradoxes/types, 143, 254n14, 273n49; propositions not objects, 689; relational notions of knowledge, 478n65; self-knowledge, 341; types, 149n35, 419n35, 543; typical ambiguity, 101, 124
Ryle, Gilbert: an Aristotelian, xiii, 38n52; Aristotelian conception of dispositions, 76–78, 131–32, 194, 251, 280, 289, 375; category, 419n35; human beings as psychophysical unities, 51, 367, 371n12, 378; "if"-statements as inference-tickets, 177, 624–25; logical grammar, 78–80; mind not inner, 174, 306; polymorphous use of words, xiv, 3, 8, 121–24, 131–35, 226, 252, 281, 305; ordinary language, 520; on paramechanical theories of mind, 25, 40n60, 394, 395n63; propositions, 456n21, 480, 556n37, 567n50, 689; reasoning precedes science of reasoning, 40n60, 275n51; relation to Dennett, 296n1, 300; role of names secondary, 428n50, 479; sentence-factors, 86–87, 112, 163n10, 186, 400, 407, 410; speech/language divide, 75, 163, 174, 186, 209, 483n78; topic-neutrality, 125; what is implicit in a thought, 612n68

Sag, Ivan, 55, 640n115
Sapir, Edward, 54, 116, 162, 192n47
Saporta, Sol, 151n38
Saussure, F. de, 7, 13, 63, 75, 80, 172, 173, 193n49, 196–200, 207, 220–21, 367, 606
Schlesinger, I. M., 45
Searle, 9n7, 164n11, 212–14, 218n97, 286, 292,

Searle (*cont.*)
378, 447–48, 453n16, 454, 473, 475, 481, 484–86
Sells, Peter, 608–9
Shewmon, Alan, 53n82
Shieber, Stuart M., 640n115, 642
Shoemaker, Sydney, 367
Silverstein, Michael, 527
Skinner, B. F., 16n23, 173, 207, 377
Smith, L. B., 353n17
Smith, Neil, 54n88
Sommers, Fred, 419n35
Speas, M., 647n9, 728n20, 732
Spencer, Andrew, 153n41
Sperber, Dan, 171, 211, 214, 215, 323, 349n9
Sportiche, D., 608
Stanley, Jason, 158n1, 164n11
Stein and Meredith, 18, 208, 353
Steiner, George, 137n28, 188–89, 191n45, 238n29, 607n62
Stern, Daniel, 355
Stock, Guy, 454
Stoljar, Daniel, 182n27
Stowell, T., 737
Strawson, P. F., 175, 209n84, 367, 371n12, 542–43
Suzuki, Akira, 650
Szabó, Zoltán Gendler, 9n7

Talmy, Leonard, 61n108, 586n25
Tarski, Alfred, 23, 124–25, 254, 272–73, 285
Taylor, Charles, 3n2, 51, 251, 367, 379–80
Taylor, Richard, 270
Tesnière, Lucien, 653n16
Thelen, E., 353n17
Thompson, Sandra, 62, 493, 499, 518
Thrainsson, H., 503n27, 510, 702n72
Tolkien, J. R. R., 608
Tolman, E. C. 199n63
Tomasello, Michael, 61, 429–35, 437–38
Tomassi, Paul 381n66
Tomlin, Russell S., 594n38
Tsimpli, Ianthi-Maria, 54n88
Turing, 49, 53, 111, 255n15, 262, 278, 282, 287, 292, 372–73

Uchida, Keiichi, 650n11
Uhlenbeck, E. M., 194, 200–201, 207n80

Van der Gaaf, W., 604n55
Van Eynde, Frank, 733n34
Van Gelder, Timothy, 296n2, 307n16, 311, 337n71
Van Gelderen, E., 64n115, 239n31
Van Roojen, Mark, 471n42
Van Valin, Robert D., Jr., xiv; heads, 56n94; on layering of the clause, 22, 29, 30, 33, 35, 400; on modality, 40, 704; on negation, 30, 33, 440; neglect of logical role of notion of subject, 57, 400n1, 430, 490n8, 493n13, 499n, 503n28, 518; notion of pivot, 525; prepositions, 661; structural functionalism, 12, 13n16, 40, 56, 162, 166, 193n49, 207, 500, 525, 577, 633, 638–39; on X-Bar theory, 706n1
Vendler, Zeno, 38, 40
Von Humboldt, Wilhelm, 8, 9, 11, 60, 63n113, 75n1, 198, 200, 237n28, 606

Webelhuth, G. *See* Ackerman and Webelhuth
Wedekind, Jürgen, 640n115
Weinreich, Uriel, 60n106, 220n3
Wiggins, David, 8n5, 427–28
Wiles, Andrew, 270
Wilson, Deirdre, 171, 211, 214, 215, 323, 349n9
Wittgenstein, Ludwig, xiv, 20, 32; comparison of sense to direction, 176n2, 215, 447, 454–56, 479, 648; contextualism of word-meaning, 177, 185, 407, 478; criticism of Locke, 384; family-resemblance, 74, 92–93, 122–24, 132–34, 252, 280; grammar, 368; 377; harmony of grammar and world, 392–93; language-game, 122, 368, 388n47, 406; on naming, 406; nature of later philosophy, 390–91; proposition as a nexus, 402n5, 404n14; questioning isomorphism and representationalism, 180n26, 386–89, 390–91; ridicule of innatism, 40n60, 51, 79, 89n17, 111, 122-23, 133, 174–75; reference, 408; rejection of constructional model of humans, 394–95; rule interpretation, 251, 253, 435; view of human nature not anti-realist, 367–71, 378. *See also* Anscombe; Baker and Hacker; Hacker; Quine
Woodworth, R. S., 354n20
Woolford, E., 430n53
Wright, Crispin, 205n76, 260, 279n53, 374n15, 388–89

Yamadam, Jeni, 54n88

Zermelo, Ernst, 8, 106
Ziff, Paul, 9n8, 111n50

Subject Index

absolutive case, 500–501, 518, 522, 584. *See also* accusative case; ergative languages
abstractions/abstract entities/types: in Aristotle, 421–22; collections, 420; events/situations corresponding to statements, 539–47; interpretations of terms, 12–13, 166, 193, 420, 424; Plato's universals corresponding to predicates, 384n41, 538–43; reality of in Grice's theory of meaning, 217-18. *See also* collections; events; paralinguistic objects; particularity; Platonism; universals
abstract subject-matters, 43, 46, 47, 125, 129, 139, 143, 193n49, 266, 273, 400, 412, 414, 493, 507, 516, 524. *See also* topic-neutrality
Accessibility Hierarchy, 616–17
accusative case, 521, 522, 528, 554–55, 565, 575; default for object in nominative/accusative languages, 488, 496, 499, 521–24, 526–27, 584, 587, 732; ergative languages contrasted, 500–501, 518; term "object" ambiguous, 519–27
acts of judgment and understanding: expressed not embodied, 20–21, 67, 396, 751, 753; materially isomorphic representation impossible, 20, 213, 384–85, 387–89, 390–92, 393–94, 396; realization not in brain and not requiring natural expression, 67, 753; simplicity of intellectual acts, 385–86, 394–95; transcendence of the body, 3, 20–21, 67, 753. *See also* computer simulation; intellect
actualilties distinguished from facts, 567–68
Actualilty: as a thematic role, 580
adjectives and adjectival phrases, 43, 48, 116, 118, 119, 155, 421, 422–23, 530, 539, 551–52, 592, 621, 650, 655, 659–60, 678–79, 706, 709, 715–24, 727; and agreement, 596; as attributes, 692–93; eager/easy contrast, 691n56, 699; underlie modal expressions, 33, 661. *See also* adverbs
adjunct/complement distinction, 429, 553, 576, 646, 652–54. *See also* adverbial clauses; adverbs
adpositions. *See* prepositions and other adpositions; postpositions
adverbial clauses: absolute participial phrases, 26–27, 534, 698–99; as adjuncts to clauses, 534, 601–3; applied *de re* or *de dicto*, 703; six kinds of nonconditional, 675. *See also* conditional statements; spatial clauses and phrases
adverbial expressions, 649, 651, 665–66, 678–79; introducing peripheral arguments, 511, 518, 576, 646n6; kinds of, 675–77; in Theme position, 742; treatment in X-Bar theory, 678–79, 723–24, 727–29, 731, 737. *See also* adverbial clauses; adverbs
adverbs, 60, 87, 119, 399, 445, 488; cannot have adjuncts, 722; chains of, 648, 720–22; kinds of, 581, 675–77; prepositions in diachronic relations with, 583, 585–87; relation to adjectives, 414, 534–35, 539, 549–50, 654n17, 660, 663, 709, 717–22; when adjunctive to clause, 581, 632, 668; when parts of verb expression, 496, 528, 614n73, 662, 682; when pronominal, 505, 517
agglutinative languages, 2n1, 94n22, 115, 118n7, 120, 153, 155–57, 605, 639, 746
analogy, xiii, xv, 8, 122–23; extrinisic analogy, 123, 131; formal analogy, 8, 93, 124–27, 128, 129; 130; intrinsic analogy, 122–23, 127, 129, 130–31, 143
anaphor, 61n109, 63, 489, 507, 575, 600–612. *See also* pragmatic anaphor; reference

animal communication systems: area of ignorance, 3n, 242; chimpanzees, 241–42; sublinguistic, 233–34, 237n28
anomalous monism, 378. *See also* theories of human nature
anti-realism: as repudiation of metaphysical, 377–78
"any" and "a certain" statements: "a certain" expressing definiteness, 628; "any" expressing indiscriminateness, 626–28; correspond with free variable formulae in formal logic, 627–28
applicatives, 413, 418, 421, 429, 653. *See also* determiners; predicate application controller; quantifier
Argument: logical term derived from mathematics, 87, 136, 161, 290, 406n9, 418, 422, 429–30, 433–34, 438, 487–93; uses in logic and grammar in family relationship, 494–98
aspect of verbs: auxiliaries of aspect, 666; indication of posture of state or act in time, 38, 40, 62, 63, 197, 222–23, 411, 432, 453n13, 479n71, 580n31, 603–4, 645n5, 646, 648, 651, 653, 657–58, 661, 662, 749
atomism: Aristotelian and other objections to, 51–52, 205–6, 219, 227, 263, 307n16, 316–18
attributive statements, 93, 129, 412n27, 414–15, 420–23, 494, 500, 508, 524–25, 580, 596, 621, 654, 660–63, 665; expressed using the copula, 571–73, 692–95, 705, 707, 714
autonomy of grammar, 14, 16, 37, 43, 60-61, 203, 206, 207, 581, 609–10, 635–37, 706, 731, 733, 736, 747, 748; as discussed by Newmeyer, 14–15n17
autonomy of human intellectual operation, 1, 2, 18–19, 20–21; made possible by malleability of the brain, 360–65, 394–96; metaphor of intellect in command, 20, 21, 128, 399, 751–53
auxiliaries of time, aspect, and structure: "be" expressing continuous action, 115, 222; "be" and "have" expressing perfect, 115, 222, 521n49; "do" giving emphasis or affecting structure, 65, 445, 590n31, 662n25, 666–69, 729; formation of passive with "be", 525, 534, 595, 597, 604, 615, 666, 668, 684n44, 685, 694; idioms of imminent action, 651n, 666, 669, 693; "will" and "shall", 606, 659, 662n25, 666, 667, 668n30, 669, 671
axiomatizability of theory of meaning, 8n5, 250n6, 279n53

basis of philosophy: Aristotelian conception, 38–39, 44, 76, 389, 392–93; in epistemology, 389; in philosophy of language, 389; Socratic or dialectical approach, 79–80, 183n30; Wittgenstein's late approach, 20, 79–80, 368, 390–93
behaviorism, 47, 51, 173, 195, 205, 207, 253, 261, 278, 292, 367, 370–71, 377, 380
biological evolution and language, 2, 19, 48, 208–9, 234–37, 247, 277, 295, 312, 327–28, 349n10, 749–50; many things not to be ascribed to evolution, 288. *See also* emergence of *Homo sapiens*; linguistic developments
Borer-Chomsky Conjecture, 730n22. *See also* heads and phrases in Chomskyan grammar
bracketing, 87, 184, 198, 419, 594–602, 610, 638, 646, 670, 672, 734–35; embedded clauses, 598–600. *See also* parsing; scope

Cartesian dualism: incoherent as causal account, 310–11
Cartesian internalization of the mind and its avoidance, 50–51, 173–75, 247, 299–300, 303, 306, 307–11, 322–24, 344–45, 349–50, 367–74
case and other noun markers, 60, 115, 585–86, 663, 710; Chomskyan conceptions of Abstract Case and Case Filter, 498, 505, 733; *karakas* of Panini, 583; localist theory of case, 105; morphological case, 120, 150–52, 198, 406, 421, 422, 500. *See also* absolutive case; accusative case; dative subjects; ergative case; thematic roles
categorematic terms: as content-introducing, 119–20, 431n58. *See also* syncategorematic
causal explanation. *See also* explanation, types of
causative verbs, 62n111, 452, 521, 526, 651n13, 666, 667, 671, 691, 700–701, 711
chiasmus, 190
Chinese room: Searle's thought experiment, 286, 292
Chômeur: downgraded object of verb with adjunct status, 683–85; nominal and adverbial adjuncts distinguished, 687–88
Chomskyan framework, 47–50, 199–203; abstractness of grammatical conceptions, 12–16, 36, 83, 166, 195–96, 200–201, 296, 362; autonomy of grammar, 14; compositional conception of grammatical formation, 5, 24, 31, 49, 205, 634, 643–44, 649, 730; conception of the mental, 52–53, 202; conception of a sentence, 5, 9, 13, 15, 20, 24, 136, 568; conception of sentence-meaning, 5, 20n25, 24–25, 205, 348n8, 384, 385, 394, 634; grammar part of psychology or neuroscience, 15–17, 48–49, 58–59, 172, 202, 207, 348–50, 360; grammatical nativism, 40–41, 46n67; "languages" as static theoretical objects, 64–66, 81; neurological functionalism, 14–15. *See also* autonomy of grammar; competence;

Internalized Language; nativism; neurological functionalism
Chomskyan grammar: development, 47–50, 199–203, 633–35, 728–34; grammatical atomization of the verb, 644, 730; idea of Abstract case, 498, 505, 638, 733; other proposals, 413n30, 415; subject and object as derived notions, 57, 489, 497–98. *See also* complementizers; heads and phrases in Chomskyan grammar; Minimalist Program; Movement theory; Principles and Parameters theory; Subjacency theory; X-Bar theory
Chomskyan weaknesses, 14, 17, 52–53, 58, 59, 172, 292, 497–98, 635, 735–36, 742–43, 747–48; credibility depends on concord with tradition, 498; dependence on adult intuitions of grammaticality, 54, 173, 381; epicycles, 55, 59, 498, 516n42, 638–39, 738, 740, 741; inattention to parsing and hearer's problems, 9n7, 55, 349–50, 638, 737; lack of empirical support, 54–55, 207–8, 497n20, 635n7, 636–37; neglect of adjuncts, 55, 723; theories to be tested only as wholes, 15–16, 644n3; treatment of early critics, 194, 200–203; treatment of nominalization and resulting contrivances, 724, 730–31; treatment of relation of logic and grammar, 37–38, 41, 63, 361, 580–82, 612–21, 748. *See also* compositionalism amongst linguists; lexical atoms; naturalism; nominalization; representationalism
Church/Kleene formulae, 255n15, 269n41
Church's thesis, 262, 278, 282
clause-markers, 156, 654–57, 674, 690, 695–700, 728n20; as connectives, 654; following relatives and conjunctions, 619, 621, 655, 695–96, 697–98. *See also* complementizers
clauses: relation to sentences, 25–26, 28, 32, 62, 163, 166–67, 206, 400, 447–49; sentential-potential from link to communication, 449; verb has same integrative role as in sentence, 489–90. *See also* subordinate clauses
code: inadequate model of language, 14, 81–83, 88, 169, 213–15, 323, 403
cognate: in relation to cognate-terms, 531, 536–38; examples, 88, 169, 230, 290, 446, 452, 466–68, 479, 522, as thematic role, 576–77
cognate/object distinction, 169, 290, 537, 548, 553–54, 572–73
cognitional cognate, 554–56, 564, 566–74; sense and its expression as co-cognates of speech-act, 88, 169, 215
collective terms 420, 514–15, 664, 692; collections, 38, 60, 131, 140–41, 143, 146, 419, 508, 581, 747
comment: functionalist term for what is said about a topic, 31, 62, 399, 487, 488, 493
competence: in Chomsky, 11n11, 14–16, 58, 75n2, 199–203, 617, 634, 646; in Lashley and Tolman, 199n63
complementizers (clause-markers): connective role, 509, 619n84, 522, 654–55, 690, 695–96, 714; in LFG, 726; interpretation in Chomskyan grammar, 730, 742; introduced by Rosenbaum and Bresnan, 728n20
complements: of adjectives and nouns when verb-rooted, 26, 33, 429, 491, 511, 653, 705–10, 724; attributive complements, 93, 530, 552, 571–73, 654, 692–95; clausal complements, 673–75, 690–92, 695–704; object complements of verbs, 26, 56, 494, 503n25, 515, 516, 517, 518–23, 576, 587, 596, 598, 619–20, 688–91; peculiarities of cognitional cognates, 491, 565, 567; semantic and morphosyntactic complements distinguished, 495, 499, 502, 505, 507, 509–13, 516–17, 521, 526, 637, 655, 656, 677, 706–7, 711; three-tier isomorphism consequent on verbal rooting, 719–24
complements, functional, 26, 429, 485, 491, 494, 496, 497, 503n25, 515, 530, 552, 565, 567, 576
complements to nouns, 677–79; two kinds, 705–10, 712–14; variations with verb-rooted nouns, 715–19, 721. *See also* Chomskyan grammar
compositionalism amongst linguists, 5, 8–9, 24, 49, 61, 205–6, 258, 605, 649, 730; bottom-up in character, 28, 49; requires decomposition before recomposition, 730; treatment of sentences as constructs, 3, 15–16; 31
compositionalism in philosophy, 5, 90–91, impossibilities from contextual influences on sense, 8–9, 110, 178, 209; para-mechanical interpretation, 24–25
computer simulation, 52, 72–73, 296, 369; of analogous and unformalizable use of most general concepts, 10, 253–60, 281–82, 284–85, 363, 369; of any use of general concepts, 383, 384–85; of language in unitary and integrated semantic structure, 234, 241, 749–50; of natural arithmetic, 255, 265–70, 369; of reliable mutual intelligibility, 280–83, 285–86, 297, of self-reflective capacities, 247–48, 285, 363, 750
Conceptual Structure: Jackendoff's conception, 50, 174n19, 201n68, 203
conditional statements: logic of, 29, 47n69, 177, 464–65, 625–27. *See also* epistemic modality; involution; supposing
conjunctions and conjunctive expressions, 77, 100n30, 119n9, 180, 228n12, 454, 499, 550, 585–86, 655, 681, 697n84, 739, 741

connectives: in Aristotle, 583, 622, 650; heads only morphosyntactically, 654–55. *See also* clause markers; conjunctions; linking elements; prepositions and other adpositions; structurizers

constitutive verbs: definition, 657, 662, 666; examples, 169, 521n49, 537, 569

constructivity of proofs and definitions, 10, 30, 94, 108, 125, 147, 148, 149n36, 229, 255n15, 264, 267n36, 271, 273, 274n49, 443, 626n97

content-introducing expressions, 114, 119–20, 128, 156, 188, 429–30, 438–39, 528, 542, 578, 582–83, 600, 645, 647, 648, 651, 657, 659–60, 661–64, 666, 669, 676, 678, 685, 689, 709, 727

context of whole language as determining meaning, 9, 186–87; Davidson's semantic holism, 90–91, 186, 220, 230. *See also* axiomatizability of theory of meaning; Saussure's structuralism

Context Principle ("Frege's principle"): a word has meaning only in context of a proposition, 177, 478; in Frege, 8n5, 185; in Wittgenstein, 185; no definite limits to contextuality of sense, 110, 133–34, 176–78. *See also* syntagmatic relations

continuity, 140–44, 146–47, 148–49n36, 266n35; in Aristotle and Newton, 38–39, 108n43, 273, 274n50; holistic implication, 307n16; as part of general logic and grammar, 43–44, 59–60, 62–63, 197, 222, 223, 413–14, 534–36, 538, 603–4, 666, 749–50; unnoticed by Davidson, 549

conventions of writing: Cobbett's explicit concern with, 160n3, 660; as distorting grammatical ideas, 157, 159, 160, 660; uniqueness of Chinese grapheme, 157n48

convergence of psychological and logical processing, 348, 361, 598–99, 609–21, 626–28

conversational implicatures, 158n1, 162, 164n11, 165, 182, 612n68, 625n96; pragmatic aspect important for Sperber and Wilson, 211, 214, 215, 323n41

creativity in thought: dynamism from multi-potential sense of each word, 6, 8, 9–11, 112, 114; in morphology, 529; in new metaphors, 96, 101, 134, 137–40; new sense constituted in act of expressing it, 86, 88, 149, 172, 569; in number theory, 140–48; same power exercised in generation of thought and speech, 11n11. *See also* intellect

cross-modal functioning in hearing and speech, 352–56; roles in imitation, 352–57; superior colliculus, 353–60

de dicto/distinction: *de re*, 702–4; "seem" and "appear" said *de dicto* of judgements, 702–3; "look", "sound", "appear" as perceptual verbs used *de re*, 702. *See also* epistemic modality

defeasible concepts, 77n4, 98, 162, 194n52

defects in speech and sense: aphasia, 313, 350–51, 746n1; illusions and delusions, 328–36; results of isolated development, age, injury, 237, 238; systems of visual perception, 313

definitions in use, 177, 185n34, 408n23

dependents of the verb, 26, 56, 576; dependent-marking and head-marking languages contrasted, 56, 491n9, 653n15

deponent verbs, 519, 522, 524, 689n52

Determiner Phrases. *See* heads and phrases in Chomskyan grammar

Determiners: as Bloomfield understood them, 413–14, 444, 532n7, 590, 592, 672n35, 693; broad application, 414–15, 677; morphological properties, 654n17, 710n4; synlexical character, 660; as topics numerals have lexical character, 664; treatment in Chomsky, 415, 739n46

disjoint elements of sentences, 26–27, 406, 488, 491, 493, 510, 518, 605, 698

dispositions and states (habits): in Jespersen, Hockett, Reichling, Uhlenbeck, 194; rival Humean conception in Kripke, 78, 375–77, 380; in Ryle and Aristotle, 75–78, 123, 131–32, 226, 251, 289, 303, 325, 370, 374–75; Ryle's single-track/many-track distinction, 77–78, 375; in Wittgenstein, 375n18, 376

distributionalist methods, 11–12, 54, 114, 116, 198, 205, 502, 534, 637

Dynamical Systems Theory, 296n2, 307n16, 311, 352–53

effectiveness, 108, 109, 112, 134, 226, 243, 373; Church's thesis and consensus as to application to formal proofs, 244, 261–62, 277–78; limits to formal, 250–57; underlying role of the understanding, 243–49; wider epistemological notion, 260–61, 262–64, 271–77, 279, 286–87, 292, 379. *See also* mechanically applicable rules; Turing-machine computability

ellipsis, 433, 620–22, 686

emergence of *Homo sapiens*: discontinuity underlying apparent continuity, 233–36; language differentiation within, 236–37; linguistic capacity unitary, 236, 237–38, 240–41, 242. *See also* biological evolution and language; unitary semantic structure

emergentism, 24n29, 51

epistemic modality, 29–30, 39, 40, 242, 433, 506, 569–71, 622–23, 628–31, 652, 697, 699–700;

attributed *de dicto,* 703; subjunctive and "conditional" moods, 452n12
equivocation (homonymy), 91n20, 92, 121, 123, 195, 421, 643, 657
ergative case, 500–501, 518, 521, 524, 526, 584, 675, 684
ergative languages, 489, 496, 500–501, 518, 521–22, 524–27, 584, 616n78, 667, 684n45; roots of ergativity and instability of voice systems, 500–501, 525–27
events: as basic objects, 44n63, 546; event and state causality, 314, 368, 546; figment of logical argumentation, 539–41, 543–50; as giving rise to infinite regress, 540–42, 543–44; status as objects of imagination, 436–37. *See also* abstractions
existential presuppositions, 30, 34, 104–5, 272, 276, 441, 443–44, 494–95, 515
existential statements: grammatical treatment of, 41, 104–5, 130; three uses of in logic, 254, 257, 508–10
explanation, types of: a priori and empirical contrasted, 245–49, 273–74nn48–49; holistic, teleological, or agent causality, 51, 78, 276–77, 368, 378–79; Humean, "causal," or anti-teleological event-and-state causality, 51, 53, 277, 306, 338, 363, 377, 546; integrating types of explanation, 245–49, 295, 315–18
expressing a sense, 3, 5, 19, 30, 67, 73, 82–86; as distinct from expressing emotions, 88
expressivism. *See* moral objectivism
extended logic. *See* general logic

facts: distinguishing from actualities, 567–68; not objects, 382–84, 386–91, 436–37, 471, 477, 564–67, 571–74
family: resemblance, 4, 45, 74, 92–93, 122, 124, 131–34, 252, 280; relationships between uses of logical and grammatical terms, 488–89, 494–98
Fermat's last theorem, 105n38, 270–71, 304–5
Fermat's least time principle, 379
figures of speech, 101–5, 127
finitariness, 248, 256n17, 263, 264, 267n36, 270, 274n49
focalized subjects, 297–98, 303, 306–7, 309, 314, 352
focal meaning. *See* relation-based connections of word use
Focus: in functionalist grammar, 35, 59, 60, 487, 506, 508–9, 512, 522, 526n58; not opposite of topic, 490–91, 525
focuses of meaning, 7, 74, 90–96, 98, 99–100, 103, 108, 109, 112, 116–17, 118, 120, 122, 123, 126–28, 129–30, 135, 137–39, 143–46, 149–51, 156, 161, 746
force (*Kraft*), 27–32, 62, 400, 404, as an aspect of sense, 162–64, 168, 216, 242, 387, 748; false separation from force, 391, 393, 447–54, 458–75, 480–82. *See also* illocutionary force
formal grammars. *See* Chomskyan grammar; distributionalist methods; Generalized Phrase Structure Grammar; Head-Driven Phrase Structure Grammar; Lexical Functional Grammar; Minimalist Program
French and English: asymmetries between, 589–91, 634n103, 698, 729, 734n37, 738
Functional Grammar. *See in Index of Names* Dik
functionalism in linguistics, 206–9; generative functionalism of Kuno and Prince, 14n16
functionalist grammars, 13n16, 207, 706; functional explanation for morphosyntactic phenomena, 502, 509, 607–9, 644, 748; functional parallels recognized absent morphosyntactic parallels, 56, 638. *See also* Functional grammar; Lexical Functional Grammar; Prague school; Role and Reference Grammar; semantic syntax; Systemic Functional Grammar

Generalized Phrase Structure Grammar (GPSG): initiated by Gazdar, 55; X-Bar theory applies only to lexical phrases, 706n1
general logic, 2, 17, 18, 21, 37, 38–40, 41, 42, 45, 59–63, 67, 75, 392, 749–50; key components of, 38–40, 43, 221–26. *See also* semantic syntax
general terms, 43, 74, 227, 384, 407, 409, 412–13, 417, 418–22, 423, 439–40, 489–90, 492, 493n13, 494–95, 499, 501, 510, 512, 514–16, 551–53, 647, 653, 660, 664, 745; importance of the most general terms, 4n3, 10, 21, 101, 130, 257–59, 285, 746–47, 752
gerund, 32, 422n38, 434n61, 439, 529, 531, 534, 604n55, 696n63, 698, 707, 717, 719; many meanings of, 535–38; mixed behavior and semantic similarity to modern English infinitive, 534–35, 551n32, 567, 607, 666, 669, 700, 707, 719; reference to products, 536–37; terminology obscured in English and French sources, 531n5, 604n55, 672n35
gerundive in Latin, 604, 694
Gödel's incompleteness theorem and its significance, 99, 134n24, 226n, 244n2, 247–48, 255, 256–57, 263, 265–70, 285; corollaries, 270
Goodstein's theorem, 270
Government and Binding theory. *See* Principles and Parameters theory
grammaticality as a property of speech, 209–10, 372

grammaticalization: definition, 2, 67, 488, 575, 578, 748–49; in development of children's speech, 32, 60, 63–64, 364–65, 406, 429, 577–79; discourse role of topic or subject, 56, 62, 487, 493, 497, 499, 518, 523, 637–38, 732–33; Meillet's account of, 578; Quine misled by superficial differences in, 184–85, 517; in sign-language, 235; as system of gluing or integrating parts of sentence, 31, 489, 582–83, 647, 650. *See also* impersonal constructions; linking elements; partitive and possessive phrases; semantic syntax

Harmonic Grammar, 641n117; sets goal to Optimality Theory, 641. *See also* optimization
Head: ambiguity of term, 56, 643, 654–55, 656–57, 659, 723; avenue to decomposition of verb, 728–31. *See also* prepositions; heads and phrases in Chomskyan grammar; heads of phrase; Lexical Functional Grammar; lexical heads
Head-Driven Phrase Structure Grammar (HPSG): concern with machine translation, 55; influenced by Shieber and context dependence, 640n115
head-marking and dependent-marking languages, 56, 491n9, 653n15
heads and phrases in Chomskyan grammar, 31–32, 64, 591, 600n50, 634, 723; error in treating nominalizations formally not functionally, 531, 655, 706–9, 724, 732–33; functional heads and phrases, 31, 64–65, 415, 444, 591, 632, 633–34, 638, 643, 656, 706, 723, 724, 728–31, 737, 738, 742; Inflection phrase, 550–51, 727–29, 732; nominal Determiner phrase, 415, 647, 696, 730, 732, 733n34; Predicate phrase, 658n19; term "functional head" attributed to Borer and Fukui, 728n20; types of lexical head, 48, 724, 737. *See also in Index of Names* Fukui; Pollock
heads of phrase: informal use of term, 410, 498, 517, 585, 592–93, 599, 608, 621, 654, 659. *See also* lexical heads, verb phrases
holism: general conception, 13, 51, 219; in biological systems, 321–22; in "framework holism", 220–28, 230–33; in human nature and language use, 20, 51–53, 174, 363–65; in perception, 20, 325–32; in physics, 13, 108n43, 206, 307n16, 316, 339, 366; in Saussure's structuralism, 219–20; in semantic holism as attacked by Dummett, 186–87, 220, 228
human beings as subjects of understanding, thought, speech, 1, 20, 67, 87, 283, 306, 309, 345, 352, 357, 366–67, 370–74
human nature, theories of: Cartesian dualism, 51, 309–11, 367; epiphenomenalism, 292, 379, 380; functional theory of mind, 203–4, 296; physicalism and its impossibility, 52, 202–3, 205, 270, 348, 362–63, 378, 380–81, 396; psychophysical holism, 51, 367; "real patterns" theory, 378–79. *See also* anomalous monism; behaviorism; psychophysical nature
human transcendence of body, 3, 18, 20–21, 67, 239, 396, 744, 752–53. *See also* computer simulation; self-reflection and criticism; theories of human nature; unitary semantic structure

identity statements, 416, 417, 422, 508, 512–13, 571–73, 582n11, 613–16, 622, 659, 662–64, 683, 692; predicate logic with identity, 141, 246, 256, 407, 545, 553; variety of concerns, 663n26. *See also wh*-questions
illocutionary force, 29, 32, 33, 162–63, 169, 174–75, 215, 388n47, 448–49, 453–54, 457, 483–85
illusions, 332–334; Ames's room, 332n60; hemiaopic vision with visual completion; Muller-Lyer, 332–33; Poggendorff, 333n65; Ponzo, 333n63; reversed hollow mask, 332; Rubin vase, 332, 333, 332; Titchener circles, 333n61
imagination: character of, 386–87, 389, 435–37, 491–92
imitation: role in language learning, 352–57, 430, 437–39
immanent objects of verbs and immanent activities, 501, 521, 523–24, 526, 553n34, 591, 689, 691, 712, 721. *See also* deponent verbs; middle voice; transeunt activities
impersonal constructions, 105n37, 185, 495, 502, 503n25, 504–9, 524, 525, 648, 689n, 697, 738–39
indefiniteness: as defined by Zermelo, 8, 106; as key to explanations of "infinite use of finite means", 6–11, 78, 90–91, 94–96, 101, 105–12, 125, 129, 134, 140, 147, 149, 179, 229, 232, 269–70, 272n48, 284, 285, 287, 289, 443, 746
indefiniteness in number, 7, 21, 78, 90–91, 94–96, 101, 105–12, 125, 129, 134, 140, 147, 149, 179, 201n68, 229, 232, 269–70, 272n48, 284, 285, 287, 289, 291, 443, 679, 746. *See also* constructivity
indirect perception: theory of stimuli (sensations) in external sensory receptors, 325–26; world construction from such stimuli, 326-27, 334-35,
induction: intuitive, 265, 267n36; mathematical, 264-65, 267-68, 270; transfinite, 149n36, 267n36, 270n45. *See also* involution
infinite Ramsey theorem, 270

infinite use of finite means, 8, 9–10, 90, 105–6, 109–12, 114, 259, 746; interpretation of Von Humboldt's dictum, 11n11, 200
infinity: ambiguity of the term, 7–11, 101, 107–9, 444; inductive, 9, 107, 125; non-denumerable, 107, 147, 444; potentially, 91, 94, 109, 241; term "actually infinite", 109, 241. *See also* constructivity; indefiniteness in number; non-enumerability
inflectional and noninflectional word-formatives, 113, 119, 150–53, 155–56, 531, 534, 545
inflections: in Aristotle, 421, 603; differences between languages, 184, 259, 405–6, 518, 526, 587–95, 604–6; inflectional morphology, 114–15, 118n7, 119, 150–57, 534, 566; among other devices in grammaticalization: 2, 60, 77, 120; place in general grammar, 422–23, 429–30, 458, 499–500, 501, 516, 531, 575, 583–89, 648–50, 653–54, 675–78, 683–84, 688, 693, 709; psychological processing of, 172, 198, 212, 234, 322, 351, 396; "verbal inflections" and "concord-inflections", 603–4. *See also* heads of phrases; language learning; one-word utterances
intellect: capacity for inquiry and discovery, 227–28, 271–74, 287–89, 747; capacity for new paradigms, 9, 10, 21, 108, 187, 192, 228, 258, 262, 282, 287, 369, 380, 747, 752; capacity for translation and mutual intelligibility, 187–192, 228; discovery and advance in natural science, 248, 263; examples in mathematics, 263–71; no restriction in use of general concepts, 10, 253–60, 747; reliance on understanding and judgment, 5, 73, 226, 244, 251, 253, 260, 296–97. *See also* general logic; self-reflection and criticism; semantic syntax
intellect and sense compared: language shaped by pragmatics and intellectual challenges, 360–65, 369–70; no restriction on intellect being shaped by its objects. 21, 37, 41–43, 45–46, 751, sensory system shaped by adaptation to external objects, 307–10, 322–26, 352–56; systems shaped by appropriate objects, 20, 323–36, 382–90, 393–94. *See also* mutual intelligibility; resonance; tuning
intensional isomorphism: in Carnap, 179; extending use of the term, 180, 184–85, 188, 190, 542, 556n36, 621
intentionality: as characteristic of the mental, 378, 379; Internalized Language described as "intensional" or "intentional", 53
intentionality in Aquinas: 359, 362, 383; implies immateriality, 383, 751
intentional objects (in Brentano's sense), 169n13, 383, 417, 425, 436, 441, 495n17, 513, 522, 553n, 573; link to referential opacity. 495n16, 562n45, 570n55, 704n74
intentional stance (phenomenological "reduction" or "bracketing"), 300, 306, 345. *See also in Index of Names* Dennett
interconnected senses of words. *See* analogy; equivocation; family resemblance; metaphor and other figures of speech; polymorphousness; relation-based connections of word use
Internalized Language: in Bloomfield, 173; Chomsky's conception of, 16, 20n25, 173; implied by mind-brain identification, 202; in Jackendoff, 203; in Quine, 173; reasons for rejection, 50–51, 58–59, 173–74, 322–23, 348–50, 367–68, 381–82, 634–35, 750
intuitionistic logic and mathematics, 10, 78n5, 94, 106, 108, 109n45, 112, 147–50, 180, 229, 257, 264, 271, 273n48, 442–44, 488, 626n97
involution, 442, 623–24
isolating languages, 115, 156, 605, 639; dry stone masonry, 27, 445, 458, 582, 605, 649, 658, 678. *See also* lexical atomism; linking elements
iterability of linguistic operations (recursiveness): secondary importance of, 9–10, 105–6, 110–11, 239, 259, 635n107, 746–47

Japanese grammatical theory, 650. *See also in Index of Names* Makino; Uchida

kinds of negation: in different places in the core, 33–34; proper (core) distinguished from nuclear (morphological), 30n37, 33; second-order, 30
knowledge, forms of, 97–98, 131–34, 231, 239, 257–58

language acquisition and use, 7, 75–78, 80–81, 374, 375n18; Chomsky's approach, 16–17, 48, 54, 748; Gibson's treatment of perception extended to language, 18–19, 22, 67, 208–9, 354–55, 356–61, 363–65, 750–51; human speech expressing a content to be reflected upon, 19, 215, 745; hypotheses on prehistoric development, 223-37, 639, 741, 749–51; infant perception of speech, 18–19, 352–56; infant speech pregnant with adult speech structures, 27, 240–41, 577–78; learning by training to adapt contrasted with learning by drill, 77–78, 290–91; LFG's advantages in explaining acquisition, 45, 54–55, 635–38; limits to developmental capacity in apes, 241–42; priority of verb in language learning, 429–34, 437–39; role of optimization in

language acquisition and use (*cont.*)
learning, 743–44; semantics and pragmatics the keys to language learning, 17, 42, 204, 207–10, 360–65, 396, 399–400, 635–38; studies in children's language learning, 45–46, 429, 431–35, 437–38, 500–501, 577–79; superior colliculus exemplifies the malleability of brain, 18–19, 208, 353, 357–60; unitary semantic syntax shaping variability in language and processing, 2, 19, 42–44, 45–47, 220, 242, 364–65, 745–46. *See also* role of brain in use of language
language as specifically human form of intellectuality, 3; adaptation to community of language-users, 356–65; integration of bodily speech with thinking expressed, 3; mode of concept-formation, 35–36, 40n58, 104, 127–28, 128–29, 240–41, 242, 406, 432, 445, 578–79, 753; psychophysical character of linguistic sign, 196, 219, 367; support of the imagination, 10, 67, 101, 140, 142, 187, 189, 191–92, 240, 434–37, 753. *See also* semantic syntax
language change and evolution, 63–66, 444–45; grammatical development, 239, 242, 525–27, 600–601, 605–7, 639. *See also in Index of Names* Lodge; Harris, Martin
language learning, 17–18, 22, 32, 45–46, 58, 60–61, 63–64, 75, 80, 132, 135, 138, 192, 206, 221, 235–36, 240–41, 429–39; in Chomsky, 16–17, 48, 54, 58, 202
language-system, 14–16, 31, 49, 165–66, 186, 200, 634, avoiding overuse of term, 12–13, 166, 197, 209n84
Langue: exercised and exhibited in *parole*, 7, 81, 95, 113–14, 118, 151, 193–94, 196–97, 375n18, 528–29, 533, 745–76; individual and communal, 80–81; knowledge grows progressively, 75, 80, 137–38
Law of Bivalence, 229, 232, 444
Law of Non-Contradiction, 183n30, 440, 442–44
Law of the Excluded Middle, 30, 34, 225, 229, 232, 440, 442–44, 623
layering of the sentence, 22, 25, 29–30, 33, 35
Least Upper Bound Theorem, 108n43, 109n46, 148, 274n50
lexical atomism: approach of sentences composed by joining lexical atoms, 12, 28, 49, 74, 205–6; in Chomsky, 634, 643–44, 649, 725n16, 730; in Jackendoff, 206, 644n2, 725n16; semantic and syntactic principle, 48–49, 730; theory alien to Plato, Frege, Jespersen, 401–4, 411–12, 644–45, 730. *See also* dry stone masonry; linking elements; Minimalist Program
lexical atomism as "one lexical item, one meaning": in Chomskyan grammar, 5; in philosophy, 5, 159, 205n76. *See also* axiomatizability of theory of meaning; context of whole language as determining meaning
lexical factor: need for concept wider than word, 2, 113–14, 115–16, 118, 150–58, 403n9, 746. *See also* inflection; morpheme; word-stem
Lexical Functional Grammar (LFG), 549n28, 594, 632–33; functional and formal interpretations and inspiration, 13n15, 57–58, 637; functional heads given non-Chomskyan interpretation, 56, 638; kinship with functional grammars, 56–58, 638; non-lexical functional heads in, 632, 725–27, 737–38; in psycholinguistics, 45, 54; verbs as functional heads in, 56, 491n9, 653n15. *See also in Index of Names* Bresnan
lexical heads of phrase: prepositions classified as by Cobbett and Chomsky, 48; three kinds, 517, 650, 654, 656–57, 660–62
lexicon: components of. *See* content-introducing expressions; synlexical expressions
LFG. *See* Lexical Functional Grammar
linguistic developments, 64–66, 91, 132, 151n37, 154–55, 235–36, 444–45, 487, 503nn25–28, 507–8, 524, 525–27, 534, 553n34, 585, 589–91, 604–9, 616n78, 628–29n98, 671n32, 680n40, 697, 699-700, 739n47, 750–51. *See also* biological evolution and language
linking elements making syntactic connection explicit, 27, 31, 115, 401–2, 489, 582–83, 586–87, 600, 603, 647, 648–50, 654–56, 673, 676, 695, 708. *See also* grammaticalization; lexical atomism; structurizers
literal meaning: ambiguous expression, 96, 102, 122, 125, 127, 138n29, 285, 484; in Aquinas, 122n14, 182n28; Carnap's criterion, 179; role of word-by-word translation, 190–91. *See also* translation

malleability of the brain, 1, 18–19, 49, 208, 277, 360, 395, 751. *See also* resonance; tuning
mathematical function: difficulties of applying notion in logic, 418, 465–67, 556–62
meaning-nominalism, 212–13, 217n95, 401. *See also in Index of Names* Beebe; Bennett, Jonathan
mechanical: as ambiguous, 312, 319–22, 348; as mathematical concept, 270, 277–78
mechanically applicable rules, 1, 4, 9, 64, 72–73, 78, 91, 97–98, 99, 101, 108, 109, 112n53, 131, 186, 221, 227–28, 243–44, 248, 250, 251, 252, 254–59, 262–64, 266, 268–69, 271, 274, 279–80, 285–87, 291, 747, 753

mechanism as form of metaphysical materialism, 51, 53, 195, 205, 379
mechanisms in psychology, 3, 19–20, 53, 199n63, 202, 212, 245, 346–48, 362; in Martin Braine, 249; need to be seen teleologically, 315–22, 334, 369–70, 379; in Pinker, Jackendoff, Boden, Dennett, and difficulties, 280–83, 312–13, 314–15, 350–51; place for a priori explanation, 245–49; Wittgenstein's objections to, 375, 377
mediums of speech, 21, 22, 113, 159, 165, 328, 447
Mental ("the language of thought"), 25, 39n56, 408n22; Chomsky's Internalized Language reminiscent of Ockham's Mental, 24–25, 634–35
metalanguage: formal/material (*suppositio formalis/suppositio materialis*) mode of speech, 530; and object-language, 101, 124–25, 254n14, 561
metaphor, xv, 4, 21, 35, 40n58, 74, 96, 101–5, 114, 116, 121–23, 127–28, 134–39, 177, 197, 215, 231, 258–59, 277, 283, 422n38, 733n35; indispensable metaphors, 127–28
metaphors for dynamic character of verb: *chi (ki)*, 31, 649, 662, 727; interweaving verbs with nouns, 30, 402n7; ion with open valence bonds, 403; "living" or "live" character, 31, 193, 410–11, 449, 479, 481, 509, 648, 650, 662, 692, 748; *nephesh* (desire or soul), 555, 650n11; nexus or drama, 30, 62, 383, 402, 479n71, 508, 522, 717, 721, 748; not captured by "finite", 479n71
middle voice, 500, 519, 522, 524, 667
Minimalist Program, 9n8, 28, 31, 48–49, 55, 632–35, 735–36; bare structure theory, 49, 633, 732n31; lack of evidence for, 207, 497n20, 632; the operation Merge, 9n8, 31–32, 49n74, 633–34, 705, 730, 747
modality, three types of, 4n3, 38–40, 63, 231, 630–31, 703–4, 709, 749; deontic and real (natural) as root modality, 33–34; epistemic modality, 29–30; imperative mood deontic, 387, 694–95, 702; real as "objective", epistemic as "subjective", 631. *See also* epistemic modality
modality (mood) and modal expressions, 38n51, 115, 120, 190, 197, 231, 392, 411, 422, 433, 452–53, 603, 644, 645n5, 648, 651, 658, 661, 666, 727; categorized with semi-auxiliaries, 658, 667–69, 670–71; in Chomskyan grammar, 643, 723–24, 727; interconnection with time-order, 223, 231, 630–31, 703–4; in LFG, 726; negation and problems of scope, 597, 667–69, 703–4; modal clauses, 695–700, 703; sortal modality, 673–75; synlexical with lexical content, 33, 661
modifiers of nouns, 135, 414, 588, 591–93, 621, 660, 677–79, 688–89, 695, 719, 720, 739–40. *See also* adjectives and adjectival phrases; complements of nouns; possessives and possessive phrases; relative clauses
modularity in psychology: module as engineering concept, 346; each module a restricted role, 352, 362–63; hiatus between input and output modules, 348–52
modus ponens, 29, 163, 183, 247, 248, 253n13, 260, 274, 443, 462, 467, 623–25
Molière's "dormitive power", 73, 252–53, 377
monomorphic and polymorphic axiom-sets, 268
mood as kind of emotion irrelevant to modality, 88, 138n29, 671n30
moral objectivism, 468–71
morpheme: capable of different senses and content, 95, 113–14, 118, 135; definition and distinction, 2, 13, 42, 81, 150–54, 549; distinguished from morphs, 154; grammatically distinguished, 114, 116, 154–55; non-significant, 154–55, 529n1; zero, 151, 414, 418. *See* inflectional and noninflectional word-formatives
morphologically primitive general names, 551–53
motivational element in perception, 303; affordance in Gibson, 303n12, 357n24; estimative power in Aquinas, 303n12; functional value in Merleau-Ponty, 303n12
Movement theory, 498, 503n26, 505, 506, 572, 595, 602, 619, 632, 635, 638, 698n65, 705–6, 729, 732–35, 736n40, 738, 740, 742; limitations and alternatives, 38n51, 55n91, 64, 203, 594–97; movement paradoxes, 491, 734; term "move" as empty metaphor, 733n35
mutual intelligibility, 81, 112, 169–71, 173–75, 187, 192, 210, 244, 250, 279n53, 295, 296, 371

nativism, 16–17, 40–47, 58, 208, 249, 292, 329, 348, 358, 364, 395, 432, 578n6, 640, 745–46
natural deduction: in Aristotle, 275; in Gentzen, 29, 443, 623, 627; natural reasoning procedures in Martin Braine, 249, 440, 625n95
naturalism: Chomsky's conception of, 52–53, 194, 202, 252, 377, 380n35, 741, 747
natural kinds and species, 16, 18, 43, 48, 197–98, 199, 235–36, 242, 306, 317, 330, 345, 360, 395, 409, 414, 424–28, 516, 532–33, 542n19, 718
natural language, 4, 9n8, 10, 30, 53, 55, 109, 124–25, 180, 205n76, 226–27, 253–54, 259,

natural language (*cont.*)
272–73, 282, 285–87, 440, 443, 473, 488, 561, 600, 610, 626–27, 633, 640n115, 642, 680n22. *See also* metalanguage; pure languages
negation, 10, 29, 30, 33–35, 59, 62–63, 128, 154, 156, 180, 224, 229, 232, 400, 431n58, 439–45, 446–48, 443n15, 454–57, 472n48, 483, 494, 507, 583n16, 596–97, 601–2, 606, 612–13, 625–26, 629, 634, 642, 644, 648, 651, 659, 666–68, 674–75, 703, 725n16, 726–30, 738. *See also* intuitionist logic; kinds of negation; Law of the Excluded Middle; presupposition; scope
neurological functionalism: in Chomsky 14–17, 47–48, 199–206, 296, 362; in Jackendoff, 15, 203–6, 208, 310–11, 315; neurology better at explaining malfunction, 351, 381, 746n1; opposed perspective in Bresnan, 55; radical criticism 17, 58, 172, 194–95, 205–9, 750
nominalization: noun-like expressions formed from verbal, 32, 44, 529–33, 535–38, 539–40, 544–49, 553–54, 574, 581, 664; strategic aim but prime mistake in Chomskyan treatment of, 724; tactics of Fukui in response, 732–33. *See also* heads and phrases in Chomskyan grammar
non-enumerability, 77, 96, 100, 109, 134, 186, 264, 265, 273, 278n, 280, 284, 611. *See also* indefiniteness in number; infinity
nonlinguistic communication, 25. *See also* knowledge; signaling and communication
noun clauses as complements of verbs. *See* complements
number, interpretations of: marking order, 147; as measures of cardinality, 146–47; as measures of size, 108, 140, 141–45, as objects algebraically distinguished, 145–46, 148
number, types of, 38n53; algebraic, 142–46; complex, 144–46, 148; natural, 9, 38, 41–42, 94, 101, 106, 107, 109, 111, 112n53, 125, 126, 140–41, 145–47, 148n36, 176, 236n, 229, 254–56, 264–71, 409, 443, 493, 530, 542n19, 552–53; negative, 38n53, 144–46; nonstandard, 38n53, 149n36; rational, 9, 145, 146, 148n35; real, 10, 94, 107–9, 112n51, 142–43, 145–48, 266n35, 271, 294, 626n97. *See also* infinity; ordinals and order-types; transfinite cardinal numbers; transfinite ordinal numbers; zero
Nunberg's ham sandwich, 100, 636

objects of verbs, 56, 57, 429, 445, 497–98, 502–4, 516, 518–26, 527n61, 535–38, 589–91, 594–95, 598–600, 603–5, 613–14, 617, 619, 632, 634, 643, 646, 649, 653, 662, 667, 670, 672, 683–86, 688–91, 698, 699–701, 708–12, 715–17, 720–22, 726, 728–31, 735–36, 739–40, 743n61; direct, indirect, and oblique, 518, 617, 646, 683, 688, 710; objects of immanent and transeunt activities, 501, 521–24, 526, 591, 689–91, 711–12, 721. *See also* absolutive case; ergative languages; undergoer
one-word utterances, 89, 238, 240, 404–6, 430–32, 438–39; inflection in, 404n14, 405, 431, 433; in Quine, 83, 167, 184–85, 407
Optimality theory, 55, 365, 633n101
optimization: seeking harmony in modes of expression and interpretation, 55n91, 364, 400, 639–42, 741, 743
ordinals and order-types, 140, 147–48, 255n15, 267n36, 269. *See also* non-enumerability; transfinite ordinal numbers
ordinary language: grammatical expectations, 209–10, 650; ordinary language philosophy, 3, 4, 205n76, 209n84, 476, 480, 483n79; negative views of, 520; phonetic expectations, 152; scrutinizing, 228–33
ostension, 215, 392, 431, 439, 506, 553, 582

pandemonium theory of mind, 298–302, 347–48
paradigmatic relations, 12, 117, 156, 196–98, 205, 221, 231; called associative relations by Saussure, 196
paradigms of thought. *See* intellect
paradoxes and their resolution, 4n3, 8, 10, 101, 106, 118–19, 124, 227, 248, 253–54, 272–74, 285, 303, 752; ad hoc responses, 143, 148, 272-73; paradoxes of saying and naming, 476–78; Ramsey's distinction between logical and semantic paradoxes, 124, 221, 248, 254n14
paradoxes by name: Berry, 107n42, 112n53; Reach's, 557; Richard, 107, 109, 112n53; Russell's and his response, 101, 124, 143, 148n35, 254n14, 273n49, 543; Zeno's and other paradoxes of continuity, 108n41, 119, 227, 260n22, 273
paralinguistic objects: status of, 167, 467–68, 480, 556, 571
Parameter: adoption of term by Chomsky, 591; wider use by Hawkins, 591–93. *See also* Chomskyan grammar
parameters, 48, 56n91, 64–65, 591–93, 601, 617, 633–35, 643, 706, 723, 730n22, 735–41
parasentential level, 622–28, 703. *See also* epistemic modality
parsing and grammatical ambiguities, 55, 349, 350, 351n13, 640–42; Gazdar's preoccupation with, 55, 737; pragmatics as guide, 597–98, 601–3, 612, 614n115, 617–20, 668. *See* scope
particularity, 130; the concrete, 13, 36, 43, 44,

56, 63, 124, 129, 131, 140, 143, 145, 200, 202, 206, 257–59, 274n50, 424
perception in Gibson's ecological view: activity and sensory operation coordinated, 18, 208, 303n12, 308, 354–58; conception of sense-organs, 307; conception of stimulus, 16, 116, 154, 171; ideas reflected in Hamlyn, 330n56; model for approach to language, 19–20, 295. *See also* resonance; tuning
perceptual patterns: importance for language, 363–64
performative and constative utterances, 29–30, 453, 482, 628, 629, 652
perlocutionary and illocutionary acts contrasted, 79n7, 85, 90, 102, 159, 160, 162, 166, 168, 169, 174, 186, 207n80, 214–15, 407, 410, 457, 482–84. *See also* illocutionary force
personal and animal identity, 315–16, 345, 351–52; implications of identity through time, 302–7, focalized subjects, 297–98, 303–7, 314, 325, 350; functional adaptation of a psychophysical organism involves fallibility, 329–34, 339–42, 343; narrative identity in Dennett and Gazzaniga, 298–302, 309–10, 314–15, 347–48
personal identity over time, 300–303; over extended time, 304–5, 369
Platonism, 217–18, 250–51, 269n42, 384, 388n49, 538–43, 546, 569; bolstered by Ramsey's view of propositions, 542–43
Polish logicians, 39, 401, 402, 418. *See also in Index of Names* Ajdukiewicz; Leśniewski
Polish notation, 63, 488
polymorphousness, 8, 79, 121, 123–24, 127, 129–31, 226, 252, 281, 305
polysemy, 91n20, 92; ambiguous term, 121
polysynthetic languages, 2n1, 115, 639, 746
possessive pronouns and phrases as attributes, 693, 713–14
possessives and possessive phrases as modifiers of nouns, 13, 413, 414, 514, 585, 588, 592–93, 713–14
possible worlds, 569–71, 625n95
postpositions, 585–86, 600n50. *See also* adpositions
poverty of the stimulus argument, 16, 207, 377; multiple criticism of, 16n23. *See also* behaviorism; *and in Index of Names* Skinner
pragmatic anaphor, 26, 180, 575, 582, 612. *See also* ostension
pragmatics: in Chomskyan conception 14, 15n18, 49, 65, 103–4, 158, 211, 215, 568; coherent definition of, 23–24, 158–59, 488, connections with predicate logic, reference, *wh*-questions, 399–400, 439, 575–77, 609–10, 612–18, 620, 638–39, 648; determining sentence identity, 26–28, 594, 644, 698, 724; force and the verbal, 30–33, 404, 162–64, 431, 434, 437, 448, 450, 483; in gauging generality of terms, 35–36; integral to semantics and shaping syntax, 16, 17–21, 25–31, 32–35, 41–44, 59, 61, 64, 67, 75, 116, 172, 178, 204, 306, 328, 369–70, 394, 396, 575, 635–37, 684, 686, 696, 725n16, 731, 736, 738, 741, 743–44, 747–51; jumble resulting from compartmentalizing, 14, 23, 158; key to notion of subject, 47n69, 416, 429–30, 433, 489–90, 493, 495, 498, 499–500, 504–5, 512, 518, 525; in learning and shaping brain function, 208–9, 210, 235, 360–64; in LFG, 14n16, 497, 633; objects of, 21–23; sentence interpretation, 33–34, 167, 458, 642, 725n16; as shaping constituent order, 598–601, 605, 735. *See also* parsing and grammatical ambiguities; private-circle pragmatics; semantic categories
Prague school, 66, 194, 207, 487, 511, 595; Vachek, Garvin, and Uhlenbeck's general accounts of, 207n80. *See also* functionalist grammars; *and in Index of Names* Jakobson; Karcevskij; Malhesius
predicate: concept of, 400, 402–4, 408–11, 412–13, 490, 493, 494–97, 646–47; concept (*rhēma*) in Plato and Aristotle as much logical as grammatical, 30, 162, 402, 410–11, 431, 450; in Frege, Geach, and modern logic, 87, 401–3, 408–9; in Martin Braine, 46, 440n71; tensions between logic and grammar and variants of idiom, 494–96
predicate application controllers, 413–15, 417, 419, 421, 422, 515, 528, 593, 647–48, 651–53, 660, 668n30; called syntactic operators by Chomsky, 413n30
Preference Rules System (Jackendoff), 258, 281
prepositions and other adpositions: heads only morphosyntactically, 655, 656, 659, 706–7, 737; predicative and nonpredicative, 661–62; synlexical character, 586–87, 600, 650, 654–55, 656, 724. *See* connectives; postpositions
presupposition, 30, 34, 62, 104–5, 232, 241, 272, 439–44, 494, 529, 628
primacy of assertion, 451–53
Principles and Parameters theory (PPT), 37, 48, 591–92; 643, 735–41; in apparent decay, 633, 634, 635, 706. *See also* Minimalist Program
private-circle pragmatics, 24, 159, 164–66, 168, 174
problem of a finite vocabulary, 7–11, 90–91, 746–47
proposition (statement), 4, 8, 20, 22, 31, 41, 60, 71–72, 132–33, 171, 224, 442–44, 450–53,

proposition (statement) (*cont.*) 457–58, 459–62, 467–68, 475–80, 556–57; Ramsey's view of, 542–43
psychophysical nature of human beings, 3, 51, 175, 204n75, 303, 309–11, 317–18, 367, 378–79, 396; of language, 1, 174, 324, 366–74; of linguistic sign in Saussure, 367; seen in integration of mechanisms, 312–15, 317–18. *See also in Index of Names* Gibson; Taylor, C.; Ryle
public character of *langue,* 7–8, 13, 36, 74, 75, 80–81
pure languages, 63–66, 80–81, 608–9. *See also* linguistic developments

quantifiers, 41, 106, 140–41, 148, 254, 257, 266, 407, 409, 413, 419, 440n72, 441, 444, 488, 494–95, 510, 517, 528, 530, 542n19, 549, 550, 552–53, 590, 592, 610, 627–28, 651, 669–70, 672n35, 731n25
quantity and identity indicators, 413–15, 419, 477, 514, 517, 599, 663, 664, 677, 679, 680, 693, 709, 719–21, 731, 733, 740
quotation, 557–64; effects of lack of quotation marks, 529, 558n4, 563, 636; Geach's treatment, 563–64; Quine's position, 564; Wittgenstein on how to quote is not to designate, 478

real numbers as Dedekind cuts, 142; point as Aristotelian cut in a line, 39n54, 125
recursiveness. *See* iterability
reductio ad absurdum, 442–45, 465, 623. *See also* Law of the Excluded Middle; negation
reference, referring, 8, 23, 26, 35n48, 58, 61n109, 63, 100, 103, 124, 126, 132, 149, 167, 171, 176, 178, 179n25, 180, 197, 202, 209n, 217–18, 225, 257, 290, 316, 318, 402, 406, 413, 432, 434–35, 489, 507; and sense, 136, 172, 407–12, 416–20, 423-28, 472, 512
registers of speech, 63, 64, 157, 605
Relational Grammar, 57, 499n21, 683n43
relation-based connections of word use, 8, 121, 123, 127, 131–35, 136
relations between senses: systematic account of, 126–39, theories of, 120–26
relative clauses, 328, 361, 415, 449, 525, 592, 598–99, 613–22, 638, 649, 654, 658, 695, 697–98, 733n35, 734; relatives as formatives, 656, 694, 698
representationalism, 20–21, 748–49, 751–52, 753; in Chomsky, 20, 348, 362, 394; cross-modal character, 352–56; in Dummett, 382–84, 388–90, 391–92; Jackendoff's representational modularity, 204, 359; in Locke and Plato, 384–85; in perception, 315, 323, 325–26, 334, 349; summary of objections to, 393–94; ultimately rejected by Putnam, 204n75; undermined by object/cognate distinction, 556, 568–74; Wittgenstein's disproof of, 386–89, 390–91
resonance: in Gibson's and allied theories, 67, 208–9, 315, 354, 358, 360, 658n20; in other theories, 393. *See also* tuning
Role and Reference Grammar (RRG), 14n16, 40, 56, 207, 503n28, 638, 661n24, 706n1. *See also in Index of Names* Blake; Foley; Van Valin
role of brain in use of language, 17, 18, 20, 67, 208–9, 234–35, 239, 242, 295–96, 322, 358–59, 360–61, 363–65, 396, 743–44, 750–51, 753
rule: conception of, 72–73, 209–10, 250–53, 274–76; application requires understanding, 253, 260
Russell's typical ambiguity, 101, 124–25, 254n14, 273

Sapir/Whorf hypothesis, 200n65; related discussion, 191–92
satellites, 494, 586n25, 646, 683, 687, 715, 729n21
Saussure's structuralism, 13, 63, 80, 196–98, 200, 219–21
Saying character: of sentences as speech-units, 21–23, 26–28, 30–32; of verb, predicate, and comment in sentences, 31, 62, 399–400, 410–11, 449–50, 488–90. *See also* clauses; metaphors for dynamic character of the verb; predicate
scientific method: Aristotelian conception, 121–22, 292, 381, 246n3, 262–63. *See also* explanation, types of; naturalism
scope: as logical concern, 29, 33, 34, 63, 488, 598, 601, 610, 612, 618, 626, 638, 648, 651, 656, 675–76, 699, 722; and negation 440, 445, 597, 667–70. *See also* bracketing
segmentability of speech, 118–19, 186–87, 229–31
self-reflection and criticism, 2, 224–26, 241, 254–55, 272–73, 284–85, 363, 752. *See also* Gödel; intellect; human transcendence of the body; paradoxes; Tarski; unitary semantic structure
semantic categories, 10, 44, 46, 62, 63, 135, 148, 416, 543–46, 577; in Aristotle, 38, 43, 44, 392–93, 581; hierarchy of, 580–82; in Polish logic, 418–20; relation of semantic to grammatical categories, 10, 40–46, 63, 745–46
semantic conventions governing sense and force supposedly distinct, 214n89, 218n97, 448–49, 473, 474–75, 485–86

semantic syntax: encompassing general logic, 59; not understood by Quine, 184–85, 517; shaping children's speech 60, 63, 240, 364, 431; as underlying grammaticalization, 2, 19–20, 32, 38–39, 59, 60, 72, 88, 63–64, 75, 128, 159–60, 221, 227, 228, 230, 232, 234, 236, 238, 239, 241, 362, 371–72

semi-auxiliary verb forms, 445, 651, 658–59, 661–62, 666–75, 676, 680, 723–24; expressing propensity, 666, 669–73, 687; psychological, 666, 671–73; types of, 666, 670–72. *See also* causative verbs; modality (mood) and modal expressions

senses of sentences: as discourse-significances, 5, 19–20, 22–23, 25–26, 28–30, 32, 36, 71, 73, 82–86, 88–89, 143, 149, 158–59, 161–62, 163–65, 167–69, 172, 175–79, 185–87, 205, 210–11, 238, 244–45, 257–60, 280–82, 284–86, 288, 290–91, 336, 366–68, 371–74, 382, 487; and force, 446–75, 480–82, 485–86; as requiring expression, not just identification, 5, 7, 19, 20, 30, 72–73, 74, 81–86. *See also* force; representationalism; translation

senses of words and other sentence-constituents: as discourse-significances, 2, 3, 5, 7–9, 73–74, 81, 84–88, 90–97, 100–112, 116–18, 120–39, 149–50, 176–78; as forming a spread and indefinite in number, 4, 8, 10, 90, 94, 106, 121–23, 139, 149, 248, 285, 394; and integration of sentence, 401–3, 477–79; sense and reference, 407–12, 416–20, 423–28. *See also* figures of speech; relations between senses; translation

sentences: as constructs of grammar: 15–16, 17, 83, 136, 161, 166, 200–201, 206, 399, 485, 636, 644, 748; as context-free, 20n25, 58, 351, 393, 399, 633, 634, 635, 637, 639-40, 642, 644, 737; as context-independent, 16, 17, 31, 58, 748; unnecesary to linguistic methodology, 13, 172, 194, 197, 211

sentences: as expressing sense, 86, 90; in linguistic tradition, 22–23, not representations, 20–21, 386–91; number and length, 9n8; pragmatic identification of, 25–28; as primarily speech-units, 7, 13, 158–60, 165–68; relation to clauses as potential sentences, 28, 32, 62, 166–67, 447–49, 594; shared objects of logic, semantics, grammar, and pragmatics, 21–23; "text-sentences" in Lyons, 16; unitary and articulated, 20. *See also* metaphors for dynamic character of the verb; one-word utterances; representationalism; unity of the thought

signaling and communication: among animals, 19, 242; chimpanzees, 241–42; Grice as providing a theory of, 23, 212–17; requires only transfer of coded signal, 23–24, 73, 74, 81–85, 86, 88, 169; signaling in Beebe, 401

sign-language, 21, 22, 88–89, 113, 159, 238n30, 360, 380

singular terms, 34, 43, 74, 100n29, 129, 224–25, 254, 257, 407–9, 411–22, 424, 439–41, 473, 489, 494–95, 543, 545, 559, 581, 647, 648, 653, 660; Dummett's remarks, 473. *See also* applicatives; general terms; predicate.

spatial clauses and phrases: when adverbial modifiers, 93, 580, 661, 675, 687–88; when attributes, 93, 580, 661

Specifiers: anomalous notion without traditional meaning, 679, 723, 731; closing growth of any given kind of phrase, 723, 731; place marker to fulfill many roles, 731–33; position as target of movement, 737–38, 739–40, 741–42; position for subject, 613–14

specious present, 337–38

speech (*parole, Sprache*): definition, 7, 75–76, 78–79, 113, 149; grammar concerned with sentences as speech-units, 21–23, 25–28, 81; require expression of sense, 19, 30–31, 84–87, 88, 89–90, 161

speech-act, 26–29, 59, 82, 102, 158–60, 167–69, 173, 210, 279, 292, 387, 391, 426; coordinate with act of understanding, 169–71, defects of Grice's account, 212–17, described as illocutionary act, 89–90, 482; possessors of force, 446–47; sense and its expression as co-cognates of, 88, 169, 215. *See also* force

speech-constituents: distinguished according to rank, 113; distinguished from speech-components, 86–87, 163n10; sentence-constituents called sentence-factors in Ryle, 87n12, 400–401. *See also* senses of words and other sentence-constituents

Sprache, as speech, 75n1; Jespersen, 193; Von Humboldt, 9, 11n11, 200, 209, 606; Wittgenstein, 456, 462n32

spread, as notion in intuitionist mathematics, 10, 94, 108–9, 112, 257; extension of intuitionist ideas, 149; usefulness in other cases, 77, 78n5, 257. *See also* constructivity

states. *See* dispositions; verbal predications

structurizers, 36, 119, 156, 622, 644, 645, 648–49, 658, 676, 682

subjacency theory and variants, 617–20, 638, 738. *See also* convergence of psychological and logical processing.

subject in grammar and logic: ambiguities in term, 44–45, 488–89, 494–95, 497–98; assumed correlate of predicate, 400, 406, 407, 412, 493; a complement or dependent of verb, 653, 660, 683, 687, 688; dative subjects, 502–4; grammaticalized topic and argument

subject in grammar and logic (*cont.*)
to verb in Bresnan and LFG, 62, 492–93, 497n19, 499, 502–3, 504–6, 565, 637; grammaticalized topic in Li and Thompson, 62, 493, 499, 518; lexical functional conception developed, 490–93, 495, 502–18; partitive and possessive phrases, 413, 440, 504, 516–19, 588–89, 626, 664; privileged syntactic arguments and primary pragmatic pivots in Van Valin, 493, 503n58, 525; problem of morphosyntactic impersonal subjects, 105n37, 502, 504–11, 513; residual problems, 525–27; singular and general subjects distinguished, 408, 413, 416–17; in traditional logic, Aristotle and Aquinas (*hypokeimenon, subjectum, suppositum*), 413, 421–22. *See also* general terms; presupposition; singular terms; topic
subjective and objective genitives, 591, 709–10, 715
subordinate clauses, 654, 695–99. *See also* adverbial clauses; noun clauses; relative clauses
superior colliculus, 353–60; Stein and Meredith on, 18–19, 208
supposing, 29, 235, 451, 454, 459, 623–24, 627. *See also* conditional statements
syncategorematic. *See also* categorematic; synlexical expressions
synchronic/diachronic approach to language, 63–66, 74, 80–81, 91–92, 94, 220, 533n, 662; diachronic as instructive for synchronic, 502–3, 506–8, 525, 526–27, 583, 585, 589, 589–90, 603–6, 696–98; language as system always in motion, 66, 750; speech as cradle of linguistic development, 606
synlexical expressions, 77, 116, 119–20, 128, 153, 156, 533–34, 578, 587, 600, 650–51, 656–58, 660–62, 666–67, 672, 679, 682, 706, 711, 721, 725–28, 749; ambivalent character of modal expressions, 33, 661; problem of adpositions, 661; structural expressions synlexical, 120, 257, 445, 589, 634, 683; synlexical verbs, 656–58, 662–63
synsentential, 27, 89, 215n91
syntagmatic relations, 12, 117, 156, 196–98, 205, 221, 231
Systemic Functional Grammar, 207n80. *See also in Index of Names* Halliday

teleology, 20, 28, 51, 53, 276–77, 295, 315, 348, 374–75; involved in functional explanation, 315–20, 325, 332–34, 352–54, 357–58, 360–63, 363–65; required, 78, 274–76, 366–70, 379, 380, 394–96
temporal order amongst events: simple and weak, 337–38; time in relativity theory, 338; timing acts of thinking, 338, 385, 753; timing physical and conscious events, 337–42
tense, 38n51, 39, 63, 64, 114, 117, 120, 150–52, 177–78, 190, 197, 222, 223, 229–31, 235, 241, 359, 361, 405, 408, 411, 422, 432, 434, 439, 444, 453, 458, 479n71, 521n49, 525, 534, 603, 604, 606–7, 609, 629–32, 634, 640, 643–45, 651–53, 657, 658, 661, 667, 669, 671n32, 672, 692, 703–4, 725, 727, 728, 730, 732, 738, 739n44, 749
thematic role, 400, 413, 414, 429, 488, 493–94, 522–23, 524, 549, 550, 565n49, 575–81, 582–84, 633, 637n110, 646, 722
Theme, 487, 509–11, 518, 565, 595, 600, 613, 621, 640, 741–42; pre-subject topic position, 62, 487, 491; other technical uses of term, 519n45
topic, 399–400, 487; basis of definition of subject, 62; creating a new ranges of subject, 10, 44, 46, 63; independent of the notion of focus, 490–91; subject as default, 56, 489; topic and subject not psychological, 34–35, 416, 490–93. *See also* subject; Theme
topic-neutrality, 43, 125, 126, 130, 140, 186, 419
topic-prominence, 492, 494n13, 510–11, 613, 615n75, 619
transeunt activities, 521, 591n33, 711, 712
transfinite cardinal numbers, 107–9, 111, 146
transfinite induction, 149n36, 267n36, 270n45
transfinite ordinal numbers, 147, 269
transformational grammar. *See* Movement Theory.
transformations. *See* Movement
translation, 93, 104, 171, 177; faithful translation, 182, 187–91; literal translation, extent of 179–90, 197–98; possibility of mutual understanding, 292; radical translation, 187, 189, 190–92, 228–30, 232–33; supposed indeterminacy of translation in Quine, 182–85; translation by machine, 50, 55, 287–89, 305n14, 372–73, 640n115, 725. *See also* mutual intelligibility
True, the, and the False as objects in Frege, 466, 473, 479n67, 480, 643
truth, theories of, 180–82; deflationary and relaxed deflationary, 181–82; truth, knowledge, proof as evaluative concepts, 99, 274–75, 450–51, 460–61
truth-tables, 462–65
tuning in Gibson's and allied theories, 18, 22, 43, 67, 208, 234–35, 239, 277, 330, 336, 356, 358,

360–61, 363–64, 636, 658n20, 750–51. *See also* resonance
Turing machine, 262, 266, 269, 278, 282
Turing-machine computability, 202, 262, 266, 278, 281, 282, 290, 315, 319–21, 641n115
Turing test: inadequacy of, 372–73

undergoer, 400, 493n13, 500–501, 519–20, 522–26, 684n45, 732, 735
unitary semantic structure: analogous and informal use of words, 4, 8, 9–10, 21, 73–74, components of general logic, 2, 38–40, 43, 221–26; control of informality avoiding paradox, 227–28; indivisibility and integratedness of, 220, 221, 226, 227–28, 233, 241, 242; presupposed earlier, 72, 75, 159–60. *See also* computer simulation; holism; intellect; self-reflection and criticism; semantic syntax
unity of the thought, 20, 338–39, 385–86, 753; expressed through articulatedness of sentence, 30–31, 88, 113–14, 159–60, 226, 400–404, 479, 582–83, 644–45, 649–50, 748
use of general concepts, 383, 384–85, 747; of the most general concepts, 10, 253–60, 281–82, 363, 369, 752

verbal predications: Aristotle's fourfold distinction, 38; mark differences of posture in time, 392, 749. *See also* aspect of verbs; *and in Index of Names* Vendler
verb kernel (*noyau*): definition, 645–46, 649–50; complements as in *rapport* with it, 653; learning of, 405–6, 432–34, 437–39; in parsing problems, 445, 597, 601, 670, 676, 699, 722; simple or structured of (semi) auxiliary with terminal verb, 590, 648, 650–51, 657–59, 660–61, 666–69, 670–73
verbless clauses ("nexus without a verb"), 411, 654, 609, 657–58, 658; clauses expressed with participle, 688–99; clauses expressed with infinitive, 699–702; "Predicate" as functional head in, 658n19. *See also* disjoint elements of sentences
verb phrases, 30–32, 410–11, 440, 498, 594, 596, 599, 608, 634, 646, 651; peculiarities of, 645, 657, 724
verbs, types of. *See* attributive statements; auxiliary verb forms; constitutive verbs; epistemic modality; modality (mood) and modal expressions; semi-auxiliary verb forms
verbs taking attributive complements: copula, 692–95; "seem" and "appear" used *de dicto,* 702; similar verbs, 692;
verb "to be": expressing existence, 662; expressing identity, 662; four uses of as copula, 508, 662, 692. *See also* attributive statements; auxiliary verb forms; existential statements; identity statements
voice, 38n51, 190, 422, 432, 496, 500, 523, 603, 646, 651, 653, 657, 658, 661, 667; active as default form of verb, 504, 509, 524–25; active, passive, middle, 500, 503, 521–24, 527, 577, 604, 632, 694, 698–99, 700, 733, 734; intransitive as anti-causative compared with anti-passive, 667, 684n45; link with reflexiveness, 500, 522, 604n56, 667. *See also* causative verbs
voluntariness 89, 98, 170, 303, 305, 314, 323n41, 340–41

wh-questions (Q-questions), 35n47, 62, 613–20, 736n40, 738; logical and grammatical links with identity statements, 62, 613–16, 622; relation to relative clauses, 621–22
word-formatives and word formation, 113, 115, 150–57; composition and blending, 115–16, 153; Item and Arrangement, 115, 153, 585–86, 676; Item and Process, 115, 153n41, 198; Word Paradigm model, 115, 152
words and lexical factors, 2, 114–15; double standing as at once *langue* items and speech-constituents, 118–19, 211; each focus of meaning a distinct *langue*-meaning, 74, 92–94; each *langue*-meaning a vehicle of many senses, 2, 7–10, 71, 94–97, 176–79; as experienced at level of *langue,* 7, 113–14, 116; interrelated uses of term in linguistics, 116–17; learning of, 109–10, 291, 355–56, 375n18, 405–6, 431–34, 437–39, 578–79; as loci of linguistic stability, 114; not mere ciphers, 7, 90; as roots of linguistic creativity, 8–11, 114; as sense-expressors, 7, 73, 74, 82, 84–86, 88, 90–91, 112, 114, 176, 210, 211; unrelated uses of term "word", 73–74. *See also* senses of words and other sentence-constituents
word-stem, 150, 152, 421, 515, 533, 549, 566, 593, 603

X-Bar theory, 48, 56, 531n6, 591, 632, 638, 643, 644, 646, 656, 678–79, 705, 706, 709, 723–25; logically vicious origin of, 724; multiple roles of "Specifiers" in, 731–33, verbs misrepresented in, 728–31

zero: in mathematics, 38n53, 144, 508; in morphology, 151, 414, 418; use in grammar, 508, 647, 660

Language & Human Understanding: The Roots of Creativity in Speech and Thought was designed in Arno and composed by Kachergis Book Design of Pittsboro, North Carolina. It was printed on 50-pound House Natural Smooth and bound by Sheridan Books of Ann Arbor, Michigan.